RESOLVING TRANSFER
PRICING DISPUTES

Via a global analysis of more than 180 transfer pricing cases from 20 representative jurisdictions, *Resolving Transfer Pricing Disputes* explains how the law on transfer pricing operates in practice and examines how disputes between taxpayers and tax administrations are dealt with around the world.

It has been designed to be an essential complement to the *OECD Transfer Pricing Guidelines for Multinational Enterprises and Tax Administrations*, which focus on transfer pricing issues but do not refer to specific transfer pricing disputes. All of the transfer pricing cases discussed in the book are linked to the relevant paragraphs of the OECD Guidelines by means of a 'Golden Bridge', i.e., a table listing the cases according to the paragraphs of the Guidelines to which they refer. It therefore provides examples of the application of the arm's length principle in many settings on all continents.

EDUARDO BAISTROCCHI is a Lecturer in Law in the Law Department at the London School of Economics and Political Science, and an Adjunct Professor at Universidad Torcuato Di Tella, Buenos Aires.

IAN ROXAN is a Senior Lecturer in Law and Director of the Tax Programme in the Law Department at the London School of Economics and Political Science.

CAMBRIDGE TAX LAW SERIES

Tax law is a growing area of interest, as it is included as a subdivision in many areas of study and is a key consideration in business needs throughout the world. Books in this series will expose the theoretical underpinning behind the law to shed light on the taxation systems, so that the questions to be asked when addressing an issue become clear. These academic books, written by leading scholars, will be a central port of call for information on tax law. The content will be illustrated by case law and legislation.

The books will be of interest for those studying law, business, economics, accounting and finance courses.

Series Editor
Dr Peter Harris,
Law Faculty, University of Cambridge,
Director of the Centre for Tax Law.
Dr Harris brings a wealth of experience to the Series. He has taught and presented tax courses at a dozen different universities in nearly as many countries and has acted as an external tax consultant for the International Monetary Fund for more than a decade.

RESOLVING TRANSFER PRICING DISPUTES

A Global Analysis

Edited by

EDUARDO BAISTROCCHI

and

IAN ROXAN

CAMBRIDGE
UNIVERSITY PRESS

CAMBRIDGE UNIVERSITY PRESS
Cambridge, New York, Melbourne, Madrid, Cape Town,
Singapore, São Paulo, Delhi, Mexico City

Cambridge University Press
The Edinburgh Building, Cambridge CB2 8RU, UK

Published in the United States of America by Cambridge University Press, New York

www.cambridge.org
Information on this title: www.cambridge.org/9781107026599

First published 2012

Printed and bound in the United Kingdom by the MPG Books Group

A catalogue record for this publication is available from the British Library

Library of Congress Cataloging-in-Publication Data

Resolving transfer pricing disputes : a global analysis / edited by Eduardo Baistrocchi, Ian Roxan.
    pages cm. – (Cambridge tax law series)
    ISBN 978-1-107-02659-9
1. International business enterprises–Taxation–Law and legislation.   2. Transfer pricing–Law
    and legislation.   3. Corporations–Taxation–Law and legislation.
        I. Baistrocchi, Eduardo.   II. Roxan, Ian.
                    K4544.R47 2012
                    338.8′8–dc23
                    2012014620

ISBN 978-1-107-02659-9 Hardback

To our families,
B, J, A and J; K and M

CONTENTS

FIGURES

TABLES

CONTRIBUTORS

REUVEN S. AVI-YONAH (United States) is the Irwin I. Cohn Professor of Law and Director of the International Tax LLM Program at the University of Michigan Law School. He teaches the basic course on taxation and courses on international taxation, corporate taxation, tax treaties and transnational law. He has published numerous articles on domestic and international tax issues, and is the author of *International Tax as International Law: US Tax Law and the International Tax Regime* (Cambridge University Press, 2007) and *US International Taxation: Cases and Materials* (2005, with Brauner and Ring), and co-editor of *Comparative Fiscal Federalism: Comparing the US Supreme Court and European Court of Justice Tax Jurisprudence* (2007). He graduated *summa cum laude* from the Hebrew University in 1983, received a Ph.D in History from Harvard University in 1986, and received a JD *magna cum laude* from Harvard Law School in 1989. From 1989 to 1993, he practised tax law in Boston and New York, specialising in the international tax aspects of mergers and acquisitions. From 1994 to 2000 he was Assistant Professor of Law at Harvard Law School. He has served as consultant to the US Treasury and the OECD on tax competition issues and has been a member of the executive committee of the New York State Bar Association Tax Section and of the Advisory Board of Tax Management, Inc. He is currently a member of the Steering Group of the OECD International Network for Tax Research and Chair of the ABA Tax Section Tax Policy Committee, an International Research Fellow of the Oxford University Centre for Business Taxation and a Trustee of the American Tax Policy Institute.

EDUARDO BAISTROCCHI (Argentina) is a Lecturer in Law at the London School of Economics and Political Science (LSE) since 2009. He teaches the course on UK business taxation and courses on international taxation and tax treaties. Before joining the LSE, he was Associate Professor of Law at Universidad Torcuato Di Tella in Buenos Aires. He studied law at the Universidad de Buenos Aires before obtaining an LLM at Harvard Law

School, and later an LLM on Tax Law at LSE. He has been a Fulbright Scholar and a Chevening Scholar. He has also been a Distinguished Visiting Professor at Northwestern University and University of Toronto. His research and publications are focused on international taxation, with a particular emphasis in the emerging world. His representative publications include 'The Transfer Pricing Problem: A Global Proposal for Simplification', *Tax Lawyer* (Summer 2006); 'The Use and Interpretation of Tax Treaties in the Emerging World: Theory and Implications' 4 *British Tax Review*, 24 September 2008; and 'Tax Disputes under Institutional Instability: Theory and Implications' (2012) 75(4) *Modern Law Review* 547. His current areas of research include the tax treaty network and BRIC countries (Brazil, Russia, India and China).

BYRON BESWICK (Canada) is a senior manager in Ernst & Young's transaction tax practice and is also a tax lawyer with Couzin Taylor LLP. He has over ten years of tax experience both as a chartered accountant and a lawyer, having formerly practised with a national accounting firm and a national law firm in Calgary and Toronto. He has extensive experience with structuring and implementing public and private mergers, acquisitions, financings and reorganisations in a variety of industries. He has also had significant experience with inbound and outbound cross-border taxation issues and transfer pricing matters. He has written on a number of taxation matters, including for *Tax Notes International*, and has spoken at various events, including the Canadian Tax Foundation's 'Young Practitioners' sessions.

MUKESH BUTANI (India) is based in Taxand, India, where he is a partner and tax practice leader of BMR Advisors, India's leading independent firm of tax advisors. He is an acknowledged expert in international tax and transfer pricing, with more than twenty-three years' experience advising several Fortune 500 multinationals on various cross-border tax structuring, transfer pricing, mergers and acquisitions, and investment structuring matters. He regularly interacts with India's Central Board of Direct Taxes, and is a member of OECD's Business Restructuring Advisory Group and ICC's Paris Taxation Commission. He actively participates in Indian affairs of the International Fiscal Association and has been its Secretary General. He is a regular speaker at significant national and international tax conferences. He regularly contributes to leading tax journals, including the *International Tax Review* and the Asia-Pacific guide of IBFD. He is also the author of *Transfer Pricing: An Indian Perspective* (2007). He is actively associated with IFA India's International Fiscal Academy. For the past four years, he has been consistently rated amongst the leading individual tax advisors in India by the *ITR* and the World Tax 2006 and 2007 guides to leading tax firms have also rated him as a leading tax advisor; he is also noted in Legal Media Group Expert Guides to the World's Leading Tax and Transfer Pricing Advisors. He has a BA in Commerce from the University of Bombay and qualified as a chartered accountant in 1985.

ISABEL CALICH (Brazil) holds a Ph.D from the London School of Economics and Political Science (LSE). Her LSE Ph.D thesis examines the relationship between international taxation and development. In 2007, she concluded her Master of Laws at LSE, with specialisation in Taxation. She graduated in Sao Paulo, Brazil, at the Law School of University Mackenzie in 2004 and at the Business School of Fundacao Getulio Vargas in 1999. She began her career practising tax law at Lilla, Huck, Otranto, Camargo Advogados, a law firm headquartered in Sao Paulo, Brazil, where she became a partner.

LEE CORRICK (Africa) is the Senior Specialist for Transfer Pricing at the Large Business Centre of the South African Revenue Service (SARS). He previously worked for the UK's HMRC as Assistant Director (Transfer Pricing) where he was responsible for ensuring that UK transfer pricing legislation was fit for purpose and that it was being implemented effectively. He led HMRC's transfer pricing Mutual Agreement Procedure and Advanced Pricing Agreement Programme. He also led the HMRC litigation in *DSG Retail Ltd and others* v. *HMRC*. He is now responsible at the SARS for ensuring the effective implementation of transfer pricing legislation and for providing specialist advice on the largest and most complex transfer pricing cases being dealt with by the SARS. He also represents South Africa on OECD Working Party 6, having previously been the UK delegate.

DAVID G. DUFF (Canada) is a Professor, Co-Director of National Centre for Business Law and Associate Dean of Academic Affairs at the University of British Columbia. From 1996 to 2008, he taught tax law and policy at the University of Toronto, Faculty of Law. Prior to this, he was a tax associate at the Toronto office of Stikeman, Elliott. He also served as a researcher with the Ontario Fair Tax Commission from 1991 to 1993 and as a tax policy analyst with the Ontario Ministry of Finance from 1993 to 1994. His teaching and research interests are in the areas of tax law and policy, environmental taxation, comparative and international taxation, and distributive justice. He has published numerous articles in the areas of tax law and policy, accident law and family law, and environmental taxation and policy, has co-authored a book on accident law and a textbook/casebook on Canadian income tax law, and has co-edited books on tax avoidance in Canada and Canadian climate change policy. He has also served as a consultant to the Canadian Department of Justice, the Alberta Department of Justice, the Ontario Panel on the Role of Government, and the Commission of Inquiry into the Investigation of the Bombing of Air India Flight 182.

PHILIP GILLETT (European Union) has over thirty years of experience in tax and Treasury matters, having worked in both the accounting profession, where he was a senior tax and financial services partner with Price Waterhouse, and in industry, as Finance Director and Director of Tax and Treasury with Courage Ltd, and then as Group Tax Controller and Group VP Tax and Treasury at ICI PLC. He was a member of the EU Commission's Panel of Experts in Business Taxation set up in 1999 to assist the European Commission in the preparation of its report on *Company Taxation in the Internal Market*, which was published in October 2001, and was a member of the EU Joint Transfer Pricing Forum from its formation in 2002 until 2006. He is a former Chairman of the Tax Committee of the Confederation of British Industry, a Past President of the Association of Corporate Treasurers and a former Hon. Treasurer of the Chartered Institute of Taxation. He is also a UK Tax Tribunal Member and a Visiting Fellow at the London School of Economics.

OFER GRANOT (Israel) is a Tax and Governmental Incentives Associate with Herzog, Fox & Neeman Law Firm. He served as a law clerk at the Supreme Court of Israel. His publications include *Purposive Interpretation in Tax Law: From Declaration of Principles to Practical Agenda* (2004), *Depreciation Based on Actual Amortizaton: Deduction by Way of Interpretation* (2006), and *Business Conducted by a Sub-contractor: Is it a 'Business' within the Meaning of the Israeli Income Tax Ordinance?* (2003).

JUAN PABLO GUERRERO DAW (Chile) is a Managing Director for KPMG Global Transfer Pricing Services in Chile. Prior to joining KPMG, he worked as an associate in transfer pricing services for Ernst & Young in Mexico. He has more than nine years of experience in a wide variety of planning and compliance transfer pricing projects as well as intangible assets valuation. He has acted as a speaker at several conferences in the most important cities in Mexico's Mid-West Region and in Santiago, Chile. He has published numerous articles in the areas of transfer pricing and restructuring. He has given presentations at Universidad Mayor on the subject of transfer pricing to MBA students. He is a man proud of his family and in love with his wife and son.

JINYAN LI (China) served as a Professor and Interim Dean of Osgoode Hall Law School from 1 July 2009 to 30 June 2010. She is currently Chair of Osgoode Faculty Council as well as the Faculty Recruitment Committee. She joined Osgoode in 1999, having previously taught for eight years at the Faculty of Law at the University of Western Ontario. She was also a Visiting Scholar at Harvard Law School, a Greenwoods and Freehills Visiting Professor of International Taxation at the University of Sydney, Australia, and a Visiting Professor at Kenneth Wang Law School, Suzhou University, China. She has served as a legal consultant to the International Monetary Fund, the Organisation for Economic Co-operation and Development, the Auditor General of Canada, the Department of Justice of Canada, as well as several leading law firms. She was also a member of an advisory committee for the Minister of National Revenue on the issue of e-commerce taxation. In 1999, she received the Douglas J. Sherbaniuk Distinguished Writing Award. She has been awarded numerous research grants, including two from the Social Science and Humanities Research Council of Canada. Her research interests include taxation law and policy, social security law, pension law, and Chinese law.

YORAM MARGALIOTH (Israel) studied law at the Hebrew University, LLM in taxation and JSD at New York University. He clerked for Supreme Court Justice Shoshana Nethanyahu and worked as a State tax attorney representing the government in tax cases before the Supreme Court. Prior to joining Tel Aviv Law Faculty, he was a faculty member at the Interdisciplinary Center, Herzliya. He previously served as a visiting professor at NYU School of Law and Northwestern University of Law and as a deputy director of the International Tax Program at Harvard Law School. He serves as an outside director of IDB Development Corp. Ltd, one of the largest and most influential holding companies in Israel. His research interests include tax law, tax policy, welfare and social policy, employee benefits, pension law and climate change.

TOSHIO MIYATAKE (Japan) is an attorney-at-law and a partner of Adachi, Henderson, Miyatake & Fujita in Tokyo, Japan. He has more than thirty years of experience in international tax practice. His tax practice ranges from tax planning to handling of tax audits and tax litigation in various tax fields. He has also handled a considerable number of transfer pricing cases. He taught Japanese international taxation at the Harvard Law School as a visiting professor in 1983, and taught at the Law Faculty of Sophia University and the Chuo University Graduate Course of Accounting for a number of years. His writings include the textbook *Kokusai Sozei Ho (International Tax Law)* in Japanese and various tax articles in Japanese and English. He was the former Chairman of the Japanese Branch of the International Fiscal Association. He is a former chairman of the Tax System Committee of the Federation of Japanese Bars, the Taxation and Legislation Committee of the American Chamber of Commerce in Japan and the Tax Law Committee of the Inter-Pacific Bar Association.

ANDREAS OESTREICHER (Germany) holds a Chair at the University of Göttingen, Faculty of Economic Sciences, and is Director of the Faculty's Tax Division. He graduated from the University of Mannheim, where he also obtained his Ph.D (1992) and post-doctoral lecture qualification (1999) in business administration. He joined PricewaterhouseCoopers in Frankfurt as a tax advisor (Steuerberater) in 1999, where he specialised in tax transfer pricing and gained considerable experience in value chain transformation projects and (multilateral) advance pricing procedures. He was appointed as a university professor in 2001. His work has been published in numerous leading economic and management journals, such as *Public Finance Analysis, Review of Managerial Sciences* and the *Schmalenbach Business Review*. He has also authored several books in this field. In 2005, he was appointed as one of the five German 'Independent Persons of Standing', eligible to become members of the Advisory Commission as referred to in the EU Arbitration Convention. Since 2011, he is among the select group of experts selected to chair arbitration panels to resolve mutual agreement procedure cases under consideration by Canada and the United States.

HUN PARK (Korea) is an Assistant Commissioner for Taxpayer Advocacy at the National Tax Service of the Republic of Korea (2011–12). He served as a Visiting Scholar at the University of Tokyo (2010); Tax Judge at the Korean Tax Tribunal (2009–10); and Associate Professor at the University of Seoul City (2003–9, currently on leave of absence). His area of interest includes inheritance tax, non-profit association, donation and taxation and the rights of the taxpayer. He has written *Gift Tax and Inheritance Tax* (2010) and published articles including 'Is there a Permanent Establishment?' in

(2009) 94a *Cahiers de Droit Fiscal International* (June) and 'The Recent Issues of Dispute Resolution by Mutual Agreement Procedure (MAP)' in (2007) 13(2) *Seoul Tax Law Review* (Korean Tax Law Association, August).

STEPHEN L. H. PHUA (Singapore) is an Associate Professor with the Faculty of Law at the National University of Singapore and is a consultant with the tax practice group at Rajah & Tann LLP. He has taught in the areas of tax law for over twenty years and has served as a Sub-Dean (1995–7) as well as the Director of the Centre for Commercial Law Studies (2001–5). Besides a study visit to the GST Division of IRAS in 1994, he has held many visiting/teaching positions in foreign universities including Harvard University, New York University, University of British Columbia, Kyushu University and University of Tasmania in the last ten years. He has been a member of the Steering Group of the INTR, Centre for Tax Policy and Administration, OECD, Paris, since 2004. He has also served on the Ministry of Finance's Tax Advisory Group. In 2007, he was appointed an Examiner at the Chartered Institute of Taxation, London, and a Programme Advisor to the International Tax and Investment Centre, Washington DC. In addition to his numerous conference papers and articles in journals, his publications include being editor of two books, *Recent Developments in Financial Regulation and Capital Markets* (2003) and *Excise Taxation in Asia* (2007).

JOÃO DÁCIO ROLIM (Brazil) is a lecturer in taxation at Fundação Getúlio Vargas and tax partner at Rolim, Godoi, Viotti & Leite Campos Advogados in Brazil. He served part-time as Fellow Researcher at Queen Mary, University of London (2006–9), and has a Ph.D in Tax Law (Federal University of the State of Minas Gerais, Brazil). He is Director of the Ibero-American Tax Arbitration in Brazil (AIBAT), Director of the IFA Brazilian branch and arbiter at CAMARB (Chamber of Arbitration in Brazil). His professional memberships also include Institute of Fiscal Studies (Founder Counsellor), Brazilian Association of Financial Law, Member of the International Fiscal Association and International Tax Ring (Coordinator).

IAN ROXAN (United Kingdom) is Director of the Tax Programme in the Law Department of the London School of Economics and Political Science (LSE). He has been a Senior Lecturer in Law since 2003, having joined LSE as a Lecturer in Law in 1995. He is a non-practising solicitor in England and is a barrister and solicitor in Ontario, Canada. He began his career practising trust and tax law with a firm in Toronto. He has also worked in the Tax

Policy Branch of the Canadian Department of Finance, where he was involved in developing tax policy and drafting legislation for three Budgets. He specialised in international, European and US tax planning, European corporate law, and value added tax, looking at a wide range of issues. He has participated in tax reform projects in developing countries in Africa and Asia for the World Bank and the Harvard Law School International Tax Program. In 2000 he won the Wedderburn Prize for his article 'Assuring Real Freedom of Movement in Direct Taxation' in the *Modern Law Review*. Ian's current research interests extend to international taxation, including the implications of taxation for development; European taxation and the influence of the European Court of Justice; corporate taxation; value added tax, including the application of the EC VAT Directives, the theory of VAT and the comparative development of VAT internationally; and tax avoidance and its implications for the development of tax systems.

VIOLETA RUIZ ALMENDRAL (Spain) is Associate Professor (Profesora Titular) at the Universidad Carlos III de Madrid, where she teaches Tax Law and courses on International and European Taxation, Sub-national Taxation and Public Spending (Budget Law). She has been a Visiting Fellow at the Westfälische Wilhelms-Universität zu Münster (Münster, 2003–4), the International Bureau for Fiscal Documentation (Amsterdam, 2005), the James Rogers College of Law (Tucson, 2006), the European University Institute (Florence, 2008) and the London School of Economics (2010). She is a recipient of post-doctoral scholarships from the Jean Monnet and Deutscher Akademischer Austauschdienst programmes and has been awarded, *inter alia*, the leading tax law prize in Spain (Premio Estudios Financieros, 2000, 2004, 2008, 2010) and the 'Award of Excellence' (Premio de Excelencia, 2009) by the Fundación Universidad Carlos III for Professors aged under 45. Her main lines of research cover fiscal federalism and sub-national taxation, tax avoidance in the European and international arena and European tax harmonisation, and her publications include *Die neue spanische Umgehungs-vorschrift des Art. 15 Ley General Tributaria (LGT) Ist der deutsche SS. 42 AO als Vorbild geeignet?* (2003), *Tax Avoidance and the European Court of Justice: What is at Stake for European GAARs?* (2005) and *An Ever Distant Union: The Cross-border Loss Relief Conundrum in EU Law* (2010). She is also a consultant on different tax issues for political institutions (municipalities and autonomous communities) and private companies.

ANDREY SHPAK (Russian Federation) is a tax partner with Goltsblat BLP Tax Practice in Moscow. He has fifteen years of experience in helping Russian and foreign multinationals operating in the Russian market streamline their tax and legal structures, in defending clients against assessments by Russian tax authorities, as well as in successfully resolving various complex cross-border tax issues, including assisting multinational clients in adapting their global service and supply arrangements to the requirements of Russian transfer pricing regulations. He graduated with honours from the Finance Academy in Moscow and holds a Ph.D in Accounting from the Russian Finance and Economics Institute in Moscow.

RICHARD VANN (Australia) is Challis Professor of Law at the University of Sydney, Consultant, Greenwoods and Freehills, Sydney. In 2006 he was William K. Jacobs Jr Visiting Professor at Harvard Law School and has taught regularly at New York University School of Law. He specialises in corporate, comparative and international taxation. He is a graduate of the University of Queensland, Australia and Oxford University, United Kingdom. He has held many government consultancies in Australia, including on the Review of Business Taxation (1998–9), the Review of International Taxation (2002–3) and the Australian Taxation Office Public Rulings Panels on international and indirect taxation (1995–2007). He has worked extensively for international organisations for over twenty years, including two full-time periods as Counsel (Taxation) in the Legal Department of the International Monetary Fund, Washington DC (1990–1) and as Head, Central and Eastern Europe and NIS Program, Fiscal Affairs Division, Organisation for Economic Co-operation and Development, Paris (1992–5). He is a member of the Permanent Scientific Committee of the International Fiscal Association and an International Research Fellow of the Centre for Business Taxation at the Said Business School of Oxford University. He participates in a number of international groups which publish books and articles on comparative and international taxation and has also published broadly on Australian taxation.

ACKNOWLEDGEMENTS

We owe the greatest thanks to our colleagues at the Law Department of the London School of Economics and Political Science (LSE) for creating a vibrant, interdisciplinary atmosphere that has inspired us to produce this book. Special thanks go to Julia Black, Neil Duxbury, Philip Gillett, Pablo Ibáñez-Colomo, Martin Loughlin, Niamh Moloney, David Oliver and Edmund Schuster. We acknowledge the financial support provided by the Law Department. We also wish to thank the prominent authors from every continent who have worked so assiduously to describe and analyse transfer pricing dispute resolution in their own jurisdictions since the inception of corporate income taxation there. Their contributions have provided a vital element in the global analysis of transfer pricing dispute resolution offered in this book. The LSE seminar that brought together the contributors to compare experiences and learn from the comments of colleagues, including very notably Eric Zolt of UCLA, helped to crystallise our understanding of the global trends. We wish to thank Amanda Tinnams of the LSE Law Department for her tireless assistance in making the seminar happen.

The OECD has generously given permission to use the Table of Contents of the *OECD Transfer Pricing Guidelines for Multinational Enterprises and Tax Administrations* (Paris: OECD Publishing, 2010) in order to make the content of the book as transparent as possible. Over 180 transfer pricing cases analysed in the book are linked to the relevant paragraphs of this key OECD document in order to provide worldwide examples of the issues it identifies. The Universidad Torcuato Di Tella Law School in Buenos Aires has also been a source of inspiration for the book. Alejandro Chehtman, Hernán Gullco, Martin Hevia, Eduardo Rivera Lopez, Celia Lerman, Sergio Muro, Ezequiel Spector and Horacio Spector have provided important feedback to key sections of the book. Last but not least, we thank the enthusiastic contribution offered by our research assistants S. Jacqueline Park, Liliana Lerchundi and Demian Macedo. Without Jacqueline Park's indefatigable editing, this book would not have seen the light of day.

Eduardo Baistrocchi and Ian Roxan
London, 30 December 2011

THE GOLDEN BRIDGE: ANALYTICAL TABLE OF CASES BY TOPICS IN THE OECD GUIDELINES

The Golden Bridge aims to link each transfer pricing dispute discussed in the book with the relevant paragraphs of the OECD Guidelines. It lists the disputes according to the headings in the Table of Contents of the 2010 edition of the *OECD Transfer Pricing Guidelines for Multinational Enterprises and Tax Administrations.* Each entry shows: (i) the specific paragraph number(s) of the OECD Guidelines referred to in the dispute (where relevant); (ii) the country; (iii) the number or name of the transfer pricing dispute as referred to in the country chapter; (iv) the page(s) where the case is referred to in the country chapter.[1] The Table of Cases by jurisdiction includes a complete list of the cases referred to in the book, including those that do not relate to any specific entry in the OECD Guidelines, or that do not concern a transfer pricing dispute.

The example below illustrates the structure of the Golden Bridge:

Chapter I   The Arm's Length Principle

A.   Introduction

[...]

D.3   Losses

¶1.70–172 – Australia – *Roche Products* v. *Commissioner of Taxation* [2008] AATA 639, (2008) 70 ATR 703   371–4, 378, 381

Preface

¶6 – UK – *Test Claimants in the Thin Cap Group Litigation* v. *HMRC* [2011] EWCA Civ 127; [2011] STC 738   329

---

[1] This book focuses on both OECD and non-OECD member countries. Although the OECD Guidelines are not necessarily applied in non-OECD countries, there are key common concepts in the domestic transfer pricing law of all countries explored here which will make the link offered by the Golden Bridge mechanism helpful in understanding how these concepts are being interpreted in all the countries considered.

Chapter I   The Arm's Length Principle

A.   Introduction

B.   Statement of the arm's length principle

B.1   Article 9 of the OECD Model Tax Convention

B.2   Maintaining the arm's length principle as the international consensus

[. . .]

D.1   Comparability analysis

D.1.1   Significance of the comparability analysis and meaning of 'comparable'

D.2   Recognition of the actual transactions undertaken

D.3   Losses

D.5   Use of customs valuations

Chapter II   Transfer Pricing Methods

Part I: Selection of the transfer pricing method

A.   Selection of the most appropriate transfer pricing method to the circumstances of the case

B.   Use of more than one method

Part II: Traditional transaction methods

A.   Introduction

B.   Comparable uncontrolled price method

B.1   In general

B.2   Examples of the application of the CUP method

C.   Resale price method

C.1   In general

C.2   Examples of the application of the resale price method

D.   Cost plus method

D.1   In general

D.2   Examples of the application of the cost plus method

Part III: Transactional profit methods

A.   Introduction

B. Transactional net margin method

B.1   General

B.3.6   Other guidance

B.4   Examples of the application of the transactional net margin method

C.   Transactional profit split method

C.1   In general

A.5   Selecting or rejecting potential comparables

A.6   Comparability adjustments

A.7   Arm's length range

A.7.1   In general

B.   Timing issues in comparability

B.3   Penalties

C.   Corresponding adjustments and the mutual agreement procedure

Articles 9 and 25 of the OECD Model Tax Convention

[. . .]

D.   Simultaneous tax examinations

E.   Safe harbours

Chapter V   Documentation

B.   Guidance on documentation rules and procedures

Chapter VI   Special Considerations for Intangible Property

B.   Commercial intangibles

B.2   Examples: patents and trademarks

C.   Applying the arm's length principle

[. . .]

C.2   *Identifying arrangements made for the transfer of intangible property*

C.3   *Calculation of an arm's length consideration*

Chapter VII   Special Considerations for Intra-Group Services

A.   Introduction

B.   Main issues

B.1   *Determining whether intra-group services have been rendered*

B.2   *Determining an arm's length charge*

B.2.1   In general

B.2.2   Identifying actual arrangements for charging for intra-group services

Chapter VIII   Cost Contribution Arrangements

[. . .]

C.   Applying the arm's length principle

Chapter IX   Transfer Pricing Aspects of Business Restructurings

[. . .]

D.2   *Intangible assets*

D.3   *Transfer of activity*

Part IV: Recognition of the actual transactions undertaken

[. . .]

TABLE OF CASES

1

ABBREVIATIONS

ADR	alternative dispute resolution
ALP	arm's length principle*
ALS	arm's length standard*
APA	advance pricing agreement (Australia: advance pricing arrangement)
ATAF	African Tax Administration Forum
ATCA	advance thin capitalisation agreement
BALRM	basic arm's length return method
BAPA	bilateral advance pricing agreement
BMR	best method rule
BRIC	Brazil, Russia, India, China
CAPM	capital asset pricing model
CAT	comparable adjustable transaction
CFC	controlled foreign corporation
CIT	corporate income tax
CPI	comparable profit interval
CPM	comparable profit method
CSA	cost sharing agreement
CT	corporate tax
CUP	comparable uncontrolled price
CUT	comparable uncontrolled transaction
DIA	direct investment abroad
DTA	double taxation agreement
DTC	double tax convention
ECJ	European Court of Justice
FA	formulary apportionment
FDI	foreign direct investment
FIE	foreign investment enterprise
FTA	free trade agreement
GAAR	general anti-avoidance rule
GDP	gross domestic product
IC	Information Circular
ITA	Income Tax Act
MAP	mutual agreement procedure

MNE	multinational enterprise
MOU	memorandum of understanding
OECD	Organisation for Economic Co-operation and Development
PATA	Pacific Association of Tax Administrators
PE	permanent establishment
PIC	comparable independent price
PIT	personal income tax
RPM	resale price method
SAP	separate accounting principle
SEZ	special economic zone
TNMM	transactional net margin method
TPM	transfer pricing method
TPO	transfer pricing officer
UNCTAD	United Nations Conference on Trade and Development

Argentina

CTA	Capital Tax Act
IRS	Internal Revenue Service
ITL	Income Tax Law

Australia

AAT	Administrative Appeals Tribunal
ATO	Australian Taxation Office
ITAA 1936	Income Tax Assessment Act 1936
NTLG	National Tax Liaison Group

Canada

CRA	Canada Revenue Agency
IWTA	Income War Tax Act
TPRC	Transfer Pricing Review Committee

China

EIT Law	Enterprise Income Tax Law
FIET Law	Income Tax Law for Enterprises with Foreign Investment and Foreign Enterprises
NPC	National People's Congress

Egypt

ETA	Egyptian Tax Authority

European Union

CCCTB	Common Consolidated Corporate Tax Base
JTPF	Joint Transfer Pricing Forum
TFEU	Treaty on the Functioning of the European Union

Germany

CPFC	Code of Procedure of Fiscal Courts
CTA	Corporate Tax Act
FC	Fiscal Code
FTA	Foreign Tax Act

India

AAR	Authority for Advance Rulings
CBDT	Central Board of Direct Taxes
DRP	Dispute Resolution Panel
DTC 2010	Direct Tax Code 2010

Israel

ITA	Israeli Tax Authority

Japan

LSRTT	Law concerning the Special Rules (etc.) incidental to the Enforcement of Tax Treaties
NTA	National Tax Agency
NTCRL	National Tax Common Rules Law
NTT	National Tax Tribunal
STML	Special Taxation Measures Law
STMLC	Special Taxation Measures Law Circulars
STMLEO	Special Taxation Measures Law Enforcement Order
STMLER	Special Taxation Measures Law Enforcement Regulations

Kenya

KRA	Kenya Revenue Authority

Korea

CITA	Corporate Income Tax Act
IITA	Individual Income Tax Act
LCITA	Law for the Coordination of International Tax Affairs
NTBA	National Tax Basic Act
NTS	National Tax Service

Singapore

CPFA	Central Provident Fund Act
FA	Finance Act
GSTA	Goods and Services Tax Act
IRAS	Inland Revenue Authority of Singapore
ITBR	Income Tax Board of Review
SDA	Stamp Duties Act

South Africa

| SARS | South African Revenue Service |
| STC | secondary tax on companies |

Spain

AEAT	Agencia Estatal de Administración Tributaria (National Tax Collection Agency)
GTC	General Tax Code
GTL	General Tax Law
LATF	Law 36/2006 for the Avoidance of Tax Fraud
LCIT	Law establishing the Corporation Income Tax
RCIT	Regulations on the Corporate Income Tax
RTEAC	Resolution of the Economic-Administrative Tribunal
TEAC	Economic-Administrative Tribunal

Tanzania

| TRA | Tanzania Revenue Authority |

United Kingdom

CTA 2010	Corporation Tax Act 2010
HMRC	Her Majesty's Revenue and Customs
ICTA 1988	Income and Corporation Taxes Act 1988
ITTOIA 2005	Income Tax (Trading and Other Income) Act 2005
TIOPA 2010	Taxation (International and Other Provisions) Act 2010
TMA 1970	Taxes Management Act 1970

United States

| IRS | Internal Revenue Service |
| TEFRA | Tax Equity and Fiscal Responsibility Act |

Zambia

| ZRA | Zambia Revenue Authority |

* The expressions 'arm's length principle' and 'arm's length standard' are used with the same meaning in this book, as encapsulated in Article 9 of the OECD Model. See Chapter 2.

PART I

The context of transfer pricing disputes

Introduction

IAN ROXAN

1.1 A transfer pricing dispute

Pharmaceutical companies need to have a continuing supply of good research developments to maintain their future profits. Their ability to profit from this research depends on exploiting patents based on the results of the research, but patents expire after a number of years, allowing other companies to compete with the developer, and some drugs are simply superseded by later developments.

In the 1960s, one major US pharmaceutical company had developed a number of valuable patents. The company naturally wanted to limit the amount of tax it would have to pay to exploit these patents. So in 1965 it established a subsidiary in Puerto Rico (a United States' dependency). At the time, US tax law permitted the transfer of patents to a Puerto Rican subsidiary tax free, and Puerto Rico offered tax haven treatment on the returns from exploiting the patents. The US parent therefore transferred the patents to the subsidiary without receiving any payment or royalties in return. The subsidiary relied on the patents in manufacturing the drugs they covered, and sold the products to the US parent.

Not unsurprisingly, the US Internal Revenue Service (IRS) was not satisfied with this, and reallocated all of the income of the subsidiary from the patents to the parent, on the basis that the subsidiary was only a contract manufacturer and that it should not be treated as the true owner of the patents.[1]

Here we have a striking example of a transfer pricing dispute. The taxpayer and the tax authority take different views of the basis on which related companies should deal with each other. The subject of this book is how such disputes are actually resolved around the world.

---

[1] *Eli Lilly & Co. v. Commissioner*, 84 T.C. 996 (1985), aff'd in part, rev'd in part, 856 F.2d 855 (7th Cir. 1988), discussed in Chapter 3, 'United States'.

Transfer pricing is the most challenging issue in international taxation for multinational enterprises and tax administrators at the beginning of the twenty-first century. It is also a fundamental problem for tax policy-makers. After the publication of the first major revision to the *OECD Transfer Pricing Guidelines for Multinational Enterprises and Tax Administrations* since they were first issued in 1995,[2] this book seeks to present new and novel insights into the resolution of transfer pricing disputes. These insights will be immediately useful to experts working on transfer pricing issues, and will also greatly interest anyone studying transfer pricing in a broader context.

1.2   Objective and scope: the range of transfer pricing disputes

The objective of the book is to describe and analyse how the law on transfer pricing operates in practice by explaining how transfer pricing issues are dealt with in disputes between taxpayers and the tax adminis-tration. The book looks at how the resolution of transfer pricing disputes has developed since transfer pricing rules were first introduced to income tax systems, tracing their origins back to the start of the modern income tax in the United Kingdom in 1842. It describes how the resolution of transfer pricing disputes has responded to and helped to develop the arm's length principle (ALP) that forms the basis of the OECD Guidelines, used to a greater or lesser degree worldwide. And it builds on this analysis to explain how transfer pricing disputes are being resolved around the world today.

In the *Eli Lilly* case, described above, the dispute was decided in the US courts, first in the specialised Tax Court, and then in the Seventh Circuit of the US Courts of Appeals. This was a case where only one jurisdiction involved imposed tax on the transactions. Very often two, or even more countries, seek to impose tax, leaving the taxpayer facing double taxation, rather than the successful tax planning it may have sought. Today, the mutual agreement procedure (MAP) available under most double tax conventions (DTCs) is extensively used by many coun-tries to help resolve transfer pricing disputes through negotiation between the tax authorities involved. Unfortunately, negotiation is not always enough, but the alternative of arbitration under the MAP or a separate treaty, as in the case of the European Union Arbitration

---

[2] *OECD Transfer Pricing Guidelines for Multinational Enterprises and Tax Administrations* (Paris: OECD Publishing, 2010) ('OECD Guidelines').

Convention,[3] has started to become more available, and it looks likely that it will become a major element in resolving transfer pricing disputes in the future.

Taxpayers now also often have the option of trying to resolve transfer pricing disputes before they develop by entering into advance pricing agreements (APAs) with one or more tax authorities. An APA can be a valuable alternative, at least when two (or more) tax authorities have agreed to the pricing regime, but it can require much time and documentation to settle the APA, and future events may make it less applicable than the parties expected.

Finally, even complex transfer pricing disputes are often settled by negotiation between the taxpayer and the tax authority. Indeed, this has often been the predominant method of settling transfer pricing disputes.

However, the dominance of different methods of resolution of disputes has changed over time, and still differs between countries. The book seeks to explain these differences and to enable practitioners to take advantage of the most effective ways of dealing with transfer pricing issues in a range of twenty countries around the world. This includes both developed and developing countries from all five continents.

1.3   Span of countries and disputes covered

The book provides details of transfer pricing explained through dispute resolution in twenty countries, using a representative selection of jurisdictions in transfer pricing on all continents. It covers over 180 transfer pricing disputes from representative countries from: (i) North America and Europe,[4] (ii) the Asia–Pacific region,[5] (iii) the BRIC countries,[6] and (iv) South America, Middle East and Africa.[7]

The countries included extend from developed countries with a long history of transfer pricing rules, such as Germany, Japan, the United Kingdom and the United States, to emerging countries that are in the forefront of transfer pricing developments, such as Brazil, Russia, India and China.

---

[3] See Chapter 5 'European Union'.
[4] Canada, Germany, Spain, United Kingdom and United States.
[5] Australia, Japan, Korea and Singapore.
[6] Brazil, Russia, India and China. The BRIC countries are analysed together here to identify any common trends in transfer pricing dispute resolution among these leading emerging countries.
[7] Argentina, Chile, Israel, Kenya, Namibia, South Africa and Tanzania.

1.4 Approach and outline

In describing how the law actually operates in each country, the book uses the OECD Guidelines as a baseline. For countries where there has already been official reaction to the 2010 revision of the OECD Guidelines, the practical implications of the revision are also examined.

In order to understand current transfer pricing practice, it is important to examine it in perspective and see how it has developed over time. The analysis of what is happening and what happened in the past – understanding historical approaches to transfer pricing law and tax dispute resolution – is often very useful to understanding what happens today. This view is reflected throughout the book.

The book is organised in three main sections. The first section (Chapters 1 and 2) outlines the root of the transfer pricing problem. It includes an analysis of the central role that the ALP has played and continues to play in resolving transfer pricing disputes, as well as how the meaning and role of the ALP has developed over time.

The second section (Chapters 3 to 20) discusses the practice of transfer pricing dispute resolution in the twenty countries as it has developed since the introduction of corporate income tax in each tax system. All the country chapters broadly share the same general structure. They have been written by local experts – tax practitioners, tax scholars and tax administrators. The List of Contributors gives full details of each of the contributing authors.

The country authors started from seven questions drafted by Eduardo Baistrocchi regarding transfer pricing dispute resolution in the country at different points in time. The questions are listed at the end of this chapter. The final section of each country chapter gives the answers to the questionnaire in order to show further how the processes of transfer pricing dispute resolution have developed in the country.

All of the contributors participated in a global conference at the London School of Economics to discuss their initial findings. The country reporters had the opportunity to present their chapters and to obtain feedback from other country reporters and regional discussants, including other participants and Eric Zolt of UCLA.

The third section of the book (Chapters 21 and 22) offers a broader analysis of the issues. Chapter 21 presents the cross-country evolutionary path of transfer pricing dispute resolution since the United Kingdom introduced income tax in 1799. It shows that the ALP is a US invention with German origins. It also shows that central driving forces for the emergence and evolution of the ALP have been two technological innovations related to globalisation: the emergence of multinational enterprises (MNEs) after the first globalisation boom (1820–1914) and the emergence of international trade in intangibles as of the second globalisation boom (1945–present). Chapter 22 considers the current state of how transfer pricing disputes are resolved and the present and future challenges in transfer pricing dispute resolution.

1.5 Interaction with the OECD Guidelines

The book offers the first global analysis of more than 180 transfer pricing cases emerging from the five continents. The book has been designed in such a way as to be an essential complement to the OECD Guidelines, which focus on transfer pricing issues, but do not refer to specific transfer pricing disputes. In order to achieve this, all of the transfer pricing cases discussed are linked to the relevant paragraphs of the OECD Guidelines by means of an Analytical Table of Cases called the Golden Bridge. The Golden Bridge lists each transfer pricing dispute discussed in the book according to the section or paragraph(s) of the Guidelines to which it refers, thus effectively providing examples of the application of the ALP in many settings. A more detailed explanation of the format is provided at the beginning of the Golden Bridge. The Table of Cases by Jurisdiction includes a complete list of the cases referred to in the book, including those that do not relate to any specific entry in the OECD Guidelines, or that do not concern a transfer pricing dispute.

1.6 Questionnaire answered by country experts

1. The structure of the law for solving transfer pricing disputes. What is the structure of the law of the country for solving transfer pricing disputes? For example, is the mutual agreement procedure (MAP), as regulated in the relevant tax treaty, the standard method for solving transfer pricing disputes?

2. Policy for solving transfer pricing disputes. Is there a gap between the nominal and effective method for solving transfer pricing disputes in the country? For example, has the country a strategic policy not to

enforce the arm's length standard (ALS) for fear of driving foreign direct investment to other competing jurisdictions?[8]

3. The prevailing dispute resolution method.   Which is the most frequent method for solving transfer pricing disputes in the country? Does it have a positive externality? For example, is the MAP the most frequent method, and if so, to what extent have successful MAPs been used as a proxy for transfer pricing case law?[9] The case of a US MNE successfully extending its bilateral advance pricing agreement (APA) concluded between two developed countries to a number of countries of the emerging world is a good example.[10]

4. Transfer pricing case law.   What is the evolution path of transfer pricing litigation in the country? For example: (i) Is transfer pricing litigation being gradually replaced by either MAPs or APAs, as regulated in the relevant tax treaties? (ii) Are foreign/local transfer pricing precedents and/or published MAPs increasingly relevant as a source of law for solving transfer pricing disputes?[11]

---

[8] For examples of strategic interpretations of tax treaty law in India and South America, see E. Baistrocchi, 'The Use and Interpretation of Tax Treaties in the Emerging World: Theory and Implications' (2008) *British Tax Review* 352, available at SSRN: ssrn.com/abstract=1273089.

[9] For a seminal paper suggesting using APAs as a proxy for transfer pricing case law in order to provide an increasingly precise meaning to the arm's length standard (ALS), see R. Vann, 'Reflections on Business Profits and the Arm's Length Principle' in B. J. Arnold, J. Sasseville and E. M. Zolt (eds.), *The Taxation of Business Profits Under Tax Treaties* (Toronto: Canadian Tax Foundation, 2004), pp. 133–68.

[10] An official of Procter & Gamble said: 'We believe that our APA strategy gives us greater predictability and financial statement precision not only in markets where we have obtained rulings, but also in other countries with similar circumstances where we have [not] yet pursued a ruling. Essentially, because the business model is the same and the circumstances are similar, our rulings give us the ability to ask the next government why shouldn't the new audit produce the same tax result as the 15 APAs that we have already obtained on substantially similar facts. When we couple this strategy with our general corporate transparency, and global consistency in execution of our planning, and strong internal controls, we have a strategy that delivers more risk management certainty.' An interview with Tim McDonald, Vice President Finance & Accounting, Global Taxes in Procter & Gamble, *Tax Policy and Controversy Briefing, A Quarterly Review of Global Tax Policy and Controversy Development*, Issue 3 (February 2010) 2–6.

[11] For an example of an analysis of the evolution of transfer pricing case law in a developed economy, see R. S. Avi-Yonah, *The Rise and Fall of Arm's Length: A Study in the Evolution of U.S. International Taxation*, University of Michigan Law and Economics Olin Working Paper no. 07–017 (27 September 2007); University of Michigan Public Law Working Paper no. 92, available at papers.ssrn.com/sol3/papers.cfm?abstract_id=1017524.

5. Customary international law and international tax procedure. Has customary international law been applied in the country to govern the relevant methods for solving transfer pricing disputes (such as the MAP)? For example, has the OECD *Manual on Effective Mutual Agreement Procedure* 'OECD Manual'[12] been deemed customary international tax law in the MAP arena for filling procedural gaps (for example, time limit for implementation of relief where treaties deviate from the OECD Model Tax Convention)?[13]

6. Procedural setting and strategic interaction. Does strategic interaction between taxpayers and tax authorities depend on the procedural setting in which they interact when trying to solve transfer pricing disputes? For example, which procedural setting in the country prompts the relevant parties to cooperate with each other the most for solving this sort of dispute, and why?[14]

7. The future of transfer pricing disputes resolution. Which is the best available proposal in light of the interests of the country for facilitating the global resolution of transfer pricing disputes, and why?[15]

---

[12] The OECD Manual is available at www.oecd.org/document/45/0,3343,en_2649_33753_36156141_1_1_1_1,00.html.

[13] On the relevance of customary international law on international tax law, see R. S. Avi-Yonah, 'International Tax as International Law' (2004) 57 *Tax Law Review* 483. An early version of this paper is available at SSRN: papers.ssrn.com/sol3/papers.cfm?abstract_id=516382.

[14] For a comprehensive discussion on the strategic behaviour of lawyers in contexts arguably similar to transfer pricing litigation (such as large commercial litigation), see R. Gilson and R. H. Mnookin, 'Disputing Through Agents: Cooperation and Conflicts Between Lawyers in Litigation' (1994) 94 *Colum. Law Rev.* 509.

[15] Global proposals for simplifying the transfer pricing problem in both the developed and emerging world include the following options:

Option 1: improved methods for solving transfer pricing disputes. See the 2007 OECD Report, *Improving the Resolution of Tax Treaty Disputes*, available at www.oecd.org/dataoecd/17/59/38055311.pdf.

Option 2: improved methods for solving tax treaty disputes in which certain MAPs are used as a proxy for transfer pricing case law. See Vann, 'Reflections on Business Profits and the Arm's Length Principle', note 9 above.

Option 3: See R. S. Avi-Yonah and K. A. Clausing, *A Proposal to Adopt Formulary Apportionment for Corporate Income Taxation: The Hamilton Project*, University of Michigan Law and Economics Olin Working Paper no. 07–009 (April 2007); University of Michigan Public Law Working Paper no. 85, available at ssrn.com/abstract=995202.

2

The transfer pricing problem

EDUARDO BAISTROCCHI

2.1 Introduction

Imagine the following scenario. A French multinational (FM) manufactures cars in France and owns a valuable intangible: the specific industry know-how in marketing its cars. FM is willing to expand its business to country X, where intellectual property rights are not properly enforced. In order to minimise the transaction costs in safeguarding the rights, FM decides to create a wholly-owned subsidiary in X which will be in charge of selling its vehicles (FM Sub.), instead of supplying its intangible know-how to an independent reseller in country X (Indep Co.). This strategy allows FM to expand its business to country X, minimising the risk of compromising its intangible via internalisation of these transactions costs.

This example shows that FM is able to replace the FM–Indep Co. relationship with the FM–FM Sub. model. More generally, this way, multinational enterprises (MNEs) are able to replace the arm's length market (the external market) for products and services with an internal market of inputs.

The external and internal markets of inputs differ at least in one significant aspect in that the open pricing mechanism only applies to the external market.[1] Conversely, a system called *transfer pricing* operates in the internal market only. Here, transfer prices refer to prices at which an enterprise transfers physical goods and intangible properties or provides services to associated enterprises.[2] Such differences in price between internal and external markets are relevant because, although

---

[1] R. G. Eccles, *The Transfer Pricing Problem: A Theory for Practice* (Lexington, MA: Lexington Books, 1986), p. 19.

[2] *OECD Transfer Pricing Guidelines for Multinational Enterprises and Tax Administrations* (Paris: OECD, 2010) ('OECD Guidelines'), p. 19, para. 11. The OECD Guidelines are available at www.oecd.org/document/34/0,3746,en_2649_34889_1915490_1_1_1_1,00.html; see also A. Gabor, *Pricing: Concepts and Methods for Effective Marketing* (Cambridge: Cambridge University Press, 1988), pp. 113–14.

MNEs do not control market prices in principle, they are relatively free to set transfer prices for their intra-firm transactions. Consequently, MNEs may use this discretion for implementing international tax planning techniques, illustrated as follows.[3]

Let's go back to the FM case above. FM is a manufacturer of cars which is a resident in France; and FM Sub., its wholly-owned subsidiary in charge of reselling its cars to independent customers in X, is a resident in country X. The taxable income of the subsidiary is then determined by the following three variables: (i) the reselling price of the cars to independent customers; (ii) the expenses paid for all its inputs (except for the cars); and (iii) the expenses incurred for purchasing the cars from the manufacturer. The market generally determines the first two variables. By contrast, the third variable (the price paid by the subsidiary for buying the cars) is under the manufacturer's control. Therefore, if the effective tax rate of the manufacturer's jurisdiction is higher than that of its subsidiary, then the manufacturer can charge the lowest possible transfer price to its subsidiary in order to channel the profits of the MNE to the lowest tax jurisdiction. Conversely, if the manufacturer's effective tax rate is lower than that of its subsidiary, the manufacturer can charge the highest possible price to its subsidiary. The net effect of this transfer pricing strategy is to increase the after-tax profit of the MNE.[4]

Transfer pricing manipulation produces at least two consequences. First, as the last example shows, it may trigger a harmful competition at a global level among tax jurisdictions, as the MNEs are encouraged to seek ways in which their after-tax profits can be maximised by channelling their taxable income to relatively low-tax jurisdictions.[5] Thus, countries may attempt to gradually lower their tax rates in order to attract MNEs to their own jurisdictions. Second, it provides a substantial advantage to MNEs in comparison with non-multinational firms, because only the former can use this type of international tax planning strategy.

Since 1915, when the United Kingdom implemented its first regulation in this area, tax jurisdictions have been exploring the ways in which such transfer-pricing abuses can be curbed in order to minimise the

---

[3] The risk of using transfer pricing as an abusive international tax planning technique has been acknowledged in many settings. See OECD Guidelines, note 2 above, p. 31, para. 1.2.

[4] R. Avi-Yonah, 'The Rise and the Fall of the Arm's Length: A Study in the Evolution of U.S. International Taxation' (1995) 89 *Virginia Tax Review* 89; P. Muchlinski, *Multinational Enterprises and the Law* (Oxford / Cambridge: Blackwell, 1995), p. 289.

[5] *Harmful Tax Competition: An Emerging Global Issue* (Paris: OECD, 2008), available at www.oecd.org/dataoecd/33/0/1904176.pdf.

adverse consequences pointed out in the previous paragraph.[6] From this exploration, a regulation has emerged that now enjoys a fairly wide international consensus: the arm's length principle (ALP).[7]

The ALP attempts to replicate 'the working of the open market in cases where goods and services are transferred between associated enterprises'.[8] Hence, the ALP requires an MNE to set the price of its internal transactions (transfer pricing) in such a way as if they were entered into by independent parties in similar circumstances. In other words, the role of the ALP is to compare an intra-firm transaction with a crucial element, a *comparable* from the open market. The ALP assumes that there will always be an available comparable. Thus, if a given intra-firm transaction is inconsistent with the comparable, tax authorities are generally empowered to adjust the relevant transfer price in order to achieve consistency with that comparable.[9] Disagreements between taxpayers and tax authorities on this adjustment (which includes disagreements as to what constitutes a correct comparable) are the root of transfer pricing disputes around the world.[10]

This chapter is organised into seven sections. Following the introduction, section 2.2 focuses on the core driving forces that explain the demand for a regulation such as the ALP since the early twentieth century. Section 2.3 outlines the 'rule versus standard' conceptual framework. Section 2.4 suggests that the ALP was largely a rule-based regulation by the mid 1930s, that is before the emergence of international trade of intangibles. Section 2.5 shows that a crucial role of the *OECD Transfer Pricing Guidelines for Multinational Enterprises and Tax Administrations* and other similar documents is to facilitate the transition of the ALP from being a self-enforcing rule into a standard-based procedural principle. Section 2.6 focuses on an example of the increasing ALP procedural meaning: the minimum threshold for procedural fairness that the local tax administration should meet when enforcing the ALP, as provided for by the OECD Guidelines. Section 2.7 concludes.

2.2   Demand for the arm's length principle

International trade and institutions are closely related. Empirical research has shown a strong positive correlation between a nation's exposure to

---

[6] See Chapter 8 'United Kingdom'.   [7] See OECD Guidelines, note 2 above, pp. 31–2.
[8] *Ibid.* pp. 31–2.   [9] *Ibid.* p. 32, para. 1.3.
[10] See, e.g., *U.S. Steel Corp. v. Commissioner*, 617 F.2d 942 (2d Cir. 1980). It is analysed in Chapter 3 'United States'.

international trade and the size of its governmental institutions from the 1870s onwards.[11] One possible explanation of this correlation can be termed the 'social insurance motive'. Taxpayers normally demand compensation against risks when their nation's economy is at its most exposed against international economic forces. Governments, in turn, respond by implementing safety nets, for example, social programmes, public employment (more frequent in poor nations) and cross-border institutional frameworks. These institutional frameworks include the tax treaty network which is currently based on the OECD Model Tax Convention on Income and Capital ('OECD Model').[12] The tax treaty network is, in turn, a core building block of the international tax regime.[13]

---

[11] D. Rodrik, *The Globalization Paradox* (Oxford: Oxford University Press, 2011), pp. 16–19. Rodrik argues that, 'Around 1870, the share of government expenditures in the economies of today's advanced economies averaged around 11 per cent. By 1920, this share had almost doubled, to 20 per cent. It increased further, to 28 per cent, in 1960. In the post-1945 period, it stood at more than 40 per cent, and has continued to rise since then. The increase has not been uniform across different countries. Governments are considerably smaller today in the United States, Japan, and Australia [with expenditure shares below 35 per cent] than they are in Sweden or the Netherlands [55–60 per cent], with most of the other European countries in-between.'

[12] R. S. Avi Yonah, *Double Tax Treaties: An Introduction* (University of Michigan Law School, 3 December 2007), available at ssrn.com/abstract=1048441.

[13] The literature on the international tax regime is immense and can be highlighted here. Excellent surveys follow. R. S. Avi–Yonah, *International Tax as International Law: An Analysis of the International Tax Regime* (Cambridge: Cambridge University Press, 2007). Avi–Yonah offers a comprehensive analysis of the international tax regime and its relationship with public international law. Y. Brauner, 'An International Tax Regime in Crystallisation: Realities, Experiences and Opportunities' (2003) 56 *Tax Law Review* 259. Brauner outlines a general conceptual framework to achieve a world tax regime through a multilateral tax treaty that might be implemented in stages. I. Roxan, 'Limits to Globalization: Some Implications for Taxation in the Developing World' (2003). This unpublished paper does not share the negative view of the effects of globalisation on taxation in the developing world. M. Graetz, 'Taxing International Income: Inadequate Principles, Outdated Concepts, and Unsatisfactory Policies' (2001) 54 *Tax Law Review* 261. Graetz argues that the current international income tax regime lacks a satisfactory normative basis. R. Vann, 'International Aspects of Income Tax' in V. Thurongi (ed.), *Tax Law Design and Drafting* (Washington, DC: IMF, 1988), vol. II, ch. 18. Vann provides a detailed discussion of policy, design and drafting issues in international income tax. Tax Law Design and Drafting' in *International Monetary Fund* (1998), vol. 2. R. S. Avi–Yonah, 'The Structure of International Taxation: A Proposal for Simplification' (1996) 74 *Texas Law Review* 1301. Avi–Yonah identifies the structure of international taxation and its normative underpinnings. S. Piccioto, *International Business Taxation: A Study in the Internationalization of Business Regulations* (London: Weidenfeld and Nicolson, 1992). Piccioto offers an historical account of the evolution of corporate income taxation. A. Ogley, *The Principles of International Tax: A Multinational Perspective* (International Information Services Inc., 1993). Ogley provides a brief and illuminating general overview.

International trade entails inherently higher transaction costs than domestic exchanges. The risk of international double taxation is one such example that results in an unforeseen transaction cost. The arm's length principle (ALP), as encapsulated in the tax treaty network, is arguably an attempt to address this transaction cost issue. Indeed, the ALP and connected documents[14] offer a model for a cross-border institutional framework that aims to be functionally equivalent to the safety net in one particular area of international trade: foreign direct investments (FDIs). In other words, the ALP seeks to avoid double taxation in the FDI area as a way to minimise transaction costs in international trade.[15]

Examples of taxpayers' demand for regulations to alleviate international double taxation are found, for instance, in the appeals in 1919 of the International Chamber of Commerce, and at the Brussels Financial Conference in 1920, where it was argued that the newly created League of Nations should do something to eliminate the 'evils' of double taxation.[16] The ALP emerged as a product of these types of demands and pressures exerted by taxpayers.[17]

The ALP is currently provided for in the following two provisions of the OECD Model. Article 9, which is the focus of this book, addresses the problem of transfer pricing in the context of associated enterprises.

---

[14] These include the OECD Guidelines.

[15] See OECD Guidelines, note 2 above, paras. 4.2 and 4.3 (stating that double taxation constitutes a potential barrier to the development of international trade and that the OECD Guidelines aim to avoid this in the area of transfer pricing). Similarly, para. 5.15 states that the documentation requirement should not be construed in such a way as to 'impede international trade and foreign investment'. As Chapter 21 shows, the role of the ALP is also to curb international tax avoidance and evasion.

[16] M.B. Carroll, *Global Perspectives of an International Tax Lawyer* (New York: Exposition Press, 1978), p. 29.

[17] The League of Nations recommended using the ALP as the international standard for addressing the transfer pricing problem. See, e.g., M. B. Carroll, 'Taxation of Foreign and National Enterprises' in *Methods of Allocating Taxable Income* (Geneva: League of Nations, 1933), vol. IV ('Carroll Report'). Indeed, the Carroll Report recommended the ALP as the best available regulation as follows: 'As the conduct of business between a corporation and its subsidiaries on the basis of dealings with an independent enterprise obviates all problems of allocation, it is recommended that, in principle, subsidiaries be not regarded as permanent establishments of an enterprise but treated as independent legal entities; and if it is shown that inter-company transactions have been carried on in such a manner as to divert profits from a subsidiary, the diverted income should be allocated to the subsidiary on the basis of what it would have earned had it been dealing with an independent enterprise.' Carroll Report, para. 628. See also Chapter 21.

The transfer pricing problem where branches are involved is addressed by Article 7 and connected documents.[18]

Article 9 of the OECD Model states the following regarding associated enterprises:

1. Where a) an enterprise of a Contracting State participates directly or indirectly in the management, control or capital of an enterprise of the other Contracting State; or b) the same persons participate directly or indirectly in the management, control or capital of an enterprise of a Contracting State and an enterprise of the other Contracting State, and in either case conditions are made or imposed between the two enterprises in their commercial or financial relations which differ from those which would be made between independent enterprises, then any profits which would, but for those conditions, have accrued to one of the enterprises, but, by reason of those conditions, have not so accrued, may be included in the profits of that enterprise and taxed accordingly.

2. Where a Contracting State includes in the profits of an enterprise of that State – and taxes accordingly – profits on which an enterprise of the other Contracting State has been charged to tax in that other State, and the profits so included are profits which would have accrued to the enterprise of the first-mentioned State if the conditions made between the two enterprises had been those which would have been made between independent enterprises, then that other State shall make an appropriate adjustment to the amount of the tax charged therein on those profits. In determining such adjustment, due regard shall be had to the other provisions of this Convention and the competent authorities of the Contracting States shall, if necessary, consult each other.

Article 9.1 creates a norm that has the following logical structure:

(a) if associated enterprises conclude a transfer pricing transaction;
(b) and that transfer pricing is not consistent with the arm's length principle;
(c) then, the tax authority has jurisdiction to adjust that transfer pricing to make it consistent with the arm's length principle.

The next section explores the logical structure of the ALP in the light of the 'rule and standard' conceptual framework. This analysis aims to determine why the ALP has an evolving meaning over time. This analysis is developed further in Chapter 21 using twenty countries as a case study.

---

[18] *2010 Report on the Attribution of Profits to Permanent Establishment* (OECD, 2010). It is available at www.oecd.org/dataoecd/23/41/45689524.pdf.

2.3   The ALP, rules and standards

All legal systems can be seen as information products because they aim to provide information on the norms applicable to a given society.[19] Interestingly, the government can provide contents to these norms at different times. On the one hand, as is the case for a rule, the content can be provided before an individual act is committed. On the other hand, as is the case for a standard, the content can be prescribed after a certain act, for instance, via case law or something functionally equivalent to case law.[20] Hence, the two different times at which contents to the norms can be given can be said to constitute either an *ex ante* or an *ex post* determination.

Examples of rules can be found in many settings. For instance, a norm requesting 'not to drive in excess of 55 miles per hour' is a rule because its meaning is precise before an individual drives a vehicle. Conversely, the norm 'drive carefully' is a standard because its meaning can only be determined *ex post*.

Rules and standards are different in at least three different dimensions: (i) cost structure; (ii) distribution of power within a legal system; and (iii) institutional assumptions. These three dimensions are discussed below.

First, rules and standards have different cost structures in terms of promulgation costs (i.e., the expenses incurred in the enactment of a norm) and enforcement costs (i.e., the costs arising from applying a norm to a given set of facts). On the one hand, rules normally face high promulgation costs and low enforcement costs. An example of a rule is a tax norm that clearly specifies *ex ante* the taxpayer's expected behaviour. In this sense, rules are expensive to create, but are relatively cheap to apply, given their self-enforcing character.[21] On the other hand,

---

[19] This section is largely based on the following articles: L. Kaplow, 'Rules versus Standards: An Economic Analysis' (1992) 42 *Duke Law Journal* 557; L. Kaplow, 'The Value of Accuracy in Adjudication: An Economic Analysis' (1994) 23 *Journal of Legal Studies* 307.

[20] This includes innovative procedures normally provided for in the tax treaty network for solving international tax disputes, such as the advance pricing agreement. See OECD Guidelines, note 2 above, pp. 23–30.

[21] The concept of self-enforcing normative systems has been applied in different areas of the law. See, e.g., B. Blank and R. Kraakman, 'A Self-Enforcing Model of Corporate Law' (1996) 109 *Harvard Law Review* 8, 1911–82. The self-enforcing normative system minimises the need to rely on administrative agencies and courts for enforcement (*ibid.* 1932).

standards normally face low promulgation costs, but high enforcement costs. An example of a standard is the norm requesting drivers to drive carefully. The enforcement costs of standards are high relative to promulgation costs, because, as said, their content can be determined *ex post* via case law only or something functionally equivalent to case law.[22]

Second, rules and standards imply a different distribution of power within a legal system. While rules originate from a centralised creation of the law (e.g., at the legislative level), standards imply a decentralised creation of the law, for example, where they are created by a decentralised network of judges. By contrast, standards (unlike rules) presuppose a legal system capable of producing case law with public good features, such as case law with a certain minimum of precedential value.[23]

Hence, the 'rule vs standard' conceptual framework includes a dynamic, rather than static, dimension. Indeed, a standard may mutate into a rule (and *vice versa*). For example, the concept 'good faith' in US contract law originally developed as a standard given its lack of precise *ex ante* meaning. Interestingly, the good faith *standard* has gradually transformed into a *rule* given the existence of growing case law which had provided the concept of 'good faith' an increasingly precise *ex ante* meaning.[24]

Conversely, the arm's length principle was a largely self-enforcing, rule-based norm until the late 1960s. It then gradually transformed into a standard-based norm following the emergence of international trade of intangibles and other similar exogenous forces which made finding comparables (a vital element of the rule-based version of the ALP) an increasingly difficult task.[25]

---

[22] An example of sources functionally equivalent to case law are advance pricing agreements. See D. M. Ring, 'On the Frontier of Procedural Innovation: Advance Pricing Agreements and the Struggle to Allocate Income for Cross Border Taxation' (2000) 21 *Michigan Journal of International Law* 192.

[23] Case law is a public good (rather than a private good) if it allows a representative person to predict the probable outcome of a future court's decision. See James M. Buchanan, 'The Limits of Liberty: Between Anarchy and Leviathan' (1974) in *The Collected Works of James M. Buchanan* (Indianapolis: Liberty Fund, 1999–2002), vol. VII, especially in ch. 6 (arguing that legal precedent is a form of social capital having public good characteristics). See also W. Landes and R. Posner, 'Legal Precedent: A Theoretical and Empirical Analysis' (1976) 19 *Journal of Law and Economics* 249 (arguing that the body of legal precedents is a capital stock that yields a flow of information services).

[24] L. Kaplow, 'Rules versus Standards: An Economic Analysis' (1992) 42 *Duke Law Journal* 557.

[25] See Chapter 21.

2.4   The ALP over a century: from a rule to a standard-based norm

As Chapter 21 shows, the ALP has evolved over time. It was first considered a self-enforcing, rule-based norm in the early twentieth century. For example, by the mid 1930s, the Carroll Report had stated the following regarding the character of the ALP:

> As the conduct of business between a corporation and its subsidiaries on the basis of dealings with an independent enterprise obviates all problems of allocation, it is recommended that, in principle, subsidiaries be not regarded as permanent establishments of an enterprise, but treated as independent legal entities; and if it is shown that inter-company transactions have been carried on in such a manner as to divert profits from a subsidiary, the diverted income should be allocated to the subsidiary on the basis of what it would have earned had it been dealing with an independent enterprise.[26]

Carroll's words suggest that the ALP was a largely self-enforcing, rule-based norm, given that finding comparables was a relatively easy task by the mid 1930s when the Carroll Report was published.

Seventy-five years after the publication of the Carroll Report, in 2010, the context had changed substantially given the emergence of exogenous (rather than endogenous) elements, such as the international trade of intangibles; and the OECD Guidelines have consequently acknowledged the increasingly non-self-enforcing character of the ALP.[27] For example, the OECD Guidelines state that: 'applying the arm's length principle can be a fact-intensive process and can require proper judgment. It may present uncertainty and may impose a heavy administrative burden on taxpayers and tax administrations that can be exacerbated by both legislative and compliance complexity.'[28] This uncertainty is in part triggered by the OECD Model failing to provide for a precise *ex ante* meaning to fundamental elements of Article 9.1, such as an 'associated enterprise' or an 'arm's length standard'.

To sum up, the ALP, which was originally a self-enforcing, rule-based norm by the early twentieth century, has transformed into a standard-based procedural regulation. This transformation was a product of increasing difficulty in finding the required comparables, probably owing to the expanding relevance of intangibles in international trade since the emergence of the information economy.[29] This context ultimately created the

---

[26] See Carroll Report note 17 above, para. 628.   [27] See OECD Guidelines, note 2 above.
[28] See *Ibid.* para. 4.93.
[29] See Chapter 21. On the information economy and intangibles, see C. Shapiro and H. R. Varian, *Information Rules* (Boston, MA: Harvard Business School Press, 1999), p. 13.

need for information products aimed at facilitating the ALP transition from a rule to a standard-based procedural principle. The OECD Guidelines is a good example of this.

2.5 OECD Guidelines: towards a procedural meaning for the ALP

The OECD Guidelines lay down the most comprehensive model of legal regulation on transfer pricing to date since the inception of corporate income tax systems at the beginning of the twentieth century. The Guidelines aim to provide an increasingly procedural (rather than substantive) meaning to the ALP as encapsulated in Article 9 of the OECD Model. Indeed, they suggest a model legal regime aimed at facilitating the administration of the ALP, which includes innovative procedures for resolving transfer pricing disputes, such as advance pricing agreements (APAs), mutual agreement procedures, simultaneous tax examinations and tax arbitration.[30]

The OECD Guidelines' institutional framework has been created, and is periodically amended, in a centralised manner by an international institution, the OECD, which aims to reflect overall trends in this area at a global level.[31] After being transplanted to local law, a decentralised network of domestic tax administrations around the world has the role of administering OECD Guidelines-based transfer pricing legal systems.[32] They include a

---

[30] See OECD Guidelines, note 2 above, Glossary 23–30. The APA process is an alternative to the standard taxpayer path of doing the transactions, filing a return, facing an audit (some level of auditing is more likely with larger taxpayers) and, finally, a possible appeal with settlement or litigation. The taxpayer initiates the APA process by approaching the local tax administration (and typically the corresponding tax authority in the other relevant jurisdiction) before engaging in the related party transactions potentially at issue. At this point, the taxpayer voluntarily provides detailed information to the government regarding its business activities, plans, competitors, market conditions and prior tax circumstances. The critical piece of this presentation is the taxpayer's explanation of its planned pricing methods. Following discussion and negotiation, the parties hopefully reach an agreement on how the taxpayer should handle the pricing of these anticipated related transactions. This understanding is embodied in the APA agreement which typically runs for a certain number of years. See Ring, 'On the Frontier of Procedural Innovation', note 22 above.

[31] R. J. Vann, 'Taxing International Business Income: Hard-boiled Wonderland and the End of the World' (2010) *World Tax Journal* 291.

[32] J. M. Josselin and A. Marciano, 'The Making of the French Civil Code: An Economic Interpretation' (2002) 14 *European Journal of Law and Economics* 193. Also R. Cooter, 'Structural Adjudication and the New Law Merchant: A Model of Decentralised Law' (1994) 14 *International Review of Law and Economics* 215.

network of standards setting the minimum thresholds of procedural fairness that local tax administrators are expected to adhere to when enforcing the OECD Guidelines in their jurisdictions.[33]

2.6   OECD Guidelines: the minimum threshold of procedural fairness in transfer pricing disputes

Theories of procedural fairness and procedural rights fall into two broad categories: process-based and outcome-based. Process-based theories evaluate fairness by the ways in which procedures treat litigants within the litigation process itself, independent of the quality of an outcome. Outcome-based theories evaluate fairness against the quality of outcomes the procedural system generates.[34]

The OECD Guidelines set out the minimum threshold of procedural fairness for the proper enforcement of OECD-based transfer pricing legal systems. The OECD-based minimum threshold includes both process-based and outcome-based procedural fairness in this arena. Examples of core process-based fairness elements assumed by the OECD Guidelines include the following four principles:

1. *Equal protection methodology.* This has two strands. The first is focused on equality before the law, e.g., 'taxpayers in identical situations should not be treated differently'.[35] The second strand deals with the proper level of scrutiny in transfer pricing disputes. It is grounded on the prudent business management principle as follows, 'The taxpayer's process of considering whether transfer pricing is appropriate for tax purposes should be determined in accordance with the same prudent business management principle that would govern the process of evaluating a business decision of a similar level of complexity'.[36]
2. *Principle of good faith showing in transfer pricing administration.* This principle is predicated on the assumption that 'a tax administration should be prepared to make a good faith showing to prove that its determination of transfer pricing is consistent with the arm's length principle even when the burden of proof is on the taxpayer'.[37]

---

[33] See E. Baistrocchi, 'Tax Disputes Under Institutional Instability: Theory and Implications' (2012) 75(4) *Modern Law Review* 547.

[34] R. G. Bone, *Civil Procedure: The Economics of Civil Procedure* (New York: Foundation Press, 2003), pp. 189–97.

[35] See OECD Guidelines, note 2 above, p. 179, para. 4.163.   [36] *Ibid.* p. 182, para. 5.4.

[37] *Ibid.* p. 136, para. 4.16.

This principle has both a local and an international dimension. Indeed, the Guidelines provide that tax jurisdictions should administer their transfer pricing rules in a manner that is fair to taxpayers and to other jurisdictions.[38] One implication of this good faith principle is that the tax authorities should properly ground their decisions on transfer pricing. For example, a taxpayer's request for a mutual agreement procedure (MAP) 'should not be rejected without good reason'.[39]

3. *Fairness and proportionality in the application of penalties.* This states that penalties can only be applied if the principle of reasonable effort in good faith is not met. This principle is defined as follows: 'it would be unfair to impose sizeable penalties on taxpayers who have made a reasonable effort in good faith to set the terms of their transactions with associated enterprises in a manner consistent with the ALP'.[40]

4. *Confidentiality.* The Guidelines state the principle of no public disclosure with listed exceptions in the following words: 'Tax administrations should be careful to ensure that there is no public disclosure of trade secrets, scientific secrets, or other confidential data. Tax administrations, therefore, should use discretion in requesting this type of information and should do so only if they can undertake that the information will be kept confidential from outside parties, except to the extent disclosure is required in public court proceedings or judicial decisions. Every endeavour should be made to ensure that confidentiality is maintained to the extent possible in such proceedings and decisions.'[41]

The four principles listed above are the core elements of the system of process-based fairness assumed by the OECD Guidelines for administering OECD-based transfer pricing regimes. They aim to evaluate fairness by the ways in which different procedures treat taxpayers within the transfer pricing dispute resolution process itself, independent of the quality of the outcome. In a similar vein, the OECD Guidelines also assume outcome-based fairness. The focus of this second strand of procedural fairness is the quality of individual outcomes. The OECD Guidelines include one fundamental test here: that tax authorities' decisions on transfer pricing disputes should avoid both double taxation[42] and double non-taxation.[43]

---

[38] *Ibid.* p. 133, para. 4.5.   [39] *Ibid.* p. 148, para. 4.55.   [40] *Ibid.* p. 139, para. 4.28.
[41] *Ibid.* p. 185, para. 5.13.
[42] *Ibid.* p. 145, para. 4.44. For example, para. 4.44 of the OECD Guidelines states that: 'the existence of such time limits and the fact that they vary from country to country should be considered in order to minimise double taxation'.
[43] *Ibid.* p. 175, para. 4.150.

In sum, the OECD Guidelines have laid down the minimum threshold of procedural fairness (both process- and outcome-based) with which a decentralised network of tax administrations around the world should comply when enforcing OECD-based transfer pricing legal systems. Such thresholds of procedural fairness delegate a substantial degree of power to tax administrators through the core principles listed above, which lack clear *ex ante* meanings. The principle of reasonable effort in good faith in the area of the application of penalties illustrates this delegation neatly.

2.7   Conclusion

The process of cross-border corporate decentralisation, which led to the creation of multinational enterprises (MNEs), began in the nineteenth century.[44] MNEs are the consequence of a market failure: the relatively high cost of certain market transactions like the one exemplified above in the area of intangibles. Thus, MNEs attempt to solve such a failure through the internalisation and reduction of these transaction costs.[45]

The arm's length principle offers a model of a cross-border institutional framework that aims to be functionally equivalent to a safety net in one particular area of international trade: foreign direct investments (FDIs). It seeks to avoid international double taxation in the FDI area as a way of minimising transaction costs in international trade.

The ALP has been transforming its character since the beginning of the twentieth century due to exogenous forces. Indeed, it was first a self-enforcing, rule-based regime by the 1930s. As time passed, the character of the ALP has changed substantially due to the exogenous (rather than

---

[44] Picciotto, *International Business Taxation*, note 13 above.

[45] R. Coase, 'The Nature of the Firm' (1937) 4 *Economica* 386, available at onlinelibrary. wiley.com/doi/10.1111/j.1468–0335.1937.tb00002.x/full (last visited 20 June 2011). See also C. N. Pielis and R. Sugden, 'On the Theory of the Transactional Firm' in C. N. Pielis and R. Sugden (eds.), *The Nature of the Transnational Firm* (London / New York: Routledge, 1996), pp. 9–15. There is a theory on why MNEs emerge that differs from the market failure one. This alternative theory maintains that a 'multinational corporation arises not out of the failure of markets for the buying and selling of knowledge, but because of its superior efficiency as an organizational vehicle by which to transfer this knowledge across borders'. See B. Kogut and U. Zander, 'Knowledge of the Firm and the Evolutionary Theory of the Multinational Corporation' (2003) 516 *Journal of International Business Studies* 516 (the cross-border transfer of knowledge theory). The analysis of transfer pricing that follows has similar implications for both the market failure and the cross-border transfer of knowledge theories because the strategic use of transfer pricing could contribute both to solving the market problem issue and facilitating the cross-border transfer of knowledge within the relevant MNE.

endogenous) elements such as the international trade of intangibles.[46] Hence, the ALP is now increasingly a standard-based procedural regime. The ALP is currently grounded on innovative procedures for resolving transfer pricing disputes. The bilateral advance pricing agreement (APA) is a neat example. Moreover, APAs and similar procedures should be applied by a decentralised network of tax administrators around the world meeting the minimum threshold of procedural fairness provided by the OECD Guidelines.

Chapters 3 to 20 offer examples of the evolutionary path of transfer pricing dispute resolution, and the successive versions of the arm's length principle, in twenty countries from the five continents since the inception of corporate income taxation. Chapter 21 then offers a cross-country comparison of this evolutionary path and its core driving forces.

[46] See Chapter 21.

PART II

North America and Europe

Transfer pricing disputes in the United States

REUVEN S. AVI-YONAH

3.1 Introduction

In 1988, the US Treasury Department published a study of inter-company pricing (the 'White Paper') that included the following endorsement of the so-called arm's length standard (ALS) for examining the reasonableness of transactions between related parties for tax purposes:

> The arm's length standard is embodied in all U.S. tax treaties; it is in each major model treaty, including the U.S. Model Convention; it is incorporated into most tax treaties to which the United States is not a party; it has been explicitly adopted by international organizations that have addressed themselves to transfer pricing issues; and virtually every major industrial nation takes the arm's length standard as its frame of reference in transfer pricing cases. The United States should continue to adhere to the arm's length standard.[1]

What is the ALS, and why did the Treasury seek to defend it in these terms? The problem for which the ALS attempts to provide the solution may be illustrated by a simple example. Suppose that a product (e.g., computers) is manufactured by a corporation in country A, and then sold to a wholly-owned subsidiary of the manufacturer in country B, which proceeds to resell it to unrelated customers. In this common situation, the taxable profit of the subsidiary is determined by three factors: (i) the price at which it resells the computers to the unrelated customers, (ii) its expenses other than cost of goods sold, and (iii) the price which it pays its parent corporation for the computers. The first two of these factors are governed by market forces outside the control of the parent or the subsidiary. However, because the parent controls the

---

[1] I.R.S. Notice 88–123, 1988–2 C.B. 458, 475 ('White Paper') (footnotes omitted). For examples of more recent statements along the same lines, see J. Iekel, 'Samuels Defends Revenue Estimating, Arm's Length Standard', 65 *Tax Notes* 1587 (16 December 1994); J. Turro, 'Treasury Continues to Champion Worldwide Arm's Length Standard' 66 *Tax Notes* 316 (16 January 1995).

subsidiary, the third factor (the price for which the manufacturer sells the computers to the reseller, or the 'transfer price') is wholly within the control of the related parties. Accordingly, the potential for abuse arises because the related parties will seek to increase after-tax profits by manipulating the transfer price. If the effective tax rate in the manufacturer's country is higher, the price will be set as low as possible so as to channel all taxable profit to the reseller. Conversely, if the effective tax rate in the reseller's jurisdiction is higher, the transfer price will be as high as possible, so as to eliminate any taxable profit of the reseller and concentrate the entire profit in the hands of the manufacturer. But for tax considerations, the affiliated parties do not care what the transfer price is, since it merely reallocates profits within the affiliated group.

Given these facts, it is understandable that transfer pricing manipulation is one of the most common techniques of tax avoidance. This is especially true in the international sphere, as there are great differences in effective tax rates among jurisdictions. Indeed, some economists have argued that the ability to manipulate transfer prices is a major reason for the existence of multinational enterprises (MNEs), which are groups of affiliated corporations operating in more than one country.[2] It is estimated that trading among such affiliates encompasses about one-third of world manufacturing trade,[3] and that percentage is constantly increasing. The transfer pricing problem is, therefore, one of the major international tax policy challenges for the coming century.

The ALS, as traditionally conceived, responds to the transfer pricing problem by seeking to determine whether transactions between related taxpayers reflect their 'true' tax liability by comparing them to similar transactions between unrelated taxpayers dealing at arm's length. This was the definition of the ALS that was understood when the White Paper was published in 1988.[4] However, as is reflected in the defensive tone of the Treasury's pronouncements, the White Paper was written at a time when this traditional conception of the ALS was coming under increasing criticism and suggestions for its replacement were rampant. In particular, the legislative history of the Tax Reform Act of 1986 indicates

[2] R. Gordon and J. Mackie-Mason, *Why is there Corporate Taxation in a Small Open Economy? The Rule of Transfer Pricing and Income Shifting*, National Bureau of Economic Research Working Paper No. 4690 (1994).

[3] U.S. General Accounting Office, *International Taxation: Problems Persist in Determining Tax Effects of Intercompany Prices* (1992), pp. 62–3.

[4] White Paper, note 1 above, pp. 459–61.

that Congress had mandated that the Treasury Department re-evaluate the continued viability of the ALS.[5] The White Paper was issued in response to this mandate. However, despite the Treasury's findings, the process begun by the Congressional mandate eventually resulted in the abandonment of the ALS, as it was understood in 1988. Its replacement, in the United States and elsewhere, was a broader and more flexible method of determining the allocation of taxable profits between related entities. Although this broader method may also be characterised as 'arm's length', it is a different type of arm's length standard than the one defended by the White Paper. Indeed, the White Paper itself played a major part in the demise of the traditional ALS.

This chapter explores the process by which the traditional ALS became the dominant method for determining transfer prices for tax purposes, the reasons for its eventual downfall, and methods that can be used in its place. First, a few definitional points are in order. The traditional ALS refers primarily to a process by which the transfer price between affiliated taxpayers is determined by using comparables – either of the same product sold by one of the affiliated parties to an unrelated party, or the same product bought by an affiliated party from an unrelated party, or of the same product sold between two parties unrelated to the affiliated parties and to each other. This method of comparison is usually called the 'comparable uncontrolled price', or CUP method.[6] In addition, the traditional ALS also encompasses two methods that likewise rely on comparables, but do not require a transaction in the same product. Under the 'cost plus' method, the transfer price is determined by comparing the manufacturer to a similar entity (under a more relaxed standard of comparability than under the CUP method), which is dealing with unrelated parties, and allocating to the manufacturer the costs borne by the unrelated comparable, plus the unrelated party's profit margin.[7] The 'resale price' method is identical to the cost plus method except that it applies to the reseller rather than the manufacturer.[8]

The ALS, as traditionally conceived, is frequently contrasted with 'unitary', 'global' or 'formulary apportionment' methods, such as those used by some states. Here the entire profit of an affiliated group is allocated among its constituent entities by means of a formula (e.g., based

---

[5] H.R. Conf. Rep. No. 99–841, 99th Cong., 2d Sess. II-638 (1986).
[6] See, e.g., Treas. Reg. s. 1.482–2(e)(2); Treas. Reg. s. 1.482–3(b).
[7] See, e.g., Treas. Reg. s. 1.482–2(e)(4); Treas. Reg. s. 1.482–3(d).
[8] See, e.g., Treas. Reg. s. 1.482–2(e)(3); Treas. Reg. s. 1.482–3(c).

on each entity's assets, payroll and sales).[9] The major difference between the ALS and the formulary method is that the ALS starts by treating each entity in an affiliated group as a separate taxpayer, hypothetically dealing with each other entity in the group at arm's length. Conversely, the formulary approach starts with the entire affiliated group as one unitary enterprise.

This chapter proposes that despite the common practice of contrasting the ALS and the formulary methods of dealing with the transfer pricing problem, they are actually not dichotomous. Instead, they form the two extreme ends of a continuum.[10] The cost plus and resale price methods, which are included in the traditional ALS, already represent one step away from pure separate treatment of each entity in the group. This is because they involve taking the group's profits as a whole, subtracting the profit margin allocable to the manufacturer or the reseller on the basis of the comparables, and then allocating the residual profit to the other party.

Next on the continuum comes the 'comparable profit method' (CPM), which is a major innovation of the recent regulations under

---

[9] For examples of recent contributions to the debate about the ALS and formulary methods, see B. F. Miller, 'None are So Blind as Those Who Will Not See' 66 *Tax Notes* 1023 (13 February 1995); J. Turro, 'The Battle over Arm's Length and Formulary Apportionment' 65 *Tax Notes* 1595 (26 December 1994); W. I. Wilkins and K. W. Gideon, 'Memorandum to Worldwide Formulary Apportionment' 65 *Tax Notes* 1259 (5 December 1994); J. R. Hellerstein, 'Federal Income Taxation of Multinationals: Replacement of Separate Accounting with Formulary Apportionment' 60 *Tax Notes* 1131 (23 August 1993); L. M. Kauder, 'The Unspecific Federal Tax Policy of Arm's Length: A Comment on the Continuing Vitality of Formulary Apportionment at the Federal Level' 60 *Tax Notes* 1147 (23 August 1993); E. J. Coffill and P. Wilson, Jr, 'Federal Formulary Apportionment as an Alternative to Arm's Length Pricing: From the Frying Pan to the Fire?' 59 *Tax Notes* 1103 (24 May 1993); B. F. Miller, 'A Reply to "From the Frying Pan to the Fire"' 61 *Tax Notes* 241 (11 October 1993); R. Avi-Yonah, 'Slicing the Shadow: A Proposal for Updating U.S. International Taxation' 58 *Tax Notes* 1511 (15 March 1993); and L. M. Kauder, 'Intercompany Pricing and Section 482: A Proposal to Shift from Uncontrolled Comparables to Formulary Apportionment Now' 58 *Tax Notes* 485 (25 January 1993). For a recent proposal to implement formulary methods in the context of NAFTA, see P. R. McDaniel, 'Formulary Taxation in the North American Free Trade Zone: A Policy Perspective' (1993–4) 49 *Tax L Rev.* 691.

[10] This idea is stated briefly in B. J. Arnold and T. E. McDonnell, 'Report on the Invitational Conference on Transfer Pricing: The Allocation of Income and Expenses Among Countries' (1993) 61 *Tax Notes* 177, 1381, but is not fully developed there or elsewhere. See Amicus Brief of Council of State Governments, *Barclays Bank PLC* v. *Franchise Tax Board*, 114 S.Ct. 2268 (No. 92–1384) (1994) (a brief by the present writer, outlining this idea in the context of a recent case over the constitutionality of state formulary methods).

section 482 of the Internal Revenue Code ('the Code'), under which the profit of either the manufacturer or the reseller is set by comparing it to the average profit earned by a very broad group of corporations operating in the same or a similar industry.[11] The standard of comparison in this case is very relaxed, and one may indeed regard the CPM as a type of formula designed to ensure that the profits of the related party do not fall outside a reasonable range of profit margins earned by other corporations which are not truly comparable with the related party.[12] As will be shown below, the CPM falls outside the traditional or narrow definition of the ALS, but it still uses some form of comparables.

Even further along on the continuum of possible methods of determining transfer prices is the 'profit split' method. This method was first introduced in the 1988 White Paper.[13] Here, the allocation of profits is determined in two steps. First, the functions performed by each of the related parties are analysed and a market rate of return is allocated to each function on the basis of comparables.[14] Then, the residual profit is split between the related parties on the basis of a formula, without using comparables.[15] The profit split method is very close to the pure formulary apportionment end of the transfer pricing continuum, because it starts with the enterprise as a whole and allocates the profits in a formulary fashion. The only differences are that some of the profits are allocated on the basis of comparables, and that the formula used to split the rest is more flexible than the traditional assets, payroll and sales-based formula used by the states.

Consequently, the words 'arm's length' can be used in two ways to refer to two different possible ranges of solutions to the transfer pricing problem. Under the traditional or narrow definition, 'arm's length' refers to methods of determining transfer prices by using comparables, and encompasses only the CUP, cost plus and resale price methods.[16] On the other hand, 'arm's length' can also be used to refer to any method of determining transfer prices that reaches results (i.e., a profit allocation) that are the same as those that would have been reached between unrelated parties. In this latter, broader sense, 'arm's length' can be used

---

[11] Treas. Reg. s. 1.482–5.   [12] Treas. Reg. s. 1.482–5(c).

[13] White Paper, note 1 above, p. 490. The profit split method has since been adopted as part of the current Treasury Regulations. See Treas. Reg. s. 1.482–6.

[14] Treas. Reg. s. 1.482–6(b).   [15] Treas. Reg. s. 1.482–6(c).

[16] 'Arm's length' does not refer to CPM, because the standard of comparability for CPM is so loose that it is doubtful whether it can truly be regarded as relying on comparables, and it has therefore been excluded from the traditional definition of the ALS.

to refer to the entire transfer pricing continuum, because even pure formulary apportionment may result in the same profit allocation as that which unrelated parties would have reached.

The next four parts of this chapter analyse the origins, rise, decline and fall of the traditional or narrow ALS, as applied to international transactions between related parties under section 482 of the Code and its predecessors.[17] The analysis will show that despite the Treasury's affirmation of the traditional ALS in its 1988 White Paper,[18] this narrow conception of the standard was already obsolete by 1988 in the large majority of cases, insofar as the United States' approach to international taxation was concerned. Subsequent developments, especially the 1992–1995 proposed, temporary and final regulations under section 482 of the Code, merely strengthened the nails in its coffin. The last sections of the chapter will focus on post-1995 litigation and then on the following questions: (1) Why has the traditional ALS proven so inadequate? (2) What methods are now used to supplement it? and (3) What additional improvements can be made in resolving the transfer pricing problem?

3.2   Origins (1917–1928)

Transfer pricing manipulation is one of the simplest ways to avoid taxation. It is, thus, not surprising that the predecessors of section 482 of the Code, legislation designed to combat such manipulation, date back almost as far as the modern income tax itself. They originated in regulation 41, chapters 77 and 78, of the War Revenue Act of 1917, which gave the Commissioner authority to require related corporations to file consolidated returns 'whenever necessary to more equitably determine the invested capital or taxable income'.[19] The earliest direct predecessor of section 482 of the Code dates to 1921, when the Commissioner

[17] The literature on s. 482 is immense. Some major contributions include J. P. Fuller, 'Section 482 Revisited' (1976) 31 *Tax L Rev.* 475; James P. Fuller, 'Section 482: Revisited Again' (1990) 45 *Tax L Rev.* 421; Richard O. Loengard, 'The Section 482 Pot Boils On: Comments on Recent Developments' (1991) 469 *Tax Forum*; Dale W. Wickham, 'The New U.S. Transfer Pricing Tax Penalty: A Solution, or a Symptom of the Cause, of the International Transfer Pricing Puzzle?' (1991) 18 *Int'l Tax J* 1. The best historical survey of the ALS up to 1986 is contained in Stanley I. Langbein, 'The Unitary Method and the Myth of Arm's Length' 30 *Tax Notes* 625 (17 February 1986) (focusing on the development of the ALS in the international context).

[18] See note 1 above and accompanying texts.

[19] T.D. 2694, 20 Treas. Dec. Int. Rev. 294, 321 (1918). See also War Revenue Act of 1917, Ch. 63, 40 Stat. 300 (1917).

was authorised to consolidate the accounts of affiliated corporations 'for the purpose of making an accurate distribution or apportionment of gains, profits, income, deductions, or capital between or among such related trades or business'.[20] This legislation was enacted, in part, because of the tax avoidance opportunities afforded by possessions corporations, which were ineligible to file consolidated returns with their domestic affiliates.[21] Thus, the problem of international tax avoidance through related corporations was one of the original motives for the enactment of the earliest predecessor of section 482 of the Code.[22] In 1928, the provision was removed from the consolidated return provisions (which were eliminated).

3.2.1   Section 45: allocation of income and deductions

In any case of two or more trades or businesses (whether or not incorporated, whether or not organised in the United States, and whether or not affiliated) owned or controlled directly or indirectly by the same interests, the Commissioner is authorised to distribute, apportion or allocate gross income or deductions between or among such trades or businesses, if he determines that such distribution, apportionment or allocation is necessary in order to prevent evasion of taxes or clearly to reflect the income of any of such trades or businesses.[23]

This language is almost identical to section 482 of the Code as it read prior to the Tax Reform Act of 1986.[24] The legislative history of section 45 of the Code, in its entirety, is as follows.

Section 45 is based upon section 240(f) of the 1926 Act, broadened considerably in order to afford adequate protection to the government

---

[20] Revenue Act of 1921, Ch. 136, s. 240(d), 42 Stat. 260 (1921) (re-enacted in Revenue Act of 1924, Ch. 234, s. 240(d), 43 Stat. 288 (1924), and Revenue Act of 1926, Ch. 27, s. 240 (f), 44 Stat. 46 (1926)). Unlike the current IRC s. 482, these earlier provisions allowed taxpayers to request that the Commissioner permit consolidation.

[21] 'Subsidiary corporations, particularly foreign subsidiaries, are sometimes employed to "milk" the parent corporation, or otherwise improperly manipulate the financial accounts of the parent company.' H.R. Rep. No. 350, 67th Cong., 1st Sess. 14 (1921); see also S. Rep. No. 275, 67th Cong., 1st Sess. 20 (1921).

[22] For surveys of the history of IRC s. 482, see White Paper, note 1 above, ch. 2; *Eli Lilly & Co. v. Commissioner*, 84 T.C. 996, 1114–15 (1985).

[23] Revenue Act of 1928, Ch. 852, s. 45, 45 Stat. 806 (1928).

[24] Among the few changes, 'Organizations' was added to 'trades or businesses', 'credits or allowances' were added to 'gross income or deductions', and 'the Secretary or his delegate may' was substituted for 'the Commissioner is authorized to'. See IRC s. 482.

made necessary by the elimination of the consolidated return provisions of the 1926 Act. The section of the new bill provides that the Commissioner may, in the case of two or more trades or businesses owned or controlled by the same interests, apportion, allocate or distribute the income or deductions between or among them, as may be necessary in order to prevent evasion (by the shifting of profits, the making of fictitious sales and other methods frequently adopted for the purpose of 'milking'), and in order clearly to reflect their true tax liability.[25]

Senator Gifford stated on the floor that 'what worries us is that any two of these corporations can get together and take advantage of questionable sales to each other to get deductions'.[26] Senator Green replied that 'Section 45 permits the bureau to allocate the income where it belongs. It ... does not permit these corporations to place the expenses just where they want to put them.'[27]

Congress' focus in enacting the predecessor of section 482 of the Code was, thus, to prevent tax evasion and to clearly reflect 'true' tax liability. However, there was no discussion of what the standard of 'true' liability was. In 1935, the Service issued regulations under section 45 of the Code, which stated that the following standards would govern its application.

3.2.2   Scope and purpose

The purpose of section 45 is to place a controlled taxpayer on a tax parity with an uncontrolled taxpayer, by determining, according to the standard of an uncontrolled taxpayer, the true net income from the property and business of a controlled taxpayer. The interests controlling a group of controlled taxpayers are assumed to have complete power to cause each controlled taxpayer so to conduct its affairs that its transactions and accounting records truly reflect the net income from the property and business of each of the controlled taxpayers. If, however, this has not been done, and the taxable net incomes are thereby understated, the statute contemplates that the Commissioner shall intervene, and, by making such distributions, apportionments or allocations as he may deem necessary of gross income or deductions, or of any item or element

---

[25] H.R. Rep. No. 2, 70th Cong., 1st Sess. 16–17 (1927); see also S. Rep. No. 960, 70th Cong., 1st Sess. 24 (1928).

[26] 69 Cong. Rec. 605, cited in J. Seidman, *Legislative History of Federal Income Tax Laws 1938–1861* (1938), p. 522.

[27] *Ibid.*

affecting net income, between or among the controlled taxpayers constituting the group, shall determine the true net income of each controlled
taxpayer. The standard to be applied in every case is that of an uncontrolled taxpayer dealing at arm's length with another uncontrolled
taxpayer.[28]

Thus, the ALS, under US tax law, was born. This section of the
regulations, in very similar language, remained in effect under section
482 of the Code until the recently-issued modifications.[29]

However, the regulations were not modified to explain what methods
should be used to arrive at an arm's length price until 1968. Previously,
this task was left to the courts.

3.3   Rise (1928–1972)

The early cases applying section 45 of the Code did not mention the
ALS. Instead, they focused on the statutory terms 'evasion of taxes' and
'clear reflection of income'.[30] It was not until the 1935 regulations were
issued, that the arm's length nature of the transaction between related
parties came into focus.[31] However, for a long period thereafter, the
courts applied a wide variety of standards to determine what constituted
a transaction that clearly reflected the taxpayer's income.[32]

Seminole Flavor Co. v. *Commissioner*[33] is a good example of these early
cases. The issue was whether transactions between a corporation and a
partnership organised to market the corporation's products should
be adjusted to shift income from the partnership to the corporation.[34]

---

[28] Art. 45–1(c) of Reg. 86 (1935) (Revenue Act of 1934). The entire regulation is quoted in
Essex Broadcasters, Inc. v. *Commissioner*, 2 T.C. 523, 528 (1943).

[29] Treas. Reg. s. 1.482–1(b)(1) redesignated as Treas. Reg. s. 1.482–1A(b)(1); cf.
Temp. Treas. Reg. s. 1.482–1T(a)(1) and (b) (1993); Treas. Reg. s. 1.482–1(b)(1). See
generally discussion in section 3.5 below. The ALS was adopted under the influence of
concurrent developments in international taxation and the initial evolution of model
standards. See S. I. Langbein, 'The Unitary Method and the Myth of Arm's Length'
(1986) 30 *Tax Notes* 625, 628–34.

[30] See, e.g., *Asiatic Petroleum Co.* v. *Commissioner*, 31 B.T.A. 1152, 1159 (1935) (stating that
a sale was not 'arm's length' but not focusing on this issue); aff'd 79 F.2d 234 (1935).

[31] See, e.g., *G.U.R. Co.* v. *Commissioner*, 41 B.T.A. 223 (1940) (sale of stock at seven times its
market value not arm's length); aff'd 117 F.2d 187 (1940).

[32] See, e.g., *National Securities Corp.* v. *Commissioner*, 137 F.2d 600 (3rd Cir. 1943); cert.
denied 320 U.S. 794 (1943). This leading case for the application of section 45 to tax-free
transfers to corporations surveys the history of s. 45 but does not mention the ALS.

[33] 4 T.C. 1215 (1945).   [34] *Ibid.* 1229.

The Tax Court, in holding for the taxpayer, stated that the arm's length nature of the transaction should be determined by whether it was 'fair and reasonable', and that the question of whether unrelated parties would have entered into the same agreement was irrelevant.[35] It then went on to hold that:

> The commission fixed does not appear to be out of line with petitioner's own experience [i.e., its expenses for marketing prior to forming the partnership]. On this basis the transaction would seem to be fair and entitled to classification as an arm's length transaction. Whether any such business agreement would have been entered into by petitioner with total strangers is wholly problematical.[36]

Other cases from the same period show similar tendencies to apply a variety of standards and to ignore the question of whether comparables exist. The standards employed included whether the transaction was 'fair' on the basis of the functions performed by the parties;[37] whether the related party paid 'full fair value';[38] and whether the prices paid would have been considered 'fair and reasonable' in the trade.[39]

On the other hand, in *Hall* v. *Commissioner*,[40] a somewhat later Tax Court case, a comparable was used to establish the arm's length price. Hall involved sales to a Venezuelan marketing affiliate at cost plus 10 per cent (a price which amounted to a discount of over 90 per cent from the regular list price) when unrelated distributors of the same product received a discount of only 20 per cent.[41] The Tax Court held that gross income had been arbitrarily shifted to the Venezuelan corporation, and that the Commissioner's allocation 'reflected Hall's income as if he had been dealing with unrelated parties. That, of course, was the purpose of the statute.'[42]

The early cases, thus, appear inconsistent in their application of arm's length. The question of whether the ALS should always be applied was

---

[35] *Ibid.* 1232.

[36] *Ibid.* 1233; see also *Palm Beach Aero Corp.* v. *Commissioner*, 17 T.C. 1169, 1176 (1952) ('fair consideration which reflects arm's length dealing').

[37] *Grenada Industries, Inc.* v. *Commissioner*, 17 T.C. 231, 260 (1951), aff'd 202 F.2d 873 (5th Cir. 1953); aff'd 346 U.S 819 (1953).

[38] *Friedlander Corp.* v. *Commissioner*, 25 T.C. 70, 77 (1955); *Motors Securities Co., Inc.* v. *Commissioner*, 11 T.C.M. 1074, 1082 (1952).

[39] *Polak's Frutal Works, Inc.* v. *Commissioner*, 21 T.C. 953, 976 (1954).

[40] 32 T.C. 390 (1959), aff'd 294 F.2d 82 (5th Cir. 1961).   [41] *Ibid.* 410.

[42] *Ibid.* (citing *Asiatic Petroleum Co.* v. *Commissioner*, 31 B.T.A. 1152 (1935), which did not, however, involve a direct application of the ALS).

finally raised in *Frank* v. *International Canadian Corporation*,[43] decided in 1962, which was twenty-seven years after the initial promulgation of the standard in regulations.[44] The case involved transfer prices for sales of chemicals by a US parent to a Western hemisphere trade corporation (WHTC). The parties stipulated that the sales reflected a 'reasonable price and profit' between the two corporations, and the District Court found that the Commissioner had thereby stipulated himself out of court on the section 45 issue.[45] The Commissioner appealed, arguing that the District Court used the 'reasonable return' standard instead of the proper arm's length standard. The Court of Appeals for the Ninth Circuit affirmed in the following terms:

> We do not agree with the Commissioner's contention that 'arm's length bargaining' is the sole criterion for applying the statutory language of section 45 in determining what the 'true net income' is of each 'controlled taxpayer'. Many decisions have been reached under section 45 without reference to the phrase 'arm's length bargaining' and without reference to Treasury Department Regulations and Rulings which state that the talismanic combination of words – 'arm's length' – is the 'standard to be applied in every case'. For example, it was not any less proper for the District Court to use here the 'reasonable return' standard than it was for other courts to use 'full fair value', 'fair price, including a reasonable profit', 'method which seems not unreasonable', 'fair consideration which reflects arm's length dealing', 'fair and reasonable', 'fair and reasonable' or 'fair and fairly arrived at', or 'judged as to fairness', all used in interpreting section 45.[46]

Thus, the Ninth Circuit essentially invalidated the regulations, and held that it was not necessary to establish what unrelated taxpayers would have done in order to clearly reflect the 'true' income and correct tax liability of related parties.[47]

One can only speculate as to what would have happened had the courts been left free to develop their own definition of 'fair' or

---

[43] 308 F.2d 520 (9th Cir. 1962).   [44] See note 28 above and accompanying texts.

[45] *Frank*, note 43 above, 308 F.2d at 528.

[46] *Ibid.* 528–9 (citations omitted) (citing *Friedlander Corp.* v. *Commissioner*, 25 T.C. 70, 77 (1955); *Grenada Industries, Inc.* v. *Commissioner*, 17 T.C. 231, 260 (1951); *Motors Securities Co., Inc.* v. *Commissioner*, 11 T.C.M. 1074, 1082 (1952); *Palm Beach Aero Corp.* v. *Commissioner*, 17 T.C. 1169, 1176 (1952); *Polak's Frutal Works, Inc.* v. *Commissioner*, 21 T.C. 953, 975–6 (1954); and *Seminole Flavor Co.* v. *Commissioner*, 4 T.C. 1215, 1232 (1945).

[47] Cf. Treas. Reg. 86, s. 45–1(b) (1935).

'reasonable' without having to adhere to the ALS.[48] During the same era as the *Frank* decision, major developments were taking place in Washington that would ultimately lead to the establishment of standards under section 482 of the Code (as section 45 of the Code had now been renumbered). The early 1960s were marked by a rise in concern on the part of the Treasury that domestic corporations were achieving deferral through transfer pricing practices with tax haven affiliates, and that foreign corporations were avoiding taxes altogether by artificially lowering the profits of their US affiliates. The Treasury contended that section 482 of the Code was not effectively protecting the US tax jurisdiction.[49]

Congress responded with legislation intended to stop these perceived abuses. Section 6 of H.R. 10650, as introduced by the House Committee on Ways and Means, provided for a new Code section, section 482(b).[50] Under the House proposal, in section 482 cases involving international transfers of tangibles, unless the taxpayer could demonstrate an arm's length price (defined, in accordance with the traditional view, as a price based on a matching or comparable adjustable transaction), or unless the taxpayer and the IRS could agree on a different method, the transfer

---

[48] See, e.g., *Nestle Company, Inc.* v. *Commissioner*, 22 T.C.M. 46, 62 (1963), decided just after *Frank* and before *Oil Base, Inc.* v. *Commissioner*, 23 T.C.M. 1838 (1964), discussed at note 56 below, in which the Tax Court analysed the royalty rate for a valuable intangible (for which no comparables could in any case be found) in an eminently sensible way under a 'reasonableness' standard, including a renegotiation of the rate to reflect profitability, without having to resort to an 'arm's length' analysis. See also *Ballentine Motor Co., Inc.* v. *Commissioner*, 39 T.C. 348, 357 (1962), aff'd 321 F.2d 796 (4th Cir. 1963) ('taxpayers owned or controlled by the same interests may enter into transactions inter se and if fair, or resulting from arm's length bargaining, such transactions will be undisturbed'). This decision was also rendered shortly after *Frank.*

[49] Hearings on the President's 1961 Tax Recommendations Before the Committee on Ways and Means, 87th Cong., 1st Sess., vol. 4 at 3549 (1961) (statement of Commissioner Caplin); see Langbein, 'The Unitary Method and the Myth of Arm's Length', note 17 above, 643–4. These concerns are remarkably similar to those voiced currently. See, e.g., R. L. Kaplan, 'Treasury Blasted over Alleged Transfer Pricing Shenanigans', 55 *Tax Notes* 150 (13 April 1992); R. L. Kaplan, 'International Tax Enforcement and the Special Challenge of Transfer Pricing' (1990) *U Ill. L Rev.* 299.

[50] H.R. 10650, 87th Cong., 2d Sess. s. 6 (1962). Important among the other provisions that were introduced to curb transfer pricing abuses was subpart F, adopted in 1962. IRC s. 952–64. This provision defines the income of controlled foreign corporations that is not eligible for tax deferral and for which dividends to the US parent must be imputed. For a brief overview of the relationship between IRC s. 482 and subpart F, see Kaplan, 'International Tax Enforcement' note 49 above, 307–11.

price would be determined under a formula based on assets, compensation and expenses related to the transferred tangible property.[51]

The House Report explained the intent of section 6 of the bill as follows:

> Present law in section 482 authorizes the Secretary of the Treasury to allocate income between related organizations where he determines this allocation is necessary 'in order to prevent evasion of taxes or clearly to reflect the income of any such organizations'. This provision appears to give the Secretary the necessary authority to allocate income between a domestic parent and its foreign subsidiary. However, in practice the difficulties in determining a fair price under the provision severely limit the usefulness of this power especially where there are thousands of different transactions engaged in between a domestic company and its foreign subsidiary.
>
> Because of the difficulty in using the present section 482, your committee has added a subsection to this provision authorizing the Secretary of the Treasury or his delegate to allocate income in the case of sales or purchases between a U.S. corporation and its controlled foreign subsidiary on the basis of the proportion of the assets, compensation of the officers and employees, and advertising, selling and promotion expenses attributable to the United States and attributable to the foreign country or countries involved. This will enable the Secretary to make an allocation of the taxable income of the group involved (to the extent it is attributable to the sales in question) whereas in the past under the existing section 482 he has attempted only to determine the fair market sales price of the goods in question and build up from this to the taxable income – a process much more difficult and requiring more detailed computations than the allocation rule permitted by this bill.
>
> The bill provides, however, that the allocation referred to will not be used where a fair market price for the product can be determined. It also provides that other factors besides those named can be taken into account. In addition, it provides that entirely different allocation rules may be used where this can be worked out to mutual agreement of the Treasury Department and the taxpayer.[52]

Predictably, the taxpayer community responded by lobbying Congress to remove section 6 from H.R. 10650, claiming that the regulatory authority under section 482 of the Code was sufficient to curb abuses.[53] Their efforts were rewarded in the Senate version of the bill, which

---

[51] H.R. 10650, 87th Cong., 2d Sess. s. 6 (1962).

[52] H.R. Rep. No. 1447, 87th Cong., 2d Sess. 28 (1962).

[53] See, e.g., Hearings on H.R. 10650 before the Senate Committee on Finance, 87th Cong., 2d Sess. 560–1, 725–6 (1962) ('Hearings') (statements by W. Slowinski and R. Landolt).

omitted the section. In conference, the House receded. The Conference Report states the reasons as follows:

> The conferees on the part of both the House and the Senate believe that the objectives of section 6 of the bill as passed by the House can be accomplished by amendment of the regulations under present section 482. Section 482 already contains broad authority to the Secretary of the Treasury or his delegate to allocate income and deductions. It is believed that the Treasury should explore the possibility of developing and promulgating regulations under this authority which would provide additional guidelines and formulas for the allocation of income and deductions in cases involving foreign income.[54]

The Treasury took three years to respond to this invitation.[55] In the meantime, however, significant new developments were taking place in the courts. *Oil Base, Inc.* v. *Commissioner*[56] represented a classic case of the application of the ALS to sales commissions paid by a US corporation to its Venezuelan marketing affiliate. These commissions were about twice the amount that the same corporation had paid its previous unaffiliated distributor of the same product in Venezuela, and were twice the amount it was currently paying to distributors in other countries. The taxpayer, however, argued that the *Frank* standard should be applied instead of arm's length, and that since it still retained higher profits from export sales to Venezuela even after the double commission than from domestic sales, the commissions were 'reasonable' under *Frank*. The Tax Court, in a memorandum decision, disagreed. It held that:

> It is unnecessary for us to decide whether the sole standard in cases under section 482 is one of an amount which would be arrived at in arm's length transactions between unrelated parties. The commissioner has been given much latitude in his use of section 482 when necessary to prevent the evasion of Federal income tax by shifting of profits between taxpayers subject to common control. The burden is on petitioner to show error in respondent's allocation. There is no evidence to show that the percentage return retained by petitioner on domestic sales would represent a

---

[54] H.R. Rep. No. 2508, 87th Cong, 2d Sess. 18–19, reprinted in 1962 U.S.C.C.A.N. 3732, 3739.

[55] Regulations, which did not accept the invitation to use a formula approach, were proposed in 1965, Prop. Treas. Reg. ss. 1.482–1(d) and 2, 30 Fed. Reg. 4256 (31 March 1965) (these regulations did not include any provisions on sales of tangibles), withdrawn and reproposed in 1966, Prop. Treas. Reg. ss. 1.482–1(d) and 2, 31 Fed. Reg. 10394 (31 March 1966), and issued in final form in 1968, Treas. Reg. s. 1.482. See discussion at note 71 below.

[56] *Oil Base, Inc.* v. *Commissioner*, 23 T.C.M. 1838 (1964).

reasonable return on export sales. There is likewise no evidence to show that the amount of commissions and discounts paid to Oil Base, Vene-zuela, represented a reasonable amount, a fair amount, or an amount which would meet any of the other criteria referred to by the Court in *Frank*. Certainly the fact that these commissions are almost double those paid by petitioner to unrelated persons in arm's length transactions is evidence that they were not fair and reasonable.[57]

Presumably, the taxpayer in *Oil Base* was encouraged to litigate, despite the egregious facts, because appeal lay to the Ninth Circuit. On appeal, the taxpayer, citing *Frank*, repeated the argument that the Commissioner erred in applying a standard of arm's length bargaining that was not in the statute. The Court of Appeals, however, held that the application of arm's length was appropriate:

> We cannot agree. Where, as here, the extent of the income in question is largely determined by the terms of business transactions entered into between two controlled corporations it is not unreasonable to construe 'true' taxable income as that which would have resulted if the transactions had taken place upon such terms as would have applied had the dealings been at arm's length between unrelated parties.
>
> *Frank* v. *International Canadian Corporation* [308 F.2d. 520 (9th Cir. 1962)], did not hold that the arm's length standard established by regu-lation was improper. It held that it was not 'the sole criterion' for determining the true net income of each controlled taxpayer. However, permissible departure from the regulation's arm's length standard was, under the facts of that case, very narrowly limited and the holding has no application to the facts before us.
>
> We conclude that the arm's length bargaining standard was properly applied pursuant to regulation. *Hall* v. *Comm'r*, 294 F.2d 82 (5th Cir. 1961).[58]

In a footnote, the Ninth Circuit specified that Frank only applied in cases where (a) there was no evidence of an arm's length price, and (b) because of the 'complexity of the circumstances ... it would have been difficult for the court to hypothesize an arm's length transaction.'[59] It is difficult to reconcile this reading of *Frank* with the list of possible standards given by the *Frank* panel four years earlier, which relegated the ALS to a very minor role. In effect, the Ninth Circuit overruled *Frank*, holding that the ALS must be applied not only when comparables exist,

[57] *Ibid.* 1845–6 (citations omitted).
[58] *Oil Base, Inc.* v. *Commissioner*, 362 F.2d 212, 214 (9th Cir. 1966) (footnote omitted).
[59] *Ibid.* 214; see also note 5 above.

but also when they do not exist, as the court can 'hypothesise' a comparable. This abrupt reversal was very likely influenced by the egregious facts of *Oil Base* and by the difficulties in applying a 'reasonableness' standard. It also seems likely that the Tax Court and the Ninth Circuit were influenced by the perception of widespread abuse as a result of the Washington hearings on the Revenue Act of 1962, and by the endorsement of the Commissioner's powers in the legislative history of that Act.[60]

The Commissioner's victory in *Oil Base* was followed by a series of cases which applied the ALS, although not always to the Commissioner's satisfaction. In *Johnson Bronze Co. v. Commissioner*,[61] the taxpayer formed an international marketing subsidiary in Panama for the majority of its foreign sales accounts. The Commissioner reallocated 100 per cent of the subsidiary's income to the parent under section 482 of the Code. The Tax Court held that the 100 per cent allocation was arbitrary and unreasonable.[62] In determining the proper allocation, the court held that 'the standard to be applied in every case is that of an uncontrolled taxpayer dealing at arm's length with another uncontrolled taxpayer'.[63] In a footnote, the court referred to *Frank* as requiring a choice between the 'reasonable' and 'arm's length' standards, but stated that 'on this subject we shall only say that, on the facts of this case, the only reasonable price charged by petitioner would be one which would have been arrived at if the parties were at arm's length'.[64] The court then held that the allocation should be based on the prices charged by unrelated parties that bought the same products from the taxpayer for resale in foreign markets.[65]

Eli Lilly & Co. v. Commissioner,[66] the first of several section 482 cases involving pharmaceutical manufacturers, involved transfer pricing between Eli Lilly & Co. (Lilly) and its subsidiary which qualified as a WHTC. The Commissioner based his reallocation on the profit earned by Lilly on sales to domestic distributors, arbitrarily divided in half to reflect volume discount. The Claims Court agreed, holding that Lilly's contention that it should be allowed to benefit from the tax subsidy to

---

[60] See Hearings, note 53 above, 3549; Langbein, 'The Unitary Method and The Myth of Arm's Length', note 17 above, 643–4.
[61] 24 T.C.M. (CCH) 1542 (1965).   [62] *Ibid.* 1556.
[63] *Ibid.* (citing Treas. Reg. s. 1.482–(b)(1)).
[64] *Ibid.* 1556 and see note 3 above (1965) (*Oil Base* is not cited).
[65] *Ibid.* 1557.   [66] 372 F.2d 990 (1967).

WHTCs 'would require the court to ignore the provisions of Treas. Reg. 1.482–1', requiring the application of the ALS. This is because if the subsidiary were unrelated it would not have been able to retain all the profit on the sales.[67]

Lilly then cited *Frank*, in arguing that its allocation was motivated by business purposes and was 'fair' and 'reasonable', and thus that the ALS should not control. The Court of Claims disagreed:

> The Ninth Circuit has since indicated that only a very narrow departure from the arm's length standard was allowed in the particular circumstances of *Frank* [citing *Oil Base*]. Moreover, even accepting Eli Lilly's interpretation that *Frank* establishes a criterion of a fair and reasonable price, such a price can best be determined by hypothesizing to an arm's length transaction. The thrust of section 482 is to put controlled taxpayers on a parity with uncontrolled taxpayers. Consequently, any measure such as 'fair and reasonable' or 'fair and fairly arrived at' must be defined within the framework of 'reasonable' or 'fair' as among unrelated taxpayers. Simply because a price might be considered 'reasonable' or 'fair' as a business incentive in transactions among controlled corporations, does not mean that unrelated taxpayers would so consider it. Thus, even if the arm's length standard is not the sole criterion, it is certainly the most significant yardstick.[68]

The problem, as the taxpayer pointed out, is that in the absence of any comparables, it is unclear how the arm's length price should be 'hypothesised'. To this question, the Court of Claims gave no answer. It rejected the comparables offered by Lilly (bulk sales to government agencies) because the market was not comparable, yet accepted the revenue agent's arbitrary decision to cut the profits of the Western hemisphere trade affiliates by half because the results were 'reasonable'.[69] When examining the outcome, it is hard to see what relevance the ALS had to the court's ultimate determination.[70]

In 1968, the regulations under section 482 of the Code were finalised, and thereafter, they formed the starting point of the analysis in the courts.[71] With few changes, these regulations applied to transfer pricing until the temporary regulations became effective in April 1993.[72] Despite

---

[67] *Ibid.* 997.   [68] *Ibid.* 1000.   [69] *Ibid.* 997.

[70] See also *Young & Rubicam, Inc.* v. *United States*, 410 F.2d 1233 (1969) (applying the ALS to services on the basis of *Eli Lilly* and *Oil Base*, but doing so without comparables).

[71] T.D. 6952, 1968–1 C.B. 218 (1968). See S. S. Surrey, 'Treasury's Need to Curb Tax Avoidance in Foreign Business Through Use of 482' (1968) 28 *J. Taxation* 75 (discussing the policy behind these regulations).

[72] See T.D. 8470, 1993–1 C.B. 90 (1993).

the invitation in the legislative history of the 1962 Act, the Treasury made no attempt to devise 'formulas' to apply section 482 of the Code.[73] Instead, for the first time, the regulations attempted to establish rules for applying the ALS to specific types of transactions, but with different degrees of specificity.[74] For services, the regulations merely recited the ALS without any guidance as to its application in the absence of comparables.[75] For intangibles, the regulations contemplated a failure to find comparables. They list twelve factors to be taken into account, but without establishing any priority or relative weight among them.[76]

The greatest detail was given for transfers of tangible property. Treasury Regulation section 1.482–2(e) described the three methods that should be used in determining an arm's length price: the comparable uncontrolled price (CUP) method, the resale price method, and the cost plus method, in that order of priority.[77] All three methods relied on finding comparable transactions, either directly or by reference to appropriate mark-ups.[78] In the absence of comparables, the regulations stated that:

> Where none of the three methods of pricing . . . can reasonably be applied under the facts and circumstances as they exist in a particular case, some appropriate method of pricing other than those described in subdivision (ii) of this subparagraph, or variations on such methods, can be used.[79]

The courts were, therefore, left free to determine their own 'fourth methods' in the absence of comparables.

These regulations effectively ensured that the courts would apply the ALS. A 1970 case, *Woodward Governor Co.* v. *Commissioner*,[80] may have represented the last challenge to the standard. The taxpayer organised foreign subsidiaries to act as marketing agents for overseas sales of

---

[73] This may have been the result of Assistant Secretary Surrey's adherence to the ALS. The Treasury may also have felt that it lacked the authority to promulgate a formulary system. See Langbein, 'The Unitary Method and the Myth of Arm's Length', note 17 above, 648.

[74] On the 'radical' nature of the regulations and their departure from earlier models see Langbein, *ibid*. 645–6. These regulations underlay the successful US attempt to establish the ALS as the international 'norm', as reflected in the White Paper, note 1 above and accompanying texts. See Langbein, *ibid*. 646–54.

[75] Treas. Reg. s. 1.482–2(b)(3).   [76] Treas. Reg. s. 1.482–2(d)(2).

[77] Treas. Reg. s. 1.482(e)(1)(ii).   [78] Treas. Reg. s. 1.482–2(e)(2)–(4).

[79] Treas. Reg. s. 1.482–2(e)(1)(iii). This language did not appear in the 1966 version of the regulations, which did not say what should be done in the absence of comparables. See Prop. Treas. Reg. s. 1.482–2, 31 Fed. Reg. 10394 (1966).

[80] 55 T.C. 56 (1970).

aircraft parts. The Commissioner applied the resale price method in reallocating income to the taxpayer. The taxpayer argued that the regulations were invalid in their requirement that the ALS should govern all cases. In the alternative, they argued that if the ALS should be applied, the CUP method should be used on the basis of sales of the same parts to General Electric. The Tax Court accepted the latter argument and therefore did not reach the former.[81]

In the meantime, other courts were finding that the ALS must be applied in section 482 cases. *Baldwin-Lima-Hamilton Corp.* v. *United States*[82] involved transfer pricing between the taxpayer and its WHTC subsidiary. The Commissioner reallocated all of the income of the subsidiary to the taxpayer. The district court held that the reallocation was arbitrary, and upheld the taxpayer's allocation based on pricing studies using assumptions that were 'tipped in the taxpayer's favor', by using inappropriate comparables.[83] The Court of Appeals reversed in part, and remanded to the district court for partial reallocation on the basis of the ALS, stating that the district court 'should reject those aspects of the [taxpayer's] theories which do not meet the arm's length standard'.[84]

United States Gypsum Co. v. *United States*,[85] involved two section 482 issues: shipping fees paid by the taxpayer to its Panamanian subsidiary and transfer pricing for goods sold by the taxpayer to its WHTC. The district court held for the taxpayer on both issues. On the shipping issue, it held that the amounts were 'reasonable and ... equal to an arm's length charge' because they were 'within the range' of unrelated party prices (based on comparables).[86] On the transfer pricing issue, the district court held that even though the prices were arbitrarily set to shift income to the WHTC, on the basis of cases like *Frank* and *Polak's Frutal* which allowed similar mark-ups, the prices were 'not unreasonable' (which the district court considered to be automatically equivalent to arm's length).[87]

The Court of Appeals for the Seventh Circuit affirmed the first holding and reversed the second.[88] On the shipping issue, the Seventh Circuit had considerable misgivings as to whether the alleged

---

[81] *Ibid.* 65–8.   [82] 435 F.2d 182 (1970).   [83] *Ibid.* 186–7.   [84] *Ibid.*
[85] 304 F.Supp. 627 (N.D. Ill. 1969), aff'd in part and rev'd in part, 452 F.2d 445 (7th Cir. 1971).
[86] *Ibid.* 634.   [87] *Ibid.* 644–5.
[88] *U.S. Gypsum Co.* v. *United States*, 452 F.2d 445, 449 (7th Cir. 1971).

comparables were indeed comparable, and whether unrelated parties would not have adjusted the terms of the contract once the profits that the shipping subsidiary was making became clear, but affirmed under a 'clearly erroneous' standard.[89] On the transfer pricing issue, the Seventh Circuit reversed, rejecting the district court's reliance on *Frank* and its predecessors and its application of a 'reasonableness' standard:

> We do not consider the cited cases helpful in deciding whether, as a matter of fact, USG's prices to [the WHTC] were the same as would have been reached in arm's length dealing. Insofar as these cases support a proposition that there may be 'reasonable' prices, different from those which would have been reached in arm's length dealing, which will result in clearly reflecting the income of controlled taxpayers, we respectfully decline to follow them.[90]

Thus, the Seventh Circuit held, as argued by the Commissioner, that applying the ALS was mandatory in all section 482 cases.[91] Two other cases from approximately the same period illustrate the courts' determination to adhere to the ALS even when the Commissioner attempted to apply a different standard. *PPG Industries, Inc.* v. *Commissioner*[92] involved the application of section 482 of the Code to a Swiss marketing subsidiary of a US manufacturer of glass, paint and chemical products. The Tax Court held for the taxpayer on the grounds that (a) the Commissioner's original allocation, based on the *Source Book of Statistics of Income*, was arbitrary and did not meet the ALS;[93] (b) most of the taxpayer's sales were at arm's length prices based on comparables;[94] and (c) the Commissioner's comparable for the remaining sales was inappropriate, and the taxpayer's allocation was 'fair' and 'reasonable' and therefore met the arm's length standard.[95]

Ross Glove Co. v. *Commissioner*[96] represents the application of section 482 of the Code to an inbound transaction, involving the sale of sheepskins to the taxpayer by a Bahamian corporation which also provided sewing services. The Commissioner attempted to hold the taxpayer to its representations to the Philippine authorities, regarding the mark-up on

---

[89] *Ibid.* 448–9.   [90] *Ibid.* 449.   [91] *Ibid.*   [92] 55 T.C. 928 (1970).
[93] *Ibid.* 993.   [94] *Ibid.* 994–5.
[95] *Ibid.* 997–8. The *PPG Industries* case is significant in two other respects: it represents an early attempt by the Commissioner to deviate from the ALS and to use industry statistics (prefiguring the current Treasury regulations), and it represents an early case of functional analysis and profit split by the court (prefiguring the White Paper).
[96] 60 T.C. 569 (1973).

its costs for currency control purposes. The Tax Court rejected this argument and held that 'there is nothing in section 482 or the regulations thereunder to indicate that the arm's length standard of section 482 is to be ignored simply because of representations made in foreign countries'.[97] The court then determined the transfer price on the basis of arbitrary adjustments to an approximate comparable.[98]

Finally, perhaps the greatest triumph for the ALS came in *Lufkin Foundry and Machine Co. v. Commissioner.*[99] The case involved transfer pricing between the taxpayer and its WHTC. The taxpayer introduced evidence regarding the reasonableness of its marketing arrangements, and the Tax Court held for it on that basis.[100] The Commissioner appealed, citing the need to meet the ALS and arguing that no evidence regarding a taxpayer's internal operations could satisfy the standard on its own.[101] The Fifth Circuit held for the Commissioner, stating that:

> No amount of self-examination of the taxpayer's internal transactions alone could make it possible to know what prices or terms unrelated parties would have charged or demanded. We think it palpable that, if the [arm's length] standard set by these unquestioned regulations is to be met, evidence of transactions between uncontrolled corporations unrelated to Lufkin must be adduced in order to determine what charge would have been negotiated for the performance of such marketing services.[102]

The courts came a long way. A mere decade before *Lufkin*, the *Frank* court had declared that, contrary to the regulations, the ALS was only one of many possible criteria under section 482.[103] It then became the sole criterion, set by 'unquestioned' regulations, and any attempt to establish transfer prices without referring to comparables was invalid. Little guidance, however, was given on what to do in the absence of comparables; and in light of his failed attempts in *PPG Industries* and *Ross Gloves* to use evidence that was not based on the ALS, the Commissioner may well have wondered whether his victory in *Lufkin* could turn out to be a pyrrhic one.

---

[97] *Ibid.* 599. Note that the ALS has by now, in the view of the Tax Court, been incorporated into the statute. This is also evidenced by a series of related cases in which the Commissioner attempted unsuccessfully to hold the taxpayer to customs valuations. See, e.g., *Brittingham v. Commissioner*, 66 T.C. 373 (1976), aff'd 598 F.2d 1375 (5th Cir. 1979); *Dallas Ceramic Co. v. United States*, 74–2 USTC (CCH) 19830 (N.D. Tex. 1974), rev'd 598 F.2d 1382 (5th Cir. 1979).

[98] *Ross Glove Co.*, note 96 above, 60 T.C. at 602.   [99] 468 F.2d 805 (5th Cir. 1972).

[100] *Ibid.* 806–7.   [101] *Ibid.*   [102] *Ibid.* 808.

[103] See note 46 above and accompanying texts.

3.4   Decline (1972–1992)

The period between 1972 (when *Lufkin* was decided) and 1992 (when the proposed section 482 regulations were issued) can be described as a gradual realisation by all parties concerned, but especially Congress and the IRS, that the ALS, firmly established by 1972 as the sole standard under section 482, did not work in a large number of cases, and in other cases its misguided application produced inappropriate results. The result was a deliberate decision to retreat from the standard while still paying lip service to it. This process, which began with the 1986 amendments to section 482, was exacerbated by the White Paper in 1988, and culminated in the proposed section 482 regulations of 1992, the temporary section 482 regulations of 1993, and the final section 482 regulations of 1994, which essentially eliminated the traditional ALS for the great majority of section 482 cases.

The decline of arm's length can be illustrated by comparing major international section 482 cases decided prior to 1973, with major cases decided after 1973 and prior to 1993. Relative to the cases of the pre-1973 era, comparables were infrequently found in the later cases.[104]

---

[104] If one takes only the cases surveyed in the White Paper, note 1 above, and the few major cases decided between 1988 and 1992, one finds that up to 1973, the ALS based on comparable transactions was employed in nine of fourteen cases (64%). From 1974 onward, comparables were found only in four of thirteen major s. 482 cases (31%). In all of these four cases (*Eli Lilly & Co.* v. *Commissioner*, 856 F.2d 855 (7th Cir. 1988); *Paccar, Inc.* v. *Commissioner*, 85 T.C. 754 (1985); *U.S. Steel Corp.* v. *Commissioner*, 617 F.2d. 942 (2d Cir. 1980); and *Bausch & Lomb Inc.* v. *Commissioner*, 933 F.2d 1084 (2d Cir. 1991)) the Service argued that the comparable was inappropriate, and in *U.S. Steel* and *Bausch & Lomb*, it attempted to reverse the result in the proposed and temporary regulations. The White Paper cites the following cases decided prior to 1973: *National Securities Corp.* v. *Commissioner*, 137 F.2d 600 (3rd Cir. 1943), cert. denied, 320 U.S. 794 (1943); *Hall* v. *Commissioner* 294 F.2d 82 (5th Cir. 1961); *Nestle Co., Inc.* v. *Commissioner*, 22 T.C.M. 46 (1963); *Oil Base, Inc.*, 362 F.2d 212 (9th Cir. 1966); *Johnson Bronze Co.*, 24 T.C.M. 1542 (1965); *Eli Lilly & Co.*, 372 F.2d 990 (1967); *Young & Rubicam, Inc.* v. *United States*, 410 F.2d 1223 (1969); *U.S. Gypsum Co.*, 452 F.2d 445 (7th Cir. 1971); *Woodward Governor Co.*, 55 T.C. 56; *Baldwin-Lima-Hamilton Corp.*, 435 F.2d 182 (1970); *PPG Industries Inc.*, 55 T.C. 928 (1970); *Lufkin Foundry and Machine Co.*, 468 F.2d 805 (5th Cir. 1972); *Ross Glove Co.*, 60 T.C. 569 (1973); and *R.T. French Co.* v. *Commissioner*, 60 T.C. 836 (1973). The White Paper cites the following cases decided after 1974: *Dallas Ceramic Co.* v. *United States*, 598 F.2d 1382 (5th Cir. 1979); *Cadillac Textiles, Inc.* v. *Commissioner*, 34 T.C.M. 295 (1975); *Edwards* v. *Commissioner*, 67 T.C. 224 (1976); *E.I. DuPont de Nemours & Co.* v. *United States*, 608 F.2d 445 (Ct. Cl. 1979); *U.S. Steel Corp.* v. *Commissioner*, 617 F.2d 942 (2d Cir. 1980); *Hospital Corp. of America* v. *Commissioner*, 81 T.C. 520 (1983); *Eli Lilly & Co.* v. *Commissioner*, 856 F.2d 855 (7th

The causes for this decline in the application of arm's length are complex, and are discussed more fully in section 3.5. Part of the explanation, of course, is that after the courts accepted the ALS, cases where comparables could easily be found were less likely to get litigated. But the fact that litigation proliferated nonetheless suggests that in too many cases the ALS was not workable. In order to understand why, it is necessary to examine the major section 482 cases from the last two decades.[105]

Consider first some major cases in which a comparable was found. *R.T. French Co.* v. *Commissioner*,[106] decided in 1973, illustrates one type of problem that the IRS encountered in applying arm's length. In *French*, the taxpayer, a US subsidiary of a UK parent, negotiated a royalty rate for the parent's valuable patented process for producing instant mashed potatoes in 1946, for a twenty-one-year period. This was before the profitability of the process was known and when there was an unrelated 49 per cent minority shareholder in the parent. In 1960, when the minority shareholder had been bought out and the process had proved extremely profitable, the licensing contract was amended, but the royalty rate remained unchanged for the duration of the contract.[107]

Cir. 1988); *Ciba-Geigy Corp.* v. *Commissioner*, 85 T.C. 172 (1985); *Paccar, Inc.* v. *Commissioner*, 85 T.C. 754 (1985); *G.D. Searle & Co.* v. *Commissioner*, 88 T.C. 252 (1987). Major cases decided between 1988 and the issuance of the proposed regulations in 1992 are *Bausch & Lomb, Inc.* v. *Commissioner*, 933 F.2d 1084 (1989); *Sunstrand Corp.* v. *Commissioner*, 96 T.C. 226 (1991); *Merck & Co. Inc.* v. *United States*, 24 Cl.Ct 73, 91–2 USTC 150,456, at 89,736 (1991). Of these cases, comparables were used only in *U.S. Steel*, *Eli Lilly* (for one year), *Paccar* and *Bausch & Lomb*.

The White Paper reports that in international examinations generally, 'fourth methods' were used 36 per cent of the time, see White Paper, note 1 above, p. 502, and that other estimates of this figure range from 14 per cent to 47 per cent. *Ibid.* 463. However, the most telling number is that in an astounding 91 per cent of the cases examined, the taxpayers did not use comparables in establishing transfer prices. *Ibid.* 502. See also US General Accounting Office, *IRS Could Better Protect U.S. Tax Interests in Determining the Income of Multinational Corporations* (1981) pp. 29 (finding that of 403 cases studied, in dollar terms, the CUP method based on direct comparables accounted for only 3 per cent of the adjustments).

[105] The following discussion is based on cases decided between 1973 and the issuance of the proposed regulations in 1992. Since 1992, there have been several more s. 482 cases based on the old regulations, and the results have been similar to those described in the text. However, the IRS has been slightly more successful, as the litigating skills utilised in s. 482 cases have improved. See, e.g., *Perkin-Elmer Corp.* v. *Commissioner*, 66 T.C.M. (CCH) 634 (1993); *Seagate Technology, Inc.* v. *Commissioner*, 102 T.C. 149 (1994); and *National Semiconductor Corp.* v. *Commissioner*, 67 T.C.M. (CCH) 2849 (1994).

[106] 60 T.C. 836 (1973).   [107] *Ibid.* 838–9.

The Service argued that unrelated parties would have amended the royalty rate so that it would be commensurate with the income derived from the patent, and that the low rates of the contract resulted in constructive dividends to the UK parent, which should be subject to withholding.[108] The Tax Court disagreed. It held that the original 1946 contract was negotiated at arm's length because of the 49 per cent minority shareholder in the UK parent: 'The position of [the minority shareholder] in the scheme of things in all likelihood assured the arm's length character of the transaction.'[109] Thereafter, the fact that profitability changed 'in no way detracted from the reasonableness of the agreement when it was made', and there was no basis for a section 482 adjustment 'so long as the "arm's length" test is met. There is no reason to believe that an unrelated party in [the parent's] position would have permitted petitioner to avoid its contractual obligations.'[110]

French illustrates the fallacy of relying entirely on the arm's length nature of the original contract, when the economic results are clearly disproportionate to the parties' expectations when that contract was signed. The Service found itself in the position of having to argue against the ALS it had espoused for so long, citing as its primary authority a case (*Nestle*) that was decided in the short interval between *Frank* and *Oil Base*, when the standard was not established as the main criterion for section 482. Not surprisingly, the Tax Court found this hard to accept after the Service had worked so hard to establish arm's length as the standard in all section 482 cases.[111] It took thirteen years and the 1986 Tax Reform Act to reverse the result of *French*.

U.S. Steel Corp. v. *Commissioner*[112] illustrates another type of problem that is recurrent in applying arm's length: the difficulty of comparing intragroup with outside transactions, even when the same product or service is involved. U.S. Steel owned a Liberian subsidiary, Navios, which it used to ship steel from Venezuela to the United States. The prices charged by Navios were set at a level that would make the steel price equal to the price of domestic steel manufactured by U.S. Steel, and the same price was charged by Navios for shipping for unrelated corporations, albeit at much lower quantities.[113] As a result Navios had high profits which were totally exempt from tax. In Tax Court, the Service successfully upheld its reallocation of US $52 million in profits to the taxpayer.[114]

---

[108] *Ibid.* 836–7 (citing *Nestle Co., Inc.* v. *Commissioner*, 22 T.C.M. (CCH) 46 (1963)) (the Service was in the unusual position of arguing that royalties to a foreign parent were too low).

[109] *Ibid.* 851.   [110] *Ibid.* 852–4.   [111] *Ibid.* 849–50.

[112] 617 F.2d 942 (2d Cir. 1980).   [113] *Ibid.* 945.   [114] *Ibid.* 942.

The taxpayer appealed and the Court of Appeals for the Second Circuit reversed. The court held:

> We are constrained to reverse because, in our view, the Commissioner has failed to make the necessary showings that justify reallocation under the broad language of section 482 ... The Treasury Regulations provide a guide for interpreting this section's broad delegation of power to the Secretary, and they are binding on the Commissioner ... [citing the ALS] This 'arm's length' standard ... is meant to be an objective standard that does not depend on the absence or presence of any intent on the part of the taxpayer to distort his income ... We think it is clear that if a taxpayer can show that the price he paid or was charged for a service is 'the amount which was charged or would have been charged for the same or similar services in independent transactions with or between unrelated parties' it has earned the right, under the Regulations, to be free from a section 482 reallocation despite other evidence tending to show that its activities have resulted in a shifting of tax liability among controlled corporations.[115]

The court thus concluded that the only issue was the comparability of Navios' transactions with those of unrelated parties. It held that they were comparable, despite the differences in volume and the assurance of continued service as a result of the parties' relationship, and despite the taxpayer's ability to manipulate the prices of the steel so as to leave a larger profit to the tax exempt shipper.[116] The court stated that:

> Attractive as this argument is in the abstract, it is a distortion of the kind of inquiry the Regulations direct us to undertake. The Regulations make it clear that if the taxpayer can show that the amount it paid was equal to 'the amount which was charged ... for the same or similar services in independent transactions' he can defeat the Commissioner's effort to invoke section 482 against him.[117]

The court rejected the Commissioner's argument that transactions with 'independent' parties are only relevant in a competitive market and not where U.S. Steel had a *de facto* monopoly, holding that this would impose an 'unfair' burden on the taxpayer. Finally, it addressed the Tax Court's attempt to return to a reasonableness standard:

> In at least one portion of Judge Quealy's opinion, however, it appears that the reason he relied upon to hold Navios' charges too high is not at all a matter involving the comparison of rates Steel paid to those paid by other steel companies. He said that what the rates paid by Steel must be measured

---

[115] *Ibid.* 947.   [116] *Ibid.* 949–50.   [117] *Ibid.* 949.

against in order to see if a section 482 reallocation is justified is 'what might be a reasonable charge for a continuing relationship involving the transportation of more than 10 million tons of iron ore per year'. If this is indeed the inquiry, then the fact that other steel companies paid Navios the same rates Steel did is irrelevant. We are constrained to reject this argument. Although certain factors make the operations undertaken by Navios for Steel unique – at one point, for example, Navios' ore carriers were the largest of their kind in the world – the approach taken by the Tax Court would lead to a highly undesirable uncertainty if accepted. In very few industries are transactions truly comparable in the strict sense used by Judge Quealy. To say that Pittsburgh Steel was buying a service from Navios with one set of expectations about duration and risk, and Steel another, may be to recognize economic reality; but it is also to engraft a crippling degree of economic sophistication onto a broadly drawn statute, which – if 'comparable' is taken to mean 'identical', as Judge Quealy would read it – would allow the taxpayer no safe harbor from the Commissioner's virtually unrestricted discretion to reallocate.[118]

Given the history of the ALS, it is hard to see how the court could have reached a different conclusion; the 'reasonableness' standard used by the Tax Court had, by 1980, been officially pronounced dead for sixteen years.[119] However, the Service's frustration at being thus hoist by its own petard is understandable, as is its subsequent attempt to reverse *U.S. Steel* in regulations.[120] The continued vitality and extensive effect of both *French* and *U.S. Steel* was illustrated in one of the major recent section 482 cases, *Bausch & Lomb, Inc.* v. *Commissioner.*[121] In *Bausch & Lomb*, the taxpayer (B&L) licensed its unique process for manufacturing soft contact lenses to an Irish tax haven manufacturer (B&L Ireland) and charged a royalty of 5 per cent. The Irish subsidiary manufactured the lenses for US $1.50 each and sold them to the taxpayer for US $7.50 each – the same price charged by unrelated parties with much higher manufacturing costs for the same product.[122]

The Commissioner's proposed adjustments included eliminating the royalty (on the theory that B&L Ireland was a contract manufacturer assured of a market for its sales) but adjusting the income to give B&L Ireland its costs plus a profit of 20 per cent.[123] The Tax Court held that

---

[118] *Ibid.* 950–1 (footnotes omitted).
[119] *Oil Base, Inc.* v. *Commissioner*, 23 T.C.M. (CCH) 1838, 1845–6 (1964); see notes 58–9 above and accompanying text.
[120] See Prop. Treas. Reg. s. 1.482–2(e)(2)(ii); Temp. Treas. Reg. s. 1.482–1T(e)(3)(iii); Temp. Treas. Reg. s. 1.482–3T(b)(2)(ii)(B), (iv); Treas. Reg. s. 1.482–1(d)(3)(ii)(C).
[121] 92 T.C. 525 (1989).   [122] *Ibid.* 525, 580.   [123] *Ibid.* 580–1.

these adjustments were an abuse of discretion. In an 86-page long opinion it first rejected the Service's 'contract manufacturer' analysis on the grounds that there was no contractual obligation by B&L to purchase the product (as if such an obligation was needed between related parties!).[124] Then, the Tax Court held that the transfer price was correct on the basis of the unrelated sales, despite the economic differences (volume differences, integrated business differences, and the fact that B&L had much lower production costs than its competitors) between the alleged comparables:

> We find that use of the comparable uncontrolled price method of determining an arm's length price is mandatory. The third-party transactions identified by petitioner provide ample evidence that the $7.50 per-lens price charged by B&L Ireland is equal or below prices which would be charged for similar lenses in uncontrolled transactions. We place particular reliance on the Second Circuit's opinion in *U.S. Steel*. To posit that B&L, the world's largest marketer of soft contact lenses, would be able to secure a more favorable price from an independent manufacturer who hoped to establish a long-term relationship with a high volume customer may be to recognize economic reality, but to do so would cripple a taxpayer's ability to rely on the comparable uncontrolled price method in establishing transfer pricing by introducing to it a degree of economic sophistication which appears reasonable in theory, but which defies quantification in practice.[125]

The court then rejected the argument from disparities of volume and from the taxpayer's lower costs, holding that the US $7.50 price was 'a market price' and therefore the taxpayer had 'earned the right to be free of adjustment' under *U.S. Steel*.[126] In the second part of its opinion, the Tax Court applied *French* and held that the subsequent profitability of the intangible was irrelevant for establishing a royalty rate, even though the licensing agreement in *Bausch & Lomb* (unlike the one in *French*) was terminable at will.[127] Accordingly, the court rejected the taxpayer's 5 per cent and the Service's 27–33 per cent rates and, since there were predictably no comparables, arbitrarily set its own rate at 20 per cent.[128]

The Commissioner appealed and the Second Circuit affirmed.[129] It admitted that 'the Commissioner's position is not without force', but held that under the regulations and the ALS, applying the

---

[124] *Ibid.* 584.   [125] *Ibid.* 589–91.   [126] *Ibid.* 592–3.   [127] *Ibid.* 601.
[128] *Ibid.* 594–611.   [129] *Bausch & Lomb*, note 121 above, 933 F.2d at 1084.

comparable uncontrolled price method was mandatory, even though economic reality may differ:

> The position urged by the Commissioner would preclude comparability precisely because the relationship between B&L and B&L Ireland was different from that between independent buyers and sellers operating at arm's length. This, however, will always be the case when transactions between commonly controlled entities are compared to transactions between independent entities.[130]

The IRS position would, in effect, 'nullify' the CUP method. The court thus felt compelled to affirm that, under the regulations, as long as the ALS governed, uneconomic results would have to be upheld even though transactions between related parties cannot realistically be compared to arm's length transactions. But if that is the case, why should the ALS apply?[131]

French, U.S. Steel and *Bausch & Lomb* illustrate a major problem in applying the ALS: if inexact comparables are used because the market had changed,[132] or because the relationship between the parties makes for a different nature of transaction,[133] the ALS leads to results that are completely unrealistic as an economic matter.[134] Why, then, were the courts in these cases so avid to find that comparables were controlling? The regulations and precedents applying the ALS provide only partial answers. The main reason was the courts' stated awareness of the morass they would be getting into by seeking to determine transfer prices in the absence of comparables. Decisions (not based on comparables) that

---

[130] *Ibid.* 1091.

[131] The Second Circuit also affirmed the Tax Court's 'best judgment' royalty determination under a 'not clearly erroneous' standard. The Second Circuit's opinion in *Bausch & Lomb*, as well as the Claims Court's opinion in *Merck & Co.* v. *United States*, 24 Cl. Ct. 73 (1991), 91–2 USTC 150,456, in effect declare that the ALS is economically if not legally inapplicable to an integrated multinational. See below.

[132] See *R.T. French Co.*, note 106 above, 60 T.C. at 836; *Bausch & Lomb*, note 121 above, 933 F.2d at 1084.

[133] See *U.S. Steel Corp.*, note 112 above, 617 F.2d at 942; *Bausch & Lomb*, note 121 above, 933 F.2d at 1084.

[134] Even when the comparables are closer, many adjustments are usually needed. In *Eli Lilly & Co.* v. *Commissioner*, 84 T.C. 996, 1176–86 (1985), for the one year in which a comparable existed, the Tax Court discussed the necessary adjustments over 11 pages, and reached the conclusion that a 66 per cent discount from the 'comparable' price was needed! But cf. *Paccar, Inc.* v. *Commissioner*, 85 T.C. 754 (1985) (Tax Court accepted the taxpayer's proposed comparable with only minimal adjustments).

cover hundreds of pages only to reach unpredictable and arbitrary results seem to justify this conclusion.

Cadillac Textiles v. *Commissioner*[135] is an early example of the courts' predicament in a domestic section 482 case. The case involved commissions paid by the taxpayer to a related entity for weaving. The taxpayer relied on the comparability of these commissions to those paid to unrelated entities.[136] The Tax Court, in a memorandum opinion, held that the alleged comparables were dissimilar because of volume differences and because there was no commitment for a continuing relationship – precisely the same factors that should have been applied in *U.S. Steel* and *Bausch & Lomb*.[137] However, having properly struck down the comparables, and having rejected the Commissioner's allocation as 'heavy handed', the court was faced with the necessity of making an arbitrary determination of the transfer price:

> Where some allocation is justified, if the respondent fails to follow a reasonable method in making such allocation, the Court must substitute its judgment ... Unfortunately, this places upon the Court the burden of decision without having all the facts ... Looking to the combined profits of both enterprises, and applying [a value added] factor, it is the Court's conclusion that there should be allocated to the petitioner under section 482 ... the sum of $100,000 [instead of $193,045.37, as proposed by the Commissioner].[138]

The Tax Court thus applied a 'profit split', the method later advocated by the White Paper[139] and ultimately specified in the current regulations.[140] However, as the round figures indicate,[141] the result was largely arbitrary. In the absence of any guidance in the regulations, the court had little choice. This explains why other courts were so reluctant to abandon any comparable, if one could be found.[142]

---

[135] 34 T.C.M. (CCH) 295 (1975).

[136] *Ibid.* 305 (citing Treas. Reg. s. 1.482–2(b)) (defining the arm's length allocation for the performance of services).

[137] *Ibid.* 305–6.

[138] *Ibid.* 306.   [139] White Paper, note 1 above, p. 490.   [140] Treas. Reg. s. 1.482–6.

[141] *Cadillac Textiles Inc.*, note 135 above, 34 T.C.M. at 306.

[142] See, e.g., *Edwards* v. *Commissioner*, 67 T.C. 224 (1976). In *Edwards*, another domestic s. 482 case, the Commissioner argued for a profit split, and the Tax Court rejected this suggestion as incompatible with the ALS, but relied on profits from an uncontrolled sale: 'The focus is not, as suggested by respondent, on determining an acceptable or reasonable overall gross profit percentage, but is on determining an arm's length price for the sale or sales in question by using the gross profit percentage established in an uncontrolled sale.' *Ibid.* 236–7.

The first major international section 482 case from this period, *E.I. DuPont de Nemours & Co. v. United States*,[143] was a major victory for the Service. The facts in *DuPont* were particularly favourable to the Service, since the taxpayer admitted that it had set transfer prices with its tax haven (Swiss) marketing subsidiary, DISA, with no reference to anything but maximising DISA's profitability. An internal *DuPont* memo discovered by the Service read:

> It would seem to be desirable to bill the tax haven subsidiary at less than an 'arm's length' price because: (1) the pricing might not be challenged by the revenue agent; (2) if the pricing is challenged, we might sustain such transfer prices; (3) if we cannot sustain the prices used, a transfer price will be negotiated which should not be more than an 'arm's length' price and might well be less; thus we would be no worse off than we would have been had we billed at the higher price.[144]

In the face of these facts, the taxpayer attempted to show that DISA met the resale price method of the regulation. The court easily rejected this argument:

> We have itemized the special status of DISA – as a subsidiary intended and operated to accumulate profits without much regard to the functions it performed or their real worth – not as direct proof, in itself, supporting the Commissioner's reallocation of profits under Section 482, but instead as suggesting the basic reason why plaintiff's sales to DISA were unique and without any direct comparable in the real world … the vital prerequisite for applying the resale price method is the existence of substantially comparable uncontrolled resellers … there is nothing in the record showing the degree of similarity called for by the regulation.[145]

The court, having rejected the taxpayer's comparables (drawn largely from general industry averages and the IRS *Sourcebook of Statistics of Income*), was faced with the necessity of either determining its own transfer price, or accepting the Service's allocation. Unlike the court in *Cadillac Textiles*, this court decided to take the easier route and accept the Service's position:

> The amount of reallocation would not be easy for us to calculate if we were called upon to do it ourselves, but Section 482 gives that power to the Commissioner and we are content that his amount (totaling some $18 million) was within the zone of reasonableness.[146]

---

[143] 608 F.2d 445 (Ct. Cl. 1979).   [144] *Ibid.* 447.
[145] *Ibid.* 449–51.   [146] *Ibid.* 455.

In determining reasonableness, the court relied on ratios of gross income to total operating costs for functionally similar corporations, and on rates of return for 1,100 corporations in general,[147] thus prefiguring the methods of the recently issued proposed, temporary and final regulations.[148] However, there was no suggestion that this reallocation constituted an application of the ALS. The opinion drew a spirited concurrence from Judge Nichols, who pointed out some of the problems with the court's approach:

> The evidence referred to supports [the result] in the weakest possible way, [we are] making bricks without straw. Assuming, still, that no formula prescribed by regulation can be used, if the Commissioner adheres in court to his original method, it would seem we would have to affirm him unless we thought his choice of method arbitrary and capricious. It is not surprising, therefore, that taxpayer's able counsel here put all his chips on the regulatory resale price method, to the virtual exclusion of any reliance on any 'fourth method', really a chaos of any and all methods. Whether the involved regulations leave too many cases for the fourth method is a question the court touches on lightly. The congressional request to write regulations to govern these section 482 reallocations is one sentence long: [']It is believed that the Treasury should explore the possibility of developing and promulgating regulations under this authority [section 482] which would provide additional guidelines and formulas for the allocation of income and deductions in cases involving foreign income.['] Clearly the result of our decision is that this has not been done in respect to the reallocation here involved, and it remains in the almost if not wholly unreviewable discretion of the Treasury, as it was when the suggestion was made. [The Treasury] should not have discretion to decide how much money anyone should have to pay to support the government.[149]

DuPont was the last major international section 482 decision in which the Service was the clear victor. The 1980s, starting with the Second Circuit's reversal in *U.S. Steel*, saw a series of section 482 related disasters for the IRS. In 1983, for instance, the Tax Court decided *Hospital Corp. of America v. Commissioner*.[150] Here, the taxpayer formed a Cayman Islands subsidiary to perform a contract to manage a hospital in Saudi Arabia. The subsidiary (LTD) performed 'minimal' functions, and all the

---

[147] *Ibid.* 456.
[148] Treas. Reg. s. 1.482–5; Temp. Treas. Reg. s. 1.482–5T (1993); Prop. Treas. Reg. s. 1.4822 (f), 57 Fed. Reg. 3571 (30 January 1992).
[149] *E.I. DuPont de Nemours & Co.*, note 104 above, 608 F.2d at 461–2.
[150] 81 T.C. 520 (1983).

substantial work on the contract was done by the taxpayer. The Commissioner argued that LTD was a sham, or alternatively, that all of its income should be allocated to the taxpayer.[151] The Tax Court, in an 82-page opinion, rejected both arguments. It held that LTD was not a sham because it 'actually carried on some minimal amount of business activity' and had officers and directors who negotiated the contract, even though the same persons were also officers and directors of the taxpayer.[152] On the section 482 issue, the court held that the Commissioner abused his discretion by the 100 per cent allocation, because this represented a repetition of the 'sham' argument.[153] Since there were no comparables suggested by any side, the court was forced to make an arbitrary profit split determination:

> Even though we have rejected respondent's 100 percent allocation of taxable income from LTD to petitioner, the evidence indicates overwhelmingly that an allocation is necessary and proper in this case. Unfortunately, there is little quantitative evidence in this record upon which we can determine what a reasonable allocation of profits would be. Neither party has been particularly helpful to the Court in this regard. However, we must do the best with what we have. Using our best judgment on the lengthy and inconclusive record before us, we have concluded and found as a fact that 75 percent of the taxable income of LTD in 1973 was attributable to petitioner.[154]

While a 75 per cent allocation may seem favourable to the Service, on the facts of the case, a 100 per cent allocation would have been justified, since LTD, in effect, performed no economic functions whatsoever. Not surprisingly, the proposed regulations attempted to reverse the result in this case.[155] The next debacle for the Service was *Eli Lilly & Co.* v. *Commissioner*,[156] which resulted in a particularly length Tax Court opinion of 196 pages. *Lilly* was one of a series of cases concerning transfers, by pharmaceutical giants, of valuable patents developed as a result of extensive domestic research and development in the United States. Thereafter, the patents were transferred on a tax-free basis to Puerto Rican subsidiaries who could reap their rewards and benefit from

---

[151] *Ibid.* 577.   [152] *Ibid.* 578–87.   [153] *Ibid.* 592–5.   [154] *Ibid.* 596–601.

[155] See Treas. Reg. s. 1.482–2(b)(8) (intangible regulations should apply in such cases of services combined with know-how); Preamble to Prop. Treas. Reg. s. 1.482–2(e) (30 January 1992).

[156] 84 T.C. 996 (1985), aff'd in part, rev'd in part and remanded, 856 F.2d 855 (7th Cir. 1988).

Puerto Rico's tax haven status. As an economic matter, there was no justification for letting the Puerto Rican subsidiary reap the rewards of the research done by the taxpayer without paying any royalty or other consideration for the patents.[157]

The taxpayer organised the subsidiary, Lilly P.R., in 1965, after having developed certain extremely lucrative patented processes. It transferred the patents to Lilly P.R., which relied on the patents to become the sole manufacturer of two drugs, Darvon and Darvon-N. Lilly P.R. then sold these drugs to the taxpayer, who in turn marketed the products throughout the United States.[158] The Commissioner reallocated the entire income from the patents to the taxpayer, arguing that Lilly P.R. was a mere contract manufacturer and that its ownership of the intangibles should be disregarded. The Tax Court rejected this approach, holding that the legal ownership of the intangibles could not be disregarded.[159] It also rejected the Commissioner's argument that the separation of income from expenses to create the patents led to a distortion, mainly because the expenses were incurred largely in the 1950s, long before the transfer, and had been recovered previously.[160]

The Tax Court then reached the issue of proper transfer pricing under the ALS. The prices paid by the taxpayer were such that it could not use the profits to fund its current R&D. The Tax Court held that this was unacceptable: 'It is inconceivable that petitioner, negotiating at arm's length, would have transferred valuable income-producing intangibles without a royalty, lump-sum payment, or other agreement that would enable petitioner to continue its general research and development activities.'[161] Thus, some section 482 allocation was necessary. However, as the drugs had been patented for two of the years in question, there were no comparables. Hence, the three regular methods (CUP, cost plus and resale price) were inapplicable. Having rejected both parties' expert witnesses, the court was obliged to determine an arbitrary 'reasonable profit split' based on the functions performed by the parties. Under the profit split, the court allocated to Lilly P.R. 100 per cent of manufacturing costs plus location savings, and 55 per cent of its income from marketing intangibles.[162] The result was a reallocation to the taxpayer

---

[157] See generally, J. T. Hexner and G. P. Jenkins, 'Puerto Rico and Section 936: A Costly Dependence' (1995) 10 *Tax Notes Int'l* 235 (discussing the relationship between transfer pricing and tax benefits for subsidiaries of US corporations, operating in Puerto Rico).

[158] *Eli Lilly & Co.*, note 156 above, 84 T.C. at 996.

[159] *Ibid.* 1123.   [160] *Ibid.* 1126.   [161] *Ibid.* 1130.   [162] *Ibid.* 1151, 1167.

of US $23 million for the 1971–2 tax years, instead of US $53 million as advocated by the Commissioner.[163]

Both parties appealed. The Court of Appeals for the Seventh Circuit reached a result which was even more favourable to the taxpayer.[164] It rejected the Tax Court's argument that Lilly would not have transferred the patents to an unrelated party without getting enough consideration to fund its ongoing R&D, holding that the stock of Lilly P.R. received by the taxpayer, together with distribution rights and technical assistance contracts, constituted sufficient consideration.[165] The Court of Appeals, nevertheless, approved the profit split method as 'not unreasonable', but remanded for an adjustment that did not require Lilly P.R. to participate in the taxpayer's R&D expenses.[166] It took the 1986 amendments to section 482 to reach a more economically reasonable result.[167]

The Service fared even worse in *G.D. Searle & Co.* v. *Commissioner,*[168] the companion case to *Lilly.* Like Lilly, Searle transferred drug patents to its Puerto Rican subsidiary (SCO) for no consideration; however, SCO subsequently manufactured and sold the drugs to unrelated parties so no transfer price issue was involved. The Tax Court rejected the Service's attempt to ignore the transfer of the intangibles and allocate the income to the taxpayer by treating SCO as a contract manufacturer.[169] The court then held that some consideration for the transfer was necessary as the intangibles accounted for 80 per cent of the taxpayer's income and transferring the patents to an unrelated party solely for stock would be 'the height of corporate mismanagement'.[170] As there were no comparables, the Tax Court was required to use its arbitrary 'best judgment' and allocated to the taxpayer US $29 and US $34 million for the two years in question (25 per cent of SCO's total net sales), compared to the US $92 and US $110 million sought by the Service.[171] Significantly, the court did not attempt to characterise this result as the product of an arm's length allocation; instead, the court reasoned 'arm's length consideration for section 482 purposes is that which results in a clear reflection of income'.[172] This remarkable tautology (the standard for clear reflection is arm's length, and arm's length is whatever results in clear reflection) marks a low point in the courts' attempts to apply the ALS in the absence of arm's length transactions.

---

[163] *Ibid.* 1107, 1167.   [164] *Eli Lilly & Co.,* note 104 above, 856 F.2d at 855.
[165] *Ibid.* 863.   [166] *Ibid.* 871–2.   [167] See discussion below.
[168] 88 T.C. 252 (1987).   [169] *Ibid.* 366–7.   [170] *Ibid.* 370.   [171] *Ibid.* 376.
[172] *Ibid.* 375.

The Service fared equally badly in its attempts to avoid the results of its own regulations in *Ciba-Geigy Corp. v. Commissioner*,[173] an inbound section 482 case. The case involved the appropriate rate of royalty to be paid by the taxpayer to its Swiss parent under an exclusive licence in which all the significant R&D had been done at the parent level. The Service argued the taxpayer was engaged in a joint venture with the parent and should have paid a lower royalty than 10 per cent or, alternatively, the arm's length rate was lower. The taxpayer argued for a higher royalty than 10 per cent. The Tax Court rejected the Service's attempts 'to deflect the thrust of his own "transfer or use of intangible property" regulations . . . which to respondent's discomfiture fit this case like a glove'.[174] Having rejected both parties' proposed comparables (because of different degrees of risk and the uniqueness of the relationship), the court held that the 10 per cent rate was reasonable, based on the 'substantial negotiations' between the related parties[175] and the testimony of an unrelated party who would have paid between 10 and 12.5 per cent for a non-exclusive licence.[176] The Service's position in this case seems unreasonable, and a higher royalty rate should have been allowed, based on the unexpected profitability of the patent, the difference between exclusive and non-exclusive licences, and the fact the parent performed the R&D.

The same arbitrariness and disregard for economic reality persists in two other recent section 482 cases which were decided, like *Bausch & Lomb*, after the publication of the White Paper: *Sundstrand Corp. v. Commissioner*[177] and *Merck & Co. Inc. v. United States*.[178] *Sundstrand* involved the licence of valuable manufacturing technology for aircraft spare parts to the taxpayer's Singapore subsidiary which in turn sold the parts to the taxpayer for distribution. The Service again attempted to apply its contract manufacturer analysis which seems appropriate because the subsidiary did not develop the product and was guaranteed, although not formally, to sell its products to the taxpayer (the airlines actually refused to buy from the subsidiary directly). The Tax Court, relying on *Bausch & Lomb*, rejected this analysis and also rejected all of the taxpayer's and the Service's proposed comparables.[179] Having criticised the parties for their 'contentiousness' and lack of cooperation,[180] the court made its own 'best estimate' of the appropriate transfer price,

---

[173] 85 T.C. 172 (1985). [174] *Ibid.* 222. [175] *Ibid.* 237. [176] *Ibid.* 226.
[177] 96 T.C. 226 (1991). [178] 24 Cl. Ct. 73 (1991).
[179] *Sundstrand*, note 104 above, 96 T.C. at 356–7. [180] *Ibid.* 374.

relying on the discounts given by the taxpayer on other products and on its representations to US Customs.[181] These bases seem both arbitrary and unrelated to the issue facing the court. With respect to the royalty, the court again rejected all comparables and arbitrarily fixed a rate of 10 per cent.[182]

Merck & Co. Inc. v. United States,[183] a case similar to G.D. Searle, is yet another recent section 482 defeat for the Service. In Merck, the taxpayer developed drugs and transferred the patents to its Puerto Rican subsidiary, MSDQ, which manufactured and sold the drugs to unrelated parties. The Service argued MSDQ should have paid the taxpayer a royalty for its R&D and marketing assistance. The Claims Court rejected the Service's position in its entirety, and ordered a refund to the taxpayer of US $5 million, plus interest.[184] The court recognised the location of the patents within the group had no business consequences,[185] but held the transfer of the intangibles valid.[186] The court found no continued royalty was required since the costs of R&D had been recovered before the transfer.[187] The court further found that the taxpayer did not provide any marketing services to MSDQ, despite the overlap of officers and directors and the functional integration between the two companies.[188] The court recognised, as an economic matter, that its decision was untenable, but felt obliged to make it in view of the 'all or nothing' positions of the parties.

For tax years 1972 through 1976, MSDQ reported taxable income that totalled US $181,802,000. Federal income tax paid was US $657,000. The pricing process that produces such disparity between costs of production and end-product prices, and permits the accumulation of retained earnings that amount to 98.82 percent of all reported taxable income, may be economically unjustified or socially unacceptable. Such results may underscore infirmities in the controls to be expected in regulated pharmaceutical markets. Such results do not establish a distortion of income as to MSDQ. Such problems cannot be addressed through section 482, under the statute and regulations as presently written.[189]

Thus, the court ignored the analysis in G.D. Searle, that no party would transfer the intangibles to an unrelated party without

---

[181] Ibid. 374–5.   [182] Ibid. 395.   [183] 24 Cl. Ct. 73 (1991).   [184] Ibid. 91.
[185] Ibid. 84–5.   [186] Ibid. 85.   [187] Ibid. 86.   [188] Ibid. 88.
[189] Ibid. 91. For another example of a court, this time the Tax Court, interposing its judgment over that of the Service in an R&D context, see Westreco, Inc. v. Commissioner, 64 T.C.M. (CCH) 849 (1992).

consideration.[190] Although this seems facially unjustifiable, any attempt to find the proper royalty rate (if required, since there could be no comparables) in the absence of 'some formula or method'[191] must have appeared equally frustrating to the court. What makes *Merck* remarkable is that arm's length analysis did not enter the court's opinion at all. The only issue discussed was whether Merck performed R&D and marketing functions for MSDQ, not whether it would have transferred the patents to an unrelated party. By ignoring arm's length, the Claims Court in effect held the standard is inapplicable to an integrated multinational enterprise like Merck, which can shift its intangibles around as it wishes.[192]

Merck and *Bausch & Lomb* thus mark the end of a process in which the ALS became increasingly irrelevant to section 482 cases. The result demonstrated that the then governing statute and regulations required changing to reflect the economic reality of multinationals. Since 1982, this task has been undertaken by Congress and the Service in the recent proposed, temporary and final regulations, leading to the abandonment of the traditional and narrow ALS for the vast majority of section 482 cases.

3.5   Fall (1992–1994)

In 1982, Congress began closing some of the loopholes that were evident in the section 482 cases. The Tax Equity and Fiscal Responsibility Act (TEFRA) altered the treatment of income attributable to intangible assets owned or leased by possessions corporations benefitting from

---

[190]   *G.D. Searle*, note 104 above, 88 T.C. at 370

[191]   *Merck*, note 178 above, 24 Cl. Ct. at 86.

[192]   In *Proctor & Gamble Co.* v. *Commissioner*, 95 T.C. 323 (1990), aff'd, 961 F.2d 1255 (6th Cir. 1992), the Tax Court reversed the Commissioner's s. 482 royalty allocation from P&G Spain to its Swiss parent, which had provided P&G Spain with substantial technical assistance, because P&G Spain was forbidden from paying royalties under Spanish law. This case illustrated the irrelevance of the ALS; clearly, no unrelated party would have provided the assistance to P&G Spain knowing it could not be paid under Spanish law. The issue under s. 482 should be the economic allocation of income, not whether a royalty could by paid. For a similar result under even more egregious circumstances, see *Exxon Corp.* v. *Commissioner*, 66 T.C.M. (CCH) 1707 (1993), where the Tax Court refused to allow the Service to allocate intercompany oil sales between Exxon subsidiaries based on Saudi Arabian price controls set, at the time, below the prevailing market price. *Ibid.* 1760. Exxon thus escaped the effect of the price restrictions on its income allocation despite demonstrations made by the Service that Exxon had flouted those restrictions. *Ibid.* 1752–60.

section 936 of the Code. TEFRA amended section 936 to provide that such income would be treated as income of the corporation's US share-holders unless the corporation elected to make cost sharing payments to its parent or to split the profit from products produced in the possession of the parent on an equal basis.[193] In passing TEFRA, Congress sought to redress the distortion of income resulting from the separation of R&D activity and the income derived from the intangible.[194] Thus, the specific Puerto Rican affiliate problem of *Lilly, G.D. Searle* and *Merck* was addressed, but only for post-1982 transfers with no inference regarding prior law.

The next step was taken in the Deficit Reduction Act of 1984, which amended section 367(d) to treat a tax-free transfer of intangibles to related foreign corporations as a sale of the intangible for annual pay-ments over the useful life of the property contingent on its productivity, use or disposition.[195] However, no inference was intended for licences of intangibles, which continued to be governed by section 482. By 1985, Congress realised *U.S. Steel* and *Lilly* indicated something should be done about the general application of section 482 of the Code, beyond the specific issues of Puerto Rican corporations or transfers to foreign affiliates. The House Report on House Bill 3838 states the problem as follows:

> Many observers have questioned the effectiveness of the 'arm's length' approach of the regulations under section 482. A recurrent problem is the absence of comparable arm's length transactions between unrelated parties, and the inconsistent results of attempting to impose an arm's length concept in the absence of comparables.
>
> A fundamental problem is the fact that the relationship between related parties is different from that of unrelated parties. Observers have noted that multinational companies operate as an economic unit, and not 'as if' they were unrelated to their foreign subsidiaries. In addition, a parent corporation that transfers potentially valuable property to its subsidiary is not faced with the same risks as if it were dealing with an unrelated party. Its equity interest assures it of the ability ultimately to obtain the benefit of future anticipated or unanticipated profits, without regard to the price it sets. The relationship similarly would enable the parent to adjust its arrangement each year, if it wished to

---

[193] IRC s. 936(h)(5).

[194] Joint Comm. on Taxation, 97th Cong., 2d Sess., General Explanation of the Revenue Provisions of the Tax Equity and Fiscal Responsibility Act of 1982, 82–96 (Comm. Print 1983).

[195] IRC s. 367(d)(2)(A).

do so, to take account of major variations in the revenue produced by a transferred item.

Certain judicial interpretations of section 482 suggest that pricing arrangements between unrelated parties for items of the same apparent general category as those involved in the related party transfer may in some circumstances be considered a 'safe harbor' for related party pricing arrangements, even though there are significant differences in the volume and risks involved, or in other factors. See, e.g., *United States Steel*. While the committee is concerned that such decisions may unduly emphasize the concept of comparables even in situations involving highly standardized commodities or services, it believes that such an approach is sufficiently troublesome where transfers of intangibles are concerned that a statutory modification to the intercompany pricing rules regarding transfers of intangibles is necessary.[196]

The specific solution proposed by the House bill, however, was relatively narrow. It would have added the following sentence to section 482: 'in the case of any transfer (or license) of intangible property (within the meaning of section 936(h)(3)(B)), the income with respect to such transfer or license shall be commensurate with the income attributable to the intangible'.[197] Other than rejecting the approaches of *French* and *U.S. Steel*, no attempt to modify section 482 more extensively along the lines suggested in the House Report was forthcoming.

Nevertheless, it is noticeable that the House did not pretend that the 'commensurate with income' standard was compatible with the ALS. The Report states the transferor of intangibles in a multinational was looking to its equity investment, 'rather than to "arm's length" factors', to recuperate its cost[198] and that 'industry norms or other unrelated party transactions do not provide a safe harbor minimum payment for related party intangible transfers'.[199] Thus, even if a perfect comparable could be found in which the same intangible was transferred to an unrelated party in the same circumstances for a fixed royalty rate, the provision would still require the allocation of 'super-royalties' to a related party transferor.

The conference agreement on the Tax Reform Act of 1986 followed the House bill except for the expansion of the 'commensurate with income'

---

[196] H.R. Rep. No. 426, 99th Cong., 1st Sess. 423–4 (1985) (footnote omitted).

[197] H.R. 3838, 99th Cong., 1st Sess. (1985). A similar 'commensurate with income' standard was applied to s. 367(d) transfers of intangibles and to s. 936(h) cost sharing payments.

[198] H.R. Rep. No. 426 at 424.   [199] *Ibid.* 425.

provisions to apply to inbound as well as outbound transfers[200] such as
the transfer in *Ciba-Geigy*. However, the report added the following
significant language:

> The conferees are also aware that many important and difficult issues
> under section 482 are left unresolved by this legislation. The conferees
> believe that a comprehensive study of intercompany pricing rules by the
> Internal Revenue Service should be conducted and that careful consider-
> ation should be given to whether the existing regulations could be
> modified in any respect.[201]

In light of this language, the report should be seen as an invitation to
the Service to shift the focus of the regulations away from the ALS. The
result of this invitation was the 1988 White Paper,[202] the 1992 proposed
regulations,[203] the 1993 temporary regulations,[204] and the 1994 final
regulations under section 482 of the Code.[205]

In discussing the White Paper, it is necessary to distinguish between
what it does and what it says it does. First, the White Paper does contain
an excellent analysis of the evolution of the statute, the regulations, and
the case law under section 482 of the Code,[206] as well as an overview of
the Service's experience in administering the law and regulations.[207] The
analysis suggests that the regulations rely too heavily on finding comparables,[208] that the case law indicates that the regulations 'fail to resolve the
most significant and potentially abusive fact patterns',[209] and that the
'fourth method' developed in the courts has been inadequate.[210]

After explaining the 1986 changes,[211] the White Paper reaches the
heart of the matter: determining what method should apply to section
482 issues in the absence of comparables. It rejects the applicability of
safe harbours because they will only serve as a 'floor' for taxpayers
unable to obtain better results otherwise.[212] The White Paper instead

---

[200] H.R. Conf. Rep. No. 841, 99th Cong., 2nd Sess. II–637 (1986), reprinted in 1986 U.S.C.C.
A.N. 4075, 4725. The conference also adopted a Senate provision, enacted as s. 1059A of
the Code, which aimed to prevent the disparities between high transfer prices and low
custom valuations at issue in *Brittingham* v. *Commissioner*, 598 F.2d 1375 (5th Cir. 1979).

[201] H.R. Conf. Rep. No. 841 at II–638, reprinted in U.S.C.C.A.N. at 4726.

[202] White Paper, note 1 above.

[203] Prop. Treas. Reg. s. 1.482, 57 Fed. Reg. 3571 (30 January 1992).

[204] Temp. Treas. Reg. s. 1.482.p. Treas. Reg. s. 1.482T (1993).

[205] Treas. Reg. s. 1.482.   [206] White Paper, note 1 above, pp. 459–61.

[207] *Ibid.* pp. 461–5.   [208] *Ibid.* pp. 464–5.   [209] *Ibid.* pp. 466–8.

[210] *Ibid.* pp. 469–71.   [211] *Ibid.* pp. 472–80.   [212] *Ibid.* p. 481.

suggests two methods based on determining appropriate returns from a functional analysis of the parties' respective economic contributions.[213] The first or 'basic' method applies when one party does not use significant intangibles of its own.[214] The economic functions of that party are analysed and appropriate rates of return are identified based on the rates of return of unrelated parties performing similar activities and assuming similar risks.[215] The residual is then assigned to the other party.[216]

The second or 'profit split' method applies when both parties per-form complex economic functions, bear significant economic risks, and use significant self-developed intangibles.[217] After applying the basic method to the measurable assets of both parties, the residual is allo-cated between them by splitting the profits based on the relative values of each party's intangibles.[218] The White Paper acknowledges that 'splitting the intangible income in such cases will largely be a matter of judgment'.[219]

This is what the White Paper proposes. The Paper, however, also has another agenda: to portray its suggested methods as compatible with the traditional ALS.[220] This agenda developed because of the strong objec-tions by our trading partners to the language contained in the 1986 legislative history advocating the abandonment of the ALS.[221] Thus, as we saw above, the White Paper recommends that the United States continue to adhere to the ALS.[222] Furthermore, the methods summar-ised above (including profit split) were given the name 'basic arm's length return method' (BALRM).[223] Finally, the White Paper contains one chapter devoted to demonstrating the compatibility of the 'com-mensurate with income' standard and the BALRM method with the ALS,[224] one chapter defending the ALS on economic grounds,[225] and an appendix attempting to demonstrate that other countries use methods which are similar to BALRM.[226]

The White Paper also contains one real concession to the ALS in that it permits taxpayers to avoid periodic adjustments to a royalty rate for intangibles if they can find a comparable lacking such adjustments.[227] This provision flies in the face of the statutory language and the

---

[213] *Ibid.* p. 488.   [214] *Ibid.* pp. 488–9.   [215] *Ibid.* p. 489.   [216] *Ibid.*
[217] *Ibid.* p. 490.   [218] *Ibid.*   [219] *Ibid.*
[220] See Loengard, 'The Section 482 Pot Boils On', note 17 above.
[221] White Paper, note 1 above, p. 475.   [222] *Ibid.*   [223] *Ibid.* p. 488.
[224] *Ibid.* pp. 475–7.   [225] *Ibid.* pp. 483–5.   [226] *Ibid.* app. C.   [227] *Ibid.* pp. 477–8.

legislative history of the 1986 amendments,[228] but the Treasury presumably felt it could not claim to be adhering to the ALS without allowing taxpayers to use comparables if they found them. Indeed, under the White Paper's proposed 'clear and convincing evidence' standard, such comparables in practice will be hard to find.[229] Whether the BALRM itself is compatible with the ALS depends upon which definition of the ALS is used. The White Paper relies on the 1979 OECD Report on transfer pricing, which permits 'some regard to the profits of the relevant [multinational enterprise]' in determining transfer prices in the absence of comparables.[230] However, this language falls far short of endorsing the use of either the profit split method advocated by the White Paper or the industry average rates of return.[231]

It is difficult to see in what way the BALRM can meaningfully be called an ALS method in the traditional sense. First, since BALRM by definition can only be applied in the absence of comparables, it falls outside the traditional definition of the ALS, which relies on comparables. Thus, BALRM can only be called an 'arm's length method' if the definition of what constitutes 'arm's length methods' is expanded to include any method that reaches results that are the same as those that would have been reached by unrelated parties. If this is the definition, then 'arm's length' includes the entire transfer pricing continuum, including formulary apportionment, because even pure formulary apportionment may, in appropriate cases, reach the same results as would have been reached by unrelated parties dealing at arm's length.

Second, even if one assumes arm's length dealings proceed from such a functional analysis as envisaged by the BALRM, such an analysis could never lead the parties to a definite fixed transfer price. As Langbein has argued, it could only lead to a range between the minimum the selling party could expect to get based on its costs and the maximum the buying party would be willing to pay based on its resale price. In most related-party contexts, there will be a residual profit not allocable to any

---

[228] See note 195–6 above and accompanying texts.

[229] White Paper, note 1 above, pp. 477–8.

[230] Organization for Economic Co-operation and Development, *Transfer Pricing and Multinational Enterprises* (1979) ('OECD Report'), p. 52.

[231] *Ibid.* p. 54 ('The profit comparison approach thus remains more in the nature of an indication that the consideration charged for the use of intangible property may or may not be reasonable.'); see also, *ibid.* p. 52 ('It is considered that it is unlikely to be possible to construct any standard rates ... as even within a given sector of industry it is extremely difficult to discern any typical rate or range of rates.').

constituent member, but rather to the existence of the overall organisation.[232] Thus, unlike a comparable with a fixed price, applying the BALRM between unrelated parties, at best, could lead to a range of acceptable transfer prices. However, the disparity between one end of the range (advocated by the taxpayer) and the other (advocated by the Service) could still be immense. Furthermore, the disparity can only be resolved by applying profit split methods which do not depend on comparables and, hence, fall outside the traditional ALS.

Thus, the true message of the White Paper was that the traditional ALS could not be applied to the majority of section 482 cases because no comparables could be found. What the White Paper instead achieved was to substitute an expanded definition of the ALS for the traditional one: ALS was now understood to include not only CUP, cost plus and resale price but also the rest of the transfer pricing continuum, up to and including profit split, as long as the results reached were compatible with arm's length results. This expansion of the scope of arm's length was the major achievement of the White Paper and constituted a revolution in the United States' approach to transfer pricing. The full fruits of such revolution can be seen in the 1994 final regulations.[233]

The methods that the White Paper suggested as a replacement for the traditional ALS, however, have at least two flaws which have been pointed out repeatedly since 1988.[234] First, BALRM analysis is extremely complicated and requires massive input by economists and accountants, as well as access to a large fund of not easily available information.[235] Second, even where the method is applied correctly, it still leaves a substantial residual to be split in many cases, and the White Paper provided no guidance on the ways to split it. The BALRM was thus unlikely to reduce the amount of section 482 litigation or the length of the ensuing opinions because the economists of the Service and the taxpayer predictably differ. When millions of dollars are involved, as is

---

[232] See Langbein, 'The Unitary Method and the Myth of Arm's Length', note 17 above, 654–5; S. I. Langbein, 'Langbein Blasts Arm's Length Method as Unworkable', *Tax Analysts Highlights and Documents*, 24 August 1990. See also discussion below (analysing the implications of this 'continuum price problem').

[233] See Treas. Reg. s. 1.482–6. See also notes 234–52 below.

[234] See, e.g., R. L. Kaplan, 'International Tax Enforcement and the Special Challenge of Transfer Pricing', (1990) *U Ill. L Rev.* 299; R. T. Rapp, 'Pitfalls in the BALRM' (1990) 49 *Tax Notes* 703 (arguing the standards of the BALRM are not easily met in the real world).

[235] See, e.g., Rapp, *ibid.* 706–7.

the case in most major section 482 cases, the matter is likely to end up in court. In fact, functional analysis was included in the IRS manual and applied before 1988, with no discernible lessening of the section 482 litigation mess.[236]

By 1992, these drawbacks of BALRM persuaded the Service it could not be applied in practice. As a result, when, in accordance with the 1986 legislative history, the proposed regulations came out in January 1992, they made no attempt to implement the White Paper. The Preamble to the proposed regulations states that:

> Many comments on the White Paper criticised the prominent role given to BALRM, arguing that BALRM would be difficult to apply because the information BALRM required generally would not be available, would be unfair to corporations whose rates of return vary considerably from the average, and would allocate too much income to U.S. entities. The Service also was urged to assign a greater role to inexact comparable transactions and to reconsider the use of safe harbor rules. These comments were taken into account in the development of the three pricing methods described in these proposed regulations.[237]

Instead of BALRM, the proposed regulations introduced the 'comparable profit interval' (CPI) method,[238] which represented another step towards the demise of the traditional ALS as the guiding standard for applying section 482 of the Code.

The proposed regulations were divided into three parts: intangibles, tangibles and cost sharing. In the case of transfers of intangibles through transfers of tangibles or services, the intangible rules applied if the income attributable to the intangible was 'material' in relation to the income attributable to the tangible property or services.[239] In the case of intangibles, when a strictly defined 'matching transaction' involving the same intangible under the same or substantially similar economic conditions and contractual terms was lacking,[240] the next method in order of priority was the 'comparable adjustable transaction' (CAT) method.[241] Under the CAT method, the arm's length consideration was determined 'by reference to the consideration charged in an

---

[236] See White Paper, note 1 above, p. 464.

[237] Preamble to Prop. Treas. Reg. s. 1.482, 57 Fed. Reg. 3571, 3572 (30 January 1992).

[238] Prop. Treas. Reg. s. 1.482(f), 57 Fed. Reg. 3571, 3586 (30 January 1992).

[239] Prop. Treas. Reg. s. 1.482–2(d)(1)(iii), 57 Fed. Reg. 3571, 3579 (30 January 1992).

[240] Prop. Treas. Reg. s. 1.482–2(d)(3), 57 Fed. Reg. 3571, 3580 (30 January 1992).

[241] Prop. Treas. Reg. s. 1.482–2(d)(2)(iii), 57 Fed. Reg. 3571, 3579 (30 January 1992).

uncontrolled transfer involving the same or similar intangible under adjustable economic conditions and contractual terms'.[242] To be considered adjustable, the contractual terms and economic conditions must be sufficiently similar such that the effect of any material differences can be determined with reasonable accuracy;[243] however, even if all the other conditions for applying the CAT method are met, 'an uncontrolled transfer will not meet the standards [of the CAT method] if the consideration determined by reference to that transfer results in a level of operating income for the tested party ... that is outside of the comparable profit interval'.[244]

In the case of transfers of tangible property, the first method to be applied was the CUP method.[245] Under the CUP method, the consideration for tangible property was determined by considering uncontrolled transfers of the same or similar physical property in the same or similar circumstances if any differences could be reflected by a reasonable number of price adjustments.[246] The CUP method was the only method for tangibles not subject to verification by means of the CPI.[247] When the CUP method was unavailable, other methods such as resale price, cost plus or 'fourth method' could be used, but the results from these methods were all subject to testing under the CPI and the ultimate method used was supposed to reach results at the 'most appropriate point' within the CPI.[248]

The CPI itself was constructed in a series of steps. First, the tested party was selected.[249] Second, the 'applicable business classification' of the tested party was determined on the basis of the businesses whose operations most closely corresponded to the tested operations involving related parties.[250] Third, constructive operating incomes were derived by applying profit level indicators from a selection of uncontrolled taxpayers in the applicable business classification to financial data of the tested operations.[251] These profit level indicators included the rate of return on

[242] Prop Treas. Reg. s. 1.482–2(d)(4)(i), 57 Fed. Reg. 3571, 3581 (30 January 1993).
[243] Prop. Treas. Reg. s. 1.482–2(d)(4)(iii), 57 Fed. Reg. 3571, 3582 (30 January 1992).
[244] Prop. Treas. Reg. s. 1.482–2(d)(4)(i).
[245] Prop. Treas. Reg. s. 1.482–2(e)(1)(ii), 57 Fed. Reg. 3571, 3586 (30 January 1992).
[246] The CUP method described was a holdover from Treas. Reg. s. 1.482–2(e)(2)(ii), which was in force during the promulgation of the proposed regulations.
[247] Prop. Treas. Reg. s. 1.482–2(e)(1)(iii), 57 Fed. Reg. 3571, 3586 (30 January 1992).
[248] Prop. Treas. Reg. s. 1.482–2(e)(1)(iii)–(iv), 57 Fed. Reg. 3571, 3586 (30 January 1992).
[249] Treas. Reg. s. 1.482–2(f)(4), 57 Fed. Reg. 3571, 3587 (30 January 1992).
[250] Prop. Treas. Reg. s. 1.482–2(f)(5), 57 Fed. Reg. 3571, 3587 (30 January 1992).
[251] Prop. Treas. Reg. s. 1.482–2(f)(6), 57 Fed. Reg. 3571, 3587 (30 January 1992).

assets, ratio of operating income to sales, and profit splits. Fourth, the CPI was determined on the basis of profit level indicators on the basis of complex statistical techniques.[252] Fifth, the 'most appropriate point' in the CPI was determined on the basis of other statistical techniques.[253] Finally, the transfer price was determined so as to produce operating income for the tested party which equalled the constructive operating income corresponding to the most appropriate point in the CPI.[254] In general, the CPI was to be constructed based on actual, rather than projected, results from the three-year period beginning with the year prior to the one under review.[255]

Is the CPI method of the proposed regulations compatible with the traditional ALS? As our trading partners promptly pointed out, the answer is no,[256] even under the Treasury's own definition of what constitutes an ALS method.[257] This definition of an ALS method was based on the definition offered in a 1979 OECD Report which endorsed the ALS and explicitly rejected formulary approaches for allocating profits between related enterprises as 'necessarily arbitrary'.[258] It accepted, however, the possibility that 'in seeking to arrive at an arm's length price in a range of transactions, some regard to the total profits of the relevant [multinational enterprise] may ... be helpful, as a check on the assessment of the arm's length price'.[259]

As the White Paper recognised, the OECD Report endorsed methods which consider the profits of the related enterprises in making arm's length determinations.[260] The CPI method, on the other hand, looked exclusively at the profits of other taxpayers to determine the proper allocation within the controlled group.[261] The CPI then judged the results of any method of allocation which, in the case of intangibles, did not meet strict standards of comparability as a 'matching transaction',[262] or, in the case of tangibles, was not based on a 'comparable uncontrolled price'.[263]

---

[252] Prop. Treas. Reg. s. 1.482–2(f)(7), 57 Fed. Reg. 3571, 3589 (30 January 1992).

[253] Prop. Treas. Reg. s. 1.482–2(f)(8), 57 Fed. Reg. 3571, 3590 (30 January 1992).

[254] Prop. Treas. Reg. s. 1.482–2(f)(9), 57 Fed. Reg. 3571, 3590 (30 January 1992).

[255] Prop. Treas. Reg. s. 1.482–2(f)(2), 57 Fed. Reg. 3571, 3587 (30 January 1992).

[256] See note 265 below and accompanying texts.

[257] See White Paper, note 1 above, p. 476.

[258] OECD Report, note 230 above, pp. 14–15.   [259] Ibid. p. 150

[260] White Paper, note 1 above, p. 476 ('Nowhere, however, does the OECD Report suggest that the profits of the related enterprises are irrelevant to this determination'). Ibid.

[261] Prop. Treas. Reg. s. 1.482–2(d)(4)(iii), 57 Fed. Reg. 3571, 3581 (30 January 1992).

[262] Prop. Treas. Reg. s. 1.482–2(d)(4)(iii), 57 Fed. Reg. 3571, 3581 (30 January 1992).

[263] Prop. Treas. Reg. s. 1.482–2(e)(1)(ii), 57 Fed. Reg. 3571, 3585 (30 January 1992).

If the results of any such method did not fall within the CPI, the transfer price was not considered 'arm's length'.[264] The CPI method thus fell squarely within the definition of a 'global' or formulary method under the OECD Report, since it disregarded the transaction between the related parties altogether and substituted a transaction based on an analysis of the profits of third parties.[265] While the CPI method did rely on comparables (unlike the BALRM with profit split, which the proposed regulations rejected), the standard of comparison used was so loose that our trading partners refused to consider it an 'arm's length' method.[266]

The proposed regulations thus marked a further step in the decline and fall of the traditional ALS based on comparables for the majority of section 482 cases. They would have also likely led to increased double taxation in the absence of agreements with our trading partners. This alone would not necessarily have been enough to condemn them. The proposed regulations, however, were also incompatible with the legislative history of the 1986 amendments (on which they relied for authority), which clearly states 'industry norms' should not be the basis for determining transfer prices.[267] More importantly, as many commentators have pointed out, the proposed regulations suffered from other flaws as well. First, they were incredibly complex, requiring the application of statistical methods far beyond the understanding of most tax directors of even the largest corporations. This could have forced taxpayers to devote resources to employing economists and statisticians, rather than in more productive ways. Second, the proposed regulations relied on the ability of taxpayers to obtain information regarding the profitability of their competitors, which was unobtainable without breaching antitrust laws.[268] Third, these regulations were unlikely to

---

[264] Prop. Treas. Reg. s. 1.482–2(f)(1), 57 Fed. Reg. 3571, 3586 (30 January 1992).

[265] OECD Report, note 230 above, p. 19. The effect of the arm's length approach advocated by the OECD Report is 'to recognize the actual transactions as the starting point for tax assessment and not, in other than exceptional cases, to substitute other transactions for them'. *Ibid.*

[266] For an analysis of the reactions of trading partners, see 'International Chamber of Commerce Opposing Proposed Transfer Pricing Rules, 69 *Daily Tax Rep. (BNA)*, 9 April 1992, G7; 'Proposed Transfer Pricing Regulations Could Spark Tax War, Experts Say', 115 *Daily Tax Rep. (BNA)*, 15 June 1992, G1. See also 'U.S. Trading Partners Respond Favorably to Proposed Section 482 Regs' 95 *Tax Notes Today*, 11 March 1992, 55-17 (a somewhat misleading title in light of the reactions actually reported).

[267] See H.R. Rep. No. 426 at 425.

[268] 'International Chamber of Commerce Opposing Proposed Transfer Pricing Rules', note 266 above.

lead to any significant reduction in litigation, given the many subjective decisions involved in their application (e.g., the selection of the tested party) and the many undefined terms (e.g., 'material') that they include. Finally, the proposed regulations were totally useless as a planning tool for taxpayers, because in order to construct the CPI, they required a clairvoyant knowledge of actual future results.[269]

In light of this uniformly negative reaction, the IRS rapidly realised a different direction had to be taken.[270] The result was the current temporary and final regulations which, on their face, appear to signal a substantial retreat by the IRS and a reaffirmation of the viability of the ALS. These appearances are, however, misleading. Closer examination reveals the temporary and final regulations will probably ensure the CPI (renamed the comparable profit method, or CPM) will be the method applied in the majority of disputed cases by the IRS to judge whether the transfer price should be adjusted, while in other cases a profit split method similar to BALRM, which does not rely on comparables at all, will be used.[271]

The temporary regulations, like the proposed regulations, began with the required lip service to the ALS, and omitted the modifications to the ALS that attracted criticism in the proposed regulations.[272]

---

[269] See generally New York State Bar Assoc. Tax Section, Comments on Proposed Section 482 and Cost Sharing Regulations, 9 September 1992; D. Kevin Dolan, 'Proposed Transfer Pricing and Cost Sharing Regulations' (1992) 21 *Tax Mgmt Int'l J* 171; Elizabeth King, 'The Section 482 White Paper and the Proposed Regulations: A Comparison of Key Provisions' (1992) 4 *Tax Notes Int'l* 331, 334; Steven P. Hannes, 'An Examination of the New U.S. Transfer Pricing Proposals' (1992) 4 *Tax Notes Int'l* 281, 282; James P. Fuller and Ernest F. Aud, Jr, 'The Proposed Section 482 Regulations' (1992) 4 *Tax Notes Int'l* 599, 600.

[270] 'Service Promises Section 482 Review, Leniency Administrating Payroll Tax Rules' 92 *Tax Notes Today*, 3 September 1992, 180–1.

[271] For analyses of the temporary regulations see J. P. Fuller and E. F. Aud, Jr, 'The New Temporary and Proposed Section 482 Regulations: A Wolf in Sheep's Clothing?' (1993) 6 *Tax Notes Int'l* 525; S. P. Hannes, 'An Evaluation of IRS's 1993 Transfer Pricing and Related Penalty Proposals: Round Three' (1993) 6 *Tax Notes Int'l* 397; V. Zonana, *Section 482: The 1993 Regulations – Once More, With Feeling!*, Tax Club Paper (9 February 1993).

[272] Temp. Treas. Reg. s. 1.482–1T(b)(1) (1993); Treas. Reg. ss. 1.482–1(b)(1)–(2) (emphasising 'arm's length results'). Compare with Prop. Treas. Reg. s. 1.482–1(b)(1), 57 Fed. Reg. 3571, 3578 (30 January 1992), which subjected the ALS to a 'sound business judgment on the basis of reasonable levels of experience' test, the 'reasonableness' test of *Frank v. International Canadian Corp.*, 308 F.2d 520, 528–529 (9th cir. 1962), which had been rejected by the Service since 1935. See notes 43–7 above and accompanying text.

However, the temporary regulations also subjected the ALS to a 'best method rule', which is retained in the final regulations, and will be an exception that swallows the traditional ALS. The best method rule (BMR) states that when the taxpayer and the Service disagree about the pricing methods to be used in reaching ALS results, the method to be used is the one that provides the 'most accurate determination' of the arm's length result.[273] The factors to be weighed when choosing the method under BMR are the completeness and accuracy of the data, the degree of comparability with uncontrolled transactions, the number, magnitude and accuracy of adjustments, and whether the result agrees with any other method.[274]

How will the BMR be applied in practice? The answer was provided in the examples given in the temporary regulations. The first example involves a non-controversial case where the taxpayer is able to provide a comparable CUP method that fits the transaction 'with a small number of minor adjustments'.[275] In this case, the BMR will allow the CUP method to overcome the resale price method proposed by the IRS.[276] This first example presupposed an exact comparable exists, but, as the cases surveyed above indicate, no such comparable can be found in the vast majority of real-life situations involving a dispute between the Service and the taxpayer. In such a case, the second example comes into play. Here, the taxpayer argues for CUP with 'several adjustments' which are not major ones while the Service argues for the resale price method. The CPM method, which is equivalent to CPI, reaches results that are consistent with resale price; therefore, the example indicates the similar results achieved by the resale price method and the CPM overcome the taxpayer's comparable.[277]

As Fuller and Aud suggest, this example 'borders on the 1992 proposed regulations' requirement that the resale price method be tested and pass muster under the CPI'.[278] In effect, whenever the IRS

[273] Temp. Treas. Reg. s. 1.482–1T(b)(2)(iii) (1994); Treas. Reg. s. 1.482–1(c).
[274] Ibid.
[275] Temp. Treas. Reg. s. 1.482–1T(b)(2)(iii)(C), Example 1 (1993); cf. Treas. Reg. s. 1.482–8, Example 1.
[276] Ibid.   [277] Temp. Treas. Reg. s. 1.482–1T(b)(2)(iii)(C), Example 2 (1993).
[278] Fuller and Aud, 'The New Temporary and Proposed Section 482 Regulations', note 271 above, 527. The example was dropped from the final regulations, but under the examples that were included, the CUP (and CUT for intangibles) apply only where identical comparables are found, so that the CPM will apply in most cases under the BMR. See Treas. Reg. s. 1.482–8.

and the taxpayer disagree about the pricing method, which is essentially in every case in which the application of the ALS is important, the two competing methods have to be tested under the CPM. Although the temporary regulations refrained from mandating, they strongly suggested that the method that is consistent with the CPM should prevail. Thus, in the temporary regulations, as in the proposed regulations, unless the taxpayer can find an exact comparable or one that requires only minor adjustments, the CPM will be used to 'trump' any taxpayer method (including the CUP) that is inconsistent with its results.[279]

The conclusion that the temporary regulations represent only a tactical retreat by the IRS from the proposed regulations' emphasis on the CPI is bolstered by examining the precise methods used for tangible and intangible transfers. For tangible property, the temporary regulations permit the use of CUP, resale price, cost plus, CPM or 'other methods'.[280] While CUP 'ordinarily will provide the most accurate measure of an arm's length price for the transfer of tangible property',[281] the standard of comparability is that the property and the circumstances must be 'substantially the same',[282] and a 'reasonable number of adjustments' for 'minor' differences can be made only 'if such differences have a definite and reasonably ascertainable effect on prices or profits'.[283] This level of comparability will rarely be found.

The other permitted methods (resale price and cost plus) do not require such a high standard of comparability;[284] but if the taxpayer disagrees with the Service on their application, the disagreement is likely to be resolved by resorting to the CPM. Thus, in practice, the temporary regulations have the same structure as the proposed regulations because the CPM still 'trumps' the competing method used by the taxpayer in the

---

[279] See Prop. Treas. Reg. s. 1.482, 58 Fed. Reg. 5263, 5265 (Intro. to Temp. Treas. Reg.) (21 January 1993) (noting the criticism that 'elevating CPM to such a high level of priority was inconsistent with' the ALS); see also J. Turro, 'An Interview with U.S. Treasury International Tax Counsel Jim Mogle (1993) 6 *Tax Notes Int'l* 303 (the International Tax Counsel accepts the criticism).

[280] Temp. Treas. Reg. s. 1.482–3T(a)(1)–(5) (1993).

[281] Temp. Treas. Reg. s. 1.482–3T(b)(1) (1993).

[282] Temp. Treas. Reg. s. 1.482–3T(b)(2)(i) (1993).

[283] Temp. Treas. Reg. s. 1.482–1T(c)(2)(ii) (1993); cf. Treas. Reg. s. 1.482–3(b)(2)(II).

[284] Temp. Treas. Reg. ss. 1.482–3T(c)(3)(i), 1.482–3T(d)(3)(i) (1993) (both stating 'close physical similarity of the property involved in the controlled and uncontrolled transactions is not ordinarily necessary' for the resale price and cost plus methods, respectively).

absence of an exact comparable.[285] This pattern is repeated with even greater clarity in the intangibles portion of the temporary regulations. The only method that can be used other than the CPM is the 'comparable uncontrolled transaction' (CUT) method which requires that the comparable intangible be of the same class, relate to the same type of products, processes or know-how, and have 'substantially the same profit potential' as the transfer at issue.[286] The last requirement is likely to prove impossible to meet because almost by definition intangibles licensed to unrelated parties will not have the same profit potential as those retained within the related group.[287] In the absence of such a precise uncontrolled comparable, the taxpayer is practically required to use CPM.[288]

CPM itself is essentially the same as CPI in the proposed regulations, but in some ways it deviates even further from the traditional ALS. CPM is applied to the 'tested party', measured by profit level indicators derived from uncontrolled taxpayers that engage in 'similar business activities'.[289] The definition of 'similar business activities' is extremely broad. The uncontrolled taxpayers need be only 'broadly similar', while 'significant product diversity and some functional diversity between the controlled and uncontrolled transactions is acceptable'.[290] If this liberal standard is met, CPM will be applied by constructing an 'arm's length range' from the operating profits of the 'comparables'. CPM can be applied even if the 'broadly similar' standard is not met; in that case, the 'arm's length range' will 'ordinarily' consist of the interquartile range

---

[285] Temp. Treas. Reg. ss. 1.482–3T(c)–(d) (1993); cf. Treas. Reg. ss. 1.482–3(c)–(d). The taxpayer is unlikely to use 'other methods' despite the permission given in the temporary regulations, Temp. Treas. Reg. s. 1.482–3T(e) (1993), and the final regulations, Treas. Reg. s. 1.482–3(e), because such methods do not satisfy the 'reasonable belief' standard of the attendant penalty provisions. See Treas. Reg. s. 1.6662–5(j)(5)(iii), which subject the taxpayer to draconian penalties of 20 or 40 per cent of the underpayment. IRC ss. 6662(a), (h)(1).

[286] Temp. Treas. Reg. s. 1.482–4T(c) (1993); cf. Treas. Reg. s. 1.482–4(c).

[287] Temp. Treas. Reg. s. 1.482–4T(c)(2)(ii)(A) (1993); cf. Treas. Reg. section 1.482–4(c)(2)(iii). In addition, the comparable transfer must meet a stringent list of 'comparable circumstances'. Temp. Treas. Reg. s. 1.482–4T(c)(2)(ii)(B) (1993); cf. Treas. Reg. s. 1.482–4(c)(2)(iii)(B).

[288] Theoretically, the taxpayer can use 'other methods', but once again, their use is constrained by the risk of penalties. IRC s. 6662. See Fuller and Aud, 'The New Temporary and Proposed Section 482 Regulations', note 271 above, at 540 ('The effect is all too clear: since CUT is very narrow and "other" methods may not be penalty proof, the regulations have a strong bias towards the use of CPM').

[289] Temp. Treas. Reg. s. 1.482–5T(c)(1) (1993); cf. Treas. Reg. s. 1.482–5(c).

[290] Temp. Treas. Reg. s. 1.482–5T(c)(1) (1993); cf. Treas. Reg. s. 1.482–5(c).

from the 25th to the 75th percentile of the constructive operating profits derived from the profit level indicators of the 'comparable' parties.[291]

The pretence that CPM is somehow consistent with the traditional ALS because it uses some form of comparables is so thin in this case that it is hard to accept it with a straight face. The 'arm's length' result under this rule must be constructed by using the profits of other parties that are not even 'broadly similar' to the related taxpayers under an extremely liberal standard of similarity. There is no question this use of the CPM is inconsistent with the 1979 OECD Report, which, as we have seen, only allows 'some regard to the total profits of the relevant [multinational enterprise] ... as a check on the assessment of the arm's length price'.[292] The temporary regulations thus represent a return to the basic White Paper position of paying lip service to the traditional ALS while, in effect, substituting a much broader and more flexible definition of 'arm's length' for it. In practice, whenever a disagreement arises between the taxpayer and the IRS and there is no exact comparable – which is the vast majority of the cases in which the application of the ALS is significant – the winning method is the CPM, according to the Service. The CPM hardly attempts to masquerade as an ALS method.

The final regulations, issued in July 1994, are 'generally consistent' with the temporary regulations, and follow the same 'basic policies'.[293] Once again, the emphasis is on arm's length results. A controlled transaction meets the ALS 'if the results of the transaction are consistent with the results that would have been realized if uncontrolled taxpayers had engaged in the same transaction under the same circumstances (arm's length result)'.[294] The best method rule (BMR), employed in deciding which method the taxpayer and the IRS should follow, states that the method used must be the one which 'provides the most reliable measure of an arm's length result'.[295]

---

[291] Temp Treas. Reg. s. 1.482–5T(d)(2)(ii) (1993); cf. Treas. Reg. s. 1.482–1(e)(2).

[292] OECD Report, note 230 above, p. 15. Predictably, our trading partners objected that the temporary regulations 'are still not fully consistent with the internationally accepted arm's length standard'. 'Korean Finance Ministry Comments on Transfer Pricing Regs', *Tax Notes Today*, 31 August 1993. See also 'German Industry Rep Takes Aim at Proposed Regs', *Tax Notes Today*, 5 August 1993; 'Keidanren Urges IRS to Take Another Look at Proposed Regs', *Tax Notes Today*, 29 July 1993.

[293] 'Intercompany Transfer Pricing Regulations under Section 482', *Highlights and Documents*, 5 July 1994, 117. On the final regulations, see G. N. Carlson *et al.*, 'The Final Transfer Pricing Regulations: The More Things Change, The More They Stay the Same', *Tax Notes Today*, 29 July 1994; S. P. Hannes, 'IRS 1994 Transfer Pricing Rules Reward Planning and Documentation, Increase Penalty Risks', *Tax Notes Today*, 1 August 1994.

[294] Treas. Reg. s. 1.482–1(b)(1).   [295] Treas. Reg. s. 1.482–1(c)(1).

Thus, the redefinition of the ALS has been completed. A need for the use of any comparable no longer exists; if a method reaches the same result as what would have been reached on an arm's length basis without resort to comparables, it is compatible with the ALS and should be applied.

The main difference between the final and temporary regulations is the increased flexibility that the final regulations afford both the tax-payer and the Service. Instead of relying on the superiority of the CPM, the final regulations emphasise the equal status of all the specified methods, leaving the taxpayer and the Service free to argue which provides the best arm's length results under the BMR. As one commen-tator has noted, this feature of the final regulations provides taxpayers with 'flexibility that may approach that allowed under the 1968 regula-tions'.[296] However, this is hardly a great compliment, given the fate of the 1968 regulations in the courts. As the architect of the 1993 tempor-ary regulations has stated, this may well create greater controversy and litigation in the future, without an end in sight.[297] In practice, it still remains likely, in the view of many commentators, that the Service's field agents will employ the CPM as their method of choice,[298] while taxpayers will prefer other methods. The resulting dispute concerning which method really is the best estimate of arm's length results will arrive in the courts once again.

The most significant innovation of the final regulations is the elevation of profit split to a status equal with all other methods of reaching an arm's length result. The two-level analysis described below may be performed in cases where either party owns significant intangibles resulting in a residual profit higher than the profit resulting from the regular functions of the parties. First, the profits resulting from the standard functions performed by the parties are allocated on the basis of market comparables; and second, the residual profit is split according to which party bore the costs of developing the intangibles (and not which party formally owns the intangible).[299] It is likely in many of the cases reaching litigation, that the parties will have significant high-profit intangibles; therefore, the profit

---

[296] Carlson *et al.*, 'The Final Transfer Pricing Regulations', note 293 above, XIII.

[297] J. Turro, 'Mogle Comments on Finalized Transfer Pricing Regulations', *Tax Notes Today*, 6 July 1994.

[298] Hannes, 'IRS 1994 Transfer Pricing Rules', note 293 above; see also 'Foreign Tax Officials Discuss Final Transfer Pricing Regs', *Tax Notes Today*, 30 September 1994 (expressing foreign concerns regarding the United States' use of the CPM under the 1994 regulations).

[299] Treas. Reg. s. 1.482–6.

split method will be the one applied under the BMR.[300] This 'residual profit split' method, however, is clearly not within the traditional ALS because it does not rely on comparables in making the crucial determination about splitting the residual. As the Treasury observed in its release accompanying the final regulations, the United States for many years has been reluctant to permit wide use of profit split methods because they do not refer solely to results of transactions between unrelated parties in determining an arm's length result. To the extent that they do not rely on such results they may be considered to be inconsistent with the arm's length standard. There are, however, cases in which it is impossible to locate adequate data to reliably apply one of the other methods. In such a case a profit split may be the best available method.[301]

The adoption of the profit split method in the final regulations marks the culmination of the trend we have observed since 1972: the fall of the traditional comparable-based ALS and its replacement by an expanded definition of 'arm's length', which includes any method reaching arm's length results. Once the conceptual step to an expanded arm's length definition is taken, however, no logical barrier exists to accepting any method which leads to arm's length results, including formulary methods. The actions needed to take this further step are the topic of the final section of this chapter.

3.6   1994–2010

Sixteen years have passed since the new transfer pricing regulations were issued in 1994. In general, these years have been marked by the unwillingness of either the taxpayers or the IRS to challenge directly the application of the new regulations. Instead, most of the activity has been either in the APA program, which has grown to over 800 APAs concluded by 2010, in the administrative appeals process, or relating to peripheral though important issues like cost sharing. As a result, it is hard to tell what impact the new regulations have had on transfer pricing litigation.

The transfer pricing cases litigated since 1995 fall into two periods. From 1995 to 2000 there were several cases litigated, all of which still fell under the old regulations, and most of which were taxpayer victories.

---

[300] Commentators have noted that the profit split method based on comparables is unlikely to be used. See, e.g., Carlson et al., 'The Final Transfer Pricing Regulations', note 293 above, VII.

[301] Treasury Release on Final Section 482 Regulations, *Tax Notes Today*, 6 July 1994.

Then there was a hiatus, with no reported cases between 2001 and 2005, followed by the first important decision on cost sharing in 2005. This was followed by a lull, but there were another two important decisions on cost sharing in 2009, both ultimately won by the taxpayer.

The cases litigated in the period between 1995 and 2000 were under the old regulations and continued the trend of taxpayer victories in the transfer pricing area, although some split the difference between the IRS and the taxpayer. In *Altama Delta Corp.*, the Tax Court applied the cost plus method under the 1968 regulations to transfer prices charged by a Puerto Rico-based corporation electing the cost sharing method under section 936 which sold combat boot uppers to its US parent corporation, which manufactured and sold finished combat boots under a Department of Defense contract.[302] The IRS attempted to limit the subsidiary to either a 15 per cent mark-up on its non-material costs or to a 7.5 per cent mark-up on all costs. The court rejected the government's argument on the grounds that the government's purported comparables were general footwear manufacturers, whereas the taxpayer was in the combat boot industry, which enjoyed higher profits in the years in question. The court also ruled that the government's attempt to apply operating profit rather than gross profit margins was unreasonable and was not a valid application of the cost plus method. The court generally accepted the taxpayer's application to the subsidiary of gross profit margins earned by others in the combat boot industry, but it limited the gross margin because the parent faced higher risks than the subsidiary.

Inverworld, Inc. v. *Commissioner* is generally considered an IRS victory because the case involved other issues relating to the US subsidiary of a Caymans corporation controlled by Mexican principals.[303] However, the case also had a transfer pricing issue, and the Tax Court held that the IRS' method of allocating income to the US subsidiary was arbitrary and unreasonable and that the correct amount should be based on arm's length fees charged by the subsidiary to its clients.

DHL Corp. v. *Commissioner* was an important case involving intangibles. The taxpayer in 1992 sold to DHLI, its foreign affiliate, the worldwide rights to its trademark for US $20 million. At the same time, DHL sold 57.5 per cent of DHLI to three unrelated investors.[304]

---

[302] *Altama Delta Corp.* v. *Commissioner*, 104 T.C. 424 (1995).

[303] *Inverworld, Inc.* v. *Commissioner*, 71 T.C.M. 3231 (1996) and 73 T.C.M. 2777 (1997).

[304] *DHL Corp.* v. *Commissioner*, 76 T.C.M. 1122 (1998), aff'd in part and rev's in part, 285 F.3d 1210 9th Cir. 2002.

The IRS argued that the arm's length price should have been US $300 million, while the taxpayer valued it at US $50 million. The Tax Court rejected both valuation estimates, and concluded that the value of the trademark was US $150 million, or 50 per cent of the IRS valuation, and that US $50 million of that was associated with US rights and US $100 million with foreign rights. The Ninth Circuit affirmed on the valuation of the US rights, but rejected any adjustment for foreign rights because DHLI and not DHL was the owner of such rights under the 1968 regulations, since it incurred most of the expenses in developing such rights. Thus, the end-result of a US $50 million adjustment was the same as the taxpayer's position and the case should be viewed as a significant taxpayer victory in the important area of intangible valuation.

GAC Produce Co. Inc. illustrates that the IRS can win transfer pricing cases against small and medium taxpayers that do not have the litigating resources enjoyed by major multinationals.[305] The case involved a corporate distributor of fresh produce and its controlled entities in Mexico, and the Tax Court held that the commissions received by the distributor for marketing services were below arm's length because they did not even cover its costs. The taxpayer position lost because it was extreme, and it is doubtful the case can be relied upon as evidence of an improvement in the IRS' litigation record.

In *UPS* v. *Commissioner* the taxpayer transferred its profits from excess valuation charges, which are premiums paid by customers for replacement of packages lost or damaged in shipping, to a Bermuda affiliate.[306] The Tax Court rejected the transfer as a sham, because while the nominal transfer was to an unrelated party the ultimate risk and profit was to the related party, OPL. However, the Court of Appeals reversed, resulting in another significant taxpayer victory in the area of intangibles. The main rationale for the Court of Appeals decision was that the charges to unrelated customers were arm's length, but this does not explain why the significant profits should be deemed earned by OPL, rather than the taxpayer.

In *Compaq* v. *Commissioner* the taxpayer purchased about 50 per cent of its printed circuit assemblies from a Singapore subsidiary.[307] The taxpayer set its prices on a modified cost plus basis, using US standard

---

[305] *GAC Produce Co., Inc.* v. *Commissioner,* 77 T.C.M. 1890 (1999).
[306] *United Parcel Service* v. *Commissioner,* 78 T.C.M. 262 (1999), rev'd, 11th Cir.
[307] *Compaq Computer Corp.* v. *Commissioner,* 78 T.C.M. 20 (1999).

costs which were less than Singapore standard costs. The IRS rejected this method, but the Tax Court approved the taxpayer's position, and concluded that the notice of deficiency was arbitrary and capricious and that the prices should be upheld under CUP. The court accepted the taxpayer's allocation of location savings to the subsidiary and also declined to adjust the price for volume discounts because these were not required under the 1968 regulations.

After *Compaq* there are no final decisions in transfer pricing cases until 2005, when the first decision on cost sharing came down and was another major taxpayer victory. Cost sharing grew out of the super royalty rule that was enacted in 1986 to prevent royalty-free transfers of intangibles to low tax subsidiaries. Under cost sharing, the taxpayer and its foreign affiliate can enter into an agreement to share the costs of developing an intangible in a prescribed ratio, such as 20 to 80 per cent. The low tax affiliate then pays for its share of the costs of development, 80 per cent in this case, and as a result can book 80 per cent of the resulting profit without being subject to IRS challenge or to the super royalty rule. Importantly, no research and development needs to actually take place in the low tax affiliate, which just has to pay for the costs with funds contributed by the parent. If the costs are US $1 million and the profit is US $1 billion, a not unreasonable assumption for pharmaceutical patents, the low tax affiliate can shelter US $800 million from tax at a cost of US $800,000.[308]

The rationale behind the rule was that if the research and development is unsuccessful, the taxpayer gives up on the deduction of the costs allocated to the low tax affiliate, since it is a foreign source deduction. But it seems very generous to allow US $800 million to escape from tax at a potential risk of a US $800,000 deduction. In addition, taxpayers avoided even that risk by entering into the agreement only after the value of the research and development was already established, although then they had to argue with the IRS on the value of the 'buy in' payment the affiliate had to make for the established value of the intangible.

The issue in *Xilinx* v. *Commissioner* was whether in calculating the cost to be included in a cost sharing agreement, the taxpayer had to include the cost of exercising stock options granted to employees who were performing the R&D.[309] The Tax Court held that because cost sharing is covered by the ALS, the cost of options should not be included because

---

[308] Treas. Reg. s. 1.482/7.   [309] *Xilinx, Inc.* v. *Commissioner*, 125 T.C. 37 (2005).

unrelated parties would not have been willing to share the cost of the options. This case is a very pro-taxpayer result because the deduction of the option exercise frequently wipes out the US tax liability of high tech companies, so that as a result most of the profit from an intangible can remain offshore while the portion allocated to the United States under the agreement is protected from tax by deducting the option exercise costs. The case once again illustrates how unrealistic it is to rely on the ALS because these agreements are usually not entered into between unrelated parties, and thus the cost sharing issue does not arise.

On appeal, the US Court of Appeals for the Ninth Circuit initially reversed *Xilinx*.[310] By a two to one majority, the panel held that costs of employee stock options must be included in the pool of costs subject to a tax sharing agreement. However, the same panel later reversed itself and held for the taxpayer.

.The Tax Court decided *Xilinx* on the ground that unrelated parties dealing with each other at arm's length would not have shared the cost of employee stock options, and therefore the ALS requires that these costs not be shared under a cost sharing agreement either.[311] The Court of Appeals explicitly accepted this factual finding and even went further in explaining why unrelated parties would never share the costs of such options. Nevertheless, the majority decided (over a vigorous dissent by Judge Noonan) to require inclusion of the stock option costs in the sharing pool.[312]

The issue in *Xilinx* was whether to include the cost of employee stock options in the pool of costs to be shared under a cost sharing agreement with Xilinx's Irish subsidiary. In general, the more costs need to be shared, the less valuable is the cost sharing agreement to the taxpayer, because costs allocated to the Irish subsidiary cannot be deducted in the United States. Many high tech companies are able to eliminate their US tax liability by deducting the cost of stock options, while locating their foreign profits in low tax jurisdictions such as Ireland.

The Tax Court and the dissent argued that because the costs of the options would not be shared by unrelated parties, under the ALS they cannot be included in the pool of costs to be shared under the cost sharing agreement. They pointed out that Treas. Reg. 1.482–1(b)(1) requires that 'the standard to be applied in every case is that of a taxpayer dealing at arm's length with an uncontrolled taxpayer', and that of the US–Ireland tax treaties requires applying the ALS to transfer pricing

---

[310] *Xilinx, Inc.* v. *Commissioner*, No. 06–74246, 2009 Us App. LEXIS 11118 (9th Cir. 2009).
[311] *Xilinx, Inc.* v. *Commissioner*, 125 T.C. 37 (2005).   [312] *Ibid.*

cases. Judge Noonan in dissent argued that the ALS is essential to the purpose of the transfer pricing regulations, which is 'parity between taxpayers in uncontrolled transactions and taxpayers in controlled transactions. The regulations are not to be construed to stultify that purpose. If the [ALS] is trumped by [the cost sharing regulations] the purpose of the statute is frustrated.'[313]

However, the majority held that the ALS was not the purpose of IRC 482: 'Significantly, achieving an arm's length result is not itself the regulatory regime's goal; rather, its purpose is to prevent tax evasion by ensuring taxpayers accurately reflect taxable income attributable to controlled transactions.'[314] It then held that the language of Treas. Reg. 1.482–1(b) (1), incorporating the ALS, is irreconcilable with the language of Treas. Reg. 1.482–7(d)(1), which required the sharing of 'all of the costs' related to developing the shared intangible. The conflict arises because unrelated taxpayers do not share stock options costs because (i) they are hard to value because no cash outlay is involved; (ii) sharing them in an unrelated joint venture would create an incentive to minimise the value of the joint venture to reduce the cost of the options; and (iii) sharing the costs reduces the deductions available to the taxpayer.[315] For these reasons, there will be no comparables in which the costs are shared, but the court nevertheless held that the 'all of the costs' requirement governs because it is the more specific regulation. Finally, the court rejected the challenge based on the US–Ireland tax treaty because of the savings clause, which is found in every US tax treaty and states that the treaty cannot affect the ability of the United States to tax its own residents, such as Xilinx.

I believe that given the history of IRC 482 and the cost sharing regulations, the majority were clearly right, albeit not quite for the reason they give (as the dissent correctly notes, it is hard to put too much weight on canons of construction such as the one the majority relied on, i.e., that the specific trumps the general). First, IRC 482 predates the ALS by at least a decade, so that it cannot be said that the ALS is 'the purpose' of IRC 482.[316] Rather, as the majority correctly argued, the purpose of IRC 482 is to accurately reflect the taxpayer's income and prevent tax evasion, and the ALS is only a means to that end

---

[313] *Xilinx, Inc.* v. *Commissioner,* Court of Appeals decision at 6180.
[314] *Ibid.* 6167.   [315] *Ibid.* 6176.
[316] R. S. Avi-Yonah, *The Rise and Fall of Arm's Length: A Study in the Evolution of US International Taxation,* University of Michigan Law and Economics, Olin Working Paper No 07–017 (2007).

(which was not really given meaning until 1968, over four decades after the language of IRC 482 was enacted).

Second, there is a good reason why cost sharing cannot be reconciled with the ALS: cost sharing grew out of the super royalty rule, which was explicitly not based on the ALS. Thus, the majority were quite correct in viewing cost sharing as a distinct regime that is not subject to the ALS. If unrelated parties do not share costs that related parties do, that means that cost sharing between related parties cannot be governed by the ALS, and that the ALS is irrelevant to this area of transfer pricing law. That was the insight of Congress when it enacted the super royalty rule in 1986, and the same insight should be applied to cost sharing.

Third, the majority were also correct in rejecting the challenge posed by the US–Ireland treaty. However, their reasoning has interesting implications which they do not seem to appreciate. The majority stated that 'Xilinx is not a foreign entity, so applying 1.482–7(d)(1) to it does not violate the treaty, even if the regulations' all costs requirement is at odds with the treaty's arm's length standard.'[317] But this point applies to *all* transfer pricing cases, not just to those involving a US parent, because *Xilinx* also involved a foreign entity (the Irish subsidiary). If the savings clause is read to enable the IRS to apply non-ALS methods to Xilinx, it can also apply them to US subsidiaries of foreign parents, because those are also US resident corporations. In that case the only cases where the ALS applies under a treaty would be to US branches of foreign entities, as the courts held (incorrectly) in *Natwest*.[318]

Unfortunately, *Xilinx* was reversed by the same panel, because the taxpayer and its allies were able to persuade the panel that the ALS is a binding standard that must be complied with in all cases. The same result was reached in *Veritas*, another cost sharing case in which the court rejected the method used by the IRS to calculate a buy-in payment for an intangible, preferring to adopt the taxpayer's comparable uncontrolled transaction method despite clear economic differences.[319] This case is important because taxpayers frequently wait until they know that an intangible is valuable before they begin sharing costs with a foreign

[317] *Xilinx*, note 311 above, 6171.
[318] *National Westminster Bank* v. *United States*, 512 F.3d 1347 (Fed. Cir. 2008) (holding ALS in Chapter 7 of the United States–United Kingdom treaty trumps the interest allocations regulations). In my opinion this case was wrongly decided because of the long tradition of applying formulas to reach arm's length results, which is the only requirement under Art. 7 (see OECD Model, Art. 7(4)).
[319] *Veritas Software Corp.* v. *Commissioner*, 133 T.C. No. 14 (2009).

affiliate, so as not to risk losing the deduction for some of the costs if the R&D is unsuccessful. If taxpayers can minimise buy-in payments, there is no risk in entering into cost sharing agreements.

The IRS has attempted to deal with some of the issues in these cases by issuing new regulations. It now has issued regulations on transfer pricing related to both services and intangibles, which are in general similar to the 1994 regulations, with some modifications. It has also recently adopted new cost sharing regulations that would limit the advantage of the method by requiring that if the low tax affiliate only contributes cash, it only gets a normal return on the cash, with the rest of the profit allocated to the parent. However, in the final version these regulations were relaxed and the results in *Xilinx* and *Veritas* make the method more attractive. The Obama administration has proposed to limit cost sharing and other intangible transfer methods, but it is unclear whether Congress will act.

Thus, the litigation record since 1994 has not in general favoured the IRS much more than the pre-1994 record, although none of these cases except *Xilinx* and *Veritas* were litigated under the new regulations. Some taxpayers are entering APAs, but these cover only a small part of the overall transfer pricing universe. Instead, most taxpayers appear to be taking a wait and see attitude until the first major case under the new regulations is decided.

For a while, this case seemed likely to be *Glaxo. Glaxo* involved the proper allocation of the profit from selling the antacid drug Zantac in the United States between the UK parent, Glaxo-Wellcome, which did the research and development and production, and its US affiliate, which did the distribution. The IRS argued that 50 per cent of the profit should be allocated to distribution, while the United Kingdom claimed most of the profit relates to R&D and production.

If the IRS had won *Glaxo*, that would have helped drive reluctant taxpayers into the APA program, which is the best hope of resolving the transfer pricing mess in the absence of consensus on a formula. However, the IRS chose to settle, albeit for a hefty US $3.4 billion (out of about US $10 billion at stake). One can understand why, given the litigation record, but now we have to wait until the next big case.

3.7 Conclusion

Fundamentally, I have long believed that corporate taxation should be source-based, rather than residence-based. The reasons for this belief are that (a) corporate residence is not very meaningful, since unlike individuals corporations are not physically present in any country, cannot vote, and are an inappropriate subject for redistributive taxation; and that (b) source-based taxation of corporations rests on the benefits corporations receive from engaging in business activity in countries that incurred costs to enable that business activity to take place.

This argument supports the view of those who would move the United States closer to a territorial system. Territoriality has many advantages, because it eliminates the incentive not to repatriate earnings, and offers simplification potential in reducing the need for a foreign tax credit. If done properly, it is also a revenue raiser because deductions allocated to exempt foreign source income would be disallowed.

But I have also repeatedly argued against moving in the direction of territoriality in the current context, and have also supported efforts (like the current one by the Obama administration) to restrict or even repeal deferral. The reason is simple: without transfer pricing reform, territoriality will in my opinion lead to an even stronger incentive to shift profits overseas, and to further revenue losses and erosion of the US corporate tax base.[320]

Thus, I believe that the key to any international tax reform must be a transfer pricing overhaul. As my co-authors Kim Clausing and Michael Durst and I have argued, one possibility is to adopt a formula (which we suggested should be sales-based) to split profits left over after routine contributions by the related affiliates are accounted for.[321]

Such a reform can be enacted by Congress, and we have included proposed legislative language in our chapter. The original Ninth Circuit decision in *Xilinx* supports our position because it points out that the ALS cannot be applied in a key area of transfer pricing law.

However, our proposals have not so far persuaded opponents of formulary apportionment (FA). Instead, the advocates of the ALS point to a list of asserted deficiencies of FA, including:

1. FA is inherently arbitrary.
2. FA will produce double taxation because some countries will apply the ALS and others FA, and the FA countries will each have a different formula.

---

[320] See R. S. Avi-Yonah, 'Comment on Yin, Reforming the Taxation of Foreign Direct Investment by US Taxpayers' (2008) 28 *VA Tax Rev.* 281.

[321] R. S. Avi-Yonah, A. K. Clausing and M. Durst, 'Allocating Business Profits for Tax Purposes: A Proposal to Adopt a Formulary Profit Split' (2009) 9(5) *Florida Tax Rev.* 497–553.

3. FA requires an impossible-to-achieve uniformity of the tax base.
4. FA violates tax treaties.
5. FA will be impossible to enact because of the opposition of the multinationals and of countries that will lose from its implementation.

I believe that there is a good answer to each of these arguments, and have in fact replied to them at length elsewhere.[322] However, I also realise that my answers are unlikely to persuade FA opponents. Thus, I want to use this chapter to propose a more modest step forward: adopting FA only in the context of ALS (rather than replacing the ALS with FA).

The basic problem arises in situations where there are no good comparables. If good comparables exist, the traditional methods (CUP, cost plus and resale price) can be used, and that would end the story. But as the OECD Guidelines acknowledge, in many cases good comparables are hard to find.

The next possible alternative under the OECD Guidelines is the transactional net margin method (TNMM). However, TNMM requires a tougher comparability test than the US CPM, which is good because CPM has proven to be the most manipulable of the current methods: an informed economist working for a major accounting firm has told me he can achieve any result the client wants using CPM. CPM is also a huge source of transactional complexity, a boon to the large accounting firms, and a problem for those who cannot afford their services. But the tougher OECD TNMM comparability standard means that TNMM cannot be applied in many cases in which CPM is used in the United States.

This leaves profit split. Under profit split, comparables are used to allocate the return on routine functions. But that usually leaves a residual in place, which arises precisely because multinationals exist to earn a return that cannot be achieved in an arm's length relationship. That, as explained above, is why good comparables are hard to find.

---

[322] Avi-Yonah, Clausing and Durst, *ibid.*; on the treaties point see also R. Avi-Yonah and A. K. Clausing, 'Reforming Corporate Taxation in a Global Economy: A Proposal to Adopt Formulary Apportionment' in J. Furman and J. Bordoff (eds.), *Path to Prosperity: Hamilton Project Ideas on Income Security, Education, and Taxes* (Brookings Institution Press, 2008) pp. 319–44. If the *Xilinx* court was right, however, then FA does not violate Chapter 9 of the treaties because of the savings clause.

Thus, the key issue in current transfer pricing is how to allocate the residual under the profit split method. The US regulations assume that the residual is the result of high profit intangibles and allocate it to where such intangibles were developed. However, this method is not helpful because (a) the OECD and the rest of the world rejects it; (b) it penalises multinationals for conducting R&D in the United States; and (c) it encourages multinationals to enter into cost sharing agreements that artificially shift profits to low tax jurisdictions. In addition, as the *Bausch & Lomb* court stated, if the value of the intangible results from the fact that two parties are related, that added value is distinct from where it was developed.

If the US approach is rejected, the question is how to allocate the residual. The OECD Guidelines are silent on this issue. This presents an opportunity: perhaps in this context, it should be possible to adopt a formula to allocate the residual.

One needs to realise that if there are no comparables (by definition) and the residual results from the relationship between the parties and would disappear if they were unrelated, then the ALS is meaningless and any allocation is arbitrary. Under these circumstances the key is to adopt the formula that is most likely to achieve consensus.

In the unilateral US context, my co-authors and I support a sales-based formula similar to the destination-basis formula for VAT. This choice of formula favours exports and therefore is likely to be politically popular, and it favours the United States because of our trade deficit.[323] In the OECD context, I would prefer a more balanced formula with three components: payroll, tangible assets and sales.

These three components are, of course, the traditional US state FA formula. This formula has proven to be remarkably successful, since in addition to the US states, it is also the basis for the global dealing regulations in the United States and OECD, and is a leading candidate for the EU's Common Consolidated Corporate Tax Base (CCCTB) formula. I believe it makes sense because each of its elements is objective (payroll and sales are transactions with outside parties, and while tangible assets depend on valuations, there is a lot of experience with asset-based formulas, such as the US interest allocation formula). Intangibles are excluded, but in my opinion that is appropriate because (a) their value results from physical and human capital and from the market and

---

[323] Avi-Yonah and Clausing, 'Reforming Corporate Taxation in a Global Economy', note 322 above.

those elements are included, and (b) you cannot allocate their value and trying to include them invites manipulation.

Thus, I would propose that in hard transfer pricing cases, in which no comparables can be found beyond the return on routine functions, the United States should adopt and the OECD should endorse using the traditional three factor state formula to allocate the residual under the profit split method.

I believe this proposal addresses the problems with FA outlined above:

1. While the formula is arbitrary it relates to economic reality, and any allocation is arbitrary in the absence of comparables. The current OECD Guidelines are also arbitrary in not allocating residuals.
2. It is unlikely that this outcome would lead to more double taxation than what already occurs for residuals under the ALS. If the United States allocates residuals based on location of R&D and other countries disagree, double taxation is already a threat. Disputes can be resolved using the new arbitration provision under the OECD model.
3. If the OECD accepts the residual formula under ALS, it does not violate treaties and it can be handled in the context of Chapter 9.
4. Since it is only a residual formula, the base has already been defined under ALS.
5. A balanced formula is less likely to produce consistent losers.

Xilinx presents an opportunity for reforming US international taxation. It indicates yet again that the ALS is broken beyond repair. The reasons are set out at length elsewhere, and I will not repeat them.[324] I believe now is the time to reform transfer pricing, for three reasons:

1. The current debate over deferral and territoriality is unlikely to be resolved unless the Administration and Congress undertake transfer pricing reform.
2. The EU, traditionally the bulwark of the ALS, is moving toward adopting FA as part of its CCCTB project.[325]

---

[324] Avi-Yonah, Clausing and Durst, 'Allocating Business Profits for Tax Purposes', note 321 above.

[325] On CCCTB, see, e.g., J. Mintz and J. Weiner, 'Some Open Negotiation Issues Involving a Common Consolidated Corporate Tax Base in the European Union' (2008) 62 *Tax L Rev.* 81.

3. Even the OECD, also a bulwark of ALS, is showing some flexibility toward adopting formulas in the context of profit split, and is about to designate profit split as a method on par with the traditional ALS-based methods.[326]

Thus, I believe this a propitious time for reform, and that the Administration and Congress should use the current debate over deferral and territoriality to engage in transfer pricing reform along the lines outlined above.

Appendix: Questionnaire (United States)

1. The structure of the law for solving transfer pricing disputes. *What is the structure of the law of the country for solving transfer pricing disputes? For example, is the mutual agreement procedure (MAP), as regulated in the relevant tax treaty, the standard method for solving transfer pricing disputes?*

The law is based on a single section of the Internal Revenue Code (section 482) which is very brief but until 1968 was the only basis for judicial decisions. In 1968 and again in 1995 there were elaborate regulatory structures added which are the basis for subsequent decisions. MAP is of limited usefulness because until recently there was no binding arbitration in US tax treaties. APAs are more useful.

2. Policy for solving transfer pricing disputes. *Is there a gap between the nominal and effective method for solving transfer pricing disputes in the country? For example, has the country a strategic policy not to enforce the arm's length standard (ALS) for fear of driving foreign direct investment to other competing jurisdictions?*

APAs are frequently based on methods that are not ALS (e.g., formulas). There is a lot of emphasis on profit methods. Otherwise ALS is followed.

3. The prevailing dispute resolution method. *Which is the most frequent method for solving transfer pricing disputes in the country? Does it have a positive externality? For example, is the MAP the most frequent method, and if so, to what extent have successful MAPs been used as a proxy for*

---

[326] See R. S. Avi-Yonah, 'Between Formulary Apportionment and the OECD Guidelines: A Proposal for Reconciliation' (2010) 2 *World Tax Journal* 3.

transfer pricing case law? For instance, Procter & Gamble (P&G) obtained a bilateral advance pricing agreement (APA) in Europe, and it was then extended to a third (Asian) country when P&G made this request to the relevant Asian tax authorities.

Most common traditionally is litigation. After 1991 APAs become more important but a lot of taxpayers refuse to engage in them because they have been winning most of the cases after 1980.

4. Transfer pricing case law. *What is the evolution path of transfer pricing litigation in the country? For example: (i) Is transfer pricing litigation being gradually replaced by either MAPs or APAs, as regulated in the relevant tax treaties? (ii) Are foreign/local transfer pricing precedents and/ or published MAPs increasingly relevant as a source of law for solving transfer pricing disputes?*

Before 1995 the most important method was litigation with taxpayers being generally very successful. Under new regulations most cases are settled in appeals and there is increasing importance of APAs but many taxpayers will not engage in the APA process. MAP is of limited usefulness.

5. Customary international law and international tax procedure. *Has customary international law been applied in the country to govern the relevant methods for solving transfer pricing disputes (such as the MAP)? For example, has the OECD Manual on Effective Mutual Agreement Procedure ('OECD Manual') been deemed customary international tax law in the MAP arena for filling procedural gaps (for example, time limit for implementation of relief where treaties deviate from the OECD Model Tax Convention)?*

No.

6. Procedural setting and strategic interaction. *Does strategic interaction between taxpayers and tax authorities depend on the procedural setting in which they interact when trying to solve transfer pricing disputes? For example, which procedural setting in the country prompts the relevant parties to cooperate with each other the most for solving this sort of dispute, and why?*

Taxpayers face a choice between going for an APA and litigating. Many taxpayers refuse to enter the APA process because they tend to prevail in litigation. For smaller taxpayers, however, both APAs and litigation are prohibitively expensive.

7. The future of transfer pricing disputes resolution. *Which is the best available proposal in light of the interests of the country for facilitating the global resolution of transfer pricing disputes, and why?*

Some combination of profit split with formulas would seem the best option because it resolves the toughest issue, which is what to do with residual profits after normal returns are accounted for.

Transfer pricing disputes in Canada

DAVID G. DUFF AND BYRON BESWICK

4.1 Introduction

Canadian income tax law has included transfer pricing rules of one form or another since the early twentieth century.[1] Despite this lengthy statutory history, however, the number of transfer pricing cases in Canada is quite small, comprising only twelve reported judgments over the past sixty years.[2] While some of these decisions involve relatively straightforward applications of conventional transfer pricing methodologies, others address important issues in the application of judicial and statutory anti-avoidance rules as well as the arm's length standard.

This chapter reviews these transfer pricing cases as well as alternative methods for resolving transfer pricing disputes through advance pricing agreements (APAs) or treaty provisions establishing mutual agreement procedures (MAPs) or mandatory arbitration. Section 4.2 provides economic context for understanding transfer pricing in Canada, explaining

---

We are indebted to E. Ian Wiebe and Liam Bath for assistance in the preparation of this chapter.

[1] See section 4.3 below.

[2] *Central Canada Forest Products Ltd* v. *MNR* (1952) 7 Tax A.B.C. 161; *J. Hofert Ltd* v. *MNR* (1962) 28 Tax A.B.C. 270; *Dominion Bridge Co.* v. *The Queen* [1975] C.T.C. 263, 75 D.T.C. 5150 (FCTD), aff'd [1977] C.T.C. 554, 77 D.T.C. 53677 (FCA); *Spur Oil Ltd* v. *The Queen* [1980] C.T.C. 1707, 80 D.T.C. 6105 (FCTD), rev'd [1981] C.T.C. 336, 81 D.T.C. 5168 (FCA); *Indalex Ltd* v. *The Queen* [1986] 1 C.T.C. 219, 86 D.T.C. 6039 (FCTD), aff'd [1988] 1 C.T.C. 60, 88 D.T.C. 6053 (FCA); *Irving Oil Ltd* v. *The Queen* [1988] 1 C.T.C. 263, 88 D.T.C. 61328 (FCTD), aff'd [1991] 1 C.T.C. 350, 91 D.T.C. 5106 (FCA); *Safety Boss Ltd* v. *The Queen* [2000] 3 C.T.C. 2497, 2000 D.T.C. 1767 (TCC); *World Corp.* v. *The Queen* [2003] 4 C.T.C. 3009, 2003 D.T.C. 951 (TCC); *1143132 Ontario Inc.* v. *The Queen* [2010] 1 C.T.C. 2109, 2009 D.T.C. 1772 (TCC); *General Electric Capital Canada Inc.* v. *The Queen* [2010] 2 C.T.C. 2198, 2010 D.T.C. 2521 (TCC), aff'd 2010 FCA 344; *GlaxoSmithKline Inc.* v. *The Queen* 2008 D.T.C. 3957 (TCC), rev'd 2010 D.T.C. 7053 (FCA); and *Alberta Printed Circuits Ltd* v. *The Queen* 2011 T.C.C. 232. This list disregards cases in which transfer pricing transactions have been the context for criminal proceedings for tax evasion.

the importance of international trade and investment to the Canadian economy, the role of Canadian and foreign multinational enterprises (MNEs) in the Canadian economy, and the relationship between Canadian corporate income tax rates and rates in other countries with which Canada has significant trade and investment relationships. Section 4.3 explains the statutory framework for transfer pricing in Canada, providing a historical account of specific statutory provisions governing transfer pricing. Section 4.4 outlines the administrative framework for transfer pricing in Canada, reviewing administrative guidelines that elaborate upon and give more specific meaning to the general language of the statutory provisions governing transfer pricing. Section 4.5 examines transfer pricing cases in Canada, considering decided, settled and ongoing cases. Section 4.6 summarises Canadian experience with alternative methods for resolving transfer pricing disputes, including advance pricing arrangements (APAs), mutual agreement procedures (MAPs) under Canada's tax treaties, and the mandatory arbitration procedure introduced in the Fifth Protocol to the Canada–United States Treaty. Section 4.7 concludes.

4.2   Economic context

The Canadian economy is the fifteenth largest in the world,[3] and like that of most developed countries is dominated by the service sector (generating over 70 per cent of the country's gross domestic product (GDP)).[4] Though a primarily rural agrarian nation before the Second World War, Canada has followed other developed nations in transitioning from a resource-based to manufacturing-based economy, then again to a service-based economy. Notwithstanding this transition, the manufacturing and resource sectors continue to play an important role in the Canadian economy, accounting respectively for 13 and 7 per cent of GDP,[5] and more importantly for 37 and 61 per cent of exports.[6]

Regionally diverse, different industries tend to dominate in each region of the country. Manufacturing and financial services are

---

[3] Central Intelligence Agency, *World Factbook* (last updated 5 July 2011), available at www.cia.gov/library/publications/the-world-factbook/rankorder/2001rank.html. Countries ranked by gross domestic product at purchasing power parity exchange rates, based on 2010 estimates.

[4] Statistics Canada, *Gross Domestic Product by Industry*, Catalogue no. 15–001-X (May 2011), p. 13 (Table 1–1), available at www.statcan.gc.ca/pub/15–001-x/15–001-x2011005-eng.pdf.

[5] *Ibid.*

[6] Statistics Canada, *Exports of Goods on a Balance-of-Payment Basis, by Product* (May 2011), available at www.statcan.gc.ca/tables-tableaux/sum-som/101/cst01/gblec04-eng.htm.

concentrated in central Canada, agriculture dominates in the Prairie provinces, marine resources are naturally located on the east and west coasts of the country, and the oil and gas and mining industries are found mostly in the western provinces, Atlantic Canada, and the territories in the North. Although foreign-controlled enterprises play a significant role in Canadian manufacturing (particularly metals and automobiles) and some resource industries (e.g., forestry), Canadian-controlled enterprises predominate in financial services, insurance, telecommunications and media, oil and gas and mining. Canadian-controlled enterprises account for 27 of the top 500 MNEs by market capitalisation as reported by the *Financial Times*.[7]

As an open economy, international trade and investment play a substantial role in Canada's economy. In 2010, exports accounted for approximately 29.4 per cent of Canada's GDP,[8] while the stock of foreign direct investment (FDI) as a percentage of GDP was 35.6 per cent for inward FDI and 39.1 per cent for outward FDI.[9] Not surprisingly, given its proximity and the size of its economy, the United States accounts for the vast majority of exports as well as a substantial share of inward and outward FDI – accounting in 2010 for 70.3 per cent of exports,[10] 54.5 per cent

---

[7] *Financial Times, FT Global 500 2011*, available at http://media.ft.com/cms/33558890-98d4-11e0-bd66-00144feab49a.pdf. Listed banks are the Royal Bank of Canada (66), the Toronto-Dominion Bank (83), the Bank of Nova Scotia (104), the Bank of Montreal (233) and CIBC (254); insurance companies are Manulife Financial (282), Great West Lifeco (348) and Power Financial (404); telecommunications and media companies are Thomson Reuters (266), BCE (334) and Rogers Communications (464); oil and gas producers are Imperial Oil (185), EnCana (361), Canadian Natural Resources (139), Cenovus Energy (304), Suncor Energy (95), Husky Energy (336) and Talisman Energy (362); oil equipment and service providers are TransCanada (321) and Enbridge (390); and mining companies are Teck Resources (286), Barrick Gold (145), Goldcorp (204) and Potash Corporation of Saskatchewan (151). Also listed are Canadian National Railway (249), Blackberry manufacturer Research in Motion (306) and financial services provider Brookfield Asset Management (466).

[8] Department of Foreign Affairs and International Trade Canada, Economic Indicators, Annual Economic Indicators, available at www.international.gc.ca/economist-economiste/statistics-statistiques/indicators-indicateurs.aspx?menu_id=28&view=d.

[9] United Nations Conference on Trade and Development (UNCTAD), *World Investment Report 2011*, 'Country Fact Sheets: Canada', available at www.unctad.org/Templates/Page.asp?intItemID=2441&lang=1. Canada became a net capital exporting country in the mid 1990s.

[10] Foreign Affairs and International Trade Canada, Canada's State of Trade: Trade and Investment Update 2011, available at www.international.gc.ca/economist-economiste/performance/state-point/state_2011_point/2011_4.aspx?lang=eng&view=d. Canada (quarterly trade and economic indicators) 1st quarter 2011, available at www.international.gc.ca/economist-economiste/assets/pdfs/Quarterly_Ec_Indicators-ENG.pdf.

of inward FDI,[11] and 40.5 per cent of outward FDI.[12] While countries in the European Union accounted for only 10.4 per cent of Canadian exports in 2010,[13] they accounted for a much larger share of inward and outward FDI.[14] Other significant sources of inward FDI include Brazil, Japan and the People's Republic of China,[15] while other major destinations for outward FDI include low-tax jurisdictions like Barbados, Ireland, the Cayman Islands, Bermuda, Hungary and the Bahamas.[16]

Given the significant role of FDI in the Canadian economy, it is not surprising that a substantial share of international trade to and from Canada occurs between affiliated enterprises. In recent years, for example, intra-firm trade has accounted for approximately three-quarters of Canadian exports, as well as a significant portion of imports.[17]

While trade and investment between Canada and other countries creates the potential for profit shifting through transfer pricing, incentives for profit shifting depend on the relationship between corporate income tax rates in Canada and those in other jurisdictions, as well as the particular tax attributes of the transacting parties. Throughout most of the 1980s and 1990s, Canadian corporate income tax rates were higher than those in the United States and many other trading partners,

---

[11] Foreign Affairs and International Trade Canada, Canada's State of Trade: Trade and Investment Update 2011, Chapter VI Overview of Canada's Investment Performance, Table 6.3, available at www.international.gc.ca/economist-economiste/performance/state-point/state_2011_point/2011_6.aspx?lang=eng&view=d.

[12] Ibid. Table 6.6.

[13] See note 10 above.

[14] See notes 11 and 12 above, reporting that the stock of inward FDI in 2010 was 7.5 per cent from the United Kingdom, 3.4 per cent from France, 9.2 per cent from the Netherlands, 3.6 per cent from Switzerland and 1.8 per cent from Germany, while the stock of outward FDI in 2010 was 11.4 per cent to the United Kingdom, 1.4 per cent to France, 1.0 per cent to the Netherlands and 1.4 per cent to Germany.

[15] In 2009, Brazil accounted for 2.7 per cent of inward FDI, Japan for 2.4 per cent and China for 1.6 per cent. Statistics Canada, see note 11 above.

[16] In 2010, Barbados accounted for 8.4 per cent of outward FDI, Ireland for 3.8 per cent, the Cayman Islands for 3.3 per cent, Bermuda for 3.1 per cent, Hungary for 2.1 per cent and the Bahamas for 2 per cent. Statistics Canada, see note 12 above.

[17] DFAIT, Canada's State of Trade: Trade and Investment Update 2010, available at www.international.gc.ca/economist-economiste/performance/state-point/state_2010_point/2010_6.aspx?lang=eng&view=d. The intra-firm trade ratio is much lower for exports to and imports from the United States. Thus, while transfer pricing is a significant issue for trade between Canada and the United States, its relative importance may not be commensurate with relative jurisdictional trade figures.

creating a strong incentive to shift profits out of Canada. Since 2000, however, Canadian corporate rates have approached the OECD average, from over 40 per cent to 25 per cent in some provinces.[18] Canadian corporate rates are now substantially lower than those in the United States, making Canada the more attractive destination for profit shifting between the two countries.

4.3 Legislative framework for transfer pricing in Canada

4.3.1 Historical development of Canada's transfer pricing rules

The first statutory provision in Canada to address transfer pricing manipulation was paragraph 3(2)(a) of the Income War Tax Act (IWTA),[19] which was introduced in 1924 to 'prevent associated or holding companies making fictitious expenses a vehicle for evading the Income Tax Act'.[20] In its original form, the provision read as follows:

> Where any corporation carrying on business in Canada purchases any commodity from a parent, subsidiary or associated corporation at a price in excess of the fair market price, or where it sells any commodity to such a corporation at a price less than the fair market price, the Minister may, for the purpose of determining the income of such corporation, determine the fair price at which such purchase or sale shall be taken into the accounts of such corporation.

This paragraph subsequently became section 23 of the 1927 version of the IWTA,[21] section 17(1) and (2) of the 1948 and 1952 versions of the Income Tax Act (ITA),[22] and section 69(1) of the current version of the ITA, which was enacted in 1972.[23] According to the text of the current provision:

> Except as expressly otherwise provided in this Act,
>
> (a) where a taxpayer has acquired anything from a person with whom the taxpayer was not dealing at arm's length at an amount in excess of

---

[18] Canada Revenue Agency, Corporation Tax Rates, available at www.cra-arc.gc.ca/tx/bsnss/tpcs/crprtns/rts-eng.html.

[19] Income War Tax Act, S.C. 1917, c. 28.

[20] House of Commons Debates, vol. III, 1924 (10 June 1924), 3027 (Sir Henry Drayton and Mr Robb).

[21] Income War Tax Act, R.S.C. 1927, ch. 97.

[22] Income Tax Act, S.C. 1948, c. 52, and R.S.C. 1952, c. 148.

[23] Income Tax Act, S.C. 1970–71–72, c. 63.

the fair market value thereof at the time the taxpayer so acquired it, the taxpayer shall be deemed to have acquired it at that fair market value; [and]

(b) where the taxpayer has disposed of anything . . . to a person with whom the taxpayer was not dealing at arm's length for no proceeds or for proceeds less than the fair market value thereof at the time the taxpayer so disposed of it, . . . the taxpayer shall be deemed to have received proceeds of disposition therefore equal to that fair market value.

For the purpose of this and other provisions of the ITA, section 251(1) deems 'related persons' not to deal with each other at arm's length and stipulates that 'it is a question of fact whether persons not related to each other are at a particular time dealing with each other at arm's length'.[24] Section 251(2) contains a detailed definition of 'related persons' which need not be considered for the purpose of this chapter.

In addition to this statutory rule, which applies to transactions between Canadian residents as well as transactions with non-residents, two more provisions were enacted in the 1930s to apply specifically to transactions with non-residents. Enacted in 1934, section 23A of the IWTA provided that:

Whenever a Canadian company advances or has advanced moneys to a non-resident company and such advances remain outstanding for a period of one year without any interest or a reasonable rate of interest having been paid or credited to the Canadian company, the Minister may for the purposes of this Act, determine the amount of interest on such moneys which shall be deemed to have been received as income by the Canadian company.

This provision, the first of several statutory rules that supplement Canada's main transfer pricing provisions by addressing specific types of arrangements with non-residents,[25] subsequently became section 19(1) of the 1948 and 1952 versions of the ITA, and section 17(1) of the current ITA in 1972. Although it is relevant to the statutory scheme for transfer pricing, this chapter does not consider this provision in detail or any of the cases in which it has been considered.

---

[24] This definition was first introduced in 1948, when the provision was amended to apply to transactions between persons not dealing with each other at arm's length.

[25] Other transfer pricing related provisions currently found in the ITA include s. 18(4), the 'thin capitalisation' rules; s. 212(1)(a), which imposes a withholding tax on management fees paid to non-residents; and s. 95(2)(a.1) through (b), which treat certain income derived by a controlled foreign affiliate as foreign accrual property income which is included in the Canadian shareholder's income on an accrual basis.

The first direct predecessor to Canada's current transfer pricing rules was introduced in 1939 as section 23B of the IWTA. In its original form, section 23B stated that:

> Where any person carrying on business in Canada pays to a non-resident as price, rental, royalty or other payment for the use of any property or reproduction thereof, or for any right, an amount which is not in conformity with similar payments made by other persons in the same kind of business, then such payment may, for the purposes of determining the income of such person, be adjusted by the Minister accordingly, unless he is satisfied that the payor and the recipient are not associated, controlled one by the other, or controlled by the same interests.[26]

This provision became section 17(3) in 1948 and 1952, and section 69(2) in 1972. With the enactment in 1998 of Canada's current transfer pricing rules in section 247, section 69(2) was repealed.

Although specifically enacted to 'prevent collusion' between certain related parties,[27] section 23B of the IWTA was relatively narrow in scope: applying only to payments 'for the use of any property or ... any right' (generally lease and royalty payments), not to the purchase of a property or right itself, nor to payments for services; and applying only to payments *to* non-residents, not payments *from* non-residents.[28] Curiously, moreover, the provision referred to 'an amount which is not in conformity with similar payments made by other persons in the same kind of business' rather than a 'fair market price' that appeared in paragraph 3(2)(a) and subsequently section 23 of the Income War Tax Act.

The limitation in section 23A and its successors to amounts that are paid only *to* non-residents was addressed in 1949, when section 17(3A)

---

[26] No definition of control or associated corporations was present in the IWTA at this time. It is likely that, given the absence of an extended definition, 'control' in section 23B referred to *de jure* control (see, e.g., *Buckerfield's Ltd* v. *MNR* [1964] C.T.C. 504, 64 D.T.C. 5301). 'Associated' corporations may have referred to corporations mutually controlled by the same entity.

[27] House of Commons Debates, vol. IV, 1939 (24 May 1939), 4483 (Mr Cahan and Mr Ilsley).

[28] Section 23B appears to have been introduced in response to specific instances of transfer pricing abuse involving inflated rental payments by Canadians to affiliated US film production companies for the use of motion picture films. See House of Commons Debates, vol. II, 1939 (24 March 1939), 2276 (Mr Esling); vol. III, 1939 (1 May 1939), 3429 (Mr Esling); and vol. IV, 1939 (24 May 1939), 4482–3 (Mr Esling). Notwithstanding this specific motivation, however, it is clear that section 23B was intended to apply to payments for the use of all types of property and rights, not only payments for motion picture films. House of Commons Debates, vol. IV, 1939 (24 May 1939), 4483 (Mr Ilsley).

was enacted to allow the revenue authorities to increase the amount of any rental and royalty payment received by a person carrying on a business in Canada from a non-resident with whom the person was not dealing at arm's length.[29] This provision became section 17(4) in 1952 and section 69(3) in 1972. Like section 69(2), this rule was repealed in 1998 with the enactment of Canada's current transfer pricing rules in section 247.

Payments for services were included in 1952, when then section 17(3) and (4) were amended to apply to 'consideration for the carriage of goods or passengers or for other services' as well as payments for the use of property.[30] At this time, both provisions were also amended by replacing the original reference to amounts 'not in conformity with similar payments made by other persons in the same kind of business' with a reference to 'the amount (... referred to as "the reasonable amount") that would have been reasonable in the circumstances if the non-resident person and the taxpayer had been dealing at arm's length'.[31] According to the Minister of Finance at the time, this amendment was designed to create a more flexible rule that would accord greater discretion to the courts to address transfer pricing disputes.[32] It also brought Canada's domestic rules into conformity with the emerging international standard for addressing transfer pricing disputes, which was subsequently adopted in Article 9 of the OECD Model Convention.[33]

Payments for property itself were not included in these provisions until 1972, when section 69(2) and (3) were drafted so as to include payments for property as well as payments for the use or reproduction of property and consideration for services.[34] However, since sales and purchase transactions could also be challenged under the general rule

---

[29] Income Tax Act, S.C. 1949, c. 25, s. 6(1).

[30] Income Tax Act, R.S.C. 1952, c. 148. For an explanation of the purpose of this amendment, see House of Commons Debates, vol. III, 1952 (27 May 1952), 2627-8 (Mr Abbott).

[31] Income Tax Act, R.S.C. 1952, c. 148. It is interesting that s. 23B as originally drafted included a reasonability test, such that an amount was to be adjusted 'to a reasonable basis' where it was not 'in conformity with similar payments made by other persons in the same kind of business or which is unreasonable' (emphasis added). References to reasonability were ultimately excluded from s. 23B, because it was suggested that 'similar payments made by other persons in the same kind of business' was a clearer test than the term 'reasonable amount'. House of Commons Debates, vol. IV, 1939 (24 May 1939), 4482 (Mr Cahan).

[32] House of Commons Debates, vol. III, 1952 (27 May 1952), 2627-8 (Mr Abbott).

[33] OECD, Draft Double Taxation Convention on Income and Capital (Paris: OECD, 1963).

[34] Income Tax Act, S.C. 1970-71-72, c. 63.

for non-arm's length transactions in section 69(1) and its predecessors,[35] the effect of the 1972 amendments was not to broaden the scope of the statutory scheme for transfer pricing, but to consolidate all rules governing payments to and from non-residents within section 69(2) and (3). Since 1972, therefore, section 69(1) is generally applied only to non-arm's length transactions between Canadian residents, while non-arm's length transactions with non-residents are addressed under section 69(2) or (3) or the more recent rules in section 247.

4.3.2 Canada's current transfer pricing rules in section 247

Section 247 came into effect on 18 June 1998 and generally applies to taxation years beginning after 1997.[36] The main thrust for the introduction of section 247 appears to have been the increasingly robust transfer pricing rules, administrative guidelines and audit practices adopted by other countries, particularly the United States.[37] By the mid-1990s, it was apparent that multinational enterprises with US operations were generally complying only with US documentation and other rules, with few multinationals preparing documentation for non-US purposes.[38] In response, the 1997 Federal Budget announced that Canada's transfer pricing rules would be updated 'to bring Canadian law and practices in line with the evolving international standard to improve taxpayer compliance and to facilitate audits' by the revenue department.[39] According to the Budget:

> These changes will preserve the fairness of Canada's tax system by ensuring that profits earned by taxpayers in connection with international transactions with non-resident related parties are properly measured and taxed in Canada.[40]

---

[35] This was confirmed in 1949 when the enactment of s. 17(3A) was justified on the basis that it would ensure that then s. 17 would 'cover a lease both ways' as well as 'a sale both ways'. House of Commons Debates, vol. III, 1949 (5 December 1949), 2728 (Mr Abbott).

[36] Section 247(3) and (4), discussed below, apply to adjustments made under s. 247(2) for tax years that begin after 1998. The penalty provisions in s. 247 do not apply to transactions completed before 11 September 1997.

[37] Canada, Technical Committee on Business Taxation, *Report of the Technical Committee on Business Taxation* (Ottawa: Department of Finance, 1997), para. 6.33.

[38] Robert Turner, *Study on Transfer Pricing*, Working Paper 96–10 (Toronto: Department of Finance, 1996), para. 10.

[39] Department of Finance, *Budget 1997, Building the Future for Canadians: Tax Fairness* (Ottawa: Department of Finance, 1997), para. 28.

[40] *Ibid.*

As a result, the Budget explained, the purpose of its initiatives on transfer pricing were to (i) update the Canadian rules to conform with the revised 1995 OECD transfer pricing guidelines (and in particular, to clarify that transactions with related non-residents were to conform with the terms and conditions that would have prevailed had the parties been acting at arm's length); (ii) require adequate documentation of transactions with related non-residents; (iii) introduce new penalty provisions related to transfer pricing adjustments; and (iv) increase resources to support transfer pricing audits.[41]

Within section 247, the substantive transfer pricing provision appears in section 247(2). According to this provision, the transfer pricing rule applies where a taxpayer or partnership and a non-resident person with whom the taxpayer or partnership, or a member of the partnership, does not deal at arm's length participate in a 'transaction' or 'series of transactions' and either: (a) the terms or conditions made in respect of the transaction or series differ from those that would have been made between arm's length persons; or (b) the transaction or series would not have been entered into between arm's length persons and it can reasonably be considered that the transaction or series was not entered into primarily for *bona fide* purposes other than to obtain a tax benefit.

Where paragraph (a) applies, paragraph 247(2)(c) (together with the midamble to section 247(2)) provides that any amounts that would otherwise be determined for purposes of the ITA in respect of the taxpayer or the partnership shall be adjusted to the quantum or nature of the amounts that would have been determined if the terms and conditions made or imposed in respect of the transaction or series had been those that would have been made between persons dealing at arm's length. Where paragraph (b) applies, paragraph 247 (2)(d) (again together with the midamble to section 247(2)) grants the Minister the authority to adjust amounts to the quantum or nature of the amounts that would have existed if the transaction or series entered into between the participants had been that which would have been entered into between persons dealing at arm's length under arm's length terms and conditions. Thus, section 247(2)(b) and

---

[41] *Ibid.*

(d) essentially permit the recharacterisation of transactions (or series of transactions) where the conditions in section 247(2)(b) are met.[42]

For the purpose of this provision, section 247(1) defines a 'transaction' to include an 'arrangement or event', while section 248(10) defines a series of transactions to include 'any related transactions or events completed in contemplation of the series'.[43] By referring to the definition of the words in section 245(1), section 247(1) also defines a 'tax benefit' as 'a reduction, avoidance, or deferral of tax or other amount payable under this Act or an increase in a refund of tax or other amount under this Act', including 'a reduction, avoidance or deferral of tax or other amount that would be payable under this Act but for a tax treaty or an increase in a refund of tax or other amount under this Act as a result of a tax treaty'.

Section 247(2) allows for both upwards and downwards transfer pricing adjustments (downwards adjustments being those that reduce the taxpayer's Canadian profits). However, downwards adjustments are made at the discretion of the Minister and are available only where 'the circumstances are such that it would be appropriate that the adjustment be made'.[44]

---

[42] It is noteworthy that the Technical Committee on Business Taxation recommended in 1997 that the actual transactions as undertaken by non-arm's length parties should be respected, since the recharacterisation of transactions would be arbitrary and would increase the risk of double taxation: see note 37 above, paras. 6.32–6.34. The Technical Committee further suggested that the existing statutory anti-avoidance provisions in the ITA were sufficient to deal with circumstances where it was appropriate to disregard the structure of a transaction as adopted by the parties. However, the requirements for the application of the anti-avoidance provisions are more onerous than those for the application of the transfer pricing provisions. Specifically, the anti-avoidance provisions incorporate 'misuse or abuse' requirements that are not found in s. 247. It is perhaps for this reason that the 1997 amended transfer pricing provisions did indeed provide for a specific recharacterisation power in certain circumstances.

[43] In *OSFC Holdings Ltd* v. *The Queen* [2001] C.T.C. 82, 2001 D.T.C. 5471 (FCA), the Federal Court of Appeal discussed at length the meaning of a 'series of transactions', concluding at para. 36 that the ordinary meaning of the words includes only 'pre-ordained transactions which are practically certain to occur', whereas the extended definition in s. 248(10) includes additional transactions that are not pre-ordained, but have some connection to the series, provided that these transactions were completed in contemplation of the series: in *Canada Trustco Mortgage Co.* v. *The Queen* [2005] C.T.C. 215, 2005 D.T.C. 5523, the Supreme Court of Canada accepted the interpretation of s. 248(10) set out in *OSFC Holdings*, adding at para. 26 that a series as defined in s. 248(10) can include events arising either before or after the common law series.

[44] See s. 247(10). Downward transfer pricing adjustments are discussed to a limited extent in IC 87–2R, see section 4.4 below.

The Minister may decide not to exercise its discretion to make a downward adjustment where, for example, the taxpayer has the right to request, or has requested, relief from double taxation under the mutual agreement procedure of a tax treaty. The Minister may also decide not to allow a downwards adjustment where the taxpayer's request for the adjustment can be considered abusive.[45] Transfer Pricing Memorandum 03, 'Downward transfer pricing adjustments under subsection 247(2)',[46] provides further guidance on circumstances that may be considered 'abusive', which include situations where the taxpayer has requested a downwards adjustment but does not repatriate funds to the relevant foreign party within a reasonable time.[47]

Section 247(3) imposes a penalty of 10 per cent on the total of any upwards adjustments made under section 247(2) that exceeds the lesser of 10 per cent of the taxpayer's gross revenue for the year and CAN $5 million. However, the penalty base is reduced by both upwards and downwards adjustments for which the taxpayer has made 'reasonable efforts' to determine and use arm's length transfer prices. Thus, the penalty under section 247(3) applies essentially only to transactions where the taxpayer has not made reasonable efforts to determine and use arm's length transfer prices.[48] For the purpose of this provision, section 247(4) deems a taxpayer or partnership *not* to have made reasonable efforts to determine and use arm's length transfer prices unless the taxpayer or partnership makes or obtains, before the date when its tax return is due for the taxation year or fiscal period in which the transaction is entered into, 'records or documents' providing a description that is 'complete and accurate in all material respects' of the following:

(i) the property or services to which the transaction relates;
(ii) the terms and conditions of the transaction and their relationship, if any, to the terms and conditions of each other transaction entered into between the participants in the transaction;

---

[45] IC 87–2R, para. 26.

[46] 20 October 2003, available at www.cra-arc.gc.ca/tx/nnrsdnts/cmmn/trns/tpm03-eng.html.

[47] Such a situation may not be considered abusive if certain other provisions of the ITA, such as s. 15(1), operate to include the amount of the adjustment in the taxpayer's income. Refer to Transfer Pricing Memorandum 03 for further guidance.

[48] The penalty also does not apply to adjustments relating to a transaction that is a 'qualifying cost contribution arrangement' as defined in s. 247(1).

(iii) the identity of the participants in the transaction and their relationship to each other at the time the transaction was entered into;

(iv) the functions performed, the property used or contributed, and the
risks assumed by the participants in the transaction;

 (v) the data and methods considered and the analysis performed to
determine the transfer prices or the allocations of profits or losses
or contributions to costs, as the case may be, in respect of the
transaction; and

(vi) the assumptions, strategies and policies, if any, that influenced the
determination of the transfer prices or the allocations of profits or
losses or contributions to costs, as the case may be, in respect of the
transaction.

Where the taxpayer or partnership does not provide this information to the
revenue authorities within three months of a request to do so, this provision
also deems the taxpayer or partnership not to have made reasonable efforts
to fulfil the contemporaneous documentation requirement.

Where transfer pricing adjustments are made under section 247, other
cross-border tax implications may arise. For example, an excess amount
considered to have been paid by a Canadian subsidiary to a foreign
parent could be included in the latter's income under section 15(1) and
deemed to be a dividend pursuant to section 214(3)(a), in turn giving
rise to withholding tax implications for the Canadian subsidiary and the
non-resident recipient.[49]

4.4   Administrative guidelines

4.4.1   Overview of transfer pricing administration in Canada

The transfer pricing rules in section 247 are intended to be a broad and
flexible tool.[50] As a result, no guidance with respect to the arm's length
standard is contained within the provision itself. Nor did former section
69(2) or (3) provide any guidance on the meaning of an amount that
'would have been reasonable in the circumstances if the non-resident
person and the taxpayer had been dealing at arm's length'. While the

---

[49] IC 87–2R states at para. 212 that the Minister may grant relief from withholding tax
obligations in certain circumstances where the underlying transactions are not considered abusive.

[50] See, e.g., the discussion of broad versus specific transfer pricing rules in Turner, *Study on
Transfer Pricing*, see note 38 above, paras. 17–18.

United States has introduced detailed regulations to supplement general statutory provisions governing transfer pricing,[51] Canada has relied on administrative documents for this purpose.

The OECD's Model Convention on Income and on Capital ('OECD Model Convention') and related commentary ('OECD Commentary'),[52] as well as OECD transfer pricing guidelines, are particularly important to the application of transfer pricing rules in Canada. Canadian administrative transfer pricing documents have traditionally been explicitly modelled on OECD guidance. In addition, it is now apparent that Canadian courts consider the OECD Model Convention, Commentary and transfer pricing guidance persuasive in applying the Canadian domestic transfer pricing provisions. In *Crown Forest Industries Ltd* v. *Canada*,[53] the Supreme Court of Canada referred to the OECD Model Convention as highly persuasive and relied on the Convention and Commentary in interpreting the provisions of the Canada–United States Tax Convention (1980). In the transfer pricing context specifically, the Federal Court of Appeal has stated that '[i]t appears to be common ground that the OECD Guidelines inform or should inform the interpretation and application of subsection 69(2) of the Income Tax Act.'[54] OECD transfer pricing guidelines were also referred to extensively in *GlaxoSmithKline Inc.* v. *The Queen*,[55] discussed in section 4.5 below.

The first major OECD transfer pricing guidelines were contained in the OECD's 1979 *Transfer Pricing and Multinational Enterprises* (the '1979 Report').[56] The major topics addressed in the 1979 Report were (i) general issues regarding transfers between non-arm's length parties; (ii) the arm's length principle and its application; and (iii) transfer pricing methods for goods, intangible property, services and loans. In 1995, the OECD released the Transfer Pricing Guidelines for Multinational Enterprises and Tax Administrations (the '1995 Guidelines').[57] The 1995 Guidelines expanded significantly the OECD's 1979 Report.

---

[51] See R. S. Avi-Yonah, 'The Rise and Fall of Arm's Length: A Study in the Evolution of US International Taxation' (1995) 15 *Virginia Tax Review* 89.

[52] OECD, *Model Convention on Income and on Capital* (Paris: OECD, 2010).

[53] *Crown Forest Industries Ltd* v. *Canada* [1995] 2 C.T.C. 64, 95 D.T.C. 5389.

[54] *SmithKline Beecham Animal Health Inc.* v. *The Queen* [2002] 4 C.T.C. 93, 2002 F.C.A. 229 (FCA), para. 8.

[55] *GlaxoSmithKline Inc.* v. *The Queen*, see note 2 above.

[56] OECD, *Transfer Pricing and Multinational Enterprises* (Paris: OECD, 1979) ('1979 Report').

[57] OECD, *Transfer Pricing Guidelines for Multinational Enterprises and Tax Administrations* (Paris: OECD, 1995) ('1995 Guidelines').

In addition to the issues discussed in the 1979 Report, the 1995 Guidelines addressed transfer pricing documentation, examination practices for tax administrations, mutual agreement procedures, advance pricing arrangements, and specific guidance with respect to intangible property. Certain subsequent revisions to the 1995 Guidelines, including revisions to guidance on intangible property and services, cost contribution arrangements, advance pricing arrangements, and administrative approaches to avoiding and resolving transfer pricing disputes, culminated in the release in September 2009 of the revised Transfer Pricing Guidelines for Multinational Enterprises and Tax Administrations (the '2009 Guidelines').[58] Chapters I–III of the 2009 Guidelines were substantially revised in 2010 with additional guidance on the selection of appropriate transfer pricing methods, the application of transactional profit methods and comparability analyses. An additional chapter was also added in 2010 dealing with the application of the arm's length principle to business restructurings and post-restructuring arrangements.

The first major transfer pricing guidelines produced by Canadian tax authorities were contained in Information Circular (IC) 87–2, the first draft of which appeared in 1984, but the final version of which was not released until 1987.[59] The purposes of IC 87–2 were to summarise the scope and application of section 69(2) and (3), provide a discussion of transfer pricing principles, and outline the revenue department's policy on auditing international non-arm's length transactions.[60] As a general rule, the transfer pricing guidelines in IC 87–2 closely followed those contained in the OECD's 1979 Report.

In 1999, the Canadian tax authorities released IC 87–2R, an updated and expanded version of IC 87–2.[61] The major additions to the revised information circular were guidelines on the new documentation and penalty provisions contained in section 247 of the ITA; competent authority procedures; and advance pricing arrangements.

---

[58] OECD, *Transfer Pricing Guidelines for Multinational Enterprises and Tax Administrations* (Paris: OECD, 2009) ('2009 Guidelines').

[59] IC 87–2, *International Transfer Pricing and Other International Transactions* (27 February 1987). The primary incentive for the preparation of IC 87–2 appears to have been the need for clarification on the application of the Canadian transfer pricing rules following an industry-wide audit of the pharmaceutical industry in the early 1980s: W. R. Lawlor, *Revenue Canada's Approach to International Transfer Pricing*, Paper presented at the Special Seminar on Issues in International Transfer Pricing, October 1986 (Don Mills: Richard De Boo, 1987). p. 1.

[60] IC 87–2, para. 3.   [61] IC 87–2R, *International Transfer Pricing* (27 September 1999).

Finally, both the OECD and the Canadian tax authorities have released a number of supplementary transfer pricing documents. In particular, the Canadian tax authorities have issued several Transfer Pricing Memoranda, ten of which are currently active (and are discussed as applicable in the sections below). Some of the OECD's more significant supplementary transfer pricing documentation includes guidance on transfer pricing in e-commerce transactions;[62] the operation of mutual agreement procedures;[63] guidance regarding the attribution of profits to permanent establishments;[64] and summary transfer pricing country profiles.[65]

The following sections review the key administrative guidelines governing the application of Canada's transfer pricing provisions, established both by the OECD and the Canada Revenue Agency (CRA).

4.4.2 Arm's length principle

The fundamental statement of the arm's length principle as discussed in the OECD's 1979 Report was contained in Article 9(1) of the OECD's Model Double Tax Convention on Income and Capital (1977):

Where

(a) an enterprise of a Contracting State participates directly or indirectly in the management, control or capital of an enterprise of the other Contracting State, or

(b) the same persons participate directly or indirectly in the management, control or capital of an enterprise of a Contracting State and an enterprise of the other Contracting State,

and in either case conditions are made or imposed between the two enterprises in their commercial or financial relations which differ from those which would be made between independent enterprises, then any profits which would, but for those conditions, have accrued to one of the enterprises, but, by reason of those conditions, have not so accrued, may be included in the profits of that enterprise and taxed accordingly.

The application of the arm's length principle as set out in the 1979 Report was based on the comparison of non-arm's length transactions

---

[62] OECD, *E-commerce: Transfer Pricing and Business Profits Taxation*, OECD Tax Policy Study No. 10 (Paris: OECD, 2005).

[63] OECD, *Manual on Effective Mutual Agreement Procedures* (Paris: OECD, 2007) (MEMAP).

[64] OECD, *Report on the Attribution of Profits to Permanent Establishments* (Paris: OECD, 2008).

[65] OECD, Transfer Pricing Country Profiles, available at www.oecd.org/document/25/0,3746,en_2649_33753_37837401_1_1_1_1,00.html.

with similar transactions between arm's length parties. In particular, the 1979 Report stated that 'prices paid for goods transferred between associated enterprises should be, for tax purposes, those which would have been paid between unrelated parties for the same or similar goods under the same or similar circumstances'.[66]

The arm's length standard discussed in the OECD's 1995 Guidelines, and carried through to the 2009 Guidelines, is in principle the same as the standard described in the 1979 Report. According to the 2009 Guidelines, transfer prices are examined 'by reference to the conditions which would have been obtained between independent enterprises in comparable transactions and comparable circumstances'.[67] Both Guidelines state that the reasons for continuing to support the arm's length standard as expressed in Article 9(1) of the OECD Model Convention are that: (i) it provides parity between multinational and independent enterprises, avoiding tax advantages or disadvantages that would otherwise distort the competitive positions of either type of entity; (ii) it is generally effective in establishing transfer prices, at least where transactions do not involve highly specialised property or services; and (iii) no superior alternative currently exists for establishing transfer prices.[68]

The Canadian statement of the arm's length principle is set out in IC 87–2R as follows:

> The arm's length principle requires that, for tax purposes, the terms and conditions agreed to between non-arm's length parties in their commercial or financial relations be those that one would have expected had the parties been dealing with each other at arm's length . . .
> [T]he arm's length principle is generally based on a comparison of the prices, or margins, used or obtained by arm's length parties with those used or obtained by arm's length parties engaged in similar transactions.[69]

The Canadian administrative guidance in ICs 87–2 and 87–2R with respect to the meaning of the arm's length principle was explicitly intended to be consistent with the guidance set out in the OECD's 1979 Report and 1995 Guidelines, respectively.[70] It is not clear, however, whether the arm's length standard that arises from section 247 is the same as the arm's length standard contained in Article 9(1) of the OECD Model Convention and interpreted by the OECD Guidelines. Examples

---

[66] OECD 1979 Report, note 56 above, para. 28.
[67] OECD 1995 Guidelines, note 57 above, and 2009 Guidelines, note 58 above, para. 1.6.
[68] *Ibid.* paras. 1.7–1.9.   [69] IC 87–2R, paras. 28 and 30.
[70] IC 87–2, para. 9; and IC 87–2R, paras. 3–4.

of differences in the formulation of the arm's length standard between the two sources are as follows:

- Article 9(1) of the OECD Model Convention refers to participation in the 'management, control or capital of an enterprise' to establish the triggering relationship between two enterprises, while section 247(2) refers to persons who do not 'deal at arm's length';
- Article 9(1) refers to conditions made or imposed between enterprises in their 'commercial or financial relations', while section 247(2)(a) more narrowly refers to terms and conditions imposed in respect of 'a transaction or a series of transactions';
- Article 9(1) operates to adjust the 'profits' of an enterprise, while section 247(2) operates to adjust the 'quantum or nature' of amounts; and
- unlike Article 9(1), section 247(2)(b) and (d) explicitly provide for the recharacterisation of transactions in certain circumstances.

Whether or not, and to what extent, these and other differences in the formulation of the arm's length standard may affect its practical application in Canada remains uncertain.

4.4.3 Transfer pricing methods

OECD's 1979 Report and IC 87–2

The 1979 Report contained the OECD's first relatively comprehensive discussion of specific transfer pricing methods. With respect to the transfer of goods, the 1979 Report stressed that, ideally, determining whether a transfer price conforms to the arm's length principle requires direct reference to prices in comparable transactions between arm's length parties. On this basis, the report concluded, the 'comparable uncontrolled price' (CUP) method was the most appropriate method for establishing transfer prices.[71]

---

[71] OECD 1979 Report, note 56 above, para. 11. Under the CUP method, a transfer price is set by direct reference to prices of comparable transactions between arm's length parties. To the extent the terms of the comparable transactions differ from the transaction under examination, adjustments to the price of the comparable transactions are required. In determining whether a particular arm's length transaction is comparable to the transaction under examination, several factors must be considered, including the market conditions at the time the transactions took place; the similarity of the goods sold; the stage of the sale (for example, wholesale versus retail); branding; any guarantees made; the volume of goods sold; the timing of the transactions; costs of transport; advertising; packaging; payment terms, etc.: *ibid.* paras. 53–5.

The 1979 Report recognised that the information necessary to apply the CUP method may not be available or may be impractical to collect; or that it may not be possible to determine whether or not arm's length transactions are in fact comparable with the related party transaction under examination.[72] In such circumstances, the report suggested that it may be necessary to use a method that provides a reasonable approximation of an arm's length price, such as the 'cost plus' method or the 'resale price' method.[73]

The 1979 Report stated that 'any other method which is found to be acceptable' may be used if that method provides the best evidence of an arm's length price in a particular case.[74] Nevertheless, alternative methods suggested in the Report all involved comparisons of some aspect of a non-arm's length transaction, such as profits or the return on capital, with those of an arm's length transaction.[75]

Global or direct methods of profit allocation were described in the 1979 Report as 'radical' and methods that 'move away from the arm's length approach'.[76] The OECD rejected the use of fixed formulary allocation methods, for the following reasons: (i) formulary methods were incompatible with the provisions of the 1979 Model Tax Convention; (ii) formulary methods are necessarily arbitrary, disregarding market conditions and the particular circumstances of the transactions between the parties involved; (iii) the information required to apply formulary methods is difficult to obtain; and (iv) formulary methods give rise to a significant risk of double taxation if countries cannot agree on the formulary factors to be used.[77] The OECD also discouraged the use of non-formulary profit allocation methods (such as the 'profit split' method discussed in the 1995 Guidelines), although the 1979 Report did state that 'some regard to the total profits of the multinational enterprise

---

[72] *Ibid.* para. 13.

[73] *Ibid.* Under the cost plus method, a transfer price is set by taking the non-arm's length seller's cost of producing the product and adding a reasonable profit mark-up. The cost plus method is useful where the related purchaser adds significant value to the product prior to resale, or where there is a significant time gap before the product is resold. Where possible, the profit mark-up is derived from comparable arm's length transactions. Under the resale price method, a transfer price is set by taking the price at which a product has been finally sold to an arm's length purchaser and subtracting a reasonable gross profit mark-up. The resale price method is appropriate where the related purchaser adds relatively little value to the profit prior to resale. Similar to the gross profit method, the profit mark-up should be derived from comparable arm's length transactions.

[74] *Ibid.* para. 46.   [75] *Ibid.* paras. 71–4.   [76] *Ibid.* para. 14.   [77] *Ibid.*

would perhaps be helpful as a check on the determination of an arm's length price where other methods were difficult to apply'.[78]

With respect to service transactions, the 1979 Report made similar recommendations regarding appropriate transfer pricing methods. Services provided to a non-arm's length party were to be priced by reference to prices paid in similar transactions between unrelated parties (similar to the CUP method for goods).[79] Where information regarding such transactions is unavailable, the 1979 Report recommended that a transfer price be established based on the cost of providing the services.[80]

Consistent with the 1979 Report, IC 87–2 recommended the use of the CUP method for transactions involving goods, followed by the cost plus and resale price methods where the application of the CUP was not possible.[81] Methods other than these were discouraged unless necessary. Possible alternative pricing methods raised in IC 87–2 were a 'check point' method, whereby a proposed transfer price could be measured against the cost of direct materials, the full cost of production, the replacement value of the goods, and/or the value of the completed product of which the transferred goods were a component;[82] and a comparison of prices with values for customs purposes.[83]

OECD's 1995 Guidelines and IC 87–2R

The OECD's 1995 Guidelines contained a more comprehensive discussion of transfer pricing methods than the 1979 Report. The guidelines continued to support the CUP, cost plus and resale price methods ('traditional transaction' methods) as the most desirable, and were of the view that in the majority of cases, it is possible to apply such methods.[84] However, the 1995 Guidelines appeared to give somewhat greater support than the 1979 Report to certain profit allocation methods. This shift likely resulted from the recognition that obtaining sufficient information to apply traditional transaction methods is frequently difficult or impossible.[85] Thus, while the 1995 Guidelines noted that profit is not a condition 'made or imposed' in a transaction and is therefore inconsistent with the arm's length comparability approach, 'in those exceptional cases in which the complexities of real-life business put practical difficulties in the way of the application of the traditional

---

[78] *Ibid.*   [79] *Ibid.* para. 164.   [80] *Ibid.* para. 165.   [81] IC 87–2, paras. 14–20.

[82] *Ibid.* para. 20.   [83] *Ibid.* para. 21.

[84] OECD 1995 Guidelines, note 57 above, para. 3.49.

[85] See, e.g., the discussion at *ibid.* para. 2.49.

transaction methods and provided all the safeguards ... are observed, application of the transactional profit methods ... may provide an approximation of transfer pricing in a manner consistent with the arm's length principle'.[86]

The primary profit methods endorsed in the 1995 Guidelines were the 'profit split' method and the transactional net margin method (TNMM). The guidelines described two branches of the profit split method: a 'contribution' approach, whereby the entire profits resulting from a particular transaction are allocated based on a functional analysis of the parties involved, taking into account assets used and risks assumed;[87] and a 'residual profit' approach, whereby each party to the transaction is allocated a basic return determined by reference to market returns for similar types of transactions between independent enterprises, and the remaining profit (resulting from the transfer of unique intangibles, for example) are allocated based on the facts and circumstances of the case.[88] Benefits of the profit split method noted in the guidelines included the fact that all parties to the transaction are considered and the total profits of a transaction are allocated, such that economies of scale or other joint efficiencies are included in the division of profits (which cannot in principle be accomplished under traditional transaction methods).[89] However, the profit split method raised the significant difficulty of having to measure combined revenues and costs and determining which costs are applicable to the transaction.[90]

The TNMM differs from the profit split method in that it is applied only to one side of a related party transaction. In this respect, the 1995 Guidelines noted that the TNMM is similar to the cost plus and resale price methods.[91] The TNMM is applied by examining the net profit margin relating to the controlled transaction relative to a chosen base, such as costs, sales or assets.[92] The net margin from the controlled transaction is ideally established by reference to the net margin the same taxpayer earns in comparable uncontrolled transactions. However, where this is not possible, the net margin that would have been earned in comparable transactions by an independent enterprise can serve as a guide.[93] Although only one side of a transaction is assessed under the TNMM, making it easier to apply than the profit split method, the guidelines note that the one-sided nature of the TNMM risks attributing

---

[86] *Ibid.* para. 3.2.   [87] *Ibid.* paras. 3.5 and 3.17.   [88] *Ibid.* para. 3.19.
[89] *Ibid.* para. 3.7.   [90] *Ibid.* para. 3.9.   [91] *Ibid.* para. 3.26.   [92] *Ibid.* para. 3.26.
[93] *Ibid.* para. 3.26.

profits to one member of a related party group that implicitly leaves other members of the group with implausibly low or high profit levels.[94]

The 1995 Guidelines also stated that other profit methods are acceptable only to the extent they are consistent with the principles underlying the profit split method and the TNMM.[95]

Although the 1995 Guidelines revealed a change in attitude towards profit methods, they continued to strongly reject the use of global formulary apportionment. In particular, the 1995 Guidelines stated that formulary apportionment presents enormous political and administrative complexity, since it requires broad agreement and cooperation between tax administrations regarding the formulas to be used, the measurement of the global tax base, the details of the accounting system to be used to measure profits, the formulas to be used to apportion the tax base, the weighing of the relevant factors, and other considerations.[96] Failure to reach an agreement on these issues creates a significant risk of double taxation for multinational enterprises. Furthermore, formulary methods would necessarily be arbitrary to some degree; would involve significant compliance costs for multinational enterprises; and would be inconsistent with the single entity approach underlying traditional transaction methods.[97]

Consistent with the 1995 Guidelines, IC 87–2R recommends the use of traditional transaction methods where possible (ideally, the CUP method), and profit methods as a last resort.[98] With respect to profit methods, however, IC 87–2R adopts a clear preference for the profit split method over the TNMM.[99] According to the IC, the one-sided nature of the TNMM is more likely than the profit split method to produce inappropriate results, particularly where the transaction involves valuable or unique intangible assets.[100] With respect to the profit split method, moreover, IC 87–2R notes a preference for the residual profit split approach over a contribution analysis, since relative contributions are often difficult to quantify.[101]

OECD's 2009 Guidelines

The OECD's 2009 Guidelines represent a greater shift from traditional transaction methods to profit split methods. In particular, although the 2009 Guidelines still state a preference for a traditional transaction

---

[94] *Ibid.* para. 3.21.   [95] *Ibid.* para. 3.1.   [96] *Ibid.* para. 3.64.
[97] *Ibid.* paras. 3.67–3.71.   [98] IC 87–2R, paras. 52–4.   [99] *Ibid.* para. 60.
[100] *Ibid.* para. 94.   [101] *Ibid.* para. 105.

method over a profit split method where they can be applied in an equally reliable manner,[102] the document now proposes a 'best method' approach:

> No one method is suitable in every possible situation and the applicability of any particular method need not be disproved. The selection of a transfer pricing method always aims at finding the most appropriate method for a particular case.[103]

The 2009 Guidelines explicitly recognise the importance of profit split methods in particular circumstances:

> There are situations where transactional profit methods are found to be more appropriate than traditional transaction methods ... [W]here there is no or limited publicly available reliable gross margin information on third parties, traditional transaction methods might be difficult to apply in cases other than those where there are reasonably reliable comparables, and a transactional profit method might be the most appropriate method in view of the availability of reasonably reliable information.[104]

We are not aware of any CRA published position to date regarding potential changes to IC 87–2R or other transfer pricing guidance addressing the OECD's 2009 Guidelines.

Summary of administrative guidance on transfer pricing methods

The foregoing analysis suggests that, since 1979, the OECD and Canadian transfer pricing guidelines have exhibited a trend (albeit a gradual one) from a traditional comparability approach for transfer pricing methods to an approach more tolerant of direct profit allocation. Clearly, this trend is a result of the growing complexity and uniqueness of related party transactions. There are also indications that the profit split method and the TNMM are becoming increasingly relied on by multinational enterprises, evidenced, for example, by the Canadian experience with advance pricing agreements.[105]

4.4.4 Recharacterisation of transactions

As a number of Canadian transfer pricing cases illustrate, the characterisation of a transaction can have a significant impact on transfer pricing

---

[102] OECD 2009 Guidelines, note 58 above, para. 2.3.
[103] *Ibid.* para. 2.2.   [104] *Ibid.* para. 2.4.   [105] See section 4.6 below.

arrangements and on the definition of an arm's length price.[106] A question therefore arises as to what extent the characterisation or nature of a transaction as determined by the non-arm's length parties should be respected by tax administrations.

The OECD's 1979 Report stated that 'as a general principle, tax authorities should base their search for an arm's length price on actual transactions and should not substitute hypothetical transactions for them, thus seeming to substitute their own commercial judgment for that of the enterprise at the time when the transactions were concluded'.[107] However, the 1979 Report also stated that the form of a transaction as structured by the parties may have to be ignored. In particular, the 1979 Report recognised 'that it may be important in considering, for example, what is ostensibly interest on a loan to decide whether it is an interest payment or, in reality, a dividend or other distribution of profit'.[108]

Like the 1979 Report, the OECD's 1995 and 2009 Guidelines allow for the recharacterisation of transactions in limited circumstances.[109] The Guidelines suggest that where the economic substance of a transaction differs from its form, or where arrangements between related parties differ from those which would have been adopted by arm's length parties behaving in a rational manner, recharacterisation of the arrangements may be appropriate.[110] For example, where an entity makes a debt investment in a related party that would have been made as an equity investment in an arm's length context, it may be appropriate to treat the loan as a subscription of capital.[111] Similarly, where an entity sells an unlimited entitlement to intellectual property rights involving future research for a lump sum under a long-term contract, it may be appropriate to recharacterise the arrangement as an ongoing research agreement.[112] The OECD's rationale for recharacterisation appears to be that, because of the lack of divergence of interests among associated entities, the contracts entered into between them may be ignored in order to determine profits that reflect arrangements that would be made between persons transacting at arm's length. The OECD Guidelines state that 'it is

---

[106] See section 4.5 below.   [107] OECD 1979 Report, note 56 above, para. 15.

[108] *Ibid.* para. 23.

[109] OECD 1995 Guidelines, note 57 above, para. 1.37. Such a recharacterisation is for tax purposes only and does not affect the underlying contracts for non-tax purposes: *ibid.* para. 1.2.

[110] *Ibid.* para. 1.37.   [111] *Ibid.*   [112] *Ibid.*

therefore important to examine whether the conduct of the parties conforms to the terms of the contract or whether the parties' conduct indicates that the contractual terms have not been followed or are a sham'.[113]

It is noteworthy that both the 1979 Report and the 1995 and 2009 Guidelines state that the intention to minimise tax is irrelevant in the context of a transfer pricing analysis:

> [T]he need to adjust the actual price to an arm's length price ... arises irrespective of any contractual obligation undertaken by the parties to pay a particular price or of any intention of the parties to minimize tax. Hence, the consideration of transfer pricing problems should not be confused with the consideration of problems of tax fraud or tax avoidance, even though transfer pricing policies may be used for such purposes.[114]

This irrelevance of intent in the OECD guidelines is inconsistent with Canada's current transfer pricing rules, which stipulate that a transaction or series must have been entered into primarily for the purpose of obtaining a tax benefit in order to be recharacterised under section 247 (2)(b) and (d). It is likely that the recharacterisation provisions were tempered in this manner to limit their breadth.[115]

The guidance in IC 87–2R regarding the recharacterisation of transactions is consistent with that in the OECD's 1995 and 2009 Guidelines (except on the issue of the relevance of intent to obtain a tax benefit as a precondition to recharacterisation). IC 87–2R states that transactions as structured by the parties are generally accepted and recognises that a related party transaction may be structured in a form that would not normally be found in an arm's length context.[116] However, the IC also notes that recharacterisation may be appropriate in exceptional cases, and in particular in the situations described in the OECD's 1995 Guidelines.[117]

It is the CRA's administrative practice, as stated in its administrative guidance, to refer all proposed assessments involving the recharacterisation

---

[113] *Ibid.* para. 1.29.

[114] OECD 1979 Report, note 56 above, p. 9. This view is in marked contrast to the requirement for a tax motivation under the Canadian anti-avoidance provisions, and it is therefore curious why early Canadian transfer pricing related cases tended to be argued under the anti-avoidance provisions and not the transfer pricing provisions.

[115] A similar purpose test limitation applies in the context of the General Anti-Avoidance Rule in s. 245 of the ITA, though s. 245 includes an additional 'misuse' or 'abuse' criterion.

[116] IC 87–2R, para. 43.   [117] *Ibid.* para. 44.

of non-arm's length transactions to the Transfer Pricing Review Committee (TPRC) before any proposed reassessment relying on the recharacterisation provisions is presented to the taxpayer.[118] The TPRC must also provide final approval before a recharacterisation reassessment is made.

4.4.5   Transfer pricing documentation

The 1979 Report provided little guidance with respect to transfer pricing documentation. The report only noted generally that it 'would be reasonable . . . to require MNEs to provide in support of any important contention either the relevant legal documents and explanatory material or at any rate sufficient information to allow the tax authorities to arrive at an informed judgement in the matter'.[119]

The 1979 Report further stated that transfer pricing evidence need not necessarily be in writing; and that documentation should not be required for every transaction, if obtaining the documentation would otherwise be an unnecessary burden on multinational enterprises.[120]

The OECD's 1995 Guidelines in this area, which have been carried through to the 2009 Guidelines, provided a significantly expanded discussion of documentation requirements. The 1995 Guidelines stated that taxpayers should make reasonable efforts at the time transfer pricing is established to determine whether the transfer pricing is appropriate for tax purposes in accordance with the arm's length principle.[121] Contrary to the 1979 Report, the 1995 Guidelines noted an expectation for written support of compliance with the arm's length principle, which taxpayers should be reasonably obliged to produce to the tax administration on request.[122]

Although dependent on the facts and circumstances of each case, the documentation requirements noted in the 1995 Guidelines generally included information about the related parties involved in the controlled transaction; a description of the business, structure and strategies of each entity involved in the transaction; a functional analysis of the parties, taking into account assets used and risks assumed; information derived from independent enterprises engaged in similar transactions or businesses; the transaction at issue; the nature and terms of the transaction;

---

[118] *Ibid.* para. 46; and Transfer Pricing Memorandum 07, *Referrals to the Transfer Pricing Review Committee* (2005).
[119] OECD 1979 Report, note 56 above, para. 25.   [120] *Ibid.* para. 25.
[121] OECD 1995 Guidelines, note 57 above, para. 5.28.   [122] *Ibid.* para. 5.4.

economic conditions at the time the transaction took place; how the product or service flows among the associated enterprises; and a list of comparable companies having similar transactions.[123]

Nevertheless, the 1995 Guidelines also recognised that a balance must be achieved between required documentation and the administrative burdens of preparing such documentation. The guidelines noted that a taxpayer should be expected to prepare certain documents only if they are indispensable for a reasonable assessment of whether transfer prices satisfy the arm's length principle and they can be obtained or prepared without disproportionately high cost. Taxpayers should not be expected to have prepared or obtained documents beyond the minimum needed to make a reasonable assessment of whether the taxpayer has complied with the arm's length principle.[124]

Canadian domestic guidance on transfer pricing documentation is contained primarily in IC 87–2R.[125] As with the 1995 Guidelines, IC 87–2R states that required transfer pricing documentation depends on the facts and circumstances of the particular transaction.[126] Notably, IC 87–2R indicates that the sufficiency of a taxpayer's documentation is a major factor in determining whether the CRA will review a particular transfer pricing issue in more detail.[127] Though IC 87–2R does not provide an exhaustive list of required information, documentation should include at least information on, where applicable: the general organisation and description of the taxpayer's business; the selection of a particular transfer pricing methodology; the projection of the expected benefits as they relate to the valuation of an intangible; the scope of the search and criteria used to select comparables; an analysis of the factors determining comparability; and the assumptions, strategies and policies as they relate to the tangible property, intangible property and services being transferred.[128] Required documentation may include foreign-based documents and information to the extent they are relevant in determining arm's length prices.[129]

IC 87–2R also addresses the rules in section 247(4), which deem a taxpayer not to have made reasonable efforts to determine and use arm's length transfer prices unless certain contemporaneous documentation is prepared by the taxpayer's due date for the year in which the transaction

---

[123] *Ibid.* paras. 5.17–5.19.   [124] *Ibid.* para. 5.28.
[125] IC 87–2 did not discuss transfer pricing documentation requirements.
[126] IC 87–2R, para. 183.   [127] *Ibid.* para. 186.   [128] *Ibid.* para. 187.
[129] *Ibid.* para. 202.

took place.[130] To ensure fair and consistent application of the law, the TPRC is responsible for reviewing all cases where a transfer pricing penalty may be assessed to evaluate whether reasonable efforts have been made.[131]

With respect to documentation requirements, taxpayers should be aware of information filing obligations in section 233.1 of the ITA. Section 233.1 requires residents of Canada and non-residents who carry on business in Canada to provide information regarding transactions with non-arm's length non-residents on an annual basis, which the tax authorities use to identify potential areas of transfer pricing risk.[132] The recommendation for an annual reporting obligation with respect to non-arm's length non-residents arose initially in the 1966 Report by the Royal Commission on Taxation (Carter Commission). The Carter Commission's view in the 1966 Report was that only through the constant surveillance of inter-company pricing practices could the inappropriate shifting of profits from high tax to low tax jurisdictions be controlled.[133] Although this recommendation was made in 1966, section 233.1 was not introduced until 1988.

Additional administrative resources have been published as aids for understanding Canadian transfer pricing documentation requirements. Transfer Pricing Memorandum 09 discusses a number of issues relating to reasonable efforts to determine and use arm's length transfer prices, including what may constitute reasonable efforts; reasonable efforts related to qualifying cost contribution arrangements; and penalty referrals to the TPRC. Transfer Pricing Memorandum 05 provides information regarding audit-related requests to taxpayers for transfer pricing documentation.

4.5   Transfer pricing cases

Notwithstanding the lengthy history of statutory provisions governing transfer pricing in Canada, the number of judicial decisions in Canada that address transfer pricing transactions is remarkably small,

---

[130] This provision is discussed in section 4.3 above.

[131] Refer to Transfer Pricing Memorandum 09, *Reasonable Efforts under Section 247 of the Income Tax Act* (2006) for further information on reviews by the Transfer Pricing Review Committee relating to penalties.

[132] The form for reporting such transactions is Form T106, Information Return of Non-Arm's Length Transactions with Non-Residents.

[133] Royal Commission on Taxation (Carter Commission), *Report* (Ottawa: Queen's Printer, 1966), vol. IV, p. 561.

comprising only eleven reported judgments. The first two of these decisions, decided in 1952 and 1962, involved sales to non-arm's length non-resident corporations, and were challenged under the general provision governing non-arm's length transactions in what is now section 69(1) of the ITA. Four subsequent cases, decided between the mid 1970s and early 1990s, involved purchases from non-resident affiliates and were challenged under judicial anti-avoidance doctrines and more general statutory anti-avoidance rules. In the early 2000s, Canadian courts decided three cases involving contracts for services that were either performed by or provided to a non-arm's length non-resident, one of which was argued under the transfer pricing rule in former section 69(2), one under ordinary principles of business valuation, and the most recent under section 247. As well, in the last few years Canadian courts have released three additional transfer pricing decisions involving Canada's transfer pricing rules, two of which address important issues in the application of these rules and resulted in appellate decisions.

The following sections review each of these judicial decisions, in order to demonstrate the types of transfer pricing transactions that the Canadian revenue authorities have challenged, and the kinds of considerations that Canadian courts have determined relevant in adjudicating these types of cases. A final section discusses other transfer pricing cases that have been settled or remain ongoing and have not resulted in judicial decisions.

4.5.1   The early cases

Given the traditional perception of Canadians as 'hewers of wood and drawers of water', it is perhaps fitting that the first reported transfer pricing case in Canada involved the sale of wood pulp by a wholly-owned Canadian subsidiary (Central Canada Forest Products Ltd) to its US parent (Central Paper Company Incorporated).[134] The Canadian subsidiary in this case reported no taxable income from the sale of 17,850 cords of wood pulp in 1949. The revenue department subsequently assessed the taxpayer under the general non-arm's length transaction rule in section 17(2) of the 1948 Income Tax Act on the basis that the fair market value of the pulp was CAN $1.00 per cord, resulting in taxable income of CAN $17,850.00.[135] On appeal, the revenue

---

[134] *Central Canada Forest Products Ltd* v. *MNR*, see note 2 above.   [135] *Ibid.* para. 4.

department failed to provide any evidence to support this assessment, while the taxpayer adduced evidence indicating that the stumpage charge to purchase cutting rights represented a significant percentage of its revenues. Not surprisingly, the Tax Appeal Board allowed the taxpayer's appeal, concluding that 'the evidence adduced by the appellant amply discharged any onus cast upon it by an assessment that, as presently founded, appears . . . to be insupportable'.[136] More specifically, the Board explained:

> Why the amount per cord added by the respondent should have been $1.00 instead of 20¢, say, or some other sum, be it larger or smaller, was not explained. All that was clear was that someone in the respondent's department had seen fit to add $1.00 per cord on an undisclosed basis of calculation or computation. The factors taken into account in so doing were not revealed. No forestry engineer was called to give expert evidence. The Board was left to deal with the problem as best if could, on the strength of most unsatisfactory and flimsy evidence.[137]

Henceforth, it would seem, Canadian transfer pricing cases were destined to become battles between experts.

Notwithstanding the clear message from the *Central Canada Forest Products* judgment that expert evidence is essential to the adjudication of transfer pricing cases, the revenue department approached its next transfer pricing case without calling a single expert witness. In *J. Hofert Ltd v. M.N.R.*,[138] the taxpayer was a Canadian corporation that was controlled by the shareholders of a US corporation (J. Hofert Company) that was at the time 'probably the largest dealer in Christmas trees in the United States of America'.[139] In assessing the taxpayer's income for its 1954 to 1956 taxation years, the revenue department increased the price of Christmas trees that it sold to J. Hofert Company on the grounds that these sales 'had not been negotiated at arm's length' and were at prices below the fair market value of the trees, as indicated by the much higher prices charged to arm's length purchasers in Canada.[140] The case turned on the status of the sales to the Canadian purchasers as a comparable uncontrolled price.

---

[136] *Ibid.* para. 11.   [137] *Ibid.* para. 5.   [138] See note 2 above.   [139] *Ibid.* para. 2.
[140] *Ibid.* para. 3: 'When assessing the appellant's reported income for these years, the Minister . . . ruled that the sales to the American buyer had not been negotiated at arm's length, the price of $2.00 to $2.04 per bale was too low and that the fair market value of the trees sold was always the price obtained in Canada in any relevant year, viz. $2.75, $2.87 and $3.19 respectively.'

Relying on the evidence of two expert witnesses, the taxpayer effectively challenged the Minister's characterisation of the Canadian sales as comparable to the sales to J. Hofert Company. First, it was argued, the higher prices for sales in Canada resulted from 'a more complicated domestic marketing process, which included the payment of wages and other expenses incurred between roadside and delivery points'.[141] Furthermore, the taxpayer's witnesses observed:

> The trees bought from the appellant by J. Hofert Company were acquired for purposes of resale in American territory to distributors, wholesalers and retailers, the highest price being paid by retailers, of course. Approximately 60% of the resold trees went to retailers and the larger part of the remaining 40% went to wholesalers. The trees sold in Canada to Canadian purchasers went to retailers only.[142]

In addition, they explained:

> all bales of trees purchased by J. Hofert Company were paid for by the latter even if numbers of the bales later proved unsuitable for resale. Trees sold to Canadian purchasers, on the other hand, were not paid for if found unsatisfactory. Instead the appellant had to bear the loss involved. In addition, the appellant took back every unsold tree. Selling trees in Canada made it necessary to have a domestic organisation of some kind for the purpose. No such requirement presented itself in the case of sales to J. Hofert Company.[143]

Finally, and perhaps most significantly, the taxpayer's witnesses testified that the quantity of trees sold in Canada was a small fraction of the trees sold to J. Hofert Company.[144] For this reason, the Board affirmed, 'it was only reasonable to grant a lower price where a huge quantity of trees was saleable under contract to one and the same purchaser'.[145]

In contrast to the taxpayer, the revenue authority failed to call any 'disinterested person in the Christmas tree business' to testify,[146] failed to provide any 'cogent evidence' to support its view that the taxpayer had sold trees to J. Hofert Company at prices less than their fair market value, and failed to contradict the testimony of the taxpayer's expert witnesses.[147]

---

[141] *Ibid.* para. 5.   [142] *Ibid.* para. 7.   [143] *Ibid.*

[144] *Ibid.* para. 4: 'the quantity of bales sold in Canada in each of the 1954 and 1955 taxation years was the equivalent of only about one-seventh of the bales sold to the one American purchaser. In 1956, the proportion was less than one-ninth.'

[145] *Ibid.,* emphasizing that '[i]t has long been a recognized trade practice ... that the bigger the purchase, the lower and more attractive should be the price'.

[146] *Ibid.*   [147] *Ibid.* para. 6.

Instead, the Board complained that it 'virtually was asked to infer from figures relating to sales made in just a part of Canada by a single dealer, the appellant, that the fair market value of Christmas trees was thereby established'.[148]

Given the testimony by the taxpayer's expert witnesses and the absence of any cogent evidence by the revenue department, it is not at all surprising that the Board allowed the taxpayer's appeal. Concluding that there was 'no essential relationship between commodity prices obtained in Canada and those obtained in similar, but much larger, transactions in American territory',[149] the Board rejected the revenue department's characterisation of the Canadian sales as a comparable arm's length transaction reflecting fair market value. In addition, the Board emphasised: 'Before the fair market value can be used as a criterion in making an income tax assessment, there must at least be demonstrable certainty as to the amount of that value.'[150]

4.5.2   Anti-avoidance cases

After the decision in *Hofert*, more than a decade passed before a Canadian court ruled on another transfer pricing transaction in *Dominion Bridge Co. v. The Queen*.[151] On this occasion, the revenue department decided to challenge the transaction not under specific statutory rules governing transactions with non-residents and non-arm's length persons, but under judicial anti-avoidance doctrines and an anti-avoidance rule disallowing the deduction of expenses incurred in respect of transactions that, if allowed, would 'unduly or artificially reduce the [taxpayer's] income'.[152] A similar strategy was adopted in each of the next three transfer pricing cases in Canada: *Spur Oil Ltd v. The Queen*,[153] *Indalex Ltd v. The Queen*,[154] and *Irving Oil Ltd v. The Queen*.[155] Like *Dominion Bridge*, each of these cases involved the purchase of commodities by Canadian resident companies from non-arm's length non-resident affiliates at amounts that the Minister argued exceeded their fair market value. Although the profits of these affiliates would now under current

---

[148] *Ibid.* para. 4.   [149] *Ibid.* para. 6.   [150] *Ibid.* para. 6.   [151] See note 2 above.

[152] Income Tax Act, R.S.C. 1952, c. 148, s. 137(1). This provision became s. 245(1) in 1972 and was repealed with the enactment of a more general anti-avoidance rule (GAAR) in 1988.

[153] See note 2 above.   [154] See note 2 above.   [155] See note 2 above.

law be subject to taxation in Canada under ITA rules governing controlled foreign corporations,[156] the specific rule including these profits in a resident shareholder's 'foreign accrual property income' (FAPI) was not enacted until 1994.[157]

Dominion Bridge

In *Dominion Bridge*, the taxpayer was a Canadian manufacturer which acquired approximately 85 per cent of its steel in Canada and the United States, and the remainder from offshore steel mills either directly or through an agent or broker representing the offshore mill.[158] In order to minimise costs and maintain more control over these purchases, and taking tax consequences into consideration, the taxpayer incorporated a wholly-owned subsidiary in the Bahamas (Span), which acquired steel from offshore mills on the taxpayer's behalf and sold this steel to the taxpayer at a mark-up. According to evidence adduced at trial, Span was grossly undercapitalised and all essential operations were carried out from the taxpayer's head office.[159]

Alleging that Span had no independent existence from the taxpayer and that the taxpayer had paid inflated amounts for steel that it had purchased from Span during the taxpayer's 1967, 1968 and 1969 taxation years, the revenue authority included all of Span's profits in computing the taxpayer's income. The basis for the revenue authority's assessment was that Span's business was really that of the taxpayer, and that the deduction of expenses allegedly incurred by the taxpayer to acquire steel from Span were in respect of transactions that, if allowed, would unduly or artificially reduce the taxpayer's income within the meaning of the anti-avoidance rule in section 137(1).[160] The taxpayer, on the other hand, argued that Span was 'a validly constituted legal entity separate in law and in fact from the Taxpayer', that Span was 'not and has never been an agent of the Taxpayer', and that the prices the taxpayer paid for steel purchased from Span were 'not in excess of the prices paid to North American mills for similar items in similar quantities meeting similar specifications and sold under similar terms and conditions'.[161]

---

[156] ITA, ss. 91–5.   [157] ITA, s. 95(2)(a.1).
[158] *Dominion Bridge* (FCTD), note 2 above, para. 3.   [159] *Ibid.* paras. 4–5, 11.
[160] *Ibid.*   [161] *Ibid.* para. 7.

At trial, the judge dismissed the taxpayer's appeal on two grounds. First, he held that the amount the taxpayer paid to purchase steel from Span exceeded its fair market value:

> The appellant paid Span 95% of the price of domestic steel, or 95% of the fair market value of domestic steel when in fact it should have paid Span the fair market value of off-shore steel.[162]

Based on this conclusion, the taxpayer's income might reasonably have been adjusted under specific rules governing transactions with non-residents or non-arm's length persons. However, the trial judge also held that the extent to which the taxpayer controlled the operations of Span supported the revenue department's argument that Span's operations were not its own but those of the taxpayer:

> The means resorted to by the appellant for the operations of the business of Span and the manner in which Span was controlled and managed by the appellant preclude my being able to find that the business of Span was its own and not that of the appellant.[163]

On this basis, he characterised the incorporation and operation of Span as a sham,[164] and held that the profits that Span reported on the sale of steel to the taxpayer were properly included in the taxpayer's income under general principles of income attribution, without any 'need to have recourse to the provisions of the Income Tax Act for deciding the issue'.[165] By disregarding the separate legal existence of Span, therefore, the judge concluded that the deductible price to the taxpayer should be the amount that Span had paid on the taxpayer's behalf.[166]

---

[162] *Ibid.* para. 19, explaining that: 'The off-shore steel of Span sold to the appellant did not become domestic by the mere fact that a copy of the relevant papers was sent by the off-shore mills to Span at Nassau.'

[163] *Ibid.* para. 17. See also *ibid.* para. 25: 'I believe that in the instance at hand the relationship between the appellant and Span is so close as to be in fact that of a single entity. Span was used solely as a vehicle to obtain steel at a profitable price, it was a mere agent, a puppet in the hands of the appellant.'

[164] *Ibid.* paras. 21–23.   [165] *Ibid.* para. 14.

[166] Curiously, however, the trial judge also suggested that the result 'might have been different' if 'the appellant had been content with paying the fair market value of off-shore steel plus a customary commission to Span for the services rendered'. *Ibid.* para. 43. As a result, it seems, the tax motivation reflected in the price at which the taxpayer purchased steel from Span contributed to the Court's characterisation of its operations as a sham and in reality those of the taxpayer.

On appeal, the Federal Court of Appeal affirmed the trial decision in a very brief judgment.[167] According to the Court, the trial judge's conclusion that Span's operations were really carried on by the taxpayer was 'a finding of fact that was open to the ... judge on the evidence before him and there is no ground for interfering with it'.[168] As a result, the Court concluded, 'the appellant's costs of the steel in question must be computed by reference to the costs incurred by Span on behalf of the appellant and not by reference to amounts shown by the companies' books and papers as having been paid by the appellant to Span for it'.[169]

Spur Oil

In *Spur Oil*, the taxpayer was a wholly-owned Canadian subsidiary of another Canadian corporation ('the Canadian parent') which was itself a partially-owned subsidiary of a US corporation ('the US parent'). While the taxpayer carried on a business exploring for crude oil and natural gas in the province of Alberta and refining and marketing petroleum products in the province of Quebec, the US parent carried on the business of a fully integrated oil company exploring for, producing and selling petroleum products through various subsidiary companies.[170] In 1969, the Canadian parent acquired a Bermuda corporation called Tepwin Company Ltd (Tepwin), which had been incorporated in 1969 by Bermuda lawyers as a shelf company.[171]

Until 1 February 1970, the taxpayer purchased crude oil directly from the US parent at an agreed upon price of US $1.9876 per barrel. Thereafter, Tepwin purchased crude oil from the US parent at this price and sold it to the taxpayer for US $2.25 per barrel. Alleging that the operations of Tepwin were actually carried on by the taxpayer, that the taxpayer purchased crude oil from Tepwin at price greater than its fair market value, and that the deduction of amounts exceeding US $1.9876 per barrel would unduly and artificially reduce the taxpayer's income, the revenue department disallowed approximately US $1.6 million of expenses incurred by the taxpayer in its 1970 taxation year, representing the difference between the amount that the taxpayer paid to Tepwin and the amount that Tepwin paid to the US parent.[172] In response, the taxpayer argued that the taxpayer had not paid an amount in excess of the fair market value of a like quantity and quality of crude oil on the open market, and that the favourable rates at

---

[167] *Dominion Bridge*, note 2 above (FCA).   [168] *Ibid.* para. 4.   [169] *Ibid.* para. 5.
[170] *Spur Oil* (FCA), note 2 above, para. 1.   [171] *Spur Oil* (FCTD), note 2 above, para. 11.
[172] *Ibid.* para. 40.

which Tepwin purchased oil from the US parent after 1 February 1970 had at no time 'been offered to or otherwise made available to' the taxpayer.[173] As a result, the case turned both on the nature of the legal relationships among the taxpayer, Tepwin and the US parent, and on the not unrelated definition of a comparable uncontrolled price.

Concluding that the agreement whereby the taxpayer could purchase crude oil from the US parent for US $1.9876 per barrel was 'a valid and subsisting contract' throughout 1970,[174] the trial judge upheld the assessment on the basis that the taxpayer's decision to purchase crude oil from Tepwin for US $2.25 per barrel unduly and artificially reduced the taxpayer's income within the meaning of the anti-avoidance rule in then section 137(1) of the Act. According to the trial judge:

> The evidence ... conclusively established that [the US parent] prior to and up to February 1, 1970, did in fact sell crude oil to Spur Oil Ltd. at $1,9876 US per barrel ... and [that] this contract ... was never formally or informally abrogated.[175]

As a result, it followed, the transactions entered into between the taxpayer, Tepwin and the US parent were 'artificial within the meaning of subsection 137(1) of the Income Tax Act'.[176] Accordingly, he held, 'the excess cost of petroleum products sold ... is not an allowable expense'.[177] For the trial judge, therefore, the continuing contractual relationship between the taxpayer and the US parent suggested that the appropriate arm's length price for the crude oil remained US $1.9876 per barrel, not US $2.25 per barrel.

Rejecting the trial judge's finding that the taxpayer's arrangement with the US parent was a valid and subsisting contract, the Federal Court of Appeal allowed the taxpayer's appeal. First, the Court held, because the taxpayer had not given any consideration for the US parent's offer to sell crude oil for US $1.9876 per barrel up to 30 April 1973, this offer could not be regarded as an enforceable contract that bound the US parent.[178] Second, it continued, because the market value of crude oil in 1970 exceeded US $2.25 per barrel, it could not be said that the transactions unduly or artificially reduced the taxpayer's income within the meaning of section 137(1) of the Act.[179] More generally, the Court declared:

> Subsection 137(1) ... does not ... prevent someone in the position of either [the US parent] or Tepwin from generating the same profit from a transaction with an affiliate like the appellant as it would from a similar

[173] Ibid. para. 8.   [174] Ibid. para. 60.   [175] Ibid. para. 59.   [176] Ibid. para. 61.
[177] Ibid.   [178] Spur Oil (FCA), note 2 above, para. 9.   [179] Ibid. para. 12.

transaction with a third party with whom it was dealing at arm's length. Such a transaction would ... only attract the prohibition of subsection 137(1) ... when appellant's cost of crude oil supply, by reason of an act of the appellant, or those controlling it, increased above the cost prevailing in the industry at the same time and under similar circumstances.[180]

Concluding that the taxpayer had no contractual right to purchase oil directly from the US parent, therefore, the Federal Court of Appeal allowed the deduction on the basis that the appropriate arm's length price for crude oil was its market value in 1970, not the lower price at which the US parent had sold the crude oil to the taxpayer and continued to sell the crude oil to Tepwin.

Indalex

In *Indalex*, the taxpayer was a wholly-owned Canadian subsidiary of another Canadian corporation which was controlled by a UK corporation called Pillar Ltd (Pillar) which had subsidiaries in several countries. The taxpayer's business involved the extrusion (moulding) of aluminium billet (the metal in its primary state) in the manufacture of products such as aluminium doors, windows and ladders. During the years at issue, its sole supplier for aluminium billet was Alcan Ingot, a subsidiary of Alcan Aluminum of Canada Ltd (Alcan).[181]

In 1965, Pillar and Alcan entered into an agreement whereby the former agreed that its subsidiaries would acquire at least 50 per cent of their aluminium billet requirements from Alcan, in exchange for which Alcan would pay Pillar a discount equal to 1.5 per cent of the value of all purchases from Alcan by its subsidiaries during the previous year. In 1967, this discount was increased to 5 per cent. In 1969, Pillar acquired a Bermuda corporation, which was renamed Pillar International Services Limited (Pillar International). On 1 January 1970, the agreement between Alcan and Pillar was amended and replaced by an agreement between Alcan and Pillar International.

During the years 1971 to 1974, the taxpayer acquired aluminium billet directly from Alcan smelters in the Province of Quebec.[182] The purchase orders for the billet, however, were placed through Pillar International, which forwarded these orders to Alcan Ingot. Once Alcan Ingot had delivered the billet to the taxpayer, it invoiced Pillar International at the Alcan list price, and Pillar International invoiced the taxpayer at the

[180] *Ibid.* para. 15.   [181] *Indalex* (FCTD), note 2 above, para. 3.   [182] *Ibid.*

same price.[183] When payment was subsequently made, the taxpayer credited Pillar International's Bermuda bank with the invoiced price, Pillar International credited Alcan Ingot's Montreal Bank with the identical amount, and Alcan paid to Pillar International's Bermuda bank a discount attributable to the purchase price.[184] This discount was paid partly in US dollars, which were retained by Pillar International, and partly in Canadian dollars, which were forwarded to the taxpayer's bank account in Toronto.[185] During the taxpayer's taxation years from 1971 to 1974, Pillar International received aggregate discounts totalling over US $6.2 million, approximately US $3.6 million of which it remitted to the taxpayer and US $2.6 million of which it retained.[186]

In computing the taxpayer's income for its 1971 to 1974 taxation years, the revenue department included the US dollar discounts on three grounds: first, that the involvement of Pillar International was a sham and the discounts were in reality earned by the taxpayer; second, that the amounts that the taxpayer paid to Pillar International for aluminium billet were expenses in respect of a transaction that if allowed would unduly or artificially reduce the taxpayer's income; and, third, that these amounts were paid to a non-arm's length person at an amount in excess of fair market value and were therefore deemed to have been made at fair market value under section 69(1) of the Act.[187] The taxpayer, not surprisingly, challenged each of these assumptions.

At trial, the judge rejected the argument that the transactions were a sham on the basis that the transactions created a real contractual relationship between the taxpayer and Pillar International,[188] but characterised the purchases from Pillar International as 'artificial transactions' within the meaning of what was then section 245(1) of the ITA.[189] Noting that the application of this anti-avoidance rule also required a reduction of income, however, the judge explained that the key question was the reasonableness of the price paid for the aluminum billet determined by its relationship to their fair market value.[190] For this purpose,

---

[183] *Ibid.* para. 4.   [184] *Ibid.* para. 5.   [185] *Ibid.*

[186] *Indalex* (FCA), note 2 above, para. 9.   [187] *Indalex* (FCTD), note 2 above, para. 8.

[188] *Ibid.* paras. 33–5, explaining that 'the evidence indicates that Indalex did not directly negotiate price with either Alcan or Alcan Ingot' even though it was 'a fair inference' that 'Pillar International did not perform much more than a collating or post office function'.

[189] *Ibid.* para. 44.

[190] *Ibid.* para. 45, citing the rules for transactions with non-arm's length and non-resident persons in then s. 69(1) and (2) of the ITA, and a more general rule in s. 67 limiting all deductions to amounts that are 'reasonable in the circumstances'.

the judge considered expert evidence with respect to the relevant market in which the taxpayer purchased aluminium billet,[191] evidence on arm's length comparables for the purchase of aluminium billet,[192] and evidence on other methods for assessing the reasonableness of the purchase price paid by the taxpayer.[193]

Beginning with the relevant market, evidence suggested that 'the market from which Indalex would purchase aluminum billet was North American (Canada and the United States) if not smaller in geographical size' due to factors like transportation costs and trade restrictions.[194] As a result, the judge concluded, the price that Pillar International paid to various Alcan companies was 'negotiated on a market by market basis'.[195] Crucially, for the trial judge, this conclusion appeared to suggest that any discount paid by Alcan companies to Pillar companies related to purchases in specific markets rather than global sales.

With respect to arm's length comparables, the judge began by stating that the aluminium industry is 'highly integrated' with 'few instances of arm's length purchases for aluminium billet'.[196] Although evidence was adduced regarding the price paid for aluminium billet by two independent companies, the judge held that neither transaction constituted a valid comparable.[197] Instead, she concluded, 'the closest arm's length comparable to a sale by Pillar International to Indalex is that by Alcan to Pillar International'.[198] At the same time, she acknowledged, 'some adjustment should be made' in order to equate an Indalex purchase from Pillar International to a Pillar International purchase from Alcan.[199]

For the purpose of this adjustment, the trial judge considered arguments by the revenue department and the taxpayer. From the revenue department's perspective, an expert witness suggested that the

---

[191] *Ibid.* paras. 49–52.   [192] *Ibid.* paras. 53–9.   [193] *Ibid.* paras. 60–89.
[194] *Ibid.* para. 49.   [195] *Ibid.* para. 50.   [196] *Ibid.* para. 53.
[197] *Ibid.* paras. 54–6. In the first case, where prices were lower, the company had been in 'considerable financial difficulty' causing Alcan to acquire an interest in the company and grant retroactive price rebates in order to ensure the collection of its accounts receivable. In the second case, where prices were slightly higher, the company purchased much less aluminium billet from Alcan than the taxpayer.
[198] *Ibid.* para. 58, explaining that: 'Each shipment of billet to Indalex was in fact purchased at arm's length by Pillar International under circumstances that are virtually identical to the purchases of the same billet by Indalex: same product; same quantities; same shipping destination; same transportation logistics; same credit terms; same scrap return arrangements.'
[199] *Ibid.* para. 59.

reasonableness of the price charged to Indalex by Pillar International might be assessed 'by reference to the profit margin on sales to the [taxpayer] and by making a direct comparison between such and the mark-ups received by firms performing similar functions but dealing at arm's length in a competitive setting' – in other words, a cost plus method.[200] Alternatively, it was suggested, 'the same could be ascertained by indirect comparison to the return on investment required by those firms'[201] – a form of comparable profit method. Given the uniqueness of Pillar International's functions, the expert witness relied on this indirect method,[202] concluding that an appropriate profit margin would be between 0.4 per cent and 0.8 per cent of sales.[203] Since Pillar International's profit margin ranged between 3.13 per cent and 5.27 per cent during the period, the revenue department argued that the price charged was not reasonable.[204]

The taxpayer, on the other hand, advanced two arguments to support the reasonableness of the purchase price: first, that the discounts were attributable to Pillar's 'worldwide purchasing power' and were therefore 'properly earned by it and not by the [taxpayer]';[205] second, that the contract with Pillar International provided various additional economic benefits to Indalex such as 'the possibility of metal switches with other members of the Pillar extruder group (if Indalex should over-estimate or under-estimate is requirements)' and extended credit terms.[206]

Although the trial judge regarded the revenue department's alternative transfer pricing methodologies as 'useful as a bottom line approach' showing 'what profit margin would have been required to sustain a company such as Pillar International in business (with a reasonable return on investment)',[207] she was unwilling to endorse either method

---

[200] *Ibid.* para. 61.   [201] *Ibid.*

[202] *Ibid.* According to the judge, this involved: '(1) determining an appropriate rate of return on investment for an enterprise with risk characteristics of Pillar International; (2) determining the amount of capital needed to support Pillar International's sales; (3) using the aforementioned factors to determine an appropriate profit margin as a percentage of sales'.

[203] *Ibid.* para. 62.   [204] *Ibid.* para. 63.   [205] *Ibid.* para. 68.

[206] *Ibid.* para. 80, mentioning also: 'the extension of the billet purchase contracts by Alcan in 4 December 1973 in tight market conditions; refusal in 1974 to allow Alcan to call *force majeure* because of a strike at Arvida Quebec . . .; discount payments on billet upcharges as well as on the base metal price; . . . excellent scrap return terms; simultaneous settlement of invoice payments and discounts; [and] regular efforts by Pillar to prevent or defer price increases or increases in scrap tolling charge or reduction in the credit terms'.

[207] *Ibid.* para. 65.

as demonstrating, 'without more, a lack of reasonableness in the price charged'.[208] Nor, however, was she persuaded by the taxpayer's arguments, finding no support for the taxpayer's claim that the discounts reflected Pillar's global purchasing power,[209] and little evidence that the taxpayer could not have obtained the alleged 'additional economic benefits' on its own.[210] Nonetheless, she concluded, while the taxpayer had not proven that the price for aluminium billet purchased from Pillar International was reasonable in the circumstances,[211] it was possible to find that 'a one per cent or less differential was the additional discount obtained by Pillar International over that the [taxpayer] could have negotiated on its own'.[212]

On appeal, the Federal Court of Appeal agreed with all findings of the trial judge with one important qualification. Explaining that Pillar International's ability to obtain a larger discount was 'due to the pooling of the purchasing power of a number of members of the Pillar group to which the appellant was an important contributor', the Court rejected the trial judge's apparent conclusion that Pillar International was entitled to the benefit of this increased discount.[213] On the contrary, the Court emphasised:

> Where non-arm's length parties combine to obtain an advantage from an outsider not available to them individually, any allocation of the advantage among them except on a pro rata basis has to be justified.[214]

Since there was no evidence that Pillar International itself contributed to the discounts that it obtained from the pooled purchasing power of the Pillar group, it followed that it was not itself entitled to any portion of the discounts that it received on the purchase of aluminium billet for

---

[208] Ibid.

[209] Ibid. para. 69. On the contrary, the judge stated on the basis of expert testimony, 'sales to Pillar International were not at a single price for a combined volume' but were 'negotiated on a market by market basis with reference to the conditions prevailing in each market separately'. Ibid. para. 86. Because Alcan had to be competitive in each market, the judge concluded, '[i]t is simply not reasonable to conclude that in those circumstances Alcan would give to Pillar International an additional discount or concession, of the magnitude claimed here, over that which it would give to Indalex negotiating on its own'.

[210] Ibid. para. 81.   [211] Ibid. para. 89.   [212] Ibid.

[213] Indalex (FCA), note 2 above, para. 24, stating that: 'Nothing in the evidence or in the findings of fact by the learned trial judge support the allocation of any part of that advantage to Pillar International.'

[214] Ibid.

the taxpayer, and any deduction by the taxpayer in respect of these discounts would unduly or artificially reduce its income. For this reason, the Court set aside the trial judgment and restored the initial assessment disallowing any deduction in respect of the discounts.[215]

Irving Oil

The facts in *Irving Oil* are similar to those in *Spur Oil*, except that the non-resident company from which the taxpayer purchased the oil at issue was a wholly-owned subsidiary rather than a sister company, as was the case in *Spur Oil.* Until 9 August 1971, the taxpayer, which was owned by the Irving family and Standard Oil of California (Socal), purchased crude oil directly from Socal under an exclusive supply agreement that the parties had entered into in 1957. After this date, the taxpayer purchased crude oil from a wholly-owned Bermuda subsidiary (Irvcal), which purchased this oil from Socal at a lower price than Irvcal charged to the taxpayer. Arguing that Irvcal was acquired as 'an instrumentality for the accumulation off-shore, in a tax free jurisdiction, of the savings resulting from the reduced cost of the crude oil' acquired from Socal, that the transactions through which Irvcal was interposed between the taxpayer and Socal 'lacked a *bona fide* business purpose and were shams', that the taxpayer had 'in fact and in substance' purchased the oil directly from Socal, and that the profits reported by Irvcal were 'in substance the profits of the plaintiff', the revenue department disallowed the deduction of the allegedly overstated price of crude oil purchased by the taxpayer during its 1971 to 1975 taxation years on the grounds that the expense was not reasonable in the circumstances and would unduly or artificially reduce the taxpayer's income.[216]

Following the Federal Court of Appeal decision in *Spur Oil*,[217] the trial judge rejected the revenue department's arguments and allowed the taxpayer's appeal for two reasons. First, he held, the contractual documents and the acts of the parties confirmed that the transactions were not shams according to the established definition of the term,[218] but created real legal relationships through which the production and

---

[215] *Ibid.* para. 27.   [216] *Irving Oil* (FCTD), note 2 above, para. 12.

[217] *Ibid.* para. 115: 'The Court considers that the *Spur Oil* case is practically indistinguishable from the case here at bar, and therefore whatever the validity of all the foregoing reasons, *stare decisis* exacts that the Appeal Division's unanimous decision in, and disposition of, *Spur Oil* must be followed here.'

[218] *Ibid.* paras. 74–7.

transportation profits from non-Canadian activities that had formerly
accrued to Socal alone were effectively shared between Socal and the
Irving family through Irvcal.[219] As a result, he declared:

> Irvcal, not the plaintiff, earned the profits, despite the metaphysically
> sequential, even if apparently simultaneous, shifts of ownership 'at ship's
> permanent hose connections at the loading port'.[220]

Second, the trial judge continued, because Irvcal's profits were 'plainly
generated by non-Canadian production and the transportation of crude
oil',[221] and the price at which the taxpayer acquired crude oil from Irvcal
was 'within the range of competitively determined arm's length prices' at
the time,[222] it followed that the deduction was 'reasonable in the circumstances'[223] and did not unduly or artificially reduce the taxpayer's
income.[224] On the contrary, he emphasised, 'a fair, competitive market
price or one within the reasonable range . . . is the quintessence of what is
"reasonable in the circumstances" of the real world',[225] and 'quintessen-
tially "in accordance with normality" rather than artificial.[226]

On appeal, the Federal Court of Appeal concluded that the transactions were purely tax-motivated,[227] but upheld the trial decision
nonetheless on the grounds that it could not dispute the lower court's
factual determinations that the production and transportation profits
were earned by Irvcal,[228] and that the price paid by the taxpayer for the
crude oil was its fair market value.[229] According to the Court:

> In view of the finding of fact that the price paid by the [taxpayer] for the
> crude was its fair market value, . . . the learned trial judge did not err in
> holding that the [amount paid to Irvcal] . . . was reasonable in the
> circumstances.[230]

---

[219] *Ibid.* paras. 79–80, explaining that 'Irvcal did perform the functions for which it was
created by serving to garner the non-Canadian profits of production and transportation
of the crude oil in question.'

[220] *Ibid.* para. 86.   [221] *Ibid.* para. 107.   [222] *Ibid.* para. 69. See also *ibid.* para. 70.

[223] *Ibid.* paras. 64 and 102.   [224] *Ibid.* para. 106.   [225] *Ibid.* para. 102.

[226] *Ibid.* para. 106. See also *ibid.* para. 107, stating that 'the notion of normality . . .
contemplates the realization of such profits outside of Canada'.

[227] *Irving Oil* (FCA), paras. 27 and 36, explaining that 'what was concocted and carried out
was a tax avoidance scheme, pure and simple', and that 'having no *bona fide* business
purpose . . . [t]he transactions through Irvcal were artificial'.

[228] *Ibid.* para. 35: 'The learned trial judge found, as a fact, that the production and
transportation profits were Irvcal's . . . [I]t is not a conclusion which was plainly wrong.
The finding that they had been earned outside Canada was not irrelevant to it.'

[229] *Ibid.* para. 30, stating that this finding of fact was 'not open to question on this appeal'.

[230] *Ibid.*

Likewise, it explained:

> Since the [taxpayer] paid Irvcal fair market value, it cannot be said that
> payment resulted in an excessive reduction of income. There was nothing
> fictitious or simulated in the reduction of the [taxpayer's] income as a
> result of paying Irvcal 66¢ more per barrel of crude than the crude cost
> Irvcal. It was very real.[231]

As a result, because Irvcal's profits were legitimately earned outside
Canada, it followed that the arm's length price was an appropriate
comparable which could not be challenged on the grounds advanced
by the revenue department.

4.5.3   Cases involving services contracts

After the appellate decision in *Irving Oil,* another decade passed before a
Canadian court released another judgment in a transfer pricing case. In
Safety Boss Ltd v. The Queen,[232] the revenue authority challenged the
amounts paid by a Canadian corporation for services provided by a
non-resident individual and corporation with whom the Canadian
corporation did not deal at arm's length. In *World Corp. v. The Queen,*[233]
the revenue authority challenged the amount paid by a non-arm's length
non-resident for the assignment of a commission agreement entered into
by a Canadian corporation. Most recently, in *Alberta Printed Circuits Ltd* v.
The Queen,[234] the revenue authority challenged amounts paid by a
Canadian corporation for services provided by a non-arm's length non-
resident corporation. While the first of these cases was argued under
former section 69(2), and the second under ordinary principles of business
valuation, the third was decided under section 247 and includes a detailed
discussion of transfer pricing methodologies. In each case, the Tax Court
allowed the taxpayer's appeal.

Safety Boss

In *Safety Boss,* the taxpayer was a Canadian corporation, 99 per cent of
the shares of which were held by Michael Miller, an oilfield firefighter
who had carried on an oilfield firefighting business through the company since he acquired it from his father in 1979. According to the
judgment, Mr Miller had thirty years of oilfield experience, had

---

[231] *Ibid.* para. 38.   [232] See note 2 above.   [233] See note 2 above.
[234] See note 2 above.

developed skills and a personal reputation worldwide, and was solely responsible for the goodwill of the company.

At the end of the 1991 war in the Persian Gulf, Mr Miller's company entered into a contract with the Government of Kuwait to extinguish oilfield fires that were set by the retreating Iraqi army. According to the Court, '[t]here is no doubt that the contract with Kuwait was obtained through Mr. Miller's initiative and contacts, as well as his reputation and skill',[235] and clearly apparent that 'the substantial earnings of the [taxpayer] from this work in Kuwait was the direct result of Mr. Miller's leadership, initiative, intelligences and business acumen'.[236]

On 28 June 1991, Safety Boss International Ltd (SBIL) was incorporated in Bermuda, with Mr Miller owning 11,996 of 12,000 issued shares. On 2 August 1991, Mr Miller himself moved to Bermuda, where it was admitted by the revenue authorities that he became a non-resident of Canada and a resident of Bermuda.[237] On 30 August 1991, the taxpayer paid a bonus of CAN $3 million to Mr Miller, which it declared to have been earned by Mr Miller pro rata from 28 February 1991 to 30 August 1991.[238] Also on 30 August 1991, Mr Miller resigned as president and director of the taxpayer, and commenced an exclusive employment contract with SBIL, under which SBIL would pay him CAN $800,000 per month. On 1 September 1991, SBIL entered into an agreement with the taxpayer to make Mr Miller's services available to the taxpayer at a rate of CAN $800,000 per month. Pursuant to this contract, the taxpayer paid SBIL approximately CAN $2 million before the taxpayer's contract with Kuwait terminated on 14 November 1991.

In computing Canadian tax payable for his 1991 taxation year, Mr Miller included CAN $2.5 million of the bonus, representing the proportion of the bonus that was earned while he was a resident of Canada. In computing its income for the relevant fiscal period, the taxpayer deducted the CAN $3 million paid to Mr Miller and the CAN $2 million paid to SBIL. The revenue authority allowed the deduction of the CAN $2.5 million bonus that Mr Miller included in computing his income but reduced the remaining CAN $500,000 to CAN $67,500 and the CAN $2 million paid to SBIL to CAN $126,000 under the transfer pricing rule in section 69(2) of the ITA on the basis that any amount in excess of these amounts would be greater than the amount that would have been reasonable in the circumstances if the taxpayer had been dealing

---

[235] *Safety Boss*, note 2 above, para. 11.   [236] *Ibid.* para. 12.   [237] *Ibid.* para. 14.
[238] *Ibid.* paras. 15–16.

at arm's length with Mr Miller and SBIL.[239] According to the revenue authority, Mr Miller's remuneration (whether paid directly or through fees to SBIL) should not exceed CAN $2,250 per day when he was in Kuwait and CAN $750 per day otherwise, since another employee was paid CAN $1,500 per day and CAN $750 per day represented a reasonable arm's length fee for any managerial duties performed by Mr Miller.[240]

Rejecting the revenue authority's characterisation of an appropriate arm's length comparable, the Tax Court allowed the taxpayer's appeal. First, it noted, the comparison to another employee and an ordinary manager ignored the facts that the contract with Kuwait and the substantial profits received by the taxpayer were attributable solely to Mr Miller.[241] As a result, the Court declared:

> To relegate Mr Miller to the position of just another employee, when he was the driving force behind the company without which neither the company nor its contract with Kuwait would have existed, is both demeaning to Mr Miller and commercially unrealistic.[242]

Second, it continued, the assessments failed to acknowledge that Mr Miller had struggled to keep the company afloat in previous years, during which he accepted little or no remuneration, and that it is a common commercial practice 'to reward valued employees in profitable years in recognition of services in prior years'.[243] As a result, the Court concluded, the fees paid to Mr Miller and SBIL 'were fully commensurate with the services rendered by Mr Miller and were not in excess of amounts that it would have been reasonable to pay had the parties been at arm's length'.[244]

World Corp.

In *World Corp.*, the taxpayer was a Canadian corporation, through which its president Alexander O, a resident of the Cayman Islands, carried on business in Canada as a licensed dealer in securities. Shares of the taxpayer were wholly owned by another Canadian company, 51 per cent of the shares of which were held by the taxpayer's office manager and 49 per cent of which were held by O.[245]

In the fall of 1989, O was approached by a builder and developer named Gerry Farantatos, who wanted to raise CAN $49 million through the sale of limited partnership units in order to finance the construction

---

[239] *Ibid.* paras. 20 and 23.   [240] *Ibid.* para. 38.   [241] *Ibid.* para. 39.   [242] *Ibid.*
[243] *Ibid.*   [244] *Ibid.* para. 53.   [245] *World Corp.*, note 2 above, para. 2.

of an office tower on property controlled by him. On behalf of the taxpayer, O offered to act as agent to sell these limited partnership units in exchange for CAN $3.9 million.[246] On 29 December 1989, the taxpayer assigned this commission to a Cayman Islands company controlled by O for CAN $41,300.[247] The revenue authority reassessed the taxpayer on the basis that the fair market value of the commission was CAN $2.5 million.[248] The taxpayer appealed on the grounds that the taxpayer's entitlement to any fees remained contingent until June 1990 and no commission agreement had been signed when the commission was assigned.[249]

At trial, the taxpayer called expert evidence challenging the revenue authority's valuation of the commission on 29 December 1989.[250] In contrast, according to the Court, the revenue authority 'adduced no evidence, ordinary or expert' to explain how it arrived at or supported the CAN $2.5 million amount at which it valued the commission receivable.[251] Not surprisingly, therefore, the Tax Court allowed the taxpayer's appeal. Concluding that the taxpayer's right to enforce payment of the commission on 29 December 1989 was 'so remote as to be worthless', the trial judge concluded that 'I am unable, in the circumstances, to ascribe any value greater than the sum of $41,300 to that right.'[252] As in the early transfer pricing cases, therefore, the decision turned on the expert evidence adduced at trial.

Alberta Printed Circuits

Alberta Printed Circuits involved a private Canadian corporation (API) which manufactured custom circuit boards for designers. Although API was originally owned exclusively by its founders, Wayne and Geraldine Bamber, shares were subsequently issued to Daniel McMuldroch, who became an employee and director of the company and performed various services for it including network administration, web development, software development and the preparation of customer data for use in manufacturing ('set up').[253]

In 1995, after attending a seminar about doing business in Barbados, Mr McMuldroch and the Bambers decided to move the set up operations to Barbados to be carried on by a Barbados corporation.[254] To this end, Mr McMuldroch resigned as a director of API, sold his API shares

---

[246] *Ibid.* para. 3.   [247] *Ibid.* para. 1.   [248] *Ibid.*   [249] *Ibid.* paras. 33–43.
[250] *Ibid.* paras. 19–32.   [251] *Ibid.* para. 56.   [252] *Ibid.* para. 66.
[253] *Alberta Printed Circuits*, note 2 above, paras. 8–12.   [254] *Ibid.* para. 13.

to a private company owned by Mr and Mrs Bamber, incorporated a Barbados International Business Company (APCI), severed his ties with Canada and became a resident of Barbados.[255] Pursuant to annual contracts that continued from February 1997 to January 2001, APCI performed three kinds of services for API: (i) database software development and maintenance; (ii) website development and maintenance; and (iii) set up operations.[256] On the grounds that the taxpayer and APCI did not deal at arm's length, that the set up fees that API paid to APCI were the same or more than set up fees that API invoiced its customers, and that the taxpayer continued to perform some set up operations itself, the revenue authority reassessed the taxpayer under section 247(2)(a), reducing the deductible amount of service payments to APCI. The taxpayer appealed, arguing that API and APCI dealt with each other at arm's length and that the fees paid under the contracts were reasonable amounts that would be agreed to by parties dealing at arm's length.

Beginning with the first of these arguments, the Tax Court held that Mr Bamber exercised *de facto* control over APCI by virtue of an arrangement whereby he and Mrs Bamber received two-thirds of its profits,[257] that this arrangement demonstrated that the two companies acted in concert without separate interests,[258] and that Mr Bamber and Mr McMuldroch directed the negotiations between the companies according to a common plan.[259] For these reasons, it concluded that API and APCI did not deal with each other at arm's length as a factual matter, even though they were not related under the statutory definition in section 251(2) of the ITA.

On the question of the reasonableness of the fees, however, the Tax Court found largely for the taxpayer and reduced the amount of the transfer pricing adjustment assessed by the revenue authority. Although the court's decision turned mostly on its factual findings that API did not continue to perform set up operations and that the set up fees paid to APCI did not exceed amounts that API charged its customers, the judgment also considered different transfer pricing methodologies and the comparability of uncontrolled transactions.

With respect to transfer pricing methodologies, the court adopted the hierarchy of methods set out in the OECD 1995 Guidelines, favouring traditional transaction methods over transactional profit methods and

---

[255] *Ibid.* paras. 14–40.   [256] *Ibid.* paras. 41–9.   [257] *Ibid.* paras. 84–96.
[258] *Ibid.* paras. 74–80.   [259] *Ibid.* paras. 81–3.

the comparable uncontrolled price (CUP) method as the preferred method for determining a reasonable arm's length price.[260] Since the taxpayer relied on the CUP method while the revenue authority's argument was based on the transactional net margin method (TNMM),[261] it is not surprising that the court preferred the taxpayer's argument to that of the revenue authority. Indeed, the court found it 'perplexing to say the least' that the revenue authority sought 'comparables for the lowest ranking method of establishing an arm's length price and not for the highest method'[262] and criticised counsel for the revenue authority for 'a fundamental abdication of her duties under the transfer pricing rules' for making 'no attempt to analyze either the applicability of the CUP or differences in the factors for determining what, if any, adjustments to the prices used could be justified'.[263]

Regarding the comparability of transactions, the court also referred to the OECD guidelines, listing five 'comparability factors' identified by the OECD,[264] and emphasising that this list 'is not intended to be exhaustive, as consideration of all relevant factors is mandated'.[265] Rejecting the revenue authority's argument that there were no comparable transactions since APCI provided set up services only for API and API did not purchase set up services from an arm's length party during the years at issue,[266] the court held that it was reasonable to compare the set up fees that API charged its customers with the set up fees that APCI charged API on the grounds that 'it makes perfect business sense to treat services provided to a client through outsourcing in the same market as if they were supplied directly to the customer'.[267] In addition to this 'internal CUP' the court also accepted evidence of comparable uncontrolled

---

[260] *Ibid.* paras. 146–55 (refusing to consider the OECD's 2010 update to the Transfer Pricing Guidelines since it 'is well beyond the taxation years at issue').

[261] *Ibid.* para. 178. [262] *Ibid.* para. 211. [263] *Ibid.* para. 192.

[264] *Ibid.* para. 162. The five factors are: (1) the characteristics of property or services being purchased or sold; (2) the functions defined by the parties to the transaction; (3) contractual terms between the parties; (4) the economic circumstances of the parties; and (5) the business strategies pursued by the parties.

[265] *Ibid.* para. 162. [266] *Ibid.* para. 184.

[267] *Ibid.* para. 186. Responding to the revenue authority's further argument (at para. 189) that it made no business sense for API to give up profits at the set up level, which it estimated at approximately 40 per cent, the court reasoned (at para. 190) that Mr and Mrs Bamber had little knowledge of or affinity for the set up function of the business, which changed substantially from when they first founded the business, so that it made sense to contract out this operation to Mr McMuldroch so that they could 'focus on their core business of manufacturing while still controlling the client by providing the client with both the service of set up and the product of manufacturing'.

prices between other parties, suggesting that the set up fees charged by APCI were not unreasonable.[268] On this basis, the court concluded that amounts paid under the contracts for set up services represented arm's length prices,[269] though it upheld a portion of the overall transfer pricing adjustment on the grounds that the taxpayer did not meet the onus of establishing that it had not overpaid for the development and maintenance of its website and database software.[270]

4.5.4   Other recent cases

In addition to *Alberta Printed Circuits*, Canadian courts have at the time of writing released three more transfer pricing decisions, two of which have attracted considerable international attention. In *1143132 Ontario Ltd v. The Queen*,[271] where the taxpayer channelled sales to purchasers in the United States through a wholly-controlled company incorporated in Barbados, the court applied the transfer pricing rule in section 247 on the basis that the subsidiary performed limited functions and assumed no risks, so that comparable arm's length prices were those paid by the ultimate US purchasers. In *General Electric Capital Inc. v. The Queen*,[272] on the other hand, the Tax Court of Canada refused to apply the transfer pricing rules in former section 69(2) and new section 247 to disallow the deduction of guarantee fees paid by the taxpayer to a non-resident parent. In *GlaxoSmithKline Inc. v. The Queen*,[273] the Federal Court of Appeal reversed a Tax Court of Canada decision which had applied the transfer pricing rule in former section 69(2) to reduce the transfer price of an active pharmaceutical ingredient that the taxpayer acquired from an associated company at prices much greater than those paid by other Canadian drug companies for an ingredient with identical chemical and biological characteristics. As the decision in *1143132 Ontario Ltd* is relatively straightforward, the following sections review only the decisions in *GE Electric* and *GlaxoSmithKline*.

GE Capital

In the *GE Capital* case, the revenue authority challenged the deductibility of guarantee fees paid by the taxpayer to a US parent company on the grounds that the taxpayer's credit rating would have been equalised with

---

[268] *Ibid.* paras. 201–12.   [269] *Ibid.* para. 229.   [270] *Ibid.* para. 243.
[271] See note 2 above.   [272] See note 2 above.   [273] See note 2 above.

that of the parent by reason of its affiliation in the absence of the guarantee arrangement.[274] On this basis, it argued, the taxpayer received no economic benefit from the guarantee, as a consequence of which the arm's length price would have been nil.[275] Alternatively, it argued, in the event that the taxpayer's credit rating would not have been the same as that of the parent, the arm's length price for the guarantee fee should be based on the difference between the interest rate spread that would have existed on amounts borrowed by the taxpayer and the parent in the absence of the guarantee and the interest rate differential with the guarantee arrangement (the 'yield approach').[276] In response, the taxpayer not only challenged the revenue authority's factual conclusion that the guarantee had no economic value,[277] but also argued that application of the arm's length standard under the applicable statutory rules precluded consideration of any affiliation benefit that might have been enjoyed by the taxpayer by virtue of its non-arm's length relationship with its US parent.[278]

Beginning with the taxpayer's second argument that application of the arm's length standard precludes the consideration of any affiliation benefit, the court rejected this view on the basis that any implicit support to the taxpayer resulted not from 'the exercise *de facto* or *de jure* control which defines a non-arm's length relationship' but from 'reputational pressure' that would be exerted by the parent company's debt holders if the taxpayer were to default on its debts.[279] Further, it concluded, to the extent that the arm's length standard mandates the adjustment of profits 'by reference to the conditions which would have been obtained between independent enterprises in comparable transactions in comparable circumstances,'[280] it follows that it is essential to consider 'the relevant economic characteristics of the controlled transaction in order to ensure the reliability of the comparisons with uncontrolled transactions'.[281]

Notwithstanding this conclusion, however, the court found for the taxpayer on the basis that it had indeed obtained an economic benefit from the guarantee. Accepting the revenue authority's yield approach as

---

[274] *GE Capital*, note 2 above, para. 168.   [275] *Ibid.*   [276] *Ibid.* para. 172.
[277] *Ibid.* paras. 176–7.
[278] *Ibid.* para. 173 (arguing that '[a]ll distortions that arise from the parties' relationship must be eliminated to arrive at an arm's length result').
[279] *Ibid.* para. 199.
[280] OECD Guidelines, para. 1.6, cited in *GE Capital*, note 2 above, para. 204.
[281] *Ibid.* para. 205 (referring to para. 1.5 of the OECD Guidelines).

the most suitable transfer pricing methodology in the circumstances,[282] it nonetheless accepted the taxpayer's argument that the guarantee provided additional protection to the taxpayer's creditors beyond the implicit support resulting from affiliation with its parent.[283] Indeed, it observed, since a third-party guarantor would have had less control than the US parent over the timing, terms and payments of the taxpayer's debt offerings, it would have assumed a greater risk and demanded a higher guarantee fee than the US parent.[284] As a result, the court concluded, the 1 per cent guarantee fee paid by the taxpayer was 'equal to or below an arm's length price in the circumstances, as the [taxpayer] received a significant net economic benefit from the transaction'.[285]

The Federal Court of Appeal upheld the Tax Court's conclusions regarding both the application of the arm's length standard and the use of the yield approach in pricing the guarantee. In addressing the application of section 69(2) and section 247(2)(a) and (c), the Court stated that it is necessary to take into account 'all the circumstances which bear on the price whether they arise from the relationship or otherwise'.[286] Since, in the context of the yield method, implicit support is a factor an arm's length person would find relevant in pricing a guarantee, such implicit support must be considered in establishing an arm's length price.[287]

GlaxoSmithKline

In *GlaxoSmithKline*, the Federal Court of Appeal addressed the transfer price of an active pharmaceutical ingredient (API) called ranitidine which the taxpayer acquired from a non-resident affiliate at prices much higher than the prices that other Canadian drug companies paid to acquire ranitidine from arm's length producers. Ranitidine was the API

---

[282] *Ibid.* paras. 259–62. The parties had acknowledged that there were no comparable uncontrolled transactions, and agreed that the resale price and cost plus methods were inapplicable, but presented competing pricing methodologies – with the taxpayer advancing an insurance-based model and a credit default swap methodology as alternative methods, and the revenue authority favouring the yield approach. *Ibid.* paras. 252–3.

[283] *Ibid.* para. 281 (concluding that '[i]mplicit support is nothing more than one's expectation as to how someone will behave in the future because economic reasons will cause the person to act in a certain manner' whereas a guarantee 'is a much more effective form of protection').

[284] *Ibid.* para. 304.   [285] *Ibid.* para. 305.

[286] *GE Capital* (FCA), note 2 above, para. 54.   [287] *Ibid.* para. 56.

in a drug called Zantac, which the taxpayer and other members of a multinational group of companies (Glaxo World) promoted as a more effective treatment for stomach ulcers than surgery or a competing drug called Tagamet.[288] Although Glaxo World held a patent on Zantac, Canadian law allowed other companies to sell generic versions of patented drugs in exchange for a royalty of 4 per cent to the patent owner.[289] During the years at issue (1990–3), the taxpayer acquired ranitidine from a non-arm's length distributor at prices ranging from CAN $1,512 to $1,651 per kilogram, while generic drug companies acquired ranitidine for prices ranging from CAN $193 to $304 per kilogram.[290] The CRA reassessed the taxpayer under former section 69(2) of the ITA on the basis that the amount that it had paid for the ranitidine exceeded the amount that it would have paid to an arm's length supplier, and for non-resident withholding tax under Part XIII of the ITA on the basis that it was deemed to have paid a dividend to its UK parent in an amount equal to the difference between the amount it paid for the ranitidine and the amount it would have paid to an arm's length supplier.[291]

At trial, the Minister argued that the generic companies' purchases of ranitidine from arm's length manufacturers established a comparable uncontrolled price,[292] while the taxpayer argued that its circumstances differed from those of the generic drug companies because its business model depended on Zantac's brand image as a superior product and because the ranitidine that it purchased from its non-arm's length supplier was manufactured according to Glaxo World's standards of good manufacturing practice, granulated to Glaxo World's standards, and produced in accordance with Glaxo World's health, safety and environmental standards.[293] On this basis, the taxpayer argued, independent licensees in Europe were a better comparator than the generic drug companies because they purchased ranitidine under the same business circumstances as the taxpayer.[294] In order to support their arguments, the Minister also relied on the cost plus method, while the taxpayer relied on the resale price method.[295]

Concluding that the arm's length purchases by the generic companies established a comparable uncontrolled price, the Tax Court of Canada dismissed the taxpayer's appeal. First, it concluded, although the

[288] *GlaxoSmithKline* (TCC), note 2 above, para. 3.   [289] *Ibid.* para. 19.
[290] *Ibid.* paras. 5–6.   [291] *Ibid.* para. 1.   [292] *Ibid.* para. 67.   [293] *Ibid.* para. 68.
[294] *Ibid.* para. 69.   [295] *Ibid.* paras. 67 and 69.

taxpayer had entered into a licence agreement with Glaxo World in addition to a supply agreement with its non-arm's length supplier, the agreements had to be considered separately.[296] On this basis, the judge declared, the issue before him was 'whether the purchase price of the ranitidine was reasonable' not whether the profits of the taxpayer or other Glaxo World companies were reasonable.[297] Second, the court continued, although there is no doubt that the taxpayer's marketing and pricing strategies differed from those of the generic drug companies, this difference had no bearing on the reasonableness of the price that it paid for ranitidine: 'Any difference in the business strategy between the appellant and the generic companies relates to the end selling price of the finished product, not the purchase price of the API'.[298] Third, it held, regardless of Glaxo World's manufacturing practices and health, safety and environmental standards, the fact that 'the generic ranitidine was bioequivalent and chemically equivalent to Glaxo's ranitidine'[299] meant that they were functionally comparable.[300] Similarly, because the taxpayer and the generic companies competed in the same market,[301] purchased ranitidine at the wholesale level on similar contractual terms,[302] and performed similar economic functions of secondary manufacture, sales and distribution, and research and development,[303] it followed that the price at which generic companies purchased ranitidine from arm's length suppliers constituted a comparable uncontrolled price for the purchase of ranitidine by the taxpayer.[304] In contrast, the court held that the European licensees were inappropriate comparators for the CUP method because the European markets and European transactions differed significantly from the Canadian market and Canadian transactions.[305] For the same reason, the court found that the resale price method was also inappropriate.[306] The cost plus method, on the other hand, generally supported the reasonableness of the Crown's CUP analysis and was largely unchallenged on cross-examination.[307] As a result, the court concluded, the price that would have been reasonable for the taxpayer to pay to its non-arm's length supplier was the price that the generic companies paid, subject to a slight increase of CAN $25 per kilogram to account for the fact that the ranitidine that was purchased by the taxpayer was granulated,[308] and the difference between this price

---

[296] *Ibid.* paras. 72–8.   [297] *Ibid.* para. 78.   [298] *Ibid.* para. 90.   [299] *Ibid.* para. 101.
[300] *Ibid.* paras. 118 and 127.   [301] *Ibid.* paras. 120–5.   [302] *Ibid.* paras. 128 and 131.
[303] *Ibid.* paras. 129–30.   [304] *Ibid.* para. 161.   [305] *Ibid.* paras. 132–42.
[306] *Ibid.* paras. 145–51.   [307] *Ibid.* paras. 157–60.   [308] *Ibid.* para. 161.

and the amount paid by the taxpayer was a deemed dividend subject to non-resident withholding tax.[309]

On appeal, the Federal Court of Appeal accepted the taxpayer's argument that an arm's length price had to be determined in light of all economically relevant circumstances, including the licence agreement and the fact that the taxpayer's business strategy depended on the sale of Zantac, not generic ranitidine. According to the Court, proper application of the arm's length standard 'requires an inquiry into those circumstances which an arm's length purchaser, *standing in the shoes of the appellant*, would consider relevant' in deciding how much to pay for ranitidine.[310] Because the trial judge had failed to consider the circumstances which would have made it possible for an arm's length purchaser to 'obtain the rights to make and sell Zantac',[311] the Court referred the matter back to the trial judge to decide upon an arm's length price in light of its judgment.[312]

The Crown applied for leave to appeal to the Supreme Court of Canada, which was granted on 24 March, 2011.[313] The Crown is asking the Court for a 'definitive statement of the legal principles to be applied in transfer pricing cases', including whether the benefits of licence agreements can be taken into account when determining arm's length pricing.[314] The taxpayer has sought leave to cross-appeal the Federal Court of Appeal's decision to return the matter to the Tax Court, thereby allowing the Minister to raise new arguments twelve years after the commencement of litigation.[315]

4.5.5   Settled and ongoing cases

In addition to these decided cases, several transfer pricing cases have been settled or remain ongoing.[316] Of these cases, a significant number

---

[309] *Ibid.* paras. 162–76.

[310] *GlaxoSmithKline* (FCA), note 2 above, para. 3 (emphasis added).

[311] *Ibid.* para. 78.   [312] *Ibid.* para. 83.

[313] Supreme Court of Canada, *Bulletin of Proceedings* (25 March 2011), p. 416, available at scc.lexum.org/en/bulletin/2011/2011–03–25.bul/2011–03–25.bul.pdf.

[314] Fasken Martineau, 'GlaxoSmithKline Transfer Pricing Case Heads to Supreme Court', *Taxation Bulletin* (25 March 2011), available at www.fasken.com/en/glaxosmithkline-transfer-pricing-case-heads-to-supreme-court.

[315] *Ibid.*

[316] For a useful review of these cases up to 2004, see F. Vincent, *Transfer Pricing in Canada* (2nd edn, Toronto: Thomson Carswell, 2004).

have involved pharmaceutical companies, which have been reassessed on the value of chemical ingredients for the manufacture of drugs in Canada acquired by Canadian companies from non-resident affiliates. The following sections discuss these pharmaceutical cases as well as other important transfer pricing cases that have been settled or remain ongoing.

Pharmaceutical cases

As in other countries,[317] some of the most protracted transfer pricing litigation in Canada has involved transactions within multinational drug companies. In addition to *GlaxoSmithKline*, the Canadian revenue authority has pursued at least three other pharmaceutical cases. The first of these cases involved purchases by Squibb Canada Inc. of ingredients from affiliates in the United States, Puerto Rico and Ireland.[318] Referring to comparable prices for ingredients sold by generic manufacturers, the revenue authorities reassessed the taxpayer under the transfer pricing rule in section 69(2) of the ITA on the basis that it has paid approximately CAN $6.4 million more than the arm's length price over the years 1975 to 1978.[319] The case was settled in 1987 with a reduction in the adjustment to CAN $1.4 million or 22 per cent of the initial assessment.[320]

The second pharmaceutical company transfer pricing case involved SmithKline Beecham Animal Health Inc., which was also reassessed on the basis that it had paid an inflated amount to non-resident affiliates in Bermuda and Ireland for a chemical ingredient that it used to manufacture a drug in Canada.[321] Covering a seven-year period, the amount of the reassessment totalled almost CAN $67 million.[322] Following nearly a decade of procedural wrangling after the case was filed in March 1995,[323] the case was settled in early 2004, with the taxpayer accepting the reassessment for the last five of the seven years at issue.[324] Interestingly,

---

[317] See R. S. Avi-Yonah's Chapter 3 'United States', discussing the *Glaxo* case.
[318] *Squibb Canada Inc.* v. *The Queen*, Federal Court Trial Division, Doc. T-3637–82.
[319] Vincent, *Transfer Pricing in Canada*, note 316 above, p. 68.
[320] *Ibid.*   [321] *Ibid.* p. 79.   [322] *Ibid.* p. 80.
[323] See *SmithKline Beecham Animal Health Inc.* v. *The Queen* [1998] 4 C.T.C. 2331, 98 D.T. C. 1929 (TCC); *SmithKline Beecham Animal Health Inc.* v. *The Queen* [2000] 1 C.T.C. 2552, 2000 D.T.C. 1526 (TCC), aff'd [2000] 2 C.T.C. 329, 2000 D.T.C. 6141 (FCA); and *SmithKline Beecham Animal Health Inc.* v. *The Queen* [2001] 2 C.T.C. 2086, 2001 D.T.C. 192 (TCC), aff'd [2003] 4 C.T.C. 93 (FCA).
[324] Vincent, *Transfer Pricing in Canada*, note 316 above, p. 83.

the taxpayer also agreed to pay CAN $3.2 million in expenses incurred by the revenue authority in order to obtain expert evidence, making the settlement a significant victory for the revenue authority.[325]

In addition to these cases, similar transfer pricing reassessments prompted an appeal by Hoffmann-LaRoche Ltd. In the case of Hoffmann-LaRoche, the facts involved the acquisition of chemical ingredients from a Bermuda affiliate at prices exceeding those charged by arm's length companies to Canadian generic manufacturers.[326] Here, as in *GlaxoSmithKline*, a key question involves the relevance of prices paid by generic manufacturers. While the taxpayer challenged the comparability of transactions entered into by generic manufacturers on the basis that these do not include support and services, the revenue authority argued that the transactions at issue should be unbundled by separating payments for the chemical ingredients from payments for services and/or royalties.[327] The Federal Court of Appeal decision in *GlaxoSmithKline* represents a major victory for taxpayers in these circumstances.

Other settled cases

In addition to these pharmaceutical cases, other transfer pricing cases that have settled have involved the following factual scenarios:[328]

(a) the sale of pulp and paper by a Canadian subsidiary, Crestbrook Forest Industries Inc. (Crestbrook) to its Japanese parents;

(b) the sale of ammonia by a Canadian company, Pacific Ammonia Inc. (Pacific Ammonia) through a foreign affiliate in Hong Kong;

(c) the sale of blueberries by a Canadian grower, Bridge Brothers Ltd (Bridge Brothers) to a non-arm's length broker in the United States;

(d) the transfer of contractual rights from a Canadian company, Denim Pipeline Inc. (Denim Pipeline) to a Barbados subsidiary specifically incorporated in order to carry out the contract;

---

[325] *Ibid.* pp. 83–4.   [326] *Ibid.* p. 86.   [327] *Ibid.* pp. 86–7.

[328] The discussion herein of these settled cases is derived from Vincent, *Transfer Pricing in Canada*, note 316 above; KPMG, 'Update on Transfer Pricing Cases Before the Courts', *Transfer Pricing in 60 Seconds*, No. 2006–06 (31 May 2006), available at www.kpmg.ca/en/services/tax/tp6006–06.html; and KPMG, 'CRA Targets Small Business in Transfer Pricing Case', *Transfer Pricing in 60 Seconds*, No. 2007–02 (5 March 2007), available at www.kpmg.ca/en/services/tax/tp60/tp60_0702.html.

(e) the establishment of a wholly-owned subsidiary in Trinidad and Tobago as the worldwide distributor for fireplaces and fixtures manufactured by the Canadian parent, FPI Fireplace Products International Ltd (FPI);

(f) the sale of welding guns to a non-arm's length distributor in Barbados;

(g) the purchase of television commercials by toy company Mattel Canada Inc. (Mattel) from its US parent;

(h) the purchase of produce and floral goods by a Canadian grocery retailer, Canada Safeway Ltd (Canada Safeway) from its US parent;

(i) the distribution of computer products in Canada by a permanent establishment of the US developer and manufacturer Norand Data Systems Ltd (Norand Data);

(j) the payment of guarantee fees, quality control fees and royalties to a Turkish company by a Canadian subsidiary, Attila Dogan Design & Construction Ltd (Attila Dogan), which was incorporated in order to secure financing from the Canadian Export Development Corporation (EDC); and

(k) the payment of service fees and interest to its US parent by a Canadian company providing tax return filing services.

The first three of these cases (*Crestbrook, Pacific Ammonia* and *Bridge Brothers*) are similar to the early Canadian transfer pricing decisions in *Central Canadian Forest Products* and *Hofert*,[329] and turned on the characterisation of comparable uncontrolled prices. Since *Crestbrook* and *Pacific Ammonia* were settled by consent to judgment with the revenue authority vacating the assessments,[330] and *Bridge Brothers* was settled with a significant reduction in the amount assessed, it appears that the revenue authority continues to have a difficult time with these kinds of cases.

The next three cases (*Denim Pipeline, FPI* and the welding gun case) are similar to *Safety Boss, World Corp.* and *Alberta Printed Circuits*,[331] in that they involved the incorporation of offshore subsidiaries in low-tax jurisdictions in order to carry out functions originally performed by the

---

[329] See the summary of these cases at notes 134–50 above.

[330] Vincent, *Transfer Pricing in Canada*, note 316 above, para. 73; *Pacific Ammonia Inc. v. The Queen*, TCC file no. 2002–81(IT)G (20 January 2005).

[331] See the summary of these cases at notes 232–270 above.

Canadian parent, and similar to the anti-avoidance cases in that the arrangements in each case were challenged not only under transfer pricing provisions, but also on the basis that the offshore subsidiary had no independent existence and operated as an agent of the Canadian parent. Despite the judgments in *Safety Boss* and *World Corp.*, a settlement in FPI for two-thirds of the transfer pricing adjustment under section 69(3) of the ITA suggests that the revenue authorities may have greater prospects for success in these types of cases.

The next three cases (*Mattel, Canada Safeway* and *Norand Data*) differ from most of the decided transfer pricing cases in Canada, since they do not involve a possible shift in profits to a low-tax jurisdiction. In each case, however, the facts appear to have given rise to questions about the appropriate transfer pricing methodology that should be applied, with the revenue authority in *Mattel* arguing that payment for the commercials should have been by way of a management fee or administrative charge, the taxpayer in *Canada Safeway* defending a cost plus methodology reflected in a 'buying charge' mark-up, and the revenue authority in *Norand Data* employing a profit split method to attribute profits to the Canadian permanent establishment. In *Mattel* and *Canada Safeway,* the taxpayer also appealed through the competent authority procedure established under the Canada–United States Income Tax Convention ('Canada–United States Treaty').

The final two cases (*Attila Dogan,* and the tax return filing service case) involved the payment of fees by Canadian subsidiaries to their non-resident parents. Although these payments are also subject to non-resident withholding tax in Canada,[332] the revenue authority appears to have concluded that transfer pricing provisions should also apply where the payments at issue exceed a reasonable amount that would be negotiated between arm's length parties. In the *Attila Dogan* case, the revenue authority argued that payments at issue were almost CAN $14 million greater than the amount that would have been reasonable in the circumstances had the parties been at arm's length.[333] The *Attila Dogan* case was settled in January 2005, with the taxpayer assenting to the assessment.[334]

---

[332] ITA, s. 212(1) (a) (management fees), (b) (interest), and (d) (royalties). See also ITA s. 214(15)(a), which deems guarantee fees to be interest for the purpose of s. 212(1)(b).

[333] Vincent, *Transfer Pricing in Canada*, note 316 above, p. 91.

[334] *Attila Dogan Design & Construction Ltd* v. *The Queen,* TCC file nos. 2002–3833(IT)G and 2002–3836(IT)G (14 January 2005).

Ongoing cases

There are a number of ongoing Canadian transfer pricing cases that have yet to be heard. These cases involve the following subject matters:

- inter-company sales of various tangible goods;[335]
- inter-company sales of software services;[336]
- inter-company purchases and sales of intangibles (trademarks, goodwill and other property) in the context of global asset divestitures;[337]
- inter-company sales of administrative services;[338]
- allocations of, or payments in respect of, marketing costs;[339]
- guarantee fees;[340] and
- inter-company sales of trade accounts receivable.[341]

It is anticipated that these cases, to the extent they proceed to trial, will provide additional much needed judicial guidance on the application of Canada's current transfer pricing rules.

4.6   Alternative dispute resolution

As the previous section of this chapter demonstrates, most transfer pricing cases in Canada have turned on the characterisation of a comparable uncontrolled price against which to measure the transaction at issue. In several of these cases, this question is also associated with a

---

[335] *AREVA Resources Canada Inc.*, TCC file no. 2010–305(IT)G and *Cameco Corporation*, TCC file no. 2009–2430(IT)G, both involving sales of uranium; *Federal White Cement Ltd*, TCC file no. 2004–2281(IT)G, involving sales of cement; *Good Earth Canada Ltd*, TCC file no. 2008–317(IT)G, involving sales of peat moss; *M. V. Osprey Ltd*, TCC file no. 2009–2996(IT)G, involving sales of seafood and related administrative expenses; *Nabors Drilling Ltd*, TCC file no. 2006–3567(IT)G and *Smith International Canada Ltd*, TCC file no. 2007–4644(IT)G, both involving sales of oil and gas equipment; and *Schering-Plough Canada Inc.*, TCC file no. 2008–3087(IT)G, involving sales of drug ingredients.

[336] *Alberta Printed Circuits Ltd*, TCC file no. 2008–714(IT).

[337] *Dow Chemical Finance Company Inc.*, TCC file no. 2007–4580(IT)G; and *Philips Electronics Ltd*, TCC file no. 2008–4088(IT)G.

[338] *Priority Management Systems (Canada) Inc.*, TCC file no. 2009–2278(IT)G; and *Sundog Distributing Inc.*, TCC file no. 2009–647(IT)G.

[339] *Four Star Distribution (Canada) Ltd*, TCC file no. 2008–1264(IT)G; *Marzen Artistic Aluminum Ltd*, TCC file no. 2010–860(IT)G; *Starline Architectural Windows Ltd*, TCC file no. 2010–866(IT)G; *Starline Window (2001) Ltd*, TCC file no. 2010–861(IT)G; and *Vitrum Holdings Ltd*, TCC file no. 2010–1489(IT)G.

[340] *HSBC Bank Canada*, TCC file no. 2006–3579(IT)G.

[341] *McKesson Canada Corp.*, TCC file no. 2008–2949(IT)G.

more fundamental issue concerning the characterisation of the legal relationships among the relevant parties. In most of these cases, the resolution of these issues has involved detailed expert evidence and lengthy litigation.[342] As a general rule, moreover, the Canadian revenue authorities prefer transaction-based methods of determining appropriate transfer prices, rather than profit-based methods such as the profit split or transactional net margin methods.

For these reasons, it is perhaps not surprising that the revenue authorities and multinational enterprises have increasingly resorted to alternative methods to resolve transfer pricing disputes, such as advance pricing arrangements (APAs), the mutual agreement procedures under tax treaties (MAPs), and mandatory arbitration. The following sections review Canadian experience with each of these alternatives to the litigation of transfer pricing disputes.

4.6.1   Advance pricing agreements

In contrast to litigation, APAs represent a cooperative approach to the resolution of transfer pricing disputes, whereby taxpayers and the revenue authority jointly agree on an acceptable transfer pricing methodology to govern transactions entered into by the taxpayer for a fixed period, usually three to five years.[343] According to the Canadian revenue authority, the APA must correspond to its administrative guidelines as well as the OECD guidelines for applying the arm's length standard, and must be appropriate to the taxpayer's situation.[344] Once entered into, the revenue authority regards an APA as 'binding' between it and the taxpayer.[345]

First established in Canada between 1990 and 1992 as a joint pilot project with the Office of the Chief Counsel in the United States,[346] the APA programme has grown dramatically in Canada over the subsequent two

---

[342] In the *Glaxo* case, for example, the revenue authority is reported to have asked over 32,000 questions and obtained 1,900 undertakings and 1,410 written answers, excluding questions and answers provided during the audit. KPMG, '*Glaxo* Update – CRA Seeks to Unbundle Transfer Price', *Transfer Pricing in 60 Seconds*, No. 2005–12 (26 October 2005), available at www.kpmg.ca/en/services/tax/tp6012–05.html.

[343] IC 94–4R, *International Transfer Pricing: Advance Pricing Arrangements (APAs)* (16 March 2001), para. 55.

[344] *Ibid.* para. 43.   [345] *Ibid.* para. 73.

[346] Canada Revenue Agency, *APA Program Report, 2004–2005* (Ottawa: Canada Revenue Agency, 2005), para. 8.

decades, and comprised 142 completed APAs by 31 March 2010.[347] The vast majority of these agreements are bilateral or multilateral APAs entered into with the competent authorities of Canada's tax treaty partners, particularly the United States (Canada's most important trading partner).[348]

Of the 142 completed APAs concluded in Canada by 31 March 2010, 54 per cent involve tangible property, compared to 20 per cent for intangible property, 21 per cent for intra-group services, and 4 per cent for financial transactions.[349] Among agreements currently under negotiation, however, there is an increase in the proportion of transactions involving intangibles (29 per cent), for which comparable arm's length prices are notoriously difficult to determine, and a decrease in the number involving tangible property (49 per cent).[350] Most interestingly, perhaps, the predominant transfer pricing methodology employed in the APAs that were concluded by 31 March 2010 is the transactional net margin method (TNMM), followed by the profit split method.[351] The predominance of the TNMM is more pronounced in the APAs listed as 'in progress' in the 2009–10 *APA Program Report*; TNMM is employed in 39 per cent of these cases.[352] As these methodologies are generally considered more appropriate for transactions within highly integrated multinational corporations, the statistics suggest that these kinds of enterprises are more likely to enter into an APA than other enterprises. For many multinationals, APAs have already displaced litigation as the preferred route to resolving transfer pricing disputes. The Canadian revenue authority also views the APA program as its transfer pricing 'compliance tool of choice'.[353]

4.6.2 Mutual agreement procedure: process and statistics

Where a revenue authority readjusts or recharacterises a cross-border non-arm's length transaction, it raises the possibility of double taxation.

---

[347] Canada Revenue Agency, *APA Program Report, 2009–2010* (Ottawa: Canada Revenue Agency, 2010), para. 9.

[348] *Ibid.* paras. 4 and 22, reporting that 113 of Canada's APAs were bilateral or multilateral APAs and that 87 of these APAs were concluded with the competent authority of the United States.

[349] *Ibid.* para. 18.   [350] *Ibid.* para. 18.

[351] *Ibid.* para. 19, reporting that fifty-six APAs employed the transactional net margin method, thirty-four the profit split method, twenty-two the comparable uncontrolled price method, nineteen the cost plus method, and eleven the resale price method.

[352] *Ibid.* para. 19.   [353] CRA, *APA Program Report, 2004–2005*, note 346 above, para. 6.

Where Canada has entered into a tax convention with the other taxing state, the taxpayer may seek relief from double taxation through the mutual agreement procedure (MAP) programme that is incorporated into Canada's network of bilateral tax conventions, in accordance with the OECD's Model Tax Convention on Income and on Capital. Through the MAP process, competent authorities from each tax authority work to negotiate a resolution to the tax dispute. The CRA's IC 71–17R5 notes that the negotiations are government-to-government interactions, with taxpayer involvement generally limited to assistance with fact-finding and a presentation of the taxpayer's position.[354] Where the two competent authorities have reached an agreement, the taxpayer can accept or reject it.[355]

To initiate the MAP process, the taxpayer (if resident in Canada) must request assistance from the Competent Authority Service Division of the CRA. Such a request must include specific information regarding the dispute.[356] The Competent Authority Division will not negotiate cases where the assessment or adjustment is based on the General Anti-Avoidance Rule contained in section 245 of the ITA or other anti-avoidance provisions.[357]

In Canada, the MAP process is the most commonly-used avenue for resolving transfer pricing disputes. According to figures from the CRA's annual *MAP Program Reports*, 535 transfer pricing cases have been completed through the MAP programme since 2001, an average of just over fifty completed cases a year.[358] Although there was a marked

---

[354] CRA, *Guidance on Competent Authority Assistance under Canada's Tax Conventions*, IC-71–17R5, (1 January 2005), para. 36.

[355] *Ibid.* para. 55.   [356] *Ibid.* para. 19.   [357] *Ibid.* para. 27.

[358] For year-on-year figures, see Canada Revenue Agency, *Mutual Agreement Procedure Program Report 1 April 2010–31 March 2011* (2011), para. 16; Canada Revenue Agency, *Mutual Agreement Procedure Program Report 1 April 2009–31 March 2010* (2010), para. 16; Canada Revenue Agency, *Mutual Agreement Procedure Program Report 1 April 2008–31 March 2009* (2009), para. 16; Canada Revenue Agency, *Mutual Agreement Procedure Program Report 1 April 2007–31 March 2008* (2008), para. 16; Canada Revenue Agency, *Mutual Agreement Procedure Program Report 1 April 2006–31 March 2007* (2007), para. 16; Canada Revenue Agency, *Mutual Agreement Procedure Program Report 1 April 2005–31 March 2006* (2006), para. 16; Canada Revenue Agency, *Mutual Agreement Procedure Program Report 1 April 2004–31 March 2005* (2005), para. 16; Canada Revenue Agency, *Mutual Agreement Procedure Program Report 1 April 2008–31 March 2009* (2009), para. 15; Canada Revenue Agency, *Mutual Agreement Procedure Program Report 1 April 2008–31 March 2009* (2009), para. 15; Canada Revenue Agency, *Mutual Agreement Procedure Program Report 1 April 2001–31 March 2004* (2004), para. 14; NB the CRA uses the term 'associated enterprises' cases to designate transfer pricing cases.

decrease in completed transfer pricing cases from 2004–5 (seventy transfer pricing cases completed) to 2007–8 (twenty-eight transfer pricing
cases completed),[359] the number of completed transfer pricing negotiations has risen to seventy-four by 2010–11.[360]

The CRA has a target completion time of twenty-four months for
negotiable MAP cases. For Canadian-initiated cases, the CRA has been
largely successful in meeting this target, with average completion times
being lower than twenty-four months in 2003–4, 2005–6, 2007–8 and
2009–10; average completion times for Canadian-initiated cases
exceeded the twenty-four-month target in 2006–7 (25.86 months average completion time), 2008–9 (28.14 months average completion time),
and 2010–11 (32.16 months average completion time).[361] The CRA
has been less successful in meeting this completion target for foreign-
initiated cases, with the exception being the most recent year where
Canadian-initiated cases outstripped foreign-initiated cases by 32.16
months to 20.39.[362]

As is the case with APAs, the most commonly used transfer pricing
methodology in MAP cases is the transactional net margin method,
which in 2010–11 was used in 45 per cent of cases, followed by the
cost plus method in 20 per cent of cases, the CUP method in 11 per
cent, the resale method in 1 per cent, and the profit split method in
0 per cent.[363] The United States is the most common foreign tax
jurisdiction involved in MAP negotiations with the CRA (involved in
over 80 per cent of completed MAP cases in 2008–9), followed by
the United Kingdom (6 per cent), Netherlands, Japan, Germany and
France (2.4 per cent each), and Mexico and Poland (1.2 per cent each).
Most transfer pricing cases are resolved so as to eliminate double
taxation.[364]

---

[359] This decline has been attributed in part to a lack of trained competent authority
analysts. J. Hejazi, *Transfer Pricing: The Basics from a Canadian Perspective* (Markham,
ON: LexisNexis, 2010), p. 57.

[360] Canada Revenue Agency, *Mutual Agreement Procedure Program Report 2010–2011*,
note 358 above, para. 16.

[361] *Ibid.* para. 11.   [362] *Ibid.*

[363] *Ibid.* para. 19. 23 per cent of cases have no method ascribed to them. The CRA states
that this occurs where the MAP case 'involves an issue of taxation contrary to a
convention or an allocation of costs between related parties'.

[364] Hejazi, *Transfer Pricing: The Basics from a Canadian Perspective*, note 359 above, p. 54
(reporting that over 90 per cent of transfer cases between the United States and Canada
are resolved without any double taxation).

4.6.3 Canada–United States Treaty and mandatory arbitration

The Fifth Protocol to the Canada–United States Treaty introduced mandatory binding arbitration provisions for transfer pricing disputes not resolved under a mutual agreement procedure. The mandatory arbitration provisions are applicable for cases arising after, or under consideration by the competent authorities on, 15 December 2008, and replace non-mandatory arbitration provisions in place prior to the Fifth Protocol.

Paragraph 6 of Article XXVI of the Canada–US Treaty (subject to certain rules and definitions for implementing the arbitration procedures in paragraph 7 of Article XXVI) provides that a dispute is subject to arbitration proceedings if certain conditions are met, including that the taxpayer must have filed tax returns in at least one of the two states for the tax years at issue; the case must not be one which the competent authorities from both states agree is not suitable for resolution through arbitration; and the taxpayer and other parties 'whose tax liability would be directly affected by the result of the arbitration process' ('concerned persons') must accede in writing to a confidentiality agreement covering all information exchanged during the arbitration process (excluding the final determination of the arbitration board). The arbitration procedure is a 'baseball-style' arbitration model, in that the arbitration board must choose between the proposals offered by the Canadian and US tax authorities without alteration or compromise. Taxpayers are not granted the opportunity to present their own proposals or to influence the arbitration board.

Pursuant to Annex A to the Canada–United States Treaty (the 'Arbitration Note'), the arbitration board must deliver a determination in writing within six months of the appointment of the board's chair. For taxpayers, this arbitration timetable 'is very encouraging given that a matter that has been languishing for a long period under a competent authority procedure has now found a way to closure'.[365] The Arbitration Note also states that in making its determination, the arbitration board shall apply, as necessary, (i) the provisions of the Canada–United States Treaty; (ii) any agreed commentaries or explanations concerning the Treaty; (iii) US and Canadian laws to the extent that they are not inconsistent with each other; and (iv) any OECD commentary, guidelines and reports regarding relevant analogous provisions of the OECD Model Convention.

---

[365] *Ibid.* para. 39.

If a concerned person does not accept an arbitration board's determination, the determination does not constitute a resolution under the mutual agreement procedure and is not binding. Further, a concerned person is entitled to terminate the arbitration proceedings at any time. However, the competent authorities have no unilateral right to terminate a proceeding, such that the competent authorities' approach to transfer pricing disputes may now be significantly altered:

> It is quite possible that the competent authorities will have more incentive to try and arrive at a mutual understanding [as a result of mandatory arbitration]. First, leaving the decision to the arbitration team may downplay the role of the competent authorities and could serve to reduce the level of credibility they have. Secondly, the risk that their proposal would be outright discarded by the arbitration team could be a great deterrent to having the case leave their control.[366]

It will be interesting to see if the new arbitration provisions achieve the desired goal of increasing the incentive for tax authorities to reach agreement, rather than risk all in arbitration.

4.7   Conclusion

Despite a lengthy history of statutory provisions governing transfer pricing in Canada, very few Canadian judicial decisions have considered transactions involving transfer pricing. Although this chapter has not considered the reasons for this experience, plausible explanations might include: the revenue authority's early failures in *Central Canada Forest Products* and *Hofert*, which may have discouraged reassessments under the transfer pricing provisions; limited auditing of international transactions, which have only relatively recently become a priority for the Canadian revenue authority; the availability of an alternative remedy in the form of mutual agreement procedures (MAPs) under bilateral tax treaties; and the recent growth of APAs as a further alternative to transfer pricing litigation.

While the availability of MAPs and APAs are likely to ensure that the number of transfer pricing cases in Canada will remain relatively small, three factors suggest that transfer pricing litigation may become more frequent than has been the case thus far in Canada. First, the growth of international trade and multinational enterprises means that the

---

[366] *Ibid.* para. 38.

universe of potential disputes from which litigation may arise has grown considerably over the last few decades. Second, recent increases in international audit staff indicate that the Canadian revenue authority is taking transfer pricing more seriously. Third, the enactment of new section 247 of the ITA in 1998 gives the revenue authorities a more powerful statutory provision with which to challenge transfer pricing transactions.

Although most decided transfer pricing cases in Canada all involve statutory provisions other than section 247, they indicate the kinds of transactions that the revenue authorities are likely to challenge and the kinds of considerations that courts have considered relevant in adjudicating transfer pricing cases. To the extent that section 247 incorporates an arm's length standard for appropriate prices and transactional forms, earlier judicial decisions are likely to remain relevant to the application of this new transfer pricing rule.

Appendix: Questionnaire (Canada)

1. The structure of the law for solving transfer pricing disputes. *What is the structure of the law of the country for solving transfer pricing disputes? For example, is the mutual agreement procedure (MAP), as regulated in the relevant tax treaty, the standard method for solving transfer pricing disputes?*

Taxpayers have a number of options when considering how to resolve a transfer pricing dispute. The MAP programme is incorporated into Canada's network of bilateral tax conventions, in accordance with the OECD's Model Tax Convention on Income and on Capital. Dispute resolution processes such as MAP, APAs and arbitration are governed by CRA policy rather than through statute. As discussed above, MAP negotiations are the most commonly used method of resolving transfer pricing disputes, with 535 transfer pricing cases concluded between 2001 and 2011.[367]

2. Policy for solving transfer pricing disputes. *Is there a gap between the nominal and effective method for solving transfer pricing disputes in the country? For example, has the country a strategic policy not to enforce*

---

[367] See note 358 above.

the arm's length standard (ALS) for fear of driving foreign direct invest-
ment to other competing jurisdictions?

There does not appear to be a noticeable gap between Canada's transfer
pricing policy and the methods by which transfer pricing disputes are
resolved. Certainly, we have not seen any evidence to suggest that the
CRA is soft-balling its approach to transfer pricing disputes for fear of
driving away foreign direct investment. Indeed, Hejazi notes that in the
past decade the CRA has increased the amount of resources and man-
power directed at transfer pricing issues.[368]

3. The prevailing dispute resolution method. *Which is the most frequent*
method for solving transfer pricing disputes in the country? Does it have a
positive externality? For example, is the MAP the most frequent method,
and if so, to what extent have successful MAPs been used as a proxy for
transfer pricing case law? For instance, Procter & Gamble (P&G) obtained
a bilateral advance pricing agreement (APA) in Europe, and it was then
extended to a third (Asian) country when P&G made this request to the
relevant Asian tax authorities.

As discussed above, the MAP has been by far the most utilised dispute
resolution method over the last decade, with APAs also playing an
important role. These dispute resolution tools do not serve a public good
function,[369] as they are not released publicly. In its Information Circulars
regarding MAP and APAs, the CRA stresses that information gathered or
generated through these dispute resolution processes is protected by the
confidentiality provisions of both the applicable tax conventions and the
ITA.[370] The only information released by the CRA regarding MAP or
APAs is general statistics relating to each programme (e.g., number of
completed cases, transfer pricing methods used, industries involved, etc.).

4. Transfer pricing case law. *What is the evolution path of transfer pricing*
litigation in the country? For example: (i) Is transfer pricing litigation being
gradually replaced by either MAPs or APAs, as regulated in the relevant tax

---

[368] Hejazi, *Transfer Pricing: The Basics from a Canadian Perspective*, note 359 above,
pp. 6–8.

[369] For a discussion of the concept of public good function of case law and other transfer
pricing dispute resolution mechanisms, see E. Baistrocchi, 'The Transfer Pricing Problem: A Global Proposal for Simplification' (2005–6) 59 *Tax Lawyer* 941.

[370] CRA, *Guidance on Competent Authority Assistance under Canada's Tax Conventions*, IC
71–17R5 (1 January 2005), para. 9; CRA, *International Transfer Pricing: Advance Pricing*
Arrangements (APAs), IC 94–4R (16 March 2001), paras. 75–7.

treaties? (ii) Are foreign/local transfer pricing precedents and/or published MAPs increasingly relevant as a source of law for solving transfer pricing disputes?

As discussed above, there is not a great deal of case law in Canada regarding transfer pricing disputes, and in particular regarding the modern transfer pricing rules in section 247. In contrast, again as discussed above, MAP negotiations and APAs have played a very large role in resolving transfer pricing disputes over the past decade. As such, it seems reasonable to conclude that such negotiated dispute resolution methods have to a great extent replaced litigation as the preferred method of resolving transfer pricing disputes. The introduction into the Canada–United States Treaty of an arbitration procedure to resolve intractable MAP cases (discussed above) is likely to enhance this trend. However, as APAs and MAPs are confidential, they do not act as sources of law for resolving future disputes.

5. Customary international law and international tax procedure. *Has customary international law been applied in the country to govern the relevant methods for solving transfer pricing disputes (such as the MAP)? For example, has the* OECD Manual on Effective Mutual Agreement Procedure *('OECD Manual') been deemed customary international tax law in the MAP arena for filling procedural gaps (for example, time limit for implementation of relief where treaties deviate from the OECD Model Tax Convention)?*

Judicial decisions have relied on OECD Guidelines and Model Treaties as persuasive interpretive aids. For example, in *GE Capital* and *GlaxoSmithKline*, courts relied in part on OECD transfer pricing guidelines in order to determine which transfer pricing methodology was most appropriate and to insist that all economically relevant circumstances be taken into account in assessing an arm's length price. Additionally, the CRA's own administrative documents relating to transfer pricing refer to and endorse the OECD's 1995 Guidelines.[371] However, it does not appear that such instruments have been taken either by the courts or by the revenue authority to represent binding international law.

6. Procedural setting and strategic interaction. *Does strategic interaction between taxpayers and tax authorities depend on the procedural setting in*

---

[371] CRA, *International Transfer Pricing*, IC 87–2R (27 September 1999).

which they interact when trying to solve transfer pricing disputes? For example, which procedural setting in the country prompts the relevant parties to cooperate with each other the most for solving this sort of dispute, and why?

It seems likely where taxpayers and tax authorities attempt to resolve transfer pricing disputes through negotiation-based methods (e.g., APAs and MAP), there will be more incentive for compromise than in adversarial arenas like the courts. Hejazi has written that the advent of mandatory arbitration for intractable MAP negotiations might lead to a greater incentive for completing cases by negotiations, as each tax authority will be wary of risking the chance that the arbitration panel selects the opposite authority's proposal.[372]

7. The future of transfer pricing disputes resolution.   *Which is the best available proposal in light of the interests of the country for facilitating the global resolution of transfer pricing disputes, and why?*

The increasing use of alternative processes to litigation (e.g., APAs, MAP and mandatory arbitration) to resolve transfer pricing disputes is a positive step. The time and cost to have a complex transfer pricing case decided through litigation is considerable. For example, the *GlaxoSmithKline* case, which involved reassessments for the taxation years between 1990 and 1993, was only decided by the Tax Court of Canada in 2008 and the Federal Court of Appeal in 2010, twenty years after the first taxation year in dispute. The pending appeal to the Supreme Court of Canada will drag on the litigation even further. Speed and cost considerations favour a greater emphasis on alternative dispute resolution to resolve transfer pricing disputes.

---

[372] Hejazi, *Transfer Pricing: The Basics from a Canadian Perspective*, note 359 above, p. 38.

Transfer pricing disputes in the European Union

PHILIP GILLETT

5.1 Background

Over the last twenty-five years the European Union has instigated two major initiatives aimed at producing a more coherent direct tax framework for Europe in order to support its key objective of creating a single economic market.

In 1990 the European Commission asked a Committee of Independent Experts on Company Taxation, under the chairmanship of Onno Ruding (Ruding Committee) to determine whether differences in business taxation among Member States led to major distortions which might affect the functioning of the single market, and to examine possible remedial measures. The Report, which was produced in 1992, made a large number of recommendations for improvements in the functioning of business taxation across the EU, including such then far-reaching ideas as cross-border loss relief, but for a variety of reasons, many of them perhaps associated with the desire for the retention of sovereignty over direct tax policy prevalent in many Member States, very little progress was made on any of the key recommendations.

Then, at the Ecofin Council in December 1998, the European Commission was asked to carry out an analytical study on company taxation within the EU and in particular to focus on the effective levels of corporate taxation in the different Member States and to identify the main tax obstacles that might restrict cross-border economic activity in the single market. This request was refined into a formal mandate for the Commission in July 1999, which resulted in the publication, in October 2001, of a Commission staff working paper entitled *Company Taxation in the Internal Market* ('2001 Report'). The conclusions of this paper can be seen to have driven EU policy on direct taxation since that time.

It is difficult to understand precisely why such significant progress has been made following the 2001 Report as compared with the Report of the Ruding Committee but perhaps one of the key drivers was the dramatic change in the nature of international business activity in the intervening years. In the years leading up to 1990, the majority of business activities within international companies were carried out within territorial structures. The internal organisation of the major international trading companies still followed essentially national dividing lines, such that national tax boundaries were broadly in line with the internal boundaries within the companies. Within each country in which a group operated there would usually be something approaching a full stand-alone trading entity, containing all the necessary functions of a trading operation, manufacturing, purchasing, sales, distribution, etc.

The decade following the publication of the Ruding Report, however, saw a dramatic shift in the way in which business operated internationally. Businesses started to be managed on global, or at least on pan-European lines, with centralised European functions, and the individual national companies within groups became less important. In fact the national company structures within groups sometimes came to be seen as an obstacle to a well-managed international business. Much of this was driven by simple economics. Manufacturing facilities became rationalised and larger, in order to achieve the desired economies of scale. Suppliers and customers were also becoming global or pan-European in nature, and, as a consequence, it was essential to trade with them in a consistent manner across the globe or region. National variations, whether in price or service or design, were inefficient and no longer acceptable within a modern business environment.

Within the EU, there was also a concern that taxation might drive location decisions between different Member States, or even cause businesses to locate outside the EU. There are certainly empirical studies that show that there is a correlation between taxation and location decisions, and there are some high profile examples of businesses relocating to Ireland, for example, primarily, it would seem, in order to take advantage of the low corporate tax rate there. The more informed view, however, is that generally such decisions are considerably more complex than simple tax rates, and that there are many other factors at work, such as the availability of an appropriately skilled and educated workforce, but clearly low tax rates can be a significant factor in deciding between otherwise similar potential locations.

It was a key feature of the 2001 Report that although it was produced by the Commission, it was produced with the assistance of two panels: a panel of academics, who assisted the Commission in determining the variations in tax burdens across EU Member States, and a panel of business representatives, who were able to explain how the different tax systems interacted with, and frequently constrained, modern business operations. The paper therefore had the support of many business organisations, which perhaps has given the Commission the confidence necessary to press ahead with the suggested initiatives in the subsequent years.

5.2   Key conclusions of the 2001 Report

The 2001 Report came up with four key causes of the main additional tax and compliance burdens which might be created by the existence of, then, fifteen separate tax systems, within what was intended to be a single economic market:

(a) the difficulty of allocating profits to each taxing jurisdiction on an arm's length basis;

(b) the 'reluctance' of Member States to permit cross-border loss offset;

(c) the tax charges which might arise on a cross-border business reorganisation, which was designed to create a more efficient operating structure; and

(d) double taxation which might occur as a result of conflicting taxing rights.

It can be seen, therefore, that transfer pricing would inevitably be a key focus of the report's recommendations.

The report also recognised the difficulties of complying with the different sets of tax rules existing between the Member States, and although this is something which most large business organisations could handle, albeit at additional cost, it was felt that the need to comply with so many different rules might deter small and medium-sized enterprises from engaging in cross-border activity, and thus significantly harm the longer term development of the EU.

It is true to say, of course, that the EU had already taken a number of initiatives to address some of these concerns – the Merger Directive 90/434/EEC, the Parent/Subsidiary Directive 90/435/EEC and the Arbitration Convention 90/436/EEC – but for a variety of reasons, some created by the different ways in which these initiatives had been implemented by the Member States, these were in practice of relatively limited impact, and were not widely used or valued by business.

Because of the new global and regional operational trade flows in international businesses, transfer pricing had clearly become a much more troublesome issue. It is perhaps an oversimplification, but, at that time, many EU Member States did not have extensive experience of international transfer pricing issues, and a number of Member States did not even have fully developed transfer pricing legislation. Those

Member States which had developed transfer pricing provisions had in many instances developed them because they feared manipulation of transfer prices by businesses who might be tempted to 'overcomply' with countries which had what might be perceived as more aggressive transfer pricing policies. Such, essentially defensive, concerns do not tend to develop systems conducive to efficient business practices.

It was a common complaint from business that they were being required to calculate internal transfer prices, in order to comply with the tax systems of the individual Member States, which were of no relevance whatsoever to the manner in which they conducted their business, and therefore served no underlying commercial purpose.

Transfer pricing compliance also presented particular difficulties as new technologies and new business practices developed. Transfer pricing practices as applied to traditional goods and services within traditional trading models were well developed in a number of key trading nations and there were therefore useful precedents as regards transfer pricing methodology in this context. This was, however, of very limited use when it came to pricing intellectual property, and the new business structures threw up new types of trading entity, which might only provide services such as distribution planning, which had not previously existed as a separate and independent trade. The report therefore also highlighted the key problem for business of uncertainty.

Certainty of execution is a vital business requirement. The thought of a substantial business cost such as taxation being uncertain for many years after transactions had taken place, and, even worse, the possibility that the end-result might be that the same profits would be taxed twice, was quite simply unacceptable in the modern business environment. In earlier times taxation might have been regarded by some businesses as a government impost and therefore outside the mainstream of business activity, and not subject to normal business disciplines. This is no longer the case. Taxation is a business cost, to be managed and controlled just like any other business cost. Uncertainty on the scale that could arise from transfer pricing issues, especially in the context of the hoped for single market, clearly needed to be eliminated.

The 2001 Report put forward two separate approaches for tackling the issues which it had identified:

(i) targeted short-term solutions aimed at individual obstacles; and
(ii) more comprehensive solutions designed to address the underlying causes of those obstacles.

The more comprehensive solution suggested by the Report was the introduction of a single common consolidated tax base for a business group's EU activities, which it was believed would address most if not all of the problems identified. Such a solution has both its supporters and detractors amongst the Member States, and it may not become a practical reality for all EU Member States in the short term, if at all, but it is now (in 2011) undoubtedly much closer to becoming a reality than was ever envisaged by many Member States, with the proposed Directive tabled by the Commission in March 2011.

The targeted measures proposed were of a more short-term and practical nature and included the following.

5.2.1   EU Directives

The 2001 Report recognised that the EU Directives referred to above had not been as effective as hoped and suggested that much of this might be due to the different ways in which the various Directives had been implemented by the Member States. It therefore suggested that progress could be made by more cooperation between the Member States as regards the exchange of best practice, etc.

5.2.2   Cross-border offset of losses

On the cross-border offset of losses the 2001 Report suggested that research should be carried out on such systems as the Danish system of joint taxation, which appeared to offer some advantages over the system proposed by the Commission in response to the Report of the Ruding Committee.

5.2.3   Transfer pricing

In the area of transfer pricing the 2001 Report focused on the application of the Arbitration Convention and proposed more coordination on the question of documentation requirements. In this context it suggested the formation of an EU working group, a joint forum on transfer pricing, comprising representatives of tax authorities and business which 'might allow the currently conflicting perspectives of the two sides to be reconciled'. It summarised the problem as follows: 'While on the one hand tax administrations view transfer pricing as a common vehicle for tax avoidance or evasion by companies and as a source of harmful tax competition between Member States, business on the other hand considers that tax authorities are imposing disproportionate compliance costs.' The Report concluded that both sides had legitimate concerns.

5.3   EU Joint Transfer Pricing Forum

On 19 July 2002 the European Commission announced the formation of the EU Joint Transfer Pricing Forum under the Chairmanship of Bruno Gibert, who had considerable experience of working in both the French tax administration and as a private sector tax professional. He proved to be an excellent choice.

The Forum was to consist of representatives of the tax administrations of the then fifteen Member States and ten representatives from the European business community. Of these private sector members five were from the tax profession and five from business. There were two representatives from each of the United Kingdom and Germany and one each from Belgium, France, Italy, Luxembourg, the Netherlands and Spain. The Forum would also be attended by representatives of the tax administrations of the ten countries who were due to join the EU in the near future, initially in an observer capacity, but in due course as full members of the Forum.

The Forum met for the first time on 3 October 2002.

In some Member States the concept of face-to-face dialogue between tax administrations and business was well established, but in others it was totally unknown. This was therefore a somewhat revolutionary, and possibly uncomfortable, idea for some Member States. In addition a number of Member States had relatively little experience of international transfer pricing disputes in practice and therefore the Member States started from very different viewpoints.

The initial work programme of the Forum focused on turning the Arbitration Convention from a theoretical agreement into a working reality. As has been stated above, the uncertainty arising from transfer pricing disputes and the time taken to resolve them is very unsatisfactory from a business viewpoint. However, such concerns pale into insignificance beside the possibility of the same profits being subject to taxation twice, in two different Member States. The Arbitration Convention was therefore potentially a key protection against this unacceptable outcome.

Most double tax conventions do, of course, contain mutual agreement provisions, which provide for tax administrations to discuss situations where double taxation might potentially arise and to try to come to a reasonable agreement as to how profits should be divided between two states. Problems can arise, however in that in most double tax conventions there is no binding legal requirement for the two states to come to an agreement which does in fact avoid double taxation. They are merely required to try to do so. The fact that such negotiations can take a great deal of time and can sometimes fail to come to a conclusion which is acceptable to the taxpayer involved is more due to the complexity of the subject than any lack of goodwill or effort on the part of the tax administrations, but the simple fact is that a route which leads from the mutual agreement procedure to a binding arbitration process, with defined timescales, is likely to lead to quicker outcomes for the taxpayer, and outcomes in which double taxation is avoided in all cases, usually without the need to invoke the arbitration provisions themselves.

5.3.1   EU Arbitration Convention

At the time the Joint Transfer Pricing Forum was established there were a number of practical issues with the Arbitration Convention which prevented it from being used in most real-life situations.

The Convention had its origins in the Commission's 1976 proposal for a Directive to eliminate double taxation within the EU, and the White Paper of 1985 on the completion of the Internal Market. The Arbitration Convention was signed on 23 July 1990 and was in force for an initial period of five years, from 1 January 1995 until 31 December 1999. This initial period was extended for additional periods of five years, unless a Member State opposed it, by a Protocol signed on 25 May 1999. In spite of this Protocol having been signed by all fifteen Member States, before the expiry of the initial five-year period of the Convention, it had not actually been ratified by all fifteen Member States at the time the Forum was established. In addition, of course, when the ten new members joined, none of them had either signed or ratified the Convention.

The question of signature and ratification of the Convention was therefore a key item in the initial work of the Forum, and indeed became a standing first item of the agenda for every meeting of the Forum until the Convention was finally ratified by all Member States. Undoubtedly a significant part of the driving force behind this achievement after so many years of limited progress was the simple expedient of peer pressure.

The next key concern to be tackled within the Arbitration Convention was the thorny issue of time limits. The Convention contains two key time limits:

1. There is a three-year deadline for submitting the request for the case to be considered under the Convention, which starts from 'the first tax assessment notice or equivalent which results or is likely to result in double taxation'.
2. There is a two-year period after which the tax authorities must set up an arbitration hearing if they have not reached agreement under the normal mutual agreement procedures. This two-year period starts on the later of:

    (a) the date of the final court of appeal, tribunal or tax authority determination, and
    (b) the date on which the formal request (as per 1 above) was properly submitted to the tax authority.

As can be seen, these definitions contain many potential uncertainties, not least the fact that the Member States have widely varying local legal processes and practices for the issuing of tax assessments and that there will not therefore be direct equivalents of a 'tax assessment notice' in all Member State jurisdictions. In addition there was much opportunity for debate as to the proper form in which a request should be made, and how much information was required to accompany the request for it to be considered properly made.

In addition the differing interpretations as to the starting points for these two vital time periods, and the considerable length of time which it often took to determine transfer pricing disputes, might mean that a key specified time period may have expired under the interpretation of one of the relevant tax authorities even though it had not even commenced under the definition of another relevant tax authority.

The Convention also contained many other provisions which it was considered were not sufficiently well defined to make the Convention a living reality, including such practical issues as to how an arbitration hearing would be funded.

All these issues were debated at great length, and in great detail, at the Forum, but eventually the Forum produced a Draft Code of Conduct for the effective implementation of the Arbitration Convention. This set out the Forum's recommendations as to how the various Convention provisions should be interpreted in practice, by reference to the legal processes and practices of all the then fifteen Member States and four of the acceding states (the Czech Republic, Malta, Poland and Slovakia) set out in both English and the language of the relevant state. This was presented to the EU Council of Ministers in a report from the European Commission dated 23 April 2004, describing the activities of the Forum from October 2003 up to December 2003, and containing the recommendation of the Commission that the Code of Conduct should be adopted. The Code of Conduct was formally adopted by the Council of Ministers on 7 December 2004.

This Code of Conduct was an essentially practical document and it was therefore considered that it would be better if it took the form of a Code of Conduct rather than specific EU legislation. Whatever the precise legal mechanism, however, its main purpose was to turn the Arbitration Convention into a living, working reality, not necessarily in the expectation that it would be used frequently, but more in the hope that its existence would encourage the competent authorities of the Member States to conclude transfer pricing disputes in the conventional manner, through the normal mutual agreement procedure, but more expeditiously and effectively than had always been the case in the past.

Interestingly, since this time, it has become increasingly common for arbitration provisions to be incorporated into normal bilateral double tax conventions, and there is now a much wider acceptance of the value which arbitration can bring to transfer pricing disputes. Indeed, it may be considered that the EU showed the way forward to the OECD which, in 2008, introduced a provision on arbitration in its Model Tax Convention.

5.3.2   Documentation

The next issue on the Forum's work programme was documentation.

Documentation has long been a bone of contention between taxpayers and tax authorities. Some tax authorities seemed to believe that an extensive set of documentation would resolve all transfer pricing disputes and thereby eliminate one of the main opportunities for tax avoidance, whereas taxpayers considered onerous documentation requirements an unnecessary and costly administrative burden on normal business activities. As was noted in the Commission Report of October 2001, both parties may have had a point.

However, not only was there significant disagreement between taxpayers and tax authorities as to the value of transfer pricing documentation, there were also different points of view amongst the Member States. Those Member States with more extensive experience of transfer pricing disputes tended to believe that although good documentation was important, and enabled tax authorities to identify major intra-group trade flows, and assess the consequent revenue risks, it was far from being the complete solution to transfer pricing disputes in practice. Those Member States tended to favour lighter documentation requirements, focusing on the key issues of identification and quantification of intra-group trade flows, rather than the substantial transfer pricing studies prevalent in some other countries.

On the other hand, those Member States with less practical experience of transfer pricing disputes felt the need for as much information as possible to be available immediately to the tax authority, perhaps believing that the need to prepare extensive (possibly contemporaneous) documentation would of itself encourage better compliance with the arm's length principle.

Not surprisingly, Forum members from the private sector tended to agree with those Member States advocating a lighter approach.

One of the problems facing business as more and more countries adopted a more thorough approach to transfer pricing, and therefore developed their own documentation requirements, was the simple proliferation of a large number of different documentation requirements. Business generally accepted the need to prepare reasonable transfer pricing documentation, but to have to prepare documentation in different forms, and to different levels of detail, for each country in which it operated was a major problem.

This problem had been addressed before, by the PATA (Pacific Association of Tax Administrators) group of nations, primarily the United States, Japan and Australia. They had produced a recommendation for a single documentation package which, if completed properly, would be acceptable in all PATA countries. Unfortunately, this was perceived by many as being merely an aggregation of all the transfer pricing documentation requirements of all PATA countries, and therefore, although it was only necessary to produce a single package of documentation, it would need to contain all the same information, and therefore require as much administrative effort, as preparing individual documentation packages for each country. It was the view of the Forum that it should try to avoid the PATA outcome.

Therefore, although there was full agreement within the Forum that the production of a single transfer pricing documentation package for the EU was a desirable objective, there remained considerable disagreement as to precisely what the main purposes of a documentation package were, and therefore how extensive the documentation requirements should be. After much debate, one of the private sector members agreed to present its own internal transfer pricing documentation to the Forum, and although this was considerably more extensive than most private sector members would have preferred, it provided an essential starting point for discussions as to how a documentation package might be structured.

The conclusion of the Forum included in the official report from the Commission was that the agreed documentation package should provide for 'standardisation of the documentation requirements necessary for a tax administration as a risk assessment tool and to obtain sufficient information for the assessment of the MNE group's transfer prices'. Clearly this objective owed much to the influence of those Member States who felt that a good documentation package could provide a high proportion of the answers to a transfer pricing dispute. This was not a view generally shared by the private sector members but it was important that a consensus could be reached so that progress could be made.

The eventual form of the agreed documentation package was a two-part package, consisting of a central file, a 'masterfile', containing information applicable across the trading group, and a separate file for each country in the EU with which the group traded. Importantly, all these documents would be in a standardised format, containing the same specified information, for all countries.

The masterfile should contain the following items:

(a) a general description of the business and business strategy, including changes in the business strategy compared to the previous tax year;
(b) a general description of the MNE group's organisational, legal and operational structure (including an organisation chart, a list of group members and a description of the participation (ownership) of the parent company in the subsidiaries);
(c) the general identification of the associated enterprises engaged in controlled transactions involving enterprises in the EU;
(d) a general description of the controlled transactions involving associated enterprises in the EU, i.e., a general description of:
    (i) flows of transactions (tangible and intangible assets, services, financial);
    (ii) invoice flows; and
    (iii) amounts of transaction flows;

(e) a general description of functions performed, risks assumed and a description of changes in functions and risks compared to the previous tax year, e.g., change from a fully-fledged distributor to a commissionaire;

(f) the ownership of intangibles (patents, trademarks, brand names, know-how, etc.) and royalties paid or received;

(g) the MNE group's inter-company transfer pricing policy or a description of the group's transfer pricing system that explains the arm's length nature of the company's transfer prices;

(h) a list of cost contribution agreements, advance pricing agreements and rulings covering transfer pricing aspects as far as group members in the EU are affected; and

(i) an undertaking by each domestic taxpayer to provide supplementary information upon request and within a reasonable time frame in accordance with national rules.

The country specific documentation was required to contain in addition:

(a) a detailed description of the business and business strategy, including changes in the business strategy compared to the previous tax year;

(b) information, i.e., description and explanation, on country-specific controlled transactions including:
   (i) flows of transactions (tangible and intangible assets, services, financial);
   (ii) invoice flows; and
   (iii) amounts of transaction flows;

(c) a comparability analysis, i.e.:
   (i) characteristics of property and services;
   (ii) functional analysis (functions performed, assets used, risks assumed);
   (iii) contractual terms;
   (iv) economic circumstances; and
   (v) specific business strategies;

(d) an explanation about the selection and application of the transfer pricing method[s], i.e., why a specific transfer pricing method was selected and how it was applied;

(e) relevant information on internal and/or external comparables, if available; and

(f) a description of the implementation and application of the group's inter-company transfer pricing policy.

Although this sounds like a rather extensive package, upon examination the detailed requirements are significantly less extensive than the documentation requirements of some other countries. In addition, the information was only required to be submitted at the commencement of a tax audit or at the specific request of a tax authority. There was no specific requirement that the documentation should have been prepared at the same time as the transactions were carried out, and it was made clear that if a Member State required taxpayers to submit transfer pricing documentation with its normal tax return then that information should be no more than a short questionnaire or an appropriate risk assessment form. It was therefore clearly left up to taxpayers to decide when they prepared this documentation.

It was also made clear that this was an optional package for business and if they wished to continue with their own approaches to compliance with individual countries requirements as they had done previously then they were free to do so.

Again, these conclusions were put forward as a Code of Conduct by the Commission in a communication dated 7 November 2005, with a view to their being adopted by the Council of Ministers on 27 June 2006.

5.3.3   Advance pricing agreements

The next subject to be addressed by the Joint Transfer Pricing Forum was advance pricing agreements (APAs).

Again, there were significant differences in the views held by the Member States regarding APAs. Some of the Member States, including some with less experience of APAs, thought that they might offer a complete solution to transfer pricing problems, and in particular that they offered a way for tax authorities to get much closer to the detail of business activities, thus gaining an invaluable understanding of business methods, which many would see as an advantage for both taxpayer and tax authority.

The private sector members, on the other hand, generally believed that although APAs had potential to add value in transfer pricing disputes, in practice many had been the subject of long drawn out negotiations, sometimes resulting in agreements of limited value, especially in the more complex situations in which they were potentially of most value. There were frequent stories of negotiations lasting three or more years, and involving considerable administrative effort, in order to deliver an APA with a three-year life. Most APAs in practice up to that time had related to relatively straightforward administrative services, which were not usually a serious problem in the absence of an APA. The areas of greatest uncertainty for business, those involving intellectual property, had not generally been the subject of successful APAs other than in a limited number of cases.

It is interesting to note that, as part of its deliberations on APAs and the different methods of transfer pricing dispute resolution, the Forum concluded that one of the most effective methods of avoiding transfer pricing disputes might be a requirement that, *before* finalising a transfer pricing adjustment, Member States would be required to consult with any other Member States involved, with a view to coming to a prior agreement on the adjustments to be made. This, to quote the formal communication from the Commission dated 26 February 2007, would 'prevent a dispute from coming into existence in the first place'. Having considered this approach, the Forum came to the conclusion that this might unfortunately require fundamental changes in domestic laws, which it thought might be beyond its remit, but, in its formal communication on the subject, the Commission came to the conclusion that 'a system of prior agreement would eliminate *all* double taxation within the EU and therefore is of the opinion that this issue could usefully be deepened in the future' (emphasis added).

The Forum fairly rapidly agreed that a unilateral APA was of very limited value in practice as a method of resolving disputes. It obviously only involved one tax authority and could not therefore be used to bind any other tax authority.

Moving on to bilateral APAs, the Forum outlined a number of potential advantages of APAs as follows:

- Taxpayers benefit from the certainty and, because of this, the taxpayer may be in a better position to predict its tax liabilities, thus helping to provide a more favourable tax environment for investment. When the term of an APA expires, the opportunity may also exist for the relevant tax administrations and enterprises to renew the APA, thus prolonging the advantages.
- In addition, the taxpayer participates in an APA by presenting and discussing its case with tax administrations to a greater degree than in the conventional mutual agreement procedure. Due to this involvement, there is an opportunity for taxpayers and tax administrations to consult and cooperate in a non-adversarial spirit and environment.

- The opportunity to discuss complex tax issues in a less confrontational atmosphere than in a transfer pricing examination can stimulate a free flow of information and agreement between all parties. This cooperative environment may also result in a more flexible review of the facts than in a more adversarial context.
- Since in an APA discussion future events have yet to take place due to the prospective nature of the APA, there is more flexibility than in a transfer pricing examination or mutual agreement procedure (MAP). This increased flexibility can only help secure an outcome beneficial to all parties.
- An APA may prevent costly and time-consuming examinations and litigation of major transfer pricing issues for taxpayers and tax administrations and thus reduce the exposure to interest payments and penalties. Once an APA has been agreed, fewer resources may be needed for subsequent examination of the taxpayer's return. It is still necessary, however, to monitor the application of the agreement and this right is maintained by the tax administration. The APA process itself may also present time savings for both enterprises and tax administrations over the time that would be spent in a conventional tax examination and subsequent MAP.
- A bilateral or multilateral APA, which agrees the tax treatment between a taxpayer and more than one tax administration, also averts the risk of double taxation. This too will encourage agreement.
- Increased flexibility in an APA procedure might also help to provide solutions to more traditional transfer pricing problems. For instance, a lack of data on comparable companies does not necessarily need to be an insurmountable problem in bilateral negotiations between tax administrations. If the taxpayers and the tax administrations can agree on an outcome which would be expected at arm's length, perhaps through a profit split based on the added value of the functions performed, it might not prove necessary to complete a database search.
- In addition, a tax administration can enjoy the benefit of enhanced taxpayer compliance which will result from an APA.
- APAs therefore have many advantages. However, APAs cannot be a cure for all transfer pricing problems and cross-border disputes. Even if an APA procedure is organised as efficiently as possible, APAs might still prove time-consuming and resource intensive due to the complexity of the issues under review, even if overall there is a resource saving compared to an audit and MAP. But these limitations or disadvantages of an APA become less serious when an APA procedure is organised and conducted more efficiently.

Few would disagree with these potential advantages of APAs. As always, however, the problem lies in the practicalities of delivering APAs within a reasonable time frame and with sufficient longevity to justify the time and effort expended by both taxpayers and the relevant tax authorities.

The Forum therefore produced some guidelines for APAs within the EU, which were published with the Commission's paper of 26 February 2007 and adopted by the EU Council of Ministers on 5 June 2007. For the most part these guidelines concentrated on describing best practice in the area, with particular regard to pre-filing discussions, complexity thresholds and timelines, but the Forum also focused on some less predictable ideas which were designed to improve the outcome for both parties.

Critical assumptions

One of the key problems with APAs is their relatively short life span compared to the time spent negotiating them. The Forum therefore focused on ways of extending this life span in an acceptable manner and recommended the use of 'critical assumptions'. It suggested that: 'Taxpayers and tax administrations should attempt to identify Critical Assumptions that are based where possible on observable, reliable and independent data', the aim being that transfer prices would be agreed by reference to these critical assumptions. If in practice the critical assumptions stayed within prescribed limits, then there would be no need to terminate the APA unless and until the critical assumptions diverged from those agreed limits, at which point the parties would agree to renegotiate the APA by reference to the new levels of the critical assumptions.

Rollback

One of the less acceptable aspects of APAs is what was termed by the Forum as rollback. This described the situation where information emerged during the APA process which led one of the tax authorities involved to conclude that incorrect transfer prices had been used in earlier years, and therefore led to the reopening of earlier years' tax liabilities. This was seen as a significant potential downside for the taxpayer, especially as it was possible that the tax liabilities for the year or years in question had already been agreed with other tax authorities and that therefore they could not be reopened in those countries. In the circumstances a unilateral reopening of the company's tax affairs by one tax authority alone would almost always lead to double taxation.

In response, a number of the Member States pointed out that if they discovered information which indicated that tax had been underpaid in earlier years they were under a statutory duty in their country to adjust the tax paid accordingly. This was not, therefore, a matter of choice, even though they might accept that the outcome was unduly harsh.

The Forum guidelines therefore came to some firm conclusions on rollback:

1. rollback, when provided for in domestic legislation, can be considered where it will resolve disputes or remove the possibility of disputes in earlier periods.
2. Rollback should only be a secondary result of the APA and should only be carried out where it is appropriate to the facts of the case. Similar facts and circumstances to those in the APA should have existed for previous periods in order for rollback to be appropriate.
3. Rollback of the APA should only be applied with the taxpayer's consent.
4. A tax administration has recourse to the usual domestic measures if, as part of the APA process, it discovers information which would affect the taxation of earlier periods. But tax administrations should advise the taxpayer of any such intended action to give the taxpayer the opportunity of explaining any apparent inconsistency before making a tax reassessment concerning previous periods.

It will be noted that point 3 might be considered potentially at odds with some of the other conclusions, but nevertheless, the guidelines are there.

The Joint Transfer Pricing Forum continues in existence and has discussed a number of other issues surrounding transfer pricing. It has also focused on further monitoring and effective implementation of the Arbitration Convention.

Many will question the effectiveness and impact of its work but a key point which should not be forgotten is that it provided a forum for all EU Member States to get together with representatives of the private sector and to exchange knowledge and understanding during a critical period in the development of transfer pricing practices in EU Member States. Given the enormous differences in understanding and experience across the EU when the Forum was established in 2002, this fact should not be underestimated.

5.4   The comprehensive solution

The reader will recall that the Commission Report of October 2001 suggested a twin-track approach to removing tax obstacles within the EU. It suggested a number of targeted short-term measures, including the formation of the Joint Transfer Pricing Forum, and the more comprehensive solution of Common Consolidated Corporate Tax Base (CCCTB). In the view of the Commission, CCCTB would offer solutions to a significant number of the tax obstacles identified in the report, including automatic offset of profits and losses within the EU. Most importantly, however, in the context of this book, it would also mean the end of transfer pricing disputes within the EU because internal transfer prices would be irrelevant. That is not to say that it would not create a whole new area for potential disagreement between taxpayer and tax authorities, but it was hoped and believed that the perceived opportunity for wide-scale manipulation of corporate profits offered by transfer pricing would be significantly reduced.

In its earlier work the Commission and the advisory panel had discussed two possible approaches to CCCTB. The first, Home State Taxation, was an idea which had been put forward by Malcolm Gammie, Sven-Olof Lodin and others some years previously, and involved using the tax base rules of the state of residence of the parent company of a group. The profits of the group would be consolidated using this single set of rules and the total group profit would then be allocated across the countries in which the group traded using a suitable formula, based on sales, assets, payroll or a combination of all three, possibly with different weightings. The profit thus allocated would then be taxed in the country concerned by applying the *local* tax rate to the profits allocated to that country.

The alternative was to create an entirely new set of tax rules which would be used to calculate the total group profits for all activities in the EU in this case, and then to allocate the profits and tax them as described above for Home State Taxation.

At first sight, Home State Taxation would seem to have a number of advantages, not the least of which was the existence of a well-established set of rules, complete with legal precedents, which had been developed over many years, to support difficult points of interpretation. However, the Commission identified a potential problem with Home State Taxation in that, for it to be accepted by all countries adopting the system, all tax systems involved would need to be subject to mutual recognition by all participating countries. In other words, all participating countries would have to accept that the tax systems of all the other participating countries were comparable to its own, and only differed in matters of irrelevant detail.

This need for mutual recognition meant that the 'well established pre-existing set of rules' would not be totally ready for use without, perhaps significant, further work. Even more of a problem was that most countries have a tendency to change, or at least tinker with, their tax systems on an annual basis. It might be, therefore, that a country's freedom to change its tax system on an annual basis would effectively also need to be subject to a mutual recognition procedure, thus potentially infringing an important part of a country's tax sovereignty.

A set of rules which might constitute CCCTB on the other hand, could be agreed upon at EU level, and would not need changing every year to suit an individual country's fiscal objectives. Given the well-known sensitivities over tax sovereignty it was not perhaps surprising that the Commission recommended the CCCTB approach.

The Commission, working with some of the Member States, has now produced a set of CCCTB rules. There remain a number of practical issues, primarily the fact that not all Member States are enthusiastic about an EU-wide tax system, and the potential loss of tax sovereignty it might entail. Possible solutions to this problem exist, in the form of enhanced cooperation, which might permit a limited number of EU states to adopt CCCTB without involving all Member States. Such approaches, however, are not yet well tried and tested, and certainly not in the minefield which is taxation within the EU.

In addition there are technical problems, such as the treatment of profits earned outside the participating Member States, especially if they are earned through a branch of, or are remitted to, a company resident within a participating Member State. Simple problems such as which double tax treaty is relevant can cause significant problems, bearing in mind that the provisions of double tax treaties tend to be designed closely around the provisions of the domestic tax legislation of the relevant Member State and do not therefore necessarily interact easily with the structure of the agreed CCCTB system.

There is also the problem of acceptance by business. Business has complained at great length, and over many years, about the administrative burden presented by transfer pricing compliance, which led to much of the support from business for the 2001 Report and its conclusions. However, many in business are concerned that a CCCTB offers significantly less opportunity for the reallocation of profits between

Member States, or for other tax arbitrage possibilities. In practice, therefore, they may well prefer to stick with the devil they know.

Unexpectedly perhaps, some of the main potential beneficiaries of a CCCTB system might be in the SME sector, such as smaller companies who trade in a few countries, within a relatively small area, perhaps on the borders of three or four central EU Member States. For them, compliance with the tax requirements of three or four Member States is a major administrative burden. The opportunity to render a single tax return, on a single tax base, to a single tax authority, leaving it up to the tax authorities to divide up the spoils, might be an attractive solution.

There is also much talk of the problems as to which formula to use for the apportionment process. Considerable work has been done on the use of allocation formulas in the United States for state tax purposes. Proponents of CCCTB would argue that the US states have been using formulary apportionment for many years without major disputes or manipulation, and would therefore suggest that this should not be a significant problem. Others, however, would argue that it works within the United States because state tax rates are generally very similar and, most importantly, very low. They are not therefore the focus of such substantial planning exercises as is the norm for national and inter-national tax planning, and they are certainly not in general likely to influence location decisions, other than for very specific types of oper-ation which are perhaps favoured by some unusual state jurisdictions.

The key, however, as to whether or not CCCTB becomes a feature of the EU tax scene will undoubtedly be politics. There have been concerns for some years over the low corporate tax rate in Ireland, and it has even been described as unacceptable tax competition by some other Member States. For Ireland it is clearly a key part of their economic plan for the country, but this view is not considered compatible with the 'European vision' by all Member States. CCCTB might therefore offer some Member States the opportunity to create a more consolidated European economic community, in line with their longer term vision for Europe.

The fortunes of CCCTB have therefore waxed and waned over recent years, depending on the politics of the time, and only time will tell if and when it will become a working reality.

5.5   Conclusions

The aim of this chapter has been to give the reader an insight into the impact of the EU, and in particular the European Commission, on transfer pricing. As it was once so succinctly put by a senior official, do you want your transfer pricing policy to be decided in Paris or in Brussels, i.e., by the OECD or by the EU?

Many would argue that overall the EU has thus far had relatively little influence on transfer pricing, even within the EU. That would seem to be a harsh judgement.

The work of the Joint Transfer Pricing Forum did a great deal to enhance the knowledge and understanding of many EU Member States, i.e., twenty-seven countries, a significant proportion of OECD membership, during a critical period in the development of transfer pricing theory. It also helped to turn arbitration from an irrelevant sideshow, talked about only in business circles, into a serious proposition which could be incorporated into many modern double tax treaties. Such developments should not be dismissed lightly.

Some would also argue that the arm's length standard, which is so fundamental to the OECD's approach to transfer pricing, is creaking under the pressure of modern business structures. The comparative freedom with which international businesses can allocate profits across the members of a trading group, according to contracts which would not be seen outside an integrated group under common ownership, cannot be universally acceptable to the tax authorities of the world.

The 2010 amendments to the OECD Transfer Pricing Guidelines preserved the arm's length concept, but the freedom given to business by these amendments might be considered a high price to pay for the continued preservation of that principle. Could the limitations of the arm's length principle lead to its eventual demise and its replacement by formulary apportionment?

Of course, at the end of the day, it can only be thought somewhat ironic that two organisations, the EU and the OECD, which were brought into existence to enhance international trade, should, in the tax arena, spend so much of their time trying to protect the tax revenues of their member countries, and in doing so place countless obstacles in the way of businesses which are becoming increasingly global, and completely transnational, in their outlook, in their drive for greater efficiency. From that perspective, perhaps the 2010 amendments to the OECD Transfer Pricing Guidelines represent the first steps down a path to a lighter touch on multinational corporations, and to a more enlightened approach where maximising the size of the pie is seen as more important than maximising an individual country's share of that pie, but perhaps this is too much to ask.

5.6   Future of transfer pricing dispute resolution

For some time to come it is likely that the most commonly used method for the resolution of transfer pricing disputes within the EU will be the mutual agreement procedures embedded within bilateral double tax treaties. Hopefully, the operation of these mutual agreement procedures will be enhanced by the use of common methodology between the Member States, much of which commonality will have been derived from their participation in the Joint Transfer Pricing Forum.

There is no doubt that in theory advance pricing agreements have much to offer both taxpayers and tax administrations but in practice they are beset by difficulties. Tax administrations are understandably reluctant to agree to long-term settlements covering many years into the future in such a fast-changing business world and therefore the time and effort required to achieve such agreements sometimes looks like too high a price to pay. The use of critical assumptions to support longer-term agreements, so that the agreement can be revisited if these critical assumptions move outside certain pre-agreed limitations, as suggested by the Forum's work, may offer a way forward, but it is suggested that tax administrations will want to see long-term experience of such agreements in practice before this approach will be widely adopted.

In the meantime, APAs will probably be limited to shorter-term agreements covering relatively simple, low value administrative functions and those very high value transactions involving complex intellectual property where the risks of incorrect transfer pricing of such assets can lead to unacceptably high levels of financial uncertainty, as evidenced by recent high profile settlements in the pharmaceutical industry.

Litigation is unlikely to provide a satisfactory way forward. Transfer pricing is by its nature an area where there is no right or wrong answer. There is always a range of possible acceptable answers and agreement is nearly always reached by compromise. This makes transfer pricing generally unsuitable for litigation and we must look for alternative forms of dispute resolution.

There are a number of groups looking at alternative dispute resolution techniques, mostly outside the tax arena, which is not generally well suited to such techniques, but transfer pricing is one area of taxation where compromise is usually the best solution, and this work therefore looks potentially very helpful.

This leads naturally to the idea of arbitration. As has been stated above, arbitration has, over recent years, moved from a theoretical topic only discussed in business circles to something which has now become acceptable to many of the major trading nations. It has been incorporated into a number of recent double tax treaties and clearly has much to offer. However, one of the main benefits of having arbitration as a potential solution is that it inevitably encourages those involved in normal mutual agreement procedures to come to an agreement.

It has long been a complaint from the business sector that the mutual agreement procedures in most treaties only require the participating tax authorities to use their best endeavours to come to an agreement. If it is too difficult to reach an agreement they can simply walk away from the process and leave the taxpayer to seek other remedies. It is suggested that the existence of arbitration mechanisms, either in the EU Arbitration Convention or in the relevant bilateral tax treaty, has done much to improve the success rates of mutual agreement procedures in recent years.

This then brings us to the EU's 'comprehensive solution', the Common Consolidated Corporate Tax Base. The rules for this already exist for the most part, and although some technical issues remain, it is clear that, with sufficient political will, these issues are soluble. The key area for doubt, therefore, is the political dimension, and in particular, that for many EU Member States, fiscal policy is one of their few remaining financial levers, especially for those Member States who are also part of the euro-zone. Inevitably, therefore, many Member States will be very reluctant to give up sovereignty over their domestic tax policy in the way which is envisaged by CCCTB. There is clearly a core group of countries for whom the adoption of CCCTB would be a natural extension of their membership of the EU, but there are many more for whom this one remaining freedom is very important.

It is interesting to note that as part of the potential solutions to the euro-zone debt crisis of 2010 and 2011 it was at times suggested that full fiscal unity might be the only long-term answer in the struggle to manage the economy of the EU as a single economic entity. It is difficult not to wonder if CCCTB might play a part in that possible fiscal unity, but clearly, whether or not CCCTB becomes the long-term comprehensive solution to transfer pricing disputes within the EU is essentially a matter of politics, rather than tax theory. It may not happen in the immediate future but if we look ten or twenty years forward it would be difficult to rule it out as a serious possibility.

6

Transfer pricing in Germany

ANDREAS OESTREICHER

6.1 Introduction

This chapter provides an analysis of dispute resolution procedures in the area of international profit attribution as seen from the perspective of the Federal Republic of Germany. It will become apparent that in this country, differences of opinion existing with regard to transfer pricing can in many cases be resolved by means of a kind of consensus between the taxpayer and the tax authorities. There is a tradition of legal provisions designed to prevent international profit shifting using inappropriate contractual arrangements in the case of substantial participation in a foreign company. But the number of judgments actually handed down by the German Bundesfinanzhof (Federal Tax Court) dealing with 'adjustment of income' (section 1 of the German Foreign Tax Act) resulting from disputes in the area of international profit attribution is surprisingly low. Although the number of rulings with respect to 'hidden profit distributions' and 'hidden capital contributions' concerning a shifting of profits between a company and its shareholders in the primarily domestic scene appears infinite, in the international transfer pricing domain it is much more common for the taxpayer and the tax authorities to come to an agreement out of court ('tax audit bazaar'). Such an agreement between taxpayer and tax authorities does not, however, guarantee freedom from double taxation. In order to prevent the occurrence of double taxation in this context, German taxpayers increasingly turn to the bi- or multilateral dispute resolution possibilities employing mutual agreement procedures and advance pricing agreements. Only in recent years has the German tax administration been giving these procedures their active support.

This chapter is structured as follows. After a brief round-up of the economic and institutional context of transfer pricing in Germany, section 6.3 will set out the historical background of the German transfer pricing rules. Section 6.4 sums up the main aspects of Germany's transfer pricing legislation. Against the background of these introductory considerations, the core topic of this contribution is dealt with in sections 6.5 to 6.7. The domestic approaches to resolving transfer pricing disputes in Germany are discussed in section 6.5, while section 6.6 complements the domestic view with a survey of bilateral and multilateral approaches. In section 6.7 advance pricing agreements are explored. The chapter is rounded off with some concluding remarks.

6.2 Economic and institutional context

Germany is regarded as having the highest-performing economy in Europe. Taking GDP as the basis, in 2010 Germany occupied fourth position in the worldwide comparison. In that year its GDP amounted to 2,497.6 billion euro.[1] Among the most essential reasons for Germany's strong performance are high productivity of labour, a first-class infrastructure in an advantageous setting within the EU, and marked innovatory strength associated with a high percentage of research-intensive industries, above-average spending on research and development, numerous patents and world leading sectors both in terms of market volume and growth potential (information and communication, the chemical industry and plastics, transport and logistics, photovoltaic and medical technology). Adding to these factors are legal certainty, an efficient legal system and a transparent, independent judiciary. A fact also of relevance to foreign investors is that Germany constitutes a market consisting of more than 80 million consumers (20 per cent of the European market), disposing over a high per capita income. Based on a per capita purchasing power of 19,684 euro (2010), Germany ranks among the top ten countries in the European comparison.

The German economy is focused on industry-produced goods and services, whereas raw materials and agricultural production are of only minor economic significance. The major trading partners are other industrialised countries, a considerable overall surplus arising from foreign trade. In 2010 the rise in German exports ran into double figures. 2011 is exhibiting a similarly dynamic development in this respect. Specialised products of high quality secure the position of German companies in their particular export markets. Among the most important

---

[1] Statistisches Bundesamt, Gross domestic product 2010 for Germany, supporting documentation for the press conference on 12 January 2011 in Wiesbaden.

export products are those of the automobile industry while raw materials for energy generation figure most strongly on the import side.

Consolidated German (directly and indirectly) held investments abroad (stock of FDI assets, all sectors, in million euros) are shown in Table 6.1.

German investments in further European countries such as the Netherlands, Belgium, Luxembourg, France and Italy follow in this order with smaller investment volumes.[2]

Consolidated foreign (directly and indirectly) held investments in Germany (stock of FDI liabilities, all sectors, in million euros) are shown in Table 6.2.

Again, foreign investments by further European countries follow with smaller investment volumes. In the case of foreign direct investment

Table 6.1 *Consolidated German (directly and indirectly) held investments abroad*

Stock of FDI assets, all sectors (in million euros)	2007	Per cent of GDP	2008	Per cent of GDP	2009	Per cent of GDP
Total	904,661	37.3	953,505	38.3	984,540	40.9
EU 27	504,263	20.8	542,943	21.8	561,610	23.4
United States	207,578	8.6	211,607	8.5	217,040	9.0
United Kingdom	119,761	4.9	99,679	4.0	120,894	5.0

Table 6.2 *Consolidated foreign (directly and indirectly) held investments in Germany*

Stock of FDI liabilities, all sectors (in million euros)	2007	Per cent of GDP	2008	Per cent of GDP	2009	Per cent of GDP
Total	472,453	19.5	479,808	19.3	469,745	19.5
EU 27	348,824	14.4	358,915	14.4	361,422	15.0
United States	54,186	2.2	47,242	1.9	36,133	1.5
The Netherlands	105,501	4.4	107,962	4.3	110,621	4.6

[2] Deutsche Bundesbank/Eurosystem, Survey on direct investments, Special publication: Statistics, 10 April 2011, p. 6 *et seq.*

(FDI) liabilities, these countries are Luxembourg, the United Kingdom, France and Italy (in this order).[3] These figures place Germany sixth in the UNCTAD ranking 2009, characterising Germany as an investment location of worldwide significance. In the years 2000 to 2009, FDI liabilities rose annually by an average of 5 per cent. The leading important sectors for foreign investment include information and communication technology, software, services, motor vehicles, engineering and the chemical industry.

Germany's favourable location conditions do have their price. Besides a major share in the federal budget that is spent on social security (54.2 per cent), the largest items on the budget agenda are general services (17.0 per cent), business enterprises[4] (5.12 per cent), education and research (4.8 per cent) and transport and telecommunications (3.9 per cent)[5] which are financed to a very great extent by taxes. Accordingly, in 2010 federal expenditure amounting to 303.7 billion euros was funded by tax revenue totalling 226.2 billion euros, administrative income of 33.1 billion euros, coin income of 0.3 billion euros and a net borrowing of 44.0 billion euros.[6] These figures illustrate the importance of taxes in funding federal expenditure and Germany's international competitiveness.

The role played by federal taxes (above all consumer taxes) in the federal tax revenue as a whole (article 106 I of the Basic Law (Grundgesetz, GG)) is relatively small (36.1 per cent). A greater role in the federal tax revenue is played by the taxes accrued jointly to the Federation, the Länder, and the municipalities (income tax, corporate income tax and value added tax) and the federal share in the trade tax (making up 74.2 per cent in total).[7] The joint taxes (article 106 III GG), Länder taxes (article 106 II GG) and the municipal taxes (article 106 VI GG) also serve to finance tasks allocated by the German Basic Law to the Länder and the municipalities (article 104a GG), with the result that with regard to the significance of tax in Germany the development of total tax revenue in the Federal Republic is of interest. This total tax revenue is created in the Federal Republic from a total of more than 40 individual types of tax, which generate significant levels of revenue only in part. Important types of tax in the area of direct taxation are in particular

---

[3] *Ibid.* p. 42 *et seq.*   [4] These enterprises operate primarily in the transport sector.
[5] Federal Ministry of Finance, Overview of the Federal Budget 2010, p. 17 *et seq.*
[6] Federal Ministry of Finance, Press Communication No. 1/2011, 13 January 2011.
[7] Please note that negative income from EU payments is to be deducted; in 2010 this amounted to 11.3 per cent of the Federal Republic's tax revenue.

Table 6.3 Development of German tax revenue 1970 to 2010*

	1970	1980	1990	2000	2004	2005	2006	2007	2008	2009	2010
Income tax	26.0 (7.2)	75.8 (9.6)	109.1 (8.3)	147.9 (7.2)	129.3 (5.9)	128.7 (5.8)	140.2 (6.1)	156.8 (6.5)	174.6 (7.0)	161.6 (6.7)	159.1 (6.4)
Corporate income tax	4.5 (1.2)	10.9 (1.4)	15.4 (1.2)	23.5 (1.1)	13.1 (0.6)	16.3 (0.7)	22.9 (1.0)	22.9 (0.9)	15.9 (0.6)	7.2 (0.2)	12.0 (0.5)
Value added tax	19.5 (5.4)	47.8 (6.1)	75.5 (5.8)	140.8 (5.1)	137.4 (6.3)	139.7 (6.3)	146.7 (6.3)	169.6 (7.0)	176.0 (7.1)	177.0 (7.4)	180.0 (7.2)
Trade tax	5.5 (1.5)	13.9 (1.8)	19.8 (1.5)	27.0 (1.3)	28.4 (1.3)	31.0 (1.4)	38.4 (1.7)	40.1 (1.7)	41.0 (1.6)	32.4 (1.3)	34.6 (1.4)
Mineral oil and energy taxes	5.9 (1.6)	10.9 (1.4)	17.7 (1.4)	37.8 (1.8)	41.8 (1.9)	40.1 (1.8)	39.9 (1.7)	39.0 (1.6)	39.2 (1.6)	39.8 (1.7)	39.8 (1.6)

* Figures in billion euros. The figures in brackets indicate the level of revenue as a percentage of GDP.

income tax, corporate income tax and trade tax. As far as indirect taxes are concerned, value added tax and taxes on mineral oil and other sources of energy produce the highest revenue. The development of tax revenue over the past thirty years is shown in Table 6.3 (in billion euros).

As can be seen from Table 6.3, income tax and value added tax carry the greatest weight in this context. Income tax is due on income of natural persons having their residence or habitual place of abode in Germany. This group of taxpayers includes sole traders and partners in a partnership with business operations. Value added tax is payable on goods and services within Germany, import of goods and intra-community acquisitions. Corporate entities and, in particular, companies limited by shares, are subject to corporate tax. Their contribution to total tax revenue is low, amounting to approximately 0.5 per cent of GDP. However, this figure should not lead to the conclusion that the correct determination of income with respect to these companies (including examination of transfer prices *vis-à-vis* affiliated companies) is of subordinate significance. Correct determination carries significance for reasons of equal taxation of companies operating in the legal form of limited companies and sole traders and partnerships alone.

Intra-group transfer pricing also features centrally in Germany because cross-border business activities are carried out primarily by enterprises in the legal form of limited companies. Taking the information provided in financial statements as a basis, foreign direct investments are carried out first and foremost by limited companies (93.9 per cent of all companies involved), whereas only a small fraction of the relevant shareholdings are held by partnerships (6.1 per cent). In both cases, the lion's share of these assets is held by large enterprises. Here, the number of limited companies accounts for 86.1 per cent, whereas the relevant fraction is 5.1 per cent in the case of partnerships.[8] In this context, Table 6.4 illustrates the volume of German FDI in terms of the number and size of FDI companies.

As far as FDI liabilities are concerned, the share of investments carried out in the legal form of a limited company is even higher (95.4 per cent), whereas the number of partnerships held by foreign investors accounts for only 4.6 per cent. As a result, it emerges that tax transfer pricing may exercise a large impact on corporate tax revenue in the first instance. Moreover, since corporate tax revenue is derived from a relatively small

---

[8] Bureau van Dijk, Database AMADEUS, update 172, 2009.

Table 6.4 *Volume of German FDI in terms of the number and size of FDI companies*

	Number of companies	Net equity	Balance sheet total	Sales revenues
Directly held FDI[a]	20,156	40.7	241.6	43.5
Indirectly held FDI	11,118	50.1	187.0	81.2
German limited companies[b]	59,072	9.38	32.03	46.39

[a] Deutsche Bundesbank/Eurosystem, Survey on Direct Investments, Special publication: Statistics, 10 April 2011, p. 6 *et seq.*; this information refers to the year 2009.

[b] Deutsche Bundesbank, Verhältniszahlen aus Jahresabschlüssen deutscher Unternehmen von 2007 bis 2008, März 2011 (Ratios taken from financial statements of German enterprises 2007 to 2008); the year referred to here is 2007.

number of enterprises, the focus is on large companies. Corporate tax statistics show that approximately 10 per cent of all German limited companies contribute some 90 per cent of the corporate tax budget.[9]

6.3   Historical background of transfer pricing rules

6.3.1   Beginnings in Germany

In the international context, the prime purpose of tax transfer prices today is to attribute tax jurisdiction between or among contracting states. Their goal is to avoid the shifting of enterprises' profits to affiliated companies subject to taxation in a different jurisdiction. In Germany, the topic 'shifting profits abroad' was already dealt with in income tax legislation dating from 1925 and 1934. Section 33 of the Income Tax Act (ITA) 1925 reads:[10]

> (1) If, as a result of special agreements between the taxpayer and a party not subject to unlimited taxation, the profit of a domestic trade or business is clearly not in proportion with the profit that would otherwise be achieved in business transactions of comparable or similar nature, said profit, or at least the usual return on capital

---

[9] Statistisches Bundesamt, Corporate Tax Statistics 2004.

[10] German Reichstag, Drucksache dated 27 April 1925 III 1924/25 No. 795, *Reichssteuerblatt* (*German Tax Gazette*, RStBl) 1925, 196.

serving this trade or business, can be taken as the basis for determining the income of the domestic trade or business. In the meaning of this provision, in addition to fixed assets, capital is deemed to include also current assets, in particular goods, products, and inventory.

(2) The provision given in section 1 of ITA 1925 does not apply if the taxpayer provides evidence that neither does he hold a share in the assets or profit of the foreign trade or business, nor does the owner of said foreign entity participate significantly in the profit or the assets of his trade or business.

Application of these provisions had proven inadequate, since in part they entailed processes that took place mainly abroad. As a consequence, they failed to be effective in cases where the taxpayer was not willing to cooperate in terms of clarifying details of events possibly incurring taxation. A further practical difficulty was that it was also necessary to determine profits that would have accrued without these particular foreign relationships.[11] It was the intention of section 30 of the ITA 1934 to overcome these difficulties by simplifying considerably the preconditions and implementation. It reads:

Taxation in the event of foreign business connections: The tax authorities of the German federal state (Land) can, in the case of income from agriculture and forestry, from trade or business, or from self-employment, determine the income tax as a fixed amount without reference to the result reported, if particular direct or indirect connections of the trade or business to a person who is either not subject to domestic taxation or only subject to limited domestic taxation make a reduction of profit possible. The authorities of the German federal state decide in their own discretion.

According to the grounds stated for this legislation, by virtue of being placed under the discretion of the tax office at the level of the Land (federal state), this provision grants these offices an additional competence. This discretion was to be exercised in such a way that the Reich (Germany) received as income tax any portion of the profits to which it was rightfully due. For these purposes, the provision was only to be applied in cases where there were indications that the profit had indeed been reduced. This provision was not to be applied if the actual business situation called for profit reductions of this kind (for example, as a consequence of 'export prices set strategically for market penetration

[11] Reichsfinanzministerium, Explanations regarding the Income Tax Act of 16 October 1934, published in Reichsgesetzblatt (German Law Gazette, RGBl) I 1934, 1005, Berlin, 8 January 1935, RStBl No. 3, 1935, 48.

purposes'). Unlike the previous regulation which only referred to income from trade or business, the specific taxation of foreign business transactions according to section 30 of the ITA 1934 had also to be applied to income from agriculture and forestry as well as to profit income accruing to self-employed persons (i.e., all types of profit income).

In 1938, the Reichsfinanzhof (Supreme Tax Court) had to hand down a ruling on the prerequisites of the 'fixed amount taxation' in the case of foreign business relationships according to section 30 of the ITA 1934. Here, the tax office entrusted with the case (the tax office at the level of the federal state) came to the conclusion that the profits of the company involved were noticeably lower than the results achieved by comparable companies. Moreover, they saw a possibility that shifting of profits abroad had taken place by way of specific transfer pricing. The German Tax Court confirmed that based on the wording of the law, the tax office was not required to provide evidence that such a shifting of profits had indeed taken place if this was deemed probable according to 'experience of life'. The court, however, ruled the taxpayer was entitled to provide evidence to the contrary. It thus pointed out that the tax office was not permitted to 'ignore without more ado' the evidence that might counter its conclusions.[12] As a consequence the German Tax Court handed back the case to the tax office for further deliberation.

In applying these limitations to the provisions of section 30 of the ITA 1934 the Supreme Tax Court was approaching the principles that still govern the way in which estimates for tax purposes have to be carried out in Germany today. The more difficult it is for the tax authorities to identify without doubt the basis for taxation, the stricter the demands made on the taxpayer to contribute information leading to clarification of the case. It was, and remains, incompatible with the principles of equal taxation, however, to base taxation in the form of a fixed amount only on the condition that a profit reduction might have taken place as a result of foreign business relationships, irrespective of whether any profit reductions actually occurred.

Nevertheless, for reasons of legal protection, the German Bundesfinanzhof (Federal Tax Court) found in 1959 that section 30 of the ITA 1934 was not compatible with the Basic Law of the Federal Republic of Germany as later enacted.[13] For the German Federal Tax Court, the

---

[12] Cf. Reichsfinanzhof, ruling of 21 December 1938 VI 537/38, RStBl 1939, 308.

[13] Bundesfinanzhof, ruling of 7 April 1959 I 2/58 S, *Bundessteuerblatt* (*Federal Tax Gazette*, BStBl) III 1959, 233.

specific nature of this provision lay not only in the fact that the tax (rather than the profit) was to be determined by way of estimates. It regarded it as being of greater significance that tax assessment was shifted from the local tax office to the tax office of the federal state. The consequence of this shift of competence to the tax office of the federal state (now Oberfinanzdirektion, regional fiscal office) was that the taxpayers' recourse to the law was reduced. The only possibility available was appeal to the German Federal Tax Court. The task of this highest Federal Court is scrutinising decisions only with respect to proper application of the law, whereas it is not entitled to undertake its own evaluation of the actual facts of the case. Since recourse to the law in Germany requires at least one appellate instance entitled to examine whether the actual facts and circumstances of a case have been properly taken into account (article 19(4) of the Basic Law) the German Federal Tax Court found section 30 of the ITA 1934 to be no longer applicable. The authority of the German Federal Tax Court for non-application of this provision arose from the fact that it was promulgated prior to the enactment of the Basic Law and had not been subject to further parliamentary debate since.

6.3.2 Development of current rules

At the same time, the tax differentials between the Federal Republic of Germany and 'some states'[14] presented strong incentives to use special structuring measures in the international arena to produce tax advantages that could not be effectively countered via the law applicable at that time in Germany. Combating the exploitation of unjustified tax advantages was also held back by the fact that the German tax authorities' sovereign powers of investigation did not extend beyond the German borders and the low-tax states concerned steadfastly rejected the idea of concluding agreements on administrative and legal assistance or providing other states with tax information. In a report of the German Federal government to the German parliament explicitly naming the tax differentials *vis-à-vis* Switzerland and Liechtenstein, Luxembourg, the Bahamas, Bermuda, the Netherlands Antilles and Panama, these attempts to circumnavigate unlimited liability to taxation were

---

[14] Report of the Federal Government to the German Bundestag of 23 June 1964 on the distortions of competition arising from transfer of seat abroad and from tax differentials between states, German Bundestag, Drucksache IV/2412, 25.

registered. Moreover the observation was made that relocation of income and assets had increased also due to the fact that income was being shifted to base companies abroad with the help of tax transfer price planning.[15]

The finance ministries of the German Länder reacted to this report from the German government by issuing a coordinated decree, with the same wording in each case (Steueroasenerlass, Tax Haven Decree).[16] According to this decree, in the event of income or assets being shifted to associated companies or other independent legal entities in tax haven countries by persons subject to unlimited tax liability, the tax authorities were asked to scrutinise whether the contracts, business transactions or asset transfers as reported indeed corresponded to the facts of the case. If not, they could not be recognised for tax purposes. This order was to be applied in particular if there was no exchange of goods or services. It referred, however, explicitly also to those cases in which remuneration was paid or received for goods or services in an amount exceeding or falling below the amount an independent third party would have paid or demanded.

As this order to correct profits lacked the necessary legal basis, however,[17] the finance ministry called for preparation of a legal regulation. This took as its basis a report by the Tax Reform Commission on the tax law pertaining to foreign transactions[18] which culminated in a German governmental resolution on 'principles for a law to preserve tax equality within foreign business connections and to enhance the situation with respect to tax competition in the context of investing abroad.[19] These principles formed a first basis for the later enacted legal

---

[15] *Ibid.* 10, 13 *et seq.*, 19 *et seq.*, 21, 23 *et seq.*

[16] Cf. e.g., Decree of the Finance Minister of Lower Saxony of 14 June 1965 S 1301–99–31 1, BStBl II 1965, 74.

[17] Cf. Wassermeyer, in Flick, Wassermeyer and Baumhoff, *Kommentar zum Außensteuerrecht*, 1973/2009, s. 1 of the Foreign Tax Act (FTA) No. 18.

[18] See Federal Ministry of Finance, *Report by the Tax Reform Commission on the Tax Law Pertaining to Foreign Transactions*, Issue 16 (Bonn, 1970); this Tax Reform Committee came to the conclusion that the national tax provisions which are based on the legal relationship of domestic enterprises had proved to be insufficient for correct taxation of foreign enterprises with interests in Germany; for business transactions between a domestic enterprise and a controlled foreign corporation, an appropriate correction on request was already guaranteed by law already in force. But it was seen as necessary to impose by way of procedural legislation a more extensive duty to provide information and evidence on domestic shareholders in foreign corporations, see *ibid.* p. 38 *et seq.*, p. 66 *et seq.*

[19] These principles and grounds for the legislation can be read, for example, in *Der Betrieb* 1971, 16 *et seq.*

provisions on 'adjustment of income' (section 1 of the Act on Taxation in respect of Connections Abroad (Foreign Tax Act), Gesetz über die Besteuerung bei Auslandsbeziehungen (Außensteuergesetz) (FTA)).[20] Section 1 of this regulation reads:

> (1) If the income of a taxpayer from foreign business relationships with a related party has been reduced, in that within the framework of such foreign business relationships he agrees terms other than those on which mutually independent third parties would have agreed in similar or comparable circumstances, it is to be adjusted, other provisions notwithstanding, to that which would have resulted from those terms as would have been agreed between mutually independent third parties.

Two further sections state:

(a) the conditions deeming the parties to be 'related'; and
(b) that a necessary estimate is to be based, in the absence of other appropriate indications, on the interest on the capital employed in the business or the net profit on turnover normally to be expected under usual circumstances.

While the conditions deeming the parties to be 'related' continue to apply today without any change, the regulations applying to estimates were revised with effect from the 2008 assessment period. The new version of the law makes it clear that in assessing the net profit on turnover normally to be expected, or the interest on the capital employed in the business, the functions carried out, the assets employed and the risks assumed have to be taken into consideration.

Over the course of time, the norm has also been subject to changes with respect to its scope of application. On the one hand, Bundesfinanzhof rulings concerning the term 'business relationship' caused the legislator to regulate which transactions are covered by the norm. On the other hand, changes also arose with respect to the type of income involved. Whereas in this connection the norm was originally applicable to relationships forming part of an activity carried out independently, sustainably, with the intention of achieving profit, and within general business operations (not applicable to 'private' loans of a natural person

---

[20] Gesetz zur Wahrung der steuerlichen Gleichmäßigkeit bei Auslandsbeziehungen und zur Verbe-serung der steuerlichen Wettbewerbslage bei Auslandsinvestitionen, Law to preserve tax equality within foreign business connections and to enhance the situation with respect to tax competition in the context of investing abroad of 8 September 1972, BGBl I 1972 No. 98, 1713.

holding their participation in the foreign corporation in private prop-erty),[21] in 1992 the legislator inserted a further section (section 4, now section 5) in which the term 'business relationship' was defined.[22] This determined that a business relationship in the sense of section 1 of the FTA must lead to income from business activities (agriculture and forestry, sale or trade or self-employed activity) or rent or lease either on the part of the taxpayer or on that of the related party.

The German Federal Tax Court's interpretation of the norm, according to which business relationships do not include such transac-tions leading to the fact that the domestic taxpayer and the foreign corporation constitute related parties, gave rise to a further change. As a consequence, the German Federal Tax Court regarded the assumption of guarantees without remuneration or interest-free loans of a German parent company to its foreign subsidiary as not fulfilling the prerequis-ites of a business relationship if, according to the foreign company law, the guarantee or loan was to be deemed equity (substituting for equity).[23] Where this was not the case, granting an interest-free loan could be treated as a business relationship.[24] In order to cover all business relationships contractually agreed, the definition of the term 'business relationship' was extended in 1993 such that it now covers 'any contractual relationship affecting income, other than an agreement between a company and its shareholders'.[25] Accordingly, it is essential that apart from the shareholding there is an exchange of goods or

---

[21] Cf. Bundesfinanzhof, ruling of 5 December 1990 I R 94/88, BStBl II 1991, 287; however, where business loans are concerned, this regulation was and continues to be applicable even in the case that the income of the foreign controlled company is taxed at the level of its parent company (application of CFC rules), cf. Bundesfinanzhof, ruling of 19 March 2002 I R 4/01, BStBl II 2002, 644.

[22] Gesetz zur Entlastung der Familien und zur Verbesserung der Rahmenbedingungen für Investitionen und Arbeitsplätze, Law to provide relief for families and to improve the climate for investment and jobs of 25 February 1992, BGBl I 1992 No. 9, S 324.

[23] See Bundesfinanzhof, resolution and rulings of 29 April 2009 I R 26/08, BFH/NV 2009, 1648; of 27 August 2008 I R 28/07, BFH/NV 2009/123; of 29 November 2000 I R 85/99, BStBl II 2002, 720; and already ruling of 30 May 1990 I R 97/88, BStBl II 1990, 875. In the more recent cases the Bundesfinanzhof has repeatedly made clear that its interpretation did not require change although the legislator defined the term 'business relationship' (new s. 4) in 1992; the tax authorities accepted this interpretation, see Federal Ministry of Finance, communication of 12 January 2010, BStBl I 2010, 34.

[24] Vgl. Bundesfinanzhof, ruling of 23 June 2010 IR 37/09, BStBl II 2010, 895.

[25] Gesetz zum Abbau von Steuervergünstigungen und Ausnahmeregelungen (Steuerver-günstigungsabbaugesetz), Tax Preference Reduction Act of 16 May 2003, BGBl I 2003 No. 19, 666.

services. This applies also if the contractual agreement (for example the granting of a guarantee by a parent company for the benefit of a subsidiary) is taken up in the bylaws or has the character of substituting equity (due to the foreign company being undercapitalised). However, if the transaction (for example, the granting of a guarantee or a letter of comfort) has its basis in the shareholder relationship the transaction does not constitute a business relationship.

In 2008 the regulations concerning 'adjustment of income' were again revised and a new section (as section 3) was included. Section 1(1) of the FTA currently reads as follows:

> (1) If the income of a taxpayer from a foreign business relationship with a related party has been reduced by basing its determination on terms, especially on pricing (transfer pricing), other than those on which mutually independent third parties would have agreed in similar or comparable circumstances (arm's length principle), it is to be adjusted, other provisions notwithstanding, to that which would have resulted from those terms as would have been agreed between mutually independent third parties. The arm's length principle is to be applied on the assumption that the mutually independent third parties had knowledge of all significant factors of the business relationship and were guided by the principles of orderly and conscientious business managers. Where the application of the arm's length principle leads to farther-reaching adjustments than under other provisions, the farther-reaching adjustments are to be made in addition to the consequences from those other provisions

In this version the 'adjustment of income' refers explicitly also to pricing (transfer pricing). It is also assumed that the contracting parties know of all significant factors of the business relationship and are acting in a 'prudent' manner. Finally, it is determined how this norm stands in relation to other adjustment norms and laid down that the various adjustments are to be applied in parallel manner.

The new section 3 regulates the order of priority of the admissible transfer pricing methods and prescribes how to apply price and margin ranges. It also brings the 'hypothetical arm's length comparison' into the canon of transfer pricing methods, supplements this method with subsequent adjustments and regulates how the hypothetical arm's length comparison is to be applied to business transactions forming a transfer of function. Finally, this section gives the government (and not the legislator) the power to regulate the details of applying the arm's length principle via decree law. These regulations will be subject to closer elaboration in the following section.

6.4   Main aspects of Germany's transfer pricing legislation

6.4.1   Corrective instruments

In order to prevent affiliated companies from shifting taxable profits or deductible expenses out of or into Germany by way of inappropriate transfer pricing arrangements of business conditions, the German tax legislator has created five basic defence mechanisms with respect to adjustment of income. The following instruments have to be taken into account in this context:

- general provisions on the attribution of assets and income and on the determination of tax base (sections 39 to 42 of the Fiscal Code (Abgabenordnung) (FC));
- hidden profit distribution (section 8(3) of the Corporate Tax Act (Körperschaftsteuergesetz), (CTA));
- hidden capital contribution (section 8(1) of the CTA in connection with section 4(1) sentences 3, 7 of the Income Tax Act (Einkommensteuergesetz) (ITA));
- deduction of interest costs for corporate entities (interest stripping rule) (section 8a of the CTA in connection with section 4h of the ITA); and
- adjustment of income in the case of business connections abroad (section 1 of the Foreign Tax Act (Außensteuergesetz) (FTA)).

The general provisions on the attribution of assets and income and on the determination of tax base apply to all areas of tax law and prohibit all manner of abusive arrangements. Of particular importance here is the fact that assets may not be attributed to the legal owner if someone other than the legal owner ('the economic owner') in fact exercises control over the asset in such a way that he can exclude the legal owner from having influence over the asset (section 39(1) of the FC).[26] It is also significant that it is irrelevant in the taxation context whether legal transactions are or become invalid. A comparable situation applies in connection with paper transactions. If a paper transaction is to cover up another transaction the latter is relevant for tax purposes (section 41 of the FC). But for practical purposes it is most relevant that tax laws may not be circumvented by using legal planning possibilities in abusive

---

[26] Examples of this are trust relationships, ownership reservation and particular leasing arrangements.

ways. Abuse is deemed to exist where an inappropriate legal planning option is chosen leading to a tax advantage for the taxpayer or a third party compared to the result of an appropriate arrangement, in a manner not intended by the law. In cases such as these the tax authorities are entitled to levy tax corresponding to that arising from business transactions with appropriate legal arrangements (section 42 of the FC). Shifting income to a controlled company can be abusive if the company has no economic substance because no offices exist and the company does not dispose of other necessary resources, for example. In the individual case, however, it needs to be examined whether particular tax laws contain special relevant provision. In this sense, with regard to the above example, the regulations concerning controlled foreign companies as set out in the Foreign Tax Act take precedence (section 7 *et seq.* of the FTA). Likewise, in respect to transfer prices or business conditions, the provisions of the particular tax laws take priority. In this context, the general legal instruments for adjusting income are 'hidden profit distributions' and 'hidden capital contributions'.

Profit distributions or dividend payments of all kinds cannot be deducted from taxable income. This also applies to 'hidden distributions' usually resulting from profit shifts between related parties. The Corporate Tax Act mentions, but does not define, the term 'hidden distribution'. According to the definition by the Federal Tax Court, a hidden distribution is 'a loss in net assets or prevention of an increase in net assets as a result of the corporate relationship which affects the level of income and is not the consequence of a resolution drawn up in accordance with company law for the distribution of profits'. It is to be added back to profit. A hidden distribution will be assumed wherever a company appears to have accepted business or financial disadvantages in favour of one or more of its shareholders or their related parties, unless an 'orderly and conscientious business manager' would also have done so within a third-party relationship under otherwise similar circumstances. Payment of excess prices for goods or services purchased by the company/subsidiary is an example. Another example of a hidden profit distribution is the charging of inappropriately low prices for goods and services rendered to the shareholder/parent company.

The corollary of a 'hidden distribution' of profits is the 'hidden contribution' of capital. Hidden contributions do not increase the profit of the recipient, but are also not deductible expenses for the (domestic) contributor. A hidden capital contribution must be a tangible benefit granted by a shareholder in that capacity (section 4(1) sentence 7 of the

ITA). If these grants increased the profit, they are to be deducted when the income of the company is determined. Whether or not this contribution is a result of the corporate relationship is gauged by reference to the same yardstick: Would an orderly and conscientious business manager have given the same benefit to a third party? Examples of such hidden contributions are supply of goods to a company/subsidiary at subnormal prices, and supply or rendering of goods and services to the shareholder/parent company at excessive prices. Intangible benefits, however, do not qualify as contributable assets.[27] The effect on profit of rendering services or loans at sub-par rates cannot, therefore, be adjusted with the help of the legal instrument of the hidden capital contribution.

Unlike the hidden profit distribution, the interest stripping rule places particular weight on combating profit shifting via group finance. Its aim is, in principle, the limitation of shareholder debt financing. The legal basis of the corresponding provision is to be found in corporate tax law and applies only to inbound cases. According to the interest stripping rule, which is also applicable for corporations (section 8a(1) of the CTA), net interest expenses paid by German taxpayers are only deductible for tax purposes up to 30 per cent of an entity's EBITDA (earnings before interests, taxes, depreciation and amortisation). In general, the interest expense can, however, be deducted without restriction, if:

(a) the net interest expenses of the company are lower than 3 million euros in the relevant tax period (section 4h(2a) of the ITA); or
(b) the company is not, or only in part, a member of a corporate group ('corporate group clause') (section 4h(2b) of the ITA); or
(c) the company is a member of a corporate group and the company's equity ratio equals (with a 2 per cent tolerance) or exceeds the equity ratio of the controlled group as a whole ('escape clause') (section 4h (2c) of the ITA).

In order to prevent income shifting, the exception rules of this regulation are somewhat stronger for corporations than for individual taxpayers. The 'corporate group clause' applies only if the corporation's interest payment for shareholder debt does not exceed 10 per cent of the corporation's total net interest expense. Shareholder debt is assumed when the debt is granted (i) by a substantial shareholder (shareholding

---

[27] See, e.g., Bundesfinanzhof, Judgment of 24 May 1984 I R 166/78, BStBl II 1984, 747.

of more than 25 per cent); (ii) by a related party of the substantial shareholder; or (iii) by a third person who has rights of recourse over one of the persons mentioned above (section 8a(2) of the CTA). By the same token, the 'escape clause' applies only if the corporation's interest payment or the interest payment of another affiliated company for shareholder debt does not exceed 10 per cent of the corporation's total net interest expense. Interest payments are only relevant for this purpose if the corresponding loans are shown as liabilities in the fully consolidated accounts of the relevant corporate group (section 8a(3) of the CTA).

6.4.2 How German law defines the arm's length principle

Section 1 of the FTA deals with the 'adjustment of income'. This provision does not interfere with the other corrective instruments and gives them priority. This applies in particular in the case of hidden profit distributions and hidden capital contributions. Unlike the hidden profit distribution and hidden capital contribution, the 'adjustment of income' which transforms the arm's length principle of international double taxation treaties into German law, is limited to cross-border cases and business relationships with related parties. The currently valid version of the arm's length principle according to German law (section 1(1) of the FTA) has already been presented in the course of the section on historical background.

In order to guarantee uniform application of the law, executive authorities (in tax matters, the German Ministry of Finance) can with the approval with the Bundesrat (Federal Council) be empowered by law to set details of application for these legal provisions. In the area of transfer prices, the legislator has made use of this possibility in the determination of type, context and scope of the documentation required[28] and in connection with the cross-border transfer of functions.[29] Further reference will be made to this below. The tax administration has no other powers to issue legally binding regulations.

Irrespective of this, however, the authorities are able to issue administrative regulations in the interests of achieving equal application of the

---

[28] Ordinance regarding the Documentation of Profit Attributions of 13 November 2003, BGBl I 2003, 2296, most recently revised by art. 9 of the Company Tax Reform 2008 of 14 August 2007, BGBl I 2007, S 1912.

[29] Ordinance regarding the Transfer of Functions of 12 August 2008, BGBl I 2008, S 1680.

laws. Such administrative regulations consist of the Federal government's guidelines, the communications of the Ministry of Finance, the decrees of the State Finance Ministries, and the orders of the Higher Tax Offices. Although these are not legally binding for the individual taxpayer, they exert a *de facto* binding effect. They contain orders of an authority to a lower authority or an official within an authority, are binding on the officers of the tax authorities, and reflect the position of the tax administration with respect to individual cases or questions of doubt.

Among the most important administrative regulations in the area of transfer pricing, interpreting the legal provisions on the 'adjustment of income' (section 1(1) of the FTA) from the perspective of the tax authorities, are:

- Grundsätze zur Anwendung des Außensteuergesetzes,[30] Principles regarding the Application of the Foreign Tax Act;
- Grundsätze für die Prüfung der Einkunftsabgrenzung bei international verbundenen Unternehmen (Verwaltungsgrundsätze),[31] Principles regarding the Audit of the Attribution of Income in Internationally Affiliated Companies ('Administrative Principles');
- Grundsätze für die Prüfung der Einkunftsabgrenzung durch Umlageverträge zwischen international verbundenen Unternehmen,[32] Principles regarding the Audit of Profit Allocation using Cost Sharing Agreements by Internationally Affiliated Companies;
- Grundsätze für die Prüfung der Einkunftsabgrenzung zwischen international verbundenen Unternehmen in Fällen der Arbeitnehmerentsendung (Verwaltungsgrundsätze – Arbeitnehmerentsendung),[33] Principles regarding the Audit of the Attribution of Income among

---

[30] Federal Ministry of Finance, Communication of 14 May 2004, IV B 4–S 1340–11/04, BStBl I 2004, 3 Special Issue 1; replaces Federal Ministry of Finance, Communication of 2 December 1994, VI C 7–S 1340–20/94, BStBl I 1995, Special Issue 1; replaces Federal Ministry of Finance, Communication of 11 July 1974, IV C 1–S 1340–32/74, BStBl I 1974, 442.

[31] Federal Ministry of Finance, Communication of 23 February 1983, IV C 5–S 1341–4/83, BStBl I 1983, S 218; repealed in part by the Administrative Principles regarding Procedures, Federal Ministry of Finance, Communication of 12 April 2005, IV B 4–S 1341–1/05, BStBl I 2005, 570.

[32] Federal Ministry of Finance, Communication of 30 December 1999, IV B 4–S 1341–14/99, BStBl I 1999, 1122.

[33] Federal Ministry of Finance, Communication of 9 November 2001, IV B 4–S 1341–20/01, BStBl I 2001, 796.

Internationally Affiliated Companies in Cases of the Posting of Workers ('Administrative Principles regarding the Posting of Workers').

Of central importance here are the Administrative Principles dating from 1983. This is underlined by the fact that today's version of the older principles regarding the application of the Foreign Tax Act contains no regulations of its own with respect to related persons, the corrective yardstick (arm's length principle), and the treatment of adjustments, but simply refers to the Administrative Principles. The principles regarding the application of the Foreign Tax Act only provide interpretations as to the form of adjustment and the term 'business relationship'.

The Administrative Principles give a detailed interpretation of the legal provisions regarding international attribution of income and include positions on various types of inter-company transactions. Originally, these principles provided guidelines on cost sharing arrangements, adjustment methods and related procedural aspects. In the course of revising and adjusting these principles in line with developments at the level of the OECD, the Federal Ministry of Finance issued regulations governing these areas in a separate communication. The communication regarding cost sharing arrangements deals with details concerning application of the arm's length principle as far as they affect general prerequisites for application, the allocable amount, the allocation mechanism, special cases, documentation and provision of evidence. The Administrative Principles regarding the Posting of Workers regulate in particular the attribution of expenses associated with the posting of staff, relevant qualification criteria, special arrangements, questions of treatment for tax purposes, and the procedure and duties concerning provision of evidence and cooperation.

In the aftermath of a Federal Tax Court case in 2001 which will be discussed in the following section, section 1 of the FTA has been supplemented with documentation and penalty provisions. These are:

- documentation requirements for cross-border transactions with related parties including permanent establishments (section 90(3) of the Fiscal Code);
- consequences of inadequate or missing documentation, including in particular the rebuttable assumption of a need for profit adjustments and the allowance to estimate income by use of least favourable point in a price range (section 162(4) of the FC); and

- penalties (5 to 10 per cent of profit adjustment with certain ceilings and restrictions) in the case that the taxpayer is non-compliant with documentation requirements (section 162(4) of the FC).

Additional detail to the latter provisions were laid down in a legal ordinance and explained in the context of administrative principles (binding for subordinate authorities). These provisions and regulations comprise:

- Verordnung zu Art, Inhalt und Umfang von Aufzeichnungen im Sinne des § 90 Abs. 3 der Abgabenordnung (Gewinnabgrenzungsaufzeich-nungsverordnung – GAufzV), Ordinance regarding the type, content and scope of records in the meaning of section 90(3) of the FC (Ordin-ance regarding the Documentation of Profit Attributions);[34] and
- Grundsätze für die Prüfung der Einkunftsabgrenzung zwischen nahe stehenden Personen mit grenzüberschreitenden Geschäftsbeziehungen in Bezug auf Ermittlungs- und Mitwirkungspflichten, Berichtigungen sowie auf Verständigungs- und EU-Schiedsverfahren (Verwaltungs-grundsätze-Verfahren),[35] Principles for the audit of the attribution of income between related parties with cross-border business relation-ships with reference to the obligation to determine transfer prices and to cooperate with the tax administration, adjustments as well as their implications in terms of competent authority and EU arbitration procedures (Administrative Principles regarding Procedures).

The ordinance governs the type, content and scope of records in the case of ordinary, specific and exceptional business transactions. Besides a duty to document the facts and circumstances on which the transactions between related parties are based, the ordinance explicitly demands also evidence on the appropriateness of transfer prices applied (grounds for the suitability of the transfer pricing methods used, calculations and comparable data). In addition, the administrative principles regarding procedure reflect the position of the tax authorities regarding questions dealing with duties of the tax authorities, participants' duties to cooper-ate, legal consequences of failure to cooperate, implementation of

---

[34] Ordinance regarding the Documentation of Profit Attributions of 13 November 2003, BGBl I 2003, 2296, most recently amended by art. 9 of the 2008 Company Tax Reform Act of 14 August 2007, BGBl I 2007, 1912.

[35] Federal Ministry of Finance, Communication of 12 April 2005, IV B 4–S 1341–1/05, BStBl I 2005, 570.

adjustments and process of transfer price corrections and mutual agreement or arbitration procedures. The details of this communication, which runs to more than 70 pages in length, cannot be given here. But for practical purposes the statements it includes on choice of method and application of database analyses and benchmarking studies are of particular relevance.

Under the 2008 Company Tax Reform Act, section 1 of the FTA obtained a new subsection determining the order and the prerequisites for applying the internationally accepted transfer pricing methods in accordance with German law. Moreover, the 'hypothetical arm's length comparison' was specified in more detail, as were its application in cases of the transfer of functions, and the possibilities of retrospective price adjustments.

The focus of the changes to the arm's length principle in German tax law (section 1 of the FTA) is on the determination of a hierarchy and the terms of application for individual transfer-pricing methods. Consequently, for intra-group cross-border business transactions, the German Foreign Tax Act requires the transfer price to be determined primarily according to the comparable uncontrolled price method, the resale price method or the cost plus method. The condition for this is that arm's length values can be found that, after adjustment as appropriate in view of the functions performed, the assets employed and the opportunities and risks assumed are comparable without limitation to those methods; several such values form a range. If no such arm's length values can be found, the application of a suitable transfer pricing method is to be based on values of limited comparability as appropriately adjusted. If no third party values of at least limited comparability can be found, the taxpayer is to base his income determination on a hypothetical third-party comparison. For this, he is to estimate the lowest price for the seller and the highest price for the buyer on the basis of a functional analysis and internal planning calculations. This scope for agreement is to follow from the profit expectations (profit potential) of each party. The price to be taken is that most likely to accord with the arm's length principle. If no other value is plausibly put forward, the mean of the scope for agreement is to be taken.

Where a function including the related opportunities and risks is transferred, accompanied by assets and other advantages transferred or lent for which no arm's length value of even limited comparability can be found, the taxpayer shall determine the scope for agreement on the basis of the transfer of the function as a whole (transfer package). This has to be done on the basis of capitalisation at adequate interest rates. The piece-meal determination of the transfer prices for all assets and services transferred, as appropriately adjusted, is to be accepted if the taxpayer can show convincingly either that no important intangibles or advantages, or the use thereof, were transferred with the function or that the sum of the piece-meal prices is equivalent to the arm's length price for the transfer package as a whole.

Where significant intangibles and advantages derive from a business connection and the future profitability varies significantly from the assumption on which the transfer price was based, there is to be a refutable presumption that, at the time of the contract, there was uncertainty as to future profits, and independent third parties would have agreed on a suitable price adjustment provision. If no such provision was agreed and there is a significant variance during the first ten years from the date of the contract, the adjustment is to be made in an appropriate lump sum amount as a correction to the original transfer price with tax effect for the business year following that in which the variance occurred.

Like the documentation provisions, this addition to the application of the arm's length principle in Germany has also been supplemented by a legal ordinance dealing with the taxation of transfer of functions, and has been explained in corresponding administrative principles. These are:

- Verordnung zur Anwendung des Fremdvergleichsgrundsatzes nach § 1 Abs. 1 des Außensteuergesetzes in Fällen grenzüberschreitender Funktionsverlagerungen (Funktionsverlagerungsverordnung – FVerlV), Ordinance on the application of the arm's length principle pursuant to section 1(1) of the FTA in cases of cross-border transfer of functions (Ordinance regarding the Transfer of Functions);[36]
- Grundsätze für die Prüfung der Einkunftsabgrenzung zwischen nahe stehenden Personen in Fällen von grenzüberschreitenden Funktionsverlagerungen (Verwaltungsgrundsätze Funktionsverlagerung),[37] Administrative Principles regarding the Transfer of Functions.

At the core of this ordinance and these administrative principles are the new terms 'function', 'transfer of function' and 'transfer

[36] Ordinance regarding the Transfer of Functions of 12 August 2008, BGBl I 2008, 1680.
[37] Federal Ministry of Finance, Communication of 13 October 2010, IV B 5–S 1341/08/10003, BStBl I 2010, 774.

package', which are discussed in the international arena under the headings of 'business reorganisation', 'transfer of an activity' and 'transfer of something of value'. In the context of the German regulations, the spotlight is on provisions regarding the determination of the value associated with the assets and other advantages bundled in a 'transfer package' (assets and other advantages such as goodwill forming an integrated part of a business), and on the conclusion resulting for the determination of respective transfer prices. Setting arm's length prices for intangible assets and transfer packages will be discussed in greater detail in the next section as these currently have no OECD parallels.

Ultimately, in 2011 the Ministry of Finance issued a decree regarding bad debt losses on a receivable from a foreign related party. This is:

- Anwendung des § 1 AStG auf Fälle von Teilwertabschreibungen und andere Wertminderungen auf Darlehen an verbundene ausländische Unternehmen,[38] Application of section 1 of the FTA to write-downs to going concern value and to other impairments regarding loans to foreign related companies.

The Ministry made it clear that a bad debt loss on a receivable from a foreign related party is only allowable where the taxpayer can show that a third party would not have taken steps beforehand to recover or secure the outstanding sum. It suggests that this could be the case where it was clearly in the business interests of the lender not to pursue debt recovery vigorously in order to maintain trading relationships. However, it offers no other examples of an acceptable write-down. The Ministry's reasoning is based on the arm's length requirement of the Foreign Tax Act which includes adequate security for a related party debt. Adequate security can, however, be seen in overall group support to enable a subsidiary to meet its debts as they fall due. Accordingly, no charge can be made for enhanced risk of default within a group. On the other hand, a default itself demonstrates the failure of that support. Hence the debt would have arisen, or been allowed to remain, in other than arm's length circumstances. Its write-off is therefore per se disallowable.

---

[38] Federal Ministry of Finance, Communication of 29 March 2011, IV B 5–S 1341/09/ 10004, BStBl I 2011, 277.

6.4.3 Determining the arm's length price for intangible assets and transfer packages according to the concepts of the hypothetical arm's length method

Steps

In order to determine the values of the relevant profit potentials, it is necessary to:

(i) identify the anticipated future benefits associated with the transferred asset or transfer package;

(ii) determine the useful lives of the corresponding assets; and

(iii) establish the required rate of return for purposes of calculating the net present value of the profit potential associated with the assets or transfer packages transferred.

The minimum and maximum prices are further determined by action alternatives as well as the transaction costs including, but not limited to, taxes on capital gains arising in the course of the transfer or sale of assets or other benefits (e.g., goodwill).

(i)   Determination of anticipated future benefits

According to the guidelines provided by the German tax authorities, the relevant income for determining the net present value of anticipated future benefits refers to the financial surpluses net of expenses, interest on debt capital and taxes flowing to the enterprise over the useful life of the asset or transfer package transferred. Typically, these cash flows are derived from planned results.

As taxes on income typically reduce to varying extent the cash flows attributable to the asset or transfer package and the cash flows of an investment alternative (represented by the cost of capital), corporate taxes have to be taken into account as expenses on the level of the corporate entity. Relevant amounts are those taxes that will presumably be assessed or have actually been assessed, paid and, as the case may be, already reduced by a given tax relief. Different views exist on whether or not to take personal taxes on corporate dividends into account.

From the perspective of the acquiring enterprise, it is to be noted that the acquisition of (a bundle of) assets is associated with tax amortisation benefits. The need to take this benefit on board results from the fact that the corporate tax to be paid is calculated on the basis of cash flows (whereas the tax base is corporate income). If looking at (parts of) an enterprise as a whole, it is not uncommon to factor in the corresponding tax benefits on a global basis. This global procedure, however, is not without difficulties as it does not allow for an appropriate allocation of the purchase price to the individual assets transferred. Instead, it would be more consistent to differentiate between the assets involved in the transfer when adding the tax amortisation benefit to the net present value of the anticipated cash flows.

(ii) Determination of the discount period/useful lives

Regarding transfer of activities, the German administrative guidelines require us to act on the assumption that the useful lives of the assets involved are not limited (i.e., to calculate the net present value based on an infinite capitalisation period) when determining the profit potential of an enterprise as a whole. This does not hold if reasons speaking in favour of a shorter capitalisation period exist or can credibly be shown.

(iii) Determination of the required rate of return

In order to determine the required rate of return, the customary interest rate regarding a quasi-riskless investment serves as a point of departure. More precisely, the calculation is to be based on riskless investments, the duration of which is equivalent to the expected term of the activity or the useful lives of significant intangible assets. Where capitalisation is to be based on an unlimited period of time, the rate of return regarding a comparable investment of a term as long as possible should be decisive.

The basic interest rate is to be increased by a premium reflecting the risk of the underlying investment. Where the subjects of valuation are activities, such premiums are to be determined by looking at the customary market return which may be earned when carrying out comparable activities.

Determination of the arm's length price

The scope for agreement is determined by minimum and maximum prices that the seller and acquirer wish to achieve or are prepared to pay. Such a scope for agreement results if the minimum price of the seller falls below the maximum price of the acquirer. In determining the minimum price, the seller looks at the profit potential associated with the asset(s) and other benefits transferred. Moreover, the expected costs arising as a consequence of the transfer (e.g., costs associated with closing down an enterprise or terminating an activity but also possible taxes on capital gains relating to the asset transfer) factor into this calculation. In this context, options realistically available to the seller (e.g., outsourcing a production activity by way of contract manufacturing) are to be taken into account.

When determining the maximum price, the acquiring company looks at the profit potential that it expects to realise through making use of the asset to be transferred or the activity to be carried out. In this context, options realistically available to the acquiring company are to be taken into account, assuming that the acquiring company is independent from the seller and is able to make use of complete information.

Regarding the scope for agreement, the price to be taken is that most likely to accord with the arm's length principle. If no other value is plausibly put forward, the mean of the scope for agreement is to be taken. This 'mean solution' is based on the assumption that (1) the benefit accruing to the contracting parties corresponds to the difference between the mean value and their minimum or maximum price and (2) the allocation of related benefits for the parties is fair if these benefits are of equal weight. Among third parties, moreover, bargaining skills, bargaining power, haste and other impacting factors may play a role.

According to the German administrative principles, a 'significant determination' justifying a later price adjustment is given if a retrospective calculation based on the actual development of profits shows that the true transfer price is outside the original scope for agreement. In reconsidering this true transfer price, however, it is only correct to take those developments into account for which uncertainty existed at the time of the transfer, thus leading to some flawed assessment regarding later developments. On the other hand, those changes in future developments resulting from post-transaction activities (later investments or reorganisation measures) should not be taken into account when retrospectively calculating the 'true' transfer price.

6.5   Transfer pricing disputes: domestic approaches

6.5.1   Final meeting in tax audits

In the interests of an equitable determination and assessment of tax relevant facts and circumstances, tax authorities in Germany can order tax audits to be carried out. The tax authorities decide with due discretion whether and, if so, when a tax audit is to be conducted. Taxable parties subject to tax audits are put into categories in terms of size which distinguish between large businesses, medium-sized businesses, small

Table 6.5 *Taxable parties subject to tax audits in Germany over the period 2007 to 2010*

Numbers of businesses	2007	2008	2009	2010
Large businesses	170,060	170,060	170,060	191,638
Medium-sized businesses	758,051	758,051	758,051	799,135
Small businesses	1,141,147	1,141,147	1,141,147	1,189,727
Very small businesses	6,321,466	6,321,466	6,321,466	6,391,015

Table 6.6 *Additional revenue and interest as a result of tax audits in Germany over the period 2007 to 2010*[*]

Additional revenue and interest	2007	2008	2009	2010
Large businesses	13,196	13,974	15,292	11,916
Medium-sized businesses	1,387	1,330	1,253	1,349
Small businesses	626	666	690	679
Very small businesses	817	1,018	1,058	972

[*] Indications in billion euros

businesses and very small businesses. The determination of the number of businesses and classification into size categories takes place, as a rule, every three years. As of 1 January 2010 the figures shown in Table 6.5 resulted.

In 2010, audits of trading or business enterprises, the businesses of self-employed persons, agricultural of forestry businesses of all sizes and associations of builder-owners, loss-allocating companies and other taxable parties have led to additional tax and interest amounting to approximately 16.8 billion euros. Broken down according to the various size categories the results are as shown in Table 6.6.

Even though the greater part of additional tax (2010: 71.1 per cent) arises from audit of the large businesses, for reasons of equitability these audits cannot be limited to this category. For the years 2007 to 2010 the number of audits and audit cycles within the size categories were as shown in Table 6.7.

As a general rule no special audits are carried out for transfer prices. Instead, transfer price auditing is carried out in the framework of the regular tax audit which normally covers a period of three to five years. However, the tax audit of interest has, over recent years, increasingly been focused on the area of transfer pricing, with relevant training of the

Table 6.7 *Number of audits and audit cycles in Germany over the period 2007 to 2010 within the categories in terms of size*

Number of tax audits and audit cycles	2007	2008	2009	2010
Large businesses	38,662	39,885	38,988	40,502
Audit cycle	4.4	4.3	4.4	4.7
Medium-sized businesses	59,068	56,999	55,157	55,315
Audit cycle	12.8	13.3	13.7	14.5
Small and very small businesses	115,645	113,752	112,379	108,086

Table 6.8 *Numbers of tax auditors in Germany over the period 2007 to 2010*

	2007	2008	2009	2010
Numbers of tax auditors	13,646	13,337	13,332	13,210

auditors and the involvement of specialists from the Federal Central Tax Office and the Regional Tax Offices. For the purposes of conducting tax audits, more than 13,000 auditors were employed over recent years (see Table 6.8).

Furthermore, 173 auditors from the Federal Central Tax Office took part in a total of 601 tax audits supported by Regional Tax Offices and completed in 2010.

Experience shows that personal exchange between the authorities and the taxpayers has dispute-arbitrating effect. This is why a meeting concerning the result of the tax audit is to be held at the end of the process (final meeting), unless, as a result of the tax audit, there is no change to the tax base, or if the taxpayer decides to forego such a meeting. In the course of a final meeting, as well as disputed matters, the legal assessment of the results of the audit and its tax consequences will be discussed (section 201 of the FC). Although this event is sometimes described as a kind of 'oriental bazaar', in many cases the final meeting results in the tax authority and the taxpayer reaching consensus on the tax treatment. This is particularly true in the area of transfer pricing. In cases where the taxpayer and the tax authorities cannot agree on a common view in the course of the tax audit, the taxpayer is entitled to take legal recourse with respect to the tax assessment.

6.5.2 Appeals procedure

In Germany, administrative courts have the task of protecting subjects in the case of official action. In tax matters, the tax courts are called upon to judge as specialised administrative courts. In order to prevent tax courts being flooded with law suits, the court procedure is proceeded by an administrative appeals procedure which gives the tax authority the opportunity to scrutinise the cases once again ('preliminary procedure'). Unlike the courts the tax authorities are bound by administrative regulations (guidelines, communications, orders and decrees).

In tax matters, the administrative appeals procedure is termed *Einspruch* (objection). If such an objection is admissible,[39] the tax authorities are required not only to reassess the initial decision in its entire scope, but also to clarify the facts and circumstances of the case. Upon application or (in certain circumstances) *ex officio*, the authorities are required to open the tax documentation and may (*ex officio*) or should (upon application by the applicant) discuss the facts and legal status of the case prior to making the appeal decision (hearing). This regulation serves, on the one hand, to realise the principle of '*rechtliches Gehör*' (legal hearing) (section 91(1) of the FC) and, on the other hand, has the further aim of promoting mutual solution of the appeal, thereby reducing the number of disputes to be dealt with in court.[40]

Should the objection be found to be (partly) justified, the tax authorities can take remedial action by (partly) withdrawing, amending or waiving the contested administrative act (section 367 of the FC). A formal decision is only needed if the tax authorities provide no remedy to the appeal. If, from the perspective of the tax authorities, the appeal is unjustified or inadmissible, it is rejected as being unfounded (section 366 of the FC) or is formally declared to be inadmissible (section 358 of the FC).

If the out-of-court legal remedy fails to bring success, in disputes concerning tax matters the taxpayer can take recourse to the fiscal

---

[39] The preconditions for this are that the objection is available by law in the case at hand, the taxpayer is permitted to make an objection because he is burdened by an administrative act as a result of a breach of the law, a flawed application of the law or inappropriate exercising of discretion, that he has legal and tax capacity, that he has observed the prescribed form and period of objection, that he is in need of legal protection and the objection has not been withdrawn.

[40] So explicitly Deutscher Bundestag, printed matter 12/6959, on s. 364a of the FC, 131, printed matter 12/7427, on s. 264a of the FC, 37.

court.[41] The tax jurisdiction is an independent arm of the national jurisdiction exercised through specific administrative courts. Unlike the general administrative jurisdiction, it is structured on two levels. The tax courts decide in a first legal action as an interlocutory hearing (section 35 of the Finanzgerichtsordnung (Code of Procedure of Fiscal Courts, CPFC) whereas the Federal Tax Court deals explicitly with court of appeals proceedings for appeals and complaints against initial decisions of the tax courts (section 36 of the CPFC). But review of the facts and circumstances by the tax courts requires the fulfilment of admissibility conditions. In addition to the formal preconditions (admissibility of recourse to the tax courts, courts jurisdiction, proper commencement of the action, observation of compliance with the time period), they include the right of action, the legal capacity as an involved party and legal capacity to act, and in particular also a legitimate interest to take legal action.

In tax court proceedings, the tax court is required *ex officio* to investigate the facts and circumstances ('investigative principle'). Court rulings result in principle from an oral hearing. Irrespective of this, all persons have a right to be legally heard (article 103(1) of the Basic Law). This right includes in particular the fact that a judgment can only be based on facts and evidence concerning which the participating parties were able to express themselves ('right of expression'). With regard to the standard of evidence, the Code of Procedure of Fiscal Courts favours a cooperative division of responsibility between the participating parties. A possible breach of legal procedural duties (duties relating to recording, to storage, presentation and cooperation) has to be taken into account. According to this distribution, a taxpayer may not gain advantage as a result of violating his duties to cooperate. In this sense the law is geared to the participants' sphere of responsibility. If the deficit in clarification stems from insufficient or lacking cooperation on the part of the taxpayer, the standard of evidence in the case of facts giving rise to or raising tax is lowered. Here, the tax authority is required to carry the objective burden of proof. But the standard of evidence remains high if tax-relieving or tax-diminishing facts are not clarified due to lack of cooperation (section 162 of the FC). For facts relieving or limiting the authorities' claim to tax, the burden of proof lies with the taxpayer.

---

[41] Unlike actions for rescission or actions requesting a change of a legal right or status, aiming at the annulment or amendment of an administrative decision, general actions for injunction or actions for a declaratory judgment need no preliminary procedure (s. 40 of the Finanzgerichtsordnung, Code of Procedure of Fiscal Courts).

Legal remedies are the revision appeal and complaint to the Federal Tax Court. Revision appeals are directed against judgments whereas complaints can be made in the context of all other decisions or resolutions of the tax court. Revision appeals have to be admitted as a general principle. The tax court or, in the event of a complaint being laid before the Federal Tax Court in respect to the denial of admissibility, the Federal Tax Court may only admit a revision appeal if:

(a) the legal matter is of significance in principle (revision appeal on a matter of principle);
(b) the further development of law requires a decision by the Federal Tax Court (revision appeal on a matter of further development of law);
(c) ensuring uniform rulings makes a decision by the Federal Tax Court necessary (revision appeal for uniformity of rulings); or
(d) a procedural flaw exists upon which the decision could have formed the basis of the ruling (revision appeal on procedural matters).

The revision appeal is decided by the Federal Tax Court. If there are deemed to be grounds for the revision appeal, the court has to reach decision itself. The precondition for this is that the legal matter is ready for decision. Otherwise the decision of the (lower) tax court is to be cancelled and the legal matter is to be referred back to the tax court for hearing, negotiation and decision. This referral back is necessary in particular where further determination of facts has to be carried out since the Federal Tax Court is not an interlocutory instance (no new facts and evidence may be presented to the Federal Tax Court which is bound by the findings of the lower tax court).

If the basic rights of a taxpayer who has exhausted the possibilities of legal recourse to the specific courts are violated, an appeal before the Federal Constitutional Court is admissible. In a similar way, the legal matter may be referred to the European Court of Justice if there is a question of European law being violated.

6.5.3   Important court rulings with respect to transfer pricing

Overview

As presented when discussing the corrective instruments, in Germany five basic defence mechanisms with respect to the adjustment of income exist. In this context, the general legal instruments for adjusting income are 'hidden profit distributions' and 'hidden capital contributions'. section 1 of the FTA ('adjustment of income') does not interfere with these corrective instruments and gives them priority. As a consequence, it comes as no surprise that in the area of profit attribution, by far the greatest number of rulings handed down by the Federal Tax Court dealt with questions regarding 'hidden profit distribution'. In relation to a controlling business manager, hidden profit distributions already emerge if the underlying transaction lacks a clear and seriously agreed, written agreement set up in advance.[42] As a consequence, the courts typically verify whether transactions between affiliated parties are based on upfront (written) agreements and result in an income allocation comparable to that arising from transactions between third parties. In comparison to 'hidden profit distributions', court rulings on 'hidden capital contributions' are less numerous. But court rulings on the adjustments of income according to section 1 of the FTA show the lowest level of distribution.

Concerning the attribution of profits to affiliated companies, the rulings of the Federal Tax Court relating to:

- the transfer of a market and a customer base;
- the interpretation of the legal term 'business relationship';
- the interest rate to be applied;
- permanent loss situations;
- licensing a trade and a company name;
- cooperative duties; and
- transfer prices concerning goods

are of particular importance for the determination of transfer prices in Germany.

---

[42] See, e.g., Bundesfinanzhof, Judgment of 6 December 1995 I R 88/94, BStBl II 1996, 383 (with reference to payment of management remuneration), Judgment of 17 May 1995 I R 147/93, BStBl II 1996, 204 (with reference to the terms of a pension agreement). The arm's length principle does not address formal criteria. Where an exchange of goods or services has taken place, the only question to deal with in the framework of the arm's length principle is the remuneration as usual in third party transactions. According to the wording of the arm's length principle it is not of significance whether the terms of the transaction were influenced by a related party. This was made clear in Germany by the Cologne Tax Court which had to rule concerning the relationship between the hidden profit distributions and the arm's length principle as set out in Article 9 of double taxation treaties. The Tax Court of Cologne takes the view that the double taxation treaty as provided in Article 9 of the OECD Model Agreement develops a blocking effect against hidden profit distributions in cases in which according to domestic law the profit adjustment is based on purely formal criteria, cf. Tax Court of Cologne of 22 August 2007, *Deutsches Steuerrecht, Entscheidungsdienst* (journal) 2008, 696; of different opinion Administrative Principles, Federal Ministry of Finance, Communication of 12 April 2005, BStBl 2005 I, p. 570, No. 6.1.1.

(i) Transfer of a market and a customer base

The court ruling I R 152/82 concerned the transfer of an 'export market' free of charge by a lower-tier subsidiary to a higher-tier subsidiary.[43] As this 'export market' failed to fulfil the criteria of a '*Teilbetrieb*' (operating unit) the local tax office came to the conclusion that the transfer of this 'market' did not constitute a transfer of goodwill. However, the tax office assessed this as a hidden distribution (transfer) of an asset comparable to goodwill, 'market and customer base'. The Federal Tax Court made it clear that the lower tax court had not given due consideration to the fact that according to the taxpayer the customers of the lower-tier subsidiary consisted only of two group companies. If a hidden profit distribution was to be assumed, the higher-tier subsidiary would have had to have been in receipt of an asset value which it had not previously held. On the other hand, the Federal Tax Court found that the lower-tier subsidiary could have granted an advantage to the higher-tier subsidiary in that it agreed to cancel immediately an existing contractual relationship without demanding any compensation. Since this called for further clarification of the facts, the revision appeal led to the cancellation of the ruling of the lower tax court and the referral back to the lower tax court.

In contrast to the decision I R 152/82, the decision I R 150/82 of the same date dealt with the transfer of an operating unit between sister companies without compensation for the goodwill actually concerned.[44] The Federal Tax Court saw this process as constituting a hidden distribution of the goodwill to the common parent company and its subsequent contribution to the sister company receiving the advantage. In more recent decisions, the Federal Tax Court no longer maintained the idea that for tax purposes the transfer of goodwill could only be carried out in the context of an operation or an operating unit.[45]

---

[43] Bundesfinanzhof, Judgment of 20 August 1986 I R 152/82, *Bundesfinanzhof Rulings/not to be published* (journal) 1987, 471.

[44] Bundesfinanzhof, Judgment of 20 August 1986 I R 150/82, BStBl II 1987, 455.

[45] Cf. Bundesfinanzhof, Judgment of 16 June 2004 X R 34/03, *Bundesfinanzhof Rulings/not to be published* (journal) 2004, 1701; Judgment of 27 March 2001 I R 42/00, BStBl II 2001, 771.

(ii)   Interpretation of 'Geschäftsbeziehung' (business relationship) as a legal term

The interpretation of the term 'business relationship' by the Federal Tax Court (I R 97/88, I R 94/88, I R 85/99, I R 5–6/02, I R 28/07, I R 26/08)[46] has been discussed above in the course of describing the historical development of section 1 of the FTA.[47] The term 'business relationship' now covers 'any contractual relationship affecting income, other than an agreement between a company and its shareholders'.

(iii)   Interest rate to be applied

Judgment I R 93/93 concerned a loan agreement between German shareholders and a Canadian corporation.[48] The local tax office found the agreed interest rate to be inappropriately low and adjusted the profit of the German shareholders on the basis of section 1 of the FTA. For the purposes of this adjustment the local tax office took as its orientation the average interest rates payable in the year of dispute for current account overdrafts, taking as a basis an interest rate of 14 per cent. The Federal Tax Court ruled that in the case of loans of private individuals, the decisive interest rate is in the first place the bank borrowing rate. When taking the usual borrowing rate as a basis, it has to be borne in mind, they found, that the loan was granted by private persons. It was to be taken into account with interest-raising effect if insufficient collateral was available for the loan. In the case that such circumstances justify no other result, the tax court can, according to the Federal Tax Court, take it as a guiding basis that the loan granter and the loan recipient will in case of doubt share equally the range between the usual bank lending rate and borrowing rate.

A similar result was already achieved in the Federal Tax Court's decision I R 83/87.[49] The court ruled that the interest rate being appropriate for the individual case is to be determined by estimate within the range between the usual bank lending rate and borrowing rate, giving

---

[46] Bundesfinanzhof, Judgment of 30 May 1990 I R 97/88, BStBl II 1990, 875; Judgment of 5 December 1990 I R 94/88, BStBl II 1991, 287; Judgment of 29 November 2000 I R 85/99, BStBl II 2002, 720; Judgment of 28 April 2004 I R 5–6/02, BStBl II 2005, 516; Judgment of 27 August 2008 I R 28/07, *Bundesfinanzhof Rulings/not to be published* (journal) 2009, 123.

[47] See section 6.3 above.

[48] Bundesfinanzhof, Judgment of 19 January 1994 I R 93/93, BStBl II 1994, 725.

[49] Bundesfinanzhof, Judgment of 28 February 1990 I R 83/87, BStBl II 1990, 649.

particular weight to the risk that the loan may not be repaid. The court believes that, as a general rule, employing the bank lending rate is not justified, in particular if the company in question is not operating a bank business and, therefore, is not burdened with the corresponding expenses. Where no other evidence is perceptible, the arm's length principle does not preclude an assessment being based on the empirical judgement that private loan granter and loan recipients share equally the range between the usual bank lending rate and borrowing rate.

(iv)   Long-term losses

The decision I R 3/92 concerned a German distributor company suffering from long-term losses resulting from the distribution of branded goods of its Danish parent company.[50] The tax auditors objected to the fact that since the launch of these products in Germany the Danish parent company did not participate in the considerable expenses that arose at the level of the German company from advertising and introducing the products on the German market. As the auditors expected the parent company to compensate its subsidiary for these expenses, they treated the corresponding 'waiver' as hidden profit distribution. The Tax Court decided in favour of the taxpayer and permitted revision appeal to the Federal Tax Court. This latter court set the decision of the tax court aside and, for purposes of further determination of the facts and circumstances, referred the legal matter back to the tax court. The Federal Tax Court found that an orderly and diligent business manager of a distributor company would introduce and sell products in the market if, based on a careful forecast, he can expect an appropriate total profit. In this context, it was to be assumed that in the start-up phase the loss period does not exceed a horizon of three years. But the conclusion reached by the tax court went no further than the assumption that in the context of a long-term market strategy, the distributor company achieves an appropriate profit. It did not, however, state in concrete terms that in a long-term market strategy the company will accrue an appropriate profit without participation of the producer in the advertising and introductory costs. As the Federal Tax Court could not itself scrutinise the considerations of the tax court, it deemed it necessary for the facts and circumstances to be further clarified by the latter court.

---

[50] Bundesfinanzhof, Judgment of 17 February 1993 I R 3/92, BStBl II 1993, 457.

The case I R 92/00 dealt with the treatment of expenses in connection with the activities of a company suffering from long-term losses.[51] The Federal Tax Court stated that it cannot be decisive whether the activity had promised to be successful when viewed in retrospect. It was further to be taken into account that the profit outlook for a new business activity can only be assessed after a start-up phase has occurred, and that losses cannot constitute grounds for assuming that there is no intention of achieving profit, provided that the company reacts by taking suitable measures. This would only be otherwise if it can be concluded that no viable business plan exists, or that the activity serves, from the outset, private interests or the interests of the shareholder.

Losses also constitute the issue in question in the legal matter I R 22/04.[52] The case concerned a distributor company which, after a price rise, achieved only below-average yield from marketing the products of its Swiss sister group company, and in the year of dispute even had negative income. Following on from the judgment I R 3/92, the Federal Tax Court ruled that a distributor company will not normally accept purchase prices which will only allow the products concerned to be sold at a loss. The taxpayer was able to show that the intra-group pricing was based on a price list applying equally in relation to other buyers from the foreign sister company. But according to the decision of the Federal Tax Court the employment of this 'comparable uncontrolled price method' requires that the price under consideration and the comparable price must be derived from at least essentially similar exchange of goods or services. This is not the case if on the basis of the prices stated, the distributor company has no possibility of making an appropriate distributing profit (disregarding short-term, temporary 'lean periods'). No fixed rules apply, but it is one of the acknowledged principles that the cost price paid by a distributor company can be checked with the help of the resale price method. In this context, where companies distribute both products of an associated company and comparable goods from other manufacturers, looking at the margins earned on products from other manufacturers can supply important reference information.

---

[51] Bundesfinanzhof, Judgment of 15 May 2001 I R 92/00, *Bundesfinanzhof Rulings* (journal) 199, 217.

[52] Bundesfinanzhof, Judgment of 6 April 2005 I R 22/04, BStBl II 2007, 658; see also Judgment of 17 October 2001 I R 103/00, BStBl II 2004, 171.

In the decision I R 103/00,[53] the Federal Tax Court ruled that substantial losses over a three-year period elicit a refutable presumption that the agreed transfer price is inappropriate and motivated by the company relationship. This applies in particular if the trading of group-internally manufactured products constitutes more or less the entire business activity of the distributor company. In the context of its onus to present evidence, the taxpayer can demonstrate why the development is in fact due to other reasons. If the presentation of such evidence is successful, losses can be allowed even beyond the period of three years, provided that the taxpayer implements any adjustment measures that may be necessary.

(v) Passing on right of use of a group and brand name

The decision I R 12/99 concerned payment for the right of a group-affiliated company to use the group name and logo.[54] The tax authorities treated the licence charge paid as a hidden profit distribution. The tax court dismissed the action brought against this decision since it recognised no deductibility of payments within the group constellation. The Federal Tax Court overruled this decision and referred the case back to the tax court for further clarification of the facts. In its decision, the Federal Tax Court was following a point of differentiation discussed in German specialist literature which resulted in the view that rights to use of names and company names, on the one hand, are to be distinguished from brand names and trademark rights, on the other. Trademark rights as product-identifying designations are to be distinguished from company names. This is necessary even when brand and company names are identical; the right to use of the name must then be subordinate at least to a certain extent to the right of trademark. It is thus decisive whether the payment is made for granting entitlement to use of the company name or for the brand name. The right of use to brand names stands in the foreground if the rights connected with the granting of the brand are suited to promoting sales. If the licence recipient is able to improve his own position, irrespective of holding a good reputation of his own, he will be prepared to pay for the granting of the trademark rights.

(vi) Duty to cooperate

The judgment I R 103/00 caused the German legislator to undertake a comprehensive overhaul of the regulations concerning taxpayer documentation and cooperation in the area of transfer prices. The crux of the

---

[53] See section 6.5.3 below.
[54] Bundesfinanzhof, Judgment of 9 August 2000 I R 12/99, BStBl II 2001, 140.

decision was determination of arm's length price for products that a German distributor company had purchased intra-group. In addition to the questions of how these prices are to be set, what data is to be referred to or used as the basis for the setting of the transfer prices, and how to deal with a possible range of different products, the prime issue here concerned clarification of the cooperation duties to be met by the taxpayer. The significance of this judgment was underlined not only by its length. It was also apparent in the fact that it took four years for the tax authorities to recognise it officially[55] and put forward a proposal for legislation.[56]

The case concerned a group-affiliated distributor company generating gross profit margins on product sales in Germany of 18 to 24 per cent. The tax authorities saw fit to adjust the margins to 26 to 28 per cent. The Federal Tax Court criticised this on the grounds that the estimate by the tax court was in breach of the rules of procedure in that the tax court saw the use of anonymous data as generally impermissible. According to the court rulings of the Federal Tax Court the utilisation of anonymous data is permissible. Should doubt exist as to the quality of data collection, however, the legal relevance of this data can be lowered.

Moreover, the Federal Tax Court denied the duty of the taxpayer to provide evidence for appropriate transfer prices in the disputed case, stating that at the time of the ruling, no specified documentation and recording duties were in place. These statements have since become obsolete in Germany, the legislator having introduced new regulations in this respect in 2003.

In respect to methodology, the Federal Tax Court declared that an in-house arm's length comparison cannot be carried out on the basis of the resale price method if the comparison involves only three non-affiliated manufacturers, the purchases do not cover all the relevant years, and the purchases constitute a maximum of 5 per cent of the overall turnover. And the Federal Tax Court also addressed the question as to whether, in the event of a range of possible transfer prices resulting, the estimate must be oriented to the high end, the low end or a median value. For the setting of transfer prices in Germany the considerations of the Federal Tax Court on this matter have been superseded, as the German legislator

---

[55] Bundesfinanzhof, Judgment of 17 October 2001 I R 103/00, BStBl II 2004, 171; resolution of 10 May 2001, *Bundesfinanhof Rulings* (journal) 194, 360.

[56] See sections 6.3.2 and 6.4.2 above with respect to the initiative regarding documentation and penalty provisions.

set out detailed regulations on this in the 2008 Corporate Tax Reform.[57] Pursuant to these, the margin of possible arm's length values, for example, must be narrowed down if the setting of transfer prices is to be based on values of limited comparability. The pronouncements concerning losses given in the Federal Tax Court judgment I R 103/00 have already been dealt with above.[58]

(vii) Transfer prices for goods

As far as is apparent, the Federal Tax Court has made statements on transfer prices for goods in only three recent judgments. These were discussed above in the context of sustained losses (I R 3/92, I R 22/04, I R 103/00), so that the reader may be referred here to those judgments.[59]

(viii) Concerns based on European law

In view of the sense of 'adjustment of income', discussions have been in progress in Germany concerning a possible conflict of section 1 of the FTA, not only since the decision of the European Court of Justice in the *SGI* matter.[60] The 'adjustment of income' (section 1 of the FTA) is limited to business transactions with foreign countries, so that due to the existing differences between the various correction formulas both in application and also in their legal consequences, many doubts exist as to whether the regulations of section 1 of the FTA are compatible with European law. Particularly apparent is the difference in connection with transfers of right of use, which in the cross-border context are covered by section 1 of the FTA, while in the domestic context these are exempted from correction. In addition, also reference to the arm's length principle and its implementation in detail (median value, the required transparency of information, and the provisions for subsequent price adjustment) give rise to unequal treatment of comparable facts and circumstances which differ only in their domestic or foreign context. These differences are particularly striking in connection with the regulations on shift of functions. If no third party values of limited

---

[57] See section 6.4 above.   [58] See section 6.5.3 above.

[59] Bundesfinanzhof, Judgment of 17 February 1993 I R 3/92, BStBl II 1993, 457; Judgment of 17 October 2001 I R 103/00, BStBl II 2004, 171; Judgment of 6 April 2005 I R 22/04, BStBl II 2007, 658.

[60] *Société de Gestion Industrielle (SGI)* v. *État belge* (C-311/08), European Court of Justice, Judgment of the Court (Third Chamber) of 21 January 2010 (reference for a preliminary ruling from the Tribunal de première instance de Mons, Belgium) [2010] OJ C63/8.

comparability can be found, the taxpayer is to base his transfer pricing on a hypothetical third-party comparison looking at the profit potential for each party for the function to be transferred. Moreover, it should not be overlooked that business relationships involving foreign transactions between related parties are subject to higher documentation obligations while also standing under particular sanctioning mechanisms (section 90(3) of the FC; section 162(3), (4) of the FC; and Ordinance regarding the Documentation of Profit Attributions). Doubts concerning the compatibility of section 1 of the FTA with European law have also been expressed by the Federal Tax Court[61] and the Tax Courts of Düsseldorf and Münster,[62] though from the German perspective no presentation has yet been made before the European Court of Justice.

6.6   Transfer pricing disputes: bilateral and multilateral approaches

6.6.1   Approaches employed

DTA mutual agreement and arbitration procedures

According to the relevant double taxation agreement (DTA) articles, a mutual agreement procedure (MAP) can be initiated if there is a possibility of double taxation occurring which the nation concerned cannot prevent through unilateral measures (mutual agreement procedure in the narrower sense). Such procedures are designed to avoid double taxation and in cases of transfer prices are aimed at achieving bilateral agreement in contractually determining an adjustment of profit. Initiation of a MAP is also possible in order to remove (i) difficulties or doubts arising in the interpretation or application of a DTA ('consultation procedure') or (ii) cases of double taxation which are not dealt with by double taxation agreements.[63] A MAP may further be initiated if

---

[61] Bundesfinanzhof, Judgment of 29 November 2000, BStBl II 2002, 720; Bundesfinanzhof, Judgment of 21 June 2001, *Bundesfinanzhof Rulings/not to be published* (journal) 2001, 1169.

[62] Tax Court of Düsseldorf, Judgment of 19 February 2008, *Tax Court Rulings* (journal) 2008, 1006; court case waived by Bundesfinanzhof, Judgment of 29 April 2009, *Bundesfinanzhof Rulings/not to be published* (journal) 2009, 1648; Tax Court of Münster, Judgment of 22 February 2008, *Tax Court Rulings* (journal) 2008, 923, revision withdrawn.

[63] Ministry of Finance, Memorandum on international mutual agreement and arbitration procedures in the field of taxes on income and capital, Communication of 13 July 2006 IV B 6–B 1300–340/06, BStBl I 2006, S 461, No. 1.2.1; in comparison to the mutual agreement procedures, consultation procedures are of considerably lower significance.

a DTA does not include a corresponding article. However, MAPs may not result in the case being resolved, although from a German perspective in many cases they lead to a successful outcome.[64] It is possible for the negotiations to end without a result or for the outcomes achieved to be implemented incompletely or not at all. A problem commonly apparent in this process is that the procedures frequently last too long and there is no obligation for the parties to come to a consensus.

Arbitration procedures provide for the extension of a MAP in the form of a 'procedure for the binding resolution of disputes concerning the interpretation or application of DTAs by one or several arbitrators' on application by the taxpayer. This only applies if the competent authorities are not able to come to an agreement within a certain given period. The OECD gives this process a maximum duration of two years. The period normally begins when the case in dispute (and its associated documents) is submitted. However, this can only happen once double taxation has actually occurred.

According to the OECD model, arbitration procedures can be applied to all unresolved issues of the case. However, this does not hold for issues already decided upon by a court in one of the nations involved. Nor is it possible to pursue an arbitration procedure and domestic appeal in parallel. Rather, the domestic appeal proceedings have to be interrupted until the arbitration court has come to a decision. The taxpayer then has the possibility of either accepting the arbitration decision and waiving the domestic appeal or rejecting it and continuing with the domestic appeal procedure.

EU arbitration procedure

The articles of the EU Arbitration Convention provide for a MAP in the narrower sense only with respect to profit allocation issues between associated enterprises and profit attribution to permanent establishments. This includes also profit adjustments arising from financial transactions including loans and loan conditions provided that they are based on the arm's length principle.[65] If the contracting states are unable to come to an agreement in a MAP based on the Arbitration Convention (phase 1), the procedure has then to be continued under the conditions of an arbitration procedure according to the provisions of the Arbitration Convention (phase 2).

---

[64] German Bundestag, printed matter 16/8027 of 11 February 2008, p. 7.
[65] Revised Code of Conduct, 2009/C322/01/01, [2009] OJ C322/2, no. 2.

Table 6.9 German MAP statistics for the 2009 reporting period

Year MAP case was initiated	Opening inventory on first day of reporting period		Initiated during reporting period		Completed during reporting period		Closed or withdrawn with double taxation during reporting period		Ending inventory on last day of reporting period		Average cycle time for cases completed, closed or withdrawn during reporting period (in months)	
	OECD	Non-OECD	OECD	Non-OECD	OECD	Non-OECD	OECD	Non-OECD	OECD	Non-OECD	OECD	Non-OECD
2003 or prior	39	11			18	2	1	1	20	8	N/A	N/A
2004	25	2			3	0	1	0	21	2		
2005	44	4			8	1	2	0	34	3		
2006	96	4			27	1	3	0	66	3		
2007	123	5			38	0	0	0	85	5		
2008	162	4			24	0	3	0	121	4		
2009			174	3	5	0	1	0	167	4		
Total	489	30	174	3	123	4	11	1	514	29		

6.6.2 Mutual agreement and arbitration procedures according to DTAs

Germany has included the possibility of applying for the initiation of a MAP in numerous DTAs.[66] Here, the application can be submitted to the tax authority locally responsible or to the Bundeszentralamt für Steuern (Federal Central Tax Office).[67] The application can be made also if an appeal is pending according to German tax law or the law of another nation or legal redress has not yet been exhausted, and has to be made without delay. Many DTAs contain specific time limitations which have to be taken into account. Where no time limitation is stated in a DTA, the German tax authorities do not in principle accept the initiation of a MAP if a period of more than four years has elapsed between notification of taxation and application by the taxpayer (see Table 6.9).

The precondition for making an application to initiate a MAP is that taxation is not in line with the terms of a DTA. Where the application is addressed to the German tax authorities, the tax administration first has to examine whether the double taxation can be removed by way of a domestic measure. If so, the German tax authorities are required to undertake such measures. Otherwise, the Federal Central Tax Office has to initiate a MAP, provided the relevant prerequisites are given. In the case that the MAP is initiated by a foreign tax authority, the German Federal Central Tax Office only examines the formal preconditions (see Table 6.10).

Assuming that a MAP goes ahead, the necessary facts and circumstances are to be determined *ex officio* by the locally responsible tax authorities. The applicant is obliged to cooperate in this process. Moreover, the results of the investigations by the foreign tax authority are to be considered. Over and above this, the DTA exchange of information clauses and the provisions of the EG Amtshilfegesetz (European

---

[66] Ministry of Finance, Memorandum on international mutual agreement and arbitration procedures in the field of taxes on income and capital, Communication of 13 July 2006 IV B 6–B 1300–340/06, BStBl I 2006, S 461, no. 2.

[67] The Federal Ministry of Finance has transferred the responsibilities for tasks of a competent authority with respect to MAPs according to DTA and the Arbitration Convention to the Federal Tax Office (s. 5(1) no. 5 of the Finanzverwaltungsgesetz, Tax Administration Act (TMA)). See Federal Ministry of Finance, tasks of the Central Federal Tax Office according to s. 5(1) no. 5 of the TMA; Communication of 20 June 2011 IV B 5–O 1000/09/10507–04, BStBl I 2011, S 674. The Federal Tax Office acts in agreement with the responsible local authorities. It is the task of these authorities to implement the MAP domestically.

Table 6.10 *Development of German MAP inventory for the period from 2006 to 2009*

Reporting period	Opening inventory on first day of reporting period	Initiated during reporting period	Completed during reporting period	Closed or withdrawn with double taxation during reporting period	Ending inventory on last day of reporting period
2006	444	212	155	25	476
2007	476	186	125	11	526
2008	527	177	171	14	519
2009	519	179	127	12	543

Communities Administrative Assistance Act) are also to be taken into account in the MAP. The tax authorities concerned can draw up together a joint report on the result of these investigations proposing also a joint assessment of the facts and circumstances and basic figures for obtaining a solution. If it is possible for mutual agreement to be found with the taxpayer by other channels, it is not necessary for a report to be prepared. Irrespective of this, the taxpayer can submit applications in the framework of the MAP and make statements on the facts and legal questions under consideration. The participants in the MAP, however, are only the tax authorities of the contracting states. They are responsible for achieving mutual agreement and notifying the taxpayer covered by the DTA about the outcomes.

In order to implement the results of the MAP, the tax assessment notice has, if necessary, to be amended. In this context, the German Abgabenordnung (Fiscal Code) states that the period in which the tax assessment notice can be subject to amendment shall not be deemed to terminate before the end of one year following the effective date of mutual agreement (section 175 of the Fiscal Code). The precondition for amendments is that the applicant declares his consent to the implementation of the MAP, pending appeals are withdrawn and the applicant agrees to forego making any appeals with respect to the outcome of the MAP itself. In the event of a MAP failing to reach agreement, the locally responsible tax authority is obliged to examine whether double taxation can be avoided by reference to factual inequity. German tax authorities will not consider measures to achieve equitable treatment if the taxpayer has not properly observed formal administrative requirements, has failed to observe duties of cooperation, or has made false statements contributing to the double taxation that has occurred.

In a (small) number of its DTAs, Germany has included mutual agreement provisions entailing binding arbitration. A first example of this is the DTA with France,[68] according to which an arbitration panel can be consulted if no mutual agreement can be found within two years following submission of the application concerned (Article 25a of the France DTA). A similar option is available also in the case of the Canada DTA.[69] According to this treaty, difficulties or doubts concerning its interpretation or application which cannot be dealt with by the competent authorities can, by mutual consent of the competent authorities, be submitted to an arbitration panel (Article 25(6) of the Canada DTA).

The DTA arbitration clauses negotiated with Austria, Sweden and the United States, however, are different. According to the Austria DTA,[70] when it comes to arbitration the contracting states are required to refer the case to the European Court of Justice if difficulties or doubts arising in interpreting the DTA cannot be resolved by the competent authorities within three years of initiating the process on application by the taxpayer. In a comparable way, the United States DTA prescribes a mandatory arbitration procedure. However, in contrast to Austria, the United States DTA details regulations for performing the obligatory arbitration procedure. It begins in principle two years after initiation of the procedure unless the competent authorities have previously agreed on a different point in time (Article 25(6) of the United States DTA).[71]

According to the Sweden DTA,[72] application of the 'European Convention for the Peaceful Settlement of Disputes'[73] is prescribed in the event that the contracting states cannot come to any agreement in the MAP (Article 41(5) of the Sweden DTA). Accordingly, disputes under international law are in principle resolved before the International

---

[68] France DTA of 20 December 2001, BGBl II 2002, S 2372.

[69] Canada DTA of 19 April 2001, BGBl II 2002, S 671.

[70] Austria DTA of 24 August 2000, BGBl II 2002, S 735.

[71] United States DTA of 4 June 2008, BStBl I 2008, S 766.

[72] Sweden DTA of 14 July 1992, BStBl I 1994, S 422.

[73] Council of Europe, ETS No. 023, European Convention for the Peaceful Settlement of Disputes, Strasbourg, 29 April 1957.

Court of Justice in The Hague. But the contracting states can equally agree to convene an arbitration court.

6.6.3   *Mutual agreement and arbitration procedures according to the EU Arbitration Convention*

Within the EU the initiation of a mutual agreement or arbitration procedure can also be based on the EU Arbitration Convention in the case of profit adjustments between associated enterprises or the attribution of profits to permanent establishments.[74] Legally, the arbitration agreement has the status of a multilateral treaty under international law standing at the same level as a bilateral DTA.[75] As a consequence, disputes concerning transfer pricing may be resolved by both the Arbitration Convention and the DTA arbitration provision. As these procedures cannot be pursued in parallel, the (first) initiated process should have priority. This priority is normally without significance for the conducting and implementation of the procedure since the German Federal Ministry of Finance applies the relevant rules likewise for both procedures.[76] In terms of content, however, the provisions of the DTAs and the Arbitration Convention are identical with the result that the taxpayer may consider whether to base his application on potentially more favourable provisions of a DTA. In this case a change to the more favourable procedure should be possible as long as it is within the relevant limitations period.[77]

From the German perspective, dispute resolution on the basis of the EU Arbitration Convention has proved to be a real success story. As far

---

[74] See Chapter 5 'European Union'.

[75] Federal Ministry of Finance, Memorandum on international mutual agreement and arbitration procedures in the field of taxes on income and capital, dated 13 July 2006 IV B 6–B 1300–340/06, BStBl I 2006, S 461, 1.1.2.

[76] *Ibid.* 12.1.2.

[77] Where no deadline for application has been laid down in the applicable DTA the German tax authorities do not approve initiation of an arbitration agreement if a taxpayer has allowed a period of more than four years from notification of taxation to elapse before applying if no specific circumstances have ruled out earlier application, see Federal Ministry of Finance, Communication of 13 July 2006, BStBl I 2006, 461, no. 2.2.3; according to the Arbitration Convention this application is to be submitted within a period of three years from first notification of the taxation that has led to or could lead to double taxation. This period starts upon receipt of the first tax assessment notice leading to double taxation (Art. 6(1) sentence 2 of the Arbitration Convention); moreover see Federal Ministry of Finance, Communication of 13 July 2006, BStBl I 2006, 461, no. 11.2.1.

as is known, there have only been three cases in the EU which have proceeded to the second level of the relevant procedure (arbitration level). Although the number of mutual agreement procedures has remained consistently high, mutual agreement in the EU is achieved within the prescribed period by almost all parties entering into a MAP. This means that for all those opting for the procedure according to the EU Arbitration Convention, double taxation is effectively cancelled out.

6.7   Pricing agreements

6.7.1   Subject matter

To minimise time-consuming disputes regarding the appropriateness of tax transfer prices between the taxpayer and the tax authorities, for the past few years the Federal Republic of Germany has made available the instrument of the advance pricing agreement (APA). With binding effect within the agreed terms, an APA makes it possible to fix:

(a) the transfer pricing method(s) to be employed,
(b) for a particular type of transaction, and
(c) for a particular period of time,

with reference to the international allocation of income among the affiliated companies of a multinational enterprise. The same applies in the case of APAs regarding the attribution of profits to permanent establishments based on the arm's length principle. Generally, the parties to an APA agree on a range of appropriate transfer prices or margins that are acceptable if the enterprise makes use of the agreed transfer pricing method. With a view to future transactions it is furthermore necessary to lay down certain conditions which affect the nature of the business transactions under consideration significantly, as 'critical assumptions'. Such critical assumptions constitute a specific agreed contractual basis in the relationship between the contracting parties to the APA. These critical assumptions can include, for example, consistent shareholding ratios, and consistent market conditions, market shares, business volumes and sales prices.

Provided that the conditions laid down in an APA are fulfilled, the transfer prices applied are seen as being appropriate. As a result, subsequent audits are limited in scope to the question of whether the taxpayer has kept to the conditions agreed upon and fulfilled his corresponding reporting duties.

Unlike the practice commonly found internationally, the German system does not allow tax agreements between taxpayers and the German tax authorities. However, on the basis of a DTA containing a clause on mutual agreement procedures in line with Article 25 of the OECD Model Tax Convention or Article 6 of the EU Arbitration Convention, concluding a mutual agreement is not only permissible in order to resolve disputes concerning transactions that have already taken place (see section 6.6 above) but may also cover future transactions and be concluded in advance.[78]

Under international law, mutual agreements between Germany and a foreign state are binding with the result that the terms of a mutual agreement and the agreed provisions have to be observed. The instrument at hand in Germany to implement the mutual agreement procedure (in advance) is the binding (advance) ruling. Parties to the application procedure for an APA are the taxpayer (applicant) and the Federal Central Tax Office as 'competent authority'. Parties to the advance agreement procedure itself are the 'competent authorities' of the contracting states and not the taxpayer with the associated enterprise. Parties to the advance ruling are the taxpayer (applicant) and the locally responsible tax office.

Since 2006, Germany has had concrete procedural regulations for carrying out an APA. According to the German perception, the mutual agreement between the competent authorities and the advance ruling between the taxpayer and the locally responsible tax office form together the APA ('Doppelpack'). As a consequence, transfer price rulings can in principle only be given if prior to this a mutual agreement has been concluded. However, in the absence of a DTA the tax authorities may, upon application, make a unilateral commitment if the circumstances appear to allow this and there is justified interest in obtaining such ruling.[79] A unilateral APA agreed by the taxpayer with a foreign tax authority is not binding for the German tax authorities. The taxpayer, however, can make an application for the German tax authorities to commit themselves correspondingly in the same unilateral way.

---

[78] Cf. Federal Ministry of Finance, Communication of 13 July 2006 IV B 6–S 1300–340/06, BStBl I 2006, 461.
[79] Cf. Federal Ministry of Finance, Communication of 29 December 2003, BStBl I 2003, 742.

6.7.2   Procedure

Since 1 September 2004, the Federal Central Tax Office as competent authority has been responsible for carrying out the APA procedure in Germany (section 5(1) No. 5 of the Finanzverwaltungsgesetz).[80] This is the office that also concludes the APA with the foreign tax authorities. With respect to the taxpayer, the local tax authorities of the Länder hold responsibility. They give the advance ruling and issue the tax assessment notices accordingly.

APAs are application-dependent. For the purpose of appropriate examination of transfer prices, applicants must inform the tax authorities fully of important facts known to them and assist them in the further clarification of all facts and circumstances of the case. An application requires justified interest on the part of the taxpayer in the conducting and concluding of the APA procedure.

Among the documents and records required in many cases for purposes of carrying out an APA are a description of shareholding ratios, a description of the organisational and operative structure of the group, a description of the operative areas, insofar as is required for the APA, a description of the business relations with associated enterprises (planned contractual arrangements), a description and explanation of the functions and risks assumed, a list and brief description of the main assets (in particular intangibles) of significance to the business relations at issue, a description of the market situation, competition and the business strategy/strategies chosen, a description and assessment of the planned value-added chains, and contributions from the companies involved, and a list of all outstanding tax issues (also in relation to other tax administrations) connected with the transactions to be covered by the APA.

Prior to making the decision on whether to file for initiation of an APA, 'pre-filing meetings' may be helpful. In such a prior meeting, the subject and content of an APA are agreed upon. A further point of discussion concerns the documents that will be required for conducting the procedure. Moreover, the time frame and prospects of agreement with the foreign tax authorities can be explored. Consultants can act in such pre-filing on a no-name basis on behalf

---

[80] Moreover, see Federal Ministry of Finance, Tasks of the Federal Central Tax Office according to s. 5(1) no. 5 of the Finanzverwaltungsgesetz (Tax Administration Law), Communication of 20 June 2011 IV B 5–O 1000/09/10507–04, BStBl I 2011, S 674.

of their clients. In cases such as these, however, any statements made by the tax authorities are not binding.

Decisions with regard to content and area of application lie with the taxpayer. As a result, the taxpayer can make his application in terms of functions, persons or regions, making reference to transactions with particular parties or countries. Any limitations must not be made arbitrarily. Implications for taxpayers in third countries have also to be taken into account. As a rule, the subject matter of an APA relates to agreement on employment of one or several transfer pricing methods for certain transactions or types of transactions. In addition, the prices or margins, arrangements for extrapolation of the agreement within the duration of the APA, or adjustment measures can also be taken up in the agreement. However, the tax authorities make provisions that go beyond the methodology for determining transfer prices dependent on the fact that they are underpinned by critical assumptions.

Example: Enterprise A applies to fix in advance the loan interest rate for an intra-group loan with the help of an APA. If, for example, A is planning to set a variable interest rate based on the development of a particular index such as LIBOR, the premium is dependent on A's creditworthiness. Here, it can be agreed upon that the relevant premium is to be made dependent on the condition that A's rating or creditworthiness does not change. This can be built in via critical assumptions.[81]

Typical 'critical assumptions' are, for example, consistent shareholding ratios and consistent market conditions, market shares, business volumes, sales prices (e.g., no drastic changes due to new technology), giving a framework in each case. The German codes of practice also cite consistent conditions, e.g., relating to supervisory rights, customs duties, import and export restrictions, international payment transactions, consistent allocation of functions and risks, consistent capital structure, consistent business model, consistent exchange rates and interest rates, tax levied in accordance with the APA in the other country, no substantial changes to the tax circumstances prevailing in the other country, and corrections to transfer prices by a third-party country not involved in the APA, which have an effect on the APA. In the German view, the taxpayer should put forward suggestions as to the critical assumptions applying to the APA from his perspective. He should also elucidate to

---

[81] Cf. *OECD Transfer Pricing Guidelines for Multinational Enterprises and Tax Administrations* (July 2010) para. 4.125.

what extent the proposed transfer price method allows changes to the critical assumptions to be taken into account. Critical assumptions and the subject matter of the APA must be so interdependent that changes to the critical assumptions are likely to influence or place in question the material agreements of the APA.

In principle, APAs apply to a future time period. They therefore normally begin with the start of the business year in which the APA application is made. Under certain circumstances, the German tax authorities approve an earlier starting point. Negotiations with the foreign authorities on a roll back of the agreement to a period preceding contractual terms are also possible.

The Federal Central Tax Office takes the decision to open an APA procedure. This decision must take appropriate account of the taxpayer's interest. The application's compatibility with German accounting principles, the international enforceability and consistency with economic reality are also factors that play a role. If, for example, it becomes clear that the taxpayer's application is based primarily on an interest in tax avoidance, the Federal Central Tax Office can, in mutual agreement with the highest responsible authority in the Land, reject it. The same applies if the taxpayer refuses to cooperate to the required extent or fails to supply information.

Cooperation, information and flexibility in terms of time are significant not only at the opening of the procedure but for the success of the entire course of an APA. Although the applicant does not actually participate in the agreement as the procedure is in the hands of the Federal Central Tax Office (who concludes the agreement) and the tax authorities of the Länder (which are involved in scrutinising it and deciding upon it), he has a duty to cooperate, to provide information, and to submit documents.

Once an APA has been concluded, it is binding for the tax authorities involved. This depends on the fulfilment of the facts and circumstances constituting the basis of the APA and the critical assumptions. The tax authorities are, therefore, entitled to check whether these conditions are being met in the framework of a (regular) tax audit. If the conditions as set out in the critical assumptions are not fulfilled, the tax authorities are no longer bound by the agreement. On the other hand, the tax authorities are not permitted to deviate from the results of the APA if the audit reveals that the taxpayer has applied it properly. They are also bound by the provisions agreed in the APA even if the taxpayer chooses to employ deviating prices, margins and transfer pricing methods (and therefore have a right to make corresponding adjustments). The taxpayer, however, is not obliged to realise the transaction as planned and on the basis of which the APA has been concluded. In this case, the APA has no legal consequence.

6.8   Concluding remarks

The arm's length principle as developed at the level of the OECD has long been established in German tax law and will be 'celebrating its fortieth anniversary' in 2012. Unlike the various domestic corrective instruments (in particular the 'hidden profit distribution' and the 'hidden capital contribution') where the legal prerequisites and individual conditions result in large part from corresponding rulings of the Federal Tax Court, over the last forty years this principle has been elaborated in parallel with the work of the OECD by means of general guidelines and specific regulations. The specific regulations concern in particular the application of the arm's length principle to permanent establishments, cost sharing agreements, the posting of employees and the transfer of functions (business reorganisations). Moreover, the obligations of a German national regarding records and cooperation with the tax administration with respect to foreign business relationships are regulated and explained in detail. For these purposes, the legal basis of the arm's length principle in Germany (section 1 of the FTA) to some extent called for correction and amendment. Currently (November 2011) the legislator is working on a further extension of the 'adjustment of income' provision aiming at implementing in German tax law the '2010 Authorised OECD Approach' regarding the attribution of profits to permanent establishments.

Although the constituent elements of the arm's length principle are regulated in detail, the application of this principle to the individual case remains difficult. It is not unusual for taxpayer and tax administration to be of a different opinion with respect to this application in a given situation. According to experience gained in the past, however, in most cases these disputes can be resolved in consultation with representatives of the local tax office or the representatives of the Federal Central Tax Office during final meetings of a field audit. From interviews of tax directors it is known that companies seek to avoid the often long-lasting and cost-intensive domestic court procedures, especially since the result of such disputes is often uncertain. In this context, however, Germany constitutes no exception. A comprehensive survey of all transfer pricing cases dealt with over the past decade by the courts in Australia, Canada, the United Kingdom and the United States shows that in this period no more than sixteen cases were decided in court.[82]

More succesful instruments appear to be advance pricing agreements and mutual agreement procedures. Following the implementation of a formal APA process in 2005, the APA team at the Federal Central Tax Office has received an increasing number of APA requests from taxpayers per year. Although the average duration of an APA is some two to three years, such a process makes it possible to fix the relevant conditions of a cross-border business relationship with binding effect within the agreed terms.

Additionally, a consistently high number of double taxation issues are resolved annually under the mutual agreement procedure. Here, the average duration of such proceedings ranges between three and four years. Even if it is not known externally to what extent these proceedings indeed result in resolving the underlying transfer pricing disputes, the reported figures at EU level make it clear that dispute resolution on the basis of the EU Arbitration Convention has proved to be a real success story. Against this background and as is apparent from more recent double taxation agreements (although not all),[83] it appears to best serve the practical issues of corporate taxpayers that Germany places particular emphasis on providing for the extension of mutual agreement procedures in the form of a binding resolution of disputes (arbitration procedures).

---

[82] Cf. J. Roin, 'Transfer Pricing in the Courts: A Cross-Country Comparison' in W. Schön and K. A. Konrad, *Fundamentals of International Transfer Pricing in Law and Economics* (Berlin/Heidelberg, 2012); A. Oestreicher, 'Comments on Julie Roin "Transfer Pricing in the Courts: A Cross-Country Comparison", in *ibid.*

[83] See, e.g., Agreement between the Federal Republic of Germany and the Principality of Liechtenstein for the Avoidance of Double Taxation and Tax Evasion with respect to Taxes on Income and Property of 17 November 2011; this, however, is not the case in respect of the Agreement between the Federal Republic of Germany and the Republic of Turkey for the Avoidance of Double Taxation and Tax Evasion with respect to Taxes on Income of 19 September 2011, the Agreement between the Federal Republic of Germany and the Republic of Hungary for the Avoidance of Double Taxation and Tax Evasion with respect to Taxes on Income and Property of 28 February 2011, and the Agreement between the Federal Republic of Germany and the Kingdom of Spain for the Avoidance of Double Taxation and Tax Evasion with respect to Taxes on Income of 3 February 2011.

Appendix: Questionnaire (Germany)

1. The structure of the law for solving transfer pricing disputes. *What is the structure of the law of the country for solving transfer pricing disputes? For example, is the mutual agreement procedure (MAP), as regulated in the relevant tax treaty, the standard method for solving transfer pricing disputes?*

In Germany, administrative courts have the task of protecting subjects in the case of official action. In tax matters, the tax courts are called upon to judge as specialised administrative courts. In order to prevent tax courts being flooded with law suits, the court procedure is preceded by an administrative appeals procedure which gives the tax authority the opportunity to scrutinise the cases once again ('preliminary procedure'). However, the tax authorities in Germany can order tax audits to be carried out even before the tax notice is issued. They decide with due discretion whether and, if so, when a tax audit is to be conducted. For these purposes, taxable parties subject to tax audits are put into categories in terms of size which distinguish between large businesses, medium-sized businesses, small businesses and very small businesses. Even though the large part of additional tax arises from audit of the large businesses, for reasons of equitability these audits cannot be limited to this category. Experience shows that personal exchange between the authorities and the taxpayers has dispute-arbitrating effect. This is why a meeting concerning the result of the tax audit is to be held at the end of the process (final meeting), unless, as a result of the tax audit, there is no change to the tax base, or if the taxpayer decides to forego such a meeting. In the course of a final meeting, as well as disputed matters, the legal assessment of the results of the audit and its tax consequences will be discussed. In cases where the taxpayer and the tax authorities cannot agree on a common view in the case of the tax audit, the taxpayer is entitled to take legal recourse with respect to the tax assessment. In tax matters, the administrative appeals procedure is termed *Einspruch* (objection). If such an objection is admissible, the tax authorities are required not only to reassess the initial decision in its entire scope, but also to clarify the facts and circumstances of the case. Upon application or (in certain circumstances) *ex officio*, the authorities are required to open the tax documentation and may (*ex officio*) or should (upon application by the applicant) discuss the facts and legal status of the case prior to making the appeal decision (hearing). This regulation serves, on the one hand, to realise the principle of '*rechtliches Gehör*' (legal hearing) and, on the other hand, has the further aim of promoting mutual solution of the appeal, thereby reducing the number of disputes to be dealt with in court. If the out-of-court legal remedy fails to bring success, in disputes concerning tax matters, the taxpayer can take recourse to the fiscal court. The tax courts decide in a first legal action as an interlocutory hearing whereas the Federal Tax Court functions explicitly as a court of appeals proceeding for appeals and complaints against initial decisions of the tax courts. But review of the facts and circumstances by the tax courts requires the fulfilment of admissibility conditions. Legal remedies are the revision appeal and complaint to the Federal Tax Court. Revision appeals are directed against judgments whereas complaints can be made in the context of all other decisions or resolutions of the tax court. Revision appeals have to be admitted as a general principle. As an alternative measure to taking recourse to the fiscal court, according to the relevant double taxation agreement articles, a mutual agreement procedure can be initiated if there is a possibility of double taxation occurring which the nation concerned cannot prevent through unilateral measures (mutual agreement procedure in the narrower sense). Germany has included the possibility of applying for the initiation of a mutual agreement procedure in numerous double taxation agreements. However, mutual agreement procedures may not result in the case being resolved, although from a German perspective in many cases they lead to a successful outcome. Arbitration procedures provide for the extension of a mutual agreement procedure in the form of a 'procedure for the binding resolution of disputes concerning the interpretation or application of double taxation agreements by one or several arbitrators' on application by the taxpayer. In a (small) number of its double taxation agreements, Germany has included mutual agreement provisions entailing binding arbitration. Within the EU, the initiation of a mutual agreement or arbitration procedure can also be based on the EU Arbitration Convention in the case of profit adjustments between associated enterprises or the attribution of profits to permanent establishments.

2. Policy for solving transfer pricing disputes. *Is there a gap between the nominal and effective method for solving transfer pricing disputes in the country? For example, has the country a strategic policy not to enforce the arm's length standard (ALS) for fear of driving foreign direct investment to other competing jurisdictions?*

There is no gap between the nominal and effective method for solving transfer pricing disputes in Germany. In particular, Germany does not pursue any strategic policy not to enforce the arm's length standard for fear of driving foreign direct investment to other competing jurisdictions.

3. The prevailing dispute resolution method. *Which is the most frequent method for solving transfer pricing disputes in the country? Does it have a positive externality? For example, is the MAP the most frequent method, and if so, to what extent have successful MAPs been used as a proxy for transfer pricing case law? For instance, Procter & Gamble (P&G) obtained a bilateral advance pricing agreement (APA) in Europe, and it was then extended to a third (Asian) country when P&G made this request to the relevant Asian tax authorities.*

Although no exact figures are publicly available, the most frequent method for solving transfer pricing disputes in Germany is probably dispute resolution in the course of final meetings in the context of field audits. In cases where existing differences of opinion between the taxpayer and the tax authorities cannot be resolved in this way, taxpayers in Germany frequently make recourse to the courts. The very large number of proceedings before the tax courts dealing with the issue of hidden profit distributions and (more rarely) hidden capital contributions provide clear evidence of this. Legal recourse is also commonly taken to solve German disputes in cross-border cases. In the great majority of cases, the taxpayer has to defend himself against assessment indicating profit distributions also in the international context. Up to now, there have been fewer transfer pricing cases based on the 'adjustment of income' provisions. In recent years, many taxpayers have also made use of the possibility to initiate a mutual agreement procedure, as is shown by the long list of proceedings reported. The APA instrument has also become increasingly evident over the last few years.

4. Transfer pricing case law. *What is the evolution path of transfer pricing litigation in the country? For example: (i) Is transfer pricing litigation being gradually replaced by either MAPs or APAs, as regulated in the relevant tax treaties? (ii) Are foreign/local transfer pricing precedents and/ or published MAPs increasingly relevant as a source of law for solving transfer pricing disputes?*

The possibility of dispute resolution by way of mutual agreement procedure has led to a slight decline in the number of cases going to court. It must be noted in this context that in Germany a MAP and a court procedure can be pursued in parallel. How frequently this occurs cannot be assessed from an outside view. When implementing the MAP, however, a prerequisite is that the applicant declares its agreement to implementation in writing, any pending appeals are completed, and following notification of the advice implementing the mutual agreement, the applicant waives a corresponding appeal (partial waiver). Local (no-name) transfer pricing precedents are relevant as a source of law for solving transfer pricing disputes. But the outcomes of mutual agreement procedures are not made public in Germany. These results and the content of advance pricing agreements are subject to tax confidentiality in Germany. Foreign transfer pricing precedents and published MAPs may serve as reference points, but do not have the feature of chargeable 'source of law'.

5. Customary international law and international tax procedure. *Has customary international law been applied in the country to govern the relevant methods for solving transfer pricing disputes (such as the MAP)? For example, has the* OECD Manual on Effective Mutual Agreement Procedure *('OECD Manual') been deemed customary international tax law in the MAP arena for filling procedural gaps (for example, time limit for implementation of relief where treaties deviate from the OECD Model Tax Convention)?*

Germany always implements without major delay the OECD recommendations into domestic law. In such implementation these recommendations do have the character of guidelines relevant for the resolution of transfer pricing disputes in Germany. Direct application of the OECD recommendations is not possible, however, as application requires prior implementation into domestic law. At the same time these 'principles' serve as guidelines, for example in the context of international mutual agreement procedures or bi- or multilateral advance pricing agreements.

6. Procedural setting and strategic interaction. *Does strategic interaction between taxpayers and tax authorities depend on the procedural setting in which they interact when trying to solve transfer pricing disputes? For example, which procedural setting in the country prompts the relevant parties to cooperate with each other the most for solving this sort of dispute, and why?*

Strategic interaction between taxpayers and tax authorities does depend on the procedural setting in which they interact when trying to solve transfer pricing disputes. In this context, the mutual agreement procedure and the advance pricing agreement constitute the strongest incentive to cooperate since the tax authorities are not obliged to pursue these proceedings to their conclusion.

7. The Future of transfer pricing disputes resolution.   *Which is the best available proposal in light of the interests of the country for facilitating the global resolution of transfer pricing disputes, and why?*

Looking ahead, it appears that general application of mutual agreement procedures with subsequent arbitration if needed would best serve the practical issues arising in cross-border transfer pricing, since in arbitration proceedings the parties concerned are obliged to resolve cases within a tightly set time frame. Experience in Germany shows that, up to now, all such procedures have already reached resolution in the course of the first phase (mutual agreement phase for which basically a total of two years is given, unless the responsible authorities extend this two-year limit by agreement with the enterprises involved) in order for the parties to avoid going to arbitration, in which they must accept the decision of the arbitrators.

Transfer pricing in Spain

The tax problem for the next ten years

VIOLETA RUIZ ALMENDRAL

7.1 Introduction

Until recently, transfer pricing was not an issue for the Spanish taxpayers operating internationally,[1] at least not a serious one, even if it was problematic for those operating on a domestic plane.[2] This started to

I sincerely thank David Ramos Muñoz and Juan Zornoza Pérez for patiently revising this chapter and making very useful suggestions. I also thank Aitor Navarro. I would also like to thank the numerous professionals, both high ranking officials from the Tax Administration (in particular, many thanks to María Coronado, of the AEAT), as well as tax auditors from the main Spanish law firms which, on condition of anonymity, have participated in the 'Informal Survey' undertaken by the author. Because the specifics of how transfer pricing in Spain is applied still remain closed to public knowledge, as most controversies begin and end in a tax audit, without their help, both in the questionnaire and informal interviews, it would have been very difficult to give an accurate view of this area. Needless to say, the usual disclaimer applies, so that all remaining errors are my own and cannot be attributed to anyone else.

This work has been completed in the framework of two publicly funded research projects: Project no. CCG10-UC3M/HUM-5181, 'Domestic Anti-avoidance Rules in the EU and International Law Setting' ('Las medidas anti-elusión nacionales y su compatibilidad con el Derecho Comunitario y el Derecho Tributario Internacional'), financed by the Comunidad de Madrid and directed by the author; and the project 'Direct Tax Harmonization in the European Union' ('La fiscalidad directa en la Unión Europea: entre competencia y convergencia'), financed by the Spanish Ministry of Science and Innovation (ref. DER 2010–20000, Dir. Juan Zornoza). Finally, this work has also benefited from a post-maternity research grant from my University available to all Professors (male or female) who have been on maternity/paternity leave (2009–11).

[1] A. M. Janschek and D. Oosterhoff, 'Transfer Pricing Trends and Perceptions in Europe' (2002) *International Transfer Pricing Journal* (March/April) 46; J. M. Calderón Carrero, *Precios de transferencia e impuesto sobre sociedades* (Barcelona: Tirant lo blanch, 2006), p. 32.

[2] See V. E. Combarros Villanueva, *Régimen tributario de las operaciones entre sociedades vinculadas en el impuesto sobre sociedades* (Madrid: Tecnos, 1988); M. L. Esteve Pardo, *Fiscalidad de las operaciones entre sociedades vinculadas y distribuciones encubiertas de beneficios* (Valencia: Tirant lo blanc, 1996).

change radically in 2006,[3] when a new regime, including its particularly burdensome documentation requirements, came into force. The first tax filing following the new transfer pricing rules took place in July 2010.[4]

For this reason the year of writing, 2011, is either a perfect year to write about transfer pricing in Spain – as there is a great deal of room for speculation, given that there is virtually no case law on the new rules – or, for the same reason, a terrible year. I will assume it is the first possibility and dedicate the following pages to report what has happened until now; how the law of transfer pricing has actually been implemented and what may happen in the following years, considering the substantial changes that transfer pricing in Spain has undergone.

In 2006, Law 36/2006 for the Avoidance of Tax Fraud (LATF) substantially amended article 16 of Law 61/1978 establishing the Corporate Income Tax[5] (LCIT), which in practice entailed an overhaul of the existing transfer pricing regime. After two subsequent reforms, this new regime entered into force in different phases, between 2008 and 2010. The main result is that there is now, for the first time in Spain, a complete transfer pricing regime which is, in principle, aligned with the (1995, not the 2010) OECD guidelines and with the recent developments in the European Union.

But transfer pricing is still relatively new to the Spanish tax culture. This becomes obvious when we analyse some of the main aspects of its implementation, namely, the post-valuation procedures undertaken by the tax authorities and the mutual agreement procedures. The purpose of this chapter is to offer a complete picture of the status quo of transfer pricing in Spain, underlining what in my view are, and will be in the coming years, the main problems of its functioning.

With this objective in mind, I will first describe the economic situation in Spain and its recent evolution, and the previous transfer pricing regimes as well as their effects. Then I will concentrate on the current

---

[3] See the findings of the 2010 Global Transfer Pricing Survey, conducted by Ernst & Young (p. 45 for Spain).

[4] This is the date when generally the fiscal year 2009 was filed. According to the Law establishing the Corporate Income Tax (LCIT), the fiscal year cannot exceed twelve months, but entities are free to establish the duration date of their fiscal years. In practice, most if not all entities establish the natural year as fiscal year (1 January to 31 December), which is why the month of July is typically the 'closing' month and the filing month for the CIT.

[5] Royal Legislative Decree (Real Decreto Legislativo) 4/2004 of 5 March 2004 establishing the Law of the Corporate Income Tax. Regulations on the Corporate Income Tax (RCIT) are in Royal Decree 1777/2004 of 30 July 2004.

rules, underlining what in my opinion are the most problematic issues as well as assessing the extent to which such rules are aligned with the OECD guidelines. My intention is both to offer a 'snapshot' of transfer pricing rules in Spain today and to underline the problematic areas.

In order to fully assess the current implementation of the OECD guidelines in Spain, while simultaneously addressing what should be expected of the new transfer pricing regime, the author has undertaken a small survey, targeted at two groups: practitioners and lawyers from the main Spanish firms dealing with the transfer pricing issues[6] and officials of the Tax Administration. A total of twenty-five questionnaires have been submitted.

The survey is, of course, biased in the sense that it was personally conducted by the author, and even when confidentiality was assured, not every subject felt comfortable disclosing certain aspects of their practice. However, it did provide a general idea of how transfer pricing is viewed in practice. Given the limited scope, it is an informal survey,[7] but one which nevertheless offers a general impression of transfer pricing implementation in Spain and which, together with the major Ernst & Young survey, completes the picture.

The survey's main results were as follows.[8]

BOX 7.1 INFORMAL TRANSFER PRICING SURVEY 2011		
Questions	Answers provided by lawyers and practitioners	Answers provided by Tax Administration officials
Given the current situation (transfer pricing reform in 2006, plus new CIT Regulations and	Yes (all respondents)	Yes (all respondents)

---

[6] I have also had the opportunity to conduct a number of follow-up interviews with different officials (who helped on condition of anonymity), which has substantially helped clarify the findings of the survey.

[7] I will refer to this survey as 'Informal Transfer Pricing Survey 2011'.

[8] Given the asymmetry of the answers, with some respondents giving long explanations and others responding with monosyllables, I have listed the issues that were mentioned in more than 50 per cent of the questionnaire and in general tried to outline the majority answer. The similarities are noteworthy, with tax officials and private sector lawyers and economists agreeing in many aspects, including what the most contentious areas may be in the future.

BOX 7.1 (*cont.*)

Questions	Answers provided by lawyers and practitioners	Answers provided by Tax Administration officials
amendment of the OECD Model Tax Convention and the transfer pricing guidelines: Do you believe there will be an increase in the number of conflicts in transfer pricing?		
What do you think will be the most problematic areas of the new (Spanish) regime?	Intangibles intra-group methods and in particular the TNMM business restructuring penalty regime	Transfer pricing methods and in particular the TNMM secondary adjustment
Do you think the new art. 16.8 of the LCIT (secondary adjustment) is an anti-abuse provision and if so what may be its relationship with arts. 13, 15 and 16 of the GTC?[a]	Yes	No. It is a special rule of the general rule established in art. 13 of the GTL
What do you think is currently the APA policy of the Tax Administration? (Please give your opinion regarding the speed of the response, how well prepared tax inspectors are, how different methods are dealt with and how well known they are)	It should be improved	It should be improved

BOX 7.1 (*cont.*)

Questions	Answers provided by lawyers and practitioners	Answers provided by Tax Administration officials
How effective are mutual agreement procedures in Spain? (Is it a good solution, would you advise it? If not, do you think it may improve in the future?)	Not a good solution yet as too slow, maybe in the future	Not a good solution yet as too slow, maybe in the future
Before 2006, were Spanish transfer pricing rules aligned with OECD guidelines?	Only in some aspects	Only in some aspects
Are they now?	Yes	Yes
Do you think the current transfer pricing rules *should* be interpreted according to the new 2010 OECD rules?	Yes	Yes[b]
Do you think the current transfer pricing rules *will* be interpreted by the Tax Administration according to the new 2010 OECD rules?	Yes	Yes
After the 2006 reform, has new personnel been hired for the transfer pricing department?	Yes	Yes
Do you expect the number of specialised staff will continue to grow in the next years?	Yes	Yes

BOX 7.1 (cont.)

Questions	Answers provided by lawyers and practitioners	Answers provided by Tax Administration officials
Can you offer an estimation of how many people currently work in your transfer pricing department?	No	No[c]

[a] General anti-avoidance rules established in the General Tax Code, (Law 58/2003 of 17 December 2003 (General Tributaria).

[b] In both groups the answer was either yes or 'yes, it would not make sense otherwise'.

[c] None of the respondents wanted to offer a given number, even if many of them spoke of a substantial increase in hiring or even the creation of a transfer pricing department.

7.2 Spanish economic and institutional context

On 20 November 1975, Francisco Franco, Spanish dictator since 1939, died. Three years later, on 6 December 1978, Spaniards voted in favour of the longest lasting constitution in their history. On 1 January 1986, Spain became a Member of the European Union. In about twenty years, Spain was radically transformed, in many more ways than I can humbly convey here.

It is not an exaggeration to say that until the late 1970s Spain did not have a *tax system* as such, at least not one that was universally implemented and enforced (the levels of tax fraud under Franco cannot be overstated) or one that followed the general structure of the tax systems of other OECD countries. The first modern personal income tax (PIT) was established in 1978, as was the first corporate income tax (CIT). The tax reform undertaken between 1978 and 1985 entailed a substantial increase of the tax pressure. Tax revenues in fact quadrupled between 1975 and 1980[9] and yet this was generally accepted, i.e., there was no tax

---

[9] OECD Tax Statistics, 'Revenue Statistics: Spain' *OECD Tax Statistics*, doi: 10.1787/data-00253-en.

Table 7.1 *Decentralisation in Spain (public spending) (% share of total public expenditure)*

Year	State	Autonomous Communities	Municipalities
1978	89.0	—	11.0
1984	72.6	14.4	13.0
1987	66.7	18.7	14.6
1990	59.6	23.9	16.5
1992	57.0	26.6	16.4
1998	51.0	32.5	16.5
2007	50.0	35.9	17.0

revolt and most taxpayers footed the bill as part of the price to pay for democracy.

Part of the reform of the tax system was a direct consequence of joining the European Union, which was also of paramount importance for Spain.[10] Finally, at the same time, Spain underwent a decentralisation process between 1978 and 1982 which resulted in seventeen Autonomous Communities,[11] a new territorial political entity. One of the most striking aspects of Spain's decentralisation is the speed at which it has developed. While in 1978, the State was in charge of 89 per cent of the public expenditure, today it manages about 50 per cent (see Table 7.1)[12]

[10] The EU was, in fact, Spain's Project. See, in this regard, C. Closa and P. M. Heywood, *Spain and the European Union* (Palgrave Macmillan, 2004).

[11] Andalusia, Aragon, Asturias, the Balearic Islands, the Basque Country, the Canary Islands, Cantabria, Castilla-La Mancha, Castilla-Leon, Catalonia, Extremadura, Galicia, Madrid, Murcia, Navarre, La Rioja and Valencia. Basque Country and Navarra have broader tax powers than the rest of the regions. In the case of the Basque Country, these powers rest in the *provincias* (Álava, Guipúzcoa and Vizcaya) that hold tax powers to regulate the Corporate Income Tax Law. The attribution of tax powers rests on a mixture of domicile and source, so that, for instance, regional tax provisions will apply when a company is domiciled in those territories but only if at least 25 per cent of its turnover is also derived there (unless turnover is lower than 7 million euros).

[12] See on these systems V. Ruiz Almendral, 'The Asymmetric Distribution of Taxation Powers in the Spanish State of Autonomies: the Common System and the *Foral* Tax Regimes' (Regional and Federal Studies Editorial) (2003) 13(4) *Frank Cass Journal* 41 and, more recently, V. Ruiz Almendral *Sharing Taxes and Sharing the Deficit in Spanish Fiscal Federalism* (Sydney: ATAX Sydney, 2012). See also, C. Colino, 'The Spanish Model of Devolution and Regional Governance: Evolution, Motivations and Effects on Policy Making' (2008) 36(4) *Policy & Politics* 573.

Part of the process of creating a tax system in Spain entailed substantially reforming its tax administration. This process took several years and it was finalised with the creation of a new administrative body in 1990, the National Tax Collection Agency (Agencia Estatal de Administración Tributaria, AEAT), which is in charge of collecting the main taxes of the system, including the PIT, CIT and value added tax (VAT).

BOX 7.2 NATIONAL TAX COLLECTION AGENCY: STATISTICS

The Agency had a 2009 budget of 1,414.3 million euros and a total of 27,755 employees.

The total number of registered taxpayers is 47,999,499, of which 1,682,509 are registered as small companies,[a] 5,154,706 are individual business people and professionals and 41,477 are large companies.

The AEAT's results in 2009 were a total net collection of 144,023 million euros.

The number of tax returns processed in 2009 for the main taxes of the system (i.e., in terms of revenue) were:

personal income tax: 19,467,138
corporate income tax: 1,389,514
value added tax: 3,525,821
excise duties: 9,130,549

[a] Small companies are those whose net revenue (as filed the previous year) does not exceed 8 million euros. Such companies benefit from a special regime, established in art. 108–114 of the LCIT, which includes several tax benefits, among others, a lower tax rate (25–30 per cent as opposed to the general rate of 35 per cent) (art. 28 of the LCIT).

Source: the author and Memoria AEAT 2009, 'Key figures for 2009', p. 7 et seq. English version available at www.aeat.es

---

Data on the economic situation is currently changing almost by the week. According to the latest figures, foreign direct investment (FDI)[13] is slowly beginning to grow again, after having fallen sharply in 2009. In fact, in 2010 there was a 41.5 per cent increase with a total volume of 23,415 million euros. It is important to note that the main element behind that FDI increase was operations in the Spanish holding regime

---

[13] See latest official data in 'Note on 2010 inward FDI data: Investment Registry, March 2011', available at www.investinspain.org/icex/cda/controller/interes/0,5464,5322992_6275487_6299039_4469127_0,00.html. Strategy and Development Office.

(Entidades de Tenencia de Valores Extranjeros, ETVE),[14] which increased by 174 per cent and was worth 11,778 million euros.

The main investors in Spain in 2010 were: the Netherlands (21.4 per cent of the total), France (18.5 per cent) and the United Kingdom (16.5 per cent), which together accounted for 56.4 per cent of total investment. Practically all foreign investment in 2010 came from the OECD countries (95.1 per cent). The two main areas of FDI in 2010 were: transport (1,983 million euros) and real estate (1,980 million euros), and these sectors accounted for 17 per cent of the total FDI. By Autonomous Community, the three leading regions by inward FDI were Madrid, Catalonia and Andalusia (4,986, 3,952 and 1,140 million euros, respectively or 42.8 per cent, 34 per cent and 9.8 per cent of total gross inward FDI, respectively).

The current[15] main indicators of the Spanish economy are shown in Table 7.2.

Finally, it is relevant to point out that the launching of a broad and ambitious Fraud Prevention Plan in 2005 substantially increased tax collection (see Table 7.3). In fact, the reform of transfer pricing legislation is part of that Plan, and officials expect collection to continue to increase as the new rules are implemented and assessed by the Tax Administration. Still, tax fraud and unreported economic activities remain a major issue in Spain. At the moment, there is no reliable estimation, but some calculations suggest that the size of the black economy in Spain is about 20 per cent of GDP.[16]

---

[14] This regime is a preferential tax treatment regime, bestowed on non-residents. It is currently regulated in art. 116–119 of the LCIT. It was introduced in the 1990s, reformed in 2003 and then again by Law 35/2006, of 28 November 2006 with the obvious purpose of capturing foreign capital.

[15] The Spanish economic forecast is changing at the time of writing (November 2011). The author prefers to leave Table 7.2 as given and advise readers that part of its content may, sadly, be outdated.

[16] It should be made clear that, to date, there is no official data on the amount of the informal economy, so that it is then correct to say that nobody really knows what it amounts too. There are, however, some estimates. For example, FUNCAS (Fundación de las Cajas de Ahorros), a think-tank, has estimated the size of this informal economy to be about 23.7 per cent of GDP between 2005 and 2008. Study available at www.funcas.es, and referred to in *El País*, 1 June.2011, digital edition at www.elpais.com/articulo/economia/Funcas/afirma/economia/sumergida/Espana/asciende/24/PIB/elpepueco/20110601elpepueco_8/Tes.

Table 7.2 Annual data and forecast for Spain (2 June 2011)

	2006[a]	2007[a]	2008[a]	2009[a]	2010[a]	2011[b]	2012[b]
GDP							
Nominal GDP (US$ bn)	1,235.9	1,444.0	1,600.2	1,468.4	1,409.9	1,529.4	1,454.8
Nominal GDP (bn euros)	984	1,054	1,088	1,054	1,063	1,119	1,152
Real GDP growth (%)	4.0	3.6	0.9	-3.7	-0.1	0.9	1.3
Expenditure on GDP (% real change)							
Private consumption	3.8	3.7	-0.6	-4.3	1.2	0.7	1.3
Government consumption	4.6	5.5	5.8	3.2	-0.7	-1.0	-1.6
Gross fixed investment	7.2	4.5	-4.8	-16.0	-7.6	-1.9	2.8
Exports of goods and services	6.7	6.7	-1.1	-11.6	10.3	8.6	3.7
Imports of goods and services	10.2	8.0	-5.3	-17.8	5.4	4.3	2.7
Origin of GDP (% real change)							
Agriculture	5.4	5.4	-2.0	-0.6	-1.2	0.3	0.3
Industry	2.9	1.3	-1.5	-9.8	-1.4	1.0	1.5
Services	4.4	4.4	2.0	-1.4	0.3	0.9	1.2
Population and income							
Population (m)	44.7	45.2	45.5	45.8[c]	45.9[c]	46.1	46.3
GDP per head (US$ at PPP)	29,213	31,266	31,488	30,643[c]	30,782[c]	31,446	32,610
Recorded unemployment (av. %)	8.5	8.3	11.4	18.0	20.1	20.6	19.7
Fiscal indicators (% of GDP)							
General government budget revenue	40.4	41.1	37.1	34.7	35.7[c]	35.9	36.3
General government budget expenditure	38.4	39.2	41.3	45.8	45.0[c]	42.7	42.0
General government budget balance	2.0	1.9	-4.2	-11.1	-9.2[c]	-6.8	-5.6
Public debt	39.6	36.1	39.8	53.2	60.1[c]	67.1	69.0

Prices and financial indicators

Exchange rate US$: euro (end-period)	0.76	0.68	0.72	0.70	0.74	0.76	0.82
Exchange rate ¥: euro (end-period)	157.07	163.13	126.21	133.40	112.13	107.50	98.82
Consumer prices (av. % change; EU harmonised measure)	3.6	2.8	4.1	-0.2	2.0	3.1	1.9
Producer prices (av. %)	5.4	3.6	6.5	-3.4	3.2	6.0	1.7
Lending interest rate (av. %)	5.8	6.6	7.4	7.0	7.2	8.3	9.3
Current account (US$ bn)							
Trade balance	-104.6	-125.2	-126.6	-59.0	-62.3	-55.0	-43.3
Goods: exports fob	220.7	264.1	284.7	228.7	253.0	321.9	319.9
Goods: imports fob	-325.3	-389.3	-411.3	-287.7	-315.2	-376.9	-363.2
Services balance	28.1	31.7	38.2	35.7	36.7	40.5	38.4
Income balance	-26.2	-41.4	-52.1	-41.1	-28.7	-37.1	-37.6
Current transfers balance	-8.1	-9.6	-14.0	-10.9	-9.4	-9.9	-9.4
Current-account balance	-110.9	-144.5	-154.5	-75.3	-63.6	-61.5	-51.9

[a] Actual.

[b] Economist Intelligence Unit forecasts.

[c] Economist Intelligence Unit estimates.

Source: The Economist, Intelligence Unit, quoting a number of sources: OECD, Main Economic Indicators; Banco de España, *Boletín Estadístico*; Instituto Nacional de Estadística; IMF, International Financial Statistics

Table 7.3 *Audit activity and results 2008/2009*

	2008	2009	% change 2008/2009
Number of taxpayers audited	25,046	25,926	3.5
Number of audit reports	56,758	61,137	7.7
Settled debt	3,719.76 m euros	4,518 m euros	21.4[a]

[a]According to the 2009 AEAT Report, the average debt settled by every taxpayer that was subject to an audit increased from 116,712.5 euros in 2005 to 174,245 euros in 2009.

Source: Memoria AEAT 2009. Available (in English) at www.aeat.es

7.3   Beginning of the use of arm's length standard

7.3.1   *Spain as a new international player: 1936–2011 in a nutshell*

Transfer pricing is primarily an international issue, and this has many consequences. The most obvious one is that it arises in the international arena and it can only be resolved via international cooperation, so both the problem and the solution have a prevailing international element. Therefore, the less international relations a country has, the lower the level of exposure its tax system will have to transfer pricing issues.

The main purpose of transfer pricing rules is to determine how much income, deriving from international transactions, should be attributed to each jurisdiction, so as to promote a seemingly fair competition setting as well as to prevent multinational entities from shifting their tax bases conveniently to avoid or minimise taxation (tax arbitrage).[17] In order to solve this problem cooperatively, the OECD has proposed a set of international rules and guidelines which are followed by most OECD countries, as well as a growing number of non-OECD countries.[18] It is debatable whether this set of rules

---

[17] See W. Schön, *Transfer Pricing: Business Incentives, International Taxation and Corporate Law*, Max Planck Institute for Tax Law and Public Finance Paper 2011/05 (2011), p. 3 *et seq.*, and W. Schön, 'International Tax Coordination for a Second-Best World (Part III)' (2010) 2 *World Tax Journal* 229.

[18] See, in this regard, E. Baistrocchi, 'The Use and Interpretation of Tax Treaties in the Emerging World: Theory and Implications', (2008) 4 *British Tax Review* 353.

amounts to a transfer pricing *regime*, as has often been claimed,[19] especially since the practice of transfer pricing shows growing dissonances in its application around the world.[20]

But transfer pricing is also a European Union issue, in particular, since the European Commission Communication of 23 October 2001[21] acknowledged its relevance and announced the creation of the EU transfer pricing guidelines alongside continuing efforts to improve the application of the Arbitration Convention 90/436/EC.[22] Of course, the culmination of that process, or rather of a different route, is the Common Consolidated Corporate Tax Base (CCCTB) project, which was formally proposed by the Commission on 16 March 2011.[23]

Spain takes a particular view on transfer pricing, which can be partially explained by the fact that it is a relatively new player in the international arena. In 1978, the year the Constitution was approved, Spain had agreed five double taxation conventions (DTCs). Today there are eighty DTCs.[24]

This explains Spain's very limited scope of experience with transfer pricing. As anyone familiar with recent Spanish history would know, the civil war (1936–9) left the country in a substantial economic depression that lasted until well into the 1950s. The Franco dictatorial regime (1939–75) was isolationist, and this resulted in Spain having practically no international relations during most of this period, although there was a short period of economic openness at the end of the 1950s.

Implementation of a transfer pricing regime in Spain is summarised in Table 7.4.

---

[19] See, in general, the controversial theory on the existence of an authentic *tax regime* by R. S. Avi-Yonah, 'International Tax as International Law' (2004) 57 *Tax Law Review* 498, and more recently, R. S. Avi-Yonah, *International Tax as International Law: An Analysis of the International Tax Regime* (New York: Cambridge University Press, 2007), p. 8 *et seq*.

[20] See J. Wittendorff, *Transfer Pricing and the Arm's Length Principle in International Tax Law* (The Hague: Kluwer Law International, 2010), p. 14 *et seq* and p. 779 *et seq*.

[21] COM 2001, 582 final.

[22] Calderón Carrero, *Precios de transferencia e impuesto sobre sociedades*, note 1 above, p. 27.

[23] See ec.europa.eu/taxation_customs/taxation/company_tax/common_tax_base/index_en.htm#practical.

[24] There are eighty DTCs in force, and a further thirteen are in different stages of the negotiation process (see www.meh.es/es-ES/Normativa%20y%20doctrina/Normativa/CDI/Paginas/CDI_crono.aspx).

Table 7.4 *Stages of transfer pricing implementation*

Year	Transfer pricing legislation	OECD Guidelines	Leading cases[a]
1967–78	Decree 3359/1967 of 23 December 1967	—	No cases, all solved in audits
1978–95	Law 61/1978 establishing the Corporate Income Tax	1977 OECD Transfer Pricing Guidelines (partially followed)	Limited cases, mostly dealing with avoidance issues
1995–2006	Law 43/1995 establishing the Corporate Income Tax	Semi-independent system (did not follow the OECD Guidelines)	Limited cases, mostly dealing with avoidance issues. Problematic use of OECD Guidelines directly by courts. Disputes solved internally (tax audits)
2006–11	Law 36/2006 for the Avoidance of Tax Fraud	1995 OECD Transfer Pricing Guidelines	One case, challenging the penalty regime before the Constitutional Court. Disputes solved internally (tax audits)

[a]All Spanish experts (academic, practitioners and public administrators) are unanimous on this: to date, *there are no leading cases* on transfer pricing. What we find are cases where transfer pricing is an issue, albeit not the central one. As insisted throughout this chapter, Spain is a new player in transfer pricing issues, and was relatively isolated during a good part of the twentieth century.

7.3.2   Transfer pricing legislation and administrative practice

Rudiments of transfer pricing: 1967 and 1978

The first tax that remotely resembles a tax on the income of entities can be traced back to the Contribución de Utilidades de la Riqueza Mobiliaria, introduced by the Budget Law of 1889–90. The author of this law, the then Minister of the Treasury Raimundo Fernández Villaverde, was a visionary who substantially contributed to implementing the rudiments of a tax system in Spain.[25] The Laws of 22 December 1922, 31 December 1946, 31 December 1954 and 26 December 1958 are sometimes mentioned as first 'drafts' of the arm's length standard (ALS) in Spain's tax regime.[26] It is the author's opinion that they were too limited in scope to actually resemble the ALS much. Even the 1964 legislation is hardly a draft, for under Franco's (so-called) tax system there was no general corporate income tax, but a limited 'charge' or tax levy for certain operations.

A first mention of the arm's length standard in Spanish law can be found in Decree 3359/1967 of 23 December 1967, which coincided with an economic 'opening' of the Franco dictatorship. Articles 17.16 and 20.1 of the 3359 Decree implemented the ALS in a very limited way, only in order to accept the deductibility of certain transnational operations.

In fact, only after the 1977–8 tax reforms did it become possible to talk about the existence of a tax system in Spain that is more or less aligned with EU and OECD countries.[27] Furthermore, there were no relevant transfer pricing cases or disputes during that period (unless the notion of 'transfer pricing dispute' is substantially expanded to include any disputes where the value of an operation is challenged).

The first real implementation did not occur until Law 61/1978 establishing the Corporate Income Tax (LCIT). Article 16 of the LCIT established the ALS with a wide scope, comprising both international and domestic dealings.[28]

---

[25] A. Gota Losada, *Tratado del Impuesto de Sociedades*, vol. I, *Nociones fundamentales del Impuesto sobre Sociedades e historia del tributo en España* (Madrid: Banco Exterior de España, Servicio de Estudios Económicos, 1988), p. 264 *et seq.*

[26] See C. García-Herrera, *Precios de transferencia y otras operaciones vinculadas en el Impuesto sobre Sociedades* (Madrid: Instituto de Estudios Fiscales, 2001), p. 31 *et seq.*

[27] A comprehensive analysis of the evolution of the tax system regarding corporations in Spain can be found in Gota Losada, *Tratado del Impuesto de Sociedades*, vol. I, *Nociones fundamentales*, note 25 above, pp. 261–418. See also the leading work by G. Sala Galvañ, *Los precios de transferencia internacionales. Su tratamiento tributario* (Valencia: Tirant lo blanch, 2003), p. 233 *et seq.*

[28] The leading work on this regime is V. E. Combarros, *Régimen tributario de las operaciones entre sociedades vinculadas en el impuesto sobre sociedades* (Madrid: Tecnos, 1988).

This regime was to a certain extent in line with the 1977 OECD Transfer Pricing Guidelines (the '1977 Guidelines'), at least in theory, for it was predominantly an anti-abuse regime, which created a high level of litigation and conflicts. It was also a regime that generated various inconsistencies; for instance, the interpretation of the tax authorities, and the wording itself of Law 61/1978, made it very difficult (in fact impossible in most cases) to undertake a correlative adjustment. In practice, only the transfer prices of the entity that had been undertaxed in Spain would be corrected, but then the pricing applied to the other party (which had actually paid more than its due debt) was not corrected, at least not until the courts began to change the prevailing administrative interpretation that was contrary to the corresponding adjustment.[29]

BOX 7.3 EXAMPLES OF CASES FROM THE LAW 61/1978 REGIME

RTEAC[a] of 10 September 1986

     RTEAC of 3 February 1987

     Both cases are similar and state the need to undertake corresponding adjustments following a tax audit in transfer pricing cases. The Court also considers transfer pricing legislation to have an anti-avoidance objective.

     The Supreme Court has dealt with the interpretation of the new regime in several cases, of which the most relevant are the cases where the system is explained and defined, by stressing its nature of a valuation system, rather than an indirect measurement of the taxable base (in particular decisions of the Supreme Court of 18 June 1992, 26 March 1992).

[a] The Tribunal Económico-Administrativo Central (TEAC) is an administrative court, an administrative body that deals with tax conflicts as a previous step to a purely judicial review. Its opinions (Resolutions) will be referred to as RTEAC.

1995 transfer pricing regime as an 'independent' (non-OECD) regime

In the same year that the OECD's 1977 Guidelines were amended, Spain approved a major reform of the CIT which, in terms of transfer pricing, in practice substantially deviated from the OECD Guidelines that had been (to a certain extent) followed before then. Law 43/1995 establishing

---

[29] See J. M. Calderón Carrero, 'Spanish Tax Courts Address Transfer Pricing Legislation', *Tax Notes International*, April 2002. See also, Sala Galvañ, *Los precios de transferencia internacionales*, note 27 above, p. 239.

the Corporate Income Tax (LCIT 1995) marked the start of an 11-year period during which the Spanish tax regime significantly deviated from the OECD Transfer Pricing Guidelines. Of course, if one takes a strict interpretation of the Preamble to the Law, the conclusion would be the opposite, for it expressly mentions the Transfer Pricing Guidelines and announces that the intention of the law was aligned with international practice. The reality of the law was, however, quite different.[30]

The main deviation from the guidelines was the fact that article 16 of the LCIT 1995 regarded transfer pricing mainly and almost exclusively as a tax-planning tool that had to be corrected by the tax authorities. This correction, however, would not take place in all cases, but only when two circumstances existed: the price was not market-based (which did not follow the ALS) *and* this caused a decrease in tax revenues for the Spanish Treasury.[31]

There were at least five aspects in which the 1995 transfer pricing regime deviated from the OECD Guidelines:

1. The transfer pricing rules were directed at the tax authorities, not taxpayers, who were not generally obliged to set values at arm's length and could not, among other things, establish post-accounting tax adjustments in order to comply with the ALS.
2. The ALS did not really shape the regime, which was driven by the need to safeguard tax revenues, so that tax authorities would only correct the tax base when transactions not only did not comply with the ALS but also implied a reduction of the tax burden to be borne in Spain. It was, in a way, an anti-abuse regime that used the ALS as a vehicle.[32]
3. Valuation methods were not properly described but only mentioned.
4. No documentation was required.
5. The 1995 regime (partly because of the above) made it very difficult, if not impossible, to undertake corresponding adjustments in an international setting.

Even if the 1995 regime did not follow the OECD Guidelines, it would be inaccurate to state that these were not present at all in the

---

[30] As Spanish commentators have consistently pointed out; see, among others, Calderón Carrero, *Precios de transferencia e impuesto sobre sociedades*, note 1 above, p. 101.

[31] See a critic in N. Carmona, 'Introducción: operaciones vinculadas y precios de transfer-encia' in N. Carmona (ed.), *Operaciones Vinculadas* (Valencia: CISS, 2009), pp. 31–2.

[32] Even if the regime could not completely fulfil its anti-abuse aspirations, given the absence of documentation, which made it very difficult to reassess the taxpayer's filing and whether or not the transfer pricing concept had been complied with; see Calderón Carrero, 'Spanish Courts Address Transfer Pricing Legislation', note 29 above.

practice of transfer pricing. In fact, they were increasingly applied by the tax authorities and also by judges as the system developed. In the process of 'judicial creep'[33] of transfer pricing, the rules were widely extended, and it may not be an overstatement to affirm that the OECD Guidelines were in fact the real transfer pricing legislation behind the Spanish domestic regulation. The Economic-Administrative Tribunal (TEAC), a semi-independent[34] administrative body that resolves tax disputes (a pre-court instance), has referred to the OECD Transfer Pricing Guidelines in an extensive body of case law, in many cases directly applying the Guidelines and the methods included therein. The Spanish Supreme Court (Tribunal Supremo) and the National Superior Court (Audiencia Nacional) have also in some cases taken the view that the Transfer Pricing Guidelines could be directly applied.

BOX 7.4 EXAMPLES OF CASES FROM THE 1995 REGIME

RTEAC no. 00/3987/2004 of 14 June 2007 and Audiencia Nacional, Sala de lo Contencioso-administrativo, Sección 2a, decision of 27 September 2007, rec. 501/2004 (claim no. 501/2004) support the direct application of the Transfer Pricing Guidelines to transactions, that is, before Spanish law can be applied.

RTEAC of 25 July 2007 and RTEAC of 10 October 2007 both admit that the valuation undertaken by the tax audit cannot be substantially modified if it has formally mentioned the different methods. In other words, the tax auditor has considerable leeway to interpret the methods as long as it is formally justified.

This practice is consistent with the way the Commentaries to the OECD Model Tax Convention have often been referred to in case law. In this regard, it is not difficult to find references to the purported character of 'authorised interpretation' of the double taxation conventions[35] as well as to imply that they are somehow directly applicable. This runs contrary to the role the Commentaries themselves consider appropriate (para. 29: 'the Commentaries are not designed to be annexed in any manner to the conventions signed

---

[33] Calderón Carrero, *Precios de transferencia e impuesto sobre sociedades*, note 1 above, p. 118.

[34] It is independent from tax inspectors, but not from the Ministry of the Treasury.

[35] There are many examples of this misconception: among others, Spanish Supreme Court cases of 29 July, 3 June and 8 April 2000, or 12 February 2003, all state that the OECD Model Tax Convention Commentaries constitute an 'authentic interpretation' of DTCs.

by member countries, which unlike the Model are legally binding international instruments').[36]

This blunt use of the Transfer Pricing Guidelines by some Spanish courts and tax officials could be partially forgiven by taking into account the European Court of Justice case law. The ECJ has actually referred to the arm's length standard as an 'internationally recognised principle' (*Lankhorst* (C-324/00)). Furthermore, the court has also made references to the OECD Model Convention and its Commentaries, which may sometimes reflect an implicit acceptance of the conventional regime in international tax law (*Gerritse* (C-234/01), ECJ, 12 June 2003, para. 45). It can be debated whether or not this is accurate, and the answer will in part depend on whether we assume that there is in fact an international tax regime.

But to apply the Transfer Pricing Guidelines in a direct manner, as Spanish courts and tax authorities often do, is quite a different matter. To the extent that it entails conferring the nature of law on an instrument of *soft law* there is a serious breach of the rule of law, which for tax purposes is clearly stated in article 31.3 of the Spanish Constitution ('Personal or property contributions for public purposes may only be imposed in accordance with the law').[37] To the extent that the Transfer Pricing Guidelines are referred to as if they were law, and for the purposes of reconstructing the tax base of the CIT, the rule of law,[38] as currently defined by the Constitutional Court, is not respected.[39]

The OECD Transfer Pricing Guidelines are not a source of law, not even soft law,[40] even if it can be argued that states are to some extent informally bound by them, to the extent that they have agreed to be so.[41]

---

[36] F. A. García Prats, 'Los Modelos de Convenio, sus principios rectores y su influencia sobre los Convenios de Doble Imposición' (2009) 133 *Crónica Tributaria* 107.

[37] See the official version of the Spanish Constitution in English at www.constitucion.es.

[38] See, in that regard, the account of the extent of the concept and its consequences today in T. Bingham, *The Rule of Law* (Allen Lane, 2010).

[39] There is an extensive body of Constitutional Court case law on the scope of the rule of law with regard to the creation and regulation of taxes. See, among others Decisions 179/1985, 19/1987 or 221/1992; see, in this regard, V. Ruiz Almendral and J. Zornoza Pérez, 'Sistema tributario y Constitución' in J. Zornoza Pérez (ed.), *Finanzas Públicas y Constitución* (Quito: Corporación Editora Nacional, 2004), pp. 103–51.

[40] J. Zornoza Pérez, 'La problemática expansión del "soft law": un análisis desde el Derecho tributario' (*mimeo*, 2011).

[41] Carmona, 'Introducción: operaciones vinculadas y precios de transferencia', note 31 above pp. 46–7.

Furthermore, the Guidelines are not officially published – in fact full access to them (in a printable version) is not provided for free – and they are not available in Spanish, which is no small matter when one takes article 9.3 of the Spanish Constitution into account which guarantees 'the publicity of legal statutes'. This problem is not exclusive to tax law. The use of all sorts of guidelines in ever more complicated areas of law usually disregards a basic aspect of the rule of law. Law, and the current economy, are so complicated that any clarification is welcome. But, in the best of scenarios such guidelines often become a substitute for common sense. At worst, they become a substitute for the rule of law itself, which lies at the heart of democracy.

Despite the fact that the Guidelines were often directly applied, it is generally agreed that before 2006 Spain remained one of the OECD countries where the practice of transfer pricing had been least developed.[42]

2006 reform: enter (officially) the OECD Guidelines

The current transfer pricing regime was introduced by Law 36/2006 of 29 November 2006 for the Avoidance of Tax Fraud (LATF), which clearly states in the Preamble its intention to align transfer pricing in Spain with the relevant provisions contained in the European Transfer Pricing Code of Conduct and the OECD Guidelines.

This immediately poses the question of what value, if any, should the reference to the Transfer Pricing Guidelines have, since they are now mentioned in the Preamble? Preambles are not, according to consistent Constitutional Court case law, part of a law itself and therefore are not of a binding nature.[43]

Moreover, the fact that the Preamble may serve as an interpretative tool should not automatically transfer that authoritative character to the Guidelines. First, as mentioned above, the Guidelines are not officially published and so they do not meet the standard laid down in article 9 of the Spanish Constitution.[44] Second, they cannot be considered to be soft

---

[42] Janschek and Oosterhoff, 'Transfer Pricing Trends and Perceptions in Europe', note 1 above, p. 46 et seq.; Calderón Carrero, *Precios de transferencia e impuesto sobre sociedades*, note 1 above, p. 32.

[43] Preambles cannot be deemed unconstitutional (STC 36/1981, 132/1989, 150/1990) even if they do have a certain 'interpretive value' (31/2010).

[44] Article 9.3 of the Spanish Constitution states: '3. The Constitution guarantees the principle of legality, the hierarchy of legal provisions, the publicity of legal statutes, the

law in the sense that EU law sometimes is considered to be (such as the Codes of Conduct). Third, the wording of the Guidelines themselves makes it very difficult to use them as a 'guiding principle', as they actually contain rules and precise indications as to how transfer pricing should be interpreted, regulated and applied in general. Finally, even if all these arguments were to be rejected, the reference in the Preamble would still refer to the 1995 Transfer Pricing Guidelines, since the LATF was approved in 2006 and it has not been significantly amended to adapt it to the OECD's 2010 Guidelines (in fact, the reforms undertaken since 2006 have been limited to reducing the documentation requirements).

However, the prevailing, or even the official, view is quite different, so that at the moment, some commentators, including tax inspectors, have suggested that the reference to the Transfer Pricing Guidelines which is included in the LATF Preamble should entail the automatic adoption of the 2010 (not 1995) Guidelines in Spanish domestic law.[45] In fact, the Tax Administration has already referred to the central role that the Guidelines should now play in transfer pricing legislation, clearly stating, in a binding ruling ('consulta vinculante'), that the transfer pricing regime should be interpreted according to the *current* OECD Guidelines, because that is how the Preamble to the LATF should be interpreted.[46]

This poses other problems, apart from the afore-mentioned rule of law issues; namely, that the new transfer pricing regime does not follow the 2010 Guidelines but, loosely, the 1995 ones. Because there are significant differences between the 1995 and 2010 versions, the adaptation of the new Guidelines is extremely difficult, unless either the law is amended or the Guidelines are applied in a direct manner (which is likely to happen again).

---

non-retroactivity of punitive provisions that are not favourable to or restrictive of individual rights, the certainty that the rule of law shall prevail, the accountability of public authorities, and the prohibition of arbitrary action of public authorities.'

[45] This seems to be the opinion of Tax Inspector L. Jones Rodríguez, 'Precios de transferencia: comparabilidad y métodos del beneficio; últimos avances de la OCDE', 18 *Carta Tributaria – Monografías*, 16–31 October 2010. Also, most respondents to the Informal Transfer Pricing Survey 2011 seem to have taken that view.

[46] Consulta vinculante V1384–07, of 26 June 2007, of the Subdirección General de Impuestos sobre las Personas Jurídicas. Similarly, the binding ruling of the Bizkaia government (Basque Country) does not explain what role the OECD Guidelines should play; it simply applies them as if they were part of the law (Consulta no. 5743 of 11 April 2011, of the Hacienda Foral de Bizkaia).

3. Furthermore, the understanding of the relevant European law as to what the ALS is and how it should be interpreted is not always perfectly aligned with the OECD Guidelines. This is particularly true if we analyse the ECJ's case law. In particular, the Court's focus on the relevant commercial reasons, even where the ALS has not been followed, is highly problematic,[47] inasmuch as it seems to add an anti-avoidance test to the ALS, which was something that had not been originally envisaged when the transfer pricing regime was designed.[48] In this regard, note the case decided in February 2011, where the Court of Appeal concluded that the United Kingdom's thin capitalisation legislation is compatible with EU law.[49]

In the following paragraphs, I will focus on the 2006 regime. At the same time, I will explain generally the current implementation of the ALS, which will also require references to pre-2006 cases, as the new law is still too recent to have generated much case law. Also, it is reasonable to expect that the tax authorities may, for the time being, follow the pre-2006 logic, which was largely based on transfer pricing being an abuse-prone situation that had to be corrected in order to protect tax revenues. The double justification of transfer pricing – as a fair competition tool as well as an anti-abuse regime – was thus largely ignored in favour of a domestic revenue-based approach.

7.4   Current implementation of the ALS

The implementation of the ALS has grown substantially in the past years (in particular since 2007), with law firms hiring new lawyers for their

---

[47] See, in this regard, A. Martín Jiménez, 'Transfer Pricing and EU Law Following the ECJ Judgment in *SGI*: Some Thoughts on Controversial Issues' (2011) *Bulletin for International Taxation* (May) 277.

[48] See V. Ruiz Almendral, 'Tiene futuro el test de los "motivos económicos válidos" en las normas anti-abuso? (sobre la planificación fiscal y las normas anti-abuso en el Derecho de la Unión Europea)' (2010) 329–30 *Revista Estudios Financieros* (August–September) 5; V. Ruiz Almendral, 'Tax Avoidance and the European Court of Justice: What is at Stake for European GAARs?' (2005) 33(12) *Intertax* 562.

[49] *Test Claimants in the Thin Cap Group Litigation* v. *HM Revenue and Customs* [2011] EWCA Civ 127 (18 February 2011), available at www.bailii.org/ew/cases/EWCA/Civ/2011/127.html. The case is also interesting because it interpreted the ECJ *Test Claimants* case, but it did so in the light of subsequent cases, namely, *Oy AA and SGI* (C-231/05 (2008), *Société de Gestion Industrielle SA (SGI) v. État Belge* (C-311/08) (2010), rather than on the basis of *Test Claimants in the Thin Cap Group Litigation* (C-524/04), which led the UK court to consider that the ECJ case law had in fact been changed (the court said *clarified*) and that specific rules that follow the arm's length test are not contrary to the freedom of establishment.

transfer pricing departments[50] and the Tax Administration dedicating more personnel to its Corporate Income Tax Department.

7.4.1   2006 transfer pricing reform in Spain (the first thorough implementation of the ALS)

The new regime in fact represents a substantial reform and an overhaul of transfer pricing implementation. Instead of being a revision process, whereby the tax authorities applied the ALS only to control tax revenues, taxpayers must now determine and use arm's length prices in all transactions between related parties ('operaciones vinculadas').

This is a significant shift of the paradigm for transfer pricing in Spain and reflects a change of philosophy in the law that abandons the anti-abuse objective of the regime in favour of an objective system based on whether the ALS has been complied with.[51] Before the 2006 reform, taxpayers were not required to value their transactions at arm's length; it was only for the tax authorities to prove that the taxable income in Spain had been either deferred or understated as a result of non-arm's length pricing. This resulted in the ALS not being widely used and tax audits were made difficult, especially in certain complicated operations where, absent documentation (the old regime did not make it compulsory), it was very difficult for the tax authorities to determine the pricing of a given transaction.

Furthermore, the fact that taxpayers were not generally required to value transactions at arm's length, and that the burden of proof was considered to lie with the tax authorities, added to the lack of provisions allowing them to undertake a 'secondary adjustment', eventually led to a system that was difficult to enforce, and where the imposition of penalties was rare. In most cases, the result of a tax audit in transfer pricing would be to require payment of the unpaid tax together with interest for late payment, but with no penalties. Because documentation was also not required, it was in practice very difficult even to complete the tax audit in a manner coherent with the appropriate methods of valuation.

---

[50] Frustratingly, it has been impossible to come up with a figure, although all respondents insist that their transfer pricing departments are currently growing and that further hiring is to be expected.

[51] J. M. Calderón and A. Martín Jiménez, 'Presupuestos y limitaciones del ajuste valorativo del artículo 16 TRLIS' in N. Carmona (ed.), Operaciones Vinculadas (Valencia: CISS, 2009), pp. 75–6.

The 2006 reforms radically changed this, introducing the following changes:

1. Related individuals and persons must value their transactions at market price (ALS).
2. Methods are described in the law, with an outline explanation of what they entail (until 2006, methods were merely mentioned, not described).
3. Taxpayers must also thoroughly justify the valuation methods employed by keeping relevant documentation (the documentation requirements follow the proposals presented by the Forum of the European Union on Transfer Pricing and specifically the Code of Conduct).
4. Tax authorities may undertake a secondary adjustment.
5. There is now a very strict penalty regime, mainly linked to the failure to keep documentation.

The transfer pricing regime now applies to both domestic and international transactions. This is probably inconsistent with one of the objectives of transfer pricing: to mitigate tax base shifting among different jurisdictions (countries). This will hardly ever occur within a single jurisdiction, so applying transfer pricing both to internal and international dealings seems odd. The reason lies in the ECJ case law, which oftentimes has caused a loss in the neutrality that it purportedly was trying to protect.[52]

Before Law 36/2006, critics of the transfer pricing regime argued, quite rightly, that the Spanish regime did not comply with EU law as it was harsher to international dealings, something probably (as it was never challenged before the ECJ) inconsistent with the ECJ's case law and, in particular, *Lankhorst* (C-324/00) and *Test Claimants in the Thin Cap Group Litigation* (C-524/04). After the *SGI* case (C-311/08), it is possible to argue that there has been a shift in ECJ case law (albeit not a shift that has been acknowledged by the Court), so that it is now acceptable that some provisions will only be applicable to international dealings, because they *only make sense* in an international setting. Many Spanish commentators have since argued that the Spanish transfer pricing regime should be amended to reflect the new ECJ case law, thereby making it applicable only to purely international transactions. Some have even

---

[52] V. Ruiz Almendral, 'An Ever Distant Union: The Cross-border Loss Relief Conundrum in EU Law' (2010) 38(10) *Intertax* (October) 495.

gone as far as to argue that the fact that the transfer pricing regime also applies to purely domestic dealings may be counter to ECJ case law inasmuch as it implies an 'unnecessary burden' for taxpayers.[53] In fact, the broad scope of associated persons, which includes many different scenarios apart from the 'natural' transfer pricing scenario of intra-group dealings, adds significant weight to what is already a heavy burden of transfer pricing documentation in Spain.

The Spanish legislator intended to apply a transfer pricing regulation across the board. The goal was to reinstate the legitimacy of the system, since the situation before 2006 displayed a worrying lack of alignment with the OECD recommendations and international practices. But to go from a regime with almost no duties (certainly no documentation duties) to the current regime is probably too fast an acceleration in a very short time span.[54]

7.4.2 'Associated persons'

One salient feature of the Spanish transfer pricing regime, and an important deviation from both the 1995 and the 2010 OECD Guidelines, is the broad notion of 'associated persons'. It includes both individuals and entities in many different scenarios. The long list of associated persons is currently contained in article 16.3 of the LCIT, which did not represent a significant departure from the pre-2006 version:

(a) an entity and the owners of its equity (at least 5 per cent, 1 per cent when the company is listed in the stock market), including the spouse, ascendants or descendants;

(b) an entity and the members of its board of directors or their adminis-trators, including the spouse, ascendants or descendants of such member or administrator;

(c) two entities of the same group;

(d) an entity and the partners of an entity of the same group;

(e) an entity and the members of the board of directors of an entity of the same group, or their administrators;

---

[53] Martín Jiménez, 'Transfer Pricing and EU Law Following the ECJ Judgment in *SGI*', note 47 above, p. 279.

[54] Commentators have harshly critised this total symmetry of the transfer pricing regime and suggested it should be amended in order to be applied only to domestic dealings; among others see C. García Novoa, 'La necesaria modificación de la regulación de las operaciones vinculadas' (2010) 1 *Quincena Fiscal* (Westlaw.es).

(f) two entities where one of them owns, indirectly, at least 25 per cent of the other one;

(g) two entities when the same person (or the spouse, ascendants or descendants) or entity owns, directly or indirectly, 25 per cent of the entity;

(h) an entity resident in Spain and its permanent establishment located in another country;

(i) an entity resident in another country and its permanent establishment located in Spain.

The scope of the Spanish transfer pricing rules is also particularly wide as they also extend to domestic operations, not just to transnational ones. In addition, they also extend to individuals and their families and the result is a large number of taxpayers that are expected to bear a very heavy documentation burden, even if it has been reduced in the 2008 and 2010 reforms.

7.4.3   Determining the price: ALS and valuation methods

Market value: accounting rules versus tax law

Article 16 of the LCIT establishes the general rule to the effect that dealings and transactions must be valued at market price. The Spanish CIT, as is the case in many other corporate income taxes in OECD countries, takes the accounting result as a basis (article 10.3) upon which tax adjustments must be applied. Accounting rules, for their part, largely follow international accounting standards in order to reflect the market value. Specifically, valuation rule 21 of the General Accounting Plan (*Plan General de Contabilidad*, PGC) established by Royal Decree 1514/2007 of 17 November 2007, refers to the need to account by the 'normal market value' in operations undertaken by associated entities. The problem is that the notion of *associated entities* is not identical in accounting rules and tax law (article 16 of the LCIT).

Furthermore, the valuation methods reflected in accounting rules are more flexible than those contained in article 16.2 of the LCIT. The Preamble to the LATF, however, expressly reflects the aim of the new transfer pricing tax rules to be aligned with accounting rules. In most cases, this objective will be fulfilled, as the accounting result of a transfer pricing transaction will reflect a similar value to the tax result,[55] but not in all cases. Thus, a question arises as to whether the taxpayer *may* or in fact *must* adjust the accounting result, by way of a compensating adjustment, in order to reflect the market value *as established* in the tax rules. The Transfer Pricing Guidelines deal with this issue (paras. 4.38 and 4.39) and acknowledge that most OECD countries do not recognise compensating adjustments 'on the grounds that the tax return should reflect the actual transactions'.

In Spain, the law is not entirely clear on what the most adequate solution should be. Tax authorities have already taken the view that a compensating adjustment would not be admissible,[56] and this view has been endorsed by several commentators.[57] Others have criticised this view[58], arguing that article 16 of the LCIT establishes the obligation for taxpayers to ensure that their tax assessment complies with the ALS. To the extent that Spanish accounting rules are not completely aligned with tax rules and have their own (sometimes competing) objectives, compensating adjustments are not only *allowed* but should be *required*. Of course in these cases the taxpayer will have to properly document the reason for the adjustment.[59]

The main problem, regardless of one's viewpoint, is that neither the law nor the regulations expressly mention this situation, and this by itself is bound to increase conflicts in the future.

The methods

As a first step in the valuation process, taxpayers are required to undertake a comparability analysis of the elements that surround a given dealing or transaction (article 16.1 and 2 of the RCIT). This regulation is aligned with the OECD Guidelines (paras. 1.38–1.62), so that Spanish

---

[55] See M. Trapé, 'Ajustes valorativos y normas de contabilidad' in N. Carmona (ed.), *Régimen fiscal de las operaciones vinculadas: valoración y documentación* (Madrid: CISS, 2011), p. 106 *et seq.*

[56] The Spanish tax authorities have expressed that view in two binding rulings ('*consultas vinculantes*'), one of 7 February 2008 (ref. V0249/08) and a more recent one, on 10 November 2010 (ref. V2401/10).

[57] E. Sanz Gadea, 'Contabilización de las operaciones vinculadas y su relación con la regulación fiscal' in *Fiscalidad de los precios de transferencia (operaciones vinculadas)* (Madrid: CEF, 2010), p. 293 *et seq.*

[58] J. M. Calderón, 'Algunas consideraciones sobre la prestación de servicios intragrupo en el marco de la nueva regulación de operaciones vinculadas', (2008) *Carta Tributaria.*

[59] As suggested by the EU Joint Transfer Pricing Forum in their Code of Conduct on Documenting Transfer Pricing Transactions.

regulations simply set out the following five elements, which must be taken into account:

(a) the specific characteristics of the goods or services that are the object of the transfer prices;

(b) the functions performed by the associated parties with regard to the dealing or transaction at stake; in particular, the risks assumed and the assets used should be identified;

(c) the contractual reflection of the dealings and transactions, taking into account the responsibilities, risks and benefits deriving from them;

(d) the particularities of the markets in which dealings/transactions take place or other economic elements that may be affecting them; and

(e) any other circumstance that may be relevant to each case, including commercial strategies. When there are no data of comparable independent entities, or when the data is not reliable enough, the taxpayer should mention it in the documentation.

Because the RCIT does not elaborate further on these elements, it is reasonable to assume that the Tax Administration will, as it has done before, use the OECD Guidelines to 'complete' what is missing in the Spanish regulation. In fact, article 16.2 of the RCIT closely follows the Guidelines. In this regard, many questions arise that will need to be resolved in the coming years. One of the questions that remains unanswered is whether the Spanish tax authorities may employ secret comparables, as in some other jurisdictions. To date, no case law or ruling has addressed the problem of secret comparables. The LCIT, on the other hand, does not seem to forbid it. However, the Spanish Supreme Court has consistently rejected the use of secret data for the reassessment of other taxes, at least to the extent that it was not freely available to the taxpayer.[60]

The comparative analysis is the necessary step in choosing the most adequate method, departing from the obvious assumption that being comparable entails that none of the differences with the entity that serves as the comparator are relevant enough to determine different prices. Comparable information is currently available in different formats. First, the annual accounts of companies registered in Spain are officially listed at the Mercantile Registry (Registro Mercantil) and are therefore publicly available. More generally, a general database on Spanish companies is

---

[60] Among others, judgments of 26 May 1989, 19 October 1995 and 3 December 1999.

also available. In this regard, tax authorities confirm using different transfer pricing databases, such as Amadeus (European scope) or SABI.[61] How comparables are used in practice will be important and will have a constitutional relevance. It is settled in case law that the use of indices and indirect elements for the construction of the taxable base does not comply with the rule of law (Constitutional Court Cases (STC) 146/1994, 255/2004).

Paradoxically, using the more detailed guidelines employed by the OECD in the 2010 version could provide both taxpayers and the Tax Administration with better tools to determine the best instruments to apply the method, at the same time as fulfilling the legitimate expectations of the taxpayer. But, of course, it would be necessary that the Transfer Pricing Guidelines were in one way or another enacted in Spanish law.

While valuation methods were merely mentioned in the 1995 transfer pricing system, the 2006 reform introduced a brief description of their functions. It also established the transactional net margin method (TNMM) for the first time in the Spanish system.

The new article 16 of the LCIT also modifies the hierarchy of the transfer pricing methods. Before 2006, the comparable uncontrolled price (CUP) was the preferred method, while the cost plus method and the resale price method occupied a secondary position in the hierarchy. Finally, the profit split method was considered subsidiary.

After 2006, CUP, cost plus and resale price are all in the first position. Only when a taxpayer cannot apply any of them, will she then be able to resort to the profit split or to the TNMM. These two methods are now subsidiary.

The inclusion of the methods in the LCIT deviates from the OECD Guidelines in two basic aspects: first, the methods are pre-ordained and secondly, the TNMM method is considered to be subsidiary, something which sits at odds with the current situation where it is, by far, the method employed most often.

The current (2010) OECD Guidelines show a paradigm shift towards a 'best method' rule, even if the US system[62] is not endorsed or suggested.[63] This change is reflected in para. 2.2, which states that 'no one method is suitable in every possible situation and the applicability of any

---

[61] The Bureau Van Dijk database listing companies located within the Iberian peninsula.
[62] See Regs. 1.482–1(c); Chapter 1, II, C (887 T.M.).
[63] In fact, the US system is criticised in para. 1.69.

particular method need not be disproved'. It also actively encourages the tax authorities to undertake 'minor or marginal" adjustments as needed. At the same time, the Guidelines also 'allow' taxpayers to go beyond the OECD methods as long as this deviation is justified.

The question in Spain is whether the Tax Administration may in fact make use of this greater flexibility in terms of correcting the taxpayer's valuation, and whether it will show the same flexibility when allowing taxpayers to deviate from the methods as required by the LCIT. Considering the law in isolation, and in particular article 16, none of the two flexibilities seems plausible, even if, as para. 1.70 of the Guidelines states, clearly it is 'not possible to provide specific rules that will cover every case'.

The introduction of the TNMM is one of the new elements of Law 36/2006 and so there is, to date, no case law regarding its actual implementation.

First and foremost, the question is whether a taxpayer may use the TNMM directly, without exhausting the first three preferred methods. The Law does not provide much information, which in fact may result in some flexibility; thus, article 16.4.2º of the LCIT states that taxpayers may use the two subsidiary methods (profit split and TNMM) when 'given the complexity of the dealings/transactions or the information that is available the first three methods cannot be applied satisfactorily'. This should allow enough leeway for taxpayers to discard the first three methods by giving a reasonable explanation for it.

Partly owing to the extension of commercial databases for finding comparables and in general the increase of available data in the past few years, the TNMM is currently the most frequently employed method;[64] it is both easy to employ and certainly more cost-effective.

The Spanish CIT regulations have also introduced what can be regarded as the 'sixth method'. In fact, article 16.6 of the RCIT establishes a special rule for transactions or dealings entered into by professionals. Thus, a taxpayer may consider the transaction to be at arm's length when a number of conditions are met that actually show the dealing to be a

---

[64] The current publicly available information on APAs does not give much information about what methods were used, but both the Informal Transfer Pricing Survey 2011 and the opinions of most Spanish commentators and practitioners suggest that this is true, something consistent with the trend in other OECD countries. See L. Jones Rodríguez, 'Métodos para determinar el valor normal de mercado de las operaciones vinculadas' in N. Carmona (ed.), *Operaciones Vinculadas* (Valencia: CISS, 2009), pp.189–90.

professional service. That a method is established in the regulations, and not in the law, is also problematic in terms of the rule of law and its interpretation by the Constitutional Court.

A further problem regarding the valuation of transactions is relatively recent and remains unresolved: it has been questioned whether the customs value should or should not coincide with the transfer pricing value, at least in those cases where the tax authorities have actually corrected the customs value to align it to market value. There are solid arguments to deny this assimilation. The main one is that customs regulations have their own objective that is served by determining the customs value. Of course, the different value may create problems in some cases, but these would not be solved by aligning the values but by enhancing the exchange of information. This is the view expressed by the Transfer Pricing Guidelines (paras. 1.78 and 1.79)[65] and also the view largely followed by the Spanish tax authorities and by the courts. However, two relatively recent Supreme Court opinions (of 30 November 2009 and 11 December 2009) challenge the prevailing view and require the tax authorities to follow, for a CIT assessment, the customs value that had been amended for the purpose of customs duties. It remains to be seen whether this view holds in the future or whether these are merely two isolated cases.

Intra-group services and cost-sharing agreements

The tax treatment of intra-group services has also been substantially changed in the new transfer pricing regime. Before 2006, only management fees were deductible, when certain requirements were met, such as the conclusion of a contract before the services were rendered. Those requirements made deducing the cost very difficult in many situations, and were certainly not aligned with the OECD Guidelines or international practice in that regard. The new article 16 of the LCIT (section 5) establishes that intra-group services will be tax deductible

---

[65] '[C]ooperation between income tax and customs administrations within a country in evaluating transfer prices is becoming more common and this should help to reduce the number of cases where customs valuations are found unacceptable for tax purposes or vice versa. Greater cooperation in the area of exchange of information would be particularly useful, and should not be difficult to achieve in countries that already have integrated administrations for income taxes and customs duties. Countries that have separate administrations may wish to consider modifying the exchange of information rules so that the information can flow more easily between the different administrations.'

as long as the taxpayer is able to show that the beneficiary obtains an advantage or utility from the rendering of such services.

When they are rendered in favour of more than one entity and a simple division is not possible, a rational criterion for distributing their cost will be accepted. In this regard, the LCIT establishes that a criterion will meet the rationality standard if the nature of the services, the circumstances under which they are rendered and the eventual benefits obtained are all taken into account.

On 17 May 2011, ECOFIN adopted the guidelines drafted by the EU Joint Transfer Pricing Forum (JTPF)[66] on low value adding intra-group services, which when (if) followed by Spanish law (as they should, at least according to the LATF's Preamble), should imply a lighter burden in documentation requirements, as well as less litigation, since intra-group dealings and their valuation are one of the most disputed areas of transfer pricing, and not just in Spain. This is logical considering their existence is already quite hard to prove, as is their valuation, so that only indirect indicators, with a rationale criterion, will normally serve as proof.

The increasing importance of intellectual property and its exponential increase in the past few years contribute to cost-sharing agreements, entered into for the development of intangibles, which have become more and more relevant in the area of transfer pricing. Spanish tax authorities are particularly worried about the potential for tax avoidance that intangibles may offer in transfer pricing.

Currently, expenses will be deducted if three conditions are met:

(a) the individuals or entities party to the agreement have access to property rights, or rights with similar economic effects, which are a direct consequence of or have been developed as part of the agreement;

(b) the contribution of the related party has taken into account the foreseen advantages or utilities that may be expected from it, according to rational criteria; and

(c) the agreements address changes in the circumstances or the parties to it and provide for the corresponding adjustment should the case arrive.

The main problem with the Spanish regulation of cost-sharing agreements is similar to other areas of transfer pricing: the regulations are

---

[66] See guidelines drafted by the EU Joint Transfer Pricing Forum on low value adding intra-group services.

scarce and do not completely regulate these issues that are becoming more and more complex. Directly applying the Guidelines completes the regulations, but this takes us back to the rule of law issues that were pointed out above.

Thin capitalisation rules and transfer pricing

Thin capitalisation rules are fully developed in Spain, in the sense that there is consistent case law and clear indications as to how they are to be applied. However, the thin capitalisation rule, currently in article 20 of the LCIT, is particularly simple and not very useful in practice. According to this provision, when the total indebtedness (be it direct or indirect) of a Spanish resident (entity) with a non-EU resident is in excess of a 3 to 1 ratio,[67] with respect to the fiscal capital of the entity, the excess accrued interest will be treated as a dividend. The main consequence is that the payments will not be deductible for the payer and that a withholding tax will be applied.

The thin capitalisation rule is connected to the transfer pricing rules in many aspects, in particular, for the rule to apply there must be an association as defined in article 16 of the LCIT and the taxpayer may apply for an APA to deal with his particular indebted situation. Furthermore, the rule consists of a secondary adjustment.

The thin capitalisation rule was enacted in 1992, and was practically stripped of any effect on 1 January 2004, as EU operations are now excluded from it, even if a general anti-avoidance rule (GAAR) may still be applicable.[68] In fact, article 20 is not only quite ineffective, but it is also not in line with the ALS. There are many problems with this provision,[69] that can be summed up in four issues: (i) the fact that it is not applicable to EU residents probably saves it from a breach of EU law, but renders it quite useless, as it will only apply to non-EU cross-borders situations; (ii) both the bluntness and the simplicity of the ratio make it very easy to circumvent; (iii) at the same time, the taxpayer is not given an opportunity to prove that there is a commercial reason for indebtedness; (iv) the rule may even be contrary to some double

---

[67] A higher ratio may be authorised by the tax authorities upon request, in those cases where a taxpayer is able to prove that he would have benefited from a higher ratio under normal market conditions.

[68] In fact, a GAAR is likely more consistent with the ECJ case law on tax avoidance.

[69] V. Ruiz Almendral, 'Subcapitalización y libertad de establecimiento: el caso *Test Claimants in the Thin Cap Group Litigation* como una oportunidad para rehabilitar el artículo 20 del TRLIS' (2008) 283 *Noticias de la Unión Europea* 125.

taxation treaties signed by Spain, to the extent that it ultimately implies a heavier burden on transnational dealings than on domestic ones and may therefore be contrary to the non-discrimination principle.[70]

The current wording of article 20 of the LCIT reflects a more fundamental problem: the effects that the ECJ's case law has on the tax systems of Member States, in particular, on anti-abuse or tax control rules. The Court can only decide on the basis of the relevant treaties, which currently bestow direct taxation powers on Member States (according to the subsidiarity principle).

In practice, when Member States are faced with an EU compatibility problem of their tax systems, they do one of three things, all of them damaging to the internal coherence of tax systems, and in the end, to neutrality in the EU: first, they may increase the scope of the rule. Thus, when the problem is an anti-abuse rule that is stricter for transnational situations, the rule may be changed so that it is also applied in domestic situations. This is exactly what has happened with thin capitalisation rules, originally designed for an international setting.[71] Second, when the problematic provision is some type of tax advantage or benefit which was only available for domestic operations or agents, the solution may be either to extend it to other EU members, or, third, simply to eliminate it altogether, which will be less challenging for tax revenues. In all cases, the result may be equally unsatisfactory, for at least some of the agents lose the benefit, with nobody gaining it.

7.4.4   Documentation requirements

In line with other European systems, such as the German or the French, the Spanish transfer pricing regime now requires taxpayers to keep extensive documentation of their transfer prices. The documentation regime largely follows the EU JTPF Code of Conduct, so the master file prepared by taxpayers should follow this Code.

But the broad scope of the Spanish transfer pricing regime, caused by the large list of related or associated persons, has made it necessary to amend the system in order to ease the documentation requirements.

---

[70] That was the conclusion reached by the Spanish Supreme Court in its Ruling of 1 October 2009.

[71] I elaborate on this point in Ruiz Almendral, 'Subcapitalización y libertad de establecimiento', note 69 above, 129 et seq.; and V. Ruiz Almendral, 'Entre la discriminación y la armonización: el régimen fiscal del no residente en España a la luz del Derecho Comunitario' (2008) 307 Estudios Financieros 3.

Thus, the documentation regime originally established by Royal Decree 1793/2008 (which amended the RCIT), was first amended (by Royal Decree 897/2010) in order to lighten the burden of documentation requirements. The current obligations are in force for entities that cannot be considered small or medium only since 19 February 2009. It was amended a second time for small and medium-sized entities (by Royal Decree 13/2010 that entered into force on 1 January 2011).[72]

This (double) reform has been generally welcomed by commentators who feared that the burdensome system of documentation, established in the middle of one of the worst economic crises in Spain, may impose too high a cost on small and medium-sized entities, and even on individuals, given the broad personal scope of Spanish transfer pricing rules.

Currently, the basic documentation requirements are set out in the CIT Regulations (arts. 18–20). Article 16.2 of the LCIT merely establishes who should keep that documentation: all associated individuals or entities. But it also establishes the exemptions listed below, together with a number of exceptions to the exemptions. This complexity mirrors the regime itself, not always easy to assess.

First, as a general rule, the documentation requirements will not be applicable to individuals or entities that have made a net profit, in the previous fiscal year, under 10 million euros, as long as the amount of the operations subject to transfer pricing rules does not exceed the amount of 100,000 euros. This limit will not be applicable to dealings undertaken with individuals or entities that are resident in an offshore territory or low tax country,[73] unless such a low tax country is in the European Union and the taxpayer is able to prove that the dealings have a 'valid economic motive' and that the individuals and entities with which the dealing took place undertake 'economic activities', as opposed to being a 'passive income' dealing.

The second amendment (enacted in 2010) of the documentation regime establishes an exemption from the documentation regime for all persons and entities, regardless of their net benefit (whether they are a big multinational or a small enterprise). As long as the dealings are

---

[72] The documentation obligations must be deemed to apply to transactions performed on or after 19 February 2009.

[73] Spain has a strict regime in relation to offshore countries. There is currently a 'black list' of offshore territories established in Royal Decree 1080/1991 of 5 July 1991 (por el que se determinan los países o territorios a que se refieren los artículos 2, apartado 3, número 4, de la Ley 17/1991, de 27 de mayo, de Medidas Fiscales Urgentes, y 62 de la Ley 31/1990, de 27 de diciembre, de Presupuestos Generales del Estado para 1991).

undertaken with one and the same person or entity and they amount to a figure not higher than 250,000 euros (article 18.4.e of the RCIT) there will be no need to document them. This exemption has several exceptions: (i) transactions carried out with tax havens; (ii) transactions concerning business transfers; (iii) share deals or transfers of real estate; and, finally, (iv) transactions related to intangible property.

7.4.5   Assessment regime and procedures to revise the taxpayer's valuation: corresponding adjustments

As mentioned above, one of the most salient features of the new transfer pricing regime is that taxpayers are now required by law to value transactions between associated parties at arm's length. The Tax Administration may then revise that value in a regular audit procedure, as provided by article 16.1.2° of the LCIT. Of course, the assessed value will be also applicable to the rest of the parties (not initially subject to the audit, as this will be done on an individual basis). The other associated parties may then challenge the revision undertaken by the tax authorities.

The audit procedure in Spain[74] will normally be initiated by a tax inspector, either because he was ordered to, because it was included in his Personal Confidential Tax Audit Plan for the fiscal year or because he came across relevant data in the course of another procedure. Once the audit process begins, the taxpayer will be informed of the nature, the scope (what taxes, what fiscal years, what transactions, etc.) and his rights and obligations throughout the proceedings. Generally, the audit must be concluded in no more than twelve months, but if certain conditions are met (complex nature of transactions, international transactions, etc.) it may be extended to a maximum of another twelve months.[75] In the course of the procedure, the taxpayer normally has the opportunity, and the obligation, to submit documentation and add relevant data for the eventual reassessment proposal. Once this proposal is adopted by the tax inspector it may be accepted or not by the taxpayer. Lowering the possible sanction will reward acceptance by the taxpayer, together with the forfeiture of future claims.

When a transfer pricing transaction is at stake, the procedure will be basically the same, except that the tax inspector must file a separate

---

[74] The procedure is regulated in art. 141–159 of the General Tax Code.
[75] Article 150 of the GTC.

reassessment containing all data relevant to the transaction and stating why, if that is the case, it is not at arm's length value, how it should be reassessed to meet the ALS, etc. (article 21 of the RCIT).

Should the taxpayer not agree with the proposal of the tax inspector, he may present a writ of allegations to the inspector's superior body, who will then decide to do one of three things: uphold the initial proposal, modify it or revoke it altogether. If the taxpayer is still not satisfied with the result, he may then do one of the two following things: (i) challenge the valuation by way of the '*tasación pericial contradictoria*', a procedure designed specifically for that purpose (article 135 of the General Tax Code (GTC)); or (ii) appeal directly to the TEAC (in that case, the possible result of the assessment must be either paid or guaranteed).

One of the main problems that the transfer pricing assessment regime poses is the restricted opportunities for other associated individuals or entities to take part in the assessment process. Thus, the other associated parties that are not the subject of an audit cannot actually participate in the valuation process. Only once the Tax Administration has reached a correcting value, with the possible assistance of the audited party, may the associated party challenge the resulting assessment. This may seem a matter of time – the important issue is that associated parties are in fact able to challenge the valuation – but in fact is of paramount importance, as the associated party will not be part of the valuation process and therefore will not be able to challenge the methods employed until a later time, when the process is finished. It may then be harder to impose a different version, which ultimately will entail a longer, costlier litigation.[76]

The situation is different when the related party is also a tax resident in Spain. In that case, the other party will be notified and given an opportunity to present facts or additional arguments that they consider relevant to the matter.

This asymmetry in the associated parties' opportunities within an assessment process poses a number of problems: first, the assessment system is, as a result, less efficient, as it may take longer and be more conflict-prone. Furthermore, at least according to some commentators,

---

[76] See criticism by J. M. Calderón and A. Martín Jiménez, 'El procedimiento de comprobación del valor normal de mercado de las operaciones vinculadas' in N. Carmona (ed.), *Operaciones Vinculadas* (Valencia: CISS, 2009), p. 444 *et seq.*

this may ultimately be a breach of the right to due process, contemplated in article 24 of the Spanish Constitution.[77]

On the other hand, it must be borne in mind that transfer pricing audit activity has substantially increased under the new regime and is very likely to rise in the future. Until the 2006 reform, transfer pricing issues would normally be a part of a general tax audit. This is no longer so as the Tax Administration is currently undertaking an internal reorganisation in order to fulfil the obligations of the new regime.[78]

A corresponding (bilateral) adjustment, as the 'adjustment to the tax liability of the associated enterprise in a second tax jurisdiction made by the tax administration of that jurisdiction, corresponding to a primary adjustment made by the tax administration in a first tax jurisdiction, so that the allocation of profits by the two jurisdictions is consistent'[79] is key to the adequate functioning of a transfer pricing regime, and is the only way to correctly implement the ALS in a sound manner, as well as to avoid double taxation, which is why it is reflected in Article 9.2 of the OECD Model Tax Convention:

> Where a Contracting State includes in the profits of an enterprise of that State – and taxes accordingly – profits on which an enterprise of the other Contracting State has been charged to tax in that other State and the profits so included are profits which would have accrued to the enterprise of the first-mentioned State if the conditions made between the two enterprises had been those which would have been made between independent enterprises, then that other State shall make an appropriate adjustment to the amount of the tax charged therein on those profits. In determining such adjustment, due regard shall be had to the other provisions of this Convention and the competent authorities of the Contracting States shall if necessary consult each other.

Of course, Article 9.2 was not intended to be applied directly, and ultimately its effectiveness is contingent on how access to the mutual agreement procedure is granted.[80]

---

[77] J. M. Calderón and A. Martín Jiménez, 'El procedimiento aplicable tras la regularización tributaria del valor normal de mercado de las operaciones vinculadas' in N. Carmona (ed.), *Régimen Fiscal de las operaciones vinculadas* (Madrid: CISS/Wolters Kluwer, 2010), p. 577.

[78] See Informal Transfer Pricing Survey 2011.

[79] OECD Transfer Pricing Guidelines, Glossary, p. 25.

[80] K. Vogel, *Klaus Vogel on Dobule Taxation Conventions* (The Hague: Kluwer Law International, 1997), p. 555; A. García Prats, 'Artículo 9 MC OCDE. Empresas asociadas' in

The regulation of corresponding adjustments is highly problematic in Spanish law, as many commentators have pointed out.[81] First, not all DTCs currently include Article 9.2,[82] although in case of DTCs entered into with EU Member States, the Arbitration Convention 90/436/(EC) will apply.[83]

Before 2006, primary adjustments would only be undertaken when the overall result of the operation, which deviates from the ALS, resulted in less taxation in Spain than would have occurred had the ALS been correctly applied. Since the Tax Administration would only correct a transfer price in those cases, only positive primary adjustments would be undertaken (that is, adjustments that increased the price after adjusting it).

As for corresponding adjustments, they would only be automatically applied in domestic operations. For international operations, corresponding adjustments would be excluded if no double taxation convention were applicable. Even when a DTC was applicable, the adjustment would not be automatically applied, and certainly could not be undertaken by the taxpayers directly. The non-resident was forced to initiate the mutual agreement procedure.

There is solid basis to argue that this asymmetric treatment of domestic and international situations was most likely contrary to the non-discrimination principle, as envisaged in Article 24 of the DTCs that follow the OECD Model, as well as contrary to the non-discrimination principle that stems from European law.

The situation, in this particular aspect, has not fundamentally changed after 2006.[84] According to article 16.9 of the LCIT and article

J. R. Ruiz and J. M. Calderón (eds.), *Comentarios a los convenios para evitar la doble imposición y prevenir la evasión fiscal concluidos por España*, Fundación Pedro Barrié de la Maza-Instituto de Estudios Económicos de Galicia (A Coruña, 2004), p. 561.

[81] It was also problematic before the 2006 reform; see criticism in J. M. Calderón and A. Martín Jiménez, 'Presupuestos y limitaciones del ajuste valorativo del artículo 16 TRLIS' in N. Carmona (ed.), *Operaciones Vinculadas* (Valencia: CISS, 2009), p. 87 *et seq.*

[82] In fact, the following DTCs do not: Germany, Austria, Brazil, Bulgaria, South Korea, Ecuador, Finland, Hungary, India, Indonesia, Italy, Japan, Luxembourg, Morocco, Mexico, The Netherlands, United Kingdom, Switzerland, Thailand and Tunisia.

[83] Commentators have harshly criticised the fact that a mere Convention is used, when a Directive would have been more effective; in Spain see P. R. Falcón v Tella and E. Pulido Guerra, *Derecho Fiscal Internacional* (Madrid: Marcial Pons, 2010), p. 237.

[84] As some commentators have already pointed out; see, among others, Calderón and Martín Jiménez, 'Presupuestos y limitaciones del ajuste valorativo del artículo 16 TRLIS', note 81 above, p. 87 *et seq.*

21 of the RCIT, non-residents will continue to be in a significantly worse position than residents. In particular, non-residents without a permanent establishment located in Spain will not be able to apply a correlative adjustment automatically applicable. If the non-resident has a DTC, he will be able to initiate the mutual agreement procedure, following the procedure established in Decree 1794/2008.[85] The basic problem lies in article 8.2.e of this Decree, that denies the possibility of the process in those cases where it can be ascertained that the taxpayer is in fact trying to avoid taxation in one of the two Member States (party to the DTC). This limitation on claiming the corresponding adjustment is not present in a purely domestic operation.[86]

7.4.6 'Non-recognition of a transaction' and 'recharacterisation' as anti-abuse rules

The new transfer pricing regime includes, for the first time in the Spanish tax system, a specific rule to recharacterise the tax base as a consequence of a transfer pricing assessment. Thus, articles 16.8 of the LCIT (and article 21bis of the RCIT) establish the so-called 'secondary adjustment'. The purpose of the rule is to ensure the correct tax treatment of the differences in valuation that arise once the ALS has been applied to a transaction or dealing (that previously had not been valued at arm's length). Article 16.8 will then be applicable to 'operations in which the agreed amount or consideration differs from the normal market value'. Should that situation occur, 'the difference between the two values [the actual value and the ALS value] will be taxed according to its nature'. This recharacterisation, for the purpose of the tax assessment, will result in a corresponding adjustment to all associated parties. Should the difference in value arise in a partner–enterprise relationship, the difference will be treated as a capital contribution (when it favours the entity) or as a profit distribution (when it is the partner/shareholder that is benefited).

---

[85] Real Decreto 1794/2008 of 3 November 2008 (BOE 278 of 18 November 2008), por el que se aprueba el Reglamento de procedimientos amistosos en materia de imposición directa. See on this process and how it does (or does not) comply with the OECD Guidelines, S. López Rivas, 'Procedimientos amistosos en materia de imposición directa' (2009) 131 *Crónica Tributaria* 36.

[86] Calderón and Martín Jiménez, 'Presupuestos y limitaciones del ajuste valorativo del artículo 16 TRLIS', note 81 above, p. 89.

The process is relatively simple: first, the Tax Administration audits the tax base and detects an inconsistency between the fair market value (ALS) and the actual transaction price reflected in the tax base. This inconsistency is corrected by amending the values and, should there be an excess income deemed to one of the associated parties, it would be recharacterised accordingly for tax purposes. This provision follows the OECD Guidelines, and specifically the main objective attributed to secondary adjustments: 'to account for the difference between the re-determined taxable profits and the originally booked profits' (para. 4.66). It is also only relatively new in the Spanish tax system; article 13 of the General Tax Law 58/2003 (*General Tributaria*, GTL) establishes the general 'characterisation' principle, by establishing that the tax debt shall arise according to the real economic nature of the dealing or transaction, regardless of the name or characterisation given to it by taxpayers.

Absent article 16.8 of the LCIT, article 13 of the GTL would provide sufficient legal cover for the tax authorities to recharacterise the income for tax purposes. It should finally be noted that neither article 16.8 of the LCIT nor article 13 of the GTL are anti-abuse rules, but merely reflect the general principle that tax laws have their own object-ives. In reality, however, article 13 has been applied time and again by the tax authorities as a general anti-avoidance rule.[87]

Spanish commentators, some even claiming that the regime may be unconstitutional, have harshly criticised this new provision.[88] The basic problem lies in whether these adjustments will be applied in an auto-matic manner, or whether the taxpayer will be given the opportunity to prove that there are commercial reasons for the deviation in value. If the *SGI* case law is taken into account, then the analysis of commercial reasons must be allowed. The author submits that this should be correct if we consider article 16.8 to be an anti-abuse rule. But this is not the case, at least according to the current wording of the provision.

Ultimately the problem lies in what interpretation the Spanish courts and tax authorities decide to give to this provision. In this regard,

---

[87] V. Ruiz Almendral, *El Fraude a la Ley Tributaria a examen* (Pamplona: Aranzadi, 2006), p. 56 *et seq.*

[88] Martín Jiménez, 'Transfer Pricing and EU Law Following the ECJ Judgment in *SGI*', note 47 above, p. 279. See also J.M. Calderón and A. Martín Jiménez, 'Los ajustes secundarios en la nueva regulación de las operaciones vinculadas' in N. Carmona (ed.), *Operaciones Vinculadas* (Valencia: CISS, 2009).

existing case law on article 13 is not very promising. Even if there are no cases yet dealing with the application of article 16.8 of the LCIT, the case law suggests that the courts may use their current case law on tax avoidance as a basis to apply article 16.8. In fact, in some cases the courts have disregarded whole transactions on two bases: (i) that they would not have occurred had the parties been unrelated, and (ii) that the only purpose was a tax purpose. This was the approach taken in the case decided by the National High Court on 3 May 2009, where the whole transaction was disregarded on the basis of the assignment of risks, the functions that had been carried out and the agreed economic compensations. This should only happen in extreme cases, but the question is whether it makes sense for the Tax Administration and the courts to apply tax avoidance doctrine to valuation/transfer pricing issues in all cases where the transactions are not consistent with the ALS – in other words, whether transforming the absence of arm's length prices into presumptions of avoidance is not actually a *recharacterisation* and a disregard of the purpose and objectives of transfer pricing rules. In this regard, the National High Court in a judgment issued on 21 May 2009 and the Central Economic-Administrative Court in a resolution issued on 22 October 2009, have respectively supported recharacterisation with the argument that an independent party would not have entered into a similar transaction.

In any event, the introduction of a secondary adjustment in Spanish transfer pricing rules has been harshly criticised. Thus, for example, some commentators have criticised the system on the grounds that secondary adjustments are deemed to be automatic in the law, which would run counter to their being an anti-abuse measure to be used only in extreme circumstances, and on the grounds that the legal provision is not sufficiently developed in the regulations.[89] I submit that none of these arguments can be accepted: article 16.8 is not primarily an anti-abuse provision, even if it may prevent abuse in some cases (something entirely different). On the other hand, the law sufficiently regulates the adjustment and its consequences so no problem with the rule of law should arise. Incidentally, this is one of the few areas of Spanish transfer pricing regulations when the law actually regulates most of the issue. Other aspects of article 16 of the LCIT are left for the RCIT, or even the

---

[89] Calderón and Martín Jiménez, *ibid.* pp. 507–18.

OECD Guidelines. Other authors have even gone as far as suggesting that article 16.8 of the LCIT may be unconstitutional.[90]

There is no specific rule in the LCIT allowing for the disregard of the transaction, as suggested by para. 1.64 to 1.69 of the Guidelines. However, in the Spanish tax system there are two general anti-avoidance rules that would meet the goal set in the Guidelines. The first rule, article 15 of the GTL, establishes a typical anti-avoidance rule and has elements common to both the German rule (article 42 of the Abgabenordnung) and the US business purpose test doctrines.[91] Section 15 of the GTL mainly refers to a problem of interpretation, where the way in which the taxpayer has interpreted a certain provision differs, 'conflicts', with that intended by the purpose of the law. Such a conflict[92] will arise:

> when the taxpayer succeeds in totally or partially avoiding the tax, or obtains a tax benefit of any kind through acts or arrangements in which both the following circumstances occur:
>
> (a) individually considered or, as a group such acts are clearly artificial or improper for attaining the pursued economic objective;
> (b) that no other substantial consequences arise from the adoption of this legal form or arrangement as would have arisen had the normal, proper form been used.

Article 16 of the GTC is an anti-sham rule and is intended to apply to the most egregious cases of tax avoidance. Article 16 is thus designed for clear abusive cases where there is virtually no transaction. It remains to be seen to what extent the tax authorities use this provision in order to disregard transactions that substantially differ from the ALS, for example, in a case where the risks assigned to the parties, the functions carried out or the agreed economic

---

[90] C. García Novoa, 'El ajuste secundario en las operaciones vinculadas' (2008) 12 *Quincena Fiscal* 57. Other Spanish commentators have actually welcomed the provision, on the grounds that it fosters legal certainty: C. García-Herrera, 'Algunas reflexiones sobre la nueva regulación de las operaciones vinculadas del Impuesto sobre Sociedades' (2007) 7 *Quincena Fiscal* 37; E. Sanz Gadea, 'Modificaciones introducidas en el IS por las Leyes 35/2006 y 36/2006' (2007) 287 *Revista Contabilidad y Tributación* 3.

[91] As the author concluded in V. Ruiz Almendral and G. Seitz, 'Die neue spanische Umgehungsvorschrift des Art. 15 Ley General Tributaria (LGT) – Ist der deutsche SS. 42 AO als Vorbild geeignet?' (2004) 4 *Steuer und Wirtschaft* 328.

[92] The term 'conflict', employed for the first time by the GTL 2003, is somewhat deceptive, in that it may mislead as to the interpretation of the provision, which is an anti-avoidance provision in its own right, not a mere description of a conflict.

compensations established among companies of a group would never have occurred had the parties been independent.[93]

The main difference between these two rules lies in the consequences. While article 15 of the GTC entails merely the recharacterization, or disregard, of the transaction undertaken by the taxpayer, as well as the payment of interest, article 16 will normally entail the imposition of sanctions and may well be grounds for a criminal conviction for tax fraud. The dramatic differences in the consequences that applying either of these two rules may have are not consistent with the similarities among them. In fact the tax authorities seem to treat them as inter-changeable rules, and end up applying article 16 even in cases where article 15 may be more suitable.

On the other hand, it is important to note that transfer pricing is by and large regarded as a 'high risk area' in terms of tax abuse and tax fraud. In fact, the Plan de Control Tributario 2011[94] lists as one of the high priorities the abuse of transfer pricing.

7.4.7   Penalty regime

In practice, as mentioned above, in the pre-2006 regime it was legally very difficult to impose penalties for breaches of the transfer pricing regime, as taxpayers were not required to value at arm's length and the tax authorities generally lacked the necessary information to prove that the taxpayer had not complied with his obligations.

One of the most salient novelties of the current transfer pricing regime is the establishment, also for the first time in Spain, of a specific penalty regime for transfer pricing transactions. The penalty regime is very severe and is directly linked to failure to comply with the documentation regime. Failure to provide the tax authorities with the complete documentation is

---

[93] As J. Zornoza points out, the anti-fraud provision has been and continues to be frequently abused by the tax authorities, which tend to apply it beyond the scope of the provision to transactions that are closer to the tax avoidance rule (art. 15 of the GTL). J. Zornoza, 'La simulación en Derecho tributario', in J. Arrieta, M. Collado and J. Zornoza (eds.), *Tratado sobre la Ley General Tributaria. Estudios en Homenaje a Alvaro Rodríguez Bereijo* (Thomson-Aranzadi, TI, 2010), p. 520 *et seq.*

[94] The 'Tax Control Plan' is the title of the guidelines that the tax authorities must make public every year, in order to prevent an arbitrary selection of those taxpayers who would potentially be subject to an audit. Of course, the plan only provides general guidelines, so as not to provide information that would eventually make useless a possible auditing process.

in itself an infringement, the sanction being greater depending on whether and to what amount a tax adjustment is also necessary.

There are different types of penalties depending on whether the tax audit results or not in a tax adjustment. When the tax base is not modified by the tax authorities, i.e., no tax adjustments, the penalty will be of 15,000 euros for every element of information that has been omitted, is inaccurate or is false.

Should, on the other hand, the tax audit reveal a need to adjust the tax base, the penalty will rise to 15 per cent of the given tax adjustment, with a minimum penalty of 30,000 euros per omitted, inaccurate or false data.

The penalty regime is not actually fully regulated in the GTL, but rather in the Regulations. This has recently been put into question by the Spanish Supreme Court (*Auto* 8 February 2011[95]), which on a prejudicial question on constitutionality sent to the Constitutional Court[96] enquired whether this situation complies with the rule of law and specifically with the constitutional obligation that Parliament must establish the basic regime of penalties (article 25 of the Constitution).

7.5   Transfer pricing disputes

The juiciest problems in the application of transfer pricing rules in Spain have not seen the light as yet. Several reasons explain this.

First, until 2006, the transfer pricing regime was to be applied only by the tax authorities, when correcting or re-evaluating a given assessment. This, of course, shaped the whole assessment practice and the subsequent, only eventual, evaluation by the tax authorities. Litigation will therefore now be focused on the audits undertaken on the basis of what the taxpayers have documented. In this regard, taxpayers may conclude the assessment procedure by helping define the taxable event and agreeing to the consequences, in what is a form of transaction accepted in article 155 of the GTL. The main consequence for the taxpayer is that sanctions will be automatically reduced by 50 per cent.

Second, because the 2006 transfer pricing regime entered into force in different phases, many taxpayers have not had the chance to challenge the results of the tax audits in court. Even before 2006, most of the disputes

---

[95] See on this case J. M. Calderón Carrero and M. Díaz-Moro Paraja, 'Decision Raises Doubts about Transfer Pricing Law', *Tax Notes International*, 25 April 2011, 284.

[96] When a given court is unsure about the constitutionality of a regime, it may 'request' the opinion of the Constitutional Court.

began and ended with a tax audit, so that it is very difficult, even misleading, to link the existing cases to the current 2010 OECD Guidelines. In fact, the vast majority of the cases deal with valuation issues, but do so from an anti-avoidance perspective, specifically trying to determine if the operation resulted in a lower tax burden in Spain. This is because, until 2006, transfer pricing rules were mainly internal rules.

BOX 7.5 STRUCTURE OF RESOLVING TRANSFER PRICING DISPUTES

Administrative level
Taxpayer files his tax assessment disclosing all relevant information and paying the corresponding tax debt.

Within the next four years (Spanish Statute of Limitations) a tax audit may investigate the taxpayer. If the tax auditor finds information sufficient to reassess the declared tax position, a tax file (*acta de inspección*) will declare that result.

The taxpayer may then challenge the final tax file, normally (in transfer pricing cases) before the TEAC which will then issue a Resolution (RTEAC).

Judicial level
The RTEAC may be challenged in court. Depending on the type of case, and the circumstances, a different type of court will decide – Regional High Court (Tribunal Superior de Justicia); High Court (Audiencia Nacional); or Supreme Court (Tribunal Supremo).

Constitutional level
The Constitutional Court is not part of the Judiciary system but stands above all state powers (judicial, legislative, executive). Laws may be challenged before the Court, either directly or by a court that needs to apply them – hence the Supreme Court's ruling asking the Constitutional Court whether the penalty regime complies with the rule of law.

Transfer pricing disputes around the world are increasing for reasons other than the transfer pricing regulations themselves: increased budgets dedicated to the control of transfer pricing; increased sophistication of databases; more options to develop new forms of globalised business-making. Furthermore, as taxpayers initiate bilateral or multilateral procedures, they may also be spurring the increase of tax audits and subsequent tax litigation.

According to OECD data, in 2009 there were more than 3,000 pending mutual agreement procedures (MAPs), of which 109 had one party in Spain (see Tables 7.5 and 7.6). This number is bound to grow in Spain, as

Table 7.5 *Pending MAP cases in OECD member countries*

Country	2006		2007	
	Number of new cases in 2006	Inventory of cases at end of 2006	Number of new cases in 2007	Inventory of cases at end of 2007
Australia	8	16	10	21
Austria	29	144	26	152
Belgium	31	81	30	95
Canada	76	134	70	153
Czech Republic	5	13	10	13
Denmark	15	82	18	82
Finland	1	12	11	22
France	104	254	100	233
Germany	212	476	186	526
Greece	1	4	2	5
Hungary	4	12	3	7
Iceland	1	1	0	1
Ireland	3	4	3	6
Italy	14	52	20	63
Japan	37	67	49	85
Korea	8	28	9	30
Luxembourg	22	31	31	34
Mexico	13	20	9	20
The Netherlands	80	120	57	151
New Zealand	4	2	5	4
Norway	15	25	21	32
Poland	11	26	7	26
Portugal	10	43	7	45
Slovak Republic	0	1	—	—
Spain	18	55	67	109
Sweden	80	101	61	100
Switzerland	—	—	45	33
Turkey	0	1	1	1
United Kingdom	55	109	44	106
United States	240	430	257	500
Total	**1097**	**2344**	**1159**	**2655**

Source: OECD Dispute Resolution, Country Mutual Agreement Procedure Statistics (2009), available at www.oecd.org/document/7/0,3746, en_2649_37989739_43754119_1_1_1_1,00.html

Table 7.6 *Pending MAPs in Spain*

Year MAP case was initiated	Opening inventory on first day of reporting year	Initiated during reporting year	Completed during reporting year	Ending inventory on last day of reporting year	Closed or withdrawn with double taxation during reporting year	Average cycle time for cases completed, closed or withdrawn during reporting year (in months)
2001 or prior	6	—	1	2	3	
2002	5	—	1	4	0	
2003	7	—	2	5	0	
2004	7	—	0	7	0	
2005	13	—	4	8	1	
2006	17	—	0	17	0	
2007	—	67	1	66	0	
Total	**55**	**67**	**9**	**109**	**4**	—

Source: OECD Dispute Resolution, Country Mutual Agreement Procedure Statistics (2009), available at www.oecd.org/document/7/0,3746, en_2649_37989739_43754119_1_1_1_1,00.html

the new system of transfer pricing is applicable to potentially many more taxpayers, and as other countries also initiate MAP procedures. In fact, as Table 7.6 shows, final data is not available on the MAPs undertaken under the new regime.

Furthermore, the number is also bound to grow after a recent legislative amendment of the Convention on Mutual Administrative Assistance in Tax Matters, to which Spain is party.[97]

---

[97] On 11 March 2011 Spain became the nineteenth country to sign the Protocol amending this multilateral Convention. This Protocol updates the standard on exchange of information and opens the amended Convention to all countries. The amended Convention entered into force on 1 June 2011.

7.6   Advance pricing agreements in Spain

One declared purpose of the LCIT 2006 is to foster the use of advance pricing agreements (APAs) for resolving transfer pricing disputes. This is expressly stated in the Preamble to LCIT 2006. In particular, article 16.7 of the LCIT and the regulations that develop it (Royal Decree 1794/2008) have introduced a certain level of flexibility in the APA procedure. In this aspect, the regime has become more effective, but it is not an aspect that has been overhauled in the Spanish tax regime. In fact, APA regulations have existed since 1995.[98]

The duration of the APA has been increased and may now be valid for up to four years after it is approved (before 2006, an APA was valid for up to three years). An APA may also have retroactive effects, to the fiscal year previous to its signature, as long as the taxpayer has not filed the CIT yet.

All associated individuals or entities party to the transaction for which the price needs to be established must file the APA proposal jointly. An APA may thus be bilateral or multilateral.

The procedure, to be filed before the Spanish Tax Collection Agency (Agencia Estatal de Administración Tributaria, AEAT) is relatively simple and straightforward. First, the taxpayer(s) will pre-file for an APA and after a waiting period of a month (maximum) he will be informed of the basic elements of the procedure and the effects that may be derived from it. Second, the filing process will begin (maximum duration: six months in the case of a unilateral APA). Crucially, all information that the taxpayer provides the AEAT during the pre-filing and filing stages of the procedure shall only be used for the purpose of the APA.

Should the taxpayer's proposal fail to be approved, the decision is not subject to appeal. Normally, the taxpayer may file another APA, after discussing the most problematic elements with the tax authorities, in an informal transaction process.

In recent times, Spanish tax authorities have had a cooperative attitude towards the signing of APAs. In fact, in 2009, the AEAT created a special working group for large companies (Foro de Grandes Empresas[99]) precisely in order to incentivise these taxpayers to request

---

[98] See, in this regard, M. L. González-Cuéllar Serrano, *Los procedimientos tributarios: su terminación transaccional* (Madrid: Colex, 1996), pp. 288–331.

[99] See www.aeat.es/AEAT.internet/Inicio_es_ES/_Segmentos_/Empresas_y_profesionales/ Foro_Grandes_Empresas/Foro_Grandes_Empresas.shtml. See also conclusions at

Table 7.7 *APAs in Spain*

	2006	2007	2008	2009	2010
Total requested	17	18	27	26	36
Domestic	6	8	11	12	20
International	11	10	16	14	16
Total filings	15	19	12	24	23
Accepted	11	15	8	19	16
Not accepted	2	0	0	4	4
Withdrawn by taxpayer	2	4	4	1	3

Source: Memorias AEAT 2006, 2007, 2008, 2009, 2010, available at www.aeat.es

an APA. A number of measures have been taken to encourage the use of that procedure, but to date it is still seldom used.

The expectation is that this should be substantially increased in the coming years. Already a small increase can be observed (see Table 7.7).

These numbers should increase in the coming years. The *Plan de Control Tributario*, published on 7 February 2011 in the *Boletín Oficial del Estado*, establishes transfer pricing to be one of the main areas to be subject to audits[100] and expressly mentions that APAs will be encouraged.

7.7   Concluding remarks: summary of the problems of the current implementation of the ALS in Spain

The main conclusion from this chapter coincides with the title: transfer pricing is *the* tax problem of the next ten years in Spain. The current transfer pricing regime poses a number of problems that may be cause of conflict in the following years; in fact, in the case of the penalty regime, the conflict has already arisen.

These problems must be added to the existing problems that have not been resolved in the transfer pricing reform. The main reason for the current problems probably arose from the acceleration, from zero to full

---

www.agenciatributaria.es/static_files/AEAT/Contenidos_Comunes/La_Agencia_Tributaria/ Segmentos_Usuarios/Empresas_y_profesionales/Foro_grandes_empresas/Grupos_Trabajo_ precios_transferencia_es_es.pdf.

[100] In particular, the Plan refers to the following areas as problematic: transfer pricing in general and three types of operations in particular, business restructuring, intangibles (valuation issues) and losses.

speed, resulting from the overhaul of the transfer pricing system in 2006, which is still being digested and will continue to be so for at least three or four years, particularly since the 2006 system has been partially reformed twice already. Simply put, there is not a widespread culture of taxpayers documenting their transfer pricing operations and presenting their CIT assessments accordingly. Also, because Spanish transfer pricing rules potentially apply to a large number of taxpayers (given the extended notion of what a related party is), the impact of the new regime is massive: major law firms are all hiring new staff in order to enlarge their transfer pricing departments, while the Tax Administration is also dedicating more personnel to transfer pricing issues.

The Spanish method of adopting the OECD Transfer Pricing Guidelines is also highly problematic. Politely put, Spanish tax authorities and courts have a worrying tendency to apply the OECD Guidelines *directly*, including the amended versions that could not possibly have been taken into account by the legislator.

Furthermore, one obvious problem of Spanish transfer pricing legislation is that it purportedly tries to serve two masters: the OECD Transfer Pricing Guidelines and the EUTPF Code of Conduct, and in general, the EU law (as any other Spanish legislation must). To the extent that the OECD transfer pricing concept is not perfectly aligned with the EU law concept, and in particular with the notion that seems to stem from the recent *SGI* case, applying transfer pricing rules in a coherent manner may be difficult.

Of course, this is part of a larger problem, which is the well-known issue of the divorce of tax treaty law and Community law. As the 2005 European Commission report on *EC Law and Tax Treaties*[101] explains, the origin of this separation lies in the initial focus by Community law on indirect taxation, at the same time that double tax agreements (DTAs) normally deal only with direct taxes (usually, taxes on income and capital, sometimes also gift and inheritance taxes as well as wealth taxes). But the main difference lies in the goals pursued by each area of law. It may then be the case that the way the questions are being posed is determining the outcome in a way that is seriously misleading: tax treaties are just another type of domestic law. A specific one, true, and one that is partly coordinated by a think-tank such as the OECD, in the case of DTAs concluded by Member States. But domestic law,

---

[101] TAXUD E1/FR DOC (05) 2306 (9 June 2005).

nevertheless. So the question is not so much international law vs. Community law, but specific domestic law vs. Community law.

On the other hand, both the current legislation of transfer pricing in Spain and the practice of the tax authorities (and often, the courts) pose constitutional problems that will need to be addressed sooner or later. First, the current model of implementing and applying the OECD Guidelines is at odds with the rule of law. The way article 16 of the LCIT and articles 16 to 29 *nonies* of the RCIT are drafted, they can hardly be effectively applied without also using the Guidelines. The Transfer Pricing Guidelines then become a basic cornerstone of the regime. Simply put, the law has designed a system whereby a substantial part of the taxable base may be determined and/or corrected by the tax authorities and the courts on the basis of the suggestion put forward by a think-tank.

Another salient issue of the Spanish transfer pricing regime is its prevailing anti-tax-avoidance approach. According to the logic of the OECD Guidelines, transfer pricing rules are not mainly rules to prevent tax avoidance or tax abuse, but rules to prevent tax base shifting (tax arbitrage) at the same time that they ensure the perfect competition ideal, which is why the central element is the *separate entity approach*, which entails treating enterprises as if they were not related. This fiction shapes the transfer pricing regime, which revolves around the objective of providing an objective, competition-based value. In this regard, the OECD Transfer Pricing Guidelines remind states that '[t]ax administrations should not automatically assume that associated enterprises have sought to manipulate their profits ... the consideration of transfer pricing should not be confused with the consideration of problems of tax fraud or tax avoidance, even though transfer pricing policies may be used for such purposes'. But tax administrators do not always share that view and transfer pricing legislation is often skewed towards the prevention of tax abuse. Spain is no exception, even if the 2006 reform purportedly intended to establish an objective rule. Different elements of the transfer pricing regime, however, point in the opposite direction, namely, that it has not abandoned the nature of being primarily an anti-abuse regime. This derives from different aspects mentioned in different places in article 16: the restrictive access of non-residents to the transfer pricing assessment and review procedure, the generalised opinion that article 16.8 (secondary adjustment) can be used automatically.

Furthermore, there are a number of unresolved issues in the current transfer pricing legislation. Thus, several aspects of the current transfer pricing regime will need further clarification as it is progressively implemented. Briefly put, at least the following four issues will need to be addressed sometime soon: (a) the relationship between accounting and tax rules (and whether compensating adjustments will be accepted/required); (b) the implementation of the methods and to what extent (and using what tools) may the tax administration correct the taxpayer's choice; (c) the assessment and revision procedure and the options for non-residents to take part in the eventual process, as well as the correct use of corresponding adjustments; and (d) the Constitutional Court will need to address the penalty regime, as requested by the Spanish Supreme Court in December 2010.

Finally, despite the direct application of the OECD Guidelines, the fact remains that the practice of transfer pricing in Spain shows a particular interpretation of the Guidelines, which is not fully aligned with the OECD. This is problematic for many reasons: first, it makes it harder for multinational enterprises to invest in or through Spain, to the extent that the Transfer Pricing Guidelines still represent an international standard employed also by non OECD countries.[102] Second, it clearly runs counter to the Spanish practice of signing double taxation treaties on the basis of the OECD Model.[103] Finally, this deviation from the OECD Guidelines may even pose problems from the European law perspective. Applying the ALS with a substantial deviation from the Guidelines, for example by using non-transparent private rulings, may even constitute a state aid.[104]

Of course, it is questionable whether the transfer pricing regime is actually an 'international tax regime', especially since that thesis seems to be based on the fact that it is a set of rules largely followed by OECD and non-OECD countries. The reality is more complex. Transfer pricing around the world is in a relative crisis, probably as a consequence of its success, with more countries than merely OECD members adapting their legislations to comply with the Transfer Pricing Guidelines. As more agents implement the rules, divergence in their interpretation or

---

[102] J. M. Calderón Carrero, 'The OECD Transfer Pricing Guidelines as a Source of Tax Law: Is Globalization Reaching the Tax Law?' (2007) 35 *Intertax* 6. See also Martín Jovanovich *et al.*, 'Transfer Pricing in Latin America' (2004) 34(5) *Tax Notes International* 505.

[103] Calderón Carrero, *Precios de transferencia e impuesto sobre sociedades*, note 1 above, p. 103.

[104] F. De Hosson, 'Codification of the Arm's Length Principle in the Netherlands Corporate Income Tax Act' (2002) 30(5) *Intertax* 189; see also Calderón Carrero, *Precios de transferencia e impuesto sobre sociedades*, note 1 above, pp. 41–2.

effects is hardly avoidable, so that there is a growing tendency towards establishing a 'customised' transfer pricing regime by OECD members (and non-members which nominally claim to follow the Transfer Pricing Guidelines).[105] This poses a fundamental question: to what extent do transfer pricing regimes still serve their initial purpose of coordinating and correctly slicing the tax base cake? It also runs counter to the idea that there is in fact a transfer pricing *regime*. There is, rather, a loose idea that transfer pricing serves to allocate the tax base and that it should be regulated. How this is done is far from uniform.

At the same time, as technology evolves and the use of databases becomes more sophisticated, it is easier than ever to justify almost any transfer price structure – the choice of comparables and method being then skewed and easily manipulated to serve whatever allocation of the tax base is considered desirable. In this regard, and for many different reasons that exceed the scope of this chapter, criticism of the ALS generally, and of the OECD Transfer Pricing Guidelines in particular, has grown exponentially in recent years, and the arguments cannot easily be ignored.[106]

Appendix: Questionnaire (Spain)

1. The structure of the law for solving transfer pricing disputes.   *What is the structure of the law of the country for solving transfer pricing disputes?*

To date, transfer pricing disputes begin and end as part of an auditing process. Joint audits are not envisaged in the law.

Structure of solving transfer pricing disputes: administrative level

1. Taxpayer files his tax assessment disclosing all relevant information and paying the corresponding tax debt.

2. Within the next four years (Spanish Statute of Limitations) a tax audit may investigate the taxpayer. If the tax auditor finds information

---

[105] See Ernst & Young 2010 survey as a good example.

[106] See, e.g., the arguments of the Testimony of Prof. Reuven S. Avi-Yonah, Hearing on Transfer Pricing Issues, given before the Committee on Ways and Means (22 July 2010) in the US Congress. See also R. S. Avi-Yonah, A. K. Clausing and M. Durst, 'Allocating Business Profits for Tax Purposes: A Proposal to Adopt a Formulary Profit Split' (2009) *Florida Tax Rev.* 497; Michael C. Durst, 'Memo to Congress: Reform Transfer Pricing *and* Protect U.S. Competitiveness' *Tax Notes*, 26 July 2010.

sufficient to reassess the declared tax position, a tax file (*acta de inspección*) will declare that result.

3. The taxpayer may then challenge the final tax file, normally (in transfer pricing cases) before the TEAC which will then issue a Resolution (RTEAC).

Judicial level: The RTEAC may be challenged in court. Depending on the type of a case and its circumstances, a different type of court will decide – Regional High Court (Tribunal Superior de Justicia); High Court (Audiencia Nacional); or Supreme Court (Tribunal Supremo).

Constitutional level: The Constitutional Court is not part of the Judiciary system but stands above all state powers (judicial, legislative and executive). Laws may be challenged before the court, either directly or by a court that needs to apply them – hence the Supreme Court's ruling asking the Constitutional Court whether the penalty regime complies with the rule of law.

For example, is the mutual agreement procedure (MAP), as regulated in the relevant tax treaty, the standard method for solving transfer pricing disputes?

The MAP method still is neither the standard method for resolving transfer pricing disputes nor is it widely used in Spain.

2. Policy for solving transfer pricing disputes. *Is there a gap between the nominal and effective method for solving transfer pricing disputes in the country? For example, has the country a strategic policy not to enforce the arm's length standard (ALS) for fear of driving foreign direct investment to other competing jurisdictions?*

No, that is not the case at all. There is in fact a policy of enforcing the ALS aggressively. Until 2006, transfer pricing legislation was primarily an anti-abuse legislation and was enforced accordingly.

3. The prevailing dispute resolution method. *Which is the most frequent method for solving transfer pricing disputes in the country? Does it have a positive externality? For example, is the MAP the most frequent method, and if so, to what extent have successful MAPs been used as a proxy for transfer pricing case law? For instance, Procter & Gamble (P&G) obtained a bilateral advance pricing agreement (APA) in Europe, and it was then extended to a third (Asian) country when P&G made this request to the relevant Asian tax authorities.*

Transfer pricing disputes are mostly resolved at an administrative level, normally via an auditing procedure (*procedimiento inspector*). If contested, the dispute may be resolved at the court level.

4. Transfer pricing case law.   *What is the evolution path of transfer pricing litigation in the country? For example: (i) Is transfer pricing litigation being gradually replaced by either MAPs or APAs, as regulated in the relevant tax treaties? (ii) Are foreign/local transfer pricing precedents and/ or published MAPs increasingly relevant as a source of law for solving transfer pricing disputes?*

Litigation is increasing but it will not be replaced by either MAPs or APAs any time soon. MAPs, on the other hand, are never published.

5. Customary international law and international tax procedure.   *Has customary international law been applied in the country to govern the relevant methods for solving transfer pricing disputes (such as the MAP)?*

Yes, the Spanish courts as well as the Spanish Tax Administration frequently refer to the OECD Manual and the Transfer Pricing Guidelines. In fact, the courts have in some cases applied the Guidelines directly.

6. Procedural setting and strategic interaction.   *Does strategic interaction between taxpayers and tax authorities depend on the procedural setting in which they interact when trying to solve transfer pricing disputes? For example, which procedural setting in the country prompts the relevant parties to cooperate with each other the most for solving this sort of dispute, and why?*

Too early to tell, as the new system was substantially changed in 2006, but my intuition is that advanced pricing agreements will be increasingly employed from now on.

7. The future of transfer pricing disputes resolution.   *Which is the best available proposal in light of the interests of the country for facilitating the global resolution of transfer pricing disputes, and why?*

MAP, perhaps in five or ten years, certainly not now.

Transfer pricing disputes in the United Kingdom

IAN ROXAN

8.1 Introduction

The experience of the United Kingdom in transfer pricing disputes is striking. On the one hand, due to the age of its income tax system, the United Kingdom has some of the earliest legislation that can be seen to have been addressed against transfer pricing. On the other hand, despite now having very modern legislation on transfer pricing, there are very few recorded transfer pricing disputes. Until the introduction of the modern rules in 1999, this appears to have been due to the strong administrative role played by the Inland Revenue as the tax authority at the time.[1]

To some extent, a similar attitude, accepting administrative contacts as the appropriate means to resolve transfer pricing disputes, appears to have persisted since then. However, there are signs that taxpayers are now more willing to litigate transfer pricing disputes, although it seems that cases are still mostly resolved before any judicial hearing.

Section 8.2 below reviews the development of transfer pricing rules in the United Kingdom to the present day. Section 8.3 looks at the United Kingdom's domestic approaches to resolving transfer pricing disputes, while section 8.4 examines the United Kingdom's use of bilateral approaches and section 8.5 looks at the use of advance pricing agreements (APAs) in the United Kingdom. Section 8.6 concludes. It should be noted that the discussion of the historical development is not only significant in understanding the current practice, since the early UK rules have been followed by a number of other countries, especially in the Commonwealth.

---

[1] The Commissioners of Inland Revenue were merged with the other UK tax authority, HM (Her Majesty's) Customs and Excise, in 2005 to form the Commissioners for HM Revenue and Customs (HMRC) by the Commissioners for Revenue and Customs Act 2005.

8.2   Development of transfer pricing rules in the United Kingdom

8.2.1   Early transfer pricing rules

Income tax was first introduced in Great Britain[2] in 1799 to finance the war against the French Emperor Napoleon.[3] The tax was repealed in 1802 on the Peace of Amiens, but revived in revised form in 1803,[4] bringing in extensive use of taxation at source (withholding tax) and the schedular system of taxation, which was still in use, at least in form, until the rewrite of the legislation over the last ten years. The 1803 tax made a distinction between residents and non-residents within Schedule D, which taxed a range of sources of income, from trades and employments to foreign income, and included a miscellaneous income category. Non-residents were only taxed on income from property and other sources in Great Britain.[5] Following the ending of the Napoleonic Wars at the Battle of Waterloo, the tax was repealed in 1816,[6] but it was again revived in 1842.[7] Where income of a non-resident was not taxable at source, the Income Tax Act 1842, section 41, provided that 'an agent in the United Kingdom receiving the income for the non-resident would be charged with tax for the non-resident: the non-resident would be chargeable to tax in the name of . . . any factor, agent, or receiver, having the receipt of any profits or gains arising as herein mentioned, and belonging to such person, in the like manner and to the like amount as would be charged if such person were resident in Great Britain,[8] and in the actual receipt thereof'.

---

[2] Great Britain was formed by the union of England (and Wales) with Scotland by the Union with Scotland Act 1706 (England) and the Union with England Act 1707 (Scotland). The United Kingdom was formed by the union of Great Britain with Ireland by the Union with Ireland Act 1800 (Great Britain) and the Act of Union (Ireland) 1800 (Ireland).

[3] An Act to repeal the Duties imposed by an Act, made in the last Session of Parliament, for granting an Aid and Contribution for the Prosecution of the War; and to make more effectual Provision for the like Purpose, by granting certain Duties upon Income, in lieu of the said Duties, 39 Geo. III, c. 13.

[4] An Act for granting to His Majesty, until the sixth day of May next after the ratification of a definitive Treaty of Peace, a Contribution on the Profits arising from Property, Professions, Trades and Offices, 43 Geo. III, c. 122.

[5] S. Dowell, *The Acts Relating to the Income Tax* (7th edn. revised by J. E. Piper, London: Butterworth & Co., 1913), pp. 2–4.

[6] HMRC, 'A Tax to Beat Napoleon', available at www.hmrc.gov.uk/history/taxhis1.htm.

[7] Income Tax Act 1842, 5 & 6 Vict. c. 85.

[8] The tax was subsequently extended to the whole of the United Kingdom by the Income Tax Act 1853, s. 5.

Income tax has remained in force ever since 1842, even though it was reintroduced then for three years only.[9] Until 1965, income tax was payable by companies as well as individuals, but companies paid income tax only at the basic rate; they were not liable to surtax (originally called super-tax). Income tax was withheld at source on dividends, but the company could set the tax collected against its own income tax liability. The first separate tax on companies was excess profits duty, introduced in 1915 to help pay for the cost of the First World War. It was charged (imposed) on profits in excess of the pre-war standard for the company. It continued until 1921.[10] Corporation profits tax applied generally to profits of companies (in addition to income tax) from 1920 to 1924. The National Defence Contribution was a new tax on company profits introduced in 1937, later renamed profits tax, which could not be set off against income tax.[11] From 1965 the liability of companies to both income tax and profits tax was replaced with liability to a new tax, corporation tax, charged on both the income and capital gains of companies.[12]

The first transfer pricing legislation in the UK tax system dates back to 1915. The Finance (No. 2) Act 1915, section 31(3), provided[13] that where a resident earned no profits or lower profits than otherwise, and this was due to the manner in which the business with a non-British non-resident was and could be arranged because of a close connection between the resident and the non-resident and because of the 'substantial control exercised by the non-resident over the resident', the non-resident could be taxed in the name of the resident as if the resident were an agent of the non-resident. In effect, the non-resident could be charged to UK income

---

[9] The long title of the Income Tax Act 1842 was 'An Act for granting to Her Majesty Duties on Profits arising from Property, Professions, Trades and Offices until 6 April 1845', quoted in M. Daunton, *Trusting Leviathan: The Politics of Taxation in Britain, 1799–1914* (Cambridge: Cambridge University Press, 2001), p. 191. Income tax still needs to be reimposed each year in the annual Finance Act – the standing legislation merely provides the rules applicable if income tax is imposed: see now s. 4(1) of the Income Tax Act 2007 and, e.g., s. 1(1) of the Finance Act 2011.

[10] A. J. Arnold, 'Profitability and Capital Accumulation in British Industry during the Transwar Period, 1913–1924' (1999) 52 *Economic History Review* (New Series) 45, 53.

[11] J. Tiley, *Revenue Law* (6th edn, Oxford and Portland: Hart Publishing, 2008), p. 828.

[12] Part IV of the Finance Act 1965. Capital gains tax was charged on individuals from the same year under Part III of the Finance Act 1965.

[13] Section 31(1) and (2) amended s. 41 of the 1842 Act by extending it to branches and to all chargeable income arising directly or indirectly to the non-resident (UK-source income) whether or not received by the branch, etc.

tax on non-UK-source profits (or turnover) to the extent that they reduced the profits of the resident. So this was a transfer pricing rule based directly on income shifting rather than on a transaction-based arm's length test. The test was 'no profits or profits less than the ordinary profits which might be expected to arise from [the resident's] business'. Otherwise, transfer pricing type situations could only be controlled by relying on principles of agency law.[14] In addition, section 31(4) provided that if the income of any non-resident chargeable in the name of a resident could not be readily ascertained (as it appeared to the Inland Revenue) the Revenue would have the discretion to tax the non-resident on a percentage of the turnover done through the resident. The percentage was to be determined 'having regard to the nature of the business'. There were limited rights of appeal under section 31(5) to the General or Special Commissioners, with the possibility of a final appeal to a referee or board of referees appointed by the Treasury. These rights of appeal are discussed further below. It should be noted that section 31(4) could apply both in the control case addressed by section 31(3) and in any other case where a non-resident was subject to tax. Thus, any non-resident carrying on business in the United Kingdom could be taxed on this presumptive basis, even if not dealing with any person in the United Kingdom other than their local agent. Sections 31(3), (4) and (5) were consolidated as Rules 7, 8 and 9 of the General Rules Applicable to Schedules A, B, C, D and E in the Income Tax Act 1918.

An example of how the provisions were applied can be found in *Gillette Safety Razor Ltd* v. *IRC*.[15] The appellant taxpayer was an English company formed in 1915 by Gaines, the former manager of the English operations of Gillette US, to take over selling Gillette razors and blades in the United Kingdom and a number of other countries. Previously, Gillette US had manufactured razors and blades in that market, first through a branch, then through a UK subsidiary, and finally through the branch of another US subsidiary, which were in each case managed by Gaines. The appellant company sold razors manufactured by Gillette US and by Gillette US's Canadian subsidiary. The agreement between Gillette US and the appellant provided for the terms on which the appellant was to sell Gillette razors and blades, including the selling prices and minimum quantities. The appellant was to sell no other

[14] J. F. Avery Jones, 'The History of the United Kingdom's First Comprehensive Double Taxation Agreement' (2007) *British Tax Review* 211, 242.

[15] *Gillette Safety Razor Ltd* v. *IRC* [1920] 3 KB 358 (KBD).

similar razors or blades. The items were sold to the appellant at a 45 to 50 per cent discount from the list prices, but the appellant was responsible for the cost of shipping and insurance, as well as advertising material. Its gross profit before working expenses was 6.37 per cent of sales.

On appeal to the Special Commissioners, they concluded that there was a close connection between the appellant and Gillette US and that the latter exercised substantial control over the appellant, so that, in the terms of section 31 of the Finance (No. 2) Act 1915 the course of business of the appellant was so arranged as to produce less than an ordinary profit. Applying section 31(4), the Special Commissioners applied a rate of 12.5 per cent of sales to determine the profit of the appellant.[16] This percentage was lower than it otherwise might have been as the Gillette name was thought to make it easier to sell the products in the United Kingdom. No indication is given whether this conclusion was based on any evidence heard, but the percentage appears to have been less than that applied by the Inland Revenue in the assessment appealed from.[17]

This is the only reported case on these provisions. One reason for this may be that they were seen as an adjunct to the agency provisions in section 41 of the 1842 Act as extended by section 31(1) and (2) of the 1915 Act. In *Greenwood* v. *F. L. Smidth* it was held that the latter provisions did not apply if the principal did not trade within the United Kingdom, but merely had an agent in the United Kingdom.[18] In contrast, in *Firestone Tyre & Rubber,* a UK subsidiary, which was in effect engaged in contract manufacturing under a master agreement entered into by its US parent, the UK company was held to be acting as the agent of the parent.[19] Given the terms of the master agreement, orders placed by a distributor with the subsidiary were held to create a contract between the distributor and the parent, which the subsidiary was obliged to fulfil. The parent was therefore trading in the United Kingdom and was taxable on the profits of that trade in the name of the subsidiary under General Rule 5 of the Schedule to the Income Tax Act 1918, which consolidated section 41 of the 1842 Act as amended by section 31 of the

---

[16] *Ibid.* 367–8.

[17] The case actually concerned excess profits tax, rather than income tax. On appeal to the High Court Rowlatt J held that the Inland Revenue's regulation-making power did not permit it to apply s. 31 to excess profits tax. He did not, therefore, discuss the substance of s. 31.

[18] *Greenwood* v. *F. L. Smidth & Co.* [1922] 1 AC 417; 8 TC 193 (HL).

[19] *Firestone Tyre & Rubber Co. Ltd* v. *Llewellin* [1957] 1 All ER 561; 37 TC 111 (HL).

1915 Act. The effect of this decision was comparable to that of a transfer pricing decision, but relied purely on agency concepts. Instead of deeming income of the foreign parent to have been earned by the subsidiary, the parent was held to be taxable in the name of the subsidiary on its own income.

The characterisation of the early legislation described is, in fact, not unanimous. Avery Jones refers to the 1915 provision as an 'arm's length rule', but does not elaborate.[20] The Inland Revenue even regarded the arm's length principle as going back to the agency provisions in section 41 of the 1842 Act.[21] They refer to a case from 1886 as supporting it; however, that is a case about a branch in the United Kingdom run by an agent. The Revenue's reference is to a remark that an attribution of profits to the branch could be done by using a fair valuation of goods when they arrived in the United Kingdom, but it is not expressed in terms of a comparison to independent enterprises.[22] As *Gillette* shows, it is not apparent that such evidence would be used in determining a fair valuation at that time. Similarly, *Gillette* shows directly that it was not apparent that the reference in section 31(3) of the 1915 Act to a resident earning 'no profits or lower profits than otherwise' would be applied by looking at evidence of dealings with or between independent enterprises.

8.2.2   Initial ALS transfer pricing rules

The United Kingdom entered into its first international double tax convention in 1945 with its treaty with the United States.[23] It included a provision similar in its terms to the first paragraph of what is now Article 9 of the OECD Model.[24] Section 51(1) of the Finance (No. 2)

---

[20] See note 14 above.

[21] Inland Revenue, 'Non-Residents Trading in the UK: The Arm's Length Principle' (1995) 18 *Inland Revenue Tax Bulletin*, available at www.hmrc.gov.uk/bulletins/tb18.htm#non-residents.

[22] *Pommery and Greno v. Apthorpe* (1886) 56 LJQB 155; 2 TC 182, 189.

[23] There was an earlier agreement with the Irish Free State in 1926 (Agreement between the British Government and the Government of the Irish Free State in respect of Double Income Tax (Dublin: The Stationery Office, 1926)), but it was unusual in basing relief on exemption by the country of source, and by credit only in the case of dual residence. It contained no transfer pricing provision.

[24] Convention and Protocol between the Government of the United Kingdom of Great Britain and Northern Ireland and the Government of the United States of America for the Avoidance of Double Taxation and the Prevention of Fiscal Evasion with respect to Taxes on Income, Washington, 16 April 1945, (1946) UKTS 26, Cmd 6902. The wording

Act 1945 gave effect in UK law to this provision and to similar provisions in subsequent double tax treaties. Section 51(1) provided in particular that the treaty provisions should, 'notwithstanding anything in any enactment, have effect ... so far as they provide for ... determining the income to be attributed to persons resident in the United Kingdom who have special relationships with persons not so resident'.[25]

Concerns arose, however, that section 51(1) might not permit upward adjustments to profits by the UK Inland Revenue under the terms of the authorising legislation.[26] In 1951, a domestic provision based on arm's

---

of the transfer pricing provision, Article IV, follows that of the Canada–United States treaty of 1942 (see Avery Jones, 'History of the UK's First Comprehensive Double Taxation Agreement', note 14 above, 242), but not that of the then current League of Nations Models, nor that of the later OECD Models. The League of Nations version can be found in Article VII of the Protocols to the Mexico and London Models, made in 1943 and 1946, respectively (Model Bilateral Convention for the Prevention of the Double Taxation of Income: Mexico Draft, and Model Bilateral Convention for the Prevention of the Double Taxation of Income and Property: London Draft, reprinted in League of Nations Fiscal Committee, *London and Mexico Model Tax Conventions: Commentary and Text*, Doc. 1946. II.A.7 (Geneva: League of Nations, 1946)), which follow the text of the 1935 Revised Draft Convention for the Allocation of Business Income Between States for the Purposes of Taxation (League of Nations Fiscal Committee, *Report to the Council on the Fifth Session of the Committee*, C.252.M.124.1935.II.A (Geneva: League of Nations, 1935), Annex I).

By 1948, the United Kingdom was using the wording that later appeared in Article 9 of the OECD 1963 Draft Double Taxation Convention on Income and Capital, and the subsequent OECD Model Tax Conventions on Income and Capital. See, e.g., Article IV of the original Netherlands–United Kingdom tax treaty of 1948 (1950) UKTS 43, Cmd 8015.

[25] The section applied to any double tax treaty given effect by Order in Council. The equivalent of s. 51(1) today is ss. 2 and 6 of the Taxation (International and Other Provisions) Act (TIOPA) 2010, formerly s. 788(1) of the Income and Corporation Taxes Act (ICTA) 1988. The equivalent of the words quoted is now to be found in s. 6(f) of the TIOPA 2010, formerly s. 788(1)(c)(ii) of the ICTA 1988.

[26] See the concerns of the Treasury recorded by the Attorney General, Sir Frank Soskice, *Hansard*, HC, vol. 489, col. 2077, 2 July 1951. (Interestingly, the Attorney General described the new provision as following provisions in 'the League of Nations Model Double Taxation Convention, which was made in 1945'.) David Oliver originally thought that the quoted portion of s. 51(1) was sufficient to give effect to the treaty 'Associated enterprises' Articles (see J. D. B. Oliver, 'Double Tax Treaties in United Kingdom Tax Law' (1970) *British Tax Review* 388, 396–8); however, the Treasury had received high-level government legal advice as to the inadequacy of s. 51(1): see J. D. B. Oliver, 'Ship-money' (1998) *British Tax Review* 1, 2. The advice was that s. 51(1) could not charge tax because it was in general aimed at relieving tax. In addition, it should be noted that s. 51(1) provided for 'charging' UK income sources to non-residents, in contrast to the neutral wording used in relation to transfer pricing. An example of this restricted approach to determining what is a charging section can be found in *Greenwood* v. *F. L. Smidth & Co.* [1922] 1 AC 417; 8 TC 193 (HL).

length prices was adopted in section 37 of the Finance Act 1951, replacing Rule 7 of the General Rules (originally section 31(3) of the 1915 Act), the old income shifting-based transfer pricing rule. This provision remained in force essentially unchanged until 1999.[27] In fact, section 37 was narrower in its terms than the treaty provisions. It only applied where one party controlled the other or both were under common control in the sense of control through shareholdings, voting power or powers conferred by the articles of association, etc. of the company, or similarly of a partnership.[28] In addition it only applied to adjust the prices of individual transactions (sales, lettings, grants and transfers of rights, etc.) that took place at a price other than that which 'might have been expected . . . . if the parties to the transaction had been independent persons dealing at arm's length'.[29] It was thus thought that it could not apply to other conditions of a transaction, and thus not, for example, to thin capitalisation.[30]

Section 37 was framed to apply to both residents and non-residents (one of the parties to the transaction had to be a body of persons, essentially either a company or a partnership), but it was excluded in cases where both parties to the transaction would bring it into account for UK tax purposes,[31] either as a receipt or as deductible expenditure. Thus, it applied largely, but not exclusively, to transactions involving non-residents.[32] Finally, following a government amendment during the debate on the Finance Bill, in response to concerns raised in Parliament about the potential administrative burden, it only applied in cases where the Inland Revenue issued a direction for it to apply.[33]

It should also be noted that a second line of attack on abnormal prices developed under the case law based on the House of Lords' decision in *Sharkey* v. *Wernher*.[34] Previous case law had held that the prices agreed by parties should normally be respected. While the *Sharkey* v. *Wernher*

---

[27] Section 37 was later consolidated in turn as s. 469 of the Income Tax Act 1952, s. 485, Income and Corporation Taxes Act (ICTA) 1970, and s. 770 of the ICTA 1988.

[28] This definition is now to be found in s. 1124 of the Corporation Tax Act (CTA) 2010 and s. 995 of the Income Tax Act (ITA) 2007.

[29] Finance Act 1951, s. 37(1)(b) and (2)(b).

[30] See Oliver, 'Ship-money', note 26 above, 1.

[31] The provision applied to income tax and profits tax, and subsequently to corporation tax.

[32] It could also apply to a sale between residents of an asset that would yield income treatment to one party, but be a (non-depreciable) capital asset for the other.

[33] Finance Act 1951, s. 37(3). See *Hansard*, HC, vol. 489, col. 2094, 2 July 1951.

[34] *Sharkey* v. *Wernher* [1956] AC 58; 36 TC 275 (HL).

principle upheld this, it said that market value could, nevertheless, be substituted in the case of a disposal of trading stock (inventory) outside the course of the trade of the taxpayer. This applied, on the one hand, to appropriations for personal use and gifts (self-supply), but also, as a type of transfer pricing principle, to sales at an undervalue so abnormal as to be outside the normal course of trade. This could apply to a price adopted between related parties for tax avoidance. The leading example is *Petrotim Securities* v. *Ayres*.[35]

Petrotim was a dealer in securities. It was acquired by Ridge Securities. In order to generate a loss and obtain a tax refund, Petrotim sold a large quantity of securities to Ridge for only one-quarter of their then realisable market value. The Court of Appeal held that such a sale at a gross undervalue was not in the course of trade, and that, following *Sharkey*, Petrotim should be required to account for the sale at market value.

Thus, the transfer pricing aspect of the *Sharkey* v. *Wernher* principle applies to pricing that is so unrealistic that the transaction is not considered to have been made in the course of trade. The *Sharkey* v. *Wernher* principle has now been incorporated into legislation, where it is expressly subordinated to the general transfer pricing rules.[36] It seems that the principle has never generally been strongly enforced.[37] Note that it is not restricted to international transactions. Indeed, all the leading cases on the principle concern purely domestic transactions.

8.2.3   Modern rules: introduction of the OECD Guidelines

From 1999, the Finance Act 1998 replaced section 770 of the Income and Corporation Taxes Act 1988 (ICTA 1988), the successor to section 37 of

---

[35] *Petrotim Securities Ltd* v. *Ayres* [1964] 1 All ER 269; 41 TC 389 (CA).

[36] See ss. 172A–172F of the Income Tax (Trading and Other Income) Act (ITTOIA) 2005 and ss. 156–61 of the CTA 2009. For a strong criticism of the self-supply aspect of *Sharkey* v. *Wernher*, and of the wording of the new legislation, especially the definition of 'trading stock', see R. Kerridge, 'The Rule in *Sharkey* v. *Wernher*: Time for a Reappraisal?' (2005) *British Tax Review* 287.

[37] See Kerridge, 'The Rule in *Sharkey* v. *Wernher*', note 36 above, 301. The Revenue, however, appears to have considered that it could be applicable in international transfer pricing cases, and so indicated that they would not seek to apply the rule where an advance pricing agreement had been reached: Inland Revenue, 'Advance Pricing Agreements: The Inland Revenue's Experience and Expectation of the Bilateral Process for Guidance to its Taxpayers' (1999) 43 *Tax Bulletin* 697, available at webarchive. nationalarchives.gov.uk/20101006151632/http://www.hmrc.gov.uk/bulletins/tb43.htm# anchor112710.

the Finance Act 1951, with Schedule 28AA to ICTA 1988. These provisions have now been rewritten as Part 4 of the Taxation (International and Other Provisions) Act (TIOPA) 2010.

The new rules were intended to follow Article 9 of the OECD Model much more closely. There are a few differences. In contrast to the 1951 rules, they tend if anything to be broader in scope than the OECD rules. The key operative test in Article 9(1) of the OECD Model is that: 'conditions are made or imposed between the two enterprises in their commercial or financial relations which differ from those which would be made between independent enterprises'. In contrast, the UK test is in effect that: 'provision ("the actual provision") has been made or imposed as between any two persons by means of a transaction or series of transactions, and the actual provision differs from the provision which would have been made as between independent enterprises'.[38] This substitutes 'provision made as between persons by means of a transaction or series of transactions' for 'conditions made between the two enterprises in their commercial or financial relations'. The word 'provision' may be wider than 'conditions', and HMRC appears to believe that 'as between' is wider than 'between', but this is then tied to transactions, although 'transaction' is given a broad meaning that can include arrangements of any kind even if not (intended to be) legally enforceable.[39] An adjustment must be made by an affected person if the actual provision 'confers a potential advantage in relation to United Kingdom taxation' on the person.[40]

The legislation goes a step further by requiring that the rules are 'to be read in such manner as best secures consistency' with the effect to be given to Article 9, as incorporated in whole or part in a tax treaty, 'in accordance with the [OECD] transfer pricing guidelines'.[41] The Inland Revenue had previously used the OECD Guidelines of 1995[42] and the earlier Report of 1979[43] as guides in applying the earlier legislation;[44] however, HMRC's

---

[38] ICTA 1988, Sch. 28AA, para. 1(1) and (2), now TIOPA 2010, s. 147(1).

[39] ICTA 1988, Sch. 28AA, para. 3, now TIOPA 2010, s. 150.

[40] ICTA 1988, Sch. 28AA, para. 1(2), now TIOPA 2010, s. 147.

[41] ICTA 1988, Sch. 28AA, para. 2(1), now TIOPA 2010, s. 164(1).

[42] OECD, *Transfer Pricing Guidelines for Multinational Enterprises and Tax Administrations* (Paris: OECD, 1995) ('OECD Guidelines').

[43] OECD Committee on Fiscal Affairs, *Transfer Pricing and Multinational Enterprises: Report of the OECD Committee on Fiscal Affairs* (Paris: OECD, 1979).

[44] See Inland Revenue, 'Transfer Pricing: New OECD Report: Guidance on Revenue Procedures' (1996) 25 *Tax Bulletin* 345, available at webarchive.nationalarchives.gov.uk/20101006151632/http://www.hmrc.gov.uk/bulletins/tb25.htm#transfer_pricing.

view is that the new provision means that the OECD Guidelines take precedence over other interpretations of the UK rules, and that Article 9 and the Guidelines apply whether or not there is an applicable UK tax treaty, and regardless of the specific wording of the treaty if there is one.[45] It is not yet entirely clear that the wording of para. 2 supports this view.[46] In any case, where it does apply, HMRC accept that it means that the differences in wording between these provisions and Article 9 should not be significant.[47] Nevertheless, these provisions are clearly much broader in scope than section 770 of ICTA 1988 was. They allow for the adjustment of the conditions of transactions as well as their prices. In particular, they can apply to thin capitalisation situations.[48]

A key change from the old legislation is the dropping of the requirement of a direction from the Inland Revenue for the application of the rules. In part this was the result of the introduction of self-assessment for corporation tax from 1999.[49] Under self-assessment companies are themselves required to determine the amount of tax due. The provisions apply that principle to transfer pricing: a company is obliged in the first instance to determine for itself whether it is subject to these rules, and to apply them if necessary. On the other hand, a tax inspector still needs the approval of the HMRC Commissioners (formerly the Board of the Inland Revenue, not to be confused with tribunals, the General and Special Commissioners) in order to amend a self-assessment or to make a new assessment in order to make a transfer pricing adjustment.[50]

---

[45] HMRC, *International Manual*, INTM 432030, available at www.hmrc.gov.uk/manuals/intmanual/INTM432030.htm. The definition of the guidelines in TIOPA 2010, s. 164(4) was amended with effect from April 2011 to refer to the 2010 revision of the OECD Guidelines: OECD, *Transfer Pricing Guidelines for Multinational Enterprises and Tax Administrations* (Paris: OECD Publishing, 2010).

[46] The Special Commissioners in *DSG Retail* (discussed below) recognised the ambiguity, but thought that HMRC's view was correct as it would have been more logical to structure the paragraph differently if the alternative meaning were intended: *DSG Retail Ltd and others* v. *HMRC* [2009] UKFTT 31 (TC); [2009] STC (SCD) 397 at para. 71.

[47] See HMRC, *International Manual*, note 45 above.

[48] When the provisions were introduced, simple thin capitalisation structures were dealt with by treating affected interest as a distribution (dividend) under s. 209(2)(da) of the ICTA 1988, but other structures, such as those involving parent guarantees of third party loans, could be dealt with under the transfer pricing provisions. See Inland Revenue, 'The New Transfer Pricing Legislation' (1998) 37 *Inland Revenue Tax Bulletin* available at www.hmrc.gov.uk/bulletins/tb37.htm; S. Ball, 'Thin Capitalisation' (1998) 1 *Corporate Tax Review* 299, 307.

[49] Self-assessment for income tax was introduced from 1996–7.

[50] Finance Act 1998, s. 110, now TIOPA 2010, s. 208.

The application of the legislation is based on the OECD concept of direct or indirect participation in the management, control or capital of another, but this is defined in a way that makes it much closer to the form of control required in the previous UK provisions. Direct participation means control of a company or partnership, while indirect participation is satisfied only by control under certain attribution rules or by 40 per cent control jointly with another who also controls at least 40 per cent of the controlled entity.[51]

There are also provisions defining when there is a potential UK tax advantage to trigger operation of the provisions,[52] and providing for compensating adjustments where the 'disadvantaged person' is subject to UK income or corporation tax on the profits.[53]

As with the pre-1999 rules, these rules were essentially limited to international transactions, but through a slightly different mechanism. No potential UK tax advantage arose if both parties were fully subject to UK income or corporation tax on the activities involved, were not entitled to a credit for foreign tax on profits from those activities, and did not claim a deduction for foreign tax.[54]

In 2004, in response to the decision of the European Court of Justice in the *Lankhorst-Hohorst* case,[55] the transfer pricing provisions were extended to purely domestic transactions. The case, which concerned the German thin capitalisation rules, appeared to indicate that it would be contrary to the EC Treaty freedom of movement provisions for a

---

[51] ICTA 1988, Sch. 28AA, para. 4, now TIOPA 2010, ss. 157–60. The same definition of 'control' is used as applied for the former provisions. The current provisions seem to be consistent with the OECD's understanding of the meaning of Article 9: see OECD Committee on Fiscal Affairs, *Model Tax Convention on Income and Capital*, condensed version, 17 July 2008 (Paris: OECD, 2008) ('OECD Model'); Commentary on Article 9, para. 1; and Oliver, 'Double Tax Treaties in United Kingdom Tax Law', note 26 above, p. 397.

[52] ICTA 1988, Sch. 28AA, para. 5, see now TIOPA 2010, s. 155. The provisions only apply to income tax and corporation tax on income. They do not apply to capital gains, but ss. 17 and 18 of the Taxation of Chargeable Gains Act 1992 require the substitution of market value in the case of any disposal not by way of bargain at arm's length (subject to the capital gains group rules), including any disposal between connected persons. This provision applies to domestic as well as international disposals, and makes no reference to OECD principles.

[53] ICTA 1988, Sch. 28AA, paras. 6, 7, see now TIOPA 2010, ss. 174–8, 188.

[54] ICTA 1988, Sch. 28AA, para. 5(2)–(6). There was an additional condition for insurance companies.

[55] *Lankhorst-Hohorst GmbH* v. *Finanzamt Steinfurt* (C-324/00) [2002] ECR I-11779; [2003] 2 CMLR 693; [2003] STC 607; 5 ITLR 467.

Member State to impose transfer pricing rules on transactions between a resident of the Member State and a resident of an other Member State, while not imposing the same rules on transactions between two residents of the Member State. The extension does not, however, apply to dormant enterprises, it only applies to small enterprises with respect to transactions with countries with which the United Kingdom does not have a tax treaty containing a non-discrimination provision, and it only applies to medium-sized enterprises in such a non-treaty case or where HMRC gives a notice requiring the taxpayer to apply the provisions.[56]

As a result of *Lankhorst-Hohorst*, the former thin capitalisation provisions in section 209(2)(da) of the ICTA 1988 were also dropped in favour of reliance on the transfer pricing rules. Additional provisions were added to ensure that the transfer pricing rules would have sufficient scope to cover the thin capitalisation transactions of concern.[57]

8.3   Domestic resolution of transfer pricing disputes in the United Kingdom

8.3.1   Approaches to resolving transfer pricing disputes

A notable feature of the resolution of transfer pricing disputes in the United Kingdom is that there are relatively few reported cases, and of them even fewer that deal with substantive issues concerning the application of the transfer pricing rules. It thus appears that a substantial proportion of transfer pricing disputes are resolved administratively or settled. To some extent this is a feature more generally of the UK tax system, but the trend is stronger in the case of transfer pricing.

The discussion that follows begins by outlining the general administrative procedures available for resolving transfer pricing disputes. The procedures for appeals to tribunals and courts are then explained, describing the differences brought by the new system of tribunals introduced in 2009. An examination of the reported cases shows not merely how these cases have influenced transfer pricing disputes. They also give insight into the role of administrative approaches. Finally, the approach taken by HMRC to resolving transfer pricing disputes is examined.

---

[56] ICTA 1988, Sch. 28AA, paras. 5A–5E, see now TIOPA 2010, ss. 165–173. A small enterprise is one employing fewer than fifty persons and having an annual turnover and/or total assets not exceeding 10 million euros. A medium-sized enterprise is one employing fewer than 250 persons and having an annual turnover not exceeding 50 million euros and/or total assets not exceeding 43 million euros.

[57] ICTA 1988, Sch. 28AA, paras. 1A, 1B, etc.; see now TIOPA 2010, ss. 152–4, etc.

8.3.2   Administrative procedures for resolving tax disputes

Since 1998, companies have been subject to self-assessment in the United Kingdom,[58] as individuals have since 1996.[59] A company subject to corporation tax must file a return based on its accounting period normally within twelve months after the end of the accounting period, and it must assess the amount of tax that is payable by it in the return.[60] The company may amend its return within the twelve months following the date of the return, and HMRC may correct errors in the return within nine months from the return date, but the company may reject the correction by amending its return.[61]

The more formal procedure is where HMRC opens an enquiry into the return. This can normally be done within twelve months from the filing deadline, or following an amendment to the return.[62] The enquiry can be into any matter arising out of a return.[63] During the enquiry the taxpayer may amend its return, and HMRC may amend the return to prevent a loss of tax, but, apart from the latter case, any amendments from the enquiry take effect when the enquiry is closed.[64] An enquiry is closed when an officer of HMRC issues a closure notice.[65] There is no time limit for this, but the taxpayer may apply to the tribunal (see below) for a direction that a closure notice be issued. On such an application the onus is on HMRC to give reasonable grounds for not closing the enquiry within the time proposed.[66] Once the enquiry has been closed, there can be no further enquiry, except one into an amendment to the return by the taxpayer.[67]

The enquiry procedure limits the extent to which HMRC can reopen a return filed by a company. However, there is a further power for HMRC to make what is called a discovery assessment, after the time for making an enquiry, if HMRC obtains new information as to a shortfall in tax,

---

[58] Introduced by Finance Act 1998, s. 117, effective for accounting periods ending on or after 1 July 1999: Finance Act 1994, Section 199 (Appointed Day) Order 1998 (SI 1998/ 3173).

[59] J. Tiley, *Revenue Law*, (6th edn., Oxford: Hart Publishing, 2008), p. 73.

[60] Finance Act 1998, Sch. 18, paras. 7, 14.   [61] *Ibid.* Sch. 18, paras. 15–16.

[62] See *ibid.* Sch. 18, para. 24 for the precise details of the deadlines for enquiries.

[63] *Ibid.* Sch. 18, para. 25. An enquiry into an amendment cannot be used to raise matters relating to other aspects of the return that would otherwise be out of time. Details of how HMRC conducts an enquiry can be found in the internal HMRC Manual on the topic, HMRC, *Enquiry Manual*, available at www.hmrc.gov.uk/manuals/emmanual/index.htm.

[64] Finance Act 1998, Sch. 18, paras. 30, 31, 34.   [65] *Ibid.* Sch. 18, para. 32.

[66] *Ibid.* Sch. 18, para. 3.   [67] *Ibid.* Sch. 18, para. 24(5).

or the shortfall has been brought about carelessly or deliberately.[68] A discovery assessment can be made within four years after the end of the accounting period, extended to six years in the carelessness case and to twenty years in the deliberate case.[69]

In any case (other than a self-assessment), an appeal may be made within thirty days by notice to the HMRC officer making the assessment.[70] Under the new procedures for appeals introduced in 2009 (see below), there is an option to have the appeal reviewed internally by HMRC at the request of the taxpayer or by an offer by HMRC, but after the review, or instead of the review, the taxpayer can notify the appeal to the tribunal.[71] In a review, HMRC begins by setting out its initial view of the matter, then reviews it in light of representations from the taxpayer. The review is conducted by a different officer from the one who made the decision with the objective of taking a fresh look at the matter and, if possible, resolving it without an appeal to the tribunal. The review officer will take into account HMRC's Litigation and Settlement Strategy, discussed below in section 8.3.5.[72]

8.3.3   Appeal procedures for resolving tax disputes

Ordinary appeal procedure for resolving tax disputes until 2009

Leaving to one side advance pricing agreements, transfer pricing disputes are handled through the same channels as other tax disputes. Until the reform of the system that came into effect for taxation in 2009, there were two tribunals to which a tax assessment could be appealed. The General Commissioners (in full, the Commissioners for the General Purposes of the Income Tax)[73] consisted of about 1,500 lay members organised in around 350 divisions across the United Kingdom. They sat with a legally qualified clerk, usually a local solicitor, who would advise

---

[68] *Ibid.* Sch. 18, paras. 41–4.

[69] *Ibid.* Sch. 18, paras. 46, 49. These time limits apply to assessments generally, but it appears that they do not apply to self-assessments, nor to enquiries, since an enquiry results in amendments to a self-assessment. See *Morris and another* v. *HMRC* [2007] EWHC 1181 (Ch); [2007] BTC 448, where this point was considered under the corresponding provisions for income tax in Taxes Management Act (TMA) 1970.

[70] Finance Act 1998, Sch. 18, para. 48.   [71] TMA 1970, ss. 49A–49I.

[72] See HMRC, *Appeals Reviews and Tribunals Guidance Manual*, ARTG4020–4080, available at www.hmrc.gov.uk/manuals/artgmanual/ARTG4001.htm.

[73] TMA 1970, s. 2(1).

them on the law as necessary.[74] However, they typically dealt with cases largely involving factual issues. In contrast, the Special Commissioners (in full, the Commissioners for special Purposes of the Income Tax) were legally qualified with at least ten years' experience.[75] As a result, they tended to hear more complex cases and those involving difficult issues of law.[76] They also had exclusive jurisdiction in certain areas, including issues arising out of the amendment of a taxpayer's return on a formal enquiry (started within one year of filing) respecting a claim under the double taxation relief provisions, which could include transfer pricing adjustments made on a return pursuant to a treaty transfer pricing Article.[77]

Appeals lay from the decisions of both the General and Special Commissioners to the High Court (Chancery Division).[78] An appeal could only be made on a question of law, as is still the case today, but a question of law includes the situation where the Commissioners made a factual inference that was quite unsupported by the evidence, so that no Commissioners who had properly instructed themselves as to the relevant law could have come to that conclusion.[79] Further appeals lay as of right from the High Court to the Court of Appeal and with leave from the Court of Appeal to the House of Lords.[80] There is also the possibility of referring a point of construction as to the implications of European Union legislation to the European Court of Justice at any stage of the proceedings for a preliminary ruling.[81]

---

[74] Tribunals Service, 'History of the General Commissioners', available at www.general-commissioners.gov.uk/AboutUs/aboutUs.htm. In 1987, there were about 5,000 members organised in 486 divisions: R. T. Bartlett, 'The Tax Tribunals: a Post-Keith Appraisal – Part I' (1988) *British Tax Review* 371, 387.

[75] TMA 1970, s. 4.

[76] Under the general rule the default was for a case to start before the General Commissioners, but the taxpayer could elect to have the appeal heard by the Special Commissioners under s. 31D of the TMA 1970, or the General Commissioners could transfer the appeal to the Special Commissioners on grounds of complexity or the expected length of the hearing under s. 44(3A) of the TMA 1970.

[77] TMA 1970, s. 46C. See generally TMA 1970, ss. 46B and 46C, also, ss. 28ZA, 31C.

[78] TMA 1970, ss. 56, 56A. Appeals from the General Commissioners were by way of case stated. The case, setting out the facts and conclusions at issue, would be drafted by the clerk to the Commissioners and signed by the Commissioners after considering any representations from the parties: General Commissioners (Jurisdiction and Procedure) Regulations 1994 (SI 1994 / 1812), regs. 20–2.

[79] *Edwards* v. *Bairstow and Harrison* [1956] AC 14; 36 TC 207 (HL).

[80] TMA 1970, ss. 56, 56A.

[81] Treaty on the Functioning of the European Union (TFEU), Art. 267, formerly called a preliminary reference: EC Treaty, Art. 234.

The reform of the tax tribunals that came into effect in 2009 was the culmination of a long process of reforming the UK system of administrative tribunals, but there had already been long-standing concerns about the tax tribunals. Some had been addressed in Finance (No. 2) Act 1992, following the Keith Report,[82] but certain procedural points and the possibility of merging the Special Commissioners with the VAT and Duties Tribunal remained outstanding.

The problem is that the General and Special Commissioners were not originally administrative tribunals. When income tax was first introduced at the end of the eighteenth century, to make it palatable, a system of local administration by leading taxpayers in the community was adopted. These were the General Commissioners. From the first reintroduction of income tax in 1803 they were appointed by another local body, the Land Tax Commissioners.[83] The Land Tax Commissioners were unpaid and were appointed by periodic Acts of Parliament.[84] As Lord Templemore said, in moving the second reading of the Land Tax Commissioners Bill 1938 in the House of Lords:

> The machinery is rather curious, and it is a very remarkable relic of Parliamentary patronage. It is the right of Members of Parliament ... to prepare lists for proposed appointments and to deposit them in the [House of Commons] Public Bills Office ... Then, when the Bill has passed both Houses the lists are published ... and ... the persons named therein will be Land Tax Commissioners.[85]

General Commissioners also had to meet a property qualification (as did Land Tax Commissioners). In 1952, a General Commissioner had to have real or personal property of a value of £5,000 or yielding £200 per annum,[86] not a small amount at the time. As a result they were not greatly changed from the body of gentry, professionals and merchants of

---

[82] *Report of the Committee on Enforcement Powers of the Revenue Departments*, Cmnd. 8822 and 9102 (1983).

[83] The land tax may be seen as a predecessor of income tax. It went back to 1693 and was abolished in 1963. In Scotland, London and certain other areas, local councils or other bodies appointed the General Commissioners. See Income Tax Act 1952, Sch. 1, Part I, para. 5; Daunton, *Trusting Leviathan*, note 9 above, p. 191.

[84] Parliament, 'The Land Tax and Role of Commissioners', available at www.parliament.uk/about/living-heritage/transformingsociety/private-lives/taxation/case-study/introduction1/land-tax-commissioners/.

[85] *Hansard*, HL, vol. 108, col. 401, 24 March 1938. The previous set of appointments had been made in 1927. A shortage of Commissioners had been discovered in late 1937.

[86] Income Tax Act 1952, Sch. 1, Part III.

the nineteenth century,[87] even though, through the twentieth century, the range of taxpayers became increasingly broad.

The General Commissioners originally appointed assessors and collectors to assist them, but it was the Commissioners who approved and confirmed assessments, and who also heard appeals from these assessments.[88] The activities of the General Commissioners and their officials were monitored and guided by civil servants in London under what were eventually called the Commissioners of Inland Revenue (referred to in the legislation as the 'Board', to distinguish them from the various other bodies of Commissioners), assisted by officials called surveyors.[89] While this system of local administration under the supervision of local lay notables drawn from the tax-paying class made income tax appear less like an intrusion of the state, some taxpayers might not wish to have their affairs examined in effect by their neighbours. Thus, there was the alternative of assessment by the Special Commissioners, consisting of the Board and some Treasury appointees, who also heard appeals against such assessments.[90] It should be noted, however, that, at least in later years, appeals were not heard by the same individual General or Special Commissioners who made the assessment.[91]

This system persisted into the twentieth century, despite a number of attempts to separate the functions of assessment and appeal in the nineteenth century, though was principally out of a concern that the system allowed too much evasion to take place.[92] The first significant step taken came in 1874 when appeals by either party from the General and Special Commissioners by way of case stated to the High Court were permitted on questions of law.[93] In 1891, the assessors, collectors and clerks were shifted from payments by poundage (out of tax collected) to fixed payments.[94]

---

[87] C. Stebbings, *The Victorian Taxpayer and the Law: A Study in Constitutional Conflict* (Cambridge: Cambridge University Press, 2009), p. 29.

[88] Daunton, *Trusting Leviathan*, note 9 above, p. 190. Some assessments were made instead by the Additional Commissioners, also appointed by the General Commissioners subject to a property qualification: *ibid.* p. 188. The Additional Commissioners were particularly responsible for assessments under Schedule D, which included trading income: see B. E. V. Sabine, *A History of Income Tax* (London: George Allen & Unwin, 1966), p. 28.

[89] Daunton, *Trusting Leviathan*, note 9 above, p. 189.

[90] G. McGregor, *Tax Appeals: A Study of the Tax Appeals Systems of Canada, the United States and the United Kingdom*, Canadian Tax Paper No. 22 (Toronto: Canadian Tax Foundation, 1960), p. 28. There were some particular types of assessment that were only made by the Special Commissioners.

[91] *Ibid.* p. 28.   [92] Daunton, *Trusting Leviathan*, note 9 above, pp. 195–7.

[93] *Ibid.* p. 201.   [94] *Ibid.* p. 197.

The first successful step to separate out assessment came in 1915, when the centrally appointed surveyors of taxes were given the power to make certain assessments on employees, subject to the usual right of appeal to the General Commissioners.[95] At last, in 1942, General Commissioners ceased to approve and confirm assessments, but the function was shifted to the Additional Commissioners. Not only were they appointed by the General Commissioners, but the General Commissioners also had the option of acting as Additional Commissioners themselves, instead of appointing others to the position.[96]

From 1960 the appointment of General Commissioners was transferred to the Lord Chancellor, the minister and officer of state responsible for the appointment of judges, assisted by an Advisory Committee in each county, and the property qualification for General Commissioners and Additional Commissioners was abolished;[97] however, their allowances and expenses were still paid by the Treasury until 1994.[98] The appointment of Special Commissioners was transferred to the Lord Chancellor from 1985.[99]

The assessing jurisdiction of the Additional, General and Special Commissioners was finally abolished by the Income Tax Management Act 1964, section 37, which transferred assessment to the inspectors of taxes.[100] That Act also introduced an important provision that became section 54 of the Taxes Management Act 1970. This provides that the taxpayer and the inspector can agree the settlement of a case under appeal, and the agreement will take effect as if it were a decision of the General or Special Commissioners on the appeal. After thirty days with no repudiation by the taxpayer, the agreement becomes final, and thus binding on both parties. This provision still applies after the reforms discussed below.

It should not be supposed from this account that the General and Special Commissioners were not independent of the Inland Revenue in

[95] B. E. V. Sabine, 'The McKenna Budget of 1915' (1977) British Tax Review 173, 181, regarding the powers under s. 28(3) and (5) of the Finance (No. 2) Act 1915.

[96] Finance Act 1942, Sch. 10, Part I, paras. 3–5. C. Stebbings, 'The General Commissioners of Income Tax: Assessors or Adjudicators?' (1993) British Tax Review 52, 61, is thus over optimistic in saying that the General Commissioners' only function after 1942 was appellate, though that appears to have reflected the general practice.

[97] Tribunals and Inquiries Act 1958, s. 7; McGregor, Tax Appeals, note 90 above, p. 27; Bartlett, 'The Tax Tribunals', note 74 above, 373.

[98] TMA 1970, s. 2(5), amended by Finance (No. 2) Act 1992, s. 76, Sch. 16, para. 2(1).

[99] Finance Act 1984, s. 127, Sch. 22, para. 1.

[100] See Stebbings, 'The General Commissioners of Income Tax', note 96 above, 57.

carrying out their appellate functions, but the public in fact did not always perceive their independence. This was to a large degree due to minor procedural factors, such as the fact that appeals to the Commissioners were made by giving a notice of appeal to the inspector responsible for making the assessment,[101] a procedure only changed with the reforms brought in in 2009.

New tribunals system of resolving tax disputes on appeal

The new system has introduced a two-tier administrative tribunal for the United Kingdom with each tier divided into specialist chambers.[102] The Tax Chamber of the First-tier Tribunal now generally hears tax appeals at first instance, although the Tax and Chancery Chamber of the Upper Tribunal has a limited power to hear appeals at first instance. Both consist of legally qualified judges and members with specialist tax expertise. Cases that go to full hearing will typically be heard by a panel consisting of three judges and members.

In tax cases the First-tier Tribunal effectively takes the place of both the General and Special Commissioners. The distinction is maintained by having different tracks for cases. Basic cases (likely to be mostly cases about minor penalties) can be heard by a panel consisting of members only. Standard and complex cases must be heard by a panel including at least one judge. With consent, complex cases may be referred to the Upper Tribunal.

Appeals from the First-tier Tribunal will lie to the Upper Tribunal on questions of law, but only with leave. The Upper Tribunal thus essentially takes over the role of the High Court in tax cases. Appeals will lie from the Upper Tribunal to the Court of Appeal, again only with leave, and from there with leave to the Supreme Court, which has replaced the House of Lords.[103]

The reforms have also introduced a change at the other end of the process. There is now the procedure for requesting a formal review of a

---

[101] C. Stebbings, '"A Natural Safeguard": The General Commissioners of Income Tax' (1992) *British Tax Review* 398.

[102] Created by the Tribunals, Courts and Enforcement Act 2007. Not all functions of the tribunals apply to Wales, Scotland or Northern Ireland (s. 30 of that Act), but in regards to tax matters the jurisdiction extends to the whole of the United Kingdom: see Explanatory Memorandum to the Transfer of Tribunal Functions and Revenue and Customs Appeal Order 2009 (SI 2009/56), para. 5.

[103] H. Gething, S. Paterson and J. Barker, 'Transformation of the Tax Tribunal' (2009) *British Tax Review* 250, 251–3.

case by HMRC before bringing an appeal before the Tribunal, discussed in section 8.3.2 above. Part of the reason for the introduction of this is that previously an appeal to the General or Special Commissioners was launched, not by notice to the Commissioners in question, but by notice of appeal to the inspector or other official of the Board. Not only did this give the impression that the two sets of Commissioners were perhaps (still) part of the Revenue authority, it also implicitly gave an opportunity for HMRC to review an appeal before passing it on to the appropriate Commissioners.[104]

8.3.4   Transfer pricing disputes before the courts and tribunals

Formalities of transfer pricing disputes

A transfer pricing decision that imposes tax has to be approved by the Commissioners of HMRC, unless it has been agreed in writing between the HMRC official deciding the matter and the taxpayer affected. The taxpayer has a thirty-day 'cooling-off' period within which the agreement can be repudiated.[105]

On an appeal in respect of a transfer pricing decision each of the taxpayers affected is entitled to be a party to the proceedings, and the transfer pricing issues are to be decided separately from any other issue in the appeal.[106]

Reporting of transfer pricing cases

The administrative origins of the General and Special Commissioners have been a factor in the relative lack of public information about transfer pricing disputes in the United Kingdom. Decisions of the General Commissioners were never published except when there was a case stated to the High Court that resulted in a court decision that was published. Indeed, being a lay body, it was not practical to require the General Commissioners to produce written reasons in every case, even for the use of the parties.[107] Decisions of the Special Commissioners

---

[104] In one case, after this transfer took ten years and the Revenue withdrew its case after a hearing had been scheduled, the Special Commissioners went on to conclude that the Revenue had acted 'wholly unreasonably' once the matter had reached the tribunal: see *Carvill* v. *Frost* [2005] STC (SCD) 208 at paras. 10 and 77 (not itself a transfer pricing case).

[105] TIOPA 2010, ss. 208–10.   [106] *Ibid.* s. 212.

[107] Bartlett, 'The Tax Tribunals', note 74 above, 378–9.

were also not published until the reforms brought in in 1994. In addition to shifting appeals from the Special Commissioners away from the stated case procedure,[108] they permitted the Special Commissioners to publish their decisions, in anonymised form if the hearing had been held in private.[109]

Nevertheless, it does appear that, as Dawn Primarolo, a Treasury Minister, stated in reply to a written question in Parliament, most transfer pricing issues raised by HMRC are resolved 'without the need of formal proceedings'.[110] The reported cases confirm that HMRC is active in pursuing transfer pricing issues. Indeed, a number of cases are appealed, but the substantive issues are almost always settled. Since *Gillette Safety Razor Ltd* v. *IRC*, discussed above, was reported in 1920, there are only two reported cases that have considered the substance of applying the transfer pricing provisions, and only the most recent, *DSG Retail Ltd* v. *HMRC*, has done so at any length.

It is, however, clear that HMRC has regularly raised transfer pricing issues in assessing taxpayers. Indeed, the concern as to whether section 51(1) of the Finance (No. 2) Act 1945 was sufficient authority for upward transfer pricing adjustments arose in an appeal of a treaty-based arm's length transfer pricing assessment.[111] Moreover, the amount of tax recovered as a result of transfer pricing enquiries has increased substantially in recent years, rising from £35 million on large businesses alone in 1999–2000 to £87 million in 2001–2, £118 million in 2003–4 and £473 million in 2006–7.[112]

There are nine cases prior to *DSG Retail* that refer to transfer pricing disputes. Of these only two were heard by the courts. The remainder were heard by the Special Commissioners after 1994 or by the First-tier Tribunal. However, the first two court cases were heard in the 1990s and relate to the same underlying procedural issue. This suggests that the Special Commissioners similarly decided a number of transfer pricing appeals before 1994, though there is no indication that any of them would have provided any detailed guidance on how to apply the transfer pricing provisions.

---

[108] TMA 1970, s. 56A, substituted by SI 1994 / 1813, Sch. 1, para. 11.

[109] *Ibid.* s. 56D; Special Commissioners (Jurisdiction and Procedure) Regulations 1994 (SI 1994 / 1811), reg. 20.

[110] *Hansard*, HC, vol. 387, col. 137W, 17 June 2002.

[111] Oliver, 'Ship-money', note 26 above, 2.

[112] *Hansard*, HC, vol. 411, col. 9–10W, 7 October 2003, and *Reports from the Select Committee on Public Accounts* (2008 HC 302), para. 20.

The timing of the first OECD Report on transfer pricing in 1979 suggests that international tax interest in transfer pricing was increasing at that time, but it was also the year in which exchange control was abolished in the United Kingdom. This gave new opportunities for UK companies to shift profits abroad, particularly to tax havens.[113] It also resulted in the adoption of the UK legislation on controlled foreign corporations (CFCs) in 1984.[114] The concerns that gave rise to the CFC legislation included the use of captive insurance companies and offshore companies used to hold intellectual property.[115] Both of these are issues that could also be seen as transfer pricing issues, but the CFC legislation has in many cases provided HMRC with a simpler approach, avoiding the difficulties of determining appropriate arm's length transfer prices in such cases. Thus the CFC legislation has also helped to reduce the number of contentious transfer pricing disputes.

HMRC and the Treasury have been consulting on a new CFC regime to respond to concerns about the validity of the original regime raised before the European Court of Justice and English courts, and out of a desire to make the UK tax system more internationally competitive. New legislation is being introduced in the Finance Act 2012.[116]

The early ALS cases

The early cases were mostly concerned with procedural issues or with the scope of the transfer pricing provisions in question. Nevertheless, they give a good sense of the way in which transfer pricing questions have been dealt with.

Beecham Group plc v. *IRC* arose in the context of an appeal to the Special Commissioners regarding an assessment against a leading pharmaceutical company apparently not concerning transfer pricing.[117] The Inland Revenue sought to obtain documents from Beecham relating

---

[113] R. Bramwell, M. Hardwick, A. James and J. Lindsay, *Taxation of Companies and Company Reconstructions* (8th edn., London: Sweet & Maxwell, 2002), pp. C3–103.

[114] Originally Finance Act 1984, ss. 82–108, consolidated as ICTA 1984, ss. 747–56.

[115] See Inland Revenue, *Taxation of International Business*, Consultative Document (London: Board of Inland Revenue, 1982).

[116] See the draft of Finance Bill 2012 published on 6 December 2011, available at www. hmrc.gov.uk/budget-updates/march2011/draft-tax-finance-bill-2012.htm#5. For further details of the background to the proposals see HM Treasury, 'Consultation on Controlled Foreign Companies (CFC) Reform: Detailed Proposals', available at www. hm-treasury.gov.uk/consult_controlled_foreign_companies_reform.htm.

[117] *Beecham Group plc* v. *IRC* (1992) 65 TC 219 (Ch D).

to transfer pricing issues from a number of years previously. Since the time for making a new assessment had expired, the Revenue planned to implement any resulting direction of the Board under section 485(3) of the ICTA 1970 (which later became section 770(3) of the ICTA 1988) for a transfer pricing adjustment by amending the assessment already under appeal. Beecham brought an application in the High Court seeking to prevent the Revenue from requiring production of the documents on the grounds that any resulting transfer pricing direction could only be implemented by making a new assessment, which would be out of time. In the High Court, Mervyn Davies J decided that the application should proceed. It is understood that the matter was eventually settled without a further hearing in the High Court or before the Special Commissioners.

In *Glaxo Group Ltd* v. *IRC* the Court of Appeal returned to the question whether a transfer pricing direction under section 485(3) could be implemented by asking the Special Commissioners to increase an assessment already under appeal.[118] A new assessment would again have been out of time. The Court of Appeal held that the provisions in section 485(3) of the ICTA 1970 for implementing a transfer pricing direction by assessment, repayment of tax or otherwise were indeed sufficient to authorise an increase ordered by the General Commissioners on an appeal to them, whether or not that amounted to an assessment. This decision is presumably still applicable to the similar wording regarding how a transfer pricing adjustment is to be made now to be found in section 215 of the TIOPA 2010. Indeed, the reverse situation may be said to have arisen in *Sun Chemical Ltd* v. *Smith*.[119] An appeal had not been settled in connection with an assessment for a past year. Since it was too late to make a new assessment for that year, the Inland Revenue sought to take advantage of the not yet settled appeal to increase the previous assessment in relation to a new, unrelated issue that had arisen. The Special Commissioner, John Avery Jones, agreed with the Revenue on the basis that *Glaxo* decided that 'while an original assessment is open the inspector can raise new points which have the effect of increasing it even though they are raised out of time for making a further assessment'.[120]

---

[118] *Glaxo Group Ltd and others* v. *IRC* [1996] STC 191; 68 TC 166 (CA). Glaxo and Beecham were predecessors of the two companies that merged in 2000 to form GlaxoSmithKline plc after merging with two other pharmaceutical groups, Wellcome plc and SmithKline Beckman.

[119] *Sun Chemical Ltd* v. *Smith* [2002] STC (SCD) 510.   [120] *Ibid.* para. 13.

One of the issues on the earlier assessment under appeal was a transfer pricing inquiry; however, as has often happened with transfer pricing issues, that part of the appeal was settled in 1999.

Ametalco UK v. *IRC* concerned another aspect of the scope of section 770, how far it could be extended by analogy to transactions other than sales of goods as provided for in section 773(4) of the ICTA 1988. The Special Commissioners held that the phrase 'the giving of business facilities of whatever kind' could include the case where a UK subsidiary gave interest-free loans to sister subsidiaries in other countries, in situations comparable to thin capitalisation.[121]

Newidgets Manufacturing Ltd v. *Jones* involved a royalty paid to a foreign parent.[122] Estimated assessments of the company's tax liability were appealed and settled under section 54 of the Taxes Management Act (TMA) 1970, which provides that an agreement between a taxpayer and the tax inspector settling an appeal before the tribunal has decided the appeal is treated as having the same binding effect as an order of the tribunal deciding the appeal. After this, the Inland Revenue made a direction under section 770 of the ICTA 1988, and made an additional assessment on the taxpayer. The Special Commissioners held that, where the Revenue has received full information from the taxpayer, it could not reopen a section 54 agreement. The inspector had enough information at the time to have raised the transfer pricing issue. There was no substantive discussion of the transfer pricing issues.

Like *Ametalco*, *Waterloo plc* v. *IRC* concerned the applicability of section 770 of the ICTA 1988 to loans in a situation comparable to thin capitalisation, this time given to a trustee in order to fund a share option scheme for employees of non-UK subsidiaries of the taxpayer company.[123] The Special Commissioners held this situation also to fall within the 'business facilities' extension of section 770 by section 773(4). Although there was no transaction between the parent and the subsidiaries, it could be seen as the giving of business facilities to the subsidiaries, since the scheme was intended to incentivise their employees. In this case there was actually some consideration of how an arm's length price might be calculated. It was, however, little more sophisticated than

---

[121] *Ametalco UK* v. *IRC* [1996] STC (SCD) 399

[122] *Newidgets Manufacturing Ltd* v. *Jones* [1999] STC (SCD) 193, an anonymised decision.

[123] *Waterloo plc* v. *IRC* [2002] STC (SCD) 95, also an anonymised decision. 'Waterloo plc' was a UK-based multinational with 185 subsidiaries in 26 countries: *ibid.* para. 17.

that in *Gillette Safety Razor*. The test was what independent companies would have paid for the facilities of increased employee benefits:

> Without having heard argument on the point it would seem to us that it would be relatively simple to calculate a price at which a third party would consider it economically beneficial to agree to provide a similar facility. The cost for a third party of providing the facility could be calculated. It would presumably consist of such expenditure as the borrowing cost of acquiring sufficient funds to purchase the shares available to meet the options, trustee fees, a management and administrative cost and any other reasonable costs to meet the needs of providing the facility ... a fee of a suitable margin over cost could be agreed.[124]

Meditor Capital Management Ltd v. *Feighan* is another procedural transfer pricing case, but here transfer pricing principles were referred to in resolving the procedural issue.[125] In connection with the application of Schedule 28AA of the ICTA 1988 to transfer pricing between a UK investment advisory company and its 100 per cent non-UK fund manager parent company, the Inland Revenue issued a notice for the production of certain documents. The taxpayer appealed to the Special Commissioners against the notice. One of the grounds of appeal was that some of the documents were not relevant to the transfer pricing enquiry. Both sides referred to the OECD Guidelines on this point. The taxpayer objected that the information referred to on this point related principally to its parent. It argued that it had provided evidence for the application of the comparable uncontrolled price methodology, as the preferred method under the Guidelines, which was therefore sufficient. The Revenue responded that to apply the arm's length principle properly required a functional analysis, in accordance with the Guidelines, which had to compare the functions performed by the parent in comparison with other clients of the taxpayer.

The Special Commissioner agreed that the functional analysis required by para. 1.21 of the OECD Guidelines[126] needed to consider the relative positions of both associated companies. This might 'show that the provision of services by [the taxpayer] to [the parent] is not at arm's length if [the parent] has no use for the relevant services supplied'.[127]

---

[124] *Ibid.* paras. 99–102.
[125] *Meditor Capital Management Ltd* v. *Feighan* [2004] STC (SCD) 273.
[126] 2010 revision of the Guidelines, para. 1.43.
[127] *Meditor Capital Management*, note 125 above, para. 51.

It is also worth mentioning that *Carvill* v. *Frost*, referred to above, and decided in the same year as *Meditor*, also contained a reference to a transfer pricing issue involving two related companies. Here, the Revenue's investigations were resolved in favour of the taxpayer, this time without an appeal.

Test Claimants in the Thin Cap Group Litigation v. *HMRC*

The *Thin Cap Group Litigation* case again took up the theme of thin capitalisation,[128] but has more to say about how transfer pricing disputes are resolved in the United Kingdom. It raised the question of whether the United Kingdom's various thin capitalisation provisions since 1995, including the use since 1999 of the new transfer pricing regime originally in Schedule 28AA of the ICTA 1988 prior to the extension to resident companies in 2004, complied with the EU freedom of movement requirements.[129] As with many of the recent cases concerning the compatibility of UK tax rules with the freedom of movement provisions, this case was brought as an action in the High Court for restitution or damages. The claims of a large number of taxpayers were consolidated under a group litigation order (comparable to a class action). The claims of five groups were selected as representative test cases and referred to the European Court of Justice.

The ECJ concluded that all the versions of the UK thin cap rules over the period restricted the freedom of movement of EU parent companies since they did not apply to resident parent companies, but also concluded that thin cap legislation can be a justified infringement if it uses 'objective and verifiable elements' to identify 'purely artificial arrangements', and if it 'allows taxpayers to produce ... evidence as to the commercial justification for the transaction in question, and only disqualifies non-arm's length interest amounts'. The OECD arm's length principle, and tests based on it would be appropriate 'objective and verifiable elements'.[130]

The case returned to the English High Court. A central issue was whether the reference to allowing taxpayers to produce 'evidence as to

---

[128] *Test Claimants in the Thin Cap Group Litigation* v. *HMRC* [2011] EWCA Civ 127; [2011] STC 738, rev'g [2009] EWHC 2908 (Ch); [2010] STC 301, considering / *Test Claimants in the Thin Cap Group Litigation* v. *IRC* (C-524/04) [2007] ECR I-2107; [2007] STC 906; 9 ITLR 877 ('*Thin Cap Group Litigation*').

[129] In particular, freedom of establishment under Art. 43 EC, now Art. 43 TFEU.

[130] *Thin Cap Group Litigation*, ECJ, note 128 above, paras. 81–3, 92.

the commercial justification for the transaction' required that the legislation needed to have an additional 'subjective' element beyond the arm's length principle. Henderson J concluded that they did not comply with EU law because they did not permit a defence of commercial justification.[131] The Court of Appeal overruled him on the basis that the subsequent case law of the ECJ indicated that evidence of commercial justification could only go to whether the arm's length test was satisfied. There was no second test.[132]

Having concluded that the taxpayers were entitled to this defence under EU law, Henderson J considered the facts in the five test cases, and found that there was commercial justification in each case. Even though his reasoning has been rejected, his review of the cases provides useful examples of how transfer pricing cases are resolved in the United Kingdom.[133] These were five cases involving major multinational groups (Volvo, Lafarge, IBM, Siemens and Standard Bank). Each of them had been settled without any regular appeal being brought. The circumstances in which the problematic loans had been made were either to finance an acquisition by the UK company or a corporate reorganisation of the group, or to assist the UK company in dealing with losses. As a result Henderson J concluded that all of the transactions had commercial justification in the sense required by a separate defence of commercial justification.[134]

Henderson J gave a brief review of the facts in each of the test cases, and how the disputes with the Inland Revenue that arose in four of them developed (Standard Bank made capital contributions to its UK subsidiaries to ensure that no thin cap problem would arise). In addition, two Revenue officials gave evidence on the Revenue's general approach to thin cap legislation. They said that in general the Revenue would be concerned if a UK company or group of UK companies had a debt–equity ratio of less than 1:1 and interest cover of income at least three times interest payable. These were taken to be a typical approximation to

---

[131] *Thin Cap Group Litigation*, EWHC, note 128 above, paras. 65–73, 75.

[132] See *Thin Cap Group Litigation*, EWCA, note 128 above, para. 62. Arden LJ dissented (though agreeing in the overall result on other grounds), arguing that the conclusion of the majority would mean that the continued applicability of the ECJ decision in *Lankhorst-Hohorst GmbH* v. *Finanzamt Steinfurt* (C-324/00) [2002] ECR I-11779 was cast in doubt. The Supreme Court refused leave to appeal on 28 June 2011, and in November 2011 refused an application to refer the case back to the ECJ.

[133] *Thin Cap Group Litigation*, EWCA, note 128 above, paras. 104–187.

[134] *Ibid.* para. 100.

arm's length debt and interest levels based on the experience of tax inspectors, but they were not the only factors taken into account and were only general guides. Henderson J's brief description of the disputes includes no reference to there having been any discussion of the direct application of arm's length principles. He appears to have taken the supposed commercial justification test as being a purely factual test. In most of the cases a Revenue official acknowledged that the transaction, at least the transaction for which the financing was provided, was commercially justified, and this appears to have been the basis for Henderson J's conclusion. As Arden LJ's dissent in the Court of Appeal notes, this can be seen as consistent with the basis on which the ECJ decided *Lankhorst-Hohorst*; however, as Advocate-General Geelhoed noted in his Opinion in the *Thin Cap Group* case, it was likely that such justifications for thin capitalisation would be 'relatively exceptional'.[135]

In part Henderson J's view appears to have been influenced by the argument, made explicitly by a witness in the *IBM* case, that the thin cap restrictions did not reflect the reality of commercial borrowing, since a UK subsidiary would be able to borrow from a third party on terms that would take into account the credit of the whole group. On the other hand, he did not accept the taxpayers' argument that this made the UK approach inconsistent with the OECD arm's length principle.[136] Stanley Burnton LJ, who gave the first judgment in the Court of Appeal, thought that the ECJ had also considered the UK approach to be consistent with the OECD version, and remarked that the restriction to looking at the creditworthiness of the UK companies in isolation was consistent with the OECD's 'functionally separate entity' approach.[137]

DSG Retail Ltd v. HMRC

DSG Retail Ltd v. *HMRC* is striking because it contains a detailed discussion and analysis of both the complicated fact situation in the case and how the transfer pricing provisions should be applied to it. The case concerned the provision of extended warranties and service contracts on consumer goods sold under the 'Dixons' and related brands over a number of years. Almost all of the risk on the transactions (initially as reinsurance and later as insurance) was taken by DISL, an Isle of Man company in the same group, but the warranties were sold to

---

[135] *Thin Cap Group Litigation*, ECJ, note 128 above, AG's Opinion, para. 67.
[136] *Thin Cap Group Litigation*, EWHC, note 128 above, para. 74.
[137] *Thin Cap Group Litigation*, EWCA, note 128 above, paras. 60–61.

consumers at the time of sale of the products by a group company in the United Kingdom acting as agent for an independent insurer or service company reinsured or insured by DISL. The contention of HMRC was that DISL benefited from overly generous terms and that the profit of DSG should be increased.

The Special Commissioners, John Avery Jones and Charles Hellier, outlined the law on transfer pricing, identifying that the key difference between section 770 and Schedule 28AA of the ICTA 1988 is that under section 770 only the price at which the transaction (or equivalent giving of facilities) occurred can be adjusted, on the basis that the terms and conditions are otherwise fixed, whereas under Schedule 28AA, the terms can also be adjusted to arm's length terms. They also discuss how to apply the OECD Transfer Pricing Guidelines, noting that, while the legislation requires them to be taken into account only under Schedule 28AA, they are also relevant to the interpretation of section 770 as 'the approach of the OECD model is a useful aid which we should apply in the absence of any other guidance as they are the best evidence of international thinking on the topic'.[138]

Making extensive use of the testimony of expert witnesses, economists and insurance experts, the Special Commissioners considered the alternatives of applying the comparable uncontrolled price and profit split methods. They considered and rejected a range of proposed comparables: companies and sources of statistics. The most comparable company was in a significantly different position in terms of bargaining power, for which it was considered that no adjustment was possible. The accepted approach to applying the profit split method was based on determining rates of return on capital in principle, using a formula based on the capital asset pricing model (CAPM). This approach does not look like a typical application of the OECD Guidelines on the profit split method, and was criticised by one expert as missing the functional analysis required by the OECD Guidelines. However, the Special Commissioners concluded that the Guidelines were satisfied:

> [W]e consider that Mr Gaysford [an expert witness for HMRC] is using a profit split method based on the total profit with a mixture of contribution analysis and residual analysis approach. This looks to the functions of the parties, DISL providing insurance in circumstances where Cornhill, an independent party, had previously agreed a return which to a large degree represented its capital employed; and the Appellant Group

---

[138] *DSG Retail Ltd* v. *HMRC*, note 46 above, para. 77.

providing the whole business by virtue of its point of sale advantage in circumstances where it has particularly strong bargaining power. External data in the form of the cost of equity is used to assess the value of DISL's contribution rather than to determine directly the division of profit. It is a mixture of the contribution analysis and residual analysis . . . The result . . . replicates the outcome of bargaining between independent enterprises in the free market (para 3.21 of the Guidelines) . . . We therefore consider that Mr Gaysford's approach is in principle in accordance with the OECD Guidelines.[139]

Mr Gaysford was an economist. Counsel for the taxpayers criticised part of his evidence on the application of the profit split method as 'economic analysis divorced from reality', but the Special Commissioners noted that the OECD Guidelines require 'an economically valid basis' for the application of this method.[140]

Rather than developing their own calculations based on their conclusions, the Special Commissioners provide a decision in principle explaining how the transfer pricing adjustment should be calculated, and leaving it to the parties to agree the actual numbers if possible, or to return to the tribunal if not. The result accepted a goodly portion of the position argued by HMRC. This approach of the decision in principle is a standard element of the procedure before the Special Commissioners, often used very effectively, and enabling the parties to have decisions from the tribunal on the broad issues (often issues of law), sufficient to enable the parties to agree the technical details without troubling the Special Commissioners further.[141] (In fact, it is understood that the parties have agreed on the numbers, and the decision is now final.)

8.3.5   Administrative resolution of transfer pricing disputes

This thin record of litigation should not be read as meaning that HMRC and the Inland Revenue before it have taken little interest in transfer

---

[139] *Ibid.* para. 153. Paragraph 3.21 is revised as para. 2.122 in the 2010 revision of the Guidelines.

[140] *DSG Retail Ltd* v. *HMRC*, note 46 above, para. 126, referring to para. 3.5 of the Guidelines, para. 2.108 in the 2010 revision.

[141] Special Commissioners (Jurisdiction and Procedure) Regulations 1994 (SI 1994 / 1811), reg. 18. The First-tier Tribunal Tax Chamber has the power to make a decision on a preliminary issue and to adjourn a hearing (Tribunal Procedure (First-Tier Tribunal) (Tax Chamber) Rules 2009 (SI 2009 / 273), rule 5), and continues the practice of making decisions in principle. See, e.g., *Masterlease Ltd* v. *HMRC* [2010] UKFTT 339 (TC), not a transfer pricing case.

pricing issues. Indeed the periodic renewal of the legislation, and the broad language used in the 1915 legislation, can be taken as evidence of an abiding concern with the effect of transfer pricing on UK tax revenues. Rather, it appears that the Revenue has preferred to deal with such questions administratively, and would appear to have been largely successful at resolving transfer pricing issues satisfactorily in this way, with what is satisfactory being qualified by the information available to HMRC. Interestingly, it appears that the power to make a direction under section 770 and its predecessors had a strong *in terrorem* effect.[142] Thus, in the six years to 1976 only eleven directions were made, of which atypically seven had been made in 1974 and only the last one remained to be settled. As the Minister said in presenting these figures in response to a parliamentary question: 'The existence of the power to make a direction is normally sufficient to enable appropriate adjustments to be negotiated without a formal direction being made.'[143] A 1998 questionnaire surveying fifty-one UK and non-UK groups found that nineteen of the groups had faced transfer pricing audits in the preceding five years.[144] While this does not look like many audits, it covers 37 per cent of the respondents.

It is also interesting to see that in each of the test cases in the *Thin Cap Group Litigation* where there was a dispute, there were (often lengthy) negotiations between the taxpayer group and the Inland Revenue.[145] These negotiations resulted in agreements about the amount of interest that would be disallowed, and about conditions that the group had to maintain to ensure comparable treatment in the future for the loans within the term of the agreement, such as interest cover and debt to equity ratios. Although these agreements were forward looking, they arose out of investigations by the Revenue of existing arrangements, so they are not advance pricing agreements (considered further in section 8.5 below). Nevertheless, they describe an environment where the Revenue is ready to enter into lengthy negotiations on transfer pricing issues and to settle them on pragmatic terms that enforce the rules while also offering the taxpayer some assurance as to the future

---

[142] R. White, 'Section 485: The Law' (1978) *British Tax Review* 85, 86.

[143] *Hansard*, HC, vol. 924, col. 238W, 19 January 1977. An example of this strategy may be the unfruitful two and a half year transfer pricing investigation referred to in *Carvill* v. *Frost*, note 104 above, para. 26.

[144] J. Elliott, *International Transfer Pricing: A Survey of UK and Non-UK Groups* (London: Chartered Institute of Management Accountants, 1998), p. 29.

[145] *Thin Cap Group Litigation*, EWHC, note 128 above, paras. 104–179.

treatment of related transactions. This helps to explain why few transfer pricing disputes have reached the courts.

It is worth asking why the first transfer pricing case has reached the tribunal system now. It has been commented that this may suggest a change in the willingness of HMRC to litigate transfer pricing issues.[146] This is part of a wider concern that HMRC is becoming less willing to settle in cases where it has decided on litigation.[147] As part of a reorganisation over the last few years of the way in which it deals with businesses, especially large businesses, HMRC has introduced practices such as providing single points of contact for such 'customers', and using risk assessment to reduce the level of contact for more reliable taxpayers. However, a recent survey suggests that despite a general improvement in relations between HMRC and large businesses, there was concern about the adoption of an 'all or nothing' approach to disputes that go to litigation.

This is interesting because the document in which HMRC announced its new litigation strategy[148] does not really substantiate this view, particularly as regards transfer pricing, although the survey may, of course, give a better indication of how the strategy is operating on the ground. In any event, the strategy was 'refreshed' in June 2011,[149] to ensure that all HMRC staff appreciated the emphasis on a non-confrontational approach where possible.[150] The new version, which is accompanied by draft Practical Guidance for HMRC Staff and a comment on the use of alternative dispute resolution (ADR) in tax cases (principally mediation),[151] seeks to emphasise the importance of starting with a non-confrontational and collaborative approach to avoid

---

[146] See C. Roche, 'Landmark Case on UK Transfer Pricing Rules: *DSG Retail* v. *HMRC*', online article, Bird & Bird, available at www.twobirds.com/english/news/articles/pages/landmark_case_uk_transfer_pricing_rules.aspx.

[147] V. Houlder, 'Litigation Still Sours Business View of HMRC', *Financial Times*, 6 July 2010, p. 4.

[148] HMRC, 'Litigation and Settlements Strategy', introduced at Business Tax Forum meeting 2 July 2007, webarchive.nationalarchives.gov.uk/20101019055120/http://www.hmrc.gov.uk/practitioners/lss.pdf.

[149] HMRC, 'Litigation and Settlements Strategy', available at www.hmrc.gov.uk/practitioners/lss.pdf.

[150] V. Houlder, 'Watchdog Backs Revenue on Tax Disputes', *Financial Times*, 8 July 2011, available at www.ft.com/cms/s/0/e899c1ac-a98d-11e0-a04a-00144feabdc0.html.

[151] HMRC, 'Publication of Draft Litigation and Settlement Strategy Guidance and Accompanying Draft Alternative Dispute Resolution Guidance', available at www.hmrc.gov.uk/practitioners/lss-intro.htm.

disputes. Mediation is seen as potentially useful in 'fact heavy' cases, such as many transfer pricing cases. It is also seen as an aid to defining issues, or to finding alternative approaches to cases that appear to be 'all or nothing' or to revolve purely around a legal question.[152] In each case the value of mediation is seen as being in improving the chances of reaching a settlement. The Guidance gives the example of a case involving a transfer pricing issue combined with an international VAT issue:

> In this case, mediation could be useful in untangling the facts surrounding the transfer pricing, or could be useful in helping the parties come to agreement regarding what information is relevant, what is available and how best it can be provided. It could also assist the parties in agreeing a transfer pricing methodology.
>
> Mediation might help the parties agree on the point of law . . . for VAT purposes. But even if the parties eventually could not agree on the substantive issue, mediation could be useful in identifying the underlying needs and interests of both parties . . . It could also be useful in setting a roadmap as to how the disputes with . . . other clients could be resolved.[153]

An ADR Panel has been established within HMRC to decide whether individual cases are suitable for ADR. Once the taxpayer and HMRC have agreed to try mediation, an ADR process agreement would need to be settled. The Guidance includes a template for such an agreement.

Settlement is encouraged, but must be in accordance with the law. This means that HMRC will not agree to a settlement that merely splits the difference on a number of issues. Transfer pricing disputes are typically seen as cases where there are a range of methods and values that the courts might approve of. The draft Practical Guidance indicates that 'HMRC would not generally take the case on to the Tribunal unless a potential settlement offered by the customer fell outside HMRC's reasonable expectation of the range of possible findings that the Tribunal might come to.'[154] However, it may also consider other factors, such as the importance of setting a precedent for compliance, the amount of revenue involved, and the priority of the case relative to other potential litigation cases.

---

[152] HMRC, 'Draft Practical Guidance for HMRC Staff on the Use of Alternative Dispute Resolution in Large or Complex Cases', available at www.hmrc.gov.uk/practitioners/adr-draft-guidance.pdf, section 5.

[153] *Ibid.* section 5, p. 8.

[154] HMRC, 'Resolving Tax Disputes: Draft Practical Guidance for HMRC Staff on the Litigation and Settlement Strategy', available at www.hmrc.gov.uk/practitioners/lss-draft-guidance.pdf, p. 34.

What this strategy does seem to suggest is a desire to enter into litigation in a carefully thought out, strategic way. This approach might well imply a greater willingness to begin litigation in cases with a substantial amount at issue and where HMRC foresees good prospects of success. Indeed, it appears that a transfer pricing case against a major UK multinational, which might well have rivaled *DSG Retail* for size and significance, had been scheduled for hearing before being settled at the end of June 2010. Even if only a small number of cases result in reported decisions, it may reflect a significant shift from trying to resolve transfer pricing issues at a pre-dispute administrative level to a readiness to take them down the formal litigation route. It is likely that this would at least result in discussions between HMRC and taxpayers based on more rigorous attempts to apply the legal principles and the OECD Guidelines.

To understand this better it is necessary to look at it in the context of the new transfer pricing governance system that HMRC adopted in 2008.[155] This created a Transfer Pricing Group including specialists from across HMRC led by a Transfer Pricing Board (TPB), which provides strategic direction on transfer pricing and makes decisions on high risk cases. Operational decisions are handled by two Transfer Pricing Panels, one for the Large Business Service (LBS), and one for the local offices that handle other cases: Local Compliance (LC). Each Panel makes decisions about opening formal transfer pricing enquiries, and determining how and within what parameters each case should be settled – negotiation, litigation, etc. Under each panel there are groups of transfer pricing specialists, who advise and assist the usual LBS and LC officials, ensuring continuity of the relationships with taxpayers. Central strategy, advice and coordination is provided by Business International, which is described as the 'transfer pricing product and process owner'.[156] No approach that might be construed as a transfer pricing enquiry may be made without the approval of the Transfer Pricing Board or the appropriate Transfer Pricing Panel. Deciding which cases to pursue is subject to detailed risk assessment. 'Risk assessment is as much about preventing the take-up of unsuitable cases as it is about identifying the high risk ones and, where an enquiry does result from the process, effort put in at the risk assessment stage will speed up the working of the case.'[157] Both

---

[155] Described in HMRC, *International Manual*, INTM450000, available at www.hmrc.gov.uk/manuals/intmanual/Index.htm.

[156] HMRC, *International Manual*, INTM452040.

[157] HMRC, *International Manual*, INTM461200.

advance pricing agreements and mutual agreement procedures (MAPs) are subject to separate governance. In the latter case this ensures that MAP will be handled by officials separate from those who conducted any related internal enquiry. HMRC's new approach to transfer pricing is also discussed in a 2002 *Tax Bulletin* article.[158]

Much of HMRC's view of how the transfer pricing rules should operate is explained in the *International Manual,* one of the HMRC Staff Manuals made available to the public online. The Manuals are written to provide guidance to inspectors on the issues covered. They are neither comprehensive nor definitive and are subject to changing views of HMRC. 'Subject to these qualifications readers may assume that the guidance given will be applied in the normal case; but where HMRC considers that there is, or may have been, avoidance of tax the guidance will not necessarily apply.'[159] The sections dealing with transfer pricing present HMRC's current interpretation of the OECD Guidelines subject to UK law.[160]

8.4   Bilateral resolution of transfer pricing disputes in the United Kingdom: mutual agreement

8.4.1   Mutual agreement procedure in UK treaties and legislation

For a country with one of the world's most extensive tax treaty networks, the United Kingdom accepted the mutual agreement procedure with surprising reluctance. Although the United Kingdom's first regular tax treaty, that with the United States in 1945, included an associated enterprises Article, it did not include a mutual agreement provision, until one was added by the 1966 Protocol.[161] In fact, it seems this was no accident. Other early UK treaties also lack a mutual agreement Article. In contrast, the Canada–United States treaty of 1942, from which the text for the associated enterprises Article in the 1945 United Kingdom–United States treaty was taken, did have a primitive mutual agreement provision. The second paragraph of Article XVIII provided: 'The

---

[158] HMRC, 'Review of Links with Business: International Tax Issues' (2002) 60 *Tax Bulletin* (TB08/02–1).

[159] HMRC, 'HMRC Guidance Manuals: Introduction', available at www.hmrc.gov.uk/ manuals/advisory.htm.

[160] See HMRC, *International Manual,* INTM430000 to INTM460000, available at www. hmrc.gov.uk/manuals/intmanual/Index.htm.

[161] Avery Jones, 'The History of the United Kingdom's First Comprehensive Double Taxation Agreement', note 14 above, 243.

competent authorities of the two contracting States may communicate with each other directly for the purpose of giving effect to the provisions of the present Convention.'[162]

Before 1966 there were a few UK treaties with mutual agreement provisions that were slightly more sophisticated versions of that in the 1942 Canada–United States treaty. Article XXV of the Sweden–United Kingdom treaty of 1960 added 'and for resolving any difficulty or doubt as to the application of the Convention',[163] words that now appear in Article 25(3) of the OECD Model. The same wording was used in the 1962 treaty with Israel,[164] but the 1960 treaty with Italy contained no mutual agreement provision.[165]

The Protocol with the United States seems to have been the first UK tax treaty provision with a mutual agreement provision comparable to that in the OECD Model. New Article XXA added by the 1966 Protocol covered in substance, though not in wording, most of the scope of Article 25 of the 1963 OECD Draft Convention.[166] Article XXA included a specific reference to using what has been termed the interpretative power (the first sentence of Article 25(3) of the OECD Model) to resolve transfer pricing disputes. It also contained two paragraphs providing for

---

[162] Canada–United States Reciprocal Tax Convention, Washington, 4 March 1942, in force 1 January 1941, reprinted in Canadian Income Tax Act S.C. 1970–71–72, c. 63, as amended with Income Tax Regulations Consolidated to April 19, 1973 (43rd edn, Don Mills, Ont.: CCH Canadian, 1973), pp. 612–23. Note that this was significantly less detailed than the provisions in Arts. XVI and XVII of the Protocol to the Mexico Draft and Arts. XVII and XIX of the Protocol to the London Draft.

[163] Convention between the Government of the United Kingdom of Great Britain and Northern Ireland and the Government of the Kingdom of Sweden for the Avoidance of Double Taxation with respect to Taxes on Income, London, 28 July 1960, (1961) UKTS 38, Cmnd 1378.

[164] Convention between the Government of the United Kingdom of Great Britain and Northern Ireland and the Government of the State of Israel for the Avoidance of Double Taxation with respect to Taxes on Income, London, 26 September 1962, (1963) UKTS 36, Cmnd 2046.

[165] Convention between the Government of the United Kingdom of Great Britain and Northern Ireland and the Government of the Italian Republic for the Avoidance of Double Taxation with respect to Taxes on Income, London, 4 July 1960, (1963) UKTS 14, Cmnd 1967.

[166] Inserted by the Supplementary Protocol between the Government of the United Kingdom of Great Britain and Northern Ireland and the Government of the United States of America amending the Convention for the Avoidance of Double Taxation and the Prevention of Fiscal Evasion with respect to Taxes on Income signed at Washington on 16 April 1945, as modified by the Supplementary Protocols signed at Washington on 6 June 1946, 25 May 1954 and 19 August 1957, London, 17 March 1966, (1966) UKTS 65, Cmnd 3128, Art. 15.

compensating adjustment mechanisms for each country. The first Canada–United Kingdom tax treaty was entered into in December 1965 and contained no mutual agreement provision;[167] however, the parties entered into a replacement treaty the following year,[168] and this one contained a mutual agreement procedure in Article 24 (with the marginal note 'Claim adjustments'), which followed the wording of the US Protocol, but without the compensating adjustment provisions. The current practice is for UK tax treaties to contain a relatively standard mutual agreement Article.

This is not, however, the end of the story. The United Kingdom is notorious for implementing tax treaties in domestic law in a limited way.[169] A legislative basis for mutual agreements was not provided until 2000 with the addition of section 815AA of the ICTA 1988.[170] The status of a mutual agreement provision before this addition was unclear. In *IRC v. Commerzbank* the High Court held that an agreement under Article XXA(2) of the United Kingdom–United States treaty was not binding on the UK courts, but that was because the provision itself only provided for the governments to consult, and did not give the result any binding effect.[171] As Avery Jones points out, however, this depended on the wording used in this paragraph, empowering the competent authorities to 'communicate with each other directly … to assure [the treaty's] consistent interpretation and application'.[172] In contrast, Article 25(3) of

---

[167] Agreement between the Government of the United Kingdom of Great Britain and Northern Ireland and the Government of Canada for the Avoidance of Double Taxation with respect to Taxes on Certain Classes of Income, Ottawa, 6 December 1965, (1966) UKTS 18, Cmnd 3033.

[168] Agreement between the Government of the United Kingdom of Great Britain and Northern Ireland and the Government of Canada for the Avoidance of Double Taxation and the Prevention of Fiscal Evasion with respect to Taxes on Income and Capital Gains, Ottawa, 12 December 1966, (1967) UKTS 32, Cmnd 3283. Presumably the renegotiation was necessitated by the introduction of capital gains tax in the United Kingdom in 1965. The same wording was used in the New Zealand–United Kingdom treaty signed in June of that year: Agreement between the Government of the United Kingdom of Great Britain and Northern Ireland and the Government of New Zealand for the Avoidance of Double Taxation and the Prevention of Fiscal Evasion with respect to Taxes on Income, Wellington, 13 June 1966, (1966) UKTS 61, Cmnd 3132.

[169] See *NEC Semi-Conductors Ltd* v. *HMRC* [2006] EWCA Civ 25; [2006] STC 606; 8 ITLR 819, aff'd on other grounds *sub nom. Boake Allen Ltd* v. *HMRC* [2007] UKHL 25; [2007] 1 WLR 1386; [2007] 3 All ER 605; [2007] STC 1265; 9 ITLR 995.

[170] See now ss. 124, 125 of the TIOPA 2010.

[171] *IRC* v. *Commerzbank AG* [1990] STC 285 (Ch D) at 302.

[172] J. F. Avery Jones, 'The Mutual Agreement Procedure' (2001) *British Tax Review* 9, 11.

the OECD Model provides that they 'shall endeavour to resolve by mutual agreement any difficulties or doubts arising as to the interpretation of the Convention'. Avery Jones thought that this could be seen as a valid delegation of power under a tax treaty, and thus within the provisions implementing the treaty in UK domestic law, but that following the addition of section 815AA, which only deals with the specific case of mutual agreement power under Article 25(1) and (2) of the OECD Model, UK courts might well be unwilling to give effect to these provisions without specific legislative authority.[173]

This leaves open the question of the status of the specific-case mutual agreement provisions prior to section 815AA. The post-1965 provisions in UK treaties use the 'shall endeavour' wording for specific case mutual agreement procedures. The view that this is a valid delegation, at least in the case of transfer pricing disputes, seems to have merit. The effect in the United Kingdom of a transfer pricing mutual agreement would typically have been an adjustment to the UK income of a UK resident company, which would appear to be within the scope of section 788(3) (c)(ii) of the ICTA 1988.[174] However, if, as discussed above, this provision was not sufficient to charge an additional amount of income to a resident, so that the enactment of what became section 770 was required, the legal basis for a mutual agreement that did not relieve the UK resident would remain doubtful.[175] It is possible that section 54 of the TMA 1970 in effect provides a statutory basis for the implementation of a transfer pricing mutual agreement accepted by the taxpayer. This would be available provided a domestic appeal was launched within the normal six-year time limit without a final decision of the

---

[173] *Ibid.* 12.

[174] Providing that the treaty provisions 'shall, notwithstanding anything in any enactment, have effect in relation to income tax and corporation tax in so far as they provide: ... (c) for determining the income or chargeable gains to be attributed: ... (ii) to persons resident in the United Kingdom who have special relationships with persons not so resident'.

[175] Avery Jones thought that the version of Art. 25(3) in the 1975 United Kingdom–United States treaty (based on the OECD Model), which included a list of six items on which the authorities 'may reach agreement', might be taken to imply that agreements on those topics were intended to be binding on taxpayers: Avery Jones, 'The Mutual Agreement Procedure', note 172 above, fn. 17. A similar argument might be made, though on the basis of less strong wording, with regard to the second sentence of Article XXA in the 1966 Protocol providing that the authorities 'may consult together to resolve disputes' regarding transfer pricing and two other topics.

Commissioners having been handed down.[176] The Inland Revenue was willing to accept 'protective' claims within the limitation period, and would reopen a section 54 settlement to implement a corresponding adjustment within the limitation period.[177] Section 815AA of the ICTA 1988, and now section 124 of the TIOPA 2010, are striking for the bold extent to which they give effect to mutual agreements. Section 124(2) provides: 'The Commissioners are to give effect to the solution or mutual agreement despite anything in any enactment, and any such adjustment as is appropriate in consequence may be made.' This means that in the United Kingdom, a mutual agreement may override a previous decision of the courts in a dispute. In principle, this could permit an agreement that took rights from a taxpayer that had previously been recognised in the case by a court.[178] The provisions also set out time limits for bringing a MAP claim (the longer of six years after the end of the tax period and the period allowed by the treaty) and for claiming an adjustment to implement a MAP agreement (twelve months after notification of the agreement).[179]

8.4.2   Use of MAP in UK transfer pricing disputes

The United Kingdom has recently expanded the guidance on how it applies the MAP, particularly in connection with transfer pricing. At the time of the introduction of section 815AA, the UK and US governments published Administrative Arrangements regarding the United Kingdom–United States MAP provisions.[180] In addition, there is some

---

[176] The basic limitation period has been shortened to four years for both claims by taxpayers and assessments: ss. 34, 43 of the TMA 1970. The six-year limit remains for assessments where there is a loss of tax brought about carelessly, and it is still twenty years in case of certain deliberate acts: s. 36 of the TMA 1970. A claim may be made within the year following a subsequent assessment, s. 43A of the TMA 1970.

[177] Chartered Institute of Taxation, Technical Release CIOT/TIR/7/97, cited in CCH, British Tax Library (CCH, online), 'Other material on s. 54'.

[178] Avery Jones, 'The Mutual Agreement Procedure', note 172 above, 10.

[179] TIOPA 2010, ss. 125(3) and 124(4), formerly ICTA 1988, s. 815AA(6) and (3).

[180] Administrative Arrangements for the Implementation of the Mutual Agreement Procedure (Article 25) of the Convention between the Government of the United Kingdom of Great Britain and Northern Ireland and the Government of the United States of America for the Avoidance of Double Taxation and the Prevention of Fiscal Evasion with respect to Taxes on Income and Capital Gains signed on 31 December 1975, as amended by Protocols (2000), available at www.hmrc.gov.uk/international/us_uk_map_arrangements.pdf. This document takes the form of a MAP agreement made under Art. 25 of the 1975 treaty. Although it was adopted under the 1975 treaty, it would appear that it is still applicable.

guidance given in the HMRC *International Manual*. Neither is very detailed. HMRC provided further guidance in February 2011 in Statement of Practice 1/11.[181] The United Kingdom does not publish information about either the level of use of the MAP or about individual agreements. Only occasionally has any information been published about the content of interpretive or legislative MAPs entered into by the United Kingdom, one example being the UK–US Administrative Arrangements. Up to 1980 a MAP with the Netherlands and one with the United States had been published, in both cases having become available in the other country.[182]

HMRC does not require any particular format for a taxpayer to initiate a MAP process, but it is important to take account of any formalities that the other country may require. For HMRC, the taxpayer needs to state the nature of the action that is, or is expected to be, not in accordance with the treaty and the relevant year, and to identify itself fully.[183] The United Kingdom generally follows the guidance in the Commentary on Article 25 of the OECD Model.[184] Most treaties provide that the MAP process has to be invoked by a taxpayer within three years of the first notification of the action resulting in double taxation. This is the 'longer period' under section 125(3) of the TIOPA 2010, referred to above. HMRC seeks to interpret this period favourably to the taxpayer, and permits a taxpayer to start the process before the period runs. For UK tax purposes, HMRC considers first notification to be the closure of a transfer pricing enquiry resulting in or threatening double taxation.[185] It appears that the United Kingdom would accept a MAP claim within six years if that were longer than the period given under the treaty, but the other country might not agree to conduct a MAP in that case.

The Administrative Arrangements set out target time limits for action by the governments: the aim is the delivery of an initial position by the requested country within 120 days of a documented request, and an agreement within eighteen months after that. Although the process is

---

[181] HMRC, 'Transfer Pricing, Mutual Agreement Procedure and Arbitration', Statement of Practice SP1/11 (2011). The current edition of the Statements of Practice is available at www.hmrc.gov.uk/agents/sop.pdf.

[182] J. F. Avery Jones *et al.*, 'The Legal Nature of the Mutual Agreement Procedure under the OECD Model Convention – II' (1980) *British Tax Review* 13, 22, 26, 27. There was also a 1965 agreement with the Netherlands published there, but it was not made pursuant to the treaty as the treaty contained no mutual agreement Article at the time.

[183] SP1/11, note 181 above, paras. 12–13.   [184] *Ibid.* para. 32.

[185] *Ibid.* para. 29.

seen as being solely between the governments, they have agreed to keep the taxpayer informed and to invite further submissions where appropriate. They also commit to coordinating the MAP process with domestic appeals and ensuring that neither government withdraws from a MAP process without discussion.

HMRC takes the view that the MAP process is secondary to ordinary domestic dispute resolution in transfer pricing cases. While a company can present a case to the competent authority at any point in the investigation and resolution process to get the MAP process started and preserve a claim, HMRC will not normally pursue it until the domestic remedies have been exhausted.[186] In a sense that means that for HMRC a MAP is principally about the compensating adjustment. Thus, there are two key themes in the advice to inspectors faced with a MAP claim. The first is to stick to aiming for a resolution within the arm's length principle, in order to have a position that is most likely to be sustained in the MAP. Short-cuts, such as bundling several years' adjustments into one or rolling interest on tax into the adjustment proper, are to be avoided. The second is to leave granting UK compensating adjustments to the MAP process.[187] A compensating adjustment can only be claimed once the potentially tax advantaged person's adjustment has been made, whether in their return or an amendment to their return, or by an assessment. On the other hand, HMRC recommends that taxpayers invoke the MAP process at an early stage, as it may make it possible to resolve any emerging conflicts between the two tax authorities before unrelievable double taxation results.[188] In an international setting this must be done by the MAP procedure, so it is only available when the United Kingdom has a treaty with the other country.[189]

---

[186] HMRC, *International Manual*, INTM470010, available at www.hmrc.gov.uk/manuals/intmanual/INTM470010.htm.

[187] HMRC, *International Manual*, INTM470020.

[188] SP1/11, note 181 above, para. 18.

[189] Where the transfer pricing rules have to be applied to a domestic situation, for instance between two UK-resident large companies, the equivalent of a compensating adjustment can be claimed under what is now s. 174 of the TIOPA 2010. In an international situation no compensating adjustment is available under the United Kingdom's unilateral double taxation relief. Before being rewritten into TIOPA 2010, Part 2, unilateral relief operated by granting relief as if there were a treaty with the territory in question having the terms specified in the unilateral relief rules: s. 790(3) of the ICTA 1988, but they did not include any provision for a MAP. Under s. 18 of the TIOPA 2010 credit is now available either under a treaty or under the unilateral relief arrangements (ss. 9–17 of the TIOPA 2010: see s. 8(1)).

The limitations of the 'shall endeavour' wording of MAP Articles in treaties, as well as their uncertain domestic law status before 2000, have meant that they were not seen by taxpayers as a highly valuable method of dispute resolution.[190] The prospect of future improvement in that came with the signing in 1990 of the EU (then EEC) Arbitration Convention, which offered the possibility of arbitration for transfer pricing disputes arising between EU Member States.[191] The United Kingdom adopted legislation to give domestic effect to decisions under the Convention in 1992,[192] although the Convention did not come into force until 1995.

Up to 1997, the United Kingdom had 'negligible experience' with the operation of the Arbitration Convention. Since then the experience has been that most cases where the Convention is invoked are settled without an arbitration panel hearing the matter.[193] The United Kingdom is fully ready to cooperate in setting up an advisory commission (the arbitrating body under the Convention in the case of a request at the end of the pre-arbitration time limit for MAP negotiation, two years under the Convention),[194] and follows the EU Code of Conduct on the Arbitration Convention.[195]

The United Kingdom has recently started including arbitration provisions in new double tax treaties, and has added arbitration provisions to a few existing ones. Arbitration provisions came into effect in 2010 under the treaties with France and Switzerland, and in 2011 under the treaties with Germany, the Netherlands and Qatar. A number of other arbitration provisions are either under negotiation or have been signed but are not yet in force.[196] Unusually, the United Kingdom's treaty with

---

[190] See, e.g., I. P. A. Stitt, 'International Tax: Avoiding Parochialism' (1997) *British Tax Review* 19, 30.

[191] Convention 90/436/EC of 23 July 1990 on the elimination of double taxation in connection with the adjustment of profits of associated enterprises [1990] OJ L225/10.

[192] ICTA 1988, s. 815B, enacted by Finance (No. 2) Act, s. 51(1). See now TIOPA 2010, ss. 126–8.

[193] SP1/11, note 181 above, para. 48.   [194] *Ibid.* para. 39.

[195] Revised Code of Conduct for the effective implementation of the Convention on the elimination of double taxation in connection with the adjustment of profits of associated enterprises, [2009] OJ C322/1. See SP1/11, note 181 above, para. 47.

[196] Details of the treaties in force can be found at www.hmrc.gov.uk/taxtreaties/in-force/index.htm, where there are also links to further information about treaty developments. For the Statutory Instruments implementing the treaties, see www.hmrc.gov.uk/tax-treaties/si.htm.

Mexico has included an arbitration provision in force since 1994.[197] However, since the provision requires the taxpayer and both competent authorities to agree to arbitration and has no time limit for invocation, it is of much less use than the more recent provisions. There are as yet few details as to how these treaty arbitration provisions will operate in practice, except in the case of Germany, where the two countries have agreed a Memorandum of Understanding.[198]

8.5   Advance pricing agreements

When the first UK transfer pricing provisions based on the arm's length principle were introduced in 1951, the Attorney General, speaking in support of the Finance Bill on an amendment that would have author-ised the Treasury to sanction transactions or classes of transactions, excluding them from the operation of the provisions, said: 'It would be very difficult to give an advance kind of sanction in respect of particular sales, and it would be equally difficult, as a matter of drafting, to take out old proofs of sales.'[199] This can almost be read as a rejection in advance of the idea of an advance pricing agreement. Nevertheless, the Inland Revenue started entering into advance pricing agreements (APAs) at least as early as the 1990s,[200] on the basis of treaty mutual agreement provisions.[201] As it happens, it was not until 1999 that the United Kingdom made legislative provision for APAs.

---

[197] Convention for the Avoidance of Double Taxation and the Prevention of Fiscal Evasion with respect to Taxes on Income and Capital Gains, Mexico City, 2 June 1994, effective 1 or 6 April 1994, pursuant to SI 1994/3212, art. 26(5).

[198] Mutual Agreement of 20 September 2011 between the Competent Authorities of the United Kingdom and the Federal Republic of Germany in order to settle the mode of application of the arbitration process provided by paragraph 5 of Article 26 of the Convention between the United Kingdom of Great Britain and Northern Ireland and the Federal Republic of Germany for the Avoidance of Double Taxation and the Prevention of Fiscal Evasion with respect to Taxes on Income and on Capital, signed at London on 30 March 2010, available at www.hmrc.gov.uk/taxtreaties/in-force/g.htm.

[199] *Hansard*, HC, vol. 489, col. 2097, 2 July 1951.

[200] Three APAs were entered into in the year to 31 March 1996, but that brought the total in force to eight. Over the next five years, a further twenty-eight were entered into. All thirty-six were still in force on 31 March 2001. Written answer, *Hansard*, HC, vol. 387, col. 137W, 17 June 2002.

[201] Inland Revenue, 'The Mutual Agreement Procedure in UK Double Taxation Conven-tions' (1996) 25 *Tax Bulletin* 345, available at webarchive.nationalarchives.gov.uk/20101006151632/http://www.hmrc.gov.uk/bulletins/tb25.htm#transfer_pricing; HMRC, 'Advance Pricing Agreements (APAs)', Statement of Practice SP3/99 (1999), para. 15.

Section 85 of the Finance Act 1999 gave effect to an agreement made between the Inland Revenue and a taxpayer dealing with 'the treatment for tax purposes of any provision made or imposed (whether before or after the date of the agreement) as between the taxpayer and any associate of his', or with matters concerning the attribution of income to a permanent establishment of the taxpayer (or to a branch or agency if the taxpayer is not a company and is carrying on a trade); however, an APA will not normally cover whether a permanent establishment exists. Thin capitalisation issues are normally dealt with separately in an advance thin capitalisation agreement (ATCA).[202] The tax consequences of matters within the proper scope of the agreement are then governed by the agreement instead of the terms of the transfer pricing legislation that would otherwise apply.[203] There are provisions for revocation of the APA under its terms or for failure of the taxpayer to meet a significant provision or key condition.[204] If the other party to a transaction is also subject to UK tax, it will be able to claim a compensating adjustment calculated in the same way under that agreement (subject to any UK APA that it has entered into).[205] The application for an APA must state the questions to be determined and the provisions the effect of which is to be clarified, as well as the reason why clarification is necessary.[206] The legislation also includes rules on the term of an APA, amendment or modification by HMRC, annulment and penalties for misrepresentation by the taxpayer, and that a mutual agreement under the relevant treaty will override the APA.[207]

HMRC has provided guidance on its practice regarding APAs in Statement of Practice SP2/10, which recently updated the original Statement of Practice SP3/99. There is also guidance on entering into bilateral APAs in a *Tax Bulletin* article from October 1999,[208] and in the 2002 *Tax Bulletin* article on international transfer pricing generally.[209]

The 1999 *Tax Bulletin* article reflects HMRC's experience in concluding APAs with treaty partners, notably the United States. Basic principles

---

[202] HMRC, 'Advance Pricing Agreements', Statement of Practice SP2/10 (2010), paras. 4–5.

[203] Finance Act 1999, s. 85. Note that ss. 85–7 of the Finance Act 1999 have been rewritten as Part 5 of TIOPA 2010 (ss. 218–30).

[204] TIOPA 2010, s. 221.   [205] *Ibid*. s. 222.   [206] *Ibid*. s. 223.   [207] *Ibid*. ss. 224–9.

[208] HMRC, 'Advance Pricing Agreements: The Inland Revenue's Experience and Expectation of the Bilateral Process for Guidance to its Taxpayers' (1999) 43 *Tax Bulletin* (TB10/99–5).

[209] HMRC, 'Review of Links with Business: International Tax Issues' (2002) 60 *Tax Bulletin* (TB 08/02–1).

are that applications should be made to both administrations simultaneously or nearly so (within four weeks). The tax administrations can be expected to coordinate their responses, agree a timetable and maintain continuous contact through the application process. Taxpayers need to be able to respond to requests for information in a timely manner. The negotiations are conducted at competent authority level and confidentiality is protected by the exchange of information treaty Articles. A pre-filing meeting can be arranged, but it is preferable that this should be done with both authorities, or at least a meeting should be arranged with the second authority as soon as possible to provide the same information. The Article sets out an eighteen-month schedule for the negotiation of an APA. The UK APA legislation provides for transfer pricing APAs only to override the Schedule 28AA transfer pricing rules (now Part 4 of the TIOPA 2010). During the term of an APA HMRC will agree not to rely on other rules, such as section 788(3)(c)(ii) (now section 6(2)(f) of the TIOPA 2010) or the principle in *Sharkey* v. *Wernher*.[210]

Statement of Practice SP2/10 provides guidance on the possible scope of an APA; the choice of unilateral, bilateral or multilateral APAs (HMRC prefers bilateral APAs); eligibility to apply for an APA (the taxpayer's transfer pricing affairs should be complex or not low risk without an APA, or the taxpayer should be seeking to implement a highly customised pricing method); how to express interest in an APA and then to make a formal application; the information required in an application, including the identification of assumptions critical to the reliability of the proposed transfer pricing method; the basis on which applications are evaluated; the process of finalising an agreement, including the requirement for the taxpayer to commit to implementing the agreed pricing method, verified in an annual report; how APAs are monitored and reviewed; changes, revocations and renewals; and penalties. An Annex provides guidance on the terms that an APA should typically cover.

Where the transactions raise a question of thin capitalisation, the taxpayer can obtain an advance thin capitalisation agreement (ATCA) under the same legislative authority. ATCAs are discussed in a separate Statement of Practice from 2007, SP04/07.[211] An ATCA will be available

---

[210] See text to note 34 above. This principle has since been given legislative effect in ITTOIA 2005, Part 2, ch. 11A, and CTA 2009, Part 3, ch. 10.

[211] HMRC, 'Advance Thin Capitalisation Agreements under the APA Legislation', Statement of Practice SP04/07 (2007).

in respect of financing arrangements affected by double tax treaty provisions, or affected by the 'acting together' provisions of schedule 28AA, para. 4A of the ICTA 1988,[212] and in respect of other types of intra-group financing, e.g., involving a quoted Eurobond. However, the arrangements should have commercial significance for the company, and the application should explain the financial strategy and commercial motivations and advantages behind the arrangements.[213] The process is less formal than that for a regular APA, but the application should normally contain the proposed terms for the ATCA. ATCAs do not cover withholding tax reductions, since they need to be applied for by the beneficial owner of the interest under the provisions of the relevant treaty. Thin cap clearance and a withholding tax reduction application can be combined under the pre-1999 'treaty route', but that will not benefit from the new protections of the APA process.[214] Other issues that may arise in parallel with thin cap issues, such as the application of the avoidance through arbitrage legislation (Part 6 of the TIOPA 2010) or the unallowable purposes rules in the loan relationships legislation (section 441 of the corporation Tax Act 2009) are also not covered by ATCAs, and are not dealt with by the Transfer Pricing Group, but HMRC will endeavour to coordinate discussions in a useful way.

8.6   Conclusion

Transfer pricing rules have a long history in the UK tax system, which reflects the facts that the origins of income tax in the United Kingdom go back over 200 years, and that the United Kingdom has long been a trading nation, so that the tax system had to take steps to control the taxation of the cross-border income flows at an early stage. Thus, the first proper transfer pricing rules can be traced back to 1915, even though the United Kingdom did not adopt the transaction-based arm's length principle until the conclusion of its first double tax treaty with the United States in 1945.

Despite this long history, there is almost no record of transfer pricing disputes coming before the courts. A number of factors can be identified

---

[212] Now see ss. 161 and 162 of the TIOPA 2010.

[213] SP04/07, note 211 above, para. 16, and HMRC, *International Manual*, INTM573050. It is interesting to compare these requirements to the defence of commercial justification discussed by Henderson J and rejected by the Court of Appeal in *Thin Cap Group Litigation*, note 128 above.

[214] SP 04/07, note 211 above, paras. 35–9.

to explain this in the early stages of the development of the transfer pricing rules. One is the nature of the first instance tribunals for direct tax cases, the General and Special Commissioners, which started in the early nineteenth century as principally administrative bodies, and only gradually became proper judicial tribunals. Moreover, until 1995 their decisions were only publically reported in cases that were appealed to the High Court. It is possible that they heard some transfer pricing cases of which there is no record.

A more important factor in this period appears to have been the optional nature of the transfer pricing rules. The 1915 rules were part of a system of taxing foreign traders in the name of UK agents and other representatives. These agency provisions could be quite powerful and had their origins in 1842, so it may well be that the transfer pricing rules were seen as merely a supplementary tool available to the tax authorities. Similarly, the first domestic arm's length transfer pricing rules of 1951 only operated if the Inland Revenue issued a direction for them to apply, and it appears that many potential transfer pricing issues were settled without a direction being issued.

Thus, by the time that the modern rules were introduced in 1999, the Revenue had long experience of negotiating and settling transfer pricing disputes. Moreover, the Revenue informally started applying the OECD guidance on transfer pricing from the issuance of the 1979 Report. This provided an element of transparency, which was enhanced with the adoption of the OECD Guidelines of 1995 as a legislated standard in 1999. However, legislating the standard has provided taxpayers with a clearer basis on which to argue transfer pricing issues in a judicial setting. The single substantive transfer pricing decision in *DSG Retail* in 2009 demonstrates how effectively this can be done by both taxpayers and the Revenue, as does the procedural reference to the OECD Guidelines in *Meditor Capital Management* five years earlier. Nevertheless, the developing HMRC litigation and settlement strategy shows a continuing commitment to resolving disputes without litigation where possible, and makes it clear that cases such as transfer pricing cases will often provide opportunities for settlement.

HMRC also has a well-developed APA system. Since it grew out of the treaty mutual agreement system, HMRC is well disposed to bilateral APAs. The main constraint on the expansion of the programme is one of resources. Not all companies consider that the cost of an APA, in terms of the level of disclosure and the length of negotiation, makes it worthwhile.

One particular feature of the UK system is the use of the transfer pricing rules to control thin capitalisation since 1999. This has resulted in the development of a special type of APA to deal with thin cap issues, the ATCA. The apparent commitment of HMRC to making the ATCA a flexible and effective instrument is a significant feature of the system.

The present UK government has the 'ambition ... to create the most competitive tax system in the G20'.[215] Given the financial constraints that the United Kingdom currently faces, and a number of related forthcoming developments in the tax system, such as new CFC rules and the possible introduction of a general anti-avoidance rule, it is to be hoped that the stability of the transfer pricing regime will be maintained, along with continued increasing openness on the part of HMRC to ensuring that its operation reflects the commercial realities of international business.

Appendix: Questionnaire (United Kingdom)

1. The structure of the law for solving transfer pricing disputes. *What is the structure of the law of the country for solving transfer pricing disputes? For example, is the mutual agreement procedure (MAP), as regulated in the relevant tax treaty, the standard method for solving transfer pricing disputes?*

1935: Income-shifting domestic transfer pricing legislation (1915) and taxation on agency principles (1842), with disputes largely resolved by administrative settlement.

1955: Treaty-based arm's length transfer pricing provisions starting in 1945 supported by more limited domestic arm's length pricing legislation (1951), with disputes largely resolved by administrative settlement.

1975: Same legislation as in 1955; increasing numbers of treaties since 1960 include MAP Article; administrative or MAP settlement remains important.

1995: Legislative provision to recognise decisions made pursuant to the EU (then EEC) Arbitration Convention added in 1992 (Convention in force from 1995); by 1995 reported cases indicate that the tax tribunals (and courts) are being used at least for issues of procedure and regarding the scope of the transfer pricing provisions; bilateral

---

[215] Speech by David Gauke MP, Exchequer Secretary to the Treasury to the Tax Journal Conference, 9 November 2011, available at www.hm-treasury.gov.uk/speech_xst_091111.htm.

treaty-based (MAP-based) advance pricing agreements in (limited) use – it is likely that the importance of the transfer pricing provisions increase following the abolition of exchange controls in 1979.

2009: Broad domestic transfer pricing legislation introduced 1999 to be interpreted in accordance with the OECD Guidelines; extended to domestic transactions of 'large' companies (and others in limited circumstances) in 2004; domestic legislation introduced to confirm domestic status of MAP agreements (2000) and APAs (1999); some greater use of tribunals and courts to resolve transfer pricing disputes is evident, possibly in response to ability to rely on OECD Guidelines.

2. Policy for solving transfer pricing disputes. *Is there a gap between the nominal and effective method for solving transfer pricing disputes in the country? For example, has the country a strategic policy not to enforce the arm's length standard (ALS) for fear of driving foreign direct investment to other competing jurisdictions?*

1935, 1955: consistent use of transfer pricing and agency legislation/ treaty provisions to control erosion of profits subject to UK tax.

1975: around this time Inland Revenue interest in enforcing transfer pricing rules begins to increase: reflected in the adoption of the 1979 OECD *Report on Transfer Pricing*; likely to have been greater following the abolition of exchange controls in 1979.

1995, 2009: continued active use of transfer pricing provisions, with updates to legislation (see Q1 above) to support policy; CFC legislation (introduced 1984) also used in conjunction with transfer pricing legislation in some outbound investment situations.

3. The prevailing dispute resolution method. *Which is the most frequent method for solving transfer pricing disputes in the country? Does it have a positive externality? For example, is the MAP the most frequent method, and if so, to what extent have successful MAPs been used as a proxy for transfer pricing case law? For instance, Procter & Gamble (P&G) obtained a bilateral advance pricing agreement (APA) in Europe, and it was then extended to a third (Asian) country when P&G made this request to the relevant Asian tax authorities.*

1935, 1955: disputes mostly resolved administratively; limited use of tribunals, only one reported case before the courts (1920).

1975, 1995: previous situation remains prevalent; MAP Articles increasingly available in tax treaties since 1960, but without express recognition in domestic law; level of use of MAP in transfer pricing disputes not public.

1995: generally as 1975; increasing number of transfer pricing cases considered by tribunals and courts, but largely regarding procedural issues or the scope of the transfer pricing legislation; issues of substantial application generally settled without a hearing; APAs starting to be used, normally as bilateral APAs under MAP provisions.

2009: legislative basis for MAP since 2000; HMRC appears to regard MAP as secondary method of resolution of transfer pricing disputes relevant only where a corresponding adjustment (by the United Kingdom or a treaty partner) is disputed; more cases being reported; first case with detailed discussion of substantive application reported; no reporting of or regular statistics on UK MAP agreements; legislative basis for APAs since 1999; additional guidance on APA and ATCAs (thin capitalisation), but level of use is not disclosed.

4. Transfer pricing case law. *What is the evolution path of transfer pricing litigation in the country? For example: (i) Is transfer pricing litigation being gradually replaced by either MAPs or APAs, as regulated in the relevant tax treaties? (ii) Are foreign/local transfer pricing precedents and/ or published MAPs increasingly relevant as a source of law for solving transfer pricing disputes?*

(i) Transfer pricing litigation remains less important than the administrative resolution of transfer pricing disputes. Since MAP Articles were introduced into UK treaties around 1960, they have become increasingly important, notably when corresponding adjustments are in issue. HMRC is more interested in bilateral than in unilateral APAs. Indeed, APAs were initially made under MAP Articles, domestic legislation not being introduced to support them until 1999.

(ii) No MAPs have been published by the United Kingdom, so they are not a source of law. There are relatively few reported transfer pricing cases, and only one, from 1999, that discusses the substantive application of transfer pricing rules.

5. Customary international law and international tax procedure. *Has customary international law been applied in the country to govern the relevant methods for solving transfer pricing disputes (such as the MAP)? For example, has the* OECD Manual on Effective Mutual Agreement Procedure *('OECD Manual') been deemed customary international tax*

law in the MAP arena for filling procedural gaps (for example, time limit for implementation of relief where treaties deviate from the OECD Model Tax Convention)?

The new HMRC Statement of Practice on the transfer pricing and the mutual agreement procedure, SP1/11, expressly refers to both the Commentary on Article 25 of the OECD Model, and to the OECD Guidelines as relevant sources of guidance; however, the Statement of Practice, which does not have the status of law, emphasises that the operation of MAP treaty Articles depends on the wording of the particular treaty, and the positions of both contracting states.

6. Procedural setting and strategic interaction.   *Does strategic interaction between taxpayers and tax authorities depend on the procedural setting in which they interact when trying to solve transfer pricing disputes? For example, which procedural setting in the country prompts the relevant parties to cooperate with each other the most for solving this sort of dispute, and why?*

1935: Transfer pricing rules of limited importance, used as a supplement to the older agency rules; lack of detail and lack of frequency of application may have encouraged administrative resolution.

1955, 1975, 1995: Requirement in 1951 transfer pricing legislation for a centrally approved direction in order to apply transfer pricing legislation limited its application to cases where this discretion was exercised, encouraging pragmatic administrative solutions, often without a direction being issued.

2009: Basing new 1999 legislation on interpretation following the OECD Guidelines has made the application of transfer pricing rules in the United Kingdom subject to a more transparent process; the increasing importance of transfer pricing and the increasing value of transfer pricing tax adjustments also provides an incentive to litigation, a trend which has been observed. On the other hand, the commitment of HMRC to a litigation strategy that focuses on settlement where possible on the basis of the legal framework, combined with an emphasis on developing continuing and constructive relations with large businesses, helps to reassert the traditional trend to administrative resolution of transfer pricing disputes. Which tendency will dominate is not yet clear.

7. The future of transfer pricing disputes resolution.   *Which is the best available proposal in light of the interests of the country for facilitating the global resolution of transfer pricing disputes, and why?*

Currently, the United Kingdom appears to show a definite openness to the use of international arbitration in transfer pricing disputes where a treaty basis for arbitration can be established. HMRC is also starting to look at alternative forms of dispute resolution, such as mediation, for domestic dispute resolution. It does not appear likely that the United Kingdom would develop MAPs or APAs as a proxy for case law in the near future, nor does the United Kingdom appear to support formulary apportionment – the United Kingdom does not currently support the development of the EU's proposed Common Consolidated Corporate Tax Base (CCCTB).

PART III

Asia-Pacific

9

Transfer pricing disputes in Australia

RICHARD VANN

Australia has a relatively long history in adopting and applying transfer pricing rules. Australia introduced a transfer pricing rule early on and there were some lengthy tribunal decisions in the area in the 1950s and 1960s. More recently, Australia has devoted significant resources to transfer pricing issues, including at the Organisation for Economic Co-operation and Development (OECD) level and in domestic development of administrative guidance and enforcement by the Australian Taxation Office (ATO).

Considerable controversy has attended this activity and led to a number of disputes and cases which have reached the public arena. The ATO has largely been unsuccessful on substantive transfer pricing issues in litigation (which is likely to lead to law changes) but successful in matters of procedure (leading to settlement of disputes after taxpayers lost the procedural contest). In addition the ATO has a large advanced pricing arrangements (APAs) programme and is actively involved in the mutual agreement procedure (MAP) on transfer pricing matters but otherwise does not seem to have a specially developed dispute resolution procedure for transfer pricing.

This chapter will start with the history, context and description of transfer pricing rules in Australia. The chapter will then review the recent case law in Australia on substantive transfer pricing issues to see what lessons may be learned about dispute resolution on such matters in the courts. Next, the procedural side of dispute resolution in the area will be considered, including the more extensive litigation experience there. Finally, alternative methods of resolving disputes will be canvassed, both those in place and those in prospect, such as arbitration and other alternative methods, followed by the overall conclusion based on the Australian experience.

9.1   History, context and current law

9.1.1   History

Australia adopted the federal income tax in 1915 and legislation on transfer pricing in 1921 based closely on the UK legislation of 1918.[1] The legislation was apparently applied with some effectiveness, especially to foreign oil companies (in a period when Australia was entirely dependent on imported oil), to judge by the number of High Court and tribunal decisions on them.[2] The court litigation was largely

---

[1] P. A. Harris, *Metamorphosis of the Australasian Income Tax: 1866–1922* (Sydney, 2002), p. 197. Although the chapter is based on Australia's federal income tax, there were colonial and then state income taxes from 1884 (when South Australia introduced an income tax with three other Australian colonies following over the next fifteen years). The federation was created in 1901 and the colonial taxes continued as state income taxes. Queensland and Western Australia did not get their income taxes until 1902 and 1907, respectively, though Queensland had previously had a dividend tax and Western Australia a company profits tax. These taxes were largely source only taxes and issues arose over the source of income which in some sense involved transfer pricing as the courts had to decide how to divide up income of the same taxpayer on a source basis when produced from activities in more than one colony/state. The first important case was *Commissioner of Taxation* v. *Kirk* [1900] AC 588 in the Privy Council on appeal from New South Wales which held that where minerals were mined in one state and then sold in another, the income had to be apportioned across the two states for taxation on a source basis. This was followed by the High Court of Australia in *Commissioner of Taxation (New South Wales)* v. *Meeks* (1915) 19 CLR 568 on similar facts. So there were multinationals in the sense of companies operating in more than one colony before the federal income tax was enacted in 1915. The state income taxes disappeared in the Second World War when the federal government took over the income tax entirely, which remains the position today. Both these cases preceded the enactment of the federal income tax in 1915, but as it was a source-based tax it also raised these kinds of issues and similar principles were applied to it (see *Australian Machinery and Investment Co. Ltd* v. *Deputy Commissioner of Taxation* (1946) 180 CLR 9, 17). It became a worldwide tax in 1930 but with a broad exemption for foreign source income which continues in a different form today so that similar kinds of source issues continue to arise for both resident and non-resident taxpayers. There was a brief period 1987–90 when double tax relief was by way of foreign tax credit almost exclusively.

[2] For example, *British Imperial Oil Company* v. *Federal Commissioner of Taxation* (1925) 35 CLR 422; *Federal Commissioner of Taxation* v. *British Imperial Oil Company* (1926) 38 CLR 153; *Shell Company of Australia* v. *Federal Commissioner of Taxation* (1930) 44 CLR 530; *Texas Company (Australasia)* v. *Federal Commissioner of Taxation* (1940) 63 CLR 382; *Mobil Oil Australia* v. *Commissioner of Taxation* (1963) 113 CLR 475; *Case 39* (1937) 7 Decisions of the Income Tax Board of Review 118; *Case 40* (1936) 7 Decisions of the Income Tax Board of Review 118; *Case 6* (1940) 9 Decisions of the Income Tax Board of Review 16. The first of these cases followed very quickly on the enactment of the provision, suggesting that issues in the oil industry prompted it, which is confirmed by the parliamentary debates. Prime Minister Hughes, in *Commonwealth of Australia*

constitutional and procedural rather than concerning the substance of adjustments that were made. The tribunal decisions concerned a formula accepted by the ATO for transfer pricing of oil and its interaction with the statutory provision, which only applied where the normal calculation of taxable income produced a lower amount. The first substantive decisions came in administrative tribunals in the 1950s and 1960s, concerning in one case what would now be called a business restructure (and was on permanent establishment (PE) issues) and in the other case the appropriate transfer price for imported oil. This last case was the first where the influence of the international agreement on the separate enterprise at arm's length is clearly evident.[3]

Parliamentary Debates 1902–1946, House of Representatives, 8 December 1921, vol. 98, p. 14132 said, 'I come now to another important clause. I refer to clause 9, which is to impose income tax upon profits derived by ex-Australian principals from the sale of their goods in Australia. Honorable members perhaps have had their attention drawn to a practice which is becoming common, and is notorious in the case of one particular company, where an Australian branch house is believed to be debited by the foreign house for goods at a price which leaves little margin for profit on the sale of such goods in Australia. These allegations have been made from time to time in this House. It has been said that one company in particular has resorted to some such method in order to escape the Australian tax. The proposed new section will give the Commissioner power to assess and charge tax upon what appear to be the real profits.' Although he does not mention oil companies, later in the debate one member said, p. 14137, 'With regard to the amendment dealing with companies trading outside the Commonwealth, who, by reason of various devices, have been able in the past to escape the payment of income taxation – as, for instance, the various oil companies to which reference has been previously made – I am glad that at last the Government are taking steps to stop this leakage. All I regret is that this proposed amendment is not to be made retrospective, as, apparently, some other provisions in the Bill are to be, so that some of the money that has been lost might be recovered.' The very company concerned in the first cases was named later in the debate, p.14251. Indeed questions were being asked about lack of tax payments by British Imperial Oil Company in Parliament on a regular basis from early 1917 which seem to have been linked with questions whether, despite its name, it was in fact an enemy-owned company.

[3] *Case 110* (1955) 5 Commonwealth Taxation Board of Review (New Series) 656 discussed in R. Vann, 'Tax Treaties: The Secret Agent's Secrets' (2006) *BTR* 345; *Case 52* (1963) 11 Commonwealth Taxation Board of Review (New Series) 261. Although the arm's length principle had not been adopted explicitly in the domestic income tax statute at this time, the case involved the first Australian tax treaty of 1946 with the United Kingdom. The ATO has long taken the view that the transfer pricing rules in tax treaties which are enacted as part of Australia's domestic tax law, confer an independent power to make transfer pricing adjustments, as noted below (see *Case 52* at 272–84 for a lengthy analysis of these issues) and the arm's length principle was thus raised in the case. The tribunal noted at 274–5 that the matter had been dealt with in the international tax literature in terms which seem to be a clear reference to the work by Mitchell Carroll for the League of Nations that led to the formulation of the arm's length principle as the international

Australia adopted its current legislation on transfer pricing in 1982. There were three main influences underlying the change from the earlier legislation. First, the Asprey Report which had reviewed the Australian tax system in the 1970s considered that the existing rules were defective in a number of ways.[4] Second, the first version of the OECD *Report on Transfer Pricing* had appeared in 1979 and the legislation was designed to align Australian law more clearly and directly with the international consensus.[5] Third, Australia had experienced an outbreak of tax avoidance activity in the 1970s, including transfer pricing, which substantially

standard, see in particular M. B. Carroll, *Taxation of Foreign and National Enterprises*, vol. IV, *Methods of Allocating Taxable Income* (Geneva, 1933), available at setis.library.usyd. edu.au/oztexts/parsons.html, item 5. The tribunal also referred to other rules which existed in the Australian federal income tax from 1936–2006 for businesses carried on partly in Australia and partly outside Australia in Income Tax Assessment Act 1936, ss. 38–43. These sections were inserted as part of a process of aligning the federal and state income tax laws on the subject and were generally intended to give effect to the principles established by court decisions on source of income, note 1 above. Section 38 contained a power to determine profits made in Australia on goods manufactured abroad and sold in Australia by subtracting from the sale price in Australia the wholesale price in the country of export and costs of transport and sale, while under s. 39 a merchant who sold goods in Australia imported from abroad deducted the purchase price and costs of transport and sale. The rule for exports from Australia in s. 42 did not contain any express rules and the determination of the profit was left to the discretion of the ATO. They were thus another form of transfer pricing rule for allocation of income between Australia and abroad of the same taxpayer.

[4] Taxation Review Committee (Asprey J, chair), *Full Report* (Canberra, 1975), pp. 266–9. The Explanatory Memorandum accompanying the Income Tax Assessment Amendment Bill 1982 states the defects as follows (available on the ATO legal database at /law. ato.gov.au/atolaw/index.htm): '(a) the section, in general, only applies to non-residents that engage in international profit shifting and does not set out to deal with Australian residents engaging in such activities; (b) the limitation to business income may preclude application of the section to rents, interest, or other transactions not clearly linked to a business; (c) the section may only apply to companies and not to other entities such as individuals and trusts; (d) the section is inadequate to impute the derivation of income in a transaction which would produce income if it were one between independent parties, such as an interest-free loan to an offshore associate; (e) the section's link with total receipts could be unduly restrictive – it could mean that even where total receipts have been reduced by a tax avoidance arrangement, the Commissioner would be unable to look beyond the reduced amount in determining taxable income.'

[5] OECD, *Transfer Pricing and Multinational Enterprises* (Paris: OECD, 1979); see the Treasurer's second reading speech when introducing the legislation into Parliament (available on the ATO legal database, note 4 above): 'At the international level, it is appropriate to recognise the valuable work of the Organization for Economic Cooperation and Development – the OECD – which has formulated guidelines for dealing with transfer pricing in its various forms.'

eroded tax revenues.[6] The transfer pricing rules were enacted as part of a broad response to tax avoidance, including in 1981 the revision of the general anti-avoidance rules which share some features with the transfer pricing rules.[7]

Despite this activity on the legislative front, administrative action was largely directed in the early 1980s to cleaning up other areas of tax avoidance. The ATO began in the mid 1980s to use a special attachment to tax returns to collect information on international transactions and transfer pricing[8] but little use seems initially to have been made of this information. A report by the Australian Audit Office and an ensuing parliamentary enquiry into the ATO enforcement of international rules, especially transfer pricing, in the late 1980s were somewhat critical of the ATO's activities in the area.[9] International taxation in this period began to receive close legislative attention with the enactment of the foreign tax credit, controlled foreign corporation (CFC) and foreign investment fund rules which combined accrual taxation of foreign income of foreign entities in which residents had relevant interests with a mixed exemption and credit system for double tax relief. The CFC rules, as was common, included base company rules directed at transfer pricing out of Australia.[10]

Reflecting these developments from the early 1990s, the ATO became extremely active on transfer pricing in a variety of ways, including the

---

[6] Court decisions that showed directly or indirectly the weaknesses in the previous transfer pricing legislation were *Commissioner of Taxation* v. *Commonwealth Aluminium Corporation* (1980) 143 CLR 646; *Federal Commissioner of Taxation* v. *Ishwerwood & Dreyfus* (1979) 46 FLR 1.

[7] The new transfer pricing rules were announced at the same time as the general anti-avoidance rules were introduced into Parliament in 1981 (see the Treasurer's second reading speech to the Income Tax Laws Amendment Bill (No. 2) 1981 available on the ATO legal database, note 4 above), the same special administrative procedure for issuing an assessment applies under both sets of provisions and they share a special penalty regime. For an insider's account by a former Commissioner of Taxation of the genesis of the legislation, see T. P. W. Boucher, *Blatant, Artificial and Contrived: Tax Schemes of the 70s and 80s* (Canberra, 2010), pp. 166–73, 349–53.

[8] See ATO Ruling IT 2514 available on the ATO legal database, note 4 above.

[9] Australian Audit Office, *Australian Taxation Office: International Profit Shifting* (Canberra, 1987); House of Representatives Standing Committee on Finance and Public Administration, *Shifting the Tax Burden* (Canberra, 1988); House of Representatives Standing Committee on Finance and Public Administration, *Tax Payers or Tax Players?* (Canberra, 1989).

[10] The CFC rules commenced operation in 1990; the base company rules are found in Income Tax Assessment Act 1936, ss.447, 448; the base company rules are due to be repealed as part of recent reviews of the CFC rules.

Table 9.1 *Stock of foreign direct investment (US$ billion)*

Year	1990		2000		2007	
Country	Australia	UK	Australia	UK	Australia	UK
Inward (I)	74	204	111	439	342	1264
Outward (O)	30	229	85	898	290	1841
Ratio I:O	2.4	0.98	1.3	0.49	1.2	0.69
I&O as %GDP	32.8	43.7	50.6	92.7	69.6	110.4

Source: UNCTAD, *World Investment Report 2009* country fact sheets, available at www.unctad.org/Templates/Page.asp?intItemID=2441&lang=1. The year 2007 is used to avoid the distortions in FDI statistics flowing from the global financial crisis.

issue of administrative guidance,[11] extensive participation in OECD activities and significant enforcement activities. As in many other countries, a separate transfer pricing area of private professional practice developed as a result, largely in the big accounting firms. Since then transfer pricing has been a central issue for multinational enterprises (MNEs) with involvement in Australia.

9.1.2   Context

By way of context for the following discussion, comparative data for Australia and the United Kingdom is provided, in Table 9.1.

The UK economy is about 2.5 times larger than Australia; the United Kingdom has fifteen of the top 100 multinationals by foreign assets outside the finance sector and Australia two. From Table 9.1 it will be evident that throughout the 1990–2007 period, the UK economy has been more exposed internationally compared to Australia, as shown by the total of inward and outward foreign direct investment (FDI) stocks as a percentage of GDP. The United Kingdom has more outward than inward FDI during the period, while for Australia initially inward FDI was more important but FDI flows are now almost in balance. Most importantly for both countries, FDI has become much more important to the economy and with it transfer pricing problems.

---

[11] The voluminous ATO guidance which can only be touched upon in this chapter is referred to in footnotes. The ATO has an excellent general website, www.ato.gov.au, containing non-technical material on transfer pricing and a legal website, note 4 above, on which the legislation, legislative history and administrative guidance can be found.

Australia collects 23.1 per cent of total tax revenue from the corporate income tax, the second highest in the OECD, while the United Kingdom collects only 9.4 per cent of total revenue from the corporate tax.[12] This suggests that Australia is more vulnerable to transfer pricing which largely affects the corporate tax. On the other hand, the Australian imputation system, which only grants imputation credits for Australian corporate tax paid, encourages transfer pricing by Australian-based MNEs into Australia rather than out of it (as this increases tax credits available to Australian resident shareholders) and may offset the risk to corporate tax revenue from transfer pricing by resident multinationals.

9.1.3   Current Australian law

Domestic transfer pricing rules

The current transfer pricing rules are found in Income Tax Assessment Act (ITAA) 1936, Part III, Division 13, sections 136AA–136AF.[13] These use a definition of international agreement to ensure that the transfer pricing rules apply only in an international context which may be contrasted with some recent developments in EU countries. The rules apply to the supply or acquisition of property, which is very broadly defined to cover all forms of goods and services. The operative rules for separate enterprises are in the following form (using section 136AD(3) as an example):

Where:

(a) a taxpayer has acquired property under an international agreement;
(b) the [ATO], having regard to any connection between any 2 or more of the parties to the agreement or to any other relevant circumstances, is satisfied that the parties to the agreement, or any 2 or more of those parties, were not dealing at arm's length with each other in relation to the acquisition;
(c) the taxpayer gave or agreed to give consideration in respect of the acquisition and the amount of that consideration exceeded the arm's length consideration in respect of the acquisition; and
(d) the [ATO] determines that this subsection should apply in relation to the taxpayer in relation to the acquisition,

---

[12] OECD, *Revenue Statistics* (Paris: OECD, 2009), p. 89, Table 13 for the 2007 year which again is chosen to avoid distortions arising from the global financial crisis.

[13] For the foundation ATO ruling on transfer pricing which also includes a thorough analysis of Division 13, see Ruling TR 94/18, available on ATO legal website, note 4 above.

then, for all purposes of the application of this Act in relation to the taxpayer, consideration equal to the arm's length consideration in respect of the acquisition shall be deemed to be the consideration given or agreed to be given by the taxpayer in respect of the acquisition.

Equivalent rules are provided for supply of property at an undervalue or for no consideration in section 136AD(1) and (2), respectively. The rules interact with the way in which international agreement is defined to ensure that they generally apply where Australia would lose revenue. The phrase 'the arm's length consideration' is explained in section 136AA(3)(c) and (d) in terms which identify what might reasonably be expected to have been received or given under an agreement between independent parties dealing at arm's length.

An important aspect of the rules which is not so obvious is that they may apply between parties who are not associated in the sense of tax treaties. This extension was deliberate to deal with a concern that unrelated parties could structure related international transactions in such a way that one is underpriced and the other overpriced while together they reflect a market price, but only one of the transactions comes within the tax jurisdiction of a particular country and erodes its revenue base because of the under- or overpricing.[14]

An additional power to specify the source of the restated income is also provided in section 136AE(1)–(3), as the operation of Australian law in the international context directly adopts residence and source concepts for business income.[15] The source rules are not generally spelt out in legislation and are susceptible to manipulation in a transfer pricing context.

[14] The Explanatory Memorandum to Income Tax Assessment Amendment Bill 1982 which enacted the rules (available on ATO legal database, note 4 above) states: 'The reference to any connection between parties to the agreement means that it would be appropriate, for example where the parties concerned are companies, to take into account whether they were members of the one company group or had substantially the same persons as shareholders or directors, or had other links. However, the fact that parties to an agreement were related would not of itself require the Commissioner to conclude that the parties were not dealing at arm's length in relation to a particular supply or acquisition of property.

'On the other hand, just as related parties to an agreement may deal with one another on an arm's length basis, there can be cases where formally unrelated parties to an agreement do not deal with one another on an arm's length basis, viewed simply in relation to a particular supply or acquisition of property. This could be the case where the particular transaction which reduces a taxpayer's Australian income is offset by benefits under another seemingly unrelated agreement, which may accrue abroad, and perhaps to an associate of the taxpayer.'

[15] Income Tax Assessment Act 1997, ss.6-5, 6-10.

In the case of a permanent establishment (PE) the Australian law adopts what the OECD now describes as the relevant business activity approach to profit attribution rather than the OECD authorised functionally separate entity approach.[16] That is, Australia does not have direct regard to notional dealings between the PE and the rest of the enterprise but rather allocates the revenue and expenses of the enterprise and uses the arm's length principle in that allocation. As it is only in rare cases that there is a difference in outcome, Australia's approach is not elaborated further.[17] It was recommended in 1999 that Australia gradually move to what has become the OECD authorised approach and that is already occurring in other parts of the legislation but not yet directly in the transfer pricing rules.[18]

Finally, the rules in section 136AF provide for adjustments to the tax position of (usually) other taxpayers in appropriate cases. For example, if it is found that an Australian subsidiary has paid a higher interest rate on borrowings from its foreign parent than justified on the arm's length principle and the interest deduction of the subsidiary is adjusted down, the interest withholding tax levied on the parent with respect to the excessive amount is in effect refunded in the adjustment process. These adjustments, of course, can only deal with the Australian tax position of the various parties. It is necessary to rely on tax treaty provisions to bring about appropriate tax adjustments in another country.

Tax treaty transfer pricing rules

Australia has generally followed international model treaties since entering into its first treaty with the United Kingdom in 1946 and now has over forty full tax treaties. The main additions and alterations that Australia makes to the provisions in Articles 7 and 9 of the OECD Model[19] have to do with administrative matters and are

---

[16] OECD, *Report on the Attribution of Profits to Permanent Establishments* (Paris: OECD, 2008), paras. 59–79, available at www.oecd.org/dataoecd/20/36/41031455.pdf.

[17] For more detail, see R. Vann, 'Reflections on Business Profits and the Arm's-Length Principle' in B. J. Arnold, J. Sasseville and E. M. Zolt (eds.), *The Taxation of Business Profits under Tax Treaties* (Toronto, 2003), pp. 133, 157–60; ATO Ruling TR 2001/11 available on the ATO legal website, note 4 above; see also TR 2005/11, TD 2002/28 concerning bank branches.

[18] Review of Business Taxation, *A Tax System Redesigned* (Canberra, 1999), Recommendation 22.11(a), available at www.rbt.treasury.gov.au.

[19] OECD, *Model Tax Convention on Income and on Capital* (Paris: OECD 2010, condensed version), pp. 26–8; in common with most other countries, Australia still uses the pre-2010 version of Article 7, p. 154.

dealt with below under that heading. In terms of substance Australia makes two apparently minor changes.

In Article 7, the deduction rule is changed to make clear that deductions are only available to PEs where they would be available to a domestic enterprise in similar circumstances, which is designed to ensure specific deduction denial rules in domestic law, such as on entertainment expense, are not overridden.[20] Consistently with domestic transfer pricing law, until 2005 Australia maintained an Observation in the OECD Commentary on Article 7 to the effect that it used the relevant business activity approach and did not directly recognise intra-entity transactions.[21] The Observation was probably dropped because Australia has been moving towards the functionally separate entity approach and in any event the approach did not produce differences in outcomes in most cases.

In Article 9, Australia adds words to preclude any argument that independent enterprises may enter into transactions which do not adopt market prices.[22] In terms of corresponding adjustments, Australia's treaties generally contain such a power along the lines of the OECD Model, Article 9(2). Some early treaties did not include the power and a few used an express foreign tax credit mechanism for making the adjustment. Whatever the treaty mechanism, the adjustment mechanism under domestic law was through tax credits rather than to revenue or expenses which could have adverse implications for taxpayers. Domestic law was recently amended so that in treaty cases corresponding adjustments are now made to revenue and expenses.[23] Australian law has no secondary adjustment mechanism in transfer pricing cases. In relation to

---

[20] The added words typically are, 'which would be deductible if the permanent establishment were an independent enterprise which paid those expenses'. The OECD has omitted the business profits deduction rule from the new version of Article 7 adopted in 2010, OECD Model, note 19 above. It is not clear whether that will work for all countries; as the Australian addition to the provision makes clear it is effectively a specific non-discrimination rule, R. Vann, 'Do We Need 7(3): The History and Purpose of the Business Profits Deduction Rule in Tax Treaties' in J. Tiley (ed.), *Studies in the History of Tax Law*, vol. 5 (Oxford: Hart Publishing, 2011).

[21] OECD, *Model Tax Convention on Income and on Capital* (Paris: OECD 2003 condensed version), p. 128.

[22] The added words are 'dealing wholly independently with one another'. The purpose here is not to extend Article 9 beyond associated enterprises (as occurs under domestic law) but to ensure that independent pricing does not take account of any other transactions between the parties which may affect the transaction in question.

[23] Corresponding adjustments are dealt with in ATO Ruling TR 2000/16 available on the ATO legal database, note 4 above; for the recent amendment see International Tax Agreements Act 1953, s.24.

treaties, this has the effect that if the excessive interest or royalties provision is activated (see OECD Model, Articles 11(6), 12(4)), the excess is not recharacterised and taxed under another Article.

Other arm's length rules

The Australian tax legislation is littered with variants on the kind of language (arm's length consideration, dealing at arm's length) which is found in the domestic law transfer pricing rules.[24] Even where that language is not used, the tax legislation has rules employing market value concepts to deal with mispricing of transactions between related parties, gifts and other situations. In most cases these rules do not have a specific international focus but at least some of them are intended for international situations.[25]

9.2   Recent case law on substantive transfer pricing issues

The centrepiece of transfer pricing rules is the methodology used to establish transfer prices. Internationally this been the subject of evolution since the first OECD Report in 1979 and the work since the 1990s. Both the ATO and the courts have recognised the importance of this work but with very different results.

9.2.1   ATO guidance

The ATO commenced a programme of lengthy public rulings on transfer pricing in 1994 which is still ongoing.[26] These rulings have generally tracked the OECD guidance as it has developed.[27] In a number of

---

[24] Treaties no longer use the 'arm's length' terminology, see Vann, note 17 above, pp. 150–1, note 48. For rulings dealing with other provisions of this type, see TR 2002/2, TD 2002/20 available on the ATO legal database, note 4 above.

[25] The most important example is Income Tax Assessment Act 1997, Division 820 on thin capitalisation. The relationship with the transfer pricing rules is a matter of ongoing controversy, see ATO Ruling TR 2010/7 available on the ATO legal database, note 4 above, and also TR 2003/1.

[26] The main rulings for transfer pricing between separate enterprises are TR 97/20 (methodologies), TR 1999/1 (services), TR 2004/1 (cost contribution arrangements) available on the ATO legal database, note 4 above. There is also a series of booklets on transfer pricing produced by the ATO on a range of transfer pricing issues that are available on the ATO general website, note 11 above.

[27] The most recent ATO Ruling is TR 2011/1 on business restructures available on the ATO legal database, note 4 above, which reflects OECD work finalised in 2010, see OECD, *Transfer Pricing Guidelines for Multinational Enterprises and Tax Administrations* (Paris: OECD, 2010), ch. 10.

respects the rulings have been in advance of the OECD, for example, in relation to methodologies generally, there is greater stress on profit methods than was the case at the time at the OECD, and on the importance of a two-sided analysis; an emphasis on bargaining in establishing prices; and the overriding requirement to reach a conclusion on the transfer price even when data or other limitations mean that it is very difficult to arrive at a firm conclusion on the price.

The process of developing these rulings was very controversial in the private sector, especially as the ATO constantly seemed to be pushing the OECD boundaries. Partly as a result of this controversy and partly as a result of processes under way in the ATO in any event, two consultative mechanisms were created for private sector input. First, a transfer pricing subcommittee of the National Tax Liaison Group (NTLG) was created. The NTLG is the means by which the ATO consults with the tax profession and has representatives on it of all the major associations of tax professionals. This group is not only consulted on rulings as they are being developed but also on administrative and other matters in the transfer pricing area.[28]

Second, the International Tax Rulings Panel was created in 1995. The ATO uses Panels of this type to engage (on a remunerated basis) private sector consultants to help in the development of its public rulings. The Panel process does not require agreement of the external members, as the rulings are ultimately the responsibility of the ATO, but it does test the reasoning and conformity with the general understanding of the tax law. The private sector members involved in the transfer pricing area for the first decade of the Panel's operation were an academic economist, an academic lawyer and a retired practising lawyer.[29] By that time the major international rulings had been processed and in 2007 the Panel was merged with the other Panels dealing with public rulings.

From the late 1990s it became evident that the ATO was actively litigating transfer pricing cases, but until 2008 the litigation was largely on procedural issues.[30] Recently two important cases on substantive transfer pricing issues, particularly methodologies, have been decided, including an appeal in the second case.

---

[28] The minutes of its meetings and various other information may be obtained from the ATO general website, note 11 above.

[29] The author was the external academic lawyer on the Panel in this period.

[30] See discussion in section 9.3 below.

9.2.2   Roche Products

The decision[31] of the Administrative Appeals Tribunal *in Roche Products* v. *Commissioner of Taxation* was the first Australian case in forty-five years on the substantive issue which lies at the heart of all transfer pricing disputes: the appropriate method (or methods) to be used to determine arm's length prices and their application. But the judgment also demonstrates why so few transfer pricing cases are litigated – the tribunal had a great deal of difficulty in resolving that issue in the face of the competing opinions of four experts, each of whom produced a range of prices using slightly different information, assumptions, methodologies and adjustments.

Evidence in the case suggests that the matter came to be litigated because of the ATO's impression that the Australian subsidiary of the Swiss Roche pharmaceutical group was insufficiently profitable – that the group's profit margin worldwide from the sale of branded prescription drugs was 75 per cent, but in Australia it was only 36 per cent.

Facts and decision

The ATO assessed Roche Products, the Australian subsidiary of the Roche group, to further tax for the calendar years 1992–2002. The assessments were based on the ATO's view that Roche Products had overpaid other Roche group companies located in Switzerland and Singapore for purchases of:

- branded prescription drugs, for example, Valium, Mogadon and Rohypnol; most were patented although some patents had expired;
- non-prescription medicines, for example, Aspro and Berocca; and
- medical equipment and consumables used in pathology and other diagnostic procedures.

There was some minor manufacturing and packaging carried out in Australia, mainly for the second category. The ATO abandoned a claim for assessment of further profits in relation to work on clinical trials carried out by Roche Products for overseas associates.

The judge found the ATO's assessments for purchases of non-prescription medicines and medical equipment excessive and discharged them to that extent, but increased the taxpayer's assessable income from

---

[31] *Roche Products* v. *Commissioner of Taxation* [2008] AATA 639, (2008) 70 ATR 703 (Downes J). Some of the material here is drawn from a comment by the author on the case, (2008) 10 *International Tax Law Reports* 681, 682–87.

the sale of prescription drugs by over AUS $40 million. The taxpayer may, however, feel that it largely won the case. On many issues its expert witnesses were clearly preferred by the judge over the ATO's experts and it won in all areas in dispute but one (though it was the major one).[32] The figure which the judge arrived at (it was not taken from the reports of any of the experts) has the appearance of a split-the-difference outcome which is not uncommon in transfer pricing cases.

Argument and reasons

It was conceded that Roche Products was not purchasing at arm's length from the offshore Roche group companies (in the sense that the parties were not independent) and so the only issue in the case was the determination of the arm's length price. Much of the evidence in the case (and much of the judgment) revolved around the differing approaches and opinions of the US economists engaged by the parties.

In trying to determine the arm's length price, the judge considered the meaning, applicability and consequences of the pricing methods discussed in the OECD's Transfer Pricing Guidelines. These methods were used by the various experts on either side. With regard to the branded and usually patented prescription drugs, all of the experts and the tribunal faced the common problem which the judge described at the outset of his opinion, that '[p]harmaceutical companies rarely sell their products through third parties ... [so that] there is generally no free market in which the products in question are sold ... [nor even a market in] potentially comparable products'.[33] Nevertheless, the judge observed that 'the way to evaluate transfer prices is to look at comparable prices at arm's length, rather than comparing different aspects of the subject's business to a range of other businesses',[34] the approach which had been taken by one of the commissioner's experts. Because of this, the judge largely rejected the opinion of one of the ATO's experts who had undertaken an analysis of the profits of companies which undertook similar activities to Roche Products (a transactional net margin method (TNMM) type profit based comparison) rather than an analysis of sales by the Roche group of comparable products in uncontrolled transactions.

---

[32] This is not the figure on which additional tax was paid. In some years tax losses were incurred and in others there was positive taxable income. It is not possible to tell from the judgment exactly how much the ATO assessed the taxpayer on, and accordingly what the reduction resulting from the judgment is, though it would seem to be substantial.

[33] [2008] AATA 639, (2008) 70 ATR 703, para. 8.   [34] Ibid. para. 115.

It seems that the expert had proceeded in this fashion because her report was prepared at a time before any comparable sales had been identified. While the judge was sympathetic to the dilemma, he was also critical of the largely unexplained way in which the comparable companies were selected in a number of respects and in which adjustments were made or points in ranges chosen. For example, in relation to the marketing activities of Roche Products for pharmaceutical products which were very different from general marketing techniques because of restrictions on advertising such products, the expert used margins derived from major advertising agencies in the United States and Canada. The judge was particularly unimpressed when the expert resorted to anecdotes and knowledge of the lore of the pharmaceutical industry to justify the choice of particular margins.

So, much of the judgment considers evidence of actual transactions undertaken by members of the Roche group, trying to isolate those sales that could be regarded as sufficiently 'comparable' though not for the purpose of the comparable uncontrolled price (CUP) method but rather for deriving gross margins to be applied in the retail price method. The expert for the taxpayer had access to a limited number of such sales prepared by another expert on behalf of the taxpayer from which it was concluded that the prices in all respects were arm's length. The ATO had a fourth expert provide an analysis in response which agreed in the broad with the taxpayer's expert but criticised the report in a number of respects, some of which were accepted by the taxpayer's expert. For example:

- the company argued that the comparison should include sales by the Roche group of generic drugs to independent drug wholesalers in Australia; the ATO argued that the only comparable transaction was sales by the Roche group of just one newly-patented drug to an unrelated drug company in Australia;
- the ATO argued that the comparison should exclude the sale of one drug because the sales volume was low; the company argued it should not be excluded. (The evidence showed that Roche Products was actually paying more for this drug than one of the independent drug wholesalers in Australia!)

Similarly, other parts of the judgment considered what adjustments should be made to the prices of actual transactions to make them more 'comparable':

- there was evidence that the Roche group's terms of trade with subsidiaries differed from the terms for sales to third parties;

• generic drugs were sold by the kilo while patented drugs were sold in blister packs.

The judge took the view that all sales should be considered unless the sale was unrepresentative, and appeared generally content with the way that these two experts made adjustments to account for marketing differences.

   In the end, he increased the taxpayer's income from the sale of prescription drugs on the basis that Roche Products should have reported its taxable income using a gross profit margin of 40 per cent, rather than the 31–40 per cent it had been reporting over the period. With regard to the sale of non-prescription medicines and medical equipment, both sides agreed that there were no comparable transactions and so a profit-based method was to be used. But the judge did not disturb the taxpayer's prices in either case. He observed that the low profit appeared largely due to operating costs, particularly the significant (and in some cases unproductive) advertising expenses incurred in Australia, rather than the price charged by the offshore Roche companies – according to the judge, one drug 'would still have been a disaster if it had been given to Roche Australia.'[35]

Importance of the case

Along the way and amidst all the detail, several important points emerge. The first is the strong and clear preference that the judge expressed for using evidence of comparable transactions by the taxpayer to determine the appropriate transfer price. As the judge put it, the task is 'identifying the comparable sales and making appropriate adjustments'.[36] It is noteworthy that he referred to general valuation principles to be applied in determining market prices as well as the specialist and voluminous material relating to transfer pricing. Second, the range of comparables should extend widely. As the judge put it, '[a]ll arm's length transactions are included' unless they are 'anomalous or atypical'.[37] The judge was unwilling to exclude either the sales of generic drugs (as the ATO had wanted) or the single patented drug (as the company had wanted). That is why the judge mainly preferred the taxpayer's expert as he had insisted on using the widest range of transactions by the Roche group with unrelated parties as possible.

---

[35] *Ibid.* para. 178.   [36] *Ibid.* para. 125.   [37] *Ibid.* para. 146.

Third, the judge was unpersuaded by the mere fact of the apparently low profitability of the Australian subsidiary compared to the position of the worldwide group. The judge commented that it was the Swiss parent which owned, and was entitled to a profit from, the intellectual property in the various drugs. Fourth, the analysis of the sales of non-prescription medicines and medical equipment shows that the judge was not prepared to allow a simple and uncritical application of profit methodologies, and was clearly uncomfortable with them. He focused on the significance of the operating costs in reducing the profit of the Australian subsidiary and cautioned that 'one of the problems of profit based methodology is that ... it inevitably attributes any loss to the pricing'[38] a conclusion he was not prepared to accept. Of the use of the profit methods by one expert he said it required 'multiple subjective determinations which admit of error at every step'.

Fifth, it seems clear that the judge was slightly frustrated by the case. The various experts each had access to different information, they elaborated their initial positions when a competing report appeared from the other side and, according to the judge, '[t]heir approach to the issues before me must have been coloured by their United States experience'.[39] For example, the US experts constantly used the interquartile range (which eliminates the data in the bottom 25 per cent and top 25 per cent of the sample as a means of removing outliers) which is sanctioned under US regulations but which has no equivalent in Australian law. Similarly, he was concerned about the experts not isolating the different years involved in their analysis. Early on in the judgment he commented that after the ATO audit began in 1998 the prices paid by the taxpayer increased marginally.

The judge also appeared concerned by the parties treating the OECD's Transfer Pricing Guidelines as if they were the law to be applied rather than the provisions of the Income Tax Assessment Act 1936 and the two tax treaties involved (Australia's treaties with Switzerland and Singapore). The judge remarked on more than one occasion that Australian law requires (in this instance) ascertaining an appropriate purchase price for particular property and this should be the focus of the inquiry (and not, as one of the experts asserted, whether an arm's length owner would consider the Australian division as a whole sufficiently profitable).

Finally, the judge dealt with the issue of the relationship of the treaty provisions and domestic law. The ATO view is that the treaty rules

---

[38] *Ibid.* para. 185.   [39] *Ibid.* para. 33.

provide an independent source of adjustment power in addition to the domestic transfer pricing rules. Hence, in cases where the treaty rule is broader than the domestic rule, the ATO can apply the treaty and *vice versa*. This ATO view has been a particular irritant to the private sector which seems to want to fight it at every opportunity even when it does not seem to make any difference in the particular case. Although the parties agreed in this case that no differences arose between the treaty and domestic law, the judge was not sure that this was correct (as one concerned profits and the other prices) and tentatively expressed the view that treaties did not confer an independent adjustment power.

9.2.3   SNF *at first instance*

The decision of the Federal Court of Australia at first instance in *SNF (Australia)* v. *Commissioner of Taxation*[40] was also largely unfavourable to the ATO's views and approaches on transfer pricing.

Facts and decision

The case concerned an Australian resident company (SNF Australia) that was a distributor of flocculents and coagulants predominantly to end-users in the mining, paper and sewage treatment industries in Australia. The products were purchased from related manufacturing companies in China, France, Korea and the United States. The parent of the SNF group was based in France and was pursuing an aggressive worldwide expansion strategy with the objective of 50 per cent of the world market in its products and having 38 per cent at the time of the case. The market share in Australia in 2002 was 18 per cent. SNF's experience was that its strategy required suffering losses in new countries as part of its market penetration strategy, including selling its products to distributors at less than their manufacturing cost, which sometimes meant overall losses for the group.

The Australian operations were established in 1990 and up to the period 2004 had only made profits in the 1994 and 1996 years, with the rest of the years involving losses. As a result of previous losses no tax was paid in the profitable years by SNF Australia or in any other years. The French parent had propped up SNF Australia with equity injections and loans to cover its losses. It generally expected to provide such support for

---

[40] *SNF (Australia)* v. *Commissioner of Taxation* [2010] FCA 635, (2010) 79 ATR 193 (Middleton J).

six years in a new market but in the Australian case the period had been longer due to 'intense competition, poor management, defalcations by an employee, excessive stock levels, an insufficiently high level of sales per sales person, and a series of bad debts'.[41] The evidence showed that the SNF group worldwide sold significant amounts of the same products to the same level and type of independent (unrelated) distributors as SNF Australia, including to some major multinationals, and that there was a small number of such sales to independent Australian-based distributors.

The ATO claimed that the SNF group was making profits worldwide on manufacture and sale of its products and that a reasonable independent firm in the position of SNF Australia would have demanded a purchase price that allowed it to make a profit. Over the period 1998–2004 it was achieving a net selling price of AUS $71.43 for AUS $100 of sales yet paying AUS $82.88 in purchases, producing a loss of AUS $11.45. There were purchases of AUS $71.3 million in this period; the adjustments made by the ATO related to purchases from the Chinese, French and US affiliates for the years 1998–2004.

The court at first instance accepted the taxpayer's evidence as to the comparable uncontrolled prices and discharged the assessments. In the multinational world of transfer pricing the actual amounts at stake were very small beer. The additional primary tax assessed for the seven-year period 1998–2004 was just over AUS $1 million which with interest and penalties almost doubled to a little over AUS $2 million. The costs of the litigation alone (not including the audit and compliance costs over the years) are likely to have been much more. Presumably, an ATO success would have had a much greater impact on later years.

Arguments and reasons

The taxpayer relied on the evidence of comparable uncontrolled prices to justify its position, producing an expert with a number of reports and three executives of the SNF group, the managing director of SNF Australia who had been appointed in 2002 to overcome the problems referred to above that were impeding its performance, the customer service manager for the group and a director and more or less sole shareholder of the group responsible for the group strategy. Their evidence was to the effect that SNF Australia was paying less than or

---

[41] *Ibid.* para. 13.

equal to the amounts charged to independent third parties in comparable transactions and also provided an explanation for the poor overall performance of SNF Australia even though its sales were growing substantially over the period.

The ATO sought to counter this approach in three ways. First, it challenged that the prices were comparable as they were worldwide not local Australian prices. Second, it argued that the evidence for the prices was defective in various ways and did not discharge the taxpayer's burden of proof (a matter discussed at more length in relation to procedure below). Third, it apparently claimed that the wrong methodology had been used and produced an expert report using TNMM and claiming that the taxpayer should have been producing a net margin of 1.7 per cent per AUS $100 of sales (based on the average of a number of comparable firms).

The ATO also argued that the treaty was the starting point for the analysis of the law (as the China, France and United States treaties were engaged in the case). However, as the taxpayer argued that the treaty only operated through domestic law and the ATO did not wish to pursue its treaty argument on this occasion, it accepted for the purpose of the case that it was relying on section 136AD of the ITAA 1936 for the adjustment. The judge accepted this position, though like the judge in *Roche Products* expressed a tentative view on the issue, this time in favour of the ATO position that tax treaties confer an independent adjustment power.

The judge approached the case by analysing the law, discussing methodologies and dissecting the evidence on both sides. In relation to the law, the judge rejected the ATO's argument that the arm's length consideration was to be determined by considering a party in the position of the taxpayer. He said:[42]

> Section 136AD(3)(c) [which has been quoted above] is concerned with the consideration in respect of the acquisition of particular property. The proper application of s. 136AD requires that the deemed arm's length consideration be determined in respect of the acquisition of the particular property by considering the arm's length consideration as 'an objective fact in the real world' ... The essential task is to determine the arm's length consideration in respect of the acquisition. One way to do this is to find truly comparable transactions involving the acquisition of the same or sufficiently similar products in the same or similar circumstances, where those transactions are undertaken at arm's length, or if not taken

---

[42] *Ibid.* paras. 41, 44.

at arm's length, where suitable adjustment can be made to determine the arm's length consideration that would have taken place if the acquisition was at arm's length. Just as in a valuation, the focus is not on the subjective or special factors of the parties involved in the transaction (e.g., whether they were financially sound or not), but is on the transaction itself and the consideration paid. In this sense, the task is not dissimilar to that undertaken in a valuation.

It will be noted that the rules appear to be transactional and so issues are raised as to how they can deal with profit methods. The ATO approach in such cases is to work backwards from a profit method into price and then to determine the price accordingly so that they comply with the legislative structure. The judge does not seem to consider this approach possible and makes clear at various points in his judgment his rejection of profit methods, it seems entirely.

He also rejected reliance of the OECD Guidelines as if they were the law, and in that sense distinguished the UK decision in *DSG Retail* [43] where the law explicitly required application of the Guidelines. He did not consider it relevant that an independent party would have gone out of business rather than incurring the long series of losses that SNF Australia suffered because the sole enquiry was whether the acquisition price of the particular property was for an arm's length consideration, not whether such a price would produce a profit. Though such losses required close scrutiny, they could not be used to call the prices into question if they were supported by comparable transactions. Although it did not matter in the final analysis, he found on the evidence that the losses were otherwise explained here by the strategy of the SNF group and the particular circumstances of SNF Australia.

In relation to the application of methodologies he noted that Division 13 of the ITAA 1936 did not prescribe any particular methodology which was thus for the court to determine. The judge quoted the Explanatory Memorandum to the Bill that introduced the legislation which referred to the CUP, cost plus, retail price and other (unspecified) methods. He also referred to both the 1979 and 1995 Guidelines in some detail, including the profits methods, and the functional and comparability analysis. He did not see any difference between the 1979 and 1995 versions, just that the latter were more detailed. He added:[44]

---

[43] *DSG Retail v. HMRC* [2009] UKFTT 31 (TC), (2009) 11 International Tax Law Reports 869.

[44] [2010] FCA 635, (2010) 79 ATR 193, paras. 58, 62, 65, 66.

> However, the 1995 Guidelines do not dictate to the court any one or
> more appropriate methods, and are just what they purport to be, guide-
> lines ... The guidelines confirm that the ideal approach to determining
> arm's length prices is to use comparable transactions. In most instances,
> this is the most appropriate method and in theory the easiest ... How-
> ever, not all of the factors referred to in the 1995 Guidelines are of the
> same importance or are to be given the same weight. This will depend
> upon the evidence presented by the taxpayer in support of its case ... In
> discussing all the factors below, I am not to be taken as imposing on the
> taxpayer the need to apply with exactness the CUP method as described
> in the 1995 Guidelines in satisfying the burden imposed upon it under
> Division 13.

Finally, on the evidence, the judge found that SNF Australia had
submitted sufficient evidence to prove that the market for the relevant
products was worldwide and so reliance could be placed on all the
transactions with unrelated parties, not just the relatively small number
that involved Australia. He found that the prices paid by SNF Australia
were in some cases equal to and in other cases less than the prices paid by
unrelated parties (and in that sense the related suppliers were bearing
some of the burden of helping establish the SNF group in Australia). He
rejected the expert report tendered by the ATO as it relied on TNMM
which did not fit with the applicable Australian domestic law.

9.2.4   SNF *on appeal*

The ATO appealed against the decision to the Full Federal Court.
Although the appeal court found that there were several errors made
by the trial judge in dealing with the evidence, overall they supported his
approach and dismissed the appeal.[45]

Status of the OECD Guidelines

While the court accepted that the OECD Commentaries were relevant to
the interpretation of tax treaties, it was the OECD Transfer Pricing
Guidelines that were mainly in issue in this case. Although the Guidelines are referred to in the Commentary on Article 9, the court did not
regard this as sufficient to make them applicable as they only purported
to be 'guidelines' which governments and taxpayers are 'encouraged' to

---

[45] *Commissioner of Taxation* v. *SNF (Australia)* [2011] FCAFC 74, (2011) 193 FCR 149
(Ryan, Jessup and Perram JJ). Some of the material here is drawn from a comment by the
author on the case, (2011) 13 International Tax Law Reports 954, 965–61.

apply. The court required evidence that both countries under a relevant tax treaty adopted the Guidelines for transfer pricing purposes and evidence was lacking in this case, though they left the door open for such evidence to be introduced in subsequent cases. Presumably, in future cases this approach will require yet more expert witnesses in the transfer pricing area.

The court seemed to regard the onus as being on the ATO to produce such evidence as it was the party seeking to use the Guidelines. Perhaps oddly, the court analysed and accepted the evidence of the taxpayer's expert witness on transfer pricing in the full knowledge that he was relying on the approach in the Guidelines without requiring any other evidence in support of that use of the Guidelines.

Transfer pricing in domestic law and treaties

The *Roche Products* case and the trial judge in *SNF* suggested that the transfer pricing exercise is 'like' a market valuation. The court on appeal indicated that transfer pricing is not a market valuation exercise but rejected criticism of the trial judge who had only made an analogy, not said that it was a market valuation.

That leaves the question of what the difference is. The ATO argued that the transfer pricing exercise requires the change of only one fact – the relationship of the parties – and that otherwise the taxpayer was to be regarded as having all its other characteristics, including in this case that the taxpayer was in perennial loss. The ATO argued that an unrelated party in loss would not have accepted pricing that kept it in loss, relying on the Guidelines for that approach, but the court rejected the ATO approach. It has already been noted that the court did not accept the authority of the Guidelines in this case, but it held in any event that the ATO approach was not mandated by the Guidelines because they only used the actual position of the taxpayer in question as the basis for adjusting alleged comparable transactions to ensure that they were comparable in terms etc. with transactions entered into by the taxpayer. The ATO also sought to introduce foreign court decisions in support of its position but the court held that the UK decision relied on, *DSG Retail*, was in line with its approach while two Canadian decisions were based on differently worded legislation which specifically included the circumstances of the taxpayer.[46]

---

[46] See note 44 above; *GlaxosmithKline* v. *R* [2010] FCA 201; *R* v. *General Electric Capital Canada* [2010] FCA 344.

One consequence of the court accepting that transfer pricing is not a simple market valuation relates to transfer pricing methodologies. The trial judge appeared to take the position that Australian domestic law was expressed in purely transactional terms and thus only permitted transactional methods for transfer pricing purposes and not profit methods – the ATO was relying on a profit method under domestic law in this case. While the appeal court does not address the matter directly, the tenor of its judgment is that profit methods are permitted under Australian domestic transfer pricing law in appropriate cases.

The trial judge had also expressed a tentative view favourable to the ATO on the issue of whether tax treaties in Australia confer a power to adjust transfer prices in addition to the domestic law transfer pricing provisions. The appeal touched on this matter only in an indirect sense by holding that the provisions of domestic law could be illuminated by the meaning of transfer pricing rules in tax treaties if the domestic rules were obscure or unclear. The court noted that one route to this conclusion is that, 'since [domestic law] is evidently intended to give effect to the equivalent of Article 9 of the various double taxation treaties, it is appropriate to interpret it consistently with Australia's obligations under those agreements'. This seems to lean against a separate treaty power and in any event consistency in interpretation would be unlikely to produce any differences in result.

Choice of transfer pricing methodology and evidence

Like *Roche Products*, *SNF* is very much a battle of experts. While the ATO fared better on appeal in *SNF* in relation to its expert (whom the trial judge seemed to rule out entirely), it remains the case that the ATO is being outgunned in the expert department in transfer pricing.

On more substantive issues, the ATO argued that there was no world market for the chemicals and hence evidence from sales in other countries was not comparable. To like effect it also argued that the terms and nature of the transactions were different. The court comprehensively rejected the ATO position, holding that there was a world market and that the taxpayer's expert and its group executives had made appropriate adjustments to third party transactions to reflect differences so that they amounted to satisfactory comparables. They thus supported the trial judge on these issues and dismissed the appeal.

Importance of the case

The *SNF* case at first instance and on appeal reflects similar difficulties as *Roche Products* and the points referred to above on that case are equally applicable here, though there are some differences of emphasis and views among the judgments. The status of profit methods is under a cloud (though only one judge has suggested that they are ruled out entirely under domestic law) and the ATO argument on the independent treaty power to make adjustments remains unresolved. Further, the Australian courts will not it seems apply the OECD Guidelines as if they are the law in Australia. They will simply be referred to as useful guidance but there is a strong overall preference for using a CUP method when evidence is available on comparable transactions of the taxpayer in applying the cost plus and retail price methods.

One wonders what China, France and the United States will make of the *SNF* decisions. In effect the court at both levels has held that the foreign suppliers are not charging enough under transfer pricing rules for the chemicals. Will those countries amend their tax assessments of the foreign suppliers and then will the SNF group through the mutual agreement procedure seek a corresponding adjustment in Australia in future tax assessments of SNF Australia if and when it becomes profitable?

9.2.5 Consequences of decisions

The decisions have revealed considerable interpretive issues in Australia's transfer pricing rules both at domestic law and treaty levels. One reaction, also taking into account other events, could be a rewrite of Australia's transfer pricing rules in domestic law and treaties.

An official review recommended rewriting various aspects of the Australian transfer pricing rules in 1999[47] and the OECD Report on Attribution of Profits to Permanent Establishments means that Australia's treaties and domestic law are now out of line with OECD thinking in the permanent establishment area.[48] The 2010 version of the OECD Guidelines have moved the emphasis towards profit methods and the OECD has released suggested transfer pricing legislation for adoption by countries.[49] Many countries have been active in revising their domestic law in recent years. These factors may be enough to prompt Australian

---

[47] Review of Business Taxation, note 18 above, pp. 670–3.

[48] See notes 17–19 and text above.

[49] OECD, *Transfer Pricing Legislation: A Suggested Approach* (Paris: OECD, 2011), available at www.oecd.org/dataoecd/41/6/45765682.pdf.

legislative action and, as will be seen in relation to procedural matters, further issues there point in the same direction.

In response to these issues in late 2011 the federal government announced that it would legislate the ATO view that tax treaties conferred powers of adjustment in transfer pricing cases and released a Treasury Consultation Paper on reforming the transfer pricing law more generally.[50] Because the issues have not been publicly ventilated by the government previously, the Consultation Paper raises areas for possible law change with some indicators of direction but makes few real commitments. It is likely to be some time before the outcome of this consultation process is finalised in legislation.

The Consultation Paper generally endorses the OECD approach to transfer pricing and wants to incorporate it more fully into Australian law for conformity with international norms and securing certainty for investors. This would likely be achieved by a two-step process. First, the tax law, drawing on the OECD specimen statute for transfer pricing and current legislation in similar countries like the United Kingdom and New Zealand, would legislate the transfer pricing concepts of tax treaties and the OECD Guidelines as rules at a high level and would then refer to the Guidelines for assistance in interpretation of the rules. Second, there would be a formal process of applying OECD updates in interpretation of the domestic law.

At the same time, in some places the Consultation Paper seems to go beyond OECD views. For example, it generally endorses the functions,

---

[50] Assistant Treasurer, 'Robust Transfer Pricing Rules for Multinationals' (1 November 2011), available at assistant.treasurer.gov.au/DisplayDocs.aspx?doc=pressreleases/2011/145.htm&pageID=003&min=brs&Year=&DocType=0; Australian Treasury, *Consultation Paper: Income Tax Cross Border Profit Allocation – Reform of Transfer Pricing Rules* (1 November 2011), available at www.treasury.gov.au/contentitem.asp?NavId=037&ContentID=2219. The ATO also released its Decision Impact Statement on the *SNF* case a few days later as part of this coordinated response, see ATO legal database, note 4 above. The ATO has tried to minimise the precedential impact of the case in a variety of ways though accepting a number of propositions for which it stands, including that the mere existence of losses does not prevent transactions being at arm's length. The ATO, contrary to the author's view, considers as a result of the case that profit methods are not permitted under Australian domestic law. In the future it is indicated that the ATO will use two alternative arguments for its position in this kind of case: that the transactions may in appropriate case be disregarded entirely and that, in market penetration cases, a service is being provided by the company carrying out that activity to other members of the group whose products are being sold by the company. Possible changes to the ATO's major public rulings are being considered. The Consultation Paper will overcome a number of the ATO's concerns with the *SNF* decision if acted upon. Legislation endorsing the ATO's view on treaties conferring a separate power was enacted by Tax Laws Amendment (Cross-Border Transfer Pricing) Act (No. 1) 2012.

assets and risks approach of the OECD but at one point adds a caveat that, '[o]ne possible qualification to this objective might arise where the actual allocation of functions, assets and risks differs from that which would have been made by independent parties behaving in a commercially rational manner'. This reflects a theme of many years in public rulings of the ATO pushing the OECD envelope. This is to be contrasted with the Paper's recognition of the need to avoid overreaching and to achieve balance in transfer pricing rules in income tax so that other countries are likely to accept Australia's approach.

The Consultation Paper notes one difference between domestic law and tax treaties that will continue: the extension of transfer pricing rules in domestic law to cases involving unrelated parties which nonetheless do not deal at arm's length.

The Consultation Paper proposes that the legislation (like treaties) focus on profits of taxpayers rather than prices of specific transactions in order to ensure that the suggestion in the *SNF Australia* case at first instance that profit methods are not permitted by current domestic law is overcome. The 2010 OECD Guidelines no longer give complete priority to transactional methods but support a most appropriate method approach, though with the gloss that, if a transactional method and a profit method are equally reliable, the transactional method is to be preferred. While the most appropriate method approach is endorsed several times in the Paper, the OECD gloss is nowhere mentioned and the overall tenor of the Paper is a clear preference for profit methods.

Similarly, the Consultation Paper refers on a number of occasions to reflecting the business outcomes that would be achieved by independent parties and taking account of the particular commercial positions of the parties. These in part are a reference to the point which the ATO lost in the *SNF* case that an independent party would not purchase at prices that kept it in perennial loss even if they reflected market prices. The Court could find no warrant for this view in the 1995 OECD Guidelines. The Paper suggests in effect rejecting the *SNF* case approach even if it is supported by the Guidelines.

Although part of domestic law and tax treaties, the transfer pricing (profit allocation) rules for PEs are identified in the Consultation Paper as a separate policy question that it is to be progressed more slowly. There are a number of reasons for the greater reticence here. First, Australian law does not currently follow the OECD authorised functionally separate entity approach, as noted above, and that approach may require greater modification of domestic law than for associated enterprises. Second, not all countries have accepted the OECD work in this area, as reflected in the UN decision not to include the new OECD work in its Model and Commentary. Third, in this context only in the Paper, there is reference to potential revenue loss arising from adopting the OECD approach.

9.2.6 Lessons for resolving transfer pricing disputes

Apart from such changes resulting from the cases, there have been some specific lessons for the ATO and taxpayers about how to run transfer pricing litigation in Australia (get the best experts and evidence and lay the ground for the use of the OECD Guidelines). The cases on substantive transfer pricing issues also suggest a number of broader lessons in relation to dispute resolution.

First and most importantly, the courts have struggled to resolve the cases. The cases are long and involve voluminous evidence, including difficult expert evidence. As a result the cases are very expensive for all the parties involved to run – taxpayers, the ATO and the courts. None of the judges who have heard the cases have a long background in tax, let alone transfer pricing, which may partly explain the difficulties the judges have had in coming to grips with the issues in the cases.

It may be possible to overcome some of these issues by appointing judges with the background expertise (though they would not often get to use it) and for the parties to refine the issues in dispute more clearly. But the fault largely resides in the transfer pricing rules themselves. One issue thrown up by the cases is whether transfer pricing is mainly a market valuation exercise (as the CUP method in particular would suggest) or involves something different (and if so, precisely what the differences are). Increasingly over time the OECD Guidelines have moved away from simple market valuations but they still fail to articulate the issues involved. The author has written at length on these kinds of issues elsewhere[51] and so will not pursue them here, but until the rules are more coherent, the difficulties evidenced in the Australian cases will continue (such as what the differences from market valuation are, how residual profit is identified and allocated, what part the particular attributes of the parties to the transactions in question play in pricing).

---

[51] Vann, notes 3, 17 above; R. J. Vann, 'Taxing International Business Income: Hard-Boiled Wonderland and the End of the World' (2010) 2 *World Tax Journal* 291.

Another set of issues concerns the fact that transfer pricing disputes can arise in very different factual scenarios which may or may not involve tax avoidance or some form of deliberate abuse. For example, the Australian cases considered above involved Australia, on the one side, and China, France, Korea, Singapore, Switzerland and the United States, on the other side. There are no traditional tax havens with zero taxes on the other side and so, to go by the judgments, no sense that tax avoidance or abuse was involved. This is to be compared, for example, with the *DSG Retail* case in the United Kingdom where there was a recognised tax haven on the other side and so it is not perhaps surprising that the tribunal there was more prepared to find against the taxpayer compared to the Australian cases. The issue of whether transfer pricing rules are systemic or anti-avoidance has been clarified in Australia at the legal level (as discussed below they are systemic), but it is not clear whether the issue of avoidance or not is having a subconscious effect on judges. The author suspects that the judges may well be influenced by this kind of issue in how they approach particular cases. If so, it will be very difficult to achieve consistency in judgments and thus more certainty for taxpayers in the operation of the rules.[52]

Finally, even if one particular transfer pricing dispute is resolved by litigation, it does not provide much guidance except in a very general sense for future transfer pricing litigation.[53] The cases are intensely fact specific and the principles (such as they are) are relatively agreed and settled through OECD processes. Litigation can be helpful for settling disputed issues of interpretation of tax

---

[52] Similarly, there seems to be inconsistent levels of enforcement of transfer pricing rules across countries even when the countries concerned nominally adopt the same rules, for a variety of reasons including the level of development, the attitude to tax competition (lax enforcement of transfer pricing can be a form of tax competition) and the desire for revenue. It is likely to be difficult for taxpayers, tax administrators and even judges not to be affected by these kinds of issues, even though they are bordering on politics rather than law.

[53] The ATO Decision Impact Statement on *Roche Products* available on the ATO legal database, note 4 above, states: 'While this decision has assumed some importance as the first substantive consideration of the application of the present form of Division 13 of the ITAA 1936, in essence it concerns the determination of the arm's length consideration for the acquisition of property under an international agreement in the particular circumstances of this case. All things considered it is seen as having limited significance for the administration of transfer pricing laws generally.' By contrast the ATO Decision Impact Statement on the *SNF* case could not take such a narrow view, note 50 above.

legislation as this generates future guidance for taxpayers, but not generally for deciding complex one-off factual questions.

Whatever the precise causes, it is hard to avoid the conclusion in Australia that courts do not seem to be as effective in resolving transfer pricing tax disputes as they are in other areas of tax law where the issues are likely to be more technical and confined.

9.3   Transfer pricing procedure and dispute resolution

Australia has a number of special rules that apply in the area of dispute resolution for transfer pricing. In addition, a number of general rules need to be understood to appreciate the dynamics of transfer pricing disputes in Australia. This section discusses the procedural aspects of transfer pricing disputes, indicating how important they have been in relation to dispute resolution (or lack of it) in this area. There have been more cases in the Australian courts on these issues than substantive issues and these are discussed in chronological sequence after describing the rules, following which further lessons are drawn. A number of procedural issues were raised in the *Roche Products* and *SNF* cases – these are noted in the course of the discussion of the current rules.

After the discussion of the cases, various other forms of dispute resolution in the transfer pricing area are considered to see whether they provide a useful alternative to litigation before domestic courts and tribunals.

9.3.1   *Transfer pricing procedure and dispute resolution in courts and tribunals*

As with substantive issues, the ATO has produced substantial guidance on the procedural side of transfer pricing on matters such as documentation (for which Australia does not have particular rules, instead relying on general record-keeping requirements), audit procedure[54] and to some degree dispute resolution. The focus here is not on general administration of transfer pricing rules but on dispute resolution through domestic tribunal and courts.

---

[54] The main ruling on documentation, audit, etc. is TR 98/11 available on the ATO legal database, note 4 above.

Special procedure for transfer pricing adjustments

It will be noted that, under the typical adjustment provision in Australia quoted earlier, the ATO is required to 'determine' that the provisions will apply. Although not apparent on its face, the determination is a formal and separate procedure for making transfer pricing adjustments which confers a form of discretion on the ATO as to whether the power should be exercised in a given case.[55] Further, it is provided in section 136AD(4) of the ITAA 1936 that if for any reason (including an insufficiency of information available), it is not possible or not practicable to ascertain the arm's length consideration in respect of the supply or acquisition of property, the ATO may determine the amount in its discretion.

The rule in section 136AD(4) is protected by Australia's tax treaties in case it could otherwise be argued that it is contrary to Article 9(1). Typically treaties provide:[56]

> Nothing in this Article shall affect the application of any law of a Contracting State relating to the determination of the tax liability of a person, including determinations in cases where the information available to the competent authority of that State is inadequate to determine the profits accruing to an enterprise, provided that that law shall be applied, so far as it is practicable to do so, consistently with the principles of this Article.

A similar provision usually appears in the business profits Article even though there is no rule in domestic law of a similar kind that applies in that case, although there is power in section 136AE(7) to take into account 'such other matters as the [ATO] considers relevant' in addition to the arm's length separate enterprise principle in determining the profits of PEs. Apart from the possible effect on the burden of proof discussed below, it is doubtful if such rules are needed in domestic law or treaties in any event – if information is simply not available then the tax administration will always have to do the best that it can to arrive at an appropriate price.

In many cases the ATO makes its determinations under all possible provisions (including tax treaty provisions pursuant to the ATO view discussed above that treaties confer separate power to adjust). Although there may be multiple determinations, they will be for the same amount,

---

[55] TR 2007/1 (replacing TR 1999/8) available on the ATO legal database, note 4 above, discusses the determination process.

[56] Australia–New Zealand Tax Treaty [2010] Australian Treaty Series 10, Art. 9(2).

and one assessment is issued off the back of the determinations (assessment is the term used for determining tax liability).[57] In turn this
procedure has prompted in taxpayers the desire to know what has caused
the ATO to act under the various powers. Taxpayers have also sought to
attack determinations on the basis that the exercise of discretion has
miscarried. Together these taxpayer concerns have led to a number of
instances of litigation.

Australia adopts a full self-assessment system for the kinds of taxpayers which are involved in transfer pricing issues under which the filing of
the tax return is deemed to be an assessment based on the amount of
taxable income disclosed in that return. This triggers several consequences. First, it lays the ground for recovery action by the ATO if the
taxpayer does not pay the amount of tax due as acknowledged in
the taxpayer's return. Second, it starts limitation periods running for
amendment of assessments on audit.

Limitation periods

Australia has a general limitation period of four years for the kinds of
taxpayers likely to be involved in transfer pricing issues. However, for
transfer pricing cases there is currently no limitation period for adjustment (which is generally achieved by way of an amended assessment), a
position that has existed since the current transfer pricing rules were
enacted in 1982.[58] Not surprisingly, this causes considerable angst
among taxpayers and the ATO does little to reduce the resentment since,
to judge by the cases to date, it often issues transfer pricing adjustments
going far back in time. For example, in the *Roche Products* case, the years
in question were 1992–2002, the amended assessments were issued in the
period 2004–2006, and audit action was first notified in late 1998.[59]

---

[57] The determination process also has an effect on the interaction of other domestic arm's
length rules and the transfer pricing rules. Provided the other rules are not directly
inconsistent with the transfer pricing rules it is not usually necessary to have an order of
priority. This is because the other rules are systemic and do not depend on the making of
a formal determination by the ATO. Hence, they apply in the absence of a transfer
pricing determination. If a determination is made then as evident in the sample of the
transfer pricing rules quoted above, the rule applies for all income tax purposes in
determining the consideration for the supply or acquisition of the relevant property
and so will normally trump the other rules, if it matters.

[58] Income Tax Assessment Act 1936, s.170.

[59] It was held in that case that a further amendment of an amended assessment was not
possible if outside the four-year period that normally applies dating from the original
deemed assessment when the tax return was filed and no further change to the

A 2007 review of the self-assessment system has included limitation periods and the current proposal for transfer pricing is to set an eight-year limitation period.[60] No real justification is put forward for why the period should be twice as long as normal other than that transfer pricing cases are difficult, but that is true of any complex corporate tax case. Some recent treaties have begun to include a seven-year period so it seems likely that this will become the treaty norm in due course.

Penalties and interest

There is also a special penalty regime applicable to the transfer pricing rules. If there is deliberate tax avoidance behaviour, the base penalty is 50 per cent of the understatement of tax or 25 per cent if the taxpayer had a reasonably arguable position that its return was correct. If there is no deliberate tax avoidance purpose, then the base penalty amount is 25 per cent, or 10 per cent if there is a reasonably arguable position.[61] These are higher than normal penalty rates but are subject to the normal discount for voluntary disclosure or uplift for deliberate obstruction. The interest charge in relation to transfer pricing cases is the same as for other tax understatements (interest is in addition to the penalty).

Because of the higher basic penalty rate and the lack of a general limitation period for transfer pricing leading to adjustments far back into the past, it is not unusual for penalties and interest to double the extra tax payable arising from the transfer pricing adjustment. The special penalty rules are also found in the same place as the extra penalties for cases where the general anti-avoidance rule in Australia is applied, which again creates additional resentment among taxpayers about the transfer pricing regime. In the *SNF* case, such a doubling occurred, though as noted above the total amounts were small by transfer pricing standards. In the *Roche Products* case, no information was provided about penalties and interest.

---

assessment for the 1996 calendar year could thus be made though it could occur in 2006 for the 2001 and 2002 calendar years. It is possible that such second amendments may occur in the first stage of the appeal process, as noted below. The law has subsequently changed in this area and the ATO has indicated that the position may not be the same under the changes, Decision Impact Statement, note 53 above.

60 Treasury Discussion Paper, *Review of Unlimited Amendment Periods in the Income Tax Laws* (Canberra, 2007), p. 11, available at www.treasury.gov.au/contentitem.asp?NavId=037&ContentID=1298.

61 Taxation Administration Act 1953, Sch. 1, ss.284-145, 284-160. Penalties are further discussed in TR 98/16 available on the ATO legal database, note 4 above.

Objection and appeal

The first step in appealing against an assessment or amended assessment is to object to the assessment. This generates an internal review process within the ATO to reconsider the assessment which may lead to further assessments adjusting the increase downwards, or affirming of the assessment. In the *Roche Products* case, there were further adjustments in the objection process which had the consequence that for one year the amendment was out of time. Once the ATO has decided the objection, the taxpayer is then free to appeal.[62]

In Australia there are two main avenues of appeal in tax cases: to the Administrative Appeals Tribunal (AAT) and to the Federal Court of Australia. The former, as its name suggests, is an administrative tribunal, not a court (which has various constitutional and other implications). It in effect stands in the shoes of the ATO and makes findings of fact, can re-exercise ATO discretions on the merits of the case and forms its own view on the correct interpretation of the law. As the transfer pricing area can involve the exercise of discretions in making adjustments, it can be an advantage to take transfer pricing cases to the AAT in the first instance. Moreover, the AAT is not bound by the rules of evidence and proceeds much less formally than a court.[63]

The Federal Court of Australia has similar powers in relation to findings of fact and the law, but applies the rules of evidence and the exercise of discretions is only open to judicial review on the normal grounds for challenging the exercise of discretions, such as being beyond power. The court cannot stand in the shoes of the ATO and exercise discretions on the merits. On the other hand, it is generally felt that the court is more competent in interpreting and applying the law.

There are two further complications in making the choice between AAT and court. First, an appeal from the AAT to the Federal Court is on matters of law only – hence a judgement has to be made as to which forum the taxpayer wishes to have deciding the facts. Second, the AAT, as well as normal tribunal members, has judicial members who are also Federal Court judges, so that it may be possible to appear before a judge in the AAT, which a taxpayer may regard as the best of both worlds The *Roche Products* case was decided by the AAT with a judicial member sitting. *SNF* was decided by the Federal Court. The two decisions are

---

[62] Taxation Administration Act 1953, Part IVC.
[63] Administrative Appeals Tribunal Act 1975, s.33.

very similar in approach (subject to what is said on the burden of proof below) and so it may not matter much which forum is chosen for the initial appeal. In the former, the tribunal held that standing in the shoes of the ATO meant it could increase the assessments made by the ATO for two of the years because the 40 per cent gross margin the tribunal decided on was more than the ATO had applied to those years, though for years where the taxpayer had returned income that involved a higher than 40 per cent gross margin, no adjustment was made. This suggests that the ATO may prefer to go to the tribunal but it is the taxpayer's, not the ATO's, choice.

Burden of proof

A more important matter is the burden in proof. In Australia the burden is always on the taxpayer[64] to disprove the assessment on the balance of probabilities. In the *Roche Products* case, the judge repeated a common proposition that once all the evidence, is in, the court or tribunal decides the outcome based on the evidence, with the result that the burden of proof has little part to play. Nonetheless, in the *SNF* case the ATO in effect tried to use the burden of proof to defeat the taxpayer.

The ATO took exception in one way or another to much of the evidence of the executives of the taxpayer's parent company and of its expert witness in relation to sale prices to unrelated third parties, particularly on the basis that there was insufficient evidence about the third parties to test whether the transactions were comparable. Many of the objections were of a technical nature, relying heavily on the hearsay rule (a rule of evidence that applies in the Federal Court but not the AAT) and the taxpayer's burden of proof, in response to which the taxpayer introduced annual reports of the third parties to assist in proving comparability.

The judge at first instance was not very sympathetic to this approach by the ATO. In the appeal court, it was found that the trial judge had made a number of errors in his handling of the evidence. That court dealt with each of the issues individually at length and on their merits but ultimately came to the conclusion that any errors did not vitiate the decision of the trial judge. Again, the overwhelming impression is that the appeal court was less than impressed by this line of attack by the ATO. It remains to be seen whether the ATO will adopt this negative strategy in future cases given its reception here. If

---

[64] Taxation Administration Act 1953, s.14ZZO.

not, it is likely that one potential difference between appeals to the Federal Court and to the AAT has been minimised.

The *SNF* case on appeal also dealt with what exactly the taxpayer needed to establish. The court accepted that there is not necessarily one 'right' transfer price in a particular transaction. The ATO argued that the taxpayer had to show an exact transfer price as being correct but the court rejected this as an impossible burden. Relatedly, the court noted that the assessment in this case was based on section 136AD(4) of the ITAA 1936, discussed above, and said that this allowed the ATO to pick one among a number of possible transfer prices in such cases but the taxpayer could discharge its burden of proof by showing 'that it paid less than *an* arm's length price'.[65] It is unclear if this means that the taxpayer must show that its price is equal to or less than the *lowest* possible arm's length price, but apparently not.

Both the ATO and the taxpayer can be at an evidentiary disadvantage in a transfer pricing case. In the *Roche Products* case, the ATO was unaware of the comparable sales that the taxpayer had made to third parties and so its first expert prepared her report without this evidence. This put the ATO on the back foot when it received the expert report on behalf of the taxpayer containing the comparables, from which it never really recovered in the case, as discussed above. In the *SNF* case, the lesson may have been learnt as the ATO seemed to have access to the taxpayer's comparables from early on.

For taxpayers, the main concern is the secret comparable, that is, information that the ATO has on other taxpayers and transactions through audit or other activity which tax secrecy laws generally prevent it from disclosing to the taxpayer. This issue was raised very early on in Australia in one of the cases concerning oil companies before an administrative tribunal. The tribunal referred various questions on procedure in relation to this issue to the High Court of Australia.[66] The court held that tax secrecy rules did not prevent such evidence being given and that it was for the tribunal to decide, balancing fairness and natural justice, whether it wished to hear the evidence and, if so, whether the taxpayer and/or its representatives could be present while the evidence was heard. It was also held that, subject to similar considerations, the tribunal could compel a witness who worked for another oil company to provide evidence even though the information was confidential.

---

[65] [2011] FCAFC 74, (2011) 193 FCR 149, para. 128.
[66] *Mobil Oil Australia* v. *Commissioner of Taxation* (1963) 113 CLR 475.

While a number of the rules concerned have undergone considerable change since that time, it is likely that a similar approach would be taken before the AAT or Federal Court today. Although the issue remains of concern to taxpayers, it does not seem to have surfaced again in the more recent cases.

Collateral attack

It will be apparent that taxpayers have a number of concerns about the procedural rules and the way they operate in transfer pricing litigation. Accordingly, a fairly common tactic has been to mount a collateral attack on the administrative process in the hope that some failure can be shown which will cause determinations or assessments by the ATO to be ruled invalid without getting to the substance of the case. This kind of attack can occur within or outside the procedural framework outlined above.

Within the framework, it will usually consist of an attempt to obtain evidence through discovery or a similar process of the actual mechanics of the determination and assessment process or the motivations of the ATO staff involved, with a view to mounting a challenge on administrative law grounds (no reasonable administrator could have come to the decision, the administrator took into account irrelevant considerations or ignored relevant considerations, the administrator acted outside power, etc.). Because the tax law provides that an assessment once made cannot be invalidated on procedural grounds,[67] the courts have found for the ATO when challenges of this kind are mounted and refused discovery, etc.

The Australian courts have long held, however, that the provision preventing challenge to process is subject to implicit exceptions on constitutional grounds as otherwise it could make a tax incontestable. The exceptions are that the decision was not a *bona fide* attempt to exercise the power, did not relate to the subject matter of the legislation in question or was not reasonably capable of reference to the power. Although taxpayers have had some success in obtaining copies of ATO files in such proceedings, they have had no ultimate success in using this form of challenge outside the usual process in the transfer pricing context.

Possible reform 2011

The Treasury Consultation Paper released in late 2011[68] canvasses a number of possible changes to the current procedural side of transfer pricing. Currently, the special determination procedure for transfer

---

[67] Income Tax Assessment Act 1936, ss.175, 177.   [68] See note 50 above.

pricing adjustments does not sit comfortably in a self-assessment environment for transfer pricing rules, which the Paper makes clear are not
intended to depend on a determination of avoidance purpose for their
operation. Accordingly it is suggested that transfer pricing move to a
self-assessment approach. As most taxpayers treat the current rules as in
effect self-executing, this should not make a significant difference in
practice.

In this context, it is suggested that the current residual discretion for
the ATO in section 136AD(4) to determine the arm's length consideration where there are information or other problems can be limited,
though perhaps retained in a reduced form. It is not clear why there
should be a special rule in this area – the ATO has no great difficulty
assessing in other areas where information is lacking (such as asset
betterment assessments in cash economy situations, which the courts
have generally upheld). Dropping or significantly reducing the scope of
this power may also lead to adoption of a separate possibility in the
Consultation Paper of omitting the special treaty rule that Australia
currently insists on to cover the situation.

Similarly, it is suggested that a reconstruction power may be necessary
in cases where it is desired to disregard the parties' transactions under
transfer pricing rules. The OECD has reinforced in 2010 that the scope for
doing so is very limited to be consistent with the general treaty rule. If the
legislation follows treaty rules and the Guidelines, that should be sufficient in Australia. Conferring a specific power to disregard transactions
will open up questions whether it goes beyond what the OECD accepts.

The Consultation Paper says that there should be a documentation
regime similar to Canada and the United States. Those regimes set the
bar very high. There is a caveat that the rules should not be overpre-
scriptive and the more detailed discussion suggests perhaps greater
flexibility (e.g., as to whether the documents must be strictly contemporaneous or completed by the time of filing a tax return). A less rigorous
small business rule also is contemplated. It seems a full-blown Australian
transfer pricing analysis will be required in the documentation, rather
than a global policy and documentation along with some national add-
ons as is used by a number of multinationals. This is because it is
contemplated that the analysis would specifically be required to address
some of the suggested features referred to above that may go beyond the
OECD Guidelines.

The Consultation Paper also follows the United States and Canada in
making a link between documentation and penalties, though proper

documentation seems to show up as a penalty reduction mechanism. On penalties more broadly, it seems to be contemplated that the current special regime for transfer pricing will remain, which does not seem consistent with the reasons for moving transfer pricing to a self-assessment basis (as noted above, the current penalty regime is linked to that for application of the general anti-avoidance rules). It is also suggested that the 20 per cent penalty increase for obstruction be extended to cases of lack of reasonable cooperation. No clear justification is provided why normal self-assessment penalties are not sufficient for transfer pricing.

One justification put forward for specific documentation require-ments is to speed up dispute resolution but the Consultation Paper merely repeats the suggestion for an eight-year limitation period in the earlier review of unlimited periods referred to above. Moreover, the Paper contemplates that it will be necessary to provide for extension of that period to address delays by taxpayers, etc. The only additional justification for a longer period in the Paper is failure by another country, such as a tax haven, to exchange information, which does not indicate a great deal of confidence in Australia's burgeoning network of information exchange treaties with tax havens. The Paper notes that recent Australian treaties have included a seven-year limit and indicates that Australia will continue to propose the position in negotiations. The comment is made that this provision is not generally used by other governments – but not the reason, which is that Australia is probably the only important country which has no limitation period for transfer pricing cases.

9.3.2   Recent cases on procedural issues

As already noted there have been more cases in this area in recent times than substantive transfer pricing cases. They are considered briefly here for the light they throw on the dispute resolution process. They often concern the details of Australian law set out in the previous section but the purpose here is not to get too far into these details, as they are peculiar to Australia and are not likely to provide general lessons about transfer pricing dispute resolution.

San Remo Macaroni

The case of *San Remo Macaroni* involved administrative challenges outside the normal appeal process even though an appeal was proceed-ing within that process. The taxpayer was an Australian supplier of pasta products. It had made products in Australia but wished to source products from Italy to meet competition. It developed links with unrelated Italian suppliers but then sought advice from a Swiss tax firm which suggested that the taxpayer use a Swiss company apparently owned and managed by the tax firm to buy the products and then to resell them to the taxpayer at a considerable mark-up.

The 1984 agreement between the taxpayer and the Swiss company setting up the arrangement lacked the kind of detail and pricing structure that would be expected in an arm's length commercial contract and also provided for the Swiss company to make substantial loans to the taxpayer at high interest rates (which in turn led to large claims for deductions of interest and exchange losses by the taxpayer). In fact, the taxpayer dealt primarily directly with the Italian suppliers though the paperwork was processed through the Swiss company. The facts had all the hallmarks of a fairly simple reinvoicing operation. The ATO sought to get information from the Italian tax authorities and the Swiss tax firm without much success and so was unable to prove directly that the taxpayer or its associates directly or indirectly owned the Swiss company or benefited (apart from the loans from the Swiss company) from its profits. In 1995 the ATO adjusted the profits of the taxpayer for the years 1985–93 on the basis that the arm's length price for purchase by the taxpayer was that being paid by the Swiss company to the Italian supplier.

The taxpayer sought declarations outside the normal appeal processes that the determinations and assessments by the ATO were invalid as the officer making them had not acted *bona fide*. The ATO parried with a motion to dismiss[69] on the grounds of abuse of process and no reasonable cause of action because the ATO did not need to prove that the conditions in section 136AD(3)(a)–(c) quoted above were fulfilled before exercising the power in paragraph (d) to make the determination. The ATO's motion was dismissed because the law in the area was not clear and therefore should be tested. The taxpayer then sought discovery of the documents before the ATO officer who made the decision which the ATO resisted.[70] The court ordered discovery and rejected the usual objection that the taxpayer was fishing for information to support its case.

[69] *San Remo Macaroni v. Commissioner of Taxation* [1998] FCA 634, (1998) 39 A.T.R. 261 (Foster J).
[70] *San Remo Macaroni v. Commissioner of Taxation* [1998] FCA 610, (1998) 39 ATR 274 (Hill J).

After production of the documents the matter finally came to hearing.[71] The ATO file showed the facts above, the ATO dealings with the taxpayer and its obtaining of price and other information from Australian Customs and third parties such as other Australian importers of Italian pasta. The ATO officer concluded that the Swiss company was a 'straw/paper' reinvoicer. The ATO then took legal advice and issued the determinations and assessments. As Australian law does not limit transfer pricing adjustments only to cases of related parties, as noted above, the fact that the ATO could not prove an ownership or similar connection between the taxpayer and the Swiss company did not prevent the adjustment and the evidence was overwhelming in the judge's view that the ATO officer had acted *bona fide*.

The judge concluded with some critical comments suggesting that the proceeding was simply to gain more time to pay for the taxpayer and that the deferral of the appeal within the normal procedure to await the outcome of the collateral attack should not have occurred. One assumes that the taxpayer then settled the case as the other proceedings did not go ahead so far as can be gleaned from public information.

Daihatsu

The case of *Daihatsu* followed a somewhat similar pattern. The taxpayer was the Australian subsidiary and distributor for the Japanese motor vehicle manufacturer. In 1998 the ATO carried out a tax strategy review of the taxpayer which was essentially to identify whether there were any issues that should be audited by the ATO. The taxpayer cooperated during this process. It was decided to proceed to audit on royalty and other payments by the taxpayer to its parent which commenced in 1999 but matters proceeded slowly and there was increasing friction between the ATO and the taxpayer (including its professional advisors).

The ATO issued a series of formal notices to various company officers to provide documents and attend for an examination under the ATO's formal investigatory powers. After a number of such notices were issued, followed by negotiations and withdrawal of notices (and further aggravation between the parties), four final notices were issued in March 2000. The taxpayer and the staff concerned challenged the notices on various administrative law grounds including intimidation, bad faith

---

[71] *San Remo Macaroni* v. *Commissioner of Taxation* [1999] FCA 1468, (1999) 43 ATR 274 (Hill J), approved by the High Court of Australia in *Federal Commissioner of Taxation* v. *Futuris Corporation* [2008] HCA 32, (2008) 237 CLR 146, para. 60.

and unreasonableness. The ATO records were made available on discovery and while they made clear the worsening relations, the judge held on 20 November 2000 that there were no grounds made out for setting aside the notices.[72]

By this point matters were hotting up. The ATO had issued determinations and assessments for over AUS $21 million over the years 1992–6 in relation to the price paid for imported vehicles and commenced recovery proceedings (as it appeared that the taxpayer may cease its Australian operations). Recovery by the ATO of tax due under an assessment in Australia is not prevented even if there is an appeal under the normal proceedings on foot. The taxpayer responded with a collateral attack outside the normal appeal processes, as in the *San Remo Macaroni* case.

That attack and the ATO's motion for summary judgment in its recovery action were set down for hearing on 27 November 2000 and the taxpayer sought an order for the ATO to answer various detailed questions (interrogatories) prior to the hearing. The ATO resisted, perhaps because the cases to this time had shown that the ATO internal material was being used by taxpayers to mount cases based on bad faith, etc. On 23 November 2000, the court held against the taxpayer[73] on the basis that the questions involved 'fishing', that they went to the merits of the assessments which cannot be challenged in a collateral attack of this kind (requiring proof of bad faith), and the lateness of the request by the taxpayer.

The taxpayer's collateral attack equally failed.[74] The ATO had obtained independent expert advice which, in the absence of any comparable transactions being found, used TNMM based on four comparable firms. The median net profit margin averaged over the years in question was 3.3 per cent and the ATO officer who made the determinations and issued the assessments used this figure for the purpose of the adjustment. He was concerned about averaging across years, causing him to do some validity checks, and about whether enough work had been done on the economic analysis. In view of the pending closure of the taxpayer's

---

[72] *Daihatsu Australia* v. *Commissioner of Taxation* [2000] FCA 1658, (2000) 46 ATR 129 (Lehane J).

[73] *Daihatsu Australia* v. *Commissioner of Taxation* [2000] FCA 1718, (2000) 46 ATR 153 (Lindgren J).

[74] *Daihatsu Australia* v. *Commissioner of Taxation* [2001] FCA 588, (2001) 47 ATR 156 (Finn J).

Australian operation the ATO felt that speed and secrecy were necessary so the officer also decided that the determinations and assessments would issue without putting a position paper to the taxpayer, which the ATO's substantial ruling on transfer pricing processes indicated was the normal procedure unless there were exceptional circumstances.

Although the taxpayer's motion for interrogatories had failed, the ATO had provided it with substantial internal information. The ATO officer also was subpoenaed by the taxpayer at the hearing to give evidence. The taxpayer produced an expert witness who questioned the ATO comparability analysis and the use of an average median net margin across all years, as well as evidence from an employee.

In terms which may spell the end of collateral challenges of this kind to transfer pricing assessments, the judge said that it will be a rare and extreme case where such a challenge to an assessment will succeed. The factors said to show the lack of a *bona fide* attempt to exercise the power here were the lack of a position paper, the speedy issue of an assessment to bolster the position of the ATO as a creditor of the taxpayer and the concerns of the ATO officer with respect to the assessments. All of these were dismissed with the comment that they amounted to an 'adventurous' claim by the taxpayer of a kind which makes judges 'restive with the slightness of allegations'.[75] The taxpayer also raised the issue of the ATO assessment under an alleged treaty power (reflecting the standard ATO approach discussed above) to show that the exercise was not referable to the power (as the taxpayer denied the existence of a treaty power) to which the judge responded that the issue of determinations under other heads of power solved the problem, if there were one.

Syngenta Crop Protection and American Express

The cases of *Syngenta Crop Protection* and *American Express*,[76] involving two unrelated taxpayers, were heard together as they raised a common issue on motions that the ATO provide further particulars and discovery to the taxpayer about the circumstances surrounding the issue of transfer pricing determinations and assessments. They arose in the course of appeal within the normal appeal process, the taxpayers apparently having learned the lesson of the *Daihatsu* cases. The ATO had already provided each taxpayer with the required statement of facts, issues and

---

[75] [2001] FCA 588, (2001) 47 ATR 156, paras. 55, 56.
[76] *Syngenta Crop Protection* v. *Commissioner of Taxation*; *American Express International* v. *Commissioner of Taxation* [2005] FCA 1646, (2005) 61 ATR 186 (Gyles J).

contentions under court rules. The taxpayers contended that the details of the basis for the transfer pricing adjustments were insufficient.

The judge doubted that the taxpayers needed to know the processes by which the assessments came to be made (it seems that the kind of evidence of ATO processes which had been on show in the *San Remo Macaroni* and *Daihatsu* cases was being sought). The judge's answer was brief and to the point:[77]

> The question as to whether the consideration is that which might reason-ably be expected to have been received or receivable as consideration in either a supply or acquisition if the property had been supplied or acquired under an agreement between independent parties dealing at arm's length is an objective question. It does not depend upon anybody's opinion, save that of the court or body making that decision. It is a matter for evidence. In cases such as the present, the taxpayer is very much better equipped to cope with such a question than the Commissioner, the taxpayer being in the trade itself. Furthermore, the burden of showing that the consideration nominated by the Commissioner is excessive or inadequate as the case may be is not, in my view, a very high burden as it is to be decided on the balance of probabilities. I am not suggesting that the factual question may not be difficult and may not involve contestable questions of fact, but they are the types of questions with which courts commonly deal. I can see no disadvantage to a taxpayer in addressing itself to that issue. If this is correct, it renders irrelevant almost all of the contentions in the submis-sions before me which have complicated these matters.

Accordingly, the taxpayer's applications were dismissed. The fate of the substantive cases is not otherwise recorded.

WR Carpenter

The case of *WR Carpenter* was similar to the *Syngenta Crop Protection* and *American Express* cases – appeals against transfer pricing adjustments within the normal appeal process in the course of which applications were made by two related taxpayers for better particulars from the ATO in respect of the assessments. The outcome was also the same, although the taxpayers fought the case to the highest court in Australia.[78] The case involved two transactions, one in 1988 and one in 1993, in which the ATO claimed loans were created by the Australian resident taxpayers to

---

[77] [2005] FCA 1646, (2005) 61 ATR 186, para. 15.

[78] *WR Carpenter Holdings* v. *Federal Commissioner of Taxation* [2008] HCA 33, (2008) 237 CLR 198, 201–13 (High Court of Australia); [2007] FCAFC 103, (2007) 161 FCR 1 (Full Federal Court); [2006] FCA 1252, (2006) 63 ATR 577 (Lindgren J).

non-residents in respect of which the non-residents should have paid interest under arm's length principles. The assessments were issued in 2004 after a lengthy audit (many adjustments relating to other companies in the group also were made but were not the subject of this litigation).

The purpose of the procedure was again to obtain evidence to try to bring down the ATO determinations on administrative law grounds and with them the assessments. The grounds were that the transactions were at arm's length and so no ground for making the adjustment had been laid and that the ATO did not take into account relevant considerations in making the determinations. The trial judge considered a long line of authorities and concluded that the taxpayers could not attack determinations under section 136AD on administrative law grounds going to the state of mind of the ATO officer involved as the section specified objective criteria for the making of a determination. Such an attack would involve procedural issues in making the assessment which were precluded by the rules outlined earlier. His reasoning was similar to that in *Syngenta Crop Protection* which he applied to refuse an order for provision of particulars by the ATO. Particulars would only be available if the ATO proposed to assert something about its state of mind, which was not the case here as the ATO was relying on the burden of proof to require the taxpayers to prove the assessments were excessive.

In the Full Federal Court there was some small disagreement with the analysis of the trial judge of the authorities but not in the conclusion that the objective criteria involved here did not involve a discretion in the sense that the ATO was positively required to exercise a discretionary judgment by the legislation before making an assessment – the determination process was simply a procedural step required in the issue of an assessment, not a discretion in the relevant sense.[79]

The taxpayers argued that the ATO should, in exercising the discretion, take account of fairness and reasonableness to them, and absence of a tax avoidance purpose and of profit shifting, partly because of the association of the rules in their enactment with the general

---

[79] In discussing the transfer pricing legislation the Full Federal Court said [2007] FCAFC 103, (2007) 161 FCR 1, para. 33, that in cases where a determination is made under s.136AD(4) it is necessary for the taxpayer to prove the actual amount of the arm's length consideration and not just that the assessment was excessive. In *SNF*, the Full Federal Court disagreed as this would impose an 'impossible onus' on the taxpayer. As discussed at note 65 and text above, it said the taxpayer was only required to show that it had paid more or less (as relevant) than *an* arm's length price given that there was not necessarily one right arm's length price.

anti-avoidance rule. The appeal court rejected this limitation on the discretion. It noted that, despite the links of the transfer pricing regime with the general anti-avoidance rule, it is not necessary for the ATO to form views on these matters before a determination could be made under section 136AD. This argument received very short shrift from the court.

On appeal to the High Court, this was the major point at issue. The court also rejected the view that the ATO had to take into account the fairness and reasonableness to the taxpayer in making a determination and assessment under section 136AD (based on the long lapse of time involved before the ATO took action), and whether the taxpayer was motivated by tax avoidance or profit shifting. It noted that the further adjustment power under section 136AF expressly involved considerations of fairness and reasonableness and hence such matters would only enter at that point.

The court accepted that the ATO could appropriately take into account whether a determination would lead to an increase in taxable income or not but refused to speculate what other matters could affect the making of a determination in response to the ATO submission that this was the only additional consideration that it could consider in making a determination. It affirmed the decisions of the lower courts and considered that the taxpayers request for particulars was a fishing expedition for information that was not relevant to the real issue of the arm's length consideration.

Thus, it has finally been established by the highest court in Australia that the transfer pricing rules are systemic and the determination process objective, which will probably bring to an end the procedural attempts by taxpayers to demonstrate in one way or another that the ATO was acting improperly in transfer pricing matters.

Although directions were given for the hearing of the substantive appeals in the case after the procedural skirmishing was over,[80] the matter was settled before the hearing eventuated.

Lessons for resolving transfer pricing disputes

It is apparent from this case law that taxpayers have felt that the rules of the game are stacked against them in the transfer pricing dispute

---

[80] *WR Carpenter* v. *Commissioner of Taxation* [2008] FCA 625 (Edmonds J). There was a large number of appeals involved concerning a wide range of companies in the group, with some of the appeals in the AAT and some in the Federal Court. The judge joined some of the AAT and Federal Court appeals with himself to sit as a judicial member of the AAT for this purpose. This again suggests that there is little difference between transfer pricing appeals proceeding in the AAT or the Federal Court.

resolution area and so they have used a number of procedural tactics to try to direct attention to the administration of the law rather than its substance. Transfer pricing is not alone in this regard but it is probably fair to say that taxpayers are more prone to use procedural attacks in this area than in others. The courts have made abundantly clear since 1999 that they do not regard these tactics as productive for resolving transfer pricing disputes and have largely forestalled their use in future.

Nonetheless, various aspects of the law and procedure could be improved to facilitate dispute resolution and to deal with taxpayer's concerns about fairness. These would include fully recognising that transfer pricing rules are systemic by bringing them fully into the self-assessment system through removing the determination procedure and breaking the current link for penalties with the general anti-avoidance rule. Similarly, a limitation period should be introduced and, if it is to be longer than the general period, the reasons should be clearly articulated. The 2011 Treasury Consultation Paper suggests that some of these changes are likely to occur.

The underlying procedural concerns of taxpayers about the difficulties of succeeding on the substance should have been allayed by the *Roche Products* and *SNF* cases, in the sense that the burden of proof is not such an issue as taxpayers seemed to consider but, on the other hand, those cases confirm that running transfer pricing litigation will be extremely expensive for all concerned. As already noted, the cases are not a good advertisement for traditional forms of litigation for dealing with transfer pricing disputes. Hence the next section looks at possible alternative forms of dispute resolution for transfer pricing.

9.3.3 *Alternative forms of transfer pricing dispute resolution*

Internationally, the long established mutual agreement procedure (MAP) has been available for many years and the advanced pricing arrangements (APA) programme built in part on MAP has a twenty-year history, while arbitration of tax disputes is just now slowly coming on line. MAP and APAs are widely used, primarily (exclusively in the case of APAs) for resolving transfer pricing disputes. The OECD has made considerable efforts in recent years to improve all these dispute resolution processes, including a rewrite and significant expansion of the Commentary on Article 25 of the OECD Model in 2008. Within Australia there is renewed interest in alternative dispute resolution for tax disputes but no clear evidence that this is being deployed successfully in transfer pricing cases.

Table 9.2 *MAP cases involving Australia*

Year	2006	2007	2008	2009
New cases	9	13	8	19
Finalised cases	16	5	10	16
Closing inventory	16	23	22	23

Source: OECD

Mutual agreement procedure

Although Australia is active in resolving transfer pricing disputes through MAP, the OECD data[81] suggest that much less use is made of the procedure in cases involving Australia both absolutely and in terms of economic size, compared to Europe and North America. The explanation may be that Australia's distance from the rest of the world means that cross-border interaction is likely to be confined to fewer but larger multinationals. Certainly that is true of the inbound transfer pricing cases that have reached the courts (*Roche Products, SNF, Daihatsu, American Express* and *Syngenta Crop Protection*) but not the outbound cases (*San Remo Macaroni* and *WR Carpenter*, which are mid- to large-sized private companies rather than enormous multinationals).

The basic OECD data for the number of MAPs involving Australia is shown in Table 9.2. Average completion time is around two years but the period varies widely and up to five years is not uncommon. Two cases are recorded in OECD data for 2006–9 where cases were not able to be resolved leading to double taxation.

A number of Australian studies have been made of the local use of MAP in earlier periods, including in transfer pricing cases which account for over 80 per cent of total cases.[82] The data in those studies show that most cases occurred with Japan and the United States (twelve of twenty-eight cases in the period reviewed) followed by Canada and Germany (eight cases). They also indicate that MAP cases over time are initiated as to about half by Australia.

Australia, Canada, Japan and the United States have formed the Pacific Association of Tax Administrators (PATA) which has as a

---

[81] Available at www.oecd.org/tax/disputeresolution/46464971.pdf, not including MAPs involving APAs.

[82] C. Burnett, 'International Tax Arbitration' (2007) 36 *Australian Tax Review* 173; M. Friezer, 'The Mutual Agreement Procedure in Australia' (1990) 7 *Australian Tax Forum* 63.

particular focus the handling of transfer pricing cases. PATA has agreed a common transfer pricing documentation format (that is, documents in the format will satisfy documentation requirements for all countries) and more detailed procedures on MAP and APAs.[83] The ATO has also issued a ruling on MAP which sets out procedures for operating the MAP in transfer pricing cases, as well as its views on the relationship with domestic appeal rights and how to deal with interest, particularly where double taxation has occurred prior to resolution of the MAP.[84] The procedure is run relatively informally but seems generally to work (in the author's limited experience) though there may be an element of split-the-difference in settlements.

At this point it is not clear if the recent efforts by the OECD to improve the MAP procedure have had an impact in the rate of utilisation, speed of resolution or taxpayer and tax administrator satisfaction with the process within Australia.

Advance pricing arrangements

Australia entered into the first ever bilateral APA with the United States in relation to Apple Computers in 1990 and has been active in the field ever since.[85] The ATO early on produced a public ruling on the APA process now replaced by a practice statement and is a party to the PATA agreement on APAs; it has published general information on APAs for years since 2002.[86]

According to the latest report for the period ending 30 June 2010, thirty-nine APAs were concluded including twenty-one renewals, twelve new APAs 'encouraged' by compliance activity and nine new unprompted APAs, taking an average of twelve months to complete. APAs involving MAPs constitute 41 per cent of the total since the beginning but only 33 per cent in the latest period, reflecting the increase in applications from medium-sized enterprises. Most unilateral APAs in the latest period are for medium-sized enterprises and most bi- or multilateral APAs for large enterprises. The methodology was

---

[83] PATA MAP Guidelines, PATA Documentation Guidelines, PATA APA Guidelines, all available from the ATO general website, note 11 above.

[84] TR 2000/16, available on the ATO legal database, note 4 above.

[85] See D. D. Damon, 'To What Extent Do APAs Confer Greater Certainty with respect to Transfer Pricing Issues' (2005) 15 *Revenue Law Journal* 111.

[86] Ruling TR 95/23 has been replaced by Practice Statement PSLA 2011/1, both available on the ATO legal database, note 4 above. The annual reports on APAs are available on the ATO general website, note 11 above.

overwhelmingly profit methods (thirty out of thirty-nine, mainly TNMM), with cost plus making up the rest. There was an inventory of seventy-seven applications at the end of the last reporting period.

In 2009 the APA programme was subject to an external review which was generally favourable, though there is an impression that the ATO is tough in APA negotiations, similarly to the US Internal Revenue Service.[87] As a result various initiatives, mainly of a management kind, are in train.

By way of comparison, the United States completed sixty-nine APAs in 2010 including thirty-two renewals and forty-nine involving MAPs. It had an inventory of 400 applications on hand and average completion times of twenty-two months for unilateral and forty-two and a half months for bilateral APAs.[88] In terms of the MAP data above, Australia is much more successful in completing APAs, both unilateral and bilateral, than MAPs in comparison with the United States (which according to OECD data completed 180 MAP cases in 2009).[89] This suggests that the greatest success in transfer pricing dispute resolution in Australia has been in the area of APAs.

In the author's view, the bilateral APA is the greatest innovation in transfer pricing dispute resolution and indeed in international dispute resolution, which could be developed further to the great benefit of taxpayers and tax administrations alike. It is further discussed in the conclusion.

Arbitration

Australia recently agreed its first tax treaty arbitration provision in its 2009 treaty with New Zealand following the form of the provision added to the OECD Model in 2008. Unlike the OECD Model, the provision is limited to questions of fact but it can be extended by an Exchange of Notes to other issues.[90] It is not yet clear if the provision will become a standard part of Australian tax treaty policy.

Australia currently has no experience with international arbitration in tax cases. Whether arbitration will prove a significant advance in the

---

[87] PricewaterhouseCoopers Legal, *Australian Taxation Office Review of Advance Pricing Arrangement Program* (Sydney, 2008) and the ATO Response are available on the ATO general website, note 11 above. The ATO and US stance in negotiations is suggested in interview research undertaken by M. Walpole and N. Riedel, *The Role of Tax in Choice of Location of Intellectual Property: Report for the Oxford University Centre for Business Taxation* (2011), pp. 12–13.

[88] Internal Revenue Service, *Announcement and Report concerning Advance Pricing Agreements* (Washington DC, 2011), available at www.irs.gov/irb/2011–16_IRB/ar11.html.

[89] See note 81 above.

[90] Australia–New Zealand Tax Treaty, note 56 above, Article 25(6), (7); OECD Model, note 19 above, Article 25(5), p. 37.

international armoury for transfer pricing dispute resolution (which would mainly show up as an increased resolution under MAP rather than through numbers of arbitrations)[91] is as yet an unanswered question.

Other domestic dispute resolution mechanisms

Although the ATO has expressed a willingness in the past to engage in other forms of dispute resolution under domestic law apart from the objection and appeal system outlined above (negotiation, mediation, conciliation and arbitration),[92] the general impression is that it uses this approach sparingly.[93]

The matter is becoming a priority, with the ATO flagging the need to improve dispute resolution in its most recent annual report.[94] In the analysis of large cases settled by the ATO, two factors noted in favour of settlement are complex factual issues with limited precedential value and different valuation methodologies for a unique asset. These suggest that the ATO sees transfer pricing cases as very suitable for settlement, though nothing is said on this particular issue in the report. Recently, the AAT and Federal Court procedures have been amended to try to resolve disputes by alternative means.[95]

As with arbitration, it may be in future that alternative dispute resolution mechanisms will be increasingly applied in transfer pricing cases but there is still a long way to go as the current activity is directed to dispute resolution generally and not the particular problems of transfer pricing dispute resolution.

[91] International tax arbitration is a supplement to MAP and not a replacement of it and is largely designed to improve the MAP process.

[92] Practice Statement PSLA 2007/23 on alternative dispute resolution, available on the ATO legal database, note 4 above.

[93] The Inspector General of Taxation, who is responsible for investigating systemic administrative issues in the ATO has, with the encouragement of the ATO, commenced an investigation into ATO use of early and alternative dispute resolution. The terms of reference, available at www.igt.gov.au/content/work_program/20110726.asp, provide a good summary of private sector views and the current position on the issue.

[94] ATO, *2009–10 Commissioner of Taxation Annual Report* (Canberra, 2010), pp. 29–35, available on the ATO general website, note 11 above.

[95] Administrative Appeals Tribunal Act 1975, Part IV Division 3 'Alternative Dispute Resolution Processes', largely dating from 2005. The Civil Dispute Resolution Act 2011, which came into effect on 1 August 2011, requires applicants who institute certain civil proceedings in the Federal Court (including proceedings concerning taxation disputes) to file a 'genuine steps statement' detailing steps taken to resolve the dispute prior to commencing proceedings, or providing reasons as to why no such steps had been taken. The respondent must file a 'genuine steps statement' in response indicating whether it agrees with the applicant's statement and if not, the reasons for the disagreement.

9.4 Conclusion

It will be evident from the previous discussion that litigation is not a suitable way of settling transfer pricing disputes in the author's view based on the Australian experience. The reasons have been outlined above in sections 9.2.6 and 9.3.2 where it has also been noted that some improvements could be made in Australian substantive and procedural law in relation to transfer pricing disputes. It is not intended to repeat that material here.

It will also be evident from the analysis of alternative dispute resolution mechanisms in Australia that the major success to date has been the APA process. While development of general dispute resolution mechanisms and a variety of transfer pricing specific mechanisms may improve future transfer pricing dispute resolution, there is not sufficient experience yet to determine what the appropriate mechanisms are and how to improve them, apart from APAs.

The twenty-year experience of APAs suggests that they have been the most successful mechanism of transfer pricing dispute resolution in that period (though not without their own difficulties in Australia) and how they may be significantly improved. The author and others have been proposing for a number of years that more work should be done on this front and recently both the OECD and the ATO have started to do so.[96]

There are two particular issues that need to be resolved for APAs to become a more useful tool for transfer pricing dispute resolution. First, the information they generate about appropriate methods has to be collected and made publicly available in some suitably anonymous form which generates precedential guidance for the treatment of the myriad situations which international transfer pricing cases throw up. Second, the price of the process has to be considerably reduced so that APAs are not solely the realm of the largest multinationals. Public information will assist on this front and the cost can be reduced for medium-sized firms by encouraging them to use unilateral APAs which build on an

---

[96] Vann, note 17 above, p. 168. For recent ATO developments, see note 87 and text above. The OECD has been overhauling general treaty dispute resolution processes in recent years and has now embarked on a review of the administrative processes in relation to transfer pricing including APAs, see www.oecd.org/department/0,3355,en_2649_33753_1_1_1_1_1,00.html for recent development including a study of simplification methods for transfer pricing submissions on administrative processes. Chile has recently proposed legislation to disclose publicly the substantive content of APAs.

internationally accepted series of benchmarks (or safe harbours) generated out of that information. The current OECD work is the appropriate forum for this process to begin.

Appendix: Questionnaire (Australia)

1. The structure of the law for solving transfer pricing disputes. *What is the structure of the law of the country for solving transfer pricing disputes? For example, is the mutual agreement procedure (MAP), as regulated in the relevant tax treaty, the standard method for solving transfer pricing disputes?*

Taxpayers have a number of options when considering how to resolve a transfer pricing dispute. The MAP programme is incorporated into Australia's network of bilateral tax conventions, in accordance with the OECD Model Tax Convention on Income and on Capital. Dispute resolution processes such as MAP, APAs, and arbitration are governed by Australian Taxation Office (ATO) policy and practice rather than through statute. APAs are the most commonly used method of resolving transfer pricing disputes, with thirty-nine concluded in the year to 30 June 2010[97] compared to sixteen MAPs concluded in the last reported period (30 June 2009).[98]

2. Policy for solving transfer pricing disputes. *Is there a gap between the nominal and effective method for solving transfer pricing disputes in the country? For example, has the country a strategic policy not to enforce the arm's length standard (ALS) for fear of driving foreign direct investment to other competing jurisdictions?*

There does not appear to be a noticeable gap between Australia's transfer pricing policy and the methods by which transfer pricing disputes are resolved. There does not seem to be any evidence to suggest that the ATO is going soft on its approach to transfer pricing disputes for fear of driving away foreign direct investment. Indeed, the ATO devotes considerable resources to transfer pricing issues and enforcement as indicated in the Australian chapter.

---

[97] Available at www.ato.gov.au/download.asp?file=/content/downloads/bus00261650nat 73225102010.pdf.

[98] Available at www.oecd.org/tax/disputeresolution/4646971.pdf, not including MAPs involving APAs.

3. The prevailing dispute resolution method. *Which is the most frequent method for solving transfer pricing disputes in the country? Does it have a positive externality? For example, is the MAP the most frequent method, and if so, to what extent have successful MAPs been used as a proxy for transfer pricing case law? For instance, Procter & Gamble (P&G) obtained a bilateral advance pricing agreement (APA) in Europe, and it was then extended to a third (Asian) country when P&G made this request to the relevant Asian tax authorities.*

APAs have been by far the most utilised dispute resolution method over the last decade, with MAPs also playing an important role. These dispute resolution tools do not serve a public good function,[99] as they are not released publicly. In its ruling regarding MAP and practice statement on APAs, the ATO indicates that information gathered or generated through these dispute resolution processes is protected by the confidentiality provisions of tax treaties.[100] The only information released by the ATO regarding MAP or APAs is general statistics relating to each programme (e.g., number of completed cases, transfer pricing methods used, industries involved, etc.).

4. Transfer pricing case law. *What is the evolution path of transfer pricing litigation in the country? For example: (i) Is transfer pricing litigation being gradually replaced by either MAPs or APAs, as regulated in the relevant tax treaties? (ii) Are foreign/local transfer pricing precedents and/or published MAPs increasingly relevant as a source of law for solving transfer pricing disputes?*

There is not a great deal of case law in Australia regarding transfer pricing disputes. There have been two substantive cases in the last forty years and four procedural cases. In contrast, again as discussed above, APAs and MAP negotiations have played a very large role in resolving transfer pricing disputes recently. As such, it seems reasonable to conclude that such negotiated dispute resolution methods have to a great extent replaced litigation as the preferred method of resolving transfer pricing disputes.

---

[99] For a discussion of the concept of public good function of case law and other transfer pricing dispute resolution mechanisms, see E. Baistrocchi, 'The Transfer Pricing Problem: A Global Proposal for Simplification' (2005–6) 59 *Tax Lawyer* 941.

[100] TR 2000/16, PSLA 2011/1, available on the ATO legal database, note 4 above.

5. Customary international law and international tax procedure. *Has customary international law been applied in the country to govern the relevant methods for solving transfer pricing disputes (such as the MAP)? For example, has the* OECD *Manual on Effective Mutual Agreement Procedure ('OECD Manual') been deemed customary international tax law in the MAP arena for filling procedural gaps (for example, time limit for implementation of relief where treaties deviate from the OECD Model Tax Convention)?*

Judicial decisions have placed some reliance on the OECD Guidelines and Model as interpretive aides but the most recent case held that it was necessary to show that both countries concerned in a treaty case adhere to the Guidelines before they can be relied on.[101] Additionally, the ATO's own administrative documents relating to transfer pricing refer to and endorse the OECD's 1995 Transfer Pricing Guidelines.[102] However, it does not appear that such instruments have been taken either by the courts or by the revenue authority to represent binding international law.

6. Procedural setting and strategic interaction. *Does strategic interaction between taxpayers and tax authorities depend on the procedural setting in which they interact when trying to solve transfer pricing disputes? For example, which procedural setting in the country prompts the relevant parties to cooperate with each other the most for solving this sort of dispute, and why?*

It seems likely where taxpayers and tax authorities attempt to resolve transfer pricing disputes through negotiation-based methods (e.g., APAs and MAP), there will be more incentive for compromise than in adversarial arenas like the courts. Procedure has played a considerable part in transfer pricing litigation in Australia – there are more cases in this area than on substantive issues. The courts, however, have sent a clear message that they will not allow procedural tactics to undermine transfer pricing adjustments, as outlined in the Australian chapter.

---

[101] *Commissioner of Taxation* v. *SNF (Australia)* [2011] FCAFC 74, (2011) 193 FCR 149 (Ryan, Jessup and Perram JJ).

[102] Particularly TR 97/20, available on the ATO legal database, note 4 above.

7. The future of transfer pricing disputes resolution. *Which is the best available proposal in light of the interests of the country for facilitating the global resolution of transfer pricing disputes, and why?*

The increasing use of alternative processes to litigation (e.g., APAs and MAP) to resolve transfer pricing disputes is a positive step. The time and cost to have a complex transfer pricing case decided through litigation is considerable. For example, the *Roche Products* case, which involved reassessments for the taxation years between 1992 and 2002, was only decided by the Administrative Appeals Tribunal in 2008. The lack of a limitation period in domestic tax law of transfer pricing adjustments contributes to the very slow resolution of cases. Speed and cost considerations favour a greater emphasis on alternative dispute resolution to resolve transfer pricing disputes. In the Australian context, APAs have been the most successful way of dealing with disputes over a twenty-year period.

10

Transfer pricing disputes in Japan

TOSHIO MIYATAKE

10.1 Introduction

In December 1985 the Tax Commission, an advisory body to the Prime Minister, submitted its report on the revision of the tax system for 1986, recommending as follows:

> As the recent internationalization of business progresses, the shifting of income abroad by manipulating prices in transactions with overseas specially related enterprises, that is, the problem of transfer pricing, has become important in the area of international taxation. It is difficult to deal with this matter sufficiently under the present law. Leaving this situation as is would be problematical from the viewpoint of proper, equitable taxation. Considering the fact that foreign countries are already equipped with a tax system to deal with such shifting of income overseas, it would be appropriate to stand on common ground with these foreign countries and to formulate provisions concerning the computation of taxable income to apply to corporations' transactions with their specifically related enterprises abroad, as well as to create measures contributing to the smooth operation of such a system, such as the collection of data, in order to realize proper international taxation.

Based on this recommendation, the Japanese international transfer pricing rules were enacted and codified as article 66-5 (later renumbered as article 66-4) of the Special Taxation Measures Law (STML) on 28 March 1986, with two principal purposes: to cope with the shifting of income abroad and to put Japan's tax system on a common ground with those of other nations.

In the drafting stage, the transfer pricing rules of the United States as well as those of the United Kingdom, Germany and France were studied. The drafters also closely studied the reports on *Transfer Pricing and Multinational Enterprises* (1979) and *Transfer Pricing and Multinational Enterprises: Three Taxation Issues* (1984), issued by the OECD Committee on Fiscal Affairs, in the belief that these reports set forth the consensus of the OECD member countries and should, therefore, form the basis for Japan's new tax legislation.

Subsequently, article 66-4-2 was added when the suspension of tax payment due to the filing of an application for mutual agreement procedure was provided.

Article 66-4 of the STML is supplemented by article 39-12 of the Special Taxation Measures Law Enforcement Order (STMLEO) and article 22-10 of the Special Taxation Measures Law Enforcement Regulations (STMLER). The tax administration's interpretation of the above law and operational guidelines are expressed in the Special Taxation Measures Law Circulars (STMLC) and the Commissioner's Directive on the Operation of Transfer Pricing ('TP Administrative Guidelines').

In 1987, the National Tax Agency (NTA) of Japan introduced advance pricing agreement (APA) (called 'Pre-confirmation' in Japan) for the first time in the world through a tax circular which is now contained in the Administrative Guidelines.[1]

10.2   Methods of resolving transfer pricing disputes

There are principally three methods of resolving transfer pricing disputes; (i) administrative appeals, (ii) judicial remedy, and (iii) mutual agreement procedure. Arbitration was not a recognised method of resolving transfer pricing disputes in Japan, but is now emerging as the fourth resolution method in the event that the competent authorities cannot agree on a mutual agreement procedure.[2]

10.2.1   Administrative appeals

In Japan, transfer pricing assessments are made by the director of a district tax office by issuing a correction notice based on a tax audit conducted by the staff of the regional taxation bureau, which is the organisation with authority for the district tax office. The practice with respect to tax audits is that the tax examiners show their interim opinions to the taxpayer after they have completed their audit and ask whether or not the taxpayer will accept their interim opinions. This gives the taxpayer an opportunity to respond to the examiners' interim

---

[1] In 1991, the IRS of the United States introduced the APA by Revenue Procedure 91-22. The IRS expressly expanded the use of the APA for bilateral APA under the mutual agreement procedure. Since then, the APA system has spread rapidly to many other countries.

[2] See section 10.2.3 (xi) below.

opinions. After hearing the taxpayer's opinion, the examiners will make a final determination and issue a correction notice if their opinion has not changed. If the taxpayer accepts their conclusions, the examiners may let the taxpayer amend its tax return rather than issuing a correction notice.

A transfer pricing assessment is made by issuing a written determination entitled 'Correction notice of corporation tax amount, etc.' The issuing authority is the director of the district tax office or the regional commissioner of the regional taxation bureau that conducted the tax audit. Ordinarily, the director of the district tax office issues it. The tax due as a result of the assessment must be paid within one month from the date the notice is issued (the payment date specified in the notice) whether or not the taxpayer disputes the assessment, unless the payment of the principal tax, as well as of the penalty and the unpaid tax, is suspended by filing an application for suspension which is permitted when the mutual agreement procedure is applied for.

There are two procedures for administrative appeals: the request for reinvestigation and the request for reconsideration.

Request for reinvestigation

Within two months after receipt of the correction notice, the taxpayer may file a request for reinvestigation with the district tax office or the regional taxation bureau which issued the correction notice (National Tax Common Rules Law (NTCRL), article 75(1)). However, if the staff of a regional taxation bureau conducted the examination for a correction notice issued by a district tax office, which is the ordinary situation in the case of transfer pricing adjustment, the taxpayer is required to file the request for reinvestigation with the regional taxation bureau (NTCRL, article 75(2)).

Request for reconsideration

If the district tax office or the regional taxation bureau denies a request for reinvestigation or does not make a determination on the request for reinvestigation within three months after such request is filed, the taxpayer may file a request for reconsideration with the National Tax Tribunal (NTT), which is a quasi-judicial organ within the NTA (NTCRL, article 77(2); article 75(3)). In the case of a denial, the request for reconsideration must be filed within one month from the date on which the taxpayer receives a certified copy of the determination of denial of the request for reinvestigation from the district tax office or the regional taxation bureau (NTCRL, article 77(2)).

A blue tax return filer[3] may skip the request for reinvestigation phase and file a request for reconsideration directly with the NTT within two months from the date on which such taxpayer receives a correction notice (NTCRL, article 75(4)(i)).

A proceeding before the NTT ordinarily takes a couple of years to complete, although the length of time varies depending on the nature and complexity of the case.

10.2.2   Judicial remedies

A taxpayer cannot go to the court directly when he has an objection to a correction notice. He is required to seek administrative remedies first either (i) by going through the request for reinvestigation and thereafter the request for the consideration, or (ii) by going through the request for reconsideration.

If a taxpayer's request for reconsideration is dismissed, the taxpayer may file with a district court a complaint seeking rescission of the correction notice within six months from the date on which the taxpayer receives a certified copy of the NTT's decision of denial of the request for reconsideration. The taxpayer can file a complaint with a district court if the NTT does not decide on the request for reconsideration within three months after its filing.

Tax litigation ordinarily takes two to three years at the district court level, depending on the nature and complexity of the case. There are three levels within the Japanese judicial system for tax suits: the district courts, the high courts and the Supreme Court. There is no court specially designed to handle tax cases. Tax litigation is handled by courts in exactly the same way as ordinary civil suits. However, a tax suit is considered to be one of the administrative law suits, and if a district

---

[3] A 'blue tax return' is a tax return (coloured blue) filed in respect of national income taxes on the basis of the designated double entry bookkeeping method. An application for approval to file a blue tax return must be submitted to the district tax office by the day before the beginning of the first year for which a blue tax return is required to be filed. This system was originally introduced in 1950 to induce taxpayers to keep correct accounting books which form the basis for tax returns. Although it achieved the initial purpose, it still continues to exist. Important benefits are available to corporations and individuals which file blue tax returns, including the carry over and back of losses, the availability of certain reserves, special depreciation and certain tax credits. A blue tax return cannot be corrected by the tax authorities without examining the accounting books, and the reasons for correcting a blue tax return must be given.

court has a special department for handling administrative law suits, a tax suit will be handled by that department.

10.2.3 Mutual agreement procedure

(i) General

All income tax treaties to which Japan is a signatory provide for a mutual agreement procedure (MAP).[4] Japanese income tax treaties are basically patterned after the OECD Model Convention. Since the NTA allows a corresponding arrangement only when a mutual agreement is reached under the MAP between the relevant competent authorities, the existence of a tax treaty providing for the mutual agreement procedure provision is important.

The mutual agreement procedure is by far the most frequently used remedy pursued by Japanese taxpayers for resolving transfer pricing adjustments. The principal reason for resorting to it is that the taxpayers can avoid international double taxation by MAP even if the original transfer pricing assessments are not entirely rescinded.

A mutual agreement procedure involves three kinds of dialogue between the competent authorities. First, if a person believes that the actions of one or both of the contracting states result in or will result in 'taxation not in accordance with the provisions of the convention', the person may present his case to the competent authority of his home state, and the competent authority has an obligation to endeavour to resolve the case by mutual agreement with the competent authority of the other contracting state (OECD Model Convention, Article 25(1) and (2)). This may be called 'the individual case mutual agreement procedure'.

Second, if any difficulties or doubts arise as to the interpretation or application of the treaty, the competent authorities of the contracting states are required to endeavour to resolve such difficulties or doubts by mutual agreement (OECD Model Convention, Article 25(3) first sentence). This may be called 'the interpretation mutual agreement procedure'. Third, the competent authorities of the contracting states may consult with each other to eliminate double taxation in cases not provided for in the treaty (OECD Model Convention, Article 25(3)

---

[4] Japan has fifty-three full fledged income tax treaties in force as of 30 April 2012 which are applicable to sixty-four countries or territories.

second sentence). This may be called 'the legislative resolution mutual agreement procedure'.

In the latter two types of mutual agreement procedure a taxpayer does not need to apply for the MAP, and it is left to the competent authorities to decide whether or not to conduct the MAP. However, in the first type, the individual case mutual agreement procedure, once a taxpayer applies for a MAP, the competent authority that receives the application has an obligation to conduct the mutual agreement procedure and to try to reach an agreement, though it has no obligation to reach agreement under the MAP. The individual case mutual agreement procedure is useful to a taxpayer in resolving any transfer pricing problems.

(ii)   Taxation not in accordance with the Convention

The threshold requirement for invoking a mutual agreement procedure is the occurrence of 'taxation not in accordance with the provisions of the convention'. Article 25(1) of the OECD Model Convention provides as follows:

> Where a person considers that the actions of one or both of the Contracting States result or will result for him in taxation not in accordance with the provisions of this Convention, he may, irrespective of the remedies provided by the domestic law of those States, present his case to the competent authority of the Contracting State of which he is a resident or, if his case comes under paragraph 1 of Article 24, to that of the Contracting State of which he is a national. The case must be presented within three years from the first notification of the action resulting in taxation not in accordance with the provisions of the Convention.

All Japanese income tax treaties have a similar provision, although a number of them, especially older tax treaties, do not have the time limitation provision.

The theoretical question is whether the assessment of additional tax by the other contracting state under its transfer pricing rules will constitute 'taxation not in accordance with the provisions of the convention'. In this regard, Japan is in a special situation. Many of the Japanese income tax treaties do not contain a provision equivalent to Article 9(2) of the OECD Model Convention which specifically requires a corresponding adjustment in transfer pricing cases. That provision states as follows:

> Where a Contracting State includes in the profits of an enterprise of that State – and taxes accordingly – profits on which an enterprise of the other

Contracting State has been charged to tax in that other State and the profits so included are profits which would have accrued to the enterprise of the first-mentioned State if the conditions made between the two enterprises had been those which would have been made between independent enterprises, then that other State shall make an appropriate adjustment to the amount of the tax charged therein on those profits. In determining such adjustment, due regard shall be had to the other provisions of this Convention and the competent authorities of the Contracting States shall if necessary consult each other.

If the relevant Japanese income tax treaty contains the same provision as Article 9(2) of the OECD Model Convention, there is no question that a mutual agreement procedure can be invoked because the provision specifically provides that the competent authorities of the contracting states shall if necessary consult each other.

A number of Japanese income tax treaties lack a provision corresponding to Article 9(2) of the OECD Model Convention. This creates a special situation for Japan and raises a question as to the theoretical basis for invoking a mutual agreement procedure for transfer pricing cases. Nevertheless, a taxpayer is considered to have the right to request a MAP if tax is assessed under the transfer pricing rules. The theoretical grounds for this right are considered below.

All the income tax treaties to which Japan is a party contain a provision on associated enterprises that is similar to Article 9(1) of the OECD Model Convention, which states:

Where:

(a) an enterprise of a Contracting State participates directly or indirectly in the management, control or capital of an enterprise of the other Contracting State, or

(b) the same persons participate directly or indirectly in the management, control or capital of an enterprise of a Contracting State and an enterprise of the other Contracting State,

and in either case conditions are made or imposed between the two enterprises in their commercial or financial relations which differ from those which would be made between independent enterprises, then any profits which would, but for those conditions, have accrued to one of the enterprises, but, by reason of those conditions, have not so accrued, may be included in the profits of that enterprise and taxed accordingly.

The above provision establishes the arm's length principle and presupposes that there is only one independent enterprise principle to be applied to a particular transaction. Taxation not in accordance with the convention would result if the two contracting states have adopted different versions of an arm's length principle. Therefore, if a contracting state taxes the profits of an enterprise under its own arm's length principle, the taxpayer in question may request the competent authority of his state to conduct a mutual agreement procedure so that both competent authorities will apply the same arm's length principle.

(iii) Application requirements for MAP

The NTA has issued a tax circular for the mutual agreement procedure.[5] The acceptable reasons for an application for MAP include the following two reasons (MAP Circular, section 3):

(i) cases in which a domestic corporation requests mutual consultations because the corporation has been subjected to transfer pricing taxation or it is recognised that the corporation will be subjected to transfer pricing taxation in Japan or in a treaty partner nation regarding transactions between the domestic corporation and its foreign related person;

(ii) cases in which a domestic corporation requests mutual consultations because the corporation has submitted an APA request prescribed in the Commissioner's Directive on the Operation of Transfer Pricing or in the Commissioner's Directive on the Operation of Transfer Pricing for Consolidated Corporations related to transactions between the domestic corporation and its foreign related person, and requests mutual consultations for such an APA.

The mutual agreement procedure may be terminated in the following cases (MAP Circular, section 20):

(i) cases in which it has been determined, after mutual consultations have begun, that the subject of the request for mutual consultations is not a subject to be discussed in mutual consultations under the applicable tax treaty;

(ii) cases in which the applicant has withdrawn the request for the APA when the request for mutual consultations is related to an APA;

(iii) cases in which the application for mutual consultations or the attachments thereto are found to contain false entries;

---

[5] Commissioner's Directive on Mutual Agreement Procedures (*sogo kyogi tetsuzuki nit tsuite*), 25 June 2001, as amended ('MAP Circular').

(iv) cases in which the applicant does not cooperate in providing the documents necessary for mutual consultations;

(v) cases in which it is impossible to assemble the documents necessary for mutual consultations because a significant time has elapsed since the assessment of taxes in Japan or in the treaty partner nation, or because of other reasons;

(vi) cases in which the applicant does not accept the proposed agreement in response to the inquiry described in MAP Circular, section 18(1);

(vii) cases in which it is recognised that the continuation of mutual consultations will not result in an appropriate solution.

(iv) Application for MAP

An application for the mutual agreement procedure, in the prescribed form, must be addressed to the Commissioner of the NTA and submitted to its Office of Mutual Agreement Procedures. There is no statute of limitations on the application, so unless the relevant income tax treaty provides a time limit (such as the two years' limitation in the Japan–Canada income tax treaty), a taxpayer can apply for MAP at any time if all other conditions are satisfied. As noted above, however, an application may not be accepted if the relevant tax data are not available due to the passage of a considerable period of time.

It is not clear exactly when a taxpayer can apply for the mutual agreement procedure, i.e., the point of time when 'a taxation not in accordance with the provisions of [the applicable treaty]' has occurred. Determining when an application for MAP can be made is a difficult issue, as is well known, because it is difficult to judge at what stage of the tax examination process the action of one of the contracting states will result in taxation not in accordance with the tax treaty. The NTA does not specify when an application for the MAP can be filed because of this difficulty. An application filed prior to the issuance of a notice of correction or determination will not be rejected just because it is filed before the issuance of the notice of correction or determination in cases where Japanese tax is in question. The question is whether or not the case is ready for the mutual agreement procedure. It is widely recognised that the timing of an application must be judged on a case-by-case basis.

A taxpayer can ordinarily file an application for MAP when the Japanese tax authorities issue a notice of correction or determination reassessing the tax liability and imposing an additional tax, or when the foreign tax authority issues a similar reassessment.

On the other hand, it is often a problem to determine when a taxpayer can apply for MAP while a tax audit is being conducted. A sufficient discussion on the tax issues will be needed with the tax authorities seeking the imposition of a tax. In the case of a tax audit in Japan, the case is considered ready when tax examiners present their written interim opinion to the taxpayer after examination, the issues in dispute are made clear, and a transfer pricing adjustment appears imminent.

(v)   Relationship to remedies under Japan's internal law

A taxpayer is entitled to pursue whatever remedies are available under a Japanese tax treaty or Japan's internal law, which poses a difficult question on the relationship between the mutual agreement procedure under an applicable tax treaty and such remedies available under the internal law. Japanese law is silent on this question. If a taxpayer prefers to pursue the MAP under an applicable tax treaty rather than a remedy provided by the internal law, the Japanese tax administration with which the request for reinvestigation or the request for reconsideration is filed will usually wait to see the outcome of the mutual agreement procedure. Thus, a taxpayer may petition for a remedy under the internal law in order to preserve its right to the remedy within the applicable statute of limitations, but then stay the internal law remedy procedure until the MAP is concluded.

(vi)   Payment of tax and MAP

When a notice of correction or determination is issued, the tax assessed thereby must be paid within one month of the issuance of the notice (NTCRL, article 35). If the tax is not paid, the Japanese tax authorities may attach the taxpayer's assets even if a remedy under the internal law is invoked, although the attached assets cannot be sold until such remedy procedure is completed, unless the value of the assets is likely to reduce markedly (NTCRL, article 105(1)). The Japanese tax authorities may upon application, and at their discretion, refrain from attaching the property of a taxpayer if the taxpayer offers security (NTCRL, article 105(3) and (5)).

The invocation of a mutual agreement procedure entitles a taxpayer to suspend its payment of the tax including the penalty and the unpaid tax, until one month after the recorrection is made based on the MAP agreement or when both competent authorities agree to terminate the MAP, provided that an appropriate security is offered by the taxpayer (STML, article 66-4-2; STMLEO, article 39-12-2).

(vii)   Proceedings

When the NTA receives an adequate application for a mutual agreement procedure, it has an obligation to start the MAP and to exert its efforts to reach a mutual agreement with the competent authority of the other contracting state, but it has no obligation to reach a mutual agreement.

The mutual agreement procedure is conducted only between the two competent authorities concerned, and the taxpayer in question cannot participate. However, the taxpayer may request the competent authority to inform it of the current status of the negotiations under the MAP, and it is customary for the NTA's Office of Mutual Agreement Procedures to meet with the taxpayer after every meeting of the competent authorities and to explain the outline of the negotiations at the meeting. The meetings of the competent authorities are held twice a year at most in a usual case, and three or four times a year between the NTA and the US Internal Revenue, which is the most frequent one.

The taxpayer will be requested to supply to the competent authority the data necessary for the conduct of the procedure, and the taxpayer's failure to provide such data may result in the discontinuance of the mutual agreement procedure. When the MAP is completed, whether or not an agreement is reached, the taxpayer concerned will be notified of the result in writing.

(viii)   Consent of the taxpayer to the MAP

In the event that an agreement is reached in the mutual agreement procedure, the taxpayer concerned must indicate whether or not it agrees with the competent authorities' mutual agreement; the taxpayer is free not to agree. If the taxpayer does not agree with the result, however, the taxpayer will be required to withdraw its application for the MAP and it may pursue remedies under the applicable internal law if the limitation period for such remedies has not expired.

(ix)   Implementation of MAP

If the taxpayer agrees to the contents of the mutual agreement and wants to have it implemented, the district tax office will automatically issue a recorrection notice in accordance with the contents of the mutual agreement, although the tax law requires the taxpayer to file a request for recorrection with the director of the district tax office within two months from the date on which the mutual agreement is reached between the relevant competent authorities (NTCRL, article 23(2)

(iii) and National Tax Common Rules Law Enforcement Order ((NTCRLEO), article 6(1) (iv)).

The director of a district tax office is expressly authorised by law to make a corresponding arrangement in accordance with a mutual agreement reached between the Japanese competent authority and a foreign competent authority (Law concerning the Special Rules, etc. of the Income Tax Law, Corporation Tax Law and Local Tax Law incidental to the Enforcement of Tax Treaties (LSRTT) article 7(1)). In the case of a larger corporate taxpayer that is under the jurisdiction of more than one district tax office, the NTA or a regional taxation bureau will make the corresponding arrangement.

For local income taxes (the Enterprise Tax and the Inhabitant Tax), the taxpayer customarily files an application for recorrection.

(x)   Interest on tax refunds and delinquent tax

Interest on a tax refund arising as a result of a correction being made in accordance with a mutual agreement does not accrue from the time of the payment of the tax in question but, rather, begins to accrue three months after the date the request for recorrection is filed, or one month after the date of the recorrection, whichever is earlier. Since the tax refund is made relatively quickly, interest does not ordinarily accrue on refunds. This often creates an imbalance in treatment where the other country concerned charges additional tax equivalent to the Japanese unpaid tax (which is in substance interest on the delayed tax payment).

When a corresponding arrangement is to be made in an international transfer pricing case, a persistent problem is determining how to deal with the unpaid tax in one country and interest on a tax refund in the other country. It is possible, of course, for the two competent authorities to agree on how to treat the unpaid tax in one country and the interest on the tax refund in the other, and it would be desirable to treat both the unpaid tax and interest on the refund in a consistent way. The NTA is authorised to waive the unpaid tax if it so agrees in a mutual agreement procedure (STML, article 66-4(21)). Also, in a reverse situation, the Japanese tax administration may determine not to pay interest on a tax refund resulting from a corresponding arrangement, if any, if it so agrees in a MAP (LSRTT, article 7(4)). These provisions are designed to allow for consistent treatment of unpaid tax in one country and interest on the resultant tax refund in the other.

(xi) Arbitration

From 1 January 2012, arbitration can be invoked as a resolution mechanism supplemental to a mutual agreement procedure between Japan, on the one hand, and the Netherlands and Hong Kong, on the other hand, if no agreement is reached under the mutual agreement procedure within two years after a case is presented for the MAP.[6] An arbitration decision must as a matter of principle be rendered within two years after a request for arbitration is filed.

10.3 Transfer pricing cases

Japan has had a limited number of court judgments on transfer pricing. The following four are all published cases on transfer pricing.

Imabari Zosen

Imabari Zosen, Takamatsu High Court judgment of 13 October 2006[7] appealed from Matsuyama District Court judgment of 14 April 2004.

This case involved the construction of five vessels by the appellant shipbuilding company, Imabari Zosen Co., Ltd, in 1989 to 1993 for its wholly owned subsidiary in Panama. The court applied the comparative uncontrolled price (CUP) method based on the prices of the vessels the appellant built for unrelated parties (internal comparables).

The respondent won. The further appeal to the Supreme Court was dismissed on 10 April 2007.

---

[6] The revised Japan–Netherlands tax treaty signed on 25 August 2010 introduced arbitration for the first time (see Implementing Arrangement regarding Paragraph 5 of Article 24 of the Convention between Japan and the Kingdom of the Netherlands for the Avoidance of Double Taxation and the Prevention of Fiscal Evasion with respect to Taxes on Income, signed by the two governments in conjunction with the revised tax treaty).

The Japan–Hong Kong tax treaty signed on 9 November 2010 also provides for arbitration (see Implementing Arrangement regarding Paragraph 5 of Article 24 of the Convention between Japan and the Government of the Hong Kong Special Administrative Region of the People's Republic of China for the Avoidance of Double Taxation and the Prevention of Fiscal Evasion with respect to Taxes on Income).

The above two tax treaties' provisions on arbitration (Art. 24(5)) became operative from 1 January 2012.

[7] Shomu Geppo vol. 54 no. 4 p. 875; Zeimu Sosho Shiryo (no. 250–) no. 254, 9626 Jungo.

Thai Bahts Loan

Thai Bahts Loan, Tokyo District Court judgment of 26 October 2006.[8]

The plaintiff (the Japanese parent company) lent the total amount of 128,225,000 Thai Bahts at 2.5 per cent to 3.0 per cent per annum in six loans for a period of 10 years to its 95 per cent owned subsidiary in Thailand in 1997 and 1998.

The court did not find any comparable loans to compare with the loans in question, and used Thai Bahts swap rate (swap rate between Thai Bahts LIBOR and a fixed interest rate) plus spread (short-term prime interest rate minus yen LIBOR) as the arm's length interest rate, which amounted to 10.5 per cent to 19.2 per cent per annum. It was not based on an actual transaction but based on a theoretical, hypothetical transaction.

The court said that even if it was a hypothetical transaction, there is an actual financial market behind it which establishes an objective financial indicator. The transfer pricing method used was a method similar to CUP.

The defendant won and this judgment became final without being appealed.

Adobe

Adobe, Tokyo High Court judgment of 30 October 2008[9] appealed from the Tokyo District Court judgment of 7 December 2007.

Since 1999, a Japanese affiliate of a US software maker provided supporting services, customer liaison and assistance in marketing to an unrelated local distributor (wholesaler) which bought the software from an Irish affiliate (or previously Cayman Islands affiliate) in exchange for compensation of the reimbursements of all operating expenses plus 1.5 per cent of the sales by the Irish (or Cayman Islands) affiliate to the local wholesaler.

The Japanese tax authorities applied a method similar to the resale price method by using the profit ratio of a local reseller of a competing software (a secret comparable) as the comparable.

---

[8] Shomu Geppo vol. 54, no. 4, p. 922; Zeimu Sosho Shiryo (no. 250–) no. 256, 10554 Jungo.

[9] Supreme Court, www.courts.go.jp/hanrei/pdf/20090508190658.pdf; Zeimu Sosho Shiryo (no. 250–) no. 258, 11061 Jungo (TAINS Z888–1303).

First, the three traditional methods (CUP, resale price and comparable profit) had priority at that time over the other methods under Japanese tax law. The Tokyo High Court held that the respondent had the burden of proof that it could not use any of the traditional methods in spite of the fact that it had exercised reasonable efforts, and affirmed that such burden was discharged.

Second, the court held that the respondent had the burden of proof that a particular transfer pricing method (the method similar to the resale price method in this case) chosen by the respondent was applicable to this case.

The court pointed out that the appellant did not sell the software in question but only provided services and that there was a lack of comparability between the appellant's services transactions and the comparable transactions the respondent utilised and also a difference in the risk profiles between them.

On account of the lack of comparability based on functions and risks, the Tokyo High Court reversed the lower court decision which affirmed the transfer pricing adjustments. This is the only case which the taxpayer won among the transfer pricing judgments. The respondent did not appeal and the High Court judgment became final. It is noted that the Tokyo High Court did not express its opinion on the issue of secret comparable because the tax authorities' assessment which used a secret comparable was rescinded.

Nippon Acchaku Tanshi

Nippon Acchaku Tanshi, Osaka High Court judgment of 27 January 2010[10] appealed from Osaka District Court judgment of 11 July 2008.

The appellant, Nippon Acchaku Tanshi Co., Ltd, in four taxable years from 1 April 1995 to 31 March 1999, sold connectors, etc., to its wholly owned subsidiaries in Singapore and Hong Kong. The tax authorities applied the cost plus method based on the appellant's sales of the same products to six unrelated parties in Taiwan (internal comparables).

The appellant argued that those internal comparables were not really comparable. One of the reasons for non-comparability was the difference in the sale volumes. The appellant's sales to the affiliates in

---

[10] Unreported (TAINS Z888–1588).

Singapore and Hong Kong were four times larger than those to the comparable companies. However, the court held that a difference within ten times does not damage comparability and does not require an adjustment.

The appellant's claim regarding the difference in the markets was also dismissed by the court which stated that there was no difference requiring an adjustment between the markets in Singapore and Hong Kong and the market in Taiwan for the connectors, etc.

The appellant's claim that there was a difference in the seller's function because the comparable companies in Taiwan were the group companies of a harness manufacturer while the affiliates in Singapore and Hong Kong were trading companies was also dismissed by the court, which found that the six comparable companies included trading companies.

The court dismissed the appellant's appeal. The Osaka High Court judgment became final as the appellant did not appeal it to the Supreme Court.

Although there have not been many court decisions on transfer pricing, they have established certain rules, as observed above.

10.4   APA as a method to prevent transfer pricing disputes

10.4.1   Certain statistical information

In practice, the APA has been used as the most effective method to prevent transfer pricing disputes. It is now a typical reaction to file an application for bilateral APA for subsequent years once a Japanese taxpayer has received a transfer pricing adjustment. The first bilateral APA Japan concluded was with the United States in 1992.

The NTA's recent *APA Program Report 2009* (published in November 2010) sets forth data showing the trends in the accrued and disposed numbers of bilateral APAs as shown in Figure 10.1.[11]

The number of bilateral APAs (BAPAs) is steadily on the increase. The geographical areas covered by BAPAs extend to the Americas, Asia and Oceania. Figure 10.2 shows the coverage of the regions.[12]

---

[11] NTA, *Concerning the Situation of APAs Involving the Mutual Agreement Procedure in 2009 Administrative Year* (November 2010) in Japanese and *APA Program Report 2009* (November 2010) in English.

[12] *Ibid.*

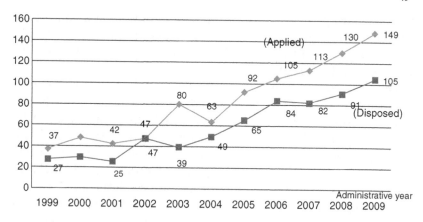

Figure 10.1 Applied and disposed numbers of BAPAs by administrative year
Note: The administrative year runs from 1 July to 30 June of the following year.

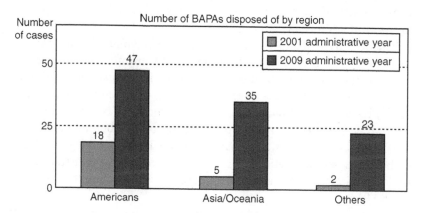

Figure 10.2 Number of BAPAs disposed of by region
Note: The treaty partners from which the NTA received the largest numbers of BAPA cases in the 2009 administrative year were (1) United States and (2) Australia.

10.4.2 Objectives of APA

The basic mechanism of transfer pricing taxation is to compute the taxable income of a corporation as if its transactions with its foreign related persons were conducted at arm's length prices.

On the other hand, an APA is a framework whereby, based on the application from a taxpayer, the tax administration confirms in advance the method of calculating the arm's length prices for transactions with its foreign related persons. Further, the tax administration will refrain from applying transfer pricing taxation to the taxpayer if the taxpayer files its tax returns in accordance with the confirmed APA conditions for the years covered by the APA.

There are three types of APA, a unilateral APA, a bilateral APA and a multilateral APA. In a unilateral APA, the NTA confirms the method of calculating the arm's length price. In a bilateral APA or multilateral APA, the NTA confirms the method of calculating the arm's length price based on an agreement on the transfer pricing method with one or more foreign tax authorities under the mutual agreement procedure. The MAP in principle is between two competent authorities (bilateral). However, occasionally multilateral mutual agreement procedure is conducted, a typical example of which is one for global trading in the financial field.

APA cases make up an absolute majority of MAP cases today; this indicates that there is an increasing need on the part of taxpayers to avoid the risk of international double taxation caused by transfer pricing taxation in advance by using APAs.

The objectives of an APA are to ensure predictability for the taxpayer in respect of transfer pricing taxation and to promote the proper and smooth enforcement of taxation. Transfer pricing adjustments can often be large, and examinations on transfer pricing often require taxpayers to commit a considerable amount of time and money. Taxpayers can avoid the burden involved in transfer pricing taxation by obtaining an APA.

With a bilateral APA, the taxpayer is assured of the legal stability of both tax administrations (or all concerned tax administrations in multilateral cases). This is why many taxpayers, including the Japanese, use BAPAs.

The contents and procedure of the APAs are set out in the TP Administrative Guidelines. Also, comprehensive guidelines for MAP, on which BAPA cases are based, are provided in the MAP Guidelines.

10.4.3   PATA guidance

On 25 June 2004, the Pacific Association of Tax Administrators (PATA) composed of the tax agencies of Japan, Australia, Canada and the United States, released the MAP Guidance and the BAPA Guidance.[13] These

---

[13] MAP Operational Guidance for Member Countries of the Pacific Association of Tax Administrators and BAPA Operational Guidance for Member Countries of the Pacific Association of Tax Administrators.

were intended to deal with the increasing use of MAPs and BAPAs, and to respond to the growing demand from taxpayers for international guidance.

Both sets of Guidance establish targets for the execution of MAP and BAPAs among PATA members, but are not binding on the members.

One of the points made in each set of Guidance is to establish a time frame under which members should endeavour to complete MAP and BAPA cases within two years. This two-year time frame does not apply to certain cases, such as cases in which a taxpayer does not cooperate. Although MAP is a government-level negotiation, taxpayers who file APA requests are permitted to participate in some sessions to provide factual information.

The MAP Guidance also applies not only to transfer pricing adjustments, but to all mutual agreement procedures.

The BAPA Guidance declares that the member countries will cooperate to deal with BAPAs under the common understanding that BAPAs are more desirable than unilateral APAs.

It should be noted that the PATA has since been reconstituted as the Leeds Castle Group. In January 2007, at the Commissioners' meeting held at Leeds Castle near London and involving Japan, United States, Canada, Australia, United Kingdom, France, China and India, it was agreed to set up a Commissioners' meeting (named the 'Leeds Castle Group') including the above eight countries, Germany and South Korea. However, the MAP Guidance and BAPA Guidance remain as useful guidelines.

10.4.4   OECD Guidelines

The OECD released the *Manual on Effective Mutual Agreement Procedures* in February 2007, as part of a broader project to improve the functioning of existing international tax dispute resolution procedures. This is a guide to increase awareness of the MAP process and function, and will provide basic information on the operation of MAP and identify best practices for MAP.

10.4.5   Relationship between APA and transfer pricing examination

Confirmation of the method of calculating the arm's length price in future years

An APA is designed to confirm the appropriateness of the method of calculating the arm's length price and of the arm's length profit level for future transactions based on past financial data, whereas a transfer pricing examination deals with transactions over the past years.

Use of range

In a transfer pricing examination, an arm's length price is calculated at a particular point. In contrast, an APA often sets a range of profit ratio which satisfies the arm's length principle that does not bring about any income shifting.

Comparable transactions

In a transfer pricing examination, tax auditors select comparable transactions. In order to confirm the appropriateness of the method of calculating the arm's length price for an APA, comparable transactions are selected on the basis of information available to the taxpayer (public data, taxpayer's internal data, etc.), although comparable transactions may be modified by the competent authorities.

Relationship between APA request and tax examination

Ongoing examinations are not interrupted as a result of an APA request.

In order to ensure confidence in the APA system, documents (other than factual documents such as financial statements, capital relationship diagrams and summary statements of business) received from a taxpayer corporation for an APA review may not be used for tax examination.

While an APA is in progress, a tax examination on the transfer pricing aspects will not be conducted for the years to be covered by the APA application (including the rollback years).

10.4.6   Application and review procedures

(i)   Due date of filing APA application

An applicant is required to file a request concerning the confirmation of the method of calculating the arm's length price along with the necessary documents no later than the day before the first day of the taxpayer's business year to be covered by the APA. When the applicant requests a BAPA, the applicant must also submit an Application for mutual agreement procedure. Although there is no deadline provided for requesting a MAP in relation to APA cases, the MAP request is usually submitted together with the APA request.

(ii)   Documents to be attached to APA application

The following documents must be attached to an APA application:

(a) documents describing the outline of the foreign-related transactions and the organisations conducting the transactions to be confirmed;

(b) documents describing the transfer pricing method (TPM) to be confirmed and specific details thereof, and an explanation as to why it is the most reasonable method;

(c) documents describing material business and economic conditions essential to the APA;

(d) documents providing a detailed explanation of the transactions to be confirmed, flows of funds, currencies used, etc.;

(e) documents regarding direct or indirect capital relationships or relationships of substantial control between the foreign-related entity/entities pertaining to the transactions to be confirmed and the APA applicant;

(f) documents regarding the functions performed by the APA applicant and the applicable foreign-related entity/entities in the transactions to be confirmed;

(g) operational and accounting information for the prior three taxable years;

(h) documents describing any transfer pricing examinations, appeals, lawsuits, etc., involving the foreign-related entity/entities, and details of past taxation in its/their home country/countries;

(i) documents describing the results of applying the proposed TPM to the prior three taxable years;

(j) Other reference documents useful for the APA.

(iii)   Taxable years to be confirmed

In principle, three to five taxable years are to be confirmed.

(iv)   Review of APA application

The review is carried out based on the following:

(a) information about the business conditions of the APA applicant and its foreign-related entity/entities, and about the foreign-related transactions;

(b) an analysis of the probability of any income transfer being made in past years that constitute the basic data for review;

(c) an analysis of the appropriateness of the method of calculating the arm's length price;

(d) an analysis of the comparability of the comparable transactions (e.g., the comparability of the items listed below):

   (i) types of inventory assets, nature of services rendered, etc.;
  (ii) stage of transactions;
 (iii) volume of transactions;
 (iv) terms and conditions of the transactions;
  (v) functions performed and risks assumed by the party/parties concerned;
 (vi) intangible assets;
(vii) business strategy;
(viii) timing of market entry;
 (ix) market conditions.

(v)   Effects of APA

When a taxpayer files its tax returns in compliance with a confirmed APA, the confirmed transactions are treated as having been concluded at the arm's length price. If the taxpayer's income of any past APA period turns out to be less than the appropriate figure calculated using the confirmed TPM, the taxpayer must file an amended tax return for that year. However, no penalties will be imposed under such circumstances. If such discrepancy is found before filing the relevant tax return, the taxpayer must make a complaint adjustment in the tax return to be filed.

(vi)   Annual report

Within the tax return filing period (usually two months) after the end of each year, the taxpayer is required to file an annual report for the tax authorities to determine whether the taxpayer complied with the APA.

10.5   Conclusion

In Japan, the mutual agreement procedure is the predominant method of resolving transfer pricing disputes. If there is no applicable income tax treaty, the mutual agreement procedure is not available. In such event, the administrative and judicial remedies will be the second preferred method. Arbitration has been available as a resolution mechanism from 1 January 2012 only when the Japanese competent authority cannot agree with the competent authorities of the Netherlands and Hong Kong in a mutual agreement procedure. Mediation is not a choice for resolving transfer pricing disputes in Japan. The bilateral APA is the most effective method of preventing transfer pricing disputes.

Appendix: Questionnaire (Japan)

1. The structure of the law for solving transfer pricing disputes. *What is the structure of the law of the country for solving transfer pricing disputes? For example, is the mutual agreement procedure (MAP), as regulated in the relevant tax treaty, the standard method for solving transfer pricing disputes?*

There are three structures for solving transfer pricing disputes: (a) administrative remedy; (b) judicial remedy; and (c) mutual agreement procedure.

The administrative remedy consists of (i) the request for reinvestigation to the Regional Commissioner of the Regional Taxation Bureau and (ii) the request for reconsideration to the National Tax Tribunal which is a part of the National Tax Agency (NTA) and acts as the final appeals office within the NTA.

The MAP is the standard method for solving transfer pricing disputes.

2. Policy for solving transfer pricing disputes. *Is there a gap between the nominal and effective method for solving transfer pricing disputes in the country? For example, has the country a strategic policy not to enforce the arm's length standard (ALS) for fear of driving foreign direct investment to other competing jurisdictions?*

No, there is no such gap.

3. The Prevailing Dispute Resolution Method. *Which is the most frequent method for solving transfer pricing disputes in the country? Does it have a positive externality? For example, is the MAP the most frequent method, and if so, to what extent have successful MAPs been used as a proxy for transfer pricing case law? For instance, Procter & Gamble (P&G) obtained a bilateral advance pricing agreement (APA) in Europe, and it was then extended to a third (Asian) country when P&G made this request to the relevant Asian tax authorities.*

It is the mutual agreement procedure in Japan. However, the contents of agreement under the MAP may not be objectively ascertainable so as to establish transfer pricing case law.

4. Transfer pricing case law. *What is the evolution path of transfer pricing litigation in the country? For example: (i) Is transfer pricing litigation being gradually replaced by either MAPs or APAs, as regulated in the relevant tax treaties? (ii) Are foreign/local transfer pricing precedents and/ or published MAPs increasingly relevant as a source of law for solving transfer pricing disputes?*

Litigation may be a path when the mutual agreement procedure is not available or acceptable.

5. Customary international law and international tax procedure. *Has customary international law been applied in the country to govern the relevant methods for solving transfer pricing disputes (such as the MAP)? For example, has the OECD Manual on Effective Mutual Agreement Procedure ('OECD Manual') been deemed customary international tax law in the MAP arena for filling procedural gaps (for example, time limit for implementation of relief where treaties deviate from the OECD Model Tax Convention)?*

No customary international law has been applied in Japan to govern any relevant methods for solving transfer pricing disputes.

6. Procedural setting and strategic interaction. *Does strategic interaction between taxpayers and tax authorities depend on the procedural setting in which they interact when trying to solve transfer pricing disputes? For example, which procedural setting in the country prompts the relevant parties to cooperate with each other the most for solving this sort of dispute, and why?*

In litigation, the relation between taxpayers and tax administration is very formalistic and the least cooperative.

In administrative relief, meetings have a more informal atmosphere and negotiated settlements may be possible (especially in the request for reinvestigation).

In MAPs, taxpayers are not directly involved. A MAP is a negotiation between two competent authorities. There is a possibility of 'horse trading' in the negotiations.

As a MAP case cannot be finally resolved unless the taxpayer accepts the competent authorities' agreement under the MAP, the competent authorities request the taxpayer's opinions when the negotiation is in progress.

7. The future of transfer pricing disputes resolution. *Which is the best available proposal in light of the interests of the country for facilitating the global resolution of transfer pricing disputes, and why?*

Simplifying the transfer pricing substantive rules may be a practical choice.

11

Transfer pricing disputes in the Republic of Korea

11.1 Introduction

The Republic of Korea has adopted the civil law system. Korea became a member of the OECD in 1996, but even before then, it had been under the influence of the OECD Model Tax Convention and various reports on transfer pricing in the international tax arena.

The Convention between the Republic of Korea and Japan for the Avoidance of Double Taxation and the Prevention of Fiscal Evasion with respect to Taxes on Income ('Korea–Japan Tax Treaty'),[1] entered into force in March 1970, is the first bilateral tax treaty for Korea, which was influenced by the 1963 draft of the OECD Model Tax Convention. The origin of the Korea–Japan Tax Treaty was the result of the efforts made by both countries since 1964 to solve the problems which had arisen where Japanese trading companies had been imposing high estimated taxes when providing goods to the Korean Public Procurement Service.[2] Since the conclusion of the Korea–Japan Tax Treaty, Korea has successively signed tax treaties with other countries and, as of 15 July 2011, seventy-seven tax treaties are in force.[3]

I appreciate the valuable comments from Seongtae Kang (former officer at the National Tax Service), Hyejung Byun (Assistant Professor at the University of Seoul City), Sangwoo Song (Senior CPA at Yulchon), Jueun Chung and Sunyoung Kim.

[1] The full text of the treaty is available at www.mofat.qo.kr/trade/treatylaw.

[2] Murai Tadashi, 'Problems of Japan–Korea Tax Treaty from the Perspective of a Japanese Scholar' (1997) 3 *Tax Law Study* (September), 92. It was in August 1916 that corporate income was first taxed in Korea, and on 7 November 1949 corporate income tax was separated from individual income tax, as the corporate tax law had been enacted. Korea was under Japanese rule (1910–45) when corporate income was first taxed. It was under US military rule between 1945 and 1948. In 1950, the year after the first enforcement of the corporate tax law, the Korean War broke out, which continued for three years. The importance of international corporate taxation has been recognised since Korea's National Tax Service was founded in 1966.

[3] See www.nts.go.kr.

Korea's bilateral tax treaties have been influenced by the 1963 OECD Model Tax Convention, the 1977 OECD Model Tax Convention and the 1979 UN Model Tax Convention; but since Korea joined the OECD in 1996, the importance of the OECD Model Tax Convention has become more prominent. For example, when the 1970 Korea–Japan Tax Treaty was amended on 16 November 1999, it adopted the OECD Model Tax Convention provisions, including those on corresponding adjustments among related companies and the principle of taxing real property income in the situs country of the real property.

Aside from signing general tax treaties, how was the transfer pricing system introduced in the tax treaties? The arm's length principle existed in the 1933 League of Nations Model Tax Convention (Article 6). The OECD Model Tax Convention and the UN Model Tax Convention also had transfer pricing provisions (Article 9). The 1970 Korea–Japan Tax Treaty had a similar transfer pricing provision (Article 8) as well, and so did the subsequent tax treaties of Korea. Since the late 1980s, price manipulation by multinational corporations using overseas related companies in their cross-border transactions became a full–fledged problem in Korea, which was a phenomenon caused by the rapid opening of the Korean economy. To prevent such cases of price manipulation, which had been designed to reduce the overall tax liabilities, the Korean government introduced the transfer pricing system applicable to cross-border transactions by amending article 46 of the Corporate Income Tax Act (CITA) Enforcement Decree of 31 December 1988. The amendment involved administration of the transfer pricing system within the framework of the 'Disallowance of Tax Deduction for Unfair Transactions' provision under article 20 of the CITA, which applied to domestic corporations.

However, the transfer pricing rule applied under the framework of existing income tax laws focused solely on the prevention of tax evasion and thereby failed to attribute multinational corporations' income among their relevant countries. As a rare example of legislative efforts to solve these problems,[4] on 6 December 1995, Korea enacted a separate domestic tax statute on the taxation of cross-border transactions, the Law for the Coordination of International Tax Affairs (LCITA), separate

---

[4] In Japan, article 66-4 ('Special cases of taxation related to transactions with an overseas related party') of the Special Tax Treatment Act was enacted in 1986. In Germany, the Foreign Transaction Taxation Act (Aussensteuergesetz) containing provisions on the principles applied to transactions among independent companies was separately enacted in 1972.

from, *inter alia*, the CITA and the Individual Income Tax Act (IITA). The LCITA, unlike tax treaties, even offered specific methods for calculating the arm's length price and provided practical details on transfer pricing. The LCITA was largely influenced by the OECD's 1995 *Transfer Pricing Guidelines for Multinational Enterprises and Tax Administrations* ('OECD Transfer Pricing Guidelines').

The LCITA provides provisions for the taxation of thin capitalisation (chapter III), taxation of tax shelter prevention (chapter IV), special gift tax cases for cross-border gifts (chapter V), and cooperation among countries in tax administration (chapter VII) as well as the taxation of transfer pricing (chapter II). As a method of resolving disputes on the taxation of international transactions, it provides for a mutual agreement procedure (MAP) in a separate chapter (chapter VI), but it does not have separate provisions regarding an arbitration procedure. Article 25 of the OECD Model Tax Convention provides for the MAP and, therefore, Korea's tax treaties mostly have these provisions. The MAP provisions under the LCITA are considered domestic statutory provisions when implementing the MAP under Korea's tax treaties.[5]

The transfer pricing provisions of the LCITA not only provide the arm's length price calculation methods (i.e., transfer pricing methods) but also address advance pricing agreement (APA), whereby a taxpayer and the Commissioner of the National Tax Service (NTS) can decide in advance the transfer pricing method and pricing criteria before filing final tax returns, which provides an opportunity for advance relief measures for transfer pricing. The NTS signed its first APA with the United States in May 1997; there have been 212 APA applications filed since then until the end of 2009 and 133 cases were finalised.[6] The NTS has been issuing advance rulings on the interpretation of Korea's tax law, akin to the advance rulings of the United States, since 1 October 2008 (articles 16 to 26 of the Legislative Matters Handling Regulation (NTS Directive no. 1803)).[7] Taxpayers can obtain advance rulings by submitting specific facts with respect to transfer pricing issues. Such submissions and requests for advance rulings must be made with their actual names and the NTS provides responses within the statutory deadline for filing tax returns.

---

[5] Taero Lee and Mansu Han, *Lectures on Tax Law* (Pak-Young Publishing, 2010), p. 992.

[6] The Full text can be found in the NTS *APA Annual Report 2009*, (NTS, August 2010), p. 10, available at www.nts.go.kr. The relevant material is available in Korean and English.

[7] For more details, see www.nts.go.kr/info/info_14_02_01.html.

There are no fees required. An APA can also be considered to constitute a type of advance ruling on the transfer pricing method, but the advance ruling system described above can be differentiated from an APA, because the advance ruling system allows an inquiry not only about the transfer pricing method but also about other legal issues of transfer pricing.[8]

As explained above, Korea has specific provisions on transfer pricing in the LCITA, a separate domestic tax statute, as well as in its tax treaties. Dispute resolution methods for transfer pricing include the advance ruling system for tax law interpretations, the APA system and the MAP. Furthermore, administrative appeal procedures such as objection, request for review, request for ruling by a tax appeal bureau and the judicial procedure, which is a three-instance system of administrative litigation, are also available following tax assessments.

Korea's dispute resolution methods on transfer pricing are summarised in the following order. Section 2 will cover the transfer pricing rule by operation of the LCITA. To understand the universality and particularity of dispute resolution procedures in Korea's transfer pricing provisions, the main parts of the LCITA need to be explored first. Section 3 introduces the details and the actual operations of the MAP as a dispute resolution procedure and summarises the relevant discussions about the introduction of an arbitration procedure in Korea. Section 4 introduces the advance transfer pricing agreement as well as the details and the actual practice of the interpretation of its tax law in the area of advance ruling. In particular, the APA, where it operates in connection with the MAP, is explained in detail. Section 5 looks at the basic structure and major cases of the administrative appeal procedure and the judicial procedure as Korea's tax dispute resolution procedure. Section 6, the conclusion of this chapter, summarises the special features of Korea's transfer pricing rule and the resulting dispute resolution methods.

11.2. Transfer pricing rule under LCITA

11.2.1 Transfer pricing rule before LCITA

With the introduction of the LCITA on 6 December 1995, Korea has a separate domestic tax law on transfer pricing. Before the LCITA was enacted, article 46(4) of the CITA Enforcement Decree, enacted on

---

[8] Kyung-geun Lee and Beom-Jun Kim, 'Introduction to Tax Law-Interpreting Advance Rulings' (2008) 14(2) *Tax Law Study* 120.

31 December 1988, applied to transfer pricing cases. The development of transfer pricing rules prior to the LCITA is described below.

Prior to article 46(4) of the CITA Enforcement Decree

Prior to the enactment of article 46(4) of the CITA Enforcement Decree on 31 December 1988, there were no separate provisions for transfer pricing. Under these circumstances, there was no choice but to apply article 20 (the 'Disallowance of Tax Deduction for Unfair Transactions' provisions) of the CITA, by which the government could reassess the amount of tax due where a related-party transaction unfairly reduced the tax burden of the taxpayer concerned. However, the provision was originally designed to apply to domestic related-party transactions and it was very difficult to apply to overseas related-party transactions.

At that time, tax treaties had transfer pricing provisions but not a specific transfer pricing method, which meant that it was difficult to administer the transfer pricing system in practice by tax treaties alone. Article 8 of the 1970 Korea–Japan Tax Treaty, Korea's first tax treaty, contained a transfer pricing provision, and Korea have since established the transfer pricing provisions in all of its seventy-seven tax treaties as of 30 June 2010, although they still fail to provide for specific arm's length price calculation methods.

After article 46(4) of the CITA Enforcement Decree

The arm's length price calculation method for overseas related-party transactions was introduced by article 46(4) of the CITA Enforcement Decree on 31 December 1988. Korea seems to have been expressly providing for a transfer pricing rule in its domestic tax law. The provision was influenced by the US Treasury Regulation section 1.482–2A(e)(1) and the 1979 OECD report entitled *Transfer Pricing and Multinational Enterprises*. The provision followed the US Treasury Regulation in that the priority among arm's length price calculation methods was given to the comparable uncontrolled price method; in addition the resale price method, the cost plus method and any other methods deemed reasonable are also included.[9] However, article 22-2 of the CITA Enforcement Rule (Ministry of Finance Decree no. 1780, partly amended on 6 March 1989) only addresses the comparable

---

[9] It is restricted to the transfer or purchase of inventory assets, instead of all transactions with foreign investors, etc. (art. 46(4) of the CITA Enforcement Decree).

uncontrolled price method, the resale price method and the cost plus method for calculating the market price, and does not address either the profit split method or the transactional net margin method.

In the amendment of the Enforcement Decree, a provision was also enacted by which the relevant corporation bore the burden of proving that the transaction price with the overseas related party was fair and reasonable (article 46(5) of the CITA Enforcement Decree). Matters related to transfer pricing, with the exception of the arm's length price calculation method or the burden of proof, were addressed in the NTS Directive 'Regulation on the Operation of Transfer Pricing Taxation' (in force on 25 January 1990). On 31 December 1990, article 20-2 of the CITA and article 55-2 of the IITA were enacted, enabling a corresponding adjustment of the income amount in accordance with the mutual agreement under tax treaties. According to the 'Disallowance of Tax Deduction for Unfair Transactions' provision of article 20 of the CITA, a corresponding adjustment was not available in principle.

Article 46(4) of the CITA Enforcement Decree enacted on 31 December 1988 was important in that the transfer pricing rules were clearly codified into the domestic tax statute; but certain problems nevertheless persisted given that the provision was placed within the framework of article 20 of the CITA,[10] and it did not provide any details of the transfer pricing rules except for the arm's length price calculation methods.

In practice, there were few cases where the provisions were applied to cross-border transactions among foreign subsidiaries of a Korean company (i.e., outbound transactions);[11] they were more often applied to cross-border transactions among overseas affiliates of a foreign-invested Korean company, all of which were under the ownership of a foreign

---

[10] When the CITA was amended on 28 December 1998, the 'Refusal of Unfair Act and Calculation' provision was moved from art. 20 to art. 52 of the CITA.

[11] *Guk-i* 46523-98 (18 February 1994), an NTS-established rule, decided that: (i) in applying art. 20 of the CITA in connection with the transaction of selling of goods to a domestic parent company's wholly-owned US subsidiary, the question of whether the tax burden was unfairly reduced depends on whether the relevant sale price had been set below the market price according to art. 46(2) (4) of the CITA Enforcement Decree; and (ii) the resale price method under art. 46(4)(1) (b) of the CITA Enforcement Decree applies where market price cannot be calculated by the comparable uncontrolled price method under (a), but the resale price and the ordinary profit may be calculated and, in such cases, the amount resulting from subtracting the ordinary profit from the resale price will be deemed the market price. This case concerned a transaction between a domestic parent company and a foreign subsidiary (outbound transaction) before the enactment of the Act.

parent company (i.e., inbound transactions),[12] albeit on a limited basis. In order to solve this problem, the LCITA, a collection of provisions on transfer pricing as a separate statute, was enacted on 6 December 1995. It closely reflects the 1995 OECD Transfer Pricing Guidelines.

11.2.2   Transfer pricing provisions under LCITA

Background and framework of LCITA

The LCITA was enacted on 6 December 1995. The legislative goal for its enactment was to:

> offer a legal basis for tax adjustments with respect to cross-border transactions among related parties in line with the launch of the WTO and as part of the preparation to join the OECD, by adopting internationally accepted and practiced standards, and provide for cooperation in tax administration and procedures thereof among countries to solve tax problems occurring in international transactions among companies.[13]

The LCITA became Korea's first separate domestic tax legislation addressing transfer pricing rules.

Once the LCITA was introduced, the provisions of the arm's length price calculation method, the obligation to submit basic data to calculate transaction prices and other provisions related to international transactions were all removed from article 46 of the preceding CITA Enforcement Decree, article 55 of the preceding IITA. Thus, the LCITA applied to cross-border transactions with overseas related parties, and the CITA applied only to transactions among related parties except for cross-border transactions. After the enactment of the LCITA, there was some controversy over the relationship between the LCITA and the CITA; to

---

[12] The National Tax Tribunal (which used to be an agency under the Ministry of Finance and Economy in charge of administrative appeals but has been renamed the National Tax Tribunal under the Prime Minister's Office) in applying the market price calculation method for overseas transactions to a transaction between a domestic subsidiary and a Hong Kong parent company, decided that an inclusion of the gross income was allowed by calculating the size of the transfer pricing adjustment, and the use of other methods was reasonable (the last in the order of priority), instead of relying on the order of priority under article 46(4) of the CITA Enforcement Decree (CUP method → resale price method → cost plus method) (*Guk-sim* 94 *Seo* 1287, 30 August 1995). This case concerned a transaction between a domestic subsidiary and a foreign parent company (inbound transaction) before the enactment of the Act.

[13] The legislative history and goals for its enactment are explained at www.law.go.kr, the government website containing Korea's present and past statutes.

address this issue, article 3(2) of the LCITA was enacted on 18 December 2002 to expressly provide that only the transfer pricing provisions, not 'Disallowance of Tax Deduction for Unfair Transactions' provisions under the IITA and the CITA, apply to cross-border transactions.

At the time of its enactment, the LCITA consisted of seven chapters and thirty-three articles. The chapters included: chapter I (general provisions); chapter II (tax adjustments on transactions with overseas related parties); chapter III (tax adjustments on interest paid to foreign controlling shareholders); chapter IV (tax adjustments on corporate income in tax havens); chapter V (special cases of gift taxes on overseas gifts); chapter VI (mutual agreement procedure), and chapter VII (international cooperation in tax matters). The LCITA, according to its addenda, came into force as of 1 January 1996; but the advance pricing agreement for the arm's length price calculation method, the taxation of thin capitalisation in chapter III and the taxation of tax havens in chapter IV, all came into force on 1 January 1997, as a longer preparation period was required in introducing the new system.

Transfer pricing: meaning and requirements

Since the LCITA was enacted on 6 December 1995, it has been amended several times. The meaning of transfer pricing in Korea and its requirements are summarised as follows, with focus on chapter II (tax adjustments on transactions with overseas related parties) of the current Act (Act no. 10410, as amended on 27 December 2010).

Transfer pricing means where a resident (including a domestic corporation and a domestic place of business) transfers taxable income overseas by paying more than the arm's length price *or* receives a lower amount than the arm's length price in its cross-border transaction with an overseas related party. The tax authority rejects this manipulated pricing (transfer pricing) for the relevant cross-border transaction and taxes the resident based on the arm's length price (article 4(1) of the LCITA). Transfer pricing taxation under the LCITA, unlike the 'Disallowance of Tax Deduction for Unfair Transactions' provisions of the CITA, does not require that it be committed with the goal of unfairly reducing the tax burden.[14]

In the LCITA, the transfer pricing rules apply to residents. The definition of resident includes both a foreign corporation's domestic place of business and a domestic corporation (article 4(1) of the LCITA).

---

[14] LCITA Basic Rules 4–0.1.

In principle, the transfer pricing rule only applies to cross-border transactions between residents and their overseas related party. The term 'overseas related party' means a non-resident having a special relationship with a resident, a domestic corporation or a domestic place of business, a foreign corporation or its foreign place of business (article 2(1)(8) of the LCITA). A foreign corporation's domestic place of business was excluded from the application of the transfer pricing rule by the amendment of the LCITA on 26 December 2008. As a transaction between a domestic corporation and a domestic place of business is a domestic transaction subject to the domestic taxing authority, it is subject to the 'Disallowance of Tax Deduction for Unfair Transactions' provisions. Thus, a foreign corporation's domestic place of business was excluded from the concept of the overseas related party and, when one party to the transaction is a domestic place of business, the transaction creating domestic-source income under article 119 of the IITA or article 93 of the CITA is excluded from the definition of a cross-border transaction (article 4(1) of the LCITA).

A 'special relationship' refers to a shareholding relationship or a *de facto* control relationship (article 2(1)(8) of the LCITA). A *shareholding relationship* exists between the parties to a transaction whenever: (i) one party to the transaction directly or indirectly owns 50/100 or more of another party's voting shares; or (ii) a third party directly or indirectly owns 50/100 or more of both parties' voting shares (article 2(1)(8)(a) and (b) of the LCITA). A *de facto control relationship* means a relationship where: (i) both parties to the transaction have a common interest and either of them can substantially decide the other's business policies due to capital contributions, goods/services transactions, loans, etc.; or (ii) the parties have a common interest and a third party can substantially decide both parties' business policies, due to capital contributions, goods/services transactions, loans, etc. (article 2(1)(8) (c) and (d) of the LCITA). The scope of a related party in the LCITA is much narrower than under the 'Disallowance of Tax Deduction for Unfair Transactions' provisions of the CITA.

When a clear reason is presented which explains why a given *de facto* control relationship does *not* fall under the special relationship, the transfer pricing rules do not apply (article 4(2) of the LCITA). This provision was adopted in order to prevent the violation of taxpayer's rights, so as to provide them with an opportunity to prove the lack of a special relationship, as the expansion of the scope of a related party, as amended on 18 December, 2002, can be over-used and it is relatively easy to establish a special relationship based on a common interest.

There exist different opinions as to whether the transfer pricing rules apply to transactions between a head office and its branches,[15] but the tax authority is of the position that it should apply.[16]

'Cross-border transaction', to which the transfer pricing rules apply, refers to any transaction in which either party is, or both parties are, non-resident(s) or foreign corporation(s), and which is related to the sale/lease of tangible or intangible assets, provision of services, lending/borrowing of money or other loss/profit and asset of the transacting party (article 2(1)(1) of the LCITA). However, as a gift or in capital transactions, the 'Disallowance of Tax Deduction for Unfair Transactions' provisions of the CITA or the IITA apply, whereas the transfer pricing rules do not (article 3(2) of the LCITA, and article 3-2 of the LCITA Enforcement Decree).

It is possible to transfer taxable income to an overseas related party by interposing a third party between the resident and the overseas related party; in such cases, in order to apply the transfer pricing rule, the resident is sometimes deemed to have conducted a cross-border transaction with the overseas related party even if, in reality, the resident has conducted a cross-border transaction with a non-overseas related party (article 7 of the LCITA). To effect such a transaction, the following requirements must first be met: (i) there must be a contract executed in advance concerning the relevant transaction between the resident and the overseas related party (including the case where a *de facto* agreement is deemed to exist in advance due to transaction-related evidence); and (ii) the terms of the relevant transaction must be substantially decided between the resident and the overseas related party. Since many prior contracts are entered into orally or otherwise informally (e.g., via emails) and not often in a written form, the amendment to the LCITA on 18 December 2002 expanded the meaning of the 'prior contract' in this respect.

Sometimes, it is even possible to correct transactions between overseas related parties within the scope of the arm's length price through other transactions with the same overseas related party. Where there is a prior

---

[15] Regarding this controversy, see Chang-hee Lee, 'Taxation of Fixed Place of Business' (2007) 13(2) *Tax Law Study* (August). This article points to the problems that may arise from treating transactions between the main office and its branches as between separate entities discussed in the OECD *Report on the Attribution of Profits to Permanent Establishments* (December 2006).

[16] National Tax 46017-48, 22 December 2001.

agreement to set off the difference in amount by other international transactions with the same overseas related party in the same taxable year, and the resident proves the contents and facts of the transaction, then all the international transactions being set off are deemed to be a single international transaction (article 8(1) of the LCITA). Even where the set-off transactions are recognised in the adjustment of the transfer pricing rules, when there is income subject to the withholding tax, the withholding has to be made by accounting that there is no set-off transaction (article 8(2) of the LCITA). The amendment introduced in the LCITA on 24 May 2006 established this restriction so that the taxing power which can be justly exercised in Korea can be secured even if a set-off transaction is recognised.

Method of calculating arm's length price

The 'arm's length price' refers to a price applied or determined as applicable to an ordinary transaction with a non-overseas related party by a resident, domestic corporation or domestic place of business (article 2(1)(10) of the LCITA). According to the LCITA, the arm's length price calculation methods (i.e., transfer pricing methods) include comparable uncontrolled price (CUP), the resale price method (RPM), the cost plus method, the profit split method, the transactional net margin method (TNMM) and other methods deemed reasonable which take into account the substance and practice of the transaction (article 5(1) of the LCITA and article 4(1) of the LCITA Enforcement Decree). This reflects the 1995 OECD Transfer Pricing Guidelines.

There have been a number of changes in terms of the priority given among the transfer pricing methods. When the LCITA was enacted on 30 December 1996, the hierarchy among the transfer pricing methods was established as follows: CUP (priority no. 1), RPM and cost plus (priority no. 2), profit split (priority no. 3), TNMM (priority no. 4) and other methods (priority no. 5) (article 5(1) of the LCITA, article 5(4) of the LCITA Enforcement Decree). When the LCITA Enforcement Decree was amended on 29 December 2000, priority among CUP, RPM and cost plus was eliminated. Thus, priority was given in the following order: CUP, RPM and cost plus (priority no. 1, these three have the same priority), profit split (priority no. 2), TNMM (priority no. 3) and other methods (priority no. 4) (article 5(1) of the LCITA, article 5(4) of the LCITA Enforcement Decree). When the LCITA Enforcement Decree was amended on 30 December 2002, the priority between profit split and TNMM was eliminated. Thus, priority was given as CUP, RPM and cost plus (ranked no. 1, these three have the same priority), profit split and TNMM (ranked no. 2, these two have the same priority) and other methods (priority no. 3), (article 5(1) of the LCITA and article 5(4) of the LCITA Enforcement Decree). When one of the other methods, the operating expense to the gross profit ratio (called the Berry Ratio method)[17] became an acceptable transfer pricing method, priority was as follows: CUP, RPM and cost plus (equally ranked no. 1 with the same priority), profit split, TNMM and the Berry Ratio method (equally ranked no. 2 with the same priority) and other methods (priority no. 3). When the LCITA Enforcement Decree was amended on 4 February 2009, the Berry Ratio method was classified as the profitability index of the TNMM. Consequently, the priority among the current transfer pricing methods is given in the order of: CUP, RPM and cost plus (equally ranked no. 1), profit split and TNMM (equally ranked no. 2) and other methods (priority no. 3).

However, under the amendment of the LCITA on 27 December 2010, the priority among the transfer pricing methods was abolished altogether. In other words, instead of these past priority schemes, the 'most reasonable' transfer pricing method must be selected and used by the taxpayer (article 5 of the LCITA and articles 4 and 5 of the LCITA Enforcement Decree). Among the 133 cases handled by APAs from 1997 to 2009, TNMM was the most frequently used transfer pricing method (in 112 cases, accounting for 84 per cent). Among the types of TNMM, the method using the operating profit ratio as a profit level index was used most frequently (53 cases), followed by the Berry Ratio method (40 cases).[18]

The Berry Ratio method was classified as the profitability index of TNMM by the amended Enforcement Decree of 4 February 2009, a method that analyses the actual operating profit, which reflects the positions of the US federal tax laws and the OECD Center for Tax Policy and Administration.[19] Regarding 'other methods deemed reasonable considering the substance and practice of the transaction', the Berry Ratio method appeared most prominent before the Enforcement Decree

---

[17] Argued by Professor Charles Berry of the United States in his testimony during the Dupont Corporation transfer pricing litigation.

[18] NTS *APA Annual Report 2009* (NTS, August 2010), p. 42.

[19] Internal Revenue Service, Treasury 482-5(b)(4)(ii)(B) prescribes it as a financial ratio in the comparable profit method. 'Transactional Profit Methods: Discussion Draft Public Comment' (OECD CTPA, 08.1.25) introduces it as a financial ratio in the transactional net margin method (TNMM).

amendment on 24 August 2006; but at present, where the Berry Ratio method is classified as one of the profitability indices of the TNMM, the statutes do not propose a specific method.

To prevent the abuse of the Berry Ratio method, the amendment of the Enforcement Decree on 18 February 2010 specified its requirements. The Berry Ratio method may be applied whenever a resident conducts a simple sales activity or provides services without the burden of inventory when the following requirements are met: (i) proportionality between the operating expenses and the gross profit; (ii) the value of products sold does not seriously influence the gross profit; and (iii) there are no other important functions, such as manufacturing, to which another arm's length price calculation method may be applicable (article 5(3) of the LCITA Enforcement Decree). The OECD Finance Committee W6 reached an agreement to specify the requirements of the OECD Transfer Pricing Guidelines in order to prevent abuse of the Berry Ratio method and such agreement was reflected here.

With respect to an *intangible asset*, its definition and other issues to consider in calculating the arm's length price are contained in statutes (articles 6(6) and 14-2(1) of the LCITA Enforcement Decree).[20] The LCITA Enforcement Decree was amended on 24 August 2006 to reflect the guidance provided by the OECD Transfer Pricing Guidelines. The term 'intangible asset' in this respect includes patent rights, utility model rights, design rights, trademark rights or service mark rights, copyrights[21] and other valuable intangible assets such as design, model and know-how, which may be used on their own or can be transferred or licensed to others (article 14-2(1) of the LCITA Enforcement Decree). In calculating the arm's length price of an intangible asset, according to its characteristics, additional revenue or saved expenses expected from the intangible asset, restrictions on the exercise of rights, possibility of transfer or licensing to others, etc., are to be considered (article 6(6) of the LCITA Enforcement Decree).

There is a separate clause addressing the arm's length price calculation for intra-group services (article 3-2 of the LCITA Enforcement Decree).

---

[20] As regards the arm's length price calculation method for intangible assets in Korea, see Hun Park and Seong Kwon Song, 'Transfer Pricing and Intangibles: Republic of Korea' (2007) 92a *Cahiers de Droit Fiscal International* 401.

[21] Initially, a computer program copyright under the Computer Program Protection Act was prescribed separately from copyright but this was omitted when the Copyright Act and the Computer Program Protection Act were combined.

The LCITA Enforcement Decree was amended on 24 August 2006 to reflect the relevant guidance provided by the OECD Transfer Pricing Guidelines in order to complement the criteria for determining the fairness of taxation of the intra-group service income, as providing intra-group services became more prominent as a result of an increasing number of multinational enterprises coming to Korea and Korean companies going overseas.

It is possible to obtain an advance approval of the NTS for the transfer pricing method to prevent transfer pricing-related disputes (article 6 of the LCITA). Such a prior approval of the arm's length price calculation method will be covered in detail below.

In a large-scale transaction, in principle, a system is in place for the NTS to work out the transfer pricing method selected by the taxpayer. A resident should choose the most reasonable transfer pricing method and submit the selected method and reasons for the choice along with the final return to the head of a district tax office (article 7(1) of the LCITA Enforcement Decree). This submission is not mandatory where, out of all the relevant business year's cross-border transactions, the total number of goods transactions is KRW 5 billion or less, and the total number of service transactions is KRW 500 million or less, or where the total number of goods transactions per overseas related party is KRW 1 billion or less, and the total number of service transactions per overseas related party is KRW 100 million or less (article 7(1) of the LCITA Enforcement Decree). Where the actual transaction price differs from the arm's length price based on the transfer pricing method, the resident may report, or request a change, by attaching the transaction price adjustment report, which adjusts the tax base and tax amount by treating the arm's length price as the transaction price (article 7(2) of the LCITA Enforcement Decree).

Tax adjustment, income disposal and corresponding adjustment for application of transfer pricing rule

Where the transaction price between related parties differs from the arm's length price, the tax base and tax amount of a resident (including domestic corporation and domestic place of business) may be adjusted based on the arm's length price (article 4 of the LCITA). There is a special provision for sharing the cost of intangible asset acquisitions. When the LCITA was amended on 24 May 2006, article 6-2 was inserted, reflecting the global standard, whereby a resident may verify the adequacy of cost/expense/risk to be shared with the overseas related party to co-develop intangible assets. Where a resident enters into a prior agreement with an overseas related party to share the cost of co-developing or securing intangible assets and conduct co-developments, and if the cost, etc., shared by the resident is less or more than the amount of the normal cost share, the tax authority may decide to change the resident's tax base and tax amount by adjusting the resident's share of cost, etc., based on the normal cost share (article 6-2(1) of the LCITA). Where a resident's expected benefit, out of the total benefit expected at the time of signing the agreement, increases or decreases by 20 per cent or more in comparison with the expected benefit realised after the development of the intangible asset, the tax authority may recalculate the resident's tax base and tax amount by adjusting the original share of each participant according to the modified expected benefit. However, in such cases, the resident's tax base and tax amount cannot be adjusted in excess of five years from the day following the deadline for filing return of tax base for the taxable year containing the intangible asset's co-development date (article 6-2(2) of the LCITA, article 14-4(1) and (4) of the LCITA Enforcement Decree).

Where the amount included in a domestic corporation's gross income according to the tax adjustment by the arm's length price is not confirmed to return to the domestic corporation from its overseas related party, this amount is to be disposed of according to any of the following three criteria: (1) as a dividend if the overseas related party is the domestic corporation's shareholder; (2) as an increase in investments in the corporation if the overseas related party is a company to which the domestic corporation has contributed capital; and (3) as a dividend if the overseas related party is any other person (article 9 of the LCITA and article 16(1) of the LCITA Enforcement Decree). Where a treaty counterpart adjusts the transaction price between a resident and its overseas related party according to the arm's length price and the relevant MAP ends, the tax authority may adjust and calculate the resident's income amount and the determined tax amount for each taxable year according to the agreement (article 10(1) of the LCITA).

Considering the fact that it may be difficult for the tax authority to collect all the necessary information as certain information about transactions between a resident and its overseas related party may not be readily available in Korea, the LCITA has a mandatory data submission provision for international transactions and a civil penalty provision for its violation (articles 11 and 12 of the LCITA). Meanwhile, since the transfer pricing rules require a difficult and time-consuming process of finding transaction prices among related companies, the National Tax Basic Act (NTBA) has a special provision for penalty tax on under-declarations (article 13 of the LCITA) in order to reduce taxpayers' burden.

11.3   MAP and arbitration

11.3.1   MAP

MAP is provided for in a number of tax treaties and domestic statutes including the LCITA, IITA, CITA, NTBA, the National Tax Collection Act and the Local Tax Basic Act.[22] In Korea, a tax treaty is a special type of law, which is considered inferior to its Constitution, but is considered superior to its domestic tax statutes in force.[23] Tax treaties do not require separate legislation to have the force of domestic law.

Korea's tax treaties sit within the general framework of the OECD Model Tax Convention, and their mutual agreement procedure closely follows Article 25 of the OECD Model Tax Convention. However, the OECD Model Tax Convention began to limit the time period for MAP application only in 2005.[24] Thus, tax treaties signed before that year usually contain no limitation on the period. The examples include Korea's tax treaties with Japan (pre-amendment), the United States, the United Kingdom, Turkey, Denmark and Brazil. According to article 22(2)(4) of the LCITA, however, an application for commencement of a MAP is not allowed 'if filed after three years from the day the applicant first learned of the taxation'. In Korea's tax treaties with Canada, the Philippines and Portugal, among others, providing for a two-year period, this two-year period is applicable; however, for tax treaties with no provision on this matter, a three-year period applies, according to the interpretation of the LCITA.

Article 25(5) of the OECD Model Tax Convention providing for instances of arbitration was added in 2008; however, in Korea, tax

---

[22] On 31 March 2010, the Local Tax Act was divided into the following separate statutes: the Basic Local Tax Act, the Local Tax Act, and the Local Tax Special Treatment Restriction Act. These statutes took effect on 1 January 2011. This chapter is based on the provisions of the Basic Local Tax Act.

[23] Article 6(1) of the Constitution. See Taero Lee and Mansu Han, *Lectures on Tax Law* (Pak-Young Publishing, 2010), p. 869.

[24] Article 25(1) second sentence of the OECD Model Tax Treaty includes the words 'within three (3) years from the first notification of the action resulting in taxation not in accordance with provisions of the Convention'.

treaties or domestic tax statutes have so far disregarded this provision, which will be discussed separately below.

Even though most tax treaties have provisions for the MAP, a detailed procedure is provided for in the LCITA. The following discussion of the MAP is based on the LCITA specifications.

(i) Meaning and current state of MAP

MAP is a procedure aimed at solving matters of tax treaty interpretation, unfair taxation or taxable income adjustment when disputes arise between Korea's competent authorities and those of its treaty counterparts (article 2(1)(5) of the LCITA). A MAP is commenced when the Ministry of Strategy and Finance, or the Commissioner of the NTS, contacts the treaty counterpart's competent authorities by means of a taxpayer's application or *ex officio* (article 22 of the LCITA). But even if an application to commence the MAP is filed, not all cases proceed to a MAP. The MAP, once commenced, proceeds between both parties to the treaty. However, even if the MAP is commenced by both of the competent authorities, there is no absolute obligation for either party to reach agreement.

A MAP under the LCITA is similar to the administrative appeal procedure (e.g., pre-taxation review of appeal, objection, request for review and request for ruling) under the NTBA, in that taxpayers aim to obtain relief measures for their rights. It is, however, different from the administrative appeal procedure such as objection, in that taxpayers file the application for the MAP not with the source country's tax authorities that impose taxes, but with the resident country's tax authorities, and that the application may be filed even if no tax has been levied.[25] The MAP can proceed in conjunction with an administrative appeal procedure, and also with a lawsuit.

A MAP may also be used for the prior approval of the arm's length price calculation method (i.e., APA) (article 6(2) of the LCITA). The NTS has been publishing the use of APAs in its annual report since 2008. APAs can be categorised into unilateral APAs in which a mutual agreement is not used and bilateral APAs in which a mutual agreement is utilised. The NTS signed its first APA with the United States in May 1997, received 212 applications for an APA by the end of 2009 and has completed 133 APAs to date. Among them, 116 applications were for

---

[25] However, the pre-tax assessment review is a pre-taxation administrative appeal procedure.

bilateral APAs and 63 of these were completed, whereas 96 applications were received for unilateral APAs and 70 of these were completed.[26] Details of the APA will be separately covered below.

The overall state of the MAP is not included in the national tax statistics annually published by the NTS. The OECD's per country MAP statistics data is the only source where one can find, in part, the number of applications received by Korea, their completion and the average completion period.[27] As of December 2007, seven mutual agreements out of the accumulated total of thirty-seven applications received have been completed and the average completion period for the seven cases has been twenty-four months. In 2007 alone, nine applications were received and one mutual agreement was completed, with a completion period of six months. Among the thirty applications received in total, eight applications have been pending four years or longer, and fourteen applications two years or longer. The MAP statistics are not identical to those for bilateral APAs. For bilateral APAs, thirteen applications were received, seven bilateral APAs were completed and thirty-one applications were handled in 2007 alone. Not all bilateral APAs accompany a MAP,[28] and not all MAP cases are APAs; therefore, the statistics for MAPs and bilateral APAs cannot be considered identical.

(ii)   Requirements to commence MAP

A Korean national/resident or a domestic corporation and non-resident or foreign corporation (limited to a non-resident or foreign corporation with place of business in Korea) can apply for the commencement of a MAP (article 22(1) of the LCITA). When the LCITA was amended on 24 May 2006, the scope of applicants who can apply for the commencement of the MAP was expanded to include the non-resident and foreign corporation with place of business in Korea as they are both taxed in the same manner as the resident and domestic corporation.

An application to commence the MAP may be filed whenever: (i) there is a need to discuss the application and interpretation of a tax treaty with a treaty counterpart; (ii) there is taxation in violation of tax treaty provisions or there is a risk that the treaty counterpart's tax authorities might commit a violation; and (iii) there is a need for

---

[26] NTS *APA Annual Report 2009*, (NTS, August 2010), p. 30.
[27] See www.oecd.org/tax/disputeresolution/43771245.pdf.
[28] It may be rejected by an APA review (arts. 10 and 11(1) of the LCITA Enforcement Decree).

tax adjustment between Korea and its treaty counterpart according to the tax treaty (article 22(1) of the LCITA). An application should be filed to the Ministry of Strategy and Finance in the first two cases, and before the Commissioner of the NTS in the remaining case (article 22(1)(1) to (3) of the LCITA). In the above-mentioned cases, the Ministry of Strategy and Finance or the Commissioner of the NTS may request the commencement of the procedure *ex officio* (article 22(4) and (5) of the LCITA).

The Ministry of Strategy and Finance or the Commissioner of the NTS, upon receiving an application for the commencement of the MAP, will request the treaty counterpart's competent authorities to commence the MAP in principle and will notify the applicant of the commencement (article 22(2) of the LCITA). But this will not apply if: (i) a domestic or foreign court has issued a final decision; (ii) the applicant is not entitled to apply under the tax treaty; (iii) it is deemed that the taxpayer is trying to use the MAP for purposes of tax evasion; or (iv) the application is filed after three years of being served the taxation notice (article 22(2)(1) to (3) of the LCITA).

(iii)   Commencement date and closing date of MAP

The commencement date of the MAP is determined as follows: (a) where a request to commence the MAP has been received *from* the treaty counterpart's competent authorities, it is the date on which the treaty counterpart's competent authorities are notified of the intent to accept this request; or (b) where a request to commence the MAP has been made *to* the treaty counterpart's competent authorities, it is the date on which the treaty counterpart's competent authorities serve notice of the intent to accept this request (article 23(1) of the LCITA).

The closing date of the MAP is the date on which an agreement in writing is reached between Korea's and the concerned treaty counterpart's competent authorities. But where there is no such mutual agreement, the closing date of the MAP will be the date on which five years have elapsed from the day following the commencing date (article 23(2) of the LCITA). This is a provision designed to lead to an early end to any mutual agreement procedure where there has been no progress for a long time.

When Korea's and the treaty counterpart's competent authorities agree to continue with the MAP, the procedure will not end even if five years have elapsed from the day following the commencing date, although it may not continue any longer than eight years as from the same date (article 23(3) of the LCITA). The LCITA was amended on 18 December 2002 to allow the MAP to last in excess of five years when both countries' tax authorities make efforts to reach a mutual agreement. When there is a final court decision during the MAP, the date of the final court decision is considered the closing date of the MAP (article 23(4) of the LCITA).

(iv)   Special cases including appeal period
and deferred collection

When the MAP is commenced, the period from its commencing date to its closing date is not included in the period for requesting a review or ruling, or filing for an administrative litigation for national tax (articles 56(3), 61 and 68 of the NTBA),[29] the period for requesting a review or ruling for local tax (article 119 of the Local Tax Basic Act), the period for making a decision on national tax review or ruling (articles 65 and 81 of the NTBA) or the period for making a decision on the local tax review or ruling (article 123 of the Local Tax Basic Act and article 24(1) of the LCITA).[30] Therefore, even after the end of the MAP, one can proceed with the domestic tax appeal procedure; and anyone who has filed an application for the MAP may have these special provisions applied without filing for a separate application. Prior to the amendment of the LCITA on 24 May 2006, an application by a taxpayer had been required; in this sense the amendment was made for the benefit of the taxpayers.

During the period of the MAP, suspension of issuance of tax assessment notices, divided notices, suspension of payments and suspension of payment of unpaid taxes are granted (article 24(2), (3) of the LCITA) when the treaty counterpart so permits during the MAP (article 24(4) of the LCITA). Interest accrues for such a deferred period (article 24(5) of the LCITA) to prevent taxpayers from abusing the MAP to extend the period of paying taxes.

Such suspensions and deferments are available for local taxes without effecting a separate procedure where such local taxes are imposed based on the amount of income tax or corporate income tax (article 24(6) of the LCITA). This was enacted when the LCITA was amended on 29 December 2000 in order to avoid the unreasonableness of repeating

---

[29] Special provisions were added to the administrative litigation period by statutory amendment on 29 December 2000, in respect of national tax reviews and rulings. This amendment was intended to expand opportunities to enforce taxpayers' rights.

[30] This period is ninety days.

a similar procedure, although the resident tax (currently a local income tax) is automatically levied when the income tax/corporate income tax is imposed.

(v)   Special cases of statute of limitation for tax imposition

Where a MAP has commenced with a treaty counterpart, a national tax cannot be levied after the end of a one-year period from the day following the MAP closing date, or after the end of the period provided for in article 26-2(1) of the NTBA, whichever falls later in time (article 25(1) of the LCITA). Where a MAP has commenced with a treaty counterpart, the local tax cannot be imposed after the end of a one-year period from the day following the MAP closing date, or after the end of the period provided for in article 38(1) of the Local Tax Basic Act, whichever is later in time (article 25(2) of the LCITA). A MAP often takes a long time but the above-mentioned provisions, despite a five-year statute of limitation period for tax imposition in general, has enabled the tax authority to levy taxes according to the result of the MAP within one year of the MAP closing date.

(vi)   Taxpayer's obligation to cooperate

The Ministry of Strategy and Finance or the Commissioner of the NTS may request that a taxpayer who has applied to commence the MAP should submit documents necessary for the MAP (article 26(1) of the LCITA). Where the taxpayer fails to cooperate faithfully in this request, the Ministry of Strategy and Finance or the Commissioner of the NTS may, *ex officio*, terminate the MAP (article 26(2) of the LCITA). These provisions aim to streamline the processing of the MAP.

(vii)   Implementing MAP result

The subsequent procedure after the closing of the MAP is described as follows. The Commissioner of the NTS, where the MAP has been completed, reports the MAP result to the Ministry of Strategy and Finance (article 27(1) of the LCITA). Within fifteen days of the day following the MAP closing date, the Ministry of Strategy and Finance or the Commissioner of the NTS, where the MAP has been completed, notifies the tax authority, the head of local government, the head of the tax court, other related agencies and the applicant who commenced the MAP, of the MAP result (article 27(2) of the LCITA). Depending on the result of the MAP, the heads of the tax authority and local government may levy taxes, amend any tax decisions, or take any other applicable tax law measures (article 27(3) of the LCITA). Where a final court decision is issued after the end of the MAP, and the decision differs from the MAP result, the mutual agreement is deemed non-existent from the beginning (article 27(4) of the LCITA).

(viii) Expanded application of the MAP result, etc.

The MAP result may also apply to transactions with a related party located in a country other than that relevant to the MAP (article 27-2(1) of the LCITA). This provision was introduced by the amendment of the LCITA on 24 May 2006.

Any person who has commenced a MAP may apply for the expanded application of the MAP result. The period to apply for this request is three years from the date on which the notice of the end of the MAP is served. The application should meet the following requirements: (1) the transaction should be of the same type as that in the MAP result; (2) the tax should have been levied in the same manner as in the MAP result; (3) the ordinary profit or transactional net margin should be the same as the one applied in the calculation of the arm's length price (article 27-2(1) (1) to (3) of the LCITA, and article 42-2(2) of the Enforcement Decree of the same Act).

For example, 'A Inc.', a company founded in Korea, purchased hundreds of different kinds of products from overseas related companies and resold them to unrelated parties. In 2005, A Inc. purchased products from 'B Inc.', an American company, 'C Inc.', a Canadian company and 'D Inc.', a Brazilian company, which all are related to A Inc., and with turnover earnings amounting to KRW 30 billion (approximately USD $30 million), KRW 60 billion and KRW 10 billion, respectively. A Inc. had calculated the arm's length price on the basis of the resale price, to which a 3 per cent profit was added. The tax authority, however, determined the ordinary profit ratio of A Inc. at 5 per cent; its previous income, therefore, was adjusted. Korea agreed with the United States to calculate the normal price on the basis of the resale price, to which a 4 per cent profit was added; and the previous income was also adjusted. If A Inc. were to file an application, the Korean tax authority may adjust the previous income between A Inc. and C Inc. or D Inc. in accordance with the Korea–United States APA, and neither the APA with Canada, nor the one with Brazil, would apply. Before the 2006 amendment, the tax should have been levied at the ordinary 5 per cent profit notwithstanding the Korea–United States agreement. After the 2006 amendment, however, the tax may be levied at 4 per cent if the taxpayer files an application. Nonetheless, this is only based on the position of the Korean tax authorities in relation to A Inc., so that neither Canada nor Brazil is under any obligation to accept this outcome. This is based on the criteria explained in *A Summary of the Tax Law Amended in 2006* (Korean Ministry of Finance and Economy, June 2007), p. 453.

11.3.2   Arbitration

The amended OECD Model Tax Convention of 2008 expressly dealt with some of the main issues relating to arbitration. Arbitration, included in Article 25(5) of the OECD Model Tax Convention, was introduced as a dispute resolution procedure to supplement, and not replace, the MAP (Comment no. 46 to Article 25 of the OECD Model Tax Convention). The 2009 OECD Transfer Pricing Taxation Guidelines, as modified after the above-mentioned amendment of the OECD Model Tax Convention, also reflect this.

In Korea, such amendments of the OECD Model Tax Convention and the 2009 OECD Transfer Pricing Taxation Guidelines are not reflected anywhere in the LCITA or tax treaties. Even if arbitration provisions have not been expressly included in the tax treaties, relevant tax authorities may establish legally binding arbitration procedures through MAPs. In addition, given that Korea is an OECD member, even where it has not expressly introduced arbitration clauses into its domestic law, arbitration can actually proceed according to this OECD position.

'Arbitration is a dispute resolution procedure leading to an agreement, through an arbitrator having expert knowledge and experience acting as a third party. One cannot say that arbitration, an out-of-court dispute resolution procedure, is not used at all in Korea. International commercial arbitrations by the Korean Commercial Arbitration Board or the Paris-based ICC Arbitration Court mostly involve arbitration cases among corporations and are already in fairly strong demand. Arbitration in the tax arena, from the perspective of the tax authority, has the problem of surrendering taxation powers to a third party. Unless tax treaties or the LCITA expressly stipulate arbitration clauses, it seems that it would be difficult to utilise arbitration in practice in the area of taxation in Korea.[31]

---

[31] See Sun-Young Kim, 'Arbitration as Institution of International Tax Dispute Resolution', paper presented at the 2009 joint symposium of tax associations, International Fiscal Association of Korea, 5 December 2009.

Some actively argue for introducing arbitration in Korea, but most are reluctant to do so.

Meanwhile, Chapter 11 of the Korea–United States Free Trade Agreement (FTA) includes an international arbitration clause (Article 11.16).[32] If the FTA clauses were to affect tax treaties, as according to the Korea–United States FTA international arbitration clause, arbitration would become mandatory in the MAP. Under the Korea–United States FTA, taxation measures are excluded from international arbitration in principle, and international arbitration can only be requested in exceptional cases such as indirect expropriation, violation of investment contracts and investment approvals due to taxation measures. For ordinary taxation matters, it is difficult to apply the international arbitration clause.

11.4 Advance pricing agreements and advance ruling confirmation

11.4.1 Advance pricing agreements

(i) APAs: meaning and current state

An advance pricing agreement (APA) is a procedure whereby a taxpayer and tax authority jointly reach an advance agreement on the proper transfer pricing determination method to calculate the arm's length price. APAs include both a bilateral APA (also called APA by mutual agreement) requiring consultation between both countries' tax authorities related to the international transaction, and a unilateral APA which can be effected by the tax authority of one country. Korea allows for both.

In Korea, APAs were first prescribed in the LCITA enacted on 6 December 1995 and, given the need for a preparation period, came into force some time later on 1 January 1997 (article 1 proviso of the addenda). APAs in Korea reflected the APAs introduced in the United States in 1991. One of the main differences, however, is that a retroactive application of the transfer pricing method was allowed in the United States,[33] although not in Korea until 2001. Through statutory amendment, a retroactive application has been permitted for bilateral APAs since 2001 and for both types of APAs since 24 May 2006. Furthermore, Korea, unlike the United

---

[32] The full text is available at www.fta.go.kr/new/ftakorea/kor_usa.asp?country_idx=19.

[33] Revenue Procedure 91-22, 1991-1 C.B. 526. In the United States, APA provisions continued to be amended thereafter. Rev. Proc. 96-53, 1996-2 C.B. 375; Rev. Proc. 2004-40, 2004-2 C.B. 50; Rev. Proc. 2006-9, 2006-1 C.B. 278; Rev. Proc. 2008-31, 2008-23 IRB are examples of these.

States, does not charge fees for APAs, even though applicants may have to pay fees for obtaining expert opinion (article 10 of the LCITA Enforcement Decree).

The LCITA only provides a single clause, article 6,[34] on APAs, but articles 9 to 14 of the LCITA Enforcement Decree establish in detail the requirements, procedures and effects of APAs. Currently, all work related to the receipt, review and approval of APAs is conducted by the International Tax Management Office and the International Tax Cooperation Office of the NTS. Typical APA work requires expertise in various areas of highly specialised tax law, such as transfer pricing. In most cases, therefore, law firms and accounting firms, among others, typically represent taxpayers.[35] For bilateral APAs, countries like the United States and Japan, where in-person meetings are customary, hold both in-person meetings and written communications in parallel, but in other countries, the mutual agreement procedure is conducted by written communications only.[36]

---

[34] LCITA, art. 6 ('Advance Pricing Agreement, etc. of Arm's Length Price Computation Method'): '(1) A resident may, where he/she intends to apply the arm's length price computation method to the taxable years for a specific period, file an application for approval with the Commissioner of the NTS not later than the end of the first taxable year for a specific period in which he/she intends to apply the arm's length price computation method, as prescribed by Presidential Decree. (2) The Commissioner of the NTS may, where a resident applies for approval of the arm's length price computation method under paragraph (1), grant approval for such method, if agreed with the competent authority of the Contracting State through mutual agreement procedures as prescribed by Presidential Decree: Provided that, in such cases as prescribed by Presidential Decree, he/she may grant Advance Pricing Agreement (hereinafter referred to as "unilateral APA" in this Article) for the arm's length price computation method without going through the mutual agreement procedures. (3) The Commissioner of the NTS, when a resident files an application for the retroactive application of the arm's length price computation method to the taxable year before the period subject to the application for approval, may approve a retroactive application within five years preceding the period to apply retroactively to the applied period: Provided that, such approval for the retroactive application may be granted for a retroactive application within three years preceding the period to apply retroactively. (4) The Commissioner of the NTS and a resident shall, where the arm's length price computation method is approved pursuant to paragraphs (2) and (3), comply with the method approved: Provided that, the same shall not apply to cases prescribed by Presidential Decree. (5) Where the arm's length price computation method is approved pursuant to paragraphs (2) and (3), a resident shall submit a report containing the arm's length price computed according to it, procedures of computation, etc. to the Commissioner of the National Tax Service as prescribed by Presidential Decree.'

[35] NTS, *Explanation of Korea's Transfer Pricing Taxation (TP) and Advance Pricing Agreement (APA)* (2002), p. 9.

[36] *Ibid.* p. 9.

In May 1997, Korea's first APA was signed with the United States. The total number of APA applications received was thirty-two in 2007, thirty-five in 2008 and forty in 2009 and, compared to the nine applications for MPAs received in 2007, it can be said that APAs are actively used. Out of the 212 applications received from 1997 to 2009, 116 (55 per cent) were for bilateral APAs, exceeding unilateral APA applications totalling 96 (45 per cent). In addition, the completion period for the 133 cases (out of the total 212 applications) from 1997 to 2009 was, on average, two years and five months for bilateral APAs and one year and eight months for unilateral APAs. All of the seventy unilateral APAs took two years or less, but less than half (thirty-one cases) of the sixty-three bilateral APAs took two years or less, and as many as fifteen cases (24 per cent) took more than three years.

With respect to the transfer pricing method accepted by the tax authorities in APAs, out of the 133 cases completed by the end of 2009, the TNMM (112 cases) was accepted most frequently, while the CUP method (one case) was rarely accepted. The CUP method might be used widely in practice, but since its calculation is clearer than other methods, taxpayers are not required to obtain the NTS's separate approval in advance. Furthermore, the resale price method has been adopted only in the cases of bilateral APAs.[37]

(ii)   Application of transfer pricing method for APAs

All international transactions to which transfer pricing rules apply can be the subject of APAs. It is also possible to file an application for APA for part of international transactions (article 6(1) of the LCITA). An APA application does not end a tax audit but may defer it. Even if a taxpayer is selected for an audit, whenever an APA application is filed to ascertain which transfer pricing method is to be applied to all or part of the transactions with an overseas related party before prior notice of the audit, the said audit may be deferred with regard to the transfer pricing method of the relevant transaction whilst the APA is in process (article 78 of the International Taxation Handling Regulation).[38]

---

[37] APA statistics in this chapter are based on the NTS *APA Annual Report 2009* (NTS, August 2010).

[38] International Tax Matters Handling Regulation is an NTS Directive and prescribes the details of APAs in Chapter V ('Prior Approval of the Arm's Length Price Calculation Method').

Items needed for an APA application include, *inter alia*, the most reasonable method that a taxpayer may resort to and the data necessary to prove that the relevant method adopted by the taxpayer is the most reasonable method. Specifically, four copies of the following documents should be submitted to the Commissioner of the NTS (article 9(1) of the Enforcement Decree of the LCITA):

(a) application for prior approval of the transfer pricing method stating the relevant period, relevant international transaction and/or transaction party, transfer pricing method, etc.;

(b) explanatory data on the transaction party's history of business and/ or content of business and/or organisation, shareholding relationship, etc.;

(c) copies of the transaction party's financial statements, tax returns, international transaction contracts and incidental documents for the previous three years;

(d) the following data specifically explaining details of the calculation method for the arm's length price applied:

    (i) comparability evaluation method and per element difference adjustment method;

    (ii) when a compared company's financial statements are used, the difference in accounting standards applied and the method to adjust them;

    (iii) when per transaction financial or cost data is used, the criteria for preparing them;

    (iv) when two or more compared transactions are used, the scope of price deemed normal and the method of coming up with it;

    (v) explanatory data for the conditions or assumptions that are the basis for the transfer pricing method;

(e) when a resident reports, or applies for, change of the tax base and the tax amount adjusted by treating the arm's length price as a transaction price, the explanatory data on the method of adjusting the difference between the actual transaction price and the arm's length price;

(f) when a mutual agreement with the relevant treaty counterpart is requested regarding the transfer pricing method applied for approval, the application to commence a mutual agreement procedure determined by the Ministry of Strategy and Finance Decree;

(g) other data proving the adequacy of the transfer pricing method for which prior approval has been applied for.

Where the documents submitted to the treaty counterpart's competent authorities differ from the above-mentioned records, these records should also be submitted (article 9(2) of the LCITA Enforcement Decree). This provision was enacted by 29 December 2000 amendment which was designed to enable the Korean tax authority to reach mutual agreements after sufficiently considering the matter. The Commissioner of the NTS may not use the submitted data other than for the purposes of review and subsequent management of the prior approval (article 9(5) of the LCITA Enforcement Decree).

Documents have to be submitted to the Commissioner of the NTS by the last date of the initial taxable year during the period when the application for the transfer pricing method has to be made (article 6 (1) of the LCITA, article 9(1) of the LCITA Enforcement Decree). Before 2001, the application had to be made prior to the start of the taxable period for the transfer pricing method to be applied.

In addition, the prior approval application for the transfer pricing method has to be made during the period in which the taxpayer intends to receive this prior approval (article 9(3) of the LCITA Enforcement Decree). Before 2001, such period was limited to three years (a three-year extension was allowed for one time only thereafter).

The applicant may change or withdraw the original prior approval application before receiving the prior approval from the Commissioner of the NTS (article 9(4) first sentence of the LCITA Enforcement Decree). In such cases, the Commissioner of the NTS has to return all the data it received for the withdrawn application to the applicant (article 9(4) second sentence of the LCITA Enforcement Decree).

(iii)   Review of APA application

The Commissioner of the NTS, in examining APA applications, may consider an opinion of the head of the district tax office and the regional tax office that exercises a jurisdiction over the applicant's tax matters (article 10(1) of the LCITA Enforcement Decree). The Commissioner of the NTS, when examining APA applications, and only where the applicant so consents, may refer to the opinion of an expert who has a neutral relationship with the applicant as to the transfer pricing method applied in an APA application. In this case, the Commissioner of the NTS, where the applicant so consents, may require the applicant to bear part of the cost (article 10(2) of the LCITA Enforcement Decree). The expert may not provide or disclose the information related to the APA application to anyone except for the applicants themselves, their agents or the Commissioner of the NTS (article 10(3) of the LCITA Enforcement Decree).

(iv)   APA by mutual agreement

If the Commissioner of the NTS decides that the APA application is inappropriate and thereby refuses the prior approval, the Commissioner should return all the submitted data to the applicant (article 11(1) of the LCITA Enforcement Decree). The Commissioner of the NTS, where the applicant has applied to commence the MAP for the APA application, should request that the treaty counterpart's competent authorities commence the MAP and will notify the applicant accordingly (article 11(2) of the LCITA Enforcement Decree).

The Commissioner of the NTS, when an agreement with the treaty counterpart has been reached in the MAP, should notify the applicant within fifteen days following the end of the MAP. In such cases, within a period of two months from being served the notice of the agreement, the applicant should notify the Commissioner of the NTS in writing on whether she consents to the content of the notice (article 11(3) of the LCITA Enforcement Decree). The applicant will be deemed as having refused to give such consent if she fails to notify the Commissioner within the two-month time frame; in addition, the original APA application will be considered to have been withdrawn by the applicant (article 11(4) of the LCITA Enforcement Decree). Even if the agreement by the MAP is not identical to the content of the original APA application, whenever the applicant consents to the content of the agreement, the applicant is deemed to have made the application, with consent, with the content proposed later in time (article 11(5) of the LCITA Enforcement Decree).

The Commissioner of the NTS, upon receiving notification by the applicant as to whether there is any consent to the contents of the mutual agreement, will make an APA for the transfer pricing method and notify the applicant accordingly within fifteen days of being served the notice (article 11(6) of the LCITA Enforcement Decree). The methods of implementing the arm's length price under the MAP can be divided into those already reported (where the period has expired) and those whose filing deadline has not begun to run (where the period has not expired). Where the period has expired, a report, or request for change, has to be made within two months, which is the period for requesting a change due to subsequent causes (articles 11(8) and 17(1) of the LCITA Enforcement Decree). Where the period has not expired, a report has to be made to the head of the district tax office by reflecting the approved content within the deadline for filing the final return for tax base and tax amount (article 12(1) of the LCITA Enforcement Decree). The Commissioner of the NTS and the resident, whenever a transfer pricing method is approved, must comply with this approved method (article 6(4) of the LCITA).

The Commissioner of the NTS is to notify the applicant of the suspension of the MAP within fifteen days whenever either of the following situations arises: (i) a mutual agreement is not reached within three years of receiving the application for the APA and the Commissioner of the NTS suspends the MAP *ex officio*; or (ii) if an agreement by the MAP cannot be reached and thus an agreement with the treaty counterpart to end the MAP has been entered into (article 11(7) of the LCITA Enforcement Decree).

(v)   Unilateral APAs

Unilateral APAs may be made whenever: (i) a taxpayer does not request the MAP when filing an APA application for the transfer pricing method; (ii) a mutual agreement is not reached within three years of receiving the APA application and the Commissioner of the NTS suspends the MAP *ex officio*; or (iii) an agreement through the MAP cannot be reached and thus an agreement with the treaty counterpart to end the MAP has been entered into (article 6(2) proviso of the LCITA, article 11-2 (1), (2) first sentence of the LCITA Enforcement Decree). In such cases, the Commissioner of the NTS, when the MAP commences, may attach a condition to the effect that the unilateral APA can be cancelled (article 11-2(2) second sentence of the LCITA Enforcement Decree).

Whenever taxpayers fall under the above-mentioned (ii) or (iii), and thus aim to receive a unilateral APA, they should submit this intention to the Commissioner of the NTS in writing within fifteen days of being served the relevant notice. If an applicant fails to submit this intention in writing, the original APA application will be deemed to have been withdrawn (article 11-2(3) of the LCITA Enforcement Decree). The Commissioner of the NTS, whenever an applicant applies for a unilateral APA, will decide within two years of the application whether to grant the APA (article 11-2(4) of the LCITA Enforcement Decree).

Relevant provisions for the APA by mutual agreement (i.e., bilateral APA) apply *mutatis mutandis* to unilateral APAs in terms of the return of documents submitted, notification of a decision on an APA application, consents, withdrawal of an APA application and effect of modified approval of an APA, etc. (article 11-2(5) of the LCITA Enforcement Decree). Adjustment of income amount after the APA is identical to the case of the APA by mutual agreement (article 11-2(6) of the LCITA Enforcement Decree). The Commissioner of the NTS and the resident, upon approval of a transfer pricing method, must comply with the approved method (article 6(4) of the LCITA).

(vi) Submission of annual reports

A resident, who received a prior approval of the transfer pricing method, should report this on an annual basis to the head of the district tax office within the filing deadline under the IITA and the CITA. In addition, the resident should, within six months of the day following the filing deadline, submit four copies of the annual report to the Commissioner of the NTS, which will include: (i) the premises of the transfer pricing method approved in advance or whether the assumption has been realised; (ii) an arm's length price calculated by the transfer pricing method approved in advance and the process of calculation; (iii) where the actual transaction price differs from the arm's length price, the handling of this difference; and (iv) other matters that were decided to be included in the annual report by the prior approval (article 6(5) of the LCITA, article 12(1) of the LCITA Enforcement Decree). Whenever the Commissioner of the NTS considers additional data is required to consider the annual report, she may issue further requests as to the necessary documents to the resident accordingly (article 12(2) of the LCITA Enforcement Decree).

(vii) Allowing retroactive application of transfer pricing method

Whenever a resident applies for a retroactive application of a transfer pricing method to the taxable year before the period for which approval has been applied for, the Commissioner of the NTS may approve a retroactive application within five years preceding the applied period. However, when a unilateral prior approval has been made, an approval may be granted for a retroactive application within three years preceding the applied period retroactively (article 6(3) of the LCITA). The NTS and the resident, whenever a transfer pricing method is approved, are to comply with this approved method (article 6(4) of the LCITA).

Before 2001, the retroactive application of the transfer pricing method was not allowed at all for either bilateral or unilateral APAs. From 2001, retrospective application for bilateral APAs was allowed; and from 24 May 2006, retrospective application for unilateral APAs was allowed. However, in the case of unilateral APAs, considering that the actual data for prior approval mainly comes from the three years immediately preceding the application and that there is a three–year period for requesting changes, retroactivity is effectively applicable only for those cases in which three years have not passed since the application date.

(viii)   Cancellation of APAs

The Commissioner of the NTS may cancel or withdraw prior approval whenever: (i) an important part of the data is not submitted or is misrepresented in the APA application for the transfer pricing method or in the submission of the resident's annual report; (ii) a resident fails to comply with the content or condition of the APA; (iii) an important part of the condition or assumption that presupposes the calculation of the transfer pricing method approved in advance is not realised; or (iv) changes in the related statutes or tax treaties have made prior approval inappropriate (article 13(1) and (2) of the LCITA Enforcement Decree). The Commissioner of the NTS, when cancelling or withdrawing a prior approval, should immediately notify the related treaty counterpart's competent authorities of this (article 13(4) of the LCITA Enforcement Decree).

The resident, in the event that the circumstances mentioned above in either (iii) or (iv) arise, may apply for a change in the original APA for the remaining period thereafter including the relevant taxable year, within the deadline for filing the final return of tax base and tax amount for the taxable year (article 13(3) first sentence of the LCITA Enforcement Decree). The data to be submitted in relation to the APA application for the transfer pricing method is limited to the amended part (article 13(3) second sentence of the LCITA Enforcement Decree).

(ix)   Utilising APA of treaty counterpart

When a resident or the overseas related party applies to the treaty counterpart's competent authorities for the APA of the transfer pricing method, and when it becomes necessary to commence the MAP with Korea, the resident should immediately apply for the APA of the transfer pricing method to the Commissioner of the NTS (article 14 of the LCITA Enforcement Decree).

11.4.2 *Advance ruling for interpretation of tax laws*

An advance ruling is one in which taxpayers make an inquiry in advance (before the statutory filing deadline) under their real name, regarding tax-related questions in respect of their specific transactions by stating specific facts and the Commissioner of the NTS provides a reply. This 'Q&A' system was introduced on 1 October 2008, based on the NTS Directive 'Regulation for Handling the Tax Law-Interpreting Advance Ruling' (enacted on 1 October 2008 as NTS Directive no. 169viii).[39] Existing Q&As and established rules differ from the tax law-interpreting advance ruling in that: (i) applicants need not specify information as to their identities nor submit the data regarding relevant transactions; (ii) a simple Q&A of the law without assuming a specific transaction is allowed; and (iii) tax authorities may make taxation decisions different from the replies provided under the existing Q&As or established rules.

A law-interpreting advance ruling binds the NTS but not the court.[40] Tax law-interpreting advance rulings are known internationally as advance rulings but are operated somewhat differently from country to country. To a limited extent, Korea's tax law-interpreting advance ruling device is influenced by the advance ruling of the United States, but also fundamentally differs in the sense that Korea's advance ruling carries no force of law nor does it require any payment of fees for the ruling.

In Korea, even before the introduction of the tax law-interpreting advance ruling, in the case of APAs under article 6 of the LCITA or tax treaty-applied prior approvals under article 98-5 of the CITA, taxpayers could inquire, under their real names, to the Commissioner of the NTS about specific transactions and, in return, receive answers. In the case of transfer pricing, APAs acted as an advance dispute resolution method, but the tax law-interpreting advance ruling introduced in 2008 can confirm in advance the legal issues of transfer pricing except for the transfer pricing method, and thus can work as an advance dispute resolution method for non-APA transfer pricing.

---

[39] Tax Law-Interpreting Advance Ruling Regulation (NTS Directive no. 1732) was abolished by the amendment of the Legislative Matters Handling Regulation (NTS Directive no. 180iii) on 15 December 2009. It was combined into the amended Legislative Matters Handling Regulation.

[40] For methods of granting the force of law, see Yun Oh and Jin-Su Kim, 'Ways to Promote Tax Law-Interpreting Advance Rulings' in *Collection of Tax Articles* (International Fiscal Association of Korea, February 2009), vol. 25(1), pp. 152–4.

Tax law-interpreting advance rulings are required to be published in the National Tax Law Information System (article 26(1) of Legislative Matters Handling Regulation). As of July 2011, according to the National Tax Law Information System,[41] there are 203 rulings available for VAT, 96 for corporate income tax, 49 for comprehensive income tax, 18 for international tax, 12 for the Restriction of Special Taxation Act, 6 for securities transaction tax, 3 for stamp tax and 2 for capital gains tax. With regard to international taxation, none of the 18 rulings concerned transfer pricing. The majority of the cases concerned, *inter alia*, whether the income in dispute is domestic-source income or exempt income and how domestic-source income was to be classified.

In contrast, the Q&As on the transfer pricing issues are published in the National Tax Law Information System[42] only in part. There are 2,531 Q&A cases available on international tax, of which twenty-seven involve transfer pricing. Among them, selected cases on the arm's length price are discussed below, one case before and one case after the enactment of the LCITA.

Before the LCITA was enacted, the established rule relating to the arm's length price calculation was laid down in *Guk-i* 46523–98 (18 February 1994). The case arose before the LCITA was enacted. Company A (a parent company in Korea) sold Company B (a wholly-owned US subsidiary of Company A) the entire heavy equipment generators manufactured by Company A at USD$30.00 per unit, lower than its cost of USD$35.53 per unit; and Company B resold it to Company C (an independent company having no shareholding relationship with either Company A or Company B) at USD$31.525 per unit. In this case, the taxpayer's question was whether the price between Company A and Company B could be regarded as fair, and whether the market price adjusted by the amount of its income when the sale price was deemed below the market price could exceed the resale price (in this case, USD $31.525 per unit) which was the price between the independent companies.

The NTS replied:

> 1. Whether the tax burden was unfairly reduced in applying Article 20 of the CITA in connection with the goods' sale transaction to an overseas related party is decided by whether the relevant sale price is below the

---

[41] See taxinfo.nts.go.kr.

[42] As the Q&As are not required to be made public, the actual number of Q&As is likely much greater in practice.

market price under Article 46(2)(4) of the CITA Enforcement Decree.
2. The *resale price method* under Article 46(4)(1)(b) of the CITA Enforcement Decree applies whenever the market price under the *comparable uncontrolled price method* of the item (a) cannot be calculated but the resale price and the ordinary profit can and, in such case, the market price is to be the resale price minus the ordinary profit.

It does not clearly answer what the tax levy would be in that case. That is the limit of the established rule.

The established rule related to the arm's length price calculation after the LCITA was enacted is laid down in *Guk-il* 46017–99 (24 February 1998). On 14 May 1994, Company A (a domestic company invested in by foreign investors in Korea) signed a technical assistance contract in which the technical service fee was calculated as '3% of the net sales, with Company B the parent company of Company A's foreign corporate shareholder which was a technical information provider and licensor of trademarks in Japan. Subsequently, Company A, in an attempt to change the service fee calculation criteria to '1.5% of the gross sales (1% trademark fee + 0.5% technical information fee)', asked whether the royalty calculated by the amended contract could be recognised as tax-deductible expenses.

The NTS's answer was:

> where a foreign-invested company, by contracting with a foreign corporation that is an overseas related party and using reasonable criteria such as sales amount or sales volume, pays the price for the provision of technology and trademark licensing, then this price will be included in the manufacturing cost or tax-deductible expenses but, if the price paid to a foreign corporation that is an overseas related party exceeds the arm's length price, Article 4 of the LCITA was to apply.

Once again, this case does not provide a clear answer as to what the tax levy would be in the relevant case.

In both cases, the tax authority's clear position on whether the taxpayer's transaction price is within the scope of the arm's length price would be calculated by employing an APA or a tax law-interpreting advance ruling.

Other major established rules related to transfer pricing include: (i) where a foreign corporation's domestic branch is deemed a foreign-based exporter's domestic place of business, the domestic branch's overseas related party will be a foreign-based exporter in reporting the transfer pricing method (*Guk-i* 46500-24, 15 January 1998); (ii) regarding the transaction between a domestic parent company and its foreign subsidiary, the amount included in the domestic parent company's gross income due to transfer pricing adjustments, which was booked as capital increase for the same amount, should not be included in the gross income of the taxable year in which the parent company subsequently transfers the shares of the foreign subsidiary (*Guk-jo* 46017-133, 7 August 2001); (iii) the interest-equivalent amount added by article 24(5) of the LCITA falls under the surcharge or double surcharge under article 21 or 22 of the National Tax Collection Act (*Seo-i* 46017-11214, 15 June 2002); (iv) the amount included in the gross income through tax adjustment by the arm's length price is to be deemed an unfairly under-declared amount in the application of the penalty tax on underdeclaration, and the penalty tax is to be calculated accordingly (National Tax 46017-18, 21 January 2003); (v) a guarantee transaction by stand-by letter of credit is a taxable transaction subject to the arm's length price adjustment (Written, Internet and Visiting Counseling Team 2–255, 6 February 2007); (vi) where a foreign subsidiary uses any funds borrowed against a domestic corporation's guarantee for an early payment of the product price to be paid to the domestic corporation, the domestic corporation's provision of the guarantee is subject to tax adjustments according to the arm's length price under article 4 of the LCITA (International Tax Resource Management Office-70, 5 February 2010); among others.

These established rules chiefly concern legal issues of transfer pricing taxation, except for the transfer pricing method. Taxpayers may also be able to solve non-APA transfer pricing issues by using tax law-interpreting advance rulings.

11.5   Administrative appeal procedure and judicial appeal procedure

11.5.1   Administrative appeal procedure

In Korea, tax cases relating to national taxes (including tariffs) must go through the administrative appeal procedure before any tax lawsuits may be filed (article 56(2) of the NTBA, article 120(2) of the Tariff Act).[43] This is called the *doctrine of exhaustion of administrative remedies.*

---

[43] As regards local taxes, one can file a lawsuit without any mandatory administrative appeal procedure. After arts. 78(2) and 81 of the Local Tax Act, requiring the exhaustion of administrative remedies, were held unconstitutional by the Constitutional Court (Constitutional Court Decision of 28 June 2001, 200 *Heonba* 30), the Local Tax Act was amended on 29 December 2001 to delete the two articles.

By contrast, transfer pricing cases are not required to go through any special administrative appeal procedure.

The administrative appeal procedure includes a pre-tax assessment review, post-taxation objection to the tax authority, a request for NTS review,[44] a request for an audit board review, and a request for a tax tribunal ruling.[45] The administrative appeal procedure for national taxes is prescribed in the NTBA.[46] With regard to the national taxes, either a request for review or a request for a ruling may be selected, but one of them must be made before filing lawsuits (articles 55(9) and 56(2) of the NTBA). Whether or not to undergo the pre-tax assessment review or objection depends on the taxpayer (articles 81-15(1) and 55(3) of the NTBA). In principle, filing an objection, request for review or request for ruling does not affect the execution of the relevant tax assessments (article 57 of the NTBA). Even if the taxpayer appeals, a surcharge continues to accumulate in order to prevent abuse of the appeals mechanism. An appeal case concerning a property seized for non-payment of a national tax may not be disposed of by public sale before the decision for the appeal becomes final (article 61(3) main text of the National Tax Collection Act), because if the taxpayer prevails in the appeal procedure, it may be difficult to recover the property.

In administrative appeals, given that the tax authority is barred from proceeding to the next stage of the administrative appeal procedure or judicial procedure when the taxpayer prevails, it is the end of the appeal procedure. However, international tax matters require a high level of expertise and most of these situations typically involve large sums of money; therefore, tax appeals in this area tend typically to proceed to litigation. However, a typical tax litigation may take two to three years, so matters disputed owing to defects of law, among the many other issues concerning the administrative appeal procedure, may be resolved by statutory amendment prior to Supreme Court decisions in the relevant cases. Such legislative improvement can be made because major tax statutes are amended every year in Korea.

---

[44] Tariffs are subject to request for review before the Customs Service.

[45] Regarding the overall tax relief system of Korea, see Sang-guk Han and Hun Park, *Study on the Improvement of Tax Relief System* (Korean Institute of Public Finance, 2005), pp. 23–41. On 29 February 2008, following the above-mentioned report, the National Tax Tribunal under the Ministry of Finance and Economy became an agency under the Prime Minister's Office and the Tax Court took charge of part of the local tax administrative appeal procedure.

[46] Local taxes are covered by the Basic Local Tax Act and tariffs are covered by the Tariff Act.

Relevant statutes sometimes cannot provide solutions for actual cases of transfer pricing despite the LCITA, with regard to cases of international taxation. One of the reasons is that it is difficult to put the process of finding a 'comparable' transaction into statutory language, which is important to transfer pricing.[47] Therefore, although Korea has adopted the civil law system, the reviews, rulings, court decisions, etc., accumulated in the administrative appeal procedure or judicial procedure are important criteria for statute interpretation of transfer pricing provisions.

Important tax court[48] rulings include the following:

1. Foreign as well as domestic transactions may be transactions of comparison (*Guk-sim* 99 *Seo* 2601, 18 September 2000).
2. The Tax authority's calculation of the arm's length price based on non-public or unverified data is against the law (*Guk-sim* 2003 *Jung* 3619, 4 May 2004).
3. In an arm's length price calculation case for which the applicant corporation selected the CUP method and the tax authority selected the transaction of comparison (*Guk-sim* 2006 *Jeon* 1555, 21 September 2007), while the taxpayer and tax authority had no objections to accepting that the CUP was the most reasonable method to employ, as the requesting corporation reported the CUP as its method of calculating the arm's length prices, the tax authority selected the loan transaction by the requesting corporation from bank A as the transaction for comparison as a reasonable transaction for comparison because the requesting corporation did not select a transaction for comparison at all. The Tax Tribunal decided that the arm's length price presented by the tax authority must be seen as a reasonable one, unless the requesting corporation presented evidence to the contrary, as it had been determined that the responsibility to prove had been sufficiently fulfilled looking at the arm's length price calculation method presented by the tax authority, although the tax authority has the responsibility to prove arm's length prices as a general rule.
4. Existing practices which do not reduce the relevant amount when in excess of the arm's length price are against the law (*Jo-sim* 2008 *Seo*

---

[47] Kyung-geun Lee and Beom-Jun Kim, 'Practices and Major Rulings of Transfer Pricing Taxation' (2010) *Monthly Tax* (June) 79.

[48] After being newly established under the name of the National Tax Court under the Ministry of Finance in April 1975, the name was changed to National Tax Tribunal in January 2000. The name was changed to the current Tax Tribunal after the reform of the organisation under the Prime Minister in February 2008.

1588, 16 September 2009). In this case, in relation to the interpretation of article 4 of LCITA which states that 'in case the international trade prices fall short of or exceed the arm's length prices, the standard of assessment and tax amount of a resident can be determined or reassessed based on arm's length prices', the Tax Tribunal decided that the above provision cannot be interpreted as allowing discretion for the inclusion of profits only for the business year in which prices fall short of arm's length prices among many business years, as there may be business years in which prices fell short of arm's length prices and business years in which price exceeded arm's length prices existing at the same time where the tax authority has launched a verification of the adequacy of transfer prices. Accordingly, it was held that the tax authority adjusting the tax (including profits) on the transfer price of the requesting corporation in which the amount fell short of arm's length prices during business year 2003 was legitimate, but that the tax authority not adjusting tax on the amount exceeding arm's length prices during business years 2004–2005 was not legitimate.

11.5.2   Judicial appeal procedure

Korea's judicial procedure is based on a three-instance system: district court, appellate court and the Supreme Court. Korea has no separate tax courts but does have administrative courts[49] handling tax cases as well as other administrative cases. In principle, tax disposition is not discontinued during the administrative litigation and the surcharge continues to accrue even if a lawsuit is filed. There is no special litigation procedure for international tax cases. Regarding transfer pricing, a mutual agreement procedure may be used as a dispute resolution procedure, which proceeds separately from litigation. A lawsuit may still be filed even where a MAP is in progress or has been completed (article 24(1) of the LCITA). However, when there is a final court decision after the MAP is completed and this court decision differs from the mutual agreement, then the mutual agreement is deemed non-existent from the very beginning (article 27(4) of the LCITA).

Korea has a Constitutional Court which is separate from the Supreme Court and handles, *inter alia*, cases of unconstitutional statute review

---

[49] In places other than Seoul, the administrative division of a district court is in charge of such cases.

and constitutional petitions. In the early days of the Constitutional Court, established in 1998, there were several decisions holding tax statutes unconstitutional;[50] however, the LCITA or international tax issues have never been handled by the Constitutional Court.

Although it has not decided many transfer pricing cases, the Supreme Court, having final authority to interpret the law, has created important interpretation criteria for matters that are hitherto not specified in the LCITA, its Enforcement Decree or its Enforcement Rule. Not all Supreme Court decisions are published, but all published decisions and some unpublished ones are posted in full in the Supreme Court's Comprehensive Legal Information Service website.[51] Among others, major decisions on transfer pricing are explored below.

Supreme Court Decision 87 Nu[52] 332, adjudicated on 27 February 1990 (although this concerned a case before article 46(4) of the CITA Enforcement Decree came into force), proposed CUP, RPM and cost plus as the methods of determining market price for the inventory as a matter of statutory interpretation. The Supreme Court held that it could not accept the price which the plaintiff, belonging to a multinational business group, negotiated in importing circuit packs from its affiliate company, as a market price. Its rationale can be summarised as follows. First, the overstatement of the losses and understatement of the profits could easily be accomplished through manipulation of the so-called transfer price, since the usual practice within this particular type of business structure consisting of various affiliated enterprises was to trade with different costs compared to the trading prices had the same transactions been carried out with an independent party. Second, the plaintiffs imported circuit packs from the affiliated enterprise under the contract, according to which the plaintiffs were to receive only 85 per cent of import prices even if they sold unused circuit packs back to the affiliated enterprise. The Supreme Court held that whether the

---

[50] Constitutional Court Decision of 3 September 1990, 89 *Heonga* 95 (principle of priority of national tax under the NTBA); Constitutional Court Decision of 25 February 1992, 90 *Heonga* 69 (conditional gift under the Inheritance Act between spouses or direct ascendants/descendants); and Constitutional Court Decision of 23 July 1992, 90 *Heonba* 2 (period to file administrative lawsuit under the NTBA) are such examples.

[51] See glaw.scourt.go.kr/jbsonw/jbson.do.

[52] In 1998, administrative litigation, including administrative litigation for tax, was changed from the former two-instance system to the current three-instance system. Consequently, the administrative cases of the Supreme Court submitted after 1998 were changed from 'Nu' to 'Du' as regards the indication of case number.

contract price was appropriate must be evaluated against the CUP, RPM, cost plus and other methods ordinarily deemed as methods of approach for market price confirmation in case of multinational affiliated enterprises without the acceptance of 'disposal market price'.

Supreme Court Decision 99 Du 3423 was adjudicated on 23 October 2001 prior to the enactment of the LCITA but after article 46(4) of the CITA Enforcement Decree came into force, which is the first statute of its kind providing for transfer pricing taxation in Korea. This was the first Supreme Court decision on transfer pricing methods after the transfer pricing rule was prescribed by article 46(4) of the CITA Enforcement Decree. The plaintiff had received a supply of movies and videos from its respective foreign related companies and had paid royalties. The tax authority proposed the royalties of such related companies received from independent companies of other countries as a comparable uncontrolled price; the Supreme Court accepted this argument only insofar as the supply of movies was concerned, but denied it for the supply of videos.

More specifically, the plaintiff was a Korean joint investment corporation of a Dutch movie distributor A and video distributor B. The plaintiff was supplied with movie and video works from UIP and CVI established by joint investment of company A and company B in England to pay the royalty. The tax authority calculated the figure which arithmetically averaged the royalty rate which an independent business C, without special relationship distributing movie works of UIP to Hong Kong, paid to UIP and the royalty rate which a company D of Korea without special relationship paid to foreign movie suppliers as the arm's length royalty rate according to the CUP on the royalty paid by the plaintiff. In the case of the videos, on the other hand, the tax authority calculated the figure that arithmetically averaged the royalty rate which an independent business E without special relationship distributing video works of CVI to Taiwan paid to CVI and the royalty rate which a company F of Korea without special relationship paid to foreign movie suppliers as the arm's length royalty rate according to the CUP on the royalty paid by the plaintiff.

The Supreme Court's rationale for the decision on the arm's length royalty rate of the movies was as follows. As the conditions of transactions between company C and UIP were very similar to the case of the plaintiff, such as the quality of product and the royalty payment method, and the difference of transaction conditions based on the difference of geographical or cultural market conditions between Hong Kong and China was also non-existent or negligible, the royalty rate between company C and UIP could be considered the arm's length royalty rate as a comparable uncontrolled price on the royalty paid by the plaintiff without having to adjust for the difference of geographical or cultural market conditions between company C and UIP. On the other hand, as the transaction of company D had differences that could not be overcome with reasonable adjustment in the quality of product (which was the most important factor) as well as differences in the transaction conditions in respect of the royalty payment method, the transaction was regarded as one that could not be considered a comparable transaction with the royalty paid by the plaintiff.

The Supreme Court's rationale for the decision on the arm's length royalty rate of the videos was as follows. Although the video royalty rate between company E of Taiwan and CVI fell under a comparable transaction case on first consideration, as it was similar to the transaction between the plaintiff and CVI in the quality of product and various transaction conditions, the difference of geographical or economic market conditions with respect to cultural standards or living standards had great influence in the decision on the royalty rate and must be adjusted in the case of videos; there was no great difference from the case of the plaintiff in the quality of product so calculating the arithmetic average by adding the royalty rate of domestic company F while without too much difficulty adjusting for the difference of geographical or economic market conditions in royalty payment method, etc. to the royalty rate between company E and CVI was reasonable as the method of adjusting for the difference of geographical or economic market conditions. Therefore, considering the figure after the adjustment as the arm's length royalty rate (market price) on royalty paid was deemed reasonable.

Supreme Court Decision 2008 Du 14364, adjudicated on 11 December 2008, held that, to be able to recognise a foreign special relationship to which the transfer pricing rules apply, the *de facto* control relationship must be 'one in which one party can actually decide all or an important part of the other party's business policy', by using, in addition to what is prescribed in the law, the same method as those prescribed in the law.

Here, the plaintiff operated a wholesale business of importing basic chemical products from a foreign affiliate company to sell these to domestic customers, as it also operated a business manufacturing Methylene Diphenyl Diisocyanate (MDI), the main ingredient of polyurethane, as an enterprise established in Korea by 100 per cent investment of company A, having its headquarters based in the United States. The tax authority regarded this as a purchase of product from the foreign affiliate company in excess of the arm's length price as provided in article 4 of the former LCITA (prior to amendment by Law no. 7956 on 24 May 2006). Six enterprises, B1, B2, B3, B4, B5 and B6, were selected as enterprises for comparison in the process of calculating the arm's length price with the RPM in accordance with article 5(1)(2) of the LCITA. The corporate tax was assessed with transfer pricing income adjustment to the profit calculated on the basis of purchase of product in excess of the arm's length price provided in article 4. B6 was excluded from the enterprises for comparison following a national tax ruling.

The appellate court ruled that the taxation disposal of this case calculating the range of arm's length prices by selecting B1 and B2 as part of the enterprises for comparison was unlawful, given the fact that B1 was in a special relationship with company C because 53 per cent of total purchase amount was purchased from company C, which was a foreign corporation during business year 2003, and that B2 was in a special relationship with company D because its representative director held an additional position as the representative director of company D since March 1998. The Supreme Court overturned the verdict of the appellate court on the grounds that a hearing on whether the relationship between the companies came within 'the case of being able actually to decide all or important part of the business policy by one or other party' ought to have been conducted to determine whether B1 and company C or B2 and company D were to be considered to have enjoyed special relationships.

In Supreme Court Decision 2007 Du 9839, adjudicated on 25 February 2010, the Court held that the transfer pricing method adopted by the tax authority did not fall under the category of 'other methods deemed reasonable considering the transaction's substance and practice'. In this case, the plaintiff, a domestic corporation, had purchased 2 million new shares of a Bermuda corporation B as a special foreign affiliate from a special purpose corporation A as a Luxemburg corporation in July 2000. The tax authority calculated the arm's length price of B's shares by comparing it to two unrelated NASDAQ-listed companies, as these two companies had been the model companies that B had been following in pursuing the goal of becoming a public company through NASDAQ from its inception. However, the Supreme Court did not recognise this price as an arm's length price.

The Supreme Court ruled that the arm's length price calculation method on the 2 million new shares by the tax authority could not be regarded as 'the method deemed reasonable reflecting the actuality and practice of miscellaneous transactions' prescribed in article 4(3) of the former LCITA Enforcement Decree, since US corporations are the companies listed on NASDAQ and a simple comparison of stock prices with B, which was not listed on the NASDAQ market, was not reasonable, and also on the grounds that there was no basis for considering that the stock price declining rate of B and US listed corporations were identical.

11.6 Conclusion

As explained above, Korea's transfer pricing rules were initially introduced by the 1970 Korea–Japan Tax Treaty, in the form of an international tax treaty, and by article 46(4) of the 1988 CITA Enforcement Decree, in the form of a domestic tax statute. These provisions reflected the discussions held at the OECD at the time. The introduction of the transfer pricing rules in Korea's domestic tax statutes in 1988 arose from a specific need to deal with cases of price manipulation by multinational enterprises in their international transactions using overseas related companies. At the time, Korea had begun to open its economy, for instance, by hosting the 1986 Seoul Asian Games and the 1988 Seoul Olympics.

The opening of Korea's economy was accelerated by its joining the OECD in 1996. By that time, the conflict between the United States and the OECD on the profit split method, as a method for determining transfer pricing, had been concluded in 1995 following the publication of the OECD *Transfer Pricing Guidelines for Multinational Enterprise and Tax Administrations*. Under Korea's special circumstances of joining the OECD, the LCITA, a domestic tax statute reflecting the OECD Transfer Pricing Guidelines, was enacted in December 1995. Statutes on transfer pricing taxation were speedily put in place, but difficulties still remained for both the taxpayers and the tax authority in deciding whether a transaction price between related parties ought to be included within the scope of the arm's length price merely by referring to the terms of the relevant statutes.

Under these circumstances, the interpretation and application of statutes to actual transfer pricing cases have sometimes been decided through administrative appeal procedures or judicial procedures. However, the subsequent dispute resolution procedure has failed to sufficiently eliminate taxpayers' concerns over transfer pricing in international transactions. In the long term, matters discussed in the administrative appeal procedure or judicial procedure may be reflected in statutory amendment, even though this may take time. At its core, the taxpayers want to know whether a given transaction price with an overseas related party will be recognised as an arm's length price by the tax authority. In Korea, since its first APA was signed in 1997, the number of APAs has gradually increased. Given the increasing number of international transactions, the positive attitude exhibited by the NTS, the government agency in charge of APAs, has been a hugely positive influence. The APA annual reports, published in both Korean and English since 2008, will further help to enhance and inform on the use of APAs by disclosing this type of information.

Unfortunately, no accurate information is currently available as to how mutual agreements, except for the bilateral APAs, are being reached with regard to determining the arm's length price. In addition, a mutual agreement typically takes a long time to complete and the process of such completion is not straightforward, either. Arbitration clauses introduced by the 2008 amended OECD Model Tax Convention and the 2009 amended OECD Transfer Pricing Taxation Guidelines came to supplement the MAP. In Korea, however, the majority opinion displays a degree of reservation about accepting such arbitration clauses. Considering the specific circumstances under which Korea's LCITA came into effect, which reflected and accommodated the OECD discussions on transfer pricing, this may seem surprising. However, if one takes into account the fact that such arbitration may be seen as a violation of the power of the tax authority, or even the state, the majority's position is understandable. Now that arbitration is adopted by the OECD Transfer Pricing Taxation Guidelines, Korea may, in the long run, adopt arbitration in its amended tax treaties or in its mutual agreements, once sufficient trust in the efficiency of the system *and* trust in the expertise and objectivity of the arbitrators has been cultivated.

Appendix: Questionnaire (Republic of Korea)

1. The structure of the law for solving transfer pricing disputes. *What is the structure of the law of the country for solving transfer pricing disputes? For example, is the mutual agreement procedure (MAP), as regulated in the relevant tax treaty, the standard method for solving transfer pricing disputes?*

The methods of resolving transfer pricing disputes in Korea include MAPs, APAs, the administrative appeal procedure and the judicial procedure.

In Korea, the statutory basis for the MAP already existed in the 1970 Korea–Japan Tax Treaty (Article 20(2)), Korea's first bilateral tax treaty, but MAPs were first used after December 1995 when the LCITA, a separate domestic tax statute on international transactions including the transfer pricing rule, was enacted (article 22 of the LCITA). But Korea has not introduced arbitration in the field of taxes either in tax treaties or domestic statutes as yet.

APAs were introduced by article 6 of the LCITA in December 1995, when the LCITA was enacted, and came into effect in January 1997. The first APA was signed in May 1997.

Neither the administrative appeal procedure nor the judicial procedure is a separate procedure limited to solving matters of transfer pricing, but are rather both a kind of general tax appeal procedure. The administrative appeal procedure includes objection, request for review and request for ruling, and is based on the NTBA. The judicial procedure is based on the Administrative Litigation Act. As regards the administrative appeal procedure for national tax, either the request for review or the request for ruling must be filed before the judicial procedure, as expressly prescribed by the NTBA (article 56(2)).

2. Policy for solving transfer pricing disputes. *Is there a gap between the nominal and effective method for solving transfer pricing disputes in the country? For example, has the country a strategic policy not to enforce the arm's length standard (ALS) for fear of driving foreign direct investment to other competing jurisdictions?*

It is difficult to say that Korea has contradictions between its legal system and actual practice in its procedure for transfer pricing dispute resolution.

Around the time of joining the OECD in 1996, Korea actively reflected the OECD Model Treaty and the OECD Transfer Pricing Guidelines in its amended tax treaties and the LCITA, a domestic tax statute. The NTS is actively enforcing the statutes as well as introducing a legal system of transfer pricing taxation. The NTS is trying to secure its tax power by applying the transfer pricing taxation system to overseas investment of domestic capital as well as to domestic investment of overseas capital.

The government entirely removed the provision that provided an order of priority among the transfer pricing calculation methods on 27 December 2010 and thereby allowed taxpayers to choose the most suitable transfer pricing calculation method. Also, the NTS is encouraging the use of APAs to actively assist prior dispute resolution in transfer pricing. MAPs are not very much used in the area of international tax except for the transfer pricing calculation method. The reason for this, it seems, is not policy reasons of the NTS but the limitations of the MAP itself.

Neither the administrative appeal procedure nor the judicial procedure have any special policy restriction on taxpayers using either procedure.

3. The prevailing dispute resolution method. *Which is the most frequent method for solving transfer pricing disputes in the country? Does it have a positive externality? For example, is the MAP the most frequent method, and if so, to what extent have successful MAPs been used as a proxy for transfer pricing case law? For instance, Procter & Gamble (P&G) obtained a bilateral advance pricing agreement (APA) in Europe, and it was then extended to a third (Asian) country when P&G made this request to the relevant Asian tax authorities.*

APAs are the most frequently used method for resolving transfer pricing disputes in Korea. From 1997 to 2009, 212 applications for APAs were received, of which those for bilateral APAs numbered 116 (55 per cent), exceeding those for unilateral APAs numbering 96 (45 per cent).

A decision in accordance with the APA is one made by the tax authority and does not have the force of law equivalent to case law. This is even more the case for decisions under an APA in which the Korean tax authority is not directly involved. The LCITA provides that where a resident or the overseas related party applies to a treaty counterpart's competent authorities for prior approval of the transfer pricing method, and it is necessary to commence a mutual agreement procedure with Korea, this resident should immediately apply to the Commissioner of the NTS for prior approval of the transfer pricing method (article 14 of the LCITA Enforcement Decree). This means that, in order to utilise the treaty counterpart's prior approval, a certain procedure has to be implemented. It also means that decisions pursuant to the APAs of other countries are not wholly accepted.

On the other hand, the LCITA provides that the result of a mutual agreement can also apply to the transaction with a related party located in countries other than the relevant country for the MAP (article 27-2(1) of the LCITA). This was introduced by the LCITA amendment of 24 May 2006. For an expanded application of the MAP, the person who applied to commence the MAP should apply for an expanded application. Expanding the result of the MAP is allowed, but only in accordance with the statute.[53]

4. Transfer pricing case law. *What is the evolution path of transfer pricing litigation in the country? For example: (i) Is transfer pricing litigation being gradually replaced by either MAPs or APAs, as regulated in the relevant tax treaties? (ii) Are foreign/local transfer pricing precedents and/ or published MAPs increasingly relevant as a source of law for solving transfer pricing disputes?*

In Korea, the administrative appeal procedure or the judicial procedure is not used with any frequency to resolve transfer pricing disputes. There are cases where queries relating to controversial legal issues of transfer pricing are raised in advance in the form of Q&As. The tax law-

---

[53] LCITA, art. 27-2 ('Extended Application, etc. of Terms and Conditions Mutually Agreed'): (1) Upon receiving an application from a person, who had filed an application for the commencement of the mutual agreement procedure after the mutual agreement was concluded, for applying the terms and conditions mutually agreed to transactions between the applicant and a specially related party who resides in any country other than the country bound by the mutual agreement within three years from the date when the notice of conclusion of the mutual agreement is delivered, as prescribed by Presidential Decree, the head of a tax authority or a local government may apply the terms and conditions mutually agreed to the transactions with the specially related party who resides in any country other than a country bound by the mutual agreement, if all the following requirements are met: 1. The transactions are of the same type as the one upon which the terms and conditions were mutually agreed; 2. Taxes have been levied in the same manner as stipulated in the terms and conditions mutually agreed; 3. Other requirements prescribed by Presidential Decree are all met. (2) Article 27 shall apply *mutatis mutandis* to the extended application of the terms and conditions mutually agreed in accordance with paragraph (1) to a specially related party who resides in any country other than the country bound by the mutual agreement.

LCITA, art. 27 ('Enforcement of Terms and Conditions Mutually Agreed'): (1) The Commissioner of the National Tax Service shall, where the mutual agreement procedures are closed, report the terms and conditions mutually agreed to the Minister of Strategy and Finance. (2) The Minister of Strategy and Finance or the Commissioner of the National Tax Service shall, where the mutual agreement procedures are closed, notify the tax authority, head of the local government, Director of the Tax Tribunal, other relevant agencies, and the applicant for a commencement of the mutual agreement procedures of the terms and conditions mutually agreed within 15 days from the day next to the closing date of the mutual agreement procedures. (3) The tax authority or the head of the local government shall make a levying disposition, revised decision and other necessary actions under the tax laws, pursuant to the terms and conditions mutually agreed. (4) Where a final decision is made by a court after the conclusion of the mutual agreement procedures, and the contents of such final decision are different from the terms and conditions mutually agreed, the said mutual agreement shall be deemed non-existent from the beginning.

interpreting advance ruling, a more developed form of the Q&As, was introduced on 1 October 2008 and is expected to help transfer pricing dispute resolution if utilised in the area of transfer pricing. It has not been used as yet, however. Currently, transfer pricing disputes are mainly resolved by using APAs. But the details of MAPs or APAs are not made public so it would be difficult to consider them 'sources of law'.

5. Customary international law and international tax procedure. *Has customary international law been applied in the country to govern the relevant methods for solving transfer pricing disputes (such as the MAP)? For example, has the* OECD *Manual on Effective Mutual Agreement Procedure ('OECD Manual') been deemed customary international tax law in the MAP arena for filling procedural gaps (for example, time limit for implementation of relief where treaties deviate from the OECD Model Tax Convention)?*

In Korea, customary international law in itself is not applied to the methods of resolving transfer pricing disputes. Customary international law can only be applied after introduction into the LCITA by statutory amendment.

The OECD Model Treaty, for the first time in 2005, created a provision limiting the time for commencing the MAP, and Korea enacted the LCITA reflecting this provision. Many of Korea's tax treaties signed earlier, including those with Japan (pre-amendment), United States, United Kingdom, Turkey, Denmark and Brazil, did not have such a time limit. As regards tax treaties with no provision for such a time limit, a three-year period is interpreted to apply pursuant to the LCITA. This interpretation may be allowed because a domestic statute which is *lex posterior* (i.e., a statute enacted later) has priority of application over a tax treaty, apart from the question of recognising customary international law.

6. Procedural setting and strategic interaction. *Does strategic interaction between taxpayers and tax authorities depend on the procedural setting in which they interact when trying to solve transfer pricing disputes? For example, which procedural setting in the country prompts the relevant parties to cooperate with each other the most for solving this sort of dispute, and why?*

In Korea, a MAP can be pursued in parallel with an administrative appeal procedure as well as litigation. From the perspective of taxpayers, there is an incentive to use the MAP in that the positions on transfer pricing by the competent authorities of both countries can be worked out once and for all. As regards the competent authorities, they need taxpayers' cooperation and the LCITA prescribes this as one of taxpayers' duties. The Ministry of Strategy and Finance or the Commissioner of the NTS may request the taxpayer who applied to commence a MAP to submit documents necessary for the MAP (article 26(1) of the LCITA). Where a taxpayer fails to dutifully cooperate in the above-mentioned request for production of documents, the Ministry of Strategy and Finance or the Commissioner of the NTS may end the MAP *ex officio* (article 26(2) of the LCITA). These are provisions to help streamline the MAP procedures.

As regards the administrative appeal procedure and the judicial procedure, the taxpayers and tax authority, as opposing parties, can hardly be expected to cooperate with each other since the right to tax is not subject to settlements or compromises in Korea.

7. The future of transfer pricing disputes resolution.   *Which is the best available proposal in light of the interests of the country for facilitating the global resolution of transfer pricing disputes, and why?*

It is difficult for both taxpayers and the tax authority to decide whether a transaction price is within the scope of the arm's length price. Korea has progressively amended statutes so that taxpayers are allowed to choose freely the most reasonable transfer pricing calculation method. Korea is actively encouraging prior dispute resolution methods through APAs to minimise subsequent disputes regarding the transfer pricing calculation method decided by the taxpayer.

Considering that making a transfer pricing decision is not easy, that a taxpayer should be given maximum discretion in the absence of a tax evasion purpose, and that the predictability of taxes for taxpayers will thus be enhanced, an APA will gain importance as a method of resolving transfer pricing disputes. Due to the limitations and issues surrounding the MAP, provisions for arbitration were included in the amended OECD Model Treaty of 2008 and the amended OECD Transfer Pricing Guidelines of 2009. However, in Korea, it is expected that both taxpayers and the tax authority will actively utilise APAs and MAPs for transfer pricing issues, and the question of whether in the longer term to adopt arbitration according to the global standard is still to be determined.

12

Transfer pricing disputes in Singapore

STEPHEN L. H. PHUA

12.1 Introduction

Up until 2009, there had been frequent lamentations by commentators about the absence of an appropriate provision in Singapore mandating the adoption of arm's length price in related party transactions. Nevertheless, the Inland Revenue Authority of Singapore (IRAS)[1] maintains that all related party transactions must comply with the arm's length standard.[2] Especially in the context of related party transactions that involve at least one foreign entity, the IRAS takes the view that Singapore has always embraced the standard as part of its international obligations embodied in all the comprehensive Double Taxation Agreements (DTAs)[3] that have been concluded with seventy jurisdictions. All these DTAs contain a fairly uniform requirement that mandates compliance with the arm's length standard for determining the payments between associated enterprises as well as payments of interest and royalty income between entities where a special relationship exists.[4]

Notwithstanding the absence of a general provision in the Income Tax Act (ITA),[5] there is a collection of disparate provisions that require some form of market value to be adopted in specific situations where the

---

I am grateful to Danny Quah, my student assistant, for his assistance and comments on an earlier draft.

[1] Inland Revenue Authority of Singapore was formed as a statutory board under the Inland Revenue Authority of Singapore Act, cap. 138A, rev. ed. 1993. IRAS has been conferred with wide-ranging powers to discharge its main function of acting as agent of the government in the administration, assessment, collection and enforcement of income tax, property tax, estate duty, stamp duties, betting and sweepstake duties, private lotteries duty and all other taxes that may be created from time to time.

[2] IRAS Circular, *Transfer Pricing Guidelines*, 23 February 2006, para. 3.1.5.

[3] As at 15 July 2011, sixty-seven of these DTAs are in force.

[4] The Articles in these DTAs are largely similar in scope to the prevailing provisions found in Articles 5, 7, 9, 11 and 12 of the OECD Model Convention on Capital and Income at the time each of the DTAs were concluded.

[5] Cap. 134, rev. ed. 2008.

489

existence of relationships between certain parties are deemed to carry a risk that arrangements could be entered into between them to avoid the incidence of tax that would otherwise have fallen due had the parties dealt at arm's length with one another. Unfortunately, there is no general provision that defines 'related parties' or makes explicit reference to the notion of an arm's length price.

Instead, there are statutory mandates to adopt a 'reasonable' price or an 'open-market' price in specific fact situations where parties to certain relationships are regarded as 'related parties'. These situations include business trusts, exemptions, employment and research and development. They utilise a common theme involving the notion of 'control'. As a general principle, two persons are regarded as being related if they are, directly or indirectly, under the control of a common person or when one person is, directly or indirectly, controlled by the other.[6]

Unfortunately, the ITA does not define what constitutes 'control'. It may be useful to take note of a more detailed definition in the Goods and Services Tax Act (GSTA).[7] In circumstances where an 'open-market value' has to be adopted in the valuation of a supply between 'connected persons', the GSTA deems a person to have control over a company if he exercises or acquires direct or indirect control of a company's affairs. These would include cases where one or more persons have acquired or are entitled to acquire the right to a greater part of the issued shares, voting power, distributable income or assets of a company upon a winding up.

12.2   Economic and institutional context

By several measures, Singapore has been consistently recognised as one of the best cities for operating a business. The World Bank regards it as the world's easiest place to do business.[8] It was placed second for sixteen consecutive years under BERI's rankings for the city with the best investment potential.[9] In international trade and investment, it is ranked first

---

[6] See ITA, ss. 2(3), 13(16).

[7] Goods and Services Act, cap. 117A, rev. ed. 2005, ss.1, 3 and 4, sch. 3.

[8] World Bank, *Doing Business 2010* (World Bank Publications, 2010), p. 4, available at www. doingbusiness.org/documents/fullreport/2010/DB10-full-report.pdf.

[9] Business Environment Risk Intelligence, *BERI Report 2010* (Washington State: BERI, April 2010).

for having the most open economy[10] with the best business environment in the Asia Pacific and worldwide.[11]

The relatively small population of 5 million people generated a gross domestic product (GDP) in excess of S$300 billion in 2010.[12] To overcome the absence of natural resources, it adopted immediately after independence in 1965 an export-driven policy to attract foreign investments to create jobs and transfer skills. Today, it is the base for investments of more than 7,000 multinational corporations (MNCs) from the United States, Japan and Europe. Its strategy to create a competitive and conducive operating environment has succeeded to the extent that international businesses compete in virtually all sectors of the economy.[13] It has become a preferred headquarter location for over 4,000 MNCs, one-third of which are listed on the Fortune 500.[14] More than a few thousand companies from China and India locate some key global functions in Singapore as springboards for global expansion.

A significant degree of credit for the sustained real GDP growth that averaged about 8 per cent per annum since 1965 can be attributed to the success of these policies.[15] In 2010, the manufacturing and service sectors were the twin engines that accounted for 26.6 and 63.6 per cent of the GDP, respectively.[16] In particular, the financial services and trade-related industries are expected to contribute about half of the GDP growth in 2011.[17] As an open economy, Singapore is highly integrated

---

[10] Robert Z. Lawrence, Margareta Drzeniek Hanouz and John Moavenzadeh, *The Global Enabling Trade Report 2010* (World Economic Forum, 2010), p. 9, available at www3. weforum.org/docs/WEF_GlobalEnablingTrade_Report_2010.pdf.

[11] Economist Intelligence Unit, 'Economist Intelligence Unit: Country Forecast', *The Economist* (February 2011), p. 2, available at www.eiu.com/report_dl.asp?issue_id= 1267792511&mode=pdf.

[12] Singapore Department of Statistics, 'Key Demographic Indicators, 1970–2010' (current prices), available at www.singstat.gov.sg/stats/themes/people/popnindicators.pdf. See also Singapore Department of Statistics, 'National Income and Balance of Payments', available at www.singstat.gov.sg/pubn/reference/yos11/statsT-income.pdf.

[13] Angelos M. Venardos (ed.), *World's Leading Financial and Trust Centres* (London: Sweet & Maxwell/Thomson Reuters 2010), p. 1113.

[14] Economic Development Board of Singapore, 'Singapore – Industry Background', available at www.sedb.com/edb/sg/en_uk/index/industry_sectors/professional_services/ industry_background.html.

[15] Singapore Department of Statistics, 'Time Series on GDP at 2005 Market Prices and Real Economic Growth', available at www.singstat.gov.sg/stats/themes/economy/hist/gdp1.html.

[16] Singapore Department of Statistics, 'GDP by Industry', available at www.singstat.gov.sg/ stats/themes/economy/ess/essa11.pdf.

[17] *Ibid.*

into the global economy. It is a strong advocate of free trade and depends on international trade and investment to drive its economic growth. As a percentage of GDP, foreign direct investment (FDI) stood at 177 per cent in 2008, while exports and international trade accounted for 147 and 281 per cent of GDP, respectively, in 2009.[18] Singapore counted Malaysia, the European Union, People's Republic of China, United States and Indonesia as its top five trading partners in 2010.[19] Other significant trading partners in Asia include Hong Kong, Japan, South Korea, Taiwan and Thailand.

The spectacular growth of the Singapore economy can be attributed to its agility in adapting successfully to the changing needs of a dynamic global economy. In a space of less than fifty years, Singapore evolved from a 'port hub in the Straits of Malacca to an international business and financial centre, as well as a cutting-edge manufacturing destination'.[20] A major factor lies in its efforts to globalise the economy.[21] The globalisation initiative may be visualised as two concentric circles: an 'outer globalisation' which focused on attracting high value-added inward investments from developed countries and an 'inner globalisation' which drove mature Singapore companies to invest into promising markets in the region.[22] These efforts paid off handsomely. Singapore continues to register remarkable growth momentum in both FDI into Singapore and direct investment abroad (DIA) into the other regional economies. From 2005 to 2009, FDI grew from S$324 billion to S$530 billion[23] while DIA jumped from S$202 billion to S$340 billion.[24] As the economy has become more highly integrated into the global capital

---

[18] Singapore Department of Statistics, 'Key Demographic Indicators', note 12 above.

[19] Ministry of Trade and Industry, *Economic Survey of Singapore 2010* (Singapore, February 2011), p. iv.

[20] Han Fook Kwang *et al.*, *Lee Kuan Yew: Hard Truths to Keep Singapore Going* (Singapore: Straits Times Press, 2011), p. 138.

[21] In 1993, the then Senior Minister Lee Kuan Yew argued for a new approach that would leverage on the resources and attractiveness of its economic partners to achieve collective competitiveness: see Chan Chin Bock *et al.*, *Heart Work: Stories of How EDB Steered the Singapore Economy from 1961 into the 21st Century* (Singapore: Singapore Economic Development Board and EDB Society, 2002), p. 196.

[22] *Ibid.*

[23] Singapore Department of Statistics, 'Foreign Direct Investment in Singapore by Country/ Region, 2005–2009', available at www.singstat.gov.sg/stats/themes/economy/biz/foreign-investment.pdf.

[24] Singapore Department of Statistics, 'Total Direct Investment Abroad by Country/Region, 2005–2009', available at www.singstat.gov.sg/stats/themes/economy/biz/investmentabroad.pdf.

markets and supply chains, transfer pricing challenges from an increased amount of intra-group trade should take on a greater significance in Singapore in the near future.

12.3.   Legislature framework of transfer pricing

12.3.1   Before 2006: history and legal basis

Related person transactions

The ITA requires certain taxpayers to adopt market values that approximate the arm's length standard in specific transactions. These provisions generally make reference to 'market value', 'open-market price' or the reasonableness of the amount in question.

Residents and non-residents

Section 53(2A) of the ITA permits the Comptroller of Income Tax to make adjustments to the respective shares of gains or profits that arise from a business operation conducted between resident and non-resident parties under certain circumstances. The scope of the subsection is as follows:

> Where a non-resident person carries on business with a resident person and it appears to the Comptroller that owing to the close connection between the resident person and the non-resident person and to the substantial control exercised by the non-resident person over the resident person the course of business between those persons can be so arranged and is so arranged that the business done by the resident person in pursuance of his connection with the non-resident person produces to the resident person either no profits or less than the ordinary profits which might be expected to arise from that business, the non-resident person shall be assessable and chargeable to tax in the name of the resident person as if the resident person were an agent of the non-resident person.

Under the subsection, the Comptroller has to establish that the business between the two persons was conducted in a manner pursuant to an arrangement that is inexplicable by reference to ordinary business dealings except on account of the close connection between them and the substantial control that was exercised by the non-resident person over the resident. Where the business is indeed so arranged to yield little or no profit to the resident person, the non-resident person will be taxable on the deficit between the actual profit and the ordinary profit which would otherwise have accrued to the resident person from that business but for the arrangement. The income of the non-resident person chargeable as such will be assessed in the name of the resident person as if the resident were an agent of the non-resident. Where the true amount of chargeable income of the non-resident could not be readily ascertained, the Comptroller may impute a presumptive gain computed based on a fair and reasonable percentage of the turnover of the business that was executed by the non-resident person through or with the resident person.[25] Section 53(3) states that:

> Where the true amount of the gains or profits of any non-resident person chargeable with tax in the name of a resident person cannot in any case be readily ascertained the Comptroller may, if he thinks fit, assess and charge the non-resident person on a fair and reasonable percentage of the turnover of the business done by the non-resident person through or with the resident person.

The percentage is to be determined in accordance with the nature of the business in each case.[26] In certain situations, a resident person may, upon the submission of satisfactory evidence, apply to the Comptroller for the deemed gain or profit so assessed upon him to be adjusted on the basis of reasonable margins that a non-resident person dealing independently with a resident person might be expected to make in similar circumstances.[27]

Section 53 does not apply to transactions where a non-resident person carries on a business in Singapore through an independent agent or broker.[28] Neither does the presumptive taxation extend to any gain or profit attributable to other transactions between non-residents only because one of the non-resident persons has derived a gain or profit that may be chargeable under section 53.[29]

Section 53(2A)–(6) have not been subject to any judicial pronouncements in Singapore nor any legislative amendment since they first appeared in the first Income Tax Ordinance in 1947.[30] The Income Tax

---

[25] ITA, s.53(3).

[26] *Ibid.* s.53(3A). The percentage as determined by the Comptroller is subject to the usual right of appeal set out in Part XVIII of the ITA.

[27] *Ibid.* s.53(6). This applies to cases in which the goods or produce are manufactured or produced outside Singapore and sold in Singapore by a non-resident person through a Singapore attorney, factor, agent, receiver or manager.

[28] *Ibid.* s.53(4).   [29] *Ibid.* s.53(5).

[30] It was originally found in s.49 of the Income Tax Ordinance, 1947 (No. 39 of 1947). The present form incorporates minor and immaterial updates to cross-referenced

Ordinance 1947 was primarily derived from the Colonial Territories' Model Income Tax Ordinance of 1922.[31] In fact, the history of this section can be traced to section 31 of the UK Finance (No. 2) Act 1915[32] (UK FA 1915). Save for differences that are immaterial to our discussion, the wording of section 53(2A) is identical to section 31(3) of the UK FA 1915. It is therefore instructive to consult the UK jurisprudence on section 31 of the UK FA 1915.

An illustration of its scope and application can be seen in the 1920 decision of *Gillette Safety Razor Ltd* v. *IRC*.[33] Although that case subsequently ended in the High Court as a futile attempt by the UK revenue authority to enlarge the scope of excess profits duty via a statutory reference to section 31 of the UK FA 1915, it nevertheless provides a useful illustration of the potential application to situations within the contemplation of section 53(2A) of the ITA. In *Gillette's* case, the Commissioners found that the US manufacturer had exercised substantial control over the UK taxpayer and that business arrangements had been put in place that resulted in less profit being attributed to the latter than the ordinary profits that were otherwise expected in such transactions. The Commissioners applied section 31 and substituted a gross margin of 12.5 per cent of sales for the 6.37 per cent reported in the accounts.[34]

Dealings in stock-in-trade

There are specific rules that apply to dealings with stock-in-trade belonging to a trade or business. In the ordinary course of business, a trader may reduce his taxable profits by manipulating the prices at

---

section numbers and replacing the words 'colony' and 'Ordinance' with 'Singapore' and 'Act', respectively.

[31] See the Heasman Report, *Income Tax: A Report to Their Excellencies the Governors of the Malayan Union and Singapore, with recommendations, including a draft bill and proposals for administration and staffing* (Kuala Lumpur: Malayan Union Government Press, 1947), published on 19 August 1947. The final Income Tax Ordinance was modified to adopt the recommendations of the *Report of the Joint Committee appointed by the Governors of the Malayan Union and Singapore to consider Mr Heasman's recommendations for the institution of an Income Tax and to report whether, if the policy of Income Tax were adopted, the principles of the legislation, a draft of which is annexed to Mr Heasman's Report, would, in their opinion, be suitable for the purpose* (Kuala Lumpur: Government Press, 1947). See also CCH Asia Pte Ltd, *Singapore Master Tax Guide Manual 2006*, para. 1929. See also Sat Pal Khattar, 'Tax Systems and Laws of Singapore' (1981) MLJ xlvii, xlvii.

[32] Finance (No. 2) Act 1915, 5 & 6 Geo. 5, c. 89, available at www.legislation.gov.uk/ukpga/1915/89/pdfs/ukpga_19150089_en.pdf.

[33] *Gillette Safety Razor Ltd* v. *IRC* [1920] 3 KB 358.

[34] *Ibid.* 367–8. See also J. Tiley (ed.), *Studies in the History of Tax Law* (2004), vol. I, pp. 124–5.

which stock-in-trade is acquired, transferred or sold. Acquisition of stock-in-trade at higher prices than market value or undervaluing them at disposal could secure tax benefits for the taxpayer or any related party that he deals with. As a general rule, the courts have given effect to transactional prices agreed by parties in the course of trade. However, where exceptional grounds exist, the courts have departed from their approach to substitute an agreed transactional price with the market price.

In 1956, the UK House of Lords created a common law rule that requires a trader who appropriates stock from his business for private, personal or other purposes unrelated to that business to account for the value of the appropriated stock at its market price. The rule arose from the decision in *Sharkey* v. *Wernher*.[35] In that case, the taxpayer had transferred five horses from a taxable trade of operating a stud farm to her recreational horse-racing stables that did not constitute a taxable activity. The House of Lords held that a trader who trades with himself or herself is required to account for the market value of any stock-in-trade that is disposed of other than in the normal course of trade.

The rule in *Sharkey* has since been extended beyond self-suppliers. It applies to any non-commercial disposition of any stock-in-trade where the actual consideration, if any, that passed between the parties is other than the market value.[36] When the rule is applied, the market value would have to be adopted by both the seller and the buyer.[37] Nevertheless, if the parties are able to establish that the consideration represents an honest bargain at a fairly negotiated price, the rule does not apply even if the value appears to be undervalued.[38]

However, being a judge-made rule, it is subject to any statutory provision that may direct a different value to be adopted.[39] The ITA contains a provision for the valuation of stock-in-trade disposed of on the discontinuance or transfer of a trade or business. Section 32 provides that:

> (1) In computing for any purpose of this Act the gains or profits of a trade or business which has been discontinued or transferred, any trading

---

[35] *Sharkey* v. *Wernher* (1956) 36 TC 275.

[36] See *Petrotim Securities Ltd* v. *Ayres* (1964) 41 TC 389. *Petrotim* was followed in *Skinner* v. *Berry Head Lands Ltd* [1971] 1 All ER 222; 46 TC 377.

[37] *Ridge Securities Ltd.* v *IRC* [1946] 1 All ER 275.

[38] *Jacgilden* v. *Castle* [1971] Ch. 408.

[39] *Sharkey*'s case was cited with approval in the Singapore High Court decision of *HC and another* v. *Comptroller of Income Tax* [1968–70] SLR(R) 742.

stock belonging to the trade or business at the discontinuance or transfer thereof shall be valued as follows:

(a) in the case of any such trading stock –
    (i) which is sold or transferred for valuable consideration to a person who carries on or intends to carry on a trade or business in Singapore; and
    (ii) the cost whereof may be deducted by the purchaser as an expense in computing for any such purpose the gains or profits of that trade or business, the value thereof shall be taken to be the amount realised on the sale or the value of the consideration given for the transfer; and

(b) in the case of any other such trading stock, the value thereof shall be taken to be the amount which it would have realised if it had been sold in the open market at the discontinuance or transfer of the trade or business.

The only Singapore court decision interpreting section 32 is *HC and another v. Comptroller of Income Tax*.[40] In that case, the taxpayer company had conveyed land pursuant to a voluntary winding up by its parent company as a return of capital *in specie* in consideration of the cancellation of the latter's interests in the whole of the issued capital of the taxpayer amounting to S$1,757,900. As the land was the stock-in-trade of the taxpayer, the question arose as to whether section 32(1)(b) was applicable notwithstanding that no actual sale or transfer had taken place. If it was applicable, the liquidators of the taxpayer company would be required to assign the market value of the land to the transfer. The Singapore High Court, following a UK decision on a provision that was nearly identical to section 32, held that it did apply and that the Comptroller was correct to assess the value of the land as S$2,291,991, representing its market value at the date of discontinuance of the trade.[41]

Employment

In the context of employment remuneration, section 14(2) of the ITA addresses the payment of compensation and remuneration to an employee who is directly or indirectly related to the employer. An employee is deemed to be related if he or she is the spouse or child of the employer or a partner of the firm in which he or she is employed.

---

[40] *Ibid.*

[41] See *Bradshaw v. Blunden* (No. 2) (1958–61) 39 TC 73. Pennycuick J in that case was concerned with s.26 of the UK Finance Act 1938. The wording of s.26 is almost identical to that in s.32 of the ITA.

This section also applies to an employee who is a spouse or child of a person who exercises or is able to exercise control over the company in which the employee is employed. Where section 14(2) applies, the employer is only entitled to deduct any payment made to a related employee to the extent that, in the opinion of the Comptroller, it is a reasonable amount having regard to the services performed by that employee.

Last, there is a provision that prevents an employee and employers from obtaining tax advantages by making excessive mandatory contributions to the Central Provident Fund.[42] Where an employee is employed by two or more employers who are related to each other, the total remuneration paid to the employee will be deemed to have been paid by one employer.[43] One employer is deemed to be related to another when 'one of them, directly or indirectly, has the ability to control the other or where both of them, directly or indirectly, are under the control of a common person'.[44]

Disposals or deemed transfers of capital assets

These provisions are largely confined to cases involving the treatment of capital allowances that have been granted to taxpayers who have incurred capital expenditure on qualifying assets in the course of a trade, business or profession. Two instances will be highlighted. First, a writing-down allowance for capital expenditure incurred in the acquisition of certain intellectual property rights by a person is denied in circumstances where the vendor is a related party who is not subject to tax on the proceeds from the disposal.[45] Second, the disposal of a qualifying asset may result in a balancing allowance or a claw-back depending on the tax-written down value relative to the disposal proceeds. For the purposes of determining the entitlement to further allowances or the liability for any tax claw-back, the valuation for an actual disposal or deemed transfer of any qualifying plant or machinery, industrial building and structure and an indefeasible right of use must

---

[42] Under the Central Provident Fund Act (cap. 36, 2001 rev. ed.) (CPF), the amount of contributions made by employers to the accounts of the employees as prescribed by the CPF are tax exempt in the hands of the employee and deductible by the employer.

[43] Where this occurs, any excess contribution is deemed to be the income of the employee and taxed as such: ITA, s.10C(8).

[44] Ibid. s.10C(9).

[45] Ibid. s.19B(10A). This applies to intellectual property rights created by R & D activities for which deductions have been allowed under ss.14, 14D, 14DA or 14E.

conform with the open-market value.[46] Where the Comptroller is satisfied by reason of the special nature of any plant or machinery that it is not practicable to determine an open-market price, a value that appears to be reasonable in the circumstances may be adopted.

General anti-avoidance rule

The general anti-avoidance provision in the ITA can be found in section 33.[47] Section 33 provides that:

> (1) Where the Comptroller is satisfied that the purpose or effect of any arrangement is directly or indirectly:
>
> (a) to alter the incidence of any tax which is payable by or which would otherwise have been payable by any person;
> (b) to relieve any person from any liability to pay tax or to make a return under this Act; or
> (c) to reduce or avoid any liability imposed or which would otherwise have been imposed on any person by this Act,
>
> the Comptroller may, without prejudice to such validity as it may have in any other respect or for any other purpose, disregard or vary the arrangement and make such adjustments as he considers appropriate, including the computation or recomputation of gains or profits, or the imposition of liability to tax, so as to counteract any tax advantage obtained or obtainable by that person from or under that arrangement.
>
> (2) In this section, 'arrangement' means any scheme, trust, grant, covenant, agreement, disposition, transaction and includes all steps by which it is carried into effect.
> (3) This section shall not apply to:
>
> (a) any arrangement made or entered into before 29 January 1988; or
> (b) any arrangement carried out for *bona fide* commercial reasons and had not as one of its main purposes the avoidance or reduction of tax.

There are only two cases that have invoked the anti-avoidance provisions in the tax statutes. In April 2011, the Singapore Income Tax Board of Review (ITBR) handed down the first judgment on section 33 of the

---

[46] For references in the ITA to 'open-market price', see ss.17(9), 19D(7), 19D(12), 20(1A), 20(5), 20(7), 24(5) and 24(6).
[47] Irving Aw, 'Revisiting the GAAR in Singapore' (2009) *SJLS* 2; Lau Kah Hee, 'Tax Avoidance in Singapore: A Critical Analysis' (2010) *SAcLJ* 11.

ITA in *AQQ* v. *Comptroller of Income Tax.*[48] AQQ, the taxpayer, entered into a complicated cross-jurisdictional financing arrangement with a bank to obtain the benefit of tax credits available to dividends paid under the imputation system.[49] Pursuant to the arrangement, AQQ unsuccessfully claimed a deduction for the substantial interest expense incurred against the dividend income received from its subsidiaries.

Apart from the *AQQ* case, the Singapore High Court had to apply the equivalent anti-avoidance provision in the Stamp Duties Act[50] (SDA) in *UOL Development (Novena) Pte Ltd* v. *Commissioner of Stamp Duties.*[51] The *UOL* case concerned the execution of an *en bloc* acquisition of fifty-three properties by UOL, the taxpayer, via fifty-three separate sale and purchase agreements instead of a single transaction involving the collective sale and purchase of all fifty-three properties. The mode chosen by UOL resulted in relatively significant stamp duty savings. Justice Tan proceeded to apply section 33A of the SDA and held in favour of the Commissioner. The learned Judge found that:

> the plan for 53 separate contracts was mooted for the sole purpose of lessening the stamp duty payable on the *en bloc* sale. There was never any intention to create rights and obligations for the parties concerned other than those envisaged in the invitation to tender. The plan for 53 separate contracts had no sound commercial basis and was so contrived that it was clearly intended to reduce or avoid tax liabilities.[52]

One of the relevant principles that has emerged from these two decisions relates to the scope of Singapore's anti-avoidance provision. The section is not concerned with the motives and subjective intentions of the taxpayer but the objective purpose and effect of the arrangement and the overt acts by which the arrangement was carried into effect. It is not sufficient to invoke the provision if tax avoidance was no more than an incidental purpose or effect. Tax avoidance must be the main purpose for entering into the arrangement. Artificiality and contrivance are strong indicia of unacceptable tax avoidance schemes. Other relevant factors include the roles of the relevant parties, their relationships and the financial impact on the taxpayer.

Despite the clarifications on the interpretation and scope of the anti-avoidance provisions, it remains unclear as to the circumstances

---

[48] [2011] SGITBR 1.
[49] The imputation system was fully abolished from 1 January 2008.
[50] Cap. 312, rev. ed. 2006.   [51] [2008] 1 SLR(R) 126.   [52] *Ibid.* 137–8.

under which a failure to adopt the arm's length standard may be considered to be arbitrary and artificial. IRAS has not formally expressed its view on the applicability of section 33 of the ITA to non-arm's length prices adopted in transactions between related parties. However, some tax commentators appear to share a common opinion that this section may support the basis for the adoption of the arm's length standard.[53] Section 33 has been drafted in very broad terms capable of being applied to a very wide range of transactions. Undoubtedly, there are many flagrant transactions where tax advantages may be obtained through the adoption of artificial prices to achieve favourable allocations of taxable profits between related entities that are inexplicable by reference to the economic risks and substance of the transactions. For example, a lease of a rubber estate by a company to its wholly-owned subsidiary at less than one-tenth of the market rent was held to fall within the scope of a general anti-avoidance provision on the ground that it was not an ordinary transaction entered into in the course of business.[54] The transaction was found to be artificial and disregarded for the purposes of income tax.[55] Alternatively, there could be more nuanced situations where the purpose of tax avoidance is achieved through complex arrangements where the adoption of non-arm's length prices may be an integral part of a contrived transaction.

However, it is also equally clear that the failure to adopt arm's length prices per se in related party transactions or dealings may not invariably constitute an arrangement entered into for the purpose of avoiding tax. For example, the section does not apply where 'any arrangement [is] carried out for *bona fide* commercial reasons and had not one of its main

---

[53] D. Sandison, 'Asia Tax Planning and Compliance in Singapore Commentary' (CCH Asia Pte Ltd), para. SGP 15–150; L. E. Teoh, 'Current Tax Issues relating to Transfer Pricing and the Repatriation of Profits' in *Current Legal Issues in the Internationalization of Business Enterprises*, (Butterworths, 1996), pp. 218–40 and S. Sharma, 'Structuring an Appropriate Transfer Pricing Policy' (2007) 13(6) *Asia-Pacific Tax Bulletin* 460.

[54] *Comptroller of Income Tax* v. *A B Estates* [1967] 1 MLJ 89, 94. The Federal Court of Malaysia was asked to determine if the transaction fell within the scope of the general anti-avoidance provision in s.29 of the Malaysian Income Tax Ordinance 1947. The wording of s.29 is identical to the predecessor of the current s.33 of the ITA. The current s.33 came into force on 29 January 1988 through the Income Tax (Amendment Act) 1988 Act No. 1 of 1988.

[55] In holding that a transaction 'not motivated by economic consideration is unnatural and therefore artificial', the Federal Court of Malaysia cited Lord Denning MR's decision in *Petrotim Securities* with approval: *ibid*. 93.

purposes the avoidance or reduction of tax'.[56] Many independent variables drive the determination of intra-group transfer prices between its members. It may be commercially unsound to imply that it is wholly illegitimate for related persons to take into account regulatory, competitive or strategic issues in setting the prices for the transfer of goods or services between them. Similarly, it may be too simplistic to characterise transactions as being 'purely tax-driven with little or no commercial value or rationale'[57] solely because their transaction prices are at variance with the arm's length standard. On the contrary, a pricing policy actuated by rational commercial bases may, arguably at its worst, be equally consonant with sound commercial strategy as well as tax avoidance.[58] Some other examples and grounds have been offered by other commentators.[59]

Conclusion

While it is true that 'the arm's length principle is adopted by most tax jurisdictions, adopting and complying with this internationally accepted principle ... [provides]... taxpayers and tax authorities ... [with] ... a common basis to deal with related party transactions'.[60] It is worthwhile to point out that the DTA obliges but does not empower a revenue authority to make adjustments to the prices between related party transactions. The provisions in the DTAs merely empower IRAS's desire to enforce the arm's length standard. However, any actual transfer pricing adjustment, whether primary or corresponding, can only be effected by reference to the domestic laws of Singapore.

Although the ITA does not contain any typical provision mandating compliance with the arm's length standard, it would not be entirely correct to maintain that IRAS lacks the requisite domestic legal basis

---

[56] ITA, s.33(3).

[57] These were the words used by the Minister for Finance in his parliamentary speech to describe tax avoidance schemes at the second reading of the Bill that led to the introduction of s.33A of the SDA in 1999. The passage was cited with approval by Justice Tan in *UOL*, note 51, above 137.

[58] See also L. Foo and D. Bell, 'Authorities Take a Closer Interest in Transfer-Pricing Arrangements' (2004) 17 *International Tax Review* (Asia Transfer Pricing Issue) 42.

[59] J. C. See, 'Singapore Transfer Pricing', *International Bureau of Fiscal Documentation*, para. 2.2, p. 4. See also A. Raj and I. Yong, 'Rules Needed to Clarify Transfer Pricing Landscape' (2009) 20(6) *International Tax Review* 77, where the authors argue that the Malaysian Parliament had, directly or indirectly, acknowledged the inadequacies of relying on the general anti-avoidance provision to deal with transfer pricing issues at the time when transfer pricing legislation was introduced in Malaysia on 1 January 2009.

[60] IRAS Circular, *Transfer Pricing Guidelines*, note 2 above, para. 3.1.6(ii).

to uphold its tax treaty obligations. The provisions that deal with those specific circumstances permit IRAS to adjust prices if justified under those limited situations. However, it is submitted that a general statutory power to make additional assessments does not of itself justify a charge on any gain or profit.[61] A valid assessment can only be supported by a liability imposed by clear statutory authority.[62] As Lord Dunedin succinctly puts it in *Whitney* v. *Inland Revenue Commissioners*, '[l]iability does not depend on assessment. That, *ex hypothesi*, has already been fixed'.[63]

12.3.2 After 2006: the rationale for the introduction of domestic transfer pricing legislation

On 23 February 2006, IRAS took the historic step to issue the first set of transfer pricing guidelines that contain an explicit direction for related persons to adopt the arm's length principle as the standard for pricing the transactions with each other. The move came as a surprise to some as it had always been thought that Singapore has little incentive to enforce the arm's length standard. Statistics suggest that this view may not be unfounded. As Figure 12.1 shows, the headline rates started to decline steadily by an average of about 1 per cent per year after 1987 to the current 17 per cent.

Despite the relatively low tax rates, the ratio of total income tax revenues to GDP has remained relatively stable and annual budget surpluses were common. As such, it appeared that a lukewarm approach to the adoption of the arm's length principle had benefited Singapore in the last twenty-five years when it enjoyed a period of fairly sustained growth in GDP[64] (See Figure 12.2).

While is it generally true that financial incentives from aggressive transfer pricing practices are greatest in high tax jurisdictions, it does not follow that low incidence of transfer pricing is associated with low tax burdens. The factors that drive the demand for transfer pricing manipulation are as complex as the

---

[61] See ITA, ss.72 and 74 for such powers. An unquoted source cites an IRAS position that these sections provide a general power to make transfer pricing adjustments: see J. C. See 'Singapore Transfer Pricing', note 59 above, para. 2.2.

[62] *Att.-Gen.* v. *Wiltshire United Diaries* (1921) 37 TLR 884. See J. Tiley, *Revenue Law* (6th edn, Oxford: Hart Publishing, 2008), p. 29

[63] [1926] AC 37, 52.

[64] Except for a few short periods in which the domestic or world economy were in recession.

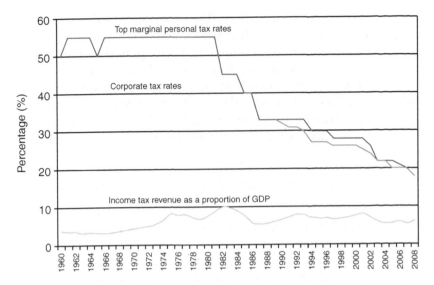

Figure 12.1   Tax rates and tax to GDP

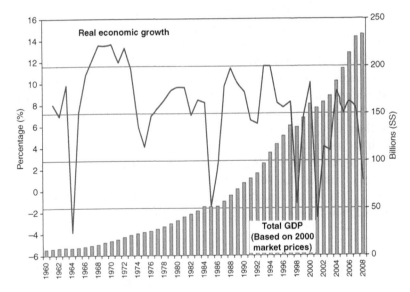

Figure 12.2   GDP growth rates and GDP

policy reasons that justify the imposition of lower tax burdens.[65] Moreover, it is worthwhile to point out that the necessity for the enactment of a transfer pricing provision is not obviated by low tax burdens.

Several reasons may be offered. First, effective tax burdens are relative and can vary significantly across jurisdictions. Second, the actual incidence of tax can be reduced or avoided in many ways. Third, unless the prevalence of tax inducements in capital-importing jurisdictions and the seduction of tax havens diminish significantly, transfer pricing in some form or other will continue to flourish in our highly integrated world economy where a large percentage of the world trade consists of intra-group transactions.[66] As such, it is not surprising that national revenue authorities, irrespective of their domestic tax rates, remain vigilant to changes in the trends in worldwide tax rates and developments in the global supply that may potentially jeopardise their fiscal sustainability.

Perhaps, IRAS deems it fit to strengthen its powers when dealing with related party transactions. While some may regard it as overdue, it is a legitimate exercise of statutory powers by a revenue authority to prioritise the allocation of limited administrative resources to maximise the overall revenue yield. In recent years, the national tax authorities in many leading jurisdictions have strengthened their enforcement powers and raised the penalties for transfer pricing violations. Thus, it is foreseeable that Singapore may have to expend substantially more resources to cope with an increasing volume of transfer pricing reviews and possibly confront inevitable revenue sacrifices for acceding to more requests for corresponding adjustments by global businesses.[67] The assumption that

---

[65] See OECD, *Choosing a Broad Base: Low Rate Approach to Taxation*, OECD Tax Policy Studies No. 19 (OECD Publishing, 2010), p.14.

[66] While there is a dearth of data on intra-firm trade across jurisdictions, the liberalisation of international goods and services in the last two decades has spawned an unprecedented growth in global value chains by MNCs. The growth in the volume of trade has outstripped GDP growth by a factor of 2 in the same period: see OECD, Working Party on International Trade in Goods and Trade in Services Statistics, *Intra-firm Trade: A Work in Progress* (2010), p. 32.

[67] More than two-thirds of the sixty-nine comprehensive DTAs that Singapore has concluded contain the equivalent of Article 9(2) of the OECD Model Convention. Article 9(2) requires a contracting state to make a corresponding adjustment to a taxpayer who has suffered a primary adjustment in the other contracting state to eliminate any unrelieved double taxation. About a quarter of the DTAs that do not contain Article 9(2) are older DTAs concluded before 1980 that were likely to have been based on the 1977 OECD Model Convention.

'MNCs are more likely to place profits into Singapore rather than out of Singapore' may no longer be valid.[68]

Despite the above, any residual uncertainty was eradicated by the promulgation of section 34D of the ITA in 2009.[69] The new section confers on IRAS the full statutory authority to make adjustments to prices in related party transactions that fall short of the arm's length standard. IRAS is no longer confined to the restrictive and limited armoury provided by the narrow provisions discussed above to deal with non-arm's length prices in related party transactions. In any event, most of the modern significant transactions are more likely to fall outside the scope of those limited provisions. Section 34D provides that:

> (1) Where 2 persons are related parties and conditions are made or imposed between the 2 persons in their commercial or financial relations which differ from those which would be made if they were not related parties, then any profits which would, but for those conditions, have accrued to one of the persons, and, by reason of those conditions, have not so accrued, may be included in the profits of that person and taxed in accordance with the provisions of this Act.
>
> (2) Where a person carries on business through a permanent establishment, this section shall apply as if the person and the permanent establishment are 2 separate and distinct persons.
>
> (3) In this section, 'related party' has the same meaning as in section 13(16).

For the purposes of section 34D, the definition of 'related party' as set out in section 13(16) is adopted. Section 13(16) provides that a 'related party' in relation to a person 'means any other person who, directly or indirectly, controls that person, or is controlled, directly or indirectly, by that person, or where he and that other person, directly or indirectly, are under the control of a common person'.

12.3.3   Tax treaty aspects

The scope of the DTAs that Singapore has concluded with the other jurisdictions plays an important role in the transfer pricing framework. First, they form the legal basis for applying domestic transfer pricing

---

[68] See H. K. Liu, 'Transfer Pricing in Singapore', 18 *CCH Tax Briefing* (May–June 2001), p. 6. The text is based on a paper presented at the Regional Conference on Transfer Pricing held in Taipei, Taiwan from 19 to 20 April 2001.

[69] Section 34D was introduced by Income Tax (Amendment) Act, Act No. 27 of 2009 and came into force on 29 December 2009.

rules to transactions between related persons operating in countries with whom Singapore has in force a DTA. Second, the application of domestic transfer pricing rules in this respect would serve to avoid or eliminate any economic double taxation that may arise from a primary adjustment by the other contracting state.

Singapore's DTAs are modelled on the OECD Model Tax Convention. The guidance in the OECD official Commentaries is generally followed.[70] All seventy DTAs contain provisions similar to Articles 7(2), 9(1), 11(6), 12(4) and 25 of the OECD Model Tax Convention.[71] These provisions authorise contracting states to make transfer pricing adjustments to trade and non-trade payments between associated enterprises or between an enterprise and its permanent establishment, interest payments in related party loans, and related party payments of royalty.

12.4 Administrative guidelines

There is no statutory prescription for the adoption of transfer pricing methodologies and parameters to ascertain the acceptable arm's length price in transactions between related persons. Besides the OECD Guidelines,[72] the principal source of guidance on the application of the arm's length principle is contained in the transfer pricing guidelines issued by IRAS. Although they are not as comprehensive as the OECD Guidelines, the IRAS transfer pricing guidelines mirror the principles and positions taken in the OECD Guidelines. As Singapore is not an OECD member, it is not obliged to comply with the OECD Guidelines. However, a voluntary adoption of the OECD Guidelines might be pragmatic as the international businesses community in Singapore may expect IRAS to endorse the international standards that most competent authorities in leading OECD member jurisdictions use.

Starting from February 2006, IRAS issued a series of guidelines on transfer pricing. The first was a main circular entitled *Transfer Pricing*

---

[70] Singapore is not a signatory to the 1969 Vienna Convention on the Law of Treaties, concluded in Vienna on 23 May 1969, entered into force 27 January 1988, 1155 UNTS 331. However, in practice Singapore regards most of the provisions of the Convention, in particular Articles 31 and 32, as reflecting rules of customary international law, which are binding on all states: see the High Court decision in *The 'Sahand' and other applications* [2011] 2 SLR 1093.

[71] Except for the DTA with Taiwan which does not contain the usual Article that deals with interest income.

[72] OECD, *Transfer Pricing Guidelines for Multinational Enterprises and Tax Administrations* (July 2010).

Guidelines[73]('Main Guidelines'). The Main Guidelines were followed shortly by another circular on *Transfer Pricing Consultation* in July 2008. That was swiftly followed by a supplementary circular on *Advance Pricing Arrangements*[74] ('APA Guidelines') in October 2008 and another on *Related Party Loans and Related Party Services*[75] ('RPL and RPS Guidelines') in February 2009.

IRAS has reassured taxpayers that it does not intend to target specific industries even though transfer pricing questionnaires are being sent to selected taxpayers. It has clarified that the exercise is part of environmental research to evaluate the general degree of compliance with a view to help focus its resources on the immediate concerns.[76] Apparently, the goal is to assess the transfer pricing risks of taxpayers, review their documentation standards and recommend changes to mitigate their risks. Logically, it might raise a red flag if the business of a taxpayer possesses any one or more of the following characteristics:[77]

(a) significant volume or percentage of cross-border transactions with related parties;
(b) sustained or inexplicable financial losses in a local member of an otherwise commercially profitable group of global companies;
(c) persistently low profit margins relative to peers operating in similar environments;
(d) the frequent use of intermediaries located in low tax jurisdictions in circumstances that do not fully accord with the true and economic substance of commercial transactions entered into by or between related parties.

12.4.1   Transfer pricing methods

The Main Guidelines restate the five methods that are contained in the OECD Transfer Pricing Guidelines. The more direct traditional transactional methods are:

---

[73] See note 2 above. This and the other circulars cited in this chapter are collectively available at www.iras.gov.sg.
[74] IRAS Supplementary Circular, *Supplementary Administrative Guidance on Advance Pricing Agreements*, 20 October 2008.
[75] IRAS Supplementary e-Tax Guide, *Transfer Pricing Guidelines for Related Party Loans and Related Party Services*, 23 February 2009.
[76] IRAS Circular, *Transfer Pricing Consultation*, 30 July 2008, para. 2.
[77] S. F. Chai, Assistant Commissioner, IRAS, 'Singapore's Approach to Transfer Pricing' (unpublished oral presentation).

(a) comparable uncontrolled price (CUP);
(b) resale price method;
(c) cost plus method.

Where the transactional methods are unsuitable, a taxpayer may rely on the transactional profit methods of:

(d) profit split method;
(e) transactional net margin method (TNMM).

IRAS has expressly stated that it endorses the presumptive best method rule because it is of the view that the reliability of the result produced by any method is dependent on the availability and quality of data as well as the precision of calibrating the comparability factor.[78] Thus, a taxpayer may utilise any one of the five methods as long as he can demonstrate that the chosen method is not only conceptually sound but yields the most accurate result in the circumstances of a given case. This position is now consistent with the recent approach taken by the OECD. The 2010 OECD Guidelines recognise that '[n]o one method is suitable in every possible situation and the applicability of any particular method need not be disproved. The selection of a transfer pricing method always aims at finding the most appropriate method for a particular case.'[79]

As the contents of the Main Guidelines largely reflect the rules articulated in the OECD Guidelines, they will not be repeated here. Instead, two other types of related party transactions will briefly be highlighted as they contain unique rules in the Singapore context. They concern related party loans and related party services. These two cases highlight IRAS's pragmatic approach to transfer pricing benchmarking. The positions adopted by IRAS reflect its appreciation of the need to strike a sensible balance between the value of complying with the arm's length standard in all cases and the attendant high costs of conducting full transfer pricing benchmarking.

12.4.2 Related party loans

There is no safe harbour rule on thin capitalisation in Singapore. For many years, however, IRAS has had a tacit practice of permitting an

---

[78] IRAS Circular, *Transfer Pricing Guidelines*, note 2 above, para. 3.2.5.3.
[79] OECD Transfer Pricing Guidelines, note 72 above, para. 2.2.

interest-free loan between related parties provided that the lender agrees to restrict its claim for deduction to any interest incurred on loans used to fund the interest-free loan. It has now been clarified in its RPL and RPS Guidelines that this practice violates the arm's length principle.[80] While the interest deduction restriction does limit the extent of possible abuse or revenue leakage, it is no substitute for the arm's length principle. In any event, the restriction has no impact in cases where the lenders do not incur any interest expense.

By way of a concession, IRAS will continue to accept interest-free loans between related domestic entities subject to the interest deduction restriction provided that the lender is not in the business of money-lending. In the case of loans between a Singapore entity and a foreign related entity, IRAS offered a two-year transition commencing on 1 January 2009 to allow affected parties more time to restructure their financial arrangements. With effect from 1 January 2011, all interest rates charged on loans between Singapore entities and their related foreign entities must comply with the arm's length price at the time of the indebtedness.

12.4.3   Related party services

Prior to the issuance of the RPL and RPS Guidelines in 2009, IRAS had an established practice of accepting a default 5 per cent mark-up for all related party services irrespective of the nature of the service or the extent of the benefits derived. It has since clarified that the 5 per cent mark-up may not be regarded as a safe harbour rule. Transfer pricing benchmarking is required for the provision of related party services unless they fall within the category of thirteen types of 'routine' services that are commonly provided solely on an intra-group basis.[81] The routine services include management, accounting, auditing, IT support, legal services, payroll and tax. In such cases, IRAS is prepared to accept the current 5 per cent mark-up as a reasonable proxy for the arm's length charge.

Where members of a group deem it mutually beneficial to enter into 'cost-pooling' arrangements to share in the costs of procuring any one or more of the thirteen categories of 'routine' services, IRAS allows a pass-through of costs without the need for a mark-up or transfer pricing

---

[80] RPL and RPS Guidelines, para. 2.1.9.   [81] RPL and RPS Guidelines, Annex A.

analysis if certain conditions are satisfied.[82] In such cases, the service has to be solely provided on an intra-group basis and the aggregate payment for such services does not exceed 15 per cent of the annual expenses of the related entity that provides the service.

12.5 Documentation

Since it is the obligation of the taxpayer to comply with the arm's length principle, he has to discharge the burden of proof that he has undertaken a robust transfer pricing evaluation of the prices adopted in all his related party transactions. In this regard, the most effective demonstration of compliance would be sound documentary evidence to substantiate the claim. Although the ITA and the Main Guidelines do not mandate concurrent submission of documents when tax returns are filed, it is imperative that the internal governance structures provide for contemporaneous documentation and robust record-keeping.

As part of the tax assessment process, IRAS has a general power under section 65 of the ITA to demand documents that fall within the usual record-keeping obligations of a taxpayer.[83] The ITA does not impose specific penalties for the failure to produce adequate transfer pricing documentation in a timely manner. However, the Main Guidelines provide a non-exhaustive list of documents that taxpayers are expected to maintain for all related party transactions. In any event, it was also highlighted that taxpayers should be mindful of different or more stringent documentation and submission requirements which the other jurisdictions in which the taxpayer operates may impose.

12.6 Corresponding adjustments

In the event that a primary adjustment is made in one contracting state, the affected taxpayer would generally expect a corresponding adjustment to be effected by the other contracting state. Of the sixty-nine DTAs that Singapore has concluded, twenty-two of them do not contain the equivalent of Article 9(2) of the OECD Model Tax Convention. Quite a number of these twenty-two DTAs are rather antiquated as some were

---

[82] RPL and RPS Guidelines, para. 3.

[83] With effect from year of assessment (YA) 2008, taxpayers who carry on a trade, business, profession or vocation are required to retain records in safe custody for a period of five years from the YA to which any income relates: s.67 of the ITA.

concluded in the 1970s and 1980s. In the absence of an equivalent to Article 9(2) in a DTA, a contracting state is strictly not obliged to make a corresponding adjustment when the other state makes a primary adjustment. As such, a failure to grant a corresponding adjustment does not amount to 'taxation not in accordance with the provisions' of a DTA that may justify relief through the mutual agreement procedure (MAP) in Article 25(1). As such, any resulting double taxation would remain unrelieved if an appropriate corresponding adjustment is not granted to the affected taxpayer.

However, based on the terms of the Official Commentary to Article 25(1), it is highly improbable that IRAS would deny a corresponding adjustment if it can be proved to its satisfaction that the primary adjustment was arrived at based on the application of sound arm's length methodologies. In any event, no reasonable competent authority would take actions that may be detrimental to the broad objectives of a DTA. It is also inconceivable that the competent authorities would approach such matters without due regard for the comity of nations, especially in cases where reciprocity is the fundamental basis on which bilateral relief is granted and applied. Subject to the merits of each case, it is known that in practice IRAS readily considers corresponding adjustment requests under the MAP Article if the taxpayer meets the standards of regular documentation records expected of a given related party transaction.

12.7   Remedies

12.7.1   Litigation and MAP

In the event that a taxpayer feels aggrieved by, or arising from, any adjustment made by any competent authority, he may seek redress through the usual channels provided by the domestic legal system of a contracting state. Where the actual or potential double taxation arising from the actions of a competent authority is deemed to be contrary to the terms of a DTA, a taxpayer may also resort to an alternative remedy provided by the MAP article in the applicable DTA. All seventy comprehensive DTAs and the seven limited DTAs that Singapore has concluded contain the standard MAP Article. If such a DTA is in force between Singapore and the jurisdiction with which a related party transaction is connected, the MAP is available if one of the affected parties is a resident of Singapore or the other contracting state. All MAP requests should comply with all the applicable procedural requirements set out in the Main Guidelines or DTA.

12.7.2   Advance pricing agreements

Although advance pricing agreements (APAs) are not strictly remedies, they are highly effective for taxpayers who wish to avoid costly and protracted litigation or highly uncertain outcomes in MAP. APAs may be unilateral or bilateral. Unilateral APAs are dealt with under the Advance Ruling procedure provided in section 108 of and Schedule 7 to the ITA.[84] A bilateral APA is implemented under the MAP procedure of a DTA. The APA Guidelines provide detailed guidance on procedural and administrative requirements for filing an APA. While the effective period of coverage of a typical bilateral APA is prospective, IRAS does accept a rollback of up to two years in appropriate cases.

As an indication of its increasing popularity, IRAS completed and documented five unilateral and five bilateral APAs in the financial year ending 31 March 2010.[85] In the preceding financial year, IRAS completed two bilateral APAs and two MAPs.[86] Currently, it is understood that IRAS has nearly twenty ongoing APAs and MAPs at different stages of progress. The time it takes to complete an APA varies according to the facts of each case. On average, each case takes about up to three years to complete.

12.8   Conclusion

It can be seen in the foregoing that the law and practice of transfer pricing is at an emerging and exciting stage. The development of the transfer pricing framework is congruent with the changes in the economic conditions in Singapore and the world over the last fifty years. The absence of enforcement measures and disputes may be readily understood by the unique fiscal conditions under which Singapore operated.

With the rapid developments in the region, the proliferation of tax inducements in capital-importing countries and the trend of falling corporate tax rates, its remains to be seen if Singapore would require a

---

[84] This was introduced by s.44 of Income Tax Amendment Act No. 34 of 2005. It came into force on 1 January 2006.

[85] IRAS *Annual Report 2009/10*, p. 25.   [86] IRAS *Annual Report 2008/09*, p. 27.

more robust transfer pricing framework or adopt more aggressive audit procedures. The outcome would be a function of the future budgetary conditions in Singapore, the demand by taxpayers for aggressive tax planning and the robustness with which other jurisdictions are pursuing transfer pricing audits.

Appendix: Questionnaire (Singapore)

1. The structure of the law for solving transfer pricing disputes. *What is the structure of the law of the country for solving transfer pricing disputes? For example, is the mutual agreement procedure (MAP), as regulated in the relevant tax treaty, the standard method for solving transfer pricing disputes?*

The MAP is incorporated into every DTA that Singapore has concluded with seventy jurisdictions. It is the standard method for addressing transfer pricing issues. Bilateral APAs are dealt with under the MAP and detailed procedural guidelines have been issued by IRAS. Unilateral APAs are dealt with under a statutory framework that applies to advance rulings.

2. Policy for solving transfer pricing disputes. *Is there a gap between the nominal and effective method for solving transfer pricing disputes in the country? For example, has the country a strategic policy not to enforce the arm's length standard (ALS) for fear of driving foreign direct investment to other competing jurisdictions?*

It is too early to predict the robustness with which IRAS will enforce the transfer pricing regulations. The outcome is contingent on the transfer pricing policies adopted by taxpayers. While it is imperative to remain competitive to attract foreign direct investments, it would be difficult for IRAS to offer any strategic value to Singapore by adopting a nominal enforcement of transfer pricing standards without jeopardising its credibility in MAP negotiations. As many of our treaty partners impose stringent, if not aggressive, transfer pricing enforcement, it would be difficult to contemplate that foreign investors would benefit from a divergent approach by Singapore.

3. The prevailing dispute resolution method. *Which is the most frequent method for solving transfer pricing disputes in the country? Does it have a positive externality? For example, is the MAP the most frequent method,*

and if so, to what extent have successful MAPs been used as a proxy for transfer pricing case law? For instance, Procter & Gamble (P&G) obtained a bilateral advance pricing agreement (APA) in Europe, and it was then extended to a third (Asian) country when P&G made this request to the relevant Asian tax authorities.

The MAP and unilateral APAs are the most utilised dispute avoidance and resolution methods in the last few years.

4. Transfer pricing case law. *What is the evolution path of transfer pricing litigation in the country? For example: (i) Is transfer pricing litigation being gradually replaced by either MAPs or APAs, as regulated in the relevant tax treaties? (ii) Are foreign/local transfer pricing precedents and/ or published MAPs increasingly relevant as a source of law for solving transfer pricing disputes?*

As the transfer pricing provision is relatively new, there is no judicial precedent on transfer pricing.

5. Customary international law and international tax procedure. *Has customary international law been applied in the country to govern the relevant methods for solving transfer pricing disputes (such as the MAP)? For example, has the OECD Manual on Effective Mutual Agreement Procedure ('OECD Manual') been deemed customary international tax law in the MAP arena for filling procedural gaps (for example, time limit for implementation of relief where treaties deviate from the OECD Model Tax Convention)?*

IRAS has issued Administrative Guidelines confirming that it adopts the OECD Transfer Pricing Guidelines when addressing transfer pricing issues and disputes. Although Singapore is not a party to the Vienna Convention on the Law of Treaties, it has traditionally accepted the position that the Vienna Convention reflects the customary rules which are applicable to the construction of terms in its treaties.[87] In addition, there is clear statutory basis for the courts to rely on any material that supports the purposive approach in the construction of statutory provisions notwithstanding that the material does not form part of the written law.[88]

---

[87] See untreaty.un.org/cod/avl/ha/vclt/vclt.html.
[88] Interpretation Act, cap. 1, 2002 rev. ed., s. 9A.

6. Procedural setting and strategic interaction. *Does strategic interaction between taxpayers and tax authorities depend on the procedural setting in which they interact when trying to solve transfer pricing disputes? For example, which procedural setting in the country prompts the relevant parties to cooperate with each other the most for solving this sort of dispute, and why?*

As long as taxpayers comply with the procedural and documentation requirements, the most significant incentive for taxpayers to cooperate with IRAS would be the quality of the outcome. Over the last few years, IRAS has allocated more internal resources to transfer pricing issues to enhance the efficiency and effectiveness of resolving disputes through MAP with its treaty-partner countries.

7. The future of transfer pricing disputes resolution. *Which is the best available proposal in light of the interests of the country for facilitating the global resolution of transfer pricing disputes, and why?*

The increasing resort by taxpayers to APAs and MAPs to avoid and resolve transfer pricing disputes is positively encouraged by IRAS. It greatly reduces the time and cost of litigation. However, the burden of compliance costs with both transfer pricing documentation and processes in APA and MAP would continue to pose significant challenges, especially for small and medium enterprises.

PART IV

BRIC Countries

13

Transfer pricing disputes in Brazil

ISABEL CALICH AND JOÃO DÁCIO ROLIM

13.1 Introduction

The objective of this chapter is to discuss the development of transfer pricing legislation in Brazil, analysing the law as well as the leading cases on transfer pricing disputes. It is important to keep in mind that the Brazilian transfer pricing legislation was enacted only in 1996 (Law no. 9.430/96). Since its enactment, there have been significant changes in the Law, fiscal authorities' interpretation and courts' decisions. This signifies that Brazilian transfer pricing rules are evolving gradually. However, there are still significant deviations between the Brazilian transfer pricing law and the arm's length principle. The arguments presented in this chapter will demonstrate that further reforms are necessary if Brazil wants to adopt rules that are closer to the international standard implemented by the OECD's member countries.

This chapter is structured as follows: (i) the economic context; (ii) the historical background of transfer pricing legislation; (iii) the main aspects of the Brazilian transfer pricing legislation; (iv) the domestic approach to transfer pricing disputes; (v) administrative procedures to minimise transfer pricing disputes; (vi) bilateral and multilateral approaches to transfer pricing disputes; (vii) recent developments in the Law; (viii) concluding remarks. Sections 13.3, 13.4 will present the economic context, historical background and the main aspects of the Brazilian transfer pricing legislation. Section 13.5 will present some leading cases on transfer pricing disputes. Sections 13.6 and 13.7 will discuss the administrative procedures adopted to minimise transfer pricing litigation, including the feasibility of adopting the advanced pricing agreement (APA) or implementing a mutual agreement procedure

The authors would like to thank Prof. E. M. Zolt and the participants in the LSE Conference on Transfer Pricing Disputes for helpful discussions and comments on previous drafts. The opinions and errors in the text are entirely the responsibility of the authors.

(MAP) through double taxation conventions (DTCs).[1] Section 13.8 will briefly analyse the recent changes introduced by Provisory Measures no. 472/09 and 478/09 and whether they reduced the gap between the Brazilian legislation and the international standard.[2] Last, in section 13.9, we will conclude by demonstrating the importance of further adjustments in the Brazilian transfer pricing legislation in order to converge to the international standard, i.e. arm's length principle.

13.2   Economic context

Brazil has received in the past years a significant amount of foreign direct investment (FDI). In 2008, the stock of FDI liabilities (inflows) was US $ 287.7 billion, whereas the stock of FDI assets (outflows) was US $ 162.2 billion.[3] Comparing these figures, it becomes clear that Brazil represents a capital importer of FDI, since inward stocks surpass outward stocks.

The significance of these stocks for the Brazilian economy can be better comprehended when compared to the Gross Domestic Product (GDP). In 2008, the Brazilian GDP was $ US 1,236.5 billion. Thus, the inward stock of FDI represented 23 per cent of GDP, while the outward stock corresponded to 13 per cent of GDP.[4]

In relation to tax revenue, Brazilian tax revenue has considerably increased since 1994. Table 13.1 summarises the figures for tax revenue,

---

[1] The income tax (and corporate tax) were implemented in Brazil in 1922 (art. 31 of Law no. 4.625, 31 December 1922). However, the first Income Tax Code was enacted only in 1924 (Decree no. 16.581, 4 September 1924). That is the reason that some books refer to the implementation of the income tax as 1924, but from our perspective the correct date is 1922. Until 1995, the territorial principle was adopted by the Brazilian legislation to tax corporation. Law no. 9.249/95 changed this situation, introducing the worldwide principle to tax foreign income of companies resident in Brazil. Very useful information is available at www.receita.fazenda.gov.br/Memoria/irpf/historia/hist1922a1924.asp. The information is provided by the Brazilian Tax Authority (Receita Federal do Brasil). Information is also available from the period that Brazil was a colony. The term 'double taxation convention' (DTC) is used in the chapter to suggest the same meaning as tax treaty.

[2] In June 2010, Provisory Measure no. 472/09 was converted into Law no. 12.249/10, whereas Provisory Measure no. 478/09 was not voted by the Congress in the legal period required (i.e., 120 days from its publication), losing its effectiveness on 1 June 2010. The changes implemented by Provisory Measure no. 478 are described in this text even though no longer in force in order to demonstrate the flaws of the transfer pricing law recognised by the Executive Power and the direction of the evolving process in the legislation.

[3] IMF, *International Financial Statistics*, Annual Series (August 2010).

[4] It is important to make clear that the stocks are composed not only by economic flows but also by valuations reflecting adjustments in exchange rates, prices, etc.

Table 13.1 *Evolution of Brazilian tax revenue in comparison with OECD tax revenue*[*]

Years	Brazil total tax revenue (1)	Brazil total tax revenue/ GDP (2)	OECD countries total tax revenue/ GDP (average) (3)	Brazil CT & CSLL revenue/Total tax revenue (4)	Brazil other taxes paid by enterprises (PIS/ Pasep+Cofins)/ Total tax revenue (5)	Brazil Enterprises' tax revenue/Total tax revenue (6) =(4)+(5)	OECD countries CT revenue/Total tax revenue (average) (7)
1994	116.39	29.46%	34.78%	7%	12%	19%	8%
1995	197.97	29.95%	34.71%	8%	11%	19%	8%
1996	217.26	28.97%	35.28%	8%	11%	19%	8%
1997	226.62	29.03%	35.41%	8%	10%	18%	9%
1998	224.98	29.73%	35.50%	7%	9%	16%	9%
1999	172.75	32.16%	35.87%	6%	13%	19%	9%
2000	183.17	32.95%	36.00%	7%	13%	21%	10%
2001	175.13	33.84%	35.52%	6%	14%	20%	9%
2002	135.40	35.53%	35.18%	9%	13%	22%	9%
2003	188.07	34.90%	35.14%	9%	13%	22%	9%
2004	239.12	35.91%	35.11%	9%	15.5%	24%	10%
2005	309.58	37.37%	35.68%	10%	14.8%	25%	10%
2006	371.61	33.51%	35.79%	10%	14.2%	24%	11%
2007	509.51	34.72%	35.84%	11%	13.9%	25%	11%
2008	442.62	35.80%	35.70%	12%	14.3%	26%	10%

[*]Columns 1 and 2 show the Brazilian total tax burden. Columns 4 and 5 show the importance of tax revenue derived from taxes on companies' profits and taxes on companies' gross income from sale of goods and services. The sum of columns 4 and 5 provided in column 6 represents the importance of tax revenue (devised from federal direct taxes) collected from enterprises in relation to Brazilian total tax revenue.

comparing the Brazilian figures[5] with the average of OECD countries.[6] All figures are presented in US $ billion.

Columns 1, 2 and 3 of Table 13.1 analyse the total tax revenue of Brazil. They demonstrate that tax revenue has not only increased in absolute figures, but also in comparison to GDP, reaching the average of OECD countries (in 2008, Brazilian tax revenue represented 35.8 per cent of Brazil's GDP, while the average for OECD countries was 35.7 per cent).

Columns 4 to 7 of Table 13.1 provide complementary information about the importance of enterprises on the total amount of tax revenue collected by the government. Column 4 expresses the percentage of tax revenue collected through corporate tax (CT) and social contribution over profits (CSLL)[7] in relation to total tax revenue collected by the Brazilian government. Both taxes are levied on companies' profits. The amount of tax collected through the levy of CT and CSLL is quite similar to the amount of tax collected through the levy of CT in OECD countries in relation to the total amount of tax revenue collected by governments (column 7). However, there are other taxes levied on enterprises by the Brazilian federal government: Cofins and Pis/Pasep.[8] These social contributions are levied on gross income from sale of goods and services. The amount of tax revenue collected through these social contributions over the total amount of tax revenue is provided in column 5. Thus, adding the percentages presented in column 4 (taxes over profits) and 5 (social contributions over gross income) allows us to identify the total tax revenue generated by enterprises in relation to the total amount of tax revenue collected by the Brazilian government. The outcomes of this sum are provided in column 6 (for instance, in 2008, enterprises in Brazil contributed 26 per cent of the total revenue collected by the government). To this extent, it becomes clear that taxation of enterprises is a sensitive issue for the Brazilian government.

Regarding this scenario, in 1999 the tax authority in Brazil published a tax study analysing the importance of large enterprises in the collection

---

[5] Brazil's data provided in Table 13.1 are available at www.receita.fazenda.gov.br/Historico/EstTributarios/Estatisticas/default.htm.

[6] OECD, *Revenue Statistics 1965–2008* (Paris: OECD, 2009).

[7] CT rate is 15 per cent, but there is a supplementary tax of 10 per cent on the amount of profits that exceeds R$20,000 per month. CSLL rate is 9 per cent.

[8] These social contributions can be levied on a cumulative or non-cumulative basis. Cofins rates are 3 per cent (cumulative) and 7.6 per cent (non-cumulative); and Pis/Pasep rates are 0.65 per cent (cumulative) and 1.65 per cent (non-cumulative).

of tax revenue.[9] Even though this study is from 1999, it provides additional arguments to understand the characteristics of the Brazilian tax system and the position of enterprises. The study demonstrated that 44 per cent of total tax revenue[10] administered by the federal tax authority was collected from 550 enterprises (500 non-financial enterprises and 50 financial enterprises), which represented only 0.02 per cent of the total number of enterprises (around 2.9 million) paying federal taxes. The study, therefore, proved that tax revenue collection is concentrated in a few large enterprises. The exact importance of multinationals is not clear in the study. However, assuming that multinationals usually have the profile of large enterprises, the study indirectly provided arguments that support the relevance of these enterprises to the Brazilian economy and, consequently, the necessity to regulate transactions with foreign associated enterprises.

13.3   Historical background of transfer pricing rules

There were two significant changes in the Brazilian tax system in the 1990s: first Brazil moved from territorial taxation of multinational enterprises (MNEs) to worldwide taxation of their income;[11] and second, Brazil enacted its first transfer pricing legislation.[12]

Regarding the first change, until 1995 any foreign income earned by an enterprise (directly through the performance of activities abroad, or indirectly through its associated enterprises) was not taxed in Brazil. The Income Tax Code of 1980, based on the territorial principle, determined that the profit generated by economic activities performed partly in Brazil and partly abroad would only be taxed on the part produced in the country.[13] Law no. 9.249/05 completely changed this scenario by establishing that profits, incomes and capital gains earned abroad were required to be included in the Brazilian tax basis. The new law went

---

[9] Brazilian Federal Tax Authority, *Analysis of tax revenue collected from big enterprises in 1999*, available at www.receita.fazenda.gov.br/Publico/estudotributarios/estatisticas/23ArrecadacaoGrandesEmpresas1999.pdf.

[10] In the referred study, tax revenue collected from enterprises includes only taxes and social contributions which economic burden is attributed to them. It is interesting to note that in Table 13.1 we analysed the percentages in relation to the total tax revenue collected by the Brazilian government, including the federal government, states and municipalities. The study developed in 1999 is focused only on federal tax revenue collected by the federal tax authority.

[11] Law no. 9.249/1995.   [12] Law no. 9.430/1996.   [13] Income Tax Code 1980, art. 268.

further than the worldwide tax principle, since it aimed to reach not only direct income earned abroad by domestic enterprises, but also indirect income earned by Brazilian corporations through associated enterprises established abroad. Thus, the law targeted the tax profits of foreign associated enterprises.[14]

In relation to the second change, until 1996 the international allocation of profits between companies was not controlled by the Brazilian tax authority, only domestic transactions that were considered 'disguised distribution of profits' were controlled. By 'disguised distribution of profits' the legislation means situations in which an enterprise performs a transaction in the domestic market, acting in the interest of the other party rather than its own interest. The objective of the transaction is to transfer taxable income to another person in order to reduce the tax burden of the enterprise. For instance, if the enterprise sells an asset to its individual shareholder for 100, but the asset is valued at 200, the gain will be taxed only when the individual sells the asset to a third person, and the taxation of capital gains by individuals is lower than for enterprises. On the other hand, if the transaction is made between two associated enterprises, the idea that underpins the transaction is to reallocate profits from one company to the other. From a tax perspective this operation makes sense, since in Brazil there are no rules for group taxation, each company represents a taxpayer, it not being possible to aggregate the profits/losses of associated enterprise. Therefore, the artificial allocation of taxable income through the transfer of an undervalued asset can reallocate taxable income that separate taxation of enterprises does not allow.

The legislation prescribes certain conditions to apply the 'disguised distribution of profits' rules: first the other party dealing with the enterprise has to be a related person defined as: (i) individual or corporate shareholder;[15] (ii) manager or director; and (iii) partner or any relative of the persons mentioned in the previous hypotheses; and second, the transaction must be performed not at market value, i.e., prices not established by the market.

As set out below, there are significant deviations between the Brazilian transfer pricing law and the arm's length principle enforced by the

---

[14] A. Xavier, *The Brazilian International Tax Law* (Rio de Janeiro: Forense, 2004), p. 439.

[15] In the case of controlling shareholder, the legislation went further by establishing that in this case even if the transaction was performed with an interposed person, the transaction is disregarded for tax purposes.

OECD. Some deviations can be justified by the domestic legislation as the rules applied to 'disguised distribution of profits'. For instance, the adoption of the concept of related persons in the transfer pricing law rather than the concept of associated enterprises reflects the idea provided in the 'disguised distribution of profits'.

The rules enacted in the 1990s demonstrate the increased importance of foreign income to the Brazilian tax system. Brazil completely changed its position in relation to international taxation by aiming to tax not only income produced in the country but also income produced abroad by resident enterprises.

13.4 Main aspects of the Brazilian transfer pricing legislation

The enactment of the Brazilian transfer pricing legislation aimed to prevent the allocation of taxable income abroad through the manipulation of prices on imports and exports between associated enterprises. Thus, the Brazilian rule intended to combat schemes of tax avoidance and tax fraud. The OECD's transfer pricing rules, on the other hand, aim to identify the price that would be agreed between independent enterprises. Therefore, whereas for the OECD, transfer pricing rules may not be anti-avoidance measures, even though transfer pricing policies may be used for such purposes,[16] Brazil incorporated the transfer pricing rules into its legislation as a mechanism to control mainly artificial tax avoidance schemes. This fact helps in understanding the reason why the Brazilian transfer pricing rules establish a maximum price for deductible expenses on imports and a minimum profit rate on exports performed between associated enterprises.

As discussed below, the Brazilian transfer pricing legislation differs significantly from the international standard, i.e., the arm's length principle adopted by the OECD member countries. A justification for this situation can be understood as an attempt to diminish the administrative and compliance costs involved in the process of determining the arm's length price. Therefore, even though Brazil aimed to adopt the arm's length principle, as set out in the official document that explained the motives of Law no. 9.430/96,[17] when the law was enacted

---

[16] OECD, *Transfer Pricing Guidelines for Multinational Enterprises and Tax Administrations* (Paris: OECD, 2009), p. 25 (OECD TPG).

[17] According to the Exposition of Motives elaborated by the Minister of Finance accompanying the project of transfer pricing law: 'in accordance with the rules adopted by OECD member countries, rules that allow the control of transfer pricing are proposed'.

the policy-maker had to consider some practical limitations of adopting the arm's length principle and opted for a law in which efficiency over-ruled fairness.

The cornerstone aspect of this difference is underpinned by the adoption of presumptions *iuris tantum* by the Brazilian legislation to determine the acceptable price charged between associated enterprises. These presumptions are in fact fixed profit margins included in the methods described in the legislation. This is the reason why the Brazilian legislation does not follow the arm's length principle, since rather than trying to identify the effective price that independent enterprises would adopt, the Brazilian legislation established parameters that work as 'safe harbours'. These fixed profit margins represent limits of tolerance formulated in advance by the Brazilian policy-maker, indicating that actual prices falling within those ranges would not be further investi-gated. The adoption of these rules may be in accordance with the Brazilian interest in preserving efficiency over fairness, even though these fixed profit margins are sometimes arbitrary, not reflecting the varying circumstances involved in each transaction performed between associ-ated enterprises.

In this context, it is possible to understand how the comparability analysis is conducted in the Brazilian transfer pricing legislation. Not all the requirements provided in the OECD TPG for conducting a compar-ability analysis are considered by Brazilian legislation. Brazilian benchmark price restrains itself to adjustments derived from the analysis of the characteristics of the property or services and of contractual terms, such as payment conditions, quantity, obligation of advertisement, promo-tion, costs of guarantee, packing costs, insurance and freight.[18] There is no requirement for applying a functional analysis, considering the economic circumstances of the markets in which the transactions under comparison were performed or the business strategy adopted by the enterprises.[19] As Brazilian legislation aims to identify the benchmark price by its own provisions, the other aspects that guide the application

---

[18] Normative Instruction no. 243/02, art. 8.

[19] There is one specific exception in relation to business strategies, i.e., strategies to compete in new markets. According to this rule even when the average export sales price does not correspond to 90 per cent of the average domestic sales price of the same goods, services or rights in the Brazilian market, the taxpayer does not need to comply with the transfer pricing legislation if the other conditions set out in this rule are fulfilled. Other aspects of business strategy are not treated in the transfer pricing legislation: Normative Instruction no. 243/02, art. 30.

of the arm's length principle are also not considered, such as evaluation of combined transactions; use of arm's length range; use of multiple year data; observation of a situation where the Brazilian enterprise has losses, but the group of enterprises is highly profitable; the existence of intentional set-offs and the effect of government policies.[20]

In relation to the methods to calculate the benchmark price, there are three methods that can be used by taxpayers in Brazil to verify whether the actual transfer price complies with the legislation. These methods correspond to the OECD's comparable uncontrolled price method (CUP),[21] cost plus method[22] and resale price method (RPM).[23] However,

---

[20] There is also an exception in relation to government policies since the Brazilian government has issued some acts (Normative Instructions nos. 602/05, 703/06, 801/07, 898/08) to mitigate the impact of the increased value of the Real (Brazilian currency). Apart from these measures, there is no other provision about the importance of government policy in determining the benchmark price under the transfer pricing legislation.

[21] For import transactions, the comparable independent price (PIC) is the Brazilian equivalent method which is defined as the average price of identical or similar goods, services and rights observed either in the Brazilian market or in a foreign market in buy and sell operations with the same conditions of payment (Law no. 9.430/96, art. 18, I).

For export transactions, the Export Sales Price (PVEx) is the Brazilian equivalent method which is defined as the average price of exports made by the enterprise to unrelated parties or by other exporters of similar or identical goods, services and rights adopting the same conditions of payment during the same fiscal year (Law no. 9.430/96, art. 19, I).

[22] For import transactions, the production cost plus profit method (CPL) is the Brazilian equivalent method which is defined as the average cost to produce identical or similar goods, services or rights in the country where they were originally produced, increased by export taxes and duties plus a fixed profit margin of 20 per cent, calculated over the obtained cost (Law no. 9.430/96, art. 18, III).

For export transactions, the purchase or production cost plus taxes and profit method (CAP) is the Brazilian equivalent method which is defined as the average cost of acquisition or production of exported goods, services or rights increased by taxes charged by the Brazilian tax authority plus a fixed profit margin of 15 per cent, calculated over the total cost plus taxes (Law no. 9.430/96, art. 19, IV).

[23] For import transactions, the resale price less profit method (PRL) is the Brazilian equivalent method which is defined as the average resale price of goods, services or rights imported less unconditional discounts, taxes over sales, commissions, fixed profit margin of 20 or 60 per cent if the imported goods were submitted to any manufacturing process (Law no. 9.430/96, art. 18, II(a)–(d), reflecting changes implemented by Law no. 9.959/00).

For export transactions, the resale price method is the Brazilian equivalent method which is defined as the average sale price of identical or similar goods, services or rights in the country of destination under similar payment conditions excluding the taxes levied and a fixed profit rate of: (i) 15 per cent, calculated by reference to the wholesale price in the country of destination (PVA); or (ii) 30 per cent, calculated by reference to the retail price in the country of destination (PVV) (Law no. 9.430/96, art. 19, II, III).

there are formulas provided in the legislation to apply the cost plus method and RPM in which the composing variables include fixed profit margins.

Notwithstanding the cases where the taxpayer needs to demonstrate that the actual price is in accordance with the benchmark price calculated through the application of fixed profit margins, the transfer pricing regulation has other provisions that allow taxpayers not to apply the transfer pricing rules if certain conditions are fulfilled. For instance, the divergence margin provision allows importers and exporters not to adjust their actual price if the difference between it and the benchmark price is less than 5 per cent.[24] There is also the safe harbour granted only to exporters, which dismisses the necessity of compliance with the legislation when the average export sale price is at least 90 per cent of the average domestic sale price of the same goods, services or rights in the Brazilian market, during the same period and under similar payment conditions.[25]

The Brazilian transfer pricing legislation makes no reference to the possibility of using third methods not set out in the law. This fact and the absence of reference in the Law to the arm's length principle curb the adoption of other methods to demonstrate the benchmark price. Furthermore, there is also a precedent[26] in the Brazilian Taxpayers' Council that expressly rejected the possibility of tax payers using third methods not provided in the Law. This indicates that the transactional profit methods are not accepted by the Brazilian tax authorities. Going further, in the context of the revision of Chapter I-III of the Transfer Pricing Guidelines[27] which changed the status of the transactional profit methods as last resort method to the same level as the traditional methods, the Brazilian legislation moves even further away from the international consensus since the profit split method and the transactional net margin method are acceptable as traditional methods by the OECD member countries, whereas Brazil does not admit of their adoption in any case.

Another peculiar aspect of the Brazilian transfer pricing rules is that there is no provision for the best method approach, or the most appropriate

---

[24] Normative Instruction no. 243/02, art. 38. It is interesting to note that this benefit is not set out in the law. It was introduced by the act issued by the tax authorities.

[25] Law no. 9.430/96, art. 19.   [26] Decision no. 103-22.016.

[27] OECD, *Review of Comparability and of Profit Method: Revision of Chapter I–III of the Transfer Pricing Guidelines* (22 July 2010), available at www.oecd.org/dataoecd/23/12/45763692.pdf.

method, where taxpayers must select the method that is apt to provide the best estimation of an arm's length price.[28] The Brazilian rules allow taxpayers to choose the method that provides the lowest tax burden even if another method would be more adequate to calculate the benchmark price.

There are other deviations in the Brazilian transfer pricing law from the OECD standard. The concept of related persons in the Brazilian transfer pricing law has a broader scope than the concept of associated enterprises set out in Article 9 of the OECD Model Tax Convention, which is adopted in the OECD Transfer Pricing Guidelines,[29] encompassing not only the concept of associated enterprises but also the following situations: (i) an individual or enterprise resident abroad which has a partnership or a joint ownership in Brazil; (ii) an individual resident abroad who is related to a director or shareholder of an enterprise resident in Brazil; (iii) an individual or enterprise which works as exclusive agent in import and export transactions. This suggests that Brazil will apply its transfer pricing rules not only to associated enterprises as defined in Article 9 of the OECD Model Tax Convention, but also to those situations. Thus, in this case, there may be a conflict on the subject aspect of its application. However, in practice, the extended concept of related persons adopted in the Brazilian legislation will not prevail over the concept of associated enterprises provided in a tax treaty, since the Brazilian Tax Code has an express disposition[30] establishing that tax treaties are *lex specialis* that are not overridden by the domestic tax laws.

Another deviation of the Brazilian transfer pricing law is its application to transactions performed between an individual or enterprise resident in Brazil and an individual or enterprise resident in a low tax jurisdiction, even if they are unrelated. The definition of low tax jurisdiction, refers to countries that do not have an income tax or levy an income tax rate less than 20 per cent, as well as to countries that allow secrecy in relation to corporate ownership.[31] In order to facilitate compliance by taxpayers, there is a list of low tax jurisdictions issued by the tax authorities.[32] The transfer pricing rules must also be applied to

---

[28] OECD Transfer Pricing Guidelines, see note 16 above, p. 49.   [29] *Ibid* p. 17.

[30] Brazilian Tax Code, art. 98.   [31] Law no. 9.430/96, art. 24.

[32] The most recent list was published in Normative Instruction no. 1037/10. The list only exemplifies some cases. If other countries present the characteristics set out above, the tax authorities will also apply the tax rules to other low tax jurisdictions even if these

transactions conducted with persons (related or unrelated) resident in countries with preferential tax regimes. The law defines 'preferential tax regimes' as tax systems that have one or more of the following characteristics: (i) has no income tax or levies an income tax rate lower than 20 per cent; (ii) grants fiscal benefits to non-resident taxpayers without requiring substantial economic activity performed in the country; or (iii) grants fiscal benefits to non-resident taxpayers which do not perform any substantial economic activity of any kind.[33] It is worth noting that while the OECD does not distinguish all preferential tax regimes, but only those considered ring-fenced (where resident taxpayers are excluded from the benefits of the regime or where the enterprise qualifying for the regime does not have access to the domestic market),[34] the Brazilian transfer pricing rules apply not only to ring-fenced regimes, but also to those regimes that impose an income tax rate below 20 per cent.

Considering the difficulties in applying the traditional methods to financial transactions and to intangible assets, there are special rules on interest on debt, royalties and technical assistance paid to foreign related persons. Until 2009, interest on loans contracted with related persons and fully registered at the Brazilian Central Bank (Bacen) were not subjected to the transfer pricing rules.[35] Interest on loans contracted with related persons not registered at the Bacen had a maximum value for deduction as expenses that corresponded to the interest rate equal to the Libor dollar rate for six-month loans plus 3 per cent per year. The amount of interest that exceeded this limit could not be deductible as expenses. The same rule applies to loans in which the Brazilian party was the lender. In these cases, if the loan were not registered at the Bacen, the lender would have to recognise as income at least the interest calculated by Libor dollar rate for six-month loans plus 3 per cent per year.

---

countries were not included in the list issued by them. To this extent, the list does not exhaust the cases; it only provides a preliminary set of countries to orient taxpayers.

[33] Law no. 9.430/96, art. 24-1A. The commentary in the previous footnote also applies to preferred tax regimes, i.e., there is a list issued by the tax authorities to guide taxpayers to identify these regimes. However, other regimes not included in the list can be treated by the tax authorities as 'preferred tax regimes' if the general characteristics that define them are identified.

[34] OECD, *The OECD's Project on Harmful Tax Practices Consolidated Application Note: Guidance in applying the 1998 Report to Preferential Tax Regimes*, available at www.oecd. org/tax/harmfultaxpractices/30901132.pdf.

[35] As discussed next, there were major changes introduced by Provisory Measure no. 472/09 which was converted into Law no. 12.249/10.

In relation to royalties and technical, scientific or administrative assistance paid to foreign related persons, the transfer pricing law expressly excluded them from its scope.[36] The applicable legislation was developed in the 1960s, having no relationship at all with the arm's length principle. According to this legislation, there can only be deducted as expenses a fixed percentage determined by the Brazilian Ministry of Finance. In the case of royalties the percentage is 5 per cent of the related revenue, whereas in the case of trademarks it is 1 per cent. These percentages are arbitrary disregarding the specific characteristics of each transaction and treating all of them in the same way.

Last, regarding the rigid aspects of the Brazilian transfer pricing rules and their narrow focus on particular characteristics of transactions performed between related persons, the rules cannot identify and take into account transactions performed with third parties that might affect a series of transactions as a whole performed between associated enterprises. For instance, the case where an enterprise (A) takes out a loan with an independent person (e.g., a bank), but this loan was only offered because there is an associated enterprise (B) acting as a guarantor.

The deviations highlighted in this section evidence the necessity for mechanisms to solve potential conflicts generated by the Brazilian transfer pricing rules. Two types of conflicts may occur: (i) domestic conflicts involving Brazilian taxpayers and local tax authorities; and (ii) international conflicts arising from the interaction of Brazilian transfer pricing law with other countries' transfer pricing rules, creating double taxation situations. All these situations are discussed in the following sections.

13.5 Transfer pricing disputes: domestic approaches

In recent years, there have been important decisions on transfer pricing cases in the administrative courts.[37] Judicial courts were not involved since most cases derived from administrative procedures conducted by tax authorities that culminated with the issue of a notice of tax assessment. According to the administrative procedure, taxpayers can present

---

[36] Law no. 9.430/96, art. 18 [9].

[37] The Administrative Taxpayers' Council is an administrative body which is part of the structure of the Ministry of Finance. In 2009, there were significant changes in the administrative instance and the designation of this court changed to Administrative Council of Tax Appeals (Portaria no. 256/09). Due to the fact that most decisions analysed in this section were made before 2009, we will use the old designation in this chapter.

a defence to the notice of tax assessment, which is then examined by an administrative judge. If not satisfied by the judge's decision, taxpayers can appeal to the Administrative Taxpayers' Council. There is a further administrative court to which taxpayers or the tax authority can appeal, the Superior Chamber of Tax Appeals; however, there are certain conditions that need to be fulfilled in order to appeal to this court.[38] Once the administrative instance is completed, the taxpayer can appeal further to the judicial instance on the grounds that the final decision of the administrative instance was not satisfactory. In practice, however, most cases have finished at the administrative instance.

Table 13.2 synthesises the main information on the final decisions of the administrative instance, i.e., the Administrative Taxpayers' Council.

Most cases set out in Table 13.2 involved the pharmaceutical and chemical industries. The years under assessment started in 1997 (the year that the transfer pricing Law entered in force) and the administrative procedure took between five and eight years to reach a final decision. Most decisions were in favour of taxpayers and, consequently, the tax authority appealed to the Superior Chamber of Tax Appeals. However, in most cases the Superior Chamber did not reverse the decision, refusing the appeal filed by the tax authorities.[39] This fact helps to explain why there has not been a significant number of cases in the judicial courts involving transfer pricing disputes. The preference for the administrative instance is also supported by the fact that it has a lower cost to taxpayers and the final decision can be reached in a shorter period of time than the judicial procedure, even though the data demonstrate that it took more than five years on average to resolve a transfer pricing litigation at the administrative instance. Nevertheless, taxpayers could also access judicial courts to determine issues that the administrative instance has no jurisdiction to examine, such as the constitutionality of the law.

Table 13.2 also makes clear that most cases of transfer pricing issues involved the discussion of domestic aspects of the law, including

---

[38] It is interesting to note that before 2009, taxpayers could only appeal to this Superior Chamber if there were precedents interpreting the law in their favour; whereas the tax authority could appeal not only in this case but also when the decision was not unanimous or against the law or against any proof presented in the administrative process. Currently, both taxpayer and tax authority can only appeal to the Superior Chamber if there are precedents interpreting the law in a different way. The right to appeal is therefore fairer nowadays.

[39] Regarding the cases set out in Table 13.2, the tax authority appealed in seven cases. The appeals were denied in six cases.

Table 13.2 *Administrative Taxpayers' Council final decisions*

Decision number	Main issue	Taxpayer	Fiscal year under dispute	Year of decision	Decision in favour of
101-97.102	Application of the RPM method set out in the transfer pricing law and restrictions created by tax authority's act	Pharmaceutical industry	1999	2009	Taxpayer
101-96.665	Application of the RPM method. Relationship between Article 9 of the Brazil–Germany DTC and the transfer pricing methods set out in the domestic legislation	Pharmaceutical industry	1997	2008	In part taxpayer
101-96.675	Application of the CUP method	Pharmaceutical industry	1998	2008	Taxpayer
101-96.677	Application of the CUP method	Film industry	2000	2008	Taxpayer
101-96.682	Application of the RPM method set out in the transfer pricing law and restrictions created by tax authority's act	Pharmaceutical industry	1998	2008	Taxpayer
105-17.077	Correct application of the transfer pricing methods set out in the domestic law. Necessity of inputting the values of freight, insurance and import duties in the benchmark price	Chemical industry	1998	2008	Tax authority
108-09.551	Application of the RPM method set out in the transfer pricing law and restrictions created by tax authority's act	Pharmaceutical industry	2000	2008	Taxpayer

Table 13.2 (*cont.*)

Decision number	Main issue	Taxpayer	Fiscal year under dispute	Year of decision	Decision in favour of
105–16.711	Taxpayer has the burden of proof to demonstrate that the actual price is in accordance with the benchmark price. Procedural aspects of calculating the benchmark price through the CUP and RPM methods	Chemical industry	2000	2007	In part to taxpayer
107–08.881	Procedural aspects to determine the benchmark price	Chemical industry	1999	2007	Tax authority
101–95.499	Existence of an independent third person between the associated enterprises	Automobile industry	1998	2006	Taxpayer
101–95.526	Application of the RPM method provided in the transfer pricing law and restrictions created by tax authority's act	Pharmaceutical industry	1999	2006	Taxpayer
101–94.859	Application of the RPM method provided in the transfer pricing law and restrictions created by tax authority's act	Pharmaceutical industry	1998	2005	Taxpayer
101–94.888	Application of the RPM method provided in the transfer pricing law and restrictions created by tax authority's act	Pharmaceutical industry	1997 and 1998	2005	Taxpayer

Table 13.2 (*cont.*)

Decision number	Main issue	Taxpayer	Fiscal year under dispute	Year of decision	Decision in favour of
101-95.107	Application of the RPM method set out in the transfer pricing law and restrictions created by tax authority's act	Pharmaceutical industry	1998	2005	Taxpayer
101-95.211	Deduction of expenses from the income tax bases in conflict with the transfer pricing rules	Packing industry	1997	2005	Tax authority
103-21.859	Application of the RPM method set out in the transfer pricing law and restrictions created by tax authority's act. Conflict between Article 9 of Brazil–Germany DTC and the domestic transfer pricing methods	Pharmaceutical industry	1997 and 1998	2005	Taxpayer
103-22.016	Application of third methods not defined in the domestic law according to the Brazil–Belgium DTC	Pharmaceutical industry	1997 and 1998	2005	In part taxpayer
103-22.017	Application of the PIC method. Procedure adopted by the tax authority to calculate the benchmark price when the taxpayer did not	Chemical industry	1998 and 1999	2005	Taxpayer
103-22.125	Application of the RPM method set out in the transfer pricing law and restrictions created by tax authority's act	Chemical industry	1998	2005	Tax authority

application of the methods, burden of proof and the interpretation of the law adopted by the tax authority. However, in order to reach their final decision, the judges at the administrative instance needed to develop a line of reasoning in which they examined the importance of the OECD's guidelines on transfer pricing rules as well as the potential conflict between Article 9 of double tax conventions following the OECD Model Convention and the methods to calculate the benchmark price provided by domestic law.

To this extent, the decisions contributed to a better understanding of the relationship between the Brazilian transfer pricing rules and the international standard established by the OECD. Brazil is not a member of the OECD and there is a grey area as to whether the OECD's understandings could be adopted to fill the gaps or even help to interpret the Brazilian legislation.

In 2005, decisions were reached by the Administrative Taxpayers' Council that significantly contributed to a better understanding on how the international standard is relevant to the application of the Brazilian transfer pricing rules. The first case[40] involved a pharmaceutical company which contested the decision reached by the first instance judge that prohibited the application of the RPM method set out in the transfer pricing law to imported goods that were further manufactured in Brazil before resale, based on an administrative act issued by the tax authority. The Administrative Taxpayers' Council reached a decision in favour of the taxpayer, revising the conclusion of the first instance judge. The Council recognised that an administrative act could not restrict the taxpayer's ability to adopt any transfer pricing method as provided in the law to calculate the benchmark price. To reach this conclusion, the Council recognised the OECD's principles and recommendations as a secondary source of law. To this extent, the Council emphasised that according to the OECD's Commentaries, the RPM method is not the most appropriate method when companies import raw material to manufacture it. However, the OECD's guidelines, as a secondary source of law, could not overrule the domestic tax law, which established that the taxpayer could choose any transfer pricing method provided by law which results in the lowest tax burden. The only requirement of the law is that taxpayers need to prove the benchmark price with current documentation.[41]

---

[40] Decision no. 101-94.888.

[41] The problem is that the legislation limits in a considerable way the use of proofs by taxpayers.

Thus, according to this decision, even when the Brazilian transfer pricing law deviates from the arm's length principle and other OECD recommendations, the domestic law should prevail. There is only one exception, i.e., when the domestic law conflicts with a provision established in a tax treaty. This exception is further discussed in relation to the next decision.

The second case[42] also involved a pharmaceutical company and the main debate referred to the limitations imposed by the tax authority's administrative act on the taxpayer's ability to choose the transfer pricing method to calculate the benchmark price. The Administrative Taxpayers' Council revised the single judge's decision and recognised that the administrative act had abusively restricted the use of the resale price method by the taxpayer. Because the parties involved were resident in Brazil and in Germany, the DTC agreed between these two countries would be applicable.[43] The Council had, therefore, also to examine the relationship between Article 9 of the Brazil–Germany DTC and the transfer pricing methods established in Brazilian domestic law. First, the judges of the Administrative Taxpayers' Council pointed out that according to the National Tax Code,[44] a tax treaty overrides domestic law, which suggested that the substance of Article 9 prevailed over domestic provisions that conflict with its content. Brazilian transfer pricing rules differ from the OECD standard. However, the judges considered the differences only partial since the arm's length principle was not rejected by the law, but was merely adapted to the Brazilian tax system. Following this line of reasoning, the Administrative Council held that the Brazilian transfer pricing methods did not conflict with the Brazil–Germany DTC. The Council also alleged that the definition of the transfer pricing methods was left for the domestic legislation of the source country applying the treaty. Based on these arguments, the Administrative Council concluded that there was no conflict between the application of the Brazilian transfer pricing methods and Article 9 of the Brazil–Germany DTC.

From a critical perspective, the main argument that sustained the application of the Brazilian transfer pricing methods even when there was a concluded DTC following the OECD Model Convention was the understanding that Brazilian law did not reject the arm's length principle, but only adapted its application to the Brazilian tax system.

---

[42] Decision no. 103-21.859.

[43] The Brazil–Germany DTC was terminated in 2005 and lost its efficacy in January 2006.

[44] National Tax Code, art. 98.

This line of reasoning may artificially circumvent the application of tax treaties. If the Council had recognised the incompatibility between the Brazilian transfer pricing methods and the arm's length principle, it would have not been able to reconcile Article 9 of the Brazil–Germany DTC with Brazilian transfer pricing methods. In theory, this hypothesis would lead to the situation in which the Brazilian methods could not be applied when there was a DTC in accordance with the OECD Model Convention, since the fact that the methods did not reflect the arm's length principle would preclude their application.

The third case[45] also involved a pharmaceutical company and the main issue debated referred to the possibility of the taxpayer applying a fourth method not set out in the domestic legislation to calculate the benchmark price when the other three methods could not be used. The Brazilian taxpayer had adopted the transactional net margin method (TNMM) and the Brazilian tax authority disregarded it based on the legal argument that this method was not allowed. The first instance judge did not allow the application of a fourth method and the taxpayer appealed to the Administrative Taxpayers' Council to enforce its rights. The taxpayer emphasised in his appeal to the Council that the adoption of a fourth method needed to be contemplated under the Belgium–Brazil DTC, since the parties involved were resident in these countries. In considering the taxpayer's position, the Council developed the following argument: first, it recognised the fact that a tax treaty prevails over domestic law in Brazil; second, it argued that the OECD's guidelines were only a secondary source of law, not binding on the Brazilian tax authority because Brazil was not a member of the OECD; third, the administrative tribunal recognised the gap between the Brazilian transfer pricing rules and the international standard adopted by the OECD member countries; fourth, the administrative judges argued that the fact that the OECD members accepted methods other than the traditional ones, such as the TNMM, did not interfere with the Brazilian law, which clearly established that the only methods accepted were the CUP, cost plus and RPM; fifth, the administrative court concluded that there was no conflict with Article 9 of the Belgium–Brazilian DTC, since the methods were not defined in that Article, being left for the domestic legislation of the country applying the treaty to define them. In sum, the understanding of the Council that there was no conflict between Article 9

---

[45] Decision no. 103-22.016.

and the methods adopted in Brazil, added to the argument that the OECD's guidelines were only a secondary source of law, allowed them to conclude that in Brazil the adoption of other methods than those provided in the law is not permitted (Law no. 9.430/96 and its amendments).

In 2008, the Administrative Taxpayers' Council reached another decision[46] analysing the relationship between Article 9 of the Brazil–Germany DTC and the domestic legislation on transfer pricing. In this case, the same pharmaceutical enterprise as in decision no. 103-21.859 was involved and the main debate focused on the discrepancies between the transfer pricing methods established by the domestic legislation and the arm's length principle provided in Article 9 of the Brazil–Germany DTC. The taxpayer alleged that the Brazilian transfer pricing law did not prohibit the adoption of the basket approach. In fact, the Brazilian transfer pricing law was not clear about this aspect, but there was an administrative regulation that expressly prohibited its adoption. The taxpayer, therefore, appealed to the Administrative Taxpayers' Council arguing for the possibility of applying the basket approach since the restriction was implemented only by an administrative act, which overruled Article 9 of the Brazil–Germany DTC.

The judges followed the precedent cases of 2005 and recognised the gap between the Brazilian transfer pricing rules and the OECD's approach. In relation to the Brazil–Germany DTC, the judges emphasised the fact that the DTC incorporated only Article 9(1) of the OECD Model Convention, leaving outside of its scope Article 9(2) which deals with adjustments required to avoid double taxation that might arise after a contracting state adjusted the profit of an associate enterprise to reflect the arm's length price. The judges interpreted the absence of Article 9(2) as the possibility of applying domestic legislation to calculate the benchmark price without conflict with Article 9. In other words, the absence of coordination between the adjustments applied by countries in which the associated enterprises were resident was considered the fundamental issue that allowed the Brazilian methods to be applied without further consequences. In our opinion, however, this interpretation is difficult to be sustained, since it is Article 9(1) that provides that the only adjustments allowed are the ones according to the arm's length principle. Therefore, the cornerstone argument that allows the application of the Brazilian transfer pricing methods (including its refusal of the basket

---

[46] Decision no. 101-96.665.

approach) under a DTC following the OECD Model Convention is the fact that the arm's length principle is respected under the domestic legislation. The recognition of the adaptation rather than the rejection of the arm's length principle is in fact the true argument that could sustain the application of the Brazilian transfer pricing methods under the Brazil–Germany DTC.

Specifically in relation to the possibility of applying the basket approach, the administrative judges understood that the acceptance by the OECD of this method did not interfere with the Brazilian legislation on transfer pricing since Brazil was not a member of the OECD and its guidelines were not binding. Furthermore, the fact that the transfer pricing law was not clear could not lead to the conclusion that the administrative act that prohibited the adoption of this approach over-extended its function. In this case, the administrative act only helped to apply a concept that was not clear in the law. It did not create a new provision, which might conflict with the law.

The content of the main decisions reached by the Administrative Taxpayers' Council have contributed to a better understanding of the relationship between the Brazilian transfer pricing rules and the international standard followed by OECD member countries.[47] Even though Brazil is not a member of the OECD, the administrative transfer pricing decisions made constant reference to the OECD's recommendations and, consequently, to the arm's length principle. From this analysis, it became clear that the reference to the OECD's recommendations is related to the application of the domestic Brazilian transfer pricing methods rather than with other aspects of the law.[48] Nevertheless, the OECD's recommendations were admitted as a secondary source of law.

Another important aspect raised by the decisions is the recognition by the Administrative Taxpayers' Council that there is a gap between the Brazilian transfer pricing rules and the international standard. However, according to the Council, the deviations were interpreted not as a rejection of the arm's length principle, but merely as an adaptation of the principle to the Brazilian tax system. The outcome of this line of reasoning was the understanding that there was no contradiction between Article 9 of tax treaties concluded in accordance with the OECD

---

[47] J. D. Rolim and G. A. Moreira, 'La experiencia de Brasil en el area de litigious de precio de transferencia' in Eduardo Baistrocchi (ed.), *Litigios de Precios de Transferencia: Teoria y Practica* (Argentina: LexisNexis, 2008), p. 188.

[48] *Ibid.* p. 182.

Model Convention and the transfer pricing methods adopted by the Brazilian domestic legislation. This may sound rather bizarre, not to say contradictory in terms, because in order to refuse the priority of the treaty over the domestic law, it is alleged that the latter is not contrary to the former. Furthermore, the fact that Article 9 of the OECD Model Convention has not established the methods to calculate the benchmark price also gave support to the Council's conclusion that the tax treaties allow the source country to define how it will apply the transfer pricing methods.

In conclusion, the Administrative Taxpayers' Council has contributed to the interpretation of the implications of the deviations between the Brazilian transfer pricing law and the international standard. However, the interpretation reflects a domestic point of view on the subject. The impact of the deviations might have a different interpretation from the perspective of a foreign tax authority. However, there is no evidence of such dispute, which might have been resolved through a mutual agreement procedure, as discussed below.

13.6   Administrative procedures to minimise transfer pricing disputes

There is no specific reference in the Brazilian transfer pricing law to advance pricing agreements (APA). However, the law establishes the possibility of dialogue between the taxpayer and the tax authority to minimise transfer pricing disputes.[49] The administrative procedures that regulate the exercise of this right of dialogue have evolved over time.

Process of Administrative Consult is a general procedure[50] that allows taxpayers to formally make enquiry of the tax authority on how to interpret the tax legislation, not restricted to transfer pricing legislation. In practice, taxpayers present a formal petition to the tax authority explaining the facts and the provision of the law related to those facts which raises doubts as to its application. The outcome of the process is a single instance decision that binds exclusively the taxpayer who made the enquiry. The taxpayer can only appeal when there are other decisions about the same subject that contradict with each other. In this case, the tax authority can provide a new decision, harmonising the understanding on the application of that provision of the law. The process, therefore, is not very flexible and the dialogue with the tax authority is limited to the

---

[49] Law no. 9.430/96, art. 21.
[50] Process of Administrative Consult established by Law no. 9.430/96, arts. 48–50.

terms of the law. This administrative mechanism has been used by many taxpayers in relation to transfer pricing legislation. Most decisions involving transfer pricing rules refer to questions on how to apply the methods described in the law. For instance, there are a considerable number of petitions requiring the opinion of the tax authority on whether certain economic activity would be regarded as manufacturing or not. This question was connected to the debate on how to apply the RPM when there was manufacturing activity performed by the Brazilian enterprise.[51] Another interesting aspect enquired about by taxpayers through this procedure was whether the methods adopted in the Brazilian legislation were compatible with Article 9 of the OECD Model Tax Convention. The Brazilian tax authority expressed their understanding that they are completely compatible.[52]

Notwithstanding the general procedure, there is another administrative procedure for transfer pricing issues. This administrative procedure[53] allows taxpayers to enter into agreement with the tax authority on the profit margin used in the methods. According to the regulation, taxpayers need to present a formal petition describing the new profit margin required and the documents that prove its requirement. The documents acceptable are (i) publications and official reports published by governments or tax authorities of countries with which Brazil has signed a DTC; or (ii) research conducted by renowned institutions in the transfer pricing area. These documents need to demonstrate that the new profit margin is underpinned by transactions conducted between independent enterprises in the Brazilian market or abroad. Data regarding transactions conducted in low tax jurisdictions and countries with preferential tax regimes are not acceptable. The outcome of this process is a definitive decision that the taxpayer cannot appeal. Thus, the procedure is very rigid and requires the presentation of a substantial amount of documents by the taxpayer who carries the burden of proof in the administrative procedure. The limitation of the evidence that can be presented by taxpayers to demonstrate the appropriate profit margin may make the process rather arbitrary.

---

[51] Process of Administrative Consult nos. 22/08, 5/06, 9/03, 13/02.

[52] Process of Administrative Consult nos. 19/00, 20/00 and 21/00.

[53] The administrative procedure on the profit margins adopted in the transfer pricing legislation is currently regulated by the Administrative Act (Portaria MP) no. 222/08. The first Administrative Act to regulate this issue was enacted in 1997 (Portaria MF no. 95/97).

Because the procedure on transfer pricing issues allows a certain dialogue between taxpayers and tax authorities on the benchmark price of transfer pricing transactions, there are some authors that associate this domestic mechanism with the APA adopted by OECD member countries. However, the difference between these two mechanisms is well known. While the Brazilian procedure has a rigid format allowing a very limited dialogue between the local tax authority and the Brazilian taxpayer on the profit margins used in the methods, the OECD's APA was conceived to allow taxpayers and tax authorities of the countries involved to reach an agreement on how to determine the most appropriate arm's length price for transactions over a certain period of time, having no prior limitation either on aspects to be discussed, or on the form of the dialogue.[54] In addition, the OECD's APA can be unilateral, bilateral or multilateral; whereas the Brazilian procedure was conceived as an unilateral agreement between a Brazilian taxpayer and the local fiscal authority. The OECD Transfer Pricing Guidelines advise countries that adopt unilateral APA to inform the other interested jurisdiction about the adjustments agreed which might create a situation of double taxation. To this extent, not only the adoption of this administrative procedure to determine different profit margins, but also the way the Brazilian legislation applies the traditional transfer pricing methods might create potential situations of double taxation, of which other jurisdictions are not usually informed.

An alternative to circumvent the absence of domestic provisions to implement an APA according to the OECD's concept would be its application through the mutual agreement procedure (MAP) provided in Article 25 of the OECD Model Convention. Under this Article, competent authorities of contracting states are allowed to conclude APAs, if transfer pricing issues will result in double taxation.[55] An agreement in these terms would bind Brazil since a tax treaty takes precedence over the Brazilian domestic law. However, Brazil has several reservations on Article 25, which will be discussed in detail below. One of these reservations refers to the second sentence of Article 25(3) which establishes the possibility of implementing a MAP to eliminate double taxation in cases not provided in the Convention.[56] Moreover, Brazil also has a reservation

---

[54] OECD Transfer Pricing Guidelines, see note 16 above, p. 126.   [55] *Ibid.*

[56] Article 25(3): 'The competent authorities of the Contracting States shall endeavour to resolve by mutual agreement any difficulties or doubts arising as to the interpretation or application of the Convention. *They may also consult together for the elimination of double taxation in cases not provided for in the Convention.*' (The sentence in italics refers to Brazil's reservation on this paragraph.)

on paragraphs 11 and 12 of the OECD's Commentaries, making clear that it does not agree with the interpretation provided in these provisions which establish that the absence of Article 9(2) does not signify that the contracting states did not want to eliminate economic double taxation arising from the application of transfer pricing rules. Examining together the Brazilian reservations on Article 25 and on its Commentaries, it is difficult to sustain the adoption of APA according to the OECD's model even through MAP. In order to have an APA established through Article 25, Brazil will have to eliminate its reservations or make it clear that in the course of negotiations with other countries, Brazil will not be bound by its position assumed in the OECD's general documentation. This position was not clearly defined by Brazil, which leaves doubts when analysing some DTCs in force since some of them have included, for instance, the last sentence of Article 25(3).[57]

It is interesting to note that even though the Brazilian transfer pricing rules have the potential to create situations of double taxation, in practice, there has been no evidence either of third countries requiring the Brazilian tax authorities to adjust the tax basis of associated enterprises in Brazil or the other way around. All enquiries involving administrative procedures were restricted to situations involving a Brazilian taxpayer and the local authority, except in the case of the Brazil–Germany DTC which was terminated for a number of different reasons, including the divergences on transfer pricing adjustments.

13.7   Bilateral and multilateral approaches to transfer pricing disputes

Transfer pricing disputes can also be solved by mechanisms provided in DTCs. To understand the effectiveness of these mechanisms it is necessary first to examine the relationship between DTCs and domestic law; and then to focus on the characteristics of transfer pricing clauses included in DTCs concluded by Brazil.

As stated above, a DTC not only overrides domestic law, but it also prevails over any further change in the legislation, as established in article 98 of the National Tax Code, which has a higher legal status in relation to federal and state legislation. In practice, the application of this provision

---

[57] For instance, the DTCs concluded with Austria (1976), China (1993), Denmark (1974), Finland (1998), among others.

signifies that in case of conflict between the domestic law and tax treaty, the latter will prevail over the former. For instance, if there was a DTC concluded between Brazil and another country and Brazil intended to apply the transfer pricing rules since the transactions were performed between an enterprise resident in Brazil and an enterprise resident abroad that had a partnership with the Brazilian enterprise, Brazil would be prevented from applying its transfer pricing rules since the concept of associated enterprises provided in the tax treaty does not encompass this situation. Only the situations comprised in the concept of associated enterprise as established in the DTC would allow the application of the Brazilian transfer pricing rules.

Brazil has twenty-nine tax treaties in force.[58] They follow the OECD Model Convention. This is the reason why, even though Brazil is not a member of the OECD, the OECD's guidelines represent an important source of law to interpret tax treaties in Brazil, although not binding since the administrative courts have already recognised the OECD's recommendations as a secondary source of law.

In relation to transfer pricing clauses provided in the OECD Model Convention, Brazil has several reservations. The first reservation is in relation to Article 9(2) which deals with adjustments required to avoid double taxation which might arise after a contracting state adjusted the profit of an associated enterprise to reflect the arm's length price. At first glance, it seems that without this paragraph, contracting states will not be able to resolve double taxation situations that might arise from adjustments of the taxable profits of associated enterprises which carried out transactions not stipulating the arm's length price. None of the DTCs concluded by Brazil include Article 9(2). In order to counteract the absence of this clause, the OECD adopted a position that the inclusion of Article 9(1) added to the provisions of Article 25 which establish the mutual agreement procedure grant to the contracting states the right to adopt measures to resolve cases of economic double taxation that might arise from the application of transfer pricing rules even in the absence of Article 9(2). However, Brazil also has reservations on Article 25.

The Brazilian reservations on Article 25 apply to (i) the last sentence of Article 25(1) because Brazil does not admit the time limit to present

---

[58] The tax treaties in force were concluded with the following countries: Argentina, Austria, Belgium, Canada, Chile, China, Czech Republic, Denmark, Ecuador, Finland, France, Hungary, India, Israel, Italy, Japan, Korea, Luxembourg, Mexico, Netherlands, Norway, Peru, Philippines, Portugal, Slovakia, South Africa, Spain, Sweden and Ukraine

the case;[59] (ii) the last sentence of Article 25(2) since Brazil considers that the implementation of reliefs and refunds following a MAP has to respect the time limit established in its domestic law;[60] (iii) the second sentence of Article 25(3) on the grounds that Brazil has no authority under domestic law to eliminate double taxation in cases not provided in the DTC;[61] and (iv) the words 'including through a Joint commission consisting of themselves or their representatives' in Article 25(4).

In addition to these reservations on Article 25, Brazil also made reservations on paragraphs 11 and 12 of the OECD Commentaries, as described previously. Analysing together these reservations on Article 9 and Article 25, we can infer that Brazil tried to avoid the use of MAP to resolve situations of double taxation that might arise from the application of transfer pricing rules. This position emphasises Brazil's understanding that the most important aspect of transfer pricing rules is to curb tax avoidance schemes rather than to resolve double taxation situations.

In practice, however, many DTCs concluded by Brazil include the last sentence of Article 25(3) which allows the use of MAP to resolve cases of double taxation not provided for in the DTC.[62] To this extent, it is not clear whether the inclusion of this provision overrides the reservations manifested by Brazil in the OECD's general documents. Therefore, when the entirety of Article 25(3) of the OECD Model Convention is included in the DTC concluded by Brazil, it would be necessary to examine what the contracting states had agreed specifically in relation to the use of MAP to resolve double taxation situations created by transfer pricing rules. Even though the Brazilian reservations indicate its resistance to resolving transfer pricing disputes through MAP, in practice this resistance might be removed through bilateral negotiations.

It is important to note that Brazil has no experience in resolving transfer pricing disputes through MAP as established in Article 25 of the OECD

---

[59] Article 25(1) last sentence: 'The case must be presented within three years from the first notification of the action resulting in taxation not in accordance with the provisions of the Convention.' OECD, 'OECD Commentary on the Model Conventions of 1977 and 1992 (incorporating the changes of 1994, 1995, 1997, 2000, 2003, 2005 and 2008)' in Kees van Raad, *Materials on International and EC Tax Law* (Leiden: International Tax Center, 2008), vol. 1, p. 447.

[60] Article 25(2) last sentence: 'Any agreement reached shall be implemented notwithstanding any time limits in the domestic law of the Contracting States.'

[61] Article 25(3) second sentence: 'They may also consult together for the elimination of double taxation in cases not provided for in the Convention.'

[62] See note 57 above for countries whose DTCs have this sentence included in the text of the Convention.

Model. In fact, there is only one example of Brazil's experience with mutual agreement procedures, which happened in the 1970s and involved a French branch of a Brazilian bank. According to the facts, the French branch raised capital in the European market to lend to Brazilian companies through the bank's head office in Brazil.[63] When the Brazilian head office paid interest to the French branch as part of the financial structure, there was a levy of withholding tax which followed the provisions of the Brazil–France DTC. However, the French authority did not authorise the use of this credit by the French branch to be offset with the corporate tax levied on the branch's profit in France. In order to resolve this double taxation situation, the Brazilian bank requested the implementation of a mutual agreement procedure. However, later the MAP was abandoned and each country tried to find a solution under its own domestic laws.[64]

Last, as regards the arbitration provision included in the 2008 updated version of the OECD Model Convention as Article 25(5), most tax treaties were concluded by Brazil before 2008, therefore they do not provide any clause relating to arbitration process. There is only one tax treaty that was concluded after 2008 (the Brazil–Peru DTC). However, the Brazil-Peru DTC did not include the new provision on arbitration process.

13.8. Recent developments in the transfer pricing legislation

In December 2009, the President of Brazil enacted two Provisory Measures[65] changing substantial aspects of the transfer pricing law (Law no. 9.430/96). There were different provisions included in these measures; some had the characteristics of tax avoidance and tax evasion rules (e.g., thin capitalisation provisions), while others only improved the methodology adopted to calculate the benchmark price (e.g., the new RPM method

---

[63] Carlos dos Santos Almeida, *The Experience of Brazil in Tax Treaties: Linkages between OECD Member Countries and Dynamic Non-member Economies* (OECD: Paris, 1996), p. 178.

[64] *Ibid.*

[65] Before analysing new legislation, it is important to understand some legal aspects of Provisory Measures. A Provisory Measure is an act issued by the President and submitted to the Congress for approval. Until its approval, this act has the authority of law and it can remain in force for sixty days extendable to an extra sixty days. If the Provisory Measure is not converted into law after the period of 120 days, it will lose its effectiveness, and a Decree will need to be issued by the Congress to regulate the provisions set out in the Provisory Measure. As already mentioned, in June 2010, Provisory Measure no. 472/09 was converted into Law no. 12.249/10, whereas Provisory Measure no. 478/09 was not voted by the Congress in the legal period required (i.e., 120 days from its publication), losing its effectiveness on 1 June 2010.

and the adoption of fixed profit margins by sector or by economic activity performed by the enterprise).[66]

As described previously, until 2009 interest on loans contracted with related persons and fully registered at the Bacen were not subjected to the transfer pricing rules. Provisory Measure no. 472/09 changed this scenario by providing new limits of deductibility for interest paid to related parties resident abroad and also special limits for interest paid to enterprises or individuals (related or unrelated) resident in low tax jurisdictions or in countries with preferential tax regimes. The new law (Law no. 12.249/10) with which Provisory Measure no. 472/09 was consolidated, established that interest paid to foreign related entities (not located in low tax jurisdictions nor in countries with preferential tax regimes) will only be deductible from the basis of income tax if three conditions apply cumulatively: (i) it represents a necessary expense;[67] (ii) the amount of indebtedness does not exceed two times the value of equity interest calculated by the equity method and held by the related person of the Brazilian entity; and (iii) the total amount of indebtedness does not exceed two times the value of equity interest calculated by the equity method and held by all related persons of the Brazilian entity. In the case of indirect participation, Law no. 12.249/10 established that the amount of indebtedness must not exceed two times the net equity of the Brazilian enterprise.[68]

In relation to interest paid to persons resident in low tax jurisdictions or countries with preferential tax regimes, the law is more severe, establishing fixed percentages of deductibility in relation to net equity of the Brazilian enterprise, independent of the value of equity interest held directly or indirectly by the foreign entities. In these cases, the

---

[66] The new RPM was defined as the weighted average sales price of goods, services or rights imported and calculated according to the following methodology: first, it was necessary to determine the proportional sales cost of imported goods represented by the division of the average weighted cost of the imported goods to the total weighted average cost of the products, in percentage terms. The calculated percentage was then multiplied by the total sales price, resulting in the amount of the sales price that was attributed to the imported goods. The outcome ('proportional sales price') was multiplied by 65 per cent (which corresponded to 100 per cent minus the fixed profit rate of 35 per cent disposed in the Provisory Measure). The final result was the benchmark price (Law no. 9.430/96, art. 18, II(a)–(e), reflecting changes implemented by Provisory Measure no. 478/09).

[67] According to the internal law, necessary expenses are those required for the performance of the enterprise's economic activity. Arbitrary expenses (i.e., those deliberately performed by the enterprise) are not deductible from the income tax basis.

[68] Law no. 12.249/10, art. 24.

requirements for the interest to be deductible from the income tax basis are (i) it represents a necessary expense; (ii) the amount of indebtedness held by the foreign entity resident in low tax jurisdictions or countries with preferential tax regimes does not exceed 30 per cent of the net equity of the Brazilian enterprise; and (iii) the total amount of indebtedness held by all foreign entities resident in low tax jurisdictions and countries with preferential tax regimes does not exceed 30 per cent of the net equity of the Brazilian entity.[69]

Law no. 12.249/10 also established further conditions that need to be fulfilled cumulatively in order for payments to persons (related or unrelated; individuals or enterprises) resident in low tax jurisdictions or in countries with preferential tax regimes to be deductible from the income tax basis in Brazil. The conditions are (i) identification of the beneficial owner; (ii) existence of an operational structure in the country where the foreign enterprise that performs the commercial transaction is located; and (iii) the existence of documents that can prove the payments made and the products/services delivered. The second condition is dispensed with if the objective of the transaction is not tax avoidance or if the profits of the foreign entity are reached by the Brazilian CFC[70] legislation.[71] In relation to these conditions established in the law, it is important to note that the Brazilian legislation neither provides a clear definition of beneficial owner nor establishes the characteristics of a transaction performed with a tax avoidance purpose. Both situations remain undefined, being left for courts to ascertain them through a case-by-case analysis.

The other main changes were introduced by Provisory Measure no. 478. However, this Provisory Measure was not voted for by the Congress in the due period, losing its effectiveness on 1 June 2010. The changes implemented by Provisory Measure no. 478, therefore, are highlighted here only to demonstrate the adjustments required in the law and already recognised by the Executive Power.

The first amendment made by Provisory Measure no. 478 consisted in the substitution of the old resale price method (RPM).[72] This provision established a different methodology to estimate the benchmark price. There was a long-term debate in the administrative courts of Brazil

---

[69] Law no. 12.249/10, art. 25.
[71] Law no. 12.249/10, art. 26.
[70] As set out in Provisory Measure no. 2158/01, art. 74.
[72] See note 66 above, for the new method.

involving the correct application of RPM.[73] The administrative court's discussion was focused on whether RPM could be adopted for transactions involving manufacturing activity in Brazil. The legislation at the beginning was not very clear on this point. Later, the law was amended introducing different parameters in the formula, depending on whether there was manufacturing activity performed in Brazil. Considering this subsequent change in the law, the administrative authority adopted the interpretation that RPM could only be applied to transactions without manufacturing activity in Brazil before the law established clear parameters for manufacturing activities. This administrative interpretation was very controversial, extending the content of the law and, consequently, it was not acceptable to taxpayers who contested it in the administrative courts. In this context, the rule introduced by Provisory Measure no. 478/09 could be understood as a government act to solve the problems of application created by the previous legislation. This background gives support to the assertion that the method introduced by Provisory Measure no. 478/09 was intended to sort out domestic problems involving the application of the RPM rather than to conform its application to the arm's length principle.

The second important modification introduced by Provisory Measure no. 478/09 was the possibility of the Minister of Finance to enact different fixed profit margins by sectors or economic activity performed by taxpayers.[74] Before this provision, the Minister of Finance could change the fixed profit margins established in the law only in special circumstances.[75] Notwithstanding the original provision, since the enactment of the transfer pricing legislation, there has been no act issued by the Minister of Finance to change the fixed profit margins provided in the law. Thus, at first glance, the enactment of this new provision would have helped to make the legislation more flexible. In practice, however, there were different aspects of this provision that compromised its effectiveness. First, the process relied on a discretionary act issued by the Minister of Finance. Second, the process adopted by the Minister of Finance that would have led to the determination of the new profit margins was not regulated in the law. The effectiveness of the measure,

---

[73] For instance, Decision no. 103-21.859 established that taxpayers had the right to use the RPM to calculate the benchmark price in import transactions since the enactment of Law no. 9.430/96. The act issued by the tax authority that restricted the application of this method to import transactions without further manufacturing in Brazil was considered illegal and, consequently, it was not accepted by the administrative court.

[74] Provisory Measure no. 478/09, art. 19-A.   [75] Law no. 9.430/96, art. 20.

therefore, relied on how logical and transparent the definition of the new profit margins would have been in practice. Otherwise, there would be no progress in the Brazilian transfer pricing legislation, which would retain the arbitrary aspects of the fixed profit margins adopted until the enactment of Provisory Measure no. 478/09. Thus, the provisions of Provisory Measure no. 478/09 also had serious flaws that need some improvement if implemented through a new act.

From a critical perspective, the major changes implemented in 2009 that were converted by the Congress into law represent a step forward in the Brazilian legislation, but it is not possible to identify a commitment to the arm's length principle. The reform was not intended to reduce the gap between the Brazilian transfer pricing law and the international standard. It was a domestic view that guided the changes implemented. Other aspects that also need to change were not dealt in the Provisory Measures, such as the application of transfer pricing rules to intangibles, the adoption of functional analysis, the evaluation of combined transactions when separate transactions are connected, etc.

13.9. Concluding remarks

Further reform is necessary on the Brazilian legislation to reduce the gap between the transfer pricing law and the international standard. The Brazilian transfer pricing rules aim to combat schemes of tax avoidance rather than to identify the arm's length price. This is the reason which justifies the adoption of parameters that determine a maximum price for deductible expenses on imports and a minimum profit rate on exports performed between associated enterprises. Double taxation that may arise from the application of the transfer pricing rules is regarded as a secondary issue in the Brazilian legislation, not receiving the necessary attention that it deserves.

Some administrative decisions have demonstrated a positive trend on the application of law in relation to the international standard. According to the administrative courts' interpretation, the deviations from the arm's length principle should not be understood as a refusal of the law to accept this principle. On the contrary, the differences derived from the necessity of adapting the arm's length principle to the Brazilian tax system. This interpretation has sustained the compatibility between the arm's length methods provided in the domestic law and Article 9 of the OECD Model Convention.

The mechanisms available in the domestic legislation and in DTCs that can be adopted to reduce transfer pricing disputes need to be improved.

The domestic legislation only allows a limited dialogue between taxpayers and the tax authority in Brazil. Better mechanisms, such as the OECD's APA, are required. APA following the OECD standard would help those Brazilian taxpayers not satisfied with the safe harbours provided in the law to request the tax authority to apply different parameters (i.e., profit margins) to identify the benchmark price. Moreover, Brazil has reservations on the transfer pricing clauses of DTCs that can curb the adoption of MAP to resolve double taxation situations that may arise from the application of contracting states' domestic rules. If Brazil aims to contribute to the global net of transfer pricing solutions, Brazil will need to improve its domestic law as well as to renounce its reservations on clauses to resolve double taxation situations derived from transfer pricing rules in DTCs.

The ideal law would be the one that respected the limitations of the Brazilian tax system regarding administrative costs and taxpayers' compliance costs and at the same time was in line with the international standard minimising potential situations of double taxation.

Appendix: Questionnaire (Brazil)

1.   The structure of the law for solving transfer pricing disputes.   *What is the structure of the law of the country for solving transfer pricing disputes? For example, is the mutual agreement procedure (MAP), as regulated in the relevant tax treaty, the standard method for solving transfer pricing disputes?*

Most transfer pricing disputes have been resolved through administrative decisions. As stated above, Brazil has several reservations on Articles 9 and 25 of the OECD Model Convention that might affect the adoption of MAP as the standard method for resolving transfer pricing disputes.

2.   Policy for solving transfer pricing disputes.   *Is there a gap between the nominal and effective method for solving transfer pricing disputes in the country? For example, has the country a strategic policy not to enforce the arm's length standard (ALS) for fear of driving foreign direct investment to other competing jurisdictions?*

No, there is no gap between the nominal and effective method for solving transfer pricing disputes in Brazil. There are significant deviations in the Brazilian transfer pricing law from the ALS, however the deviations were not created through fear of driving away FDI. In fact, the transfer pricing law is used as an instrument to combat tax evasion and avoidance rather than to attract FDI.

3. The prevailing dispute resolution method. *Which is the most frequent method for solving transfer pricing disputes in the country? Does it have a positive externality? For example, is the MAP the most frequent method, and if so, to what extent have successful MAPs been used as a proxy for transfer pricing case law? For instance, Procter & Gamble (P&G) obtained a bilateral advance pricing agreement (APA) in Europe, and it was then extended to a third (Asian) country when P&G made this request to the relevant Asian tax authorities.*

The most usual method for solving transfer pricing disputes is administrative litigation. Brazil has no experience in solving transfer pricing disputes through MAP.

4. Transfer pricing case law. *What is the evolution path of transfer pricing litigation in the country? For example: (i) Is transfer pricing litigation being gradually replaced by either MAPs or APAs, as regulated in the relevant tax treaties? (ii) Are foreign/local transfer pricing precedents and/ or published MAPs increasingly relevant as a source of law for solving transfer pricing disputes?*

At the moment the evolution of transfer pricing litigation consists in the development of administrative jurisprudence that explains the relationship between the Brazilian transfer pricing law and the arm's length principle. The adoption of administrative procedures that allow taxpayers to make enquiries of the tax authorities (i) on the interpretation of transfer pricing law, and (ii) on the fixed profit margins provided in the methods has also increased. However, these procedures of dialogue are very limited, not corresponding to the actual APA enforced by the OECD.

5. Customary international law and international tax procedure. *Has customary international law been applied in the country to govern the relevant methods for solving transfer pricing disputes (such as the MAP)? For example, has the OECD Manual on Effective Mutual Agreement Procedure ('OECD Manual') been deemed customary international tax law in the MAP arena for filling procedural gaps (for example, time limit for implementation of relief where treaties deviate from the OECD Model Tax Convention)?*

As already stated, Brazil has no experience with MAP for solving transfer pricing disputes.

6. Procedural setting and strategic interaction. *Does strategic inter-action between taxpayers and tax authorities depend on the procedural setting in which they interact when trying to solve transfer pricing disputes? For example, which procedural setting in the country prompts the relevant parties to cooperate with each other the most for solving this sort of dispute, and why?*

The procedural setting that requires the interaction between taxpayers and tax authority consists in the Administrative Process of Consult. This is a general procedure that taxpayers can use to make enquiry of the tax authorities on the interpretation of any tax law. There is also a specific procedure for transfer pricing issues. Both administrative procedures allow a very limited dialogue between taxpayers and the tax authority. In fact, the dialogue follows the parameters provided in the law. Therefore, to request the interpretation of a provision, or to request the adoption of a different profit margin in the transfer pricing methods, taxpayers need to fulfil the conditions set out in the law. For instance, in relation to the administrative process in which a taxpayer requests the opinion of the tax authority on a different profit margin, he can only prove his argument through the documents accepted by the law (e.g., (i) publications and official reports published by governments or tax authorities of countries with which Brazil has signed a DTC; or (ii) research conducted by renowned institutions in the transfer pricing area). Thus, not only is the burden of proof carried by the taxpayer, but also there are several limitations on the documents that can be adopted as proof, restricting taxpayers' rights and the dialogue with the tax authority. Furthermore, taxpayers are reluctant to provide information to the tax authority through fear that information will be used against them in the future. A procedural setting that renders the dialogue between the tax authority and taxpayers more flexible is required in order to achieve improved solution of transfer pricing issues.

7. The future of transfer pricing disputes resolution. *Which is the best available proposal in light of the interests of the country for facilitating the global resolution of transfer pricing disputes, and why?*

The introduction and practice of APA between taxpayers and fiscal authorities would represent an important achievement considering the peculiarities of the Brazilian legislation. Moreover, the abolition of the reservations on Article 9(2) and Article 25(3) of the OECD Model Convention, as well as on paragraphs 11 and 12 of the OECD's Commentaries, will also facilitate the resolution of transfer pricing disputes through mutual agreement procedures.

Transfer pricing disputes in the Russian Federation

ANDREY SHPAK

14.1 Introduction

The economic and business environment in Russia changed significantly following the fall of communism in 1991. Free market reforms (instead of transacting at predetermined regulated prices), opening foreign trade (which was monopolised by the government until then) and introduction of the modern tax system played very important roles in this transition, exposing Russia to the forces of globalisation shaping the modern economic system. Transfer pricing becomes especially important in this context.

However, it would be surprising if transfer pricing in Russia would be a developed concept given that the tax system, in the Western sense of the expression, has only a twenty-year history in modern Russia. However, transfer pricing is an important feature of the Russian tax and political landscape, especially given the commodity bias of the Russian economy.

Following this introduction, this chapter covers the following topics: (ii) economic and institutional context; (iii) historical background of transfer pricing legislation; (iv) overview of the key aspects of the Russian transfer pricing legislation; (v) administrative procedures to resolve transfer pricing disputes; (vi) trends in the domestic court practice on transfer pricing issues; (vii) bilateral and multilateral approaches to transfer pricing disputes; (viii) recent developments in the area of transfer pricing; and (ix) concluding remarks, including the author's opinion on the likely routes for future developments in this area.

14.2 Economic and institutional context

The fall of communism opened up the Russian economy in unprecedented ways: foreign trade turnover increased from US $124.9 billion in

1995 to US \$625.6 billion in 2010.[1] Foreign direct investment (FDI), which was 0.25 per cent of GDP in 1992, increased to 3 per cent of GDP in 2009 (and exceeded 4 per cent in 2007 and 2008).[2]

This growth was substantially fuelled by the growth in commodity prices, and commodity exports accounted for more than 80 per cent of total Russian exports. According to Expert 400, the major Russian annual company ranking, resource-linked companies accounted in 2010 for approximately 50 per cent of the revenues and more than 70 per cent of the profits of the largest 400 companies.[3]

The commodity-based nature of the economy also influences the nature of the Russian tax system and composition of the Russian treasury: indirect and resource-based taxes (the latter often linked to the global price of the underlying commodities) accounted for almost two-thirds of the consolidated Russian treasury[4] (approximately one-third of which related to VAT and excises), and the other third to mineral extraction tax and export duties.

Profits tax typically accounts for just 15–20 per cent of the consolidated treasury. As a result, the effect of transfer pricing on the Russian treasury is likely to be rather limited, and the impact is felt primarily at the regional, rather than federal, level (since profits tax primarily goes to the regional treasuries, whereas the federal treasury primarily collects indirect and resource-based taxes).

As a result, even though transfer pricing issues have been hotly debated in Russia for over a decade (with this debate having culminated in adoption of the new transfer pricing regulations, as discussed below), they have never been at the core of the Russian tax policy or strategy.

Although this situation may gradually change over time, with increasing globalisation of Russian companies and the economy as a whole, it is unlikely to gain the same importance as in some other major Western economies.

14.3 Historical background

Evolution of the transfer pricing concept has taken several distinct stages in Russia, which are discussed below.

---

[1] See www.gks.ru/wps/wcm/connect/rosstat/rosstatsite/main/trade/.
[2] See www.indexmundi.com/facts/russia/foreign-direct-investment.
[3] See www.raexpert.ru/ratings/expert400/2010/, Goltsblat BLP analysis.
[4] Source: Russian treasury data available at info.minfin.ru/fbdohod.php, Goltsblat BLP analysis.

14.3.1 Pre-1991

It is difficult to talk about a 'tax system' in relation to a socialist economy, which Russia was until the end of 1991 (as part of the Soviet Union). However, taxes technically also existed in the Soviet Union. During the Soviet era it is estimated that over 90 per cent of total government revenue consisted of payments collected from the state-owned enterprises. The main source of government revenues was the so-called 'turnover tax', which was assessed based on the value added net of manufacturing costs and overhead (i.e., effectively represented quasi-VAT). The calculation procedure was linked to retail prices of the manufactured products and the rates were set by different authorities who were also responsible for setting the state-controlled retail prices for these products. Distribution of unutilised profits (i.e., quasi-dividends) was also an important source of government revenues. The system had remained largely intact since it was originally introduced in the 1930s.

It is apparent that in the Soviet system, where prices were government-controlled and the public finance system was designed to centralise and redistribute all profits that were not immediately necessary at the enterprise level, transfer pricing in the Western sense of the expression was largely irrelevant (or, alternatively, can be viewed as being the extreme case of complete government control over transfer pricing).

14.3.2 1991 to 1999

The situation changed with the fall of communism in 1991 and introduction of the Western-type tax system in December 1991 that was required to move the country in the direction of a free market economy.

The system, introduced in December 1991,[5] split the taxes into three broad categories: federal (VAT, profits tax, excise taxes, import and export duties, natural resource taxes); regional (property taxes, forestry and water taxes); and local taxes (various local licence fees, special taxes, property taxes payable by individuals, etc.).

The outline of the current tax system has remained largely the same to this date, although the number of taxes and their allocation between different treasury levels (federal, regional and local) has changed over time.

---

[5] Law no. 2118-1 On the foundations of the tax system in the Russian Federation of 27 December 1991.

This new tax legislation introduced the possibility to adjust the tax base based on market prices, however, on a very limited scale. The only trigger was whether the sale was made above or below cost: companies selling products (or services) at prices below cost had to calculate the VAT tax base based on the market prices for similar products (or services), but not less than the actual cost.[6] Companies were allowed to use the actual sales price if the sales price exceeded the market levels, or if sale below cost was justified by lower product quality or consumer characteristics. However, the resulting excessive input VAT was in any case not recoverable. In case of exchange of products or services (barter) there was a requirement to calculate the VAT tax base on the basis of the average selling price of similar products (services) during the month of the transaction, or (if no sales of similar products took place in that month) based on the price of the last sale, but not below cost.

Similar provisions allowing price adjustments in case of sales below cost were also included in the profits tax legislation.[7]

In practice, this rule was often applied without taking into consideration the actual circumstances and it did not distinguish between taxpayers who were abusing their rights and manipulating prices for tax reasons versus those who acted in good faith and had to sell below cost due to deteriorating market situation.

By the end of the 1990s it became apparent that the then existing tax system was not efficient: it included too many individual tax laws with ambiguous and often conflicting provisions, blurred division of authority between the federal and regional authorities as regards introduction of new taxes, etc. This culminated in the development and introduction in 1999 of the new Tax Code, which has remained in effect until the present time.

14.3.3   1999 to 2011

The Tax Code codified the principles of the existing Russian tax system, including the list of taxes, the rights of the tax authorities and taxpayers, general definitions and tax administration and procedure (the first 'general' part of the Tax Code came into force in 1999, while the second, establishing detailed rules for individual taxes, was gradually introduced over the next few years).

---

[6] Article 4(1) of Law no. 1992-1 On Value Added Tax of 6 December 1991 (as amended by Law no. 57-FZ dated 6 December 1994).

[7] Article 2(5) of Law no. 2116-1 of 27 December 1991 On taxes on profits of enterprises and organisations of 27 December 1991.

Introduction of the Tax Code was an important step in the company's transition to a tax system based on the rule of law, since it established clear boundaries for the various government authorities in establishing tax liabilities and interpreting tax statutes.

All taxes can now be introduced only by federal laws (including the Tax Code), but some of the elements of taxation can be set by regional or local laws, as long as such powers are granted by a relevant federal law.

As a general rule, international tax treaties supersede the domestic tax legislation (this is directly provided by the Russian Constitution). However, the treaty rates and other provisions do not apply if the taxpayer is better off under the domestic tax legislation.

It can be argued that the core principles of the Russian tax system are set by the Russian Constitution adopted in 1993 (especially article 57 which pronounces the relevant rights and obligations of Russian citizens). In particular, this includes, for example:

- obligation for everyone to pay the legally established taxes and dues;
- no retroactive effect for laws introducing new taxes or deteriorating the position of taxpayers;
- requirement for general principles of taxation and rules for federal taxes to be established only by federal law;
- since taxes always mean the restriction of property rights, such a restriction should be proportionate to the constitutionally significant purposes of establishing the tax;
- when setting the tax, all key elements (including the object of taxation, tax base etc.) should be clearly defined;
- taxes cannot be discriminatory.

Numerous decisions of the Russian Constitutional Court have applied these principles to real-life situations and significantly influenced the development of the Tax Code that is currently in force. Although the Constitutional Court has rarely addressed tax issues in its decisions over the last few years, its decisions continue to be applied by regular Arbitrazh courts;[8] for example, in 2010 there were more than 100 instances of the Supreme Arbitrazh Court citing Constitutional Court decisions in its resolutions.

---

[8] This is the branch of the court system responsible for resolving disputes between entities, including the government; it also covers tax disputes between companies and the tax authorities.

As regards transfer pricing, introduction of the first part of the Tax Code (with effect from 1 January 1999) introduced different, more comprehensive rules on the possibility to adjust prices for tax purposes (discussed in more detail below), which remained in force until very recently (new, revised rules come into force with effect from 1 January 2012, as discussed below).

The transfer pricing rules that were introduced into the Russian Tax Code in 1999 were originally intended to be a temporary compromise between rudimentary provisions that existed prior to that (the 'sales below cost' rules) and OECD-type rules. The core provisions (explained in more detail below) consisted of just two articles in the Tax Code[9] comprising in total approximately four pages of printed text (out of more than 750 pages for the whole Tax Code).

As a result, the rules were relatively basic and rudimentary, and differed significantly from OECD transfer pricing guidelines. Although the rules declared arm's length price (labelled as 'market price') as the key guiding principle, they were very prescriptive in terms of the procedure, and there were too many deviations (as explained below) to consider them as being truly based on an arm's length principle.

First of all, these transfer pricing provisions were purely transaction-based. They also in certain circumstances could capture transactions between parties that were not affiliated, effectively allowing the tax authorities to use them as an anti-abuse measure. For example, the law listed the following transactions with unrelated parties as 'controlled transactions' (i.e., those subject to transfer pricing control): (i) transactions involving 'barter' (i.e., direct exchange) of goods or services; (ii) cross-border, i.e., 'foreign trade' transactions; and (iii) if there was a fluctuation of more than 20 per cent in the level of prices used by the taxpayer for identical or similar goods, works, or services over a short period of time (the term 'short period of time', while extremely important, was still undefined in the Tax Code).

The definition of interrelated parties was also significantly wider as compared to the OECD Guidelines, deeming companies with direct or indirect control of more than 20 per cent as interrelated for transfer pricing purposes. At the same time, the law technically did not capture 'sister' companies (e.g., being owned by the same foreign parent, but not having direct ownership in each other). This, however, was

---

[9] Articles 20 and 40 of the Tax Code.

viewed as a technicality, since the Tax Code gave the courts the right to deem any two parties interrelated (the Constitutional Court later limited this right to situations where the affiliation could be proved under other branches of legislation, e.g., under anti-monopoly legislation).

Special rules were introduced in respect of securities and derivatives in 2002.[10] As a general rule (with some minor exceptions), for tax purposes the tax base on securities and derivatives is linked to market price regardless of whether the transaction is carried out with a related party or not, although the rules for marketable and non-marketable securities differ.

Based on the accepted interpretation of applicable law, interest, not being a payment for product or service, was exempt from transfer pricing control.

There has been debate on whether sale of property rights (e.g., royalties or shares in Russian limited liability companies (LLCs)) was subject to transfer pricing control. The Russian courts tended to support the notion that prices for property rights could not be adjusted for tax purposes. However, there are several court cases where adjustment relating to property rights has been accepted by the court.

Also, the Tax Code requires the tax base to be applied based on the similar rules in case of gifts (free of charge transactions) between companies even if they do not fall under the four types of controllable transactions listed above.

An important feature of the rules effective during this period was the existence of the so-called '20 per cent safe-harbour deviation'. Once the transaction was a 'controlled' one, then the tax authorities had the right to adjust the price for tax purposes (effectively assessing additional profits tax, VAT and other taxes, if applicable), only if they could prove that the price used by the taxpayer in a particular transaction differed from the market price by more than 20 per cent. In other words, any deviation within 20 per cent was acceptable. This obviously significantly reduced the scope for potential application of the transfer pricing rules.

In terms of the methods, when determining the proxy for a market price, only three methods were allowed to be used:

(i)   the comparable uncontrolled price (CUP) method;
(ii) the resale price method; and
(iii) the cost plus method.

---

[10] By introduction of Chapter 25 of the Tax Code regulating application of profits tax.

The methods should technically have been used in the exact priority as they are listed, and in order to use the next method, the tax authorities had to prove that the previous method either could not be applied or did not allow the assessment of a fair proxy of the market price. At the same time, the law allowed the courts to use other information if the listed methods did not allow properly arriving at the market price.

When making the assessments, the tax authorities technically had to rely on the official sources of information. At the same time, they also had to take into account the particular characteristics of the transaction, marketing policy of the company, including discounts, etc., and prove that their assessment took this into account. These somewhat conflicting provisions made the tax authorities' task a lot more difficult if not impossible in certain circumstances.

In practice, the courts have accepted a wide range of proxies for market prices as an alternative, e.g., information on market prices from the local chambers of commerce, formal appraisals of market value, etc. At the same time, the requirement for the tax authorities to justify that they took into account all the particular elements of the challenged transaction continues to make the challenge difficult.

Under the rules effective during that period, there were no formal transfer pricing documentation requirements and most companies did not maintain transfer pricing files.

Similarly, there were no transfer pricing audits. The control of prices was performed as part of the regular tax control, i.e., regular desk or field tax audits. There was also no legal procedure for obtaining an advance pricing agreement (APA).

14.3.4   Post-2012

The Russian Parliament on 18 July 2011 adopted a new law, which represents a major step towards bringing the Russian transfer pricing rules closer to the OECD Guidelines. This new law in certain aspects is just an evolution of the previously existing rules, and, as a result, significant gaps and deviations will remain as compared to the OECD Transfer Pricing Guidelines. Details of the new rules are discussed in the next section.

14.4   Current transfer pricing rules

Deficiencies in the existing rules became apparent to both the taxpayers and the Ministry of Finance almost immediately after the rules were introduced in 1999. As a result, the Ministry of Finance began developing a new, more sophisticated and more OECD-compliant version of the transfer pricing rules since the early 2000s. This culminated in the new law ('the Law') being officially approved on 18 July 2011 by the Russian Parliament (Federal Assembly). The Law entered into force on 1 January 2012.[11] The government declared combating tax avoidance through the use of transfer prices as the key purpose of the law when it was being adopted, thus effectively accepting that the prior rules were not really effective in this regard.

The new legislation amends the definition of related persons: the required share of direct or indirect participation of one legal entity in another which provides grounds for treating persons/entities as related now amounts to 25 per cent. An important exception is that direct or indirect state (government) participation in Russian companies will not, as such, be regarded as a ground to deem the companies related. The courts retain the right to treat persons/entities as related on grounds not directly specified in the Law. However, the Constitutional Court decision (mentioned above and discussed in more detail below) that this right of the courts cannot be arbitrary and that any decision to declare persons related should have a basis in other pieces of legislation will likely continue to apply.

Most of the provisions of the new Law refer only to transactions with goods, works and services. This gave the basis for many experts to claim that (based on the historic court practice interpreting the terms 'goods, works and services') this implies that the new transfer pricing rules do not extend to interest, royalties and transactions with other objects of civil rights (property rights, etc.). However, the law contains a couple of more generic references, which allowed the Ministry of Finance to claim that both royalties and interest should also be included in the scope of transfer pricing rules (as well as any other transaction that has an impact on the tax base). It remains to be seen which interpretation will prevail, or whether any amendments will be introduced into the law to clarify this crucial aspect.

Reference to a previously allowed 20 per cent safe harbour of price fluctuations has been substituted by market price range. Accordingly, this expands the scope of transactions with related parties potentially subject to transfer pricing control.

---

[11] Federal Law no. 227-FZ of 18 July 2011 On amendments to certain legislative acts of the Russian Federation relating to development of the Rules for Price Determination for Taxation Purposes.

There is also a specific exemption for certain types of prices from transfer pricing control:

- state regulated prices (subject to certain limitations);
- prices established in line with directives by anti-monopoly bodies (subject to certain limitations);
- prices for securities and derivatives (these are subject to special transfer pricing rules in the profits tax chapter);
- prices set out by an appraiser (in cases where the appraisal is mandatory under the Russian legislation);
- prices determined under an approved APA.

The scope of controlled transactions was also significantly revised. Under the new rules, the following transactions will be regarded as controlled:

- transactions between Russian related persons, if the total sum of income (i.e., revenue) generated on such transactions:
  - exceeds RUR 1 billion in a calendar year (the threshold is set as RUR 3 billion for year 2012, and RUR 2 billion for year 2013);
  - exceeds RUR 100 million in a calendar year, and one of the parties to the transaction applies a special tax regime in the form of unified tax on imputed income or unified agricultural tax (this provision enters into force on 1 January 2014);
  - exceeds RUR 60 million in a calendar year, and one of the parties to the transaction: pays mineral extraction tax, or is exempt from profits tax or applies zero profits tax rate, or is a resident of a special economic zone;
- cross-border transactions between related parties without any threshold on the sum of income;
- cross-border transactions with unrelated parties with goods traded on global commodity exchanges, if the total amount of income (revenue) on such transactions exceeds RUR 60 million in a calendar year, with regard to:
  - oil and oil products;
  - ferrous and non-ferrous metals;
  - mineral fertilisers;
  - metals and precious stones;
- transactions with the residents of the jurisdictions and territories which are listed by the RF Ministry of Finance as low-tax and/or non-cooperative in terms of fiscal information exchange (offshores/tax havens), where the total sum of income under such transactions exceeds RUR 60 million in a calendar year.

The important development is that domestic transactions with unrelated parties are clearly exempt from transfer pricing control[12] (which was not the case under the previous regulations, which captured transactions with unrelated parties where prices significantly deviated from regular prices for the same product). The courts retain the right to consider a transaction to be controlled even in cases where the transaction does not technically fall into the list of controlled transactions due to conditions artificially created by a taxpayer.

There is also specific exemption for transactions made within a consolidated group of taxpayers[13] or between Russian legal entities, registered in one region of Russia (federation unit), provided that such entities:

- do not have any separate subdivisions either in another region of Russia (federation unit), or abroad;
- do not pay profits tax to other regional budgets (treasuries) of the RF federation units;
- do not have profits tax losses;
- do not fall into any other category of controlled transactions under the Law.

The above thresholds for a transaction to be considered controlled are based on the sums of income (revenue) under transactions in a calendar year, where such sum of income is determined as total sum of income received under such transactions with one person (related persons) in a calendar year, calculated in line with the rules for income recognition under the profits tax chapter of the Russian Tax Code.

The Law expands the number of methods available for transfer pricing purposes and now allows five methods to be used by tax authorities for the calculation of taxable income in related-party transactions:

---

[12] Except for cases where a technically independent intermediary is artifically inserted between two affiliated entities without performing any meaningful functions.

[13] The Russian Parliament has recently adopted the law on consolidated taxpayer group (Law no. 321-FZ of 16 November 2011), which introduces the possibility to create a consolidated taxpayer group for Russian companies on condition that total sales revenues and other income for the group exceeds RUR 100 billion, the total sum of taxes payable for the group exceeds RUR 10 billion, and the asset value of the group exceeds RUR 300 billion. Therefore, based on the mentioned thresholds, most companies appear to be ineligible for tax consolidation.

(i)   comparable uncontrolled price (CUP) method;
(ii)   resale price method;
(iii) cost plus method;
(iv)   transactional net margin method (TNMM);
(v)   profit split method.

The Law retains the concept of hierarchy of methods. Unlike the US and the European practice, the CUP method is treated as the main method and tax authorities can opt for other methods only if this method cannot apply. At the same time, the Law provides that the resale price method is to be used as the priority method for cases where goods are purchased from a related person and are subsequently resold without processing under a transaction with an unrelated party. Historically, the need for the tax authorities to use the CUP method has significantly complicated the task of the tax authorities in proving their case. It remains to be seen whether this will continue to be a hurdle under the new Law.

In terms of sources of information, the Law lists the following sources that can be used by the Russian tax authorities for transfer pricing purposes:

- information on prices and exchange quotations;
- customs statistics;
- information on prices and exchange quotations from official information sources of authorised state and municipal bodies;
- data from informational and price agencies;
- information on transactions made by the taxpayer.

In the absence or lack of information from the above sources, the tax authorities may turn to other publicly available information sources (including commercially available information databases). However, the priority is given to Russian sources. As a result, any foreign benchmarking studies and supporting documentation need to be adapted using Russian comparables.

Technically, there is no requirement for the taxpayers to maintain supporting documentation. Taxpayers are only required to notify local tax authorities about the controlled transactions made within a calendar year. Such notifications need include only description (subject) of the transaction, parties to the transactions and sum of income and (or) expenses. The Law does not require the taxpayer to provide any additional documents or calculations attached to the notification.

The obligation to provide transfer pricing documentation arises only upon receipt of the respective claim from the tax authorities to provide additional documents. The tax authorities are authorised to require documentation related to a transaction (or group of similar transactions). The documentation required is the document describing activities of the taxpayer, list of the parties to the transaction and their functions, description of the transaction, the transfer pricing methods used for price determination, and information on economic benefits derived by the taxpayer. Failure to provide documentation is subject to a fine of RUR 5,000; however, absence of documentation may expose the taxpayers to additional fines where the tax authorities ultimately make a transfer pricing adjustment. Until 2014 the respective provisions on notifications and documentation will apply to the cases where the sum of income under controlled transactions in a calendar year exceeds RUR 100 million in 2012 and RUR 80 million in 2013. In terms of the fines, the fines based on price adjustments will not apply with regard to the periods before 2014, a 20 per cent fine will be charged in 2014–2016, and a 40 per cent fine will apply starting from 2017.

An important development in the new Law is the introduction of the concept of corresponding adjustments. The new Law envisions the possibility to perform corresponding adjustments in cases where the tax authority in the course of a tax audit comes to a conclusion that the price applied by one of the parties to a controlled transaction does not correspond to the market range. In such case, the other party to the controlled transaction is entitled to make corresponding adjustments in its tax accounts. However, corresponding adjustments are allowed only if the party to the transaction, which was subject to the original assessment voluntarily paid such additional assessment to the tax authorities. Also, no mechanism is established for cross-border transactions.

The provisions of articles 20 and 40 of the Russian Tax Code (which outline the transfer pricing rules effective prior to introduction of the new Law) will continue to have effect with regard to transactions, income and/or expenses which are reported by taxpayers prior to the entry of the Law into force.

Although the initial version of the Law envisioned that the RF Ministry of Finance would issue guidance (methodic recommendations) on the application of the Law's provisions, the final text does not have such a provision. It is worth remembering that Russia is still not an OECD member, and that OECD transfer pricing guidance is not mandatory for Russian tax authorities, or for the courts. As a result, taxpayers will have to base their decisions and interpretation on the literal reading of the text of the Law and the evolved court case law, which will still be relevant with regard to certain provisions of the new Law (e.g., subject matter of controlled transactions, hierarchy of methods, etc., see in more detail below).

Overall, the Law contains a number of controversial provisions. For instance, the Law uses the term 'publicly available sources of information', while there is lack of definition of this term, which will inevitably result in disputes on whether certain information is derived from publicly available sources, and, thus, whether it can be used to determine the market price range; the hierarchy of methods set forth by the Law may limit application of certain transfer pricing methods in cases where there is information that is publicly available, but not acceptable for the purposes of the respective method chosen; the Law excludes from the controlled transactions those transactions between companies located in one region (federation unit) of Russia on condition they do not report losses, while it is unclear whether this exclusion may apply to cases where losses were reported by one of the parties in the respective tax period, but after the transaction was made.

Due to lack of possibility to refer to OECD guidelines, as well as differences in approaches used by OECD and Russian legislators, multinational enterprises may have to adapt their global corporate transfer pricing policy to the specific Russian legislation requirements. As an example, in certain cases the Law treats cross-border transactions between unrelated persons as controlled, which is not commonly the case for most OECD member states; the Law does not provide any special rules for cost-sharing arrangements, which is typical for most European jurisdictions. Also, in contrast to the OECD guidelines, the Law envisions a formal hierarchy of the information sources used for market price range determination, as well as making advance pricing agreements available only to Russian companies.

Another important aspect is that the law currently treats Russian entities and permanent establishments (PE) of foreign entities differently, effectively denying PEs many of the rights available to domestic companies (e.g., they cannot sign APAs). The law also does not address the allocation of profit procedures in case of a PE.

The Ministry of Finance has recently announced that it has drafted more than fifty amendments to the Law aimed at clarifying many of the unclear issues in the Law. It is expected that these amendments will be considered by the Russian Parliament in 2012.

14.5   Administrative procedure

The government authority that is responsible for ensuring tax collection and correct application of the tax legislation is the Ministry of Finance, which oversees the Federal Tax Service that is responsible for tax control and collection.

The Ministry of Finance is also authorised to issue non-binding clarifications on the application of tax laws. The public and private letters issued by the tax authorities outline the authorities' official position with respect to various controversial tax issues. However, following the constitutional principle of division of powers, such clarifications do not have the force of law (are not regarded as a source of law and may, therefore, be disregarded by taxpayers and courts) and are not binding. They could, however, be a useful indicator for the taxpayers on what position the tax authorities are likely to take on various controversial issues described in these documents.

Although technically such official letters should be obligatory guidance for the tax and other state authorities in their application of the tax law provisions, this is not necessarily the case in practice, and local tax inspectorates can take positions that differ from those outlined in the Ministry of Finance letters. There are also numerous precedents of the Ministry of Finance issuing conflicting guidance on the same issue.

The courts, as a general rule, give little weight to written clarifications issued by the Ministry of Finance for the reasons mentioned above. However, such clarifications are more readily accepted by courts when dealing with the application of double tax treaty provisions, where the Ministry of Finance is typically stated as being the competent authority.

In terms of tax control procedures, as a general rule, most taxes are self-assessed based on tax declarations filed by taxpayers to the tax authorities. Tax authorities can review tax declarations during desk tax audits (which automatically start upon submission of the tax declaration) and field tax audits (performed at the initiative of the tax office). As a general rule, the tax authorities can perform only one field tax audit in respect of the particular tax for the particular tax year.[14]

The Tax Code establishes a clear procedure for performing a tax audit (including the time limits on how long an audit should take), issuing an

---

[14] There are some exceptions to this rule (e.g., the right for a repeat tax audit in case of control procedures by the superior tax authority, or the right to perform tax audit in case of liquidation or reorganisation).

assessment and appealing the raised assessment. An assessment raised by the tax authorities as a result of the review can be objected to before a formal decision is made, although in the majority of cases this is just a formality.

Until recently, transfer pricing issues were addressed during regular tax audits. With the new transfer pricing rules coming into force on 1 January 2012, transfer pricing audits now represent a separate type of audit with different (extended) statutory periods for completing the review. Transfer pricing tax audits may cover only profits tax, personal income tax (with regard to individual entrepreneurs, advocates, notaries), mineral extraction tax and VAT (only if one party to the transaction is not a VAT taxpayer). Collection of taxes additionally assessed as a result of such transfer pricing audit may be done exclusively under a court procedure.

The general limitation period for tax audits is three calendar years preceding the year of review,[15] which also applies to transfer pricing audits.[16] As a result, the tax authorities in practice typically try to have a field audit for major taxpayers every two to three years, although there are examples of smaller taxpayers operating without a tax audit over longer periods.

Experience shows that the Russian tax authorities historically tended to have a fiscal focus during tax audits (especially in field tax audits). Recent statistics indicate that an assessment has been raised in more than 90 per cent of field tax audits. It is not clear, however, whether this fiscal focus will also affect transfer pricing audits.

Technically, the Tax Code establishes the obligation of the tax authorities to prove the violation of tax law and that the person is guilty of committing this violation (presumption of innocence principle).

In practice, however, the situation is more complex, as, for example, most disputes centre on challenges of recovery of input VAT or deduction of expenses for profits tax purposes. In such disputes the courts tend to ask not only for the tax authorities' arguments to challenge the recovery or deduction, but also for proof from the taxpayer that the taxpayer actually had the right to, and met all requirements established in the law for, such

---

[15] There is a technical possibility to extend this period in case of a criminal prosecution, however, such extensions are rarely applied in case of corporate taxes.

[16] Shorter limitation periods are established for transfer pricing audits during the transition period: audit in respect of 2012 can only be initiated during 2013; whereas audit of 2013 can only be initiated during 2014 and 2015; after that the limitation period for transfer pricing audits becomes the standard three years.

recovery. There is also at least one public transfer pricing case, where lack of proof of the market nature of a transfer price (*Mechel* case, discussed below) was an important factor in the court ruling in favour of the tax authorities.

Typically, there is very limited downside for the tax authorities in raising the assessment, as the courts historically have been reluctant to grant taxpayers recovery of the litigation costs (only recently there were several precedents that allowed recovery of reasonable amounts, but even there the amount of recovery rarely exceeds US $30,000).

The assessment must also be formally appealed to the higher tax authority prior to bringing the case to court. The tax authorities acknowledge that approximately 25 per cent of initially raised assessments are discarded following such appeal.

In case of an assessment under a regular tax audit the tax authorities typically apply a 20 per cent penalty, and are also obliged to charge interest for the period of underpayment that is linked to the Central Bank of Russia discount rate (which as of 1 August 2012 stands at 8.25 per cent per annum). There is also a possibility to impose a 40 per cent penalty (instead of 20 per cent) for intentional violation, however, this is rarely applied in practice.

In respect of separate transfer pricing audits, as mentioned above, no penalties should apply in respect of 2012 and 2013, a 20 per cent penalty will apply for 2014 to 2016, and a 40 per cent penalty will apply for the periods after 2017. Maintenance of proper transfer pricing documentation may exempt the taxpayer from this penalty.

If following the appeal procedure the taxpayer still disagrees with the assessment, then it can take the issue to court.

In many cases, going to court allows the taxpayer to obtain an injunction against the payment of the assessment until the case is ultimately settled. However, over the last several years the courts have become more reluctant to grant an automatic injunction, and this now often requires providing a bank guarantee to the court or putting a sizeable deposit (typically of at least 50 per cent of the amount of the assessment) into court.

Similar to other civil law-based legal systems, court cases in Russia do not have the force of law, although unlike many other jurisdictions the volume of tax litigation is significant (currently running at the level of 90,000 to 100,000 tax cases considered by the courts annually). It is worth noting that the current number of cases is already a sizeable reduction from a peak of more than 400,000 tax cases heard in 2005.

As a result, court practice in the tax arena has become increasingly important. The Supreme Arbitrazh Court has also put a lot of effort recently into ensuring consistency of the court cases on similar issues, emphasising that its interpretations of the law outlined in its decisions are binding for lower level courts.

A tax litigation process for the Russian corporate taxpayers typically takes six to nine months and involves three levels (first instance, appellate and cassation), as well as an opportunity subsequently to apply to the Supreme Arbitrazh Court (which, however, typically accepts less than 5 per cent of applications).

The court litigation process is generally considered to be fair, although some practitioners and litigators report that the judges sometimes apply less rigorous standards to evidence presented by the tax authorities as compared to evidence presented by taxpayers.

The process is also fairly transparent, with at least cassation level court decisions being officially published on the Supreme Arbitrazh Court website,[17] as well as available through all major commercial legal databases. The Supreme Arbitrazh Court also routinely makes its hearings available online to the general public.

Recent statistics published by the Federal Tax Services indicate that the tax authorities win approximately 70 per cent of tax litigation cases, but less than 50 per cent of amounts raised against companies. At the same time, most prominent local tax litigation firms typically advertise a win rate in excess of 90 per cent, so success in litigation may be influenced by the quality of legal help. Currently, there is no requirement to be licensed or have special legal status to represent a company in a tax litigation as long as the representative has a valid power of attorney.

The Supreme Arbitrazh Court reports a gradual decrease in tax cases filed by taxpayers against tax authorities – the current level of cases is approximately 50 per cent down from its peak in 2007.

14.6   Transfer pricing disputes: domestic approaches

First of all, transfer pricing disputes are not that common in the current Russian tax environment. For example, based on the search results in the leading Russian legal database, out of more than 250,000 tax related cases heard at the cassation (third) court level since 2001, less than 4,000 (or less than 1.5 per cent of cases) touch upon transfer pricing in one

---

[17] See kad.arbitr.ru.

form or another.[18] Also, although there are currently no exact statistics on the win-loss ratio, it is widely accepted in the professional community that taxpayers tended to win 70–80 per cent of all transfer pricing cases in Russia (it is not currently clear whether the new transfer pricing rules will meaningfully change this).

This may be the result of the historical difficulties that the Russian tax authorities faced in collecting evidence of the breach of transfer pricing rules following the procedure established by the law. As a result, the Russian tax authorities, for example, on the cost side prefer to challenge the deduction of the expense or recovery of the associated input VAT as a whole based on alleged failure to meet the 'economic justification' requirement,[19] deficiencies in VAT invoices, or following the 'unjustified tax benefit' court doctrine,[20] rather than follow the transfer pricing route.[21]

Nevertheless, the court practice plays an important role in filling the gaps in the current transfer pricing rules, which, as discussed above, until recently have been fairly rudimentary.

Since the Russian transfer pricing legislation has been rule-based rather than principle-based, the court practice in this area has historically concentrated on various technical aspects of following the specific adjustment procedure as outlined in the transfer pricing legislation. This practice will in many respects continue to be relevant even under the new rules, since many definitions and concepts are still similar.

14.6.1 Scope of application of the law

The Russian Supreme Arbitrazh Court issued its first court act in connection with the new transfer pricing rules just six months after they came into force. Joint Resolution of the Supreme Arbitrazh Court no. 41 and of the Supreme Court no. 9 of 11 June 1999 reinforced that the transfer pricing rules can apply only to the four types of the transactions specifically listed in the law.

---

[18] Goltsblat BLP analysis based on the information contained in Consultant Plus database (www.consultant.ru/).

[19] Article 252 of the Tax Code.

[20] Resolution of the Presidium of the Supreme Arbitrazh Court no. 53 of 12 October 2006.

[21] Another possible reason is that the transfer pricing rules were not explicit enough, which provided some basis for isolated precedents of courts arguing that transfer pricing rules can only apply to the revenue side and cannot be used to adjust the cost base: see, e.g., Resolution of the Federal Arbitrazh Court for the North-Western Region no. A52-2867/2008 of 13 July 2009 (*Intraflex* case). The new rules that came into force in 2012 provide a clearer basis to adjust both the revenue side and the cost side of transactions.

Another important clarification came from the Constitutional Court in response to a claim by a taxpayer that transfer pricing rules breach the Russian Constitution by making the tax burden subjective and unpredictable.[22] The Constitutional Court, however, ruled that transfer pricing rules do not breach taxpayers' constitutional rights per se. At the same time, similar to other methods for deemed estimation of the tax base, they can only apply to situations where there is reason to believe that the taxpayer deliberately understated the tax base. Unfortunately, this principle has not been widely used by Arbitrazh courts in subsequent court proceedings. It will, however, remain to be relevant even under the new transfer pricing rules that came into force from 1 January 2012.

14.6.2 Allowed sources of information

There have been many conflicting decisions on the question of allowed sources, and the court practice continues to evolve. The courts have not come to a unified conclusion of what should be considered an 'official source of information', although some courts considered the existence of official powers to collect, analyse and disseminate information as an important consideration when determining whether the information was 'official'.[23]

An important document in this respect is the Resolution of the Presidium of the Supreme Arbitrazh Court no. 11583/04 of 18 January 2005 where the Supreme Arbitrazh Court suggested that official sources of information in order to be applicable need to contain data on the market prices of comparable products sold in similar circumstances in the specific time period. As a result, information from statistics authorities, being too generic, cannot be used for transfer pricing purposes. This position has been applied in many court decisions.[24]

---

[22] Ruling of the Constitutional Court no. 441-O of 4 December 2003 (*Niva-7* case). Similar arguments are also contained in Ruling of the Constitutional Court no. 442-O of 4 December 2003 (*BAO-T* case).

[23] See, e.g., Resolution of the Federal Arbitrazh Court for the Moscow District no. KA-A40/10623–06 of 3 November 2006.

[24] See, e.g., Resolution of the Federal Arbitrazh Court for the Volgo-Vytasky District no. A82-7208/2005-37 of 17 November 2006 (*Ruskhleb* case); Resolution of the Federal Arbitrazh Court for the Povolzhsky District no. A72-7227/05-12/484 of 6 April 2006 (*Vtorchermet* case); Resolution of the Federal Arbitrazh Court for the North-Western District no. A21-12254/03-C1 of 25 January 2006 (*Kaminskaya* case).

At the same time, there are also precedents[25] where the courts followed a previous position of the Supreme Arbitrazh Court,[26] where it deemed statistical information to be acceptable for transfer pricing purposes.[27]

There is currently no consensus on whether an appraisal report from an authorised institution can be used a valid basis for transfer pricing adjustments. It appears that the courts overall do not consider such report to be acceptable as the sole basis for an adjustment, although sometimes accept it in the absence of other data.

14.6.3 Types of information on comparables eligible to be used for CUP purposes

Probably the first actual case decided by the Supreme Arbitrazh Court on transfer pricing matter was the *Yuganskneftegaz* case in 2002[28] (Yuganskneftegaz was at that time part of the infamous Yukos conglomerate).

In that case the tax authorities made a tax assessment based on deviation of the actual sale prices used by Yuganskneftegaz on sales to affiliated entities versus average oil prices indicated in a letter from the Economic Policy Department of the regional government authorities. The court deemed such approach unacceptable. It clarified that in order to be able to use a price as a comparable, the price should take into account similar parameters that formed the basis for the taxpayer's price.

The Supreme Arbitrazh Court reinforced this principle once more several years later in the *Carasan* case,[29] where it argued that any information that is used to determine market prices for transfer pricing purposes should contain information on market prices of identical or similar goods or services sold during the same period of time and in comparable circumstances. Otherwise such information cannot be used as the basis for transfer pricing adjustments.

Another example of the same logic is the fairly recent *Bolshevik Coal Mine* case.[30] In that case the tax authorities used information on coal

---

[25] Resolution of the Federal Arbitrazh Court no. Ф04-5088/2005 of 2 March 2006 (*Sibekologiya* case).

[26] Publicised by the Letter of the Ministry of Finance no. 03–02–01/1 of 16 September 2004.

[27] This is one of the examples where the Supreme Arbitrazh Court supported apparently inconsistent legal positions within a relatively short period of time.

[28] Resolution of the Supreme Arbitrazh Court no. 1369/01 of 19 November 2002.

[29] Resolution of the Supreme Arbitrazh Court no. 11583/04 of 18 January 2005.

[30] Resolution of the Supreme Arbitrazh Court no. 10280/09 of 12 January 2010.

export prices that they obtained from a local Commerce Chamber as
the basis to make a transfer pricing adjustment. However, the provided
information referred to export sales of coal of a particular grade on FCA
terms to Estonia. The court ruled that since the taxpayer sold coal of a
different grade on different commercial terms and to a different country,
that information could not form the basis for a transfer pricing
adjustment.

Obviously, such approach made the use of the CUP method very
difficult for the tax authorities in most circumstances.

14.6.4 Definition of interrelated parties

Although the Tax Code grants to the courts the right to deem any two
taxpayers interrelated for the purposes of application of transfer pricing
rules, the Constitutional Court ruled that this cannot be arbitrary and
the underlying reasons should be stated in some form in a federal law.[31]
This principle was also gradually accepted by Arbitrazh courts.[32]

The courts also ruled that existence of interrelatedness in itself is not
the reason for adjustment of prices for tax purposes and that the tax
authorities in every case need to prove deviation of more than 20 per cent
from the market price.[33]

14.6.5 Definition of a short period of time

This was an important issue since it determined when domestic transactions with independent parties may have been subject to transfer pricing
control. As a general rule, the courts understand 'short period of time' as
a period shorter than one year. However, there are precedents of the
courts deeming a period even shorter than one year as being 'too long'
for the purposes of application of transfer pricing.[34]

This aspect will become less relevant in the future, since the new
transfer pricing rules coming into force on 1 January 2012 no longer
contain a '20 per cent change in a short period of time' test.

---

[31] *Niva-7* case, note 22 above.

[32] See, e.g., Resolutions of the Federal Arbitrazh Court for the Moscow Region no. KA-A40/
8729-07 of 6 September 2007 (*Loxwell Trading* case), and no. KA-A40/7270-07 of 28
August 2007 (*Great-B* case).

[33] *Ibid.*

[34] See, e.g., Resolution of the Federal Arbitrazh Court for the Central District no. A14-632-
200837/28 of 6 October 2008 (*Agroimpuls* case) where the court deemed two transactions
that happened within nine months of one another as being insufficient for determining
the existence of a '20 per cent deviation within a short period of time'.

14.6.6 Use of methods

As mentioned above, article 40 established a strict hierarchy in application of the methods for determining a market price for tax purposes. This is one of the main reasons why historically the tax authorities were forced to try to identify a proper external comparable to be able to raise a transfer pricing adjustment. For example, analysis of court practice in 2006 and 2007[35] indicated that out of forty-four court cases during these years where the tax authorities succeeded, only six used resale or cost plus methods. The rest were based on identifying a comparable.

This, obviously, as mentioned above, complicates the task of the tax authorities, since finding a proper comparable in open sources is often very complicated, if possible at all. This is probably one of the main reasons why the tax authorities tended to lose most of the transfer pricing cases in court.

At the same time, when the tax authorities 'do their homework' properly, they significantly increase their chances of winning. A vivid example of this is a recent decision of the Supreme Arbitrazh Court[36] (so-called *Mechel* case).

In the above ruling, the Supreme Arbitrazh Court supported the lower courts in their determination that courts should not be bound by methods listed in the Tax Code, and that they may accept any other method the courts find justifiable as long as the tax authorities properly prove their case. The courts also determined that unless the company provided proof that the tax authorities' methods used to arrive at an estimate of the market price for transfer pricing purposes is incorrect (which the court determined that the Mechel's affiliate failed to do), it is free to deem the calculations made by the tax authorities to be accurate, even where methods listed in the Tax Code have not been strictly followed.

If this approach is followed by other courts, it may mean that it will become more difficult for the Russian companies to use procedural defences in transfer pricing disputes, especially in the context of new transfer pricing rules, which are less prescriptive and potentially provide

---

[35] Emelianov and Zatochny, Nalogoved, 2007, no. 9.
[36] Ruling of the Supreme Arbitrazh Court no. 2087/11 of 4 March 2011 (*Korshunovsky GOK* or *Mechel* case).

a lot more opportunities to decide transfer pricing cases based on substance rather than form.

14.7 Transfer pricing disputes: bilateral and multilateral approaches MAP/arbitration

Although most Russian double tax treaties contain Articles on mutual agreement procedure, these provisions are rarely used in practice. There are only a few public precedents of actual usage of this procedure to arrive at a mutual understanding of the relevant double tax treaty provisions. Most notable examples are discussions with the German, Cypriot and Belarus authorities, which resulted in the Ministry of Finance issuing official clarifications on the agreed interpretation of the treaties, as well as agreement of the Ministry of Finance to accept tax residence certificates from selected countries without an obligatory apostille.[37]

These cases, however, did not address transfer pricing issues. And since historically, as mentioned above, inbound transfer pricing typically has not been challenged from the tax perspective, there was no reason for and no precedents of using mutual agreement procedure in respect of individual transfer pricing cases.

14.8 Advance pricing agreements

Until recently there was no legal basis for signing advance pricing agreements (APAs) between the taxpayer and the tax authorities. Although there is anecdotal evidence of informal arrangements between the local authorities and the taxpayers on the amount of taxes expected to be paid to the local budget, such arrangements are not official, and have indeed been fiercely resisted and sometimes even officially denounced by the federal tax authorities.

The new transfer pricing Law, however, allows major Russian tax-payers (as defined by applicable Russian tax registration regulations, which include several thousand of the largest taxpayers in Russia) to conclude APAs with the tax authorities starting from 1 January 2012. In this context, signing APAs between a foreign entity (e.g., MNC's headquarters) directly and the tax authorities is technically impossible.

---

[37] See, e.g., Letter of the Moscow Department for the Federal Tax Service no. 16-15/133937 of 21 December 2010.

APAs will cover the rules for price determination and or application of transfer pricing methods in controlled transactions for tax purposes. Respectively, conclusion of APAs will exempt the taxpayer from the obligation to prove that the prices applied in controlled transactions with related parties correspond to the market price range. APAs can be concluded for a term of not more than three years.

It remains to be seen to what extent such APAs will be effective and whether the practice of their application will be as positive in Russia as it is routinely viewed in other major jurisdictions.

14.9 Concluding remarks

The Russian transfer pricing rules and the Russian tax system continue to evolve in response to the increasing integration of Russia into the world economy.

The new transfer pricing rules coming into force in 2012 represent a significant change in application of the transfer pricing rules in Russia and bring it closer to the practices common in jurisdictions with older and more developed tax systems.

However, even though these new rules are closer to OECD Transfer Pricing Guidelines, this does not necessarily mean that (a) multinationals can safely apply in Russia the methods they apply in other European countries; or that (b) the relevant transfer pricing provisions will be interpreted in a way similar to the OECD Transfer Pricing Guidelines.

This is because Russia, not being a member of the OECD, is not bound by the OECD Transfer Pricing Guidelines. The Russian tax authorities and the courts will also be using the specific Russian language in the adopted law.

The court practice that was developed under the currently existing transfer pricing rules (especially to the extent it addresses the definition of market prices, acceptability of information, definition of the related parties, rights and obligations of the taxpayers) will continue to be relevant.

The fact that Russia has a fairly developed appeal procedure and transparent court system (at least in the area of tax law) may also mean that we will likely see more and more court cases in this area, which will continue to fill the gaps left by the transfer pricing laws.

It can be expected that the Russian approach will continue to evolve in the future closer to the OECD Transfer Pricing Guidelines. However, the practical implementation will still likely have distinct features of the Russian legal system, and is unlikely to be 100 per cent identical to the approaches suggested by the OECD Transfer Pricing Guidelines.

Appendix: Questionnaire (Russia)

1. The structure of the law for solving transfer pricing disputes. *What is the structure of the law of the country for solving transfer pricing disputes? For example, is the mutual agreement procedure (MAP), as regulated in the relevant tax treaty, the standard method for solving transfer pricing disputes?*

All tax rules (including transfer pricing rules) are set by the Tax Code at the federal level. The tax authorities do not have powers to negotiate the assessment once it is raised – they can either drop the assessment altogether or insist that the issue is solved in court. In practice, however, it is sometimes possible to negotiate with the tax authorities on the issues to be covered by the assessment prior to them raising such assessment.

2. Policy for solving transfer pricing disputes. *Is there a gap between the nominal and effective method for solving transfer pricing disputes in the country? For example, has the country a strategic policy not to enforce the arm's length standard (ALS) for fear of driving foreign direct investment to other competing jurisdictions?*

Technically, there is no gap between the nominal and effective method for solving transfer pricing disputes in Russia, since both the taxpayer and the tax authorities go to court to resolve any disputes they may have, which follows from the constitutional principle that all taxpayer's liabilities can be set solely by written law adopted at the federal level. However, the Russian tax authorities could probably have used the appeal procedure (that happens prior to going to court) more extensively to resolve more cases instead of forcing them to go to court.

The new transfer pricing rules are loosely based on the OECD guidelines (with some exceptions). However, since the legislation is new, it remains to be seen to what extent the implementation practice would deviate from the European and US practice.

3. The prevailing dispute resolution method. *Which is the most frequent method for solving transfer pricing disputes in the country? Does it have a positive externality? For example, is the MAP the most frequent method, and if so, to what extent have successful MAPs been used as a proxy for transfer pricing case law? For instance, Procter & Gamble (P&G) obtained a bilateral advance pricing agreement (APA) in Europe, and it was then extended to a third (Asian) country when P&G made this request to the relevant Asian tax authorities.*

The new transfer pricing legislation has not been widely tested yet. Although there is some anecdotal evidence that the tax authorities may pay some attention to the *bona fide* transfer pricing documentation prepared in other jurisdictions (especially at the federal Minfin level and for larger taxpayers), technically, all transfer pricing disputes in Russia need to be solved purely under Russian law, and based on Russian comparables and underlying data (foreign data can be used only in some circumstances and only if it can be proved that there is no comparable Russian data available; it is also expected that adjustment to comparable Russian data can be demonstrated).

4. Transfer pricing case law. *What is the evolution path of transfer pricing litigation in the country? For example: (i) Is transfer pricing litigation being gradually replaced by either MAPs or APAs, as regulated in the relevant tax treaties? (ii) Are foreign/local transfer pricing precedents and/ or published MAPs increasingly relevant as a source of law for solving transfer pricing disputes?*

Technically, Russian authorities and courts can base their decisions solely on Russian legislation, as well as explicit provisions in international treaties signed by Russia. Since Russia is not a party to the OECD, any OECD documents (including guidelines) have no legal force in Russia, although there are precedents of Russian courts using references to OECD documents (as an indicator of international best practice) as supporting arguments. Courts also have the technical right to take into consideration any facts that they deem relevant to properly decide on the case.

5. Customary international law and international tax procedure. *Has customary international law been applied in the country to govern the relevant methods for solving transfer pricing disputes (such as the MAP)? For example, has the* OECD Manual on Effective Mutual Agreement

Procedure ('*OECD Manual*') been deemed customary international tax law in the MAP arena for filling procedural gaps (for example, time limit for implementation of relief where treaties deviate from the OECD Model Tax Convention)?

No, Russian tax procedure is based solely on the Russian legislation. The administrative procedure, however, has been evolving over the years to provide clear formal rights to the taxpayers, and the courts have been fairly strict in enforcing the rights of the taxpayers for due process in case of a tax assessment.

As mentioned in the chapter, Russia has no experience with MAP for solving transfer pricing disputes.

6. Procedural setting and strategic interaction.   *Does strategic interaction between taxpayers and tax authorities depend on the procedural setting in which they interact when trying to solve transfer pricing disputes? For example, which procedural setting in the country prompts the relevant parties to cooperate with each other the most for solving this sort of dispute, and why?*

There are no specific formal incentives for the cooperation between the taxpayer and the tax authorities. The taxpayer has an obligation to duly calculate and pay the taxes, and the tax authorities have the right to control the correctness of such calculation and payment of tax through desk and field audits. The taxpayer also has the right to apply for clarification on application of the tax law, however, such clarifications are not binding for either party and do not have the force of law.

In case of a tax assessment, the tax authorities have to follow a specific procedure (perform a formal audit, issue an assessment notice, give the right to the taxpayer to raise formal objections, etc.). The procedure itself, however, does not provide any incentive for reaching a compromise. As a result, most tax disputes are settled in court.

7. The future of transfer pricing disputes resolution.   *Which is the best available proposal in light of the interests of the country for facilitating the global resolution of transfer pricing disputes, and why?*

Practical implementation of APAs, as well as reducing the threshold for application of both APAs and domestic tax consolidation (which under Russian rules exempts from transfer pricing compliance any intra-group domestic transactions) may significantly reduce the scope for transfer pricing disputes.

In a situation where the Russian tax authorities are prohibited by law from issuing binding guidance, developing domestic court practice (case law) will also be important in providing practical guidance to taxpayers in interpretation of the new transfer pricing rules.

Transfer pricing disputes in India

MUKESH BUTANI

15.1 Introduction

The buzz of globalisation and liberalisation has engulfed nations worldwide. Companies have moved beyond local markets. Countries are no longer isolated economies. Our world, as we know, is witnessing an increasing trend towards globalisation. For businesses, this has translated into prosperity and new markets, but lurking in this opportunity is the complexity of cross-border transactions. It is a simple premise: no two economies are similar. The taxes are different and so are the laws and regulations. It is in this scenario that the role of transfer pricing has gained both importance and credence. With the unprecedented increase in cross-border transactions between various arms of global enterprises, a host of complicated tax issues have emerged. One such key issue, transfer pricing, has gained enormous attention from both the business community and tax authorities across the world.

A multinational corporation operates in different countries across the globe with its facilities expanding offshore. It is a common phenomenon for such a corporation to have production centres located in different countries, thereby allowing the transfer of stock and services from one country to another. With changes in global businesses and tax environment in different geographies, one may encounter a thicket of transfer pricing issues and challenges on the way. It is in this context that the transfer pricing laws prescribe robust mechanisms for dealing with disagreements on transfer pricing matters that may arise in the course of global business operations. With this background, this chapter discusses in detail the transfer pricing dispute resolution mechanisms and transfer pricing audit experience in India. The chapter also provides a brief glance at the significant recent developments in the Indian transfer pricing landscape.

I am indebted to Sanjiv Malhotra, Manish Khurana and Priya Bubna for assistance in the preparation of this chapter.

Before we delve into the historical background of the transfer pricing dispute resolution mechanism prevalent in India, a brief glance at the foreign direct inflows of India may be useful. Since 1991, with the liberalisation of trade and foreign exchange policy, India has started integrating its economy with the world. Increased cross-border services have led to a large inflow of foreign direct investment (FDI) in to India. The cumulative amount of FDI (equity inflows) has amounted to US$153,209 million from August 1991 to March 2011. In the financial year ending 31 March 2011 (1 April 2010 to 31 March 2011) the figure for FDI (equity inflows) has been US$20,304 million.[1] With increased FDI, the importance of implementation of anti-avoidance provisions assumed greater significance.

15.2   Emergence of transfer pricing in India

Until the early 1990s, the Indian economy remained by and large insulated from the rest of the world. Although erosion of tax base through manipulative pricing of goods and services was a possibility, with significantly fewer cross-border transactions, the threat of transferring profits was not so imminent.

The Indian legal and regulatory landscape underwent a significant change in the 1990s as India embarked upon economic reforms. In the early 1990s, the Indian economy opened up to foreign investments and there was a quantum jump in the number of cross-border transactions. While novel policies were introduced by the policy-makers to fuel the engine of economic growth, the economic reform programme and concomitant globalisation necessitated the introduction of comprehensive transfer pricing legislation in India. It was around ten years ago, in November 1999, that an expert group was set up by the government to study global transfer pricing practices and examine the need for detailed legislation specifically dealing with transfer pricing. Based on the recommendations of the group, in 2001, India enacted new provisions in the Indian Income Tax Act, 1961 ('the Act'), to counter the growing threat of tax avoidance by manipulation of transfer prices. What saw expression in the form of Chapter X of the Act were the Indian transfer pricing regulations. Legislated within the existing scheme of regulations, the transfer pricing provisions were further elucidated in rules 10A to 10E of the Indian Income Tax Rules, 1962 ('the Rules'). The Act and Rules

---

[1]   *Reserve Bank of India Bulletin* (August 2011).

simultaneously laid down parameters for determining transfer prices of tangible/intangible property transferred and services rendered in related party transactions, as well as processes for resolving transfer pricing disputes arising in the course of business operations.

In India, transfer pricing dispute resolution mechanisms can be understood in the backdrop of the domestic laws prevalent in the country and the alternate dispute resolution mechanisms contained in the tax treaties signed by India.

15.2.1   Pre-2001 scenario (1935–1961)

Prior to the introduction of comprehensive transfer pricing regulations, certain basic provisions existed within the framework of the Indian Income Tax Act, 1922, in the form of anti-avoidance measures. Under section 42(2) of the Indian Income Tax Act, 1922, it was expressly laid down that for any price set between a resident[2] and a non-resident owing to the business connection between both the parties (i.e., controlled), the typical market mechanisms that establish prices for a transaction between third parties may not be in play. Hence, the income should be recomputed to reflect reasonable and fair prices to be taxed in India. In this regard it is pertinent to note the decision of the Supreme Court[3] in *Mazagaon Dock Ltd.*[4] The case involved two non-resident enterprises engaged in shipping activities, which entered into an arrangement with its Indian counterpart for repair of the ships. In accordance with the terms of the arrangement, the Indian company was liable to recover only the cost of the services rendered without charging any profit margin. The Supreme Court observed that the dealings between the parties were in the nature of business activities warranting recovery of a mark-up, as would have been in the course of normal business dealings. Section 42(2) of the Indian Income Tax Act, 1922 was invoked, the pricing arrangement set between the transacting entities was rejected and income recomputed to reflect reasonable profits akin to what would have been earned between unrelated parties.

15.2.2   Pre-2001 scenario (1961–2001)

The Indian Income tax Act, 1922 was subsequently repealed and replaced by the Indian Income Tax Act, 1961. Section 92 of the Act

---

[2] Indian Income Tax Act, 1961, s.6.   [3] The Apex Court in India.
[4] Supreme Court of India (1958) 34 ITR 368.

contained provisions empowering the Revenue authorities to determine an appropriate transaction price in a scenario where the tax administrators believed that the transfer prices were not apt owing to the 'close connection' between the two parties (resident and a non-resident). Further, where such a business connection existed in India, the income that was 'reasonably attributable' to the business operations carried out in India was to be taxed in India. Rule 10 of the Rules outlined guidance on how the income of a non-resident taxpayer could be apportioned to the business operations carried out in India, in the event where it could not be definitely ascertained. Where the actual amount of the income accruing to any non-resident, through or from any business connection in India, could not be definitely computed, the income taxable under the Act was to be computed by adopting one of the following approaches:

- at a reasonable percentage of turnover from Indian operations;
- total profits in proportion of receipts in India compared to total receipts; and
- in any other manner considered appropriate and reasonable by the authorities.

Such principles of business connection and apportionment of income are well established by way of various judicial precedents. In *Bombay Trust Corporation Ltd* v. *CIT*[5] and *Jethabhai Javerbhai* v. *CIT*[6], the above-mentioned principles are well articulated. Similarly, there have been numerous cases in the past where business connection has been the talking point and has led to recomputation of the transfer prices of multinational corporations.

Further the courts, in various instances, have not refrained from placing reliance on independent comparables for determining the rate of return (where books of accounts were not available or were unreliable). Jurisprudence emerging from cases such as *Badri Shah Sohan Lal* v. *CIT*[7] and *CIT* v. *Abdul Aziz Sahib*,[8] clearly reflect the administration's preference for reliance on profits earned by similar players in the industry *vis-à-vis* the accounts of the taxpayer itself. This approach adopted is akin to the concept of the transfer pricing provisions introduced post-2001 in India.

---

[5] MISC(1928) 3 ITC 135.   [6] Nagpur High Court (1951) 20 ITR 331.
[7] Lahore High Court (1936) 4 ITR 303.   [8] Madras High Court (1939) 7 ITR 647.

15.2.3   Post-2001 scenario

In 2001, the Indian government introduced comprehensive transfer pricing legislation in the form of Chapter X (constituting sections 92 to 92F) of the Act. The motive was to ensure that with the increasing presence of multinational enterprises, arm's length profits are retained in India contributing to the revenue of the exchequer and preventing erosion of the tax base. The view among the policy-makers was to provide a statutory framework that could enable computation of reasonable, fair and arm's length profits in the country. To ensure fair and just tax collection in the country and address concerns of the taxpayers, transfer pricing dispute resolution mechanisms were introduced. Taxpayers in India currently can access the following available dispute resolution mechanisms:

1. Under the domestic law: various dispute resolution mechanisms are contained within the scope of the domestic tax regulations under the Act. These are discussed in the subsequent sections.
2. Under double taxation avoidance agreements (DTAAs): India has entered into DTAAs with various countries with the intention of providing relief to taxpayers in cases of double taxation. Mutual agreement procedure (MAP), an alternate dispute resolution mechanism under the DTAA, is being increasingly used for resolving transfer pricing disputes in India.

15.3   Overview of the administrative set-up for dispute resolution

The structure of domestic dispute resolution administration is depicted in Figure 15.1. The detailed process of dispute resolution among the various levels is explained in the ensuing sections.

15.4   Emergence of transfer pricing disputes

In India, taxpayers are required to follow the tax year which runs from 1 April to 31 March of the subsequent year. A taxpayer in India is required to file its return[9] of income within the stipulated time limit

---

[9] Income Tax Act, 1961, s.139(1).

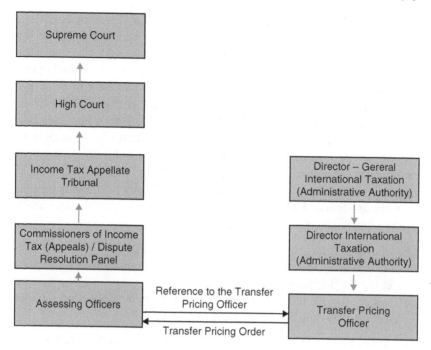

Figure 15.1 Domestic dispute resolution structure

(30 November[10] following the tax year ending 31 March for which a return is to be filed for corporate taxpayers). Further, an accountant's certificate[11] (detailing the international transactions and the arm's length nature of the same) in the prescribed form is also required to be filed by the taxpayers undertaking international transactions with their associated enterprises. While the return can be filed electronically with the Revenue, the accountant's certificate has to be filed in its physical form. The accountant's certificate is authenticated by an external chartered accountant who is authorised to do so. Non-filing of tax returns can subject the taxpayer to interest and penalty liability. Non-furnishing of the accountant's certificate may also subject the taxpayer to penal consequences.

The Act provides a comprehensive definition of the term 'associated enterprise' and covers various cases in which two enterprises will be

---

[10] New due date provided under *ibid.* s.139(1) effective from April 2011 for companies subject to transfer pricing provisions.
[11] *Ibid.* s.92E.

deemed to be 'associated'. The Direct Tax Code Bill, 2009 ('Original DTC') unveiled in August 2009 proposed significant changes in the Indian tax regime to align it with global best practices.

The Original DTC proposed to widen the scope of associated enterprises by lowering the benchmark for equity participation from 26 per cent to 10 per cent and proposing other similar changes. However, in the final bill laid out in the Indian Parliament, the Direct Tax Code Bill, 2010 ('DTC 2010'), the proposal to widen the definition of associated enterprises by lowering equity participation thresholds to 10 per cent and similar other changes have been shelved. The DTC 2010, however, in addition to the existing circumstances specified under the Act, proposes two circumstances for enterprises to qualify as associated enterprises. These additional circumstances are:

(a) where an enterprise influences the terms and price at which services are provided to another enterprise (such a condition already exists in the Act for goods); and

(b) where one of the enterprises is located in a specific or distinct location, as may be prescribed.

The second additional condition of treating an enterprise located in a specific or distinct location, as may be prescribed, is vague and requires clarification from the government on its intent.

15.4.1   Selection of cases for audit

An audit procedure is initiated in India as soon as the assessing officer[12] takes up a case for a detailed examination. The assessing officer examines the income of the taxpayer to determine if the tax offered is in compliance with the regulations laid down in the Act. In common parlance, a taxpayer will be liable to transfer pricing disputes until such time as the Revenue is in agreement with the tax offered by the taxpayer.

---

[12] The assessing officer is the authority who initiates the assessment of income under the Act. He receives income tax returns from the assessee within his jurisdiction (defined by *ibid.* s.124) and makes assessment under *ibid.* ch. XIV. Section 2(7A) of the Act defines 'assessing officer' to mean the Assistant Commissioner or Deputy Commissioner or Assistant Director or Deputy Director or the income tax officer who is vested with the relevant jurisdiction under s.120(1) or (2) or any other provision of the Act. It can even include the Additional Commissioner or Additional Director, Joint Commissioner or Joint Director who is directed under s.120(4)(b) of the Act to exercise all powers and functions conferred on an assessing officer under the Act.

The assessing officer can issue an intimation[13] selecting a case for audit within six months from the end of the tax year in which the return of income is filed. Once the case is selected for audit, in a scenario where the aggregate value of international transaction undertaken exceeds the administratively specified value (currently US$3.25 million),[14] transactions are referred by the assessing officer to a specified group of officers designated to handle transfer pricing matters. These officers, known as transfer pricing officers (TPOs), examine the international transactions to determine if the international transactions undertaken were at arm's length. The order passed by the TPO is binding on the assessing officer. In a scenario where the aggregate value of the transaction does not exceed the specified limit, the assessing officer can himself proceed to decide on the arm's length nature of the transaction or can refer the matter to the TPO.

In the changes proposed in the Original DTC, the cases were proposed to be picked up directly by the TPO for audit by undertaking a risk-based assessment. However, in the DTC 2010, the proposal for selection for audit by undertaking a risk-based assessment has been dropped and the current procedure has been restored.

It is important to note that where a reference has not been made and an order has been passed by the assessing officer, the assessing officer cannot utilise its power to rectify mistakes and make a reference to the TPO. Section 154 of the Act confers upon the officer the right to rectify mistakes apparent from the record, which he may have committed during the course of assessment proceedings. Non-reference within the stipulated time cannot be regarded as a mistake apparent from the record under section 154 and thus a reference, after the passing of an order by the assessing officer, is not possible.

Further, the assessing officer has the powers to issue notice[15] for selection of cases for audit where any income earned in the past has not been assessed, within a period of four years from the end of the assessment year. The period of four years is extended to six years if the income escaping assessment exceeds/is likely to exceed the specified limit (approximately US$2,500). These powers are provided to the assessing officer by virtue of section 148 of the Act. The section is used by the Revenue authorities to reopen audit of a year, if they have reason to believe that income for the year has escaped taxation. After a matter has

---

[13] *Ibid.* s.143(1).   [14] Assuming US $1 = INR 45.   [15] Income Tax Act, 1961, s.148.

been reopened using the provisions of section 148, the assessing officer can refer the matter to the TPO for examination from a transfer pricing perspective. In *Coca Cola India Inc.*,[16] the reopening of cases for the past year on the basis of transfer pricing adjustment in a subsequent year was held to be valid.

Akin to the power under section 148 provided to the assessing officer, the Act also grants certain powers to the Commissioners of Income Tax to undertake revisionary proceedings.[17] Under the provisions, pursuant to examining the records of an order passed by the assessing officer, the Commissioner, on his own accord, may initiate proceedings where he believes that the decision made by the assessing officer is erroneous to the extent that it is prejudicial to the Revenue. The term 'prejudicial to the Revenue' implies an action leading to a compromise in tax revenue that should fairly accrue to the Revenue authorities. The time limit for initiating the revision proceedings is two years from the end of the tax year in which the order to be revised is passed by the assessing officer.

The principles on invoking revisionary provisions have been well enunciated in *Ranbaxy Laboratories*.[18] The Income Tax Appellate Tribunal ('the Tribunal') sustained the Commissioner's action of initiating revisionary proceedings under section 263 of the Act as the assessing officer had abstained from referring the case to the TPO, even though the value of the international transaction exceeded US$1.1 million (the administratively specified limit for reference which was subsequently increased to US$3.25 million). Further, in *FabIndia Overseas Private Ltd*,[19] the Commissioner under section 263 initiated revisionary proceedings. In the instant case, the value of international transactions did not exceed the administratively specified value and thus no reference was made to the TPO. However, revisionary proceedings were initiated as the Commissioner believed that a detailed examination of the case (not undertaken by the assessing officer) was required from a transfer pricing perspective. In *Maithan International*,[20] the Tribunal held that while revisionary proceedings could be undertaken for a lack of enquiry, they could not be undertaken for inadequate enquiry. In *Sun Microsystems India*

---

[16] Punjab and Haryana High Court (2009) 309 ITR 194.
[17] Income Tax Act, 1961, s.263.   [18] Tribunal, Delhi Bench (2008) 299 ITR 175.
[19] Tribunal, Delhi Bench (2010) ITA no. 1980/Del/2009.
[20] Tribunal, Kolkata Bench (2011) TII 77.

Pvt Ltd,[21] the Commissioner initiated revisionary proceedings as the TPO and the assessing officer had accepted the taxpayer's transactions to be at arm's length without examining the comparables. The Tribunal upheld the action of the Commissioner after concluding that the order of the assessing officer was erroneous and prejudicial to the interests of the Revenue.

15.4.2 Role of transfer pricing officer

Upon the receipt of a reference by the assessing officer, the TPO is required to determine the arm's length price of an international transaction by issuing the transfer pricing order. Since the assessing officer is bound by the order of the TPO, he computes the income of the taxpayer in conformity with the price so determined by the TPO. The procedure entails collation of facts by the TPO, by serving a notice on the taxpayer requiring him to produce documentation in support of the inter-company pricing undertaken by him. The regulations mandate that the TPO should provide an opportunity to the taxpayer to submit evidence regarding the determination of the arm's length price. The TPO is expected to consider the appropriateness of the method selected and applied by the enterprise, reliability of data used and other facts and circumstances in determining the arm's length price of the international transaction. The documentation quality and the economic considerations of the transaction should also be given adequate importance. The TPO is required to provide an opportunity of being heard to the taxpayer before passing the order and may require the taxpayer to produce any additional evidence from time to time during the course of proceedings. The Delhi High Court in *Moser Baer India Ltd*[22] held that the regulations cast an obligation on the TPO to accord an oral hearing to the taxpayer before the determination of the arm's length price. The TPO may require any person to furnish information/ statements or accounts, as may be useful in the course of proceedings on the case. Further, the TPO is also empowered to undertake all actions under section 131(1) of the Act. These mostly relate to discovery and inspection of books of accounts, enforcing the attendance of any person, compelling the production of books of accounts and other documents. Further, the TPO is empowered to undertake survey

---

[21] Tribunal, Bangalore Bench (2011) TII 75.   [22] Delhi High Court (2008) 316 ITR 1.

operations[23] after entering into any business premises falling within his tax jurisdiction. Accordingly, the TPO can examine books of accounts, verify cash, stock, etc. and obtain necessary information from persons at such premises.

The Revenue authorities also have the power to require any person to furnish any information which may be useful in the course of proceedings of another taxpayer. This power is provided to the Revenue by virtue of section 133(6) of the Act. This easily paves way for the Revenue to access information which may not be normally available from the taxpayer and use the same while computing the arm's length price.

The TPO can proceed to determine the arm's length price of a transaction if, on the basis of the material/information available, he is of the opinion that:

- the price charged/paid in the international transaction has not been determined in accordance with the regulations;
- any information/document relating to the international transaction has not been maintained by the taxpayer as required by the regulations;
- the data used in computation of the arm's length price is not reliable or correct; and
- the taxpayer has failed to furnish within the specified period any information/document required to be furnished.

The TPO, after taking into account all relevant facts and data available to him, determines the arm's length price and issues an order. The transfer pricing order should contain details of the data used, reasons for arriving at a certain price and the applicability of transfer pricing methods. Subsequently, the TPO forwards the order to the assessing officer for the computation of the total income of the taxpayer in conformity with the arm's length price determined by the TPO. The assessing officer is, however, empowered to make additions to the income of the taxpayer on non-transfer pricing issues. It is imperative that the TPO provides a copy of the order to the taxpayer as well. Once the transfer pricing order is issued, the same is subsumed in the draft assessment order issued by the assessing officer.

The TPO may amend the transfer pricing order where there is any mistake[24] apparent from the record in the order. The TPO may amend

---

[23] Income Tax Act, 1961, s.92CA was amended with effect from June 2011, empowering the TPO with powers under s.133A.

[24] Ibid. s.154.

the order passed by it under provisions of the Act, either on its own motion or by rectifying mistakes which have been brought to its notice by the taxpayer. No amendment under section 154 can be made after the expiry of four years from the end of the tax year in which the order sought to be amended was passed. Further, where an application for amendment is made by the taxpayer, the TPO will pass an order (making the amendment or refusing to allow the claim) within a period of six months from the end of the month in which the application is received. An arguable matter cannot be a subject for an application under section 154 for it cannot be considered as a mistake apparent from record. The Supreme Court has succinctly explained the scope and ambit of section 154 in *TS Balram, ITO* v. *Volkart Bros.*[25]

On the issuance of a transfer pricing order, the assessing officer cannot use any other anti-avoidance measure under the Act to make any further disallowance with respect to international transactions undertaken by the taxpayer. This is evident in the rulings handed down by the Tribunal in Bangalore in *Aztec Software & Technology Services Ltd*[26] where it was held that any general provision within the framework of the Act cannot take precedence over the specific transfer pricing provisions. Such a conclusion was reiterated in a recent decision of the Delhi bench of the Tribunal in *Oracle India Pvt Ltd.*[27]

15.4.3   Audit time charter

Timelines are to be borne in mind during the course of assessment proceedings for timely adjudication of cases. Assessment timelines are depicted in Figure 15.2.

15.5   Dispute resolution mechanism under domestic law

In the context of transfer pricing, dispute resolution mechanisms are necessary tools designed and made available to taxpayers and Revenue authorities to sort out the 'fine line' between national prerogatives and restrictions on pricing arrangements. Under the Indian domestic law, a taxpayer can take recourse to the following mechanisms for transfer pricing dispute resolution.

---

[25] Supreme Court of India (1971) 82 ITR 50.
[26] Tribunal, Bangalore Bench (2007) 294 ITR 32.   [27] Tribunal, Delhi Bench TIOL 540.

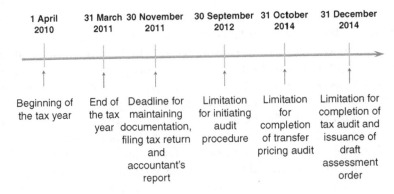

Figure 15.2   Transfer pricing assessment time lines

15.5.1   Dispute Resolution Panel

The Finance Act 2009 has introduced the Dispute Resolution Panel (DRP) under section 144C of the Act, as a fast-track alternate mode to resolve tax disputes. The DRP is available to any person in whose case a transfer pricing adjustment is made in consequence of an order of the TPO and for assessment of income of a foreign company. The DRP consists of three Commissioners of Income Tax appointed by the Central Board of Direct Taxes[28] (CBDT) and has wide-ranging powers akin to that of a court under the Code of Civil Procedure, 1908. The decisions of the Panel are based on the majority opinion of the Commissioners forming part of the panel. Panels have been established in the various prominent cities of India, having jurisdiction over different geographical areas covering the whole of the country.

As discussed earlier, the assessing officer after incorporating the order of the TPO and making additions, if any, on non-transfer pricing issues, serves a draft assessment order on the taxpayer before issuing the final order. The taxpayer is required to file its acceptance (with the assessing officer) or objections (with the assessing officer and the DRP) within thirty days from the date of receipt of the draft order. In case of acceptance or no objections being received within thirty days, the assessing officer issues the final order within one month from the end of the month in which the acceptance of the taxpayer is received or the period for filing objection expires.

[28] The most senior tax administration authority in India.

Where an objection is filed by the taxpayer, the DRP analyses the case and directs the assessing officer in the completion of the audit. The DRP examines all the relevant facts and submissions and can call for additional evidence, make further enquiries and confirm, reduce or even enhance the proposed adjustment. The taxpayer is permitted to produce additional evidence before the DRP in compliance with the rules made in this regard. However, the DRP is required to give clear directions on the reduction, enhancement or confirmation and cannot send the case back to the assessing officer, directing the officer to conduct further enquiry and redo the assessment.

The directions issued by the DRP are binding on the tax officer and cannot be appealed against by the Revenue authorities. The DRP is required to provide an opportunity of being heard to the taxpayer and the tax officer whose interest is prejudiced by the directions being given. There is a time limit of nine months (from the end of the month in which the draft order is forwarded to the taxpayer) for the DRP to issue its directions.

After issuance of directions by the DRP, the assessing officer is required to pass the final order in conformity with such directions within a period of one month from the end of the month in which such directions are received. An appeal against such an order by the taxpayer will lie only to the Tribunal.

The DRP provides a fast-track avenue for dispute resolution, without the burden of tax demand, as application to the DRP comes prior to the issuance of the final assessment order. The Act does not provide for the transfer of disputes in respect of the proceedings prior to 1 October 2009 to the DRP. However, in *HCL Technologies Ltd*,[29] the Supreme Court directed the taxpayers to approach the DRP on the transfer pricing disputes raised before it, even though the proceedings related to past periods. The Court also gave a specific direction that the DRP should not refuse to entertain the application merely for the reason that it was made after the cut-off date.

The taxpayer can chose either of the two routes, filing objections with the DRP or filing an appeal before the Commissioner (Appeals). The Commissioner (Appeals) route would be available only after the assessing officer passes the final order, once the time limit for filing objections before the DRP has expired. Thus, the two routes are alternatives not

---

[29] Supreme Court of India (2009) 225 CTR 357.

co-existent. Although the DRP constitutes a collegium of Commissioners, in practice a slight reluctance has been observed with regard to the DRP adjudicating on interpretive issues with respect to the Commissioner (Appeals), as the DRP order is binding on the Revenue and cannot be appealed against. In a recent ruling, the Karnataka High Court[30] held that unlike the Commissioner (Appeals), the power of the DRP to increase the assessment is limited to the issues arising from the draft assessment order. Accordingly, the Court held that the DRP cannot raise new issues which were not discussed in the draft assessment order and increase the assessment.

In the first round, the DRP had in many instances passed brief orders dismissing the taxpayers' objections without providing reasons for the same. In several of these cases, the Tribunal[31] has remanded the cases back to the DRP requiring it to consider the taxpayer's submissions appropriately after giving adequate opportunity of being heard.

15.5.2   Appeals before Commissioner (Appeals)

An appeal is a reconsideration of an audit by a higher authority. The transfer pricing order is incorporated in the regular tax assessment order, which can be further appealed against. As discussed above, as an alternative to approaching the DRP, the taxpayer can also adopt the route of approaching the Commissioner (Appeals), if he chooses not to file objection to the draft order proposed by the assessing officer. The availability of this route as an alternative to DRP was clarified in the Letter issued by the CBDT on 20 January 2010.

The procedure for filing an appeal application is fairly simple. Section 249 of the Act provides for the form and limitation period for the filing of an appeal. The taxpayer is required to file an appeal within thirty days from the date of receipt of the final assessment order. The application covers the grounds of appeal and a summary of facts. Usually, the taxpayer also files an application for any penalty proceedings (initiated as a result of transfer pricing adjustments) to be kept in abeyance until the appeal is disposed of. If the taxpayer and the Revenue are not in agreement with the order of the Commissioner (Appeals), they may prefer an appeal to the Tribunal.

---

[30] *GE India Technology Centre Pvt Ltd*, Karnataka High Court (2011) *TS* 462
[31] *GAP International Outsourcing India Pvt Ltd*, Tribunal, Delhi Bench (2010) TII 59.

The Commissioner (Appeals) has explicit powers in disposing of an appeal. He has the power to admit any new facts or issues, even when such matters were not raised before the tax officer during the course of the assessment proceedings. He is also empowered to admit additional grounds, during the course of the appeal proceedings, which were not originally raised at the time of filing the appeal. He can call for a report from the assessing officer, requiring him to inquire on any matter and report the result, and use such report in disposing of the appeal. The Commissioner (Appeals) can make further inquires before disposing of the appeal. In disposing of appeals, the Commissioner (Appeals) has the power to confirm the assessment order, reduce or annul an assessment. He even has the power to increase the assessment resulting in further demand against the taxpayer after giving reasonable notice to the taxpayer.

15.5.3   Revision application by taxpayer

Apart from the appellate remedy before the Commissioner (Appeals), the taxpayer has an alternative route of petitioning the Commissioner of Income Tax (an administrative authority) to revise any order passed by a subordinate authority.[32] Such application has to be made within one year from the date on which the order in question was received by the taxpayer. However, to pursue this route, the taxpayer will have to waive his right of appeal against the relevant order of the lower authority. If the Commissioner's order is not favourable to the taxpayer, the taxpayer will not be entitled to any appellate remedy under the Act. As the route is devoid of opportunity to litigate the matter further, it is not usually explored by taxpayers.

15.5.4   Appeals before the Tribunal

If the taxpayer is not in agreement with the order passed by Commissioner (Appeals) or the assessment order in consonance with the directions of the DRP, it may prefer an appeal to the Tribunal, the second level appellate authority. Such appeal is required to be filed within sixty days from the receipt of the order to be appealed against. The Revenue, on receipt of notice that such an appeal has been preferred by the other party, may

---

[32] Income Tax Act, 1961, s.264.

within thirty days of the receipt of the notice file a memorandum of cross-objections providing its line of contention. If the Revenue authorities are not in agreement with the Commissioner (Appeals) order, they also can appeal to the Tribunal. In such a case the taxpayer may, within thirty days of receipt of the notice, file a memorandum of cross-objection outlining its contention. As regards the order of the DRP, the same is binding on the Revenue and cannot be further appealed against.

Usually the Bench of the Tribunal comprises one accountant member and one judicial member. If the members of a Bench differ in opinion on any point, the view of judicial member will prevail. In the case of Benches comprising more than two members, the point will be decided according to the opinion of the majority. When the members are equally divided in terms of their opinion, they will state the point on which they differ, and the case will be referred by the President of the Tribunal for hearing on such point, by one or more of the other members of the Tribunal. In this scenario, the point will be decided according to the opinion of the majority of the members of the Tribunal who have heard the case, including those who first heard it. Wherever possible, the Tribunal will dispose of the appeal within four years from the end of the tax year in which the appeal is filed. The Tribunal may, after giving opportunity to both parties of being heard, pass such order, as it may think fit. Only those issues which were raised in the appeal and such additional grounds as may be raised with the leave of the Tribunal can be considered by the Tribunal. Recently, in numerous instances, the Tribunal has sent back cases to the assessing officers with directions to conduct a fresh analysis on the matters in question. While this may appear as a longer route, the Tribunal in some cases expedited the process of adjudication by issuing specific directions to the tax officers on the manner in which such examination should be undertaken to avoid further litigation.

Where there is any apparent mistake in an order of the Tribunal, the taxpayer can petition the Tribunal within four years from the end of the tax year in which the order was passed.[33] Thereupon, the Tribunal may accept the taxpayer's petition and rectify the error. The Tribunal functions under the jurisdiction of the Ministry of Law and Company Affairs. Whenever the Tribunal intends to express an opinion different from the one expressed by the earlier Bench, the matter would be placed

---

[33] *Ibid.* s.254.

before the President of the Tribunal, so that he could refer the case to a full Bench of the Tribunal known as a Special Bench.

15.5.5   Appeals before the High Court and Supreme Court

If the taxpayer or the tax authority is aggrieved by the order of the Tribunal, he may file an appeal with the state's jurisdictional High Court where the case involves a substantial question of law. The appeal has to be filed within 120 days from the date the order appealed against is received by the Commissioner (Appeals) or the taxpayer. An appeal will lie to the Supreme Court from any judgment of the High Court on an appeal, if the High Court certifies it to be a fit case for appeal to the Supreme Court. An independent issue not considered by the Tribunal or High Court cannot be permitted to be raised before the Supreme Court for the first time.

15.6   Alternate dispute resolution mechanisms under domestic law

In addition to the normal appellate proceedings, the taxpayer can take recourse to the following mechanisms.

15.6.1   Advance ruling

The Authority for Advance Rulings (AAR) was established in India with the intention to avoid needless litigation and to promote better taxpayer relations, particularly for transactions involving non-residents. The AAR is an authority constituted by the central government for determination of a question of law or fact in relation to a transaction undertaken or proposed to be undertaken by a non-resident.

Any non-resident desirous of obtaining an advance ruling can make an application.[34] The application process and mechanism have been provided in rules 44E to 44F of the Rules. The application can be withdrawn within a period of thirty days from the date of application. The question raised in the application should relate to the applicant. However, where the question of law or fact raised by the applicant is already pending either before the Revenue, the Tribunal or any court, the AAR will not accept the application. The AAR will also not accept the

---

[34] On Form 34C in quadruplicate.

application if the question is designed for the avoidance of tax or if it relates to the determination of fair market value of any property. The question formulated in the application cannot be modified at the time of hearing. The AAR, on receipt of the application, will send a copy to the Commissioner concerned and, whenever considered necessary, also call upon the Commissioner to furnish relevant records. The AAR has the power either to allow or reject the application. The applicant can, on request, appear either in person or can be represented through a duly authorised representative. The AAR will pronounce the order within six months from the receipt of the application.

The advance ruling is binding only on the applicant who had sought it in respect of the specific transaction in respect of which the advance ruling was sought. It is also binding on the Commissioner and the subordinates to the Commissioner who have jurisdiction over the applicant. To this extent, unlike decisions of the Tribunal or courts, the AAR rulings have a persuasive value for other taxpayers.

Further, no appeal against the ruling of the AAR is permitted to the taxpayer. That being said, it is pertinent to note that the taxpayer seeking the advance ruling has the right to file a Special Leave Petition before the Supreme Court of India against the ruling pronounced by the AAR.

With regard to transfer pricing disputes, the AAR has limited applicability. In transfer pricing cases, the dispute may be the choice of a particular method or computation of arm's length price. Since determination of fair market value of any property is outside the scope of advance ruling, the remedy available has little utility to the taxpayer. This principle draws reference from *Instrumentarium Corporation*.[35] In that case, the question before the AAR was to determine the effect of an international transaction involving the provision of an 'interest free loan' by a non-resident on the government exchequer or tax revenue of the country. The AAR declined to pronounce any ruling on the applicability of section 92 and held that as the question raised involved determination of the fair market value of a property, the issue raised fell outside the ambit of the AAR. Similarly, in *Morgan Stanley*,[36] the AAR declined to comment on the appropriateness of a transfer pricing methodology, as in its view, such question involved determination of the fair market value of property.

[35] Authority for Advance Ruling (2004) 272 ITR 499.
[36] Authority for Advance Ruling (2006) 284 ITR 260.

In the recent rulings pronounced by the AAR in *Dana Corporation*,[37] *Amiantit International Holding Ltd*,[38] *Goodyear Tire and Rubber Company*[39] and *Deere and Company*,[40] the AAR has specifically held that for an income to be subject to transfer pricing provisions, it is imperative that the charging sections of the Act should apply. The AAR held that in the event such consideration does not fall within the purview of the definition of 'income' within the Act, the transfer pricing provisions, being merely technical provisions, will not apply.

It was held that under the scheme of the Act, section 92 and the related provisions under Chapter X of the Act contain provisions for computation of income arising from international transaction(s) having regard to the arm's length price. Thus, for application of section 92 of the Act, there has to be income embedded in the international transaction. Accordingly, where an international transaction is entered into *gratis*, that is, without consideration, section 92 of the Act, not being in the nature of a charging provision, cannot be applied to impute notional income. Similar principles have been reiterated in *Vanenburg Group BV v. CIT*.[41]

The route of approaching the AAR can thus be used by the taxpayer to seek a ruling on the applicability of transfer pricing regulations to a particular transaction. However, the AAR cannot decide on the price at which a transaction should have been undertaken in light of the transfer pricing provisions.

15.6.2 Settlement Commission

The Settlement Commission ('the Commission') was formed in India to counter the malaise of tax evasion. The Commission comprises a chairman and as many vice-chairmen and other members as the central government thinks fit. The Commission has Benches with three members each.

At any stage of a case, whether at return filing stage or assessment or appeal, any taxpayer can file the application[42] to the Commission, to make a 'full and true disclosure' of his income which has not been

[37] Authority for Advance Ruling (2009) 227 CTR 441.
[38] Authority for Advance Ruling (2010) 230 CTR 19.
[39] Authority for Advance Ruling (1006 and 1031 of 2010).
[40] Authority for Advance Ruling (2011) TII 14.
[41] Authority for Advance Ruling (2007) 289 ITR 464. [42] On Form 34B.

disclosed before the tax officer. The additional income tax payable on the income disclosed in the application should exceed INR 1 million. However, if the tax officer has already discovered the income or has enough material to establish the undisclosed income, then the application cannot be proceeded with. Once an application is made by a taxpayer, it cannot be withdrawn. The Commission, after considering the material contained in the application and having regard to the nature and circumstances of the case or the complexity of the investigation involved, may allow or reject the application. The application can only be rejected after giving the taxpayer an opportunity of being heard. The Commission exercises exclusive jurisdiction in relation to the case pending before it. The order passed by the Commission is final and conclusive and cannot be rectified even for an apparent mistake. The only remedy against the order would be a Special Leave Petition under article 136 of the Constitution before the Supreme Court or a writ petition before the High Court.

15.6.3   Writ petition

A writ is a formal, legal, written order issued by the courts to an officer or to any person to do or refrain from doing something specified in the order therein. A writ petition can be filed in the jurisdictional High Courts or Supreme Court when fundamental rights are denied or when there is a violation of principles of natural justice.

The Supreme Court has power to issue writs under article 32[43] of the Constitution of India. The High Court, under article 226 of the Constitution of India, has wider power to issue writs for the purpose of enforcement not only of fundamental rights, but for the redressing of any other injury or illegality and contravention of the ordinary law as well. Courts have held that a writ is a special remedy available in exceptional circumstances and ordinarily not granted where an alternative remedy is available to the taxpayer. Nevertheless, it has been entertained when the alternative remedy involved lengthy procedures and unnecessary harassment by the executive authority acting without jurisdiction, as held in *Mercury Travels Ltd.*[44] If a writ petition filed by a party under article 226[45] is dismissed on the grounds that the petitioner has

---

[43] Right to constitutional remedy.   [44] Calcutta High Court (2002) 258 ITR 533.
[45] Writ before High Court.

an alternative remedy available to it, then the dismissal would not constitute a bar to a subsequent petition under article 32.[46]

A writ, as stated above, is a remedy in cases where the order of the lower authorities is clearly in contravention with fundamental rights enshrined in the Constitution or is contrary to principles of natural justice.

15.7   Tax treaties: what is their relevance in the Indian tax regime?

A tax treaty is a mutual agreement between two countries which governs the taxation of their residents. Also, in case of conflict of residence, tax treaties play the all important role of determining the state of residence of the taxable entity. The Vienna Convention defines a tax treaty as an 'international agreement concluded between states in written form and governed by international law, whether embodied in a single instrument or in two or more related instruments and whatever its particular designation'.

With the advent of multinational organisations, the importance of tax treaties has increased considerably as both the source country and the residence country are desirous of taxing a particular stream of income. A tax treaty acts as a codified law in resolving the tax issues and disputes arising out of activities undertaken by a resident of a state in another state. Courts have held that tax treaties have the effect of a legally binding international agreement on the states concluding the same and any digression from the provision of the treaty entered into has to be approved by both the states which have concluded the treaty.

India has entered into more than seventy comprehensive and fifteen limited agreements with different countries. While the comprehensive agreements cover different streams of income, the scope of limited agreements is limited to income from airline operations, merchant shipping, etc.

15.7.1   Applicability of tax treaties and their interplay with Indian domestic law

One of the important questions arising in jurisprudence on international tax is the applicability of tax treaties *vis-à-vis* the domestic tax laws. Section 90 of the Indian Income Tax Act empowers the government to

---

[46] Writ before Supreme Court.

enter into agreements with other states for avoidance of double taxation. Section 90(2) states as the following in the context of tax treaties having precedence over domestic tax laws:

> (2) Where the Central Government has entered into an agreement with the Government of any country outside India under subsection (1) for granting relief of tax, or as the case may be, avoidance of double taxation, then, in relation to the assessee to whom such agreement applies, the provisions of this Act shall apply to the extent they are more beneficial to that assessee.

This provision in the Indian domestic tax law clearly lays down that where the tax treaty applies in relation to a transaction entered into by a person, the provisions of the Act will apply only to the extent such provisions are beneficial.

The landmark judgment on the application of tax treaties *vis-à-vis* the domestic law was pronounced by the Indian Supreme Court in *Azadi Bachao Andolan*.[47] While upholding the validity of having a tax residency certificate as sufficient requirement for claiming treaty relief under the India–Mauritius Treaty, the Indian Apex Court, after examining existing judicial precedents, endorsed the view of the treaty having the primary application. The court observed that the judicial consensus in India has been that section 90 is specifically intended to enable and empower the central government to issue a notification for implementation of the terms of a double taxation avoidance agreement. The provisions of such an agreement, with respect to cases to which they apply, would operate even if inconsistent with the provisions of the Income Tax Act. The Apex Court went on to hold that the terms of the tax avoidance agreements would automatically override the provisions of the Income Tax Act in the matter of ascertainment of chargeability to income tax and ascertainment of total income. This decision of the Indian Supreme Court settled the debate on beneficial treaty provisions being used for planning investments in India from a direct tax perspective.

Indian courts have also laid down that the application of treaty provisions lies at the option of the assessee and the same cannot be imposed on the assessee, even if the assessing authority believes that a beneficial claim may be made in future on account of such provisions. Further, in the Indian context, specific provisions of the treaty on chargeability to tax and computation of income will override the Act

---

[47] Supreme Court of India (2003) 263 ITR 706.

even when the change in the provisions of the Act is subsequent to the treaty. As regards the rate of tax, the Act will be overridden by a specific provision in the treaty but a general provision in the treaty will not override a specific provision in domestic law.

15.7.2 Importance of tax treaty in transfer pricing policy

Article 9 of the Organisation for Economic Co-operation and Development (OECD) Model Convention enables contracting states to appropriately determine the profits of associated enterprises on an arm's length basis. Further, this Article also enables adjustments (corresponding and secondary adjustments) to avoid taxation of the same income in the hands of different entities of the same group. These adjustments may be effected through MAP under Article 25 of the Model Tax Convention. Article 9 and Article 25 of the Model Tax Convention are therefore the relevant articles in the context of transfer pricing.

The Indian tax treaties do not directly provide guidelines on the subject of transfer pricing. However, relevant Articles of treaties entered into by India on 'associated enterprises' (usually Article 9 or Article 10 of treaties entered into by India, referred to in this chapter for discussion as Article 9), provide some guidance on transactions with associated enterprises. Many tax treaties entered into by India provide for an adjustment to profit where the transaction between the associated enterprises has been entered into on terms other than 'arm's length terms'. Where the terms of the transaction are not at 'arm's length' the Indian tax treaties provide a right for a state to tax the profits accruing, on an arm's length basis, to an enterprise of that state.

Article 9(1) of the treaties (Article 9 where there are no clauses (2) and (3)) typically provides the scenario under which an adjustment can be made to the price at which a transaction has been entered into between the associated enterprises. Article 9(1)[48] of the treaties entered into by

---

[48] As provided in both the Model Conventions, Article 9(1) of treaties entered into by India provides as follows: 'Where: (a) an enterprise of a Contracting State participates directly or indirectly in the management, control or capital of an enterprise of the other Contracting State, or (b) the same persons participate directly or indirectly in the management, control or capital of an enterprise of a Contracting State and an enterprise of the other Contracting State, and in either case conditions are made or imposed between the two enterprises in their commercial or financial relations which differ from those which would be made between independent enterprises, then any profits which would, but for those conditions, have accrued to one of the enterprises, but, by reason of those conditions, have not so accrued, may be included in the profits of that enterprise and taxed accordingly.'

India is identical to Article 9(1) of the UN Model Convention and the OECD Model Convention (this Article being identical in both the Model Conventions).

Apart from Article 9(1), many treaties entered by India also have Articles 9(2) and (3). Articles 9(2) and (3) do not exist in Indian treaties with countries like France, Germany, Mauritius, Singapore, Italy, Spain, Korea, etc. Article 9(2)[49] of the treaties entered into by India is similar to Article 9(2) of the OECD Model Convention and the UN Model Convention (this also being similar in both the Model Conventions). This provision defines the scope of a corresponding adjustment to the associated enterprise (transaction which has resulted in the adjustment) in the other contracting state, thereby eliminating the economic double taxation of an adjustment made on account of transfer pricing regulation. The provision also lays down the competent authority route in deciding on the availability of the corresponding adjustment to the associated enterprise in the other contracting state.

Article 9(3) of treaties entered into by India is in line with the UN Model Convention. This provision does not form part of the OECD Model Convention. This provision restricts the applicability of Article 9 (2) by laying down certain circumstances in which Article 9(2) shall not apply, as follows:

> (3) The provisions of paragraph 2 shall not apply where judicial, administrative or other legal proceedings have resulted in a final ruling that by actions giving rise to an adjustment of profits under paragraph 1, one of the enterprises concerned is liable to penalty with respect to fraud, gross negligence or wilful default.

Article 9(3) provides for a penalty (in addition to penal provisions in the domestic Act), by stating that no corresponding adjustment shall be allowed to the associated enterprise, in a scenario where the enterprise to whose income adjustment has been made on account of applying

---

[49] Article 9(2) states as follows: 'Where a Contracting State includes in the profits of an enterprise of that State – and taxes accordingly – profits on which an enterprise of the other Contracting State has been charged to tax in that other State and the profits so included are profits which would have accrued to the enterprise of the first-mentioned State if the conditions made between the two enterprises had been those which would have been made between independent enterprises, then that other State shall make an appropriate adjustment to the amount of the tax charged therein on those profits. In determining such adjustment, due regard shall be had to the other provisions of this Convention and the competent authorities of the Contracting States shall if necessary consult each other.'

transfer pricing regulations is liable to penalty with respect to fraud, gross negligence or wilful default and there has been a final ruling in this respect.

In this context it is important to observe that for denial of the benefit of corresponding adjustment, the following three conditions should be aggregately satisfied:

(i)   imposition of penalty should be in relation to transfer pricing adjustment;

(ii) the penalty imposed should be on account of fraud, gross negligence or wilful default; and

(iii) a final ruling should have been made in respect of imposition of penalty.

It is important to note that Article 9(3) will only be operational if there has been a final ruling in respect of the levy of a penalty and not tax.

As discussed above, Article 25 on MAP is another Article which is relevant from a transfer pricing perspective. This Article provides for the competent authority route in resolving transfer pricing disputes and has been discussed in detail in the section on dispute resolution under a DTAA.

The MAP route for sorting out disputes arising out of applying transfer pricing provisions exists in almost all the tax treaties entered into by India. However, in this context, it is important to note the recent comments by India stating its position on the OECD Model Tax Convention. India has clearly in its comments stated that in the absence of any specific provision in the DTAA (i.e., Article 9(2) discussed above), adjustments to transactions between associated enterprises on account of transfer pricing adjustments will not fall under the scope of Article 25.

15.8   Dispute resolution under DTAA

Article 25 of the OECD Model Tax Convention provides for MAP as a mechanism for resolving transfer pricing disputes. This Article is adopted in almost all the DTAAs entered into by India.

15.8.1   Mutual agreement procedure

MAP is an alternative dispute resolution mechanism that may be pursued by taxpayers. In common parlance, it is simply the resolving of disputes through direct negotiation and agreement between the competent authorities of the contracting states. Article 25 of the OECD Model Tax Convention provides for MAP. It was in February 2003 that the Indian government issued a specific guidance for MAP procedure. The guidance procedures are contained in rules 44G and 44H of the Rules.

India's experience with MAP, is largely of recent times. Most MAPs that the Indian competent authority has dealt with pertain to the period after 1998 and have primarily been with the United States, Japan, and on an exceptional basis with countries in Continental Europe. Since the Indian transfer pricing law in itself is relatively new, there are very few precedents on transfer pricing related to MAP, though some transfer pricing cases are being negotiated under MAP. MAP in itself is a special procedure outside the domestic law to resolve transfer pricing disputes. The MAP mechanism is meant for the resolution of intergovernmental disputes concerning taxation under the relevant tax treaty. It is the actions of the state that may lead to double taxation, as, for example, adjustments made by Revenue authorities where transactions are not at arm's length. If the double taxation is the consequence of the taxpayer's action, the mechanism of MAP will not be available.

Dispute resolution under MAP is a two-fold procedure:

(a) presentation of the case by the taxpayer to the contracting state of which the applicant is resident;
(b) resolution by that contracting state itself, but if it is unable to do so, then by mutual agreement with the other contracting state.

15.8.2   Who can present a case?

The taxpayer may initiate the mutual agreement process by making a claim to the competent authority for the country of which he is a resident. A claim should specify the year concerned, the nature of action giving rise to taxation not in accordance with the Convention and the full names and addresses of the parties to which the procedures relate. In India, rule 44G provides for the procedure applicable to residents and, under the Rules, an application is to be made in statutory Form no. 34F. In this form the taxpayer has to identify the foreign tax authorities and describe the reasons for seeking competent authority assistance.

Rule 44H stipulates that where a reference has been received from the competent authority of a foreign country in respect of any action taken by the Indian Revenue authority, the competent authority in India shall call for and examine the relevant records with a view to giving its response. In such a case, the Indian competent authority will endeavour to arrive at a resolution in accordance with the terms of the tax treaty.

15.8.3 Time limit for presentation of the case

The presentation of the case should be made generally within three years from the date of action of one or both of the contracting states, which in the opinion of the taxpayer has resulted or will result in taxation not in accordance with the tax treaty with the country. If the taxability is affected by a series of actions or a combination of decisions, the period of three years will run from the first notification of the most recent of them. The running of the limitation commences when the concerned person becomes aware of the action taken or proposed to be taken which will have adverse effects on him and not from the date when he forms an opinion about such adverse effects.

The action giving rise to double taxation may not have taken place as yet but the taxpayer may still present the case to the competent authority if he can establish that the actions of one or both of the contracting states are likely to result in taxation which is not in accordance with the Convention. However, the likelihood of such taxation should be probable and not just a mere possibility.[50]

Indian Revenue authorities have adopted the stand that the action which results in taxation, not in accordance with the tax treaty, can be held to have occurred only when the assessing officer issues an order taxing the income of the taxpayer, in a manner which may lead to double taxation. Thus, in the view of the Indian Revenue authorities, MAP application can be filed only after passing of the assessment order.

15.8.4 MAP mechanism

The first stage of the procedure is the presentation of the case to the competent authority of the state in which the taxpayer is a resident. The competent authority on receipt is obliged to determine whether the objection is *prima facie* justified. The application of the taxpayer to set the MAP in motion should not be rejected without good reasons.[51] The Andhra Pradesh High Court in *CIT* v. *Visakhapatnam Port Trust*[52] held that Article 25 outlines a procedure which is in addition to and not in

---

[50] OECD Commentary on Article 25, para. 14.   [51] *Ibid.* para. 34.
[52] Supreme Court of India (1983) 144 ITR 146.

substitution of the remedies before the domestic courts or tribunal. Therefore, the taxpayer is entitled to seek the remedies available under the domestic laws of the states, besides taking up the matter with the competent authority. If a taxpayer has already taken up the matter with the competent authority and has also taken it up under the domestic law, in case of conflicting decisions, the decision more favourable to the taxpayer should be implemented. If the competent authority of the resident state is not able to arrive unilaterally at a satisfactory solution, it will make an endeavour to resolve the dispute by mutual agreement with the competent authority of the other state.

The resolution arrived at under MAP is communicated to the Chief Commissioner or the Director-General of Income Tax, in writing. The assessing officer gives effect to the resolution within ninety days of the receipt of the resolution, provided that the assessee gives his acceptance to the resolution taken under MAP and withdraws his appeal, if any, pending on the issue which was the subject matter for adjudication under MAP. The amount of tax, interest or penalty already determined is adjusted after giving effect to the decision taken under MAP. For the purposes of rules 44G and 44H, 'competent authority of India' means an officer authorised by the central government for the purposes of discharging the functions as such.

Under rule 44H, the taxpayer has the choice to accept the outcome of the MAP proceedings. The taxpayer may reject the outcome of MAP if a more favourable result is expected in the administrative appeal procedure. However, rule 44H also stipulates that if the MAP outcome is accepted, all rights with respect to appeal should be given up.

In cases of MAP with the competent authorities of the United States, United Kingdom and Denmark, respectively, the tax demand is suspended until the outcome of the proceedings is known. The suspension of the tax demand is subject to the furnishing of a bank guarantee. Where the consultative proceedings fail, the bank guarantee may be invoked in satisfaction of the tax demand.

The competent authorities of India and the United States entered into a Memorandum of Understanding (MOU) in 2003 in relation to suspension of collection of taxes during the pendency of MAP. Under the notification of April 2003, only a resident of the United States could apply for suspension of tax demand during MAP proceedings. In September 2007, the CBDT issued an instruction to extend the applicability of the MOU to Indian resident entities, by virtue of which Indian residents can also apply for suspension of tax liability during the course of MAP. This change benefitted Indian resident taxpayers, especially in cases involving transfer pricing, where the resident enterprise is liable to pay taxes on such income which may have been charged to tax in the hands of the associated enterprise in the United States.

15.8.5   Practical experiences

As discussed above, most MAP cases that the Indian competent authority has dealt with pertain to the period after 1998 and have been primarily with the United States and Japan and on an exceptional basis with countries in Continental Europe.

Over the past few years, several US affiliates of Indian companies operating in the software services sector have filed MAP applications. We understand that among the initial MAP applications recently concluded for software services, the US and Indian competent authorities have reached a negotiated settlement for a cost plus margin of around 18 per cent for tax year 2003–4 and around 17.5 per cent for tax year 2004–5. As regards the information technology enabled services sector, we understand that these figures are around 24 per cent for tax year 2003–4 and 17.5 per cent for tax year 2004–5.

Though the settlement is only binding for the tax years under dispute and is applicable to the specific taxpayer, the development does provide an indication of settlement expected from MAP proceedings in respect of applications filed by software services enterprises/information technology enabled service providers and would serve as a reference point for the previous year and future years in dispute.

15.8.6   Difference between MAP and normal appellate proceedings

Table 15.1 outlines the differences between the normal appellate proceedings and MAP.

15.9   Reliance on OECD Guidelines and US transfer pricing rules

Though India is not an OECD[53] Member State (although India has been offered 'enhanced engagement' status by the OECD), the *OECD Transfer Pricing Guidelines for Multinational Enterprises and Tax Administrators*

---

[53] Organisation for Economic Co-operation and Development.

Table 15.1 *Normal appellate process and MAP: a comparison*

Particulars	Appellate process	MAP
Time	Time-consuming	Time-consuming, allow at least 12–24 months for resolution
Additional material	Detailed documents required	Detailed documents required
Participation by taxpayer	Proceedings in the presence of taxpayer	Taxpayer involved in the information gathering and explanation of facts. Taxpayer not a part of actual bilateral negotiations
Payment of tax	Tax payment may not be deferred	Tax payment can be deferred, bank guarantee to be submitted
Positive factors	Good documentation with good legal counsel has a strong chance in Tribunal and higher levels. Taxpayer has the comfort of being present when the appeal is being heard	A MAP outcome generally eliminates double taxation and is a beneficial situation for both countries. Deferment of tax payment pending conclusion of MAP is a significant positive

('OECD Guidelines') play a supplementary role in transfer pricing issues on which Indian legislation is silent. Indian jurisprudence abounds with examples where the courts have endorsed reference to OECD Guidelines and Commentary for interpreting and applying domestic laws.

In this regard, a reference may be made to the ruling in *Aztec Software & Technology Services Ltd* (above) where the Tribunal held as follows:

> India is not a Member of the OECD. India, however, has an observer status and has an advanced engagement with the OECD. The organisation has been supporting efforts of tax administration in India to effectively administer and implement Transfer Pricing Policy. A useful reference can be made to OECD Guidelines, for the purposes of resolving issues provided they do not override the domestic law.

A similar view was reiterated by the Tribunal in *Mentor Graphics (Noida) Pvt Ltd*[54] where the Tribunal held:

[54] Tribunal, Delhi Bench (2007) 112 TTJ 408.

The TPO neither followed mandatory provision of rule 10B quoted above nor guidelines of OECD and his computation of ALP is patently erroneous.

Further, tax tribunals in India have frequently referred to US court decisions and the approach of European tax authorities. The Supreme Court in *Union of India* v. *Azadi Bachao Andolan* and *Ishikawajima Harima Industries Ltd* v. *Director of Income Tax*[55] made a reference to the commentaries by Klaus Vogel on double taxation conventions, in deciding the cases. In *Ranbaxy Laboratories Ltd* (above), the Tribunal relied upon the OECD Guidelines and the US regulations for articulating the principles for choice of tested party and aggregation of transactions.

Reference to the OECD Guidelines and US transfer pricing regulations are also to be noted in *Sony India Private Ltd.*[56] Such references are in fact found in most of the transfer pricing rulings in India.

In the light of the above jurisprudence, a clear view emerges that as long as the OECD Guidelines and other international commentaries are not inconsistent with the domestic law, reliance should be placed on them. Hence, while deliberating on transfer pricing issues on which Indian regulations are silent, due regard can be given to the OECD Guidelines and international commentaries.

15.10   Transfer pricing audit in India: an overview

A flurry of transfer pricing related developments in India has made it the single largest tax concern for corporations operating in India. Indian transfer pricing regulations can be regarded as at a very early stage of evolution. Given the relative infancy of the laws in India, coupled with limited guidance on the interpretation of legislation, contentions/ disputes are more likely to arise than not.

Recently concluded audits have brought to the fore various issues where the Revenue has differed with the taxpayer regarding the applicability and interpretation of the transfer pricing provisions. While each round of audit has enhanced the Revenue's experience in administration of transfer pricing regulations, with each round significant controversies have surfaced. Lack of detailed guidelines and unavailability of precedents has been the primary reason for controversies. Controversies principally surround issues such as use of the transactional net margin

[55] Supreme Court of India (2007) 288 ITR 408.
[56] Tribunal, Delhi Bench (2008) 315 ITR 150.

method (TNMM), multiple year data, and various such issues which will be discussed below. So far, during audits, the Revenue has also relied on the approach stipulated by the OECD Guidelines when applying Indian transfer pricing regulations. However, this has been done only to the extent that these guidelines were not in conflict with specific domestic transfer pricing provisions. No unified approach has been followed by the Revenue across the country and this has come as an obstruction in providing a synchronised guidance to the taxpayer. In a variety of cases, contradictory views were adopted by the Revenue over similar facts. The successive rounds of audits and aggressive industry reactions following them have thus opened up a Pandora's Box of contentious issues.

The trends in transfer pricing audits in India have exhibited an aggressive stance taken by the Revenue. In several cases, TPOs have placed greater reliance on prior orders in the previous year rather than examining the documentation afresh. Thus, in most cases, the taxpayers subjected to adjustment in the prior year face similar adjustment in the succeeding year. Predetermined revenue targets coupled with paucity of resources explain excessive reliance by the Revenue on the prior year's approach. Loss-making companies or companies with low operating margins are clearly the targets. Where the taxpayer offered justification for losses in terms of market penetration and seeding strategies, or a long-term view of the Indian market, the Revenue has required the taxpayer to furnish extensive documentation.

There are numerous technical issues (whether single or multiple year data should be used, how the arm's length range should be computed, whether foreign comparables can be used, etc.) on which no clear and consistent stand of the Revenue was discernible. Lack of departmental position has added to the uncertainty in audit. Reliance on last year's order and an inconsistent stand by the Revenue underscores the need for planning based on worse case scenarios. Susceptibility of particular industries to transfer pricing adjustments was quite clearly revealed in the successive years of audit. The Revenue closely scrutinised software services, banking and finance, and the automobile and pharmaceutical industries.

Further, the CBDT has not fixed any qualitative criteria for subjecting a case to transfer pricing audit. The TPOs generally undertook a fairly detailed analysis of the facts and circumstances and requested extensive transfer pricing information. Global cost contribution and cost allocation arrangements, intra-group services and royalty/technology transfer payments were accepted only on the basis of sound allocation keys and benefits tests, even when charged on a cost-to-cost basis. The quality of the documentation and commercial reality of the outcome of the transactions was also required to be explained in the course of the audit.

The primary concern of the Revenue has been to ensure that India's tax base was not eroded in any manner. While mapping strategies for the future, it is imperative for corporations to keep an eye on the trends revealed by the audit experience thus far. Although, only five rounds of audit have been completed, they afford valuable insights into the working of transfer pricing law. With uncertainties surrounding the arena of transfer pricing, the only escape routes for the taxpayers are the dispute resolution mechanisms, which reflect some signs of optimism.

Though nothing substantial has changed in the context of the Indian transfer pricing regulations, much more evolution is likely to come through judicial decisions and interpretations, rather than amendments to the regulations themselves. By using an 'appropriate' transfer pricing arrangement between two related parties of the same corporate group, the group may want to optimise its global tax costs. However, what is 'appropriate' is questionable. Tax planning undertaken by multinationals is not free from the Indian Revenue's reach. It is here that the interplay of dispute resolution mechanisms plays a predominant role in ironing out creases and providing answers to emerging controversies, serving as a guiding post for the future.

15.11   Indian transfer pricing controversies and principles

Five rounds of transfer pricing audit completed thus far in India have revealed several lacunae in the Indian transfer pricing legislation. So far in the chapter, we have explained the evolution of the transfer pricing regime in India and have discussed the alternatives available for the resolution of transfer pricing disputes. A brief background of the transfer pricing audit experience has also been provided. This section aims to highlight the major issues which have been the focus of contention between the Indian Revenue authorities and the taxpayers, and to define and elucidate the principles emerging out of these disputes.

15.11.1   Arm's length range

Paragraphs 1.45 to 1.48 of the OECD Guidelines recognise that transfer pricing is not an exact science and application of the most appropriate method produces a range of figures, all of which are relatively equally reliable – the differences in the figures being due to the fact that, in general, the application of the arm's length principle only produces an approximation of conditions that would have been established between independent enterprises. Under the Indian regulations, proviso to section 92C(2), prior to amendment by the Finance Act 2009 with effect from 1 October 2009 provided as follows:

> Provided that where more than one price is determined by the most appropriate method, the arm's length price shall be taken to be the arithmetic mean of such prices, or, at the option of the assessee, a price which may vary from the arithmetical mean by an amount not exceeding 5 per cent of such arithmetical mean.

A plain reading of the text of former proviso to section 92C(2) suggested that the benefit of the variation of 5 per cent should be allowed by the Revenue authorities at the option of the taxpayer. However, in the recent audit experience, a restrictive view was adopted by the Revenue suggesting that if the transaction price so determined does not fall within the 5 per cent variation from the arm's length price, no benefit would be provided to the taxpayer. This view resulted in significant controversies in the transfer pricing audit. The contrary view adopted by the taxpayer was that the arithmetic mean of various prices should be reduced by 5 per cent for determining the arm's length price as per the language of proviso to section 92C(3) of the Act. Thereafter, adjustment, if any, would need to be computed by taking the difference in the arm's length price so determined (after allowing for the 5 per cent reduction/variation) and the actual price of the international transaction as shown in the books of accounts. The view is further fortified by notes on clauses of the Finance Bill 2002 and the circulars issued by the CBDT.

The Tribunal rulings in *Sony India Private Ltd* (above) and *Philips Software Centre Private Ltd*[57] went a long way in providing the much sought after clarification in relation to the above-mentioned provision. The Tribunal in these cases affirmed that the benefit of the $(+/-)$ 5 per cent range should be available to all taxpayers and not just a few. In fact, in *Sony India Private Ltd*, the Tribunal demonstrated by an elegant argument that adjustment should be made to the range rather than to the arithmetic mean. The interpretation adopted by the Tribunal is in line with the view that taxpayers would ordinarily wish to take and with the intent of the regulations as emerging from a plain reading of the

---

[57] Tribunal, Bangalore Bench (2008) 119 TTJ 721.

proviso to section 92C(2). In the judgment in *Skoda Auto India Private Ltd*,[58] the Pune Tribunal relying on and in accordance with the decision in *Sony India Private Ltd*, adjudged the issue of (+/−) 5 per cent range in favour of the taxpayer. However, the Tribunal in *Deloitte Consulting India Pvt Ltd*[59] and *ST Micro Electronics Pvt Ltd*[60] has held that the 5 per cent adjustment would not be available when the taxpayer's transaction fell outside the 5 per cent range. These rulings contain only limited discussion on the reasons supporting such a conclusion.

The Finance Act 2009 has amended the 5 per cent adjustment provisions to override the judicial precedents discussed above. The amended proviso reads as follows:

> Provided that where more than one price is determined by the most appropriate method, the arm's length price shall be taken to be the arithmetic mean of such prices;
>
> Provided further that if the variation between the arm's length price so determined and price at which the international transaction has actually been undertaken does not exceed 5 per cent of the latter, the price at which the international transaction has actually been undertaken shall be deemed to be the arm's length price.

The amendment is effective from 1 October 2009. The memorandum explaining the provisions of the Finance Bill 2009 states that the new proviso would apply for all transfer pricing proceedings conducted on or after 1 October 2009. Such a position would mean that the 5 per cent benefit would not be available as a standard adjustment, even for earlier assessment years, where proceedings are pending.

However, an alternative view is possible that the amendment would apply only for the tax year 2009–10 onwards and not to the earlier years. This view is on the basis that the amended proviso, which restricts the right available to the taxpayer for the standard adjustment, is a substantive and not a procedural amendment. It is a settled legal principle that substantive amendments can have only prospective effect and would not apply prior to the introduction of the change.

The Revenue is of the view that the amended law would apply to all proceedings pending on 1 October 2009 and in situations where the arm's length price falls below the 5 per cent variation from the transaction price, no benefit would accrue to the taxpayer. The contrary view

---

[58] Tribunal, Pune Bench (2009) 112 TTJ 699.
[59] Tribunal, Hyderabad Bench (ITA 1082 of 2010).
[60] Tribunal, Delhi Bench (ITA 1806, 1807 of 2008).

of taxpayers, as regards the effective date of applicability of the amended position, is likely to keep the controversy in this regard alive and surely kicking.

Recently, the Tribunal has in *SAP Labs India Pvt Ltd*[61] and *I-Policy Network Pvt Ltd*[62] held that the amendment would not be applicable for the assessment years preceding the amendment, even if those years are assessed subsequently.

The Finance Act 2011 has substituted the acceptable arm's length range of 5 per cent under section 92C and has empowered the CBDT to prescribe the percentages in this regard. The CBDT is yet to notify the percentages, which are to be effective from the assessment year 2012–13.

15.11.2 Selection of the most appropriate method

In the recently concluded audits, there have been various instances of outright rejection of the methodology adopted by the taxpayers. The Indian transfer pricing regulations clearly spell out that the choice of selecting the most appropriate method to demonstrate the arm's length nature of the transaction lies with the taxpayer. A plain reading of the regulation and various circulars[63] issued by the CBDT illustrates that the primary onus to determine the arm's length price lies with the taxpayer. Where such onus is discharged by the taxpayer and the data used for determining the arm's length price is reliable and correct, there should be no intervention with such arm's length price. Under section 92CA(3) of the Act, the transfer pricing officer is empowered to determine the arm's length price in respect of an international transaction, only in

---

[61] Tribunal, Bangalore Bench (2011) 44 SOT 156.

[62] Tribunal, Delhi Bench (ITA 5504 of 2010).

[63] CBDT Circular no. 14, 20 November 2001: 'Under the new provisions the primary onus is on the taxpayer to determine an arm's length price in accordance with the rules, and to substantiate the same with the prescribed documentation. Where such onus is discharged by the taxpayer and the data used for determining the arm's length price is reliable and correct, there can be no intervention by the Assessing Officer. This is made clear by sub-section (3) of section 92C which provides that the Assessing Officer may intervene only if he is, on the basis of material or information or document in his possession, of the opinion that the price charged in the international transaction has not been determined in accordance with sub-sections (1) and (2), or information and documents relating to the international transaction have not been kept and maintained by the taxpayer in accordance with the provisions contained in sub-section (1) of section 92D and the rules made thereunder; or the information or data used in computation of the arm's length price is not reliable or correct.'

accordance with section 92C(3). Thus, the observation from the circular equally applies to the determination of the arm's length price by the TPO, when the case is referred to him. This unequivocally establishes that the onus is on the taxpayer to select the most appropriate method for the purpose of benchmarking its controlled international transactions.

Further, another circular[64] recognises the difficulties in the application of the regulations due to there being inadequate data in the public domain and the law itself being new and evolving in nature. A view may therefore be taken that where the taxpayer has discharged its burden, ordinarily it is not open to the Revenue authorities to intervene and stipulate a different method as the most appropriate method. Any such determination of arm's length price based on a different method without giving due weight to the nature of the transaction, functions performed, and availability or reliability of data would be considered erroneous and against the spirit of the regulations. The Bangalore Tribunal has fortified this view in its ruling in *Philips Software Centre Private Ltd* (above). The Tribunal stressed that the Revenue is not justified in adopting a different methodology unless it is proved that the methodology adopted by the taxpayer is erroneous.

15.11.3   Use of multiple-year data and contemporaneous data

The use of multiple-year data with respect to comparable transactions for computing the arm's length price of an international transaction has been a debatable issue in recent audits. Although the regulations do not specifically deal with it, rule 10B(4) of the Income Tax Rules provides that it is mandatory to use data relating to the tax year in which the international transaction was entered into. However, data for the preceding two years can be used, if data for the preceding years reveal facts which could have an influence on the determination of transfer prices in relation to the transactions being compared.

Interestingly, the draft transfer pricing rules circulated by the Department of Revenue, Ministry of Finance in June 2001 were rigid and inflexible with regard to the use of prior year data. Based on representations made by the industry, chambers of commerce and OECD's recommendation, the final rules were made flexible to permit the use of

---

[64] CBDT Circular no. 12, 23 August 2001: 'The tax authorities have to be circumspect while handling transfer pricing cases . . . there is a need to ensure that taxpayers are not put to avoidable hardships in the implementation of these regulations.'

multiple-year data. Taxpayers' primary argument on adopting multiple-year data is to ensure that the results for the relevant year are not unduly influenced by abnormal factors.

However, despite the aforesaid arguments for the use of multiple-year data, the Tribunal on various occasions has interpreted the regulations strictly and in line with the Revenue's view. It has been held that single-year data should be used for transfer pricing analysis unless cogent reasons for the use of prior years' data are furnished (as seen in the *Aztec Software Services* and *Mentor Graphics* decisions, above).

Recently, the Delhi Tribunal in *Customer Service India Private Ltd*[65] held that it is mandatory to use current year data for comparability analysis, even if such data was not available at the time of transfer pricing documentation. It further held that the preceding two years' data could be used, but only if it was proved that such data revealed facts which could influence the price. The Pune Tribunal in *Honeywell Automation India Ltd*[66] rejected a comparable with a financial reporting period of eighteen months, with the last six-month period therein falling beyond the taxpayer's tax year. It held that there is no scope to consider data for a subsequent period as comparable.

Further, rule 10D(4) of the Rules states as follows:

> The information and documents specified under sub-rules (1) and (2), should, as far as possible, be contemporaneous and should exist at the latest by the specified date referred to in clause (iv) of section 92F.

Therefore, in selecting the most appropriate method, regard must be given to the availability of data necessary for the application of the method. Data which is not available at the time of complying with the prescribed documentation and information requirements under rule 10D cannot reasonably be envisaged by the taxpayer, and therefore cannot be taken into consideration in determining the arm's length price. However, the Tribunal in the recent case of *Symantec Software Solutions Pvt Ltd*[67] upheld the use of current year data even when it was not accessible to the taxpayer at the time of documentation, but became available subsequently.

Recent audit experience suggests that the Revenue authorities are asking for fresh economic analyses of international transactions based on current data of comparable companies that was not available during the documentation stage. A view, however, has been taken by taxpayers

---

[65] 2009 TIOL 424.   [66] 2009 TIOL 104.   [67] Tribunal, Mumbai Bench (2011) TII 60.

that to maintain documentation based on data that was not available at the time of conducting the economic analysis would be impossible and taxpayers cannot reasonably be expected to fulfil a requirement they could not anticipate.

The regulations mandate that the prescribed information and documentation is to be maintained by the taxpayer at the latest by the due date of filing the tax return (i.e., September 30/November 30 following the tax year). Rule 10D(4) also states that the information and documentation should 'as far as possible' be contemporaneous and 'should exist at the latest by the specified date'. Therefore, where the taxpayer has made its best efforts in using and relying on the latest possible data available before the prescribed time limit, it can be argued that the taxpayer has fulfilled the requirement of maintaining contemporaneous documentation and nothing further is required. However, in light of the Tribunal ruling in *Symantec Software* as discussed above, the position could continue to be contentious.

15.11.4 Economic adjustments

Economic adjustments in the course of undertaking benchmarking analysis have been the talking point in the recent judicial cases. Several multinational corporations have set up captive outsourcing units in India that undertake services such as research and development, software development, back office support, call centres, engineering, administration and management, payroll processing and other outsourced services. Captive units operate in a virtually risk-free environment. Generally significant business risks such as capital risk, market risk, price risk, credit risk, etc., are borne by the overseas associated enterprise while the captive unit seldom faces any losses due to such risks. Captive units typically operate on a cost plus mark-up basis, i.e., the associated enterprises pay the Indian units a mark-up over the total operating costs incurred by the unit.

The margin earned by the captive units cannot be compared with other independent enterprises since there would be a wide disparity between the risks undertaken by the two. While the captive units usually are expected to continue to earn a mark-up over costs incurred in providing the services, comparable independent companies undertake a significantly wider range of risks, earning super profits or significant losses from time to time. From this stems the issue of economic adjustments to account for the differences in risk profiles of the captive unit and the identified comparables. The question in hand is not only of the need to make appropriate adjustments, it extends to the issue of accurately quantifying the risks for the purpose of adjustments and the subjectivity involved in making such adjustments. In India, although the TPOs have acknowledged the need for adjustments, the same have often been arbitrary and ad hoc due to the absence of adequate guidance. Further disagreements on the factors (capacity utilisation, fixed assets, etc.) which may necessitate an economic adjustment have also been a bone of contention in quite a few cases.

A few rulings adjudicated by the Tribunal stress the need to carry out adjustments on account of the differing functional and risk profile of comparable companies *vis-à-vis* the taxpayer. In a landmark ruling by the Tribunal, in *Mentor Graphics (Noida) Pvt Ltd* (above), the issue of risk and working capital adjustment has been addressed. The ruling reiterated the importance of undertaking a risk analysis and accordingly making an adjustment for the same, if required. Further, the Tribunal's ruling in *E-Gain Communications Private Ltd*[68] also provided that while undertaking a benchmarking analysis, suitable adjustments should be made for differences on account of function, assets, risk and other relevant factors. In the same context, in *Philips Software Centre Private Ltd* (above), it was ruled that the taxpayer was justified in carrying out an adjustment of 5.25 per cent to eliminate differences on account of risk profile. The ruling also emphasised the need for a working capital adjustment. In the ruling in *Sony India Private Ltd* (above), the Tribunal stressed that in case of material differences in functional and risk profile between the taxpayer and comparables, sufficient and appropriate adjustments are warranted. The Tribunal justified an adjustment of 20 per cent for intangibles and research and development. The principle of adjustment on account of differences in working capital was also allowed for.

However, the Tribunal in *Symantec Software Solutions Pvt Ltd*[69] held that the 5 per cent safe harbour provided under section 92C was for the differences in risk profiles as it would be impossible to have a perfect comparable without any difference or variation from the tested party. Accordingly, it rejected any further economic adjustments. The Tribunal in *Deloitte Consulting India Pvt Ltd*[70] rejected adjustments claimed for lower risk borne by a captive service provider. In that case, the Tribunal

---

[68] Tribunal, Pune Bench (2008) 118 ITD 243.
[69] Tribunal, Mumbai Bench (2011) TII 60.
[70] Tribunal, Hyderabad Bench (ITA 1082 of 2010).

held that the warranty provided by the subsidiary to its parent to deliver its work free of errors amounted to carrying a risk and accordingly rejected the claim that there were differences in risk profiles. In light of these rulings, the claim for risk adjustments could continue to be contentious.

At the level of the TPO, the adjustment on account of working capital differences is being considered in light of rulings of the Tribunal. However, with respect to other adjustments, Revenue authorities have not been amenable to the arguments put forward by the taxpayers.

15.11.5 *Principle of aggregation*

Another fundamental issue that needs to be addressed relates to aggregation of transactions. The principle of aggregation is a well established rule in transfer pricing analysis. This principle seeks to combine all functionally similar transactions, for which a blanket arm's length analysis can be conducted. This principle has been enshrined in the Rules through rule 10A(d), which provides that a 'transaction includes a number of closely linked transactions'.

The above-mentioned rule recognises that in practice, a taxpayer may be involved in controlled transactions involving numerous products, or may be involved in numerous controlled transactions with respect to the same product. Accordingly, it may prove impractical to analyse transactions individually to determine the arm's length price. Under such circumstances, it is permissible to apply an appropriate pricing method to the overall results of a given business segment.

The OECD Guidelines[71] in this regard state as follows:

> There are often situations where separate transactions are so closely linked or continuous that they cannot be evaluated adequately on a separate basis. Examples may include (1) some long-term contracts for the supply of commodities or services, (2) rights to use intangible property, and (3) pricing a range of closely-linked products (example in a product line) when it is impractical to determine pricing for each individual product or transaction. Another example would be the licensing of manufacturing know-how and the supply of vital components to an associated manufacturer. In such case it may be more reasonable to assess the arm's length terms for the two items together rather than individually. Such transactions should be evaluated together using the most appropriate arm's length method or methods.

---

[71] OECD Guidelines, para. 1.42.

Thus, in a majority of cases, testing the arm's length character of individual transactions may be impractical and hence transactions should be aggregated. In the ruling in *Development Consultants Private Ltd*,[72] the Kolkata Tribunal observed that ideally a comparison should be made on a transaction-by-transaction basis. However, an aggregation approach may be followed when transactions are so closely linked that they cannot be evaluated separately. Similarly, in *Star India Private Ltd*,[73] the Mumbai Tribunal held that aggregation can be done only when the transactions are closely linked and rejected the Revenue's approach of aggregating three independent activities of the company for the purpose of benchmarking. The Tribunal in *UCB India Pvt Ltd*[74] held that even under TNMM, the analysis has to be on a transaction to transaction basis. In that case, it rejected the use of entity-wide margins, when the taxpayer's activity comprised both manufacturing and trading.

Indian regulations do not specifically provide for situations in which an aggregation approach may be followed and hence this has led to disputes in many cases. Detailed guidance on the applicability of aggregation principles may be of great use to the taxpayers while preparing their transfer pricing documentation. Further, a judicial precedent which discusses the principle in detail may also be of great interpretational help for taxpayers.

15.11.6   Revenue's approach on attribution of profits

The principles of attribution still suffer from drawbacks as observed from the Indian transfer pricing experience. Even in the era of comprehensive transfer pricing regulations, the Revenue has been relying on the rule of thumb to attribute profits to a permanent establishment, as revealed from two cases, *Rolls Royce Private Ltd Co.*[75] and *Galileo International Inc.*[76] In both these cases, the Revenue has proceeded to hold that the overseas enterprises had a permanent establishment (PE) in India and attribute profit on a basis which can hardly be termed as reasonable and concrete.

---

[72] Tribunal, Calcutta Bench (2008) 115 TTJ 577.
[73] Tribunal, Mumbai Bench (2008) ITA no. 3585/M/2006.
[74] Tribunal, Mumbai Bench (2009) 124 TTJ 289.
[75] Tribunal, Delhi Bench (2007) 113 TTJ 446.
[76] Tribunal, Delhi Bench (2007) 116 ITD 1.

Despite the fact that the transfer pricing regulations introduced in 2001 apply to all PEs, the Revenue authorities and courts have repeatedly used the rule of thumb for attribution of profits in a situation where an overseas enterprise has been held to have a PE in India. The decisions pronounced in the above-mentioned cases relate to a period after the introduction of comprehensive transfer pricing regulations. The Revenue authorities and courts in these cases have not attempted to reach a conclusion on the arm's length return earned by the PE based on more scientific transfer pricing principles. There is no reference at all in the above decisions to the transfer pricing regulations. On the other hand, the approach adopted by the Tribunal for attributing profits is an approximate one. Moreover, the percentage of profits attributed in either case (being 35 per cent and 15 per cent) are on the higher side and appear to be arbitrary. However, in the recent case of *Excelpoint Systems PTE Ltd*,[77] the Tribunal observed that a 'transfer pricing study' would facilitate the assessing authority in determining the taxable income in a scenario where permanent establishment is held to be in existence. This case, being the solitary positive precedent in this regard, needs further support in the form of judicial opinion to ensure the attribution of profits to a PE are made on the basis of the transfer pricing rules and regulations.

As discussed above, in most of the judicial pronouncements, transfer pricing methods have not been used in attributing profits to a PE constituted as a result of activities undertaken by an overseas enterprise in India. However, certain rulings, including a decision by the Indian Supreme Court, have held that if the Indian associated enterprise is remunerated at arm's length, no further attribution is required to be made to the PE which is constituted as a result of activities of the Indian associated enterprise.[78]

15.12 Transfer pricing penalties

Though the transfer pricing regulations clearly spell out the compliance requirements, where taxpayers are non-compliant, they are exposed to

---

[77] Tribunal, Bangalore Bench (2009) ITA nos. 1233 to 1239 (Bang)/2008.

[78] *DIT* v. *Morgan Stanley and Co. Inc.*, Supreme Court (2007) 292 ITR 416; *SET Satellite (Singapore) Pte Ltd* v. *DDIT*, Mumbai High Court (2008) 307 ITR 205; and *BBC Worldwide Ltd* v. *DDIT*, Tribunal, Delhi Bench (2010) 128 TTJ 411.

Table 15.2 *Transfer pricing penalties: a snapshot*

Nature of default	Penalties
Failure to maintain such information and documents as prescribed by transfer pricing law (s.271AA)	A sum equal to 2% of the value of each international transaction entered into by taxpayer
Inability to furnish the report or information/documents (s.271G)	A sum equal to 2% of the value of the international transaction for each such failure
Concealment of income or furnishing inaccurate particulars, post-audit adjustment (s.271(1)(c))	100–300% of tax on the adjusted amount
Failure to furnish accountant's certificate (s.271BA)	INR 100,000

penal consequences. The instances in which taxpayers are subjected to penalties are shown in Table 15.2.

As regards the penalty for concealment of income, the relevant penalty provisions clearly provide that in case of a transfer pricing adjustment, it will be deemed that the transfer pricing adjustment represents income in respect of which particulars have been concealed or inaccurate particulars have been furnished by the taxpayer. This can, however, be rebutted, if the taxpayer can demonstrate that the price charged or paid in the international transaction was computed in accordance with the transfer pricing provisions in good faith and with due diligence. Thus, a transfer pricing adjustment, in more cases than not, would result in penal provisions being invoked by the Revenue.

However, in this regard, recent jurisprudence from the Tribunal provides a welcome relief to the taxpayer. In *Vertex Customer Service (India) Pvt Ltd*,[79] it was held that a penalty is not to be levied when the taxpayer has computed the arm's length price as per the law in good faith and with due diligence. It was also held that the penalty need not be imposed for a mere technical breach of the law, or when the taxpayer acted on the genuine belief that he has not breached the law. This view of the Tribunal was reinforced in *Sutron Corporation.*[80] Further, in *Firmenich Aromatics (India) Pvt Ltd,*[81]

---

[79] Tribunal, Delhi Bench (2009) 126 TTJ 184.
[80] Tribunal, Delhi Bench (2009) ITA no. 2786/Del/08.
[81] Tribunal, Mumbai Bench (2010).

it was held that additions made to the arm's length price on account of difference of opinion in selecting the method of computation between the taxpayer and the TPO does not amount to furnishing inaccurate particulars of income. Since the taxpayer had computed the arm's length price in good faith, a penalty could not be levied in such case.

15.13   Advance pricing agreement

Globally, the advance pricing agreement (APA) is an important tool to avoid and mitigate disputes arising in the arena of transfer pricing. APA can be defined as an arrangement between the taxpayer and the Revenue where the issue and methodology related to transfer pricing is settled in advance. In this sense, APA being a pre-emptive mechanism, it is not really a tool for dispute resolution but is certainly a tool to reduce uncertainties during transfer pricing audits. APAs can be divided into a unilateral arrangement (involving only one country's tax administration) or bilateral (involving tax administrations of two or more countries). The APA regime is adopted by many countries ensuring that transfer pricing disputes are kept to a minimal level.

It is hoped that the Indian government will plug the loopholes that exist in India's transfer pricing regulations and incorporate APA as a tool. At present, there is no mechanism in India for securing an APA. However, the DTC 2010, while aligning the Indian tax laws with internationally accepted taxation principles and best practices, includes a proposed section 118, which would allow taxpayers to seek an APA. Such an agreement will be binding on the taxpayer and the Revenue authorities. Under the proposed law, APAs could be entered into for a maximum period of five years. There is no proposal for renewal or roll forward of APAs. The CBDT is expected to announce detailed guidelines which will include the composition and functioning of a body to administer APAs once the provision is enacted into law.

15.14   Safe harbour provisions

A recent development under the Finance Act 2009 is the introduction of safe harbour provisions under section 92CB in the Act, enabling the CBDT to make safe harbour rules. 'Safe harbour' refers to circumstances in which the Revenue authorities will accept the transfer price declared by the assessee. While the rules are yet to be framed, they are expected to be announced soon and apply for past years. The safe harbour rules present an opportunity to resolve industry-specific issues, by prescribing a reasonable safe harbour range for specific industries. Since section 92CB provides for accepting the transactions as being at arm's length if they are within the safe harbour range, this mechanism would help reduce the transfer pricing disputes to a great extent.

15.15   Conclusion

Transfer pricing in India is regarded as amongst the most important business issues. Even though a decade old, the transfer pricing regulations in India are still evolving. Successive rounds of audits have opened up a box full of contentious issues. The recent rulings have provided some insights into what lies ahead – the road, however, is still not clear.

India, backed up by its robust economic growth and huge consumer base with high disposable income, continues to be a major global destination for businesses worldwide. It is hoped that in order to ensure a more conducive tax environment, the government will adopt global best practices in dealing with transfer pricing issues. To provide clarity on transfer pricing issues for businesses, introduction of APA could be a very significant tool. Further, judicial reforms are the need of the hour to clear the huge backlog of cases.

The litigation landscape appears to be very dynamic and full of challenges. The Revenue and the Indian taxpayers continue to ride on the same learning curve. Thus, there is a need for a cautious approach from both sides. Adequate transfer pricing planning and preparedness holds the only key for businesses.

Appendix: Questionnaire (India)

1. The structure of the law for solving transfer pricing disputes.   *What is the structure of the law of the country for solving transfer pricing disputes? For example, is the mutual agreement procedure (MAP), as regulated in the relevant tax treaty, the standard method for solving transfer pricing disputes?*

The regulations in India explicitly lay down the dispute resolution mechanism for transfer pricing disputes. The most commonly adopted route for dispute resolution is the procedure as outlined in the domestic law. Of late, taxpayers have shown an inclination towards resorting to treaty provisions under MAP for resolving transfer pricing disputes. In this context, the recent observations of India on the OECD Model Tax Convention assume importance. Very categorically, India has stated that in the absence of a specific provision in the DTAA, i.e., Article 9(2) as discussed in the chapter, adjustments to transactions between associated enterprises on account of transfer pricing will not fall under the scope of MAP.

2. Policy for solving transfer pricing disputes. *Is there a gap between the nominal and effective method for solving transfer pricing disputes in the country? For example, has the country a strategic policy not to enforce the arm's length standard (ALS) for fear of driving foreign direct investment to other competing jurisdictions?*

The Indian transfer pricing regulations were legislated with a view to providing a statutory framework for retention of arm's length profits in India. The purpose of the introduction of the regulations was to prevent erosion of the tax base. India does not have any strategic policy of not enforcing the arm's length standard for fear of diverting foreign direct investment to competing jurisdictions.

The stance adopted by the Revenue in transfer pricing audits is a clear indication that India does not consider robust transfer pricing regulations as a deterrent to foreign direct investment.

3. The prevailing dispute resolution method. *Which is the most frequent method for solving transfer pricing disputes in the country? Does it have a positive externality? For example, is the MAP the most frequent method, and if so, to what extent have successful MAPs been used as a proxy for transfer pricing case law? For instance, Procter & Gamble (P&G) obtained a bilateral advance pricing agreement (APA) in Europe, and it was then extended to a third (Asian) country when P&G made this request to the relevant Asian tax authorities.*

The regulations under the Indian domestic law are the most frequent method for resolving transfer pricing disputes. As discussed in the chapter, certain taxpayers are adopting MAP as an alternate dispute resolution mechanism. While MAP provisions allow a corresponding adjustment (subject to the existence of Article 9(2) as discussed in the chapter), there is no provision for corresponding adjustment under the domestic law. India does not currently have an APA mechanism. APA as a tool is proposed to be introduced in the Direct Tax Code 2010 (likely to be implemented from 1 April 2012) and will serve as a useful recourse for averting transfer pricing disputes going forward.

4. Transfer pricing case law.   *What is the evolution path of transfer pricing litigation in the country? For example: (i) Is transfer pricing litigation being gradually replaced by either MAPs or APAs, as regulated in the relevant tax treaties? (ii) Are foreign/local transfer pricing precedents and/or published MAPs increasingly relevant as a source of law for solving transfer pricing disputes?*

The transfer pricing provisions in India are at a stage of constant evolution. Most of the guidance is currently available in the form of judicial precedents. While MAP is a recent phenomenon which has been adopted by taxpayers, not many have been concluded as yet. As and when settlement of more cases via MAP take place, the same will serve as a guiding post for future disputes.

5. Customary international law and international tax procedure.   *Has customary international law been applied in the country to govern the relevant methods for solving transfer pricing disputes (such as the MAP)? For example, has the OECD Manual on Effective Mutual Agreement Procedure ('OECD Manual') been deemed customary international tax law in the MAP arena for filling procedural gaps (for example, time limit for implementation of relief where treaties deviate from the OECD Model Tax Convention)?*

The OECD Transfer Pricing Guidelines for Multinational Enterprises and Tax Administrators play a supplementary role in transfer pricing issues on which Indian legislation is silent. Indian jurisprudence abounds with examples where the courts have endorsed reference to the OECD Guidelines and Commentary for interpreting and applying domestic laws. Further, tax tribunals in India have frequently referred to US court decisions and the approach of European tax authorities. Thus clearly, as long as the OECD Guidelines and other international commentaries are not inconsistent with the domestic law, reliance has been placed on them for articulating transfer pricing principles.

6. Procedural setting and strategic interaction.   *Does strategic interaction between taxpayers and tax authorities depend on the procedural setting in which they interact when trying to solve transfer pricing disputes? For example, which procedural setting in the country prompts the relevant parties to cooperate with each other the most for solving this sort of dispute, and why?*

The Indian Revenue authorities have been aggressive while undertaking transfer pricing audits. In our experience, the procedural setting has had no impact on the interaction between Revenue authorities and the taxpayers, with both adopting varied interpretation of transfer pricing regulations. With the introduction of the Dispute Resolution Panel (DRP) in 2009, it was hoped that the interaction between the Revenue authorities and the taxpayer would be more effective. However, it has emerged that the DRP is reluctant to take a stand on interpretation issues (its order being binding on the Revenue authorities) resulting in a continuing lack of clarity on application of transfer pricing provisions.

7. The future of transfer pricing disputes resolution. *Which is the best available proposal in light of the interests of the country for facilitating the global resolution of transfer pricing disputes, and why?*

Globally, APA is an important tool to avoid and mitigate transfer pricing litigation. Introduction of the same in the Indian transfer pricing regulations is likely to go a long way in reducing transfer pricing disputes. As discussed, the DTC 2010 proposes to introduce the APA mechanism in India. This, when operative, would aid in providing much sought after certainty for businesses in addressing their transfer pricing issues.

Transfer pricing disputes in China

JINYAN LI

16.1 Introduction

Transfer pricing is a relatively new issue in the People's Republic of China. China opened its door to foreign investors in the late 1970s and multinational enterprises brought their transfer pricing practices to China. It was not until 1991 that China enacted the first transfer pricing law. As expected, China imported the arm's length principle to deal with the imported transfer pricing problem. Because the Chinese legal culture differs in many respects from that of OECD countries, especially the United States where the arm's length standard originated, adaptation of the OECD-based solution is inevitable. In addition, China's national interest in cross-border transfer pricing matters has changed over the past three decades, which has led to corresponding changes in China's approach to resolving transfer pricing disputes.

Following this introduction, section 16.2 provides a brief cultural and historical context for the arm's length principle in China. Section 16.3 discusses the implementation and administration of the arm's length principle. Section 16.4 examines the resolution of transfer pricing disputes in China under the domestic mechanism and the mutual agreement procedure (MAP) under bilateral tax treaties. In light of the Chinese national interests and existing legal culture, section 16.5 suggests that the future solution of the global transfer pricing problems lies in bilateral or multilateral advance pricing agreements and a pragmatic application of the arm's length principle.

16.2 Historical and cultural context for transfer pricing disputes

16.2.1 Transfer pricing's arrival in China

Transfer pricing was not an issue in China when the Chinese economy was isolated from the rest of the world. Related party transactions and the associated transfer pricing issues started to appear in China when multinational enterprises were allowed to invest in China in the form of joint ventures or wholly-owned subsidiaries (collectively known as foreign investment enterprises or FIEs). China introduced a Western style enterprise income tax in 1980[1] without any transfer pricing rules. In fact, the arm's length principle, or anything similar to it, was not mentioned in the tax legislation.

During the 1980s and early 1990s, foreign investors used transfer pricing strategies to shift profits away from China to avoid Chinese tax as well as to minimise exchange or other investment risks.[2] However, there were virtually no transfer pricing disputes, primarily because the tax authorities did not challenge the transfer pricing practices. China's main policy objective at that time was to attract FDI and to push Chinese-made products to international markets, predominantly through joint ventures, which was achieved, in part, by generous tax incentives.[3] Chinese partners in these joint ventures were not very familiar with the world market as a result of several decades of the 'closed door' policy in China. In most joint ventures, the foreign party was responsible for marketing the products overseas and for acquiring the technology, equipment and raw materials. Such arrangements generally provided opportunities for the foreign party to control the price of the sales and purchases. Chinese tax incentive measures also encouraged exports.[4] In addition to transfer pricing

---

[1] Income Tax Law of the People's Republic of China concerning Joint Ventures with Chinese and Foreign Investment adopted by National People's Congress and promulgated on 10 September 1980; Income Tax Law applicable to Foreign Enterprises, adopted by the National People's Congress in 1981. Both were abolished with the promulgation of Income Tax Law of the People's Republic of China for Enterprises with Foreign Investment and Foreign Enterprises, promulgated by the National People's Congress on 9 April 1991 ('FIET Law'). For an overview of the history of the Chinese tax system, see A. Easson and Jinyan Li, 'Taxation of Foreign Business and Investment in the People's Republic of China' (1985–6) NW J Int'l L and Bus. 666; Jinyan Li, Taxation in the People's Republic of China (New York: Preager Publishers, 1991).

[2] See Jinyan Li and A. Paisey, Transfer Pricing Audits in China (New York: Palgrave Macmillan, 2007); Jinyan Li, 'Transfer Pricing in China' (2000) Bulletin for Int'l Fiscal Doc. (November) 565; and Yongwei Liu, A Study on Legal Issues related to Transfer Pricing (Beijing: Beijing University Press, 2004).

[3] See Z. Jiang, 'China's Tax Preferences to Foreign Investment: Policy, Culture and Modern Concepts' (1998) 18 NW J Int'l L and Bus. 549; and Jian Li, 'The Rise and Fall of Chinese Tax Incentives and Implications for International Tax Debates' (2007) 8 Florida Tax Rev. 670.

[4] FIEs were required to balance their foreign exchange accounts. Chinese tax law encouraged FIEs to export at least 70 per cent of their products. Keeping the cost of goods produced by the FIEs low helped the competitiveness of these products, and shifted

transactions involving tangible goods, transfer pricing was presumably used in financing and licensing transactions.

The complexity of transfer pricing issues increased with the expansion of the types and scope of foreign direct investment (FDI) in China. China's accession to the World Trade Organization in 2001 led to the opening of China's internal markets to goods manufactured by FIEs and liberalisation of investment regulations in financial and other services. Since 2008, China has encouraged Chinese companies to make FDI overseas. Such increased integration of China's economy with the global economy meant that transfer pricing practices in China are becoming more and more like those in other countries.

When China abolished most of the tax incentives for foreign investors and lowered the standard corporate tax rate to 25 per cent in 2007, transfer pricing issues became increasingly important for the tax administration. To most investors, the new Enterprise Income Tax (EIT) Law resulted in a higher tax burden with the elimination of most preferential tax rates and holidays through the introduction of a harmonised tax rate of 25 per cent. Many companies had been subject to 15 or 24 per cent tax rates, coupled with tax holidays to eliminate or reduce the applicable tax rate by half for a number of years (depending on the specific tax incentive).[5]

Transfer pricing has also become increasingly important in China because of the use of tax havens and intangibles. Classic tax havens have already been leading sources of FDI inflow to China. British Virgin Islands, Cayman Islands, Samoa and Mauritius are among the top ten sources.[6] In 2005, for example, FDI from British Virgin Islands (US$5.96 billion) was more than five times that from the United States (US$1.03 billion).[7] Direct investment in China by foreign multinational corporations is increasingly accompanied by intangibles and services, causing complexities in transfer pricing assessment. China-based multinational corporations have been increasing investment abroad and using transfer pricing to manage their global tax liabilities.

---

profits from China to the parent or sister corporations overseas. For an overview of the FDI in China, see 'Invest in China', available at www.fdi.gov.cn/pub/FDI_EN/default.htm.

[5] See J. Eichelberger and B. Kelly, 'Tax Planning Strategies in Response to China's Changing Tax Landscape: Issues and Structures to be Considered in a Post Tax Unification China' (2007) 3 *Asia Pac. Tax Bull.* 140.

[6] For a list of origins of FDI, see *China Statistical Year Book* (2005), available at www.stats.gov.cn/tjsj/ndsj/2005/html/R1815e.htm.

[7] *Ibid.*

A significant number of Chinese enterprises use holding companies in offshore tax havens for investment overseas.[8]

Transfer pricing has been one of the most serious types of tax avoidance in terms of potential revenue loss to China. Protecting China's tax base is thus a key concern for the State Administration of Taxation (SAT). During the recent global financial crisis, in order to prevent multinational enterprises from shifting foreign losses to Chinese companies or moving profit from China to tax havens, the SAT stated in a Circular[9] that the Chinese-resident enterprises that have limited functions and risks should not assume the risks associated with the market and financial crisis, and that they are expected to earn a reasonable level of profit according to the arm's length principle.[10]

16.2.2   Transplanting the arm's length principle

The use of transfer pricing was noticed as a policy issue when it resulted in a potential 'abuse' of the Chinese tax incentives, such as tax holidays. Because tax holidays would commence after the first profitable tax year, FIEs could use transfer pricing to postpone the 'start-up' loss years. When three-quarters of FIEs were reporting tax losses in the 1980s and early 1990s,[11] transfer pricing was suspected as the main reason. In 1988, China's first

---

[8] 'Investment Outflows to Tax Havens', *China Daily*, 22 June 2004, available at People's Daily Online, english.peopledaily.com.cn/200406/22/eng20040622_147138.html. The *People's Daily* reported: 'The British Virgin Islands is a major destination for China's offshore investment . . . 10,000 out of 500,000 companies there are from China. Most China-originated money entering tax havens will re-enter China as "foreign investment", "round tripping". . . A closer examination of China's star foreign direct investment (FDI) figures reveal a large amount of capital going out of the country and returning under a different guise. The World Bank and other experts have estimated the scale of this round tripping could be as large as 20% to 30% of the total FDI inflow into China, but there is no clear definition and detailed estimation method behind the numbers . . . Even worse is that the trend is growing bigger . . . The biggest pay-off for recycling mainland-originated money through a web of companies offshore is the tax concessions that China grants to foreign firms.'

[9] See SAT Circular, 'Strengthening the Oversight and Investigation of the Cross-Border Transactions between Associated Enterprises' (*Guo Shui Han* no. 363 (2009)).

[10] Taxpayers have been advised that when it comes to transfer pricing, 'China is about as important as it gets'. 'Water-tight documentation and excellent government relations are a sine qua non, as is building up a strong local tax team, and using top-notch advisors.' See G. DeSouza, 'Structuring an Appropriate Transfer Pricing Policy' (2008) 4 *Asia Pac. Tax Bull.* 309.

[11] For an overview of Chinese tax incentives, see Li, 'The Rise and Fall of Chinese Tax Incentives', note 3 above; Jiang, 'China's Tax Preferences to Foreign Investment' note 3 above.

transfer pricing Circular was issued by the local tax authority in Shenzhen special economic zone (SEZ).[12] Shenzhen SEZ was a 'window' of China to foreign investors, and, to some extent, an 'incubator' for developing China's international tax rules. At that time, the tax authorities in Shenzhen had the most experience with FIEs and their transfer pricing practices. They were concerned not only with potential loss of tax revenue, but also with the loss of profit to the Chinese partner in the joint ventures, which were often state-owned enterprises. This was a double hit to China's national interest because the state lost tax revenue as well as its share of profit as an equity owner. The fact that some taxpayers could 'play' the tax system, which was regarded as a symbol of China's sovereignty to some extent, was disturbing to policy-makers and tax collectors. This led to the introduction of the arm's length principle in 1991[13] and in the Tax Administration Law in 1992.[14]

The introduction of the arm's length principle was no surprise. China had been keen on following the 'international tax norm', with the appropriate modifications to suit Chinese local conditions. The arm's length principle had already been included in China's tax treaties and was perceived to be the only 'realistic' solution to the transfer pricing problem.[15]

---

[12] Interim Measures for Tax Administration of Transactions between Foreign Investment Enterprises and Associated Enterprises in Shenzhen Special Economic Zone, issued by Shenzhen Government in 1988.

[13] Article 13 of the FEIT Law, note 1 above, states: 'The payment or receipt of charges or fees in business transactions between an enterprise with foreign investment, or an establishment or place set up in China by a foreign enterprise to engage in production or business operations, and its associated enterprises shall be made in the same manner as the payment or receipt of charges or fees in business transactions between independent enterprises. Where the payment or receipt of charges or fees is not made in the same manner as in business transactions between independent enterprises and results in a reduction of taxable income, the tax authorities shall have the right to make reasonable adjustments.'

[14] Law of the People's Republic of China concerning the Administration of Tax Collection ('Tax Administration Law'), adopted at the Twenty-seventh Meeting of the Standing Committee of the Seventh National People's Congress on 4 September 1992; amended in 1995, 2001; Implementation Regulations for the Tax Administration Law, effective as of 15 October 2002.

[15] China has signed tax treaties with around ninety countries, including all but one OECD member countries. China has also concluded a tax arrangement with Hong Kong and Macao special administration. All of China's tax treaties contain a rule identical to Article 9(1) of the OECD Model Convention. Article 9(2) of the OECD Model, which requires a corresponding adjustment provision, is also included in the majority of Chinese treaties. It is not included, however, in the treaties with Austria, Belgium, Brazil, Canada, France,

As in other countries, detailed transfer pricing rules are needed to implement the arm's length principle. The SAT[16] issued interpretation guidelines in 1992[17] and 1998.[18] These guidelines incorporated much of the OECD Transfer Pricing Guidelines (without explicitly acknowledging it) and reflected some of the best practices in other countries. During the period 1991–2007, the SAT's enforcement of the arm's length principle intensified in the face of growing evidence that tax incentives had questionable effects on attracting FDI and that transfer pricing was resulting in lost tax revenue.[19] Transfer pricing started to be considered a serious issue by the SAT, which began to dedicate more resources to transfer pricing audits and investigations. From 1991 to 2000, 18,000 foreign-invested enterprises were audited, and one-third of the audits resulted in positive tax adjustments. These numbers represented a very small percentage of FIEs in China, and most of the enterprises audited were small in business scale.[20]

Germany, Italy, Japan, Malaysia, Norway, Poland, Singapore, Spain, Switzerland, Thailand and the United Kingdom.

[16] The SAT is responsible for the implementation of Chinese tax laws. Its mandate includes enforcing tax laws, drafting tax legislation and setting national goals or quotas on the amount of revenue to be collected in each province. The SAT's head office in Beijing is not directly involved in the actual collection of taxes. State tax bureaus at the local level are generally responsible for processing tax returns and collecting taxes. They are located at provincial, municipal and county levels across the country.

[17] In 1992, the tax authorities published a Circular entitled 'The Implementation Measures for the Tax Administration of Transactions between Associated Enterprises' (*Guo Shui Fa* no. 237 (1992)), to explain the standards for the identification of associated enterprises, annual information to be reported and other fundamental issues.

[18] *Guo Shui Fa* no. 59 (1998) ('1998 Transfer Pricing Circular'). This Circular was comprised of fifty-two articles organised in twelve chapters. In October 2002, the State Council introduced Implementation Rules for Tax Collection and Administration Law, articles 51 to 56 of which provide detailed rules for transfer pricing, which incorporated many provisions in the 1998 Transfer Pricing Circular.

[19] Jiang, 'China's Tax Preferences to Foreign Investment', note 3 above; Li, 'The Rise and Fall of Chinese Tax Incentives', note 3 above.

[20] For a rather detailed account of the history of the Chinese transfer pricing system, see *Transfer Pricing Tax System and Its Development in China*, which was purportedly prepared by the SAT, available at www.rrojasdatabank.info/chinatrprice02.pdf ('Unofficial SAT Document on Transfer Pricing'). Presumably, the SAT did not have adequate data or resources to pursue the larger taxpayers with more complex transactions. Such problems are typical for developing countries, such as a lack of well-trained transfer pricing auditors, a lack of experience in resolving tax disputes through international cooperation (e.g., mutual agreement procedure, bilateral APA or corresponding

With further investment in transfer pricing and more experience gained, the SAT revised the transfer pricing Circular again in 2004[21] and released a new Circular on advance pricing agreements (APAs) – 'Implementation Rules for Advance Pricing Agreements governing Transactions between Related Enterprises (Trial)'.[22] In 2005, the SAT established a national anti-avoidance case monitoring and management system.[23] More detailed transfer pricing rules, along with a general anti-avoidance rule, a thin capitalisation rule, and controlled foreign corporations rule, were enacted as part of the new EIT Law and the Implementation Regulations for the EIT Law.[24] The SAT published Measures for the Implementation of Special Tax Adjustment (Trial) in 2009 ('Implementation Measures').[25]

At present, Chinese transfer pricing rules are found in four sources: (i) the EIT Law promulgated by the National People's Congress (articles 41–4) and the Administration of Tax Collection Law (article 36);[26](ii) EIT Regulations (articles 109–15) and Rules for the Implementation of Administration of Tax Collection Law (articles 51–6) promulgated by the State

---

adjustment), a lack of information infrastructure for transfer pricing data gathering and analysis, and a lack of sophisticated transfer pricing techniques and procedures.

[21] SAT Circular, *Guo Shui Fa* no. 143 (2004).

[22] SAT Circular, *Guo Shui Fa* no. 118 (2004). The year of 2004 was known in China as the year of anti-avoidance, *China Tax News*, 2 September 2009.

[23] *Ibid.* By the end of 2007, 174 taxpayers had been subjected to transfer pricing audits, 152 of which had been reassessed, resulting in over RMB 1.2 billion.

[24] Enterprise Income Tax Law of the People's Republic of China, promulgated by the Fifth Session of the Tenth National People's Congress (16 March 2007) ('EIT Law'). The Chinese text of the EIT Law is available on the State Administration of Taxation website, www.chinatax.gov.cn. See also Implementation Regulations of Enterprise Income Tax Law of the People's Republic of China, promulgated by Decree no. 512 of the State Council on 6 December 2007, effective 1 January 2008 ('EIT Regulations'). The Chinese text of the EIT Regulations is available at www.chinatax.gov.cn. For comments, see Jinyan Li, 'Fundamental Enterprise Income Tax Reform in China: Motivations and Major Changes' (2007) 61 *Bulletin for Int'l Taxation* 519; Jinyan Li and H. Huang, 'The Transformation of Chinese Enterprise Income Tax: Internationalization and Chinese Innovations' (2008) 62 *Bulletin for Int'l Fiscal Documentation* 275.

[25] SAT, *Guo shui fa* (2009) no. 2, 8 January 2009, effective on 1 January 2008. Administrative Circulars issued prior to 2008 were revoked. The SAT has issued several sets of measures related to transfer pricing, such as 'How to Deal with the Enterprise Income Tax on the Service Charges Paid to a Parent Company by a Subsidiary Company' (*Guo Shui Fa* no. 86 (2008)); 'Related Tax Policy Issues on the Pre-tax Deduction Standard of the Interest Expenses Paid to Related Parties' (*Guo Shui Fa* no. 121 (2008)); 'Trial Measures on the Application for Mutual Agreement Procedures (MAP) by Chinese Residents and Citizens' (*Guo Shui Fa* no. 115 (2005)).

[26] Tax Administration Law, note 14 above.

Council; (iii) administrative regulations/guidelines issued by the SAT; and (iv) tax treaties. They largely track the OECD Guidelines on Transfer Pricing and are very close to those found in OECD countries.[27]

16.2.3 Cultural preference for administrative resolutions

The transplantation of the arm's length principle into China took place in the broader legal culture that is very different from Western countries. Western legal culture, broadly stated, is based on the principle of the rule of law and separation of powers between the legislature, the judiciary and the government. In the area of taxation, the rule of law means that taxes must be imposed through a proper legislative process rather than through administrative discretion or judicial discretion. The government and the taxpayers must comply with tax laws. The judiciary is independent of the government and the legislature. Before the court, the government and the taxpayer are equal parties, each represented by counsel. There is a basic presumption that any ambiguity in tax legislation is generally interpreted in favour of the taxpayer and that taxpayers have the right to arrange their affairs to minimise their tax liability. The court is the final arbiter of any dispute between the taxpayer and the government. If the government dislikes the court decision, it can overrule the decision through legislative amendments.

China is a 'socialist country ruled by law' (*shehui zhuyi fazhi guojia*)[28] and has a long history of 'rule by man' in imperial China.[29] There is no Western style separation of powers. The Constitution provides that the State Council (the executive branch) and the People's Court are both subordinate to the National People's Congress (which is the legislative body). In the area of taxation, the State Council and its ministries, such as Ministry of Finance and the State Administration of Taxation, have the power to make, interpret and

---

[27] See Explanation of the EIT Regulations available at www.chinatax.gov.cn.

[28] In 1999 the Constitution was amended to state in art. 5: 'The People's Republic of China shall practice ruling the country according to law, and shall construct a socialist rule-of-law state'. The Preamble to the Constitution states that China will be guided by 'Marxism-Leninism, Mao Zedong Thought, Deng Xiaoping Theory' and that 'the Chinese people of all ethnic groups will continue to adhere to the people's democratic dictatorship and the socialist road'.

[29] R. Pereenboom, *China Modernizes: A Threat to the West or Model for the Rest?* (Oxford: Oxford University Press, 2007); P. B. Potter, *The Chinese Legal System: Globalization and Local Legal Culture* (Routledge, 2001).

enforce tax laws. In general, Chinese courts have little independent power to interpret the meaning of the law, although the Supreme People's Court can make general interpretations without actually hearing cases. The court's role is largely limited to adjudicating 'administrative cases', criminal cases and civil cases. Administrative cases involve taxpayers suing tax officials for 'misconducts' or in respect of 'specific or concrete administrative actions or decisions' of the tax administration. These conducts are generally related to actions in assessing penalties, enforcing collections or other aspects of tax administration.[30] Any disputes between taxpayers and the local tax offices arising from the interpretation of tax legislation can only be first addressed through appealing to the tax office of a higher level.[31] Occasionally, there is a case before a People's Court requiring interpretation of the meaning of the law.[32] In the only court case on transfer pricing, *ZFC Company*, the taxpayer went to the local People's Court, lost the case, and withdrew its appeal after filing the application to appeal.[33]

---

[30] In such administrative cases, taxpayers won more than two-thirds of the cases. See J. Liu et al., *Study on China's Taxation Legal System* (Beijing: Taxation Science Research Institute, 2005), pp. 85–162.

[31] Yao Meiyan and Hao Ruyu, *Study on Chinese Taxation Legal System* (China Tax Press, 2005), pp. 663–9 (in Chinese) Xing Zheng Su Song Fa (Administrative Procedure Law of the People's Republic of China) adopted on 4 April 1989 at the Second Session of the Seventh National People's Congress, effective 1 October 1990. The SAT has issued guidelines to help local tax offices prepare for the defence, make arguments in court, file appeals and enforce court decisions. See Shui Wu Xing Zheng Ying Su Gong Zuo Gui Chen (Operational Guidelines on Responding to Tax Administrative Appeals) effective on 1 January 1995. See also 'Decision of the SAT on Several Questions Concerning Establishing Disciplinary and Inspection Offices', *Zhongguo Shuiwu Bao (China Tax Newspaper)*, 15 November 1995 (in Chinese).

[32] According to art. 53 of the Administrative Procedure Law, the court only takes the SAT's interpretation as a reference. Article 53 states: 'In handling administrative cases, the people's courts shall take, as references, regulations formulated and announced by ministries or commissions under the State Council in accordance with the law and administrative rules and regulations'.

[33] See www.67786.com/caiwuhuiji/fadingzhangbu/80015.html (in Chinese); S. Shi and N. Jiang, 'Why ZFC Initiatively Withdrew the Lawsuit after Appeal?', available at www.hwuason.com. For more general discussion of the tax administrative cases, see Wu Jinsong, 'Reflections on Our Country's System of Tax Administrative Interpretation' (2010) *Theory and Practice of Tax Law* 69 (in Chinese); Xu Jimin, 'A Study on the Rules governing the Procedures and Evidence of Tax Administration' (2010) *Theory and Practice of Tax Law* 65; and the Taxation Science Research Institute of the State Administration of Taxation of China, *Study on China's Taxation Legal System*

It is true that in Western countries transfer pricing disputes are resolved predominantly through administrative means and transfer pricing litigation is infrequent. However, the fact that taxpayers can go to court influences how the parties react to each other. In law, the taxpayer and the tax administration are 'equals' before the court. In China, the absence of taxpayers' ability to go to court puts taxpayers in a subordinate position *vis-à-vis* the tax administration. Such 'top-down' relationship distinguishes the Chinese system of transfer pricing dispute resolution from that in OECD countries.

There are also fundamental features of the Chinese tax system that make it difficult for taxpayers to disagree with the tax authorities. For example, the tax authorities are empowered not only to enforce tax laws, but also to 'make' tax laws in the form of administrative rules. In China, tax legislation includes tax laws (*fa lü* or 法律) enacted by the National People's Congress (the legislature),[34] administrative regulations (*xingzheng fagui* or 行政法规) promulgated by the State Council (the executive branch),[35] as well as administrative rules introduced by the Ministry of Finance and/or State

---

(May 2005), pp. 284–95 (all in Chinese). There have been debates in China about creating a specialised tax court or broadening the jurisdiction of the court to include genuine interpretative issues. See Zhu Daqi and He Xiaxiang, 'On the Foundation of Tax Court' (2007) 3 *Contemporary Law Review* 17; Zhai Jiguang, 'On the Establishment of Tax Court in China' (2003) 4 *Journal of Heilongjiang Administrative Cadre Institute of Politics and Law* 98; Li Yan, 'On the Establishment of Tax Court in China' (2009) 4 *Journal of Liaoning Normal University* (Social Science Edition) 26 (in Chinese).

[34] The National People's Congress (NPC) is the supreme body under the Chinese Constitution. It meets once a year in Beijing. Most of the laws are passed by the Standing Committee of the NPC. The NPC often delegates legislative powers to the government (i.e., the State Council or ministries of the State Council). This power is exercised through the control over its members (the majority of members of the NPC and high-ranking government bureaucrats are members), as well as through making policy decisions. In practice, the Communist Party controls the law-making process as most members of the NPC are Communist Party members who are required to follow the Party direction.

[35] Article 89 of the Chinese Constitution provides that the State Council has power 'to adopt administrative measures, enact administrative rules and regulations and issue decisions and orders in accordance with the Constitution and the law'. Article 90 of the Constitution provides that the ministries and commissions of State Council have the power to 'issue orders, directives and regulations within the jurisdiction of their respective departments and in accordance with the law and the administrative rules and regulations, decisions and orders issued by the State Council'. The directives, regulations and measures issued by the SAT have the force of law, as long as they do not violate the legislation enacted by the State Council and the National People's

Administration of Taxation (*bumen guizhang* or部门规章).[36] As
such, the SAT Measures or rules have the force of law in China.[37]

The SAT attempts to minimise transfer pricing disputes through
transparency and incentives for cooperation. The SAT has published
detailed guidelines in the Implementation Measures to help taxpayers
manage their transfer pricing risks. Taxpayers are advised of the targets
for transfer pricing audits[38] and would presumably keep these in mind
in their compliance efforts or be motivated to negotiate an APA. Taxpayers are also provided with some 'safe harbours' based on the median
of the range of profitability established by comparable enterprises.[39]
Taxpayers engaged in certain business activities, such as manufacturing
under a related party's orders, are advised not to assume any risk and
loss associated with 'incorrect decisions, low capacity utilisation, or
sluggish sales'.[40] Because the Chinese transfer pricing rules incorporate

Congress. See Chinese Law-Making Law, promulgated by the Standing Committee of
National People's Congress, 15 March 2000 and effective 1 July 2000, art. 71.

[36] See Law-Making Law, *ibid.* In principle, a lower-level form of legislation must not deviate
from higher-level forms of legislation. In practice, many detailed rules of interpretation
and application are specified in administrative rules or administrative regulations.
'Administrative Rules' are documents issued by departments of the State Council,
including the Ministry of Finance and State Administration of Taxation. A similar system
exists at local levels. See Liu *et al.*, *Study on China's Taxation Legal System*, note 30 above,
pp. 279–99.

[37] There is a long tradition of this style of law-making in China. See W. Alford, 'The Limits
of "Grand Theory" in Comparative Law' (1986) 61 *Wash. L Rev.* 945; D. C. K. Chow, *The
History of Law in Imperial and Modern China, in the Legal System of the People's Republic
of China* (West Group Publishing, 2003), ch. 2; T. B. Stephens, *Order and Discipline in
China: the Shanghai Mixed Court, 1911–1927* (Washington, DC: University of
Washington Press, 1992); W. C. Jones, 'Trying to Understand the Current Chinese Legal
System' in C. S. Hsu (ed.), *Understanding China's Legal System: Essays in Honor of Jerome
A. Cohen* (New York: New York University Press, 2003) pp. 7–45; G. Mayeda, 'A
Normative Perspective on Legal Harmonization: China's Accession to the WTO'
(2005) 38 *UBC Law Rev.* 83; X. Ren, *Tradition of the Law and Law of the Tradition*
(Greenwood Press, 1997), pp. 17–44.

[38] Implementation Measures, note 25 above, art. 29.

[39] *Ibid.* art. 41 provides: 'When the tax authorities analyse and evaluate a taxpayer's
profitability by using the quartile method, if the taxpayer's profit level is below the
median of the range of profitability established by comparable enterprises, in principle
the taxpayer's profit should be adjusted up to a level not lower than the median of the
range established by the comparable enterprises.'

[40] *Ibid.* art. 39 states: 'Enterprises that engage in manufacturing under a related party's
orders and do not perform functions such as operational decision-making, research and
development and sales should not bear the risks and losses associated with incorrect
decisions, low capacity utilization, or sluggish sales, and should normally maintain a
certain level of profit.'

the basic concepts and principles in the OECD Transfer Pricing Guidelines, they are generally familiar to multinational corporations.[41] As discussed further below, taxpayers are provided with several opportunities to negotiate with the tax authorities before transfer pricing adjustment decisions are finalised.[42]

16.3 Transfer pricing law and administration

16.3.1 Transfer pricing law

Article 41 of the EIT Law provides that where a transaction between an enterprise and its related parties is not based on the arm's length principle, thereby reducing the taxable income of the enterprise or its related parties, the tax authorities are empowered to make reasonable adjustments to the taxable income of the enterprise or its related parties. The arm's length principle refers to 'the principle adopted by unrelated parties in carrying out transactions with each other according to a fair price and normal business practice'.[43]

The term 'associated enterprise' (*guan lian qi ye*), which is used in Article 9 of the OECD Model, is not used. Instead, the 'associated party' or 'related party' (*guan lian fang*) is used. The choice of words is important because a related party does not have to be an 'enterprise'; it can be a partnership or an individual. The characterisation of the relationship is based on the substance-over-form approach. In addition to formal legal relationships, business and operational relationships are also factors for consideration. The term 'related party' is an enterprise, organisation or individual that has one of the following relationships with a taxpayer enterprise: (a) direct or indirect control over such matters as funds, operation, purchase and sales; (b) both are directly or indirectly controlled by the same third person; or (c) other relationships due to associated interests.[44]

---

[41] 'China Creates a Legal Sword to Counter Tax Avoidance (Zhongguo Zhujiu Fan Bishui Falv Lijian)', *China Tax News*, 2 September 2009, available at 202.108.90.130/n8136506/ n8136593/n8137681/n8817331/n8817378/8818718.html (in Chinese).

[42] Transfer pricing audit and assessment are generally conducted by SAT offices located at the provincial or municipal level. The Special Tax Adjustment Measures provide guidelines for both taxpayers and local tax offices. There are also procedures for local tax offices to submit cases for review or filing by the head office in Beijing and for taxpayers to apply to the head office for reconsideration.

[43] EIT Regulations, note 24 above, art. 110. [44] *Ibid.* art. 109.

The Implementation Measures provide the following criteria for determining if an enterprise (Party A) is considered to be related to another enterprise, economic organisation or individual (Party B):

(a) where 25 per cent or more of all the shares of Party A are held directly or indirectly by Party B, or 25 per cent or more of all the shares of both parties are commonly held by a third party;

(b) debts owed by Party A to Party B (other than an independent financial institution) exceed 50 per cent of Party A's paid-up capital, or 10 per cent or above of the total debts owed by Party A is guaranteed by Party B (other than an independent financial institution);

(c) Party B appoints more than half of Party A's senior management personnel (including members of the board of directors and managers), or appoints at least one senior member of the board of directors who is able to exert control over the board of directors; or the same third party appoints more than half of the senior management personnel (including the members of the board of directors and managers), or more than one senior member of the board of directors who is able to exert control over the board of directors of Party A and Party B;

(d) more than half of Party A's senior management personnel (including board members, and managers) concurrently hold senior management positions with Party B, or at least one senior board member who is able to control the decision of the board of Party A concurrently holds a senior position in Party B; or

(e) the business of Party A depends on intangibles licensed from Party B (including industrial property rights or know-how); the purchase and sale activities of Party A are primarily controlled by Party B; Party A's provision or receipt of services is primarily controlled by Party B; or one party has substantial control over another party's production, operation and transactions, or both parties have other types of relationships in interests, including family relationships, and the relationship where Party A shares basically the same interests with major shareholders of Party B even though the 25 per cent shareholding percentage requirement is not satisfied.

The determination of 'related parties' is based more on an economic reality test as opposed to a legalistic, formal control test.

16.3.2   Transfer pricing methods

Under the Chinese law, methods that satisfy the arm's length principle include, but are not limited to, the internationally-accepted methods. Other methods may be considered 'reasonable' in transfer pricing assessment. What is 'reasonable' seems to be dictated more by the 'right outcome' rather than the 'right process or methodology'. This is consistent with the Chinese substance-over-form, holistic and pragmatic approach to tax avoidance.

The comparable uncontrolled price (CUP) method, resale price method, cost plus method, transactional net margin method (TNMM), profit split method, and any other reasonable methods can be used to determine if the arm's length principle is complied with.[45] There is no hierarchy in the application of these methods. 'Other reasonable methods' include a deeming method that determines a taxpayer's profit on the basis of (i) the profit level of enterprises that are the same or similar to the taxpayer; (ii) the taxpayer's cost plus reasonable expenses and profit margins; (iii) a reasonable proportion of the profit of the group of related companies.[46]

The selection of a method depends on the nature of transactions and the results of the comparability analysis. A comparability analysis should consider: (a) the characteristics of the property or services being purchased or sold; (b) the functions performed by the parties to the transactions (taking into account assets used and risks assumed); (c) the terms and conditions of the contract; (d) the economic circumstances of the parties, such as overall environment for the industry, geographical location, market scale, market level, market share, degree of market competition, consumer purchasing power, substitutability of the goods and services, prices of the production factors, cost of transportation, and governmental regulations; and (e) the business strategies pursued by the parties, such as strategies regarding innovation, research and development, business diversification, risks minimisation and market penetration.

There is no formal recognition of the concept of 'arm's length range' in the Chinese transfer pricing legislation. However, this concept is relevant in practice, especially in the context of APAs. The arm's length range is one of the issues to be negotiated before reaching an APA. If the

---

[45] *Ibid.* art. 111; Implementation Measures, note 25 above, art. 21.
[46] EIT Regulations, note 24 above, art. 115.

actual outcome of the taxpayer falls out of the range of arm's length prices, it is evidence of violation of an APA.

16.3.3   Documentation requirements

Taxpayers are required to file annual related party transactions information forms along with their tax return,[47] as well as contemporaneous documentation and other relevant documents. These other relevant documents include documents that provide information on related party transactions in respect of the resale (transfer) price or final sale (transfer) price of assets, right to use property, services or documents that describe comparable prices, pricing methods and profit levels.[48]

Contemporaneous documentation must cover five types of information: (i) organisational structure;[49] (ii) production and business operations of the taxpayer and its related parties; (iii) description of related party transactions; (iv) comparability analysis; and (v) selection of transfer pricing methods. With respect to contemporaneous documentation regarding production and business operations, the taxpayer must provide information on:

(a) the major economic and legal issues affecting the taxpayer and the industry, such as a summary of the enterprise's and industry's development, business strategy, industrial policy or industrial restrictions;
(b) a description of the group's supply chain arrangement and the position that the taxpayer is located in the chain; a summary showing the percentage of the enterprise's revenues and profits by business line, market and competition analysis;
(c) information regarding the functions, risks and assets of the enterprise; and
(d) the group's consolidated financial report prepared according to the group's year end.

The documentation must be in Chinese. Information on overseas related parties or transactions must be notarised or certified by certified

---

[47] EIT Law, note 24 above, art. 43.   [48] EIT Regulations, note 24 above, art. 114.
[49] Implementation Measures, note 25 above, art. 14.

public accountants. Contemporaneous documentation must be prepared by 31 May of the following year and maintained for ten years.[50] Taxpayers are required to submit their contemporaneous documentation within twenty days of the date of request by the tax bureau.

16.3.4 *Audit and investigation*

Audits are conducted by local tax authorities which are in charge of the taxpayer. Key targets for transfer pricing audits are identified as enterprises that have relatively large amounts of related party transactions or multiple types of related party transactions; long-term losses, marginal profit or fluctuating profits; profit levels lower than the industry's; profit levels lower than the related corporate group's; profit levels that do not match with the functions they perform and the risks they assume; transactions with related parties located in tax havens; failed to submit annual related party transaction disclosure forms or failed to prepare contemporaneous documents; or obviously failed to comply with the arm's length principle.[51]

A transfer pricing audit generally involves a desk audit[52] and a field audit.[53] The tax authorities can adjust a taxpayer's income retroactively for up to ten years and conduct a five-year post-audit review of taxpayers that have had a transfer pricing adjustment upon audit. Audits outside China are authorised 'if there is a real need for obtaining information and materials related to comparable prices, economic data, etc.' and such information is available outside China. The SAT can obtain the information through the exchange of information mechanism under a tax treaty, through Chinese embassies or consulates in foreign countries, or field audits in a foreign jurisdiction.

---

[50] Under the EIT Law, enterprises in China must adopt the calendar year as their taxation year. Many enterprises have their audited financial report finalised only in the first quarter of the following year. Therefore, they may face significant time pressure to prepare contemporaneous documentation before the 31 May deadline.

[51] Implementation Measures, note 25 above, art. 29.

[52] According to art. 31 of the Implementation Measures, note 25 above, desk audits are part of the tax authorities' routine collection and administrative activities. It is a screening process for the tax officials to select transfer pricing targets. During desk audits, the tax officials make an overall evaluation and analysis of the taxpayer's production and operational status and related party transactions on the basis of the taxpayer's annual tax returns, related party transactions reporting forms, and other tax related documents.

[53] A field audit is required if desk audits fail to resolve the questions concerning the information, pricing and expenses reported by the enterprise.

16.3.5   Adjustments

Upon completion of the transfer pricing audit and investigation, a Notice on Special Tax Audit Conclusion will be issued to the enterprise if related party transactions have been found not to have been conducted at arm's length. The tax authorities will then draft a preliminary special tax adjustment plan and enter into negotiations with the taxpayer about the adjustment plan. If the taxpayer disagrees with the draft preliminary adjustment plan, it can provide further information during the specified period for further consideration by the tax authorities. The tax authorities will then issue a Notice of Preliminary Special Tax Audit Adjustment. If the taxpayer disagrees with the preliminary adjustment notice, the taxpayer must inform the tax authorities in writing within seven days of receiving the notice and provide grounds for disagreement. The tax authorities will negotiate and deliberate again after receiving the enterprise's submission. The taxpayer is deemed to agree with the preliminary adjustment notice if the taxpayer does not raise any disagreements within the time limit. The tax authorities will then issue a Notice of Special Tax Audit Adjustment. A taxpayer must pay the additional taxes arising from transfer pricing adjustments within the specified time limit. In case of difficulties in making the tax payment on time, the taxpayer may apply for postponement for a period of no more than three months. Penalties are imposed on failures to pay the taxes on time.

When making the adjustments, the tax authorities are allowed to use public as well as non-public information.[54] In principle, if a taxpayer's profitability is lower than the median of the inter-quartile range established by comparable companies, the tax authorities are likely to adjust the taxpayer's profitability to at least the median of the range.[55]

There is no legislative reference to secondary adjustments. Where the transfer pricing adjustment results in a reduction in the amount of interest, rental, royalty and other similar payments subject to withholding tax, the overpaid withholding taxes will not be refunded.[56]

16.3.6   Penalties

Taxpayers who have failed to provide the relevant documentation are subject to penalties. For example, taxpayers who fail to file tax returns or submit the information within a prescribed time limit may be liable to

---

[54] Implementation Measures, note 25 above, art. 37.   [55] Ibid. art. 41.
[56] Ibid. art. 88.

pay a fine, ranging from CNY 2,000 to CNY 10,000.[57] A further penalty between CNY 2,000 and CNY 10,000 will be imposed for continued failure to submit forms before the new deadline. These penalties are relatively small.

In addition to the additional tax liabilities, interest charges, a 'penalty' of 5 per cent per annum (computed on a daily basis on the amount of underpaid tax) will be levied. This penalty may be waived if the taxpayer has prepared and submitted contemporaneous documentation according to the rules specified in the Implementation Measures.

16.4   Disputes prevention and administrative resolution

Transfer pricing disputes are resolved primarily through preventive measures, such as detailed guidelines for taxpayers, cost sharing agreements, or APAs, or negotiated settlement with the tax administration. As mentioned earlier, judicial resolution is not currently effective.

16.4.1   Guidelines on intangibles

Intangibles present unique challenges in applying the arm's length principle. The Implementation Measures clarify that ownership of intangibles must be determined on the basis of a substance-over-form approach, and that ownership is not limited to a strict legal sense but also includes ownership in an economic sense. Relevant factors for consideration include the contribution made by each party to the development, formation and maintenance of the intangible property. In the case of co-ownership, each party's share of ownership is based on the amount of fees incurred for establishing, registering and maintaining an intangible property and for developing the value of an intangible property in an emerging market. If a profit split method is used, the Implementation Measures require that each party's basic profits be determined first on the basis of its respective functions and risks, and the excess profits be split by referring to each party's contribution to the intangible property. In cases where a related Chinese entity performs

---

[57] Tax Administration Law, note 14 above, art. 62. If a taxpayer has a valid reason for not being able to file declaration forms within the prescribed time period, the taxpayer must apply for a postponement before the deadline expires. Subject to approval by the tax authority, the filing may be postponed for a maximum of thirty days. A penalty of CNY 2,000 will be imposed on failure to file the forms on time.

only limited functions and bears limited risks as opposed to having independent decision-making and price-setting powers in an intangible property transaction, the Chinese party's share in the profits produced by the intangible property is limited, but its 'normal profit' must be guaranteed.

In the case of marketing intangibles, because the Chinese market is an emerging one and its market features and consumer behaviours are largely different from those of developed countries, Western products and marketing behaviours need to be localised to a large extent in order to adapt to the Chinese market. In this 'localisation' process, the Chinese enterprise that is a party to the transaction plays an indispensable role. Therefore, even though the intangible property's legal ownership is not transferred to the Chinese enterprise, the Chinese enterprise may also have certain economic ownership and may be justified to receive its reasonable share of the intangible property's excess profits.[58]

16.4.2   Cost sharing agreements

Taxpayers are encouraged to enter into cost sharing agreements (CSAs).[59] CSAs are defined as an agreement reached concerning the sharing of common costs among related parties in accordance with the arm's length principle[60] or the principle of 'matching costs with anticipated benefits'. CSAs can be used for the joint development and transfer of intangibles, the provision of services, including group purchases and group marketing activities. Taxpayers must provide the tax authorities with relevant documentation to prove that the pricing is reasonable and that the shared costs are proportionate with the anticipated profits. The tax authorities determine if a CSA is consistent with the arm's length principle.[61] Taxpayers are advised to request a binding

---

[58]   T. Liao, 'P. R. China's Experience of Tax Administration on Transfer Pricing of Intangible Property Transactions', paper presented at United Nations Group of Experts Meeting on Tax Aspects of Domestic Resource Mobilization, 'A Discussion of Enduring and Emerging Issues', Rome, 4–5 September 2007, available at www.un.org/esa/ffd/tax/2007DRM_SEG/12TransferPricingChina.doc.

[59]   C. Holmes and K. Holmes, 'A Comparative Survey of Cost Contribution Agreements: China and International Best Practices' (2007) *Asia Pac. Tax Bull.* (July/August) 299.

[60]   EIT Regulations, note 24 above, art. 112.

[61]   Implementation Measures, note 25 above, art. 69. A qualifying CSA receives the following tax treatment: costs allocated according to the CSA are deductible for Chinese tax purposes; compensating adjustments are included in taxable income in the year the adjustment is made; and where a CSA involves intangible property development, buy-in

APA to eliminate the risks of not complying with the tax authority's interpretation and tax treatment of the CSA.

A CSA is considered inconsistent with arm's length principle if (a) it does not have a *bona fide* commercial purpose or economic substance; (b) it violates the arm's length principle; (c) the allocation of costs and benefits among the CSA participants does not comply with the 'cost and benefit matching' principle; (d) the enterprise has failed to file the CSA with the tax authorities or has not prepared, maintained and provided contemporaneous documentation for the CSA; or (e) the enterprise will not be in operation for at least twenty years from the time the CSA is signed.[62]

During the enforcement period of a CSA, taxpayers are required to prepare and maintain contemporaneous documents in addition to the documents required by the general contemporaneous documents rule.[63] These CSA-related documents include information about the cost allocation to the participants during the current taxation year and a comparison of the expected benefit and the actual results from the CSA, and the corresponding adjustments made during the current taxation year. These documents must be submitted to the tax authorities by 20 June of the following year, regardless of whether agreement is reached via an APA.

16.4.3   Advance pricing agreements

Overview

The SAT regards the APA programme as an effective method to provide certainty for both the tax authorities and taxpayers. The programme reduces the compliance costs for taxpayers by mitigating the transfer pricing audit risks and minimises the risk of double taxation. In the meantime, it helps save administration costs for tax authorities by reducing the number of audits and provides more certainty in tax revenue. The SAT encourages large enterprises to enter into APAs as the best method for resolving transfer pricing disputes.[64] About one-quarter of the Implementation Measures are dedicated to APAs.[65] In

---

or buy-out payments, or distribution of outcomes upon the termination of the agreement, should be treated as a purchase or disposal of the intangible property.

[62] *Ibid.* art. 75.   [63] *Ibid.* art. 74.

[64] Fan Xinkui, 'Difficulties in Pressing Forward Advance Pricing Agreement (APA) in China' (2008) 4(1) *Asian Social Science*, www.CCSEnet.org/journal/html.

[65] APAs were first allowed in China by Circular 59 published in 1998. The first APA was concluded in 1998 between a taxpayer and a local tax authority. In September 2004, the

Table 16.1 *Number of APAs signed*

Year	Unilateral APAs	Bilateral APAs	Multilateral APAs	Total
2005	13	1	0	14
2006	10	0	0	10
2007	7	3	0	10
2008	6	1	0	7
2009	5	7	0	12
Total	**41**	**12**	**0**	53

addition to the general advantages of APAs, China offers other incentives, such as exemptions on contemporaneous documentation for transactions covered by APAs. As a useful tool for resolving transfer pricing issues and managing risks, multinational enterprises have been receptive to the APA programme.

On 30 December 2010, SAT published its first annual report on APAs.[66] According to the report, fifty-three APAs had been concluded by the end of 2009, twelve of which are bilateral APAs, with Japan, Korea, Singapore, United States and Denmark. About fifty-one bilateral APAs are currently being negotiated or evaluated. The report provides an overview of the APA programme as shown in Tables 16.1, 16.2 and 16.3.

Concluding APAs

According to the Implementation Measures, APA candidates must have an annual volume of related party transactions exceeding RMB 40 million. An APA application might be rejected where the taxpayer intended to lower its taxable profit through an APA, the applicant (or its affiliate) is under an ongoing transfer pricing audit, has low turnover or is a new taxpayer without an audit history.

The period of time required to conclude a bilateral APA varies. The APA between Wal-Mart, SAT and the US Internal Revenue Service took six months, whereas the one with South Korea took more than two years.[67]

SAT issued formal APA rules in *Guo Shui Fa* no. 118 (2004), which were incorporated into the Implementation Measures published in 2009.

[66] SAT, *China Advance Pricing Arrangement: Annual Report*, available at www.chinatax.gov. cn/n8136506/n8136608/n9947993/. . ./n10518029.pdf.

[67] Office of the SAT, 'China and Denmark Concluded its First Bilateral APA', 30 October 2009, available at 202.108.90.130/n8136506/n8136548/n8136623/9308899.html (in Chinese). The first bilateral APA was concluded in September 2005 between a taxpayer, the

Table 16.2 *APAs by transaction type*

Accepted application Transaction type	Concluded APAs number of APAs	Percentage	Transaction type	Number of APAs	Percentage
Purchase and sale of tangible assets	11	46%	Purchase and sale of tangible assets	42	62%
Transfer or use of intangible assets	8	33%	Transfer or use of intangible assets	13	19%
Provision of services	5	21%	Provision of services	13	19%
Financing	0	–	Financing	0	–
Total	**24**	**100%**	**Total**	**68**	**100%**

Table 16.3 *APAs by transfer pricing method*

Method	CUP	Resale price	Cost plus	TNMM	Profit split	other
Number	4	0	15	35 (15 full cost mark-up; 20 return on sales)	2	2

Intra-China multilateral APAs are becoming more common. Foreign enterprises doing business in multiple Chinese provinces through

SAT and the Japanese National Tax Administration. The APA was negotiated between the taxpayer and the Shenzhen Local Tax Bureau, and approved under the mutual agreement procedure set out in the China–Japan Tax Treaty. A more recent bilateral APA was concluded between the Korean National Tax Service and SAT on 7 November 2007 regarding Samsung. The APA covers two Chinese subsidiaries of Samsung, one in Suzhou and another in Shandong. As the subsidiaries filed separate applications with their respective tax bureaus, this bilateral agreement is regarded as 'twin' APAs from China's perspective. Bilateral APAs have been concluded with Japan, Korea, the United States and Denmark.

subsidiaries have to deal with several local tax offices. Because Chinese tax law does not allow these subsidiaries to file consolidated tax returns, each subsidiary was previously required to file an APA with its respective local authorities. The SAT prescribes procedures for local tax bureaus to communicate and coordinate with each other. A group of related enterprises in China can enter into an APA to cover transactions between these multiple Chinese taxpayers and their common related foreign party or even transfer pricing for intra-China transactions between the related Chinese taxpayers.

As in other countries, there are detailed rules regulating each phase of APA negotiations.[68] For a bilateral APA, the taxpayer must submit the Formal APA Application and the Application for Initiating Mutual Agreement Procedure to the SAT and the relevant tax authority simultaneously. The main issues of negotiation include functions of the related parties, risks assumed, comparable data, assumptions, transfer pricing policy and methods and the arm's length range. The negotiation phase ends with the parties reaching an agreement on the subjects discussed. A draft APA is subsequently created. For bilateral APAs, the SAT will negotiate with the competent tax authority of the treaty partner country, and the draft APA will be prepared according to the negotiation memorandum after consensus is achieved.

The term of the APA is three to five years, which generally begins from the year in which an APA application is filed. An APA is not renewed automatically, although the taxpayer may apply for renewal within ninety days before the expiration of the initial term. During the term of the APA, the taxpayer is required to maintain adequate documents (including accounting ledgers and records) and file an annual report

---

[68] For example, at the formal application phase (which starts within three months of receiving Notice of Formal Negotiation of APA) the taxpayer must submit a Formal APA Application, which should include at least the following documents: information on group organisation, corporate structure, related parties and related party transactions; the tested taxpayer's financial and accounting statements for the past three years, product functionality and assets (including tangible and intangible assets) information; types and tax years of related parties; functions and risks of the relevant related parties, including the organisation, people, cost, equity as the dividing standard; factors considered in selecting transfer pricing method, the functional and comparability analysis that supports the selection of the transfer pricing method, and the underlying assumptions; market conditions, including the industry development trend and market competition; annual business size, performance forecasts and business plan during the period of the APA; transactional, operational and financial information such as the profit level; and issues related to domestic and international laws and tax treaties.

with the tax authorities within five months after the end of a tax year. The annual report must contain information on the operations of the taxpayer during the past year, contain proof that the APA has been strictly followed, and disclose whether the taxpayer wishes to revise or cancel the APA, and whether the taxpayer anticipates any future problems in executing the APA. The tax authorities conduct periodic audits to ensure that the APA is actually implemented. Significant violations of the APA terms by the taxpayer could result in the retroactive cancellation of the APA. If the taxpayer's actual operating results fall outside of the range of arm's length prices or profit levels as prescribed in the APA, but the non-compliance does not constitute a 'serious' or 'blanket' violation of the terms and requirements of the APA, the tax authorities will not cancel the APA, but have the power to make transfer pricing adjustments in accordance with the APA.

If there are 'fundamental changes' that affect the basis of transfer pricing determinations (e.g., changes in the assumptions), the taxpayer is required to notify the relevant tax authority within thirty days of the occurrence of such. The tax authority is required to complete the review and evaluation within sixty days of receiving a report and, through negotiations with the taxpayer, decide on whether the original APA should be cancelled or modified.

Confidential information and legal effect

Both the competent tax authorities and the taxpayer have the obligation to keep the information provided during APA negotiations confidential. If an APA negotiation fails before an agreement is reached, all materials and information must be returned to their original owner. The tax authorities cannot use any non-factual information obtained during the failed APA negotiations against the taxpayer in subsequent audits of the transactions that are the subject of the APA negotiations.

There is a dispute resolution mechanism for the APA programme. According to article 63 of the Implementation Measures, for example, during the implementation period of the APA, if there are disagreements between the relevant tax authority and the taxpayer, both parties must resolve the disputes through negotiation. If the negotiations fail, the case may be brought to the tax authorities at the higher level, or ultimately to the SAT in the case of a bilateral or multilateral APA, for coordination. If the taxpayer disagrees with the decision of the higher-level tax authority or the SAT, the APA negotiations should be terminated.

16.4.4   *Mutual agreement procedure*

It is difficult to ascertain whether the mutual agreement procedure (MAP) is the most frequent method for solving transfer pricing disputes in China. The increasing popularity of bilateral APAs indicates that MAP is an important mechanism. MAP is also used in making corresponding transfer pricing adjustments.

In the case of transfer pricing adjustments, the taxpayer in China may, within three years of receiving its transfer pricing adjustment notice, apply for corresponding adjustments to the income of its associated party in a treaty country in accordance with the MAP set forth in the applicable treaty.[69] The head office of the SAT has the ultimate power to decide whether an application for MAP should be accepted. With the exception of 'urgent situations', the head office does not directly make contact with the applicant. The applicant sends its application to the state tax bureau at the local level, which will then submit the application to the head office. In the case of transfer pricing disputes, the SAT will invoke the MAP process if there is evidence that a treaty partner country's actions have resulted in, or will result in, tax consequences inconsistent with the provisions of the tax treaty and the tax issue is related to the application for an APA, potential or actual double taxation. If the MAP results in a reduction of the taxpayer's tax liability in China, the taxpayer will receive interest in addition to a tax refund.[70]

16.5   Future of transfer pricing disputes resolution

The increasing sophistication of taxpayers and their advisors and the intensification of the SAT's efforts in transfer pricing audits will likely lead to a greater number of disputes. From China's perspective, the best approach for facilitating the global resolution of transfer pricing disputes is through bilateral or multilateral APAs as well as a pragmatic way of interpreting and applying the arm's length principle.[71]

---

[69] Implementation Measures, note 25 above, art. 98.
[70] Tax Administration Law, note 14 above, art. 51.
[71] Global proposals for simplifying the transfer pricing problem in both the developed and emerging world include the following options: option (1) improved methods for solving transfer pricing disputes (see 2007 OECD, Improving the Resolution of Tax Treaty Disputes (2007), available at www.oecd.org/dataoecd/17/59/38055311.pdf); option (2) improved methods for solving tax treaty disputes in which certain MAPs are used as a proxy for transfer pricing case law (see R. Vann, 'Reflections on Business Profits and the

16.5.1   APAs and the Chinese way

The APA programme in China developed rapidly during the past decade. Multinational corporations regard APAs as an essential strategy in managing their transfer pricing risks in China. There are some challenges in expanding APAs, such as the high cost of obtaining an APA, the amount of time required, the limited period of validity, and the concern about protecting trade secrets, which are not unique to China. Nonetheless, APAs are perhaps the only real formal mechanism for resolving transfer pricing disputes in China.

The nature of transfer pricing problems is such that it involves at least two taxpayers who are related to each other and two tax authorities. To the taxpayers, it might be a zero-sum game and it may make little difference to which government taxes are paid, as long as taxes are not overpaid. The two tax authorities need to work out a way of sharing the tax base. A bilateral APA provides certainty for taxpayers and the tax authorities. Bilateral APAs, if published, may also function as a source of informal 'common law' in international taxation.[72] Another potential advantage of bilateral or multilateral APAs is that they can indirectly deal with the problem of tax havens. Since offshore tax havens generally are not centres of economic activities, and economic profits are earned in countries with 'normal' tax systems, a bilateral APA between these countries can presumably circumvent some of the difficulties with obtaining information from tax haven jurisdictions.

Collaborative or non-adversarial style of dispute resolution is more consistent with the Chinese way. The Western style of litigation has never taken root in China.[73] In recent years, even though Western

Arm's Length Principle,' in B. J. Arnold, J. Sasseville and E. M. Zolt (eds.), *The Taxation of Business Profits Under Tax Treaties* (Toronto: Canadian Tax Foundation, 2004), p. 133; see also E. Baistrocchi, 'The Transfer Pricing Problem: A Global Proposal for Simplification' (2006) *Tax Lawyer* (Summer), papers.ssrn.com/sol3/papers.cfm?abstract_id=1276504); option (3) a global formulary apportionment (see R. S. Avi-Yonah and K. A. Clausing, *A Proposal to Adopt Formulary Apportionment for Corporate Income Taxation: The Hamilton Project*, University of Michigan Law and Economics Olin Working Paper no. 07–009 (2007); University of Michigan Public Law Working Paper no. 85 (2007)), available at ssrn.com/abstract=995202.

[72] See also Baistrocchi, 'The Transfer Pricing Problem, note 71 above and Li Qian and Cai Qinghui, 'Some Thoughts on Perfection of Chinese Transfer Pricing Tax System' (2008) 7 *Fujian Tribune (Humanities and Social Sciences Monthly)* 34.

[73] There is a rich body of literature on Chinese traditional legal culture and the Chinese way of dispute resolution. See, e.g., T. V. Lee (ed.), *Contract, Guanxi, and Dispute Resolution in China* (Taylor & Francis, 1997); R. Peerenboom, More Law, Less Courts: Legalised

style civil and criminal procedures have been transplanted into China and civil and economic disputes among private parties are increasingly resolved by Chinese courts, disputes between the state and private parties (citizens or corporations) remain largely outside the Chinese court system.[74] The Chinese value system is based on collective right and social harmony.[75] The relationship between the state and taxpayers is framed in terms of 'duty' to support the state, as opposed to a kind of 'deprivation' of private property.[76] The lack of genuine independence of the court makes it difficult for the court to be a true arbiter of disputes between the state and taxpayers, although in many administrative cases, the tax authorities have been found by the court to have failed to strictly follow the law and procedures.[77] In the meantime, however, it is in the interest of the Party-led state that the Chinese economy continues to grow. International investment and trade is crucial to economic growth. The SAT has strived to maintain the balance between adopting international anti-avoidance tax norms and maintaining the friendliness of the tax system to foreign investors. APAs are non-confrontational, non-threatening to the power of the

---

Governance, Judicialization and Dejudicialization in China, La Trobe Law School Legal Studies Research Paper no. 2008/10; R. Peerenboom, *China's Long March Toward Rule of Law* (Cambridge: Cambridge University Press, 2002); R. Peerenboom and K. Scanlon 'An Untapped Dispute Resolution Option: Mediation Offers Companies Distinct Advantages in Certain Cases' (2005) 4 *China Bus. Rev* 36.

[74] For an excellent overview of dispute resolution in China, see R. Peerenboom and X. He, 'Rule of Law in China: Chinese Law and Business Dispute Resolution in China – Patterns, Causes, and Prognosis' (2009) 4 *E Asia L Rev.* 1, www.cityu.edu.hk/slw/lib/doc/Frank_pub/5.pdf.

[75] In China, rights are more commonly associated with collectivities and claims made to community membership rather than negative freedoms *vis-à-vis* the state. See G. Wang, *The Chineseness of China* (Hong Kong: Oxford University Press, 1991); R. R. Edwards, L. Henkin and A. J. Nathan, *Human Rights in Contemporary China* (New York: Columbia University Press, 1986); see Ren, *Tradition of the Law*, note 37 above, pp. 19–35; Jones, 'Trying to Understand the Current Chinese Legal System', note 37 above, 7–45.

[76] Liu Rong and Du Jian, 'The Protection of Taxpayer's Rights and Chinese Taxation Judicial Reform' (2007) 1 *Taxation Research* 51; You Xiaoqiang and Wang Zhifang, 'Taxation Agreement and the Protection of Taxpayer's Rights' (2007) 2 *Taxation Research* 69.

[77] See Li Qian and Han Yu, 'Some Comments on General Anti-Avoidance Provisions in the Enterprise Income Tax Law of the People's Republic of China' (2008) 8 *International Taxation in China* 68; Zhou Chengjuan, 'On the Core Values of Tax Law and the Protection of Taxpayers' Rights' (2009) 4 *Taxation Research* 60; Wang Jianping, 'The Concept of Taxpayers Right and the Relationship between the Government and Taxpayers' (2008) 4 *International Taxation in China* 57.

state, and within the sole jurisdiction of the SAT. In other words, APAs can potentially offer practical solutions to the transfer pricing problems without requiring China to introduce a Western style rule of law, requiring an independent judiciary. In this sense, the tax disputes are more of an economic nature as opposed to a 'political' one.

16.5.2 Pragmatic implementation of the arm's length principle

The notion of 'arm's length' is 'foreign' to the Chinese cultural emphasis on '*guanxi*' or 'relationships'. In the Chinese culture, 'insiders' are expected to treat each other differently from 'outsiders'. Insiders value the long-term relationship and may not care about immediate cost or benefits. Expecting 'insiders' to behave like strangers in the eyes of law may require a cultural shift. Furthermore, the rules-based application of the arm's length principle is not an easy fit with the Chinese holistic, pragmatic approach to problem solving. The Chinese approach is exemplified by Deng Xiaoping's famous saying that 'It doesn't matter if a cat is black or white, so long as it catches mice.' China's approach to reforms has been guided by the philosophy of '*mo zhe shi tou guo he*', or 'crossing the river by groping the stone under foot', as opposed to a clearly-mapped route in advance. The end is known, but the means may vary, depending on the circumstances. Such gradualism and pragmatism has helped China find a way to economic development that is not modelled on any specific theory or doctrine.

The Chinese adaptation of the arm's length principle seems to be guided by the same philosophy. The arm's length principle is a means to an end, not the end by itself. China clearly declares in article 41 of the EIT Law and in Article 9 of the tax treaties that the arm's length principle is the guiding principle in transfer pricing adjustments. At the same time, article 111 of the EIT Regulations states that, in addition to the CUP, resale price, cost plus, TNMM and profit split methods, there are 'other reasonable methods' consistent with the arm's length principle. Under article 115 of the EIT Regulations, a taxpayer's profit can be assessed on the basis of a reasonable proportion of the overall profit of the enterprise group if the taxpayer has failed to provide full and accurate information on transfer pricing. The contemporaneous documentation must provide information that is relevant to the determination of the reasonable profit share of the global profit of the enterprise group, including the organisational and equity ownership structure of the corporate group, the consolidated financial statement for the corporate group, and, in selecting the profit split method, an explanation of the contributions by the taxpayer in China to the overall profit or residual profit of the group.[78] During transfer pricing audits, taxpayers are increasingly being asked to provide information and data from offshore related parties. 'Evidently, the reason for such requests is largely based on the belief that related parties should apportion their profit based on certain formulae.'[79]

The SAT has recently devoted more resources to transfer pricing audits, both in terms of increasing personnel in charge of audits, and improving audit practices and developing databases. Instead of focusing on transactions using traditional methods such as CUP, cost plus or resale price, more transfer pricing audits have been focusing on intangibles and the preference for the profit split method over traditional methods. This is likely attributable to two factors. First, it reflects China's changing status from being only a low-cost factory for the world to also supporting one of the fastest growing consumer markets. Multinational companies have restructured their Chinese investments to take advantage of the growing demand inside the country, which required them to bring significant intangibles, such as trade names and marketing intangibles, to China, an issue not previously faced in the country. The second factor is the US$3.4 billion tax settlement reached between GlaxoSmithKline and the US Internal Revenue Service that has provided further precedent for SAT inquiries into marketing intangibles.[80]

In their transfer pricing audits in the automotive industry, SAT auditors are increasingly focusing on the global operations and value chain of automotive multinationals, functions and risks borne and

---

[78] Implementation Measures, note 25 above, art. 14.

[79] American Chamber of Commerce, *White Paper: Taxation*, (2004), available at www.amcham-china.org.cn/amcham/show/content.php?Id=360.

[80] S. Chong *et al.*, 'Advance Pricing Agreements: Negotiating China's Tax System and APA Framework – Lessons from the November 2007 China–Korea Accord' in BNA International, *Tax Management Transfer Pricing Report* (January 2008). See note 44 above: '[T]he Chinese market is an emerging one. Its market features and consumer behaviors are largely different from the developed countries. Numerous cases show that Western products and marketing behaviors need to be localized to a large extent in order to adapt to the Chinese market. In this localization process, the Chinese partners have an indispensable role to play. In this case, although the intangible property's legal ownership sometimes does not belong to the Chinese enterprise, yet the Chinese enterprise may also have certain economic ownership and may be justified to get its reasonable share of the intangible property's excess profits.'

contributions made by Chinese subsidiaries as part of the global supply chain, and other unique attributes of the automotive industry in China, for example, whether any local intellectual property has been created by Chinese subsidiaries. The SAT has been advocating the economic attributes of China through discussions with taxpayers and foreign competent tax authorities in negotiating APAs. These attributes include market premium, location savings and the Chinese government's specific industry stimulus policies.[81]

These recent developments indicate the SAT's willingness to go beyond the transactional-based profit split. The 'arm's length principle' must be applied 'in China's specific practice' within the framework of the OECD Guidelines.

16.6   Conclusions

China's approach to resolving transfer pricing disputes is largely influenced by China's general legal structure, the philosophy of pragmatism, its preference for consensus-based dispute resolution, and its desire to be consistent with the so-called international tax norm. China is likely to become a major advocate for a pragmatic interpretation of the arm's length principle and use it as a means of achieving a fair allocation of the international tax base. As argued elsewhere by the author[82] and other international tax scholars,[83] the arm's length principle is capable of being interpreted to encompass a form of global profit split or formula apportionment. There is growing acceptance that 'the arm's length principle and formulary apportionment should not be seen as polar extremes; rather, they should be viewed as part of a continuum of methods ranging from CUP to

[81] 'SAT Clarifies This Year's Anti-avoidance Focus,' *China Tax News*, 9 April 2010, available at www.chinatax.gov.cn/n8136506/n8136548/n8136748/9629254.html (in Chinese).

[82] Jinyan Li, *International Taxation in the Age of Electronic Commerce: A Comparative Study* (Canadian Tax Foundation, May 2003); and 'Slicing the Digital Pie with a Traditional Knife: Effectiveness of the Arm's Length Principle in the Age of Electronic Commerce', *Tax Notes Int'l*, 19 November 2001, p. 775.

[83] See, e.g., J. M. Weiner, 'Practical Aspects of Implementing Formulary Apportionment in the European Union' (2007) 8 *Florida Tax Rev.* 630; J. Roin, 'Can the Income Tax be Saved: The Promise and Pitfalls of Adopting Worldwide Formulary Apportionment' (2007–8) 61 *Tax L Rev.* 169; R. Avi-Yonah, Between Formulary Apportionment and the OECD Guidelines: A Proposal for Reconciliation (29 May 2009) University of Michigan Law and Economics Olin Working Paper no. 09–011; University of Michigan Public Law Working Paper no. 152, available at ssrn.com/abstract=1411649.

predetermined formulas'.[84] Bilateral or multilateral APAs have been touted as effective means of resolving transfer pricing disputes.

Appendix: Questionnaire (China)

1. The structure of the law for solving transfer pricing disputes. *What is the structure of the law of the country for solving transfer pricing disputes? For example, is the mutual agreement procedure (MAP), as regulated in the relevant tax treaty, the standard method for solving transfer pricing disputes?*

In China, the structure for solving transfer pricing disputes is the administrative review procedure and the mutual agreement procedure. Bilateral APAs and MAP are becoming increasingly important.

2. Policy for solving transfer pricing disputes. *Is there a gap between the nominal and effective method for solving transfer pricing disputes in the country? For example, has the country a strategic policy not to enforce the arm's length standard (ALS) for fear of driving foreign direct investment to other competing jurisdictions?*

There was perhaps a strategic policy not to enforce the arm's length standard in the 1980s and early 1990s when China was relying on tax policies to entice FDI. The gap between the nominal and effective method for solving transfer pricing disputes in China is difficult to ascertain as the SAT effectively determines both the nominal and effective method.

3. The prevailing dispute resolution method. *Which is the most frequent method for solving transfer pricing disputes in the country? Does it have a positive externality? For example, is the MAP the most frequent method, and if so, to what extent have successful MAPs been used as a proxy for transfer pricing case law? For instance, Procter & Gamble (P&G) obtained a bilateral advance pricing agreement (APA) in Europe, and it was then extended to a third (Asian) country when P&G made this request to the relevant Asian tax authorities.*

---

[84] B. J. Arnold and T. E. McDonnell, 'Report on the Invitational Conference on Transfer Pricing: the Allocation of Income and Expenses among Countries' (1993) 13 *Tax Notes* 1377.

APAs are perhaps the most effective way of resolving transfer pricing disputes. Bilateral APAs are presumably used as a proxy for transfer pricing case law as there is no case law per se in China. However, because APAs are not officially published, their value is limited.

4. Transfer pricing case law. *What is the evolution path of transfer pricing litigation in the country? For example: (i) Is transfer pricing litigation being gradually replaced by either MAPs or APAs, as regulated in the relevant tax treaties? (ii) Are foreign/local transfer pricing precedents and/ or published MAPs increasingly relevant as a source of law for solving transfer pricing disputes?*

Not relevant in China.

5. Customary international law and international tax procedure. *Has customary international law been applied in the country to govern the relevant methods for solving transfer pricing disputes (such as the MAP)? For example, has the* OECD Manual on Effective Mutual Agreement Procedure *('OECD Manual') been deemed customary international tax law in the MAP arena for filling procedural gaps (for example, time limit for implementation of relief where treaties deviate from the OECD Model Tax Convention)?*

International tax norms or customary international law has been influential in China. The Chinese transfer pricing regime, including APAs and MAP, is largely modelled on the OECD materials.

6. Procedural setting and strategic interaction. *Does strategic interaction between taxpayers and tax authorities depend on the procedural setting in which they interact when trying to solve transfer pricing disputes? For example, which procedural setting in the country prompts the relevant parties to cooperate with each other the most for solving this sort of dispute, and why?*

Yes, taxpayers in China have only one effective way of resolving transfer pricing disputes, and that is to cooperate with the tax authorities.

7. The future of transfer pricing disputes resolution. *Which is the best available proposal in light of the interests of the country for facilitating the global resolution of transfer pricing disputes, and why?*

The best available proposal in light of the interests of China for facilitating the global resolution of transfer pricing disputes is bilateral or multilateral APAs and a more pragmatic interpretation of the arm's length principle to allow the use of global profit split based on some reasonable formulas.

PART V

South America, Middle East and Africa

Transfer pricing disputes in Argentina

EDUARDO BAISTROCCHI

17.1 Introduction

The Argentine government has been concerned about international tax avoidance techniques based on transfer pricing almost since the inception of the UK-based income tax system in 1932. A central reason for this concern has been to protect the corporate income tax base in the context of the globalisation of the food industry, in which Argentina has been a key player since the beginning of the twentieth century.[1] The two core areas on which most transfer pricing disputes have been focused in this country over the last eighty years are conduit schemes[2] and the strategic use of intangibles.[3]

This chapter aims to answer two main questions. First, what has been the evolutionary pattern of transfer pricing regulations in Argentina since the inception of corporate income taxation in 1932? Second, what is the core dynamic of transfer pricing dispute resolution in Argentina since then?

---

[1] S. Berensztein and H. Spector, 'Business, Government and the Law' in G. della Paolera and A. Taylor (eds.), *Argentina: Essays in the New Economic History* (Cambridge: Cambridge University Press, 2003), where it is argued that the growth of fresh beef exports to Britain began in the 1880s when British companies established meat packing factories in Argentina. In 1907, the growth of its home market led the United States to look for Argentine sources of chilled beef. This marked the beginning of US investments in the flourishing Argentine meat packing industry. See also J. Berlinski, 'International Trade and Commercial Policy' in della Paolera and Taylor (eds.), *Argentina: Essays in the New Economic History, ibid.*

[2] A representative conduit scheme dispute in the transfer pricing arena is *Nobleza Piccardo*, decided by Tax Court (Chamber B), 15 July 2010. It dealt with a toll manufacturer and stripped distributor arrangement as defined by the *OECD Transfer Pricing Guidelines for Multinational Enterprises and Tax Administrations* (Paris: OECD, 2010) ('OECD Guidelines'), para. 9.77. The entities involved were based in Argentina, Chile and Switzerland. The tax court decided in favour of the taxpayer. See section 17.5 below.

[3] A representative dispute in the intangibles area (e.g., payment of royalties for the use of trademarks) is *Refinerías de Maíz*, which involved entities based in Argentina and the United States. It was decided in favour of the government by the Supreme Court on 10 July 1964. See section 17.3.4 below.

The first point argued in this chapter is that the evolution of the Argentine transfer pricing regulatory framework can be divided into six periods since the inception of the income tax system. Each regulatory period is normally associated with a major local fiscal debacle. One dominant feature here is the convergence of transfer pricing law with international standards. Indeed, the Argentine legal framework has been gradually evolving in order to achieve consistency, first with the League of Nations' 1933 Carroll Report and then with the OECD recommendations on transfer pricing. The OECD Guidelines are playing a crucial role in this convergence as the Congress[4] and the courts[5] have been increasingly transplanting the OECD Guidelines into the Argentine domestic law since 1998, when the foreign direct investment (FDI) flow as a percentage of the gross domestic product (GDP) was at its highest since the 1911–1915 period.[6]

The second point argued in this chapter is the following. Transfer pricing dispute resolution in Argentina as of 1932 suggests that Argentina has been increasingly enforcing transfer pricing provisions strategically as a countercyclical measure in order to address its fiscal deficit problems on tax bases that are relatively difficult to move rapidly to competing jurisdictions, such as Brazil and Uruguay. Multinational enterprises (MNEs) from the agribusiness and automobile industries are good examples of this. Interestingly, the taxpayers have won most of the transfer pricing litigation on procedural grounds since the OECD Guidelines began to be transplanted in to Argentine local law in 1998.[7]

The chapter is organised into eight sections. Following the introduction (section 17.1), section 17.2 focuses on the context of institutional and economic instability in which transfer pricing has been enforced in Argentina since the inception of its corporate income taxation

---

[4] For example, the Congressional Committee Reports underpinning the 1998 and 1999 reforms explicitly refer to the 1995 OECD Guidelines as their main source. See the introduction to section 17.4 below.

[5] For example, the transfer pricing dispute in *Ericsson*, decided by Tax Court (Chamber C) on 15 August 2007, was solved in the light of para. 1.52 of the OECD Guidelines. This paragraph deals with the interpretation of contractual relationships where no written terms exist. The tax court said that the role of the OECD Guidelines was to fill in gaps of Argentine law to make transfer pricing regulations as clear as possible. See section 17.5 below.

[6] See Table 17.1.   [7] See section 17.5 below.

in 1932. Argentine democracy includes an eroded system of checks and balances since the 1930 military coup, the first successful military overthrow of a civilian government in Argentine history, and the electoral fraud perpetrated in the 1930s, which contributed to the emergence of Perón and subsequently to political and economic instability.[8]

Section 17.3 focuses on the start of the use of the arm's length principle (ALP) in the context of key historical background. In doing so, it explores the six Argentine statutory approaches to the transfer pricing problem since the inception of income taxation in 1932 to 1998 when the OECD Guidelines began to be transplanted into its domestic law. It further analyses the major transfer pricing disputes emerging over this period.

Section 17.4 deals with the current implementation of the ALP. It includes the substantive and procedural law (auditing and documentation).

Section 17.5 analyses transfer pricing disputes from a domestic perspective. An emphasis is given to litigation, assessment and settlement practices. It is observed that most transfer pricing disputes are resolved through litigation, rather than through alternative dispute resolution methods, such as mutual agreement procedures (MAPs) and/or advance pricing agreements (APAs).

Section 17.6 studies transfer pricing disputes from bilateral and multilateral approaches. The focus here is on the MAPs and arbitration. There is no precedent in this area in Argentina, although the MAP is provided for in most tax treaties concluded by Argentina since the 1960s.

Section 17.7 deals with APAs, including the unilateral, bilateral and multilateral dimensions. There has been no APA concluded by Argentina so far. Section 17.8 concludes the chapter's findings and offers a view on future developments in Argentina.

---

[8] L. J. Alston and A. Gallo, 'Electoral Fraud: The Rise of Peron and Demise of Checks and Balances in Argentina' (2011) 47 *Exploration in Economic History* 179, available at www.nber.org/papers/w15209. They maintain that 'The future looked bright for Argentina in the early 20th century. It had already achieved high levels of income per capita and was moving away from authoritarian government towards a more open democracy. Unfortunately, Argentina never finished the transition. The turning point occurred in the 1930s when to stay in power, the Conservatives in the Pampas resorted to electoral fraud, which neither the legislative, executive, or judicial branches checked. The decade of unchecked electoral fraud led to the support for Juan Perón and subsequently to political and economic instability.'

17.2   Economic and institutional context

Since the inception of income taxation in 1932, transfer pricing has been enforced in Argentina in the context of institutional and economic instability. A proxy to measure Argentine institutional instability is the Supreme Court's tenure. The pre-Perón tenure of Justices was nearly ten years, whereas in the post-Perón years, tenure fell to roughly six years. Oscillations between military and democratic governments matched the instability of the courts.[9] Since the first Perón Administration, Argentina's Supreme Court 'has been replaced en masse five times as of 1947'.[10]

Argentina's economic policies have been particularly volatile since 1947. For example, Argentina's economic policy from 1970 to 1990 ranked as the seventh most volatile out of 106 countries.[11]

17.2.1   Economic context

Table 17.1 shows that Argentina has been facing a chronic fiscal deficit since the Great Depression.[12] It has also been exposed to relatively high inflation rates as of the 1940s, including two separate periods of hyperinflation during the 1980s and early 1990s.[13] If the foreign direct investment (FDI) flow is deemed a proxy of a country's degree of integration into the global economy, Table 17.1 suggests that Argentina became increasingly less integrated with the global economy between the Great Depression and the 1990s.[14]

Table 17.2 indicates that Argentine corporate income taxation as a percentage of total tax collection is larger than that of the OECD countries since the 1990s. For example, whereas the corporate income tax collection was 12.64 per cent of total tax collection in Argentina in 2007, it accounted for only 10.76 per cent in the OECD countries in 2007.[15] Likewise, corporate income taxation as a percentage of the GDP has been increasingly relevant since 2004 in the country. Indeed, since 2004 corporate income taxation as per the GDP

---

[9] See Figure 17.1.

[10] W. C. Banks and A. Carrió, 'Presidential Systems in Stress: Emergency Powers in Argentina and the United States' (1993) 15 *Mich. J Int'l L* 1, 29.

[11] P. Spiller and M. Tommasi, 'The Institutional Foundation of Public Policy: A Transactions Approach with Application to Argentina' (2003) 19(2) *Journal of Law Economics and Organisation* 281.

[12] See Table 17.1 column 3.   [13] See Table 17.1 column 2.

[14] See Table 17.1 column 4.   [15] See Table 17.2 columns 3 and 6.

Table 17.1 *Policy indicators 1900–2009*

Period	Inflation	Federal deficit (% GDP)	FDI flow (% GDP)
1900–5	2.41	−4.19	6.52
1906–10	2.66	−2.21	8.44
1911–15	2	−0.67	7.71
1916–20	11.70	−1.51	0.74
1921–5	−6.23	−2.32	1.84
1926–30	−0.7	−2.94	2.24
1931–5	−3.86	−4.34	1.2
1936–40	3.01	−9.77	0.99
1941–5	5.55	−7.05	0.55
1946–50	19.86	−6.02	0.09
1951–5	18.14	−4.97	0.4
1956–60	38.25	−5.05	[−]
1961–5	23.20	−2.62	[−]
1966–70	19.33	−8.56	[−]
1971–5	64.43	−9.04	0.18
1976–80	192.89	−12.14	0.29
1981–5	322.63	−5.58	0.44
1986–90	583.80	−0.64	0.81
1991–5	32.23	−1.68	1.6
1996–2000	−0.1	−3.8	4.05
2001–5	10.64	0.042	1.95
2006–9	8.65	0.96	2.38

Source: ssrn.com/abstract=1444711

ratio in Argentina has been in the region of 3 per cent, similar to the OECD ratio in this area.[16] In sum, corporate income taxation in Argentina plays a more relevant role in the local tax system, both in terms of total tax collection and GDP terms, compared to the OECD countries.[17]

---

[16] See Table 17.2 columns 2 and 5.

[17] K. L. Sokoloff and E. M. Zolt, 'Inequality and Taxation: Evidence from the Americas on How Inequality may Influence Tax Institutions' (2006) 59(2) *Tax Law Review* 274, available at ssrn.com/abstract=985831. Sokoloff and Zolt maintain that it is not surprising that Latin American countries and other developing countries focus on revenue resources such as taxes on trade, taxes imposed on foreign corporations, and general consumption taxes.

Table 17.2 *Corporate tax: ratios*

	Argentina			OECD		
Years	Total tax/ GDP	Corporate tax/GDP	Corporate tax/Total tax	Total tax / GDP	Corporate tax/GDP	Corporate tax/Total tax
1990	16.50%	[–]	[–]	33.72%	2.59%	7.93%
1991	18.45%	[–]	[–]	34.12%	2.70%	8.10%
1992	21.60%	0.91%	4.21%	34.31%	2.39%	7.24%
1993	21.98%	1.27%	5.77%	34.78%	2.54%	7.42%
1994	21.90%	1.55%	7.06%	34.78%	2.56%	7.56%
1995	20.71%	1.67%	8.05%	34.71%	2.67%	7.80%
1996	20.01%	1.56%	7.80%	35.28%	2.79%	7.99%
1997	20.85%	1.96%	9.39%	35.41%	3.04%	8.58%
1998	21.21%	2.21%	10.44%	35.50%	3.04%	8.60%
1999	21.37%	2.21%	10.36%	35.87%	3.11%	8.76%
2000	21.74%	2.37%	10.92%	36.00%	3.54%	9.85%
2001	21.14%	2.40%	11.37%	35.52%	3.25%	9.13%
2002	20.30%	1.74%	8.55%	35.18%	3.18%	9.03%
2003	23.79%	2.61%	10.96%	35.14%	3.14%	9.04%
2004	26.70%	3.61%	13.53%	35.11%	3.31%	9.49%
2005	27.19%	3.76%	13.81%	35.68%	3.64%	10.24%
2006	27.74%	3.62%	13.05%	35.79%	3.84%	10.74%
2007	29.35%	3.71%	12.64%	35.84%	3.85%	10.76%
2008	31.01%	3.59%	11.58%	34.55%	3.53%	10.09%
2009	31.64%	3.33%	10.53%			

Source: Data on Argentine tax available at asap.org.ar and OECD tax data available at stats.oecd.org/

17.2.2   Institutional context

Figure 17.1 reflects the institutional evolution of Argentina during the 1879–1999 period. The upper left cell represents the conservative governments (i.e., a greater separation of powers given that the Supreme Court was relatively independent from the Executive, but less democracy because of problems relating to the electoral system). The upper right cell denotes the constitutional ideal (a greater separation of powers and more democracy). The lower left cell represents the five military coups faced by Argentina during the twentieth century (less democracy and less separation of powers). Finally, the

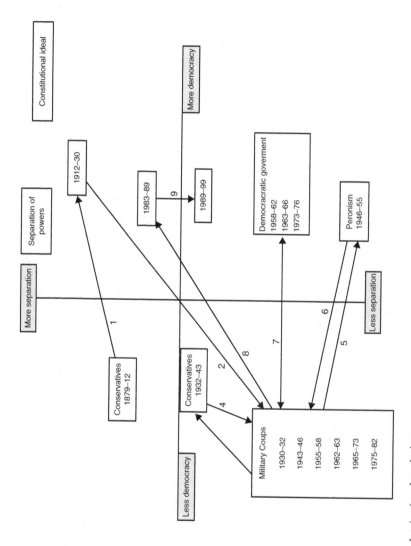

Figure 17.1 Institutional evolution

lower right cell represents the populist governments (more democracy and less separation of powers).

Figure 17.1 suggests that the 1930 military coup was a turning point in the Argentine institutional evolution. Indeed, since the Great Depression, the Argentine institutional path has been fundamentally locked into the two lower cells: either military or populist regimes. There was a short period of time during the 1980s which may be located in the constitutional ideal cell, owing to the relative independence of the Supreme Court.

In sum, the context in which the transfer pricing regulations have been enforced during the 1932–2011 period is dominated by institutional instability and volatile economic policies observed in Argentina. This has led to greater freedom for tax officials to implement rent-seeking strategies, in an incremental fashion, as a *quid pro quo* for administering the tax system.[18]

17.3   Transfer pricing in Argentina: prior to the 1998 tax reform

From 1932 up to 1997, Argentina employed five different statutory approaches to the transfer pricing problem. The 1998 reform embodies the sixth approach, which sparked the gradual transplant of the legal framework encapsulated in the 1995 OECD Guidelines to Argentine domestic law.

17.3.1   First period (1932–1942): La Anglo case

In Argentina, income tax was made law by a 1932 Decree passed by the first military government in the context of a fiscal debacle.[19] It was exclusively based on the source principle, i.e., only the income generated from a domestic source was taxable. The justification for choosing the territorial method of taxation (rather than the global one) was based on the fact that Argentina was a capital-importing country.[20] There was

---

[18] E. Baistrocchi, 'Tax Disputes under Institutional Instability: Theory and Implications' (2012) 75(4) *Modern Law Review*, 547.

[19] Act no. 11682, 12 January 1933, [1920–40] ADLA 303. See Table 17.1 column 3. It shows that the fiscal deficit in Argentina was 2.94 over the 1926–30 period. D. Rock, *Argentina 1516–1987: From Spanish Colonization to Alfonsin* (Berkeley, LA: University of California Press, 1987), pp. 214–61. See also R. T. Alemann, *Breve historia de la política económica argentina 1500–1989* (Buenos Aires: Editorial Claridad, 1997), p. 192.

[20] D. Jarach, 'Las empresas con intereses internacionales frente al impuesto a los réditos' (1946) III *Jurisprudencia Argentina* 21.

only one provision in the income tax law addressing the transfer pricing problem. Subsidiaries domiciled in Argentina were subject to article 17 as follows:

> Article 17. Income registered as sourced in Argentina in the accounting books of companies under foreign control is presumed as such, except if proven otherwise.[21]

Article 17 embodied a presumption according to which the Argentine-based subsidiaries were required to have separate accounting from their foreign head offices; it was deemed that, in principle, the local accounting books properly reflected the income sourced in Argentina. Hence, only if such a presumption was rebutted was the tax authority empowered to adjust the subsidiary's transfer pricing.

Soon after the introduction of income taxation in 1932, the tax authority began to notice that certain subsidiaries manipulated the price of their intra-firm transactions to shift the tax base to foreign jurisdictions. The government described as follows the abuse of transfer pricing carried out by some MNEs:

> According to officers of the Profit Tax Department, there are cases where certain enterprises associated with foreign companies are trying either to shift or to hide income sourced in Argentina in order to avoid paying all or part of their Argentine profit tax liabilities. The evasion is carried out by manipulating the purchase price in the case of importers, or the selling price in the case of exporters, in such a way that economic activity taking place in Argentina derives almost no profit subject to [the Argentine Profit] Tax. It is also common that a low commission is allocated to Argentine-based associated enterprises, thus minimising their income [sourced in Argentina].[22]

Article 17 proved to be ineffective in curbing this abuse because of at least three different reasons. First, the legislation provided no explicit test (such as the ALP) to determine *proper* transfer prices. Second, the burden of proof of any manipulation was carried by the tax authority, which incurred high costs to access relevant information, such as the company's foreign headquarters' accounting books. Third, article 17 required the unrestrained application of accounting standards to assess the business tax base.

---

[21] Article 17 of Act no. 11682 as consolidated in 1932 by Decree no. 112578. These and other provisions in this chapter have been translated by the author.

[22] *Modificación de leyes impositivas y creación de nuevos gravámenes* (Buenos Aires: Ministerio de Hacienda de la Nación, 1944), p. 213.

The overall effect of this normative system was to make the presumption embodied in article 17 difficult to rebut. Consequently, far from deterring transfer pricing manipulation, this system may have actually promoted aggressive international tax planning techniques based on transfer pricing. The La Anglo transfer pricing dispute is a case that best describes this point. Then-senator Lisandro de la Torre outlined the facts of the La Anglo case, which he considered a representative example of a frequent transfer pricing manipulation scheme at the time, involving the commodity industry. In his 1935 speech before the Argentine Senate, he remarked:

> [Certain Argentine] companies avoid paying [Argentine] income taxes on the grounds that they are manufacturing agencies that transfer their products at cost to their overseas holding companies. This includes La Anglo Company . . . The meatpacker La Anglo pretends to be a manufacturing company working at cost for a third entity based overseas [in Liechtenstein or Switzerland]. In fact, that manufacturing company does not exist and the profits are hidden. In Argentina, La Anglo maintains that its profits are taxed in England, and in England, Lord Vestey [La Anglo's controlling shareholder] claims that those profits are taxed in Argentina. Thus, [La Anglo] avoids paying income taxes in both countries.[23]

La Anglo's Argentine subsidiary had two sets of accounting books. The official ones submitted to the local tax authorities allocated virtually no income to the Argentine entity, whereas the real ones were hidden from their view. The real accounting records were eventually uncovered by the tax authorities at the public hearings held before the Congress. It has been argued that:

> [C]ertain businessmen had been using irregular accounting practices. They tried to hide their [accounting] books and one of them [Richard Tootell from La Anglo] went to jail for that reason. The most remarkable case happened after La Anglo had denied that it had any cost accounting books in Buenos Aires. The Special Commission appointed by Congress inspected the ship Norman Star on the basis of information obtained from two port employees. La Anglo's cost accounting books were found on board, hidden under the label 'Corned Beef', ready to depart for the United Kingdom.[24]

---

[23] *Diario de Sesiones de la Cámara de Senadores de la Nación*, Período Ordinario (1935), vols. 1, 201 and 250. The La Anglo case was the basis for a 1984 film entitled *Asesinato en el Senado de la Nación*.

[24] P. H. Smith, *Carne y política en la Argentina* (Buenos Aires: Paidós, 1968), p. 163. See also Rock, *Argentina 1516–1987*, note 19 above, p. 227. Rock argues that Lisandro de la Torre denounced a variety of fraudulent accounting practices among meat packing enterprises, including their evasion of income tax and exchange control regulations. De la Torre also alleged that members of the government had personally profited from transfer pricing

At the time, the head of the Argentine income tax administration outlined the core problem of article 17 as follows:

> The law only provides that income sourced in Argentina on the accounting books of the taxpayer is subject to income taxation here. La Anglo has declared its income according to its accounting records and has paid the tax according to the law ... This is one of the many international combinations where the form of incorporation protects businesses from the tax authority ... There is no legal method to prevent this, and I am not aware of any country where this problem has been solved. In the famous La Anglo case, not even England – according to my sources – was able to make it pay taxes on its income because it ended up in associations based in Switzerland or in countries of Central Europe.[25]

Consequently, La Anglo ended up facing no transfer pricing adjustments either in Argentina or in the United Kingdom.

All in all, transfer pricing manipulations such as the one presumably implemented by La Anglo in the 1930s suggest that the article 17 regime implicitly encapsulated a form-over-substance test which proved ineffective in deterring this type of international tax planning. The government therefore decided in 1943 to experiment with a legal framework with US origins for resolving transfer pricing disputes: a *procedural* arm's length principle, as explained below. This was the starting point of the second period.

17.3.2   Second period (1943–1946): a procedural arm's length principle

By 1943, the Argentine government's role in the economy began to increase substantially due to its rising intervention in the market, for instance the nationalisation of key public services.[26] This pressed the government to increase its tax revenue in order to cope with its increasing fiscal deficit.[27] Not surprisingly, the elimination of tax-avoidance schemes ranked high among its priorities.

---

manipulations. These accusations were debated in the Senate amid vehement denials from senior administration figures. The atmosphere of growing recrimination reached a bizarre climax when Enzo Bordabehere, De la Torre's fellow senator from Santa Fe, was shot dead on the floor of the Senate.

[25] Speech by Mr Malaccorto, Head of Income Taxation, before the Argentine Congress in *Diario de Sesiones de Senadores* (1935), vol. 1, p. 255.

[26] Rock, *Argentina 1516–1987*, note 19 above, pp. 214–61.

[27] The fiscal deficit was 7.05 as a percentage of the GDP in Argentina over the 1941–5 period. See Table 17.1.

The Ramírez military government focused on transfer pricing manipulation in the context of the export and import of goods, and left the transfer pricing problems arising from other types of transactions (such as services) to future reforms. The 1943 transfer pricing system was justified on the grounds that the demand and supply law does not apply in the area of intra-firm transactions; consequently, MNEs can determine their transfer pricing according to their own interest in order to 'evade the tax'.[28] It was suggested that these problems also put MNEs at a comparative advantage with regard to non-MNEs.[29]

Article 7 of Decree no. 18229/43 was passed in order to address the transfer pricing problem (the procedural ALP clause).[30] It provided the following:

> The determination of income derived from the export and import of goods shall be subject to the following principles:
>
> (a) Income derived from the export of goods produced, manufactured, processed, or purchased in the country shall be deemed sourced in Argentina.
>
> Net income shall be determined deducting from the wholesale price at the place of destination, the cost of such goods, the expenses of transportation and insurance to such a place, the commission and selling expenses, and the expenses incurred in Argentina. Where the price is not established, or the one declared is lower than the wholesale price at the place of destination, it shall be presumed, unless proven otherwise, that there is an economic link between the local exporter and the foreign importer, it then being necessary to take the wholesale price at the place of destination to determine the value of the exported goods.
>
> The shipping abroad of goods produced, manufactured, processed, or purchased in Argentina through subsidiaries, branches, selling agents or other intermediaries of persons or entities that are foreign residents shall also be regarded as an export.
>
> (b) Income obtained by foreign exporters by the mere introduction of their products into Argentina is deemed not sourced in Argentina. However, where the price of the sale to the local purchaser is higher than the wholesale price in the country of origin plus transport and insurance expenses to Argentina, it shall be deemed, unless proven otherwise, that there is an economic link between the Argentine

---

[28] Decree no. 18229/43, 55.   [29] *Ibid.*

[30] Article 7 of Decree no. 18229/43 passed by the military government headed by Ramírez on 31 December 1944, [IV] ADLA 49. Article 7 was mainly based on a Bill proposed to Congress by the federal Executive branch on 19 April 1941, which had been rejected by Congress. *Diario de Sesiones de la Cámara de Diputados* (1942), vol. IV, p. 1010.

importer and the foreign exporter, the balance being income sourced in Argentina, and both parties are jointly liable therefore.

In cases where, pursuant to the preceding provisions, the wholesale price governs but is not publicly and commonly known, the calculation of income sourced in Argentina shall be made on the basis of the profits obtained by independent enterprises engaged in identical or similar activities.

This is the procedural ALP clause. It establishes a general rule according to which the price attached to the export and import of goods must be equivalent to the wholesale price of comparable products at the place of destination, unless the parties prove that they are not associated.[31]

The drafters of this rule explained its rationale as follows: they were of the opinion that the wholesale price at the place of destination is a proxy of the market price which independent parties would agree to if placed under similar circumstances. This reasoning shows that they were implicitly embodying a pricing method based on comparables. The application of the procedural ALP based on the wholesale price of goods was first introduced into Argentine law in 1943.

The procedural ALP clause was probably an attempt to deter the adoption of international transfer pricing tax avoidance techniques, such as the one implemented by La Anglo. This attempt was made by introducing a procedural (rather than substantive) ALP and reversing the burden of proof onto the taxpayers.

Finally, the procedural ALP clause established a default rule for cases in which foreign wholesale prices are not available. In such circumstances, profit sourced in Argentina has to be ascertained upon the basis of the income derived by 'independent enterprises involved in identical or similar activities'. Hence, the default rule was also based on comparables as defined by the relevant international standards.[32]

---

[31] The source of art. 7 was art. 45, reg. 86 (1935) of the US Revenue Act of 1934. J. P. Crockett, 'Tax Pattern in Latin America' (1962) 15(1) *National Tax Journal* 103. The entire regulation is quoted in *Essex Broadcasters, Inc.* v. *Commissioner* (1943) 2 TC 523, 528.

[32] M. B. Carroll, 'Taxation of Foreign and National Enterprises' in *Methods of Allocating Taxable Income* (Geneva: League of Nations, 1933), vol. IV ('Carroll Report'). The Carroll Report stated the following on the role of comparables to solve transfer pricing problems, 'As the conduct of business between a corporation and its subsidiaries on the basis of dealings with an independent enterprise obviates all problems of allocation, it is recommended that, in principle, subsidiaries be not regarded as permanent establishments of an enterprise but treated as independent legal entities; and if it is shown that inter-company transactions have been carried on in such a manner as to divert profits from a subsidiary, the diverted income

The procedural ALP clause implies a substantial change from the previous La Anglo case regulatory framework. Indeed, Argentina moved from a form-over-substance test in which the tax authority had the burden of proof (encapsulated in article 17), to a substance-over-form test grounded on an objective element: the wholesale price at the place of destination. Moreover, the burden of proof was allocated to the taxpayer.

The Argentine Supreme Court applied the procedural ALP clause for the first time in *SA SIA*, decided on 6 September 1967.[33] Here, the taxpayer, a corporation resident in Argentina, had exported horses to Peru, Venezuela and the United States. It was stated in the corporation's tax return that these transactions had produced losses because the selling price had been lower than the costs. The tax authority decided to monitor the transactions under the procedural ALP, i.e., according to the wholesale price at the place of destination. The conclusion was reached that, contrary to what had been argued by the taxpayer, such transactions had indeed generated profits. The tax authority based this statement on foreign horse trade publications that explicitly referred to the horses of the taxpayer and the transactions involved in this case.

Ultimately, the government won the *SA SIA* case. The Supreme Court maintained that, since the evidence on which the tax authority based its argument was not attacked by the taxpayer, it had to be deemed that the wholesale price of the horses was correctly reflected. Thus, the transfer pricing adjustment was considered valid. The judgment in the *SA SIA* case shows that the export and import clause was precise enough during the 1960s to be put into action.

The procedural ALP was drafted probably taking into account the experience acquired in the La Anglo case. In this sense, the procedural ALP should be considered a clear improvement from the previous approach for its self-enforcing character in the context without intangibles.[34] However, the clause contained a number of faulty elements as well. In effect, soon after 1943, the government realised that this article had two main problems. First, it was based on the assumption that comparable transactions would always be available. This assumption

---

should be allocated to the subsidiary on the basis of what it would have earned had it been dealing with an independent enterprise.' See Carroll Report, para. 628.

[33] Corte Suprema de Justicia de la Nación, vol. 266, 514 (1967).

[34] The concept of self-enforcing normative systems has been applied in different areas of the law. B. Blank and R. Kraakman, 'A Self-Enforcing Model of Corporate Law' (1996) 109 *Harvard Law Review* (June) 1911. The self-enforcing normative system minimises the need to rely on administrative agencies and courts for enforcement (*ibid.* 1932).

was quickly proved wrong when the tax authority faced difficulties in finding them with the emergence of intangibles. Therefore, the question regarding the standard to be used when no comparables could be found, e.g., when intangibles were involved, remained unanswered by the procedural ALP. Second, this clause left open a loophole, i.e., transfer pricing abuses in areas other than the export and import of goods, such as services. These two main problems were the main targets considered in the third period.

17.3.3   Third period (1946–1960): an unworkable arm's length principle

In early 1946, the Farrel military administration decided to substantially amend the transfer pricing scheme in the context of the third fiscal debacle since the Great Depression.[35] No formal justification for this amendment was provided.[36] Nevertheless, from the wording of the new provisions it can be inferred that the 1946 reform sought two main goals: (i) to provide a response to import and export transfer pricing cases where no comparables could be found;[37] (ii) to extend the ALP legal system to transactions other than the import and export of goods – services are a good example of this. In addition, it can be further inferred that the extension was strongly motivated by the need to further increase the collection of tax revenue in light of the 1945 fiscal crisis and in the context of the local economy that had been becoming increasingly diversified.[38]

Unfortunately, the military government failed to implement these goals. This failure produced the erosion of the ALP, because it was introduced so vaguely that tax avoidance was made a relatively easy task. This section is devoted to explaining the reasons for the failure of the 1946 reform and its far-reaching implications in the following decades.

Export and import of goods

Neither subsection (a) nor (b) of the procedural ALP was amended. Hence, it was maintained by the 1946 reform as the primary pricing

---

[35] The fiscal deficit over the 1941–5 period was 7.05 as a percentage of GDP, the largest since at least 1900. See Table 17.1.

[36] Decree no. 14338/46 was passed on 20 May 1946, [VI] ADLA 477.

[37] The procedural ALP (as it was worded during the second 1943–6 period) was unable to solve the transfer pricing problem in a context without comparables.

[38] See Table 17.1.

mechanism for checking transfer pricing in both the export and import of goods. Yet significant changes were introduced in the default rule of this clause, probably because of increasing difficulties in finding comparables due to the emergence of intangibles. The default rule was redrafted as follows, based on an expansive definition of the comparables:

> In cases where, in accordance with the preceding provisions, the wholesale price at the place of origin must be applied but it is not publicly and commonly known, or where there are doubts about whether it refers to the same goods as imported or to similar ones, or where comparison is difficult due to other reasons, the calculation of income sourced in Argentina shall be made on the basis of the percentage of profit obtained by independent enterprises engaged in identical or similar activities. In the absence of an identical or similar activity, the tax authority is hereby empowered to apply the net percentage that it establishes on the basis of branches of trade that have certain analogies to the one under consideration.[39]

The 1946 reform to the default provision of the procedural ALP produced different consequences in the area of imports as compared to the export of goods. In effect, the *export* of goods was implicitly excluded from the scope of the default mechanism, because it only referred to the problem of absence of comparables in the context of the *import* of goods.[40]

---

[39] Last paragraph of art. 9 of Act no. 11682, as amended by the 1946 reform.

[40] Note that the default mechanism of the procedural ALP was only triggered when either of the following conditions was satisfied: (i) the wholesale price at the place of origin had to be applied but it was not publicly and commonly known; (ii) when there were doubts about whether the wholesale price referred to the same goods as imported or to similar ones.

Another novelty of the 1946 reform in the area of the import of goods was the following. This reform expanded the scope of the default mechanism because it was applicable not only when the wholesale price was unavailable (as was provided in the 1943 reform), but also when there were doubts as to whether the wholesale price referred to goods identical or similar to those involved in the import. In addition, the 1946 reform established a second default rule under a more relaxed standard of comparability than either the procedural ALP or the first default rule: 'In the absence of an identical or similar activity, the tax authority is hereby empowered to apply the net percentage that it establishes on the basis of branches of trade that have certain analogies to the one under consideration' (emphasis added). The creation of a second default method suggests that the government was dissatisfied with the performance of tests based on close comparables and, consequently, it was intending to move to alternative, more relaxed tests of comparability. This pattern shows that the classic ALP started a process of erosion, i.e., a move away from close comparables.

As a result of the 1946 reform, transfer pricing in the context of the export of goods could only be monitored through the procedural ALP method regulated under subsection (a) of the export and import clause. Consequently, this reform gave exporters room for tax planning, given that the procedural ALP is ineffective when comparable goods cannot be found. For example, if a given exporter was able to export goods with some unique features, his transfer pricing abuse was beyond the control of the Argentine tax authorities, since neither the procedural ALP nor the default mechanism could be applied.

The exclusion of exports from the scope of the default mechanism is hardly justifiable. This is because of the fact that both the import and the export of goods can easily be used to implement transfer pricing manipulation. Hence, this exclusion produced an asymmetric normative transfer pricing system between exporters and importers of goods without any clear rationale.

The unjustified exclusion of exports involving goods from the scope of the default mechanism could have resulted from either bad drafting or the pressure of exporters' interest groups in the context of the then military government. The latter explanation appears more likely given the large economic interests at stake.

Transactions other than import and export of goods

The second significant novelty introduced by the 1946 reform is article 14 of the Income Tax Act (ITA). Its main role is to establish the general rule for deterring transfer pricing abuses in the income tax arena. The scope of article 14 only excluded the export and import of goods because these transactions were regulated by the procedural ALP. Furthermore, article 14 exclusively refers to foreign MNEs that have either branches or subsidiaries based in Argentina, i.e., it does not include Argentine MNEs because they were mostly created several decades later.

Article 14 provided that:

> (1) The tax authority shall assess the net income of branches and subsidiaries or entities of foreign enterprises on the basis of their separate accounting records, making the necessary corrections to assess the real profits of these establishments.
>
> (2) In the absence of sufficient accounting records, or where such records do not accurately show the net income arising in Argentina, the tax authorities may deem, for the purpose of the tax, that the branch or subsidiary and the head office form an economic unit, and thus assess the net taxable income.

The regulations under article 14 stated:

> When the results of the activities carried out cannot be easily and
> accurately determined by the accounting records of the subsidiary or
> branch, income arising in Argentina will be determined on the basis
> of the results obtained by independent enterprises engaged in the same
> or similar line of business. The tax authority, when circumstances so
> require, may adopt other indices.[41]

Broadly speaking, article 14 establishes that the separate accounting
principle (SAP) is the primary method for allocating profits among the
profit-units of a foreign MNE.[42] In addition, both the economic unit
principle and the ALP are applied as secondary pricing methods.[43] Let us
examine some of the issues here.

The application of the SAP, as implemented by article 14, must have
been unsatisfactory. This was the case, as the Carroll Report suggested,
given that 'conflicting viewpoints as to what is a fair transfer price [are
not solved by the SAP]'.[44]

Moreover, the application of the secondary pricing methods also
proved unsatisfactory, because there was uncertainty surrounding the
scope of the two methods proposed. In effect, both of them were to be
triggered when the SAP was not applicable, even though only one of
them, the economic unit principle, was established by article 14; and
there was no provision delegating jurisdiction to the Executive branch to
pass the alternative ALP secondary pricing method. The tension between
the two secondary pricing alternatives (the economic unit principle
and the ALP) and their interaction with the primary pricing method
made the 1946 version of article 14 an unworkable legal regime.

The military government did not explain what the sources of article 14
were, although there are reasons to believe that the 1933 Carroll Report was

---

[41] Article 15 of Decree no. 10439 was passed on 18 April 1947, [VII] ADLA 608. This provision
was not substantially amended up to the 1998 reform. However, it was re-enacted in the
following seven Decrees: (i) art. 14 of Decree no. 6188, passed on 27 March 1952, [XII-A]
ADLA 411; (ii) art. 14 of Decree no. 10653, passed on 15 June 1956, [XVI-A] ADLA 546;
(iii) art. 14 of Decree no. 4778, passed on 14 June 1961 [XXI-A] ADLA 604; (iv) art. 12 of
Decree no. 786, passed on 23 July 1970; (v) art. 15 of Decree no. 2126, passed on 30 December
1974 [XXXV-A] ADLA 155; (vi) art. 19 of Decree no. 2353, passed on 2 December 1986,
[XLVII-A] ADLA 285; (vii) finally, art. 19 of Decree no. 1344, passed on 25 November 1998.

[42] See art. 14(1).

[43] The economic unit principle is embodied in art. 14(2), whereas the ALP is embodied in
the regulations under art. 14(1).

[44] *Ibid.*

the main source for article 14(1) and its regulations.[45] In effect, Carroll advocated, 'the adoption of separate accounting as the primary method of allocating income to the various countries in which an enterprise has permanent establishments',[46] and this proposition was embodied in article 14(1). He also focused on the problem that arises 'when accounts pertaining to the local establishment are insufficient, or the business is of such a nature that appropriate accounting methods to reflect its taxable income cannot readily be devised'.[47] In these circumstances, Carroll pointed out that the 'tax administration should be required to limit its assessment to what would be earned by an independent enterprise engaged in similar activities under similar circumstances'.[48] In other words, Carroll suggested the ALP as the core pricing method, a rule that the Argentine authorities later established in the regulations under article 14, although it ultimately clashed with article 14(2), which was incompatible with the ALP.

Finally, the economic unit provision embodied in article 14(2) is a rule based upon the substance-over-form doctrine specifically tailored for transfer pricing.[49] This article implies a departure from the Carroll Report, because the League of Nations' 1935 Draft Convention for the Allocation of Business Income between States for the Purposes of Taxation, which reflected Carroll's position to a great extent, seemed to reject the possibility of treating subsidiaries as part of a single unit.[50]

1946 reform: an unworkable transfer pricing scheme

The 1946 reform retained the procedural ALP as the primary pricing mechanism in the context of the import and export of goods. In addition,

---

[45] After explaining the root of the transfer pricing problem, M.B. Carroll said the following to justify why the separate accounting principle should be used as the primary pricing method (and what should be done if the SAP does not apply): 'The tax official in each country where there is an establishment has at his immediate disposal only accounts (if any) of the local establishment, and it is necessary for him to ascertain whether or not they reflect the true profit attributable to that establishment. This entails, in some cases, allotting to it the capital normally required to carry on its activities, and, in every case, billing to it or making charges at the same rates as it would to an outsider. Unfortunately, however, the local establishment is not so treated by the great majority of enterprises, and the tax inspector finds it necessary to adjust the accounts after securing whatever additional information is available, or to make an assessment on an empirical or fractional basis.' Carroll Report, note 32 above, para. 12.

[46] *Ibid.* para. 189.   [47] *Ibid.* para. 190.   [48] *Ibid.*

[49] Jarach, 'Las empresas con intereses', note 20 above, 28–9. F. Martínez, *Derecho Tributario Argentino* (Tucumán: Imprenta de la Universidad de Tucumán, 1956), p. 54.

[50] S. Piccioto, *International Business Taxation: A Study in the Internationalization of Business Regulations* (London: Weidenfeld and Nicolson, 1992).

it extended the ALP by means of article 14 to the broader area of transactions other than the export and import of goods, whereby the ALP was only given the role of a secondary pricing method without any explanation.

This reform left many questions unanswered. Article 14 failed to clarify how ALP would interact with both the separate accounting method and the economic unit principle. Key concepts for implementing the ALP remained undefined, such as comparable transactions or associated enterprises. The sources of the 1946 reform were omitted.

The obscurity of article 14 might explain, in part, why it remained a dormant clause over decades.[51] Last but not least, it was a mystery why the export of goods was subject to fewer transfer pricing controls than the import of goods.

A number of reasons may explain these shortfalls, such as a lack of political commitment[52] by the military government to effectively deter transfer pricing abuses, and the lobbying by exporters of goods. The practical consequence of this lobbying was that the transfer pricing manipulation in the context of the export of goods remained largely beyond the tax authority's control for at least twenty-seven years, from the 1946 reform up to 1973.

The overall effect of the 1946 reform was that it probably paved the way for a tax avoidance industry that came to light as of 1961 with the emergence of the first wave of transfer pricing litigation in Argentine history.[53] This status quo led to the fourth period where the courts began to search for a legal basis focusing on curbing the transfer pricing abuses, different from the ALP – the domestic general anti-avoidance rule (GAAR). This will be the focus of the next section.

17.3.4 Fourth period (1961–1976): GAAR prevails over ALP

The fourth period ran from 1961, when the tax court decided the case of *Refinerías de Maíz*, to the 1976 military coup. One of the main features of

---

[51] The courts applied art. 14(1) in only one major case in the period that runs from 1946 (when it was introduced) up to 1976 (when the text was changed). The case was *Productos Químicos CIBA*, decided in 1972 by the Tax Court (Chamber A). See section 17.3 below.

[52] On the relevance of political commitment as a factor for achieving a successful tax administration in developing countries, see M. Casanegra de Jantscher and R. M. Bird (eds.), *The Reform of Tax Administration: Improving Tax Administration in Developing Countries* (IMF, 1992), p. 13.

[53] The La Anglo case never reached the Argentine courts.

this stage was that large sectors of Argentine society had a hostile attitude towards multinational enterprises – a feeling that was first shared by most judges of the tax court, then by all of the Supreme Court Justices and, finally, by a unanimous Congress.

A number of reasons seem to explain this hostile attitude. The first was the high levels of fiscal deficit, particularly in 1958,[54] coupled with external indebtedness,[55] resulted in economic austerity policies that brought on recession and made levels of return unattractive to MNEs. This led to a general decline in MNE investments in Latin America.[56] The second was the high level of inflation, worsened by currency and foreign exchange control, which paved the way to transfer pricing abuses fostered by the poorly drafted anti-avoidance normative system analysed above. In sum, a sharp decrease in MNE investment flows and an awareness of transfer pricing abuse provided contexts within which the courts decided the cases described below.

Since 1961, most of the chambers of the tax court focused on transfer pricing cases from the standpoint of the general anti-avoidance provision, without even referring to the ALP embodied in the (obscure) regulation of article 14. This judicial pattern of avoiding the use of the ALP was also followed by the Supreme Court itself as from 1973. Thus, it is necessary to briefly explore the main features of the domestic GAAR and its relationship with the ALP.

General anti-avoidance rule: three open-ended questions

The GAAR, whose main source is German law,[57] was introduced into Argentine law in 1946.[58] The text of the GAAR was never amended and is currently stated in the Federal Act on Tax Proceedings no. 11,683, which provides:

> In determining the true substance of a taxable event, the actions, situations, and relations of an economic nature which the taxpayers actually perform, seek, or establish shall be taken into consideration. When the legal forms or structures used by taxpayers for such actions, situations, or relations are not clearly those which private law offers or authorises to

---

[54] See Table 17.1.

[55] Alemann, *Breve historia*, note 19 above, p. 298. See also Rock, *Argentina 1516–1987*, note 19 above, pp. 320–66.

[56] P. Muchlinski, *Multinational Enterprises and the Law* (Cambridge: Blackwell Publishers, 1995), p. 31.

[57] Martínez, *Derecho Tributario*, note 49 above, p. 42.

[58] Decree no. 14341/46, [VI] ADLA 49.

adequately reflect their economic purpose, the inadequate legal forms or structures shall be set aside in considering the real taxable event and the real economic situation shall be deemed to fall under the forms and structures that private law would allow taxpayers to adopt as the best suited to their real purpose.[59]

This article embodies a system similar to what is known in the common law jurisdictions as the substance-over-form doctrine.[60] It gives judges a powerful tool: if certain circumstances are met, they may disregard the juridical forms employed by taxpayers and *recharacterise* them. However, the GAAR fails to provide an accurate test to determine when it is triggered, or how such a recharacterisation is to be used.[61] The tax policy implicit in the GAAR can be worded as follows: the more obscure its scope, the wider its anti-avoidance effect.

The application of the GAAR in transfer pricing cases raises (at least) three questions: (i) how the GAAR interacts with the specific anti-avoidance rule for transfer pricing, i.e., the ALP; (ii) if the GAAR may be applied to transfer pricing cases, under what circumstances it is triggered; and (iii) how transactions are recharacterised when they are looked at in the light of the GAAR. In the next section, it will be seen how the courts responded to these three questions during the 1961–76 period.

Tax court case law: GAAR in action

The leading case, *Refinerías de Maíz*, decided on 6 December 1961, is the first transfer pricing case decided by an Argentine court. Corn Products Refining Co. was a US corporation that held 96.6 per cent of the shares of its Argentine subsidiary, Refinerías de Maíz, which was in charge of selling commodities to independent parties. They entered into a licence contract under which the subsidiary would pay royalties to the head office to be entitled to use certain trademarks within the Argentine territory. The royalties were fixed and had to be paid by the subsidiary even when it was unable to make a profit.

This case arose because the tax authority adjusted the subsidiary's tax accounts on the basis that the royalties could not be deducted because

---

[59] Article 2 of Decree no. 821/98, which consolidated the Federal Tax on Proceedings, available at www.dgi.gov.ar.

[60] G. Teijeiro, 'The Argentine Tax Treaty Network: A Safe Harbour for Foreign Taxpayers' (1999) 20 *Tax Notes International* 287.

[61] S. Le Pera and P. Lessa, 'The Disregard of a Legal Entity for Tax Purposes' (1989) 74a *Cahiers de Droit Fiscal International* 165.

they were the subsidiary's *hidden profits*. The tax authority argued that under the GAAR, such royalties had to be deemed profits because the concept 'contract' presupposes, at least, two different parties with opposing interests – a requirement not met in the instant case given that the American corporation was the controlling shareholder of the Argentine subsidiary.

The taxpayer's main argument was that the subsidiary was a legal entity independent of its head office, and that the amount of the royalty was *reasonable and normal*. Thus, it concluded, the royalties had to be considered as an allowable expense.

The tax court accepted the tax authority's view. It held that since Corn Products Refining Co. held over 90 per cent of the shares of the subsidiary, they could not be deemed independent entities. Therefore, 'the royalties paid [to the US head office] were, due to its economic effects, a way for [the head office] to obtain additional profits from its Argentine subsidiary'.

The taxpayer had implicitly referred to the ALP when it argued that the 'reasonable and normal' test should be applied to this case. However, the tax court, without giving any justification, considered it irrelevant to solving this case.

The tax court did not explicitly refer to the legal basis of its decision to disregard the legal personality of the subsidiary and to recharacterise the payment made to the head office. However, it can be inferred that the GAAR was the clear legal basis for its reasoning. This must be the case given that, in the subsequent cases, the GAAR was explicitly cited as its deciding rationale by the tax court.[62]

To conclude, in *Refinerías de Maíz*, the tax court employed the GAAR to establish a presumption, which was not rebuttable, according to which royalties remitted by subsidiaries to their head offices under licence contracts could not be deducted from the subsidiaries' tax accounts. Moreover, the tax court did not explain why the GAAR took precedence over article 14 and its regulations, which encapsulated an obscure version of the ALP.[63]

---

[62] The proposition that the tax court grounded its reasoning on the GAAR, although it made no reference to it, is also backed by the fact that the Federal Court of Appeals, when it affirmed the tax court's decision, explicitly employed the GAAR as its main legal basis.

[63] The tax court's decision in *Refinerías de Maíz* was upheld by the Federal Court of Appeals on 14 October 1963 (Derecho Fiscal XIV-332). It was also upheld by the Supreme Court on 10 July 1964 on procedural grounds (CSJN 259 Fallos 141, 1964).

Parke Davis was an extension of the *Refinerías de Maíz* rationale to the pharmaceutical industry.[64] Parke Davis Co. was a US corporation that held 99.95 per cent of the shares of Parke Davis y Cía, its Argentine subsidiary. They had entered into a licensing contract that allowed the subsidiary to use, *inter alia*, certain chemical formulas in exchange for the payment of royalties to its American head office. The contract was not a sham and the amount of the royalties was considered normal by the tax authorities.

The tax court, in a 2 to 1 decision, held that since the US corporation held practically the entire capital of the Argentine subsidiary, they could not be considered separate legal entities. Hence, under the GAAR, the parent/subsidiary relationship had to be deemed a parent/branch relationship. Thus, Parke Davis y Cía was not allowed to deduct from its tax accounts the payments made to its US head office.

Unlike the *Refinerías de Maíz* case, the GAAR was explicitly applied in *Parke Davis* to disregard the legal personality of the subsidiary and recharacterise the payment, despite the fact that the transaction was not a sham and the amount of the royalties was considered normal.

The tax court's majority vote made no explicit reference to the ALP. However, it implicitly took it into account when it accepted that the amount of the royalties had been normal under the arm's length conditions. In other words, this implicit reference shows that the tax court was aware of the tension that had existed between the GAAR and the ALP. Nevertheless, it decided to give precedence to the former over the latter without offering any justification. This decision shows the impact that hostility towards MNEs had on legal reasoning.

The dissenting opinion in the *Parke Davis* decision is noteworthy, because it was the first opportunity in which the ALP was used to solve a transfer pricing case in Argentine history. It was argued that the GAAR did not allow the legal personality of the subsidiary to be disregarded when dealing with its foreign parent corporation. This proposition was based on the fact that the GAAR had to be construed narrowly because of the economic circumstances prevailing when it was passed in 1946, which were quite different from those that existed when this case was decided. No reference was made to the economic unit principle embodied in article 14(2), despite its close relationship with the GAAR.

The dissenting judge maintained that this case had to be resolved under the normal transaction test according to which the subsidiary may

---

[64] The *Parke Davis* case was decided by the tax court on 24 March 1970.

deduct the royalties paid to its foreign parent company if two require-ments are met: first, if the licence contract is not a sham; and second, if the amount of the royalties is normal. He said in *obiter dictum* that only the excess of the royalties that does not meet the normal transaction test could be recharacterised as, for instance, profits remitted to the parent corporation. He concluded that in the present case, the royalties were allowable because the tax authority had failed to show that either the first or the second requirements had not been satisfied.

The dissenting opinion did not base its decision on article 14 of the Income Tax Act or its regulations. In fact, these provisions were not even referred to in the decision. This test was extrapolated from the regula-tions of the Capital Tax Act (CTA) that had been passed in 1965.[65] This extrapolation was probably made in order to avoid the problems of the ALP as implemented by article 14 of the ITA.[66] The National Court of Appeals upheld the *Parke Davis* decision on the grounds of GAAR similar to those developed by the tax court's majority vote.[67]

The *Productos Químicos CIBA* case was also related to the pharmaceu-tical industry with one distinguishing feature: it was the only unanimous tax court case resolved during the 1961–76 period on the grounds of the ALP.[68] It was decided by a tax court chamber that was aware of the actual source of article 14, the Carroll Report.[69]

Ciba Société Anonyme was a Swiss corporation that held over 99 per cent of the shares of its Argentine subsidiary, Productos Químicos CIBA Sociedad Anónima. They entered into both licence and loan contracts, and the issue was whether the subsidiary could deduct from its tax accounts the royalties and interest paid to the foreign head office.

The tax court held that the issue had to be decided on the grounds of the normal transaction test implicitly established in article 14(1) of the ITA. Such a test empowered the tax authority to adjust the taxpayer's account if

---

[65] This Capital Tax Act was titled 'Impuesto sustitutivo a la transmisión gratuita de bienes'. The regulation on which the dissenting opinion grounded the ALP was art. 12 of Decree no. 3745/65.

[66] Some of the problems emerging from art. 14 have been analysed above. See section 17.3 above.

[67] The Federal Court of Appeals decided the *Parke Davis* case on 31 August 1971.

[68] Tax Court (Chamber A) decided the *CIBA* case on 9 February 1972.

[69] This awareness is suggested by the fact that the only academic article that referred to this issue (i.e., Jarach, 'Las empresas con intereses', note 20 above, 28–9 was quoted in the *CIBA* case.

the accounts do not reflect the transaction that would have been 'entered between separate or independent enterprises' in similar circumstances.

The tax court then said that this case was not governed by the GAAR but by the procedural ALP as encapsulated by article 14(1). This was the case given that article 14(1) envisaged a scheme specially tailored for checking intra-group transactions on the basis of the ALP, without disregarding the legal personality of subsidiaries. This point was supported by the regulations under article 14.[70]

In light of the normal transaction test, it was decided that the royalties paid by the Argentine subsidiary to its Swiss head office could be deducted based on the following two reasons, that the transfer of a technology contract was not a sham transaction and the amount of the royalties was normal. In contrast, the interest paid to the head office was disallowed because it did not satisfy the normal transaction test (as the agreed interest was not deemed normal).

Supreme Court and the prevailing tax court approach

In early 1973, the *Parke Davis* case reached the Supreme Court in the context of the largest fiscal debacle since the 1940s.[71] It was the first opportunity for the Justices to decide on a transfer pricing litigation. They had to choose between the two competing approaches: (i) the GAAR as developed by the tax court's (Chamber B) majority vote in *Parke Davis*; and (ii) the ALP as used by the tax court (Chamber A) in the *CIBA* case. The Supreme Court decided to follow the former approach.

The reasoning of the Court was fundamentally doctrinal. The starting point was that, under the French-based Argentine Civil Code, the concept of a 'contract' assumes the existence of at least two parties with non-aligned interests. Thus, the transaction entered into between the foreign head office and its local subsidiary could not be deemed a valid contract since the former wholly owned the latter. This conclusion made the regulations under article 14 invalid as regards the paragraph referring to the ALP because, in the Supreme Court's view, the parties had wrongly assumed the existence of a contract.

Under the GAAR approach, the Supreme Court held that both parties should be deemed members of one *economic unit*. Therefore, in the *Parke Davis* case, the intellectual rights assigned by the head office to its wholly owned subsidiary had to be considered an equity contribution to the

---

[70] The text of this regulation is quoted above. See section 17.3 above.
[71] See Table 17.1.

latter. In addition, the royalties paid to the head office had to be deemed the subsidiary's profits. Consequently, the so-called royalties could not be deducted from the subsidiary's tax accounts.

The Supreme Court reinforced its holding as follows. The foreign head office received in the relevant fiscal years: (i) the royalties stemming from the assignment to its subsidiary of the right to exploit the marks and patents in Argentina; and (ii) the profits derived by its subsidiary from the exploitation of such marks and patents. The Justices pointed out that, '*Therefore, if the royalties could be deducted from the subsidiary, it would be equivalent to a tax exemption that was not established by the Income Tax Act.*'

The decision of the Supreme Court in *Parke Davis* amounted to an irrebuttable presumption according to which transactions entered into by the foreign head office with its subsidiary resident in Argentina had to be recharacterised as either equity contribution or dividends.[72] This presumption, based upon the substance-over-form doctrine, repealed the arm's length approach as embodied in the regulations under article 14.

The *Parke Davis* holding implied an absolute denial of any deductions based on charges for intra-group transactions between the foreign head office and its local subsidiary, a policy that was common in Latin America during the 1970s. A major consequence of this case was the discrimination of enterprises on the grounds of nationality. In effect, Argentine companies were put at a comparative advantage as opposed to foreign multinationals, because only the former were allowed to deduct the royalties paid to non-resident enterprises from their tax accounts.

GAAR/ALP tension in the fourth period (1961–1976)

As mentioned above, the application of the GAAR in transfer pricing cases opened three crucial questions. It is time to explore the courts' responses during the 1961–76 period.

The first question focuses on how the GAAR interacted with the specific anti-avoidance rule for transfer pricing, i.e., the ALP. The majority of the chambers of the tax court and a unanimous Supreme Court ruled to repeal (albeit implicitly) the ALP and employ the GAAR in all

---

[72] J. M. Martín, 'El principio de la realidad económica y los abusos de las estructuras societarias' (1973) *Jurisprudencia Argentina* 1039. Martín argued that the federal Constitution does not empower the Supreme Court to issue such a presumption.

types of transfer pricing cases, as developed in the *Parke Davis* case.[73] This repeal was facilitated by a number of factors. For instance, the ALP was so poorly drafted that even its legal basis was considered unclear. In this respect, it is pertinent to recall the different views that were developed in the *CIBA* case[74] and the dissenting opinion presented in the *Parke Davis* case.[75] In addition, the Argentine judges at the time were probably more familiar with the GAAR than the cryptic ALP, whose rationale was not explained by its drafters. Moreover, the only academic who wrote briefly about its sources, Professor Dino Jarach, referred to bibliography not written in Spanish but in French, English and German.[76] This language barrier surely made it difficult for both the taxpayers and the judges to improve their understanding of the ALP.

Finally, the information costs of applying the ALP were much higher than that of the GAAR. In effect, the former had to be applied on a case-by-case basis evaluating complex facts and making difficult decisions, e.g., whether a given transaction is comparable to the one at issue. In contrast, the GAAR, as construed by the Supreme Court in *Parke Davis*, could be applied on a mechanical basis. The sole fact that a given transaction was entered into between a foreign head office and its local subsidiary was enough to refuse the deduction of the payments in the subsidiary's tax account.

The second question focuses on the circumstances under which the GAAR may be applied to transfer pricing cases. Case law ruled that under the GAAR, the fact that a foreign head office held at least 80 per cent of the equity of its local subsidiary caused an irrebuttable presumption that such enterprises were members of one economic unit.[77] Hence, the subsidiary was unable to deduct the payments made to its head office from its tax accounts. The Supreme Court thus created a specific anti-avoidance rule to deal with the problem of transfer pricing in the area of intangibles. This rule was assumed to be a derivation of the domestic GAAR.

---

[73] None of the courts that employed the GAAR to transfer pricing cases attempted to explain what was the scope left to the ALP.

[74] In the *CIBA* case it was argued that the legal basis of the ALP was the regulations under art. 14 of the ITA.

[75] It was maintained that the ALP was embodied in art. 12 of the regulations under the Capital Tax Act referred to previously. See section 17.3.3 above.

[76] Jarach, 'Las empresas con intereses', note 20 above, 28–9. See also note 49 above.

[77] An 80 per cent equity requirement was established by the tax court in *Le Carbone Lorraine SC*, decided on 17 November 1969. A. R. López, 'Criteria for the Allocation of Items of Income and Expense between Related Corporations in Different States, Whether or Not Parties to Tax Conventions' (1971) 56b *Cahiers de Droit Fiscal International* II/51, II-77.

The third question focuses on how cross-border, intra-firm transactions had to be recharacterised under the GAAR. As was maintained by the Supreme Court in *Parke Davis*, they were to be considered as either equity contributions or profit remittances.

Congress backed the case law[78]

One of the main objectives of the 1973 reform under the Perón administration was to address the problems of the tax avoidance industry in the income tax area. Tax avoidance was perceived as the main reason why the income tax ratio to total tax revenues had substantially fallen since the early 1960s.[79] In addition, the Senate Committee Report described the tax system in effect at that time as 'so unfair that through its loopholes the tax burden [was] shifted from upper to lower income taxpayers'.[80] The 1973 fiscal debacle was the largest since the Great Depression.[81] Within the context of this anti–avoidance climate and fiscal debacle, the Perón administration sent to Congress the Tax Reform Bill, which explicitly addressed the transfer pricing problem.

The procedural ALP clause[82] was amended only to expand the scope of its default mechanism to include both export and import transactions, thereby eliminating the 1946 unjustified exclusion of exports.[83] A unanimous Congress passed the new wording of the procedural ALP without any comments to the contrary from the

---

[78] Income Tax Act 20628 was passed by Congress on 27 December 1973. It became effective on 1 January 1974.

[79] The House of Representative's Committee Report on the 1973 Tax Reform stated, 'By 1941 [income taxes] amounted to 13.72% of the total tax revenue; by 1942 tax revenue had gone up to 18.92%; by 1943 it had increased again to 22.86%, and from 1952 to 1959 the figure was about 30% of the total tax revenue. Since 1960, there has been a clear fall in the revenue collected from income taxes'. Libro de Sesiones de la Cámara de Diputados de la Nación (6 December 1973), p. 4675.

[80] *Libro de Sesiones de la Cámara de Senadores de la Nación* (21 December 1973), p. 3029.

[81] See Table 17.1.

[82] The procedural ALP was encapsulated in art. 8 of Act no. 20628. See section 17.3.3 above.

[83] The new default provision of the export and import clause was amended as follows, 'In the cases where, in accordance with the preceding provisions, the wholesale price at the place of origin or destination must be applied but it is not publicly and commonly known, or there are doubts about whether it refers to the same goods as imported or exported, or to similar ones, or where comparison is difficult due to other reasons, the calculation of income sourced in Argentina shall be made on the basis of the percentage of profit obtained by independent enterprises engaged in identical or similar activities. In the absence of an identical or similar activity, the tax authority is hereby empowered to apply the net percentage that it establishes on the basis of branches of trade that have certain analogies to the one under consideration'.

law-makers.[84] Hence, from the 1973 reform onwards, both the import and export of goods could be controlled by the same set of transfer pricing methods. Thus, a symmetric treatment between the export and import of goods was set up again after twenty-seven years (1946–73).

The 1973 reform of article 14 was the target of many heated arguments in Congress inflamed by hostility towards foreign multinationals.[85] The House of Representatives' Committee Report described as follows the main transfer pricing abuses in the area of services and intangibles that article 14 was intended to solve:

> A number of Argentine subsidiaries of foreign enterprises . . . shifted real income to their countries through technical assistance transactions, royalties paid as consideration for the assignment of patents, marks, formulae, etc. They also made this shift through payment of interest due to financial contributions. Therefore, they remitted to foreign jurisdictions large amounts of revenue that was deducted from their Argentine subsidiaries.[86]

Likewise:

> It is a well-known fact that by means of technology transfer agreements whose consideration is not related to the services received, enterprises under foreign control remit overseas profits that are subject to a lower tax liability than the liability that corresponds to dividends.[87]

Congress, in a unanimous vote,[88] decided that the Supreme Court judgment in *Parke Davis* was the proper approach to curb the overcharging abuses described in the previous paragraph.[89] Hence, the 1973 reform of article 14 was an attempt to embody in a legislative provision the rationale of *Parke Davis*. Article 14 was redrafted as follows:

> Branches and subsidiaries of foreign enterprises must produce their accounting records on a separate basis from their foreign parent companies, making the necessary corrections to assess the net real profits sourced in Argentina.

---

[84] *Libro de Sesiones de la Cámara de Senadores de la Nación* (6 December 1973), p. 4702.

[85] Article 14 'embodies the political philosophy of our great movement in its struggle towards independence from foreign economic ties. It is a process to regain complete control of economic decisions.' *Libro de Sesiones de la Cámara de Diputados de la Nación* (6 December 1973), p. 4683.

[86] *Libro de Sesiones de la Cámara de Diputados de la Nación* (6 December 1973), p. 4683.

[87] See the 1974 Report issued by the Perón administration on the Technology Transfer Bill that was passed by Congress as Act no. 20794. *Libro de Sesiones de la Cámara de Diputados de la Nación* (26th meeting 1974), p. 2790.

[88] *Libro de Sesiones de la Cámara de Diputados de la Nación* (6 December 1973), p. 4702.

[89] *Ibid.* p. 4683, where the full text of the *Parke Davis* decision was published.

In the absence of sufficient accounting records, or where such records do not accurately show the net income arising in Argentina, tax authorities may deem that the branch or subsidiary and the head office form an economic unit and thus assess the net taxable income.

Consideration for financial or technological contributions (including technical advice) made by the head office, an affiliate, branch or a financially related third party to a foreign enterprise in Argentina cannot be deductible in the tax balance sheets of the payer. Such payments shall receive the tax treatment that governs the profits of branches.[90]

The same rule applies even failing evidence of ties between the local enterprise or person and the foreign recipient if the analysis of the former's financial situation reveals that the centre of its decisions is not in the hands of its natural authorities, or that the contract or agreement under which the obligation arises had not been entered into with a third party under the usual practices of international trade.

Any contract between companies or persons covered by this article will have no tax effects, and the payments made shall be treated in accordance with the principles governing equity contributions and profits.

Article 14 referred to enterprises that were both explicitly under foreign control, such as subsidiaries or branches, and those over which such foreign control was implicit but could nevertheless be inferred, for instance, from the structure of its capital. Then article 14 established a rule under which interests and royalties remitted by such enterprises to their associated foreign entities had to be deemed profit remittance. Hence, these payments could not be deducted from the taxpayer's tax accounts and had to be subject to the tax treatment of branches, i.e., they were subject to a 45 per cent tax rate while the standard rate was 22 per cent.

The 1973 version of article 14 implied a substantial change of approach to the transfer pricing problem. Instead of focusing on the transfer pricing abuses upon the basis of the ALP, as was suggested by the provisions effective up to the 1973 reform, Congress decided to apply a new methodology, consisting of an absolute denial of any type of deduction based on charges for transactions entered into between an enterprise under foreign control and its associated entity.

This rule was an extension of the Supreme Court holding in *Parke Davis*. In effect, it was extended from the licence contracts concluded in the pharmaceutical industry between an Argentine subsidiary and

---

[90] Under art. 63(b) of the ITA, the tax rate applicable to branches was 45 per cent. Note that the standard rate was 22 per cent.

its foreign controlling shareholder to any type of transaction concluded in any type of industry between an Argentine-based enterprise under foreign control and its offshore associated entity. Furthermore, article 14 also implied that the separate entity approach was repealed in the area of foreign MNEs, but not in respect of Argentine MNEs.

The Argentine government was aware of this direct discrimination effect between foreign and local MNEs based on nationality. Indeed, it decided to denounce its tax treaty with West Germany which had an anti-discriminatory provision based on Article 24 of the OECD Model Tax Convention on Income and Capital.[91]

In conclusion, the 1973 reform brought about the demise of the ALP for transactions other than the import and export of goods. This demise was the direct result of extending the GAAR to transfer pricing. Indeed, the Supreme Court created a specific anti-avoidance rule to deal with the problem of transfer pricing in the area of intangibles: the prohibition of deductions of any payments made by wholly owned local subsidiaries to their foreign holding companies. This rule was based on the domestic general anti-avoidance norm. This approach was later supported by a unanimous vote of the Congress and extended to any type of intra-firm payments in the context of foreign MNEs.[92] This was probably an attempt to protect the corporate tax base in the context of the worst fiscal debacle since the Great Depression.

17.3.5   Fifth Period (1976–1998): renaissance of the ALS

Transactions other than export and import of goods

On 24 March 1976 there was another military coup in Argentina. The new government decided, less than ninety days after it took office, to repeal article 14 as amended by the Perón administration in the 1973 reform.[93] It also decided that the arm's length principle would be the

---

[91]   See C. A. Tutzer, 'Allocation of Expenses in International Arm's Length Transactions of Related Companies' (1975) 2 *Cahiers de Droit Fiscal International* 17, 27.

[92]   G. J. Glogauer argued that, 'The arm's length criteria cannot be applied since the reasoning of the Court [that was followed in the 1973 reform] does not take into consideration economic reality, even though it intends to, but prefers the organic theory [based on the domestic GAAR]'. G. J. Glogauer, 'Tax Treatment of the Importation and Exportation of Technology, Know-how, Patents, Other Intangibles and Technical Assistance' (1975) 2 *Cahiers de Droit Fiscal International* 27.

[93]   Rock, *Argentina 1516–1987*, note 19 above, pp. 367–403. The military revolution was on 24 March 1976 and the Economic Ministry announced the new transfer pricing policy

prevailing methodology to address the problem of transfer pricing abuses. This new policy was embodied in article 14 as amended by the 1976 reform.[94]

Such a substantial policy change was justified on the following grounds. It was believed that the tax legislation passed under the 1973 reform had been an attempt to curb transfer pricing manipulation. However, the argument was that it had produced a serious market distortion where there was discrimination of enterprises under foreign control as compared with national enterprises. It was argued that the practical effect thus produced was 'to try to solve an abuse by making the opposite abuse'. The military government considered that this type of discrimination deterred foreign inward investment, a point that was high on its agenda.[95]

The 1976 reform reworded article 14 to read as follows:

(1) Branches and other permanent establishments of enterprises, persons or foreign entities must keep separate accounting records from those of their parent company and other branches and other permanent establishments or subsidiaries, and must adjust them if necessary in order to assess the net income sourced in Argentina.

(2) In the absence of sufficient accounting records, or where such records do not accurately show the net income arising in Argentina, tax authorities may deem that the foreign and national entities referred to in the previous paragraph form an economic unit and thus assess the net taxable income.

(3) Transactions between a local enterprise of foreign capital and the individual or legal entity domiciled abroad that either directly or indirectly controls such an enterprise shall, for all purposes, be deemed to have been entered into between independent parties, provided that the terms and conditions of such transactions are consistent with normal market practices between independent entities, with the following limits:

A. Loans: must be consistent with article 20(1) of Act no. 21382.[96]
B. Contracts covered by the Technology Transfer Act: according to the provisions laid down by this Act.[97]

---

on 16 June 1976. See the Statement of Motives of the Foreign Investment Bill that became Act no. 21382.

[94] The Income Tax 1976 reform was passed by Act no. 21481, effective as of 5 January 1977.

[95] The justification of the new approach to the transfer pricing problem from 1976 onwards was developed by the Minister of Finance. See his statement on the Bill that became the Foreign and Investment Act no. 21382, 16 June 1976, [XXXVII-B] ADLA 894.

[96] 'Loans will be subject to [the ALP] provided they are not objected to by the Central Bank of the Republic ... on the grounds of the particular conditions of the transaction or of the borrower's improper debt/equity ratio.'

[97] The outline of this regime is discussed below.

(4) When the requirements provided [in this article], *as to considering such transactions as concluded between independent entities, are not met, they will be subject to the principles of capital contributions and profit.*

(5) For the purposes of this article, a local enterprise of foreign capital will be the enterprise that meets the requirements established in article 2(3) of Act no. 21382.[98]

The first paragraph of article 14 embodies the policy of the military government not to amend the standard by which enterprises under foreign control must have a separate account independent from the other profit-units of the MNE. This standard was transplanted from the League of Nations' 1933 Carroll Report to Argentine domestic law upon the inception of its income tax system and has been maintained since then.

The second paragraph of article 14, similar to the one introduced in the 1946 reform, was envisaged as a two-fold device: first, to encourage enterprises to have sufficient accounting records (this concept was not defined); and, second, to ensure that such records show the net income arising in Argentina. Moreover, the second paragraph also establishes a punitive device (i.e., an undefined profit-based mechanism for allocating income) that would be triggered if the separate accounting rule was not met.

The third paragraph of article 14 explicitly introduced for the first time in Argentine history an early version of the ALP in the law itself to address the transfer pricing problem in an area different from the import and export of goods, such as intangibles. The interaction between the three central elements of article 14 was made clear: (i) the separate accounting principle, (ii) the ALP, and (iii) the economic unit principle. In effect, it was established that the ALP must be used to adjust the separate accounting records of enterprises under foreign control in order to make them reflect the true profit attributable to them (i.e., enterprises under foreign control).[99] In other words, the first two elements integrate the primary pricing method of intra-firm transactions. In addition, the third element (i.e., economic unit principle) was to be considered the

---

[98] 'A local enterprise of foreign capital: enterprise domiciled in Argentina in which individuals or legal entities not domiciled in Argentina own either directly or indirectly more than 49% of the equity, or hold either directly or indirectly the voting power necessary to prevail in the shareholder meetings or partner meetings.' Foreign Investment Act no. 21382, art. 2.3.

[99] The 1976 reform did not expressly state what had been the sources of art. 14.

secondary pricing method when certain requirements regarding the separate accounting rule are not satisfied.

Hence, the 1976 version of article 14 was probably the result of the lessons learned during the first (1932–42) La Anglo case period, when no methodology was given to adjust separate accounts[100] and the third (1946–60) 'unworkable ALP period', when neither the legal basis of the ALS was clear nor its interaction with the German-based economic unit principle understood. The evolutionary path extended towards making the Argentine transfer pricing system increasingly consistent with international standards then encapsulated in the 1932 Carroll Report.

The definition of an 'enterprise under foreign control', provided in article 14(5), is precise enough to make it workable. No definition, however, was provided for the 'comparables' despite their key relevance to the ALP.[101]

The government assumed that the ALP, as defined in article 14(3), might not be effective for deterring transfer pricing manipulation in the area of loans and technology transfer. Without departing from such a standard, it established the special procedural guidelines to determine under which circumstances loans and technology transfers could be deemed to meet the ALP.

Concerning the loans, article 14 established a fixed ratio approach.[102] In effect, in order to provide clear guidance as to when a loan could be considered to be meeting the ALP, a debt/equity ratio was established, and the Argentine Central Bank was empowered to decide, within a certain period of time, whether a loan failed to meet this rule.

In the area of technology transfer, the ALP worked as follows: there had to be a *fair relationship* between the consideration paid and the transferred technology.[103] To facilitate the application of this fair relationship test, the following alternatives were provided: (a) a safe

---

[100] See section 17.3 above.

[101] 'Forty-sixth Congress of the International Fiscal Association, Cancún, 1992', (1992) 77a *Cahiers de Droit Fiscal International* 30. It is stated there that the ALP was not defined in Argentina. E. J. Reig, 'El grupo de sociedades como unidad contribuyente' (1977) 26 *Derecho Fiscal* 385, 392. The author stresses that there is a lack of precision in the regulation dealing with the meaning of the ALP.

[102] On the application of the fixed ratio approach to loans, see the OECD Model Tax Convention on Income and on Capital, updated as of 1 November 1997, vol. II, 'Thin Capitalisation Report', R(4)-14, available at www.oecd.org/dataoecd/42/20/42649592.pdf.

[103] Transfer of Technology Act no. 22426, art. 5.

harbour[104] and (b) the approval of the contract by the government justifying why the transaction at issue met the ALP.[105] Royalties paid in consideration for the use of marks were disallowed.[106]

The fourth paragraph of article 14, based on the Supreme Court judgment in *Parke Davis*,[107] was a punitive device to be triggered if the ALP was not met. In that case, any rendering of goods or services by the foreign controlling shareholder to its subsidiary would be recharacterised as a capital contribution. Conversely, any consideration paid by the latter to the former would be considered as either profit remittance or capital repatriation (the 'capital contribution and profit' rule).[108]

Export and import of goods

The 1976 military government decided not to amend the procedural ALP as amended in the 1973 reform and continued the regulations governing the export and import of goods since 1943 without substantial changes.[109] Nonetheless, the Supreme Court, whose members had been appointed by the military government, substantially narrowed its scope of application in the leading case *Eduardo Loussinian SA*, decided in 1983.[110] The facts of the case are as follows.

Loussinian SA was an enterprise resident in Argentina which was in the business of importing and selling rubber and latex. It concluded a supply contract with a non-resident subsidiary of a foreign MNE. Under

---

[104] It was presumed that the fair relationship test was met if the royalties paid did not exceed 5 per cent of the net value of the goods and service produced using this technology as input. See Decree no. 580/81, art. 5.

[105] Act no. 22426, art. 2.

[106] The rationale of this rule was based on the following grounds: 'To avoid the difficulties that would arise in the process of determining the fair valuation on a case–by–case basis.' See the Memorandum addressed to the Executive branch attached to the Technology Transfer Bill, [XXXVII-C] ADLA 2565, column 2.

[107] See para. 11 of the Supreme Court decision in *Parke Davis*. The direct source of art. 14 (4), as of 1976, was the 1973 version of art. 14(5).

[108] The scope of the 'capital contribution and profit rule' was substantially narrowed by regulations under which this rule only had to be applied to the excess of a given price over the normal price. See art. 20 of Decree no. 1344/98. The friendly treatment that enterprises under foreign control enjoyed since the 1976 reform can be inferred from the fact than none of these punitive devices was ever applied. J. Asiain, 'Forty-sixth Congress of the International Fiscal Association, Cancún, 1992' (1992) 57a *Cahiers de Droit Fiscal International* 275.

[109] Income Tax Reform Act no. 21481, *Anuario de Legislación* 1977-A 6.

[110] The *Loussinian* case was decided by the Supreme Court on 20 September 1983, *Revista Jurídica Argentina La Ley* D-559 (1983).

this contract, the parent corporation of the MNE, Israeli-based ACLI International Incorporated ('ACLI Israel'), would provide Loussinian SA with goods from early January 1974 up to the end of 1975.

After the contract was entered into, international market prices for rubber and latex fell substantially,[111] yet Loussinian SA continued to import the goods from ACLI Israel in spite of the big losses arising from the importation of these products. The tax authority decided that there was a problem with overcharging in this contract, and that the procedural ALP should control this case.[112] Thus, it considered that the difference between the wholesale price of the goods at the place of origin and the price agreed to in the contract, minus some expenses, was income that had been sourced in Argentina which Loussinian SA should have withheld when it made its payments to ACLI Israel. Both the tax court and the Court of Appeals upheld the tax authority's decision.

The Supreme Court decided the case in favour of the taxpayer, stating that even though the purchasing price was higher than the wholesale price, the latter could not be applied in this case in determining the income sourced in Argentina. Here, the Supreme Court considered that Loussinian SA had successfully rebutted the presumption under which the parties were deemed 'associated' due to the gap between the prices.

The Supreme Court argued that there was no evidence that the parties were associated because, *inter alia*, it was not proved that ACLI Israel had owned 'shares of Loussinian SA during 1974, 1975 and 1976'. In addition, the Court ruled that the fact that ACLI Israel had placed Loussinian SA in charge of selling ACLI products in Argentina was not a proof that the parties were associated. It went on to hold that, given that the parties were not associated, the procedural ALP did not compel Loussinian SA to justify a payment substantially above the wholesale price.

From an empirical perspective, the holding in *Loussinian* case has made it relatively easy for the taxpayer to rebut the presumption of control provided in the procedural ALP clause. In effect, under the rationale of the Supreme Court, only the structural control between the parties was considered relevant for applying the procedural ALP. Hence, the 1983 *Loussinian* Supreme Court decision substantially

---

[111] The Supreme Court decision does not state how substantial the decrease of the market price of the goods involved in this case actually was.

[112] Recall that under the procedural ALP, if there is a gap between the wholesale price and the agreed price, it will be presumed that the parties are associated, unless proof to the contrary is provided. See section 17.3 above.

narrowed the scope of application of the procedural ALP as an anti-avoidance mechanism from 1983 up to the 1998 reform, when Argentina decided to implement the OECD Guidelines, albeit in a gradual fashion, in its domestic law.

In sum, the 1976 reform and the 1983 *Loussinian* case created the following legal scheme to deter transfer pricing abuses. The general provision was the ALP as established in article 14(3). There were two areas, however, in which the ALP had procedural features: (i) for the import and export of goods; (ii) for loans and technology transfers. This scheme was implemented without discriminating between foreign and Argentine MNEs.

The Supreme Court's *Loussinian* precedent introduced a major distortion into the transfer pricing legal scheme, because it envisaged a concept of control in the import and export areas that was substantially narrower than the concept applied by article 14. In effect, the definition in the area of the import and export of goods only included direct structural control, such as the parent/subsidiary relationship, whereas article 14 also included non-structural control, for example, one derived from an *indirect* holding of voting power of an enterprise necessary to prevail in its meetings.

Hence, there were two different definitions of control playing out in transfer pricing regulations. The practical consequence of this asymmetry was that it was much easier to manipulate transfer pricing in the area of the import and export of goods than in any other types of cross-border transactions.

GAAR/ALP tension in the fifth period (1976–1998)

It is useful to recall that in the early 1960s, when the GAAR was first applied by the courts in the area of transfer pricing, the immediate question raised was: how does the GAAR interact with the ALP, which is the specific anti-avoidance rule for transfer pricing? The 1976 Ministry of Finance memorandum on the 1973 tax reform focused on this question. It clearly showed that the military government was committed to preventing the application of the GAAR in the area of transfer pricing. This was the case because the government considered that its application, as developed in the *Parke Davis* case, led to discrimination against enterprises under foreign control in relation to their national counterparts, thus deterring both foreign inward investment and technology transfers.[113]

---

[113] The 1976 military government did not provide a response to the 1973 Supreme Court argument in *Parke Davis* regarding the inapplicability of the concept of contract to

The military government's intention of preventing the courts from applying the GAAR to transfer pricing cases can also be inferred from the comprehensive legal scheme in 1976, described above, that left no room for its application in the transfer pricing arena. Therefore, the remaining two questions[114] are rendered irrelevant in this period.

In sum, the ALP continued through the 1976–98 period resulting in a creeping transition towards an increasingly procedural (rather than substantive) legal regime. Indeed, the 1943 version of the procedural ALP expanded from the import and export of goods to loans and the transfer of technology by the 1970s. A potential explanation of this transition is the increasing emergence of intangibles in the international trade in which Argentina was a key player.

17.4   Current implementation of the ALP: 1998 reform

Argentina began moving towards a free market economy in 1991, away from the price controls and state-owned industries of the previous decades.[115] This trend encouraged the MNEs either to start or substantially increase their investments in Argentina, which in part explains the substantial increase in FDI as a percentage of GDP since 1991.[116]

By the same token, MNEs were relatively free to manipulate their transfer pricing. In effect, the narrow scope of application of the procedural ALP clause produced by the *Loussinian* Supreme Court precedent and the lack of key definitions[117] for making article 14 workable in the area of services are likely to have encouraged tax

---

intra-group transactions. This lack of response was probably because *stare decisis* has a narrow scope at the Argentine Supreme Court level. In effect, most of its members generally feel obliged to follow case law when they themselves have participated in them. This tradition is surely the result of the frequent changes in the Supreme Court personnel since 1930. The 1976 military government appointed all the members of the Supreme Court. See section 17.2 above.

[114] The remaining two questions are the following: (a) If GAAR may be applied to transfer pricing cases, under what circumstances is its mechanism triggered?; (b) How are transactions to be recharacterised when they are considered in the light of the GAAR?.

[115] The reform was passed under Act no. 25063 which was published in the *Boletín Oficial* on 30 December 1998. See Cecilia Goldemberg (ed.), *Manual de Precios de Transferencia en Argentina* (Buenos Aires: La Ley, 2007). See also G. Gotlib and F. Vaquero, *Aspectos internacionales de la tributacion argentina* (Buenos Aires: La Ley, 2005).

[116] See Table 17.1.   [117] Such as the concept of 'comparable transaction'.

planning in this area. This was the sceneario faced by the 1998 Congress which made transfer pricing reform a compelling issue.

The 1998 reform was the starting point for a gradual implementation of the 1995 OECD Guidelines into the Argentine domestic law. Indeed, the 1998,[118] 1999[119] and 2003[120] legislative reforms have incrementally transplanted four chapters of the OECD Guidelines, with certain deviations, into the Argentine domestic law. The four chapters are Chapter I (Arm's length principle), Chapter II (Transfer pricing methods), Chapter III (Comparability analysis), and Chapter V (Documentation).

The Congressional Committee Reports on the 1998 and 1999 reforms explicitly referred to the 1995 OECD Guidelines as their main source.[121] The 2003 reform then introduced a domestic anti-avoidance provision targeted to transfer pricing manipulation in the commodity industry. Moreover, both the tax administration and the tax courts were increasingly referring to the OECD Guidelines to fill in gaps in domestic transfer pricing regulations.[122]

The Argentine domestic transfer pricing norms deviate from the OECD Guidelines in certain aspects. Three examples are shown here. First, the tested party must always be based in Argentina, which means that overseas tested parties are therefore currently excluded from the regulations.[123] Second, all comparability factors listed in the OECD Guidelines have been transplanted into Argentine domestic law, except one, business strategies.[124] Third, the definition of control is particularly broad under the local regulations. For example, exclusive agents are considered within the scope of the transfer pricing regime.[125] These deviations from the OECD Guidelines arguably aim to broaden the scope of the domestic transfer pricing regime and maximise the corporate tax base. Certain core elements of the domestic transfer pricing regime are outlined below.

---

[118] Act no. 25063.   [119] Act no. 25239.   [120] Act no. 25784.

[121] Senator Verna, who led the Committee Report, explicitly referred to the 1995 OECD Guidelines as the source of the 1998 reform during the session held on 7 December 1998. In a similar vein, the Committee Reporter Senator Capitanich also referred to the 1995 OECD Guidelines, when grounding the 2003 reform encapsulated in Act no. 25784, in order to show the source of the domestic transfer pricing regime.

[122] See section 17.5 below.   [123] Resolución General AFIP no. 1122/01, art. 9.

[124] Decree no. 916/2004, art. 21.2.   [125] Resolución General AFIP no. 1122/01, art. 7.

17.4.1 Scope: international transactions

The Argentine transfer pricing legal framework is based on two fundamental categories: international transactions between non-associated entities, on the one hand, and international transactions between associated entities, on the other. The first category, transactions between non-associated entities, normally implies that the relevant entities only have the duty to keep certain records if the *de minimis* clause is not triggered.[126] The second category, transactions between associated entities, is subject to a higher level of scrutiny, and the relevant entities have to comply with a regime largely based on the OECD Guidelines.

17.4.2 Associated enterprises

The definition of associated enterprises, or *vinculación económica* in Spanish, is particularly broad.[127] It consists of a non-exhaustive list of situations which are deemed within the associated enterprise concept, including: (i) exclusive agents; (ii) one entity assumes the losses of another entity; and (iii) the same person works for the two entities even if she is not a member of the board of directors.

The transfer pricing regime fundamentally covers international transactions between associated enterprises.[128] Transactions are deemed to be between associated entities whenever one of these companies is based in a low tax jurisdiction listed in the regulations.[129]

17.4.3 Implementation of the ALP

The implementation of the arm's length principle by the Argentine domestic law is broadly consistent with the 1995 OECD Guidelines. For example, the five transfer pricing methods listed in the Guidelines are provided for in the law[130] and defined in the regulations[131] as follows: (i) comparable uncontrolled price (CUP) method; (ii) resale price method; (iii) cost plus method; (iv) transactional net margin method (TNMM); and (v) transactional profit split method.

---

[126] *Ibid.* arts. 2 and 3.   [127] *Ibid.* art. 7.   [128] *Ibid.* art. 5.
[129] Act no. 25784, art. 8 and Decreto Reglamentario 916/2004, art. 21.
[130] Act no. 25784, art. 15.   [131] Decree no. 916/2004, art. 21.1.

Tested party

According to the OECD Guidelines, the tested party, 'is the one to which a transfer pricing method can be applied in the most reliable manner and for which the most reliable comparables can be found, i.e., it will most often be the one that has the least complex functional analysis'.[132] The Argentine transfer pricing regime deviates from this. It instead provides that the tested party should always be based in Argentina. Indeed, it states that, '[f]or the application of transfer pricing methods, comparability analysis and price justifications should be applied directly to the local entity'.[133] The potential rationale for this deviation could be to minimise the enforcement cost of the ALP given that the tax authority has greater control to monitor a local entity than one based overseas.

Comparability analysis

Argentine regulations have transplanted all the comparability factors listed in the OECD Guidelines[134] into its domestic law except for one: business strategies, which include market penetration schemes.[135] One potential justification for this omission may be the protection of the corporate tax base in the short run, given that market penetration strategies might temporarily diminish the Argentine corporate income tax base and, therefore, tax collection.

17.4.4   Reporting and documentation requirements

Associated enterprises are subject to relatively high levels of reporting and documentation requirements. For example, they are required to submit two tax returns (one at mid-fiscal year in addition to the annual tax return). They are also expected to submit a transfer pricing study on a yearly basis.[136]

A proxy to determine the level of transfer pricing enforcement in a given country is the number of experts present in the so-called 'Big Four' accounting firms, i.e., partners and managers, working full-time on transfer pricing. In Argentina, this has changed substantially since the 1998 reform brought the implementation of the OECD Guidelines into its domestic law. Deloitte and PWC are representative cases. While there

---

[132] OECD Guidelines, A.3.3, para. 3.18.
[133] Resolución General AFIP no. 1122/01, art. 9.   [134] OECD Guidelines, ch. III.
[135] Decree no. 916/2004, art. 21.2.   [136] Resolución General AFIP no. 1122/01, art. 6.

were two transfer pricing experts at Deloitte in 1998, this number had risen to seven by 2011. In a similar vein, while there were three full-time transfer pricing experts at PWC in 1998, the figure had risen to forty experts by 2011.[137]

Data rendering obligation

This obligation includes comprehensive information about all the profit units of the relevant MNE. The data requested can be divided into the following seven items: (i) the listing of all the associated enterprises (*grupo empresario* in Spanish), stating each one's role; (ii) each associated enterprise's partners or members, stating their participation in the stock; (iii) each partner's country of residence, except in the case of listed companies; (iv) the name of the chief executive officer, or similar position, during the last three years within the group (stating her country of residence); (v) the location of each enterprise; (vi) a description of each enterprise's corporate purpose; and (vii) a description of the activities of each enterprise.[138]

Assessing procedures

The assessment procedure formally starts with a letter of deficiency sent to the taxpayer by an administrative judge who is an employee of the federal tax authority. The assessment is normally based on the data previously gathered by tax inspectors in a document entitled Final Report of Inspection (*Reporte final de inspección*).[139]

---

[137] I am grateful to Manuel Diskenstein from Deloitte and Vioteta Maresca from PWC for providing this information.

[138] Resolución General AFIP no. 1122/01, Annex IV.

[139] Decree no. 821/1998, art. 16. The role of federal tax inspectors and tax administrative judges (and their limits) are discussed in the tax court's decision in *Administración Federal de Ingresos Públicos* v. *Nobleza Piccardo SACI y F,* decided by Tax Court (Chamber B) on 15 July 2010. The tax court stated that, 'The interaction of the tax inspecting role and assessment role is problematic. The inspecting role, regulated by articles 40 and 41 of Act no. 11683, entails an activity aimed at determining if the taxable event has been triggered in a given case and, if so, the tax base. This inspecting activity is governed by flexible deadlines and broad technical discretion for the tax administration in order to obtain relevant information on the basis of the duty to cooperate [with the tax administration] imposed on both taxpayers and third parties. The inspecting role has a broad scope but it has limits arising from taxpayers' rights.' The relevant information thus collected by the tax inspectors, normally set out in a document called Final Inspection Report, should be included in the letter of deficiency (*vista*, in Spanish), provided for in art. 24 of Act no. 11683. The letter of deficiency effectively starts the assessment procedure under the control of the tax

The taxpayer has up to thirty days to respond to the letter of deficiency and offer an explanation to support her case along with evidence.[140] The administrative judge then has to make a ruling (typically within 120 working days).[141] If the taxpayer is unsuccessful, she can appeal to the tax court without paying the claimed tax,[142] which is a court independent from the tax authority, but falls within the scope of the Executive branch.

The tax court decision may, in turn, be appealed by the taxpayer and/or the tax authority before the Federal Court of Appeals and, subsequently, the Supreme Court.[143] If the taxpayer loses before the tax court, she has to pay the tax claim with interest on a provisional basis in order to be able to appeal the tax court's decision before the Federal Court of Appeals and the Supreme Court.[144] Transfer pricing cases usually take, on average, more than ten years until the Supreme Court issues a final decision.

17.4.5   Domestic anti-avoidance for the commodity industry

The Argentine Congress introduced a specific anti-abuse provision in the transfer pricing arena in 2003. It was targeted to the commodity industry because of the government's perception that this industry was involved in aggressive international transfer pricing manipulation based on a report by the tax authority.[145] The anti-abuse provision states as follows:

> In the case of commodity exports to associated offshore traders who are not the effective recipients of the commodities, it will be deemed that the best method to determine income sourced in the Argentine Republic is

administrative judge. The letter should include the 'precise grounds of the tax claim'. The assessment procedure, unlike the inspecting activity, is highly regulated. Its main role is to provide the taxpayer the opportunity to show its theory of the case and offer the relevant proof. The administrative judge has jurisdiction to request new facts but the requests should be limited to the fiscal periods and charges focused on by the tax inspectors. See paras. 7.2 and 7.3 of the *Nobleza Piccardo* decision, note 139 above.

[140] Decree no. 821/1998, art. 17.   [141] *Ibid.*   [142] *Ibid.* art. 76.

[143] *Ibid.* art. 86.   [144] *Ibid.* art. 194.

[145] The Argentine Federal Tax Authority Report on Transfer Pricing Abuses (2003) stated that, 'As a result of an investigation on the seven largest Argentine traders controlling 60% of total agricultural exports, we have reached the conclusion that the income tax paid by them over the 1997–2001 period has been too low. These traders have paid ARS 19 million in income taxes on sales valued at ARS 20,000 million which represent 0.08% of the total sales.' Libro de Sesiones de la Cámara de Diputados (13 August 2003). The report was included in the speech that congressman Giubergia delivered in the House of Representatives on that date.

the market price when the goods are shipped regardless of the price agreed on with the offshore trader.

However, if the price agreed on with the offshore trader is higher than the market price at the aforementioned time [of shipping], the first price [agreed on] will be the relevant one to ascertain the transfer pricing of the transaction. This method will not be applied if the taxpayer demonstrates beyond a doubt that the offshore trader concurrently meets the following [three] requisites:

(a) to have effective presence in the [offshore] resident territory, a commercial establishment through which its businesses are administered and meet the [local] legal requirements of incorporation, registration and submission of accounting books. The assets, risks, and functions should be consistent with the volumes of the transactions;
(b) its core business should not consist in either obtaining passive income or the commercial intermediation of goods from or to the Argentine Republic with other members of the group;
(c) its international trade with other associated enterprises of the same group may not exceed 30 per cent of the annual total transactions concluded by the offshore trader.

The tax administration may limit the scope of this method when it considers that the causes that motivated its introduction have ceased.[146]

This domestic, targeted anti-avoidance rule is normally referred to as the 'sixth method',[147] because it has been added to the existing five OECD-based transfer pricing methods[148] provided for in the Argentine domestic law.[149] The sixth method aims to avoid schemes in the commodity industry similar to those implemented by La Anglo in the early 1930s.[150] It is in this area of law that the Argentine government is most likely to focus its transfer pricing enforcement efforts in the foreseeable future.[151]

17.5   Transfer pricing disputes: domestic approaches

Litigation is the most frequent method for resolving transfer pricing disputes in Argentina. Other dispute resolution methods, such as mutual agreement procedures and advance pricing agreements, are the usual

---

[146] Act no. 25784.
[147] The sixth method was introduced into Argentine federal law by Act no. 25784 as of 22 October 2003.
[148] OECD Guidelines, note 2 above, ch. II.
[149] Article 15 of the ITA (as amended by Act no. 25063).   [150] See section 17.3 above.
[151] 'Argentina accuses world's largest grain traders of huge tax evasion. Grain traders ADM, Bunge, Cargill and Dreyfus deny charges by Argentine government of substantial tax evasion', *Guardian*, 1 June 2010, available at www.guardian.co.uk/business/2011/jun/01/argentina-accuses-grain-traders-tax-evasion.

approaches to resolving transfer pricing disputes in most countries, although they have never been implemented in Argentina so far. One important explanation for this local litigation dynamic is the strong incentives tax officials have which impel them to maximise tax collection in the short term.[152] Over all, Argentina has experienced two major waves of transfer pricing litigation since 1932. The first wave, which ran from 1960–78, has been analysed above[153] and coincides with three relatively deep fiscal debacles: in 1958, 1962 and 1975 (see Table 17.1). The second wave was triggered in the context of the 2001 financial debacle.[154]

There have been eight large transfer pricing litigation cases in Argentina since the country began to incorporate the OECD Guidelines into its domestic law in 1998. In most disputes, the taxpayer won on procedural grounds based (either explicitly or implicitly) on the OECD Guidelines. An analysis of the major transfer pricing cases is given below.

The *Bagó* case dealt with two main issues: (i) the tax administration's burden of proof for adjusting the transfer pricing of an MNE;[155] and (ii) the main role of transfer pricing regulations in Argentina. The facts of this case were as follows: Bagó was a member of an Argentine-based pharmaceutical MNE. The tax authority adjustment had been made on the basis of, among others, the difference between the price charged by Bagó to local independent purchasers and the price agreed between Bagó Argentina and its offshore associated enterprises. The former price (agreed with local independent purchasers) was higher than the latter (exports to associated offshore enterprises). The relevant regulation was domestic, rather than treaty law.[156]

The tax court ruled in favour of the taxpayers. The decision was based on the fact that the tax authority had failed to meet the burden of proof relevant for a transfer pricing dispute. Ultimately, the court was of the opinion that the tax authority's objection to the taxpayer's transfer prices 'should be compelling enough, and its outcome should lead to substantial differences' with the transfer pricing under scrutiny.[157] Moreover, the

---

[152] Baistrocchi, 'Tax Disputes under Institutional Instability', note 18 above.

[153] See section 17.3 above.   [154] See Table 17.1.

[155] *Administración Federal de Ingresos Públicos* v. *Laboratorios Bagó SA*, decided by Tax Court (Chamber D) on 11 November 2006.

[156] Article 8 of the ITA in the wording in force before the 1998 reform. See section 17.3 above.

[157] Concurring opinion of Judge Porta. This point was shared by Judges Castro and Torre.

court pointed out that '[t]he taxpayer has objected to the tax authority's evidence with reasonable precision and force'.[158]

Finally, the court stated that the main role of transfer pricing legislation was to protect the corporate tax base of Argentina's source income. It maintained that the manipulation of transfer pricing was:

> normally implemented between associated companies by setting prices that do not reflect market prices, for example, by overcharging services exported from low tax countries to high tax countries. This type of tax planning that erodes the corporate tax base in many cases is difficult to prove, particularly in the area of international transactions, thus preventing the enforcement of the proper tax treatment.[159]

The *Ericsson* case dealt with two central issues: (i) loans between associated companies when no written contracts exist; and (ii) the role of transfer pricing regulations in Argentina. The facts of the case were as follows. Ericsson Treasury, a Swedish firm, lent US$12 million to its Argentine-based subsidiary. There was no written contract and the tax authority's decision to make adjustment here was based on the lack of written contract that was required by the ALP.

The tax court decided the case in favour of the taxpayer.[160] The court's decision was based on two central propositions. First, the role of the OECD Guidelines was to fill in gaps of Argentine law to make transfer pricing regulations as clear as possible. Second, the court decided this case in the light of paragraph 1.52 of the OECD Guidelines, which states that, 'Where no written terms exist, the contractual relationships of the parties must be deduced from their conduct and the economic principles that generally govern relationships between independent enterprises.' The court held that the conduct of the entities involved in this transaction, 'does not allow to infer a tax avoidance behaviour', and the relevant loan was replaced by another loan given by a local, independent financial institution under similar conditions to the loan that triggered this dispute. The tax court noted in *obiter dicta* that transfer pricing regulations aim to protect the Argentine corporate tax base.

---

[158] Concurring opinion of Judge Castro (Tax Court, Chamber C). This point was shared by Judge Torres.

[159] *Ibid.*

[160] *Compañía Ericsson SACI* v. *Administración Federal de Ingresos Públicos*, Tax Court (Chamber C), 15 August 2007. See C. Rosso Alba, 'Tax Court Overturns Transfer Pricing Assessment', *Tax Notes International*, 26 March 2007, p. 1179.

The *Daimler Chrysler* case dealt with automobile exports from Argentina to Brazil in the context of the double tax convention signed between the two countries. Two central issues were: (i) the definition of associated enterprises, and (ii) the method to determine the arm's length price. The facts of the case were as follows. Exports between Mercedes Benz Argentina and Mercedes Benz Brazil were at a lower price than the wholesale price in Argentina (which was the relevant element to reach an arm's length price according to Argentine domestic law).[161]

The tax court decided the case in favour of the government.[162] The court ruled that Mercedes Benz Argentina and Mercedes Benz Brazil were controlled by Daimler Benz AG Germany, because Mercedes Argentina had acknowledged to the Argentine tax authority that they were associated enterprises. Moreover, the court held that the transfer price had to be adjusted in such a way that makes it consistent with the pricing method provided for under the Argentine domestic law, i.e., the Argentine wholesale price.[163] Here, the court did not refer explicitly to the Argentine–Brazil Double Taxation Convention.

The *Volkswagen I* transfer pricing case dealt with the application of a general domestic anti-abuse rule to a transaction governed by a tax treaty based on the OECD Model Convention. The facts of the dispute were as follows. The Volkswagen (VW) Group consisted, among others, of three entities involved in the automobile industry. The ultimate parent company based in Germany ('VW AG'), controlled two subsidiaries based in South America: VW Argentina and VW Brazil. There was an enterprise in between VW Argentina and VW Brazil, Cotia Trading SA, incorporated in Brazil ('Cotia Brazil'). VW Argentina exported cars manufactured in Argentina to Cotia Brazil. Cotia Brazil, in turn, resold those cars to VW Brazil in such a way that all the relevant risks of the exports were borne by VW Brazil, which controlled all major decisions made by Cotia Brazil in the import of cars to Brazil.

The tax court decided the case in favour of the taxpayer on the basis of two points.[164] First, the court argued that the role of Cotia Brazil should be disregarded and set aside, and that the car exports should be characterised as effectively being between VW Argentina and VW Brazil.

---

[161] Article 8 of the ITA in the wording in force before the 1998 reform. See section 17.3 above.

[162] *Daimler Chrysler Argentina*, Tax Court (Chamber A), decided on 2 September 2009.

[163] See section 17.3.2 above for the full text of Article 8.

[164] *Volkswagen Argentina*, Tax Court (Chamber B), decided on 11 December 2009.

Cotia Brazil was to be ignored given that all the relevant risks and functions were controlled by VW Brazil. Second, the comparable used by the tax authority was inappropriate and, thus, the case was decided in favour of the taxpayer.

The *Aventis Pharma* case is a progeny of the leading case *of Bagó*. It dealt with the scope of the tax administration's burden of proof capable of successfully adjusting the transfer pricing of an MNE.[165] The facts of this case were as follows. Aventis Pharma was the Argentine subsidiary of a US pharmaceutical MNE. The tax authority adjustment had been based upon, among others, wrong selection of the comparables.

The tax court decided the case in favour of the taxpayer. Its decision was based upon two central propositions. First, the OECD Guidelines were relevant in Argentina in those areas which were not inconsistent with Argentine law. In other words, the tax court held that the role of the OECD Guidelines was to fill in gaps of Argentine law to make transfer pricing regulations as clear as possible.[166] Second, the tax court maintained that the tax authority's burden of proof in transfer pricing disputes should be based on reasons at least as rigorous as the ones developed by the taxpayer in its transfer pricing study.[167] As the tax authority had not met this burden of proof, the adjustment was rejected by the tax court.

There was a significant *obiter dictum* in the *Aventis Pharma* decision. The tax court noted that Argentine law had thus far lacked the advance pricing agreement procedure, which is the usual way for resolving transfer pricing disputes in most countries.[168]

The *Volkswagen II* case was a progeny of the *Bagó* and *Aventis Pharma* cases. It further elaborated on the scope of the tax authority's burden of proof to make valid transfer pricing adjustments.[169] The case dealt with the impact of the major Argentine financial crisis on the automobile industry during the 1999 fiscal year. The issues involved idle capacity and costs emerging from cutbacks in personnel.

The tax court decided the case in favour of Volkswagen, the German automobile MNE. The decision was based on two main

---

[165] *Administración Federal de Ingresos Públicos* v. *Aventis Pharma SA*, Tax Court (Chamber D), decided on 26 February 2010.

[166] *Administración Federal de Ingresos Públicos* v. *Aventis Pharma SA*, Tax Court (Chamber D), section X.

[167] *Ibid.*   [168] *Ibid.* section VII.

[169] Tax Court (Chamber B), decided on 12 July 2010.

rationales. First, the tax court held that the taxpayer's transfer pricing study reversed the burden of proof onto the tax authority.[170] Second, the tax authority would have been able to successfully challenge the relevant transfer pricing study only if the challenge was based on 'compelling arguments' (the 'compelling arguments test').[171] The tax court held that the tax authority had not met the compelling arguments test in this case because it was based on ungrounded propositions.

The *Nobleza Piccardo* case[172] dealt with a toll manufacturer and stripped distributor arrangement.[173] It was implemented by a triangular scheme among associated legal entities based in Argentina, Chile and Switzerland. This decision was a progeny of the *Bagó*, *Aventis Pharma* and *Volkswagen I* cases on the question of the tax administration's burden of proof in transfer pricing cases.

The facts of the case were as follows.[174] British American Tobacco Ltd ('BAT Switzerland'), a Swiss holding company, entered into a contract manufacturing agreement with Nobleza Piccardo SACI ('NP Argentina'), its Argentine subsidiary. According to this agreement, NP Argentina would produce cigarettes in Argentina, and all the relevant risks would be borne by BAT Switzerland.[175] BAT Switzerland would then sell and invoice the cigarettes to Extralan, a Chilean tobacco trader based in a free zone in Chile ('Extralan Chile'), for US$12,564,590.09. NP Argentina, in turn, would export the cigarettes to Extralan Chile for US$7,440,144.

---

[170] *Ibid.* section VII, para. 1.   [171] *Ibid.* section VIII, para. 3.

[172] *Administración Federal de Ingresos Públicos v. Nobleza Piccardo SACI y F,* Tax Court (Chamber B), decided on 15 July 2010.

[173] The OECD Guidelines defines this arrangement as follows: 'Assume the arrangement is restructured and the taxpayer now operates a so called "toll manufacturer" and "stripped distributor". As part of the restructuring, a foreign associated enterprise is established that acquires various trade and marketing intangibles from various affiliates including the taxpayer. Further to the restructuring, raw materials are to be acquired by the foreign associate enterprise, put in consignment in the premises of the taxpayer for manufacturing in exchange for a manufacturing fee. The stock of finished products will belong to the foreign associated enterprise and be acquired by the taxpayer for immediate re-sale to third party customers (i.e., the taxpayer will only purchase the finished products once it has concluded a sale with a customer). Under this new business model, the foreign associated enterprise will bear the inventory risks that were previously borne by the taxpayer.' OECD Guidelines, note 2 above, para. 9.77.

[174] The facts of the *Nobleza Piccardo* case are outlined in Judge Porta's judgment (section VI, paras. 1, 2 and 3), and in Torres' and Castro's judgment (sections 6 and 7.1).

[175] Section 7.1, para. 4 of Torres' and Castro's judgment.

The tax court's decision suggested that Extralan Chile was an independent agent representing BAT Switzerland in Chile.[176]

The Argentine tax authority considered that NP Argentina had a transfer pricing problem during the 1999 and 2000 fiscal years in its exports to Extralan Chile. Indeed, the Argentine tax authority argued that NP Argentina had actually under-invoiced US$5,124,445.99 to Extralan Chile,[177] i.e., US$12,564,590 (the sales price of cigarettes from BAT Switzerland to Extralan) minus US$7,44,144 (the export price of cigarettes from NP Argentina to Extralan Chile). NP Argentina argued that this price gap was the result of the contract manufacturing agreement that NP Argentina had concluded with BAT Switzerland during the relevant period.[178]

The tax court decided the case in favour of the taxpayer on procedural grounds. It argued that the tax authority's letter of deficiency in transfer pricing cases should be based on compelling reasons to justify a deviation of contractual prices (the compelling reason test).[179] This compelling reason test was not met in this case on the following three grounds: (a) the tax authority had based its decision on the wrong transfer pricing method;[180] (b) the tax authority had used wrong comparables that attributed to NP Argentina a profit level of 116.12 per cent, which was inconsistent with the 45.2 per cent maximum profit level of comparable entities;[181] and (c) the NP Argentina profit level over the relevant period was comparable to that of similar Argentine-based contract manufacturers.

In its *obiter dictum*, the court maintained that the OECD Guidelines may have relevance even in respect of those tax treaties that are not based on the OECD Model, such as the one concluded between Argentina and Chile, which is based on the Andean Model.[182]

The *Toepfer* case[183] focused on the temporal scope of a specific, domestic anti-avoidance rule targeted to deter transfer pricing manipulation in the Argentine agribusiness industry. This anti-avoidance rule provided that, under certain conditions, the best method to determine the transfer pricing of commodity exports between a resident exporter

---

[176] *Ibid.* section 7.1, para. 2.   [177] *Ibid.* section 6, para. 4.
[178] Section VII, para. 2 of Judge Porta's judgment.
[179] Section 8, paras 1 and 2 of Torres' and Castro's judgment.
[180] *Ibid.* section 8, para. 4 *in fine.*   [181] *Ibid.* section 12.1, para. 2.
[182] *Ibid.* sections 10.1 and 12.1.
[183] *Administración Federal de Ingresos Públicos* v. *Alfred C. Toepfer Internacional SA*, decided by Tax Court (Chamber D) on 5 July 2010.

and a non-resident associated trader was the highest of two alternative prices: (i) the market price in force when the relevant contract was entered into, or (ii) the market price when the commodities were shipped overseas. As mentioned above, this anti-avoidance rule is normally called the 'sixth method'[184] because it has been added to the five OECD-based transfer pricing methods[185] provided for in domestic law.[186]

The facts of the *Toepfer* case were the following. Alfred C. Toepfer Internacional ('Toepfer'), a subsidiary of a German MNE, was a major Argentine exporter of agricultural commodities. Its business model worked as follows during the relevant period. Toepfer had been selling commodities to two alternative non-resident associated traders: one based in Liechtenstein and the other in Brazil. On the one hand, the Liechtenstein trader was in charge of reselling the commodities to independent clients based in Europe, Africa and Asia. The Brazilian trader, on the other hand, was focused on reselling the commodities in the South American market.

Toepfer and its two offshore traders had set the relevant transfer prices in line with the market price in force when the contracts were entered into, rather than the market price existing when the commodities were shipped overseas. The market price in force when the commodities were shipped overseas, i.e., the shipping market price, was consistently higher than the price at the time the relevant contract was entered into between Toepfer and its traders, known as the contract market price. Consequently, the Argentine tax authority argued that the sixth method was applicable, i.e., the (higher) shipping market price was to prevail over the (lower) contract market price.

The main issue emerging from the *Toepfer* case dealt with the retroactive application of the sixth method. Indeed, the question was whether it was valid to apply this domestic anti-avoidance rule, which had become effective in 2003, to the *Toepfer* case, which actually pertained to the fiscal year of 1999.

The tax court decided this case in favour of the taxpayer, based on two central propositions. First, transactions beyond the scope of the sixth method were to be governed by the market price in force at the time the relevant contracts were entered into.[187] Second, the sixth method's

---

[184] The sixth method was introduced into Argentine federal law by Act no. 25784 as of 22 October 2003. See section 17.4 above.

[185] OECD Guidelines, note 2 above.

[186] Article 15 of the ITA (as amended by Act no. 25063).

[187] *Toepfer*, note 183 above, section XI.

specific domestic anti-avoidance rule could only be applied prospectively (rather than retroactively) as of the date on which the law introducing this rule had become effective, i.e., 22 October 2003. Consequently, the sixth method did not apply to any of Toepfer's transactions entered into before that date, in other words, the 1999 fiscal year. In sum, the *Toepfer* case was to be governed by the market price in force at the time the relevant contracts were entered into.[188]

The *Toepfer* case was important for four reasons. First, it was the first transfer pricing litigation concerning the agribusiness industry since the 1970s. Second, the tax court began its analysis by quoting the OECD Guidelines to determine the role and the international meaning of the ALP.[189] Third, the tax court applied the ALP to identify the Argentine-sourced corporate tax base.[190] Fourth, the decision limited the temporal scope of a domestic, specific anti-avoidance rule, without exploring the relevance, if any, of the domestic, general anti-avoidance rule. This is noteworthy because the GAAR had been predominantly applied by the tax courts during the 1960s to resolve most transfer pricing disputes.

However, the *Toepfer* decision failed to address a number of important issues and some of its propositions lacked sufficient reasoning. For example, the court did not decide on whether the sixth method was consistent with Article 9 of the Argentina–Brazil Double Tax Treaty, as it decided that the Argentina–Brazil Tax Treaty was irrelevant in this case for unclear reasons. The *Toepfer* decision has since been appealed by the government.

17.6 Transfer pricing disputes: bilateral and multilateral approaches

Mutual agreement procedures (MAP) are provided for in most Argentine tax treaties. However, Argentina has never concluded a MAP on the grounds that they are forbidden by its constitutional law. Tax arbitration clauses have not been provided for in the Argentine law so far.

17.7 Advance pricing agreements

Neither unilateral nor bilateral advance pricing agreements are included in Argentine law to date.

---

[188] *Ibid.* [189] *Ibid.* section VI, para. 1.
[190] OECD Guidelines, note 2 above, para. 1.2 *in fine*.

17.8   Concluding remarks

The evolution of the Argentine international tax system illustrates the impact of globalisation on tax convergence over the 1932–2011 period.[191] A representative example here is the gradual convergence with international standards in the area of transfer pricing. Indeed, the Argentine domestic legal framework has evolved in order to achieve greater consistency, first with the League of Nations' 1933 Carroll Report[192] and then with the 1995 OECD Guidelines.[193] This convergence has been reinforced by the implementation of the OECD version of the ALP, first to the Argentine tax treaty network in 1966.[194] The ALP later permeated Argentine domestic law from 1998, when the FDI flow, as a percentage of GDP, was at its highest since the 1911–15 period.[195] In this convergence, the OECD Guidelines are increasingly playing a crucial role, as Congress and the courts have gradually been transplanting the OECD Guidelines into domestic law since 1998.[196] This gradual implementation of the international standards is also influenced by local elements, however. For example, Argentina, like other countries such as Brazil and India, use transfer pricing law as a mechanism to control tax avoidance and evasion rather than to avoid double taxation. Thus, the main role of the ALP, as applied by the Argentine tax authorities, is to protect the corporate income tax base, even if this results in international double taxation.

In addition, it has been observed that litigation is by far the most common method employed for resolving transfer pricing disputes in Argentina. Other dispute resolution methods, such as MAPs and APAs, have never been implemented in the country. One important explanation for this is the structure of incentives that tax officials have in Argentina.[197] There have been eight large transfer pricing litigation cases since the country began implementing the OECD Guidelines into domestic law. In most disputes, the taxpayer won on procedural grounds based (either explicitly or implicitly) on the OECD Guidelines.[198]

---

[191] R. S. Avi-Yonah, *Tax Convergence and Globalization*, 214 University of Michigan Public Law Working Paper no. 214 (8 July 2010), Available at ssrn.com/abstract=1636299.

[192] See section 17.3 above.   [193] See section 17.4 above.

[194] The 1966 Argentina–Germany Tax Treaty is a good example.

[195] The FDI flow as a percentage of GDP was 4.05 over the 1996–2000 period. See Table 17.1.

[196] See section 17.5 above.

[197] Baistrocchi, 'Tax Disputes under Institutional Instability', note 18 above.

[198] See section 17.5 above.

In sum, the evolution of transfer pricing dispute resolution in Argentina since the beginning of the twentieth century has been influenced by both exogenous and endogenous driving forces. Globalisation is a clear example of the former, which explains the increasing relevance of the OECD Guidelines in this country. Experimenting with methods to minimise enforcement costs of the ALP, such as the procedural versions of the ALP, is a important example of the latter and a promising step forward.

Appendix: Questionnaire (Argentina)

1. The structure of the law for solving transfer pricing disputes. *What is the structure of the law of the country for solving transfer pricing disputes? For example, is the mutual agreement procedure (MAP), as regulated in the relevant tax treaty, the standard method for solving transfer pricing disputes?*

The structure of the law for solving transfer pricing disputes has two core dimensions in Argentina: domestic and tax treaty laws. On the domestic law front, the structure is based on the standard litigation proceeding provided for in the Federal Act on Tax Proceedings no. 11,683 (Ley de Procedimiento Tributario). It became effective as of 1933.

On the tax treaty law front, the structure is grounded on the MAP. The MAP has been included in the Argentine tax treaty network as of 1966, when Argentina concluded its first tax treaty with Germany, but it was never applied. The relevant MAP provision is based on Article 25 of the OECD Model Convention. The number of double taxation agreements which include Article 25 has substantially increased over time: from one in 1966 to fourteen in 2010. This is shown in Table 17.3.

Argentina has not agreed any MAP over the 1932–2011 period. There are two central reasons to explain this. First, the transfer pricing dispute resolution system is too prone to conflict because of certain strategic reasons.[199] On the other hand, there is no specific procedure for implementing bilateral MAPs in Argentina.

2. Policy for solving transfer pricing disputes. *Is there a gap between the nominal and effective method for solving transfer pricing disputes in the country? For example, has the country a strategic policy not to enforce*

---

[199] Baistrocchi, 'Tax Disputes under Institutional Instability', note 18 above.

Table 17.3 *Argentine double taxation agreements including Article 25*

Year	MAP provisions available in the Argentine tax treaty network	Cumulative numbers
1975	Germany, Act no. 17249, effective as of 1966	1
	Germany, Act no. 22025, effective as of 1979	
1995	Germany, Act no. 22025, effective as of 1979	8
	Austria, Act no. 22589, effective as of 1979	
	Brazil, Act no. 22675, effective as of 1980	
	Canada, Act no. 24398, effective as of 1994	
	Denmark, Act no. 24838, effective as of 1997	
	France, Act no. 22357, effective as of 1981	
	Italy, Act no. 22747, effective as of 1983	
	Spain, Act no. 24258, effective as of 1994	
2010	Austria, terminated as of 2010	14
	Australia, Act no. 25238, effective as of 1999	
	Belgium, Act no. 24850, effective as of 1999	
	Brazil, Act no. 22675, effective as of 1980	
	Canada, Act no. 24398, effective as of 1994	
	Denmark, Act no. 24838, effective as of 1997	
	Finland, Act no. 24654, effective as of 1997	
	France, Act no. 22357, effective as of 1981	
	Germany, Act no. 22025, effective as of 1979	
	Italy, Act no. 22747, effective as of 1983	
	Netherlands, Act no. 24933, effective as of 1998	
	Norway, Act no. 25461, effective as of 2001	
	Spain, Act no. 24258, effective as of 1994	
	Switzerland, not yet ratified	
	United Kingdom, Act no. 24727, effective as of 1997	

the arm's length standard (ALS) for fear of driving foreign direct invest-ment to other competing jurisdictions?

The policy for solving transfer pricing disputes tends towards litigation, rather than MAPs. This policy is the product of a number of reasons that include the tax officials' incentive structure, which increasingly induces them to maximise tax collection in the short run.

In sum, the standard method for solving transfer pricing disputes in Argentina is litigation rather than MAP. During the 1932–2011 period, there have been twelve major transfer pricing litigations, yet no MAP has been agreed.

3. The prevailing dispute resolution method. *Which is the most frequent method for solving transfer pricing disputes in the country? Does it have a positive externality? For example, is the MAP the most frequent method, and if so, to what extent have successful MAPs been used as a proxy for transfer pricing case law?*

As said, transfer pricing disputes in Argentina are mostly resolved through litigation. The twelve major disputes over the 1932–2010 period are studied in sections 17.3 and 17.5 of the chapter. Transfer pricing case law normally provides limited positive externalities. This is so because their holdings are particularly fact specific, making their extension to other situations difficult to justify.

4. Transfer Pricing Case Law. *What is the evolution path of transfer pricing litigation in the country? For example: (i) Is transfer pricing litigation being gradually replaced by either MAPs or advance pricing agreements (APAs), as regulated in the relevant tax treaties? (ii) Are foreign/local transfer pricing precedents and/or published MAPs increasingly relevant as a source of law for solving transfer pricing disputes?*

The core dynamic of transfer pricing disputes in Argentina over the 1932–2010 period has been prone to confrontation between the tax authority and the taxpayer particularly during fiscal debacles. The tax officials' structure of incentives, referred to above, is a case in point.

The evolution path of transfer pricing dispute resolution in Argentina is grounded on two core elements. On the one hand, the path is towards an increasing transfer pricing litigation rate. For example, at least five large transfer pricing litigation cases began in the 2001–3 period. This litigation rate is the highest since the income tax system was introduced in 1932. On the other hand, transfer pricing judicial proceedings increasingly last longer, as may be seen in the *Refinerías de Maíz* case, which went on for four years since the letter of deficiency was sent to the taxpayer in 1960 until it was decided by the Supreme Court in 1964. Conversely, the *Daimler Chrysler* case took six years simply to reach the tax court level. Indeed, the letter of deficiency was issued in 2003 and the tax court ruled on the *Daimler Chrysler* case in 2009. Transfer pricing precedents do not seem to have brought positive externalities to the transfer pricing arena over the 1932–2010 period. They normally have not been cited by courts or tax authorities when grounding their decisions. No MAP has been agreed to date.

In sum, the core dynamic of transfer pricing disputes in Argentina over the relevant period is towards confrontation and litigation. This strategic environment arguably explains why no bilateral MAP has been agreed in Argentina so far. A bilateral MAP presupposes a minimum threshold of cooperation between the relevant tax authorities and taxpayers, something which has not been achieved so far in Argentina.

5. Customary international law and international tax procedure. *Has customary international law been applied in the country to govern the relevant methods for solving transfer pricing disputes (such as the MAP)? For example, has the OECD Manual on Effective Mutual Agreement Procedure ('OECD Manual') been deemed customary international tax law in the MAP arena for filling procedural gaps (for example, time limit for implementation of relief where treaties deviate from the OECD Model Tax Convention)?*

Customary international law has never been used by either the tax authority or the courts to fill in gaps in the relevant methods for solving transfer pricing disputes over the 1932–2011 period. There have been at least eight large transfer pricing litigation cases in Argentina since the country began transplanting the OECD Guidelines into domestic law in 1998. In most disputes, the taxpayer won on procedural grounds based (either explicitly or implicitly) on the OECD Guidelines. Thus, the tax court has been using the OECD Guidelines as soft law to fill in gaps in domestic law since 1998.[200]

6. Procedural setting and strategic interaction. *Does strategic interaction between taxpayers and tax authorities depend on the procedural setting in which they interact when trying to solve transfer pricing disputes? For example, which procedural setting in the country prompts the relevant parties to cooperate with each other the most for solving this sort of dispute, and why?*

There has been no experimentation in the MAP arena in Argentina over the 1932–2011 period. Consequently, it is hard to compare the strategic interaction among the relevant players in a MAP in comparison with litigation settings. Transfer pricing litigation has not induced the parties to cooperate with each other (or with the judge) to solve this type of

---

[200] See section 17.5 above.

dispute. The adversarial nature of litigation and the incentive structure of tax officials to maximise tax collection in the short run are two reasons that explain this non-cooperative dynamic.[201]

7.   The future of transfer pricing disputes resolution.   *Which is the best available proposal in light of the interests of the country for facilitating the global resolution of transfer pricing disputes, and why?*

Arguably the ideal method of transfer pricing dispute resolution in Argentina should meet the following elements. First, it should be as consistent as possible with the current structure of the international tax regime in order to minimise transition costs. Second, it should deter opportunistic behaviour in both the tax authority and the taxpayer communities. Examples of opportunistic behaviour of a taxpayer and the tax authority are the La Anglo case[202] and the *Aventis Pharma* case,[203] respectively. Third, the ideal method of transfer pricing dispute resolution should be flexible to adapt to the dynamic nature of the global economy. Fourth, it should have a global reach, i.e., it should be workable in both the developed and the developing worlds.

A procedural (rather than substantive) ALP may meet the requirements listed above. It could be grounded on an optional system of published bilateral APAs that may produce a proxy for transfer pricing case law, in such a way as to create a dynamic (rather than static) network of formulas for the allocation of the international tax base. These published, bilateral APAs could then be included in the OECD Guidelines to maximise their global visibility and use.

---

[201] Baistrocchi, 'Tax Disputes under Institutional Instability', note 18 above.
[202] See section 17.3 above.   [203] See section 17.4 above.

Transfer pricing disputes in Chile

JUAN PABLO GUERRERO DAW

18.1 Introduction

In the past twenty years, Chile has begun to adopt a policy towards increasing its participation in the global markets by fostering the trade of goods and services, promoting mainly inbound foreign investments and by eliminating barriers for outbound foreign investments, thereby progressively opening its economy to the international community. This has been reflected in the increased volume of free trade agreements and double taxation agreements that Chile has concluded so far. Currently, Chile has a tax treaty network of more than twenty double taxation agreements in force, in addition to several double taxation agreements that have been signed but are pending approval.[1]

This chapter will briefly describe the recent economic and business environment in Chile, including the definition of its current tax structure, in order to understand why Chile has become an attractive country for foreign investment. The chapter will then explore the history and description of the Chilean transfer pricing regulation, established in 1997. Additionally, it recounts the low, but increasing, level of activity in the areas of transfer pricing audits and disputes in Chile, followed by a conclusion based on the Chilean experience.

18.1.1 Economic environment

Chile's recent accession to the OECD is just one example of the growing level of international acknowledgement in the past two decades during which Chile has reformed its system of democracy, its economic policies and, more importantly, its fiscal discipline. Today, it is indeed possible to

---

[1] Double taxation agreements in force with Argentina, Brazil, Belgium, Canada, Colombia, Korea, Croatia, Denmark, Ecuador, Spain, France, Ireland, Malaysia, Mexico, Norway, New Zealand, Paraguay, Peru, Poland, Portugal, United Kingdom, Thailand, Switzerland and Sweden. Double taxation agreements signed with Russia, United States and Australia.

view Chile as the highest ranking emerging economy in Latin America and, according to the *World Competitiveness Yearbook* (WCY) of the Institute for Management Development (IMD), the most competitive country in Latin America, which explains why foreign direct investment (FDI) flows have grown in the past ten years.

Chile is no longer a country known only for its mining and agricultural exports. Today, Chile has become an attractive country for foreign investment in virtually all industrial sectors; this growing trend has also meant that the FDI now forms an essential building block of the country's economic development and growth. The FDI has also contributed towards developing worthy research and development centres for new technologies and intellectual property in Chile. According to the Global Investment Trends Monitor published by the United Nations Conference on Trade and Development (UNCTAD), 10 per cent of the total FDI inflows in Latin American countries, in the past five years, were allocated to Chile. The same report shows that the sales of Chilean companies to foreign transnational corporations (without considering the sales of foreign subsidiaries in Chile) have doubled in growth.

Figure 18.1 shows FDI inflows in Latin American by country.

A similar report to that of the UNCTAD, made by the Economic Commission for Latin America (ECLA), *La inversión extranjera directa en América Latina y el Caribe – 2010* (*Foreign Direct Investment in Latin America and the Caribbean – 2010*), reveals that countries in Latin America with a higher inflow of FDI in absolute terms show a relatively low FDI as a proportion to the GDP in 2010: 2.4 per cent in Brazil and 1.7 per cent in Mexico; however, Chile stands out for its high proportion of FDI to the GDP in 2010. The Chilean Central Bank estimates that the FDI in 2010 was US$15,095 million, which represents 7.4 per cent of the GDP, and the average from 2000 to 2010 of the FDI percentage over the GDP was 6.6 per cent.[2] Figure 18.2 shows the FDI percentage over the GDP from 1998 to 2010.

The mining sector has accounted for most of the FDI in Chile; this is relevant given that Chile is one of the world's biggest copper producers. Between 1974 and 2010, the mining sector received, on average, 32.9 per cent[3] of the gross investment income under Decree Law 600;[4]

---

[2] Source: Chilean Foreign Investment Committee.   [3] *Ibid.*

[4] Decree Law 600 (DL 600) is a method for the transfer of capital to Chile. Under this voluntary system, foreign investors intending to transfer capital, physical assets or other forms of investment request to enter into a foreign investment contract with the Chilean State.

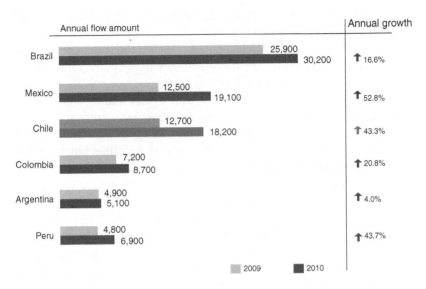

Figure 18.1 FDI in Latin America, 2009–2010
Note: Total in 2010-US$88.200 million
Source: UNCTAD (www.unctad.org)

22.1 per cent for services; 19.2 per cent for electricity, gas and water; among others, as shown in Figure 18.3.

Although the average figure between 1974 and 2010 shows that the mining sector accounted for a large proportion of the FDI, this can be explained by the removal of restrictions on private investment to explore and mine more deposits in the country which used to be in place. More specifically, until 1995, the FDI in the mining sector had represented over half the total investments. However, between 1999 and 2001, this percentage decreased significantly owing to investments made in other sectors, such as electricity, gas, water, transportation networks and communications; and further owing to the deregulation of the telephone services and the infrastructure concessions programme which allowed private capital to invest in construction and operation of motorways and airports. However, since 2002, with the boom in the global demand for copper and the new gold mining projects in Chile, the average FDI in the mining sector over the total Chilean FDI has improved to approximately 28 per cent.

On average (1974–2010), the country with the most FDI in Chile was the United States, accounting for 25.9 per cent of the total investments, followed

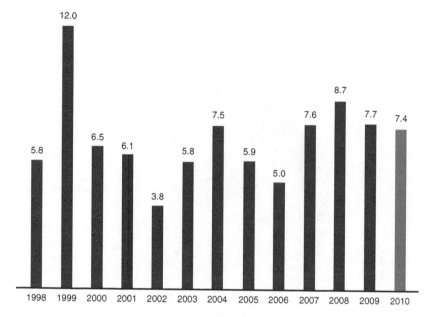

Figure 18.2   Chile: foreign direct investment (% of GDP)
Source: Central Bank of Chile (www.bcentral.cl)

by Spain (18.7 per cent), Canada (17.7 per cent), United Kingdom (8.5 per cent), Australia (4.8 per cent) and Japan (3.9 per cent).[5]

18.1.2   Tax structure

The Chilean Constitution establishes that taxes cannot have a pre-determined use or target, and the government, through the President's initiative, has the exclusive prerogative of proposing to the Congress any changes to the tax system.

Relevant dates in Chilean tax history include:[6]

1874: Stamp Duty and Legal Paper Act (Ley de Timbres y Estampillas y Papel Sellado) enacted. This law taxed sale of goods.
1912: creation of the General Tax Administration.
1969: taxpayer identification number established.

---

[5] Source: Chilean Foreign Investment Committee.   [6] Source: Chilean IRS, www.sii.cl.

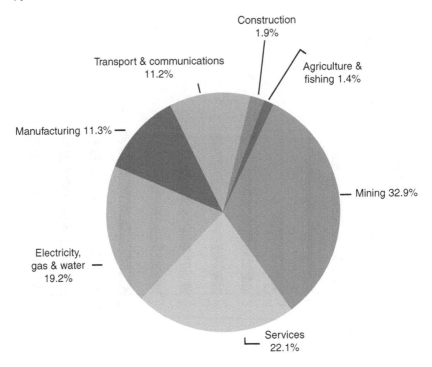

Figure 18.3   Breakdown of inflow by sector, 1974–2010
Source: Foreign Investment Committee (www.foreigninvestment.cl)

1974: introduction of the value added tax.
1984: taxes paid by company profits were integrated to personal taxes paid by the company owners.
1997: the transfer pricing regulation was incorporated into the Income Tax Law (ITL).
2005: the Chilean Internal Revenue Service (IRS) was incorporated as an observer in the working groups of the OECD Committee on Fiscal Affairs.

18.1.3   Chilean tax structure

In Chile the main applicable taxes (as shown in Figure 18.4) are:

(a) income tax;
(b) tax on sales of goods and services;
(c) specific taxes; and
(d) others.

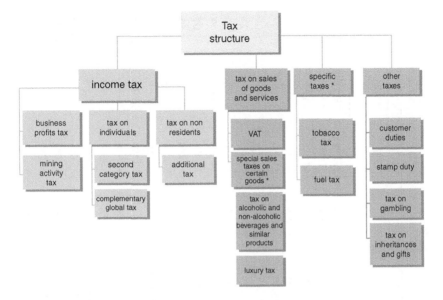

Figure 18.4 Chilean tax structure

Note: Special sales and specific taxes are internationally known as excise tax.

The Chilean income tax system taxes legal entities in two stages:

(i) first category tax: business profits (corporate tax rate);
(ii) second level tax: if profits are distributed to individuals domiciled in Chile (complementary global tax) or remitted to foreign legal entities or individuals (additional tax).

On average, in the last twenty years, the total tax revenue as a percentage of GDP has represented slightly less than 20 per cent (see Table 18.1).

As shown in Table 18.2, in Chile, VAT[7] revenues account for over one-half of the total net tax revenue.

18.2   Inception of arm's length principle

All the double taxation agreements entered into by Chile (except for its treaty with Argentina) contain the arm's length principle in Article 9, which follows the OECD Model Tax Convention.[8]

However, Chile has also simultaneously implemented transfer pricing legislation and regulations effective since the beginning of 1998. These rules,

---

[7] VAT rate is a flat 19 per cent.

[8] OECD Model Tax Convention on Income and on Capital.

Table 18.1 *Total tax revenue as percentage of GDP*

| Year | 2000 | 2001 | 2002 | 2003 | 2004 | 2005 | 2006 | 2007 | 2008 |
Country									
Australia	30.3%	28.7%	29.6%	29.8%	30.1%	29.8%	29.3%	29.5%	27.1%
Austria	43.2%	45.3%	44.0%	43.8%	43.4%	42.4%	41.9%	42.1%	42.7%
Belgium	44.7%	44.7%	44.8%	44.3%	44.5%	44.6%	44.3%	43.8%	44.2%
Canada	35.6%	34.8%	33.7%	33.7%	33.6%	33.4%	33.3%	33.0%	32.3%
Chile	19.4%	19.7%	19.7%	19.3%	19.8%	21.6%	23.2%	24.0%	22.5%
Czech Republic	35.3%	35.6%	36.3%	37.3%	37.8%	37.5%	37.0%	37.3%	36.0%
Denmark	49.4%	48.5%	47.9%	48.0%	49.0%	50.8%	49.6%	49.0%	48.2%
Finland	47.2%	44.8%	44.7%	44.1%	43.5%	43.9%	43.8%	43.0%	43.1%
France	44.4%	44.0%	43.4%	43.2%	43.5%	43.9%	44.0%	43.5%	43.2%
Germany	37.2%	36.1%	35.4%	35.5%	34.8%	34.8%	35.4%	36.0%	37.0%
Greece	34.0%	32.9%	33.6%	32.0%	31.1%	31.8%	31.7%	32.3%	32.6%
Hungary	38.5%	37.9%	37.8%	37.8%	37.4%	37.4%	37.2%	39.7%	40.2%
Iceland	37.2%	35.4%	35.3%	36.7%	38.0%	40.6%	41.5%	40.6%	36.8%
Ireland	31.3%	29.1%	27.9%	28.4%	29.9%	30.4%	31.8%	30.9%	28.8%
Israel	36.8%	36.7%	36.3%	35.4%	35.4%	35.5%	35.9%	36.3%	33.8%
Italy	42.2%	41.9%	41.3%	41.7%	41.0%	40.8%	42.3%	43.4%	43.3%
Japan	27.0%	27.3%	26.2%	25.7%	26.3%	27.4%	28.0%	28.3%	28.1%
Korea	22.6%	23.0%	23.2%	24.0%	23.3%	24.0%	25.0%	26.5%	26.5%
Luxembourg	39.1%	39.7%	39.3%	38.1%	37.3%	37.6%	35.6%	35.7%	35.5%
Mexico	16.9%	17.1%	16.5%	17.4%	17.1%	18.1%	18.2%	17.9%	21.0%
Netherlands	39.6%	38.1%	37.4%	36.9%	37.2%	38.4%	39.1%	38.7%	39.1%

Table 18.1 (*cont.*)

Year Country	2000	2001	2002	2003	2004	2005	2006	2007	2008
New Zealand	33.2%	32.7%	34.0%	33.8%	34.8%	36.7%	36.1%	35.1%	33.7%
Norway	42.6%	42.9%	43.1%	42.3%	43.3%	43.5%	44.0%	43.8%	42.6%
Poland	32.8%	32.6%	33.1%	32.6%	31.7%	33.0%	34.0%	34.8%	34.3%
Portugal	32.8%	32.6%	33.3%	33.6%	32.8%	33.7%	34.4%	35.2%	35.2%
Slovak Republic	34.1%	33.1%	33.3%	33.1%	31.7%	31.5%	29.4%	29.4%	29.3%
Slovenia	37.5%	37.7%	38.0%	38.2%	38.3%	38.6%	38.3%	37.8%	37.2%
Spain	34.2%	33.8%	34.2%	34.2%	34.6%	35.7%	36.6%	37.3%	33.3%
Sweden	51.4%	49.4%	47.5%	47.8%	48.1%	48.9%	48.3%	47.4%	46.3%
Switzerland	30.0%	29.5%	29.9%	29.2%	28.8%	29.2%	29.3%	28.9%	29.1%
Turkey	24.2%	26.1%	24.6%	25.9%	24.1%	24.3%	24.5%	24.1%	24.2%
United Kingdom	36.4%	36.2%	34.6%	34.3%	34.8%	35.7%	36.5%	36.2%	35.7%
United States	29.5%	28.4%	26.0%	25.5%	25.7%	27.1%	27.9%	27.9%	26.1%
OECD Total	35.5%	35.0%	34.7%	34.7%	34.6%	35.2%	35.4%	35.4%	34.8%

Source: OECD Statistics, available at stats.oecd.org/Index.aspx?DataSetCode=REV

Table 18.2 Chilean fiscal revenues series in Chilean pesos[*]

Concepts		2005	2006	2007	2008	2009	2010
1.	Income tax	3,448,994	4,060,323	5,119,013	4,859,011	3,649,471	4,985,748
2.	VAT	5,348,266	5,705,708	6,720,283	7,899,960	6,999,560	8,300,220
3.	Specific taxes	1,120,159	1,143,881	1,324,513	1,208,378	1,302,109	1,610,540
4.	Stamp duty	457,851	480,767	485,541	499,904	63,050	200,283
5.	Custom duties	328,347	328,583	306,504	319,533	167,103	261,453
6.	Other taxes	180,188	137,578	135,746	172,197	355,500	204,024
7.	Debtors fluctuation	(193,814)	(4,534)	(3,900)	(133,741)	(92,169)	(80,977)
Total net tax revenue		**10,689,992**	**11,852,307**	**14,087,700**	**14,825,241**	**12,444,624**	**15,481,293**

[*]Figures in million nominal Chilean pesos

Source: Chilean IRS, available at www.sii.cl/aprenda_sobre_impuestos/estudios/estadistribu/ingresos_tributarios.htm

although they broadly follow the arm's length principle as the standard for determining transfer prices between internationally related taxpayers, contain little detail as to how such a standard should be applied by either the Chilean IRS or its taxpayers. Unfortunately, administrative regulations issued by the Chilean IRS[9] do not contain much guidance on this matter, either. Under these circumstances, it is not surprising that from this date transfer pricing disputes have been reduced to only a handful of audit cases, which typically ended in their very early stages with the Chilean IRS[10] not being able to make any detailed enquiries or assessment of the tax charge.

Given the lack of clear rules and with only a few transfer pricing disputes arising, this has led to uncertainty as to how these rules will be applied by the Chilean IRS and the courts. In addition, given that Chile has only recently joined the OECD, it is very unlikely that the OECD Transfer Pricing Guidelines would have any real authority over the Chilean IRS or its courts, unless there exists a specific ruling or an amendment in the legislation in a specific direction. Despite the above, the Chilean authorities have expressed an unofficial opinion with regard to the Commentaries to the OECD Model Tax Convention, stating that they may be used as a complementary method of interpretation under Articles 31 and 32 of the Vienna Convention.[11] However, there has been no direct pronouncement as to the applicability of the OECD Transfer Pricing Guidelines.

18.2.1 Transfer pricing before 1998: amendment of article 38 of the Income Tax Law

Before the enactment of specific transfer pricing rules (which came into force through an amendment to article 38 of the ITL),[12] tax provisions of general application had existed which required transactions to be conducted at 'fair value'. These rules, which are still in force, are broader in some respects but also more limited in scope than the current article 38. For instance, these rules apply not only to international transactions but also to transactions conducted between related parties. At the same time, some of these provisions can apply in more restricted circumstances, as outlined below.

---

[9] Circular No. 3, issued on 6 January 1998. The text of these regulations can be found at www.sii.cl/documentos/circulares/1998/circu03.htm.

[10] Servicio de Impuestos Internos.

[11] 2008 OECD Commentaries on the Model Tax Convention, Commentary on Article 4 para. 11.

[12] Unless otherwise stated, all references to articles and sections are to the Income Tax Law, contained in art. 1 of Decree Law no. 824, published in the Official Gazette on 31 December 1974.

Article 64 of the Tax Code

Under article 64(3) and (6) of the Chilean Tax Code,[13] the Chilean IRS has the 'authority to appraise the value or price assigned to a sale or transfer or service, in case such price is significantly lower than its fair value or the value charged on similar operations, considering the circumstances in which the transaction is conducted'. A rule under which prices set between unrelated or independent parties may be subject to scrutiny of the relevant tax authorities is somewhat puzzling given that, by definition, such prices would normally be considered fair or a price determined at an arm's length. Another question that arises is why application of this rule is limited to situations where the price is lower than the fair value. Perhaps the answer is the same for both questions: historically, this rule was viewed as a tool for policing cases of tax evasion where parties agreed on a public or formal 'low' price while payment of the balance was made without disclosure or simply 'under the table'.

Article 17 no. 8 of the Income Tax Law

This provision extends the application of article 64 of the Tax Code to transfers of real estate, shares of stock and other assets subject to long-term capital gains tax treatment[14] to a corporate taxpayer, where the price set by the parties is substantially higher than its fair value or the value charged on similar transactions. Again, this rule does not just apply to related parties. Its purpose is to deny long-term capital gain treatment to an unreasonably inflated price where the acquirer of the asset will have a tax basis greater than the fair value for the asset.

Article 31 of the Income Tax Law: expense deduction requirements

The Chilean IRS has long maintained a position that the requirements for allowing deductions of business expenses contained in article 31 of the ITL include (although not expressly contained in the law) that the expense is reasonable both with regard to its nature

---

[13] Chilean Tax Code contained in art. 1 of Decree Law no. 830, published in the Official Gazette on 31 December 1974.

[14] In certain circumstances and if specific requirements are met, the gain on the sale or transfer of real estate obtained by an individual is not taxable. A single level of tax at the corporate tax rate may be imposed on the gain on the sale or transfer of assets, such as shares of stock, mining property, water rights, intellectual or industrial property and others, instead of two levels of tax (first category tax and second level tax).

and its amount. Through these requirements, deduction of expenses greater than the amount necessary for generating the taxable income for the taxpayer may be disallowed by the tax authority. Even though this rule does not require that a related party transaction has to be involved, in practice, the Chilean IRS usually uses this tool for challenging payments to a related party resident outside Chile whose expenses have been paid by the taxpayer.[15]

Article 36: import and export prices

Article 36 of the ITL covers business activities of importers and exporters. Under this provision, the Chilean IRS has the authority to determine the effective income of importers or exporters or both, and challenge the import and export prices, where the prices paid by the taxpayer are inconsistent with the normal prices obtained either in an internal or an external market. Additionally, this provision contains a presumption according to which the minimum net taxable income of importers and/or exporters is equal to 1 per cent to 12 per cent of their total import or export operations or the aggregate of both, conducted during the calendar year for which the tax is payable. The specific rate will be determined by the tax authority on a case-by-case basis, depending on the facts and circumstances.

18.3   Current implementation of ALP

18.3.1   Implementation of ALP in domestic legislation

Arm's length principle

Article 38 of the ITL introduced the arm's length principle in Chile and reads:

> When the prices that an agency or branch charges to its headquarters or to another agency or related company of the headquarters do not correspond to the *values that under similar transactions are charged between independent companies*, the Regional Office may, if justified, reject them ... The same rule will apply to prices paid or accrued with regard to goods or services provided by the headquarters, its agencies or related companies, when those prices do not correspond to normal market prices charged between non-related companies (emphasis added).

The Chilean IRS gave further guidance about this principle in Circular 3 of 1998:

---

[15] Private Letter Ruling no. 1118, issued on 4 March 2004. The text is available at www.sii.cl/pagina/jurisprudencia/adminis/2004/renta/ja669.htm.

> To determine the prices ... initially and as a starting point, a comparison between prices and conditions of transactions between related enterprises and prices and conditions of transactions between unrelated enterprises should be made. For these purposes, the type and nature of the goods or services and the type of operations and the economic environment must be taken into account.[16]

Transfer pricing methods

Article 38 of the ITL only explicitly considers the cost plus method, the resale price method and a third method known as one of 'reasonable profitability'. The law and the Chilean IRS regulations do not provide further detail on the reasonable profitability method; however, practitioners generally consider that this third method includes non-traditional transaction methods contained in the OECD Transfer Pricing Guidelines, i.e., the profit split method and the transactional net margin method (TNMM).

Article 38 no. 3 of the ITL provides:

> When the prices that an agency or branch charges to its headquarters or to another agency or related company of the headquarters, do not correspond to the values that under similar transactions are charged between independent companies, the Regional Office will be able to object to them justifiably, taking as a reference for those prices a *reasonable margin* according to the features of the operation, or the production costs plus a reasonable margin of profit. The same rule will apply to prices paid or accrued with regard to goods or services provided by the headquarters, its agencies or related companies, when those prices do not correspond to normal market prices charged between non-related companies, besides being able to consider the resale prices of goods acquired from a related party and sold to an independent party, less a comparable profit margin in similar transactions conducted with or by independent parties (emphasis added).

In addition, article 38 no. 4 of the ITL states:

> In case the agency does conduct the same types of operations with independent parties, the Regional Office has the authority to challenge them justifiably considering the international market values that the respective products or services have in the international market. For these purposes, the Regional Office should request information from the National Customs Service, the Central Bank of Chile and other entities who have the required information.

---

[16] Circular no. 3, issued on 6 January 1998. The text of this Circular is available at: www.sii.cl/documentos/circulares/1998/circu03.htm.

It may be argued that article 38 no. 4, makes an implicit reference to the comparable uncontrolled price (CUP), although it is the author's view that this provision contemplates a method that considers market prices in general without making reference to specific comparable transactions; therefore, it is not entirely consistent with the arm's length standard.

The law does not establish any hierarchy among the transfer pricing methods and it is not clear how the tax authorities would select the most appropriate transfer pricing method based on the different circumstances of the case.

Related party

The authority to make allocations or adjustments under transfer pricing is normally conditioned upon satisfying the requirement that a relationship must exist between the taxpayer in question and another organisation.

Article 38 is not the exception. Its application is limited to situations where 'an enterprise incorporated abroad *participates directly or indirectly in the direction, control or equity* of a business established in Chile, and vice versa ... or when the same persons *participate directly or indirectly in the direction, control or equity* of an enterprise established in Chile and an enterprise established abroad' (emphasis added).

In addition, a presumption of control exists in certain situations, for instance, the existence of exclusivity agreements, joint performance agreements, preferential treatments, financial or economic dependence and when transactions are made with companies incorporated or located in a listed tax haven.

An administrative guidance on article 38[17] considers that the concept of related or controlled taxpayers for the purposes of applying the transfer pricing rules encompasses situations described in articles 86 and 87 of the Corporations Law[18] and articles 97 and 98 of the Securities Law.[19]

Article 86 of the Corporations Law describes a situation where a company is controlled by another company, where more than 50 per cent of ownership exists or where a company has the power to elect or designate the majority of the board of directors or control the

---

[17] Circular no. 3, issued on 6 January 1998. The text of this Circular is available at www.sii.cl/documentos/circulares/1998/circu03.htm.

[18] Law no. 18.046, published in the Official Gazette on 22 October 1981.

[19] Law no. 18.045, published in the Official Gazette on 22 October 1981.

management of the other company. Article 87 describes a 'greater than 10 per cent ownership' relationship. Articles 97 and 98 of the Securities Law define the controlling person or group of persons of a company by reference to a 'facts and circumstances' test. In essence, according to these provisions, a person or a group of persons acting jointly controls a company directly or indirectly, when it participates in its ownership and may either: (i) ensure the majority of the votes in the shareholders' meetings and elect the majority of the directors in case of corporations, or ensure the majority of the votes in the partners' meetings and designate the manager or legal representative or their majority in case of other types of legal entities; or (ii) have decisive influence in the administration of the company.

With respect to the scope of the transactions covered under the provisions, no definition is provided by the law. However, the Circular[20] indicates that transfer of goods and services, transfer of technology and granting of the use or temporary enjoyment of patents and trademarks are included within the scope of article 38, as well as excessive interests, commissions and other payments made in connection with credit or financial operations with related parties.

Comparability analysis

Neither the Chilean legislation nor its regulations provide a mechanism for establishing whether there is comparability between the controlled and uncontrolled transactions. There are no rules regarding how comparability adjustments should be made, either. However, it is broadly understood that the arm's length principle contained in article 38 should be based on a comparison of the conditions in a controlled transaction with the conditions in transactions between the unrelated parties.

Other related rules

There are other related rules contained in the Income Tax Law that deal with situations in which related parties might manipulate the prices charged.

For example, article 38 no. 5 of the ITL specifically allows the Chilean IRS to reject any part of the deduction of interest, commissions or any other payments arising from credit or financial transactions executed with their headquarters or another agency of the headquarters, or with a financial institution that enjoys a level of participation of at least 10 per cent in the capital of the company's headquarters. In practice, this means that interest, commissions and other payments which are not set at

---

[20] Circular no. 3, note 17 above, p. 11.

arm's length may be disallowed as non-deductible expenses when computing a net profit.

In the case of banks which are not incorporated in Chile, article 37 of the ITL provides that the Chilean IRS may disallow the amounts paid to the headquarters for interest, commissions or any other payment arising from financial transactions as a deductible expense, where the amounts so charged are not comparable to the amounts that would ordinarily be charged under similar conditions.

Finally, article 31 no. 12 of the ITL establishes a limit on the deduction of payments made to foreign residents for the use, enjoyment or exploitation of trademarks, patents, formulas and other similar services, such as royalties or any other form of remuneration. In general terms, those payments are deductible up to a maximum amount of 4 per cent of the income on sales and services of the respective tax year. This limit does not apply if between the taxpayer and the beneficiary of the payment there is no direct or indirect relation in the capital, control or management or when in the country of residence of the beneficiary, income tax is levied at a rate of at least 30 per cent. In addition, the applicability of this provision is limited only to those cases where there is no double tax treaty in force with the country of residence of the recipient of the payments. In such cases, the limitation is provided by the arm's length principle.

18.3.2 Tax treaties

Except for the treaty with Argentina, all other Chilean tax treaties are based on the OECD Model Tax Convention and contain transfer pricing provisions similar to the ones contained in the Model Convention.

Under the 'Business Profit' Article of these treaties, Chile may attribute profits to a Chilean permanent establishment of a resident of the other contracting state consistent with the profits which it might be expected to make if it were a separate enterprise dealing independently with the enterprise. In addition, under the 'Associated Enterprises' Article, Chile may allocate profits to a Chilean enterprise conducting business activities with a related enterprise in the other contracting state, if such profits of the Chilean enterprise are inconsistent with the profits that would have been obtained by dealing with independent parties.

When a contracting state performs a transfer pricing adjustment consistent with the tax treaty, Chile is required under the treaty to make an appropriate or corresponding adjustment to take such transfer pricing adjustment into consideration.

Chile has no obligation to make a corresponding adjustment in the absence of a tax treaty. In such cases, the taxpayer affected by double taxation may amend its tax return and request a refund of taxes paid in excess. The taxpayer would be required to provide adequate supporting evidence to prove the need to modify the amount of the tax paid. Before approving the refund, the Chilean IRS has to conduct a review of the case, through an audit procedure similar to the one it employs when making a normal transfer pricing audit, and would only do so if the taxpayer can show the validity of the refund request.

18.3.3   Transfer pricing documentation

Chilean law does not require a taxpayer who carries out transactions with foreign related parties to produce a transfer pricing report. The only rule that deals with documentation requirements is article 38 of the ITL which establishes:

> Taxpayers must keep a register of persons with whom they carry out transactions or have participation in, in the terms described in the last two paragraphs [i.e., with related parties], keeping both the register and the documentation that supports those transactions available for examination upon request by the Internal Revenue Service.

Taxpayers are not required to prepare specific documentation supporting their transfer prices.

Upon audit, however, the Chilean IRS would typically request information and documentation, including (i) list of related entities; (ii) detailed description of imports and exports, or the operations subject to review; (iii) detailed description of services and intangibles; (iv) description of the activities conducted by the company in Chile and organisational chart; (v) financial statements showing segregated profit and loss statement for each business unit; and (vi) company pricing policy.[21]

18.3.4   Penalties

The gain determined by the authority as a result of its assessment tools provided by article 38 of the ITL, will be deemed as withdrawn at the end

---

[21] Chile Transfer Pricing Country Profile. 27 February 2009, available at www.oecd.org/ctp/transferpricing/38463162.pdf.

of the fiscal year for the purposes of global complementary tax, additional tax or the 35 per cent sole tax provided by article 21 no. 3 of the ITL.

Accordingly, when the income is determined for taxpayers other than by way of corporation stocks, limited by shares corporations (as regards the stockholders) or listed in article 58 no. 1 of the ITL, the income will be added to the net taxable income of the first category for the application of such taxes in the fiscal year in which they have been earned. Such income will also be subject to global complementary tax or additional tax, as such income is deemed withdrawn at the end of the said fiscal year by the owners or partners in such companies or corporations. However, if the mentioned income is determined by corporation stocks, limited by shares corporations (as regards the stockholders) or a taxpayer pursuant to Article 58 no. 1 of the ITL, it will be levied at the same time but only with the special tax established in article 21 no. 3 of the ITL. In these two situations, the taxes will be applied regardless of the balance in the taxable profits record (FUT) of the company or taxpayer.[22]

The IRS can also reject the deduction of excess expenses paid or owed abroad for interest, commissions or any other payments because of credit or financial transactions made with foreign related parties or with a financial institution in which the parent company has an interest of at least 10 per cent in the capital. Pursuant to article 33 no. 1 of the ITL, the excess expenses should be added to net taxable income subject to first category tax for the application of this tax, duly adjusted according to article 33 no. 3 of the ITL, when the disbursements have actually been made. These excess expenses will be levied with the special rate of 35 per cent under article 21 no. 3 of the ITL, as they correspond to cash disbursements not attributable to the value or cost of the assets.[23]

Transfer pricing procedure

There are no special rules for transfer pricing audit procedures, disputes or court procedures; therefore, common rules of procedure apply. The Chilean IRS is entitled to a special period of assessment when transfer pricing cases are involved.

The Chilean IRS starts an audit process with a request to the taxpayer, asking for specific information or documentation. The taxpayer must respond to this request, and if she refuses to do so, the IRS may ask the

---

[22] Ruling 57 of the IRS of 1998, ch. III.1.d. This ruling amended the corresponding rules contained in Ruling 3 of the same year.

[23] Ruling 3 of the IRS of 1998, ch. III.3.

courts to order that the information be provided. With this response, the IRS may close the audit process if it considers that the taxpayer has properly complied with her tax obligations. The taxpayer may also, at this stage, amend her tax return if she considers that the IRS' objections have merit. Where there is a disagreement, the tax administration will summon the taxpayer to provide additional information and will start a formal procedure against her.

In general, the statute of limitation is three years from the end of the term in which taxes were due. The term is six years for taxes assessed by means of returns when the return has not been filed or has been deliberately misfiled.

Transfer pricing penalties

The Chilean legislation does not provide for special transfer pricing penalties, so the general rules of penalties apply. However, the transfer pricing adjustment finally determined is subject to a 35 per cent tax in lieu of the income tax. On top of this, regular penalties and interest for underpayment of taxes may apply.

18.3.5   Alternative measures

The Chilean legislation does not provide for any other alternative measures for resolving either general or specific tax disputes, including transfer pricing disputes. Currently there are no rules governing advance pricing agreements, cost sharing arrangements or mandatory arbitration.

18.4   Transfer pricing disputes: current situation

Even though Chile has had transfer pricing legislation for more than ten years, from the beginning of 2010 to the present date, and the Chilean IRS has intensified its auditing practice with regard to companies with cross-border intercompany transactions, despite these efforts no case has ever been brought to the public arena. Agreed adjustments have been made by forestry, mining and pharmaceutical companies. In addition, it is important to mention that in many other countries the first transfer pricing audits were focused on payments sent abroad, whereas in Chile some of the assessments focused on the prices of services provided to the foreign related companies (e.g., shared service centres located in Chile) as they generated losses. This is owing to the fact that these companies were not recovering the costs involved in the provision of such services, which in turn arises from the arbitrary and manipulative cost allocation criteria (Chile allocated

Table 18.3 Exports of hazelnuts during 2009

Date	Tax ID	Exporter	Destination	Product	FOB (US$)	Units of measurement	Quantity	FOB per unit
3/31/2009	96618010–2	Fruticola Agrichile SA	Italy	Hazelnuts	359814	Net Kg.	126166	2.851909
4/30/2009	96618010–2	Fruticola Agrichile SA	Italy	Hazelnuts	50118	Net Kg.	25049	2.000798
3/31/2009	96618010–2	Fruticola Agrichile SA	Italy	Hazelnuts	143811.01	Net Kg.	50546	2.845151
3/31/2009	96618010–2	Fruticola Agrichile SA	Italy	Hazelnuts	197015.99	Net Kg.	74868	2.631511
3/31/2009	96618010–2	Fruticola Agrichile SA	Italy	Hazelnuts	72258.67	Net Kg.	25390	2.84595
3/31/2009	96618010–2	Fruticola Agrichile SA	Italy	Hazelnuts	342015.33	Net Kg.	125132	2.733236
7/30/2009	96811410–7	Exportadora Sun West SA	Argentina	Hazelnuts	14000	Net Kg.	5000	2.8
9/30/2009	96811410–7	Exportadora Sun West SA	Spain	Hazelnuts	32000	Net Kg.	12000	2.666667
10/22/2009	96811410–7	Exportadora Sun West SA	Brazil	Hazelnuts	5255.6	Net Kg.	2000	2.6278
9/28/2009	96811410–7	Exportadora Sun West SA	Germany	Hazelnuts	48344	Net Kg.	20000	2.4172
10/6/2009	96811410–7	Exportadora Sun West SA	Uruguay	Hazelnuts	3600	Net Kg.	1500	2.4
11/17/2009	96811410–7	Exportadora Sun West SA	Brazil	Hazelnuts	10000	Net Kg.	4000	2.5
10/6/2009	79759730–9	Lafrut Ltda.	Brazil	Hazelnuts	50450	Net Kg.	25000	2.018
12/18/2009	79759730–9	Lafrut Ltda.	Brazil	Hazelnuts	9990	Net Kg.	4720	2.116525

a cost which was lower than that which should be allocated) in addition to not allocating any mark-ups consistent with the arm's length principle.

Together with the audit process, the Chilean IRS is creating a database of prices for different products and services, making an official non-mandatory request for information from the taxpayer (not a notice of audit) regarding the purchase or sale price of different products either with related parties or third parties. Additionally, the Chilean National Customs Service keeps records detailing imports and exports, including the purchase date of such products, the company importing/exporting them, the number of units and the amount paid. This information is available to the public through the governmental authority, Dirección de Promoción de Exportaciones (ProChile, Export Promotion Agency). Table 18.3 provides an example of the information that ProChile provides.

18.5   Transfer pricing disputes: bilateral and multilateral approaches

18.5.1   Mutual agreement procedures

To date, Chile has not received any mutual agreement procedure (MAP) requests; however, in the near future, it is expected that the first MAP will be agreed between Argentina and Chile, despite the fact that the procedure is not defined in the double taxation treaty entered into between the two countries nor in the Chilean Income Tax Law. The agreement of the MAP is due to the fact that the two countries are cooperating in the first binational mining project in the world (with investment of approximately US$2,400 million), under which the functions, assets and risks that will be assumed by the companies in Chile and Argentina will need to be clearly defined to determine the revenues for each jurisdiction.

18.5.2   Advance pricing agreements

Despite the fact that the present regulation on transfer pricing does not contain provisions for advance pricing agreements (APAs), the taxpayer may request from the Chilean IRS, under no. 1(a) of article 6 of the Tax Code,[24] confirmation of the tax criteria applied to it through request for

---

[24] A Standard which enables the National Director administratively to interpret tax provisions, set standards, provide instructions and issue orders to charge and audit taxes.

a ruling. For instance, the Group producing methanol[25] requested from the Chilean IRS a ruling as to the correct method to be applied in calculating the amount of the consideration paid to its related party in Canada as well as the deductibility of the expenses related to these transactions. The background and resolution were set out in the 2009 ruling as follows:

> The Group's Global Marketing and Logistics department based in Vancouver maintains a database which tracks the worldwide supply and demand for methanol. Using this database to identify the periods where supply and demand are practically balanced, from time to time the Group implements strategies to buy methanol in the spot market. These strategies are implemented when it is probable that balance conditions may be maintained in the methanol market, achieving prices greater than those which would have been obtained without this program. As a rule, customers buy the total amount of its methanol requirements under contract when the price in the spot market is greater than the price in the contract, which generally occurs when the methanol market is balanced and prices are high or increasing. The Group presents losses when methanol bought in the spot market is sold to customers under contracts at a lower price. Losses for the Group resulting from these transactions destined to hinder an excessive drop in prices in the spot market is offset by the greater prices which the four plants obtain for the new contracts or price recalculations, which, as indicated above, are affected by the spot price. The follow-up of prices which the Corporation has conducted to assess the effect of these transactions in the spot market has proven that its purpose is met.
>
> However, it is a fact that the resulting price stabilization does not benefit the Corporation but the four companies that own the respective four production plants. Due to this, within the rationale of linking expenses to their respective benefits, the Group believes it is logical to recognize that the Corporation is acting on behalf of the four production plants interested in price stabilization. In order to formally indicate this reality, the Chilean Entity granted a mandate to the Corporation for the latter, on its own but on behalf of Chilean Entity, to buy and sell in the spot market as well as acquire the methanol industry production rights in the proportional amount that corresponds to Chilean Entity in these price stabilization transactions. This proportional amount is determined based on the tons produced annually by each plant. Thus, for example, if the plant in Chile produced 40% of the Group's annual tonnage, then Chilean Entity would participate, through the mandate, of 40% of the results of the transactions in the spot market. Consequently, following the example, Chilean Entity

---

[25] A multinational supplier of methanol to the major international markets of Asia Pacific, North America, Europe and Latin America.

would receive from the Corporation accountability for 40% of the losses produced that year as a result of the strategies described above.[26]

Additionally, due to the extraordinary circumstances in the market, in confirming the 2009 ruling, the following was added:

The individuals and entities that consult indicate that as a result of cut-offs in the gas supply from Argentina, starting from 2007 the Chilean Entity has significantly reduced its production of methanol, which, in its turn, has resulted in a decrease in the Group's worldwide inventories below one million tons.

To replace missing inventories and assure that customers will receive methanol committed on a timely basis and thus avoid stating to customers that this is a force majeure situation, the Group began in September 2007 a purchase process in the spot market at a level consistent with these objectives.

Obviously, the Chilean Entity is the producer which currently receives non-proportionate benefits with that part of spot purchases destined to cover its production deficit, ensuring timely supply and market retention for the time when the Chilean Entity resumes operations at full capacity.

To meet, under these different factual circumstances, with the distribution of results proportional to the benefits in the intercompany contract, the Production Entities have reformulated distribution mechanisms. The reformulation contemplates, in the first place, a distribution in an amount proportional to the sub-production of the Production Companies and, subsequently, a distribution of the balance of the results in the traditional proportional amount to the production of the Production Entities.[27]

Taxpayer Query:
That the positive or negative results, which are allocated to the Chilean Entity by the Corporation, as a result of the application of the intercompany contract according to the mechanism explained above, are for the Chilean Entity taxable income or expenses necessary to generate income, as the case may be.[28]

Tax Authority Opinion:
[T]he positive or negative results that are allocated to the Chilean Entity by the Corporation, as a result of the application of the intercompany contract per the mechanism explained above, will be for the Chilean Entity taxable income or expenses necessary to generate income, solely as long as there is clearly evidenced before the SII, compliance with the

[26] Private Letter Ruling no. 831, issued on 26 February 2001. The text is available at www.sii.cl/pagina/jurisprudencia/adminis/2001/renta/ja173.htm.

[27] Private Letter Ruling no. 271, issued on 2 February 2009. The text is available at www.sii.cl/pagina/jurisprudencia/adminis/2009/renta/ja271.htm.

[28] Ibid.

requirements established in article 31 of the Income Tax Law quoted as follows:[29]

- that it is directly related with the business or activity that is developed;
- that they are expenses that are necessary to produce the income understanding as such, those disbursements of an inevitable or obligatory nature, considering not only the nature of the expense but also its amount, that is to say, how much expense has been necessary to produce income in the financial period, whose net taxable income is being determined;
- that they have not already been discounted as an integral part of the direct cost of the goods and services required to obtain the income;
- that the taxpayer has actually incurred the expenses, whether this is paid or owed at the end of the fiscal period. In this way, for the proper fulfilment of this requirement, it is necessary that the expense should have had its origin in a real and actual acquisition or proportion and not in a mere appreciation of the taxpayer; and
- finally, that they be convincingly evidenced or justified before the Internal Revenue Service, that is to say, the taxpayer must prove the nature, need, effectiveness and amount of the expenses with the documentary support that it has, the Service being able to object to them if, for grounded reasons, they are not considered accurate, and, in particular in regard to the matter under analysis that these results correspond to actual income or actual expenses incurred by the Agency in Chile during the year.

Despite the fact that the request for the confirmation of the criteria, as presented by the methanol Group, was mostly related to the deductibility of the expenses, the calculation mechanism for the consideration amount was very relevant in the taxpayer's presentation and this was accepted by the tax authority.

18.6   Expected change in transfer pricing regulation

From the beginning of 2011, the Chilean IRS has announced, in different forums and in the press, the publication of the Draft Bill on Transfer Pricing. The Chilean IRS has repeatedly indicated that the proposed change in the law is not intended to provide a new look at the topic; on the contrary, the essence of the regulation is maintained and it is solely intended to provide greater certainty on the legal aspects and clarify the methodology for the benefit of the Chilean taxpayers. Thus:

---

[29]   *Ibid.*

Today: transactions between related parties must 'correspond to the values that under similar transactions are charged between independent companies' (article 38 of the ITL);

Draft Bill: transactions between related parties 'must be made at prices or market value' where 'Prices or market value are those that will be agreed or agreed between independent parties in similar transactions'.

According to the Chilean IRS, the new regulation on transfer pricing will include the following.

18.6.1   Clarifying the accepted methodology

Both the methodology accepted and the selection of the method will be consistent with OECD Guidelines:[30] 'The selection of a transfer pricing method always aims at finding the most appropriate method for a particular case. For this purpose, the selection process should take account of the respective strengths and weaknesses of the OECD recognised methods.'

Accepted methods will include:

- CUP;
- cost plus;
- resale price;
- TNMM;
- profit split.

However, if when considering the characteristics and circumstances of the case it is not possible to apply any of the methods indicated above, other methods can be used which allow the fair determination or estimation of prices or normal market values which have been agreed or would have been agreed by independent third parties in comparable transactions and circumstances.

18.6.2   Transfer pricing information return

Chilean taxpayers conducting transactions with foreign related entities will be required to file an information return detailing their cross-border intercompany transactions. The details of the contents of this return will be determined by the Chilean IRS through a circular.

---

[30] *OECD Transfer Pricing Guidelines for Multinational Enterprises and Tax Administrations* (July 2010), ch. 2 pt. 1.

18.6.3 Advance pricing agreements

The performance of (voluntary) APAs will be allowed. The request for agreement will have to include a transfer pricing analysis. The Chilean IRS could terminate an APA where long as there have been changes in the essential elements which determine the agreed value or price.

18.6.4 Contemporaneous transfer pricing documentation (transfer pricing report)

As a rule, transfer pricing analyses will not be an obligation on taxpayers and will have no probative value by themselves. They will only be mandatory in the case of an APA (which is itself voluntary).

Ultimately, transfer pricing analyses will be background information which companies will be able to use to determine their transfer pricing. However, this will not be required by the Chilean IRS at an audit and will not have any special probative value because of being performed. Notwithstanding this, a well-performed transfer pricing analysis will simplify the audit.

18.6.5 Corresponding adjustments

The limit for this type of sequential adjustments is likely to be five years retroactively and, therefore, companies will only be able to eliminate double taxation of an adjustment to which they have been subject in another jurisdiction during such period.

This initiative is included within the framework of the Chilean government's anti-tax evasion plan that seeks to collect US$1,300 million in four years from increasing tax audits, generally in relation to income tax. In addition, the Chilean IRS has created a specialised unit (economists, lawyers and accountants) which will be in charge of the transfer pricing audits.

18.7 Concluding remarks

Since the beginning of the application of transfer pricing regulations in 1998, transfer pricing in Chile came to be perceived as the tale of 'The Little Boy Who Cried Wolf'. Each year, rumours have gone around that the tax authorities are about to launch transfer pricing audits, but every year since then has typically ended with no such drama. However, as of

2011, I can now say that 'the wolf has finally arrived and it is indeed very hungry'. Recently, the Chilean IRS Director at an interview indicated that 'transfer pricing is no longer a myth. This year the Chilean IRS has already conducted seven specific audits'.[31]

As indicated by the tax authority, the amendment to the regulation related to transfer pricing is solely to provide taxpayers with greater legal certainty. However, this had not been the priority for the government given that current regulations allow the tax authority to review transfer pricing, which has resulted in a significant increase in transfer pricing audits.

The strategy followed by the tax authority in the audit process has been to notify the four or five leading companies of an industry to make comparison between their financial ratios and select the companies that could have a transfer pricing contingency to undergo a more intensive review. It is important to mention that many of the transfer pricing audits have been carried out on iconic companies (with important global brands).

Accordingly, and unlike any other countries in Latin America, Chile will not base the application of transfer pricing regulations on the taxpayer's obligation to submit a transfer pricing survey every year; it will simply require a taxpayer with intercompany transactions to make a transfer pricing information return, which will allow the Chilean authorities to identify those companies that might not be complying with the arm's length principle. From the author's point of view, the fact that Chile is a relative newcomer in the area of reviewing compliance matters and other related details of transfer pricing regulations has provided it with an ideal opportunity to learn from the best practices of, and errors hitherto experienced in, other jurisdictions, such as the avoidance of bureaucracy in the presentation of the transfer pricing report and building very skilled audit teams specialised by industries and by specific types of transactions.

The widespread use of APAs seems unlikely in Chile, not least in the near future, because the experience of countries which do employ APAs more frequently has shown that, unless the tax authorities provide the taxpayer with the possibility of approaching them anonymously in the first instance, no taxpayer is likely to take the risk of being the first one to request an APA and receive a negative or an unwanted response.

---

[31] Silvana Celedon and Julio Pizarro, 'SII prevé que evasión tributaria bajará en US$300 millones este año', *El Mercurio*, Economía y Negocios, 26 November 2011.

Appendix: Questionnaire (Chile)

1. The structure of the law for solving transfer pricing disputes. *What is the structure of the law of the country for solving transfer pricing disputes? For example, is the mutual agreement procedure (MAP), as regulated in the relevant tax treaty, the standard method for solving transfer pricing disputes?*

Under the Income Tax Law, in the absence of a double taxation agreement, there is no special procedure for resolving transfer pricing disputes. Therefore, all disputes will go through the general audit and court procedures. In almost all the cases where Chile has concluded a double taxation agreement, the agreement reflects the mutual agreement procedure.

2. Policy for solving transfer pricing disputes. *Is there a gap between the nominal and effective method for solving transfer pricing disputes in the country? For example, has the country a strategic policy not to enforce the arm's length standard (ALS) for fear of driving foreign direct investment to other competing jurisdictions?*

There exists a gap between the nominal and effective method for resolving transfer pricing disputes, since the law embodies the general procedure for dealing with transfer pricing assessments; however, in practice, this has not been used by the tax authorities.

3. The prevailing dispute resolution method. *Which is the most frequent method for solving transfer pricing disputes in the country? Does it have a positive externality? For example, is the MAP the most frequent method, and if so, to what extent have successful MAPs been used as a proxy for transfer pricing case law? For instance, Procter & Gamble (P&G) obtained a bilateral advance pricing agreement (APA) in Europe, and it was then extended to a third (Asian) country when P&G made this request to the relevant Asian tax authorities.*

Chile has not been faced with transfer pricing disputes.

4. Transfer pricing case law. *What is the evolution path of transfer pricing litigation in the country? For example: (i) Is transfer pricing litigation being gradually replaced by either MAPs or APAs, as regulated in the relevant tax treaties? (ii) Are foreign/local transfer pricing precedents and/*

or published MAPs increasingly relevant as a source of law for solving transfer pricing disputes?

Chile does not have transfer pricing case law.

5. Customary international law and international tax procedure.   *Has customary international law been applied in the country to govern the relevant methods for solving transfer pricing disputes (such as the MAP)? For example, has the OECD Manual on Effective Mutual Agreement Procedure ('OECD Manual')[32] been deemed customary international tax law in the MAP arena for filling procedural gaps (for example, time limit for implementation of relief where treaties deviate from the OECD Model Tax Convention)?*

Chile has no experience in the use of customary international law applied to govern the relevant methods in resolving transfer pricing disputes.

6. Procedural setting and strategic interaction.   *Does strategic interaction between taxpayers and tax authorities depend on the procedural setting in which they interact when trying to solve transfer pricing disputes? For example, which procedural setting in the country prompts the relevant parties to cooperate with each other the most for solving this sort of dispute, and why?*

There has been minimal interaction between the taxpayers and tax authorities regarding transfer pricing disputes.

7. The future of transfer pricing disputes resolution.   *Which is the best available proposal in light of the interests of the country for facilitating the global resolution of transfer pricing disputes, and why?*

The use of APAs could provide the taxpayer with greater certainty on the methodology applied to define their transfer pricing policy, particularly for complex transactions typical of the mining industry, through the mitigation of the possibility of disputes. Additionally, APAs could reduce the incidence of double taxation and also reduce the taxpayer's costs associated with audit defence and documentation preparation.

---

[32] The OECD Manual is available at www.oecd.org/ctp/transferpricing/manualoneffective mutualagreementprocedures-index.htm.

19

Transfer pricing disputes in Israel

OFER GRANOT AND YORAM MARGALIOTH

19.1 Introduction: the Israeli tax sphere

Modern Israeli income tax law developed within an archaic British colonial statutory framework. Israel's Income Tax Ordinance (New Version), 1961 (the 'Ordinance') originated in an ordinance enacted in 1941 (and later amended in 1947) by the British Mandate government, based on a Model Income Tax Ordinance prepared by the Inter-departmental Committee on Income Tax in the Colonies not Possessing Responsible Government. The Mandatory Tax Ordinance continued to apply after Israel's independence in 1948. In 1960, it was redrafted in Hebrew, without changing the substance.[1] Since then, this 'new version' has been the basis for frequent amendments of the Ordinance (195 to date). At the beginning of the twenty-first century, major fiscal reforms resulted in the modernisation of the Ordinance. A residency-based tax system replaced the earlier territorial-based system. New provisions were enacted, addressing participation exemption, taxation of REIT funds, taxation of trusts, transfer pricing for international transactions, a pre-ruling mechanism, CFCs, and more. Tax rates and various capital gains exemptions were frequently updated to attract foreign investment and human capital.

The authors would like to thank Irit Leo (Manager, Transfer Pricing Department, Israel Tax Authority), Dror Bitterman (Former Deputy-Manager, Transfer Pricing Department, Israel Tax Authority) and Ofir Levi (Former Director, International Taxation Department, State Revenue Administration, Ministry of Finance) for helpful discussions and Dr Michael Bricker for helpful comments on previous drafts. Yoram Margalioth would like to thank Paula Goldberg Fund for generous financial support. Obviously, the opinions (as well as the errors) in the text are the authors alone.

[1] Assaf Likhovski, 'Formalism and Israeli Anti-Avoidance Doctrines in the 1950s and 1960s' in John Tilley (ed.), *Studies in the History of Tax Law* (2004), pp. 339, 344–5; Yoseph Edrey, 'Introduction to the Theory of Taxation' (2008), p. 83.

On the international side, as of August 2012, Israel is signatory to fifty-one tax treaties which were ratified and are in effect.[2] In addition, Israel has signed a new tax treaty with Malta, and renewed several old treaties,[3] all of which are yet to be ratified. Most of Israel's treaties are based on the OECD Model Convention, and Israel is now acting to adjust its tax treaties to the revised 2008 OECD Model Convention.[4]

19.2   Economic and institutional context

19.2.1   Economic context

Israel's inward stock of foreign direct investment (FDI) in 2008 was US$57,481 million and its outward FDI stock was US$53,672 million.[5] Israel's gross domestic product (GDP) in 2008 was US$202 billion,[6] hence total FDI stock was about 55 per cent of GDP.

Israel's leading exports are high-technology products, cut diamonds and agricultural products (fruits and vegetables). High-tech industries account for about 80 per cent of the exports.[7] In 2008, exports of goods to the United States constituted approximately 28 per cent of total exports of Israeli goods. Exports to Europe constituted approximately 33 per cent of total exports, and exports to the remaining countries constituted approximately 39 per cent.[8]

Israel's twenty-five top multinational enterprises (MNEs) had over US$18 billion dollars in foreign assets in 2008 and employed nearly 93,000

---

[2] Treaties between Israel and Uzbekistan, Austria, Ukraine, Italy, Ireland, Ethiopia, Bulgaria, Belgium, Belarus, Brazil, United Kingdom and Northern Ireland, the United States, Jamaica, Georgia, Germany, Denmark, South Africa, South Korea, India, the Netherlands, Hungary, Turkey, Thailand, Greece, Japan, Luxemburg, Lithuania, Latvia, Moldova, Mexico, Norway, China, Singapore, Slovenia, Slovakia, Spain, Poland, Portugal, the Philippines, Finland, Czechoslovakia, France, Canada, Croatia, Romania, Russia, Sweden, Estonia, Vietnam, Taiwan and Switzerland.

[3] Treaties with the United Kingdom and Northern Ireland, Germany, Austria, Belgium.

[4] See 'Update on Changes in Israel's Tax Treaties Policy' in Meir Kapota and Ofir Levi, 'Legislation Review,' Misim 12/6 A-114, 120–123 (2008).

[5] UNCTAD, *World Investment Report 2009* (UNCTAD, 2010).

[6] CIA Factbook: Israel 2009, available at www.jewishvirtuallibrary.org/jsource/History/ciaisrael.html#Econ.

[7] See 'Trends in the Israeli Economy' (June 2009) available at www.finance.gov.il/research_e/trends2005–2009.pdf.

[8] *Ibid.*

persons abroad.[9] Being first in the world for availability of qualified scientists and engineers,[10] Israel provides multinationals with a professional and skilled labour market. And indeed some of the world's leading high-tech companies, such as Intel and HP, have their main, or most important, research and development centres in Israel.[11] Microsoft, Google, Facebook, Berkshire-Hathaway, Motorola, Intel, HP, Siemens, Samsung, GE, Philips, Lucent, AOL, Cisco, Applied Materials, Winbond, IBM and J&J, are just a few examples of multinationals that run core activities, mostly research and development, in Israel.

19.2.2   Institutional context

Increasing awareness of international taxation and the area of transfer pricing (in particular, following the recommendations of the Ben-Bassat Committee in 2000),[12] triggered the establishment of the International Taxation Unit (affiliated to the Professional Division) within the Israeli Tax Authority (ITA), including a transfer pricing desk. The desk was later separated from the International Taxation Unit and became an independent department, responsible for guiding and advising assessing officers in the transfer pricing field, issuing APAs, drafting white papers and proposals for legislative amendments, and structuring transfer pricing policy.

In practice, it seems that the Transfer Pricing Department has less effect than one would expect. The department is seriously understaffed, with only 3.5 positions. The people working there are well educated in the fields of law, accounting and economics, but the department has no enforcement powers, as only assessing officers initiate and perform audits and assessing procedures, and approach the Transfer Pricing Department for advice only if they choose to do so. Even though assessing officers do challenge transfer pricing aspects of taxpayers'

---

[9] See 'Israel's Leading Multinationals Continue to Expand Domestically and Abroad Despite the Crisis', available at www.vcc.columbia.edu/files/vale/documents/Israel-Report-March2010.pdf.

[10] IMD, *World Competitiveness Yearbook 2007* (Lausanne: IMD, 2008).

[11] See www.intel.com/jobs/israel/sites/haifa.htm. For many other examples and analysis see AnnaLee Saxenian, *The New Argonauts: Regional Advantage in a Global Economy* (2006); Dan Senor and Saul Singer, *Start-up Nation: The Story of Israel's Economic Miracle* (2009).

[12] *Report of the Public Committee for Income Tax Reform* (Ben-Bassat Committee) (Jerusalem, May 2000).

returns and issue tax demands in this regard, disputes between the taxpayers and the assessing officers over such tax demands do not generally reach the courts. It seems that taxpayers prefer to solve their transfer pricing issues by way of comprehensive compromises with assessing officers (who have no expertise in transfer pricing) over their entire tax return, rather than approaching the courts specifically on transfer pricing issues or applying to the Transfer Pricing Department for an advance pricing agreement (APA). In addition, ITA management seems not yet to acknowledge the potential of transfer pricing enforcement and deterrence and, except for the official ITA Circular 3/2008, no extensive ITA guidelines were initiated or published concerning transfer pricing.[13] It is not surprising then, that only about twenty APA applications are submitted per year (see section 19.7 below).

In May 2010 Israel became an OECD member. Even before joining the OECD Israel did its best to follow the *OECD Transfer Pricing Guidelines for Multinational Enterprises and Tax Administrations* ('OECD Guidelines') as well as the US Transfer Pricing Rules by using them as interpretative sources.

The OECD Guidelines and the US Transfer Pricing Rules are regularly used by the ITA in audits as well as in negotiations.[14] In addition, the OECD Guidelines and the US Rules are likely to be important sources of reference when Israeli courts address international transfer pricing cases.

Israel uses the OECD Model Tax Convention as the model for its tax treaties and continues to adapt and revise them accordingly.[15] Prior to the accession of Israel to the OECD, a committee on behalf of the OECD recently examined and confirmed Israeli transfer pricing legislation, policy and practice.

In addition, US law is in general a significant source of referral for Israeli tax purposes due to the United States' worldwide political and economic power, as well as its relationship with and influence on Israel.

---

[13] ITA Circular 3/2008 'Transfer Pricing' (14 July 2008) Misim 22/4.

[14] Leon Harris, 'Israel: Transfer Pricing and Intangibles' (2007) 92a *Cahiers de Droit Fiscal International* 344, 356; Jacob Houlie, *Transfer Pricing* (2006), p. 44.

[15] See a review by Israel's Ministry of Finance on Israel's accession to the OECD, available at www.oecd.org/dataoecd/44/57/41163971.pdf. See also 'Israel and OECD', available at www.oecd.org/israel; Meir Kapota, 'The OECD: VAT on International Services and Intangible Transactions', Misim 12/5 A-14, A-15 (2008) (stating that 'Israel must review the OECD recommendations as Israel is in the process of joining the OECD and has to adapt its tax policy to the policy promoted by the OECD').

Indeed, due to the significance of the OECD Guidelines and the US transfer pricing rules in markets and economies that are important to Israel,[16] the explanatory note to the transfer pricing regulations (issued by the ITA) stated that 'the Regulations set rules for transfer pricing reporting in accordance with the IRS and OECD rules',[17] aimed at reducing exposure to double taxation.[18] Moreover, even before the transfer pricing statutory regime came into force in November 2006, the Transfer Pricing Department issued transfer pricing assessments, and negotiated and signed APAs with taxpayers based on OECD Guidelines and on the provisions of US law.[19]

Regulation 6 includes a transitional provision according to which, for two years after the publication of the Regulations, taxpayers would be allowed to use transfer pricing studies prepared prior to the publication of the Regulations based on principles of the OECD or member countries of the OECD. Whereas ITA Circular 3/2008 views this provision as deviating from Israeli transfer pricing rules,[20] it is difficult to believe that the ITA would disregard transfer pricing studies that comply with OECD or US guidelines, considering the ITA's reliance on such sources prior to the enactment of the Regulations and even thereafter. Moreover, Israeli courts have acknowledged the importance of using OECD Commentary when interpreting an Israeli tax treaty based on the OECD Model Convention[21]

---

[16] ITA Circular 3/2008, para. 1.3.

[17] Original text is not available. See Houlie, *Transfer Pricing*, note 14 above, p. 44; Zemi Fliter and Sharon Shulman, 'Taxation of Credit Transactions: Tax Year 2007 Onwards' Misim 22/2 A-1 (2008).

[18] Original text is not available. See Avi Nov, *Taxation of International Transactions* (2008), p. 261.

[19] Houlie, *Transfer Pricing*, note 14 above, p. 230.   [20] ITA Circular 3/2008, para. 3.5.

[21] In *Yanko Weis* v. *Assessing Officer Holon*, Income Tax Appeal 5663/07 (District Court, Tel-Aviv) Misim 22/1 E-191, E-196 (2008), when addressing a case concerning the Israel–Belgium Treaty, the court ruled: 'Whilst the position of the OECD is not binding on Israeli courts, it has much interpretative power. That is, *inter alia*, because it expresses the views of the OECD member states and highlights the advisable interpretation also for states interested in joining the OECD. In addition, even if one of the contracting states is an OECD member, the expectation between the two contracting countries should be that the interpretation of a treaty based on the OECD Model Convention would be according to the OECD Commentary. Uniformity in the implementation of tax treaties based on the OECD Model Convention by the courts of the contracting states is an inherent need in implementing a tax treaty which is an agreement becoming a law following the ratification thereof by the contracting states. Therefore, when interpreting a concrete tax treaty, the OECD Commentary is an interpretive tool.'

or similar to it.[22] Even when addressing the Israel–United States Tax Treaty, Israeli courts examined the parallel arrangements in the OECD Model Convention.[23] This is likely to be the case when the courts address Israeli transfer pricing rules, as they are based on OECD Guidelines.

19.3   Transfer pricing in Israel: prior to 2003 tax reform

Transfer pricing provisions in the modern sense were promulgated only in a 2003 tax reform and applied only to international transactions. No similar transfer pricing legislation has been enacted with respect to local transactions. However, even before the 2003 tax reform, there has always been a general requirement that transactions between related parties should take place at arm's length. As outlined below, the Israeli legal tax sphere included few sources and provisions through which the ITA could address transfer pricing issues.

19.3.1   Income Tax Ordinance (New Version), 1961

Section 4 of the Ordinance addresses export transactions of productive enterprises. All profits of such enterprises from sale or delivery of goods abroad are deemed to have accumulated in Israel, unless it is proved that such profits were the result of actions taken abroad.[24] Furthermore, any endorsement, use or action regarding such products abroad will be disregarded by the ITA, and profits derived from such will be deemed accumulated in Israel and will be assessed based on the profits such an enterprise could have gained under 'the best conditions'.[25]

Sections 111–112 and 114 of the Ordinance address transactions between an Israeli resident and a non-Israeli resident who has a close connection to and 'actual control over' the Israeli resident. If the Israeli resident derives no profit or less profit 'than might be expected' from such a transaction, the foreign resident will be subject to Israeli tax, enforced via the Israeli resident.[26] If it is difficult to assess the income of the foreign resident from such a transaction, the assessing officer can determine it as a 'fair and reasonable portion' of the turnover of her business with the

---

[22] *Gteck Technologies* v. *Kfar Saba Assessing Officer*, Income Tax Appeal 1255/02, Misim 19/3 E-196 (2005) (discussing the Israel–Japan Tax Treaty).

[23] *Elitzur Ashkelon* v. *Assessing Officer Ashkelon*, Income Tax Appeal 5663/07 (District Court, Tel-Aviv), Misim 22/5 E-175, E-182 (2008).

[24] Section 4(1) of the Ordinance.   [25] *Ibid.* s. 4(2).   [26] *Ibid.* s. 111.

Israeli resident.[27] If the tax assessment is performed in connection with distribution of goods manufactured abroad, the assessing officer may assess the income of the Israeli and the non-Israeli residents (at their request) based on profit, which 'would have reasonably accumulated to a merchant purchasing such a good from the manufacturer'.[28]

Section 30 of the Ordinance prohibits the deduction of expenses higher than the amount necessary for generating the income of the taxpayer. Section 53 determines that a non-Israeli insurer can have made a profit of 10 per cent of the total amount of premiums paid from his Israeli insurance business, unless proved otherwise by the non-Israeli insurer. Section 73 provides that in certain circumstances, Israeli-sourced profits of a non-Israeli from transport of cargo loaded in Israel may be calculated on the basis of a 'fair portion' of the amount paid for such transport. Sections 3(i)–(j) authorise the assessing officer to apply a minimal statutory interest rate on credit transactions between related parties where the interest rate declared by the parties was lower.

Section 85 of the Ordinance provides that the business inventory taken out of the business, or transformed into a fixed asset within the business, shall be deemed sold for the amount that would have been received in a transaction between unrelated parties for a clean and free asset, unless the assessing officer is convinced that the consideration paid was not affected by the relations between the parties involved. The same approach toward consideration appears in section 88, which defines 'consideration' in the context of the sale of capital assets.

Section 86 of the Ordinance sets the general anti-avoidance rule, according to which an assessing officer may disregard a transaction if he believes that a transaction that reduces or could reduce the amount of tax paid by any person is artificial or fictitious, or that the principal purpose of the transaction is avoidance of tax or improper reduction of tax, even if the transaction is not illegal.

19.3.2   Common law powers of the ITA

The Israeli Supreme Court ruled that the ITA could reclassify transactions which are described for tax purposes in a way which does not reflect their real substance under the general law (e.g., a dividend

---

[27] *Ibid.* s. 112.

[28] *Ibid.* s. 114. See 'Section 114 – Sale of Foreign Manufacturing' in ITA, *Interpretation of the Israeli Tax Ordinance* (ITA and Ronen Press) ('Havak'), p. F-10.

distribution, which is a salary payment; a lease, which is actually a sale).[29] Following such reclassification, it would be necessary to set a new price that suits the real economic substance of the transaction.

19.3.3   Israel's tax treaties

All of Israel's tax treaties include rules similar to the transfer pricing provisions of the OECD Model Convention. Under the 'Associated Enterprises' provision,[30] Israel may set the profits of an Israeli enterprise derived from its business with a related enterprise in the other contracting state, if such profits differ from the profits that would have accrued between independent parties. When a contracting state applies its transfer pricing policy to an operation connected to Israel, Israel needs to consider making an 'appropriate adjustment'.[31] 'Business profits' provisions enable Israel to allocate incomes and expenses to a permanent establishment.[32] When the amount of interest or royalties paid is higher than the arm's length amount due to special relations between the parties involved, the limited tax rate applying on interest and royalties under the OECD Model Convention does not apply to the excess amount.[33] Exchange of information provisions, similar to Article 26 of the OECD Model Convention, can help the ITA to collect information concerning business operations outside of Israel for transfer pricing purposes as well.

Need for a change

The legal framework described above was considered too narrow, unclear, non-homogeneous and outdated to adequately cope with the transfer pricing challenges of the modern era.[34] First, the specific provisions in the Ordinance were not promulgated to deal with transfer pricing issues. Moreover, some of these provisions originated in the

---

[29] *Rochwarger Rutmentsh* v. *Assessing Officer Tel Aviv 1*, Request for Civil Appeal 8522/96, Misim J/3 E-70 (1997); *Assessing Officer for Large Enterprises* v. *Yoav Rubinstein*, Civil Appeal 3415/97, Misim 17/4 E-59, E-62 (1997).

[30] Article 9(1) of the OECD Model Covention.   [31] *Ibid.* Art. 9(2).

[32] *Ibid.* Art. 7(2) and (3).   [33] *Ibid.* Arts. 11(6) and 12(4).

[34] Harry Kirsh, 'Transfer Pricing Aspects in International Transactions' (1991) 19(75) *Israeli Tax Quarterly Magazine* 207; Houlie, *Transfer Pricing*, note 14 above, pp. 231–9; Avi Nov, *Taxation of International Transactions*, note 18 above, pp. 255–7; Amnon Rafael and Yaron Mehulal, *Income Tax* (1996), vol. IV, pp. 355–82; Avraham Alter and Ori Kalif, *International Double Taxation Conventions* (2003), vol. A/I, pp. 131–2; Avidor Avni and Gil Mizrahi, 'Transfer Pricing in International Transactions: Comparative Law' in *The Israeli Income Tax Reform Following Amendment 132 of the Income Tax Ordinance* (2002), pp. 379–85.

1940s when transfer pricing did not exist and the very nature of international business operations and international taxation and tax planning were completely different. Section 4 of the Ordinance was part of the Mandatory Tax Ordinance of 1947, whose purpose was to determine the location of income of an Israeli manufacturer. However, following the 2003 Israeli tax reform, Israeli residents pay taxes on a personal worldwide basis rather than on a territorial basis.

Section 111 of the Ordinance is not structured as a transfer pricing provision. It levies tax on a non-Israeli resident via an Israeli resident. It therefore seems to contradict Article 7(1) of the OECD Model Convention (adopted in Israel's tax treaties), which grants Israel the right to tax the business income of non-Israeli residents only if they have a permanent establishment in Israel. Since Israeli law is overridden by the tax treaties to which Israel is signatory,[35] section 111 does not apply to non-Israeli residents who have no permanent establishment in Israel.

Sections 3(i) and (j) of the Ordinance apply a minimum statutory interest rate to credit transactions between related parties, although the statutory rate may be higher than the arm's length interest rate. Moreover, applying section 3(j) in such circumstances to international credit transactions would trigger a higher withholding tax rate under Article 11 (6) of the Model Convention, which was adopted in Israel's tax treaties.[36]

Second, the above-mentioned provisions address only certain cases of transactions between related parties. For example, section 4 of the Ordinance does not apply to income from import transactions, vocation, services, various passive income (including from IP licensing) or sale of assets.[37] Section 85 is limited to taking inventory out of a business and does not apply to services, royalties or other passive income.[38] Section 111 applies only when a non-Israeli has actual control over an Israeli resident but not *vice versa*. Indeed, in *Zilberman Flumin* v. *Assessing Officer Haifa*,[39] the court held that taxpayers could provide services for consideration less than the market price or even for no consideration at all, as the Ordinance does not require otherwise.[40] Third, most of these provisions do not set

---

[35] Section 196 of the Ordinance.   [36] Houlie, *Transfer Pricing*, note 14 above, p. 235
[37] ITA Circular 3/2008.   [38] *Ibid.* para. 1.4.2.
[39] *Zilberman Flumin* v. *Assessing Officer Haifa*, Income Tax Appeal (District Court, Haifa) 149/99, Misim 16/3 E-120, E-128 (2002).
[40] The court referred to the Israeli Supreme Court judgment in *Poskalinsi* v. *Assessing Officer Tel Aviv*, according to which, unless the Ordinance states otherwise, a taxpayer is not liable for tax on income he had the right and power to get but avoided getting. See *Poskalinsi* v. *Assessing Officer Tel Aviv*, Civil Appeal 340/62, Padi 17 795, 797 (1963).

any method or mechanism for allocating profits, nor do they offer a method to measure them.

Fourth, although the ITA is of the opinion that transfer pricing issues are within the scope of section 86 of the Ordinance,[41] the application of section 86 to such matters is questionable. In *Livne Shlomo v. Assessing Officer Hadera*,[42] the court held that the assessing officer may use section 86 of the Ordinance to ignore that portion of the rental payments that exceeded the arm's length price. The court ruled that a tax return that includes such exaggerated payments is 'fictitious', and that the transaction should also be considered 'artificial', since there was no commercial ground for determining such a price. Nevertheless, it seems highly doubtful that an Israeli court would consider every transaction in which financial conditions are not arm's length as an 'artificial' or 'fictitious' transaction to which section 86 applies, in particular when the controversy is not over the substance or the classification of the transaction but rather over being at arm's length. Moreover, section 86 also applies to transactions whose principal purpose is avoidance of tax or improper reduction of tax, but it is difficult to prove that a taxpayer was not acting *bona fide* or that his intention was to avoid tax. Not surprisingly, common transfer pricing rules do not address the intentions (*mens rea*) of taxpayers with respect to the transactions under review. In any case, since the aim of section 86 was not to handle transfer pricing issues, it does not set any method to examine whether the pricing was indeed 'proper'.

Finally, the application of the OECD Model Tax Convention for transfer pricing purposes is also problematic. The 'associated enterprises' section does not set the method through which transfer pricing should be reviewed and calculated. Moreover, it is not evident that the ITA could apply the Convention's 'associated enterprises' provision without having equivalent authority under Israeli law. It is not surprising, then, that the ITA Circular published in 1981,[43] which addressed 'tax liability of cost plus entities', based on the above legal framework (mainly on section 111 of the Ordinance) was ignored and never implemented, as being too vague and insufficient.[44]

---

[41] *Ibid.* para. 1.4.4.

[42] *Livne Shlomo v. Assessing Officer Hadera*, Income Tax Appeal (District Court, Tel Aviv) 14/91, Misim 7/1 E-130, E-139–149 (1992).

[43] ITA Circular 14/81, 'Tax Liability of Cost-Plus Entities'.

[44] Boaz Tal and Udi Shostak, 'Transfer Pricing between Related Parties,' Misim 12/4 E-162 (1998); Houlie, *Transfer Pricing*, note 14 above, p. 228.

As of the early 1990s, in light of the increasing international exposure of the Israeli economy and growing globalisation, on one hand, and the legal fiscal vacuum in the area of transfer pricing, on the other, several government-appointed tax reform committees recommended enacting transfer pricing rules.[45] Although the recommendations did not mature into legislation, they did increase the ITA's awareness of the importance of international taxation and transfer pricing. Following the recommendations of the Ben-Bassat Committee in 2000,[46] an International Taxation Unit was established within the ITA, including a transfer pricing desk, which studied the field and drafted white papers and proposals for legislative amendments.

Only in August 2002, following the recommendations of the National Committee on Reform of Taxation (the Rabinovitz Committee),[47] did the Israeli Parliament (the Knesset) enact section 85A of the Ordinance, introducing a formal transfer pricing regime for the taxation of international transactions.[48] However, the statutory transfer pricing regime only came into force on 29 November 2006, with the promulgation of detailed transfer pricing regulations: the Income Tax Regulations (Determination of Market Conditions) 2006 ('Regulations').[49]

19.4   Israeli transfer pricing statutory regime (2003 onwards)

Section 85A of the Ordinance together with the Regulations established the Israeli statutory transfer pricing regime for international transactions. The transfer pricing rules adopt the arm's length principle, determining that the price and terms of international transactions between parties having special relations will be examined by way of comparison to similar transactions by unrelated parties, and will be reported and taxed accordingly (section 85A(a)). While international transactions are

---

[45] *Report of the Committee on Reform of International Taxation* (Rafael Committee) (Karan D, November 1991) suggested granting assessing officers the authority to handle transfer pricing issues. The recommendations of the Rafael Committee were adopted in the Proposal for the Amendment Income Tax Ordinance Law (no. 120), 1998, but did not become law. Similar recommendations were also made in *Report of the Public Committee for Income Tax Reform* (Ben-Bassat Committee) (Jerusalem, May 2000) but these also did not become law.

[46] *Ibid.* Ben-Bassat Committee Report, note 45 above.

[47] *Report of the Committee for Income Tax Reform* (June 2002).

[48] Amendment Income Tax Ordinance Law (no. 132), 2002, Book of Laws 1863 ('Amendment 132'), effective as of 1 January 2003.

[49] Section 98(d) of Amendment 132.

subject to broad transfer pricing rules, no such requirements apply to local transactions. The commentary on section 85A provides no explanation for limiting these rules to international transactions only. However, the legislative background clearly indicates that transfer pricing issues were initially considered within the international context of shifting revenues outside of Israel, while in domestic transfer pricing matters all revenues were (allegedly) captured by the Israeli tax net.

The limited scope of transfer pricing rules could place non-Israeli residents at a disadvantage compared to their Israeli competitors when doing business with other Israeli residents. The competitiveness of non-Israelis could be adversely affected as they are subject to arm's length standards, and are exposed to a heavy bureaucratic burden due to documentation and reporting requirements, which in Israel apply to international transactions (particularly if such requirements are broader than requirements in their place of residence). This may raise the question of whether the Israeli transfer pricing regime could be considered, in some cases, as violating the non-discrimination clause in Article 24 of the OECD Model Convention, which applies ' to any taxation or any requirement connected therewith', including 'method of assessment . . . [and] the formalities connected with the taxation (returns, payment, prescribed times, etc.)'.[50]

In *Buchris v. Assessing Officer Hadera*,[51] the Israeli Supreme Court approved imposing a tax on employers of non-Israelis, even though such a policy clearly (and deliberately) lowered the economic value of employing them. The Supreme Court ruled that the non-discrimination paragraph in the OECD Model Convention aimed to prevent the imposition of a higher tax burden on foreign nationals compared to the tax imposed on Israeli nationals. At the same time, it was not meant to achieve total equity in every aspect of taxation. According to the *Buchris* principle, it is therefore doubtful whether transfer-pricing rules would indeed be considered discriminatory, as they do not apply a different tax to non-Israeli residents, but only indirectly place them at a competitive disadvantage.[52]

---

[50] Commentary on the Articles of the 2008 OECD Model Income and Capital Tax Convention, 'Commentary on Article 24', para. 15.

[51] *Buchris v. Assessing Officer Hadera*, Bagatz 2587/04 Misim 19/4 E-115, E-118 (2005).

[52] See also Oscar Abu-Razek and Elisha Kesner, 'Transfer Pricing in Israel (Part I)', Misim 21/2 A-57, A-70 (2007).

19.4.1   International transactions

The Israeli transfer pricing rules apply to international transactions only. An 'international transaction' is defined in regulation 1 as a transaction taking place between parties, at least some of whom have a 'special relationship',[53] and where (i) one or more of the parties is a foreign resident or (ii) part or all of the income from the transaction is also taxable outside of Israel. This definition captures not only transactions between an Israeli resident and an Israeli branch of a non-Israeli corporation (if the management and control over that branch are exercised outside of Israel), but also transactions between an Israeli resident and the permanent establishment of an Israeli resident outside of Israel, on condition that the parties involved have special relations.[54]

19.4.2   Special relationship

The term 'special relationship' is broadly defined as including (but not limited to) the relationship between a person (natural or legal) and his relative; when one party to a transaction exercises control over the others; or when there is control of a single person over parties to a transaction, directly or indirectly, individually or together with another.[55] A 'relative' is defined as a spouse, sister, parent, grandparent, descendant and spouse's descendant and spouse of each of the afore-mentioned; a person and his attorney; a holder or a partner in a partnership.[56] 'Control' is defined as 'holding, directly or indirectly, at least 50 per cent of the means of control'.[57] 'Together with another' means together with a relative or a

---

[53] Houlie, *Transfer Pricing*, note 14 above, pp. 247–8, stating that the arm's length rule in s. 85A applies only to 'an international transaction [in which] the parties thereof have special relations'. Therefore, since the Regulations were to be promulgated concerning cases which fall within s. 85A(a) only (see s. 85A(e)), it is arguable that notwithstanding the definition of 'international transaction' in reg. 1, the rules would not apply to an international transaction not all of whose participating parties have special relations.

[54] ITA Circular 3/2008, para. 2.2; Abu-Razek and Kesner, 'Transfer Pricing in Israel (PtI),' note 52 above, suggest (at para. 5.3.4, p. A-72) that in the case of a transaction between an Israeli resident and an Israeli permanent establishment in a treaty country, the transfer pricing rules should not apply even though the permanent establishment is a non-Israeli resident, since the entire income derived from the transaction is taxable in Israel only.

[55] Section 85A(b) of the Ordinance.   [56] *Ibid.* s. 76(d).

[57] For the definition of 'means of control', s. 85A(b) of the Ordinance refers to s. 75B(a)(2) of the Ordinance, which in turn refers to s. 88 of the Ordinance, where 'means of control' are defined as one of the following rights, regardless of the legal source from which the right originates: (i) the right to profits; (ii) the right to appoint a director or a director general in the company or other similar functionaries in other entities; (iii) voting right

non-relative if they regularly cooperate, based on agreement with respect to the material matters of the company, directly or indirectly.[58]

As mentioned above, a special relationship is not a closed list. Apart from the cases specified in the definition, special relations could also exist in other cases. According to ITA Circular 3/2008, a special relationship would include a case where parties to an international transaction have, or are controlled directly or indirectly, by the same interest, similar to the terms of section 482 of the US Internal Revenue Code.[59]

19.4.3   Transactions covered

Section 85A applies to all kinds of transactions (except issuance of certain capital notes), of all magnitudes, with no relief for small transactions. The only relief applies to 'one-time' international transactions, approved as such by the assessing officer. Such transactions are to be reported as if the price or the terms thereof were determined between parties that have no special relationship, i.e., the transaction would still need to be reported to the ITA (according to the reporting rules in regulation 5) like any other transaction covered by transfer pricing rules, except for the requirement to perform a transfer pricing study with respect to such a transaction (unless such a transfer pricing study has already been prepared).[60]

The term 'one-time transaction' is not defined in the Ordinance or in the Regulations. ITA Circular 3/2008 defines a 'one-time' transaction as a transaction that is not usually carried out by the taxpayer with parties with whom he has special relations. The 'one-time' nature of the transaction lies in its very low frequency, its low magnitude in itself, as well as in comparison to other of the taxpayer's transactions. In addition, ITA Circular 3/2008 requires that the application to approve one-time transaction status be sent to the ITA Transfer Pricing Department (and not to

---

in the general assembly in the company or in a parallel forum in another entity; (iv) the right to distribute the remainder of the assets following payment of debts upon liquidation; (v) the right to instruct a person who has one of the afore-mentioned rights as to how to exercise his right.

[58] For the definition of 'together with another', s. 85A(b) of the Ordinance refers to s. 75B (a)(4), and broadens this definition (which is limited to Israeli residents only in the case of non-relatives) also to non-Israeli residents.

[59] ITA Circular 3/2008, para. 2.2.

[60] Income Tax Regulations 2006, reg. 5(c); ITA Circular 3/2008, para. 3.3.

the regional assessing officer) to enable the ITA to follow a consistent policy in approving such applications.[61]

Since the ITA considers capital notes as a common and important financing vehicle for Israeli businesses,[62] the Ordinance provides that under certain requirements, issuance of capital notes would be classified for the purpose of section 85A of the Ordinance, not as a credit transaction but as an investment, therefore not triggering arm's length interest.[63] Under similar conditions, also the minimum statutory interest rate under section 3(j) of the Ordinance does not apply to certain capital notes.[64]

19.4.4 Implementation of the arm's length principle

Regulation 2(b) states that the arm's length principle is to be implemented by a transfer pricing assessment that compares the reviewed transaction to similar transactions, applying one of the comparison methods set out in the Regulations. Accordingly, the minimal statutory interest rate on credit transactions between related parties set out in sections 3(i)–(j) of the Ordinance does not apply to international transactions covered by section 85A and the Regulations.[65]

If a comparison is made with similar transactions using the comparable uncontrolled price (CUP) method and no adjustments are necessary for any differences in the comparison criteria, an international transaction will be considered to be at arm's length if the result falls within the entire range of comparable transactions. If another comparison method is used, the transaction will be considered at arm's length if it falls within the inter-quartile range.

If an international transaction appears not to be at arm's length, the transaction price to be reported for Israeli tax purposes will be the median price.[66] This inflexible outcome, limited to the median price only, increases exposure to double taxation. As further elaborated below, when Israel adjusts the terms of an international transaction, the relevant contracting treaty state has to make an appropriate adjustment if it also considers the transaction not to be at arm's length (assuming the applicable tax treaty includes a

---

[61] ITA Circular 3/2008, para. 3.3.   [62] *Ibid.* para. 2.1.

[63] Section 85A(e) requires, *inter alia*, that the note is granted to a controlled party, not bearing interest or differentials and repaid only after a period of at least five years.

[64] Paragraphs (10)–(11) of the definition of 'Loan' in s. 3(j)(1) of the Ordinance.

[65] Similarly, para. (9) of the definition of 'Loan' in s. 3(j)(1) of the Ordinance provides that s. 3(j) does not apply to a loan which is an international transaction according to s. 85A. A similar provision appears in s. 3(i).

[66] Income Tax Regulations 2006, reg. 2(c).

provision similar to section 9(2) of the OECD Model Convention). However, if using the median is not a widely accepted international practice, the contracting state may refuse to make an adjustment based on median price, other than using a lower value that could also reasonably reflect arm's length terms. In case of disagreement, at present there is usually no mechanism to compel the two countries to avoid the resulting double taxation.

Tested party

The 'tested party' is a party to an international transaction that meets both of the following conditions:[67] (i) it is reasonable to assume that comparison to similar transaction(s) conducted will produce the most reliable result in determining the market value; (ii) there is more suitable, appropriate and reliable information on the tested party than on any other party. In most cases, the tested party would be the party that does not own substantial tangible or intangible assets and whose operation is easier to characterise than operations of the other parties to the transaction.[68] A 'similar party' is one whose comparison criteria are the same or similar to those of the tested party.

Similar transactions

A 'similar transaction' is a transaction between the tested party and an unrelated party whose comparison criteria are the same or similar to those of the international transaction examined. Only if no such international transaction is found can 'external' transactions be reviewed, i.e., a transaction between unrelated parties whose comparison criteria are the same or similar to those of a transaction conducted by the tested party. In both cases, when comparison criteria are not identical, the comparison would be made in such a way as to eliminate the effect that the existing differences may have on the result of the comparison.[69]

The comparison criteria are defined as (i) field of activity, including manufacturing, marketing, sales, distribution, research and development and consulting; (ii) type of product or service rendered; (iii) contractual terms; (iv) risks associated, including geographical, financial and credit risks; (v) economic climate; (vi) the effect of goodwill or other intangible assets held.[70]

Comparable similar transactions are those carried out in the three tax years preceding the examined transaction.[71] When justified, and with the

---

[67] *Ibid.* reg. 1.
[68] ITA Circular 3/2008, para. 3.2.2.   [69] Income Tax Regulations 2006, reg. 1.
[70] *Ibid.* reg. 1.   [71] *Ibid.* reg. 3(1).

approval of the ITA, older transactions may also be taken into account. All transactions of the 'similar party' in these years are taken together unless it can be shown that a material change in the comparison criteria occurred during the three-year period, following which only some of the transactions will be considered as one transaction.[72] Considering various similar transactions as one necessitates using the average of the data relevant to the comparison method used.[73]

Comparison methods

The comparison method required is one of the following, listed in declining order of preference:[74]

1. Comparable uncontrolled price (CUP), comparing the price set in the international transaction and the price set in a similar transaction. If CUP is not applicable, among the following methods, that which is most appropriate.
2. Comparing profitability: cost plus method or resale price method (RPM); and if neither applies, then the most appropriate among the following.
3. Transactional net margin methods (TNMMs): (i) operating margin (comparison of the rate of operating profit or loss according to the financial statements in similar transactions); or (ii) return on capital employed (comparing the ratio between the profit or loss and the assets, liabilities and/or capital, as applicable); or (iii) another method that is most appropriate in the circumstances.
4. Profit split method: based on the fair allocation of profits or loss between parties to a joint activity, considering the contribution of each party to the transaction, including exposure to risks and rights in assets related to the deal.
5. If none of the above is applicable, the most suitable method for the specific circumstances.

---

[72] *Ibid.* reg. 3(2). The ITA views this regulation as applying only to 'external similar transactions' and not to transactions carried out by the 'tested party' itself (see ITA Circular 3/2008, para. 3.2.2.1). However, since 'similar party' also covers the 'tested party', and with no rationale for differentiating between the two for this purpose, reg. 3(2) seems to apply to similar transactions that are both external and internal. Houlie, *Transfer Pricing*, note 14 above, p. 257 and Harris, 'Israel: Transfer Pricing and Intangibles', note 14 above, p. 344, also consider reg. 3(2) to apply in both cases.

[73] *Ibid.* reg. 3(3).

[74] Ibid. reg. 2(a) and definition of 'Profit Rate' in reg. 1. See also ITA Circular 3/2008, para. 3.2.4.c; Houlie, *Transfer Pricing*, note 14 above, pp. 254–5; Harris, 'Israel: Transfer Pricing and Intangibles', note 14 above, p. 343.

19.4.5　Reporting and documentation requirements

Annual tax return

A taxpayer is required to attach Form 1385 to her annual tax return, reporting each international transaction conducted with a related party, its price and terms and whether these conform to market terms.[75] Data reported must include: (a) names and residence of parties to the transaction; (b) the substance of the transaction; (c) the transaction price; (d) a signed statement of the company directors that the international transactions were at arm's length; (e) whether each international transaction was a 'one-time' transaction and was approved as such by the assessing officer.[76]

Data provision obligations

Upon demand from the assessing officer, the taxpayer must provide all documents and data concerning the international transaction, the foreign parties to the transaction and the way the price was determined.[77] The obligation to provide such data is not limited to the 'tested party' or even to a party to the transaction; it applies to any 'taxpayer' under the Ordinance who possesses data relevant to such a transaction. In addition, a taxpayer who is a party to the transaction (not necessarily the 'tested party') must submit to the assessing officer, upon demand and within sixty days, a report containing all of the following:[78] (i) the taxpayer's ownership structure, including any direct or indirect controlling rights holders therein, and any entity directly or indirectly held by them severally or jointly with the taxpayer; (ii) the parties to the international transaction, their residency, and the special relations between them and the taxpayer; (iii) the contractual terms of the international transaction including assets, services provided, the price, and the terms of loans, credit and guarantees; (iv) the taxpayer's field of activity and developments in this field; (v) the economic climate in which the taxpayer operates and the risks to which she is exposed; (vi) direct or indirect use of intangibles; (vii) all transactions between the taxpayer and a party to the international transaction, including loans, payment of management fees, partnerships, joint ventures, gifts, guarantees, trust agreements as well as any other agreement; (viii) similar transactions, the selected comparison method and the comparison parameters upon which the range of values and the inter-quartile range

---

[75] Section 85A(d) of the Ordinance.　　[76] ITA Circular 3/2008, para. 3.4.
[77] Section 85A(c)(1) of the Ordinance.　　[78] Income Tax Regulations 2006, reg. 5(a).

were determined, the results of the comparison, the range of values and the inter-quartile range, and the conclusions derived from the comparison; (ix) the way in which the transaction was reported in the foreign country, including in advance pricing agreements (if submitted) or in tax returns, and an explanation of any differences between the reports.

The taxpayer must also attach to the report the transaction agreement, other agreements with the parties with whom the taxpayer has special relations, other documents supporting the data provided, the transfer pricing study, tax returns or reports filed in other countries, any determinations made by a foreign tax authority, and any opinion provided by an accountant or an attorney.[79]

The above data provision obligations enable the ITA to collect information on foreign 'tested parties' through Israeli taxpayers. To date, the ITA has never approached foreign tax authorities by force of exchange of information provisions in treaties to collect information on foreign 'tested parties', but instead has required Israeli taxpayers to provide such information.

Formally, the ITA does not accept transfer pricing assessments prepared for other tax authorities, except for the two-year period following the publication of the Regulations during which (for adjustment purposes) taxpayers were allowed to use transfer pricing assessments prepared prior to the publication of the Regulations, if they conformed to the principles of the OECD or a member country of the OECD.[80] However, considering the compliance costs involved in preparing new assessments according to Israeli requirements (as well as the lack of sufficient Israeli comparables), in the case of multinationals with vast worldwide activity headquartered in the United States or in a European country, the ITA may be willing to accept transfer pricing studies based on US or OECD standards, or according to the EU Transfer Pricing Documentation Code of Conduct (EU TPD).

Assessing procedures

Other than when the taxpayer applies for an APA, the assessing officer can address transfer pricing issues when reviewing the taxpayer's annual tax returns. Within three years after the end of the tax year in which the tax return was filed, the assessing officer may review the taxpayer's self-assessment, approve it or issue a best-judgement assessment if there are

---

[79] *Ibid.* reg. 5(b).   [80] *Ibid.* reg. 6.

reasonable grounds to believe that the taxpayer's tax return is incorrect. The director of the ITA may extend the three-year period to four years.[81] However, in criminal instances (failure to report all income or filing a false return), the statute of limitations is ten years after the end of the year in which the offence was committed.[82]

19.5   Transfer pricing disputes: domestic approach

19.5.1   The burden of proof

Following the submission of all the data requested by the assessing officer and set in the Ordinance and the Regulations, the burden shifts to the assessing officer to prove that different terms must be applied to the international transaction reviewed.[83] This implies that if the taxpayer does not provide all the required data (including information on non-Israeli residents), the burden of proof is on the taxpayer. When the transfer pricing matter concerns the proper conduct of the taxpayer's books, this implied conclusion seems to contradict section 155 of the Ordinance, which explicitly states that where the issue concerns the taxpayer's books, if the taxpayer's books were not disqualified, the burden of proof would be on the assessing officer.[84]

However, in *Ideal Tours (1982) Israel Ltd* v. *Assessing Officer Jerusalem*,[85] the district court ruled that even when the burden of proof is on the taxpayer (and all the more, when it is on the assessing officer), the assessing officer cannot challenge the terms of a transaction or of a business operation without relying on studies referring to comparable operations in the relevant economic field.

It seems that, at present, the ITA does not have sufficient comparable data on transactions by Israeli corporations to challenge transfer pricing assessments on the merits. The ITA reported to the OECD that for transfer pricing purposes, the ITA uses only public information and not confidential or privileged information (such as data on other comparable transactions under the review of the ITA), nor information received from other sources (such as the Money Laundering Prohibition

---

[81] Section 145(a) of the Ordinance.   [82] *Ibid.* ss. 220 and 225.

[83] Section 85A(c)(2) of the Ordinance.

[84] *Tahanat Sherutei Rechev Romema Haifa* v. *Assessing Officer Haifa*, Income Tax Appeal (Haifa) 240/01, Misim 17/5 E-291 (2003).

[85] *Ideal Tours (1982) Israel Ltd* v. *Assessing Officer Jerusalem*, Income Tax Appeal (Jerusalem) 9054/05, Misim 22/4 E-197 (2008).

Authority). Furthermore, the ITA does not subscribe to any database that contains data on Israeli corporations, although at least one such database exists. The ITA does subscribe to a database covering the operation of European and US corporations. It is likely, then, that the ITA would consider US and European comparables as a substitute for evaluating the transfer pricing of Israeli taxpayers.

19.5.2 Tax litigation

Israel has no specialised tax courts and tax cases are heard on the district court level (where there is usually one judge who handles tax cases), with a right to appeal to the Supreme Court of Israel. Legal proceedings are therefore often prolonged (minimum two–three years before a judgment is given) and expensive. In addition, having courts using purposive interpretation of law (giving more weight to the economic rationale than to the language of the law) and the application of the substance over form doctrine makes courts less predictable. Therefore, in many cases, tax litigation is only initiated for tactical reasons vis-à-vis the ITA or as a final resort, after all other means have been exhausted.

So far, only one case, *Ideal Tours* (mentioned above), concerning an international transfer pricing matter has been discussed by an Israeli court.[86] In that matter, an Israeli company paid substantial royalties to a US company for using the name and reputation of the US company, one of whose two shareholders was the father of the directors of the Israeli company and the sole shareholder in the US parent company of the Israeli subsidiary. The ITA had refused to let the Israeli company deduct the royalty expenses, arguing that the taxpayer had not proved the need to pay such royalties nor the reasonableness of the amounts paid. The court overruled the assessing officer regarding these arguments.

The court ruled that special relations and trust between parties are not against the taxpayer, but rather these explain why the exceptional financial

---

[86] *Ibid.* In *Horvitz v. State of Israel*, Criminal Appeal 1182/99, Misim 14/5 E-76 (2000), the Supreme Court discussed the criminal liability of Israeli companies and their directors in tax avoidance due to unlawful shift of income from Israeli companies to related non-Israeli companies. The Supreme Court did not have to address the civil aspects of the tax scheme, which included transfer pricing aspects. For criminal law purposes, the court gave much weight to the corporate principle of the 'separate legal entities' of the companies involved and to the formal function they had (even if passive). At the same time, the Supreme Court ignored the fact that the royalties paid between the related companies were coordinated in a way that resulted in shifting a substantial amount of income from Israel, which, at that time, levied tax on a territorial basis.

terms of the transaction were not determined based on a thorough economic examination. This could be interpreted as rejection of the arm's length standard as the court refused to view the Israeli subsidiary as a separate entity. We do not think, however, that such interpretation is meaningful. The case predated the enactment of the Israeli transfer pricing legislation and was not informed of the importance of compliance with the international standard. It is very likely that future cases will be dealt in accordance with section 85A and its regulations which are meant to apply the OECD Guidlines and will therefore be interpreted accordingly.

Whereas transfer pricing tax demands had been issued before the transfer pricing regulatory regime came into force, the fact that only one case has been brought to court, as well as the low volume of APA applications submitted to the ITA, suggest that transfer pricing disputes are usually settled at the level of assessing officers.

Though the transfer pricing legislation came into effect only on 29 November 2006, the ITA could try to challenge international transactions carried out before that date by using the new transfer pricing regulations as an interpretative framework for the implementation of the law which existed prior to that date, a technique used by Israel's Supreme Court in other tax cases.[87] Approaching Israeli courts in the context of international transfer pricing issues is not relevant when the taxpayer's arguments refer to a non-Israeli tax authority. The question naturally has to address an assessment issued by the ITA. Taxpayers can approach the Supreme Court directly, in its role as High Court of Justice, to challenge the validity of Israeli legislation that is arguably unconstitutional or contradicts the obligations of the State of Israel under treaties (including tax treaties) to which it is a signatory.[88] However, in such cases, the Supreme Court takes a very cautious approach and is reluctant to interfere in the discretion of legislative or administrative authorities, except when the circumstances are extreme.

19.5.3   Sanctions

With no specifically designated fines or sanctions in transfer pricing matters, the general provisions set out in the Ordinance apply. The

---

[87] M. L. Hashka'ot v. Director of Betterment Tax, Civil Appeal 4271/00 Misim 17/6 E-61, E-64 (2003); Gonen v. Assessing Officer Haifa, Civil Appeal 477/02, Misim 20/1 E-71, E-78 (2006).

[88] Kaniel v. State of Israel, Bagatz 9333/03, Misim 19/3 E-76 (2005); Buchris v. Assessing Officer Hadera, Bagatz 2587104, Misim 19/4 E-115 (2005).

Ordinance does not apply major civil fines. There are no fines as a percentage of the income in dispute, except in two cases: (i) where the extra tax required by the ITA is more than 50 per cent of the total amount of tax for which the taxpayer is liable: a 15 per cent fine if the taxpayer did not prove that he was not negligible in reporting the income to the ITA, or a 30 per cent fine if the assessing officer has reasonable grounds to believe that the taxpayer deliberately tried to avoid tax payment;[89] (ii) a 30 per cent fine, when the assessing officer decided, based on section 86 of the Ordinance, to ignore a transaction the taxpayer had to report according to the Income Tax Regulations (Tax Planning to be Reported) 2006.[90]

On the other hand, criminal liability under the Ordinance is very broad; the provisions reviewed below are only the major ones. Section 215 of the Ordinance provides that any non-compliance with the provisions of the Ordinance or with the Regulations promulgated thereunder is an offence, which triggers a penalty of at least one year's imprisonment. The same applies to a failure to respond properly to any requirement issued by the ITA by force of the Ordinance; refusal to accept a notice issued under the Ordinance; failure to file a tax return; failure to properly manage tax books; destroying or hiding documents relevant to the assessment; failure to properly document income or to report income according to the Income Tax Regulations (Tax Planning to be Reported) 2006.[91] Section 217 of the Ordinance applies criminal liability to offences of negligence in reporting incomes. Section 220 of the Ordinance applies criminal liability to offences of deliberate intent to evade tax payment or to assist such evasion, where the taxpayer deliberately did not report income; provided the ITA with false data; prepared or assisted in preparing fake books; used any kind of fraud, deceit or device for evading tax; and where false data was presented to the payer of the income so as to evade or reduce the amount of tax withheld. Where corporations are liable for criminal liability under the Ordinance, their active directors are also personally liable for the same level of criminal liability, unless they prove they had no knowledge of the offence or that they took all reasonable means to prevent such an offence from occurring.[92] The explicit statement by the company's directors under Form 1385, attached to the annual tax return,[93] that the international transactions were at arm's length, also increases their exposure to criminal

---

[89] Section 131(b)–(c) of the Ordinance.   [90] *Ibid.* s. 131(c1).
[91] *Ibid.* s. 216.   [92] *Ibid.* s. 224A.   [93] See the text to note 76 above.

liability. However, it is important to note that criminal procedures are rarely activated in income tax matters, except in cases of clear attempts to evade tax by not reporting income, false reports, etc.

19.6   Transfer pricing disputes: bilateral and multilateral approaches

19.6.1   Appropriate adjustment rule under Israel's tax treaties

Section 9(2) of the OECD Model Convention provides that a contracting state shall make an appropriate adjustment following the application of transfer pricing policy by the other contracting state with respect to profits and conditions that are not at arm's length, according to section 9(1) of the OECD Model Convention. In case of disagreement between the two states with respect to the adjustment needed, a mutual agreement procedure will be implemented.

Some of Israel's tax treaties include appropriate adjustment provisions similar to section 9(2) of the OECD Model Convention.[94] Others include appropriate adjustment provisions that deliberately deviate from the OECD Model,[95] by allowing the other contracting state to make adjustments only if it considers such adjustments to be justified.[96] Under the OECD wording, the other state does not have to make an appropriate adjustment if it considers the initial adjustment improper. Therefore, the 'justification' condition not only emphasises this; it arguably broadens the discretion of the ITA not to make an appropriate adjustment for other reasons as well, even if the initial adjustment is proper. Finally, a few treaties (including some signed

---

[94]   This includes treaties between Israel and Ukraine, Japan (conditional on the consent of the competent authorities), Luxemburg, China, Philippines, Czechoslovakia (will not apply in cases of fraud or wilful default), South Korea, Canada, Switzerland (the competent authorities have to consult to reach consent regarding the adjustment of profits), Latvia and Singapore.

[95]   For example, regarding the Israel–Moldova Treaty, see Ofir Levi, 'Legislation Review', Misim 11/6 (December 2007) A-97, 106; regarding the Israel–Portugal Treaty, see Ofir Levi and Meir Kapota, 'Legislation Review', Misim 12/3 (June 2008) A-111, 122.

[96]   This includes treaties between Israel and Uzbekistan, Ireland, the United States (if there is no agreement on appropriate adjustment, a mutual agreement procedure would apply), Ethiopia, Bulgaria, Belarus, Jamaica, India, Turkey, Mexico (will not apply in case of fraud, gross negligence or wilful default), Slovakia (will not apply in cases of fraud or wilful default), Spain, Finland, France, Croatia, Russia (if there is no agreement on appropriate adjustment, a mutual agreement procedure would apply), Portugal, Moldova, Lithuania, Slovenia and Estonia.

after 1977, when Article 9 was first incorporated into the OECD Model Convention) do not include a provision similar to Article 9(2) of the OECD Model Convention.[97] To date, Israel has adjusted the tax liability of taxpayers in a few cases following the application of transfer pricing rules by treaty states.

In recent years, the Ministry of Finance has announced its willingness to adjust Israel's tax treaties to economic changes that occurred since their signing (some were signed in the 1960s and 1970s) and to changes in the OECD Model Convention.[98] Indeed, Israel's new tax treaty with Estonia includes an appropriate adjustment provision similar to Article 9(2) but with 'justification' conditions. It is expected that adjustments of other treaties will also include the incorporation of an appropriate adjustment rule, in the spirit of Article 9(2) of the OECD Model Convention.

19.6.2 Mutual agreement procedures

Mutual agreement procedure (MAP) provisions appear in all of Israel's tax treaties;[99] all are generally similar to Article 25 of the OECD Model Convention, though to date, no MAPs have been initiated in the context of transfer pricing. According to the general principles of Israeli administrative law, once the taxpayer asks to initiate a MAP, the ITA must *bona fide* exercise its discretion, taking into account all the relevant circumstances, and only the relevant ones. This rule applies to the question of whether to initiate the procedure as well as to the effort that the ITA invests in reaching an agreement once it has began negotiating with the other competent authority.

In *Gteck Technologies* v. *Kfar Saba Assessing Officer,*[100] the District Court of Tel Aviv ruled that court proceedings were to be delayed pending the application of a MAP, if initiated by the taxpayer. The court decided that the MAP should be regarded as part of the assessment procedure. If a

---

[97] These include treaties between Israel and Austria, Italy, the United Kingdom and Northern Ireland, Belgium, Brazil, Germany, Denmark, South Africa, the Netherlands, Hungary, Greece, Norway, Poland, Romania, Sweden and Thailand.

[98] Kapota and Levi, note 4 above.

[99] The current Israel–United Kingdom Tax Treaty in effect does not include mutual agreement procedure provisions. Such provisions appear in the renewed Israel–United Kingdom Treaty, which is yet to be ratified.

[100] *Gteck Technologies* v. *Kfar Saba Assessing Officer,* Income Tax Appeal 1255/02, Misim 19/3 E-196 (2005).

taxpayer were interested in initiating a MAP, the ITA had to decide whether to initiate such a procedure and to exhaust negotiations with the other tax authority before court proceedings could take place. If a court judgment was handed down before the MAP was exhausted, it would frustrate such a procedure, since the ITA would be bound by the judgment of the Israeli court and the other tax authority would most likely refuse to negotiate under such conditions even if further related issues that required negotiation remained undecided. However, failure to reach a mutual agreement would not negatively affect the possibility of carrying on legal proceedings at a later stage. Yet, in cases where a court's judgment in a case or in certain aspects thereof would not frustrate the possibility of initiating a MAP, it may be possible to bring legal proceedings prior to the exhaustion of the procedure.

In *Koltin* v. *Assessing Officer Kfar Saba*,[101] the same court ruled that court proceedings would not be delayed unless the taxpayer supplied the ITA with all the background information needed to facilitate the initiation of a MAP. In our understanding, this judgment was meant to discourage attempts to delay court proceedings for tactical reasons, merely by asking the ITA to initiate MAPs. In practice, taxpayers rarely ask the ITA to initiate MAPs, given the bureaucracy, time and expense involved, and the fact that there is no guarantee that such a procedure would result in an agreement, since the authorities only need to attempt to reach agreement.

As detailed below, Israel's tax treaties with Mexico and Ireland include voluntary arbitration clauses to which a transaction could be referred (with the consent of the taxpayer and the competent authorities), if the MAP failed. In addition, a 'suspended' mandatory arbitration clause is included in Israel's treaty with Denmark and some renewed treaties are expected to apply mandatory arbitration in such a case.

19.6.3   International tax arbitration

Israel is not a member of the European Union and therefore the EU Arbitration Convention[102] does not apply to it. Until 2009, only two of Israel's tax treaties included arbitration clauses: Article 25(5) of the

---

[101] *Koltin* v. *Assessing Officer Kfar Saba*, Income Tax Appeal 1192/04 Misim 20/3 E-126 (2006).

[102] Convention 90/436/EC on the Elimination of Double Taxation in connection with the Adjustment of Profits of Associated Enterprises.

Israel–Mexico Treaty and Article 26(6) of the Israel–Ireland Treaty, both referring to voluntary (not mandatory) arbitration. In both treaties, the arbitration provisions are part of the MAP section. Only after the MAP is exhausted and the competent authorities of the contracting states fail to reach an agreement can the case be submitted for arbitration, with the consent of both authorities and the taxpayer, provided that the taxpayer agrees in writing to be bound by the arbitration decision. The decision of the arbitration board in a particular case will be binding on both contracting states with respect to that case only. Neither treaty fixes a time limit for reaching agreement under the MAP, the exhaustion of which is required for referring the case to arbitration.[103]

Both treaties left it to the contracting countries to establish arbitration procedures through notes exchanged via diplomatic channels. However, no such procedures have been determined so far.[104] Unless otherwise determined, the taxpayer has no part in the arbitration, with the exception of the requirement for written consent to submit the case for arbitration. At the end of Article 25(5) of the Israel–Ireland Treaty, it is stated that the provisions of that paragraph shall become effective when the contracting states have so agreed through the exchange of diplomatic notes. At the time of writing, diplomatic notes had not yet been exchanged; no use has been made of the Mexico–Israel Treaty arbitration clause even though it has been in effect since January 2000.[105]

A mandatory arbitration clause was incorporated into Article 25(5) of the OECD Model Convention in 2008. It states that if within two years, the competent authorities of the two contracting states do not reach agreement, the unresolved issue would be submitted to arbitration at the taxpayer's request, unless a court or an administrative tribunal of either state had already rendered a decision on these issues. The arbitration decision would bind both states, and be implemented regardless of any time limits in the domestic laws of the contracting states. In accordance with Israel's consent to adjust Israel's tax treaties to the revised 2008 OECD Model Convention,[106] negotiations have been held with the

---

[103] Michael Bricker and Dror Levi, 'Mutual Agreement Procedure and Arbitration Clause in Tax Treaties', Misim 15/2 A-15 (2001); Yitzhak Hadari, 'Mandatory Arbitration Between States concerning Transfer Pricing', Misim 12/5 A-1 (2008).

[104] Information received from the International Taxation Department, Incomes Administration, Ministry of Finance of Israel.

[105] Information received from the International Taxation Department, Incomes Administration, Ministry of Finance of Israel.

[106] Kapota and Levi, note 4 above.

United Kingdom, Germany, Denmark and Belgium regarding the inclusion of the mandatory arbitration paragraph in its revised tax treaties.[107] To the best of our knowledge, the United Kingdom has agreed to the incorporation of Article 25(5) into the renewed tax treaty between Israel and the United Kingdom.[108] Denmark agreed only to a 'suspended inclusion' of Article 25(5) in the 2012 Israel–Denmark Treaty, to the effect that the arbitration clause will automatically apply only when Denmark incorporates such a clause in another tax treaty with a third party.

The arbitration clause in Article 25(5) of the OECD Model Convention offers two main advantages compared to the arbitration provisions in Israel's treaties with Ireland and Mexico: mandatory arbitration if the taxpayer asks for arbitration so that the submission of the case to arbitration is not at the discretion of the competent authorities, and the time limit of two years for reaching an agreement.

19.7   Advance pricing agreements

In 2005, the ITA was statutorily authorised to issue tax rulings, following the promulgation of sections 185B–185F of the Ordinance.[109] However, tax rulings were issued long before, including with respect to transfer pricing. In fact, transfer pricing rulings were issued not only before section 85A (enacted in 2002) became effective on 29 November 2006, but even years before its enactment.[110]

Section 85A of the Ordinance includes specific APA provisions.[111] It provides that a party to an international transaction may approach the director of the ITA for an APA confirming that the price of a transaction or series of transactions satisfies the arm's length standard. Such an application has to include all the material facts and details of the transactions; the method for determining the price; any document, approval, opinion, statement, evaluation, the transaction agreement or draft thereof; and any other document required by the director of the

---

[107] The renewed treaties with the United Kingdom, Belgium and Germany were signed but are not in effect.

[108] Ofir Levi, 'A New Tax Treaty with the UK' (2009) *Accountant* 84, 85.

[109] Amendment Income Tax Ordinance Law (no. 147), 2005, Book of Laws 766 ('Amendment 147').

[110] For example, ITA Circular 36/93 'Issuances of Pre-Rulings by the ITA' (22 July 1993), Misim 7/5 C-5, provides that the ITA may issue tax rulings for non-Israelis in case of transfer pricing issues.

[111] Section 85A(d) of the Ordinance.

ITA. The ITA has to notify the taxpayer of its decision in the application within 120 days, or up to 180 days if the taxpayer is notified before the 120-day period ends. If the ITA does not respond during this period, the application will be considered as satisfying the arm's length standard and as approved by the ITA.

General tax ruling provisions also apply to APAs as long as they do not contradict APA provisions.[112] An application cannot be withdrawn without the ITA director's permission.[113] The application may be anonymous but the ruling will be issued only after the applicant is identified.[114] Following an application by the taxpayer, the director of the ITA may issue a tax ruling both by way of an agreement with the taxpayer or without the consent of the taxpayer.[115] The taxpayer must be given a reasonable opportunity to be heard before a tax ruling is issued.[116] There is no appeal on a tax ruling issued by way of an agreement with the taxpayer; a tax ruling issued not by way of an agreement can be appealed as part of an appeal on an assessment issued by the ITA.[117] The ITA director is bound by a tax ruling issued unless the information or documents submitted were incomplete, false or misleading or if the circumstances relating to the ruling changed.[118] If the ruling was issued by way of an agreement, the applicant is also bound by the ruling, unless the act concerned was not carried out.[119]

There are no statutory provisions concerning applications for bilateral or multilateral APAs, nor do any ITA Circulars deal with this issue. Only about twenty APA applications are submitted per year (many of them anonymous), and the number of APAs actually issued at the request of the applicants (who consequently have to reveal their identity) is much lower. So far, there have been no applications for issuing bilateral or multilateral APAs.

19.8 Concluding remarks

Israel has only recently joined the OECD. This happened after years of anticipation during which Israel has been taking into account OECD standards in an attempt to promote its accession to the OECD. Israel is therefore very likely to do its best to comply with any transfer pricing rules adopted by the OECD. The main hurdles are practical and

---

[112] *Ibid.* s. 158D(g).   [113] *Ibid.* s. 158D(f).   [114] *Ibid.* s. 158D(e).
[115] *Ibid.* s. 158C(a).   [116] *Ibid.* s. 158C(d).   [117] *Ibid.* s. 158C(e).
[118] *Ibid.* s. 158E(a).   [119] *Ibid.* s. 158E(b).

institutional. Only assessing officers (who have no expertise in transfer pricing) initiate and perform audits and assessment procedures, and approach the Transfer Pricing Department for advice only if they choose to do so. It seems that taxpayers prefer to solve their transfer pricing issues by way of comprehensive compromises with assessing officers over their entire tax return, rather than approaching the courts specifically on transfer pricing issues or applying to the Transfer Pricing Department for an APA. In addition there are very limited Israeli comparables, making it, among other things, too costly to comply for small and medium-sized firms which cannot afford the fees charged by the local branches of the big four accounting firms.

Appendix: Questionnaire (Israel)

1. The structure of the law for solving transfer pricing disputes.   *What is the structure of the law of the country for solving transfer pricing disputes? For example, is the mutual agreement procedure (MAP), as regulated in the relevant tax treaty, the standard method for solving transfer pricing disputes?*

MAP is the only legal mechanism structured in the Israeli law for solving transfer pricing disputes. However, to date, no MAP has been initiated for solving transfer pricing disputes. In general, Israel expressed its willingness to include a mandatory arbitration clause based on Article 25(5) of the revised 2008 OECD Model Convention in future revisions of its existing tax treaties with OECD countries. Israel's renewed tax treaty with the United Kingdom (not yet in effect) includes such a mandatory arbitration clause. The renewed tax treaty with Denmark includes (at Denmark's request) a suspended mandatory arbitration clause, which will take effect only when Denmark incorporates such a clause in another tax treaty with a third party. At present, the Israel–Ireland and the Israel–Mexico Tax Treaties include an optional arbitration clause (never used to date), in case the dispute is not resolved through MAP.

2. Policy for solving transfer pricing disputes.   *Is there a gap between the nominal and effective method for solving transfer pricing disputes in the country? For example, has the country a strategic policy not to enforce the arm's length standard (ALS) for fear of driving foreign direct investment to other competing jurisdictions?*

The Israeli transfer pricing regime is in its infancy. Insofar as there are gaps between the statutory transfer pricing regime *de jure* and the implementation thereof *de facto*, these can principally be attributed to the birth pangs of the new transfer pricing rules, the learning period required for the relatively new and undermanned Transfer Pricing Department, and structural flaws that encourage taxpayers to reach settlements with assessing officers instead of applying for APAs. Israel does not view transfer pricing policy as a means to attract investments. Moreover, Israel has recently joined the OECD after many years of anticipation and, at least in the near future, is likely to be as cooperative as possible. This means that it is likely do the following: (i) use transfer pricing to assess and collect all taxes due from activity that took place within its tax jurisdiction; (ii) prevent double taxation.

3. The prevailing dispute resolution method. *Which is the most frequent method for solving transfer pricing disputes in the country? Does it have a positive externality? For example, is the MAP the most frequent method, and if so, to what extent have successful MAPs been used as a proxy for transfer pricing case law? For instance, Procter & Gamble (P&G) obtained a bilateral advance pricing agreement (APA) in Europe, and it was then extended to a third (Asian) country when P&G made this request to the relevant Asian tax authorities.*

As mentioned above, the only method for solving international transfer pricing disputes in Israel is the MAP (including arbitration). However, MAP was never exercised in the context of transfer pricing. Taxpayers do approach the ITA following the application of transfer pricing rules by other countries and, if justified, the ITA adjusts the Israeli tax liability accordingly. In addition, although the assessing officers issue transfer pricing tax demands that challenge reports made in annual tax returns, taxpayers seem to prefer not to go to court nor to approach the Transfer Pricing Department for an APA, but to solve transfer pricing disputes through a comprehensive settlement with the ITA covering all the tax issues in dispute in the relevant year. Therefore, in practice, transfer pricing rules are not fully exercised or implemented by the ITA and consequent disputes with other tax authorities in these circumstances are lessened.

4. Transfer pricing case law. *What is the evolution path of transfer pricing litigation in the country? For example: (i) Is transfer pricing*

litigation being gradually replaced by either MAPs or APAs, as regulated in the relevant tax treaties? (ii) Are foreign/local transfer pricing precedents and/or published MAPs increasingly relevant as a source of law for solving transfer pricing disputes?

Except for one case, there have been no transfer pricing court judgments (concerning international transactions) in Israel. Taxpayers seem to prefer to settle with assessing officers rather than go to court, or approach the Transfer Pricing Department of the ITA for APAs.

5. Customary international law and international tax procedure. *Has customary international law been applied in the country to govern the relevant methods for solving transfer pricing disputes (such as the MAP)? For example, has the OECD Manual on Effective Mutual Agreement Procedure ('OECD Manual') been deemed customary international tax law in the MAP arena for filling procedural gaps (for example, time limit for implementation of relief where treaties deviate from the OECD Model Tax Convention)?*

The OECD Manual is not formally deemed customary international tax law. However, Israeli transfer pricing regulations were meant to be compatible with the OECD and US transfer pricing rules to reduce exposure to double taxation in this context. In addition, Israeli courts use the OECD Commentary when interpreting an Israeli tax treaty based on the OECD Model Convention or similar thereto, and even when addressing the Israel–United States Tax Treaty (which is based on the US model). Therefore, in practice, the OECD Model Convention as well as US transfer pricing rules represent important non-binding interpretative and referral sources for Israeli tax purposes and are regularly used by the ITA in audits as well as in negotiations and are likely to be important sources of reference when Israeli courts address international transfer pricing cases.

6. Procedural setting and strategic interaction. *Does strategic interaction between taxpayers and tax authorities depend on the procedural setting in which they interact when trying to solve transfer pricing disputes? For example, which procedural setting in the country prompts the relevant parties to cooperate with each other the most for solving this sort of dispute, and why?*

As stressed throughout this chapter, transfer pricing in Israel is enforced by the assessing officers who have no expertise in transfer pricing issues.

ITA experts in this field become involved only if assessing officers ask them for advice or request an economic study to challenge transfer pricing assessments provided by the taxpayers. These are very rare.

At present, taxpayers have no incentive to approach the ITA with requests for APAs as this is likely to harm them strategically, as reaching settlements at relative low cost is feasible. Assessing officers are highly unlikely to spot the problematic aspects of taxpayers' transfer pricing practices, and even if they do, other issues with which they are more familiar are likely to take precedence in settlement negotiations. Moreover, the ITA has an inherent disadvantage in bringing these issues to court, as they require significant time, money and expertise for producing economic studies and the like. Based on the fact that with the exception of one case, there are no court precedents, we assume that the ITA will be hesitant about bringing transfer pricing issues to court for fear that losing cases would significantly decrease deterrence. The outcome of the above is that transfer pricing settlements can be reached at relatively low cost to the taxpayers; hence, no cooperation seems to be the taxpayers' preferred strategy.

We therefore think that any procedure that would increase enforcement, such as greater involvement in the audit process by the ITA's Transfer Pricing Department (which may require increasing its staff) would significantly increase taxpayers' cooperation in solving transfer pricing disputes.

7. The future of transfer pricing disputes resolution.   *Which is the best available proposal in light of the interests of the country for facilitating the global resolution of transfer pricing disputes, and why?*

Israel is a small economy. While it has no effect on global markets, it does engage in significant economic activity with both Europe and the United States. Because of its relatively small size and the significance of foreign trade to its economy, it is likely to adopt any policy suggested by its much larger economic partners. Israel would adopt whatever practices are thought to be the mainstream in an effort to benefit from harmonisation. Because the importance of its trade with Europe is about equal to that of its trade with the United States, Israel would try to satisfy both, so that its transfer pricing policy would be a compromise between the two, if their policies differed. As mentioned above, Israel has recently joined the OECD and is adjusting all relevant policies, including its transfer pricing rules, to conform to OECD requirements.

Transfer pricing disputes in Africa

LEE CORRICK

20.1 Introduction: the African tax sphere

The basis of taxation in the African continent varies quite considerably from country to country. Many African countries have a residency basis for taxation while others tax on a territoriality basis, and some such as Liberia tax on a blend of the two bases.

Turning to individual countries, companies resident in Mauritius are subject to income tax on their worldwide income. Resident companies are companies incorporated in Mauritius and companies with their central management and control in Mauritius. If a non-resident company has a branch carrying on business in Mauritius, the non-resident company is subject to tax on the income of the branch.

Likewise Nigerian resident companies are subject to tax on their worldwide profits. Non-resident companies are taxed on the profits of their operations in Nigeria only. Resident companies in Uganda are also subject to tax on their worldwide income, but tax credits are granted for tax paid on foreign-source income. Non-resident companies are subject to tax on income derived from sources in Uganda only.

Angolan companies carrying out industrial and commercial activities in Angola are subject to industrial tax (corporate income tax). An Angolan company, which is a company that has its head office or effective management and control in Angola, is subject to industrial tax on its worldwide profits.

Other African countries tax on a territorial basis. Cameroon and Congolese companies are taxed on the territoriality principle. Therefore Cameroon and Congolese companies carrying on a trade outside

Cameroon and the Congo, respectively, are not taxed in Cameroon and the Congo on their foreign source profits.

Foreign companies with activities in Cameroon are subject to Cameroon corporate tax on Cameroon source income. This is the same in the Congo where foreign companies with activities in the Congo are subject to Congolese corporate tax on Congolese source income.

Egyptian corporations are subject to corporate profits tax on their profits derived from Egypt, as well as on profits derived from abroad, unless the foreign activities are performed through a permanent establishment located abroad. Foreign companies are subject to Egyptian tax only on their profits derived from Egypt.

In Kenya, income tax is payable by companies and by unincorporated organisations and associations (excluding partnerships). Taxable trading income consists of income arising or deemed to arise in Kenya.

Prior to 1 January 2001, South African income tax had been levied on a source basis, but now all resident individuals and companies are taxed on their worldwide income. Companies are considered to be resident in South Africa if they are incorporated or have their place of effective management in South Africa.[1]

South African companies are taxed on their worldwide income, excluding branch profits derived from 'designated countries'. Non-resident companies are taxed on their South African source income only. Income is considered to be from a South African source if its originating cause is located in South Africa.

A South African resident company may also be liable for the secondary tax on companies (STC). STC was introduced in 1993 at the same time as there was a reduction in the company rate of tax.[2] Since October 2007, STC is calculated at 10 per cent of the 'net amount' of any qualifying dividend or deemed dividend distributed. Liability for STC arises when distributions of dividends are made, although exemptions apply to certain dividends made. A company that is not resident in South Africa is not liable to STC.

In Botswana, all companies operating in the country are subject to tax on earnings in Botswana.

---

[1] Income Tax Act no. 58 of 1962, s. 1.   [2] *Ibid.* s. 64B(1).

20.2   Economic and institutional context

20.2.1   Economic context

Africa has witnessed strong growth in foreign direct investment (FDI) in recent years, with inflows rising to US$36 billion in 2006 from US$2.4 billion in 1987 (Figure 20.1). African FDI inflows in 2006 were equivalent to about one-fifth of the region's gross fixed capital formation (Figure 20.1). In many countries, FDI rose in the primary and services sectors, partly because of exploitation of Africa's vast natural resources and because of a wide range of national privatisation schemes. As a result, inward FDI stock in the region rose to US$315 billion in 2006, continuing a long climb from US$42 billion in 1985.

The recent surge of FDI inflows to the Africa region, particularly over the period 2001–2007 (Figure 20.1), followed from the twin forces of an upward spiral in commodity prices and a more positive climate for investments. These changes were backed by reforms of policy frameworks for FDI, including, among other steps, changes in regulations related to natural resource exploitation.

Recent rising FDI inflows have not, however, led to an increase in Africa's share of global FDI: Africa's share essentially has matched the

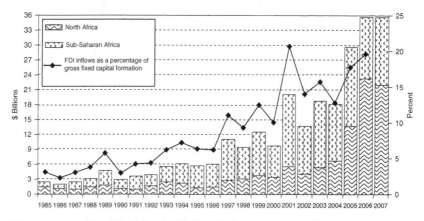

Figure 20.1   Africa: FDI inflows and their share in gross fixed capital formation, 1985–2007

Note: North Africa includes Algeria, Egypt, Libyan Arab Jamahiriya, Morocco, Sudan and Tunisia; and sub-Saharan Africa, the rest of the countries in Africa.

Source: UNCTAD, *World Investment Directory*: (2008), vol. X 'Africa' (preliminary estimates for 2007)

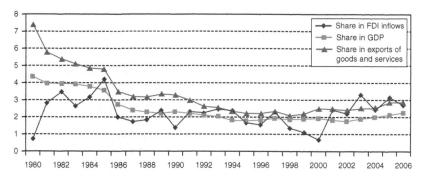

Figure 20.2 Shares of African countries in world FDI inflows, world GDP and world exports, 1980–2006
Source: UNCTAD, *World Investment Directory* (2008), vol. X 'Africa'.

continent's share of global gross domestic product (GDP) and trade (Figure 20.2). African FDI inflows remained static at about 2–3 per cent between 2000 and 2006 (2.7 per cent in 2006). The expansion of FDI into the region also was not evenly spread across the continent. In 2006, the North Africa sub-region and some of the region's largest natural resource producers, such as Angola, Nigeria and South Africa (Figure 20.3), accounted for the bulk of total FDI.

The top two FDI-recipient countries, South Africa and Nigeria, accounted for 37 per cent of the region's inward FDI stock in 2006. Moreover, their share of primary-sector inward FDI increased at the same time as their share of manufacturing-sector FDI declined (see Table 20.1). Similar changes took place in several other African countries. Only in a few countries did the share of manufacturing FDI inflows increase over the same period.[3]

The main commodities exported by African nations are palm oil, gold, diamonds, oil, cocoa, timber and precious metals. Despite the liberalisation of trade over more than the last two decades, the level and composition of Africa's exports have not substantially changed, according to the 2008 report by the United Nations Conference on Trade and Development (UNCTAD) on economic development in Africa. The principal destination for African countries' exports is still Europe. Countries that are now members of the European Union (EU) account for 40 per cent of exports from African countries.

---

[3] UNCTAD, 'Strong Performance in Foreign Direct Investment in Africa', UNCTAD Press Release, UNCTAD/PRESS/PR/Accra/2008/019, 2 April 2008.

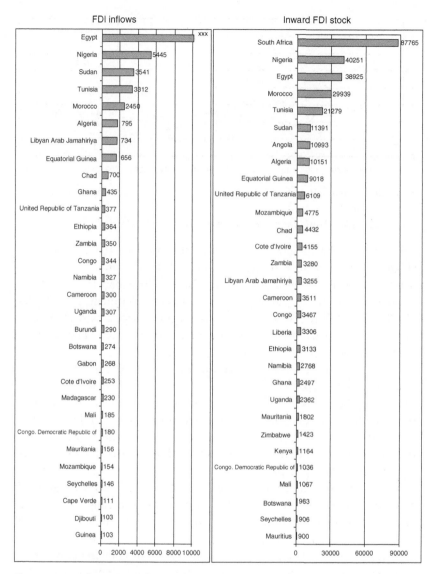

Figure 20.3   Africa: FDI inflows and inward FDI stock, 2006
Source: UNCTAD, *World Investment Directory* (2008), vol. X 'Africa'

The European market's importance has gradually been receding as the same European countries accounted for 66 per cent of Africa's export in 1960.

Table 20.1 Industrial distribution of inward FDI in selected African countries, selected years (% share in total)

Flows

SectorIndustry	Mauritania		Morocco		Mozambique		Tunisia	
	1999	2006	1996	2006	2001	2006	1995	2006
Total	100.0	100.0	100.0	100.0	100.0	100.0	100.0	100.0
Primary	38.4	1.0	8.3	0.5	2.4	62.2	80.4	21.7
Secondary	–	–	48.3	34.4	76.0	30.9	7.9	7.9
Tertiary	–	–	39.4	64.7	21.7	6.9	9.2	70.4
Unspecified	61.6	99.0	4.0	0.4	–	–	2.4	–
Memorandum								
Total ($ million)	15	155	327	2 964	255	154	323	3 308

Stock

SectorIndustry	Botswana		Madagascar		Morocco		South Africa		Swaziland		Uganda	
	1997	2005	2002	2006	2002	2006	1996	2006	2000	2006	2000	2003
Total	100.0	100.0	100.0	100.0	100.0	100.0	100.0	100.0	100.0	100.0	100.0	100.0
Primary	74.7	59.6	6.9	48.9	6.9	3.7	5.2	41.1	14.1	20.2	4.9	0.7
Secondary	6.0	3.2	13.2	22.8	22.6	30.6	40.1	27.0	70.5	62.0	36.0	26.6
Tertiary	18.7	36.8	79.2	28.3	60.9	59.7	54.7	31.9	12.1	17.8	56.5	64.6
Unspecified	0.6	0.5	0.7	–	9.6	5.9	–	–	3.4	–	2.7	8.0
Memorandum												
Total ($ million)	1 280	806	166	932	12 130	29 939	13 236	87 765	536	748	540	724

Source: UNCTAD, World Investment Directory (2008), vol. X 'Africa'.

The second largest export market for African products is North America, especially the United States. The importance of North America as an export market for African countries has grown considerably since 2002.

This is mainly as a result of increased sourcing of oil from Africa and the implementation of the US Africa Growth and Opportunity Act of 2000. The share of African exports going to North America was 24 per cent in 2006. Most significant, according to the report, was the rise of developing Asia as an important destination for African exports. The share of African exports going to developing countries in Asia had not exceeded 6 per cent between 1960 and 1992 but almost tripled between 1992 and 2006 to 16 per cent.[4]

20.2.2   Institutional context

Africa has an increasing awareness of the importance of international taxation and in particular transfer pricing. Some African countries have now established, or are establishing, specialist transfer pricing teams within their tax administrations to address transfer pricing risk in the country.

These transfer pricing teams are now starting to commence transfer pricing work in their respective countries. However, the capacity of these teams is still in many cases quite limited and further capacity building is needed is many African tax administrations.

Many African countries have started working together through the African Tax Administration Forum (ATAF) to share their experiences on different approaches to transfer pricing audits. The ATAF work is aimed at building transfer pricing capability and capacity in ATAF countries by developing an understanding of key transfer pricing issues and practices across the African continent. ATAF has set up a Transfer Pricing Working Group which will be developing plans and products to assist ATAF members to build their transfer pricing capacity. The work will enable African tax administrations to share practical experience on issues such as fact finding and audit techniques through the use of case studies.

---

[4] UNCTAD, *Economic Development in Africa, Export Performance Following Trade Liberalisation: Some Patterns and Policy Perspectives* (15 September 2008).

20.3   Transfer pricing regimes in Africa

Transfer pricing legislation is relatively new in Africa. One of the first countries to introduce transfer pricing legislation in Africa was Liberia which introduced legislation in 1977. Other African countries introduced legislation much later. For example, it was only introduced into South African law with effect from 1995[5] and in Kenya substantive transfer pricing rules were only introduced on 1 July 2006.[6] Egypt introduced transfer pricing rules effective under article 30 of Income Tax Law no. 91 in 2005.

Many African countries still do not have specific transfer pricing legislation but have general anti-abuse provisions which they use to deal with transfer pricing issues in their country.

20.3.1   South Africa

Since South Africa's re-emergence in the international market in the early 1990s there has been a marked expansion of international trade and commerce in the country. This has involved wide-ranging changes in the volume and complexity of international trade. An increasing proportion of that international activity is carried on between members of multinationals. As the globalisation of business activity continued to accelerate, protecting the South African tax base became increasingly vital to South Africa's wealth and development.

Exchange controls had historically provided some protection to South Africa against the more significant manipulation of transfer prices to transfer profits to lower tax jurisdictions. However, in anticipation of the relaxation of exchange controls and the envisaged adverse effect on the South African tax base, the Commission of Enquiry into Certain Aspects of the Tax Structure in South Africa (under the chairmanship of Prof. M. M. Katz) recommended in its first and second Interim Reports that transfer pricing provisions be introduced into the South African Income Tax Act 1962. Consequently, transfer pricing rules were introduced into the Income Tax Act in 1995.

The relevant legislation is at section 31 of the Income Tax Act and covers both transfer pricing and thin capitalisation measures. The transfer pricing rules adopt the arm's length principle which is an

---

[5] Income Tax Act no. 58 of 1962, s. 31.   [6] Income Tax Act, s. 18(3).

international standard for transfer pricing, determining that the price of cross-border transactions where any goods or services have been effected between connected persons will be examined by way of comparison to similar transactions by unrelated parties. The legislation states that the Commissioner may in determining the taxable income of either party to the transaction adjust the consideration in respect of the transaction to reflect the arm's length price for the goods or services. While cross-border transactions are within the scope of the transfer pricing rules, transactions between two South African residents are not within the scope of the legislation.

The South African transfer pricing rules apply to the cross-border supply of goods or services between connected persons. Goods are defined in the Act as including any corporeal movable thing, fixed property and any real right in any such thing or fixed property.

Services are also defined in the Act and include anything done or to be done, including:

(a) the granting, assignment, cession or surrender of any right, benefit or privilege;
(b) the making available of any facility or advantage;
(c) the granting of financial assistance, including a loan, advance or debt, and the provision of any security or guarantee;
(d) the performance of any work;
(e) an agreement of insurance; and
(f) the conferring of rights to or the use of incorporeal property.

The term 'connected person' is defined in section 1 of the Income Tax Act. Practice Note 7 sets out the definition and in relation to a company it means:

(i)   its holding company as defined in section 1 of the Companies Act 1973;
(ii)   its subsidiary as defined in section 1 of the Companies Act 1973;
(iii) any other company, where both companies are subsidiaries (as defined) of the same holding company;
(iv)   any person, other than a company as defined in section 1 of the Companies Act, who individually or jointly with any connected person in relation to such person, holds (directly or indirectly) at least 20 per cent of the company's equity share capital or voting rights. The person so contemplated could be a natural person, trust, close corporation or any entity which is not a company for the purposes of the Companies Act 1973;

(v)   any other company, if at least 20 per cent of the equity share capital of such company is held by such other company and no shareholder holds the majority voting rights of such company. This will be the case where companies B and C each hold 50 per cent of the equity share capital of company A, both companies B and C will be connected persons in relation to company A;

(vi) any other company, if such company is managed or controlled by any person (A) who or which is a connected person in relation to such company; or any person who or which is a connected person in relation to A.

Two companies will be connected persons in the event of one company being managed or controlled by a connected person in relation to the other company, as well as where the companies are managed or controlled by persons who are connected persons in relation to each other. For example, two companies, one whose shares are held by a trust and the other, whose shares are held by the beneficiary of such trust, will be connected persons in relation to each other.

In this context, references to a company in the definition are not limited to 'company' as defined in the Act.[7] Company also refers to entities which are companies or corporations according to the ordinary meaning of the word. For example, a company incorporated under the law of any country other than the Republic of South Africa, which does not carry on business in the Republic and which is not a shareholder of a South African company, could also be a connected person for the purposes of the application of the connected persons provisions.

The legislation applies to the supply of goods or services between the following:

(i)   a South African resident and any other person who is not a South African resident;

(ii)   a non-resident and a permanent establishment in South Africa of a non-resident; and

(iii) a South African resident and a permanent establishment outside of South Africa of a person who is resident in South Africa.

In all cases, the rule only applies where the persons are connected persons in relation to one another. However, it does not apply to a transaction between two South African residents whether or not they are connected.

---

[7] Income Tax Act no. 58 of 1962, s. 1.

Under section 64C(2)(e) of the Income Tax Act a transfer pricing adjustment under section 31 may be deemed to be a dividend on which secondary tax on companies is payable.

In addition, where there has been an underpayment of tax due to non-arm's length pricing the taxpayer may be liable to interest on the underpayment of tax under section 89 of the Income Tax Act and possibly penalties under section 76 if the underpayment of tax is due to an incorrect statement in its tax return. The penalty may be up to 200 per cent of the underpaid tax.

The South African Revenue Service (SARS) issues Practice Notes that provide guidance on their interpretation and application of the Income Tax Act. Practice Note 2 was published in May 1996 and deals with financial assistance provided by overseas connected parties to South African taxpayers. In August 1999, the SARS published Practice Note 7 which deals with transfer pricing. The objective of Practice Note 7 is to provide taxpayers with guidelines about the procedures to be followed in the determination of arm's length prices, taking into account the South African business environment. It also sets out the Commissioner's views on practical issues such as documentation that are relevant in setting and reviewing transfer prices.

The Practice Note has been drafted as a practical guide and is not intended to be a prescriptive or exhaustive discussion of every transfer pricing issue that might arise. The Note states that SARS decides each case on its own merits, taking into account the taxpayer's business strategy and commercial judgement.

In 2010, South Africa made changes to its transfer pricing legislation. The new legislation widens the scope of the legislation and is more closely aligned to the wording of Article 9 of the OECD Model Tax Convention.

It applies where any transaction, operation, scheme agreement or understanding has been directly or indirectly entered into or effected between or for the benefit of either or both:

(i)   a person that is a resident, and any other person that is not a resident;

(ii)   a person that is not a resident, and any other person that is not a resident that has a permanent establishment in South Africa to which the transaction, operation, scheme, agreement or understanding relates;

(iii) a person that is a resident, and any other person that is a resident that has a permanent establishment outside of South Africa to which the transaction, operation, scheme, agreement or understanding relates, and those persons are connected persons in relation to one another, and any term or condition of that transaction, operation, scheme, agreement or understanding is different from any term or condition that would have existed had those persons been independent persons dealing at arm's length; and results or will result in any tax benefit being derived by any person that is a party to that transaction, operation, scheme, agreement or understanding.

In those circumstances, the taxable income of each party to that transaction, operation, scheme, agreement or understanding that derives the tax benefit must be calculated as if that transaction, operation, scheme, agreement or understanding had been entered into on the terms and conditions that would have existed had those persons been independent persons dealing at arm's length.

20.3.2 Kenya

Kenya's transfer pricing rules are set out in section 18(3) of the Income Tax Act (ITA). These empower the Kenya Revenue Authority (KRA) Commissioner to adjust the profits accruing to a resident from a course of business conducted with related non-resident persons to reflect such profit as would have accrued if the course of business had been conducted by independent persons dealing at arm's length. This provides the KRA Commissioner with the statutory authority to adjust the transfer price in international transactions between connected parties to reflect an arm's length price. For the purposes of section 18(3) of the ITA and with specific reference to companies, a company is related to another company if:

(a) it participates directly or indirectly in the management, control or capital of the business of the other; and
(b) a third person participates directly or indirectly in the management, control or capital of the business of both of them.

Section 18(8) of the ITA makes provision for the issuance of guidelines for the determination of an arm's length value of a transaction for the purposes of section 18 and for the specification of such further requirements as the Minister may consider necessary for the better carrying out of the provisions of the section.

Such guidelines have been issued by the Minister in the form of the Income Tax (Transfer Pricing) Rules, 2006 ('TP Rules'). The stated purpose of the TP Rules is to provide guidelines to be applied by related enterprises in determining the arm's length prices of goods and services in transactions involving them and to provide administrative regulations, including the types of records and documentation to be submitted to the KRA Commissioner by a person involved in transfer pricing arrangements.

Rule 6 lists the transactions which may be subject to adjustment of prices under the TP Rules to include:

- the sale and purchase of goods;
- the sale, purchase or lease of tangible assets;
- the transfer, purchase or use of intangible assets;
- the provision of services;
- the lending or borrowing of money; and
- any other transactions which may affect the profit or loss of the enterprise involved.

Rule 10 of the TP Rules requires a person applying arm's length pricing to develop an appropriate transfer pricing policy, to determine the arm's length price in accordance with the guidelines provided in the TP Rules and to provide documentation evidencing their analysis upon request by the Commissioner. In addition to the requirements set out in rule 10, rule 9(1) gives the Commissioner powers to request information, including documents relating to transactions where transfer pricing is applied.

20.3.3   Tanzania

Tanzania introduced transfer pricing legislation in its Income Tax Act 1973. However, the legislation only applied to transactions with a non-resident. The new Income Tax Act (ITA) 2004 introduced transfer pricing rules that apply to transactions with either a resident or a non-resident.

Section 33 of the ITA 2004 requires that any arrangement between associates must be conducted at arm's length, and where the Tanzania Revenue Authority (TRA) Commissioner considers a taxpayer has failed to meet this standard, he has the authority to make adjustments to the pricing or recharacterise any amount. The Act does not specify any particular methodology for determining what constitutes an arm's length price.

The TRA has stated that it will apply internationally agreed arm's length principles as set out in the UN and OECD Transfer Pricing Guidelines. Furthermore, the TRA has indicated that it will follow the ruling in the Kenyan tax case on transfer pricing (*Unilever Kenya Ltd*, referred to in section 20.5.2 below), which applied the OECD transfer pricing principles.

In addition to section 33, the general deductibility section within the ITA 2004, section 11, provides that expenditure must be incurred wholly and exclusively in the production of income from the business. The deductibility of an expense may therefore be challenged under this section if, for example, the amount is considered to be excessive or unsupported by suitable evidence.

20.3.4   Algeria

In Algeria, articles 141*bis* (enacted by the Finance Act 2007) and 189 of the Direct Tax Code contain general provisions concerning intra-group transactions and the means by which they may be audited by the tax authorities.

Amendments were made in the Finance Act 2008 that extended the scope of the transfer pricing audit guidelines to include associated Algerian enterprises. The tax administration's authority to audit transfer prices in Algeria, therefore, is no longer limited to cross-border intra-group transactions but also covers domestic transfer pricing.

20.3.5   Tunisia

Tunisia does not have any specific transfer pricing rules in its General Tax Code. However, when carrying out tax audits, the Tunisian tax administration relies on other grounds, such as the 'abnormal act of management' doctrine, to audit transfer prices.

In some instances, an 'abnormal act of management' has been defined as any action that places the burden of an expense (or loss) on the taxpayer or that deprives the taxpayer of income without justification or proof that the action was in the interest of the taxpayer's commercial operations. Under this definition, such an act could be one that is conducted in the interest of a third party or that only provides the taxpayer with a negligible interest, one that is out of proportion with the advantage that a third party would receive from it.

20.3.6   Cameroon

In Cameroon, article L19*bis* of the Tax Procedure Code (enacted by the Finance Act 2006) provides that when the tax administration obtains evidence during the course of a tax audit which supports a presumption that the taxpayer transferred profits within the meaning of article 19 of the Code, the tax authorities may request the taxpayer to provide information and documents showing:

(a) the nature of the relationship between the companies in question;
(b) the pricing method used for the transactions in question;
(c) the activities performed by the associated companies; and
(d) the tax treatment applicable to the transactions carried out by companies located outside of Cameroon.

20.3.7 Namibia

Namibia introduced transfer pricing legislation on 14 May 2005. The legislation in section 95A to the Namibian Income Tax Act enforces the arm's length principle in cross-border transactions carried out between connected persons. During September 2006, the Directorate of Inland Revenue issued Practice Note 2 of 2006 (PN 2/2006) containing guidance on the application of the transfer pricing legislation.

Section 95A of the Namibian Income Tax Act (ITA) is essentially aimed at ensuring that cross-border transactions by companies operating in a multinational enterprise are fairly priced and that profits are not stripped out of Namibia and taxed in other tax jurisdictions. Section 95A achieves this by giving the Minister of Finance (who essentially delegates to the Directorate of Inland Revenue) the power to adjust any non-market-related prices charged or paid by Namibian entities in cross-border transactions with related parties to arm's length prices and to tax the Namibian entity as if the transactions had been carried out at market-related prices.

PN 2/2006 was issued during September 2006. The objective of this Practice Note is to provide taxpayers with guidelines about the procedures to be followed in the determination of arm's length prices, taking into account the Namibian business environment. It also sets out the Minister's views on documentation and other practical issues that are relevant in setting and reviewing transfer pricing in international agreements.

The Practice Note includes definitions for the following terms which were not initially defined in section 95A of the ITA:

- advance pricing arrangement;
- connected person;
- controlled transaction;
- uncontrolled transaction;

- multinational;
- OECD Guidelines;
- transfer prices.

The Practice Note is based on and acknowledges the principles of the OECD Guidelines. Nothing in the Practice Note is intended to be contradictory to the OECD Guidelines and in cases where there is conflict, the provisions of the Guidelines will prevail in resolving any dispute. Any amendments made to the OECD Guidelines will be deemed to be incorporated into the Practice Note.

A 'connected person' is defined in PN 2/2006. In relation to a company, the following are regarded as 'connected persons':

(i) its holding company;
(ii) its subsidiary;
(iii) any other company, where both such companies are subsidiaries of the same holding company;
(iv) any person, who individually or jointly with any connected person in relation to such person, holds (directly or indirectly) at least 20 per cent of the company's equity share capital or voting rights;
(v) any other company, if at least 20 per cent of the equity share capital of such company is held by such other company, and no shareholder holds the majority voting rights of such company; and
(vi) any other company, if such other company is managed or controlled by:
    (a) any person who or which is a connected person in relation to such company; or
    (b) any person who or which is a connected person in relation to such company.

Even though it is accepted that section 95A by definition can only apply between separate legal entities, the contents of the Practice Note will also apply to transactions between a person's head office with the branch of such person or a person's branch with another branch of such person. The OECD Guidelines' interpretation of arm's length will be followed in the application of the Practice Note.

20.3.8 Zambia

Transfer pricing legislation was first introduced in Zambia in 1999 and was subsequently amended in 2001 and 2002, respectively. The transfer pricing provisions for Zambia are contained in sections 97A to

97D of the Zambia Income Tax Act 1966 (ITA) and the Transfer Pricing Regulations, 2000 ('Regulations'). The Income Tax (Transfer Pricing) Regulations 2000 provide definitions regarding the extent of application of the transfer pricing provisions contained in the ITA. In March 2005, a draft Practice Note was issued by the Zambia Revenue Authority (ZRA) which provides detail on how the ZRA would apply the transfer pricing rules.

Zambia does not tax on a worldwide basis, and the legislation aims to counter tax losses brought about by non-arm's length pricing. Furthermore, the transfer pricing legislation only applies in situations where the effect of the associated party pricing is to understate Zambian profit or overstate Zambian losses.

Zambia's transfer pricing policy does not only apply to cross-border transactions but also to transactions between Zambian taxpayer residents who are wholly and solely within the Zambian tax jurisdiction (i.e., domestic transactions). This ensures losses are not effectively shifted between taxpayers or between sources by applying non-arm's length pricing. In addition, the transfer pricing legislation applies to partnerships and individuals as well as companies.

Section 97A(2) of the Zambia ITA states that the provisions relating to transfer pricing apply 'where actual conditions [have been] imposed instead of the arm's length conditions [and] there is, except for this section, a reduction in the amount of income taken into account in computing the income of one of the associated persons referred to in subsection (1), in this section referred to as the first taxpayer, chargeable to tax for a charge year, in this section referred to as the income year'.

The phrase 'actual conditions' is defined in section 97A(1) of the ITA as 'conditions made or imposed between any two associated persons in their commercial or financial relations'.

'Associated persons' is defined in section 97(C) of the ITA. The section states that one person associates with another if:

(a) one participates directly or indirectly in the management, control or capital of the other; or
(b) the same persons participate directly or indirectly in the management, control or capital of both of them.

The Zambia draft Practice Note states that in relation to a body corporate one participates directly in the management, control or capital of the body corporate if they have 'control' over the body corporate.

'Control' means the power of a person to secure that the affairs of the body corporate are conducted in accordance with the wishes of that person. Such power would be derived from shareholding or other powers conferred by the constitutional documents of the body corporate.

The draft Practice Note states that a person indirectly participates in a second person corporate if the first person would be a direct participant ('potential participant') due to:

(a) rights and powers which the potential participant, at a future date, is entitled to acquire or will become entitled to acquire;
(b) rights and powers that are, or may be required, to be exercised on behalf of, under the direction of, or for the benefit of the potential participant;
(c) where a loan has been made by one person to another, not confined to rights and powers conferred in relation to the property of the borrower by the terms of any security relating to the loan;
(d) rights and powers of any person with whom the potential participant is connected;
(e) rights and powers which would be attributed to another person with whom the potential participant is connected if that person were himself the potential participant.

The draft Practice Note further includes in its definition of 'indirect participation' joint ventures that are able to use non arm's length prices to shift profits overseas for their mutual benefit. The rules only apply to transactions between at least one of the joint venture parties ('major participant') and the joint venture itself and not between two joint ventures themselves unless they are under common control.

The draft Practice Note states that although sections 97A–97D of the ITA are inapplicable to transactions between branches and their head offices, the provisions are applicable to transactions between a Zambian branch of an overseas head office and associated companies of the overseas head office (wherever resident) or overseas branches of a Zambian head office and a person associated to the Zambian head office, wherever located. Section 97C(3) of the ITA states that conditions are taken to be imposed either by an arrangement or series of arrangements, or agreement or series of agreements. The definition includes:

(a) transactions, understandings and mutual practices; and
(b) an arrangement or agreement whether or not it is intended to be legally enforceable.

Further the arrangement or agreement or series of arrangements or agreements may not have to take place between two related parties, e.g., 'thinly capitalised' taxpayers paying interest to third parties under finance arrangements guaranteed by associates.

20.4   Current implementation of the arm's length principle

20.4.1   Procedural mechanisms: selection of cases for audit

South Africa

In South Africa, the tax officer in the South African Revenue Service (SARS) will review the income tax return provided by the taxpayer and if the officer identifies a potential transfer pricing risk the case will be referred to a transfer pricing auditor in the SARS Transfer Pricing Unit. The transfer pricing auditor will carry out an initial risk review. The objective of the initial risk review is to assess the level of the potential transfer pricing risk. This involves reviewing the existing information that is available to the SARS, for example, financial statements, the income tax return and information that is in the public domain. The transfer pricing auditor may decide to issue a standard questionnaire to the taxpayer for their completion. The main focus of the questionnaire is to identify the quantum and nature of the controlled transactions and the likely tax position of the other party to the transaction. The review will also aim to assess the outcome of the transactions and whether those outcomes look commercial within the context of the industry within which the entity operates.

The transfer pricing auditor will present his or her findings to a panel who will determine whether there is a material transfer pricing risk. If there is a material risk the enquiry will proceed to the next stage, called a transfer pricing record review. The panel will consist of senior members of the SARS Transfer Pricing Unit.

In the transfer pricing record review, the transfer pricing auditor will request the transfer pricing policy document from the taxpayer, if one exists. Following the transfer pricing auditor's review of the document, the auditor will present his or her further findings to the panel who will decide whether to take the matter up for a transfer pricing audit.

If the matter is audited, the transfer pricing auditor will issue a Letter of Findings once they have finished their fact finding and reviews. The Letter of Findings will set out their findings and conclusion on the matter. Subsequent to the Letter of Findings, if the SARS considers a transfer pricing adjustment is needed an assessment will be made for the additional tax. The taxpayer may object to the assessment and the matter may then go into settlement or alternative dispute resolution. If resolution cannot be reached between the SARS and the taxpayer, the matter will result in litigation.

Egypt

In Egypt, tax audits are generally carried out through a risk-based sampling process. Case selection is done electronically based on specific criteria. For transfer pricing audits the Egyptian Tax Authority (ETA) will assign a taxpayer a low risk rating if the taxpayer prepares and maintains adequate documentation demonstrating how its transfer prices have been determined.

By contrast, taxpayers giving inadequate consideration to their transfer pricing practices will be assigned a high tax risk rating. Taking into consideration that taxpayers with a high perceived risk are more likely to be audited by the ETA than those perceived to have a low risk, the ETA considers it to be in taxpayers' best interest to prepare and maintain adequate documentation demonstrating their compliance with the arm's length principle.

20.4.2   Africa's tax treaties

Many African countries are now starting to build a network of tax treaties. South Africa currently has eighteen treaties which have been ratified and are in effect with other African countries, and fifty treaties which have been ratified and are in effect with countries in the rest of the world. Other African countries are increasing the number of treaties they have in place. For example Mauritius has thirty-five in force, two for ratification, five for signature and eleven in negotiation. Most African countries base their treaties on either the OECD Model Convention on Income and on Capital or on the United Nations model. In some cases, the treaties are a blend of the two models. This is the case, for example, in Nigeria which also blends the models with its own national model.

South Africa embodies within its tax treaties the principles of both Articles 7 and 9 of the OECD Model Tax Convention on Income and on Capital. Article 7 provides, *inter alia*, for the attribution of profits to a permanent establishment of an enterprise. Article 9 of the OECD Model Tax Convention stipulates that the arm's length principle should be applied to commercial and financial relations between associated companies residing in the contracting states. In its Practice Note, SARS states that it is the view of the Commissioner that there is no inconsistency between the South African domestic law on transfer pricing and the tax treaties, as both embody the arm's length principle.

Under the OECD Model Convention,[8] Article 9(1) provides that the taxation authorities of a contracting state may, for the purposes of calculating tax liabilities of associated enterprises, tax profits which have not accrued in that state but would have accrued if the associated enterprises had been independent enterprises.

Article 9(2) provides that in these circumstances where this leads to economic double taxation, the other state will make an appropriate adjustment so as to relieve the double taxation. Most of South Africa's treaties contain both paragraph (1) and (2) of Article 9 of the Model Tax Convention. However, South Africa does have some treaties which were entered into before the introduction of Article 9(2) into the Model Treaty and no equivalent to Article 9(2) exists in such treaties. For example, this is the case in the South Africa Treaty with Germany which entered into force on 28 February 1975. The equivalent of Article 9(1) is at Article 5 of that Treaty.

Most African countries are including the transfer pricing provisions of the OECD Model Convention in their treaties which they have negotiated or are in the process of negotiating. Under the 'Associated Enterprises' provision of the model, this means African countries may recompute the profits of an enterprise of that country from its business with a related enterprise in another contracting state if those profits differ from the profits that would have accrued between independent enterprises.

20.4.3   Interaction of tax treaties and domestic tax law

One of the key questions arising in jurisprudence on international tax is the applicability of tax treaties *vis-à-vis* the domestic tax laws. In South Africa, section 108 of the Income Tax Act states that as soon as may be after the approval by Parliament of any agreement between the Republic of South Africa and the government of another country for the prevention or relief from double taxation, the arrangements must be notified by publication in the *Government Gazette* and the arrangements so notified will thereupon have effect as if enacted in the Income Tax Act.

---

[8] OECD Model Tax Convention on Income and on Capital.

20.4.4 *Need for change*

With the increased globalisation of business and the increase in intra-group cross-border transactions transfer pricing is an area of increasing risk to the tax base of all countries but particularly to developing countries, including African countries. This is leading to many African tax administrations giving more focus to transfer pricing issues and to considering bringing in transfer pricing legislation or changes to their existing transfer pricing legislation.

The Christian Aid Report in March 2009 titled *False Profits: Robbing the Poor to Keep the Rich Tax Free* alleged that 'goods from the industrial world are sold to developing countries at hugely inflated prices to enable the company that is the buyer to shift large amounts of capital abroad whilst reducing the company profit margin and minimising its tax liability'. The report refers to this and other practices as 'trade mispricing'.

African countries are working together through the ATAF[9] to tackle the risk arising from transfer pricing. ATAF was formed with the aim of promoting efficient, effective and economic tax administration to foster economic growth and improved service delivery for the improvement of living standards of people living in Africa. ATAF was inspired by the deliberations at the International Conference on Taxation, State Building and Capacity Development in Africa held in Pretoria, South Africa, from 28–29 August 2008. Commissioners, senior tax administrators and policy-makers from twenty-eight African countries resolved to work towards the establishment of ATAF.

ATAF has quickly recognised the importance of transfer pricing and this was demonstrated when its first technical event was on the issue of 'Implementation of Transfer Pricing' which was held in July 2009 in Uganda. In 2011, the ATAF Transfer Pricing Working Group was formed and it is planning to develop plans and products that will assist ATAF members to increase their transfer pricing capacity and capability.

The challenges faced by many African countries are not only in terms of bringing in legislative reforms but also in building the capability and capacity in their tax administrations to effectively implement their transfer pricing rules and address the transfer pricing risks faced in the country. The products developed by the ATAF Transfer Pricing Working Group will therefore include guidance on drafting transfer pricing and

---

[9] See www.sars.gov.za/home.asp?pid=10421.

thin capitalisation legislation, guidance on identifying transfer pricing risk and facilitating the sharing of knowledge and best practice in transfer pricing.

The South African tax administration has had a centralised team of transfer pricing specialists for a number of years. The team is located in SARS Large Business Centre which deals with all of the tax issues of the largest businesses in South Africa. The team advises SARS tax auditors on all transfer pricing issues and works with the tax auditors on all transfer pricing audits.

There are currently eleven people in the transfer pricing team and most of the team have worked in commercial transfer pricing practices before joining the SARS. The SARS is aiming to increase these resources substantially in the near future.

The Egyptian Tax Authority (ETA) recently established a centralised group in charge of international taxation affairs, including transfer pricing. The group is responsible for introducing transfer pricing guidelines. In addition, the central group will monitor the transfer pricing implementation process, including transfer pricing reviews. Transfer pricing audits will be performed by the tax offices under the supervision of the centralised group.

There are ten members in the centralised group. This level of resourcing is expected to increase based on the expected workload. In terms of background, 70 per cent of the resources are accountants, 20 per cent are economists, and the rest are lawyers. A training plan has been prepared to enhance tax auditors' transfer pricing capabilities. Therefore, a significant change is expected over the coming years in the background of these resources.

In Kenya, the Domestic Taxes Department within the KRA is responsible for conducting corporate tax enquiries and at present there is not a specialist unit for conducting transfer pricing audits. However, investment has been made in developing specialist expertise within the KRA through training both locally and abroad.

The position is similar in Tanzania where there is not currently a dedicated transfer pricing unit within the TRA. Transfer pricing issues are handled by the Large Taxpayers Department or Domestic Revenue Department as part of the normal process of reviewing a taxpayer's income tax affairs.

This is also the case in Zambia where the Domestic Taxes Department within the ZRA is responsible for conducting corporate tax enquiries and as yet there is not a specialist unit for conducting transfer pricing audits. However, investment has been made in developing specialist expertise within the ZRA through training both locally and abroad (i.e., in the United Kingdom, Australia and South Africa).

In Namibia, the Ministry of Finance is still in the process of setting up a special unit that will specifically deal with transfer pricing. Support and assistance is being provided to the Ministry of Finance by the OECD and the SARS.

On the legislative issues, most African countries base their legislation for dealing with transfer pricing risk on the arm's length principle. This is the case whether it is specific transfer pricing legislation or anti-avoidance legislation. For example, Liberia and Mauritius both have specific transfer pricing legislation which is based on the arm's length principle. Uganda and Botswana use anti-avoidance legislation to address transfer pricing risk but their anti-avoidance provisions are based on the arm's length principle.

However, some African countries consider that because their anti-avoidance rules are not specific to transfer pricing they may not be entirely effective in dealing with transfer pricing risk and bringing in specific transfer pricing rules would increase the tax administration's effectiveness in dealing with transfer pricing issues.

In its Tax Law Amendment Bill 2010,[10] South Africa proposes to amend its legislation for both transfer pricing and thin capitalisation purposes. The changes to its legislation will bring its law more in alignment with the wording of Article 9 of the Model Tax Convention. The law will move away from simply adjusting the pricing of a transaction to a rule which states that if the actual terms and conditions of a transaction differ from the terms and conditions that would have arisen if the parties had been independent enterprises and this leads to a South African tax benefit for one of the parties to the transaction, then the taxable income of that party is to be determined based on the profits that would have arisen if the arm's length terms and conditions had been entered into by the parties. The new rules will look at not only cross-border transactions entered into by the connected persons but also cross-border operations, schemes, agreements or understandings entered into by connected persons.

Changes to the thin capitalisation rules will move South Africa away from considering whether the financial assistance provided by

[10] Tax Law Amendment Bill 2010, clause 53.

connected persons is excessive in relation to the South African resident's fixed capital to determining the taxable income based on the terms and conditions that would have existed if the parties to the loan, etc., had been independent enterprises. This means looking at the level of financial assistance the South African taxpayer could and would have borrowed at arm's length.

20.4.5   Implementation of the arm's length principle

In South Africa, Practice Note 7 published by the SARS states that the first and overriding principle for determining the transfer price is that transactions between connected persons are to be conducted at arm's length. This simply means that the transactions should have the substantive financial characteristics of a transaction between independent parties where each party will strive to get the utmost benefit from the transaction.

South Africa has adopted the arm's length principle which is the international norm and the SARS Commissioner is of the opinion that application of this internationally accepted principle will minimise the potential for double taxation.

The Practice Note recognises that transfer pricing is not an exact science and that the application of the most appropriate method or methods will often result in a range of justifiable transfer prices. The Practice Note also recognises that a high level of comparability is required in order to apply one of the traditional transaction methods (comparable uncontrolled price (CUP), cost plus and resale price methods). The Note accepts that when using these methods, an outcome that falls within a properly constructed arm's length range should be regarded as being arm's length if the data used to construct the arm's length range is truly comparable. However, if the transaction falls outside the arm's length range it is a matter of judgement as to where in the range the adjustment should be affected. The Commissioner concurs with the view of the OECD that the adjustment should reflect the point in the range that best accounts for the facts and circumstances of the controlled transaction. However, in the absence of persuasive evidence for the selection of a particular point in the range, the Commissioner may select the mid-point in the range.

The Practice Note states that when applying methods other than a traditional transaction method the approximations used in applying these other methods which rely on broader measures of comparability can result in extensive ranges, some of which may not be sufficiently accurate to permit the general statement that any point in the range may be regarded as arm's length.

20.4.6 Tested party

When determining the party to be evaluated in a controlled transaction from a South African perspective, the focus should be primarily on the functions performed by the South African member, as the basis for determining and applying an appropriate pricing method.

However, there may be instances where based on a taxpayer's circumstances and the information available it would be appropriate for the foreign party to a transaction to be evaluated in determining the most reliable measure of the arm's length price. This would be the case where the foreign party does not own any intangible property or does not perform any unique functions.

However, the Commissioner generally prefers using the South African party as the party to be evaluated in appraising whether a taxpayer's transfer prices are at arm's length. It is therefore important that if a South African taxpayer uses a foreign party as the party to be evaluated, the price determined is also considered in relation to the South African operations, to ensure that it results in an appropriate return for those operations.

20.4.7 Principles of comparability

South Africa considers that comparability is fundamental to the application of the arm's length principle. It considers that the preferred arm's length methods are based on the concept of comparing the prices/margins achieved by connected persons in their dealings to those achieved by independent entities for the same or similar dealings. In order for such comparisons to be useful, the economically relevant characteristics of the situations being compared must be highly comparable.

To be comparable means that none of the differences (if any) between the situations being compared could materially affect the condition being examined in the method (e.g., price or margin) or that reasonably accurate adjustments can be made to eliminate the effect of such differences. If suitable adjustments cannot be made, then the dealings cannot be considered comparable.

The SARS Practice Note 7 states that the assessment of comparability can be affected, *inter alia*, by:

(a) the characteristics of goods and services;
(b) the relative importance of functions performed;
(c) the terms and conditions of relevant agreements;
(d) the relative risk assumed by the taxpayer, connected enterprise and any independent party where such party is considered as a possible comparable;
(e) economic and market conditions; and
(f) business strategies.

However, South Africa and other African countries experience significant difficulties in obtaining information on uncontrolled transactions in their own countries. The SARS Commissioner recognises those difficulties and at paragraph 11.2 of the SARS Practice Note 7 states that the Commissioner will accept the use of foreign country comparables (e.g., data from the Australian, UK and US markets) in taxpayers' transfer pricing analyses. However, taxpayers using such comparables would be expected to assess the expected impact of geographic differences and other factors on the price.

Thus, the Practice Note cautions that while foreign comparables might be useful, taxpayers will need to exercise caution to ensure that appropriate adjustments reflect differences between the South African and foreign markets.

The same difficulties are faced in Kenya over the search for comparables in the local market and the KRA has confirmed that it will accept the use of financial databases used elsewhere in the world, and specifically Amadeus/Orbis, provided justification for their use, such as the absence of information on local comparables, is provided.

For similar reasons, the Zambia draft Practice Note states that the ZRA will accept the use of foreign comparables, such as data from the UK, US and Australian markets. However, taxpayers using this approach are required to adjust for the expected effect on the price due to geographic and other differences in the Zambian market.

20.4.8 *Acceptable methods for determining an arm's length price*

In South Africa, neither the transfer pricing legislation nor the tax treaties entered into by South Africa prescribe any particular methodology for the purpose of ascertaining an arm's length price. Given there is no prescribed legislative preference, the SARS Practice Note sets out the methods the Commissioner would generally seek to use to determine the arms' length price.

The Note states that the most appropriate method in a given case will depend on the facts and circumstances of the case and the extent and reliability of data on which to base a comparability analysis. It should always be the intention to select the method that produces the highest degree of comparability.

The SARS Commissioner endorses the standard transfer pricing methods of comparable uncontrolled price (CUP), resale price method (RPM), cost plus, transactional net margin method (TNMM) and profit split method as acceptable transfer pricing methods. The most appropriate method will depend on the particular situation and the availability of reliable data to enable its proper application.

The South African transfer pricing rules do not impose a hierarchy on the transfer pricing methods. The Commissioner acknowledges in the Practice Note that the suitability and reliability of a method will depend on the facts and circumstances of each case. The most reliable method will be the one that requires fewer and more reliable adjustments. However, as a general rule the traditional transaction methods are preferred. Of these methods the CUP method is preferred as it looks directly to the product or service transferred and is relatively insensitive to the specific functions which are performed by the entities being compared.

20.4.9 Reporting and documentation requirements

Annual tax return

In South Africa, a taxpayer is required to address specific transfer pricing questions when filing its income tax return (IT14). The taxpayer is required to report whether it entered into any cross-border transactions with connected persons. It is also required to report in its tax return whether it has provided goods or services or anything of value (including transactions on capital account) to a non-resident connected person for no consideration.

In Kenya, for financial years ending on or after 31 December 1999, companies are required to disclose all transactions with related parties under International Accounting Standard (IAS) 24. The wide definition of related parties in IAS 24 ensures that financial statements prepared in accordance with IFRS will provide the KRA with information concerning related party transactions and this will likely be the starting point for KRA enquiries into transfer pricing.

Documentation requirements

South Africa South African transfer pricing rules set no explicit requirement on taxpayers to prepare and maintain transfer pricing documentation. However, under section 74 and section 74A of the Income Tax Act the Commissioner may require that a taxpayer furnishes such information, documents or things as the Commissioner requires for the administration of the Income Tax Act.

The SARS may require detailed transfer pricing documentation to be provided within seven days from the date of request, although in practice a longer period of time may be given to provide the information. In the Practice Note, the SARS states that it considers it is in the taxpayers' best interest to document how transfer prices have been determined.

In addition, the South African income tax return requires taxpayers to supply specific information regarding transactions entered into between connected persons. It will be difficult for a taxpayer to comply with these requirements if the taxpayer has not addressed the question of whether its dealings comply with the arm's length principle.

The Practice Note sets out documentation guidelines that broadly follow Chapter V of the OECD Guidelines.[11] According to paragraph 5.4 of the OECD Guidelines, the taxpayer's process of considering whether transfer pricing is appropriate for tax purposes should be determined in accordance with the same prudent business management principles that would govern the process of evaluating a business decision of a similar level of complexity and importance. The Commissioner would expect taxpayers to have created, referred and retained documentation in accordance with this principle.

As a general rule the Commissioner considers that taxpayers should contemporaneously document the process they have followed and their analysis in determining transfer prices in their efforts to comply with the arm's length principle. The Commissioner will rely as much as possible on documentation that should be created in the ordinary course of business and in setting a transfer price.

---

[11] *OECD Transfer Pricing Guidelines for Multinational Enterprises and Tax Administrations.*

Taxpayers may be asked to provide the Commissioner with relevant documentation created when the cross-border transaction was contemplated and at the time when the transaction was entered into.

Taxpayers under investigation would be expected to provide relevant documents, explanatory material and other information to which the company has access or could reasonably be expected to have access. The nature of documentation likely to be sought includes relevant transfer pricing policies, product profitabilities, relevant market information (such as sales forecasts and market characteristics), the profit contributions of each party and an analysis of the functions, assets, skills and the degree and nature of the risks involved for the parties.

Kenya In Kenya, the Transfer Pricing Rules do not make it a statutory requirement for taxpayers to complete transfer pricing documentation. However, rule 9(1) gives the Commissioner permission to request information, including documents relating to the transactions where the transfer pricing issues arise, and a non-comprehensive list of the documents which the Commissioner may request is provided in rule 9(2). Rule 10 similarly requires a taxpayer who avers the application of arm's length pricing to provide documentation evidencing the taxpayer's analysis upon request by the Commissioner. The requirement for taxpayers to complete transfer pricing documentation is therefore implied in the Rules and it is in the taxpayers' best interest to complete and maintain such documentation.

The documents which the Commissioner may request are required to be prepared in or to be translated into English and include documents relating to:

- the selection of the transfer pricing method and the reasons for the selection;
- the application of the method, including the calculations made and price adjustment factors considered;
- the global organisation structure of the enterprise;
- the details of the transactions under consideration;
- the assumptions, strategies and policies applied in selecting the method; and
- such other background information as may be necessary regarding the transaction.

The effect of the above express and implied statutory requirements is to place the burden of proving that prices are arm's length on the taxpayer. A taxpayer who fails to provide transfer pricing documentation to support the arm's length nature of its prices is therefore at risk that the KRA will conduct a transfer pricing audit and examine its transfer pricing policies in detail. In the event that the KRA, as a result of the examination, adjusts the transfer price adopted by the taxpayer, the lack of adequate documentation may make it difficult for the taxpayer to rebut the adjustment.

Tanzania   Tanzania has no explicit requirement in the legislation for the taxpayer to prepare transfer pricing documentation, although section 33 of the ITA 2004 does require that the persons who are involved in the relevant transaction should 'quantify, apportion and allocate amounts to be included or deducted in calculating income between the persons as is necessary to reflect the total income or tax payable that would have arisen for them if the arrangement has been conducted at arm's length'. This indicates that adequate documentation must be available to support the pricing of transactions between associates.

Morocco   In Morocco, the Finance Act 2009 includes a provision that authorises the tax authorities to require Moroccan companies that conduct transactions with related non-Moroccan companies to provide certain transfer pricing information and documentation, including:

. the nature of the relationship between the two companies;
. the type of service rendered;
. the pricing method used; and
. the tax treatment applicable to the non-Moroccan company.

Under this provision, Moroccan companies involved in intra-group transactions must be able to produce, at the tax administration's request, complete transfer pricing documentation within a thirty-day period after the request. Failure to comply with the transfer pricing documentation production request allows the Moroccan tax administration to make a tax reassessment on transfer pricing grounds.

Zambia   In Zambia, the draft Practice Note states that the following records should be kept to avoid exposure to penalties:

(a) primary accounting records;
(b) tax adjustment records; and
(c) records of transactions with associated businesses.

Namibia   In Namibia, the Practice Note states that a taxpayer is required to be in possession of transfer pricing documentation. If the Minister, as a result of this examination, substitutes an alternative arm's length amount for the one adopted by the taxpayer, the lack of adequate documentation may make it difficult for the taxpayer to rebut that substitution.

The Practice Note expressly states that a taxpayer needs to demonstrate that it has developed a sound transfer pricing policy in terms of which transfer prices are determined in accordance with the arm's length principle by documenting the policies and procedures for determining those prices. There is currently no statutory requirement that the transfer pricing policy should be submitted to the Directorate of Inland Revenue as part of the annual income tax return. Taxpayers are thus merely required to prepare and maintain a transfer pricing policy and present it as a motivation for the prices adopted in international transactions in the event that the Inland Revenue conducts a transfer pricing audit. Practice Note 2/2006 states that in the event that the taxpayer cannot present a transfer pricing policy, it will be very difficult for the taxpayer to successfully object against any transfer pricing adjustments made and corresponding assessments issued by the Directorate of Inland Revenue.

20.4.10   Assessing procedures

In South Africa, the tax officer can address transfer pricing issues when reviewing the taxpayer's annual tax returns. The Commissioner may decide that an adjustment is needed to the consideration in respect of the transaction to reflect an arm's length price for the goods or services. The assessment to make this adjustment to the taxable income of the taxpayer must be made within three years of the date of the assessment in which the transfer pricing adjustment should have been assessed to tax.[12] However, if the Commissioner is satisfied that the amount that should have been assessed was not assessed due to fraud or misrepresentation or non-disclosure of material facts, then the Commissioner may make an assessment after this three-year period.

20.5   Transfer pricing disputes: domestic approaches

20.5.1   Burden of proof

Under the South African transfer pricing rules, the discretion to adjust the consideration in respect of a transaction lies with the Commissioner. The Practice Note states that in discharging its burden of proof it is clearly in a taxpayer's best interest to:

---

[12] Income Tax Act no. 58 of 1962, s. 76.

- develop an appropriate transfer pricing policy;
- determine the arm's length amount as required by section 31 of the ITA;
- voluntarily produce documents to evidence their analysis.

Section 82 of the ITA places the burden of proof regarding exemptions, non-liability for tax, deductions and set-offs on the taxpayer.

The 2010 changes to the South African transfer pricing legislation will place the burden of proof on the taxpayer to calculate their taxable income based on the profits that would have arisen to the South African taxpayer if arm's length terms and conditions had been applied in the transaction.

In Tanzania, under the provisions of section 33 and the self-assessment regime, the burden of proof is on the taxpayer to ensure that transactions are carried out on an arm's length basis.

In Kenya, the burden of proof is on the taxpayer to demonstrate that the controlled transactions have been conducted in accordance with the arm's length standard.

Under section 97C of the Zambia Income Tax Act, the burden of proof lies with the taxpayer in Zambia to demonstrate that the transfer pricing policy complies with the relevant rules and that the transactions have been conducted in accordance with the arm's length standard.

In the Zambia draft Practice Note, the ZRA states that as a step towards discharging the burden of proof, it is in the taxpayer's best interests to:

(a) develop and apply an appropriate transfer pricing policy;
(b) determine the arm's length conditions as required by section 97A of the ITA;
(c) maintain contemporaneous documentation to support the policy and the arm's length conditions in points (a) and (b) above; and
(d) voluntarily produce the documentation when asked.

In Namibia, the burden of proof is on the taxpayer. However, PN 2/2006 states that the taxpayer may be assured that the burden of proof will not be misused by the Directorate of Inland Revenue through groundless or unverifiable assertions about transfer pricing.

20.5.2 Tax litigation

Tax litigation on transfer pricing has rarely been invoked in Africa. Litigation has taken place on two transfer pricing cases in Kenya, but a judgment has only been delivered on one case. In 2005 the High Court of Kenya held, in the case of *Unilever Kenya Ltd* v. *Commissioner for Income Tax* (Income Tax Appeal no. 753 of 2003), that in the absence of any guidelines on transfer pricing in Kenya, the OECD Guidelines were acceptable.

The facts of the case were as follows. Unilever Kenya Ltd (UKL) entered into a contract dated 28 August 1995 with Unilever Uganda (UUL) whereby UKL was to manufacture on behalf of UUL and supply to UUL such products as UUL required in accordance with orders issued by UUL. UKL supplied such products during 1995 and 1996. UKL also manufactured and sold goods to the Kenyan domestic market and export market, to customers not related to UKL.

The prices charged by UKL for identical goods in domestic export sales were different from those charged by it for local domestic sales. The prices charged by UKL to UUL differed from both the above sales and were lower than those charged in domestic sales and domestic export sales for identical goods.

The KRA Commissioner raised assessments against UKL for 1995 and 1996 in respect of sales made by UKL to UUL on the basis that UKL's sales to UUL were not at arm's length prices.

The taxpayer (UKL) argued that in the absence of specific guidelines from the KRA on section 18 of the Act the OECD Guidelines and the methods prescribed in those Guidelines for the calculation of an arm's length price are a proper, reasonable and objectively acceptable basis for the determination of an arm's length price as required under section 18(3) of the ITA.

UKL contended that the application of the CUP method by the KRA Commissioner was erroneous. In applying the CUP method, the KRA Commissioner ought to have considered whether the average price charged by UKL in domestic sales was a comparable price to that charged by UKL in the UUL sales and whether the price charged by UKL in domestic export sales was a comparable price to that charged by UKL in the UUL sales.

UKL contended that neither of these prices are comparable as there are wide differences in selling prices per unit weight of the different products and no two sales would comprise a similar mix of products in similar proportions. The KRA Commissioner had made no allowances for the costs of marketing goods in Kenya with all resultant overheads as opposed to selling goods directly to UUL for UUL to market in Uganda at its (UUL's) costs.

Similar principles were contended to apply to sales to foreign companies in countries where Unilever had no sister company so that UKL had to bear the costs of promotion of its goods in those countries. The prices charged by UKL on domestic sales in the same period were higher than the transfer prices as a result of UKL's recovery of additional costs, not as a result of any 'discount' given to UUL or as a result of the relationship between the two companies.

UKL submitted that the cost plus method, which has been endorsed by the OECD Guidelines as an appropriate method for determining an arm's length price, was the appropriate method to use in this case. This recovered the supplying company's costs plus an appropriate return on capital employed. The standard pre-tax return on capital employed applied in this case was 10 per cent, which it was contended by the taxpayer represented the average return on capital made by companies in the Unilever Group on sales to unrelated third parties.

In his response, the KRA Commissioner argued that section 18(3) of the ITA was clear and that he was bound to apply and implement the sub-section without wavering or persuasions by what other jurisdictions apply. He submitted that the OECD Convention and its related guidelines, such as the Transfer Pricing Guidelines, did not have any application in the appeal, arguing they are used to guide countries entering into double taxation agreements which was not the case here. The Guidelines cannot be part of the legislation except where the country has adopted the recommendations in a tax treaty with another country.

In response to the taxpayer's argument that it had to take into account its Kenyan overheads in selling to countries which have no sister companies and that it did not have to take into account such overheads on sales to UUL, the KRA Commissioner stated that it was of no consequence as section 18(3) of the ITA does not allow expenses incurred in another jurisdiction by a resident of that jurisdiction (Uganda).

In the judgment, Judge Alnashir Visram did not accept the argument put forward by the KRA that the wording of section 18(3) of the ITA was not ambiguous at all and must be read literally and did not allow references to foreign law and OECD principles. He stated:

> I am, therefore, unable to accept the argument that in view of the alleged clear wording of section 18(3) of the Act, no guidelines are necessary here in Kenya. That is rather simplistic and devoid of logic. We live in what is now referred to as a 'global village'. We cannot overlook or sideline what has come out of the wisdom of taxpayers and tax collectors in other countries.

He did not accept that the OECD Guidelines were germane only to countries with double taxation guidelines, quoting as an example the second item in the preface to the OECD Guidelines that reads:

These issues arise primarily from the practical difficulty, for both MNEs [multinational enterprises] and tax administrators, of determining the income and expenses of a company or a permanent establishment that is part of an MNE group that should be taken into account within a jurisdiction, particularly where the MNE Group's operations are highly integrated.

He considered the Act provided no guidelines and therefore other guidelines should be looked at and considered and that the cost plus method was appropriate for arriving at an arm's length price.

20.6   Transfer pricing disputes: bilateral and multilateral approaches

20.6.1   Appropriate adjustment rule under African tax treaties

Under the OECD Model Tax Convention, Article 9(1) deals with adjustments to profits that a contracting state may make for tax purposes where transactions have been entered into between associated enterprises on other than arm's length terms.

Such adjustments to the profits for tax purposes in one contracting state may give rise to economic double taxation (taxation of the same income in the hands of different persons). Article 9(2) of the Model Tax Convention provides that in these circumstances the other contracting state shall make an appropriate adjustment so as to relieve the double taxation. Where there is disagreement between the two states with respect to the adjustment needed, a mutual agreement procedure will be implemented.

In some cases, the tax treaties of African countries include appropriate adjustment provisions similar to Article 9(2) of the OECD Model provision. For example, all of Botswana's tax treaties contain such a provision.

Article 9(2) of the OECD Model Tax Convention provides that a contracting state must make an appropriate adjustment to the amount of tax it levies on profits, if the other contracting state has made an adjustment to the profits of a related enterprise. Furthermore, the competent authorities of the contracting states may consult each other over transfer pricing adjustments. Although South Africa's treaties generally incorporate such adjusting mechanisms the wording of the relevant Article in the treaties may not oblige South Africa to make a corresponding adjustment in all cases.

Most African countries try and resolve their transfer pricing disputes through negotiation and only resort to litigation when resolution cannot be reached through negotiation.

Often African countries have a formal process for trying to resolve transfer pricing disputes. For example, in South Africa and Mauritius if the administrations raise an assessment based on a transfer pricing adjustment, the taxpayer has a right to object to the assessment and if necessary take the matter though a formal appeals process.

In Botswana, although there is no specific transfer pricing law in place, if the dispute cannot be resolved through negotiation the dispute is dealt with by the Board of Adjudicators through the country's anti-avoidance provisions.

20.6.2   Mutual agreement procedures

Mutual agreement procedure (MAP) provisions feature in the tax treaties of many African countries. MAP appears in all of Botswana's treaties and also features in Liberia's tax treaties and many of South Africa's treaties.

South Africa's tax administration is now starting to gain some experience of the MAP process as it has met cases where taxpayers are claiming a corresponding adjustment for an adjustment by another tax administration and other cases where it has made a transfer pricing adjustment and the taxpayer has asked for a corresponding adjustment from the other tax administration. However, these cases are still in the early stages of discussion and as yet none have reached a conclusion.

20.6.3   International tax arbitration

Clearly, African countries are not members of the European Union and therefore the EU Arbitration Convention does not apply to these countries.

However, some African countries do have arbitration clauses in some of their treaties. For example, South Africa has such a provision in its treaties with the Netherlands and Switzerland and will consider the inclusion of such a clause if proposed by the other state during treaty negotiations.

20.7   Advance pricing agreements

Advance pricing agreements (APAs) are currently not used by African countries. However, some African countries have considered and continue to consider the introduction of an APA programme.

South Africa has in the past considered introducing an APA programme but due to various factors has not as yet introduced such a programme. However, the issue remains under consideration and may change at a later date.

20.7.1   OECD Guidelines as interpretative sources

The *OECD Transfer Pricing Guidelines for Multinational Enterprises and Tax Administrations* ('OECD Guidelines') are an important but non-binding interpretative source for many African countries which apply transfer pricing rules. Both Uganda and Liberia consider their domestic transfer pricing law is compatible with the OECD Guidelines and Botswana uses the OECD Guidelines to assist it in dealing with its transfer pricing disputes. Nigeria also looks to the OECD Guidelines when applying its domestic transfer pricing rules.

South Africa states in its Practice Note on transfer pricing that due to the international importance of the OECD Guidelines, its Practice Note is based, *inter alia*, on those guidelines. Although South Africa is not a member of the OECD, it acknowledges that the OECD Guidelines are an important and influential document that reflects unanimous agreement amongst the member countries reached after an extensive process of consultation with industry and tax practitioners in many countries. The OECD Guidelines are also followed by many countries which are not OECD members and are therefore becoming a globally accepted standard.

The South African Practice Note states that the OECD Guidelines should be followed in the absence of specific guidance in the Practice Note, the provisions of its transfer pricing law or its tax treaties.

20.8   Concluding remarks

African countries in the last few years have begun to take a more proactive and coordinated approach to the transfer pricing risks in their countries. The capability of African countries to deal with such transfer pricing risks varies considerably from one country to the next, with some countries not having any transfer pricing legislation while others have transfer pricing legislation, transfer pricing guidance for taxpayers and specialist transfer pricing teams with several years' experience of carrying out transfer pricing audits, often on very large MNEs.

The major challenge facing African tax administrations over the next few years will be to build their capacity to deal with transfer pricing risk. The first steps in that process are already being taken by African tax administrations, with various programmes in place to share experiences on transfer pricing audits between African countries.

Appendix: Questionnaire (Africa)

1. The structure of the law for solving transfer pricing disputes.   *What is the structure of the law of the country for solving transfer pricing disputes? For example, is the mutual agreement procedure (MAP), as regulated in the relevant tax treaty, the standard method for solving transfer pricing disputes?*

This varies across different African countries. For example, in Liberia there are other mechanisms for solving transfer pricing disputes but MAP as regulated in the tax treaty is the standard method for solving transfer pricing disputes. In Botswana, all issues where it is considered there is an avoidance or reduction of taxation through fictitious or artificial transactions are dealt with through general anti-avoidance provisions, which all appear in one section of the Botswana income tax legislation. All of Botswana's tax treaties provide for a MAP for resolving any issues that relate to any dispute in the implementation of the treaties, including Article 9 disputes. Uganda also applies its anti-avoidance provisions for resolving transfer pricing disputes.

In other African countries, such as Mauritius and South Africa, there are no specific provisions in the law to deal with transfer pricing disputes. Where the taxpayer disputes the transfer price adopted by the tax administration there is the right to object and, subsequently to appeal against any additional tax charged. In both countries, MAP may be used to resolve transfer pricing disputes.

2. Policy for solving transfer pricing disputes.   *Is there a gap between the nominal and effective method for solving transfer pricing disputes in the country? For example, has the country a strategic policy not to enforce the arm's length standard (ALS) for fear of driving foreign direct investment to other competing jurisdictions?*

Some African countries enforce the arm's length principle through their legislation. For example, South Africa has specific transfer pricing legislation (section 31 of Income Tax Act no. 58 of 1962) which states that adjustments may be made to taxable income to reflect the arm's length price. Liberia has a policy of enforcing the arm's length standard in transfer pricing disputes which is stipulated in the Liberia Transfer Pricing Regulation (Liberia Revenue Code, section 10).

In other African countries, such as Botswana, the arm's length principle is enforced through its general anti-avoidance provisions within its law. However, in some African countries such as Uganda, Mauritius and Nigeria there is no specific transfer pricing legislation, although in some cases there are sections in the general tax laws that address the application of the arm's length standard which is the generally accepted standard in the country.

3. The prevailing dispute resolution method.   *Which is the most frequent method for solving transfer pricing disputes in the country? Does it have a positive externality? For example, is the MAP the most frequent method, and if so, to what extent have successful MAPs been used as a proxy for transfer pricing case law? For instance, Procter & Gamble (P&G) obtained a bilateral advance pricing agreement (APA) in Europe, and it was then extended to a third (Asian) country when P&G made this request to the relevant Asian tax authorities.*

For many African countries, transfer pricing disputes are still a relatively new issue. Most African countries look to resolve transfer pricing disputes through negotiation and litigation is seen as a last resort. In some countries, such as Botswana and Nigeria, MAP is sometimes used to assist in resolving transfer pricing disputes. In South Africa, when assessments are made for a transfer pricing adjustment because the tax administration does not consider the pricing used by the taxpayer to calculate their taxable income is in accordance with the arm's length standard, taxpayers have preferred to seek resolution of the dispute through negotiations with the tax administration rather than opting for litigation.

4. Transfer pricing case law.   *What is the evolution path of transfer pricing litigation in the country? For example: (i) Is transfer pricing litigation being gradually replaced by either MAPs or APAs, as regulated in the relevant tax treaties? (ii) Are foreign/local transfer pricing precedents and/ or published MAPs increasingly relevant as a source of law for solving transfer pricing disputes?*

There has been very little transfer pricing litigation in Africa. Uganda has litigated one transfer pricing dispute and has another dispute which is still in the courts. Botswana also has some transfer pricing disputes which are currently in the process of litigation. In all other cases, taxpayers appear to prefer to settle such disputes through negotiation with the tax administrations.

5.   Customary international law and international tax procedure.   *Has customary international law been applied in the country to govern the relevant methods for solving transfer pricing disputes (such as the MAP)? For example, has the* OECD Manual on Effective Mutual Agreement Procedure *('OECD Manual') been deemed customary international tax law in the MAP arena for filling procedural gaps (for example, time limit for implementation of relief where treaties deviate from the OECD Model Tax Convention)?*

Due to the infancy of transfer pricing legislation and disputes in African countries, most of the countries have not applied customary international law to resolve transfer pricing disputes. However, some African countries such as Liberia do use the OECD Manual to fill procedural gaps. Botswana also uses the OECD Manual where tax treaties are applicable as these treaties are largely based on the OECD Model Convention.

6. Procedural setting and strategic interaction.   *Does strategic interaction between taxpayers and tax authorities depend on the procedural setting in which they interact when trying to solve transfer pricing disputes? For example, which procedural setting in the country prompts the relevant parties to cooperate with each other the most for solving this sort of dispute, and why?*

Many African tax administrations do not have any transfer pricing specialists and transfer pricing disputes are dealt with by tax officers with general tax experience. This puts the tax administration at a strategic disadvantage to taxpayers when trying to enforce the arm's length standard, particularly if the taxpayer is a global multinational enterprise with global transfer pricing expertise. Officers with no specific transfer pricing expertise may struggle to identify the more complex transfer pricing risks and deal with the more complex transfer pricing arguments put forward by more technically sophisticated taxpayers. This may incentivise taxpayers to under-reward the entities in the African countries.

These risks are recognised by many African countries and they are taking the first steps to training tax officers in transfer pricing matters. Other African tax administrations, such as South Africa, that already have transfer pricing specialists are working proactively to increase the size of their transfer pricing teams and to increase the technical capacity of the teams. This is in recognition of the significant risk that transfer pricing is seen to be to these countries' tax bases.

7.   The future of transfer pricing disputes resolution.   *Which is the best available proposal in light of the interests of the country for facilitating the global resolution of transfer pricing disputes, and why?*

With the increasing trading activity between South Africa and the rest of the world, the issue of transfer pricing disputes is becoming of increasing importance to South Africa. The continued and wider application of the arms' length principle and increasing use of MAP to resolve such transfer pricing disputes are viewed by South Africa as being the best way forward for resolving transfer pricing disputes.

PART VI

Conclusion

Transfer pricing dispute resolution: the global evolutionary path (1799–2011)

EDUARDO BAISTROCCHI

21.1 Introduction

The international tax regime has found itself in the midst of a creeping transition from rules to standards from the beginning of the twentieth century. The self-enforcing, rule-based arm's length principle, which by the early 1930s had obviated most problems of allocation of the international income tax base,[1] has gradually turned into a procedural, standard-based arm's length principle that has been particularly visible since the world's first bilateral advance pricing agreement (APA) was concluded between Australia and the United States in 1990.[2]

This transition entails important consequences for the structure of transfer pricing dispute resolution at the outset of the twenty-first century. It includes shifting ultimate decision-making down the legal hierarchy (by relying on APAs, tax litigation, and other similar procedures to solve international tax disputes),[3] with the consequent increasing importance of experts[4] and the quality of state intervention to enforce the arm's length principle.[5]

The global evolutionary path of transfer pricing dispute resolution consists of six stages as of the start of income taxation in the

---

[1] See section 21.4 below.

[2] A similar movement from rules to standards can be witnessed in other areas of the law. See, e.g., Daniel A., Crane, 'Rules versus Standards in Antitrust Adjudication' (2007) 64 *Washington and Lee Law Review* 49; Cardozo Legal Studies Research Paper no. 162, available at ssrn.com/abstract=927293.

[3] *OECD Transfer Pricing Guidelines for Multinational Enterprises and Tax Administrations* (Paris: OECD, 2010) ('OECD Guidelines'), pp. 23–30.

[4] For example, most recent transfer pricing litigation in Australia and Canada is very much a battle of experts. See Chapter 9 'Australia' and Chapter 4 'Canada'.

[5] E. A. Baistrocchi, 'Tax Disputes under Institutional Instability: Theory and Implications' (2012) 75(4) *Modern Law Review* 547.

United Kingdom in 1799 to finance the war against the French Emperor Napoleon. The arm's length principle (ALP) has increasingly been, in turn, the central regulatory technology[6] for solving transfer pricing disputes worldwide since its emergence in US domestic law at the beginning of the twentieth century.

The rise and evolution of the ALP are adaptations to two core technological innovations related to globalisation: first, the emergence of multinational enterprises (MNEs) and later of the international trade in intangibles. The ALP adaptation is an attempt to facilitate the resolution of transfer pricing disputes in a dynamic (rather than static) context. Indeed, the world has experienced two globalisation booms and one bust over the past two centuries. The first boom started around 1820 and lasted until the advent of the First World War. The second began at the end of the Second World War and has continued since. The inter-war years witnessed a retreat from this otherwise continuous shift towards global integration, fostered by the increasing relevance of technological innovation.[7]

The ALP was first introduced into US domestic law in 1928.[8] Its origins include an early version of the ALP encapsulated in a 1925 German regulation abrogated by Hitler in 1934.[9] The ALP was then recommended by the League of Nations Carroll Report in 1933 as the global standard to address the transfer pricing problem.[10] Since then, the ALP has been gradually transplanted to all continents, normally on the basis of a two-stage dynamic: first, from a model tax treaty to tax treaty law;[11] second, from tax treaty law into domestic law. The United

---

[6] R. Baldwin and J. Black, *Really Responsive Regulation*, LSE Law, Society and Economy Working Papers 15/2007 (2007), p. 20, available at www.lse.ac.uk/collections/law/wps/WPS15–2007BlackandBaldwin.pdf.

[7] J. G. Williamson, *Winners and Losers over Two Centuries of Globalization*, National Bureau of Economic Research Working Paper 9161 (1992), available at www.nber.org/papers/w9161.pdf. See also Dani Rodrik, *The Globalization Paradox* (Oxford: Oxford University Press, 2011).

[8] See note 34 below.   [9] See note 35 below.

[10] Mitchell B. Carroll, *Taxation of Foreign and National Enterprises*, vol. IV in *Methods of Allocating Taxable Income* (Geneva: League of Nations, 1933), paras. 627–9 ('Carroll Report').

[11] This transplant dynamic shows the crucial role the League of Nations and the OECD model tax treaties have played in international tax convergence since the early twentieth century. Indeed, model tax treaties effectively minimise collective action costs. M. Olson, *The Logic of Collective Action: Public Goods and the Theory of Groups* (Cambridge, MA: Harvard University Press, 1971).

Kingdom is an early representative example. Indeed, the United Kingdom and the United States signed their first tax treaty including the ALP in 1945. The United Kingdom then introduced the ALP into its domestic law immediately after the Second World War and detailed UK regulations were issued in 1951.[12]

The ALP was first transplanted from the United States to Europe via France in 1936,[13] then to Latin America via Argentina in 1943,[14] to Australasia via Australia in 1946,[15] to Asia via Japan in 1986,[16] and to Africa via South Africa in 1995.[17]

The global transplant of the ALP has normally been a consequence of waves of foreign direct investment (FDI) to the relevant countries and/or regions. For example, the ALP transplant from the United States to France in 1932, implemented via the France–United States Tax Treaty, was the result of the increasing expansion of US MNEs to France after the First World War.[18]

Interestingly enough, in most cases the original intent for importing the ALP to domestic law has been anti-avoidance, i.e., to protect the corporate income tax base from international tax planning techniques based on transfer pricing. For example, the anti-avoidance function of the ALP was made manifest by the US Congress in 1928,[19] by the Canadian Parliament in 1939,[20] by the Japanese Parliament in 1986,[21] and by the Brazilian Congress in 1996.[22]

Most countries explored in this book follow the same six-stage evolutionary path, starting at different points in time and going along the path at a different pace. The United Kingdom and China are clear examples. Whereas the United Kingdom took 209 years to complete

---

[12] See Chapter 8 'United Kingdom' and Appendix VI below.

[13] See France–United States DTC, Art. IV, which entered into force on 1 January 1936. M. B. Carroll, *Global Perspectives of an International Tax Lawyer* (New York: Exposition Press, 1978), pp. 35–42. See note 38 below.

[14] See Chapter 17 'Argentina'. [15] See Chapter 9 'Australia'.

[16] See Chapter 10 'Japan'. [17] See Chapter 20 'Africa'.

[18] Carroll, *Global Perspectives*, note 13 above. Carroll stated that, 'As the French were apprehensive about their ability to recapture any profit diverted from the French subsidiary to the American parent corporation, we agreed to incorporate in the treaty for bilateral application the well-known section 45 (now section 482 of the US Internal Revenue Code), which authorized the tax authorities to relocate income as if transactions had been effected on an arm's length basis' (p. 40).

[19] See Chapter 3 'United States'. [20] See Chapter 4 'Canada'.

[21] See Chapter 10 'Japan'. [22] See Chapter 13 'Brazil'.

the full cycle from 1799, China did it in just thirty years from 1991 by transplanting the regulatory technology, the ALP, first via the tax treaty signed with Japan in 1983 and then into Chinese domestic law in 1991.[23]

The way the countries studied here solve transfer pricing disputes is normally related to exogenous elements. The local endowment of natural resources is a neat example. This can be seen as a continuum. At one end, countries with large endowments of natural resources, such as Argentina, Brazil and Russia, are keen to resolve transfer pricing disputes by means of litigation. At the other end of the continuum, countries without this endowment, like Israel, Japan and the United Kingdom, normally prefer negotiations as the standard method to solve transfer pricing disputes. This pattern seems to be grounded in the relative mobility of the relevant tax base. Less mobility makes transfer pricing litigation more likely (and *vice versa*).

This chapter is organised into seven sections. After this introduction, Section 21.2 sets out the six core stages of the evolutionary path of transfer pricing dispute resolution in twenty countries from all continents since 1799 when the United Kingdom introduced its income tax system. Section 21.3 identifies the main avenues that have been used to transplant ALP regulatory technology from the United States to the rest of the world since the France–United States Tax Treaty entered into force in 1936. Section 21.4 focuses on the impact of technological innovation in the ALP structure. This includes comparing the ALP structure before and after the emergence of the international trade in intangibles from the early 1970s. Section 21.5 outlines the five versions of the ALP technology since its emergence in US domestic law in the late 1920s. Section 21.6 identifies issues emerging from the current ideal stage, stage VI, and outlines potential solutions. Section 21.7 concludes, showing that the ALP global transition from a rule-based to a procedural, standard-based regulatory technology is an adaptation to exogenous (rather than endogenous) forces, which includes technological innovations related to globalisation and international tax competition for FDI.

21.2 Transfer pricing dispute resolution: a cross-country comparison

Figure 21.1 maps the evolutionary path of transfer pricing dispute resolution in twenty countries from the five continents since 1799 onwards. The matrix consists of seven cells that represent a sequence of

[23] See Chapter 16 'China' and Appendix VI below.

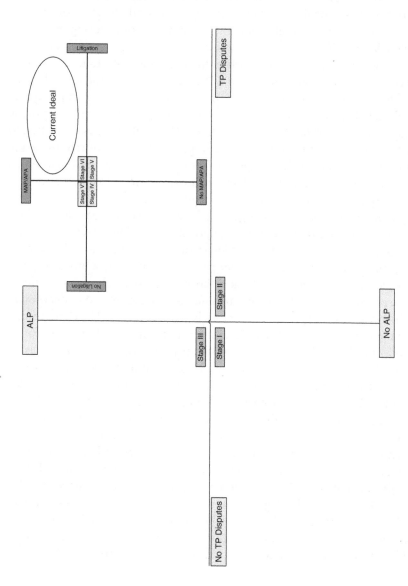

Figure 21.1 Transfer pricing dispute resolution (TPDR): the evolutionary path

evolutionary stages that are adaptations of the international tax regime to two core technological innovations: first, the emergence of multinationals over the first globalisation (1840–1914) and second, the emergence of the international trade in intangibles in the local economy during the second globalisation (1945–present). The scope of each stage is as follows.

Stage I: Denotes a context before the emergence of MNEs in the local economy, i.e., before globalisation. It is represented in the lower-left cell of the matrix. Stage I represents an absence of transfer pricing disputes (No TP Disputes) in an income tax setting without transfer pricing regulations based on the ALP (No ALP). The United States in the period between 1909 and 1921 is an example of stage I. It ran from the introduction of the US corporate income tax system in 1909, which did not include transfer pricing regulations, to 1921 when the US Congress began to notice transfer pricing abuses.[24]

Stage II: Denotes the emergence of transfer pricing disputes (TP Disputes) in a context without transfer pricing regulations based on the ALP (No ALP). It is represented in the lower-right cell of the matrix. The matrix assumes that the wording 'transfer pricing disputes' has a broad scope. It includes, for example, when local authorities complain about international tax planning techniques based on transfer pricing. 'No ALP' denotes an absence of transfer pricing regulations based on the ALP. The United States in the period from 1921 to 1928 is an example of stage II. It ran from the early phases of international transfer pricing disputes emerging as of 1921,[25] to the enactment of section 45 of the Internal Revenue Code in 1928. The wording of section 45 is almost identical to section 482 of the Code, which provides the current statutory grounding for the US ALP.[26]

Stage III: Represents the time when the ALP is largely a self-enforcing normative system given the frequent availability of comparables. It is a context before the emergence of the international trade in intangibles. Stage III is reflected in the upper-left cell of the matrix. Stage III deals with the absence of international transfer pricing disputes (No TP Disputes) in an ALP legal framework provided for in domestic law. The United States in the period between 1928 and 1935 is a case in point. It ran from the introduction of an early version of the ALP in 1928, to the emergence of early transfer pricing litigation as of 1935.[27]

---

[24] See note 41 below.   [25] *Ibid.*   [26] See note 34 below.

[27] This included *Asiatic Petroleum Co.* v. *Commissioner*, 31 B.T.A. 1152, 1159 (1935). See Chapter 3 'United States'.

Stage IV: Represents the emergence of intangibles in international trade and the consequent impact on ALP enforcement given the decreasing availability of comparables. Stage IV is reflected in the lower-left cell of the small matrix. Transfer pricing disputes normally begin and end within the local tax administration. Disputes are normally solved through administrative measures such as guidelines for taxpayers, interpretation circulars and negotiated settlements with the tax administration. Neither litigation nor bilateral APAs or MAPs are used to solve transfer pricing disputes. China from 1991 (when the ALP was introduced into Chinese domestic tax law) to 2005 (when the first bilateral APA was concluded by China with Japan) is a case in point.[28]

Stage V: Consists of transfer pricing litigation (Litigation) as the core method to solve transfer pricing disputes. The regulatory framework provides neither the mutual agreement procedure nor advance pricing agreements (No MAP/No APA). Stage V is reflected in the lower-right cell of the small matrix. The United States from 1935 (when early transfer pricing litigation emerged) to 1990 (when the United States concluded its first bilateral APA with Australia) is an example of stage V.[29]

Stage V': Refers to an environment in which all relevant transfer pricing disputes are solved in a non–litigation setting (No Litigation). Bilateral APAs and MAPs (MAP/APA) are a prominent instance of this phase. It is represented in the upper-left cell of the small matrix. China is an example of stage V' since the inception of the APA programme in 2005 until the emergence of the *ZFC* transfer pricing litigation case in 2010.[30]

Stage VI: Makes visible the transition of the ALP from a self-enforcing, rule-based regulation into a largely procedural, standard-based concept. Stage VI is reflected in the upper-right cell of the small matrix. In Stage VI, most transfer pricing disputes are solved by means of MAPs, bilateral APAs or alternative dispute resolution methods (ADR). ADR includes tax mediation and negotiation between the taxpayer and the local tax administration in areas such as intangibles. Transfer pricing arbitration and litigation are credible threats to induce both tax authorities and taxpayers, respectively, to cooperate in the MAP/APA/ADR context. Stage VI assumes that transfer pricing litigation and tax arbitration are the second best options when MAPs, bilateral APAs or ADRs are unfeasible; for example, when the other relevant state is a non-cooperative, low-tax

---

[28] See Chapter 16 'China'.   [29] See Chapter 9, 'Australia' and Chapter 3 'United States'.
[30] See Chapter 16 'China'.

country. Australia is an example of stage VI since 1990, when it signed the world's first bilateral APA with the United States, to the present.[31]

The following sections will apply Figure 21.1 in the context of five different groups of countries to further understand the core dynamic of transfer pricing dispute resolution in all continents since 1799. Figure 21.2 focuses on Europe and North America; Figure 21.3 on the Asia-Pacific region; Figure 21.4 on the BRIC countries; Figure 21.5 on the Middle East and South America. Figure 21.6 deals with Africa.

21.2.1   Europe and North America

There were two competing standards addressing the transfer pricing problem by the early twentieth century: on the one hand, the UK approach encapsulated in its 1915 domestic regulation, which was a transfer pricing rule based directly on income shifting rather than on a transaction-based arm's length principle (1915 UK approach);[32] on the other hand, the US approach, which was a transaction-based arm's length principle encapsulated in its 1928 domestic law (1928 US approach).[33] The origins of the 1928 US approach include a 1925

---

[31] See Chapter 9 'Australia' and Chapter 16 'China'.

[32] The first transfer pricing legislation in the UK tax system dates back to 1915. Finance (No. 2) Act 1915, s.31(3) provided that where a resident earned no profits or lower profits than otherwise, and this was due to the manner in which the business with a non-British non-resident was and could be arranged because of a close connection between the resident and the non-resident and because of the 'substantial control exercised by the non-resident over the resident', the non-resident could be taxed in the name of the resident as if the resident were an agent of the non-resident. In effect, the non-resident could be charged UK income taxes on non-UK-source profits (or turnover) to the extent that they reduced the profits of the resident. So this was a transfer pricing rule based directly on income shifting rather than on a transaction-based arm's length test. See Chapter 8 'United Kingdom'.

[33] The first transfer pricing legislation in the US tax system dates back to 1928. It provides the following: 'In any case of two or more trades or businesses (whether or not incorporated, whether or not organized in the United States, and whether or not affiliated) owned or controlled directly or indirectly by the same interests, the Commissioner is authorized to distribute, apportion, or allocate gross income or deductions between or among such trades or businesses, if he determines that such distribution, apportionment, or allocation is necessary in order to prevent evasion of taxes or clearly to reflect the income of any of such trades or businesses.' Revenue Act of 1928, ch. 852, s. 45, 45 Stat. 806 (1928). The transaction-based ALP was introduced into US domestic law in 1935: 'The standard to be applied in every case is that of an uncontrolled taxpayer dealing at arm's length with another uncontrolled taxpayer.' Art. 45-1(c) of reg. 86 (1935) (Revenue Act of 1934). See Chapter 3 'United States'.

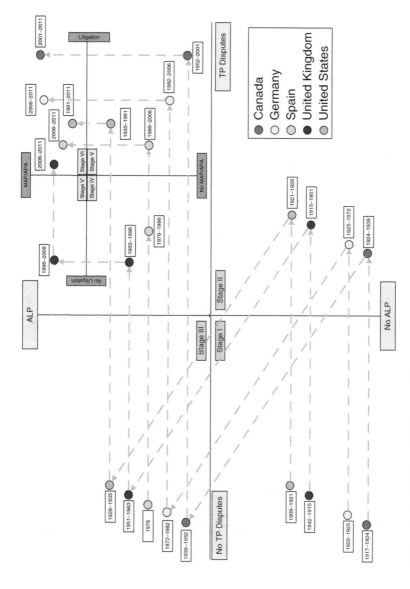

Figure 21.2 TPDR: evolutionary path in Europe and North America

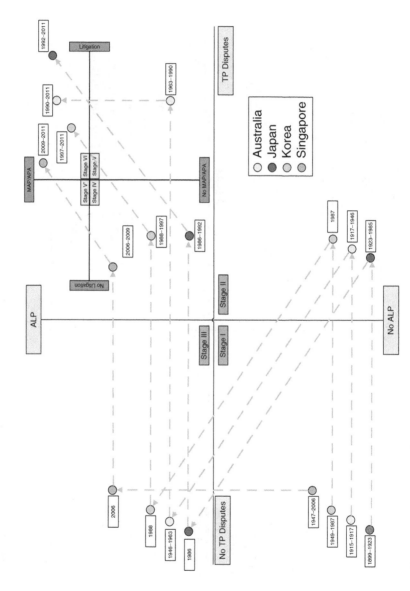

Figure 21.3 TPDR: evolutionary path in Asia-Pacific

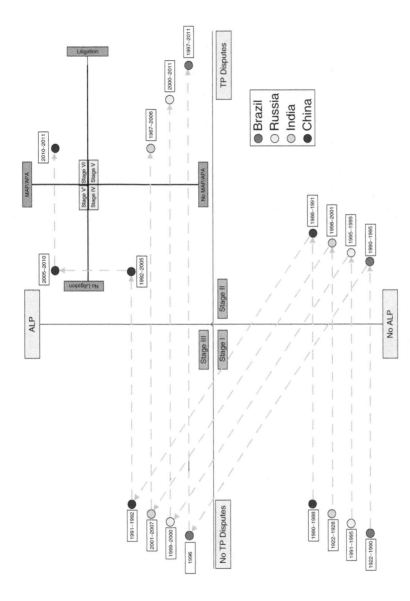

Figure 21.4 TPDR: evolutionary path in BRIC countries

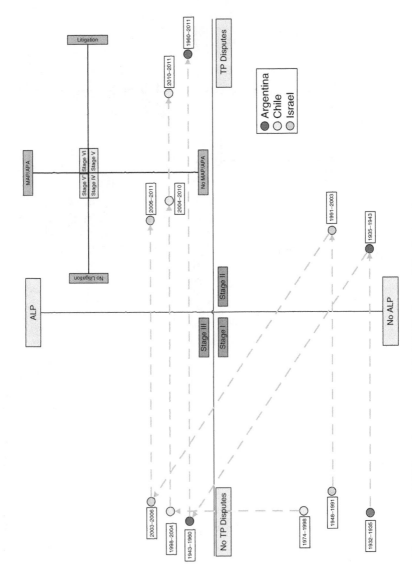

Figure 21.5 TPDR: evolutionary path in Middle East and South America

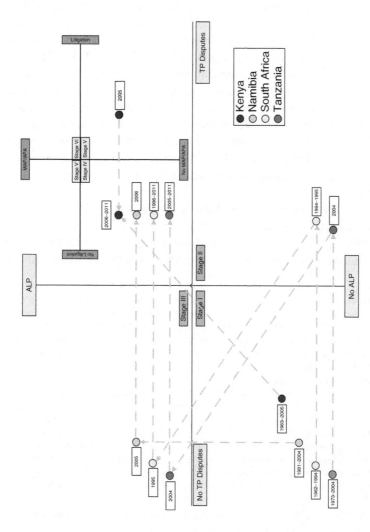

Figure 21.6 TPDR: evolutionary path in Africa

German domestic provision which was probably the first transaction-based ALP in the world.[34] Edwin R. A. Seligman, a prominent US tax scholar with a German education, might have contributed to the transplant of this 1925 German regulation to US domestic law in 1928.[35]

For a number of reasons, the 1928 US approach eventually prevailed over the 1915 UK approach. Indeed, the League of Nations Carroll Report recommended the adoption of the ALP in 1933.[36] The United States signed a double taxation convention with France that included the ALP provision and entered into force in 1936.[37] The ALP then expanded to the rest of the world. This is an early example showing the adoption of US domestic regulatory technology by the international tax regime.[38]

Figure 21.2 deals with the evolutionary path of transfer pricing dispute resolution in Europe and North America. Five countries are focused on: Canada, Germany, Spain, the United Kingdom and the United States.[39]

Figure 21.2 shows a remarkable convergence in Europe and North America as to the evolutionary path of transfer pricing dispute resolution. Canada, Germany and the United States follow the standard six-stage evolutionary path since the early twentieth century. The United Kingdom

---

[34] The first transfer pricing legislation in the German tax system dates back to 1925. The topic 'shifting profits abroad' was dealt with in German income tax legislation dating between 1925 and 1934. Section 33 of the Income Tax Act (ITA) 1925 reads: (1) 'If, as a result of special agreements between the taxpayer and a party not subject to unlimited taxation, the profit of a domestic trade or business is clearly not in proportion with the profit that would otherwise be achieved in business transactions of comparable or similar nature, said profit, or at least the usual return on capital serving this trade or business, can be taken as the basis for determining the income of the domestic trade or business. In the meaning of this provision, in addition to fixed assets, capital is deemed to include also current assets, in particular goods, products, and inventory. (2) The provision given in Section 1 of 1925 ITA does not apply if the taxpayer provides evidence that neither does he hold a share in the assets or profit of the foreign trade or business, nor does the owner of said foreign entity participate significantly in the profit or the assets of his trade or business.' See German Reichstag, Drucksache, 27 April 1925 – III 1924/25 no. 795, *Reichssteuerblatt* (*RStBl*, *German Tax Gazette*) 1925, 196. See Chapter 6 'Germany'.

[35] A. K. Mehrotra, 'Envisioning the Modern American Fiscal State: Progressive-Era Economists and the Intellectual Foundations of the U.S. Income Tax' (2005) 52 *UCLA Law Review* 1793.

[36] See note 10 above.   [37] See note 18 above.

[38] J. Wittendorff, 'The Transactional Ghost of Article 9(1) of the OECD Model' (2009) *Bulletin for International Taxation* (March) 107.

[39] The evolutionary path of each country studied in Figure 21.2 is explained in Appendix I below.

also follows the standard path since 1799, although it reached stage VI via stage V′ (rather than stage V) in order to accommodate its deeply rooted tradition of solving transfer pricing disputes through negotiations rather than litigation. Spain also followed the standard evolutionary path with the following caveat: it leapfrogged both stages I and II because it introduced the ALP at the very inception of the Spanish corporate income taxation, when it opened its economy to FDI over the second half of the twentieth century, i.e., by 1978 after the 1977 Moncloa Pact.

The United States was the first country to begin stage III by including the ALP in domestic law in 1928, followed by Canada in 1939, the United Kingdom in 1951, Germany in 1972, and then Spain in 1978.[40] In most cases, the original intent of ALP emergence and transplant was to protect the corporate income tax base from unacceptable international tax planning techniques based on transfer pricing. For example, the Committee Report submitted to the US House of Representatives argued in 1921 that, 'subsidiary corporations, particularly foreign subsidiaries, are sometimes employed to "milk" the parent corporation, or otherwise improperly manipulate the financial accounts of the parent company'.[41] In a similar vein, the German federal government complained to the German Parliament in a crucial 1964 report that relocation of income and assets had increased due to the fact that income was being shifted to companies based abroad (normally in Switzerland, Liechtenstein, Luxembourg, the Bahamas, Bermuda, the Netherlands Antilles and Panama) with the help of transfer pricing planning. In 1975, Germany introduced the ALP into domestic legislation.[42]

Another point worth mentioning in stage III is that whereas the European and North American countries explored here spent 8.6 years on average in stage III, the Asia-Pacific countries spent just 5.6 years.[43] This is probably so because most European and North American countries focused on in Figure 21.2 reached stage III before the emergence of the international trade in intangibles in the local economy (before the early 1970s in the United States). Hence, the ALP was by then a largely self-enforcing regulation. Comparables were normally available. This self-enforcing hypothesis is confirmed by the lack of transfer pricing litigation based on the lack of comparables when Europe and North America were in stage III. For example, as seen, the ALP was introduced as domestic law in the United

---

[40] See Appendix VI below.

[41] H. R. Rep. no. 350, 67th Cong., 1st Sess. 14 (1921); see also S. Rep. no. 275, 67th Cong., 1st Sess. 20 (1921). See Chapter 3 'United States' note 22.

[42] See Chapter 6 'Germany'.   [43] See Appendix VI below.

States in 1928 and taxpayers enforced it without any transfer pricing dispute triggered by comparability issues until 1973.[44] Hence, the ALP in its stage III US version was presumably a largely self-enforcing normative system until the emergence of the international trade in intangibles in the United States.

The United States was also the first country in Europe and North America to prompt stage VI by signing the first bilateral APA in the world with Australia in relation to Apple in 1990. Interestingly enough, the APA is a procedural technology first designed in Japan in the late 1980s and further improved by the United States from 1990.[45] The bilateral APA system was later adopted by Canada in 2001, Germany and Spain in 2006, and the United Kingdom in 2008.[46]

Canada, Germany, the United Kingdom and the United States completed the full six-stage cycle in a relatively long period of time (84, 86, 209 and 81 years, respectively), probably because they were the innovators of the ALP technology (and its different versions).[47] Conversely, Spain completed the full cycle in just 28 years from 1978 by transplanting ALP technology into domestic law at the very inception of a full-fledged corporate income tax system in 1978.[48] Hence, Spain is a European example of leapfrogging the ALP regulatory technology.[49] Indeed, Spain has understandably leapfrogged the first two stages, starting its path from stage III onwards.

The United Kingdom and the United States are arguably at the opposite ends of a continuum in the area of transfer pricing dispute resolution. For example, while the United States spent over half a century litigating

---

[44] Relative to the cases of the pre-1973 transfer pricing litigation era in the United States, comparables were infrequently found in the later cases. Part of the explanation, of course, is that after the courts accepted the ALP, cases where comparables could easily be found were less likely to be litigated. But the fact that litigation proliferated nonetheless suggests that in too many cases the self-enforcing ALP as encapsulated in stage III was not workable. In order to understand why, it is necessary to examine the major s. 482 cases from the 1972–92 period. *R. T. French Co.* v. *Commissioner*, decided in 1973, illustrates this problem. See Chapter 3 'United States'.

[45] See Chapter 10 'Japan'.   [46] See Appendix I below.

[47] See Appendix VI below. Section 21.5 below outlines the five different versions of the ALP regulatory technology from its emergence in US domestic law in the late 1920s.

[48] See Chapter 7 'Spain'.

[49] 'Leapfrogging' means the transplant of the best available regulatory technology when countries open their economies to FDI. Leapfrogging can be seen in many settings including international trade. See M. Motta, J. F. Thisse and A. Cabrales, *On the Persistence of Leadership or Leapfrogging in International trade* (London: London Centre for Economic Policy and Research, 1995).

transfer pricing disputes in court (the United States spent 56 years in stage V), the United Kingdom spent at least 42 years solving transfer pricing disputes at the tax administration level by negotiation. Indeed, the United Kingdom remained in stages IV, V′ and VI (they all denote different ways of resolving transfer pricing disputes by negotiation) and swapped stage V (which represents a context of solving transfer pricing disputes only by litigation) for stage V′ (denoting MAPs, APAs and ADRs as the main way for solving transfer pricing disputes).

An explanation for the different approaches adopted by the United Kingdom and the United States in solving transfer pricing disputes is based on exogenous elements. They include the degree of mobility of the corporate tax base. For example, transfer pricing litigation is normally associated with countries with relatively high endowments of natural resources such as the United States. Conversely, countries with relatively low endowments of natural resources, like the United Kingdom, tend to solve transfer pricing disputes predominantly through different types of negotiations.

In sum, the ALP orginated in the United States in the early twentieth century. It is the outcome of a competition between two incompatible standards (UK law enacted in 1915 and US law introduced in 1928) in which the US approach prevailed, particularly after the Second World War. All countries studied in this region broadly followed the same six-stage evolutionary path for solving transfer pricing disputes starting at different points in time and at a different pace. For example, innovators of the ALP technology (such as Canada, Germany, the United States and the United Kingdom) normally spent more time to complete the full cycle than early adopters (like Spain). In all countries studied in Figure 21.2, the original intent of introducing the ALP into domestic law was to protect the corporate tax base from unacceptable international tax planning techniques based on transfer pricing. The ALP then expanded to the rest of the world, fundamentally by means of the tax treaty network.

21.2.2   Asia-Pacific

Figure 21.3 focuses on the evolutionary path of transfer pricing dispute resolution in the Asia-Pacific region. The focus is on six countries: Australia, China, India,[50] Japan, Korea and Singapore.[51]

---

[50] The evolutionary path of China and India are explored further in Figure 21.4.

[51] The evolutionary path of each Asian-Pacific country included in Figure 21.3 is explained in Appendix II below.

The ALP was first transplanted from Europe and North America to the Asia-Pacific region via Australia when Australia and the United Kingdom signed the 1946 Tax Treaty incorporating the ALP, which, in turn, was followed by Australian domestic legislation on the ALP in 1982. The ALP was then transplanted to domestic law in Japan (1986), Korea (1988), and finally Singapore (2006) after the signing of the relevant bilateral tax treaties including the ALP.[52]

Interestingly enough, the length of stage III in the Asia-Pacific region was much shorter than in Europe and North America, probably because stage III fundamentally emerged in Asia from 1982, i.e., *after* the rise of the international trade in intangibles. Thus, the Asia-Pacific countries studied in Figure 21.3 moved faster than the North American and European countries from stage III to stage VI in order to be able to use the bilateral APA, MAP and ADR as the main method for solving transfer pricing disputes in an intangible-intensive international trade context. Japan is a good example. Stage III lasted just one year in Japan (1986), whereas stage IV took 6 years only (1986–92); then Japan leapfrogged stage V altogether to move on directly to stage IV, when it concluded its first bilateral APA with the United States in 1992.

This acceleration is in part explained by the fact that a number of Asia-Pacific countries leapfrogged stages to reach the best available regulatory technology when they opened their economies to FDI. Korea is a representative example in Asia as it took just 10 years (1987–2007) to get through stages II, III, IV and VI.[53] Singapore is an example of an Asian country which has leapfrogged many stages. Indeed, the Singaporean path was stages I, III, IV and VI.

Hence, the time for completing the six-stage evolutionary path in the Asia-Pacific region is much faster than in Europe and North America. Indeed, whereas Canada, Germany, Spain, the United Kingdom and the United States took an average time of 97.6 years to complete the full six-stage cycle, Australia, China, Japan, Korea and Singapore completed the cycle over an average of 62 years.[54]

Another interesting feature in Asia is the relatively invisible demise of the 1915 UK approach to the transfer pricing problem. Indeed, whereas both Australia and Singapore had transplanted the 1915 UK approach

---

[52] For example, Korea signed its first tax treaty with Japan including the ALP in 1970. This was the first Korean tax treaty. The ALP then permeated to Korean domestic law in 1988. See Chapter 11 'Korea'.

[53] See Appendix VI below.   [54] See Appendix VI below.

into domestic law in 1921 and 1947, respectively, both countries decided to transplant the US-based ALP regulatory technology in 1946 and 2006, respectively.[55]

21.2.3   BRIC countries

Figure 21.4 focuses on the evolutionary path of transfer pricing dispute resolution in the BRIC countries, i.e., Brazil, Russia, India and China.[56]

Figure 21.4 shows that China is the innovator among the BRIC countries as regards ALP regulatory technology. Indeed, the ALP was first transplanted to the BRIC world by China (1991), then Brazil (1996), later Russia (1999), and finally India (2001). China is the only BRIC country which has already completed the six-stage evolutionary path. The other three countries are still in stage V.

Let us examine China first. After 13 years in stage IV, China reached stage VI via stage V' (rather than stage V). This path was probably triggered for institutional and cultural reasons. China lacks an independent judiciary and there is a deeply rooted Chinese tradition of solving tax disputes at the tax administration level. Stages IV, V' and VI all denote different types of negotiations for solving transfer pricing disputes, in which China has spent most of the relevant time since the inception of corporate income taxation in 1980.[57]

Interestingly enough, the length of stage III in the BRIC countries is on average just 2.7 years.[58] Hence, the average length of stage III in the BRIC countries is much shorter than in Europe and North America (8.6 years) and the Asia-Pacific countries (5.6 years), probably because stage III emerged in the BRIC countries in 1991 (via China), later than in Europe, North America or the Asia-Pacific region, i.e., stage III emerged after the rise of the international trade in intangibles.

As the Asia-Pacific countries have already experienced, the BRIC countries seem to be moving towards stage VI following the lead of China, which has been in stage VI since 2010. India and Russia have recently introduced legislation on bilateral APAs, so they are expected in

---

[55] See Appendix VI below.

[56] The evolutionary path of each country focused on Figure 21.4 is explained in Appendix III below.

[57] See Appendix VI below.   [58] See Appendix VI below.

both countries soon. To date, Brazil is lagging behind this trend towards bilateral APAs for certain cultural reasons incompatible with negotiations between taxpayers and the tax authority.[59] The strategic interaction in the FDI area within the BRIC countries might induce Brazil to move towards stage VI in the near future.

The transplant of the ALP from Europe and North America to the BRIC countries was also through the tax treaty network via Japan, Greece, Spain and the United States. The first tax treaty concluded by China that included Article 9(1) of the OECD Model Convention was with Japan in 1983. The ALP was later included in Chinese domestic law in 1991. The ALP was also transplanted to Brazil via Japan in 1967.[60] Then, Brazil introduced a rule-based version of the ALP into its domestic law in 1996. A similar pattern can be seen in Russia. The Russia–Spain Double Taxation Convention (DTC), signed in 1985, was the first Russian treaty to include Article 9(1) of the OECD Model. The Russia–United States DTC, signed in 1992, was the first Russian treaty to include Article 9(2) of the OECD Model. The ALP was later introduced into Russian domestic law in 1999. Finally, the first comprehensive tax treaty entered into by India was with Greece in 1967. Article IV of the India–Greece Tax Treaty is broadly similar to Article 9 of the OECD Model. The ALP later permeated to Indian domestic law in 2001.

In sum, the BRIC countries have been swiftly importing the ALP regulatory technology since China opened its economy to FDI in the 1980s. There is a clear pattern in the BRIC countries towards stage VI, with the exception of Brazil.

---

[59] See Chapter 13 'Brazil'.

[60] The oldest DTC signed by Brazil currently in force including Article 9.1 of the OECD Model Convention was the one signed with Japan (1967). The transcription of the relevant Article reads as follows: 'Article 6: Where: an enterprise of a Contracting State participates directly or indirectly in the management control or capital of an enterprise of the other Contracting State, or the same persons participate directly or indirectly in the management, control or capital of an enterprise of a Contracting State and an enterprise of the other Contracting State, and in either case conditions are made or imposed between the two enterprises in their commercial or financial relations which differ from those which would be made between independent enterprises, then any profits which would, but for those conditions, have accrued to one of the enterprises, but, by reason of those conditions, have not so accrued, may be included in the profits of that enterprise and taxed accordingly.' See www.receita.fazenda.gov.br/Principal/Ingles/Acordo/Japan/Japan24011967.htm.

21.2.4   Middle East and South America

Figure 21.5 focuses on the evolutionary path of transfer pricing dispute resolution in the Middle East and South America. The countries studied are Argentina, Brazil,[61] Chile and Israel.[62]

Argentina, Brazil, Chile and Israel are following the six-stage evolutionary path starting at different points in time. So far, they have yet to reach stage VI. Israel is in stage IV, whereas Argentina, Brazil and Chile are in stage V.

The ALP was transplanted from Europe and North America to this region's domestic law via Argentina in 1943, then Brazil in 1996, followed by Chile in 1998, and Israel in 2003.[63] As seen in Europe and the Asia-Pacific region, the ALP transplant has normally been implemented through the tax treaty network and it has later permeated to domestic law.

South America is a region with a relatively high endowment of natural resources. For example, it offers vital inputs for the agribusiness, mining, oil and forestry industries. Countries with this endowment tend to prefer litigation as the most frequent means to solve transfer pricing disputes. That is the case of Argentina, which has been in stage V (resolution of transfer pricing disputes via litigation) since 1960, and Brazil, which has been in stage V since 1997. Chile seems to be heading towards a similar litigation approach given that it moved to stage V in 2010, when transfer pricing litigation emerged in both the mining and forestry industries. Conversely, Israel, which lacks natural resources, is in stage IV, where transfer pricing disputes normally start and end at the tax administration level.

21.2.5   Africa

Figure 21.6 concentrates on the evolutionary path of transfer pricing dispute resolution in Africa. The countries focused on are Kenya, Namibia, South Africa and Tanzania.[64]

---

[61] The Brazilian path is included in Figure 21.4.

[62] The evolutionary path of each country studied in Figure 21.5 is explained in Appendix IV below.

[63] Argentina was the first South American country to transplant the ALP into its domestic law from US domestic law in 1943. This transplant was probably triggered by the relatively high flow of US and UK FDI into the Argentinean food industry. See Chapter 17 'Argentina'.

[64] The evolutionary path of each African country studied in Figure 21.6 is explained in Appendix V below.

Figure 21.6 shows that South Africa is the innovator in Africa in ALP regulatory technology. Indeed, the ALP was first transplanted from Europe and North America into domestic law in Africa via South Africa (1995), then Tanzania (2004), later Kenya and Namibia (2005). A peculiarity here is that the judiciary (rather than parliament or congress) has played a crucial role in transplanting part of the OECD Guidelines into domestic law. Kenya is a case in point, where the Supreme Court made that transplant in the *Unilever* case by holding that the OECD Guidelines are acceptable to fill in gaps in Kenyan domestic law. The *Unilever* holding, in turn, has been transplanted to Tanzania by the local tax authority.[65]

Leapfrogging is particularly visible in Africa. For example, Kenya moved from stage I (no transfer pricing regulations) to stage V (litigation in the *Unilever* case) and then back to stage IV (negotiations at the tax administration level presumably in the light of the *Unilever* holding).

21.2.6   Transfer pricing dispute resolution: a global comparison

Figure 21.7 shows that the income tax system is a UK invention (encapsulated in stage I) and the ALP, in turn, is a US invention (encapsulated in stage III). Both inventions have been transplanted to the rest of the world at different starting points and speed. A core driving force of ALP global expansion is the timing and magnitude of FDI flows. Indeed, the emergence and evolution of ALP regulatory technology is normally a by-product of FDI flows. It aims to minimise problems of over paid and under paid international taxation as demanded by taxpayers[66] and tax authorities, respectively.[67]

The length of time a given country spends in each stage might be a proxy of the impact of exogenous forces (such as cultural traditions, institutional design, and the endowment of natural resources) on the local transfer pricing dispute resolution dynamic. For example, the United Kingdom spent over half a century in stages where different

---

[65] See Chapter 20 'Africa'.

[66] Examples of taxpayers' demand for regulations to alleviate international double taxation are found, for instance, in the appeals in 1919 of the International Chamber of Commerce and at the Brussels Financial Conference in 1920, where it was argued that the newly created League of Nations should do something to eliminate the 'evils' of double taxation. Carroll, *Global Perspectives*, note 13 above, p. 29.

[67] See section 21.1 above.

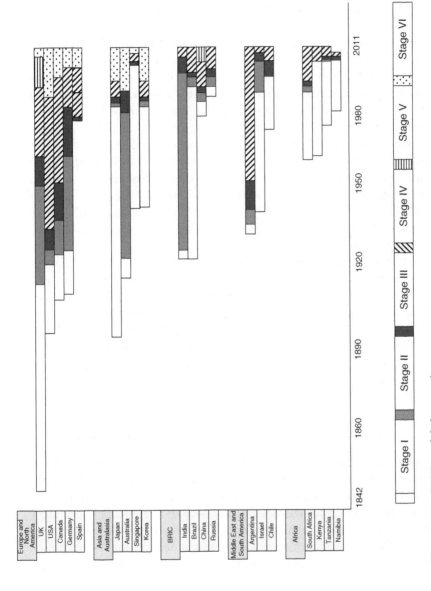

Figure 21.7 TPDR: a global comparison

types of negotiations (rather than litigation) between the taxpayer and the tax authority were crucial for solving transfer pricing disputes. These different types of negotiations are encapsulated in stages IV, V' and VI. The United Kingdom spent 36, 12 and over 4 years, respectively in these stages.[68]

Stage III has been increasingly shorter around the world as time goes by. For example, while stage III lasted an average of 8.6 years in North America and Europe, it covered an average of 5.6 years in the Asia-Pacific region, and just 2.7 years in the BRIC countries. This decreasing time period is probably a proxy for the emergence of technological innovations (such as the international trade in intangibles) and the consequent increasing difficulties of enforcing the rule-based version of the ALP (as encapsulated in stage III) because of the lack of comparables. Consequently, there is a pressing need for the relevant country to move more quickly to a new version of the ALP technology, such as those encapsulated in stages IV, V, V' or VI, which are presumably better equipped than stage III to adapt to technological innovation and international tax competition.

The timing of the emergence of each ALP version in a given country is also influenced by exogenous elements. For example, Australia was relatively late in dealing with transfer pricing issues involving intangibles because its main exports were basically primary production, whereas imports were not particularly high tech until more recently. *Roche Products*, decided in 2008, was the first case clearly involving intangible issues, even though royalty issues were already referred to as early as 2000, in the *Daihatsu* case.[69]

21.3   The ALP: core dynamic of its global transplant

There is convergence in the way the ALP has been transplanted from US domestic law to the rest of the world. Indeed, the core dynamic of the ALP transplant to most countries has normally been twofold: from model treaties and related documents (such as the OECD Guidelines) to tax treaty law, and then from tax treaty law to domestic law. In other words, the ALP has been transplanted fundamentally via the tax treaty network, and it has later permeated to a growing number of local domestic laws.

---

[68] See Appendix VI below.   [69] See Chapter 9 'Australia'.

The Republic of Korea's experience in this area is a representative example of this top-down transplant dynamic. The ALP was first included in the Japan–Korea DTC in 1970. This was the first Korean DTC. Eighteen years later, in 1988, the ALP penetrated into Korean domestic law to protect the corporate tax base.[70] A similar twofold pattern can be witnessed in Australia,[71] China,[72] Germany,[73] Japan,[74] Russia,[75] Singapore,[76] Spain[77] and the United Kingdom.[78] (A caveat is in order here. Countries such as Argentina and Chile are exceptions to this usual top-down ALP transplant pattern. They follow a bottom-up pattern. The ALP was introduced into both Argentinean and Chilean domestic law first and then into their tax treaty law.[79] A potential explanation for this infrequent bottom-up (rather than top-down) ALP transplant pattern might be the relatively close strategic interaction between this group of countries and the United States when that transplant was implemented: 1943 in Argentina and 1998 in Chile.

The OECD Guidelines have been increasingly used by domestic courts of both OECD and non-OECD member countries, at least to fill in gaps in both treaty and domestic norms encapsulating the ALP. Indeed, the OECD Guidelines, which were first launched in 1995 based on a 1979 OECD report,[80] are increasingly either hard law or soft law[81] in an

---

[70] See Chapter 11 'Korea'.   [71] See Chapter 9 'Australia'.

[72] China concluded its first OECD-based tax treaty in 1983 with Japan. The ALP was later introduced into Chinese domestic law in 1991.

[73] This first German DTC including the ALP was signed with the United States on 22 July 1954 and entered into force on 1 January 1955 (with retroactive effect as from 1 January 1954). The ALP later permeated to German domestic law in 1972. See Appendix VI below.

[74] See Chapter 10 'Japan'.   [75] See Chapter 14 'Russian Federation'.

[76] See Chapter 12 'Singapore'.   [77] See Chapter 7 'Spain'.

[78] See Chapter 18 'United Kingdom'.

[79] The ALP was first introduced into Argentine domestic law in 1943 based on a domestic US regulation in a context of substantial UK and US FDI to the country; the ALP was then included in the first Argentine tax treaty which was signed with Germany in 1966 on the basis of the 1963 OECD Model. (See Act 17.249 passed by the Argentine Congress on 7 July 1966 and Chapter 17 'Argentina'). In a similar vein, the ALP was introduced into Chilean domestic law in 1998 and then into Chilean tax treaty law when Chile signed its tax treaty with Mexico in 1999. See www.sii.cl/pagina/jurisprudencia/convenios.htm.

[80] OECD, *Transfer Pricing and Multinational Enterprises* (Paris: OECD, 1979).

[81] D. M. Ring, 'Who is Making International Tax Policy? International Organizations as Power Players in a High Stakes World' (2010) 33 *Fordham Int'l LJ* 649; Boston College Law School Legal Studies Research Paper no. 185, available at ssrn.com/abstract=1542646. Ring argues in note 10 of her paper that international relations scholars use the term 'soft law' to refer to an organisation's ability to create norms and guidelines that do not carry the force of law, but nevertheless create a sense of obligation to which states may conform. In the world of

expanding number of countries worldwide. Again, the Republic of Korea is a representative example of the increasing transplant of the OECD Guidelines into domestic and tax treaty law. A similar transplant pattern can be seen in countries such as Argentina, Chile, China, India, Japan, Russia, Spain and Singapore.[82]

21.4   The ALP in context

This section aims to show the impact of technological innovations on the structure of the ALP over time. The international trade in intangibles is used as a representative case study.

21.4.1   The ALP before the emergence of the international trade in intangibles

Mitchell B. Carroll produced the first comprehensive analysis of the methods for allocating taxable income in his seminal report under the auspices of the League of Nations in 1933 ('Carroll Report').[83] It was published when the United States was in stage III. The Carroll Report assumed that the ALP would be a largely self-enforcing normative system. Indeed, the report stated that the ALP 'obviates all problems of allocation', probably because comparables were normally available by 1933 given that international trade was not intangible-intensive at that time. For example, the ALP was introduced as domestic law in the United States in 1928 and taxpayers enforced it without any transfer pricing dispute triggered by the lack of comparables until the early 1970s.[84] A similar pattern of a lack of disputes can be seen in other countries over that period. Indeed, there is no transfer pricing litigation produced by the lack of comparables in any of the twenty countries explored here until the 1970s. Hence, the ALP was presumably a largely self-enforcing normative system until the emergence of the international trade in intangibles.

In sum, the ALP originally was functionally equivalent to a rule-based normative system as it had a largely clear *ex ante* meaning grounded in comparables. Comparables were normally available before the emergence of the information economy that increasingly brought about goods without comparables, i.e., intangibles.

---

international tax policy, the Organisation for Economic Co-operation and Development is a primary proponent of soft law power, establishing model tax treaties, which are then widely adopted by member states.

[82] See the chapters on Argentina, Chile, China, India, Japan, Russia, Spain and Singapore.

[83] See the Carroll Report, note 10 above.   [84] See note 44 above.

21.4.2 The information economy: emergence of intangibles

Since about 1969, when the first email was sent, globalisation initiated a new stage called the 'information economy', which is characterised by the increasing relevance of intangibles.[85] Individuals, or enterprises, engaged in creative or innovative activities produce intangibles as outputs. Broadly speaking, the original intangibles consist of additions to knowledge and new information of all kinds and also new creations. The formula for a new chemical is a case in point.[86]

An original is the archetypal immaterial good. It is a good because it is an entity over which ownership rights (intellectual property) can be established and which is of economic value to its owner. It is also intangible because it has no physical dimensions or coordinates in space. The producer of the original is its first owner, but the ownership may be transferred to another economic unit.[87]

The ownership right is often legally recognised through a copyright or patent, but the copyright or patent is only a legal instrument which should be clearly distinguished from the entity over which the ownership right is established. The original intangible can be bought and sold as often as required. Intangibles can be traded and retraded in the same way as material goods, both domestically and internationally.[88]

The international trade in intangibles within the same corporate groups has become increasingly relevant since the 1970s.[89] MNEs are incrementally chosen to hold intellectual property separately from both production and research.[90] For example, AstraZeneca, a leading UK pharmaceutical MNE, moved trademarks to Puerto Rico for a breast cancer drug, a migraine pill and its top-selling anti-cholesterol preparation, Crestor. The company had a factory in Puerto Rico manufacturing

---

[85] C. Shapiro and H. R. Varian, *Information Rules* (Harvard Business School Press, 1999), p. 13.

[86] P. Hill, 'Tangibles, Intangibles and Services: A New Taxonomy for the Classification of Output' (1999) 32(2) *Canadian Journal of Economics*, 'Special Issue on Service Sector Productivity and the Productivity Paradox' (April) 426.

[87] *Ibid.*   [88] *Ibid.* 426–46.

[89] R. Griffith, H. Miller and M. O'Connell, *Corporate Taxes and Intellectual Property: Simulating the Effect of Patent Boxes* (Institute for Fiscal Studies, 2010), p. 18, available at www.ifs.org.uk/publications/5361. See also 'HM Treasury Corporate Tax Reform: Delivering a More Competitive System' (November 2010), available at www.hm-treasury.gov.uk/d/corporate_tax_reform_complete_document.pdf.

[90] *Ibid.*

AstraZeneca drugs under a special low-tax regime. This implied that any additional profits from charging trademark royalties could also be attributed to Puerto Rico.[91] One net effect of this strategy could be a substantial reduction of the effective tax rate faced by the relevant MNE.

This business model based on the strategic management of intangibles makes finding comparables increasingly difficult in the transfer pricing arena, and, thus, the rule-based ALP (as encapsulated in stage III) has incrementally become unworkable since the 1970s. This is so for a number of reasons, including that transfer pricing case law cannot correct this failure of the rule-based ALP for certain strategic reasons.[92]

21.4.3   The ALP after the emergence of the international trade in intangibles

The Carroll Report had a major influence on the OECD Model in the area of transfer pricing. The 1933 Carroll Report proposition on the ALP referred to above[93] was eventually encapsulated in Article 9 of the OECD Model, which is currently the central normative system in transfer pricing around the world.[94]

The OECD Guidelines expressly acknowledge that since the 1990s, the ALP is no longer a self-enforcing normative system given the increasing difficulties in finding comparables.[95] The *practical* difficulty of enforcing the ALP has now evolved into a *conceptual* difficulty according to the

---

[91] Baistrocchi, 'Tax Disputes under Institutional Instability', note 5 above.

[92] E. A. Baistrocchi, 'The Transfer Pricing Problem: A Global Proposal for Simplification', *Tax Lawyer* (Summer 2006) available at ssrn.com/abstract=1276504.

[93] See note 10 above.

[94] The text of Article 9 of the OECD Model is set out in Chapter 2.

[95] The OECD Guidelines state the following: 'A practical difficulty in applying the arm's length principle is that associated enterprises may engage in transactions that independent enterprises would not undertake. Such transactions may not necessarily be motivated by tax avoidance but may occur because in transacting business with each other, members of an MNE group face different commercial circumstances than would independent enterprises. Where independent enterprises seldom undertake transactions of the type entered into by associated enterprises, the arm's length principle is difficult to apply because there is little or no direct evidence of what conditions would have been established by independent enterprises. The mere fact that a transaction may not be found between independent parties does not of itself mean that it is not arm's length.' See the OECD Guidelines, para. 1.11. See also Richard Vann, 'Taxing International Business Income: Hard-Boiled Wonderland and the End of the World' (2010) 2(3) *World Tax Journal* 291.

2010 version of the OECD Guidelines, which calls for 'an attempt to develop approaches that are realistic and reasonably pragmatic'.[96]

This enforcement issue of the ALP was first faced by countries whose economies rely heavily on intangibles, such as Japan and the United States. Thus, Japan and the United States have led in the creation of a procedural setting to apply the ALP, particularly when intangibles are involved: the advance pricing agreement (APA). Since 1990, APAs have become the main procedural standard to solve transfer pricing enforcement problems in countries once their economies become intangible-intensive, as denoted by stage VI.

The APA process is an alternative to the standard taxpayer path of doing the transactions, filing a return, facing an audit (some level of auditing is more likely with larger taxpayers), and, finally, a possible appeal with settlement or litigation. The taxpayer initiates the APA process by approaching the tax authority (and typically the corresponding tax authority in the other relevant jurisdiction) before engaging in the related party transactions potentially at issue. At this point, the taxpayer voluntarily provides detailed information to the government regarding its business activities, plans, competitors, market conditions and prior tax circumstances. The critical piece of this presentation is the taxpayer's explanation of its planned pricing methods. Following discussion and negotiation, the parties hopefully reach an agreement on how the taxpayer should handle the pricing of these anticipated related transactions. This understanding is embodied in a (confidential) APA agreement which typically runs for three years.[97]

APAs have over twenty years of history, which has substantially contributed to changing the character of the international tax regime from a self-enforcing normative system based on rules (as shown by stage III) into a non-self-enforcing, procedural regime (as denoted by stage VI). As seen, the world's first APA was concluded in 1990 between Australia and the United States. A section on APAs was included in the

---

[96] OECD Guidelines, para. 9.11.

[97] Diane M. Ring, 'On the Frontier of Procedural Innovation: Advance Pricing Agreements and the Struggle to Allocate Income for Cross Border Taxation' (2000) 21 *Michigan Journal of International Law* 143. In her article, Ring gives a comprehensive description and evaluation of the US APA procedure using, *inter alia*, public choice as a theoretical framework. The US APA model has been followed by many countries including Australia, Belgium, Canada, Germany, Japan, the Netherlands and Spain. For a global analysis of the APA process, see J. M. Calderon, *Advance Pricing Agreements. A Global Analysis* (Kluwer Law International, 1998).

OECD Guidelines in 1995, at a time when such approaches were still relatively novel. In 1991, the OECD Council adopted guidelines for concluding APAs under MAP procedures.[98] Since then, the OECD has been promoting bilateral APAs, i.e., APAs concluded between two states. In 2004, the Pacific Association of Tax Administrators (whose members are Australia, Canada, Japan and the United States) released operational guidance on conducting bilateral APAs, and in February 2007, the European Commission adopted a Communication containing the proposed guidelines for APAs within the European Union.[99] Today, around twenty-five countries have formal APA programmes, and the numbers are growing. Furthermore, new forms of APAs are emerging, such as multilateral APAs, joint APAs with customs authorities, and streamlined APA procedures for medium-sized enterprises.[100] China is also increasingly using APAs to enforce the ALP. By the end of 2011, at least ten bilateral APAs had been concluded with Japan, Korea, the United States and Denmark. About fifty bilateral APAs are currently being negotiated or evaluated in China.[101]

In sum, the ALP regulatory technology has been nominally the same since its inception in 1928 in US domestic law. The context has substantially changed since then and the ALP has consequently been adapted through the production of different versions of this regulatory technology.[102] These versions are explored in the next section.

21.5 Five core versions of ALP regulatory technology

Five 'versions' of the ALP regulatory technology have sequentially emerged since its rise in 1928. ALP Version 1.0 is represented in stage III (a self-enforcing, rule-based ALP before the emergence of the international trade in intangibles). ALP Version 2.0 is represented in stage IV (transfer pricing disputes normally start and end at the local tax

---

[98] The mutual agreement procedure (MAP) is regulated by Article 25 of the OECD Model Convention.

[99] See Chapter 5 'European Union'.

[100] C. Silberztein, Foreword to Gareth Green (ed.), *Transfer Pricing Manual* (BNA, 2008), p. xxxi.

[101] See Chapter 16 'China'.

[102] While stages I and II developed in North America and Europe before the emergence of international organisations, the League of Nations and the OECD were heavily involved in the ALP transition from stages III to VI.

administration level; neither litigation nor bilateral APAs or MAPs are used to solve transfer pricing disputes). ALP Version 3.0 is represented in stage V (transfer pricing disputes are usually solved by litigation). ALP Version 4.0 is represented in stage V' (transfer pricing disputes are normally solved by APAs, MAPs or ADRs without litigation). And finally, ALP Version 5.0 is encapsulated in stage VI (transfer pricing disputes are normally solved by APAs, MAPs or ADRs in which tax litigation and tax arbitration are infrequent elements). These five versions are adaptations of the ALP to exogenous forces such as technological innovations, as may be witnessed in the international trade in intangibles.

Interestingly enough, there are similarities between the evolution of the ALP and the Commerce Clause provided for in the US Constitution since 1787.[103] The Commerce Clause was originally a self-enforcing, rule-based regulation granting legislative power to the US Congress over interstate commerce in the context of a country with an economy focused on agriculture. 'Interstate commerce' originally had a clear *ex ante* meaning. Technological innovation and other exogenous factors eventually contributed to produce increasingly interconnected commercial activities among the US States. Commercial activities were no longer localised so it became difficult to imagine a purely internal commerce that affected no other States. 'Interstate commerce' gradually turned into a procedural, standard-based principle whose meaning was to be ascertained on a case-by-case basis by the US federal judiciary. In sum, both the Commerce Clause and the ALP regulatory technologies have remained nominally the same since their inception in 1787 and 1928, respectively, but they have evolved through successive 'versions' over time. Their effective structures have been transformed substantially (from rules into standards) to adapt to exogenous forces, technological innovation being a case in point.[104]

21.6   Stage VI: the last stage of the ALP?

Stage VI is considered the current ideal, albeit still unsatisfactory. It is the current ideal because it is the procedural setting with more potential to produce positive externalities in the transfer pricing arena.

---

[103] Section 8(2) grants Congress power to 'regulate Commerce with foreign Nations, and among the several States, and with the Indian Tribes'.

[104] See R. Harrison, *The Growth of Federal Power in American History* (R. Jeffreys-Jones and B. Collins (eds.), 1983).

There are four examples of positive externalities that can currently be triggered by bilateral APAs and MAPs. First, the APA system may effectively play the role of a laboratory specialised in providing a relatively clear *ex ante* meaning to the ALP with precedential value. The case of a US MNE successfully extending its bilateral APA concluded between two developed countries to a number of countries of the emerging world is a good example.[105] Second, there are a number of MAPs concluded between the United States and India in the software industry that have reached the public domain, establishing a cost plus margin of around 18 per cent for the tax year 2003–4.[106] Third, Korean domestic law specifically grants taxpayers the right to expand the application of MAPs to third countries if certain conditions are met.[107] Fourth, Germany is also granting APAs certain precedential value.[108]

Stage VI is still unsatisfactory because the APA and MAP outcomes are normally completely secret; this may be inconsistent with a well-functioning liberal democracy. For example, not all comparable taxpayers are granted their petitions for APAs – the GlaxoSmithKline dispute in the United States is a case in point.[109]

---

[105] An official of Procter & Gamble has maintained the following on its bilateral APAs global strategy: 'We believe that our APA strategy gives us greater predictability and financial statement precision not only in markets where we have obtained rulings, but also in other countries with similar circumstances where we have [not] yet pursued a ruling. Essentially, because the business model is the same and the circumstances are similar, our rulings give us the ability to ask the next government why shouldn't the new audit produce the same tax result as the 15 APAs that we have already obtained on substantially similar facts. When we couple this strategy with our general corporate transparency, and global consistency in execution of our planning, and strong internal controls, we have a strategy that delivers more risk management certainty.' An interview with Tim McDonald, Vice President Finance and Accounting, Global Taxes in Procter & Gamble, 'Tax Policy and Controversy Briefing' in *A Quarterly Review of Global Tax Policy and Controversy Development* (February 2010), 2–6.

[106] See Chapter 15 'India'.

[107] Korean law provides that the result of a mutual agreement can also apply to the transaction with a related party located in countries other than the relevant country for the MAP (art. 27–2(1) of the LCITA). This was introduced by the LCITA amendment dated 24 May 2006. For an expanded application of the MAP result, the person who applied to commence the MAP should apply for an expanded application. Expanding the result of the MAP is allowed, but only in accordance with the statute. See Chapter 11 'Korea'.

[108] Under German law, a unilateral APA agreed by the taxpayer with a foreign tax authority is not binding on the German tax authorities. The taxpayer, however, can make an application for the German tax authorities to commit themselves correspondingly in the same unilateral way. See Chapter 6 'Germany'.

[109] See Chapter 3 'United States'. See also Martin Sullivan, 'With Billions at Stake, Glaxo Puts US APA Program on Trial', *Tax Notes Int'l*, 3 May 2004, 456.

It remains to be seen if the six stages outlined in Figure 21.1 represent the whole evolutionary cycle of the ALP regulatory technology or, alternatively, whether a new stage VII will eventually emerge to resolve the issues triggered by stage VI. A system of an optional publication of anonymous bilateral APAs could be a core element of this potential new stage VII.[110]

21.7 Conclusion: towards a global convergence on transfer pricing dispute resolution

This chapter shows the evolutionary path of transfer pricing dispute resolution in twenty countries from the five continents since 1799. It consists of six core stages that encapsulate how the ALP has gradually evolved from being a rule-based regulation to a procedural, standard-based regulation over the last century. The main driving force of this transformation is probably the ALP adaptation to two central technological innovations: the emergence of multinational enterprises over the first globalisation (1850–1914), and then the emergence of the international trade in intangibles during the second globalisation (1945 to the present).

The countries analysed here can be organised into three categories. The first group of countries encompasses the ones that have already finished the six stages. They include Japan and the United States. The second group identifies countries following the standard evolutionary path, although stage VI has yet to be reached. For example, Brazil, India and Russia are still in stage V (transfer pricing litigation without any signed bilateral APA). The third group includes countries that are leapfrogging stages of the evolutionary path in the search for the best available regulatory technology when they open their economies to FDI. For example, Singapore has moved since 1947 from stage I to stage III and IV and then directly to Stage VI.

The original intent of local authorities in transplanting the ALP technology into domestic law has normally been broadly the same in all continents: the protection of the corporate tax base from aggressive international tax planning techniques based on transfer pricing in the context of an increasing flow of FDI. Indeed, the ALP has normally been considered as a specific

---

[110] See R. Vann, 'Reflections on Business Profits and the Arm's Length Principle' in B. J. Arnold, J. Sasseville and E. M. Zolt (eds), *The Taxation of Business Profits Under Tax Treaties* (Toronto: Canadian Tax Foundation, 2004), pp. 133, 168. See also E. A. Baistrocchi, 'The Transfer Pricing Problem: A Global Proposal for Simplification', 59(4) *Tax Lawyer* 941 available at ssrn.com/abstract=1276504.

anti-avoidance regulation. This original intent is particularly visible in the following countries (listed in chronological order): United States (1921),[111] Australia (1921),[112] Canada (1924),[113] France (1932),[114] Argentina (1935),[115] Japan (1986),[116] Korea (1988),[117] China (1991),[118] South Africa (1994),[119] India (2001),[120] Brazil (2005)[121] and Spain (2006).[122]

There also seems to be global convergence on how the ALP has been transplanted from the 1928 US domestic law to the rest of the world. A core dynamic of the ALP transplant has normally been twofold: from model tax treaties produced by the League of Nations and later the OECD to tax treaty law; and then from tax treaty law to domestic law. In other words, the ALP has been transplanted fundamentally via the tax treaty network, and it has later permeated to a growing number of local domestic laws. The United Kingdom[123] and Korea[124] are representative examples of the ALP global transplant.

Moreover, international tax organisations such as the League of Nations and then the OECD have contributed to minimising collective action costs emerging from the never-ending adaptation of the international tax regime to technological innovation. For example, documents produced by the League of Nations (such as the 1932 Carroll Report) and the OECD (like the 1995 version of the OECD Guidelines) have been instrumental in facilitating the ALP transplant into domestic law and its evolution over time, particularly from stage III all the way to stage VI. For instance, the OECD Guidelines on transfer pricing are frequently considered as either hard law or soft law in most of the OECD and non-OECD countries studied in this book.

The countries studied here generally started the ALP evolutionary path at different points in time and went through the stages at a different pace. The cases of United Kingdom[125] and China[126] are representative examples. While the United Kingdom took around 209 years to complete the six stages since 1799, China has done so in around 30 years since the introduction of a Western-style income tax system in 1980.

---

[111] See Chapter 3 'United States'.   [112] See Chapter 9 'Australia'.

[113] See Chapter 4 'Canada'.

[114] See Carroll, *Global Perspectives*, note 13 above, pp. 35–42.

[115] See Chapter 17 'Argentina'.   [116] See Chapter 10 'Japan'.

[117] See Chapter 11 'Korea'.   [118] See Chapter 16 'China'.   [119] See Chapter 20 'Africa'.

[120] See Chapter 15 'India'.   [121] See Chapter 13 'Brazil'.   [122] See Chapter 7 'Spain'.

[123] See Chapter 8 'United Kingdom'.   [124] See Chapter 11 'Korea'.

[125] See Chapter 8 'United Kingdom'.   [126] See Chapter 16 'China'.

Five 'versions' of the ALP regulatory technology have sequentially emerged over the last century. For example, ALP Version 1.0 is represented in stage III (a self-enforcing ALP before the emergence of the international trade in intangibles in the late 1960s).

The six-stage evolutionary path framework presented in this chapter is a two-way system. It includes the evolution of the ALP technology, as shown in section 21.2 above, as well as a regression to older versions of the ALP. For example, if most taxpayers were to win transfer pricing litigation in the United States, the US transfer pricing dispute resolution system may eventually move back from stage VI to V because there would be a weaker incentive for taxpayers to use the APA/MAP/ADR option.

The pattern of transfer pricing dispute resolution in any given country seems to be influenced by contextual elements. For example, at one end of the continuum, countries with natural resources (such as Brazil and Russia) tend to prefer solving transfer pricing disputes by litigation. At the other end of the continuum, countries without natural resources (like Japan and United Kingdom) normally prefer negotiation over litigation. The international mobility of the tax base seems to be an explanation for this divergent approach for solving transfer pricing disputes across nations. Less mobility makes transfer pricing litigation more likely (and *vice versa*).

Future research in this area includes exploring whether the emergence and global expansion of the ALP regulatory technology can be seen as a standard technology, like the railway. This research could help illuminate, for example, if this type of regulation is governed by the usual theoretical framework applied to all types of technology, such as network markets (which include competition between incompatible standards),[127] the Roger's Bell Curve (which explains the technology adoption lifecycle among innovators, early adopters, early majority, late majority and laggers), leapfrogging (as a short-cut to adopt the best available technology), and the emergence of versions of the same technology as an attempt to adapt to a dynamic, rather than static, context.[128]

---

[127] E. A. Baistrocchi, 'The Use and Interpretation of Tax Treaties in the Emerging World: Theory and Implications', 4 *British Tax Review*, 24 September 2008, available at ssrn.com/abstract=1273089.

[128] On leapfrogging in international trade law, see M. Motta, J. F. Thisse and A. Cabrales, *On the Persistence of Leadership or Leapfrogging in International Trade* (London: London Centre for Economic Policy and Research, 1995).

In sum, the ALP is a remarkable example of tax convergence and globalisation.[129] It is also a regulatory technology which has gone through different versions to adapt to technological innovation related to globalisation and international tax competition. It remains to be seen if the sixth stage is the end of the ALP history, or whether, as is desirable, a seventh stage will eventually emerge to further improve this crucial technology of the international tax regime.

Appendix I: Evolutionary path of transfer pricing dispute resolution in Europe and North America

Canada has gone through the six-stage evolutionary path since 1917, leapfrogging stage IV only. Canada is currently in stage VI. The outline of the Canadian stages is as follows. Stage I lasted 7 years (1917–24). It ran from the inception of corporate income taxation in Canada in 1917 until 1924, when there was neither transfer pricing legislation nor transfer pricing disputes. Stage II took 15 years (1924–39). It began with the introduction of a primitive version of the ALP in 1924 to 'prevent associated or holding companies from making fictitious expenses a vehicle for evading the Income Tax Act', according to the House of Commons debates.[130] Stage III lasted 13 years (1939–52). It ran from the inception of a domestic provision, which is the first direct predecessor to Canada's current ALP transfer pricing regulation, until the emergence of transfer pricing litigation in 1952. Canada leapfrogged stage IV. Stage V lasted 49 years (1952–2001). Transfer pricing disputes escalated into litigations. *Central Canada Forest Products*, decided in 1952, was the first reported transfer pricing case in Canada. Stage VI began in 2001. At least 535 MAPs and 142 bilateral APAs have been concluded in Canada by 2001. There has been mandatory binding arbitration in the Canada–United States Treaty since 2008. Cases are increasingly focused on intangibles. Only a small number of litigation cases had been initiated by 2001, including *World Corp.* and *GlaxoSmithKline Inc.*[131]

Germany has gone through the six-stage evolutionary path since 1920, reaching stage VI in 2006. Hence, Germany took 86 years to complete

---

[129] R. S. Avi-Yonah, *Tax Convergence and Globalization*, University of Michigan Law and Economics Empirical Legal Studies Center Paper no. 10–019 (8 July 2010); University of Michigan Public Law Working Paper no. 214, available at http://ssrn.com/abstract=1636299.

[130] See Chapter 4 'Canada'.   [131] *Ibid.*

the full cycle (1920–2006). The outline of each of the German stages is as follows. Stage I lasted 5 years (1920–25). It ran from 1920, when Germany introduced its corporate income tax system, until 1925, when there was neither transfer pricing legislation nor registered transfer pricing disputes. Stage II took 40 years (1925–64). It began with the introduction of an early version of the ALP in 1925. This is probably the first time in the world that the ALP, explicitly grounded on comparables, was introduced into the law. The ALP was replaced in 1934 with a standard that in a later court ruling was referred to as 'experience of life'. This peculiar standard was, in turn, invalidated by the Federal Tax Court on constitutional grounds in 1959. A 1964 official report stated that 'income was being shifted to base companies abroad with the help of transfer pricing'. Stage III lasted 10 years (1972–82). It ran from the inception of a domestic provision adopting the ALP in 1972, until the emergence of a 1982 transfer pricing litigation in an ALP regulatory context: the Bundesfinanzhof case on 'hidden profit distribution' in an international context, decided in 1986. Stage V lasted 24 years (1982–2006). Most transfer pricing disputes were resolved before the courts within a context in which no single MAP or bilateral APA was completed. Germany then moved on to stage VI in 2006. Most transfer pricing disputes are resolved at the German administration level, bilateral APAs or MAPs, with infrequent litigation.[132]

Spain has gone through the six stages of the evolutionary path in just 28 years, leapfrogging stages I and II. These two stages were leapfrogged because Spain introduced a full-fledged corporate income tax system (including the ALP) in 1978, thus beginning the cycle from stage IV (1978). Stage IV lasted 8 years (1978–86). It ran from the introduction of the ALP in 1978 to the emergence of the first transfer pricing litigation, in a context without MAPs and APAs. During stage IV, most transfer pricing disputes started and ended at the Spanish tax administration level. Spain leapfrogged stage V. Stage VI has been running since 2006, with an increasing number of transfer pricing disputes that have been solved by bilateral APAs and MAPs. There is infrequent transfer pricing litigation, such as the Spanish Supreme Court (*Auto*, 8 February 2011) on the transfer pricing penalty regime.[133]

United Kingdom has gone through the six-stage evolutionary path since 1799, reaching stage VI only in 2008. Hence, the United Kingdom took 209 years to complete the full cycle (1799–2008). There is one

---

[132] See Chapter 6 'Germany'.   [133] See Chapter 7 'Spain'.

peculiarity here. The United Kingdom took the usual path from stage I to stage VI except in the following respect. It reached stage VI via stage V' (rather than by stage V), probably because of the United Kingdom's deeply rooted tradition of solving transfer pricing disputes at the UK tax administration level. The outline of each of the UK stages is as follows. Stage I lasted 116 years (1799–1915). It ran from 1799, when the United Kingdom introduced its income tax system, until 1915 when there was neither transfer pricing legislation nor transfer pricing disputes. Stage II took 36 years (1915–51). It began with the introduction of transfer pricing regulations in 1915. It was based directly on income shifting, rather than on a transaction-based ALP test. There was one transfer pricing dispute in stage II, which escalated into litigation: *Gillette Safety Razor, Ltd* v. *IRC* (1920). Stage III lasted 12 years (1951–63). It ran from the inception of a domestic provision explicitly adopting the ALP in 1951, until the emergence of a transfer pricing dispute in an ALP regulatory context: *Petrotim Securities Ltd* v. *Ayres*. It was decided in 1963. Stage IV lasted 33 years (1963–96). All transfer pricing disputes were resolved at the UK tax administration level within a context in which no single MAP or bilateral APA was completed. The United Kingdom then moved on to stage V'. This referred to an environment in which all relevant transfer pricing disputes were resolved in a non-litigation setting through bilateral APAs and MAPs and lasted 12 years (1996–2008). It ran from the inception of the APA programme in 1996 until the emergence of the first transfer pricing litigation in *DSG Retail Ltd*, decided in 2008. Stage VI started in 2008. Most transfer pricing disputes are being resolved either by bilateral APAs or MAPs, with infrequent litigation. The *DSG Retail Ltd* case is the only example available so far.[134]

United States: See the introduction to section 21.2 above.

Appendix II: Evolutionary path of transfer pricing dispute resolution in the Asia-Pacific countries

Australia has gone through the six-stage evolutionary path starting at the federal level in 1915 (there were some disputes over the source of income under the prior colonial and state income taxes which involved transfer pricing considerations). It has completed the full cycle in 75 years. Stage

---

[134] See Chapter 8 'United Kingdom'.

I lasted 2 years (1915–17). It ran from the inception of corporate income taxation in Australia in 1915 until 1917, when questions about transfer pricing issues in respect of British Imperial Oil were being asked in Parliament. Stage II lasted 29 years (1917–46). It began over the 1917–21 period when Australia discussed and introduced the first explicit transfer pricing legislation. For example, the Australian Prime Minister had complained about international tax planning techniques based on transfer pricing by 1921.[135] This led the Australian Parliament to introduce transfer pricing legislation in 1921, based closely on the UK 1918 legislation, which in turn was based directly on income shifting, rather than on a transaction-based ALP test. There were transfer pricing disputes in a non-ALP context.[136] Stage III lasted 17 years (1946–63). It ran from 1946, when Australia entered into its first tax treaty with the United Kingdom that incorporated the arm's length principle, which was followed by domestic legislation incorporating the ALP in 1982. Stage IV was leapfrogged. Stage V lasted 27 years (1963–90). It started with the first substantive Australian transfer pricing case.[137] Stage VI began in 1990 with Australia's first bilateral APA with the United States in relation to Apple. Australia has been active in APAs and MAPs, but the local tax administration is regarded as demanding in respect to what is required before a bilateral APA can be issued. This has led to the emergence of a stage IV within stage VI. In other words, some transfer pricing disputes

---

[135] The Australian Prime Minister complained about aggressive international tax planning techniques based on transfer pricing during stage II by oil companies. Indeed, Prime Minister Hughes, in Commonwealth of Australia Parliamentary Debates 1902–1946, House of Representatives, 8 December 1921, vol. 98, p. 14132 said, 'I come now to another important clause. I refer to clause 9, which is to impose income tax upon profits derived by ex-Australian principals from the sale of their goods in Australia. Honourable members perhaps have had their attention drawn to a practice which is becoming common, and is notorious in the case of one particular company, where an Australian branch house is believed to be debited by the foreign house for goods at a price which leaves little margin for profit on the sale of such goods in Australia. These allegations have been made from time to time in this House. It has been said that one company in particular has resorted to some such method in order to escape the Australian tax. The proposed new section will give the Commissioner power to assess and charge tax upon what appear to be the real profits.' See the Australia Chapter, section 9.1.

[136] There was transfer pricing litigation over stage II, such as *British Imperial Oil Company* v *Federal Commissioner of Taxation* (1925) 35 C.L.R. 422. However, these transfer pricing cases are largely constitutional and procedural rather than concerning the substance of adjustments that were made. See Chapter 9 'Australia'.

[137] *Case 52* (1963) 11 Commonwealth Taxation Board of Review (New Series) 261.

are solved at the tax administration level in areas such as intangibles. Australia was relatively late to deal with transfer pricing issues in intangibles because its main exports were basically primary production and imports were not particularly high tech until more recently. *Roche Products*, decided in 2008, is the first case clearly involving intangible issues, although royalty issues were referred to in the *Daihatsu* case in 2000.[138]

Japan has gone through the six-stage evolutionary path since 1899, leapfrogging stage V only. Japan is currently in stage VI. Stage I lasted 24 years (1899–1923). Stage I ran from the inception of income taxation in Japan in 1899 until the emergence in 1923 of a transfer pricing regulation different from the ALP.[139] Stage II lasted about 62 years (1923–85). During this stage, for example, the 1985 Tax Commission, an advisory body to the Japanese Prime Minister, submitted a report which complained about aggressive international tax planning techniques based on transfer pricing.[140] This led the Japanese Parliament to introduce transfer pricing legislation into domestic law in 1986. Stage III lasted one year (1986), when transfer pricing legislation was introduced into Japanese domestic law. Stage IV covered six years (1986–92), when most transfer pricing disputes were resolved at the tax administration level. Japan then leapfrogged Stage V because all relevant transfer pricing litigation emerged after 1992 when Japan signed it first bilateral APA. Stage VI

---

[138] See Chapter 9 'Australia'.

[139] The 1923 Japanese transfer pricing provision was called 'denial of acts or accounting of family companies'. It effectively created the 'reasonable test' for setting transfer pricing. The Supreme Court decision of 29 May 1958 (12 MINSHU no. 8, 1254) affirmed the Tokyo High Court decision of 20 December 1951 (2 GYOSAISHU no. 12, 2196), which adopted the reasonableness approach. A majority of the court precedents thereafter have followed the reasonable approach.

[140] For example, the 1985 Tax Commission stated, 'As the recent internationalization of business progresses, the shifting of income abroad by manipulating prices in transactions with overseas specially related enterprises, that is, the problem of transfer pricing, has become important in the area of international taxation. It is difficult to deal with this matter sufficiently under the present law. Leaving this situation as is would be problematical from the viewpoint of proper, equitable taxation. Considering the fact that foreign countries are already equipped with a tax system to deal with such shifting of income overseas, it would be appropriate to stand on common ground with these foreign countries and to formulate provisions concerning the computation of taxable income to apply to corporations' transactions with their specifically related enterprises abroad, as well as to create measures contributing to the smooth operation of such a system, such as the collection of data, in order to realize proper international taxation.' See Chapter 10 'Japan'.

began when Japan signed its first bilateral APA with the United States in 1992. The *Imabari Zosen* case was heard at the Matsuyama District Court in 1996. In stage VI, most transfer pricing disputes are resolved by bilateral APAs under MAPs or at the tax administration level. At least sixty-nine bilateral APAs had been concluded by Japan by 1999. Japan signed at least one multilateral APA during that period.[141]

Republic of Korea has gone through the six stages of the evolutionary path since 1949, leapfrogging stage V only. Korea is currently in stage VI. The outline of the Korean stages is as follows. Stage I lasted 38 years (1949–87). It ran from the introduction of corporate income taxation in 1949, which did not include transfer pricing regulations, to 1987, when the Korean judiciary started to notice transfer pricing abuses.[142] Stage II lasted about one year (1987). It ran from the 1987 judicial decision, Du 332, to the introduction of the ALP into Korean domestic law in 1988. Stage III lasted one year (1988). It ran from the inception of a domestic provision explicitly adopting the ALP in 1988 until the emergence of transfer pricing disputes in an ALP context in 1988. Stage IV lasted nine years (1988–97), when most transfer pricing disputes were solved at the tax administration level in a context without APAs or MAPs. Korea leapfrogged stage V. This was so because all relevant transfer pricing litigation emerged after the introduction of the MAPs and bilateral APA options in 1997. Stage VI started in 1997 when Korea concluded its first bilateral APA with the Unites States. At least 106 applications for bilateral APAs have been submitted to Korea as of 1997. Transfer pricing litigation has been an infrequent element in Korea. It includes the 2008 Supreme Court decision, Du 14364.[143]

Singapore has gone through the six stages of the evolutionary path since 1947, leapfrogging stage II and V. The outline of the Singaporean stages is as follows. Stage I lasted 59 years (1947–2006). It ran from the introduction of corporate income taxation in 1947, which included transfer pricing regulations based on the 1915 UK regulations, until the introduction of the ALP in 2006. Singapore leapfrogged Stage II (there was only one case in 1968 in which the taxpayer won). Stage III

---

[141] *Ibid.*

[142] It has been argued that, 'Since the late 1980s, the price manipulation by multinational corporations using overseas related companies in their cross-border transactions became a full-fledged problem in Korea, which was a phenomenon caused by the rapid opening of the Korean economy.' See Chapter 11 'Korea'.

[143] *Ibid.*

lasted one year (2006). It emerged with the inception of guidelines by the tax authority explicitly adopting the ALP in 2006. Stage IV lasted 3 years (2006–9). Singapore leapfrogged Stage V. It then moved on to Stage VI in 2009, when bilateral APAs and MAPs began to be used as the main avenue for solving transfer pricing disputes.[144]

Appendix III: Evolutionary path of transfer pricing dispute resolution in the BRIC countries

Brazil has gone through the first five stages of the evolutionary path since 1922, leapfrogging stage IV only. Brazil is currently in stage V. Stage I lasted 68 years (1922–90). Stage I ran from the inception of corporate income taxation in Brazil in 1922 until 1999, when there was neither transfer pricing legislation nor transfer pricing disputes. Stage II lasted 5 years (1990–5). There was an increasing perception of transfer pricing manipulation in Brazil over this stage. This led the Brazilian Congress to introduce transfer pricing legislation in 1996 based on a rule-based version of the ALP.[145] Stage III ran from the inception of a domestic provision explicitly adopting transfer pricing in 1996 until the emergence of transfer pricing disputes in an ALP regulatory context. Stage IV was not relevant in Brazil because there was normally little room for negotiation between the taxpayer and the tax administration in the transfer pricing arena. Stage V has run from the emergence of transfer pricing litigation in Brazil in 1997 to the present. One of the first cases decided was Re 101–96.665, involving the pharmaceutical industry. At the time of writing, neither bilateral APAs nor MAPs have been concluded in Brazil.[146]

Russia has gone through the first five stages of the evolutionary path since 1991, leapfrogging stage IV only. Russia is currently in stage V. Stage I lasted 4 years (1991–95). Stage I ran from the inception of income taxation in Russia in 1991 until 1995, when there was neither transfer pricing legislation nor transfer pricing disputes. Stage II lasted 4 years (1995–9). There was a growing perception of transfer pricing

---

[144] See Chapter 12 'Singapore'.

[145] The enactment of Brazilian transfer pricing legislation aimed to prevent the allocation of taxable income abroad through the manipulation of prices on imports and exports between associated enterprises. The Brazilian rule was intended to combat schemes of tax avoidance and tax fraud.

[146] See Chapter 13 'Brazil'.

manipulation in Russia over stage II. This perception led the Russian Parliament to introduce transfer pricing legislation in 1999 based on the ALP. Stage III lasted 4 years (1999–2000). It ran from the inception of a domestic provision explicitly adopting the ALP in 1999, until the emergence of transfer pricing litigation in an ALP regulatory context. The first transfer pricing disputes emerged in the lower courts in 2000, following the results of the tax audits for the 1999 fiscal year, with some initial guidance issued by the Supreme Courts as early as 1999. At the higher courts' level, the first taxpayer's case was probably the *Yugansneftegaz* case, decided by the Supreme Arbitrazh Court in 2002, and the *Niva-7* case, decided by the Constitutional Court in 2003. Russia leapfrogged stage IV, presumably because there was normally little room for negotiations between the taxpayer and the tax administration in the transfer pricing arena. Stage V has run from 2000 to the present. At the time of writing, there have been neither bilateral APAs nor MAPs concluded by Russia. The transfer pricing reform that is to become effective in 2012 formally introduces a bilateral APA regime, which may indicate a gradual transition towards stage VI.[147]

India has gone through the first five stages of the evolutionary path since 1922, leapfrogging stage IV only. India is currently in stage V. The outline of the Indian stages is as follows. Stage I lasted 5 years (1922–27). Stage I ran from the inception of corporate income taxation in India in 1922 until 1928, when there was neither transfer pricing legislation nor transfer pricing disputes. Stage II took 73 years (1928–2001). It started with the emergence of a transfer pricing dispute that escalated into litigation: *Commissioner of Income Tax* v. *Bombay Trust Corporation Ltd*, decided in 1928. The *Bombay Trust* case was decided in favour of the taxpayer in the light of the principal/agent test as provided for in Indian domestic legislation. Stage III lasted 6 years (2001–7). It ran from the inception of a domestic provision explicitly adopting the ALP in 2001, until the emergence of transfer pricing disputes in an ALP regulatory context in 2007. *Mentor Graphics (Noida) Pvt Ltd* v. *Commissioner of Income Tax*, decided in 2007, was an early example of transfer pricing litigation in a post-2001 ALP scenario. India leapfrogged stage IV for a number of legal and cultural reasons which prevented negotiations between the tax administration and the taxpayers. Stage V started in 2007 with the *Mentor Graphics* case. At the time of writing, there have been no bilateral APAs or MAPs concluded by India.[148]

---

[147] See Chapter 14 'Russian Federation'.   [148] See Chapter 15 'India'.

China has gone through the six stages of the evolutionary path in less than three decades. There is one peculiarity here. China took the usual path from stage I to stage VI except in the following respect. China reached stage VI via stage V' (rather than via stage V), probably because of the Chinese cultural and institutional contexts that have deterred transfer pricing litigation. China is currently in stage VI. The outline of the Chinese stages is as follows. Stage I lasted 8 years (1980–8). Stage I ran from the inception of a Western style income tax in China in 1980 until 1988, when there were neither transfer pricing regulations nor transfer pricing disputes. Stage II took 3 years (1988–91). It began with the issuance of China's first transfer pricing Circular by the local tax authority in the Shenzhen special economic zone (an 'incubator' for developing China's international tax rules). This Circular was the result of the perception by Chinese policy-makers that some taxpayers could 'play' the tax system by transfer pricing manipulation. Stage II ended with the introduction of the ALP into Chinese domestic law in 1991. Stage III lasted one year (1991–2). It ran from the inception of a domestic provision explicitly adopting the ALP in 1991, until the emergence of transfer pricing disputes in an ALP regulatory context. Stage IV ran from 1992 (when the ALP was introduced into Chinese tax administration law) to 2005 (when the first bilateral APAs were concluded between China and Japan). Stage V' referred to an environment where all relevant transfer pricing disputes were solved in a non-litigation setting by APAs and MAPs. It lasted 5 years (2005–10). It ran from the inception of the APA programme in 2005 until the emergence of the first transfer pricing litigation in *ZFC* in 2010. Stage VI started in 2010. There has been one transfer pricing litigation, *ZFC*. At least twelve bilateral APAs have been signed over the 2005–2010 period.[149]

Appendix IV: Evolutionary path of transfer pricing dispute resolution in the Middle East and South America

Argentina has gone through the first five stages of the evolutionary path since 1932, leapfrogging stage IV only. This country is currently in stage V. Stage I lasted 3 years (1932–5). Stage I ran from the inception of corporate income taxation in Argentina in 1932 until 1935, when there was no transfer pricing legislation or transfer pricing disputes. Stage II

---

[149] See Chapter 16 'China'.

took 8 years (1935–43). It started with the emergence of a transfer pricing dispute in the meat industry, which triggered the appointment of a congressional committee to investigate the case.[150] Stage III lasted 17 years (1943–60). It ran from the inception of a domestic provision encapsulating an early version of the ALP in the export of goods arena until the emergence of the first transfer pricing litigation in 1960 in the agribusiness industry. Argentina skipped stage IV for a number of legal and cultural reasons which made negotiations between the tax administration and the taxpayers an infrequent procedure for solving transfer pricing disputes. Stage V started with the *Refinerías de Maíz* case in 1960 and extends to the present. Neither bilateral APAs nor MAP have been concluded so far.

Chile has leapfrogged stages of the usual evolutionary path. It has gone from stage I to III (skipping stage II). It is currently in stage V and there is a congressional bill that may move Chile to stage VI. The outline of the Chilean stages is as follows. Stage I lasted 24 years (1974–98). Stage I ran from the inception of corporate income taxation in Chile in 1974 until 1998, when there was no transfer pricing legislation or transfer pricing disputes. The Chilean path then moved on to stage III. It lasted 6 years (1998–2004). Stage III ran from the inception of domestic provisions explicitly adopting the ALP in 1998 amid a context with no transfer pricing disputes until the emergence of tax authority rulings in 2004. In stage IV, transfer pricing disputes normally began and ended within the Chilean tax administration. Disputes were normally solved through administrative measures, such as guidelines for taxpayers, interpretation circulars, and negotiated settlements with the tax administration. Private Ruling no. 1118, issued in 2004, seems to have been the starting point for stage IV. This private ruling has been used by the Chilean tax administration, for example, to challenge payments to a related party residing outside of Chile. This country then moved to stage V, when transfer pricing litigation emerged in the mining and forestry industries in 2010.

---

[150] '[Certain Argentine] companies avoid paying [Argentine] income taxes on the grounds that they are manufacturing agencies that transfer their products at cost to their overseas holding companies. This includes La Anglo Company.' Lisandro de la Torre added, 'The meatpacker La Anglo pretends to be a manufacturing company working at cost for a third entity based overseas [in Liechtenstein or Switzerland]. In fact, this so-called manufacturing company does not exist and the profits are hidden. In Argentina, La Anglo maintains that its profits are taxed in England, and in England, Lord Vestey [La Anglos' controlling shareholder] claims that those profits are taxed in Argentina. Thus, [La Anglo] avoids paying income taxes in both countries.' See Chapter 17 'Argentina'.

A congressional bill introducing bilateral APAs suggests that Chile may move on to stage VI shortly.[151]

Israel has gone through the first four stages of the evolutionary path since 1948. It is currently in stage IV. The outline of each Israeli stage is as follows. Stage I lasted 43 years (1948–91). Stage I ran from the establishment of Israel in 1948, upon which it adopted the prior British colonial framework for tax law that included no transfer pricing regulations (except for a few limited arm's length provisions), to 1991, when Israel began to notice transfer pricing abuses.

Stage II lasted 12 years (1991–2003). It ran from Israeli tax policy-makers' perception of transfer pricing manipulations in 1991, to the enactment of the 2003 reform introducing the ALP for international transactions into Israeli domestic law. Already at this stage transfer pricing rulings were issued. Stage III lasted 3 years (2003–6). It ran from the inception of a domestic provision explicitly adopting the ALP in 2003 until the time it actually came into force in November 2006, with the promulgation of detailed transfer pricing regulations. In stage IV, transfer pricing disputes in Israel normally begin and end within the tax administration. The local tax authority has issued one Circular introducing its interpretation of the transfer pricing legislation. Disputes are usually solved through administrative measures, such as negotiated settlements and transfer pricing rulings with the tax administration. No bilateral APAs or MAPs (in the context of transfer pricing) have been concluded in Israel so far.

Appendix V: Evolutionary path of transfer pricing dispute resolution in Africa

Kenya has gone through an unusual evolutionary path which effectively transplanted certain parts of the OECD Guidelines into Kenya's domestic law via a leading case in the country's highest court. The outline of each of Kenya's stages is as follows. It moved from stage I into stage V, and finally back to stage IV. Stage I lasted 31 years (1963–94). Stage I ran from the inception of corporate income taxation in Kenya in 1963 until 1994, when there was no transfer pricing legislation or transfer pricing disputes. The path then jumped to stage V. Stage V started in 1995 with the emergence of the first transfer pricing litigation in Kenya: *Unilever Kenya Ltd* v. *Commissioner for Income Tax*. The case was decided by the

---

[151] See Chapter 18 'Chile'.

High Court of Kenya in 2005 in the light of the OECD Guidelines, although there was no tax treaty involved in this case and Kenya was not an OECD member. The High Court of Kenya effectively transplanted to Kenya's domestic law the cost plus method as defined by the OECD Guidelines in order to fill in certain gaps in the domestic law. In the *Unilever* decision, the High Court of Kenya justified the transplant of this element of the OECD Guidelines to Kenya's domestic law on the following grounds: 'We live in what is now referred to as a "global village". We cannot overlook or side-line what has come out of the wisdom of taxpayers and tax collectors in other countries.' Kenya introduced comprehensive transfer pricing legislation one year later, in 2006, regulating the ALP in a more detailed manner than before. Stage IV started in 2006. Transfer pricing disputes have since generally been resolved at the Kenyan tax administration level, in a context in which no single MAP or APA has been completed so far.[152]

Namibia has gone through the four first stages of the usual evolutionary path, leapfrogging stage II. Namibia is currently in stage IV. The outline of each Namibian stage is as follows. Stage I lasted 23 years (1981–2004). Stage I ran from the inception of corporate income taxation in Namibia in 1981 until 2004, when there was neither transfer pricing legislation nor transfer pricing disputes. The path then jumped to stage III. It ran from the inception of domestic law explicitly adopting the ALP in 2005. Namibia's path then has moved on to stage IV, starting in 2006. Transfer pricing disputes have generally been resolved at the Namibian tax administration level, in a context in which no single MAP or bilateral APA has been completed. The tax authority issued a crucial Practice Note in 2006, which stated that nothing in the Practice Note was intended to be contradictory to the OECD Guidelines and, in cases where there was conflict, the provisions of the Guidelines would prevail in resolving any dispute. It also stated that any amendments made to the OECD Guidelines would be deemed to have been incorporated into this Practice Note.[153]

South Africa has gone through the first four stages of the usual evolutionary path. The country is now in stage IV. Stage I lasted 32 years

---

[152] See Chapter 20 'Africa'. Corporate tax existed at the time of independence in Kenya in 1963. See debtireland.org/download/pdf/kenya_tjn_rpt.pdf, Kenya Report Pages, pp. 14–16.

[153] See Chapter 20 'Africa'. Corporate tax was included in the Income Tax Act of 1981. Namibia declared its independence from South Africa in 1990. See www.namibian.com. na/index.php?id=28&tx_ttnews[tt_news]=14529&no_cache=1.

(1962–94). It ran from the inception of corporate income taxation in 1962, when there was no transfer pricing legislation or transfer pricing disputes. Stage II took one year (1994–5). It began with the 1994 report by Prof. M. M. Katz recommending the introduction of transfer pricing rules in order to address the problem of transfer pricing manipulation. Stage III ran from the inception of a domestic provision explicitly adopting the ALP in 1995, in a context with no transfer pricing disputes. Stage IV began when transfer pricing disputes were generally resolved at the South African tax administration level. The South African 1996 Practice Note lists the transfer pricing methodologies and states that the OECD Guidelines should be followed in the absence of specific guidance in the Practice Note, the provisions of its transfer pricing law, or its tax treaties. No single MAP or APA has been completed so far in South Africa.[154]

Tanzania has gone through the first four stages of the usual evolutionary path, leapfrogging stage II only. This country is now in stage IV. The four stages evolved as follows. Stage I lasted 31 years (1973–2004). It ran from the inception of corporate income taxation in 1973, which did not include transfer pricing provisions, until the 2004 reform. Tanzania presumably leapfrogged stage II, given that there is no data on transfer pricing disputes in a non-ALP regulatory context. Stage III lasted one year (2004). It ran from the inception of domestic law explicitly adopting the ALP in 2004 with no transfer pricing disputes. The path then moved on to stage IV in 2005. It has run from 2005 to the present. Transfer pricing disputes are generally resolved at the Tanzanian tax administration level, in a context in which no single MAP or APA has been completed. The tax authority has stated that it will apply internationally agreed arm's length standards as set out in the UN and OECD Transfer Pricing Guidelines. Furthermore, it has indicated that it will follow the ruling in the Kenyan tax case on transfer pricing (*Unilever Kenya Ltd*), which applied the OECD transfer pricing principles to domestic transfer pricing cases.[155]

---

[154] See Chapter 20 'Africa'. Corporate income tax is governed by Income Tax Act no. 58 of 1962. See www.acts.co.za/tax/index.htm.

[155] See Chapter 20 'Africa'.

Appendix VI: The global transfer pricing dispute resolution evolutionary path

	Stage I	Stage II	Stage III	Stage IV	Stage V	Stage V'	Stage VI	Full cycle
Europe and North America			Average: 8.6 years					Average: 97.6 years
Canada	1917–24	1924–39	1939–52 (13 years)	Leapfrogged	1952–2001	N/A	2001 to the present	84 years
Germany	1920–5	1925–72	1972–82 (10 years)	Leapfrogged	1982–2006	N/A	2006 to the present	86 years
Spain	Leapfrogged	Leapfrogged	1978 (1 year)	1978–86	1986–2006	N/A	2006 to the present	28 years
United Kingdom	1799–1915	1915–51	1951–63 (12 years)	1963–96	Leapfrogged	1996–2008	2008 to the present	209 years
United States	1909–21	1921–8	1928–35 (7 years)	Leapfrogged	1935–91	N/A	1991 to the present	81 years
Asia-Pacific			Average: 5.6 years					
Australia	1915–17	1917–46	1946–63 (17 years)	Leapfrogged	1963–90	N/A	1990 to the present	75 years
Japan	1899–1923	1923–85	1986 (1 year)	1986–92	Leapfrogged	N/A	1992 to the present	93 years
Korea	1949–87	1987	1988 (1 year)	1988–97	Leapfrogged	N/A	1997 to the present	48 years
Singapore	1947–2006	Leapfrogged	2006 (1 year)	2006–9	Leapfrogged	N/A	2009 to the present	62 years
BRIC countries			Average: 2.7 years					
Brazil	1922–90	1990–5	1996 (1 year)	Leapfrogged	1997 to the present			
Russia	1991–5	1995–9	1999–2000 (2 years)	Leapfrogged	2000 to the present		2011 law introduces bilateral APAs	
India	1922–8	1928–2001	2001–7 (6 years)	Leapfrogged	2007 to the present		2011 law introduces bilateral APAs	
China	1980–8	1988–91	1991–2 (2 years)	1992–2005	N/A	2005–10	2010 to the present	30 years
Middle East and South America			Average: 6.7 years					
Argentina	1932–5	1935–43	1943–60 (17 years)	N/A	1960 to the present			
Chile	1974–98	Leapfrogged	1998–2004 (6 years)	2004–10	2010 to the present			
Israel	1948–91	1991–2003	2003–6 (3 years)	2006 to the present				
Africa			Average: 1 year					
Kenya	1963–2005	Leapfrogged	Leapfrogged	Leapfrogged	2005			
Namibia	1981–2004	Leapfrogged	2005 (1 year)	2006 to the present				
South Africa	1962–94	1994–5	1995 (1 year)	1996 to the present				
Tanzania	1973–2004	2004	2004 (1 year)	2005 to the present				

Resolving the resolution of transfer pricing disputes: global trends and divergences

IAN ROXAN

22.1 Developments and divergences

The development of transfer pricing rules and dispute resolution processes around the world reflects the fact that countries' tax systems develop at different times and at different rates, and that they share experiences with each other through organisations such as the OECD, the IMF, the World Bank, the United Nations and the European Union. Problematic transfer prices are a response by taxpayers to differences between tax systems that affect the allocation of taxing rights between countries.[1] So it comes as no surprise to find countries developing similar approaches and following similar paths to transfer pricing. This observation does, however, risk obscuring some important divergences.

22.2 Divergences in the nature of transfer pricing standards

The first is in the nature of the standards that are used to deal with transfer pricing. The choice of standards is commonly seen as being between the traditional strict arm's length standard (ALS) and formulary apportionment. This reflects the two methods that have attracted attention in the United States. Avi-Yonah suggests in Chapter 3 that these approaches are merely ends of a spectrum. The material gathered by the country contributors suggests that the position is in fact more complicated.

Transfer pricing is one of those areas of tax law where it is often easier to say that an action is wrong (unfair, etc.), than it is to identify exactly

---

[1] This view of the taxpayer's perspective applies when the taxpayer is primarily seeking to obtain all available tax advantages. Taxpayers that are (part of) multinational enterprises may well also be using transfer prices to generate appropriate incentives and accounting within the organisation.

in what way it is wrong. This is why early transfer pricing legislation in countries such as the United States and United Kingdom initially just gave the tax authority power to adjust any prices between related companies that appeared to be unfair.

The obvious problem with such a formulation is that it places great discretion in the hands of the tax authority. While the courts can in principle control the tax authority in its exercise of discretions, they need a legal test against which to evaluate the tax authority's conduct. Some courts, in cases such as *Gillette*[2] and *Seminole Flavor Co.*,[3] have shown a readiness to take up this challenge, but in doing so they have rarely developed theories of transfer pricing. Rather their decisions have tended to be pragmatic and ad hoc, and their reasons have tended to be unconvincing.

Under the influence of the OECD Guidelines in particular, more precise tests have been sought. The test that seemed to offer the greatest precision was ALS, based on the idea of finding comparable transactions between unconnected parties that would provide objective evidence of the legitimate transfer price. In the 1920s and 1930s, when this approach emerged, it probably looked like an appropriate and feasible solution. One problem with it would have been information. In those days getting good information on commercial activities in far away countries could be physically difficult. Today, obtaining information on commercial activities is not itself the problem. The developments in information technology have made large amounts of information available in tax administration and commercial databases.

The problem, as Gillett highlights in Chapter 5, is that the way in which modern multinationals increasingly do business makes the concept of the comparable unconnected transaction increasingly less meaningful, because the organisation of these multinationals is not based on an allocation of functions or activities by country. The use of new calculation and comparison methods based on comparing the profitability of roughly comparable transactions in companies undertaking similar activities or functions, or on comparing the profitability of such companies themselves, has helped to make it more feasible to find a transfer price in these circumstances, as these methods do not require as strict comparables to be found as under strict ALS; however, they often only produce a range of acceptable prices, as the descriptions

---

[2] *Gillette Safety Razor Ltd* v. *IRC* [1920] 3 KB 358 (KBD).
[3] *Seminole Flavor Co.* v. *Commissioner*, 4 T.C. 1215 (1945).

of methods such as the OECD's transactional net margin method (TNMM) acknowledge,[4] based on the conclusions of expert evidence, often applying sophisticated analysis to large sets of data. The apparent precision of such analysis distracts from the fact that the final determination once again has a substantial subjective component.[5]

When such methods are considered by the courts, this subjective element is likely to lead to a return to pragmatic decisions, unless the court is presented with a clear analysis of the bases used by the competing experts in a way that makes it practicable for the court to consider their effectiveness in applying transfer pricing calculation methods. The decision in the *DSG Retail* case from the United Kingdom[6] may be seen as an example of that, but it may also suggest how much achieving that clarity of analysis depends upon clear presentation by witnesses and counsel, and relevant experience on the part of judges well versed in tax law and practice.

These problems do not just arise with the profit-based calculation methods. Trying to stretch traditional ALS methods to the new business models may require a similarly subjective evaluation. This is well illustrated by two Canadian cases. In *Alberta Printed Circuits*,[7] the concept of the 'internal comparable uncontrolled price (CUP)' was used, while in *GlaxoSmithKline*[8] there was a dispute between courts over the perspective from which to apply the CUP. These problems are even more likely to arise in applying transfer pricing legislation that adopts a simpler test than the full range available under the OECD Guidelines, which is the situation in a number of the non-OECD member countries discussed in this book.

22.3   Divergences in transfer pricing dispute resolution: the role of challenges

Such concerns highlight the important role that dispute resolution plays in the effective operation of transfer pricing rules. Indeed, a second area of divergence arises on the dispute resolution side. This is the divergence

---

[4] See the 2010 OECD Guidelines, para. 3.45. The current US regulations go further and recognise that any of the methods can result in a range, when there are several relevant comparables: Treas. Reg. s. 1.482-1(e)(1).

[5] This is acknowledged in the 2010 OECD Guidelines, para. 3.8, discussing the profit split method.

[6] *DSG Retail Ltd and others* v. *HMRC* [2009] UKFTT 31 (TC); [2009] STC (SCD) 397.

[7] *Alberta Printed Circuits Ltd* v. *The Queen* 2011 T.C.C. 232.

[8] *GlaxoSmithKline Inc.* v. *The Queen* 2008 D.T.C. 3957 (TCC), rev'd 2010 D.T.C. 7053 (FCA).

between countries with challenged transfer pricing systems and those with unchallenged systems. The challenges may be to the scope of the transfer pricing rules, and may include constitutional issues. Alternatively, they may be to the operation of the rules at a legal level, in issues such as the choice of pricing method or the criteria for applying a method, or at a procedural level, challenging, for example, documentation requirements.

The level of such challenges will be influenced by institutional issues, such as the extent to which the courts are generally used to raise constitutional challenges in tax matters. This will reflect not only the extent to which such challenges are legally available, but also the extent to which tax issues are seen in constitutional terms. In countries such as Spain, Germany and Brazil, such challenges have been more common. The impact of the EU freedom of movement provisions on direct taxation raises an additional set of quasi-constitutional issues, as Oestreicher and Ruiz Almendral have discussed in Chapters 6 and 7.

Nevertheless, the extent to which constitutional and scope challenges are used in transfer pricing will also reflect the extent to which the operation of the rules is seen as giving businesses sufficient certainty. If the rules are set out in detail, challenges are more likely to be at the operational level. Challenges to scope and constitutionality are risky in that they have an all-or-nothing element to them. Unless they are clearly well founded, they offer limited scope of relief to the taxpayer. When the rules are not well defined, when the tax authority has considerable discretion, then such challenges are also valuable as a lever in negotiations.

In contrast, challenges to the operation of the rules are an unreliable tool for taxpayers when the transfer pricing tests are not well defined, as the decision of a court becomes harder to predict and is more likely to be ad hoc. Rules that are defined in detail may thus encourage litigation, because taxpayers will have a greater chance of using an argument that has a credible foundation in the rules. Operational challenges also offer more reliable opportunities for settlement negotiations with the tax authority when the rules are well defined. These factors seem to be a good description of the path that transfer pricing has taken in the United States, and may also well describe recent developments in a number of the other countries discussed here. On the other hand, the example of the United States also reveals the disadvantage of litigation under detailed transfer pricing rules: the level of detail offers greater opportunities to present expert evidence, which typically makes transfer pricing litigation lengthy and costly.

It is also necessary to consider the interaction with the previous point about the subjective quality of detailed rules that are not congruent with modern business structures. These are the rules that particularly depend on expert evidence. Although their detail provides a good basis for such evidence, for what Duff and Beswick term a 'battle of experts', their subjective quality can mean that they provide a less reliable basis for taxpayers in the absence of litigation. The problem with procedural solutions to transfer pricing issues is thus that they do not avoid the fundamental conundrum of transfer pricing tests that do not work in the modern business environment.

22.4   Further responses

22.4.1   Alternative substantive tests

One response to this would be to consider again the alternative of formulary apportionment, rejected until now by the OECD. While full formulary apportionment offers a degree of certainty wholly lacking from ALS used in the modern commercial environment, it also presents some risk of generating distortions. First, there are the distortions to the tax system that would result from the transition to the new method, but it is also possible that other distortions would arise as taxpayers saw opportunities to take advantage of the formula used. The risk is that the nature of the corporate income tax would be significantly changed. The use of a typical apportionment formula based on sales, assets and employees could in effect convert the corporate income tax from being a tax on profits to a set of excise taxes on these factors of production. Of course, it is important not to overstate this risk. In the modern globalised world it is far from clear that corporate income taxes on multinationals operate effectively as taxes on profits now. Formulary apportionment might, in that case, simply make the incidence of corporate income tax more transparent. That would seem to be desirable as a matter of tax policy and democratic principle, although it is less clear whether it would be desirable as a matter of political reality.

Another solution would be to find a workable development of, or alternative to, the arm's length principle (ALP) that gives the element of certainty needed by business, while being robust to the risk of manipulation by taxpayers. It is beyond the scope of this book, and probably too early in any event, to assess whether the 2010 OECD Guidelines offer such a workable alternative.

22.4.2 *Alternative procedural approaches: prospects for MAPs and APAs*

If new tests do not offer an easy solution to the conundrum of transfer pricing tests that do not fit the modern business environment, it may be necessary to look again at whether procedural alternatives can assist after all. Most of the country chapters consider the benefits of advance pricing agreements (APAs) and mutual agreement procedures (MAPs). The work that has been done by the OECD and by the EU joint transfer pricing forum has helped to improve the usability of these procedures. The great advantage that MAPs and bilateral or multilateral APAs offer is, of course, that they include the agreement of tax authorities on both sides of a transaction, thus ensuring that, when the agreement applies, double taxation is eliminated. It is interesting to see that very often APAs are in practice based on calculation methods such as TNMM or the profit split. This suggests that the other great advantage that APAs offer comes from the ability to assess a business plan in advance in circumstances where a taxpayer and the affected governments are able to agree on a calculation method as part of the process of developing the agreed commercial transfer pricing strategy. Taxpayers are justifiably suspicious both of the documentation requirements of the APA process, and of the amount of otherwise confidential information that they may need to disclose to the tax authority, but the process gives the two sides an opportunity to understand better each other's concerns, and to adapt both the transfer pricing tax strategy and the commercial strategy to better reflect those concerns.

Unfortunately, it does not seem likely that operating the APA process in this way would lend itself directly to the creation of new transfer pricing precedents. Applying it with the sort of flexibility described would not directly help to elaborate a set of rules describing transfer pricing calculation methods. The tax authorities involved could be in a better position to draw insights from APAs. Such insights could be incorporated in regulations or administrative guidance; however, taxpayers would be justifiably concerned that the tax authority might attempt to draw lessons in its own favour from this process.

It is important to remember also the other key trend that emerges in relation to APAs: even in countries where the process is well established, the number of APAs is small in comparison to the number of taxpayers potentially affected by transfer pricing rules. Of course, many affected taxpayers may have relatively simple transfer pricing affairs that are easily agreed with all the tax authorities involved, without the need for the effort required to negotiate an APA. Nevertheless, while an APA is less costly than court litigation, and more reliable than the currently uncertain MAP system, it is only effectively available for a limited number of taxpayers.

The MAP process has the advantage that it is relatively simple for taxpayers to use, even though, until arbitration becomes better established, it is far from expeditious and is not certain of producing a result that eliminates double taxation. Arbitration looks like a promising improvement to the MAP process. Currently, a key benefit is that the arbitration hearing itself is unattractive to tax authorities. This makes the deadlines in the arbitration procedures provide a powerful incentive for the tax authorities to make the regular MAP process work. There is a risk that this reflects the lack of experience that governments have with transfer pricing arbitration. Should arbitration hearings prove popular, they might end up involving the complexity and levels of expert evidence that now feature in much of transfer pricing litigation before the courts.

These considerations make it important to understand what is happening in contrast in national tax systems, where transfer pricing decisions largely go unchallenged. A lack of challenges could indicate a system giving the tax authority a high level of discretion, thus leaving taxpayers hard pressed to find any justiciable grounds for challenge. However, a number of countries included in this book show that in such cases taxpayers can often turn to challenges based on scope and constitutionality. The remaining explanations for a lack of challenges would seem to be either that the tax system is like that experienced at least at certain times by a few of the countries examined in this book; or that the tax authority uses its transfer pricing powers in a limited range of cases, on the basis of standards that are well understood by taxpayers, and where taxpayers have good opportunities to present their arguments at an administrative level before the tax authority has become committed to a position, as will inevitably happen on a judicial appeal. For such an approach based on administrative negotiation to work, it is not necessary that taxpayers be content with the positions taken by the tax authority, but taxpayers should normally feel that they will have, first, a better opportunity to present arguments on complex transfer pricing issues to the tax authority than to the courts, and, second, that the tax authority will take a reasonable and reasonably predictable position that does not undermine the commercial viability of the taxpayer's affairs.

22.5   Conclusion

In summary, the challenge raised by the systems for resolving transfer pricing disputes in countries around the world, as presented in the chapters of this book, is twofold. On the one hand, the rules need to provide a way of determining an allocation of multinational profits between countries that is fair and not the result of inappropriate manipulation for a tax advantage. On the other hand, the rules also need to provide a basis in terms of substantive rules and procedures whereby any disputes that arise can be resolved cost-effectively and with a reasonable degree of predictability for both sides. Nearly all the countries discussed in this book are working towards using the OECD Guidelines as a basis for achieving this, together with MAPs in treaties and, more recently, APAs and arbitration. Given the challenges presented by the way in which multinational business is developing in the modern globalised world, it is far from clear that this combination will prove to be the best route to follow. However, the chapters of this book provide important material to assist in making that assessment.

INDEX